Human Rights Sourcebook

Human Rights Sourcebook

Edited by

Albert P. Blaustein
Roger S. Clark
Jay A. Sigler

A Washington Institute Book

Paragon House Publishers
New York

First edition, 1987
Published in the United States by

PARAGON HOUSE PUBLISHERS
90 Fifth Avenue
New York, New York 10011

A Washington Institute for Values in Public Policy Book.

Library of Congress Cataloging-in-Publication Data

Human rights sourcebook.

"A Washington Institute book."
Bibliography.
Includes index.
1. Civil rights (International law)   2. Civil
rights.   I. Blaustein, Albert P., 1921–   .
II. Clark, Roger S., 1940–   .   III. Sigler, Jay A.
K3238.H86   1987   341.4'81   86-25435
ISBN 0-88702-202-2

DEDICATED TO
The Right to be Informed

CONTENTS

INTRODUCTION

Our primary objective has been to meet the demand for a one-volume compilation of the *official* texts of *all* the fundamental human rights documents—so comprehensive that it can be relied upon without going to any other source.

But we wanted to do more. Supplementing this up-to-date compendium of official texts are explanations and commentaries, supported by a basic bibliography. Further, we have added the procedural documentation for human rights enforcement. All of this has been organized in a neutral international framework. There is no national bias; there is no advocacy of special interests.

Thus, this book is designed for the needs of scholars, lawyers, teachers and students, officials of international agencies and human rights activists throughout the world, as well as being a basic library reference work.

Of course it begins with the human rights documents of the United Nations—virtually all of them. This is followed by the comparable documentation of the International Labor Organization and Unesco, plus the regional human rights conventions of Europe, America and Africa. The collection also includes such international treaties as the Geneva Conventions on the laws of war and the Helsinki Accords. Finally, this source book includes basic human rights pronouncements from constitutions, national legislation and judicial decisions.

The significance and value of so definitive a collection cannot fully be appreciated until one tries to locate these materials from scattered library sources or directly from the national and international bodies themselves. The spadework has now been done, and the contours and parameters of human rights in the world community can be gleaned from an examination of the contents of this source book.

This work provides the resource foundation for standards to be applied to the acts of both nations and individuals when assessing claims of human rights violations. The materials here can be used by non-governmental organizatons and the human rights community in their analyses of human rights problems and in their human rights advocacy. In addition, they can be used by members of international and domestic agencies and tribunals in their deliberations. Since bibliographic references are provided, in-depth analyses are facilitated.

Teachers, students and other scholars in the human rights field should find this volume especially useful. Hours and days of research labor can be saved because of the scope of materials made available here. For this reason, it is hoped that the source book will accelerate the pace of teaching and scholarship in this vital area.

It is also the hope of the editors that this collection will influence the development and maturation of human rights in the world community; to the extent that this book is made available in libraries throughout the world. It should encourage groups and individuals who have been denied rights in the past to claim them in the future. Since this book is not organized from the vantage point of any one nation, its international character should be meaningful to all who strive for a freer, more humane and more fulfilling society—regardless of the vagaries of foreign policy.

We took as our inspiration (and guideposts) those other great documentaries which are so useful—and so much used: Stephenson and Marcham's *Sources of English Constitutional History* and Commager's *Documents of American History.* We also benefited from the experience of Blaustein and Zangrando's *Civil Rights and the Black American.* These documentaries provide the reader/user with more than just a documentary compilation. Editors' skills organized raw data to provide a philosophic approach to the growth and development of freedom and liberty. We could do no less in a documentary on human rights.

There was one other goal which guided our work, and the fact that it is listed last does not mean that it was last in our thinking. For the validity and enforcement of human rights must be subject to the fundamental right of due process—with the requirement of due notice. No one should be held guilty of an offense not provided for in international or national law at the time it was committed. Even the violator of human rights is entitled to the right of knowing in exact, precise and specific terms the rights that have been prescribed and the acts that have been proscribed. We in the human rights field who support the rule of law are under an obligation to make the rules known.

Grateful acknowledgement is made to James Coker for his contributions on the Laws of War; to Robert A. Friedlander for his contribution on the European Convention on the Suppression of Terrorism; to Richard Gittleman for his contibution on the OAU's Banjul Charter on Human and People's Rights; and to David H. Oh for his work on the materials dealing with the Organization of American States. Special thanks also go to Dana B. Epstein, Mary Ann DiConstanzo and Mark Plotkin for valued editorial assistance.

Albert P. Blaustein
Roger S. Clark
Jay A. Sigler

I. United Nations Documents

INTRODUCTION

1. THE NATURE AND AUTHORITY OF THE DOCUMENTS

The Chapters that follow concern intergovernmental activity to foster human rights. During the nineteenth century there had been sporadic *ad hoc* international efforts to deal with questions such as slavery and the treatment of victims of war. The first permanent efforts, at the global level, to deal with matters of human rights were the mandates and minorities protection arrangements of the League of Nations and the efforts of the International Labor Organization in respect of labor standards. The League and the ILO (the latter is considered in Chapter II) were formed in 1919 as part of the World War I Peace Settlement.

Article 22 of the "Covenant," the treaty setting up the League, provided that in certain German and Turkish colonies that had been detached from those countries during the War, "there should be applied the principle that the well-being and development of such peoples form a sacred trust of civilization."[1] In order to fulfill this trust, the countries administering these territories owed certain obligations to the international community which were supervised, albeit in a rudimentary way, by the Council of the League and a body of experts set up for the purpose, the Permanent Mandates Commission. Analagous procedures were to find their way into the United Nations Charter.

Also as part of the peace settlement, obligations to respect minority rights were undertaken by (or imposed upon) many of the new European states which emerged following the War. Again, certain procedures were created to enforce these obligations, but they were not notably successful. This kind of guarantee of group rights was not repeated in the United Nations Charter.

Some of the smaller countries represented at the San Francisco Conference, at which the Charter of the United Nations was adopted, wished to include a Bill of Rights, or at least precise provisions pertaining to the protection of human rights. By this means, it was argued, future sources of conflict might be diverted at their source. Such efforts were not entirely availing, but the Charter (in particular Articles 1, 13 and 55) does contain several references to the "promotion" of human rights and fundamental freedoms as one of the goals of the Organization. The notion of "promoting" was deliberately chosen to denote a weaker obligation on states than might have been the case if a strong word like "protect" had been used. Nevertheless, and this was implicit in the notion of promoting, the drafters of the Charter expected that the Organization would work actively at the spelling out of various international instruments, both to give detailed normative content to the generalizations of the Charter and to devise enforcement or supervision procedures to encourage states to abide by their obligations. Sections C through M of this Chapter and Chapter IV are primarily devoted to this concretization work of the UN. Article 1 of the Charter enshrines the "principle of equal rights and self-determination of peoples." Articles 75 through 91 made provision for a "Trusteeship" system to take the place of the League's mandate arrangements. In addition, Articles 73 and 74 of the Charter recognize that states with non-self-governing territories other than those brought under the Trusteeship system owe some international obligations in respect of even those territories. It is difficult to over-estimate the significance that the working out of the principle of self-determination has had for the UN. One need only mention the substantial time on the agenda of the General Assembly devoted over the years to decolonization matters; the transformation of the *principle* of self-determination into a *right*; the creation of machinery [in particular the Committee of 24 discussed in Chapter IV (A2)] to give concrete expression to the inchoate obligation contained in Articles 73 and 74 of the Charter; and the fact that about half of the current membership of the UN comprises states that were dependent territories when the Charter was adopted.

It is difficult to come to grips both with the nomenclature used to describe the various instruments that have been used by the UN family of organizations in its standard-setting activities and with the differing legal effects of those instruments. Some remarks on these two points may therefore be helpful.

1. Nomenclature. Basically, the instruments fall into two categories: multilateral treaties and resolutions. The treaties are variously called "Charters," "Convenants," "Conventions" and "Protocols." The effect of each of these under international law is exactly the same, in spite of the differences in name. "Charter" is the name typically given to a very important treaty, especially of an organizational nature (like the UN Charter) and "Covenant" is usually a term also reserved for especially important treaties. "Convention" is a kind of boiler-plate title used for run-of-the-mill agreements while "Protocol" is mainly used to describe an agreement that is supplementary to another (like the Optional Protocol to the International Convenant on Civil and Political Rights). Many of the resolutions in the pages that follow are called Declarations. This term is often used in UN practice when an effort is being made to show that this is a particularly important kind of resolution. Other resolutions in our sample are called just that: resolutions; others yet, are called Rules or Principles. To make things even more difficult, one 1974 resolution is called the Charter of Economic Rights and Duties of States. "Charter" is obviously meant to give some weight to the document but, unlike other Charters, it is not a treaty. At all events, the UN Charter makes no distinctions between the legal effects of these various different kinds of resolutions, and it is to the legal effect of our documents that we now turn.

2. Legal effect. Article 38.1 of the Statute of the International Court of Justice is often regarded as declaratory of what constitutes the "sources" of international law. It provides that the Court, "whose function is to decide in accordance with international law such disputes as are submitted to it,"[2] is to apply:

a. international conventions, whether general or particular, establishing rules expressly recognized by the contesting states;

b. international custom, as evidence of a general practice accepted as law;

c. the general principles of law recognized by civilized nations;

d. subject to the provisions of Article 59, [which provides that "The decision of the Court has no binding force except between the parties and in respect of that particular case"] judicial decisions and the teachings of the most highly qualified publicists of the various nations, as subsidiary means for the determination of rules of law.

Treaties, when ratified if necessary, are clearly international law under Article 38.1.a. They establish "rules expressly recognized" by the parties to them.

The effect of Resolutions is more complex. Bodies like the General Assembly of the UN and its analogues in the Specialized Agencies have been formally granted only a power to "recommend", not a power to make international "legislation" by resolution. There are certain minor exceptions to this general proposition in the case, for example, the International Monetary Fund and the International Civil Aviation Organization, which are not relevant in the present context. Thus, the argument sometimes goes, their resolutions are at best of varying degrees of moral force, the degree depending upon how substantially they were supported in the voting. This rather simple argument has to be modified by at least two considerations.

In the first place, it is increasingly recognized in international usage, although the matter is far from being uncontroversial, that widely supported resolutions like the Universal Declaration of Human Rights and the Declaration on the Granting of Independence to Colonial Countries and Peoples (and even some unratified treaties) play a legal role as:

a. Authoritative interpretations of the provisions of the Charter and the Constitutions of the Specialized Agencies and thus assimilated to conventional law under paragraph 1.a of Article 38, or

b. As examples of practice contributing to the development of international customary law (38.1.b.), or

c. As evidence of "general principles of law recognized by civilized nations" (38.1.c.).

On each of these kinds of analysis, it is important to examine the voting on the particular resolution (and the resolution's influence in subsequent usage) in order to gauge the extent to which a consensus has been reached around it. The fact that overwhelming numerical support exists may not be conclusive. This may be countered by the identity of dissenting states and their influence so far as the particular item is concerned. (This aspect is of considerable significance in international economic matters.)

Second, it is clear that in the international arena, Declarations and other resolutions perform similar functions to those rules and principles that we call "law" without hesitation. As Professor Falk has written:

A main function of law is to establish an agreed system for the communication of claims and counterclaims between international actors and thereby to structure argument in diplomatic settings. In the search for the bases of

justification or objection it is clear that the resolutions of the Assembly play a
crucial role—one independent of whether their status is to generate binding
legal rules or to embody mere recommendations.[3]

It may well be that, in light of what has just been suggested, the real difference between the two kinds of instruments is one of degree rather than one of kind— a difference in the degree of pressure for compliance and the degree, which states consider themselves obligated to comply.[4]

One final comment on the documents as "law." We have been speaking so far about the status of the documents on the international plane. It should also be remembered that in some states, treaties, at least those containing precise obligations, can be "self-executing" as a matter of domestic law and may thus be relied upon as a source of law in legal proceedings within the state. In addition, the Universal Declaration is referred to, at least as an aspirational standard, in the constitutions of several developing states. The 1960 Constitution of the Republic of the Ivory Coast, for example, says that "The people of the Ivory Coast declare their adherence to the principles of Democracy and the Rights of Man, as they have been defined by the Declaration of the Rights of Man and the Citizen of 1789, by the Universal Declaration of 1948 and as they have been guaranteed by this Constitution."[5] Again, the 1978 Constitutional Charter of the Military Committee of National Reconstruction of Mauritania records that the armed forces, which have taken over the Government, have proclaimed their intention, inter alia, to "adhere to the principles established by the Declaration of Human Rights, the Charter of the United Nations, the Organization of African Unity and the League of Arab States."[6] Such statements may be included in the constitutional documents cynically and cosmetically, but they are likely to be taken seriously in some quarters. They provide both a standard for the measurement of a Government by its citizens and some evidence of state practice that can be used to support the notion of the Universal Declaration as containing customary norms of international law.

2. RELEVANT PROVISIONS OF THE UNITED NA-TIONS CHARTER

The Charter provisions that follow constitute the framework for later UN human rights activities. They speak in general terms and we suggest you view the material subsequent to them as efforts to give concrete content to these generalities. As you read all the documents in this Chapter, you may wish to consider the extent to which they adopt an approach based on the rights of *individuals* or one based on the rights of *collectivities*. At the outset, we note that the Charter refers both to rights of individuals which are to be accorded without distinction as to race, sex, language, or religion[7] and to a very important principle affecting certain collectivities, the principle of equal rights and self-determination of peoples.[8] You will notice that the Charter speaks in much greater detail concerning the rights of peoples in territories placed under the trusteeship system than it does of the rights of the inhabitants of other non-selfgoverning territories. We shall have occasion in Section E of this

Chapter and in Chapter IV to consider efforts to remove this disparity, both at the normative and the procedural level.

In addition to the Charter provisions conferring powers on the UN, we include the provision in the Charter, Article 2 paragraph 7, that is automatically relied upon by states seeking to deny any role to the UN in a particular human rights matter. Almost as automatically, the shield of Article 2 paragraph 7 is thrust aside by a majority of the membership. Depending upon the states concerned and the issue before the organ involved, application of the paragraph is generally avoided by reliance on variants of one or more of the three following arguments: (i) Human rights, because of their inclusion in the Charter and general international law, are no longer "essentially within the domestic jurisdiction of any state." (ii) The specific action proposed in the UN does not constitute "intervention" which is said to have a technical meaning of "dictatorial interference", *i.e.*, some kind of force. (iii) In any event, Article 2.7 has no role where "massive" or "systematic" violations are concerned, particularly those likely to affect the maintenance of international peace and security. In the case of the UN action against Southern Rhodesia the Security Council applied the exception to Article 2(7) specifically dealt with in its own language ("but this principle shall not prejudice the application of enforcement measures under Chapter VII") since that was an enforcement action within Chapter VII of the Charter.[9]

ABBREVIATIONS USED

A/ . . .	General Assembly Document
Conf.	Conference
Doc.	Document
E/ . . .	Economic and Social Council Document
ECOSOC	(United Nations) Economic and Social Council
E.S.C.	(United Nations) Economic and Social Council
ESCOR	(United Nations) Economic and Social Council Records
G.A.	General Assembly
GAOR	General Assembly Official Records
G.B.	Governing Body
I.C.J.	International Court of Justice
I.L.O.	International Labor Organization
L.S.	Limited Series
OAS	Organization of American States
OAU	Organization of African Unity
Res.	Resolution
Rev.	Revision
Supp.	Supplement
T/ . . .	(United Nations) Trusteeship Council
TCOR	(United Nations) Trusteeship Council Official Records
U.N.	United Nations
UNESCO	United Nations Educational, Scientific, and Cultural Organization
U.N.T.S.	United Nations Treaty Series
Y.B.	Yearbook

A. UNITED NATIONS

1. UNITED NATIONS CHARTER (1945) (Preamble, Articles 1, 2.7, 13, 55, 56, 62, 73–74, 75–85). Signed at San Francisco, 26 June 1945. Entered into force on 24 October 1945.

WE THE PEOPLES OF THE UNITED NATIONS
DETERMINED

to save succeeding generations from the scourge of war, which twice in our lifetime has brought untold sorrow to mankind, and

to reaffirm faith in fundamental human rights, in the dignity and worth of the human person, in the equal rights of men and women and of nations large and small, and

to establish conditions under which justice and respect for the obligations arising from treaties and other sources of international law can be maintained, and

to promote social progress and better standards of life in larger freedom,

AND FOR THESE ENDS

to practice tolerance and live together in peace with one another as good neighbors, and

to unite our strength to maintain international peace and security, and

to ensure, by the acceptance of principles and the institution of methods, that armed force shall not be used, save in the common interest, and

to employ international machinery for the promotion of the economic and social advancement of all peoples,

HAVE RESOLVED TO COMBINE OUR EFFORTS TO ACCOMPLISH
THESE AIMS.

Accordingly, our respective Governments, through representatives assembled in the city of San Fransisco, who have exhibited their full powers found to be in good and due form, have agreed to the present Charter of the United Nations and do hereby establish an international organization to be known as the United Nations.

CHAPTER I. PURPOSES AND PRINCIPLES

Article 1

The Purposes of the United Nations are:

1. To maintain international peace and security, and to that end: to take effective collective measures for the prevention and removal of threats to the peace, and for the suppression of acts of aggression or other breaches of the peace, and to bring about by peaceful means, and in conformity with the

principles of justice and international law, adjustment or settlement of international disputes or situations which might lead to a breach of the peace;

2. To develop friendly relations among nations based on respect for the principle of equal rights and self-determination of peoples, and to take other appropriate measures to strengthen universal peace;

3. To achieve international cooperation in solving international problems of an economic, social, cultural, or humanitarian character, and in promoting and encouraging respect for human rights and for fundamental freedoms for all without distinction as to race, sex, language, or religion; and

4. To be a center for harmonizing the actions of nations in the attainment of these common ends.

Article 2

7. Nothing contained in the present Charter shall authorize the United Nations to intervene in matters which are essentially within the domestic jurisdiction of any state or shall require the Members to submit such matters to settlement under the present Charter; but this principle shall not prejudice the application of enforcement measures under Chapter VII.

Article 13

1. The General Assembly shall initiate studies and make recommendations for the purpose of:

a. promoting international cooperation in the political field and encouraging the progressive development of international law and its codification;

b. promoting international cooperation in the economic, social, cultural, educational, and health fields, and assisting in the realization of human rights and fundamental freedoms for all without distinction as to race, sex, language, or religion.

2. The further responsibilities, functions, and powers of the General Assembly with respect to matters mentioned in paragraph 1(b) above are set forth in Chapters IX and X.

CHAPTER IX. INTERNATIONAL ECONOMIC AND SOCIAL COOPERATION

Article 55

With a view to the creation of conditions of stability and well-being which are necessary for peaceful and friendly relations among nations based on respect for the principle of equal rights and self-determination of peoples, the United Nations shall promote:

a. higher standards of living, full employment, and conditions of economic and social progress and development;

b. solutions of international economic, social, health, and related problems; and international cultural and educational cooperation; and

c. universal respect for, and observance of, human rights and fundamental freedoms for all without distinction as to race, sex, language or religion.

Article 56

All Members pledge themselves to take joint and separate action in cooperation with the Organization for the achievement of the purposes set forth in Article 55.

CHAPTER X. THE ECONOMIC AND SOCIAL COUNCIL

Functions and Powers

Article 62

1. The Economic and Social Council may make or initiate studies and reports with respect to international economic, social, cultural, educational, health, and related matters and may make recommendations with respect to any such matters to the General Assembly, to the Members of the United Nations, and to the specialized agencies concerned.

2. It may make recommendations for the purpose of promoting respect for, and observance of, human rights and fundamental freedoms for all.

3. It may prepare draft conventions for submission to the General Assembly, with respect to matters falling within its competence.

4. It may call, in accordance with the rules prescribed by the United Nations, international conferences on matters falling within its competence.

CHAPTER XI. DECLARATION REGARDING NON-SELF-GOVERNING TERRITORIES

Article 73

Members of the United Nations which have or assume responsibilities for the administration of territories whose peoples have not yet attained a full measure of self-government recognize the principle that the interests of the inhabitants of these territories are paramount, and accept as a sacred trust the obligation to promote to the utmost, within the system of international peace and security established by the present Charter, the well-being of the inhabitants of these territories, and, to this end:

a. to ensure, with due respect for the culture of the peoples concerned, their political, economic, social, and educational advancement, their just treatment, and their protection against abuses;

b. to develop self-government to take due account of the political aspirations of the peoples, and to assist them in the progressive development of their free political institutions, according to the particular circumstances of each territory and its peoples and their varying stages of advancement;

c. to further international peace and security;

d. to promote constructive measures of development, to encourage research, and to cooperate with one another and, when and where appropriate, with specialized international bodies with a view to the practical achievement of the social, economic, and scientific purposes set forth in this Article; and

e. to transmit regularly to the Secretary-General for information purposes, subject to such limitation as security and constitutional considerations may require, statistical and other information of a technical nature relating to economic, social, and educational conditions in the territories for which they are respectively responsible other than those territories to which Chapters XII and XIII apply.

Article 74

Members of the United Nations also agree that their policy in respect of the territories to which this Chapter applies, no less than in respect of their metropolitan areas, must be based on the general principle of good-neighborliness, due account being taken of the interests and well-being of the rest of the world, in social, economic, and commercial matters.

CHAPTER XII. INTERNATIONAL TRUSTEESHIP SYSTEM

Article 75

The United Nations shall establish under its authority an international trusteeship system for the administration and supervision of such territories as may be placed thereunder by subsequent individual agreements. These territories are hereinafter referred to as trust territories.

Article 76

The basic objectives of the trusteeship system, in accordance with the Purposes of the United Nations laid down in Article 1 of the present Charter, shall be:

a. to further international peace and security;

b. to promote the political, economic, social, and educational advancement of the inhabitants of the trust territories, and their progressive development towards self-government or independence as may be appropriate to the particular circumstances of each territory and its peoples and the freely expressed wishes of the peoples concerned, and as may be provided by the terms of each trusteeship agreement;

c. to encourage respect for human rights and for fundamental freedoms for all without distinction as to race, sex, language, or religion, and to encourage recognition of the interdependence of the peoples of the world; and

d. to ensure equal treatment in social, economic, and commercial matters for all Members of the United Nations and their nationals, and also equal treatment for the latter in the administration of justice, without prejudice to the attainment of the foregoing objectives and subject to the provisions of Article 80.

Article 77

1. The trusteeship system shall apply to such territories in the following categories as may be placed thereunder by means of trusteeship agreements:
   a. territories now held under mandate;
   b. territories which may be detached from enemy states as a result of the Second World War; and
   c. territories voluntarily placed under the system by states responsible for their administration.
2. It will be a matter for subsequent agreement as to which territories in the foregoing categories will be brought under the trusteeship system and upon what terms.

Article 78

The trusteeship system shall not apply to territories which have become Members of the United Nations, relationship among which shall be based on respect for the principle of sovereign equality.

Article 79

The terms of trusteeship for each territory to be placed under the trusteeship system, including any alteration or amendment, shall be agreed upon by the states directly concerned, including the mandatory power in the case of territories held under mandate by a Member of the United Nations, and shall be approved as provided for in Articles 83 and 85.

Article 80

1. Except as may be agreed upon in individual trusteeship agreements, made under Articles 77, 79, and 81, placing each territory under the trusteeship system, and until such agreements have been concluded, nothing in this Chapter shall be construed in or of itself to alter in any manner the rights whatsoever of any states or any peoples or the terms of existing international instruments to which Members of the United Nations may respectively be parties.
2. Paragraph 1 of this Article shall not be interpreted as giving grounds for delay or postponement of the negotiation and conclusion of agreements for placing mandated and other territories under the trusteeship system as provided for in Article 77.

Article 81

The trusteeship agreement shall in each case include the terms under which the trust territory will be administered and designate the authority which will exercise the administration of the trust territory. Such authority, hereinafter called the administering authority, may be one or more states or the Organization itself.

Article 82

There may be designated, in any trusteeship agreement, a strategic area or

areas which may include part or all of the trust territory to which the agreement applies, without prejudice to any special agreement or agreements made under Article 43.

Article 83

1. All functions of the United Nations relating to strategic areas, including the approval of the terms of the trusteeship agreements and of their alteration or amendment, shall be exercised by the Security Council.

2. The basic objectives set forth in Article 76 shall be applicable to the people of each strategic area.

3. The Security Council shall, subject to the provisions of the trusteeship agreements and without prejudice to security considerations, avail itself of the assistance of the Trusteeship Council to perform those functions of the United Nations under the trusteeship system relating to political, economic, social, and educational matters in the strategic areas.

Article 84

It shall be the duty of the administering authority to ensure that the trust territory shall play its part in the maintenance of international peace and security. To this end the administering authority may make use of volunteer forces, facilities, and assistance from the trust territory in carrying out the obligations towards the Security Council undertaken in this regard by the administering authority, as well as for local defense and the maintenance of law and order within the trust territory.

Article 85

1. The functions of the United Nations with regard to trusteeship agreements for all areas not designated as strategic, including the approval of the terms of the trusteeship agreements and of their alteration or amendment, shall be exercised by the General Assembly.

2. The Trusteeship Council, operating under the authority of the General Assembly, shall assist the General Assembly in carrying out these functions.

B. THE INTERNATIONAL BILL OF RIGHTS

INTRODUCTION

The three documents that follow are often referred to collectively as the "International Bill of Rights."[10] Work commenced on drafting the Universal Declaration of Human Rights at the very beginning of the life of the UN. The Declaration codifies in solemn form not only the traditional civil and political rights such as equality before the law, freedom from arbitrary arrest, detention and exile, the presumption of innocence and freedom of speech and assembly, but also the "newer" economic, social and cultural rights—such as the right to social security, the right to work and the rights to adequate health care and education. It was adopted on December 10, 1948 without dissent by a vote of 48 to 0 with 8 abstentions (Byelorussian S.S.R., Czechoslavakia, Poland, Saudi Arabia, Ukrainian S.S.R., U.S.S.R., Union of South Africa and Yugoslavia). By the terms of its preamble, the Declaration describes itself as "a common standard of achievement for all peoples and all nations,"[11] language that hardly attests to its legal effect. Nevertheless, many scholars have argued that it has entered the body of international law, either as an authoritative interpretation of the human rights provisions of the Charter or, by virtue of its many re-citations by the General Assembly both in general and in specific cases, as part of the body of international customary law. Be that as it may, it was understood that the Declaration would be followed by the drafting of an instrument or instruments of indisputably legal effect that would also contain some enforcement procedures. (The Declaration is silent on the matter of enforcement.) In 1949, work began on what became the two Covenants and the Optional Protocol to the Covenant on Civil and Political Rights (this latter document is discussed in Chapter IV). It proved to be a long and tedious business which was not completed until December, 1966 when the Covenants were approved by the General Assembly and opened for signature and ratification. Sufficient ratifications (35) were obtained to bring both Covenants into force in 1976. At the time of writing there are 65 parties to the Covenant on Economic, Social and Cultural Rights and 63 to that on Civil and Political Rights.

The content of the two Covenants is fairly similar to that of the Universal Declaration although more detailed language is sometimes used. There are, however, a few instances of omissions of rights contained in the Universal Declaration (such as the right to own property contained in Article 17 of the Declaration) and one significant addition. The addition is common Article 1 of the two Covenants which speaks of the "right" of "all peoples" to self-determination. Its inclusion and location at the outset of the Covenants dramatically symbolized the changing forces in the United Nations and the enormous importance of decolonization in the work of the organization.

The drafting of separate Covenants reflects two important considerations. First was the feeling that the different kinds of rights involved require different kinds of supervisory procedures. (See *infra* Chapter IV on these procedures.) Second was the understanding that, while a state which becomes party to the

Covenant of Civil and Political Rights should be in a position to guarantee those rights immediately to all persons within its jurisdiction, somewhat more latitude is appropriate with regard to economic, social and cultural rights. Thus, Article 2 of the Covenant on Economic, Social and Cultural Rights, which has no counterpart in the other Covenant, obligates each state party to "take steps, individually and through international assistance and cooperation, especially economic and technical, to the maximum of its available resources, with a view to achieving progressively the full realization of the rights recognized in the present Covenant. . . . "

On the International Bill of Rights in general, *see* H. Lauterpacht, *International Law and Human Rights* (1950), (the classic work); J. Carey, *U.N. Protection of Civil and Political Rights* (1970); L. Sohn, "A Short History of United Nations Documents on Human Rights" in, *Commission to Study the Organization of Peace, the United Nations and Human Rights* 39 (1968); R. Clark and L. Nevas, "The First Twenty-Five Years of the Universal Declaration of Human Rights and the Next," 48 Conn. B.J. 111 (1974).

For an examination of the practice of the Supervisory Committee under the Covenant on Civil and Political Rights, suggesting that it seems to be content with "progressive development," *see*, F. Jhabvala, " The Practice of the Covenant's Human Rights Committee, 1976–1982: Review of State Party Reports," 6 Human Rights Q. 81 (1984).

1. UNIVERSAL DECLARATION OF HUMAN RIGHTS

(1948) G.A. Res. 217A (III), 3(1) U.N. GAOR Resolutions 71, U.N. Doc. A/810 (1948)

PREAMBLE

Whereas recognition of the inherent dignity and of the equal and inalienable rights of all members of the human family is the foundation of freedom, justice and peace in the world,

Whereas disregard and contempt for human rights have resulted in barbarous acts which have outraged the conscience of mankind, and the advent of a world in which human beings shall enjoy freedom of speech and belief and freedom from fear and want has been proclaimed as the highest aspiration of the common people,

Whereas it is essential, if man is not to be compelled to have recourse, as a last resort, to rebellion against tyranny and oppression, that human rights should be protected by the rule of law,

Whereas it is essential to promote the development of friendly relations between nations,

Whereas the peoples of the United Nations have in the Charter reaffirmed their faith in fundamental human rights, in the dignity and worth of the human person and in the equal rights of men and women and have determined to promote social progress and better standards of life in larger freedom,

Whereas Member States have pledged themselves to achieve, in co-operation with the United Nations, the promotion of universal respect for and observance of human rights and fundamental freedoms,

Whereas a common understanding of these rights and freedoms is of the greatest importance for the full realization of this pledge,

Now, therefore,

THE GENERAL ASSEMBLY

Proclaims this Universal Declaration of Human Rights as a common standard of achievement for all peoples and all nations, to the end that every individual and every organ of society, keeping this Declaration constantly in mind, shall strive by teaching and education to promote respect for these rights and freedoms and by progressive measures, national and international, to secure their universal and effective recognition and observance, both among the peoples of Member States themselves and among the peoples of territories under their jurisdiction.

Article 1

All human beings are born free and equal in dignity and rights. They are endowed with reason and conscience and should act towards one another in a spirit of brotherhood.

Article 2

Everyone is entitled to all the rights and freedoms set forth in this Declaration, without distinction of any kind, such as race, colour, sex, language, religion, political or other opinion, national or social origin, property, birth or other status.

Furthermore, no distinction shall be made on the basis of the political, jurisdictional or international status of the country or territory to which a person belongs, whether it be independent, trust, non-self-governing or under any other limitation of sovereignty.

Article 3

Everyone has the right to life, liberty and security of person.

Article 4

No one shall be held in slavery or servitude; slavery and the slave trade shall be prohibited in all their forms.

Article 5

No one shall be subjected to torture or to cruel, inhuman or degrading treatment or punishment.

Article 6

Everyone has the right to recognition everywhere as a person before the law.

Article 7

All are equal before the law and are entitled without any discrimination to equal protection of the law. All are entitled to equal protection against any discrimination in violation of this Declaration and against any incitement to such discrimination.

Article 8

Everyone has the right to an effective remedy by the competent national tribunals for acts violating the fundamental rights granted him by the constitution or by law.

Article 9

No one shall be subjected to arbitrary arrest, detention or exile.

Article 10

Everyone is entitled in full equality to a fair and public hearing by an independent and impartial tribunal, in the determination of his rights and obligations and of any criminal charge against him.

Article 11

1. Everyone charged with a penal offence has the right to be presumed innocent until proved guilty according to law in a public trial at which he has had all the guarantees necessary for his defence.
2. No one shall be held guilty of any penal offence on account of any act or omission which did not constitute a penal offence, under national or international law, at the time when it was committed. Nor shall a heavier penalty be imposed than the one that was applicable at the time the penal offence was committed.

Article 12

No one shall be subjected to arbitrary interference with his privacy, family, home or correspondence, nor to attacks upon his honour and reputation. Everyone has the right to the protection of the law against such interference or attacks.

Article 13

1. Everyone has the right to freedom of movement and residence within the borders of each State.
2. Everyone has the right to leave any country, including his own, and to return to his country.

Article 14

1. Everyone has the right to seek and to enjoy in other countries asylum from persecution.
2. This right may not be invoked in the case of prosecutions genuinely

arising from non-political crimes or from acts contrary to the purposes and principles of the United Nations.

Article 15

1. Everyone has the right to a nationality.
2. No one shall be arbitrarily deprived of his nationality nor denied the right to change his nationality.

Article 16

1. Men and women of full age, without any limitation due to race, nationality or religion, have the right to marry and to found a family. They are entitled to equal rights as to marriage, during marriage and at its dissolution.
2. Marriage shall be entered into only with the free and full consent of the intending spouses.
3. The family is the natural and fundamental group unit of society and is entitled to protection by society and the State.

Article 17

1. Everyone has the right to own property alone as well as in association with others.
2. No one shall be arbitrarily deprived of his property.

Article 18

Everyone has the right to freedom of thought, conscience and religion; this right includes freedom to change his religion or belief, and freedom, either alone or in community with others and in public or private, to manifest his religion or belief in teaching, practice, worship and observance.

Article 19

Everyone has the right to freedom of opinion and expression; this right includes freedom to hold opinions without interference and to seek, receive and impart information and ideas through any media and regardless of frontiers.

Article 20

1. Everyone has the right to freedom of peaceful assembly and association.
2. No one may be compelled to belong to an association.

Article 21

1. Everyone has the right to take part in the government of his country, directly or through freely chosen representatives.
2. Everyone has the right of equal access to public service in his country.
3. The will of the people shall be the basis of the authority of government; this will shall be expressed in periodic and genuine elections which shall be by universal and equal suffrage and shall be held by secret vote or by equivalent free voting procedures.

Article 22

Everyone, as a member of society, has the right to social security and is entitled to realization, through national effort and international co-operation and in accordance with the organization and resources of each State, of the economic, social and cultural rights indispensable for his dignity and the free development of his personality.

Article 23

1. Everyone has the right to work, to free choice of employment, to just and favourable conditions of work and to protection against unemployment.

2. Everyone, without any discrimination, has the right to equal pay for equal work.

3. Everyone who works has the right to just and favourable remuneration ensuring for himself and his family an existence worthy of human dignity, and supplemented, if necessary, by other means of social protection.

4. Everyone has the right to form and to join trade unions for the protection of his interests.

Article 24

Everyone has the right to rest and leisure, including reasonable limitation of working hours and periodic holidays with pay.

Article 25

1. Everyone has the right to a standard of living adequate for the health and well-being of himself and of his family, including food, clothing, housing and medical care and necessary social services, and the right to security in the event of unemployment, sickness, disability, widowhood, old age or other lack of livelihood in circumstances beyond his control.

2. Motherhood and childhood are entitled to special care and assistance. All children, whether born in or out of wedlock, shall enjoy the same social protection.

Article 26

1. Everyone has the right to education. Education shall be free, at least in the elementary and fundamental stages. Elementary education shall be compulsory. Technical and professional education shall be made generally available and higher education shall be equally accessible to all on the basis of merit.

2. Education shall be directed to the full development of the human personality and to the strengthening of respect for human rights and fundamental freedoms. It shall promote understanding, tolerance and friendship among all nations, racial or religious groups, and shall further the activities of the United Nations for the maintenance of peace.

3. Parents have a prior right to choose the kind of education that shall be given to their children.

Article 27

1. Everyone has the right freely to participate in the cultural life of the

community, to enjoy the arts and to share in scientific advancement and its benefits.

2. Everyone has the right to the protection of the moral and material interests resulting from any scientific, literary or artistic production of which he is the author.

Article 28

Everyone is entitled to a social and international order in which the rights and freedoms set forth in this Declaration can be fully realized.

Article 29

1. Everyone has duties to the community in which alone the free and full development of his personality is possible.

2. In the exercise of his rights and freedoms, everyone shall be subject only to such limitations as are determined by law solely for the purpose of securing due recognition and respect for the rights and freedoms of others and of meeting the just requirements of morality, public order and the general welfare in a democratic society.

3. These rights and freedoms may in no case be exercised contrary to the purposes and principles of the United Nations.

Article 30

Nothing in this Declaration may be interpreted as implying for any State, group or person any right to engage in any activity or to perform any act aimed at the destruction of any of the rights and freedoms set forth herein.

2. INTERNATIONAL COVENANT ON ECONOMIC, SOCIAL AND CULTURAL RIGHTS (1966) G.A. Res. 2200 (XXI), 21 U.N. GAOR, Supp. (No. 16) at 49, U.N. Doc. A/6316 (1966). In force 3 January 1976 in accordance with Article 27 .

PREAMBLE

THE STATES PARTIES TO THE PRESENT COVENANT,

Considering that, in accordance with the principles proclaimed in the Charter of the United Nations, recognition of the inherent dignity and of the equal and inalienable rights of all members of the human family is the foundation of freedom, justice and peace in the world,

Recognizing that these rights derive from the inherent dignity of the human person,

Recognizing that, in accordance with the Universal Declaration of Human Rights, the ideal of free human beings enjoying freedom from fear and want can only be achieved if conditions are created whereby everyone may enjoy his economic, social and cultural rights, as well as his civil and political rights,

Considering the obligation of States under the Charter of the United Nations to promote universal respect for, and observance of, human rights and freedoms,

Realizing that the individual, having duties to other individuals and to the community to which he belongs, is under a responsibility to strive for the promotion and observance of the rights recognized in the present Covenant,

Agree upon the following articles:

PART I

Article 1

1. All peoples have the right of self-determination. By virtue of that right they freely determine their political status and freely pursue their economic, social and cultural development.

2. All peoples may, for their own ends, freely dispose of their natural wealth and resources without prejudice to any obligations arising out of international economic co-operation, based upon the principle of mutual benefit, and international law. In no case may a people be deprived of its own means of subsistence.

3. The States Parties to the present Covenant, including those having responsibility for the administration of Non-Self-Governing and Trust Territories, shall promote the realization of the right of self-determination, and shall respect that right, in conformity with the provisions of the Charter of the United Nations.

PART II

Article 2

1. Each State Party to the present Covenant undertakes to take steps, individually and through international assistance and co-operation, especially economic and technical, to the maximum of its available resources, with a view to achieving progressively the full realization of the rights recognized in the present Covenant by all appropriate means, including particularly the adoption of legislative measures.

2. The States Parties to the present Covenant undertake to guarantee that the rights enunciated in the present Covenant will be exercised without discrimination of any kind as to race, colour, sex, language, religion, political or other opinion, national or social origin, property, birth or other status.

3. Developing countries, with due regard to human rights and their national economy, may determine to what extent they would guarantee the economic rights recognized in the present Covenant to non-nationals.

Article 3

The States Parties to the present Covenant undertake to ensure the equal right of men and women to the enjoyment of all economic, social and cultural rights set forth in the present Covenant.

Article 4

The States Parties to the present Covenant recognize that, in the enjoyment of those rights provided by the State in conformity with the present Covenant, the State may subject such rights only to such limitations as are determined by law only in so far as this may be compatible with the nature of these rights and solely for the purpose of promoting the general welfare in a democratic society.

Article 5

1. Nothing in the present Covenant may be interpreted as implying for any State, group or person any right to engage in any activity or to perform any act aimed at the destruction of any of the rights or freedoms recognized herein, or at their limitation to a greater extent than is provided for in the present Covenant.

2. No restriction upon or derogation from any of the fundamental human rights recognized or existing in any country in virtue of law, conventions, regulations or custom shall be admitted on the pretext that the present Covenant does not recognize such rights or that it recognizes them to a lesser extent.

PART III

Article 6

1. The States Parties to the present Covenant recognize the right to work, which includes the right of everyone to the opportunity to gain his living by work which he freely chooses or accepts, and will take appropriate steps to safeguard this right.

2. The steps to be taken by a State Party to the present Covenant to achieve the full realization of this right shall include technical and vocational guidance and training programmes, policies and techniques to achieve steady economic, social and cultural development and full and productive employment under conditions safeguarding fundamental political and economic freedoms to the individual.

Article 7

The States Parties to the present Covenant recognize the right of everyone to the enjoyment of just and favourable conditions of work which ensure, in particular:

a. Remuneration which provides all workers, as a minimum, with:

i. Fair wages and equal remuneration for work of equal value without distinction of any kind, in particular women being guaranteed conditions of work not inferior to those enjoyed by men, with equal pay for equal work;

ii. A decent living for themselves and their families in accordance with the provisions of the present Covenant;

b. Safe and healthy working conditions;

c. Equal opportunity for everyone to be promoted in his employ- ment to an appropriate higher level, subject to no considerations other than those of seniority and competence;

d. Rest, leisure and reasonable limitation of working hours and periodic holidays with pay, as well as remuneration for public holidays.

Article 8

1. The States Parties to the present Covenant undertake to ensure:

a. The right of everyone to form trade unions and join the trade union of his choice, subject only to the rules of the organization concerned, for the promotion and protection of his economic and social interests. No restrictions may be placed on the exercise of this right other than those prescribed by law and which are necessary in a democratic society in the interests of national security or public order or for the protection of the rights and freedoms of others;

b. The right of trade unions to establish national federations or confederations and the right of the latter to form or join international trade-union organizations;

c. The right of trade unions to function freely subject to no limitations other than those prescribed by law and which are necessary in a democratic society in the interests of national security or public order or for the protection of the rights and freedoms of others;

d. The right to strike, provided that it is exercised in conformity with the laws of the particular country.

2. This article shall not prevent the imposition of lawful restrictions on the exercise of these rights by members of the armed forces or of the police or of the administration of the State.

3. Nothing in this article shall authorize States Parties to the International Labour Organisation Convention of 1948 concerning Freedom of Association and Protection of the Right to Organize to take legislative measures which would prejudice, or apply the law in such a manner as would prejudice, the guarantees provided for in that Convention.

Article 9

The States Parties to the present Covenant recognize the right of everyone to social security, including social insurance.

Article 10

The States Parties to the present Covenant recognize that:

1. The widest possible protection and assistance should be accorded to the family, which is the natural and fundamental group unit of society, particularly for its establishment and while it is responsible for the care and education of dependent children. Marriage must be entered into with the free consent of the intending spouses.

2. Special protection should be accorded to mothers during a reasonable period before and after childbirth. During such period working mothers should be accorded paid leave or leave with adequate social security benefits.

3. Special measures of protection and assistance should be taken on behalf of all children and young persons without any discrimination for reasons of

parentage or other conditions. Children and young persons should be protected from economic and social exploitation. Their employment in work harmful to their morals or health or dangerous to life or likely to hamper their normal development should be punishable by law. States should also set age limits below which the paid employment of child labour should be prohibited and punishable by law.

Article 11

1. The States Parties to the present Covenant recognize the right of everyone to an adequate standard of living for himself and his family, including adequate food, clothing and housing, and to the continuous improvement of living conditions. The States Parties will take appropriate steps to ensure the realization of this right, recognizing to this effect the essential importance of international co-operation based on free consent.

2. The States Parties to the present Covenant, recognizing the fundamental right of everyone to be free from hunger, shall take, individually and through international co-operation, the measures, including specific programmes, which are needed:

a. To improve methods of production, conservation and distribution of food by making full use of technical and scientific knowledge, by disseminating knowledge of the principles of nutrition and by developing or reforming agrarian systems in such a way as to achieve the most efficient development and utilization of natural resources;

b. Taking into account the problems of both food-importing and food-exporting countries, to ensure an equitable distribution of world food supplies in relation to need.

Article 12

1. The States Parties to the present Covenant recognize the right of everyone to the enjoyment of the highest attainable standard of physical and mental health.

2. The steps to be taken by the States Parties to the present Covenant to achieve the full realization of this right shall include those necessary for:

a. The provision for the reduction of the stillbirthrate and of infant mortality and for the healthy development of the child;

b. The improvement of all aspects of environmental and industrial hygiene;

c. The prevention, treatment and control of epidemic, endemic, occupational and other diseases;

d. The creation of conditions which would assure to all medical service and medical attention in the event of sickness.

Article 13

1. The States Parties to the present Covenant recognize the right of everyone to education. They agree that education shall be directed to the full development of the human personality and the sense of its dignity, and shall strengthen the respect for human rights and fundamental freedoms. They

further agree that education shall enable all persons to participate effectively in a free society, promote understanding, tolerance and friendship among all nations and all racial, ethnic or religious groups, and further the activities of the United Nations for the maintenance of peace.

2. The States Parties to the present Covenant recognize that, with a view to achieving the full realization of this right:

a. Primary education shall be compulsory and available free to all;

b. Secondary education in its different forms, including technical and vocational secondary education, shall be made generally available and accessible to all by every appropriate means, and in particular by the progressive introduction of free education;

c. Higher education shall be made equally accessible to all, on the basis of capacity, by every appropriate means, and in particular by the progressive introduction of free education;

d. Fundamental education shall be encouraged or intensified as far as possible for those persons who have not received or completed the whole period of their primary education;

e. The development of a system of schools at all levels shall be actively pursued, an adequate fellowship system shall be established, and the material conditions of teaching staff shall be continuously improved.

3. The States Parties to the present Covenant undertake to have respect for the liberty of parents and, when applicable, legal guardians to choose for their children schools, other than those established by the public authorities, which conform to such minimum educational standards as may be laid down or approved by the State and to ensure the religious and moral education of their children in conformity with their own convictions.

4. No part of this article shall be construed so as to interfere with the liberty of individuals and bodies to establish and direct educational institutions, subject always to the observance of the principles set forth in paragraph 1 of this article and to the requirement that the education given in such institutions shall conform to such minimum standards as may be laid down by the State.

Article 14

Each State Party to the present Covenant which, at the time of becoming a Party, has not been able to secure in its metropolitan territory or other territories under its jurisdiction compulsory primary education, free of charge, undertakes, within two years, to work out and adopt a detailed plan of action for the progressive implementation, within a reasonable number of years, to be fixed in the plan, of the principle of compulsory education free of charge for all.

Article 15

1. The States Parties to the present Covenant recognize the right of everyone:

a. To take part in cultural life;

b. To enjoy the benefits of scientific progress and its applications;

c. To benefit from the protection of the moral and material interests resulting from any scientific, literary or artistic production of which he is the author.

2. The steps to be taken by the States Parties to the present Covenant to achieve the full realization of this right shall include those necessary for the conservation, the development and the diffusion of science and culture.

3. The States Parties to the present Covenant undertake to respect the freedom indispensable for scientific research and creative activity.

4. The States Parties to the present Covenant recognize the benefits to be derived from the encouragement and development of international contacts and co-operation in the scientific and cultural fields.

* * *

[For omitted procedural provisions, Articles 16–25, see below, Chapter IV.A.4.]

Article 25

Nothing in the present Covenant shall be interpreted as impairing the inherent right of all peoples to enjoy and utilize fully and freely their natural wealth and resources.

PART V

Article 26

1. The present Covenant is open for signature by any State Member of the United Nations or member of any of its specialized agencies, by any State Party to the Statute of the International Court of Justice, and by any other State which has been invited by the General Assembly of the United Nations to become a party to the present Covenant.

2. The present Covenant is subject to ratification. Instruments of ratification shall be deposited with the Secretary-General of the United Nations.

3. The present Covenant shall be open to accession by any State referred to in paragraph 1 of this article.

4. Accession shall be effected by the deposit of an instrument of accession with the Secretary-General of the United Nations.

5. The Secretary-General of the United Nations shall inform all States which have signed the present Covenant or acceded to it of the deposit of each instrument of ratification or accession.

Article 27

1. The present Covenant shall enter into force three months after the date of the deposit with the Secretary-General of the United Nations of the thirty-fifth instrument of ratification or instrument of accession.

2. For each State ratifying the present Covenant or acceding to it after the deposit of the thirty-fifth instrument of ratification or instrument of accession, the present Covenant shall enter into force three months after the date of the deposit of its own instrument of ratification or instrument of accession.

Article 28

The provisions of the present Covenant shall extend to all parts of federal States without any limitations or exceptions.

Article 29

1. Any State Party to the present Covenant may propose an amendment and file it with the Secretary-General of the United Nations. The Secretary-General shall thereupon communicate any proposed amendments to the States Parties to the present Covenant with a request that they notify him whether they favour a conference of States Parties for the purpose of considering and voting upon the proposals. In the event that at least one third of the States Parties favours such a conference, the Secretary-General shall convene the conference under the auspices of the United Nations. Any amendment adopted by a majority of the States Parties present and voting at the conference shall be submitted to the General Assembly of the United Nations for approval.

2. Amendments shall come into force when they have been approved by the General Assembly of the United Nations and accepted by a two-thirds majority of the States Parties to the present Covenant in accordance with their respective constitutional processes.

3. When amendments come into force they shall be binding on those States Parties which have accepted them, other States Parties still being bound by the provisions of the present Covenant and any earlier amendment which they have accepted.

Article 30

Irrespective of the notifications made under article 26, paragraph 5, the Secretary-General of the United Nations shall inform all States referred to in paragraph 1 of the same article of the following particulars:

a. Signatures, ratifications and accessions under article 26;

b. The date of the entry into force of the present Covenant under article 27 and the date of the entry into force of any amendments under article 29.

Article 31

1. The present Covenant, of which the Chinese, English, French, Russian and Spanish texts are equally authentic, shall be deposited in the archives of the United Nations.

2. The Secretary-General of the United Nations shall transmit certified copies of the present Covenant to all States referred to in article 26.

3. INTERNATIONAL COVENANT ON CIVIL AND POLITICAL RIGHTS (1966) G.A. Res. 2200 (XXI), 21 U.N. GAOR, Supp. (No. 16) at 52, U.N. Doc. A/6316 (1966). In force 23 March 1976 in accordance with Article 49.

PREAMBLE

THE STATES PARTIES TO THE PRESENT COVENANT,

Considering that, in accordance with the principles proclaimed in the

Charter of the United Nations, recognition of the inherent dignity and of the equal and inalienable rights of all members of the human family is the foundation of freedom, justice and peace in the world,

Recognizing that these rights derive from the inherent dignity of the human person,

Recognizing that, in accordance with the Universal Declaration of Human Rights, the ideal of free human beings enjoying civil and political freedom and freedom from fear and want can only be achieved if conditions are created whereby everyone may enjoy his civil and political rights, as well as his economic, social and cultural rights,

Considering the obligation of States under the Charter of the United Nations to promote universal respect for, and observance of, human rights and freedoms,

Realizing that the individual, having duties to other individuals and to the community to which he belongs, is under a responsibility to strive for the promotion and observance of the rights recognized in the present Covenant,

Agree upon the following articles:

PART I

Article 1

1. All peoples have the right of self-determination. By virtue of that right they freely determine their political status and freely pursue their economic, social and cultural development.

2. All peoples may, for their own ends, freely dispose of their natural wealth and resources without prejudice to any obligations arising out of international economic co-operation, based upon the principle of mutual benefit, and international law. In no case may a people be deprived of its own means of subsistence.

3. The States Parties to the present Covenant, including those having responsibility for the administration of Non-Self-Governing and Trust Territories, shall promote the realization of the right of self-determination, and shall respect that right, in conformity with the provisions of the Charter of the United Nations.

PART II

Article 2

1. Each State Party to the present Covenant undertakes to respect and to ensure to all individuals within its territory and subject to its jurisdiction the rights recognized in the present Covenant, without distinction of any kind, such as race, colour, sex, language, religion, political or other opinion, national or social origin, property, birth or other status.

2. Where not already provided for by existing legislative or other measures, each State Party to the present Covenant undertakes to take the necessary steps, in accordance with its constitutional processes and with the provisions of the

present Covenant, to adopt such legislative or other measures as may be necessary to give effect to the rights recognized in the present Covenant.

3. Each State Party to the present Covenant undertakes:

a. To ensure that any person whose rights or freedoms as herein recognized are violated shall have an effective remedy, notwithstanding that the violation has been committed by persons acting in an official capacity;

b. To ensure that any person claiming such a remedy shall have his right thereto determined by competent judicial, administrative or legislative authorities, or by any other competent authority provided for by the legal system of the State, and to develop the possibilities of judicial remedy;

c. To ensure that the competent authorities shall enforce such remedies when granted.

Article 3

The States Parties to the present Covenant undertake to ensure the equal right of men and women to the enjoyment of all civil and political rights set forth in the present Covenant.

Article 4

1. In time of public emergency which threatens the life of the nation and the existence of which is officially proclaimed, the States Parties to the present Covenant may take measures derogating from their obligations under the present Covenant to the extent strictly required by the exigencies of the situation, provided that such measures are not inconsistent with their other obligations under international law and do not involve discrimination solely on the ground of race, colour, sex, language, religion or social origin.

2. No derogation from articles 6, 7, 8 (paragraphs 1 and 2), 11, 15, 16 and 18 may be made under this provision.

3. Any State Party to the present Covenant availing itself of the right of derogation shall immediately inform the other States Parties to the present Covenant, through the intermediary of the Secretary-General of the United Nations, of the provisions from which it has derogated and of the reasons by which it was actuated. A further communication shall be made, through the same intermediary, on the date on which it terminates such derogation.

Article 5

1. Nothing in the present Covenant may be interpreted as implying for any State, group or person any right to engage in any activity or perform any act aimed at the destruction of any of the rights and freedoms recognized herein or at their limitation to a greater extent than is provided for in the present Covenant.

2. There shall be no restriction upon or derogation from any of the fundamental human rights recognized or existing in any State Party to the present Covenant pursuant to law, conventions, regulations or custom on the pretext that the present Covenant does not recognize such rights or that it recognizes them to a lesser extent.

PART III

Article 6

1. Every human being has the inherent right to life. This right shall be protected by law. No one shall be arbitrarily deprived of his life.

2. In countries which have not abolished the death penalty, sentence of death may be imposed only for the most serious crimes in accordance with the law in force at the time of the commission of the crime and not contrary to the provisions of the present Covenant and to the Convention on the Prevention and Punishment of the Crime of Genocide. This penalty can only be carried out pursuant to a final judgement rendered by a competent court.

3. When deprivation of life constitutes the crime of genocide, it is understood that nothing in this article shall authorize any State Party to the present Covenant to derogate in any way from any obligation assumed under the provisions of the Convention on the Prevention and Punishment of the Crime of Genocide.

4. Anyone sentenced to death shall have the right to seek pardon or commutation of the sentence. Amnesty, pardon or commutation of the sentence of death may be granted in all cases.

5. Sentence of death shall not be imposed for crimes committed by persons below eighteen years of age and shall not be carried out on pregnant women.

6. Nothing in this article shall be invoked to delay or to prevent the abolition of capital punishment by any State Party to the present Covenant.

Article 7

No one shall be subjected to torture or to cruel, inhuman or degrading treatment or punishment. In particular, no one shall be subjected without his free consent to medical experimentation.

Article 8

1. No one shall be held in slavery; slavery and the slave-trade in all their forms shall be prohibited.

2. No one shall be held in servitude.

3. a. No one shall be required to perform forced or compulsory labour;

   b. Paragraph 3 (*a*) shall not be held to preclude, in countries where imprisonment with hard labour may be imposed as a punishment for a crime, the performance of hard labour in pursuance of a sentence to such punishment by a competent court;

   c. For the purpose of this paragraph the term "forced or compulsory labor" shall not include:

   i. Any work or service, not referred to in subparagraph (*b*), normally required of a person who is under detention in consequence of a lawful order of a court, or of a person during conditional release from such detention;

   ii. Any service of a military character and, in countries where conscientious objection is recognized, any national service required by law of conscientious objectors;

iii. Any service exacted in cases of emergency or calamity threatening the life or well-being of the community;

iv. Any work or service which forms part of normal civil obligations.

Article 9

1. Everyone has the right to liberty and security of person. No one shall be subjected to arbitrary arrest or detention. No one shall be deprived of his liberty except on such grounds and in accordance with such procedure as are established by law.

2. Anyone who is arrested shall be informed, at the time of arrest, of the reasons for his arrest and shall be promptly informed of any charges against him.

3. Anyone arrested or detained on a criminal charge shall be brought promptly before a judge or other officer authorized by law to exercise judicial power and shall be entitled to trial within a reasonable time or to release. It shall not be the general rule that persons awaiting trial shall be detained in custody, but release may be subject to guarantees to appear for trial, at any other stage of the judicial proceedings, and, should occasion arise, for execution of the judgement.

4. Anyone who is deprived of his liberty by arrest or detention shall be entitled to take proceedings before a court, in order that that court may decide without delay on the lawfulness of his detention and order his release if the detention is not lawful.

5. Anyone who has been the victim of unlawful arrest or detention shall have an enforceable right to compensation.

Article 10

1. All persons deprived of their liberty shall be treated with humanity and with respect for the inherent dignity of the human person.

2. a. Accused persons shall, save in exceptional circumstances, be segregated from convicted persons and shall be subject to separate treatment appropriate to their status as unconvicted persons;

b. Accused juvenile persons shall be separated from adults and brought as speedily as possible for adjudication.

3. The penitentiary system shall comprise treatment of prisoners the essential aim of which shall be their reformation and social rehabilitation. Juvenile offenders shall be segregated from adults and be accorded treatment appropriate to their age and legal status.

Article 11

No one shall be imprisoned merely on the ground of inability to fulfil a contractual obligation.

Article 12

1. Everyone lawfully within the territory of a State shall, within that territory, have the right to liberty of movement and freedom to choose his residence.

2. Everyone shall be free to leave any country, including his own.

3. The above-mentioned rights shall not be subject to any restrictions except those which are provided by law, are necessary to protect national security, public order (*ordre public*), public health or morals or the rights and freedoms of others, and are consistent with the other rights recognized in the present Covenant.

4. No one shall be arbitrarily deprived of the right to enter his own country.

Article 13

An alien lawfully in the territory of a State Party to the present Covenant may be expelled therefrom only in pursuance of a decision reached in accordance with law and shall, except where compelling reasons of national security otherwise require, be allowed to submit the reasons against his expulsion and to have his case reviewed by, and be represented for the purpose before, the competent authority or a person or persons especially designated by the competent authority.

Article 14

1. All persons shall be equal before the courts and tribunals. In the determination of any criminal charge against him, or of his rights and obligations in a suit at law, everyone shall be entitled to a fair and public hearing by a competent, independent and impartial tribunal established by law. The Press and the public may be excluded from all or part of a trial for reasons of morals, public order (*ordre public*) or national security in a democratic society, or when the interest of the private lives of the parties so requires, or to the extent strictly necessary in the opinion of the court in special circumstances where publicity would prejudice the interests of justice; but any judgement rendered in a criminal case or in a suit at law shall be made public except where the interest of juvenile persons otherwise requires or the proceedings concern matrimonial disputes or the guardianship of children.

2. Everyone charged with a criminal offence shall have the right to be presumed innocent until proved guilty according to law.

3. In the determination of any criminal charge against him, everyone shall be entitled to the following minimum guarantees, in full equality:

a. To be informed promptly and in detail in a language which he understands of the nature and cause of the charge against him;

b. To have adequate time and facilities for the preparation of his defence and to communicate with counsel of his own choosing;

c. To be tried without undue delay;

d. To be tried in his presence, and to defend himself in person or through legal assistance of his own choosing; to be informed, if he does not have legal assistance, of this right; and to have legal assistance assigned to him, in any case where the interests of justice so require, and without payment by him in any such case if he does not have sufficient means to pay for it;

e. To examine, or have examined, the witnesses against him and to obtain the attendance and examination of witnesses on his behalf under the same conditions as witnesses against him;

f. To have the free assistance of an interpreter if he cannot understand or speak the language used in court;

g. Not to be compelled to testify against himself or to confess guilt.

4. In the case of juvenile persons, the procedure shall be such as will take account of their age and the desirability of promoting their rehabilitation.

5. Everyone convicted of a crime shall have the right to his conviction and sentence being reviewed by a higher tribunal according to law.

6. When a person has by a final decision been convicted of a criminal offence and when subsequently his conviction has been reversed or he has been pardoned on the ground that a new or newly discovered fact shows conclusively that there has been a miscarriage of justice, the person who has suffered punishment as a result of such conviction shall be compensated according to law, unless it is proved that the non-disclosure of the unknown fact in time is wholly or partly attributable to him.

7. No one shall be liable to be tried or punished again for an offence for which he has already been finally convicted or acquitted in accordance with the law and penal procedure of each country.

Article 15

1. No one shall be held guilty of any criminal offence on account of any act or omission which did not constitute a criminal offence, under national or international law, at the time when it was committed. Nor shall a heavier penalty be imposed than the one that was applicable at the time when the criminal offence was committed. If, subsequent to the commission of the offence, provision is made by law for the imposition of the lighter penalty, the offender shall benefit thereby.

2. Nothing in this article shall prejudice the trial and punishment of any person for any act or omission which, at the time when it was committed, was criminal according to the general principles of law recognized by the community of nations.

Article 16

Everyone shall have the right to recognition everywhere as a person before the law.

Article 17

1. No one shall be subjected to arbitrary or unlawful interference with his privacy, family, home or correspondence, nor to unlawful attacks on his honour and reputation.

2. Everyone has the right to the protection of the law against such interference or attacks.

Article 18

1. Everyone shall have the right to freedom of thought, conscience and religion. This right shall include freedom to have or to adopt a religion or belief

of his choice, and freedom, either individually or in community with others and in public or private, to manifest his religion or belief in worship, observance, practice and teaching.

2. No one shall be subject to coercion which would impair his freedom to have or to adopt a religion or belief of his choice.

3. Freedom to manifest one's religion or beliefs may be subject only to such limitations as are prescribed by law and are necessary to protect public safety, order, health, or morals or the fundamental rights and freedoms of others.

4. The States Parties to the present Covenant undertake to have respect for the liberty of parents and, when applicable, legal guardians to ensure the religious and moral education of their children in conformity with their own convictions.

Article 19

1. Everyone shall have the right to hold opinions without interference.

2. Everyone shall have the right to freedom of expression; this right shall include freedom to seek, receive and impart information and ideas of all kinds, regardless of frontiers, either orally, in writing or in print, in the form of art, or through any other media of his choice.

3. The exercise of the rights provided for in paragraph 2 of this article carries with it special duties and responsibilities. It may therefore be subject to certain restrictions, but these shall only be such as are provided by law and are necessary:

a. For respect of the rights or reputations of others;

b. For the protection of national security or of public order (*ordre public*), or of public health or morals.

Article 20

1. Any propaganda for war shall be prohibited by law.

2. Any advocacy of national, racial or religious hatred that constitutes incitement to discrimination, hostility or violence shall be prohibited by law.

Article 21

The right of peaceful assembly shall be recognized. No restrictions may be placed on the exercise of this right other than those imposed in conformity with the law and which are necessary in a democratic society in the interests of national security or public safety, public order (*ordre public*), the protection of public health or morals or the protection of the rights and freedoms of others.

Article 22

1. Everyone shall have the right to freedom of association with others, including the right to form and join trade unions for the protection of his interests.

2. No restrictions may be placed on the exercise of this right other than those which are prescribed by law and which are necessary in a democratic society in the interests of national security or public safety, public order (*ordre public*), the protection of public health or morals or the protection of the rights

and freedoms of others. This article shall not prevent the imposition of lawful restrictions on members of the armed forces and of the police in their exercise of this right.

3. Nothing in this article shall authorize States Parties to the International Labour Organisation Convention of 1948 concerning Freedom of Association and Protection of the Right to Organize to take legislative measures which would prejudice, or to apply the law in such a manner as to prejudice the guarantees provided for in that Convention.

Article 23

1. The family is the natural and fundamental group unit of society and is entitled to protection by society and the State.

2. The right of men and women of marriageable age to marry and to found a family shall be recognized.

3. No marriage shall be entered into without the free and full consent of the intending spouses.

4. States Parties to the present Covenant shall take appropriate steps to ensure equality of rights and responsibilities of spouses as to marriage, during marriage and at its dissolution. In the case of dissolution, provision shall be made for the necessary protection of any children.

Article 24

1. Every child shall have, without any discrimination as to race, colour, sex, language, religion, national or social origin, property or birth, the right to such measures of protection as are required by his status as a minor, on the part of his family, society and the State.

2. Every child shall be registered immediately after birth and shall have a name.

3. Every child has the right to acquire a nationality.

Article 25

Every citizen shall have the right and the opportunity, without any of the distinctions mentioned in article 2 and without unreasonable restrictions:

a. To take part in the conduct of public affairs, directly or through freely chosen representatives;

b. To vote and to be elected at genuine periodic elections which shall be by universal and equal suffrage and shall be held by secret ballot, guaranteeing the free expression of the will of the electors;

c. To have access, on general terms of equality, to public service in his country.

Article 26

All persons are equal before the law and are entitled without any discrimination to the equal protection of the law. In this respect, the law shall prohibit any discrimination and guarantee to all persons equal and effective protection against discrimination on any ground such as race, colour, sex, language, religion, political or other opinion, national or social origin, property, birth or other status.

Article 27

In those States in which ethnic, religious or linguistic minorities exist, persons belonging to such minorities shall not be denied the right, in community with the other members of their group, to enjoy their own culture, to profess and practise their own religion, or to use their own language.

* * *

[For omitted procedural provisions, Articles 28–45, see below, Chapter IV.A.5.]

PART V

Article 46

Nothing in the present Covenant shall be interpreted as impairing the provisions of the Charter of the United Nations and of the constitutions of the specialized agencies which define the respective responsibilities of the various organs of the United Nations and of the specialized agencies in regard to the matters dealt with in the present Covenant.

Article 47

Nothing in the present Covenant shall be interpreted as impairing the inherent right of all peoples to enjoy and utilize fully and freely their natural wealth and resources.

PART VI

Article 48

1. The present Covenant is open for signature by any State Member of the United Nations or member of any of its specialized agencies, by any State Party to the Statute of the International Court of Justice, and by any other State which has been invited by the General Assembly of the United Nations to become a party to the present Covenant.

2. The present Covenant is subject to ratification. Instruments of ratification shall be deposited with the Secretary-General of the United Nations.

3. The present Covenant shall be open to accession by any State referred to in paragraph 1 of this article.

4. Accession shall be effected by the deposit of an instrument of accession with the Secretary-General of the United Nations.

5. The Secretary-General of the United Nations shall inform all States which have signed this Covenant or acceded to it of the deposit of each instrument of ratification or accession.

Article 49

1. The present Covenant shall enter into force three months after the date of

the deposit with the Secretary-General of the United Nations of the thirty-fifth instrument of ratification or instrument of accession.

2. For each State ratifying the present Covenant or acceding to it after the deposit of the thirty-fifth instrument of ratification or instrument of accession, the present Covenant shall enter into force three months after the date of the deposit of its own instrument of ratification or instrument of accession.

Article 50

The provisions of the present Covenant shall extend to all parts of federal States without any limitations or exceptions.

Article 51

1. Any State Party to the present Covenant may propose an amendment and file it with the Secretary-General of the United Nations. The Secretary-General of the United Nations shall thereupon communicate any proposed amendments to the States Parties to the present Covenant with a request that they notify him whether they favour a conference of States Parties for the purpose of considering and voting upon the proposals. In the event that at least one third of the States Parties favours such a conference, the Secretary-General shall convene the conference under the auspices of the United Nations. Any amendment adopted by a majority of the States Parties present and voting at the conference shall be submitted to the General Assembly of the United Nations for approval.

2. Amendments shall come into force when they have been approved by the General Assembly of the United Nations and accepted by a two-thirds majority of the States Parties to the present Covenant in accordance with their respective constitutional processes.

3. When amendments come into force, they shall be binding on those States Parties which have accepted them, other States Parties still being bound by the provisions of the present Covenant and any earlier amendment which they have accepted.

Article 52

Irrespective of the notifications made under article 48, paragraph 5, the Secretary-General of the United Nations shall inform all States referred to in paragraph 1 of the same article of the following particulars:

    a. Signatures, ratifications and accessions under article 48;

    b. The date of the entry into force of the present Covenant under article 49 and the date of the entry into force of any amendments under article 51.

Article 53

1. The present Covenant, of which the Chinese, English, French, Russian and Spanish texts are equally authentic, shall be deposited in the archives of the United Nations.

2. The Secretary-General of the United Nations shall transmit certified copies of the present Covenant to all States referred to in article 48.

C. PREVENTION OF DISCRIMINATION

INTRODUCTION

The UN Charter spoke of "human rights and fundamental freedoms for all, without distinction as to race, sex, language or religion." The Universal Declaration of Human Rights added to the list of proscribed "distinctions" those based on "color" and on "political or other opinion, national or social origin, property, birth or other status." Later documents expanding upon these provisions tend to use the term "discrimination" rather than "distinction" to describe the general concept involved. They also demonstrate increased sophistication in emphasizing that it is not *all* differences in treatment on the basis of race, etc., that are prohibited, but only arbitrary or unreasonable ones. Typically the later documents on discrimination prohibit distinctions, exclusions, restrictions or preferences based on one of the prohibited grounds that have the purpose or effect of nullifying or impairing *equality of treatment*. It is also commonly recognized that special measures, particularly of a temporary nature, taken to ensure equality of treatment for particular groups or individuals ("affirmative action" in United States terms) may be justified and, in certain circumstances, obligatory.

For good discussions of the concept of discrimination *see* W. McKean, "The International Law of Non-Discrimination," in *Essays on Race Relations and the Law in New Zealand* 1 ff (McKean ed. 1971); V. Van Dyke, *Human Rights Without Discrimination*, 67 Am. Pol.Sci.Rev.1267 (1973).

It will be noted that most progress has been made in defining and responding to discrimination based on race and sex. On discrimination based on language, *see* V. Van Dyke, "Human Rights Without Distinction as to Language," 20 *Int'l Studies Q.* 3 (1976). Drafting instruments on religious discrimination has proceeded at a snail's pace but a Declaration concerning religious freedom was finally adopted in 1981. *See* R. Clark, "The United Nations and Religious Freedom," 11 *New York University Journal of International Law and Politics* 197 (1978); R. Clark, "The United Nations Declaration on the Elimination of All Forms of Intolerance and of Discrimination Based on Religion or Belief," *Chitty's Law Journal* (1984).

1. INTERNATIONAL CONVENTION ON THE ELIMINATION OF ALL FORMS OF RACIAL DISCRIMINATION (1965) G.A. Res. 2106A(XX), 20 U.N. GAOR, Supp. (No. 14) at 47, U.N. Doc. A/6014 (1965). In force 4 January 1969 in accordance with Article 19.

THE STATES PARTIES TO THIS CONVENTION,

Considering that the Charter of the United Nations is based on the principles of the dignity and equality inherent in all human beings, and that all Member States have pledged themselves to take joint and separate action, in co-operation with the Organization, for the achievement of one of the purposes of the United

Nations which is to promote and encourage universal respect for and observance of human rights and fundamental freedoms for all, without distinction as to race, sex, language or religion,

Considering that the Universal Declaration of Human Rights proclaims that all human beings are born free and equal in dignity and rights and that everyone is entitled to all the rights and freedoms set out therein, without distinction of any kind, in particular as to race, colour or national origin,

Considering that all human beings are equal before the law and are entitled to equal protection of the law against any discrimination and against any incitement to discrimination,

Considering that the United Nations has condemned colonialism and all practices of segregation and discrimination associated therewith, in whatever form and wherever they exist, and that the Declaration on the Granting of Independence to Colonial Countries and Peoples of 14 December 1960 (General Assembly resolution 1514 (XV)) has affirmed and solemnly proclaimed the necessity of bringing them to a speedy and unconditional end,

Considering that the United Nations Declaration on the Elimination of All Forms of Racial Discrimination of 20 November 1963 (General Assembly resolution 1904 (XVIII)) solemnly affirms the necessity of speedily eliminating racial discrimination throughout the world in all its forms and manifestations and of securing understanding of and respect for the dignity of the human person,

Convinced that any doctrine of superiority based on racial differentiation is scientifically false, morally condemnable, socially unjust and dangerous, and that there is no justification for racial discrimination, in theory or in practice, anywhere,

Reaffirming that discrimination between human beings on the grounds of race, colour or ethnic origin is an obstacle to friendly and peaceful relations among nations and is capable of disturbing peace and security among peoples and the harmony of persons living side by side even within one and the same State,

Convinced that the existence of racial barriers is repugnant to the ideals of any human society,

Alarmed by manifestations of racial discrimination still in evidence in some areas of the world and by governmental policies based on racial superiority or hatred, such as policies of *apartheid*, segregation or separation,

Resolved to adopt all necessary measures for speedily eliminating racial discrimination in all its forms and manifestations, and to prevent and combat racist doctrines and practices in order to promote understanding between races and to build an international community free from all forms of racial segregation and racial discrimination,

Bearing in mind the Convention concerning Discrimination in respect of Employment and Occupation adopted by the International Labour Organisation in 1958, and the Convention against Discrimination in Education adopted by the United Nations Educational, Scientific and Cultural Organization in 1960,

Desiring to implement the principles embodied in the United Nations Declaration on the Elimination of All Forms of Racial Discrimination and to secure the earliest adoption of practical measures to that end,

Have agreed as follows:

PART I

Article 1

1. In this Convention, the term "racial discrimination" shall mean any distinction, exclusion, restriction or preference based on race, colour, descent, or national or ethnic origin which has the purpose or effect of nullifying or impairing the recognition, enjoyment or exercise, on an equal footing, of human rights and fundamental freedoms in the political, economic, social, cultural or any other field of public life.

2. This Convention shall not apply to distinctions, exclusions, restrictions or preferences made by a State Party to this Convention between citizens and non-citizens.

3. Nothing in this Convention may be interpreted as affecting in any way the legal provisions of States Parties concerning nationality, citizenship or naturalization, provided that such provisions do not discriminate against any particular nationality.

4. Special measures taken for the sole purpose of securing adequate advancement of certain racial or ethnic groups or individuals requiring such protection as may be necessary in order to ensure such groups or individuals equal enjoyment or exercise of human rights and fundamental freedoms shall not be deemed racial discrimination, provided, however, that such measures do not, as a consequence, lead to the maintenance of separate rights for different racial groups and that they shall not be continued after the objectives for which they were taken have been achieved.

Article 2

1. States Parties condemn racial discrimination and undertake to pursue by all appropriate means and without delay a policy of eliminating racial discrimination in all its forms and promoting understanding among all races, and, to this end:

a. Each State Party undertakes to engage in no act or practice of racial discrimination against persons, groups of persons or institutions and to ensure that all public authorities and public institutions, national and local, shall act in conformity with this obligation;

b. Each State Party undertakes not to sponsor, defend or support racial discrimination by any persons or organizations;

c. Each State Party shall take effective measures to review governmental, national and local policies, and to amend, rescind or nullify any laws and regulations which have the effect of creating or perpetuating racial discrimination wherever it exists;

d. Each State Party shall prohibit and bring to and end, by all appropriate means, including legislation as required by circumstances, racial discrimination by any persons, group or organization;

e. Each State Party undertakes to encourage, where appropriate, integrationist multiracial organizations and movements and other means of eliminating barriers between races, and to discourage anything which tends to strengthen racial division.

2. States Parties shall, when the circumstances so warrant, take, in the social, economic, cultural and other fields, special and concrete measures to ensure the adequate development and protection of certain racial groups or individuals belonging to them, for the purpose of guaranteeing them the full and equal enjoyment of human rights and fundamental freedoms. These measures shall in no case entail as a consequence the maintenance of unequal or separate rights for different racial groups after the objectives for which they were taken have been achieved.

Article 3

States Parties particularly condemn racial segregation and *apartheid* and undertake to prevent, prohibit and eradicate all practices of this nature in territories under their jurisdiction.

Article 4

States Parties condemn all propaganda and all organizations which are based on ideas or theories of superiority of one race or group of persons of one colour or ethnic origin, or which attempt to justify or promote racial hatred and discrimination in any form, and undertake to adopt immediate and positive measures designed to eradicate all incitement to, or acts of, such discrimination and, to this end, with due regard to the principles embodied in the Universal Declaration of Human Rights and the rights expressly set forth in article 5 of this Convention, *inter alia*:

a. Shall declare an offence punishable by law all dissemination of ideas based on racial superiority or hatred, incitement to racial discrimination, as well as all acts of violence or incitement to such acts against any race or group of persons of another colour or ethnic origin, and also the provision of any assistance to racist activities, including the financing thereof;

b. Shall declare illegal and prohibit organizations, and also organized and all other propaganda activities, which promote and incite racial discrimination, and shall recognize participation in such organizations or activities as an offence punishable by law;

c. Shall not permit public authorities or public institutions, national or local, to promote or incite racial discrimination.

Article 5

In compliance with the fundamental obligations laid down in article 2 of this Convention, States Parties undertake to prohibit and to eliminate racial discrimination in all its forms and to guarantee the right of everyone, without distinction as to race, colour, or national or ethnic origin, to equality before the law, notably in the enjoyment of the following rights:

a. The right to equal treatment before the tribunals and all other organs administering justice;

b. The right to security of person and protection by the State against violence or bodily harm, whether inflicted by government officials or by any individual group or institution;

c. Political rights, in particular the rights to participate in elections—to vote and to stand for election—on the basis of universal and equal suffrage, to take part in the Government as well as in the conduct of public affairs at any level and to have equal access to public service;

d. Other civil rights, in particular:

i. The right to freedom of movement and residence within the border of the State;
ii. The right to leave any country, including one's own, and to return to one's country;
iii. The right to nationality;
iv. The right to marriage and choice of spouse;
v. The right to own property alone as well as in association with others;
vi. The right to inherit;
vii. The right to freedom of thought, conscience and religion;
viii. The right to freedom of opinion and expression;
ix. The right to freedom of peaceful assembly and association;

e. Economic, social and cultural rights, in particular:

i. The rights to work, to free choice of employment, to just and favourable conditions of work, to protection against unemployment, to equal pay for equal work, to just and favourable remuneration;
ii. The right to form and join trade unions;
iii. The right to housing;
iv. The right to public health, medical care, social security and social services;
v. The right to education and training;
vi. The right to equal participation in cultural activities;

f. The right of access to any place or service intended for use by the general public, such as transport, hotels, restaurants, cafés, theatres and parks.

Article 6

States Parties shall assure to everyone within their jurisdiction effective protection and remedies, through the competent national tribunals and other State institutions, against any acts of racial discrimination which violate his human rights and fundamental freedoms contrary to this Convention, as well as the right to seek from such tribunals just and adequate reparation or satisfaction for any damage suffered as a result of such discrimination.

Article 7

States Parties undertake to adopt immediate and effective measures, particularly in the fields of teaching, education, culture and information, with a view to combating prejudices which lead to racial discrimination and to promoting understanding, tolerance and friendship among nations and racial or ethnic groups, as well as to propagating the purposes and principles of the Charter of the United Nations, the Universal Declaration of Human Rights, the United Nations Declaration on the Elimination of All Forms of Racial Discrimination, and this Convention.

* * *

[For omitted procedural provisions, Articles 8–16, see below, Chapter IV.A.3.]

PART III

Article 17

1. This Convention is open for signature by any State Member of the United Nations or member of any of its specialized agencies, by any State Party to the Statute of the International Court of Justice, and by any other State which has been invited by the General Assembly of the United Nations to become a Party to this Convention.

2. This Convention is subject to ratification. Instruments of ratification shall be deposited with the Secretary-General of the United Nations.

Article 18

1. This Convention shall be open to accession by any State referred to in article 17, paragraph 1, of the Convention.

2. Accession shall be effected by the deposit of an instrument of accession with the Secretary-General of the United Nations.

Article 19

1. This Convention shall enter into force on the thirtieth day after the date of the deposit with the Secretary-General of the United Nations of the twenty-seventh instrument of ratification or instrument of accession.

2. For each State ratifying this Convention or acceding to it after the deposit of the twenty-seventh instrument of ratification or instrument of accession, the Convention shall enter into force on the thirtieth day after the date of the deposit of its own instrument of ratification or instrument of accession.

Article 20

1. The Secretary-General of the United Nations shall receive and circulate to all States which are or may become Parties to this Convention reservations made by States at the time of ratification or accession. Any State which objects to the reservation shall, within a period of ninety days from the date of the said communication, notify the Secretary-General that it does not accept it.

2. A reservation incompatible with the object and purpose of this Convention shall not be permitted, nor shall a reservation the effect of which would inhibit the operation of any of the bodies established by this Convention be

allowed. A reservation shall be considered incompatible or inhibitive if at least two thirds of the States Parties to this Convention object to it.

3. Reservations may be withdrawn at any time by notification to this effect addressed to the Secretary-General. Such notification shall take effect on the date on which it is received.

Article 21

A State Party may denounce this Convention by written notification to the Secretary-General of the United Nations. Denunciation shall take effect one year after the date of receipt of the notification by the Secretary-General.

* * *

[For omitted procedural provisions, Article 22, see below, Chapter IV.A.3.]

Article 23

1. A request for the revision of this Convention may be made at any time by any State Party by means of a notification in writing addressed to the Secretary-General of the United Nations.

2. The General Assembly of the United Nations shall decide upon the steps, if any, to be taken in respect of such a request.

Article 24

The Secretary-General of the United Nations shall inform all States referred to in article 17, paragraph 1, of this Convention of the following particulars:

    a. Signatures, ratifications and accessions under articles 17 and 18;

    b. The date of entry into force of this Convention under article 19;

    c. Communications and declarations received under articles 14, 20 and 23;

    d. Denunciations under article 21.

Article 25

1. This Convention, of which the Chinese, English, French, Russian and Spanish texts are equally authentic, shall be deposited in the archives of the United Nations.

2. The Secretary-General of the United Nations shall transmit certified copies of this Convention to all States belonging to any of the categories mentioned in article 17, paragraph 1, of the Convention.

2. INTERNATIONAL CONVENTION ON THE SUPPRESSION AND PUNISHMENT OF THE CRIME OF APARTHEID (1973) G.A. Res. 3068 (XXVIII), 28 U.N. GAOR, Supp. (No. 30) at 75, U.N. Doc. A/9030 (1973). In force 18 July 1976 in accordance with Article XV.

THE STATES PARTIES TO THE PRESENT CONVENTION,

Recalling the provisions of the Charter of the United Nations, in which all

Members pledged themselves to take joint and separate action in co-operation with the Organization for the achievement of universal respect for, and observance of, human rights and fundamental freedoms for all without distinction as to race, sex, language or religion,

Considering the Universal Declaration of Human Rights, which states that all human beings are born free and equal in dignity and rights and that everyone is entitled to all the rights and freedoms set forth in the Declaration, without distinction of any kind, such as race, colour or national origin,

Considering the Declaration on the Granting of Independence to Colonial Countries and Peoples, in which the General Assembly stated that the process of liberation is irresistible and irreversible and that, in the interests of human dignity, progress and justice, an end must be put to colonialism and all practices of segregation and discrimination associated therewith,

Observing that, in accordance with the International Convention on the Elimination of All Forms of Racial Discrimination, States particularly condemn racial segregation and *apartheid* and undertake to prevent, prohibit and eradicate all practices of this nature in territories under their jurisdiction,

Observing that, in the Convention on the Prevention and Punishment of the Crime of Genocide, certain acts which may also be qualified as acts of *apartheid* constitute a crime under international law,

Observing that, in the Convention on the Non-Applicability of Statutory Limitations to War Crimes and Crimes Against Humanity, "inhuman acts resulting from the policy of *apartheid*" are qualified as crimes against humanity,

Observing that the General Assembly of the United Nations has adopted a number of resolutions in which the policies and practices of *apartheid* are condemned as a crime against humanity,

Observing that the Security Council has emphasized that *apartheid* and its continued intensification and expansion seriously disturb and threaten international peace and security,

Convinced that an International Convention on the Suppression and Punishment of the Crime of *Apartheid* would make it possible to take more effective measures at the international and national levels with a view to the suppression and punishment of the crime of *apartheid*,

Have agreed as follows:

Article I

1. The States Parties to the present Convention declare that *apartheid* is a crime against humanity and that inhuman acts resulting from the policies and practices of *apartheid* and similar policies and practices of racial segregation and discrimination, as defined in article II of the Convention, are crimes violating the principles of international law, in particular the purposes and principles of the Charter of the United Nations, and constituting a serious threat to international peace and security.

2. The States Parties to the present Convention declare criminal those organizations, institutions and individuals committing the crime of *apartheid*.

Article II

For the purpose of the present Convention, the term "the crime of *apartheid*," which shall include similar policies and practices of racial segregation and discrimination as practised in southern Africa, shall apply to the following inhuman acts committed for the purpose of establishing and maintaining domination by one racial group of persons over any other racial group of persons and systematically oppressing them:

a. Denial to a member or members of a racial group or groups of the right to life and liberty of person:

i. By murder of members of a racial group or groups;

ii. By the infliction upon the members of a racial group or groups of serious bodily or mental harm, by the infringement of their freedom or dignity, or by subjecting them to torture or to cruel, inhuman or degrading treatment or punishment;

iii. By arbitrary arrest and illegal imprisonment of the members of a racial group or groups;

b. Deliberate imposition on a racial group or groups of living conditions calculated to cause its or their physical destruction in whole or in part;

c. Any legislative measures and other measures calculated to prevent a racial group or groups from participation in the political, social, economic and cultural life of the country and the deliberate creation of conditions preventing the full development of such a group or groups, in particular by denying to members of a racial group or groups basic human rights and freedoms, including the right to work, the right to form recognized trade unions, the right to education, the right to leave and to return to their country, the right to a nationality, the right to freedom of movement and residence, the right to freedom of opinion and expression, and the right to freedom of peaceful assembly and association;

d. Any measures, including legislative measures, designed to divide the population along racial lines by the creation of separate reserves and ghettos for the members of a racial group or groups, the prohibition of mixed marriages among members of various racial groups, the expropriation of landed property belonging to a racial group or groups or to members thereof;

e. Exploitation of the labour of the members of a racial group or groups, in particular by submitting them to forced labour;

f. Persecution of organizations and persons, by depriving them of fundamental rights and freedoms, because they oppose *apartheid*.

Article III

International criminal responsibility shall apply, irrespective of the motive involved, to individuals, members of organizations and institutions and representatives of the State, whether residing in the territory of the State in which the acts are perpetrated or in some other State, whenever they:

a. Commit, participate in, directly incite or conspire in the commission of the acts mentioned in article II of the present Convention;

b. Directly abet, encourage or co-operate in the commission of the crime of *apartheid*.

Article IV

The States Parties to the present Convention undertake:

a. To adopt any legislative or other measures necessary to suppress as well as to prevent any encouragement of the crime of *apartheid* and similar segregationist policies or their manifestations and to punish persons guilty of that crime;

b. To adopt legislative, judicial and administrative measures to prosecute, bring to trial and punish in accordance with their jurisdiction persons responsible for, or accused of, the acts defined in article II of the present Convention, whether or not such persons reside in the territory of the State in which the acts are committed or are nationals of that State or of some other State or are stateless persons.

Article V

Persons charged with the acts enumerated in article II of the present Convention may be tried by a competent tribunal of any State Party to the Convention which may acquire jurisdiction over the person of the accused or by an international penal tribunal having jurisdiction with respect to those States Parties which shall have accepted its jurisdiction.

Article VI

The States Parties to the present Convention undertake to accept and carry out in accordance with the Charter of the United Nations the decisions taken by the Security Council aimed at the prevention, suppression and punishment of the crime of *apartheid*, and to co-operate in the implementation of decisions adopted by other competent organs of the United Nations with a view to achieving the purposes of the Convention.

* * *

[For omitted procedural provisions, Articles VII-XII, see below, Chapter IV.A.7.]

Article XIII

The present Convention is open for signature by all States. Any State which does not sign the Convention before its entry into force may accede to it.

Article XIV

1. The present Convention is subject to ratification. Instruments of ratification shall be deposited with the Secretary-General of the United Nations.

2. Accession shall be effected by the deposit of an instrument of accession with the Secretary-General of the United Nations.

Article XV

1. The present Convention shall enter into force on the thirtieth day after the date of the deposit with the Secretary-General of the United Nations of the twentieth instrument of ratification or accession.

2. For each State ratifying the present Convention or acceding to it after the deposit of the twentieth instrument of ratification or instrument of accession, the Convention shall enter into force on the thirtieth day after the date of the deposit of its own instrument of ratification or instrument of accession.

Article XVI

A State Party may denounce the present Convention by written notification to the Secretary-General of the United Nations. Denunciation shall take effect one year after the date of receipt of the notification by the Secretary-General.

Article XVII

1. A request for the revision of the present Convention may be made at any time by any State Party by means of a notification in writing addressed to the Secretary-General of the United Nations.

2. The General Assembly of the United Nations shall decide upon the steps, if any, to be taken in respect of such request.

Article XVIII

The Secretary-General of the United Nations shall inform all States of the following particulars:

a. Signatures, ratifications and accessions under articles XIII and XIV;

b. The date of entry into force of the present Convention under article XV;

c. Denunciations under article XVI;

d. Notifications under article XVII.

Article XIX

1. The present Convention, of which the Chinese, English, French, Russian and Spanish texts are equally authentic, shall be deposited in the archives of the United Nations.

2. The Secretary-General of the United Nations shall transmit certified copies of the present Convention to all States.

3. CONVENTION ON THE POLITICAL RIGHTS OF WOMEN (1952) G.A. Res. 640(VII), 7 U.N. GAOR, Supp., (No. 20) at 27, U.N. Doc. A/2361 (1952). In force 7 July 1954 in accordance with Article VI.

THE CONTRACTING PARTIES

Desiring to implement the principle of equality of rights for men and women contained in the Charter of the United Nations.

Recognizing that everyone has the right to take part in the government of his country directly or indirectly through freely chosen representatives, and has the right to equal access to public service in his country, and desiring to equalize the status of men and women in the enjoyment and exercise of political rights, in accordance with the provisions of the Charter of the United Nations and of the Universal Declaration of Human Rights,

Having resolved to conclude a Convention for this purpose,

Hereby agree as hereinafter provided:

Article I

Women shall be entitled to vote in all elections on equal terms with men, without any discrimination.

Article II

Women shall be eligible for election to all publicly elected bodies, established by national law, on equal terms with men, without any discrimination.

Article III

Women shall be entitled to hold public office and to exercise all public functions, established by national law on equal terms with men, without any discrimination.

Article IV

1. This Convention shall be open for signature on behalf of any Member of the United Nations and also on behalf of any other State to which an invitation has been addressed by the General Assembly.

2. This Convention shall be ratified and the instruments of ratification shall be deposited with the Secretary-General of the United Nations.

Article V

1. This Convention shall be open for accession to all States referred to in paragraph 1 of article IV.

2. Accession shall be effected by the deposit of an instrument of accession with the Secretary-General of the United Nations.

Article VI

1. This Convention shall come into force on the ninetieth day following the date of deposit of the sixth instrument of ratification or accession.

2. For each State ratifying or acceding to the Convention after the deposit of the sixth instrument of ratification or accession the Convention shall enter into force on the ninetieth day after deposit by such State of its instrument of ratification or accession.

Article VII

In the event that any State submits a reservation to any of the articles of this Convention at the time of signature, ratification or accession, the Secretary-General shall communicate the text of the reservation to all States which are or may become parties to this Convention. Any State which objects to the reservation may, within a period of ninety days from the date of the said communication (or upon the date of its becoming a party to the Convention), notify the Secretary-General that it does not accept it. In such case, the Convention shall not enter into force as between such State and the State making the reservation.

Article VIII

1. Any State may denounce this Convention by written notification to the Secretary-General of the United Nations. Denunciation shall take effect one year after the date of receipt of the notification by the Secretary-General.
2. This Convention shall cease to be in force as from the date when the denunciation which reduces the number of parties to less than six becomes effective.

Article IX

Any dispute which may arise between any two or more Contracting States concerning the interpretation or application of this Convention, which is not settled by negotiation, shall at the request of any one of the parties to the dispute be referred to the International Court of Justice for decision, unless they agree to another mode of settlement.

Article X

The Secretary-General of the United Nations shall notify all Members of the United Nations and the non-member States contemplated in paragraph 1 of article IV of this Convention of the following:
    a. Signatures and instruments of ratification received in accordance with article IV;
    b. Instruments of accession received in accordance with article V;
    c. The date upon which this Convention enters into force in accordance with article VI;
    d. Communications and notifications received in accordance with article VII;
    e. Notifications of denunciation received in accordance with paragraph 1 of article VIII;
    f. Abrogation in accordance with paragraph 2 of article VIII.

Article XI

1. This Convention, of which the Chinese, English, French, Russian and Spanish texts shall be equally authentic, shall be deposited in the archives of the United Nations.
2. The Secretary-General of the United Nations shall transmit a certified copy to all Members of the United Nations and to the non-member States contemplated in paragraph 1 of article IV.

4. DECLARATION ON THE ELIMINATION OF DIS-CRIMINATION AGAINST WOMEN (1967) G.A. Res. 2263 (XXII), 22 U.N. GAOR, Supp. (No. 16) at 35, U.N. Doc. A/6716 (1967).

THE GENERAL ASSEMBLY,

Considering that the peoples of the United Nations have, in the Charter, reaffirmed their faith in fundamental human rights, in the dignity and worth of the human person and in the equal rights of men and women,

Considering that the Universal Declaration on Human Rights asserts the principle of non-discrimination and proclaims that all human beings are born free and equal in dignity and rights and that everyone is entitled to all the rights and freedoms set forth therein without distinction of any kind, including any distinction as to sex,

Taking into account the resolutions, declarations, conventions and recommendations of the United Nations and the specialized agencies designed to eliminate all forms of discrimination and to promote equal rights for men and women,

Concerned that, despite the Charter of the United Nations, the Universal Declaration of Human Rights, the International Covenants on Human Rights and other instruments of the United Nations and the specialized agencies and despite the progress made in the matter of equality of rights, there continues to exist considerable discrimination against women,

Considering that discrimination against women is incompatible with human dignity and with the welfare of the family and of society, prevents their participation, on equal terms with men, in the political, social, economic and cultural life of their countries and is an obstacle to the full development of the potentialities of women in the service of their countries and of humanity,

Bearing in mind the great contribution made by women to social, political, economic and cultural life and the part they play in the family and particularly in the rearing of children,

Convinced that the full and complete development of a country, the welfare of the world and the cause of peace require the maximum participation of women as well as men in all fields,

Considering that it is necessary to ensure the universal recognition in law and in fact of the principle of equality of men and women,

Solemnly proclaims this Declaration:

Article 1

Discrimination against women, denying or limiting as it does their equality of rights with men, is fundamentally unjust and constitutes an offence against human dignity.

Article 2

All appropriate measures shall be taken to abolish existing laws, customs, regulations and practices which are discriminatory against women, and to establish adequate legal protection for equal rights of men and women, in particular:

a. The principle of equality of rights shall be embodied in the constitution or otherwise guaranteed by law;

b. The international instruments of the United Nations and the specialized agencies relating to the elimination of discrimination against women shall be ratified or acceded to and fully implemented as soon as practicable.

Article 3

All appropriate measures shall be taken to educate public opinion and to direct national aspirations towards the eradication of prejudice and the abolition of customary and all other practices which are based on the idea of the inferiority of women.

Article 4

All appropriate measures shall be taken to ensure to women on equal terms with men, without any discrimination:

a. The right to vote in all elections and be eligible for election to all publicly elected bodies;

b. The right to vote in all public referenda;

c. The right to hold public office and to exercise all public functions.
Such rights shall be guaranteed by legislation.

Article 5

Women shall have the same rights as men to acquire, change or retain their nationality. Marriage to an alien shall not automatically affect the nationality of the wife either by rendering her stateless or by forcing upon her the nationality of her husband.

Article 6

1. Without prejudice to the safeguarding of the unity and the harmony of the family, which remains the basic unit of any society, all appropriate measures, particularly legislative measures, shall be taken to ensure to women, married or unmarried, equal rights with men in the field of civil law, and in particular:

a. The right to acquire, administer, enjoy, dispose of and inherit property, including property acquired during marriage;

b. The right to equality in legal capacity and the exercise thereof;

c. The same rights as men with regard to the law on the movement of persons.

2. All appropriate measures shall be taken to ensure the principle of equality of status of the husband and wife, and in particular:

a. Women shall have the same right as men to free choice of a spouse and to enter into marriage only with their free and full consent;

b. Women shall have equal rights with men during marriage and at its dissolution. In all cases the interest of the children shall be paramount;

c. Parents shall have equal rights and duties in matters relating to their children. In all cases the interest of the children shall be paramount.

3. Child marriage and the betrothal of young girls before puberty shall be prohibited, and effective action, including legislation, shall be taken to specify a minimum age for marriage and to make the registration of marriages in an official registry compulsory.

Article 7

All provisions of penal codes which constitute discrimination against women shall be repealed.

Article 8

All appropriate measures, including legislation, shall be taken to combat all forms of traffic in women and exploitation of prostitution of women.

Article 9

All appropriate measures shall be taken to ensure to girls and women, married or unmarried, equal rights with men in education at all levels, and in particular:

a. Equal conditions of access to, and study in, educational institutions of all types, including universities and vocational, technical and professional schools;

b. The same choice of curricula, the same examinations, teaching staff with qualifications of the same standard, and school premises and equipment of the same quality, whether the institutions are co-educational or not;

c. Equal opportunities to benefit from scholarships and other study grants;

d. Equal opportunities for access to programmes of continuing education, including adult literacy programmes;

e. Access to educational information to help in ensuring the health and well-being of families.

Article 10

1. All appropriate measures shall be taken to ensure to women, married or unmarried, equal rights with men in the field of economic and social life, and in particular:

a. The right, without discrimination on grounds of marital status or any other grounds, to receive vocational training, to work, to free choice of profession and employment, and to professional and vocational advancement;

b. The right to equal remuneration with men and to equality of treatment in respect of work of equal value;

c. The right to leave with pay, retirement privileges and provision for security in respect of unemployment, sickness, old age or other incapacity to work;

d. The right to receive family allowances on equal terms with men.

2. In order to prevent discrimination against women on account of marriage or maternity and to ensure their effective right to work, measures shall be taken to prevent their dismissal in the event of marriage or maternity and to provide paid maternity leave, with the guarantee of returning to former employment, and to provide the necessary social services, including child-care facilities.

3. Measures taken to protect women in certain types of work, for reasons inherent in their physical nature, shall not be regarded as discriminatory.

Article 11

1. The principle of equality of rights of men and women demands implementation in all States in accordance with the principles of the Charter of the United Nations and of the Universal Declaration of Human Rights.

2. Governments, non-governmental organizations and individuals are urged, therefore, to do all in their power to promote the implementation of the principles contained in this Declaration.

5. CONVENTION ON THE ELIMINATION OF ALL FORMS OF DISCRIMINATION AGAINST WOMEN

(1979) G.A. Res. 34/180, 34 U.N. GAOR, Supp. (No. 46) at 193, U.N. Doc. A/34/46 (1979). In force 3 September 1981 in accordance with Article 27.

THE STATES PARTIES TO THE PRESENT CONVENTION,

Noting that the Charter of the United Nations reaffirms faith in fundamental human rights, in the dignity and worth of the human person and in the equal rights of men and women,

Noting that the Universal Declaration of Human Rights affirms the principle of the inadmissibility of discrimination and proclaims that all human beings are born free and equal in dignity and rights and that everyone is entitled to all the rights and freedoms set forth therein, without distinction of any kind, including distinction based on sex,

Noting that the States Parties to the International Covenants on Human Rights have the obligation to ensure the equal right of men and women to enjoy all economic, social, cultural, civil and political rights,

Considering the international conventions concluded under the auspices of the United Nations and the specialized agencies promoting equality of rights of men and women,

Noting also the resolutions, declarations and recommendations adopted by the United Nations and the specialized agencies promoting equality of rights of men and women,

Concerned, however, that despite these various instruments extensive discrimination against women continues to exist,

Recalling that discrimination against women violates the principles of equality of rights and respect for human dignity, is an obstacle to the participation of women, on equal terms with men, in the political, social, economic and cultural life of their countries, hampers the growth of the prosperity of society and the family and makes more difficult the full development of the potentialities of women in the service of their countries and of humanity,

Concerned that in situations of poverty women have the least access to food, health, education, training and opportunities for employment and other needs,

Convinced that the establishment of the new international economic order based on equality and justice will contribute significantly towards the promotion of equality between men and women,

Emphasizing that the eradication of *apartheid*, all forms of racism, racial discrimination, colonialism, neo-colonialism, aggression, foreign occupation and domination and interference in the internal affairs of States is essential to the full enjoyment of the rights of men and women,

Affirming that the strengthening of international peace and security, the relaxation of international tension, mutual co-operation among all States irrespective of their social and economic systems, general and complete disarmament, in particular nuclear disarmament under strict and effective international control, the affirmation of the principles of justice, equality and mutual benefit in relations among countries and the realization of the right of peoples under alien and colonial domination and foreign occupation to self-determination and independence, as well as respect for national sovereignty and territorial integrity, will promote social progress and development and as a consequence will contribute to the attainment of full equality between men and women,

Convinced that the full and complete development of a country, the welfare of the world and the cause of peace require the maximum participation of women on equal terms with men in all fields,

Bearing in mind the great contribution of women to the welfare of the family and to the development of society, so far not fully recognized, the social significance of maternity and the role of both parents in the family and in the upbringing of children, and aware that the role of women in procreation should not be a basis for discrimination but that the upbringing of children requires a sharing of responsibility between men and women and society as a whole,

Aware that a change in the traditional role of men as well as the role of women in society and in the family is needed to achieve full equality between men and women,

Determined to implement the principles set forth in the Declaration on the Elimination of Discrimination against Women and, for that purpose, to adopt the measures required for the elimination of such discrimination in all its forms and manifestations,

Have agreed on the following:

PART I

Article 1

For the purposes of the present Convention, the term "discrimination against women" shall mean any distinction, exclusion or restriction made on the basis of sex which has the effect or purpose of impairing or nullifying the recognition, enjoyment or exercise by women, irrespective of their marital status, on a basis of equality of men and women, of human rights and fundamental freedoms in the political, economic, social, cultural, civil or any other field.

Article 2

States Parties condemn discrimination against women in all its forms, agree to pursue by all appropriate means and without delay a policy of eliminating discrimination against women and, to this end, undertake:

a. To embody the principle of the equality of men and women in their national constitutions or other appropriate legislation if not yet incorporated therein and to ensure, through law and other appropriate means, the practical realization of this principle;

b. To adopt appropriate legislative and other measures, including sanctions where appropriate, prohibiting all discrimination against women;

c. To establish legal protection of the rights of women on an equal basis with men and to ensure through competent national tribunals and other public institutions the effective protection of women against any act of discrimination;

d. To refrain from engaging in any act or practice of discrimination against women and to ensure that public authorities and institutions shall act in conformity with this obligation;

e. To take all appropriate measures to eliminate discrimination against women by any person, organization or enterprise;

f. To take all appropriate measures, including legislation, to modify or abolish existing laws, regulations, customs and practices which constitute discrimination against women;

g. To repeal all national penal provisions which constitute discrimination against women.

Article 3

States Parties shall take in all fields, in particular in the political, social, economic and cultural fields, all appropriate measures, including legislation, to ensure the full development and advancement of women, for the purpose of guaranteeing them the exercise and enjoyment of human rights and fundamental freedoms on a basis of equality with men.

Article 4

1. Adoption by States Parties of temporary special measures aimed at accelerating *de facto* equality between men and women shall not be considered discrimination as defined in the present Convention, but shall in no way entail as a consequence the maintenance of unequal or separate standards; these measures shall be discontinued when the objectives of equality of opportunity and treatment have been achieved.

2. Adoption by States Parties of special measures, including those measures contained in the present Convention, aimed at protecting maternity shall not be considered discriminatory.

Article 5

States Parties shall take all appropriate measures:

a. To modify the social and cultural patterns of conduct of men and women, with a view to achieving the elimination of prejudices and customary and all other practices which are based on the idea of the inferiority or the superiority of either of the sexes or on stereotyped roles for men and women;

b. To ensure that family education includes a proper understanding of maternity as a social function and the recognition of the common responsibility of men and women in the upbringing and development of their children, it being understood that the interest of the children is the primordial consideration in all cases.

Article 6

States Parties shall take all appropriate measures, including legislation, to suppress all forms of traffic in women and exploitation of prostitution of women.

PART II

Article 7

States Parties shall take all appropriate measures to eliminate discrimination against women in the political and public life of the country and, in particular, shall ensure to women, on equal terms with men, the right:

a. To vote in all elections and public referenda and to be eligible for election to all publicly elected bodies;

b. To participate in the formulation of government policy and the implementation thereof and to hold public office and perform all public functions at all levels of government;

c. To participate in non-governmental organizations and associations concerned with the public and political life of the country.

Article 8

States Parties shall take all appropriate measures to ensure to women, on equal terms with men and without any discrimination, the opportunity to represent their Governments at the international level and to participate in the work of international organizations.

Article 9

1. States Parties shall grant women equal rights with men to acquire, change or retain their nationality. They shall ensure in particular that neither marriage to an alien nor change of nationality by the husband during marriage shall automatically change the nationality of the wife, render her stateless or force upon her the nationality of the husband.

2. States Parties shall grant women equal rights with men in respect to the nationality of their children.

Article 10

States Parties shall take all appropriate measures to eliminate discrimination against women in order to ensure to them equal rights with men in the field of education and in particular to ensure, on a basis of equality of men and women:

a. The same conditions for career and vocational guidance, for access to studies and for the achievement of diplomas in educational establishments of all categories in rural as well as in urban areas; this equality shall be ensured in pre-school, general, technical, professional and higher technical education, as well as in all types of vocational training;

b. Access to the same curricula, the same examinations, teaching staff with qualifications of the same standard and school premises and equipment of the same quality;

c. The elimination of any stereotyped concept of the roles of men and women at all levels and in all forms of education by encouraging coeducation and other types of education which will help to achieve this aim and, in particular, by the revision of textbooks and school programmes and the adaptation of teaching methods;

d. The same opportunities to benefit from scholarships and other study grants;

e. The same opportunities for access to programmes of continuing education, including adult and functional literacy programmes, particularly those aimed at reducing, at the earliest possible time, any gap in education existing between men and women;

f. The reduction of female student drop-out rates and the organization of programmes for girls and women who have left school prematurely;

g. The same opportunities to participate actively in sports and physical education;

h. Access to specific educational information to help to ensure the health and well-being of families, including information and advice on family planning.

Article 11

1. States Parties shall take all appropriate measures to eliminate discrimination against women in the field of employment in order to ensure, on a basis of equality of men and women, the same rights, in particular:

a. The right to work as an inalienable right of all human beings;

b. The right to the same employment opportunities, including the application of the same criteria for selection in matters of employment;

c. The right to free choice of profession and employment, the right to promotion, job security and all benefits and conditions of service and the right to receive vocational training and retraining, including apprenticeships, advanced vocational training and recurrent training;

d. The right to equal remuneration, including benefits, and to equal treatment in respect of work of equal value, as well as equality of treatment in the evaluation of the quality of work;

e. The right to social security, particularly in cases of retirement, unemployment, sickness, invalidity and old age and other incapacity to work, as well as the right to paid leave;

f. The right to protection of health and to safety in working conditions, including the safeguarding of the function of reproduction.

2. In order to prevent discrimination against women on the grounds of marriage or maternity and to ensure their effective right to work, States Parties shall take appropriate measures:

a. To prohibit, subject to the imposition of sanctions, dismissal on the grounds of pregnancy or of maternity leave and discrimination in dismissals on the basis of marital status;

b. To introduce maternity leave with pay or with comparable social benefits without loss of former employment, seniority or social allowances;

c. To encourage the provision of the necessary supporting social services to enable parents to combine family obligations with work responsibilities and participation in public life, in particular through promoting the establishment and development of a network of child-care facilities;

d. To provide special protection to women during pregnancy in types of work proved to be harmful to them.

3. Protective legislation relating to matters covered in this article shall be reviewed periodically in the light of scientific and technological knowledge and shall be revised, repealed or extended as necessary.

Article 12

1. States Parties shall take all appropriate measures to eliminate discrimination against women in the field of health care in order to ensure, on a basis of equality of men and women, access to health care services, including those related to family planning.

2. Notwithstanding the provisions of paragraph 1 of this article, States Parties shall ensure to women appropriate services in connexion with pregnancy, confinement and the post-natal period, granting free services where necessary, as well as adequate nutrition during pregnancy and lactation.

Article 13

States Parties shall take all appropriate measures to eliminate discrimination against women in other areas of economic and social life in order to ensure, on a basis of equality of men and women, the same rights, in particular:

a. The right to family benefits;

b. The right to bank loans, mortgages and other forms of financial credit;

c. The right to participate in recreational activities, sports and all aspects of cultural life.

Article 14

1. States Parties shall take into account the particular problems faced by rural women and the significant roles which rural women play in the economic survival of their families, including their work in the non-monetized sectors of the economy, and shall take all appropriate measures to ensure the application of the provisions of this Convention to women in rural areas.

2. States Parties shall take all appropriate measures to eliminate discrimination against women in rural areas in order to ensure, on a basis of equality of men and women, that they participate in and benefit from rural development and, in particular, shall ensure to such women the right:

a. To participate in the elaboration and implementation of development planning at all levels;

b. To have access to adequate health care facilities, including information, counselling and services in family planning;

c. To benefit directly from social security programmes;

d. To obtain all types of training and education, formal and non-formal, including that relating to functional literacy, as well as, *inter alia*, the benefit of all community and extension services, in order to increase their technical proficiency;

e. To organize self-help groups and co-operatives in order to obtain equal access to economic opportunities through employment or self-employment;

f. To participate in all community activities;

g. To have access to agricultural credit and loans, marketing facilities, appropriate technology and equal treatment in land and agrarian reform as well as in land resettlement schemes;

h. To enjoy adequate living conditions, particularly in relation to housing, sanitation, electricity and water supply, transport and communications.

PART IV

Article 15

1. States Parties shall accord to women equality with men before the law.

2. States Parties shall accord to women, in civil matters, a legal capacity identical to that of men and the same opportunities to exercise that capacity. In particular, they shall give women equal rights to conclude contracts and to administer property and shall treat them equally in all stages of procedure in courts and tribunals.

3. States Parties agree that all contracts and all other private instruments of any kind with a legal effect which is directed at restricting the legal capacity of women shall be deemed null and void.

4. States Parties shall accord to men and women the same rights with regard to the law relating to the movement of persons and the freedom to choose their residence and domicile.

Article 16

1. States Parties shall take all appropriate measures to eliminate discrimination against women in all matters relating to marriage and family relations and in particular shall ensure, on a basis of equality of men and women:

a. The same right to enter into marriage;

b. The same right freely to choose a spouse and to enter into marriage only with their free and full consent;

c. The same rights and responsibilities during marriage and at its dissolution;

d. The same rights and responsibilities as parents, irrespective of their marital status, in matters relating to their children; in all cases the interests of the children shall be paramount;

e. The same rights to decide freely and responsibly on the number and spacing of their children and to have access to the information, education and means to enable them to exercise these rights;

f. The same rights and responsibilities with regard to guardianship, wardship, trusteeship and adoption of children, or similar institutions where these concepts exist in national legislation; in all cases the interests of the children shall be paramount;

g. The same personal rights as husband and wife, including the right to choose a family name, a profession and an occupation;

h. The same rights for both spouses in respect of the ownership, acquisition, management, administration, enjoyment and disposition of property, whether free of charge or for a valuable consideration.

2. The betrothal and the marriage of a child shall have no legal effect, and all necessary action, including legislation, shall be taken to specify a minimum age for marriage and to make the registration of marriages in an official registry compulsory.

* * *

[For omitted procedural provisions, Articles 17–22, see below, Chapter IV.A.8.]

PART VI

Article 23

Nothing in this Convention shall affect any provisions that are more conducive to the achievement of equality between men and women which may be contained:

(*a*) In the legislation of a State Party; or

(*b*) In any other international convention, treaty or agreement in force for that State.

Article 24

States Parties undertake to adopt all necessary measures at the national level aimed at achieving the full realization of the rights recognized in the present Convention.

Article 25

1. The present Convention shall be open for signature by all States.

2. The Secretary-General of the United Nations is designated as the depositary of the present Convention.

3. The present Convention is subject to ratification. Instruments of ratification shall be deposited with the Secretary-General of the United Nations.

4. The present Convention shall be open to accession by all States. Accession shall be effected by the deposit of an instrument of accession with the Secretary-General of the United Nations.

Article 26

1. A request for the revision of the present Convention may be made at any time by any State Party by means of a notification in writing addressed to the Secretary-General of the United Nations.

2. The General Assembly of the United Nations shall decide upon the steps, if any, to be taken in respect of such a request.

Article 27

1. The present Convention shall enter into force on the thirtieth day after the date of deposit with the Secretary-General of the United Nations of the twentieth instrument of ratification or accession.

2. For each State ratifying the present Convention or acceding to it after the deposit of the twentieth instrument of ratification or accession, the Convention shall enter into force on the thirtieth day after the date of the deposit of its own instrument of ratification or accession.

Article 28

1. The Secretary-General of the United Nations shall receive and circulate to all States the text of reservations made by States at the time of ratification or accession.

2. A reservation incompatible with the object and purpose of the present Convention shall not be permitted.

3. Reservations may be withdrawn at any time by notification to this effect addressed to the Secretary-General of the United Nations, who shall then inform all States thereof. Such notification shall take effect on the date on which it is received.

* * *

[For omitted procedural provisions, Article 29, see below, Chapter IV.A.8.)

Article 30

The present Convention, the Arabic, Chinese, English, French, Russian and Spanish texts of which are equally authentic, shall be deposited with the Secretary-General of the United Nations.

6. DECLARATION ON THE ELIMINATION OF ALL FORMS OF INTOLERANCE AND OF DISCRIMINA-TION BASED ON RELIGION OR BELIEF (1981) G.A. Res. 36/55, 36 U.N. GAOR, Supp. (No. 51) 171, U.N. Doc. A/36/51 (1981).

THE GENERAL ASSEMBLY,

Considering that one of the basic principles of the Charter of the United Nations is that of the dignity and equality inherent in all human beings, and that all Member States have pledged themselves to take joint and separate action in co-operation with the United Nations to promote and encourage universal respect for and observance of human rights and fundamental freedoms for all, without distinction as to race, sex, language or religion,

Considering that the Universal Declaration of Human Rights and the International Covenants on Human Rights proclaim the principles of non-discrimination and equality before the law and the right to freedom of thought, conscience, religion or belief,

Considering that the disregard and infringement of human rights and fundamental freedoms, in particular of the right to freedom of thought, conscience, religion or whatever belief, have brought, directly or indirectly, wars and great suffering to mankind, especially where they serve as a means of foreign interference in the internal affairs of other States and amount to kindling hatred between peoples and nations,

Considering that religion or belief, for anyone who professes either, is one of the fundamental elements in his conception of life and that freedom of religion or belief should be fully respected and guaranteed,

Considering that it is essential to promote understanding, tolerance and respect in matters relating to freedom of religion or belief and to ensure that the use of religion or belief for ends inconsistent with the Charter, other relevant instruments of the United Nations and the purposes and principles of the present Declaration is inadmissible,

Convinced that freedom of religion or belief should also contribute to the attainment of the goals of world peace, social justice and friendship among peoples and to the elimination of ideologies or practices of colonialism and racial discrimination,

Noting with satisfaction the adoption of several, and the coming into force of some, conventions, under the aegis of the United Nations and of the specialized agencies, for the elimination of various forms of discrimination,

Concerned by manifestations of intolerance and by the existence of discrimination in matters of religion or belief still in evidence in some areas of the world,

Resolved to adopt all necessary measures for the speedy elimination of such intolerance in all its forms and manifestations and to prevent and combat discrimination on the grounds of religion or belief,

Proclaims this Declaration on the Elimination of All Forms of Intolerance and of Discrimination Based on Religion or Belief:

Article 1

1. Everyone shall have the right to freedom of thought, conscience and religion. This right shall include freedom to have a religion or whatever belief of his choice, and freedom, either individually or in community with others and in public or private, to manifest his religion or belief in worship, observance, practice and teaching.

2. No one shall be subject to a coercion which would impair his freedom to have a religion or belief of his choice.

3. Freedom to manifest one's religion or belief may be subject only to such limitations as are prescribed by law and are necessary to protect public safety, order, health or morals or the fundamental rights and freedoms of others.

Article 2

1. No one shall be subject to discrimination by any State, institution, group of persons or person on the grounds of religion or belief.

2. For the purposes of the present Declaration, the expression "intolerance and discrimination based on religion or belief" means any distinction, exclusion, restriction or preference based on religion or belief and having as its purpose or as its effect nullification or impairment of the recognition, enjoyment or exercise of human rights and fundamental freedoms on an equal basis.

Article 3

Discrimination between human beings on the grounds of religion or belief constitutes an affront to human dignity and a disavowal of the principles of the Charter of the United Nations, and shall be condemned as a violation of the human rights and fundamental freedoms proclaimed in a Universal Declaration of Human Rights and enunciated in detail in the International Covenants on Human Rights, and as an obstacle to friendly and peaceful relations between nations.

Article 4

1. All states shall take effective measures to prevent and eliminate discrimination on the grounds of religion or belief in the recognition, exercise and enjoyment of human rights and fundamental freedoms in all fields of civil, economic, political, social and cultural life.

2. All States shall make all efforts to enact or rescind legislation where necessary to prohibit any such discrimination, and to take all appropriate measures to combat intolerance on the grounds of religion or belief in this matter.

Article 5

1. The parents or, as the case may be, the legal guardians of the child have the right to organize the life within the family in accordance with their religion or belief and bearing in mind the moral education in which they believe the child should be brought up.

2. Every child shall enjoy the right to have access to education in the matter of religion or belief in accordance with the wishes of his parents or, as the case may be, legal guardians, and shall not be compelled to receive teaching on religion or belief against the wishes of his parents or legal guardians, the best interests of the child being the guiding principle.

3. The child shall be protected from any form of discrimination on the grounds of religion or belief. He shall be brought up in a spirit of understanding, tolerance, friendship among peoples, peace and universal brotherhood, respect for freedom of religion or belief of others, and in full consciousness that his energy and talents should be devoted to the service of his fellow men.

4. In the case of a child who is not under the care either of his parents or of legal guardians, due account shall be taken of their expressed wishes or of any other proof of their wishes in the matter of religion or belief, the best interests of the child being the guiding principle.

5. Practices of a religion or belief in which a child is brought up must not be injurious to his physical or mental health or to his full development, taking into account article 1, paragraph 3, of the present Declaration.

Article 6

In accordance with article 1 of the present Declaration, and subject to the provisions of article 1, paragraph 3, the right to freedom of thought, conscience, religion or belief shall include, *inter alia*, the following freedoms:

a. To worship or assemble in connection with a religion or belief, and to establish and maintain places for these purposes;

b. To establish and maintain appropriate charitable or humanitarian institutions;

c. To make, acquire and use to an adequate extent the necessary articles and materials related to the rites or customs of a religion or belief;

d. To write, issue and disseminate relevant publications in these areas;

e. To teach a religion or belief in places suitable for these purposes;

f. To solicit and receive voluntary financial and other contributions from individuals and institutions;

g. To train, appoint, elect or designate by succession appropriate leaders called for by the requirements and standards of any religion or belief;

h. To observe days of rest and to celebrate holidays and ceremonies in accordance with the precepts of one's religion or belief;

i. To establish and maintain communications with individuals and communities in matters of religion or belief at the national and international levels.

Article 7

The rights and freedoms set forth in the present Declaration shall be accorded in national legislation in such a manner that everyone shall be able to avail himself of such rights and freedoms in practice.

Article 8

Nothing in the present Declaration shall be construed as restricting or derogating from any right defined in the Universal Declaration of Human Rights and the International Covenants on Human Rights.

7. DECLARATION ON THE PARTICIPATION OF WOMEN IN PROMOTING INTERNATIONAL PEACE AND CO-OPERATION (1982) G.A. Res. 37/63, 37 U.N. GAOR, Supp. (No. 51) at 194, U.N. Doc. A/37/51 (1983).

THE GENERAL ASSEMBLY,

Considering that the Charter of the United Nations expresses the determination of the peoples of the United Nations to reaffirm faith in the equal rights of men and women and to practise tolerance and live together in peace with one another as good neighbours,

Considering also that the Universal Declaration of Human Rights proclaims that the inherent dignity and equal and inalienable rights of all members of the human family is the foundation for freedom, justice and peace in the world,

Considering further that the International Covenants on Human Rights provide for the equal right of men and women to the enjoyment of all economic, social, cultural, civil and political rights,

Reaffirming the objectives of the United Nations Decade for Women: Equality, Development and Peace,

Taking into account the resolutions, declarations, conventions, programmes and recommendations of the United Nations and the specialized agencies and international conferences designed to eliminate all forms of discrimination and to promote equal rights for men and women,

Recalling that the Declaration of Mexico on the Equality of Women and Their Contribution to Development and Peace, 1975, states that women have a vital role to play in the promotion of peace in all spheres of life; in the family, the community, the nation and the world,

Recalling that the Convention on the Elimination of All Forms of Discrimination Against Women declares that discrimination against women violates the principles of equality of rights and respect for human dignity, is an obstacle to the participation of women, on equal terms with men, in the economic, social, cultural, civil and political life of their countries and makes more difficult the full development of the potentialities of women in the service of their countries and of humanity,

Recalling also that the Convention on the Elimination of All Forms of Discrimination against Women affirms that the strengthening of international peace and security, the relaxation of international tension, mutual co-operation among all States irrespective of their social and economic systems, general and complete disarmament and in particular, nuclear disarmament under strict and effective international control, the affirmation of the principles of justice, equality and mutual benefit in relations among countries and the realization of the right of peoples under alien and colonial domination and foreign occupation to self-determination and independence, as well as respect for national sovereignty and territorial integrity, will promote social progress and development and as a consequence, will contribute to the attainment of full equality between men and women,

Recognizing that the Convention on the Elimination of All Forms of Discrimination against Women obligates States Parties to take all appropriate measures to eliminate discrimination against women in all its forms and in every field of human endeavor, including politics, economic activities, law, employment, education, health care and domestic relations,

Noting that, despite progress towards the achievement of equality between men and women, considerable discrimination against women continues to exist, thereby impeding the active participation of women in promoting international peace and co-operation,

Welcoming the contribution which women have nevertheless made towards promoting international peace and co-operation, the struggle against colonialism, *apartheid*, all forms of racism and racial discrimination, foreign aggression and occupation and all forms of alien domination, and towards the unrestricted and effective enjoyment of human rights and fundamental freedoms,

Welcoming also the contribution of women for a just restructuring of international economic relations and the achievement of a new international economic order,

Convinced that women can play an important and increasing role in these areas,

Solemnly proclaims the Declaration on the Participation of Women in Promoting International Peace and Co-operation set forth in the annex to the present resolution.

ANNEX

Declaration on the Participation of Women in Promoting International Peace and Co-operation

PART I

Article 1

Women and men have an equal and vital interest in contributing to international peace and co-operation. To this end women must be enabled to exercise their right to participate in the economic, social, cultural, civil and political affairs of society on an equal footing with men.

Article 2

The full participation of women in the economic, social, cultural, civil and political affairs of society and in the endeavor to promote international peace and co-operation is dependent on a balanced and equitable distribution of roles between men and women in the family and in society as a whole.

Article 3

The increasing participation of women in the economic, social, cultural, civil and political affairs of society will contribute to international peace and co-operation.

Article 4

The full enjoyment of the rights of women and men and the full participation of women in promoting international peace and co-operation will contribute to the eradication of *apartheid*, of all forms of racism, racial discrimination, colonialism, neo-colonialism, aggression, foreign occupation and domination and interference in the internal affairs of States.

Article 5

Special national and international measures are necessary to increase the level of women's participation in the sphere of international relations so that women can contribute, on an equal basis, with men to national and international efforts to secure world peace and economic and social progress and to promote international co-operation.

PART II

Article 6

All appropriate measures shall be taken to intensify the national and international efforts in respect of the participation of women in promoting international peace and co-operation by ensuring the equal participation of women in the economic, social, cultural, civil and political affairs of society through a balanced and equitable distribution of roles between men and women in the domestic sphere and in society as a whole, as well as by providing an equal opportunity for women to participate in the decision-making process.

Article 7

All appropriate measures shall be taken to promote the exchange of experience at the national and international levels for the purpose of furthering the involvement of women in promoting international peace and co-operation and in solving other vital national and international problems.

Article 8

All appropriate measures shall be taken at the national and international levels to give effective publicity to the responsibility and active participation of women in promoting international peace and co-operation and in solving other vital national and international problems.

Article 9

All appropriate measures shall be taken to render solidarity and support to those women who are victims of mass and flagrant violations of human rights such as *apartheid*, all forms of racism, racial discrimination, colonialism, neo-colonialism, aggression, foreign occupation and domination and of all other violations of human rights.

Article 10

All appropriate measures shall be taken to pay tribute to the participation of women in promoting international peace and co-operation.

Article 11

All appropriate measures shall be taken to encourage women to participate in non-governmental and intergovernmental organizations aimed at the strengthening of international peace and security, the development of friendly relations among nations and the promotion of co-operation among States and, to that end, freedom of thought, conscience, expression, assembly, association, communication and movement, without distinction as to race, political or religious belief, language or ethnic origin, shall be effectively guaranteed.

Article 12

All appropriate measures shall be taken to provide practical opportunities for the effective participation of women in promoting international peace and co-operation, economic development and social progress and, to that end:

a. To promote an equitable representation of women in governmental and non-governmental functions,

b. To promote equality of opportunities for women to enter diplomatic service,

c. To appoint or nominate women, on an equal basis with men, as members of delegations to national, regional or international meetings,

d. To support increased employment of women at all levels in the secretariats of the United Nations and the specialized agencies, in conformity with Article 101 of the Charter of the United Nations.

Article 13

All appropriate measures shall be taken to establish adequate legal protection of the rights of women on an equal basis with men in order to ensure effective participation of women in the activities referred to above.

Article 14

Governments, non-governmental and international organizations, including the United Nations and the specialized agencies and individuals, are urged to do all in their power to promote the implementation of the principles contained in the present Declaration.

8. INTERNATIONAL CONVENTION AGAINST *APARTHEID* IN SPORTS G.A. Res. 40/64 (1985). Not yet in force.

THE GENERAL ASSEMBLY,

Recalling its resolution 32/105 M of 14 December 1977, by which it adopted the International Declaration against *Apartheid* in Sports,

Recalling also its resolution 39/72 D of 13 December 1984, by which it requested the *Ad Hoc* Committee on the Drafting of an International Convention against *Apartheid* in Sports to continue its work with a view to submitting the draft Convention to the General Assembly at its fortieth session,

Recalling further that the International Convention on the Suppression and Punishment of the Crime of *Apartheid 93/* declares that *apartheid* is a crime violating principles of international law, in particular the purposes and principles of the Charter of the United Nations,

Mindful of the special responsibility of the United Nations to eliminate *apartheid* and racial discrimination in sports and in society,

Convinced that *apartheid* still dominates sports and the society as a whole in South Africa and that all so-called reforms have not led to any meaningful change in sports and the society in that country,

Reaffirming its unqualified support for the Olympic principle that no discrimination be allowed on the grounds of race, religion or political affiliation and its belief that merit should be the sole criterion in sport activities,

Reaffirming the necessity to ensure an international concerted action to isolate the racist régime of South Africa from the field of international sports as well as all other fields,

Commending the efforts of the Special Committee against *Apartheid* to ensure the total isolation of *apartheid* in sports and, in particular, the publication of the *Register of Sports Contacts* with South Africa and urging Member States, pending the entry into force of the Convention, to co-operate with the Special Committee on matters relating to the isolation of *apartheid* in sports,

Commending all sports bodies, teams and individual sportsmen that have declared their determination not to engage in sports contacts with South Africa until the evil system of *apartheid* is abolished,

Convinced that the Convention would be an important instrument towards the isolation of the racist régime of South Africa and the elimination of *apartheid* sports and that it should be signed and ratified by States at the earliest possible date and its provisions implemented without delay,

Considering that the text of the Convention should be made known throughout the world,

1. *Adopts* and opens for signature and ratification the International Convention against *Apartheid* in Sports, the text of which is annexed to the present resolution;

2. *Appeals* to all States to sign and ratify the Convention as soon as possible;

3. *Requests* all Governments and intergovernmental and nongovernmental organizations to acquaint the public as widely as possible with the text of the Convention, using all the information media at their disposal;

4. *Requests* the Secretary-General to ensure the urgent and wide dissemination of the Convention and, for that purpose, to publish and circulate its text;

5. *Commends* the efforts of the Special Committee against *Apartheid* and requests it to continue to publish the *Register of Sports Contacts* with South Africa until the establishment of the Commission against *Apartheid* in Sports.

ANNEX

International Convention against Apartheid in Sports

The States Parties to the present Convention,

Recalling the provisions of the Charter of the United Nations, in which all Members pledged themselves to take joint and separate action, in co-operation with the Organization, for the achievement of universal respect for, and observance of, human rights and fundamental freedoms for all without distinction as to race, sex, language or religion,

Considering that the Universal Declaration of Human Rights proclaims that all human beings are born free and equal in dignity and rights and that everyone is entitled to all the rights and freedoms set forth in the Declaration without distinction of any kind, particularly in regard to race, colour or national origin,

Observing that, in accordance with the International Convention on the Elimination of All Forms of Racial Discrimination, States Parties to that Convention particularly condemn racial segregation and *apartheid* and undertake to prevent, prohibit and eradicate all practices of this nature in all fields,

Observing that the General Assembly of the United Nations has adopted a number of resolutions condemning the practice of *apartheid* in sports and has affirmed its unqualified support for the Olympic principle that no discrimination be allowed on the grounds of race, religion or political affiliation and that merit should be the sole criterion for participation in sports activities,

Considering that the International Declaration against *Apartheid* in Sports, which was adopted by the General Assembly of the United Nations on 14 December 1977, solemnly affirms the necessity for the speedy elimination of *apartheid* in sports,

Recalling the provisions of the International Convention on the Suppression and Punishment of the Crime of *Apartheid* and recognizing, in particular, that participation in sports exchanges with teams selected on the basis of *apartheid* directly abets and encourages the commission of the crime of *apartheid*, as defined in that Convention,

Resolved to adopt all necessary measures to eradicate the practice of *apartheid* in sports and to promote international sports contacts based on the Olympic principle,

Recognizing that sports contact with any country practising *apartheid* in sports condones and strengthens *apartheid* in violation of the Olympic principle and thereby becomes the legitimate concern of all Governments,

Desiring to implement the principles embodied in the International Declaration against *Apartheid* in Sports and to secure the earliest adoption of practical measures to that end,

Convinced that the adoption of an international convention against *apartheid* in sports would result in more effective measures at the international and national levels, with a view to eliminating *apartheid* in sports,

Have agreed as follows:

Article 1

For the purposes of the present Convention:

(*a*) The expression *"apartheid"* shall mean a system of institutionalized racial segregation and discrimination for the purpose of establishing and maintaining domination by one racial group of persons over another racial group of persons and systematically oppressing them, such as that pursued by South Africa, and *"apartheid* in sports" shall mean the application of the policies and practices of such a system in sports activities, whether organized on a professional or an amateur basis;

(*b*) The expression "national sports facilities" shall mean any sports facility operated within the framework of a sports programme conducted under the auspices of a national government;

(*c*) The expression "Olympic principle" shall mean the principle that no discrimination be allowed on the grounds of race, religion or political affiliation;

(*d*) The expression "sports contracts" shall mean any contract concluded for the organization, promotion, performance or derivative rights, including servicing, of any sports activity;

(*e*) The expression "sports bodies" shall mean any organization constituted to organize sports activities at the national level, including national Olympic committees, national sports federations or national governing sports committees;

(*f*) The expression "team" shall mean a group of sportsmen organized for the purpose of participating in sports activities in competition with other such organized groups;

(*g*) The expression "sportsmen" shall mean men and women who participate in sports activities on an individual or team basis, as well as managers, coaches, trainers and other officials whose functions are essential for the operation of a team.

Article 2

States Parties strongly condemn *apartheid* and undertake to pursue immediately by all appropriate means the policy of eliminating the practice of *apartheid* in all its forms from sports.

Article 3

States Parties shall not permit sports contact with a country practising *apartheid* and shall take appropriate action to ensure that their sports bodies, sports teams and individual sportsmen do not have such contact.

Article 4

States Parties shall take all possible measures to prevent sports contact with a country practising *apartheid* and shall ensure that effective means exist for bringing about compliance with such measures.

Article 5

States Parties shall refuse to provide financial or other assistance to enable their sports bodies, teams and individual sportsmen to participate in sports activities in a country practising *apartheid* or with teams or individual sportsmen selected on the basis of *apartheid*.

Article 6

Each State Party shall take appropriate action against its sports bodies, teams and individual sportsmen that participate in sports activities in a country practising *apartheid* or with teams representing a country practising *apartheid*, which, in particular, shall include:

(*a*) Refusal to provide financial or other assistance for any purpose to such sports bodies, teams and individual sportsmen;

(*b*) Restriction of access to national sports facilities to such sports bodies, teams and individual sportsmen;

(*c*) Non-enforceability of all sports contracts which involve sports activities in a country practising *apartheid* or with teams or individual sportsmen selected on the basis of *apartheid*;

(*d*) Denial and withdrawal of national honours or awards in sports to such teams and individual sportsmen;

(*e*) Denial of official receptions in honour of such teams or sportsmen.

Article 7

States Parties shall deny visas and/or entry to representatives of sports bodies, teams and individual sportsmen representing a country practising *apartheid*.

Article 8

States Parties shall take all appropriate action to secure the expulsion of a country practising *apartheid* from international and regional sports bodies.

Article 9

States Parties shall take all appropriate measures to prevent international sports bodies from imposing financial or other penalties on affiliated bodies which, in accordance with United Nations resolutions, the provisions of the present Convention and the spirit of the Olympic principle, refuse to participate in sports with a country practising *apartheid*.

Article 10

1. States Parties shall use their best endeavours to ensure universal compliance with the Olympic principle of non-discrimination and the provisions of this Convention.

2. Towards this end, States Parties shall prohibit entry into their countries of members of teams and individual sportsmen participating or who have participated in sports competitions in South Africa and shall prohibit entry into their countries of representatives of sports bodies, members of teams and individual sportsmen who invite on their own initiative sports bodies, teams and sportsmen officially representing a country practising *apartheid* and partic-ipating under its flag. States Parties may also prohibit entry of representatives of sports bodies, members of teams or individual sportsmen who maintain sports

contacts with sports bodies, teams or sportsmen representing a country practising *apartheid* and participating under its flag. Prohibition of entry should not violate the regulations of the relevant sports federations which support the elimination of *apartheid* in sports and shall apply only to participation in sports activities.

3. States Parties shall advise their national representatives to international sports' federations to take all possible and practical steps to prevent the participation of the sports bodies, teams and sportsmen referred to in paragraph 2 above in international sports competitions and shall, through their representatives in international sports organizations, take every possible measure to:

(*a*) Ensure the expulsion of South Africa from all federations in which it still holds membership as well as to deny South Africa reinstatement to membership of any federation from which it has been expelled; and

(*b*) In case of national federations condoning sports exchanges with a country practising *apartheid*, to impose sanctions against such national federations including, if necessary, expulsion from the relevant international sports organization and exclusion of its representatives from participation in international sports competitions.

4. In cases of flagrant violations of the provisions of this Convention, States Parties shall take appropriate action as they deem fit, including where necessary steps aimed at the exclusion of the responsible national sports governing bodies, national sports federations or sportsmen of the countries concerned from international sports competition.

5. The provisions of the present article relating specifically to South Africa shall cease to apply when the system of *apartheid* is abolished in that country.

Article 11

1. There shall be established a Commission against *Apartheid* in Sports (hereinafter referred to as the Commission) consisting of fifteen members of high moral character and committed to the struggle against *apartheid*, particular attention being paid to the participation of persons having experience in sports administration, elected by the States Parties from among their nationals, having regard to the most equitable geographical distribution and the representation of the principal legal systems.

2. The members of the Commission shall be elected by secret ballot from a list of persons nominated by the States Parties. Each State Party may nominate one person from among its own nationals.

3. The initial election shall be held six months after the date of the entry into force of the present Convention. At least three months before the date of each election, the Secretary-General of the United Nations shall address a letter to the States Parties inviting them to submit their nominations within two months. The Secretary-General shall prepare a list in alphabetical order of all persons thus nominated, indicating the States Parties which have nominated them, and shall submit it to the States Parties.

4. Elections of the members of the Commission shall be held at a meeting of States Parties convened by the Secretary-General at United Nations Headquarters. At that meeting, for which two thirds of the States Parties shall constitute

a quorum, the persons elected to the Commission shall be those nominees who obtain the largest number of votes and an absolute majority of the votes of the representatives of States Parties present and voting.

5. The members of the Commission shall be elected for a term of four years. However, the terms of nine of the members elected at the first election shall expire at the end of two years; immediately after the first election, the names of these nine members shall be chosen by lot by the Chairman of the Commission.

6. For the filling of casual vacancies, the State Party whose national has ceased to function as a member of the Commission shall appoint another person from among its nationals, subject to the approval of the Commission.

7. States Parties shall be responsible for the expenses of the members of the Commission while they are in performance of Commission duties.

Article 12

1. States Parties undertake to submit to the Secretary-General of the United Nations, for consideration by the Commission, a report on the legislative, judicial, administrative or other measure which they have adopted to give effect to the provisions of the present Convention within one year of its entry into force and thereafter every two years. The Commission may request further information from the States Parties.

2. The Commission shall report annually through the Secretary-General to the General Assembly of the United Nations on its activities and may make suggestions and general recommendations based on the examination of the reports and information received from the States Parties. Such suggestions and recommendations shall be reported to the General Assembly together with comments, if any, from States Parties concerned.

3. The Commission shall examine, in particular, the implementation of the provisions of article 10 of the present Convention and make recommendations on action to be undertaken.

4. A meeting of States Parties shall be convened by the Secretary-General at the request of a majority of the States Parties to consider further action with respect to the implementation of the provisions of article 10 of the present Convention. In cases of flagrant violation of the provisions of the present Convention, a meeting of States Parties shall be convened by the Secretary-General at the request of the Commission.

Article 13

1. Any State Party may at any time declare that it recognizes the competence of the Commission to receive and examine complaints concerning breaches of the provisions of the present Convention submitted by States Parties which have also made such a declaration. The Commission may decide on the appropriate measures to be taken in respect of breaches.

2. States Parties against which a complaint has been made, in accordance with paragraph 1 of the present article, shall be entitled to be represented and take part in the proceedings of the Commission.

Article 14

1. The Commission shall meet at least once a year.
2. The Commission shall adopt its own rules of procedure.
3. The secretariat of the Commission shall be provided by the Secretary-General of the United Nations.
4. The meetings of the Commission shall normally be held at United Nations Headquarters.
5. The Secretary-General shall convene the initial meeting of the Commission.

Article 15

The Secretary-General of the United Nations shall be the Depositary of the present Convention.

Article 16

1. The present Convention is open for signature at United Nations Headquarters by all States until its entry into force.
2. The present Convention shall be subject to ratification, acceptance or approval by the signatory States.

Article 17

The present Convention is open for accession by all States.

Article 18

1. The present Convention shall enter into force on the thirtieth day after the date of deposit with the Depositary of the twenty-seventh instrument of ratification, acceptance, approval or accession.
2. For each State ratifying, accepting, approving or acceding to the present Convention after its entry into force, the Convention shall enter into force on the thirtieth day after the date of deposit of the relevant instrument.

Article 19

Any dispute between States Parties arising out of the interpretation, application or implementation of the present Convention which is not settled by negotiation shall be brought before the International Court of Justice at the request and with the mutual consent of the States Parties to the dispute, save where the Parties to the dispute have agreed on some other form of settlement.

Article 20

1. Any State Party may propose an amendment or revision to the present Convention and file it with the Depositary. The Secretary-General shall thereupon communicate the proposed amendment or revision to the States Parties with a request that they notify him whether they favour a conference of States Parties for the purpose of considering and voting upon the proposals. In the event that at least one third of the States Parties favour such a conference, the Secretary-General shall convene the conference under the auspices of the United Nations. Any amendment or revision adopted by the majority of the States

Parties present and voting at the conference shall be submitted to the General Assembly of the United Nations for approval.

2. Amendments or revisions shall come into force when they have been approved by the General Assembly of the United Nations and accepted by a two-thirds majority of the States Parties to the present Convention, in accordance with their respective constitutional processes.

3. When amendments or revisions come into force, they shall be binding on those States Parties which have accepted them, other States Parties still being bound by the provisions of the present Convention and any earlier amendment or revision which they have accepted.

Article 21

A State Party may withdraw from the present Convention by written notification to the Depositary. Such withdrawal shall take effect one year after the date of receipt of the notification by the Depositary.

Article 22

The present Convention has been concluded in Arabic, Chinese, English, French, Russian and Spanish, all texts being equally authentic.

9. DECLARATION ON THE HUMAN RIGHTS OF INDIVIDUALS WHO ARE NOT NATIONALS OF THE COUNTRY IN WHICH THEY LIVE (1985) G.A. Res. 40.144 (1985).

THE GENERAL ASSEMBLY,

Having considered the question of the human rights of individuals who are not nationals of the country in which they live,

Decides to adopt the Declaration on the Human Rights of Indivduals who are not Nationals of the Country in which They Live, which is annexed to the present resolution.

ANNEX

Declaration on the Human Rights of Individuals who are not
Nationals of the Country in which They Live

The General Assembly,

Considering that the Charter of the United Nations encourages the promotion of universal respect for and observance of the human rights and fundamental freedoms of all human beings, without distinction as to race, sex, language or religion,

Considering that the Universal Declaration of Human Rights proclaims that all human beings are born free and equal in dignity and rights and that everyone is entitled to all the rights and freedoms set forth in the Declaration, without distinction of any kind, such as race, colour, sex, language, religion, political or other opinion, national or social origin, property, birth or other status,

Considering that the Universal Declaration of Human Rights proclaims further that everyone has the right to recognition everywhere as a person before the law, that all are equal before the law, are entitled without any discrimination to equal protection of the law, and that all are entitled to equal protection against any discrimination in violation of the aforementioned Declaration and against any incitement to such discrimination,

Being aware that the States parties to the International Covenants on Human Rights now in force undertake to guarantee that the rights enunciated in these Covenants will be exercised without discrimination of any kind as to race, colour, sex, language, religion, political or other opinion, national or social origin, property, birth or other status,

Conscious that, with improving communications and the development of peaceful and friendly relations among countries, individuals increasingly live in countries of which they are not nationals,

Reaffirming the purposes and principles of the Charter of the United Nations,

Recognizing that the protection of human rights and fundamental freedoms provided for in international instruments should also be ensured for individuals who are not nationals of the country in which they live,

Proclaims this Declaration on the Human Rights of Individuals who are not Nationals of the Country in which They Live:

Article 1

For the purposes of this Declaration, the term "alien" shall apply, with due regard to qualifications made in subsequent articles, to any individual who is not a national of the State in which he or she is present.

Article 2

1. Nothing in this Declaration shall be interpreted as legitimizing any alien's illegal entry into and presence in a State, nor shall any provision be interpreted as restricting the right of any State to promulgate laws and regulations concerning the entry of aliens and the terms and conditions of their stay or to establish differences between nationals and aliens. However, such laws and regulations shall not be incompatible with the international legal obligations of that State, including those in the field of human rights.

2. This Declaration shall not prejudice the enjoyment of the rights accorded by domestic law and of the rights which under international law a State is obliged to accord to aliens, even where the present Declaration does not recognize such rights or recognizes them to a lesser extent.

Article 3

Every State shall make public its national legislation or regulations affecting aliens.

Article 4

Aliens shall observe the laws of the State in which they reside or are present and regard with respect the customs and traditions of the people of that State.

Article 5

1. Aliens shall enjoy in accordance with domestic law and subject to the relevant international obligations of the State in which they are present, in particular the following rights:

(*a*) The right to life and security of person; no alien shall be subjected to arbitrary arrest or detention; no alien shall be deprived of his liberty except on such grounds and in accordance with such procedures as are established by law;

(*b*) The right to protection against arbitrary or unlawful interference with privacy, family, home or correspondence;

(*c*) The right to be equal before the courts, tribunals and all other organs and authorities administering justice and, when necessary, to free assistance of an interpreter in criminal proceedings and, when prescribed by law, other proceedings;

(*d*) The right to choose a spouse, to marry, to found a family;

(*e*) The right to freedom of thought, opinion, conscience and religion; the right to manifest one's religion or beliefs subject only to such limitations as are prescribed by law and are necessary to protect public safety, order, health or morals or the fundamental rights and freedoms of others;

(*f*) The right to retain their own language, culture and tradition;

(*g*) The right to transfer abroad earnings, savings or other personal monetary assets, subject to domestic currency regulations.

2. Subject to such restrictions as are prescribed by law and which are necessary in a democratic society to protect national security, public safety, public order (ordre public), public health or morals or the rights and freedoms of others, and which are consistent with the other rights recognized in the relevant international instruments and those set forth in the present Declaration, aliens shall enjoy the following rights:

(*a*) The right to leave the country;

(*b*) The right to freedom of expression;

(*c*) The right to peaceful assembly;

(*d*) The right to own property alone as well as in association with others, subject to domestic law.

3. Subject to the provisions referred to in paragraph 2, aliens lawfully in the territory of a State shall enjoy the right to liberty of movement and freedom to choose their residence within the borders of the State.

4. Subject to national legislation and due authorization, the spouse and minor or dependent children of an alien lawfully residing in the territory of a State shall be admitted to accompany, join and stay with the alien.

Article 6

No alien shall be subjected to torture or to cruel, inhuman or degrading treatment or punishment and, in particular, no alien shall be subjected without his free consent to medical or scientific experimentation.

Article 7

An alien lawfully in the territory of a State may be expelled therefrom only in pursuance of a decision reached in accordance with law and shall, except where compelling reasons of national security otherwise require, be allowed to submit the reasons against his expulsion and to have his case reviewed by, and be represented for the purpose before, the competent authority or a person or persons specially designated by the competent authority. Individual or collective expulsion of such aliens on grounds of race, colour, religion, culture, descent or national or ethnic origin is prohibited.

Article 8

1. Aliens lawfully residing in the territory of a State shall also enjoy, in accordance with the national laws, the following rights, subject to their obligations referred to in article 4:

(*a*) The right to safe and healthy working conditions, to fair wages and equal remuneration for work or equal value without distinction of any kind, in particular women being guaranteed conditions of work not inferior to those enjoyed by men, with equal pay for equal work;

(*b*) The right to join trade unions and other organizations or associations of their choice and to participate in their activities. No restrictions may be placed on the exercise of this right other than those prescribed by law and which are necessary in a democratic society in the interests of national security or public order or for the protection of the rights and freedoms of others;

(*c*) The right to health protection, medical care, social security, social service, education, rest and leisure, provided that they fulfil the requirements under the relevant regulations for participation and that undue strain is not placed on the resources of the State.

2. With a view to protecting the rights of aliens carrying on lawful paid activities in the country in which they find themselves, such rights may be specified by the Governments concerned in multilateral or bilateral conventions.

Article 9

No alien shall be arbitrarily deprived of his lawfully acquired assets.

Article 10

Any alien shall be free at any time to communicate with the consulate or diplomatic mission of the State of which he is a national or, in their absence, with the consulate or diplomatic mission of any other State entrusted with the protection of the interests of the State of which he is a national in the State where he resides.

D. SLAVERY, SERVITUDE, FORCED LABOR AND SIMILAR INSTITUTIONS AND PRACTICES

The campaign for the abolition of slavery, which began in the 1700's, was the first great effort in international human rights activity.

The Slavery Convention of 1926, originally concluded under the auspices of the League of Nations, was aimed at the prevention and suppression of the slave trade and of slavery as it was traditionally known. The functions of the League in respect of the Convention were taken over by the United Nations pursuant to the 1953 Protocol to the Convention. The Supplementary Convention of 1956 was a further effort to deal with the suppression of some of the manifestations of slavery; it also brought within the ambit of prohibition institutions such as debt bondage, serfdom, sale of women into marriage and certain child labor practices. Regretably, neither slavery itself nor some of the practices akin to slavery have been entirely eliminated.

The Convention for the Suppression of the Traffic in Persons and of the Exploitation of the Prostitution of Others (1949) is often collected along with the slavery documents. We have included it in our section on Marriage and the Family, Childhood and Youth, *infra* Section 11, where we think it more appropriately belongs.

Probably the best source of material concerning the background to the treaties and international efforts generally is the "Report of the United Nations Special Rapporteur on Slavery," Mohamed Awad, *U.N. Doc.* E/4168/Rev.1 (1966). There is much useful material in the periodical journal of the Anti-Slavery Society which is entitled *The Anti-Slavery Reporter and Aborigines' Friend.* And *see,* V. Nanda and M. Bassiouni, *Slavery and the Slave Trade: Steps Toward its Eradication,* 12 Santa Clara Lawyer 434 (1972).

See also the ILO Forced Labor Conventions, *infra* Chapter II.

1. SLAVERY CONVENTION (1926) 82 U.N.T.S. 51, 212 U.N.T.S. 17.

SIGNED AT GENEVA ON 25 SEPTEMBER 1926

ENTRY INTO FORCE: 9 March 1927, in accordance with article 12. The Convention was amended by the Protocol done at the Headquarters of the United Nations, New York, on 7 December 1953; the amended Convention entered into force on 7 July 1955; the date on which the amendments, set forth in the annex to the Protocol of 7 December 1953, entered into force in accordance with article III of the Protocol.

Whereas the signatories of the General Act of the Brussels Conference of

1889–90 declared that they were equally animated by the firm intention of putting an end to the traffic in African slaves,

Whereas the signatories of the Convention of Saint-Germain-en-Laye of 1919, to revise the General Act of Berlin of 1885, and the General Act and Declaration of Brussels of 1890, affirmed their intention of securing the complete suppression of slavery in all its forms and of the slave trade by land and sea,

Taking into consideration the report of the Temporary Slavery Commission appointed by the Council of the League of Nations on June 12th, 1924,

Desiring to complete and extend the work accomplished under the Brussels Act and to find a means of giving practical effect throughout the world to such intentions as were expressed in regard to slave trade and slavery by the signatories of the Convention of Saint-Germain-en-Laye, and recognising that it is necessary to conclude to that end more detailed arrangements than are contained in that Convention,

Considering, moreover, that it is necessary to prevent forced labour from developing into conditions analogous to slavery,

Have decided to conclude a Convention and have accordingly appointed as their Plenipotentiaries [*names omitted*]

. . . *have agreed* as follows:

Article 1

For the purpose of the present Convention, the following definitions are agreed upon:

(1) Slavery is the status or condition of a person over whom any or all of the powers attaching to the right of ownership are exercised.

(2) The slave trade includes all acts involved in the capture, acquisition or disposal of a person with intent to reduce him to slavery; all acts involved in the acquisition of a slave with a view to selling or exchanging him; all acts of disposal by sale or exchange of a slave acquired with a view to being sold or exchanged, and, in general, every act of trade or transport in slaves.

Article 2

The High Contracting Parties undertake, each in respect of the territories placed under its sovereignty, jurisdiction, protection, suzerainty or tutelage, so far as they have not already taken the necessary steps:

a. To prevent and suppress the slave trade;

b. To bring about, progressively and as soon as possible, the complete abolition of slavery in all its forms.

Article 3

The High Contracting Parties undertake to adopt all appropriate measures with a view to preventing and suppressing the embarkation, disembarkation and transport of slaves in their territorial waters and upon all vessels flying their respective flags.

The High Contracting Parties undertake to negotiate as soon as possible a general Convention with regard to the slave trade which will give them rights and impose upon them duties of the same nature as those provided for in the

Convention of June 17th, 1925, relative to the International Trade in Arms (Articles 12, 20, 21, 22, 23, 24, and paragraphs 3, 4 and 5 of Section II of Annex II), with the necessary adaptations, it being understood that this general Convention will not place the ships (even of small tonnage) of any High Contracting Parties in a position different from that of the other High Contracting Parties.

It is also understood that, before or after the coming into force of this general Convention, the High Contracting Parties are entirely free to conclude between themselves, without, however, derogating from the principles laid down in the preceding paragraph, such special agreements as, by reason of their peculiar situation, might appear to be suitable in order to bring about as soon as possible the complete disappearance of the slave trade.

Article 4

The High Contracting Parties shall give to one another every assistance with the object of securing the abolition of slavery and the slave trade.

Article 5

The High Contracting Parties recognise that recourse to compulsory or forced labour may have grave consequences and undertake, each in respect of the territories placed under its sovereignty, jurisdiction, protection, suzerainty or tutelage, to take all necessary measures to prevent compulsory or forced labour from developing into conditions analogous to slavery.

It is agreed that:

(1) Subject to the transitional provisions laid down in paragraph (2) below, compulsory or forced labour may only be exacted for public purposes.

(2) In territories in which compulsory or forced labour for other than public purposes still survives, the High Contracting Parties shall endeavour progressively and as soon as possible to put an end to the practice. So long as such forced or compulsory labour exists, this labour shall invariably be of an exceptional character, shall always receive adequate remuneration, and shall not involve the removal of the labourers from their usual place of residence.

(3) In all cases, the responsibility for any recourse to compulsory or forced labour shall rest with the competent central authorities of the territory concerned.

Article 6

Those of the High Contracting Parties whose laws do not at present make adequate provision for the punishment of infractions of laws and regulations enacted with a view to giving effect to the purposes of the present Convention undertake to adopt the necessary measures in order that severe penalties may be imposed in respect of such infractions.

Article 7

The High Contracting Parties undertake to communicate to each other and to the Secretary-General of the League of Nations any laws and regulations which they may enact with a view to the application of the provisions of the present Convention.

* * *

[For omitted procedural provisions, Article 8, see below, Chapter IV.A.16.]

Article 9

At the time of signature or of ratification or of accession, any High Contracting Party may declare that its acceptance of the present convention does not bind some or all of the territories placed under its sovereignty, jurisdiction, protection, suzerainty or tutelage in respect of all or any provisions of the Convention; it may subsequently accede separately on behalf of any one of them or in respect of any provision to which any one of them is not a party.

Article 10

In the event of a High Contracting Party wishing to denounce the present Convention, the denunciation shall be notified in writing to the Secretary-General of the League of Nations, who will at once communicate a certified true copy of the notification to all the other High Contracting Parties, informing them of the date on which it was received.

The denunciation shall only have effect in regard to the notifying State, and one year after the notification has reached the Secretary-General of the League of Nations.

Denunciation may also be made separately in respect of any territory placed under its sovereignty, jurisdiction, protection, suzerainty or tutelage.

Article 11

The present Convention, which will bear this day's date and of which the French and English texts are both authentic, will remain open for signature by the States Members of the League of Nations until April 1st, 1927.

The Secretary-General of the League of Nations will subsequently bring the present Convention to the notice of States which have not signed it, including States which are not Members of the League of Nations, and invite them to accede thereto.

A State desiring to accede to the Convention shall notify its intention in writing to the Secretary-General of the League of Nations and transmit to him the instrument of accession, which shall be deposited in the archives of the League.

The Secretary-General shall immediately transmit to all the other High Contracting Parties a certified true copy of the notification and of the instrument of accession, informing them of the date on which he received them.

Article 12

The present Convention will be ratified and the instruments of ratification shall be deposited in the office of the Secretary-General of the League of Nations. The Secretary-General will inform all the High Contracting Parties of such deposit.

The Convention will come into operation for each State on the date of the deposit of its ratification or of its accession.

IN FAITH WHEREOF the Plenipotentiaries signed the present Convention.

DONE at Geneva the twenty-fifth day of September, one thousand nine hundred and twenty-six, in one copy, which will be deposited in the archives of the League of Nations. A certified copy shall be forwarded to each signatory State.

2. PROTOCOL AMENDING THE SLAVERY CONVENTION (1953) G.A. Res. 794 (VIII), 8 U.N. GAOR, Supp. (No. 17) at 50, U.N. Doc. A/2630 (1953).

THE STATES PARTIES TO THE PRESENT PROTOCOL,

Considering that under the Slavery Convention signed at Geneva on 25 September 1926 (hereinafter called "the Convention") the League of Nations was invested with certain duties and functions, and

Considering that it is expedient that these duties and functions should be continued by the United Nations,

Have agreed as follows:

Article I

The States Parties to the present Protocol undertake that as between themselves they will, in accordance with the provisions of the Protocol, attribute full legal force and effect to and duly apply the amendments to the Convention set forth in the annex to the Protocol.

Article II

1. The present Protocol shall be open for signature or acceptance by any of the States Parties to the Convention to which the Secretary-General has communicated for this purpose a copy of the Protocol.

2. States may become Parties to the present Protocol by:
   a. Signature without reservation as to acceptance;
   b. Signature with reservation as to acceptance, followed by acceptance;
   c. Acceptance.

3. Acceptance shall be effected by the deposit of a formal instrument with the Secretary-General of the United Nations.

Article III

1. The present Protocol shall come into force on the date on which two States shall have become Parties thereto, and shall thereafter come into force in respect of each State upon the date on which it becomes a Party to the Protocol.

2. The amendments set forth in the annex to the present Protocol shall come into force when twenty-three States shall have become Parties to the Protocol,

and consequently any State becoming a Party to the Convention, after the amendments thereto have come into force, shall become a Party to the Convention as so amended.

Article IV

In accordance with paragraph I of Article 102 of the Charter of the United Nations and the regulations pursuant thereto adopted by the General Assembly, the Secretary-General of the United Nations is authorized to effect registration of the present Protocol and of the amendments made in the Convention by the Protocol on the respective dates of their entry into force and to publish the Protocol and the amended text of the Convention as soon as possible after registration.

Article V

The present Protocol, of which the Chinese, English, French, Russian and Spanish texts are equally authentic, shall be deposited in the archives of the United Nations Secretariat. The texts of the Convention to be amended in accordance with the annex being authentic in the English and French languages only, the English and French texts of the annex shall be equally authentic, and the Chinese, Russian and Spanish texts shall be translations. The Secretary-General shall prepare certified copies of the Protocol, including the annex, for communication to States Parties to the Convention, as well as to all other States Members of the United Nations. He shall likewise prepare for communication to States including States not Members of the United Nations, upon the entry into force of the amendments as provided in article III, certified copies of the Convention as so amended.

IN WITNESS WHEREOF the undersigned, being duly authorized thereto by their respective Governments, signed the present Protocol on the date appearing opposite their respective signatures.

DONE at the Headquarters of the United Nations, New York, this seventh day of December one thousand nine hundred and fifty-three.

ANNEX TO THE PROTOCOL AMENDING THE SLAVERY CONVENTION SIGNED AT GENEVA ON 25 SEPTEMBER 1926

In *article 7* "the Secretary-General of the United Nations" shall be substituted for "the Secretary-General of the League of Nations."

In *article 8* "the International Court of Justice" shall be substituted for the "Permanent Court of International Justice," and "the Statute of the International Court of Justice" shall be substituted for "the Protocol of December 16th, 1920, relating to the Permanent Court of International Justice."

In the first and second paragraphs of *article 10* "the United Nations" shall be substituted for "the League of Nations."

The last three paragraphs of *article 11* shall be deleted and the following substituted:

"The present Convention shall be open to accession by all States, including States which are not Members of the United Nations, to which the Secretary-

General of the United Nations shall have communicated a certified copy of the Convention."

"Accession shall be effected by the deposit of a formal instrument with the Secretary-General of the United Nations, who shall give notice thereof to all States Parties to the Convention and to all other States contemplated in the present article, informing them of the date on which each such instrument of accession was received in deposit."

In *article 12* "the United Nations" shall be substituted for "the League of Nations."

3. SUPPLEMENTARY CONVENTION ON THE ABOLITION OF SLAVERY, THE SLAVE TRADE, AND INSTITUTIONS AND PRACTICES SIMILAR TO SLAVERY (1956) (SEE ALSO ILO DOCUMENTS, CHAPTER II) 7 September 1956, 266 U.N.T.S. 3. Entered into force 30 April 1957 in accordance with Article 13.

PREAMBLE

The States Parties to the present Convention,

Considering that freedom is the birthright of every human being.

Mindful that the peoples of the United Nations reaffirmed in the Charter their faith in the dignity and worth of the human person.

Considering that the Universal Declaration of Human Rights, proclaimed by the General Assembly of the United Nations as a common standard of achievement for all peoples and all nations, states that no one shall be held in slavery or servitude and that slavery and the slave trade shall be prohibited in all their forms,

Recognizing that, since the conclusion of the Slavery Convention signed at Geneva on 25 September 1926, which was designed to secure the abolition of slavery and of the slave trade, further progress has been made towards this end,

Having regard to the Forced Labour Convention of 1930 and to subsequent action by the International Labour Organisation in regard to forced or compulsory labour,

Being aware, however, that slavery, the slave trade and institutions and practices similar to slavery have not yet been eliminated in all parts of the world,

Having decided, therefore, that the Convention of 1926, which remains operative, should now be augmented by the conclusion of a supplementary convention designed to intensify national as well as international efforts towards the abolition of slavery, the slave trade and institutions and practices similar to slavery,

Have agreed as follows:

SECTION I

INSTITUTIONS AND PRACTICES SIMILAR TO SLAVERY

Article 1

Each of the States Parties to this Convention shall take all practicable and necessary legislative and other measures to bring about progressively and as soon as possible the complete abolition or abandonment of the following institutions and practices, where they still exist and whether or not they are covered by the definition of slavery contained in article 1 of the Slavery Convention signed at Geneva on 25 September 1926:

a. Debt bondage, that is to say, the status or condition arising from a pledge by a debtor of his personal services or of those of a person under his control as security for a debt, if the value of those services as reasonably assessed is not applied towards the liquidation of the debt or the length and nature of those services are not respectively limited and defined;

b. Serfdom, that is to say, the condition or status of a tenant who is by law, custom or agreement bound to live and labour on land belonging to another person and to render some determinate service to such other person, whether for reward or not, and is not free to change his status;

c. Any institution or practice whereby:

i. A woman, without the right to refuse, is promised or given in marriage on payment of a consideration in money or in kind to her parents, guardian, family or any other person or group; or

ii. The husband of a woman, his family, or his clan, has the right to transfer her to another person for value received or otherwise; or

iii. A woman on the death of her husband is liable to be inherited by another person;

d. Any institution or practice whereby a child or young person under the age of 18 years, is delivered by either or both of his natural parents or by his guardian to another person, whether for reward or not, with a view to the exploitation of the child or young person or of his labour.

Article 2

With a view to bringing to an end the institutions and practices mentioned in article 1 (*c*) of this Convention, the States Parties undertake to prescribe, where appropriate, suitable minimum ages of marriage, to encourage the use of facilities whereby the consent of both parties to a marriage may be freely expressed in the presence of a competent civil or religious authority, and to encourage the registration of marriages.

SECTION II

THE SLAVE TRADE

Article 3

1. The act of conveying or attempting to convey slaves from one country to

another by whatever means of transport, or of being accessory thereto, shall be a criminal offence under the laws of the States Parties to this Convention and persons convicted thereof shall be liable to very severe penalties.

2. a. The States Parties shall take all effective measures to prevent ships and aircraft authorized to fly their flags from conveying slaves and to punish persons guilty of such acts or of using national flags for that purpose.

b. The States Parties shall take all effective measures to ensure that their ports, airfields and coasts are not used for the conveyance of slaves.

3. The States Parties to this Convention shall exchange information in order to ensure the practical co-ordination of the measures taken by them in combating the slave trade and shall inform each other of every case of the slave trade, and of every attempt to commit this criminal offence, which comes to their notice.

Article 4

Any slave who takes refuge on board any vessel of a State Party to this Convention shall *ipso facto* be free.

SECTION III

SLAVERY AND INSTITUTIONS AND PRACTICES SIMILAR TO SLAVERY

Article 5

In a country where the abolition or abandonment of slavery, or of the institutions or practices mentioned in article 1 of this Convention, is not yet complete, the act of mutilating, branding or otherwise marking a slave or a person of servile status in order to indicate his status, or as a punishment, or for any other reason, or of being accessory thereto, shall be a criminal offence under the laws of the States Parties to this Convention and persons convicted thereof shall be liable to punishment.

Article 6

1. The act of enslaving another person or of inducing another person to give himself or a person dependent upon him into slavery, or of attempting these acts, or being accessory thereto, or being a party to a conspiracy to accomplish any such acts, shall be a criminal offence under the laws of the States Parties to this Convention and persons convicted thereof shall be liable to punishment.

2. Subject to the provisions of the introductory paragraph of article 1 of this Convention, the provisions of paragraph 1 of the present article shall also apply to the act of inducing another person to place himself or a person dependent upon him into the servile status resulting from any of the institutions or practices mentioned in article 1, to any attempt to perform such acts, to bring accessory thereto, and to being a party to a conspiracy to accomplish any such acts.

SECTION IV

DEFINITIONS

Article 7

For the purposes of the present Convention:

a. "Slavery" means, as defined in the Slavery Convention of 1926, the status or condition of a person over whom any or all of the powers attaching to the right of ownership are exercised, and "slave" means a person in such condition or status;

b. "A person of servile status" means a person in the condition or status resulting from any of the institutions or practices mentioned in article 1 of this Convention;

c. "Slave trade" means and includes all acts involved in the capture, acquisition or disposal of a person with intent to reduce him to slavery; all acts involved in the acquisition of a slave with a view to selling or exchanging him; all acts of disposal by sale or exchange of a person acquired with a view to being sold or exchanged; and, in general, every act of trade or transport in slaves by whatever means of conveyance.

SECTION V

CO-OPERATION BETWEEN STATES PARTIES AND COMMUNICATION OF INFORMATION

Article 8

1. The States Parties to this Convention undertake to co-operate with each other and with the United Nations to give effect to the foregoing provisions.

2. The Parties undertake to communicate to the Secretary-General of the United Nations copies of any laws, regulations and administrative measures enacted or put into effect to implement the provisions of this Convention.

3. The Secretary-General shall communicate the information received under paragraph 2 of this article to the other Parties and to the Economic and Social Council as part of the documentation for any discussion which the Council might undertake with a view to making further recommendations for the abolition of slavery, the slave trade or the institutions and practices which are the subject of this Convention.

SECTION VI

FINAL CLAUSES

Article 9

No reservations may be made to this Convention.

* * *

[For omitted procedural provisions, Article 10, see below, Chapter IV.A.16.]

Article 11

1. This Convention shall be open until 1 July 1957 for signature by any State

Member of the United Nations or of a specialized agency. It shall be subject to ratification by the signatory States, and the instruments of ratification shall be deposited with the Secretary-General of the United Nations, who shall inform each signatory and acceding State.

2. After 1 July 1957 this Convention shall be open for accession by any State Member of the United Nations or of a specialized agency, or by any other State to which an invitation to accede has been addressed by the General Assembly of the United Nations. Accession shall be

E. RIGHT TO SELF-DETERMINATION

INTRODUCTION

Article 73 of the Charter (*see supra* Section A1) spoke of the obligation of Members of the UN which have responsibilities for non-self governing territories to "develop self-government" and to transmit to the Secretary-General certain information on those territories. Acting under the aegis of Article 73, the General Assembly has made various efforts to create machinery to supervise these obligations (*see infra* Chapter IV), as well as to determine to which territories the obligations of Article 73 apply. In the course of its efforts the Assembly has made some significant attempts to define the right to self-determination. The three Resolutions that follow constitute its most important efforts in this regard. (*See* also common Article 1 of the International Covenants, *supra*, Section 3). It is fair to say that, taken together (and in United Nations usage the 1960 Declaration is given the most weight), the documents represent strong support for the ending of "salt-water" colonialism. On the other hand, they provide little underpinning for any right of secession from independent countries including former colonies, regardless of the crazy-quilt boundaries left as a legacy by the colonial powers.

The best of the large body of literature on this topic is: R. Emerson, *Self-Determination Revisited in an Era of Decolonization* (1964); U. Umozurike, *Self-Determination in International Law* (1972); A. Sureda, *The Evolution of the Right of Self-Determination: A Study of United Nations Practice* (1973); Y. El-Ayouty, *The United Nations and Decolonization; The Role of Afro-Asia* (1971); C. Toussaint, *The Trusteeship System of the United Nations* (1956).

1. DECLARATION ON THE GRANTING OF INDEPENDENCE TO COLONIAL COUNTRIES AND PEOPLES (1960) G.A. Res. 1514 (XV), 15 U.N. GAOR, Supp. (No.16) at 66, U.N. Doc. A/4684 (1960).

THE GENERAL ASSEMBLY

Mindful of the determination proclaimed by the peoples of the world in the Charter of the United Nations to reaffirm faith in fundamental human rights, in the dignity and worth of the human person, in the equal rights of men and women and of nations large and small and to promote social progress and better standards of life in larger freedom,

Conscious of the need for the creation of conditions of stability and well-being and peaceful and friendly relations based on respect for the principles of equal rights and self-determination of all peoples, and of universal respect for, and observance of, human rights and fundamental freedoms for all without distinction as to race, sex, language or religion,

Recognizing the passionate yearning for freedom in all dependent peoples and the decisive role of such peoples in the attainment of their independence,

Aware of the increasing conflicts resulting from the denial of or impediments in the way of the freedom of such peoples, which constitute a serious threat to world peace,

Considering the important role of the United Nations in assisting the movement for independence in Trust and Non-Self-Governing Territories,

Recognizing that the peoples of the world ardently desire the end of colonialism in all its manifestations,

Convinced that the continued existence of colonialism prevents the development of international economic co-operation, impedes the social, cultural and economic development of dependent peoples and militates against the United Nations ideal of universal peace,

Affirming that peoples may, for their own ends, freely dispose of their natural wealth and resources without prejudice to any obligations arising out of international economic co-operation, based upon the principle of mutual benefit, and international law,

Believing that the process of liberation is irresistible and irreversible and that, in order to avoid serious crises, an end must be put to colonialism and all practices of segregation and discrimination associated therewith,

Welcoming the emergence in recent years of a large number of dependent territories into freedom and independence, and recognizing the increasingly powerful trends towards freedom in such territories which have not yet attained independence,

Convinced that all peoples have an inalienable right to complete freedom, the exercise of their sovereignty and the integrity of their national territory,

Solemnly proclaims the necessity of bringing to a speedy and unconditional end colonialism in all its forms and manifestations;

And to this end

Declares that:

1. The subjection of peoples to alien subjugation, domination and exploitation constitutes a denial of fundamental human rights, is contrary to the Charter of the United Nations and is an impediment to the promotion of world peace and co-operation.

2. All peoples have the right to self-determination; by virtue of that right they freely determine their political status and freely pursue their economic, social and cultural development.

3. Inadequacy of political, economic, social or educational preparedness should never serve as a pretext for delaying independence.

4. All armed action or repressive measures of all kinds directed against dependent peoples shall cease in order to enable them to exercise peacefully and freely their right to complete independence, and the integrity of their national territory shall be respected.

5. Immediate steps shall be taken, in Trust and Non-Self-Governing Territories or all other territories which have not yet attained independence, to transfer all powers to the peoples of those territories, without any conditions or reservations, in accordance with their freely expressed will and desire, without

any distinction as to race, creed or colour, in order to enable them to enjoy complete independence and freedom.

6. Any attempt aimed at the partial or total disruption of the national unity and the territorial integrity of a country is incompatible with the purposes and principles of the Charter of the United Nations.

7. All States shall observe faithfully and strictly the provisions of the Charter of the United Nations, the Universal Declaration of Human Rights, and the present Declaration on the basis of equality, non-interference in the internal affairs of all States, and respect for the sovereign rights of all peoples and their territorial integrity.

2. PRINCIPLES WHICH SHOULD GUIDE MEMBERS IN DETERMINING WHETHER OR NOT AN OBLIGATION EXISTS TO TRANSMIT THE INFORMATION CALLED FOR UNDER ARTICLE 73e OF THE CHARTER (1960) G.A. Res. 1541 (XV), 15 U.N. GAOR, Supp. (No. 16) at 29, U.N. Doc. A/4684 (1960).

THE GENERAL ASSEMBLY

Considering the objectives set forth in Chapter XI of the Charter of the United Nations,

Bearing in mind the list of factors annexed to General Assembly resolution 742 (VIII) of 27 November 1953,

Having examined the report of the Special Committee of Six on the Transmission of Information under Article 73 e of the Charter, appointed under General Assembly resolution 1467 (XIV) of 12 December 1959 to study the principles which should guide Members in determining whether or not an obligation exists to transmit the information called for in Article 73 e of the Charter and to report on the results of its study to the Assembly at its fifteenth session,

1. *Expresses its appreciation* of the work of the Special Committee of Six on the Transmission of Information under Article 73 e of the Charter;

2. *Approves* the principles set out in section V, part B, of the report of the Committee, as amended and as they appear in the annex to the present resolution;

3. *Decides* that these principles should be applied in the light of the facts and the circumstances of each case to determine whether or not an obligation exists to transmit information under Article 73 e of the Charter.

ANNEX TO GENERAL ASSEMBLY RESOLUTION 1541 (XV)

Principles which should guide Members in determining whether or not an obligation exists to transmit the information called for in Article 73 e of the Charter of the United Nations

Principle I

The authors of the Charter of the United Nations had in mind that Chapter XI should be applicable to territories which were then known to be of the colonial type. An obligation exists to transmit information under Article 73 e of the Charter in respect of such territories whose peoples have not yet attained a full measure of self-government.

Principle II

Chapter XI of the Charter embodies the concept of Non-Self-Governing Territories in a dynamic state of evolution and progress towards a "full measure of self-government". As soon as a territory and its peoples attain a full measure of self-government, the obligation ceases. Until this comes about, the obligation to transmit information under Article 73 e continues.

Principle III

The obligation to transmit information under Article 73 e of the Charter constitutes an international obligation and should be carried out with due regard to the fulfilment of international law.

Principle IV

Prima facie there is an obligation to transmit information in respect of a territory which is geographically separate and is distinct ethnically and/or culturally from the country administering it.

Principle V

Once it has been established that such a *prima facie* case of geographical and ethnical or cultural distinctness of a territory exists, other elements may then be brought into consideration. These additional elements may be, *inter alia*, of an administrative, political, juridical, economic or historical nature. If they affect the relationship between the metropolitan State and the territory concerned in a manner which arbitrarily places the latter in a position or status of subordination, they support the presumption that there is an obligation to transmit information under Article 73 e of the Charter.

Principle VI

A Non-Self-Governing Territory can be said to have reached a full measure of self-government by:
    a. Emergence as a sovereign independent State;
    b. Free association with an independent State; or
    c. Integration with an independent State.

Principle VII

    a. Free association should be the result of a free and voluntary choice by the peoples of the territory concerned expressed through informed and democratic processes. It should be one which respects the individuality and the cultural characteristics of the territory and its peoples, and retains for the peoples of the territory which is associated with an independent State the freedom to modify the status of that territory through the expression of their will by democratic means and through constitutional processes.

b. The associated territory should have the right to determine its internal constitution without outside interference, in accordance with due constitutional processes and the freely expressed wishes of the people. This does not preclude consultations as appropriate or necessary under the terms of the free associaton agreed upon.

Principle VIII

Integration with an independent State should be on the basis of complete equality between the peoples of the erstwhile Non-Self-Governing Territory and those of the independent country with which it is integrated. The peoples of both territories should have equal status and rights of citizenship and equal guarantees of fundamental rights and freedoms without any distinction or discrimination; both should have equal rights and opportunities for representation and effective participation at all levels in the executive, legislative and judicial organs of government.

Principle IX

Integration should have come about in the following circumstances:

a. The integrating territory should have attained an advanced stage of self-government with free political institutions, so that its peoples would have the capacity to make a responsible choice through informed and democratic processes;

b. The integration should be the result of the freely expressed wishes of the Territory's peoples acting with full knowledge of the change in their status, their wishes having been expressed through informed and democratic processes, impartially conducted and based on universal adult suffrage. The United Nations could, when it deems it necessary, supervise these processes.

Principle X

The transmission of information in respect of Non-Self-Governing Territories under Article 73 e of the Charter is subject to such limitation as security and constitutional considerations may require. This means that the extent of the information may be limited in certain circumstances, but the limitation in Article 73 e cannot relieve a Member State of the obligations of Chapter XI. The "limitation" can relate only to the quantum of information of economic, social and educational nature to be transmitted.

Principle XI

The only constitutional considerations to which Article 73 e of the Charter refers are those arising from constitutional relations of the territory with the Administering Member. They refer to a situation in which the constitution of the territory gives it self-government in economic, social and educational matters through freely elected institutions. Nevertheless, the responsibility for transmitting information under Article 73 e continues, unless these constitutional relations preclude the Government or parliament of the Administering Member from receiving statistical and other information of a technical nature relating to economic, social and educational conditions in the territory.

Principle XII

Security considerations have not been invoked in the past. Only in very exceptional circumstances can information on economic, social and educational conditions have any security aspect. In other circumstances, therefore, there should be no necessity to limit the transmission of information on security grounds.

3. DECLARATION ON PRINCIPLES OF INTERNATIONAL LAW CONCERNING FRIENDLY RELATIONS AND COOPERATION AMONG STATES IN ACCORDANCE WITH THE CHARTER OF THE UNITED NATIONS (1970) (THE PRINCIPLE OF EQUAL RIGHTS AND SELF-DETERMINATION OF PEOPLES) G.A. Res. 2625 (XXV), 25 U.N. GAOR, Supp. (No. 28) at 121, U.N. Doc. A/8028 (1970).

THE GENERAL ASSEMBLY,

Reaffirming in the terms of the Charter of the United Nations that the maintenance of international peace and security and the development of friendly relations and co-operation between nations are among the fundamental purposes of the United Nations,

* * *

Convinced that the subjection of peoples to alien subjugation, domination and exploitation constitutes a major obstacle to the promotion of international peace and security,

Convinced that the principle of equal rights and self-determination of peoples constitutes a significant contribution to contemporary international law, and that its effective application is of paramount importance for the promotion of friendly relations among States, based on respect for the principle of sovereign equality,

Convinced in consequence that any attempt aimed at the partial or total disruption of the national unity and territorial integrity of a State or country or at its political independence is incompatible with the purposes and principles of the Charter.

Considering the provisions of the Charter as a whole and taking into account the role of relevant resolutions adopted by the competent organs of the United Nations relating to the content of the principles,

Considering that the progressive development and codification of the following principles:

a. The principle that States shall refrain in their international relations from the threat or use of force against the territorial integrity or political independence of any State, or in any other manner inconsistent with the purposes of the United Nations.

b. The principle that States shall settle their international disputes by peaceful means in such a manner that international peace and security and justice are not endangered.

c. The duty not to intervene in matters within the domestic jurisdiction of any State, in accordance with the Charter,

d. The duty of States to co-operate with one another in accordance with the Charter.

e. The principle of equal rights and self-determination of peoples.

f. The principle of sovereign equality of States.

g. The principle that States shall fulfil in good faith the obligations assumed by them in accordance with the Charter,

so as to secure their more effective application within the international community, would promote the realization of the purposes of the United Nations,

Having considered the principles of international law relating to friendly relations and co-operation among States,

1. *SOLEMNLY PROCLAIMS* THE FOLLOWING PRINCIPLES:

THE PRINCIPLE OF EQUAL RIGHTS AND SELF-DETERMINATION OF PEOPLES

By virtue of the principle of equal rights and self-determination of peoples enshrined in the Charter of the United Nations, all peoples have the right freely to determine, without external interference, their political status and to pursue their economic, social and cultural development, and every State has the duty to respect this right in accordance with the provisions of the Charter.

Every State has the duty to promote, through joint and separate action, realization of the principle of equal rights and self-determination of peoples, in accordance with the provisions of the Charter, and to render assistance to the United Nations in carrying out the responsibilities entrusted to it by the Charter regarding the implementation of the principle, in order:

a. To promote friendly relations and co-operation among States; and

b. To bring a speedy end to colonialism, having due regard to the freely expressed will of the peoples concerned;

and bearing in mind that subjection of peoples to alien subjugation, domination and exploitation constitutes a violation of the principle, as well as a denial of fundamental human rights, and is contrary to the Charter.

Every State has the duty to promote through joint and separate action universal respect for and observance of human rights and fundamental freedoms in accordance with the Charter.

The establishment of a sovereign and independent State, the free association or integration with an independent State or the emergence into any other political status freely determined by a people constitute modes of implementing the right of self-determination by that people.

Every State has the duty to refrain from any forcible action which deprives peoples referred to above in the elaboration of the present principle of their right to self-determination and freedom and independence. In their actions against, and resistance to, such forcible action in pursuit of the exercise of their right to self-determination, such peoples are entitled to seek and to receive support in accordance with the purposes and principles of the Charter.

The territory of a colony or other Non-Self-Governing Territory has, under the Charter, a status separate and distinct from the territory of the State administering it; and such separate and distinct status under the Charter shall exist until the people of the colony or Non-Self-Governing Territory have exercised their right of self-determination in accordance with the Charter, and particularly its purposes and principles.

Nothing in the foregoing paragraphs shall be construed as authorizing or encouraging any action which would dismember or impair, totally or in part, the territorial integrity or political unity of sovereign and independent States conducting themselves in compliance with the principle of equal rights and self-determination of peoples as described above and thus possessed of a government representing the whole people belonging to the territory without distinction as to race, creed or colour.

Every State shall refrain from any action aimed at the partial or total disruption of the national unity and territorial integrity of any other State or country.

* * *

[Other Principles omitted]

F. WAR CRIMES AND CRIMES AGAINST HUMANITY

INTRODUCTION

The question of war crimes is, to a substantial extent, governed by the Geneva Conventions (Chapter VI) which were not developed under the auspices of the United Nations. The matter of crimes against humnanity has, however, been one of considerable importance to the United Nations. In large part, the human rights provisions of the Charter were a response to the Holocaust of the Second World War. It was only appropriate, therefore, that the first UN human rights treaty to be adopted was the Genocide Convention of 1948.

The prosecution of persons charged with war crimes and crimes against humanity has been facilitated by the 1968 Convention and 1973 Principles which we reproduce following the Genocide Convention.

A very useful set of further readings on this subject is *Crimes of War*, (R. Falk, G. Kolko and R. Lifton, eds. 1971).

And see *International Criminal Law*, Vol. I, *Crimes*, (M. Bassiouni ed., 1986).

1. CONVENTION ON THE PREVENTION AND PUNISHMENT OF THE CRIME OF GENOCIDE (1948) G.A. Res. 260A (III), 3 (1) U.N. GAOR at 174, U.N. Doc. A/810 (1948). In force 12 January 1951 in accordance with Article XIII.

THE CONTRACTING PARTIES,

Having considered the declaration made by the General Assembly of the United Nations in its resolution 96 (I) dated 11 December 1946 that genocide is a crime under international law, contrary to the spirit and aims of the United Nations and condemned by the civilized world,

Recognizing that at all periods of history genocide has inflicted great losses on humanity, and

Being convinced that, in order to liberate mankind from such an odious scourge, international co-operation is required,

Hereby agree as hereinafter provided:

Article I

The Contracting Parties confirm that genocide, whether committed in time of peace or in time of war, is a crime under international law which they undertake to prevent and to punish.

Article II

In the present Convention, genocide means any of the following acts committed with intent to destroy, in whole or in part, a national, ethnical, racial or religious group, as such:

    a. Killing members of the group;

    b. Causing serious bodily or mental harm to members of the group;

    c. Deliberately inflicting on the group conditions of life calculated to bring about its physical destruction in whole or in part;

    d. Imposing measures intended to prevent births within the group;

    e. Forcibly transferring children of the group to another group.

Article III

The following acts shall be punishable:

    a. Genocide;

    b. Conspiracy to commit genocide;

    c. Direct and public incitement to commit genocide;

    d. Attempt to commit genocide;

    e. Complicity in genocide.

Article IV

Persons committing genocide or any other other acts enumerated in article III shall be punished, whether they are constitutionally responsible rulers, public officials or private individuals.

Article V

The Contracting Parties undertake to enact, in accordance with their respective Constitutions, the necessary legislation to give effect to the provisions of the present Convention and, in particular, to provide effective penalties for persons guilty of genocide or any of the other acts enumerated in article III.

Article VI

Persons charged with genocide or any of the other acts enumerated in article III shall be tried by a competent tribunal of the State in the territory of which the act was committed, or by such international penal tribunal as may have jurisdiction with respect to those Contracting Parties which shall have accepted its jurisdiction.

Article VII

Genocide and the other acts enumerated in article III shall not be considered as political crimes for the purpose of extradition.

The Contracting Parties pledge themselves in such cases to grant extradition in accordance with their laws and treaties in force.

Article VIII

Any Contracting Party may call upon the competent organs of the United Nations to take such action under the Charter of the United Nations as they consider appropriate for the prevention and suppression of acts of genocide or any of the other acts enumerated in article III.

Article IX

Disputes between the Contracting Parties relating to the interpretation, application or fulfilment of the present Convention, including those relating to the responsibility of a State for genocide or for any of the other acts enumerated in article III, shall be submitted to the International Court of Justice at the request of any of the parties to the dispute.

Article X

The present Convention, of which the Chinese, English, French, Russian and Spanish texts are equally authentic, shall bear the date of 9 December 1948.

Article XI

The present Convention shall be open until 31 December 1949 for signature on behalf of any Member of the United Nations and of any non-member State to which an invitation to sign has been addressed by the General Assembly.

The present Convention shall be ratified, and the instruments of ratification shall be deposited with the Secretary-General of the United Nations.

After 1 January 1950, the present Convention may be acceded to on behalf of any Member of the United Nations and of any non-member State which has received an invitation as aforesaid.

Instruments of accession shall be deposited with the Secretary-General of the United Nations.

Article XII

Any Contracting Party may at any time, by notification addressed to the Secretary-General of the United Nations, extend the application of the present Convention to all or any of the territories for the conduct of whose foreign relations that Contracting Party is responsible.

Article XIII

On the day when the first twenty instruments of ratification or accession have been deposited, the Secretary-General shall draw up a *procès-verbal* and transmit a copy thereof to each Member of the United Nations and to each of the non-member States contemplated in article XI.

The present Convention shall come into force on the ninetieth day following the date of deposit of the twentieth instrument of ratification or accession.

Any ratification or accession effected, subsequent to the latter date shall become effective on the ninetieth day following the deposit of the instrument of ratification or accession.

Article XIV

The present Convention shall remain in effect for a period of ten years as from the date of its coming into force.

It shall thereafter remain in force for successive periods of five years for such Contracting Parties as have not denounced it at least six months before the expiration of the current period.

Denunciation shall be effected by a written notification addressed to the Secretary-General of the United Nations.

Article XV

If, as a result of denunciations, the number of Parties to the present Convention should become less than sixteen, the Convention shall cease to be in force as from the date on which the last of these denunciations shall become effective.

Article XVI

A request for the revision of the present Convention may be made at any time by any Contracting Party by means of a notification in writing addressed to the Secretary-General.

The General Assembly shall decide upon the steps, if any, to be taken in respect of such request.

Article XVII

The Secretary-General of the United Nations shall notify all Members of the United Nations and the non-member States contemplated in article XI of the following:

a. Signatures, ratifications and accessions received in accordance with article XI;

b. Notifications received in accordance with article XII:

c. The date upon which the present Convention comes into force in accordance with article XIII;

d. Denunciations received in accordance with article XIV;

e. The abrogation of the Convention in accordance with article XV;

f. Notifications received in accordance with article XVI.

Article XVIII

The original of the present Convention shall be deposited in the archives of the United Nations.

A certified copy of the Convention shall be transmitted to each Member of the United Nations and to each of the non-member States contemplated in article XI.

Article XIX

The present Convention shall be registered by the Secretary-General of the United Nations on the date of its coming into force.

2. CONVENTION ON THE NON-APPLICABILITY OF STATUTORY LIMITATIONS TO WAR CRIMES AND CRIMES AGAINST HUMANITY (1968) G.A. Res. 2391 (XXIII), 23 U.N. GAOR, Supp. (No. 18) at 40, U.N. Doc. A/7218 (1968). In force 11 November 1970 in accordance with Article VIII.

PREAMBLE

THE STATES PARTIES TO THE PRESENT CONVENTION,

Recalling resolutions of the General Assembly of the United Nations 3 (I) of 13 February 1946 and 170 (II) of 31 October 1947 on the extradition and punishment of war criminals, resolution 95 (I) of 11 December 1946 affirming the principles of international law recognized by the Charter of the International Military Tribunal, Nürnberg, and the judgement of the Tribunal, and resolutions 2184 (XXI) of 12 December 1966 and 2202 (XXI) of 16 December 1966 which expressly condemned as crimes against humanity the violation of the economic and political rights of the indigenous population on the one hand and the policies of *apartheid* on the other,

Recalling resolutions of the Economic and Social Council of the United Nations 1074 D (XXXIX) of 28 July 1965 and 1158 (XLI) of 5 August 1966 on the punishment of war criminals and of persons who have committed crimes against humanity,

Noting that none of the solemn declarations, instruments or conventions relating to the prosecution and punishment of war crimes and crimes against humanity made provision for a period of limitation,

Considering that war crimes and crimes against humanity are among the gravest crimes in international law,

Convinced that the effective punishment of war crimes and crimes against humanity is an important element in the prevention of such crimes, the protection of human rights and fundamental freedoms, the encouragement of confidence, the furtherance of co-operation among peoples and the promotion of international peace and security,

Noting that the application to war crimes and crimes against humanity of the rules of municipal law relating to the period of limitation for ordinary crimes is a matter of serious concern to world public opinion, since it prevents the prosecution and punishment of persons responsible for those crimes,

Recognizing that it is necessary and timely to affirm in international law, through this Convention, the principle that there is no period of limitation for war crimes and crimes against humanity, and to secure its universal application.

Have agreed as follows:

Article I

No statutory limitation shall apply to the following crimes, irrespective of the date of their commission:

a. War crimes as they are defined in the Charter of the International Military Tribunal, Nürnberg, of 8 August 1945 and confirmed by resolutions 3 (I) of 13 February 1946 and 95 (I) of 11 December 1946 of the General Assembly of the United Nations, particularly the "grave breaches" enumerated in the Geneva Conventions of 12 August 1949 for the protection of war victims;

b. Crimes against humanity whether committed in time of war or in time of peace as they are defined in the Charter of the International

Military Tribunal, Nürnberg, of 8 August 1945 and confirmed by resolutions 3 (I) of 13 February 1946 and 95 (I) of 11 December 1946 of the General Assembly of the United Nations, eviction by armed attack or occupation and inhuman acts resulting from the policy of *apartheid*, and the crime of genocide as defined in the 1948 Convention on the Prevention and Punishment of the Crime of Genocide, even if such acts do not constitute a violation of the domestic law of the country in which they were committed.

Article II

If any of the crimes mentioned in article I is committed, the provisions of this Convention shall apply to representatives of the State authority and private individuals who, as principals or accomplices, participate in or who directly incite others to the commission of any of those crimes, or who conspire to commit them, irrespective of the degree of completion, and to representatives of the State authority who tolerate their commission.

Article III

The States Parties to the present Convention undertake to adopt all necessary domestic measures, legislative or otherwise, with a view to making possible the extradition, in accordance with international law, of the persons referred to in article II of this Convention.

Article IV

The States Parties to the present Convention undertake to adopt, in accordance with their respective constitutional processes, any legislative or other measures necessary to ensure that statutory or other limitations shall not apply to the prosecution and punishment of the crimes referred to in articles I and II of this Convention and that, where they exist, such limitations shall be abolished.

Article V

This Convention shall, until 31 December 1969, be open for signature by any State Member of the United Nations or member of any of its specialized agencies or of the International Atomic Energy Agency, by any State Party to the Statute of the International Court of Justice, and by any other State which has been invited by the General Assembly of the United Nations to become a Party to this Convention.

Article VI

This Convention is subject to ratification. Instruments of ratification shall be deposited with the Secretary-General of the United Nations.

Article VII

This Convention shall be open to accession by any State referred to in article V. Instruments of accession shall be deposited with the Secretary-General of the United Nations.

Article VIII

1. This Convention shall enter into force on the ninetieth day after the date of the deposit with the Secretary-General of the United Nations of the tenth instrument of ratification or accession.

2. For each State ratifying this Convention or acceding to it after the deposit of the tenth instrument of ratification or accession, the Convention shall enter into force on the ninetieth day after the date of the deposit of its own instrument of ratification or accession.

Article IX

1. After the expiry of a period of ten years from the date on which this Convention enters into force, a request for the revision of the Convention may be made at any time by any Contracting Party by means of a notification in writing addressed to the Secretary-General of the United Nations.

2. The General Assembly of the United Nations shall decide upon the steps, if any, to be taken in respect of such a request.

Article X

1. This Convention shall be deposited with the Secretary-General of the United Nations.

2. The Secretary-General of the United Nations shall trnsmit certified copies of this Convention to all States referred to in article V.

3. The Secretary-General of the United Nations shall inform all States referred to in article V of the following particulars:

  a. Signatures of this Convention, and instruments of ratification and accession deposited under articles V, VI and VII;

  b. The date of entry into force of this Convention in accordance with article VIII;

  c. Communications received under article IX.

Article XI

This Convention, of which the Chinese, English, French, Russian and Spanish texts are equally authentic, shall bear the date of 26 November 1968.

IN WITNESS WHEREOF the undersigned, being duly authorized for that purpose, have signed this Convention.

3. PRINCIPLES OF INTERNATIONAL CO-OPERATION IN THE DETECTION, ARREST, EXTRADITION AND PUNISHMENT OF PERSONS GUILTY OF WAR CRIMES AND CRIMES AGAINST HUMANITY (1973) G.A. Res. 3074 (XXVIII), 28 U.N. GAOR, Supp. (No. 30) at 78, U.N. Doc. A/9030 (1973).

THE GENERAL ASSEMBLY,

Recalling its resolutions 2583 (XXIV) of 15 December 1969, 2712 (XXV) of 15 December 1970, 2840 (XXVI) of 18 December 1971 and 3020 (XXVII) of 18 December 1972,

Taking into account the special need for international action in order to ensure the prosecution and punishment of persons guilty of war crimes and crimes against humanity,

Having considered the draft principles of international co-operation in the detection, arrest, extradition and punishment of persons guilty of war crimes and crimes against humanity,

Declares that the United Nations, in pursuance of the principles and purposes set forth in the Charter concerning the promotion of co-operation between peoples and the maintenance of international peace and security, proclaims the following principles of international co-operation in the detection, arrest, extradition and punishment of persons guilty of war crimes and crimes against humanity:

1. War crimes and crimes against humanity, wherever they are committed, shall be subject to investigation and the persons against whom there is evidence that they have committed such crimes shall be subject to tracing, arrest, trial and, if found guilty, to punishment.

2. Every State has the right to try its own nationals for war crimes or crimes against humanity.

3. States shall co-operate with each other on a bilateral and multilateral basis with a view to halting and preventing war crimes and crimes against humanity, and shall take the domestic and international measures necessary for that purpose.

4. States shall assist each other in detecting, arresting and bringing to trial persons suspected of having committed such crimes and, if they are found guilty, in punishing them.

5. Persons against whom there is evidence that they have committed war crimes and crimes against humanity shall be subject to trial and, if found guilty, to punishment, as a general rule in the countries in which they committed those crimes. In that connexion, States shall co-operate on questions of extraditing such persons.

6. States shall co-operate with each other in the collection of information and evidence which would help to bring to trial the persons indicated in paragraph 5 above and shall exchange such information.

7. In accordance with article 1 of the Declaration on Territorial Asylum of 14 December 1967, States shall not grant asylum to any person with respect to whom there are serious reasons for considering that he has committed a crime against peace, a war crime or a crime against humanity.

8. States shall not take any legislative or other measures which may be prejudicial to the international obligations they have assumed in regard to the detection, arrest, extradition and punishment of persons guilty of war crimes and crimes against humanity.

9. In co-operating with a view to the detection, arrest and extradition of

persons against whom there is evidence that they have committed war crimes and crimes against humanity and, if found guilty, their punishment, States shall act in conformity with the provisions of the Charter of the United Nations and of the Declaration on Principles of International Law concerning Friendly Relations and Co-operation among States in accordance with the Charter of the United Nations.

4. CONVENTION ON THE TAKING OF HOSTAGES
(1979) G.A. Res. 34/146, 34 U.N. GAOR, Supp. (No. 46) at 245, U.N. Doc. A/34/46 (1979). In force 3 June 1983 in accordance with Article 18.

THE GENERAL ASSEMBLY,

Considering that the progressive development of international law and its codification contribute to the implementation of the purposes and principles set forth in Articles 1 and 2 of the Charter of the United Nations,

Mindful of the need to conclude, under the auspices of the United Nations, an international convention against the taking of hostages,

Recalling its resolution 31/103 of 15 December 1976, by which it established the *Ad Hoc* Committee on the Drafting of an International Convention against the Taking of Hostages and requested it to draft at the earliest possible date an international convention against the taking of hostages,

Further recalling its resolutions 32/148 of 16 December 1977 and 33/19 of 29 November 1978,

Having considered the draft Convention prepared by the *Ad Hoc* Committee in pursuance of the above-mentioned resolutions,

Adopts and opens for signature and ratification or for accession the International Convention against the Taking of Hostages, the text of which is annexed to the present resolution.

105th plenary meeting
17 December 1979

ANNEX

INTERNATIONAL CONVENTION AGAINST THE TAKING OF HOSTAGES

The States Parties to this Convention,

Having in mind the purposes and principles of the Charter of the United Nations concerning the maintenance of international peace and security and the promotion of friendly relations and co-operation among States,

Recognizing, in particular, that everyone has the right to life, liberty and security of person, as set out in the Universal Declaration of Human Rights and the International Covenant on Civil and Political Rights,

Reaffirming the principle of equal rights and self-determination of peoples as enshrined in the Charter of the United Nations and the Declaration on Principles of International Law concerning Friendly Relations and Co-operation among

States in accordance with the Charter of the United Nations, as well as in other relevant resolutions of the General Assembly,

Considering that the taking of hostages is an offence of grave concern to the international community and that, in accordance with the provisions of this Convention, any person committing an act of hostage taking shall be either prosecuted or extradited,

Being convinced that it is urgently necessary to develop international co-operation between States in devising and adopting effective measures for the prevention, prosecution and punishment of all acts of taking of hostages as manifestations of international terrorism,

Have agreed as follows:

Article 1

1. Any person who seizes or detains and threatens to kill, to injure or to continue to detain another person (hereinafter referred to as the "hostage") in order to compel a third party, namely, a State, an international inter-governmental organization, a natural or juridical person, or a group of persons, to do or abstain from doing any act as an explicit or implicit condition for the release of the hostage commits the offence of taking of hostages ("hostage-taking") within the meaning of this Convention.

2. Any person who:
   a. Attempts to commit an act of hostage-taking, or
   b. Participates as an accomplice of anyone who commits or attempts
   to commit an act of hostage-taking likewise commits an offence for the
   purposes of this Convention.

Article 2

Each State Party shall make the offences set forth in article 1 punishable by appropriate penalties which take into account the grave nature of those offences.

Article 3

1. The State party in the territory of which the hostage is held by the offender shall take all measures it considers appropriate to ease the situation of the hostage, in particular, to secure his release and, after his release, to facilitate, when relevant, his departure.

2. If any object which the offender has obtained as a result of the taking of hostages comes into the custody of a State Party, that State Party shall return it as soon as possible to the hostage or the third party referred to in article 1, as the case may be, or to the appropriate authorities thereof.

Article 4

States Parties shall co-operate in the prevention of the offences set forth in article 1, particularly by:
   a. Taking all practicable measures to prevent preparations in their
   respective territories for the commission of those offences within or
   outside their territories, including measures to prohibit in their territories illegal activities of persons, groups and organizations that

encourage, instigate, organize or engage in the perpetration of acts of taking of hostages;

b. Exchanging information and co-ordinating the taking of administrative and other measures as appropriate to prevent the commission of those offences.

Article 5

1. Each State Party shall take such measures as may be necessary to establish its jurisdiction over any of the offences set forth in article 1 which are committed:

a. In its territory or on board a ship or aircraft registered in that State;

b. By any of its nationals or, if that State considers it appropriate, by those stateless persons who have their habitual residence in its territory;

c. In order to compel that State to do or abstain from doing any act; or

d. With respect to a hostage who is a national of that State, if the State considers it appropriate.

2. Each State Party shall likewise take such measures as may be necessary to establish its jurisdiction over the offences set forth in article 1 in cases where the alleged offender is present in its territory and it does not extradite him to any of the States mentioned in paragraph 1 of this article.

3. This Convention does not exclude any criminal jurisdiction exercised in accordance with internal law.

Article 6

1. Upon being satisfied that the circumstances so warrant, any State Party in the territory of which the alleged offender is present shall, in accordance with its laws, take him into custody or take other measures to ensure his presence for such time as is necessary to enable any criminal or extradition proceedings to be instituted. That State party shall immediately make a preliminary inquiry into the facts.

2. The custody or other measures referred to in paragraph 1 of this article shall be notified without delay directly or through the Secretary-General of the United Nations to:

a. The State where the offence was committed;

b. The State against which compulsion has been directed or attempted;

c. The State of which the natural or juridical person against whom compulsion has been directed or attempted is a national;

d. The State of which the hostage is a national or in the territory of which he has his habitual residence;

e. The State of which the alleged offender is a national or, if he is a stateless person, in the territory of which he has his habitual residence;

f. The international intergovernmental organization against which compulsion has been directed or attempted;

g. All other States concerned.

3. Any person regarding whom the measures referred to in paragraph 1 of this article are being taken shall be entitled:

a. To communicate without delay with the nearest appropriate representative of the State of which he is a national or which is otherwise entitled to establish such communication or, if he is a stateless person, the State in the territory of which he has his habitual residence;

b. To be visited by a representative of that State.

4. The rights referred to in paragraph 3 of this article shall be exercised in conformity with the laws and regulations of the State in the territory of which the alleged offender is present, subject to the proviso, however, that the said laws and regulations must enable full effect to be given to the purposes for which the rights accorded under paragraph 3 of this article are intended.

5. The provisions of paragraphs 3 and 4 of this article shall be without prejudice to the right of any State Party having a claim to jurisdiction in accordance with paragraph 1 (*b*) of article 5 to invite the International Committee of the Red Cross to communicate with and visit the alleged offender.

6. The State which makes the preliminary inquiry contemplated in paragraph 1 of this article shall promptly report its findings to the States or organization referred to in paragraph 2 of this article and indicate whether it intends to exercise jurisdiction.

Article 7

The State Party where the alleged offender is prosecuted shall, in accordance with its laws, communicate the final outcome of the proceedings to the Secretary-General of the United Nations, who shall transmit the information to the other States concerned and the international intergovernmental organizations concerned.

Article 8

1. The State Party in the territory of which the alleged offender is found shall, if it does not extradite him, be obliged, without exception whatsoever and whether or not the offence was committed in its territory, to submit the case to its competent authorities for the purpose of prosecution, through proceedings in accordance with the laws of that State. Those authorities shall take their decision in the same manner as in the case of any ordinary offence of a grave nature under the law of that State.

2. Any person regarding whom proceedings are being carried out in connexion with any of the offences set forth in article 1 shall be guaranteed fair treatment at all stages of the proceedings, including enjoyment of all the rights and guarantees provided by the law of the State in the territory of which he is present.

Article 9

1. A request for the extradition of an alleged offender, pursuant to this Convention, shall not be granted if the requested State Party has substantial grounds for believing:

a. That the request for extradition for an offence set forth in article 1 has been made for the purpose of prosecuting or punishing a person on account of his race, religion, nationality, ethnic origin or political opinion; or

b. That the person's position may be prejudiced:

i. For any of the reasons mentioned in subparagraph (*a*) of this paragraph, or

ii. For the reason that communication with him by the appropriate authorities of the State entitled to exercise rights of protection cannot be effected.

2. With respect to the offences as defined in this Convention, the provisions of all extradition treaties and arrangements applicable between States Parties are modified as between States Parties to the extent that they are incompatible with this Convention.

Article 10

1. The offences set forth in article 1 shall be deemed to be included as extraditable offences in any extradition treaty existing between States Parties. States Parties undertake to include such offences as extraditable offences in every extradition treaty to be concluded between them.

2. If a State Party which makes extradition conditional on the existence of a treaty receives a request for extradition from another State Party with which it has no extradition treaty, the requested State may at its option consider this Convention as the legal basis for extradition in respect of the offences set forth in article 1. Extradition shall be subject to the other conditions provided by the law of the requested State.

3. States Parties which do not make extradition conditional on the existence of a treaty shall recognize the offences set forth in article 1 as extraditable offences between themselves, subject to the conditions provided by the law of the requested State.

4. The offences set forth in article 1 shall be treated, for the purpose of extradition between States Parties, as if they had been committed not only in the place in which they occurred but also in the territories of the States required to establish their jurisdiction in accordance with paragraph 1 of article 5.

Article 11

1. States Parties shall afford one another the greatest measure of assistance in connexion with criminal proceedings brought in respect of the offences set forth in article 1, including the supply of all evidence at their disposal necessary for the proceedings.

2. The provisions of paragraph 1 of this article shall not affect obligations concerning mutual judicial assistance embodied in any other treaty.

Article 12

In so far as the Geneva Conventions of 1949 for the protection of war victims or the Protocols Additional to those Conventions are applicable to a particular act of hostage-taking, and in so far as States Parties to this Convention are bound under those conventions to prosecute or hand over the hostage-taker, the present Convention shall not apply to an act of hostage-taking committed in the course of armed conflicts as defined in the Geneva Conventions of 1949 and the Protocols thereto, including armed conflicts, mentioned in article 1, paragraph 4, of Additional Protocol I of 1977, in which peoples are fighting against colonial domination and alien occupation and against racist régimes in the exercise of their right of self-determination, as enshrined in the Charter of the United Nations and the Declaration on Principles of International Law concerning Friendly Relations and Co-operation among States in accordance with the Charter of the United Nations.

Article 13

This Convention shall not apply where the offence is committed within a single State, the hostage and the alleged offender are nationals of that State and the alleged offender is found in the territory of that State.

Article 14

Nothing in this Convention shall be construed as justifying the violation of the territorial integrity or political independence of a State in contravention of the Charter of the United Nations.

Article 15

The provisions of this Convention shall not affect the application of the Treaties on Asylum, in force at the date of the adoption of this Convention, as between the States which are parties to those Treaties; but a State Party to this Convention may not invoke those Treaties with respect to another State Party to this Convention which is not a party to those Treaties.

Article 16

1. Any dispute between two or more States Parties concerning the interpretation or application of this Convention which is not settled by negotiation shall, at the request of one of them, be submitted to arbitration. If within six months from the date of the request for arbitration the parties are unable to agree on the organization of the arbitration, any one of those parties may refer the dispute to the International Court of Justice by request in conformity with the Statute of the Court.

2. Each State may at the time of signature or ratification of this Convention or accession thereto declare that it does not consider itself bound by paragraph 1 of this article. The other States Parties shall not be bound by paragraph 1 of this article with respect to any State Party which has made such a reservation.

3. Any State Party which has made a reservation in accordance with paragraph 2 of this article may at any time withdraw that reservation by notification to the Secretary-General of the United Nations.

Article 17

1. This Convention is open for signature by all States until 31 December 1980 at United Nations Headquarters in New York.

2. This Convention is subject to ratification. The instruments of ratification shall be deposited with the Secretary-General of the United Nations.

3. This Convention is open for accession by any State. The instruments of accession shall be deposited with the Secretary-General of the United Nations.

Article 18

1. This Convention shall enter into force on the thirtieth day following the date of deposit of the twenty-second instrument of ratification or accession with the Secretary-General of the United Nations.

2. For each State ratifying or acceding to the Convention after the deposit of the twenty-second instrument of ratification or accession, the Convention shall enter into force on the thirtieth day after deposit by such State of its instrument of ratification or accession.

Article 19

1. Any State Party may denounce this Convention by written notification to the Secretary-General of the United Nations.

2. Denunciation shall take effect one year following the date on which notification is received by the Secretary-General of the United Nations.

Article 20

The original of this Convention, of which the Arabic, Chinese, English, French, Russian and Spanish texts are equally authentic, shall be deposited with the Secretary-General of the United Nations, who shall send certified copies thereof to all States.

IN WITNESS WHEREOF, the undersigned, being duly authorized thereto by their respective Governments, have signed this Convention, opened for signature at New York on 18 December 1979.

G. PROTECTION OF PERSONS SUBJECTED TO DETENTION OR IMPRISONMENT

INTRODUCTION

This section contains several extremely important documents on a topic that is an expanding area of international concern. None of the documents is in treaty form. The Standard Minimum Rules for the Treatment of Prisoners were approved by resolutions of the Economic and Social Council and endorsed by the General Assembly in resolutions recommending implementation and adoption by Member States, G.A.Res. 2858, 26 U.N. GOAR Supp. (No. 29) at 94, U.N.Doc.A/8588 (1971) and G.A. Res. 3144, 28 U.N. GOAR Supp. (No. 30) at 85, U.N. Doc.A/9425 (1973). The Rules were originally adopted in 1957 and their scope was expanded by the addition of Rule 95 in 1977 which extends the coverage of appropriate Rules to persons arrested or imprisoned without charge ("detained"). The degree of incorporation of the Rules into domestic law has been disappointing but a case can be made that the Rules are now part of the corpus of international customary human rights law. On the Minimum Rules generally, *see* R. Lillich and F. Newman, *International Human Rights: Problems of Law and Policy* 183–261 (1979); D. Skoler, "World Implementation of the United Nations Standard Minimum Rules for the Treatment of Prisoners," 10 J.Int'l L. & Econ. 453 (1975).

The Declaration on Torture, adopted by the General Assembly, was inspired in large part by the "Campaign for the Abolition of Torture" begun by Amnesty International in 1972. Work was completed in 1984 on a Convention on Torture to put further legal sanction behind the norms of the Declaration. *See* M. Lippman, "The Protection of Universal Human Rights: The Problem of Torture," Vol. 1, No. 4, "Universal Human Rights," 25 (Oct.-Dec. 1979); Association Internationale de Droit Penal, Special Issue of the Revue Internationale de Droit Penal, 1977, Nos. 3 & 4, "The Prevention and Suppression of Torture." Like the Standard Minimum Rules, the Declaration is arguably part of international customary law.[12] It is often relied upon by international non-governmental organizations in their interventions with governments on behalf of individual prisoners or groups of prisoners.

The Code of Conduct for Law Enforcement Officials and the Principles of Medical Ethics are part of a series of efforts to develop standards for the behavior of the various types of professionals involved in the criminal justice area—police, lawyers and doctors (and, in too many countries, the military). *See* Lillich and Newman, *supra* at 245–261. The Code and Principles are too new to support any strong argument that they are part of customary international law, but it may, perhaps, be argued that their norms represent "general principles of law recognized by civilized nations."

1. STANDARD MINIMUM RULES FOR THE TREATMENT OF PRISONERS (1957 AND 1977) E.S.C. Res. 663 (XXIV) C, 24 U.N. ESCOR, Supp. (No. 1) at 11, U.N. Doc. E/3048 (1957). As Amended, 1977.

PRELIMINARY OBSERVATIONS

1. The following rules are not intended to describe in detail a model system of penal institutions. They seek only, on the basis of the general consensus of contemporary thought and the essential elements of the most adequate systems of today, to set out what is generally accepted as being good principle and practice in the treatment of prisoners and the management of institutions.

2. In view of the great variety of legal, social, economic and geographical conditions of the world, it is evident that not all of the rules are capable of application in all places and at all times. They should, however, serve to stimulate a constant endeavour to overcome practical difficulties in the way of their application, in the knowledge that they represent, as a whole, the minimum conditions which are accepted as suitable by the United Nations.

3. On the other hand, the rules cover a field in which thought is constantly developing. They are not intended to preclude experiment and practices, provided these are in harmony with the principles and seek to further the purposes which derive from the text of the rules as a whole. it will always be justifiable for the central prison administration to authorize departures from the rules in this spirit.

4. (1) Part I of the rules covers the general management of institutions, and is applicable to all categories of prisoners, criminal or civil, untried or convicted, including prisoners subject to "security measures" or corrective measures ordered by the judge.

(2) Part II contains rules applicable only to the special categories dealt with in each section. Nevertheless, the rules under section A, applicable to prisoners under sentence, shall be equally applicable to categories of prisoners dealt with in sections B, C and D, provided they do not conflict with the rules governing those categories and are for their benefit.

5. (1) The rules do not seek to regulate the management of institutions set aside for young persons such as Borstal institutions or correctional schools, but in general part I would be equally applicable in such institutions.

(2) The category of young prisoners should include at least all young persons who come within the jurisdiction of juvenile courts. As a rule, such young persons should not be sentenced to imprisonment.

PART I

RULES OF GENERAL APPLICATION

Basic Principle

6. (1) The following rules shall be applied impartiallly. There shall be no

discrimination on grounds of race, colour, sex, language, religion, political or other opinion, national or social origin, property, birth or other status.

(2) On the other hand, it is necessary to respect the religious beliefs and moral precepts of the group to which a prisoner belongs.

Register

7. (1) In every place where persons are imprisoned there shall be kept a bound registration book with numbered pages in which shall be entered in respect of each prisoner received:

a. Information concerning his identity;

b. The reasons for his commitment and the authority therefor;

c. The day and hour of his admission and release.

(2) No person shall be received in an institution without a valid commitment order of which the details shall have been previously entered in the register.

Separation of categories

8. The different categories of prisoners shall be kept in separate institutions or parts of institutions taking account of their sex, age, criminal record, the legal reason for their detention and the necessities of their treatment. Thus,

a. Men and women shall so far as possible be detained in separate institutions; in an institution which receives both men and women the whole of the premises allocated to women shall be entirely separate;

b. Untried prisoners shall be kept separate from convicted prisoners;

c. Persons imprisoned for debt and other civil prisoners shall be kept separate from persons imprisoned by reason of a criminal offence;

d. Young prisoners shall be kept separate from adults.

Accommodation

9. (1) Where sleeping accommodation is in individual cells or rooms, each prisoner shall occupy by night a cell or room by himself. If for special reasons, such as temporary overcrowding, it becomes necessary for the central prison administration to make an exception to this rule, it is not desirable to have two prisoners in a cell or room.

(2) Where dormitories are used, they shall be occupied by prisoners carefully selected as being suitable to associate with one another in those conditions. There shall be regular supervision by night, in keeping with the nature of the institution.

10. All accommodation provided for the use of prisoners and in particular all sleeping accommodation shall meet all requirements of health, due regard being paid to climatic conditions and particularly to cubic content of air, minimum floor space, lighting, heating and ventilation.

11. In all places where prisoners are required to live or work,

a. The windows shall be large enough to enable the prisoners to read or work by natural light, and shall be so constructed that they can allow the entrance of fresh air whether or not there is artificial ventilation;

b. Artificial light shall be provided sufficient for the prisoners to read or work without injury to eyesight.

12. The sanitary installations shall be adequate to enable every prisoner to comply with the needs of nature when necessary and in a clean and decent manner.

13. Adequate bathing and shower installations shall be provided so that every prisoner may be enabled and required to have a bath or shower, at a temperature suitable to the climate, as frequently as necessary for general hygiene according to season and geographical region, but at least once a week in a temperate climate.

14. All parts of an institution regularly used by prisoners shall be properly maintained and kept scrupulously clean at all times.

Personal hygiene

15. Prisoners shall be required to keep their persons clean, and to this end they shall be provided with water and with such toilet articles as are necessary for health and cleanliness.

16. In order that prisoners may maintain a good appearance compatible with their self-respect, facilities shall be provided for the proper care of the hair and beard, and men shall be enabled to shave regularly.

Clothing and bedding

17. (1) Every prisoner who is not allowed to wear his own clothing shall be provided with an outfit of clothing suitable for the climate and adequate to keep him in good health. Such clothing shall in no manner be degrading or humiliating.

(2) All clothing shall be clean and kept in proper condition. Underclothing shall be changed and washed as often as necessary for the maintenance of hygiene.

(3) In exceptional circumstances, whenever a prisoner is removed outside the institution for an authorized purpose, he shall be allowed to wear his own clothing or other inconspicuous clothing.

18. If prisoners are allowed to wear their own clothing, arrangements shall be made on their admission to the institution to ensure that it shall be clean and fit for use.

19. Every prisoner shall, in accordance with local or national standards, be provided with a separate bed, and with separate and sufficient bedding which shall be clean when issued, kept in good order and changed often enough to ensure its cleanliness.

Food

20. (1) Every prisoner shall be provided by the administration at the usual hours with food of nutritional value adequate for health and strength, of wholesome quality and well prepared and served.

(2) Drinking water shall be available to every prisoner whenever he needs it.

Exercise and sport

21. (1) Every prisoner who is not employed in outdoor work shall have at least one hour of suitable exercise in the open air daily if the weather permits.

(2) Young prisoners, and others of suitable age and physique, shall receive physical and recreational training during the period of exercise. To this end space, installations and equipment should be provided.

Medical services

22. (1) At every institution there shall be available the services of at least one qualified medical officer who should have some knowledge of psychiatry. The medical services should be organized in close relationship to the general health administration of the community or nation. They shall include a psychiatric service for the diagnosis and, in proper cases, the treatment of states of mental abnormality.

(2) Sick prisoners who require specialist treatment shall be transferred to specialized institutions or to civil hospitals. Where hospital facilities are provided in an institution, their equipment, furnishings and pharmaceutical supplies shall be proper for the medical care and treatment of sick prisoners, and there shall be a staff of suitably trained officers.

(3) The services of a qualified dental officer shall be available to every prisoner.

23. (1) In women's institutions there shall be special accommodation for all necessary pre-natal and post-natal care and treatment. Arrangements shall be made wherever practicable for children to be born in a hospital outside the institution. If a child is born in prison, this fact shall not be mentioned in the birth certificate.

(2) Where nursing infants are allowed to remain in the institution with their mothers, provision shall be made for a nursery staffed by qualified persons, where the infants shall be placed when they are not in the care of their mothers.

24. The medical officer shall see and examine every prisoner as soon as possible after his admission and thereafter as necessary, with a view particularly to the discovery of physical or mental illness and the taking of all necessary measures; the segregation of prisoners suspected of infectious or contagious conditions; the noting of physical or mental defects which might hamper rehabilitation, and the determination of the physical capacity of every prisoner for work.

25. (1) The medical officer shall have the care of the physical and mental health of the prisoners and should daily see all sick prisoners, all who complain of illness, and any prisoner to whom his attention is specially directed.

(2) The medical officer shall report to the director whenever he considers that a prisoner's physical or mental health has been or will be injuriously affected by continued imprisonment or by any condition of imprisonment.

26. (1) The medical officer shall regularly inspect and advise the director upon:

    a. The quantity, quality, preparation and service of food;

    b. The hygiene and cleanliness of the institution and the prisoners;

    c. The sanitation, heating, lighting and ventilation of the institution;

    d. The suitability and cleanliness of the prisoners' clothing and bedding;

    e. The observance of the rules concerning physical education and sports, in cases where there is no technical personnel in charge of these activities.

(2) The director shall take into consideration the reports and advice that the medical officer submits according to rules 25 (2) and 26 and, in case he concurs with the recommendations made, shall take immediate steps to give effect to those recommendations; if they are not within his competence or if he does not concur with them, he shall immediately submit his own report and the advice of the medical officer to higher authority.

Discipline and punishment

27. Discipline and order shall be maintained with firmness, but with no more restriction than is necessary for safe custody and well-ordered community life.

28. (1) No prisoner shall be employed, in the service of the institution, in any disciplinary capacity.

(2) This rule shall not, however, impede the proper functioning of systems based on self-government, under which specified social, educational or sports activities or responsibilities are entrusted, under supervision, to prisoners who are formed into groups for the purposes of treatment.

29. The following shall always be determined by the law or by the regulation of the competent administrative authority:

    a. Conduct constituting a disciplinary offence;

    b. The types and duration of punishment which may be inflicted;

    c. The authority competent to impose such punishment.

30. (1) No prisoner shall be punished except in accordance with the terms of such law or regulation, and never twice for the same offence.

(2) No prisoner shall be punished unless he has been informed of the offence alleged against him and given a proper opportunity of presenting his defence. The competent authority shall conduct a thorough examination of the case.

(3) Where necessary and practicable the prisoner shall be allowed to make his defence through an interpreter.

31. Corporal punishment, punishment by placing in a dark cell, and all cruel, inhuman or degrading punishments shall be completely prohibited as punishments for disciplinary offences.

32. (1) Punishment by close confinement or reduction of diet shall never be inflicted unless the medical officer has examined the prisoner and certified in writing that he is fit to sustain it.

(2) The same shall apply to any other punishment that may be prejudicial to the physical or mental health of a prisoner. In no case may such punishment be contrary to or depart from the principle stated in rule 31.

(3) The medical officer shall visit daily prisoners undergoing such punishments and shall advise the director if he considers the termination or alteration of the punishment necessary on grounds of physical or mental health.

Instruments of restraint

33. Instruments of restraint, such as handcuffs, chains, irons and strait-

jackets, shall never be applied as a punishment. Furthermore, chains or irons shall not be used as restraints. Other instruments of restraint shall not be used except in the following circumstances:

 a. As a precaution against escape during a transfer, provided that they shall be removed when the prisoner appears before a judicial or administrative authority;

 b. On medical grounds by direction of the medical officer;

 c. By order of the director, if other methods of control fail, in order to prevent a prisoner from injuring himself or others or from damaging property; in such instances the director shall at once consult the medical officer and report to the higher administrative authority.

34. The patterns and manner of use of instruments of restraint shall be decided by the central prison administration. Such instruments must not be applied for any longer time than is strictly necessary.

Information to and complaints by prisoners

35. (1) Every prisoner on admission shall be provided with written information about the regulations governing the treatment of prisoners of his category, the disciplinary requirements of the institution, the authorized methods of seeking information and making complaints, and all such other matters as are necessary to enable him to understand both his rights and his obligations and to adapt himself to the life of the institution.

(2) If a prisoner is illiterate, the aforesaid information shall be conveyed to him orally.

36. (1) Every prisoner shall have the opportunity each week day of making requests or complaints to the director of the institution or the officer authorized to represent him.

(2) It shall be possible to make requests or complaints to the inspector of prisons during his inspection. The prisoner shall have the opportunity to talk to the inspector or to any other inspecting officer without the director or other members of the staff being present.

(3) Ever prisoner shall be allowed to make a request or complaint, without censorship as to substance but in proper form, to the central prison administration, the judicial authority or other proper authorities through approved channels.

(4) Unless it is evidently frivolous or groundless, every request or complaint shall be promptly dealt with and replied to without undue delay.

Contact with the outside world

37. Prisoners shall be allowed under necessary supervision to communicate with their family and reputable friends at regular intervals, both by correspondence and by receiving visits.

38. (1) Prisoners who are foreign nationals shall be allowed reasonable facilities to communicate with the diplomatic and consular representatives of the State to which they belong.

(2) Prisoners who are nationals of States without diplomatic or consular representation in the country and refugees or stateless persons shall be allowed

similar facilities to communicate with the diplomatic representative of the State which takes charge of their interests or any national or international authority whose task it is to protect such persons.

39. Prisoners shall be kept informed regularly of the more important items of news by the reading of newspapers, periodicals or special institutional publications, by hearing wireless transmissions, by lectures or by any similar means as authorized or controlled by the administration.

Books

40. Every institution shall have a library for the use of all categories of prisoners, adequately stocked with both recreational and instructional books, and prisoners shall be encouraged to make full use of it.

Religion

41. (1) If the institution contains a sufficient number of prisoners of the same religion, a qualified representative of that religion shall be appointed or approved. If the number of prisoners justifies it and conditions permit, the arrangement should be on a full-time basis.

(2) A qualified representative appointed or approved under paragraph (1) shall be allowed to hold regular services and to pay pastoral visits in private to prisoners of his religion at proper times.

(3) Access to a qualified representative of any religion shall not be refused to any prisoner. On the other hand, if any prisoner should object to a visit of any religious representative, his attitude shall be fully respected.

42. So far as practicable, every prisoner shall be allowed to satisfy the needs of his religious life by attending the services provided in the institution and having in his possession the books of religious observance and instruction of his denomination.

Retention of prisoners' property

43. (1) All money, valuables, clothing and other effects belonging to a prisoner which under the regulations of the institution he is not allowed to retain shall on his admission to the institution be placed in safe custody. An inventory thereof shall be signed by the prisoner. Steps shall be taken to keep them in good condition.

(2) On the release of the prisoner all such articles and money shall be returned to him except in so far as he has been authorized to spend money or send any such property out of the institution, or it has been found necessary on hygienic grounds to destroy any article of clothing. The prisoner shall sign a receipt for the articles and money returned to him.

(3) Any money or effects received for a prisoner from outside shall be treated in the same way.

(4) If a prisoner brings in any drugs or medicine, the medical officer shall decide what use shall be made of them.

Notification of death, illness, transfer, etc.

44. (1) Upon the death or serious illness of, or serious injury to a prisoner,

or his removal to an institution for the treatment of mental affections, the director shall at once inform the spouse, if the prisoner is married, or the nearest relative and shall in any event inform any other person previously designated by the prisoner.

(2) A prisoner shall be informed at once of the death or serious illness of any near relative. In case of the critical illness of a near relative, the prisoner should be authorized, whenever circumstances allow, to go to his bedside either under escort or alone.

(3) Every prisoner shall have the right to inform at once his family of his imprisonment or his transfer to another institution.

Removal of prisoners

45. (1) When prisoners are being removed to or from an institution, they shall be exposed to public view as little as possible, and proper safeguards shall be adopted to protect them from insult, curiosity and publicity in any form.

(2) The transport of prisoners in conveyances with inadequate ventilation or light, or in any way which would subject them to unnecessary physical hardship, shall be prohibited.

(3) The transport of prisoners shall be carried out at the expense of the administration and equal conditions shall obtain for all of them.

Institutional personnel

46. (1) The prison administration, shall provide for the careful selection of every grade of the personnel, since it is on their integrity, humanity, professional capacity and personal suitability for the work that the proper administration of the institutions depends.

(2) The prison adminstration shall constantly seek to awaken and maintain in the minds both of the personnel and of the public the conviction that this work is a social service of great importance, and to this end all appropriate means of informing the public should be used.

(3) To secure the foregoing ends, personnel shall be appointed on a full-time basis as professional prison officers and have civil service status with security of tenure subject only to good conduct, efficiency and physical fitness. Salaries shall be adequate to attract and retain suitable men and women; employment benefits and conditions of service shall be favourable in view of the exacting nature of the work.

47. (1) The personnel shall possess an adequate standard of education and intelligence.

(2) Before entering on duty, the personnel shall be given a course of training in their general and specific duties and be required to pass theoretical and practical tests.

(3) After entering on duty and during their career, the personnel shall maintain and improve their knowledge and professional capacity by attending courses of in-service training to be organized at suitable intervals.

48. All members of the personnel shall at all times so conduct themselves and perform their duties as to influence the prisoners for good by their example and to command their respect.

49. (1) So far as possible, the personnel shall include a sufficient number of specialists such as psychiatrists, psychologists, social workers, teachers and trade instructors.

(2) The services of social workers, teachers and trade instructors shall be secured on a permanent basis, without thereby excluding part-time or voluntary workers.

50. (1) The director of an institution should be adequately qualified for his task by character, administrative ability, suitable training and experience.

(2) He shall devote his entire time to his official duties and shall not be appointed on a part-time basis.

(3) He shall reside on the premises of the institution or in its immediate vicinity.

(4) When two or more institutions are under the authority of one director, he shall visit each of them at frequent intervals. A responsible resident official shall be in charge of each of these institutions.

51. (1) The director, his deputy, and the majority of the other personnel of the institution shall be able to speak the language of the greatest number of prisoners, or a language understood by the greatest number of them.

(2) Whenever necessary, the services of an interpreter shall be used.

52. (1) In institutions which are large enough to require the services of one or more full-time medical officers, at least one of them shall reside on the premises of the institution or in its immediate vicinity.

(2) In other institutions the medical officer shall visit daily and shall reside near enough to be able to attend without delay in cases of urgency.

53. (1) In an institution for both men and women, the part of the institution set aside for women shall be under the authority of a responsible woman officer who shall have the custody of the keys of all that part of the institution.

(2) No male member of the staff shall enter the part of the institution set aside for women unless accompanied by a woman officer.

(3) Women prisoners shall be attended and supervised only by women officers. This does not, however, preclude male members of the staff, particularly doctors and teachers, from carrying out their professional duties in institutions or parts of institutions set aside for women.

54. (1) Officers of the institutions shall not, in their relations with the prisoners, use force except in self-defence or in cases of attempted escape, or active or passive physical resistance to an order based on law or regulations. Officers who have recourse to force must use no more than is strictly necessary and must report the incident immediately to the director of the institution.

(2) Prison officers shall be given special physical training to enable them to restrain aggressive prisoners.

(3) Except in special circumstances, staff performing duties which bring them into direct contact with prisoners should not be armed. Furthermore, staff should in no circumstances be provided with arms unless they have been trained in their use.

Inspection

55. There shall be a regular inspection of penal institutions and services by

qualified and experienced inspectors appointed by a competent authority. Their task shall be in particular to ensure that these institutions are administered in accordance with existing laws and regulations and with a view to bringing about the objectives of penal and correctional services.

PART II

RULES APPLICABLE TO SPECIAL CATEGORIES

A. Prisoners Under Sentence

Guiding principles

56. The guiding principles hereafter are intended to show the spirit in which penal institutions should be administered and the purposes at which they should aim, in accordance with the declaration made under Preliminary Observation 1 of the present text.

57. Imprisonment and other measures which result in cutting off an offender from the outside world are afflictive by the very fact of taking from the person the right of self-determination by depriving him of his liberty. Therefore the prison system shall not, except as incidental to justifiable segregation or the maintenance of discipline, aggravate the suffering inherent in such a situation.

58. The purpose and justification of a sentence of imprisonment or a similar measure deprivative of liberty is ultimately to protect society against crime. This end can only be achieved if the period of imprisonment is used to ensure, so far as possible, that upon his return to society the offender is not only willing but able to lead a law-abiding and self-supporting life.

59. To this end, the institution should utilize all the remedial, educational, moral, spiritual and other forces and forms of assistance which are appropriate and available, and should seek to apply them according to the individual treatment needs of the prisoners.

60. (1) The régime of the institution should seek to minimize any differences between prison life and life at liberty which tend to lessen the responsibility of the prisoners or the respect due to their dignity as human beings.

(2) Before the completion of the sentence, it is desirable that the necessary steps be taken to ensure for the prisoner a gradual return to life in society. This aim may be achieved, depending on the case, by a pre-release régime organized in the same institution or in another appropriate institution, or by release on trial under some kind of supervision which must not be entrusted to the police but should be combined with effective social aid.

61. The treatment of prisoners should emphasize not their exclusion from the community, but their continuing part in it. Community agencies should, therefore, be enlisted wherever possible to assist the staff of the institution in the task of social rehabilitation of the prisoners. There should be in connexion with every institution social workers charged with the duty of maintaining and

improving all desirable relations of a prisoner with his family and with valuable social agencies. Steps should be taken to safeguard, to the maximum extent compatible with the law and the sentence, the rights relating to civil interests, social security rights and other social benefits of prisoners.

62. The medical services of the institution shall seek to detect and shall treat any physical or mental illnesses or defects which may hamper a prisoner's rehabilitation. All necessary medical, surgical and psychiatric services shall be provided to that end.

63. (1) The fulfilment of these principles requires individualization of treatment and for this purpose a flexible system of classifying prisoners in groups; it is therefore desirable that such groups should be distributed in separate institutions suitable for the treatment of each group.

(2) These institutions need not provide the same degree of security for every group. It is desirable to provide varying degrees of security according to the needs of different groups. Open institutions, by the very fact that they provide no physical security against escape but rely on the self-discipline of the inmates, provide the conditions most favourable to rehabilitation for carefully selected prisoners.

(3) It is desirable that the number of prisoners in closed institutions should not be so large that the individualization of treatment is hindered. In some countries it is considered that the population of such institutions should not exceed five hundred. In open institutions the population should be as small as possible.

(4) On the other hand, it is undesirable to maintain prisons which are so small that proper facilities cannot be provided.

64. The duty of society does not end with a prisoner's release. There should, therefore, be governmental or private agencies capable of lending the released prisoner efficient after-care directed towards the lessening of prejudice against him and towards his social rehabilitation.

Treatment

65. The treatment of persons sentenced to imprisonment or a similar measure shall have as its purpose, so far as the length of the sentence permits, to establish in them the will to lead law-abiding and self-supporting lives after their release and to fit them to do so. The treatment shall be such as will encourage their self-respect and develop their sense of responsibility.

66. (1) To these ends, all appropriate means shall be used, including religious care in the countries where this is possible, education, vocational guidance and training, social casework, employment counselling, physical development and strengthening of moral character, in accordance with the individual needs of each prisoner, taking account of his social and criminal history, his physical and mental capacities and aptitudes, his personal temperament, the length of his sentence and his prospects after release.

(2) For every prisoner with a sentence of suitable length, the director shall receive, as soon as possible after his admission, full reports on all the matters

referred to in the foregoing paragraph. Such reports shall always include a report by a medical officer, wherever possible qualified in psychiatry, on the physical and mental condition of the prisoner.

(3) The reports and other relevant documents shall be placed in an individual file. This file shall be kept up to date and classified in such a way that it can be consulted by the responsible personnel whenever the need arises.

Classification and individualization

67. The purposes of classification shall be:

a. To separate from others those prisoners who, by reason of their criminal records or bad characters, are likely to exercise a bad influence;

b. To divide the prisoners into classes in order to facilitate their treatment with a view to their social rehabilitation.

68. So far as possible separate institutions or separate sections of an institution shall be used for the treatment of the different classes of prisoners.

69. As soon as possible after admission and after a study of the personality of each prisoner with a sentence of suitable length, a programme of treatment shall be prepared for him in the light of the knowledge obtained about his individual needs, his capacities and dispositions.

Privileges

70. Systems of privileges appropriate for the different classes of prisoners and the different methods of treatment shall be established at every institution, in order to encourage good conduct, develop a sense of responsibility and secure the interest and co-operation of the prisoners in their treatment.

Work

71. (1) Prison labour must not be of an afflictive nature.

(2) All prisoners under sentence shall be required to work, subject to their physical and mental fitness as determined by the medical officer.

(3) Sufficient work of a useful nature shall be provided to keep prisoners actively employed for a normal working day.

(4) So far as possible the work provided shall be such as will maintain or increase the prisoners' ability to earn an honest living after release.

(5) Vocational training in useful trades shall be provided for prisoners able to profit thereby and especially for young prisoners.

(6) Within the limits compatible with proper vocational selection and with the requirements of institutional administration and discipline, the prisoners shall be able to choose the type of work they wish to perform.

72. (1) The organization and methods of work in the institutions shall resemble as closely as possible those of similar work outside institutions, so as to prepare prisoners for the conditions of normal occupational life.

(2) The interests of the prisoners and of their vocational training, however, must not be subordinated to the purpose of making a financial profit from an industry in the institution.

73. (1) Preferably institutional industries and farms should be operated directly by the administration and not by private contractors.

(2) Where prisoners are employed in work not controlled by the administration, they shall always be under the supervision of the institution's personnel. Unless the work is for other departments of the government the full normal wages for such work shall be paid to the administration by the persons to whom the labour is supplied, account being taken of the output of the prisoners.

74. (1) The precautions laid down to protect the safety and health of free workmen shall be equally observed in institutions.

(2) Provision shall be made to indemnify prisoners against industrial injury, including occupational disease, on terms not less favourable than those extended by law to free workmen.

75. (1) The maximum daily and weekly working hours of the prisoners shall be fixed by law or by administrative regulation, taking into account local rules or custom in regard to the employment of free workmen.

(2) The hours so fixed shall leave one rest day a week and sufficient time for education and other activities required as part of the treatment and rehabilitation of the prisoners.

76. (1) There shall be a system of equitable remuneration of the work of prisoners.

(2) Under the system prisoners shall be allowed to spend at least a part of their earnings on approved articles for their own use and to send a part of their earnings to their family.

(3) The system should also provide that a part of the earnings should be set aside by the administration so as to constitute a savings fund to be handed over to the prisoner on his release.

Education and recreation

77. (1) Provision shall be made for the further education of all prisoners capable of profiting thereby, including religious instruction in the countries where this is possible. The education of illiterates and young prisoners shall be compulsory and special attention shall be paid to it by the administration.

(2) So far as practicable, the education of prisoners shall be integrated with the educational system of the country so that after their release they may continue their education without difficulty.

78. Recreational and cultural activities shall be provided in all institutions for the benefit of the mental and physical health of prisoners.

Social relations and after-care

79. Special attention shall be paid to the maintenance and improvement of such relations between a prisoner and his family as are desirable in the best interests of both.

80. From the beginning of a prisoner's sentence consideration shall be given to his future after release and he shall be encouraged and assisted to maintain or establish such relations with persons or agencies outside the institution as may promote the best interests of his family and his own social rehabilitation.

81. (1) Services and agencies, governmental or otherwise, which assist released prisoners to re-establish themselves in society shall ensure, so far as is possible and necessary, that released prisoners be provided with appropriate documents and identification papers, have suitable homes and work to go to, are suitably and adequately clothed having regard to the climate and season, and have sufficient means to reach their destination and maintain themselves in the period immediately following their release.

(2) The approved representatives of such agencies shall have all necessary access to the institution and to prisoners and shall be taken into consultation as to the future of a prisoner from the beginning of his sentence.

(3) It is desirable that the activities of such agencies shall be centralized or co-ordinated as far as possible in order to secure the best use of their efforts.

B. Insane and Mentally Abnormal Prisoners

82. (1) Persons who are found to be insane shall not be detained in prisons and arrangements shall be made to remove them to mental institutions as soon as possible.

(2) Prisoners who suffer from other mental diseases or abnormalities shall be observed and treated in specialized institutions under medical management.

(3) During their stay in a prison, such prisoners shall be placed under the special supervision of a medical officer.

(4) The medical or psychiatric service of the penal institutions shall provide for the psychiatric treatment of all other prisoners who are in need of such treatment.

83. It is desirable that steps should be taken, by arrangement with the appropriate agencies, to ensure if necessary the continuation of psychiatric treatment after release and the provision of social-psychiatric after-care.

C. Prisoners Under Arrest or Awaiting Trial

84. (1) Persons arrested or imprisoned by reason of a criminal charge against them, who are detained either in police custody or in prison custody (jail) but have not yet been tried and sentenced, will be referred to as "untried prisoners" hereinafter in these rules.

(2) Unconvicted prisoners are presumed to be innocent and shall be treated as such.

(3) Without prejudice to legal rules for the protection of individual liberty or prescribing the procedure to be observed in respect of untried prisoners, these prisoners shall benefit by a special régime which is described in the following rules in its essential requirements only.

85. (1) Untried prisoners shall be kept separate form convicted prisoners.

(2) Young untried prisoners shall be kept separate from adults and shall in principle be detained in separate institutions.

86. Untried prisoners shall sleep singly in separate rooms, with the reservation of different local custom in respect of the climate.

87. Within the limits compatible with the good order of the institution,

untried prisoners may, if they so desire, have their food procured at their own expense from the outside, either through the administration or through their family or friends. Otherwise, the administration shall provide their food.

88. (1) An untried prisoner shall be allowed to wear his own clothing if it is clean and suitable.

(2) If he wears prison dress, it shall be different from that supplied to convicted prisoners.

89. An untried prisoner shall always be offered opportunity to work, but shall not be required to work. If he chooses to work, he shall be paid for it.

90. An untried prisoner shall be allowed to procure at his own expense or at the expense of a third party such books, newspapers, writing materials and other means of occupation as are compatible with the interests of the administration of justice and the security and good order of the institution.

91. An untried prisoner shall be allowed to be visited and treated by his own doctor or dentist if there is reasonable ground for his applicaton and he is able to pay any expenses incurred.

92. An untried prisoner shall be allowed to inform immediately his family of his detention and shall be given all reasonable facilities for communicating with his family and friends, and for receiving visits from them, subject only to such restrictions and supervision as are necessary in the interests of the administration of justice and of the security and good order of the institution.

93. For the purposes of his defence, an untried prisoner shall be allowed to apply for free legal aid where such aid is available, and to receive visits from his legal adviser with a view to his defence and to prepare and hand to him confidential instructions. For these purposes, he shall if he so desires be supplied with writing material. Interviews between the prisoner and his legal adviser may be within sight but not within the hearing of a police or institution official.

D. Civil Prisoners

94. In countries where the law permits imprisonment for debt, or by order of a court under any other non-criminal process, persons so imprisoned shall not be subjected to any greater restriction or severity than is necessary to ensure safe custody and good order. Their treatment shall be not less favourable than that of untried prisoners, with the reservation, however, that they may possibly be required to work.

E. Persons Arrested or Detained Without Charge

95. Without prejudice to the provisions of article 9 of the International Covenant on Civil and Political Rights, persons arrested or imprisoned without charge shall be accorded the same protection as that accorded under part I and part II, section C. Relevant provisions of part II, secton A, shall likewise be applicable where their application may be conducive to the benefit of this special group of persons in custody, provided that no measures shall be taken implying that re-education or rehabilitation is in any way appropriate to persons not convicted of any criminal offence.

2. DECLARATION ON THE PROTECTION OF ALL PERSONS FROM BEING SUBJECTED TO TORTURE AND OTHER CRUEL, INHUMAN OR DEGRADING TREATMENT OR PUNISHMENT (1975) G.A. Res. 3452 (XXX), 30 U.N. GAOR, Supp. (No. 34) at 91, U.N. Doc. A/10034 (1975).

THE GENERAL ASSEMBLY,

Considering that, in accordance with the principles proclaimed in the Charter of the United Nations, recognition of the inherent dignity and of the equal and inalienable rights of all members of the human family is the foundation of freedom, justice and peace in the world,

Considering that these rights derive from the inherent dignity of the human person,

Considering also the obligation of States under the Charter, in particular Article 55, to promote universal respect for, and observance of, human rights and fundamental freedoms,

Having regard to article 5 of the Universal Declaration of Human Rights and article 7 of the International Covenant on Civil and Political Rights, both of which provide that no one may be subjected to torture or to cruel, inhuman or degrading treatment or punishment,

Adopts the Declaration on the Protection of All Persons from Being Subjected to Torture and Other Cruel, Inhuman or Degrading Treatment or Punishment, the text of which is annexed to the present resolution, as a guideline for all States and other entities exercising effective power.

ANNEX

DECLARATION ON THE PROTECTION OF ALL PERSONS FROM BEING SUBJECTED TO TORTURE AND OTHER CRUEL, INHUMAN OR DEGRADING TREATMENT OR PUNISHMENT

Article 1

1. For the purpose of this Declaration, torture means any act by which severe pain or suffering, whether physical or mental, is intentionally inflicted by or at the instigation of a public official on a person for such purposes as obtaining from him or a third person information or confession, punishing him for an act he has committed or is suspected of having committed, or intimidating him or other persons. It does not include pain or suffering arising only from, inherent in or incidental to, lawful sanctions to the extent consistent with the Standard Minimum Rules for the Treatment of Prisoners.

2. Torture constitutes an aggravated and deliberate form of cruel, inhuman or degrading treatment or punishment.

Article 2

Any act of torture or other cruel, inhuman or degrading treatment or punishment is an offence to human dignity and shall be condemned as a denial of the purposes of the Charter of the Untied Nations and as a violation of the human rights and fundamental freedoms proclaimed in the Universal Declaration of Human Rights.

Article 3

No State may permit or tolerate torture or other cruel, inhuman or degrading treatment or punishment. Exceptional circumstances such as a state of war or a threat of war, internal political instability or any other public emergency may not be invoked as a justification of torture or other cruel, inhuman or degrading treatment or punishment.

Article 4

Each State shall, in accordance with the provisions of this Declaration, take effective measures to prevent torture and other cruel, inhuman or degrading treatment or punishment from being practised within its jurisdiction.

Article 5

The training of law enforcement personnel and of other public officials who may be responsible for persons deprived of their liberty shall ensure that full account is taken of the prohibition against torture and other cruel, inhuman or degrading treatment or punishment. This prohibition shall also, where appropriate, be included in such general rules or instructions as are issued in regard to the duties and functions of anyone who may be involved in the custody or treatment of such persons.

Article 6

Each State shall keep under systematic review interrogation methods and practices as well as arrangements for the custody and treatment of persons deprived of their liberty in its territory, with a view to preventing any cases of torture or other cruel, inhuman or degrading treatment or punishment.

Article 7

Each State shall ensure that all acts of torture as defined in article 1 are offences under its criminal law. The same shall apply in regard to acts which constitute participation in, complicity in, incitement to or an attempt to commit torture.

Article 8

Any person who alleges that he has been subjected to torture or other cruel, inhuman or degrading treatment or punishment by or at the instigation of a public official shall have the right to complain to, and to have his case impartially examined by, the competent authorities of the State concerned.

Article 9

Wherever there is reasonable ground to believe that an act of torture as defined in article 1 has been committed, the competent authorities of the State concerned shall promptly proceed to an impartial investigation even if there has been no formal complaint.

Article 10

If an investigation under article 8 or article 9 establishes that an act of torture as defined in article 1 appears to have been committed, criminal proceedings shall be instituted against the alleged offender or offenders in accordance with national law. If an allegation of other forms of cruel, inhuman or degrading treatment or punishment is considered to be well founded, the alleged offender or offenders shall be subject to criminal, disciplinary or other appropriate proceedings.

Article 11

Where it is proved that an act of torture or other cruel, inhuman or degrading treatment or punishment has been committed by or at the instigation of a public official, the victim shall be afforded redress and compensation in accordance with national law.

Article 12

Any statement which is established to have been made as a result of torture or other cruel, inhuman or degrading treatment or punishment may not be invoked as evidence against the person concerned or against any other person in any proceedings.

3. CODE OF CONDUCT FOR LAW ENFORCEMENT OFFICIALS (1979) G.A. Res. 34/169, 34 U.N. GAOR (Supp. No. 46) at 185, U.N. Doc. A/34/36 (1979).

Article 1

Law enforcement officials shall at all times fulfil the duty imposed upon them by law, by serving the community and by protecting all persons against illegal acts, consistent with the high degree of responsibility required by their profession.

Commentary:

a. The term "law enforcement officials" includes all officers of the law, whether appointed or elected, who exercise police powers, especially the powers of arrest or detention.

b. In countries where police powers are exercised by military authorities, whether uniformed or not, or by state security forces, the definition of law enforcement officials shall be regarded as including officers of such services.

c. Service to the community is intended to include particularly the rendition of services of assistance to those members of the community who by reason of personal, economic, social or other emergencies are in need of immediate aid.

d. This provision is intended to cover not only all violent, predatory and harmful acts, but extends to the full range of prohibitions under penal statutes. It extends to conduct by persons not capable of incurring criminal liability.

Article 2

In the performance of their duty, law enforcement officials shall respect and protect human dignity and maintain and uphold the human rights of all persons.

Commentary:

a. The human rights in question are identified and protected by national and international law. Among the relevant international instruments are the Universal Declaration of Human Rights, the International Covenant on Civil and Political Rights, the Declaration on the Protection of All Persons from Being Subjected to Torture and Other Cruel, Inhuman or Degrading Treatment or Punishment, the United Nations Declaration on the Elimination of All Forms of Radial Discrimination, the International Convention on the Elimination of all Forms of Racial Discrimination, the International Convention on the Suppression and Punishment of the Crime of *Apartheid*, the Convention on the Prevention and Punishment of the Crime of Genocide, the Standard Minimum Rules for the Treatment of Prisoners and the Vienna Convention on Consular Relations.

b. National commentaries to this provision should indicate regional or national provisions identifying and protecting these rights.

Article 3

Law enforcement officials may use force only when strictly necessary and to the extent required for the performance of their duty.

Commentary:

a. This provision emphasizes that the use of force by law enforcement officials should be exceptional; while it implies that law enforcement officials may be authorized to use force as is reasonably necessary under the circumstnaces for the prevention of crime or in effecting or assisting in the lawful arrest of offenders or suspected offenders, no force going beyond that may be used.

b. National law ordinarily restricts the use of force by law enforcement officials in accordance with a principle of proportionality. It is to be understood that such national principles of proportionality are to be respected in the interpretation of this provision. In no case should this provision be interpreted to authorize the use of force which is disproportionate to the legitimate objective to be achieved.

c. The use of firearms is considered an extreme measure. Every effort should be made to exclude the use of firearms, especially against children. In general, firearms should not be used except when a suspected offender offers armed resistance or otherwise jeopardizes the lives of others and less extreme measures are not sufficient to restrain or apprehend the suspected offender. In every instance in which a firearm is discharged, a report should be made promptly to the competent authorities.

Article 4

Matters of a confidential nature in the possession of law enforcement officials shall be kept confidential, unless the performance of duty, or the needs of justice, strictly require otherwise.

Commentary:

By the nature of their duties, law enforcement officials obtain information which may relate to private lives or be potentially harmful to the interests, and especially the reputation, of others. Great care should be exercised in safeguarding and using such information, which should be disclosed only in the performance of duty or to serve the needs of justice. Any disclosure of such information for other purposes is wholly improper.

Article 5

No law enforcement official may inflict, instigate or tolerate any act of torture or other cruel, inhuman or degrading treatment or punishment, nor may any law enforcement official invoke superior orders or exceptional circumstances such as a state of war or a threat of war, a threat to national security, internal political instability or any other public emergency as a justification of torture or other cruel, inhuman or degrading treatment or punishment.

Commentary:

a. This prohibition derives from the Declaration on the Protection of All Persons from Being Subjected to Torture and Other Cruel, Inhuman or Degrading Treatment or Punishment, adopted by the General Assembly, according to which:
Such an act is "an offence to human dignity and shall be condemned as a denial of the purposes of the Charter of the United Nations and as a violation of the human rights and fundamental freedoms proclaimed in the Universal Declaration of Human Rights" and other international human rights instruments.
b. The Declaration defines torture as follows:
" . . . torture means any act by which severe pain or suffering, whether physical or mental, is intentionally inflicted by or at the instigation of a public official on a person for such purposes as obtaining from him or a third person information or confession, punishing him for an act he has committed or is suspected of having committed, or intimidating him or other persons. It does not include pain or suffering arising only from, inherent in or incidental to, lawful sanctions to the extent consistent with the Standard Minimum Rules for the Treatment of Prisoners."
c. The term "cruel, inhuman or degrading treatment or punishment" has not been defined by the General Assembly, but should be

interpreted so as to extend the widest possible protection against abuses, whether physical or mental.

Article 6

Law enforcement officials shall ensure the full protection of the health of persons in their custody and, in particular, take immediate action to secure medical attention whenever required.

Commentary:

a. "Medical attention", which refers to services rendered by any medical personnel, including certified medical practitioners and para-medics, shall be secured when needed or requested.

b. While the medical personnel are likely to be attached to the law enforcement operation, law enforcement officials must take into account the judgement of such personnel when they recommend providing the person in custody with appropriate treatment through, or in consultation with, medical personnel from outside the law enforcement operation.

c. It is understood that law enforcement officials shall also secure medical attention for victims of violations of law or of accidents occurring in the course of violations of law.

Article 7

Law enforcement officials shall not commit any act of corruption. They shall also rigorously oppose and combat all such acts.

Commentary:

a. Any act of corruption, in the same way as any other abuse of authority, is incompatible with the profession of law enforcement officials. The law must be enforced fully with respect to any law enforcement official who commits an act of corruption, as Governments cannot expect to enforce the law among their citizens if they cannot, or will not, enforce the law against their own agents and within their own agencies.

b. While the definition of corruption must be subject to national law, it should be understood to encompass the commission or omission of an act in the performance of or in connexion with one's duties, in response to gifts, promises or incentives demanded or accepted, or the wrongful receipt of these once the act has been committed or omitted.

c. The expression "act of corruption" referred to above should be understood to encompass attempted corruption.

Article 8

Law enforcement officials shall respect the law and the present Code. They shall also, to the best of their capability, prevent and rigorously oppose any violations of them.

Law enforcement officials who have reason to believe that a violation of this

Code has occurred or is about to occur shall report the matter to their superior authorities and, where necessary, to other appropriate authorities or organs vested with reviewing or remedial power.

Commentary:

a. This Code shall be observed whenever it has been incorporated into national legislation or practice. If legislation or practice contains stricter provisions than those of the present Code, those stricter provisions shall be observed.

b. The article seeks to preserve the balance between the need for internal discipline of the agency on which public safety is largely dependent, on the one hand, and the need for dealing with violations of basic human rights, on the other. Law enforcement officials shall report violations within the chain of command and take other lawful action outside the chain of command only when no other remedies are available or effective. It is understood that law enforcement officials shall not suffer administrative or other penalties because they have reported that a violation of this Code has occurred or is about to occur.

c. The terms "appropriate authorities or organs vested with reviewing or remedial power" refer to any authority or organ existing under national law, whether internal to the law enforcement agency, or independent thereof, with statutory, customary or other power to review grievances and complaints arising out of violations within the purview of this Code.

d. In some countries, the mass media may be regarded as performing complaint review functions similar to those described in commentary (*c*). Law enforcement officials may, therefore, be justified if, as a last resort and in accordance with the laws and customs of their own countries and with the provisions of article 4 of the present Code, they bring violations to the attention of public opinion through the mass media.

e. Law enforcement officials who comply with the provisions of this Code deserve the respect, the full support and the co-operation of the community and of the law enforcement agency in which they serve, as well as of the law enforcement profession.

4. PRINCIPLES OF MEDICAL ETHICS (1982) G.A. Res. 37/194, 37 U.N. GAOR, Supp. (No. 51) at 210, U.N. Doc. A/37/51 (1983).

THE GENERAL ASSEMBLY,

Recalling its resolution 31/85 of 13 December 1976, in which it invited the World Health Organization to prepare a draft Code of Medical Ethics relevant to the protection of persons subjected to any form of detention or imprisonment against torture and other cruel, inhuman or degrading treatment or punishment,

Expressing once again its appreciation to the Executive Board of the World Health Organization which, as its sixty-third session in January 1979, decided to endorse the principles set forth in a report entitled "Development of codes of medical ethics" containing, in an annex, a draft body of principles prepared by the Council for International Organizations of Medical Sciences and entitled "Principles of medical ethics relevant to the role of health personnel in the protection of persons against torture and other cruel, inhuman or degrading treatment or punishment,"

Bearing in mind Economic and Social Council resolution 1981/27 of 6 May 1981, in which the Council recommended that the General Assembly should take measures to finalize the draft Principles of Medical Ethics at its thirty-sixth session,

Recalling its resolution 36/61 of 25 November 1981, in which it decided to consider the draft Principles of Medical Ethics at its thirty-seventh session with a view to adopting them,

Alarmed that not infrequently members of the medical profession or other health personnel are engaged in activities which are difficult to reconcile with medical ethics,

Recognizing that throughout the world significant medical activities are increasingly being performed by health personnel not licensed or trained as physicians, such as physician-assistants, paramedics, physical therapists and nurse practitioners,

Taking note with appreciation of the "Guidelines for Medical Doctors concerning Torture and other Cruel, Inhuman or Degrading Treatment or Punishment in relation to Detention and Imprisonment," as adopted by the twenty-ninth World Medical Assembly, held in Tokyo in October 1975,

Noting that in accordance with the Declaration of Tokyo measures should be taken by States and by professional associations and other bodies, as appropriate, against any attempt to subject health personnel or members of their families to threats or reprisals resulting from a refusal by such personnel to condone the use of torture or other forms of cruel, inhuman or degrading treatment,

Reaffirming the Declaration on the Protection of all Persons from Being Subjected to Torture and other Cruel, Inhuman or Degrading Treatment or Punishment as unanimously adopted in its resolution 3452 (XXX) of 9 December 1975, in which it declared any act of torture or other cruel, inhuman or degrading treatment or punishment an offence to human dignity, a denial of the purposes of the Charter of the United Nations and a violation of the Universal Declaration of Human Rights,

Recalling that, in accordance with article 7 of the Declaration adopted under resolution 3452 (XXX), each State shall ensure that the commission of all acts of torture, as defined in article 1 of that Declaration, or participation in, complicity in, incitement to and attempt to commit torture, are offences under its criminal law,

Convinced that under no circumstances a person shall be punished for carrying out medical activities compatible with medical ethics regardless of the person benefiting therefrom, or shall be compelled to perform acts or to carry out work in contravention of medical ethics, but that at the same time, contravention of medical ethics for which health personnel, particularly physicians, can be held responsible should entail accountability,

Desirous to set further standards in this field which ought to be implemented by health personnel, particularly physicians, and by Government officials:

1. *Adopts* the "Principles of Medical Ethics relevant to the role of health personnel, particularly physicians, in the protection of prisoners and detainees against torture and other cruel, inhuman or degrading treatment or punishment" annexed to the present resolution;

2. *Calls upon* all Governments to give the Principles of Medical Ethics, together with the present resolution, the widest possible distribution, in particular among medical and paramedical associations, and institutions of detention or imprisonment in an official language of the State;

3. *Invites* all relevant intergovernmental organizations, in particular the World Health Organization, and non-governmental organizations concerned to bring the Principles of Medical Ethics to the attention of the widest possible group of individuals, especially those active in the medical and paramedical field.

ANNEX

PRINCIPLES OF MEDICAL ETHICS RELEVANT TO THE ROLE OF HEALTH PERSONNEL, PARTICULARLY PHYSICIANS, IN THE PROTECTION OF PRISONERS AND DETAINEES AGAINST TORTURE, AND OTHER CRUEL, INHUMAN OR DEGRADING TREATMENT OR PUNISHMENT

Principle 1

Health personnel, particularly physicians, charged with the medical care of prisoners and detainees, have a duty to provide them with protection of their physical and mental health and treatment of disease of the same quality and standard as is afforded to those who are not imprisoned or detained.

Principle 2

It is a gross contravention of medical ethics, as well as an offence under applicable international instruments, for health personnel, particularly physicians, to engage, actively or passively, in acts which constitute participation in, complicity in, incitement to or attempts to commit torture or other cruel, inhuman or degrading treatment or punishment.

Principle 3

It is a contravention of medical ethics for health personnel, particularly physicians, to be involved in any professional relationship with prisoners or detainees the purpose of which is not solely to evaluate, protect or improve their physical and mental health.

Principle 4

It is a contravention of medical ethics for health personnel, particularly physicians:

    a. To apply their knowledge and skills in order to assist in the interrogation of prisoners and detainees in a manner that may adversely affect the physical or mental health or condition of such prisoners or detainees and which is not in accordance with the relevant international instruments;

b. To certify, or to participate in the certification of, the fitness of prisoners or detainees for any form of treatment or punishment that may adversely affect their physical or mental health and which is not in accordance with the relevant international instruments, or to participate in any way in the infliction of any such treatment or punishment which is not in accordance with the relevant international instruments.

Principle 5

It is a contravention of medical ethics for health personnel, particularly physicians, to participate in any procedure for restraining a prisoner or detainee unless such a procedure is determined in accordance with purely medical criteria as being necessary for the protection of the physical or mental health or the safety of the prisoner or detainee himself, of his fellow prisoners or detainees, or of his guardians, and it presents no hazard to his physical or mental health.

Principle 6

There may be no derogation from the foregoing principles on any ground whatsoever, including public emergency.

5. CONVENTION AGAINST TORTURE AND OTHER CRUEL, INHUMAN OR DEGRADING TREATMENT OR PUNISHMENT (1984) G.A. Res. 39/46, 39 U.N. GAOR, Supp. (No. 51) at 197, U.N. Doc. A/39/51 (1984). Not yet in force.

THE STATES PARTIES TO THIS CONVENTION,

Considering that, in accordance with the principles proclaimed in the Charter of the United Nations, recognition of the equal and inalienable rights of all members of the human family is the foundation of freedom, justice and peace in the world,

Recognizing that those rights derive from the inherent dignity of the human person,

Considering the obligation of States under the Charter, in particular Article 55, to promote universal respect for, and observance of, human rights and fundamental freedoms,

Having regard to article 5 of the Universal Declaration of Human Rights[1] and article 7 of the International Covenant on Civil and Political Rights,[2] both of

[1]Resolution 217 A (III).
[2]Resolution 2200 A (XXI), annex.

which provide that no one shall be subjected to torture or to cruel, inhuman or degrading treatment or punishment,

Having regard also to the Declaration on the Protection of All Persons from Being Subjected to Torture and Other Cruel, Inhuman or Degrading Treatment or Punishment, adopted by the General Assembly on 9 December 1975,[3]

Desiring to make more effective the struggle against torture and other cruel, inhuman or degrading treatment or punishment throughout the world,

Have agreed as follows:

PART I

Article 1

1. For the purposes of this Convention, the term "torture" means any act by which severe pain or suffering, whether physical or mental, is intentionally inflicted on a person for such purposes as obtaining from him or a third person information or a confession, punishing him for an act he or a third person has committed or is suspected of having committed, or intimidating or coercing him or a third person, or for any reason based on discrimination of any kind, when such pain or suffering is inflicted by or at the instigation of or with the consent or acquiescence of a public official or other person acting in an official capacity. It does not include pain or suffering arising only from, inherent in or incidental to lawful sanctions.

2. This article is without prejudice to any international instrument or national legislation which does or may contain provisions of wider application.

Article 2

1. Each State Party shall take effective legislative, administrative, judicial or other measures to prevent acts of torture in any territory under its jurisdiction.

2. No exceptional circumstances whatsoever, whether a state of war or a threat of war, internal political instability or any other public emergency, may be invoked as a justification of torture.

3. An order from a superior officer or a public authority may not be invoked as a justification of torture.

Article 3

1. No State Party shall expel, return ("*refouler*") or extradite a person to another State where there are substantial grounds for believing that he would be in danger of being subjected to torture.

2. For the purpose of determining whether there are such grounds, the competent authorities shall take into account all relevant considerations including, where applicable, the existence in the State concerned of a consistent pattern of gross, flagrant or mass violations of human rights.

---

[3]Resolution 3452 (XXX), annex.

Article 4

1. Each State Party shall ensure that all acts of torture are offences under its criminal law. The same shall apply to an attempt to commit torture and to an act by any person which constitutes complicity or participation in torture.

2. Each State Party shall make these offences punishable by appropriate penalties which take into account their grave nature.

Article 5

1. Each State Party shall take such measures as may be necessary to establish its jurisdiction over the offences referred to in article 4 in the following cases:

    a. When the offences are committed in any territory under its jurisdiction or on board a ship cr aircraft registered in that State;

    b. When the alleged offender is a national of that State;

    c. When the victim is a national of that State if that State considers it appropriate.

2. Each State Party shall likewise take such measures as may be necessary to establish its jurisdiction over such offences in cases where the alleged offender is present in any territory under its jurisdiction and it does not extradite him pursuant to article 8 to any of the States mentioned in paragraph 1 of this article.

3. This Convention does not exclude any criminal jurisdiction exercised in accordance with internal law.

Article 6

1. Upon being satisifed, after an examination of information available to it, that the circumstances so warrant, any State Party in whose territory a person alleged to have committed any offence referred to in article 4 is present shall take him into custody or take other legal measures to ensure his presence. The custody and other legal measures shall be as provided in the law of that State but may be continued only for such time as is necessary to enable any criminal or extradition proceedings to be instituted.

2. Such State shall immediately make a preliminary inquiry into the facts.

3. Any person in custody pursuant to paragraph 1 of this article shall be assisted in communicating immediately with the nearest appropriate representative of the State of which he is a national, or, if he is a stateless person, with the representative of the State where he usually resides.

4. When a State, pursuant to this article, has taken a person into custody, it shall immediately notify the States referred to in article 5, paragraph 1, of the fact that such person is in custody and of the circumstances which warrant his detention. The State which makes the preliminary inquiry contemplated in paragraph 2 of this article shall promptly report its findings to the said States and shall indicate whether it intends to exercise jurisdiction.

Article 7

1. The State Party in the territory under whose jurisdiction a person alleged to have committed any offence referred to in article 4 is found shall in the cases

contemplated in article 5, if it does not extradite him, submit the case to its competent authorities for the purpose of prosecution.

2. These authorities shall take their decision in the same manner as in the case of any ordinary offence of a serious nature under the law of that State. In the cases referred to in article 5, paragraph 2, the standards of evidence required for prosecution and conviction shall in no way be less stringent than those which apply in the cases referred to in article 5, paragraph 1.

3. Any person regarding whom proceedings are brought in connection with any of the offences referred to in article 4 shall be guaranteed fair treatment at all stages of the proceedings.

Article 8

1. The offences referred to in article 4 shall be deemed to be included as extraditable offences in any extradition treaty existing between States Parties. States Parties undertake to include such offences as extraditable offences in every extradition treaty to be concluded between them.

2. If a State Party which makes extradition conditional on the existence of a treaty receives a request for extradition from another State Party with which it has no extradition treaty, it may consider this Convention as the legal basis for extradition in respect of such offences. Extradition shall be subject to the other conditions provided by the law of the requested State.

3. States Parties which do not make extradition conditional on the existence of a treaty shall recognize such offences as extraditable offences between themselves subject to the conditions provided by the law of the requested State.

4. Such offences shall be treated, for the purpose of extradition between States Parties, as if they had been committed not only in the place in which they occurred but also in the territories of the States required to estabilsh their jurisdiction in accordance with article 5, paragraph 1.

Article 9

1. States Parties shall afford one another the greatest measure of assistance in connection with criminal proceedings brought in respect of any of the offences referred to in article 4, including the supply of all evidence at their disposal necessary for the proceedings.

2. States Parties shall carry out their obligations under paragraph 1 of this article in conformity with any treaties on mutual judicial assistance that may exist between them.

Article 10

1. Each State Party shall ensure that education and information regarding the prohibition against torture are fully included in the training of law enforcement personnel, civil or military, medical personnel, public officials and other persons who may be involved in the custody, interrogation or treatment of any individual subjected to any form of arrest, detention or imprisonment.

2. Each State Party shall include this prohibition in the rules or instructions issued in regard to the duties and functions of any such persons.

Article 11

Each State Party shall keep under systematic review interrogation rules, instructions, methods and practices as well as arrangements for the custody and treatment of persons subjected to any form of arrest, detention or imprisonment in any territory under its jurisdiction, with a view to preventing any cases of torture.

Article 12

Each State Party shall ensure that its competent authorities proceed to a prompt and impartial investigation, wherever there is reasonable ground to believe that an act of torture has been committed in any territory under its jurisdiction.

Article 13

Each State Party shall ensure that any individual who alleges he has been subjected to torture in any territory under its jurisdiction has the right to complain to, and to have his case promptly and impartially examined by, its competent authorities. Steps shall be taken to ensure that the complainant and witnesses are protected against all ill-treatment or intimidation as a consequence of his complaint or any evidence given.

Article 14

1. Each State Party shall ensure in its legal system that the victim of an act of torture obtains redress and has an enforceable right to fair and adequate compensation, including the means for as full rehabilitation as possible. In the event of the death of the victim as a result of an act of torture, his dependants shall be entitled to compensation.

2. Nothing in this article shall affect any right of the victim or other persons to compensation which may exist under national law.

Article 15

Each State Party shall ensure that any statement which is established to have been made as a result of torture shall not be invoked as evidence in any proceedings, except against a person accused of torture as evidence that the statement was made.

Article 16

1. Each State Party shall undertake to prevent in any territory under its jurisdiction other acts of cruel, inhuman or degrading treatment or punishment which do not amount to torture as defined in article 1, when such acts are committed by or at the instigation of or with the consent or acquiescence of a public official or other person acting in an official capacity. In particular, the obligations contained in articles 10, 11, 12 and 13 shall apply with the substitu-

tion for references to torture of references to other forms of cruel, inhuman or degrading treatment or punishment.

2. The provisions of this Convention are without prejudice to the provisions of any other international instrument or national law which prohibits cruel, inhuman or degrading treatment or punishment or which relates to extradition or expulsion.

PART II

Article 17

1. There shall be established a Committee against Torture (hereinafter referred to as the Committee) which shall carry out the functions hereinafter provided. The Committee shall consist of ten experts of high moral standing and recognized competence in the field of human rights, who shall serve in their personal capacity. The experts shall be elected by the States Parties, consideration being given to equitable geographical distribution and to the usefulness of the participation of some persons having legal experience.

2. The members of the Committee shall be elected by secret ballot from a list of persons nominated by States Parties. Each State Party may nominate one person from among its own nationals. States Parties shall bear in mind the usefulness of nominating persons who are also members of the Human Rights Committee estabilshed under the International Covenant on Civil and Political Rights and who are willing to serve on the Committee against Torture.

3. Elections of the members of the Committee shall be held at biennial meetings of States Parties convened by the Secretary-General of the United Nations. At those meetings, for which two thirds of the States Parties shall constitute a quorum, the persons elected to the Committee shall be those who obtain the largest number of votes and an absolute majority of the votes of the representatives of States Parties present and voting.

4. The initial election shall be held no later than six months after the date of the entry into force of this Convention. At least four months before the date of each election, the Secretary-General of the United Nations shall address a letter to the States Parties inviting them to submit their nominations within three months. The Secretary-General shall prepare a list in alphabetical order of all persons thus nominated, indicating the States Parties which have nominated them, and shall submit it to the States Parties.

5. The members of the Committee shall be elected for a term of four years. They shall be eligible for re-election if renominated. However, the term of five of the members elected at the first election shall expire at the end of two years; immediately after the first election the names of these five members shall be chosen by lot by the chairman of the meeting referred to in paragraph 3 of this article.

6. If a member of the Committee dies or resigns or for any other cause can no longer perform his Committee duties, the State Party which nominated him shall appoint another expert from among its nationals to serve for the remainder of his term, subject to the approval of the majority of the States Parties. The

approval shall be considered given unless half or more of the States Parties respond negatively within six weeks after having been informed by the Secretary-General of the United Nations of the proposed appointment.

7. States Parties shall be responsible for the expenses of the members of the Committee while they are in performance of Committee duties.

Article 18

1. The Committee shall elect its officers for a term of two years. They may be re-elected.

2. The Committee shall establish its own rules of procedure, but these rules shall provide, *inter alia*, that:

  a. Six members shall constitute a quorum;

  b. Decisions of the Committee shall be made by a majority vote of the members present.

3. The Secretary-General of the United Nations shall provide the necessary staff and facilities for the effective performance of the functions of the Committee under this Convention.

4. The Secretary-General of the United Nations shall convene the initial meeting of the Committee. After its initial meeting, the Committee shall meet at such times as shall be provided in its rules of procedure.

5. The States Parties shall be responsible for expenses incurred in connection with the holding of meetings of the States Parties and of the Committee, including reimbursement to the United Nations for any expenses, such as the cost of staff and facilities, incurred by the United Nations pursuant to paragraph 3 of this article.

Article 19

1. The States Parties shall submit to the Committee, through the Secretary-General of the United Nations, reports on the measures they have taken to give effect to their undertakings under this Convention, within one year after the entry into force of the Convention for the State Party concerned. Thereafter the States Parties shall submit supplementary reports every four years on any new measures taken and such other reports as the Committee may request.

2. The Secretary-General of the United Nations shall transmit the reports to all States Parties.

3. Each report shall be considered by the Committee which may make such general comments on the report as it may consider appropriate and shall forward these to the State Party concerned. That State Party may respond with any observations it chooses to the Committee.

4. The Committee may, at its discretion, decide to include any comments made by it in accordance with paragraph 3 of this article, together with the observations thereon received from the State Party concerned, in its annual report made in accordance with article 24. If so requested by the State Party concerned, the Committee may also include a copy of the report submitted under paragraph 1 of this article.

Article 20

1. If the Committee receives reliable information which appears to it to contain well-founded indications that torture is being systematically practised in the territory of a State Party, the Committee shall invite that State Party to co-operate in the examination of the information and to this end to submit observations with regard to the information concerned.

2. Taking into account any observations which may have been submitted by the State Party concerned, as well as any other relevant information available to it, the Committee may, if it decides that this is warranted, designate one or more of its members to make a confidential inquiry and to report to the Committee urgently.

3. If an inquiry is made in accordance with paragraph 2 of this article, the Committee shall seek the co-operation of the State Party concerned. In agreement with that State Party, such an inquiry may include a visit to its territory.

4. After examining the findings of its member or members submitted in accordance with paragraph 2 of this article, the Committee shall transmit these findings to the State Party concerned together with any comments or suggestions which seem appropriate in view of the situation.

5. All the proceedings of the Committee referred to in paragraphs 1 to 4 of this article shall be confidential, and at all stages of the proceedings the co-operation of the State Party shall be sought. After such proceedings have been completed with regard to an inquiry made in accordance with paragraph 2, the Committee may, after consultations with the State Party concerned, decide to include a summary account of the results of the proceedings in its annual report made in accordance with article 24.

Article 21

1. A State Party to this Convention may at any time declare under this article that it recognizes the competence of the Committee to receive and consider communications to the effect that a State Party claims that another State Party is not fulfilling its obligations under this Convention. Such communications may be received and considered according to the procedures laid down in this article only if submitted by a State Party which has made a declaration recognizing in regard to itself the competence of the Committee. No communication shall be dealt with by the Committee under this article if it concerns a State Party which has not made such a declaration. Communications received under this article shall be dealt with in accordance with the following procedure:

    a. If a State Party considers that another State Party is not giving effect to the provisions of this Convention, it may, by written communication, bring the matter to the attention of that State Party. Within three months after the receipt of the communication the receiving State shall afford the State which sent the communication an explanation or any other statement in writing clarifying the matter, which should include, to the extent possible and pertinent, reference to domestic procedures and remedies taken, pending or available in the matter;

    b. If the matter is not adjusted to the satisfaction of both States

Parties concerned within six months after the receipt by the receiving State of the initial communication, either State shall have the right to refer the matter to the Committee, by notice given to the Committee and to the other State;

c. The Committee shall deal with a matter referred to it under this article only after it has ascertained that all domestic remedies have been invoked and exhausted in the matter, in conformity with the generally recognized principles of international law. This shall not be the rule where the application of the remedies is unreasonably prolonged or is unlikely to bring effective relief to the person who is the victim of the violation of this Convention;

d. The Committee shall hold closed meetings when examining communications under this article;

e. Subject to the provisions of subparagraph (c), the Committee shall make available its good offices to the States Parties concerned with a view to a friendly solution of the matter on the basis of respect for the obligations provided for in this Convention. For this purpose, the Committee may, when appropriate, set up an *ad hoc* conciliation commission;

f. In any matter referred to it under this article, the Committee may call upon the States Parties concerned, referred to in subparagraph (b), to supply any relevant information;

g. The States Parties concerned, referred to in subparagraph (b), shall have the right to be represented when the matter is being considered by the Committee and to make submissions orally and/or in writing;

h. The Committee shall, within twelve months after the date of receipt of notice under subparagraph (b), submit a report:

    i. If a solution within the terms of subparagraph (e) is reached, the Committee shall confine its report to a brief statement of the facts and of the solution reached;

    ii. If a solution within the terms of subparagraph (e) is not reached, the Committee shall confine its report to a brief statement of the facts; the written submissions and record of the oral submissions made by the States Parties concerned shall be attached to the report.

In every matter, the report shall be communicated to the States Parties concerned.

2. The provisions of this article shall come into force when five States Parties to this Convention have made declarations under paragraph 1 of this article. Such declarations shall be deposited by the States Parties with the Secretary-General of the United Nations, who shall transmit copies thereof to the other States Parties. A declaration may be withdrawn at any time by notification to the Secretary-General. Such a withdrawal shall not prejudice the consideration of any matter which is the subject of a communication already transmitted under this article; no further communication by any State Party shall be received under this article after the notification of withdrawal of the declaration has been

received by the Secretary-General, unless the State Party concerned has made a new declaration.

Article 22

1. A State Party to this Convention may at any time declare under this article that it recognizes the competence of the Committee to receive and consider communications from or on behalf of individuals subject to its jurisdiction who claim to be victims of a violation by a State Party of the provisions of the Convention. No communication shall be received by the Committee if it concerns a State Party which has not made such a declaration.

2. The Committee shall consider inadmissible any communication under this article which is anonymous or which it considers to be an abuse of the right of submission of such communications or to be incompatible with the provisions of this Convention.

3. Subject to the provisions of paragraph 2, the Committee shall bring any communications submitted to it under this article to the attention of the State Party to this Convention which has made a declaration under paragraph 1 and is alleged to be violating any provisions of the Convention. Within six months, the receiving State shall submit to the Committee written explanations or statements clarifying the matter and the remedy, if any, that may have been taken by that State.

4. The Committee shall consider communications received under this article in the light of all information made available to it by or on behalf of the individual and by the State Party concerned.

5. The Committee shall not consider any communications from an individual under this article unless it has ascertained that:

    a. The same matter has not been, and is not being, examined under another procedure of international investigation or settlement;

    b. The individual has exhausted all available domestic remedies; this shall not be the rule where the application of the remedies is unreasonably prolonged or is unlikely to bring effective relief to the person who is the victim of the violation of this Convention.

6. The Committee shall hold closed meetings when examining communications under this article.

7. The Committee shall forward its views to the State Party concerned and to the individual.

8. The provisions of this article shall come into force when five States Parties to this Convention have made declarations under paragraph 1 of this article. Such declarations shall be deposited by the States Parties with the Secretary-General of the United Nations, who shall transmit copies thereof to the other States Parties. A declaration may be withdrawn at any time by notification to the Secretary-General. Such a withdrawal shall not prejudice the consideration of any matter which is the subject of a communication already transmitted under this article; no further communication by or on behalf of an individual shall be received under this article after the notification of withdrawal of the declaration has been received by the Secretary-General, unless the State Party has made a new declaration.

Article 23

The members of the Committee and of the *ad hoc* conciliation commissions which may be appointed under article 21, paragraph 1 (*e*), shall be entitled to the facilities, privileges and immunities of experts on mission for the United Nations as laid down in the relevant sections of the Convention on the Privileges and Immunities of the United Nations.*

Article 24

The Committee shall submit an annual report on its activities under this Convention to the States Parties and to the General Assembly of the United Nations.

PART III

Article 25

1. This Convention is open for signature by all States.
2. This Convention is subject to ratification. Instruments of ratification shall be deposited with the Secretary-General of the United Nations.

Article 26

This Convention is open to accession by all States. Accession shall be effected by the deposit of an instrument of accession with the Secretary-General of the United Nations.

Article 27

1. This Convention shall enter into force on the thirtieth day after the date of the deposit with the Secretary-General of the United Nations of the twentieth instrument of ratification or accession.
2. For each State ratifying this Convention or acceding to it after the deposit of the twentieth instrument of ratification or accession, the Convention shall enter into force on the thirtieth day after the date of the deposit of its own instrument of ratification or accession.

Article 28

1. Each State may, at the time of signature or ratification of this Convention or accession thereto, declare that it does not recognize the competence of the Committee provided for in article 20.
2. Any State Party having made a reservation in accordance with paragraph 1 of this article may, at any time, withdraw this reservation by notification to the Secretary-General of the United Nations.

Article 29

1. Any State Party to this Convention may propose an amendment and file

---

*Resolution 22 A (I).

it with the Secretary-General of the United Nations. The Secretary-General shall thereupon communicate the proposed amendment to the States Parties with a request that they notify him whether they favour a conference of States Parties for the purpose of considering and voting upon the proposal. In the event that within four months from the date of such communication at least one third of the States Parties favours such a conference, the Sectretary-General shall convene the conference under the auspices of the United Nations. Any amendment adopted by a majority of the States Parties present and voting at the conference shall be submitted by the Secretary-General to all the States Parties for acceptance.

2. An amendment adopted in accordance with paragraph 1 of this article shall enter into force when two thirds of the States Parties to this Convention have notified the Secretary-General of the United Nations that they have accepted it in accordance with their respective constitutional processes.

3. When amendments enter into force, they shall be binding on those States Parties which have accepted them, other States Parties still being bound by the provisions of this Convention and any earlier amendments which they have accepted.

Article 30

1. Any dispute between two or more States Parties concerning the inter-pretation or application of this Convention which cannot be settled through negotiation shall, at the request of one of them, be submitted to arbitration. If within six months from the date of the request for arbitration the Parties are unable to agree on the organization of the arbitration, any one of those Parties may refer the dispute to the International Court of Justice by request in conformity with the Statute of the Court.

2. Each State may, at the time of signature or ratification of this Convention or accession thereto, declare that it does not consider itself bound by paragraph 1 of this article. The other States Parties shall not be bound by paragraph 1 of this article with respect to any State Party having made such a reservation.

3. Any State Party having made a reservation in accordance with paragraph 2 of this article may at any time withdraw this reservation by notification to the Secretary-General of the United Nations.

Article 31

1. A State Party may denounce this Convention by written notification to the Secretary-General of the United Nations. Denunciation becomes effective one year after the date of receipt of the notification by the Secretary-General.

2. Such a denunciation shall not have the effect of releasing the State Party from its obligations under this Convention in regard to any act or omission which occurs prior to the date at which the denunciation becomes effective, nor shall denunciation prejudice in any way the continued consideration of any matter which is already under consideration by the Committee prior to the date at which the denunciation becomes effective.

3. Following the date at which the denunciation of a State Party becomes effective, the Committee shall not commence consideration of any new matter regarding that State.

Article 32

The Secretary-General of the United Nations shall inform all States Members of the United Nations and all States which have signed this Convention or acceded to it of the following:

    a. Signatures, ratifications and accessions under articles 25 and 26;

    b. The date of entry into force of this Convention under article 27 and the date of the entry into force of any amendments under article 29;

    c. Denunciations under article 31.

Article 33

1. This Convention, of which the Arabic, Chinese, English, French, Russian and Spanish texts are equally authentic, shall be deposited with the Secretary-General of the United Nations.

2. The Secretary-General of the United Nations shall transmit certified copies of this Convention to all States.

H. NATIONALITY, STATELESSNESS, ASYLUM AND REFUGEES

INTRODUCTION

This batch of documents deals with problems created by transnational movement of persons. Such movement may take place voluntarily, as when a woman marries a man of different nationality and citizenship and migrates to his country. It may happen involuntarily as a result of war, political upheaval or changes in national boundaries. The treaties and Declaration that follow constitute attempts to solve some of the difficult status questions that ensue.

There are useful discussions of this area in J. Stoessinger, *The Refugee and the World Community* (1956); L. Holborn, *Refugees: A Problem of Our Time. The Work of the United Nations High Commissioner for Refugees 1951–1972* (1975); A. Mutharika, *The Regulation of Statelessness Under International and National Law* (1976 with 1978 Supp.); J. Claydon, "Internationally Uprooted People and the Transnational Protection of Minority Culture," 24 *N.Y. Law Sch. L. Rev.*, 125 (1978).

See especially A. Grahl-Madsen, *The Status of Refugees in International Law* (1966).

1. CONVENTION ON THE NATIONALITY OF MARRIED WOMEN (1957) G.A. Res. 1040 (XI), 11 U.N. GAOR, Supp. (No. 17) at 18, U.N. Doc. A/3572 (1957). In force 11 August 1958 in accordance with Article 6.

THE CONTRACTING STATES,

Recognizing that, conflicts in law in practice with reference to nationality arise as a result of provisions concerning the loss or acquisition of nationality by women as a result of marriage, of its dissolution or of the change of nationality by the husband during marriage,

Recognizing that, in article 15 of the Universal Declaration of Human Rights, the General Assembly of the United Nations has proclaimed that "everyone has the right to a nationality" and that "no one shall be arbitrarily deprived of his nationality nor denied the right to change his nationality,"

Desiring to co-operate with the United Nations in promoting universal respect for, and observance of, human rights and fundamental freedoms for all without distinction as to sex,

Hereby agree as hereinafter provided:

Article 1

Each Contracting State agrees that neither the celebration nor the dissolution of a marriage between one of its nationals and an alien, nor the change of nationality by the husband during marriage, shall automatically affect the nationality of the wife.

Article 2

Each Contracting State agrees that neither the voluntary acquisition of the nationality of another State nor the renunciation of its nationality by one of its nationals shall prevent the retention of its nationality by the wife of such national.

Article 3

1. Each Contracting State agrees that the alien wife of one of its nationals may, at her request, acquire the nationality of her husband through specially privileged naturalization procedures; the grant of such nationality may be subject to such limitations as may be imposed in the interests of national security or public policy.

2. Each Contracting State agrees that the present Convention shall not be construed as affecting any legislation or judicial practice by which the alien wife of one of its nationals may, at her request, acquire her husband's nationality as a matter of right.

Article 4

1. The present Convention shall be open for signature and ratification on behalf of any State Member of the United Nations and also on behalf of any other State which is or hereafter becomes a member of any specialized agency of the United Nations, or which is or hereafter becomes a Party to the Statute of the International Court of Justice, or any other State to which an invitation has been addressed by the General Assembly of the United Nations.

2. The present Convention shall be ratified and the instruments of ratification shall be deposited with the Secretary-General of the United Nations.

Article 5

1. The present Convention shall be open for accession to all States referred to in paragraph 1 of article 4.

2. Accession shall be effected by the deposit of an instrument of accession with the Secretary-General of the United Nations.

Article 6

1. The present Convention shall come into force on the ninetieth day following the date of deposit of the sixth instrument of ratification or accession.

2. For each State ratifying or acceding to the Convention after the deposit of the sixth instrument of ratification or accession, the Convention shall enter into force on the ninetieth day after deposit by such State of its instrument of ratification or accession.

Article 7

1. The present Convention shall apply to all non-self-governing, trust, colonial and other non-metropolitan territories for the international relations of

which any Contracting State is responsible; the Contracting State concerned shall, subject to the provisions of paragraph 2 of the present article, at the time of signature, ratification or accession declare the non-metropolitan territory or territories to which the Convention shall apply *ipso facto* as a result of such signature, ratification or accession.

2. In any case in which, for the purpose of nationality, a non-metropolitan territory is not treated as one with the metropolitan territory, or in any case in which the previous consent of a non-metropolitan territory is required by the constitutional laws or pratices of the Contracting State or of the non-metropolitan territory for the application of the Convention to that territory, that Contracting State shall endeavour to secure the needed consent of the non-metropolitan territory within the period of twelve months from the date of signature of the Convention by that Contracting State, and when such consent has been obtained the Contracting State shall notify the Secretary-General of the United Nations. The present Convention shall apply to the territory or territories named in such notification from the date of its receipt by the Secretary-General.

3. After the expiry of the twelve-month period mentioned in paragraph 2 of the present article, the Contracting States concerned shall inform the Secretary-General of the results of the consultations with those non-metropolitan territories for whose international relations they are responsible and whose consent to the application of the present Convention may have been withheld.

Article 8

1. At the time of signature, ratification or accession, any State may make reservations to any article of the present Convention other than articles 1 and 2.

2. If any State makes a reservation in accordance with paragraph 1 of the present article, the Convention, with the exception of those provisions to which the reservations relates, shall have effect as between the reserving State and the other Parties. The Secretary-General of the United Nations shall communicate the text of the reservation to all States which are or may become Parties to the Convention. Any State Party to the Convention or which thereafter becomes a Party may notify the Secretary-General that it does not agree to consider itself bound by the Convention with respect to the State making the reservation. This notification must be made, in the case of a State already a Party, within ninety days from the date of the communication by the Secretary-General; and, in the case of a State subsequently becoming a Party, within ninety days from the date when the instrument of ratification or accession is deposited. In the event that such a notification is made, the Convention shall not be deemed to be in effect as between the State making the notification and the State making the reservation.

3. Any State making a reservation in accordance with paragraph 1 of the present article may at any time withdraw the reservation, in whole or in part, after it has been accepted, by a notification to this effect addressed to the Secretary-General of the United Nations. Such notification shall take effect on the date on which it is received.

Article 9

1. Any Contracting State may denounce the present Convention by written

notification to the Secretary-General of the United Nations. Denunciation shall take effect one year after the date of receipt of the notification by the Secretary-General.

2. The present Convention shall cease to be in force as from the date when the denunciation which reduces the number of Parties to less than six becomes effective.

* * *

[For omitted procedural provision, Article 10, see below, Chapter IV.A.16.]

Article 11

The Secretary-General of the United Nations shall notify all States Members of the United Nations and the non-member States contemplated in paragraph 1 of article 4 of the present Convention of the following:

a. Signatures and instruments of ratification received in accordance with article 4;

b. Instruments of accession received in accordance with article 5;

c. The date upon which the present Convention enters into force in accordance with article 6;

d. Communications and notifications received in accordance with article 8;

e. Notifications of denunciation received in accordance with paragraph 1 of article 9;

f. Abrogation in accordance with paragraph 2 of article 9.

Article 12

1. The present Convention, of which the Chinese, English, French, Russian and Spanish texts shall be equally authentic, shall be deposited in the archives of the United Nations.

2. The Secretary-General of the United Nations shall transmit a certified copy of the Convention to all States Members of the United Nations and to the non-member States contemplated in paragraph 1 of article 4.

2. CONVENTION ON THE REDUCTION OF STATE-LESSNESS (1954) G.A. Res. 896 (IX), 9 U.N. GAOR, Supp. (No. 21) at 49, U.N. Doc. A/2890 (1954). In force 13 December 1975 in accordance with Article 18.

THE CONTRACTING STATES,

Acting in pursuance of resolution 896 (IX), adopted by the General Assembly of the United Nations on 4 December 1954,

Considering it desirable to reduce statelessness by international agreement,

Have agreed as follows:

Article 1

1. A Contracting State shall grant its nationality to a person born in its territory who would otherwise be stateless. Such nationality shall be granted:
    a. At birth, by operation of law, or
    b. Upon an application being lodged with the appropriate authority, by or on behalf of the person concerned, in the manner prescribed by the national law. Subject to the provisions of paragraph 2 of this article, no such application may be rejected.
A Contracting State which provides for the grant of its nationality in accordance with sub-paragraph (*b*) of this paragraph may also provide for the grant of its nationality by operation of law at such age and subject to such conditions as may be prescribed by the national law.

2. A Contracting State may make the grant of its nationality in accordance with sub-paragraph (*b*) of paragraph 1 of this article subject to one or more of the following conditions:
    a. That the application is lodged during a period, fixed by the Contracting State, beginning not later than at the age of eighteen years and ending not earlier than at the age of twenty-one years, so, however, that the person concerned shall be allowed at least one year during which he may himself make the appication without having to obtain legal authorization to do so;
    b. That the person concerned has habitually resided in the territory of the Contracting State for such period as may be fixed by that State, not exceeding five years immediately preceding the lodging of the application nor ten years in all;
    c. That the person concerned has neither been convicted of an offence against national security nor has been sentenced to imprisonment for a term of five years or more on a criminal charge,
    d. That the person concerned has always been stateless.

3. Notwithstanding the provisions of paragraphs 1 (*b*) and 2 of this article, a child born in wedlock in the territory of a Contracting State, whose mother has the nationality of that State, shall acquire at birth that nationality if it otherwise would be stateless.

4. A Contracting State shall grant its nationality to a person who would otherwise be stateless and who is unable to acquire the nationality of the Contracting State in whose territory he was born because he has passed the age for lodging his application or has not fulfilled the required residence conditions, if the nationality of one of his parents at the time of the person's birth was that of the Contracting State first above mentioned. If his parents did not possess the same nationality at the time of his birth, the question whether the nationality of the person concerned should follow that of the father or that of the mother shall be determined by the national law of such Contracting State. If application for such nationality is required, the application shall be made to the appropriate authority by or on behalf of the applicant in the manner prescribed by the national law. Subject to the provisions of paragraph 5 of this article, such application shall not be refused.

5. The Contracting State may make the grant of its nationality in accordance with the provisions of paragraph 4 of this article subject to one or more of the following conditions:

a. That the application is lodged before the applicant reaches an age, being not less than twenty-three years, fixed by the Contracting State,

b. That the person concerned has habitually resided in the territory of the Contracting State for such period immediately preceding the lodging of the application, not exceeding three years, as may be fixed by that State;

c. That the person concerned has always been stateless.

Article 2

A foundling found in the territory of a Contracting State shall, in the absence of proof to the contrary, be considered to have been born within that territory of parents possessing the nationality of that State.

Article 3

For the purpose of determining the obligations of Contracting States under this Convention, birth on a ship or in an aircraft shall be deemed to have taken place in the territory of the State whose flag the ship flies or in the territory of the State in which the aircraft is registered, as the case may be.

Article 4

1. A Contracting State shall grant its nationality to a person, not born in the territory of a Contracting State, who would otherwise be stateless, if the nationality of one of his parents at the time of the person's birth was that of that State. If his parents did not possess the same nationality at the time of his birth, the question whether the nationality of the person concerned should follow that of the father or that of the mother shall be determined by the national law of such Contracting State. Nationality granted in accordance with the provisions of this paragraph shall be granted:

a. At birth, by operation of law, or

b. Upon an application being lodged with the appropriate authority, by or on behalf of the person concerned, in the manner prescribed by the national law. Subject to the provisions of paragraph 2 of this article, no such application may be rejected.

2. A Contracting State may make the grant of its nationality in accordance with the provisions of paragraph 1 of this article subject to one or more of the following conditions:

a. That the application is lodged beofre the applicant reaches an age, being not less than twenty-three years, fixed by the Contracting State;

b. That the person concerned has habitually resided in the territory of the Contracting State for such period immediately preceding the lodging of the application, not exceeding three years, as may be fixed by that State;

c. That the person concerned has not been convicted of an offence against national security;

d. That the person concerned has always been stateless.

Article 5

1. If the law of a Contracting State entails loss of nationality as a consequence of any change in the personal status of a person such as marriage,
termination of marriage, legitimation, recognition or adoption, such loss shall be
conditional upon possession or acquisition of another nationality.

2. If, under the law of a Contracting State, a child born out of wedlock loses
the nationality of that State in consequence of a recognition of affiliation, he shall
be given an opportunity to recover that nationality by written application to the
appropriate authority, and the conditions governing such application shall not
be more rigorous than those laid down in paragraph 2 of article 1 of this
Convention.

Article 6

If the law of a Contracting State provides for loss of its nationality by a
person's spouse or children as a consequence of that person losing or being
deprived of that nationality, such loss shall be conditional upon their possession
or acquisition of another nationality.

Article 7

1. a. If the law of a Contracting State entails loss or renunciation of
nationality, such renunciation shall not result in loss of nationality
unless the person concerned possesses or acquires another nationality.

b. The provisions of sub-paragraph (*a*) of this paragraph shall not
apply where their application would be inconsistent with the principles stated in articles 13 and 14 of the Universal Declaration of Human
Rights approved on 10 December 1948 by the General Assembly of the
United Nations.

2. A national of a Contracting State who seeks naturalization in a foreign
country shall not lose his nationality unless he acquires or has been accorded
assurance of acquiring the nationality of that foreign country.

3. Subject to the provisions of paragraphs 4 and 5 of this article, a national
of a Contracting State shall not lose his nationality, so as to become stateless, on
the ground of departure, residence abroad, failure to register or on any similar
ground.

4. A naturalized person may lose his nationality on account of residence
abroad for a period, not less than seven consecutive years, specified by the law
of the Contract State concerned if he fails to declare to the appropriate authority
his intention to retain his nationality.

5. In the case of a national of a Contracting State, born outside its territory,
the law of that State may make the retention of its nationality after the expiry of
one year from his attaining his majority conditional upon residence at that time
in the territory of the State or registration with the appropriate authority.

6. Except in the circumstances mentioned in this article, a person shall not
lose the nationality of a Contracting State, if such loss would render him
stateless, notwithstanding that such loss is not expressly prohibited by any other
provision of this Convention.

Article 8

1. A Contracting State shall not deprive a person of his nationality if such deprivation would render him stateless.

2. Notwithstanding the provisions of paragraph 1 of this article, a person may be deprived of the nationality of a Contracting State:

a. In the circumstances in which, under paragraphs 4 and 5 of article 7, it is permissible that a person should lose his nationality;

b. Where the nationality has been obtained by misrepresentation or fraud.

3. Notwithstanding the provisions of paragraph 1 of this article, a Contracting State may retain the right to deprive a person of his nationality, if at the time of signature, ratification or accession it specifies its retention of such right on one or more of the following grounds, being grounds existing in its national law at that time:

a. That, inconsistently with his duty of loyalty to the Contracting State, the person:

i. Has, in disregard of an express prohibition by the Contracting State rendered or continued to render services to, or received or continued to receive emoluments from, another State, or

ii. Has conducted himself in a manner seriously prejudicial to the vital interests of the State;

b. That the person has taken an oath, or made a formal declaration, of allegiance to another State, or given definite evidence of his determination to repudiate his allegiance to the Contracting State.

4. A Contracting State shall not exercise a power of deprivation permitted by paragraphs 2 or 3 of this article except in accordance with law, which shall provide for the person concerned the right to a fair hearing by a court or other independent body.

Article 9

A Contracting State may not deprive any person or group of persons of their nationality on racial, ethnic, religious or political grounds.

Article 10

1. Every treaty between Contracting States providing for the transfer of territory shall include provisions designed to secure that no person shall become stateless as a result of the transfer. A Contracting State shall use its best endeavours to secure that any such treaty made by it with a State which is not a party to this Convention includes such provisions.

2. In the absence of such provisions a Contracting State to which territory is transferred or which otherwise acquires territory shall confer its nationality on such persons as would otherwise become stateless as a result of the transfer or acquisition.

Article 11

The Contracting States shall promote the establishment within the framework of the United Nations, as soon as may be after the deposit of the sixth instrument of ratification or accession, of a body to which a person claiming the benefit of this Convention may apply for the examination of his claim and for assistance in presenting it to the appropriate authority.

Article 12

1. In relation to a Contracting State which does not, in accordance with the provisions of paragraph 1 of article 1 or of article 4 of this Convention, grant its nationality at birth by operation of law, the provisions of paragraph 1 of article 1 or of article 4, as the case may be, shall apply to persons born before as well as to persons born after the entry into force of this Convention.

2. The provisions of paragraph 4 of article 1 of this Convention shall apply to persons born before as well as to persons born after its entry into force.

3. The provisions of article 2 of this Convention shall apply only to foundlings found in the territory of a Contracting State after the entry into force of the Convention for that State.

Article 13

This Convention shall not be construed as affecting any provisions more conducive to the reduction of statelessness which may be contained in the law of any Contracting State now or hereafter in force, or may be contained in any other convention, treaty or agreement now or hereafter in force between two or more Contracting States.

* * *

[For omitted procedural provision, Article 14, see below, Chapter IV.A.16.]

Article 15

1. This Convention shall apply to all non-self-governing, trust, colonial and other non-metropolitan territories for the international relations of which any Contracting State is responsible; the Contracting State concerned shall, subject to the provisions of paragraph 2 of this article, at the time of signature, ratification or accession, declare the non-metropolitan territory or territories to which the Convention shall apply *ipso facto* as a result of such signature, ratification or accession.

2. In any case in which, for the purpose of nationality, a non-metropolitan territory is not treated as one with the metropolitan territory, or in any case in which the previous consent of a non-metropolitan territory is required by the constitutional laws or practices of the Contracting State or of the non-metropolitan territory for the application of the Convention to that territory, that Contracting State shall endeavour to secure the needed consent of the non-metropolitan territory within the period of twelve months from the date of signature of the Convention by that Contracting State, and when such consent has been obtained the Contracting State shall notify the Secretary-General of the

United Nations. This Convention shall apply to the territory or territories named in such notification from the date of its receipt by the Secretary-General.

3. After the expiry of the twelve-month period mentioned in paragraph 2 of this article, the Contracting States concerned shall inform the Secretary-General of the results of the consultations with those non-metropolitan territories for whose international relations they are responsible and whose consent to the application of this Convention may have been withheld.

Article 16

1. This Convention shall be open for signature at the headquarters of the United Nations from 30 August 1961 to 31 May 1962.

2. This Convention shall be open for signature on behalf of:

a. Any State Member of the United Nations:

b. Any other State invited to attend the United Nations Conference on the Elimination or Reduction of Future Statelessness;

c. Any State to which an invitation to sign or to accede may be addressed by the General Assembly of the United Nations.

3. This Convention shall be ratified and the instruments of ratification shall be deposited with the Secretary-General of the United Nations.

4. This Convention shall be open for accession by the States referred to in paragraph 2 of this article. Accesson shall be effected by the deposit of an instrument of accession with the Secretary-General of the United Nations.

Article 17

1. At the time of signature, ratification or accession any State may make a reservation in respect of articles 11, 14 or 15.

2. No other reservations to this Convention shall be admissible.

Article 18

1. This Convention shall enter into force two years after the date of the deposit of the sixth instrument of ratification or accession.

2. For each State ratifying or acceding to this Convention after the deposit of the sixth instrument of ratification or accession, it shall enter into force on the ninetieth day after the deposit by such State of its instrument of ratification or accession or on the date on which this Convention enters into force in accordance with the provisions of paragraph 1 of this article, whichever is the later.

Article 19

1. Any Contracting State may denounce this Convention at any time by a written notification addressed to the Secretary-General of the United Nations. Such denunciation shall take effect for the Contracting State concerned one year after the date of its receipt by the Secretary-General.

2. In cases where, in accordance with the provisions of article 15, this Convention has become applicable to a non-metropolitan territory of a Contracting State, that State may at any time thereafter, with the consent of the territory concerned, give notice to the Secretary-General of the United Nations denouncing this Convention separately in respect to that territory. The denunciation shall take effect one year after the date of the receipt of such notice by the

Secretary-General, who shall notify all other Contracting States of such notice and the date of receipt thereof.

Article 20

1. The Secretary-General of the United Nations shall notify all Members of the United Nations and the non-member States referred to in article 16 of the following particulars:
   a. Signtures, ratifications and accessions under article 16;
   b. Reservations under article 17;
   c. The date upon which this Convention enters into force in pursuance of article 18;
   d. Denunciations under article 19.
2. The Secretary-General of the United Nations shall, after the deposit of the sixth instrument of ratification or accession at the latest, bring to the attention of the General Assembly the question of the establishment, in accordance with article 11, of such a body as therein mentioned.

Article 21

This Convention shall be registered by the Secretary-General of the United Nations on the date of its entry into force.

IN WITNESS WHEREOF the undersigned Plenipotentiaries have signed this Convention.

DONE at New York, this thirtieth day of August, one thousand nine hundred and sixty-one, in a single copy, of which the Chinese, English, French, Russian and Spanish texts are equally authentic and which shall be deposited in the archives of the United Nations, and certified copies of which shall be delivered by the Secretary-General of the United Nations to all Members of the United Nations and to the non-member States referred to in article 16 of this Convention.

3. CONVENTION RELATING TO THE STATUS OF STATELESS PERSONS (1954) 28 September 1954, 360 U.N.T.S. 130. In force 6 June 1960 in accordance with Article 39.

PREAMBLE

THE HIGH CONTRACTING PARTIES,

Considering that the Charter of the United Nations and the Universal Declaration of Human Rights approved on 10 December 1948 by the General Assembly of the United Nations have affirmed the principle that human beings shall enjoy fundamental rights and freedoms without discrimination,

Considering that the United Nations has, on various occasions, manifested its profound concern for stateless persons and endeavoured to assure stateless persons the widest possible exercise of these fundamental rights and freedoms,

Considering that only those stateless persons who are also refugees are covered by the Convention relating to the Status of Refugees of 28 July 1951, and that there are many stateless persons who are not covered by that Convention,

Considering that it is desirable to regulate and improve the status of stateless persons by an international agreement,

Have agreed as follows:

CHAPTER I

GENERAL PROVISIONS

Article 1

Definition of the Term "Stateless Person"

1. For the purpose of this Convention, the term "stateless person" means a person who is not considered as a national by any State under the operation of its law.

2. This Convention shall not apply:

   i. To persons who are at present receiving from organs or agencies of the United Nations other than the United Nations High Commissioner for Refugees protection or assistance so long as they are receiving such protection or assistance;

   ii. To persons who are recognized by the competent authorities of the country in which they have taken residence as having the rights and obligations which are attached to the possessionof the nationality of that country;

   iii. To persons with respect to whom there are serious reasons for considering that:

   a. They have committed a crime against peace, a war crime, or a crime against humanity, as defined in the international intruments drawn up to make provisions in respect of such crimes.

   b. They have committed a serious non-political crime outside the country of their residence prior to their admission to that country;

   c. They have been guility of acts contrary to the purposes and principles of the United Nations.

Article 2

General Obligations

Every stateless person has duties to the country in which he finds himself, which require in particular that he conform to its laws and regulations as well as to measures taken for the maintenance of public order.

Article 3

Non-Discrimination

The Contracting States shall apply the provisions of this Convention to stateless persons without discrimination as to race, religion or country of origin.

Article 4

Religion

The Contracting States shall accord to stateless persons within their territories treatment at least as favourable as that accorded to their nationals with respect to freedom to practise their religion and freedom as regards the religious education of their children.

Article 5

Rights Granted Apart from this Convention

Nothing in this Convention shall be deemed to impair any rights and benefits granted by a Contracting State to stateless persons apart from this Convention.

Article 6

The Term "In the Same Circumstances"

For the purpose of this Convention, the term "in the same circumstances" implies that any requirements (including requirements as to length and conditions of sojourn or residence) which the particular individual would have to fulfil for the enjoyment of the right in question, if he were not a stateless person, must be fulfilled by him, with the exception of requirements which by their nature a stateless person is incapable of fulfilling.

Article 7

Exemption from Reciprocity

1. Except where this Convention contains more favourable provisions, a Contracting State shall accord to stateless persons the same treatment as is accorded to aliens generally.

2. After a period of three years' residence, all stateless persons shall enjoy exemption from legislative reciprocity in the territory of the Contracting States.

3. Each Contracting State shall continue to accord to stateless persons the rights and benefits to which they were already entitled, in the absence of reciprocity, at the date of entry into force of this Convention for that State.

4. The Contracting States shall consider favourably the possibility of according to stateless persons, in the absence of reciprocity, rights and benefits beyond those to which they are entitled according to paragraphs 2 and 3, and to extending exemption from reciprocity to stateless persons who do not fulfil the conditions provided for in paragraphs 2 and 3.

5. The provisions of paragraphs 2 and 3 apply both to the rights and benefits referred to in articles 13, 18, 19, 21 and 22 of this Convention and to rights and benefits for which this Convention does not provide.

Article 8

Exemption from Exceptional Measures

With regard to exceptional measures which may be taken against the person, property or interests of nationals or former nationals of a foreign State, the Contracting States shall not apply such measures to a stateless person solely on account of his having previously possessed the nationality of the foreign State in question. Contracting States which, under their legislation, are prevented from applying the general principle expressed in this article shall, in appropriate cases, grant exemptions in favour of such stateless persons.

Article 9

Provisional Measures

Nothing in this Convention shall prevent a Contracting State, in time of war or other grave and exceptional circumstances, from taking provisionally measures which it considers to be essential to the national security in the case of a particular person, pending a determination by the Contracting State that that person is in fact a stateless person and that the continuance of such measures is necessary in his case in the interests of national security.

Article 10

Continuity of Residence

1. Where a stateless person has been forcibly displaced during the Second World War and removed to the territory of a Contracting State, and is resident there, the period of such enforced sojourn shall be considered to have been lawful residence within that territory.

2. Where a stateless person has been forcibly displaced during the Second World War from the territory of a Contracting State and has, prior to the date of entry into force of this Convention, returned there for the purpose of taking up residence, the period of residence before and after such enforced displacement shall be regarded as one uninterrupted period for any purposes for which uninterrupted residence is required.

Article 11

Stateless Seamen

In the case of stateless persons regularly serving as crew members on board a ship flying the flag of a Contracting State, that State shall give sympathetic consideration to their establishment on its territory and the issue of travel documents to them or their temporary admission to its territory particularly with a view to facilitating their establishment in another country.

CHAPTER II

JURIDICAL STATUS

Article 12

Personal Status

1. The personal status of a stateless person shall be governed by the law of the country of his domicile or, if he has no domicile, by the law of the country of his residence.

2. Rights previously acquired by a stateless person and dependent on personal status, more particularly rights attaching to marriage, shall be respected by a Contracting State, subject to compliance, if this be necessary, with the formalities required by the law of that State, provided that the right in question is one which would have been recognized by the law of that State had he not become stateless.

Article 13

Movable and Immovable Property

The Contracting States shall accord to a stateless person treatment as favourable as possible and, in any event, not less favourable than that accorded to aliens generally in the same circumstances, as regards the acquisition of movable and immovable property and other rights pertaining thereto, and to leases and other contracts relating to movable and immovable property.

Article 14

Artistic Rights and Industrial Property

In respect of the protection of industrial property, such as inventions, designs or models, trade marks, trade names, and of rights in literary, artistic and scientific works, a stateless person shall be accorded in the country in which he has his habitual residence the same protection as is accorded to nationals of that country. In the territory of any other Contracting State, he shall be accorded the same protection as is accorded in that territory to nationals of the country in which he has his habitual residence.

Article 15

Right of Association

As regards non-political and non-profit-making associations and trade unions the Contracting States shall accord to stateless persons lawfully staying in their territory treatment as favourable as possible, and in any event, not less favourable than that accorded to aliens generally in the same circumstances.

Article 16

Access to Courts

1. A stateless person shall have free access to the courts of law on the territory of all Contracting States.

2. A stateless person shall enjoy in the Contracting State in which he has his habitual residence the same treatment as a national in matters pertaining to access to the courts, including legal assistance and exemption from *cautio judicatum solvi*.

3. A stateless person shall be accorded in the matters referred to in paragraph 2 in countries other than that in which he has his habitual residence the treatment granted to a national of the country of his habitual residence.

CHAPTER III

GAINFUL EMPLOYMENT

Article 17

Wage-Earning Employment

1. The Contracting States shall accord to stateless persons lawfully staying in their territory treatment as favourable as possible and, in any event, not less favourable that that accorded to aliens generally in the same circumstances, as regards the right to engage in wage-earning employment.

2. The Contracting States shall give sympathetic consideration to assimilating the rights of all stateless persons with regard to wage-earning employment to those of nationals, and in particular of those stateless persons who have entered their territory pursuant to programmes of labour recruitment or under immigration schemes.

Article 18

Self-Employment

The Contracting States shall accord to a stateless person lawfully in their territory treatment as favourable as possible and, in any event, not less favourable than that accorded to aliens generally in the same circumstances, as regards the right to engage on his own account in agriculture, industry, handicrafts and commerce and to establish commercial and industrial companies.

Article 19

Liberal Professions

Each Contracting State shall accord to stateless persons lawfully staying in their territory who hold diplomas recognized by the competent authorities of that State, and who are desirous of practising a liberal profession, treatment as favourable as possible and, in any event, not less favourable than that accorded to aliens generally in the same circumstances.

CHAPTER IV

WELFARE

Article 20

Rationing

Where a rationing system exists, which applies to the population at large and regulates the general distribution of products in short supply, stateless persons shall be accorded the same treatment as nationals.

Article 21

Housing

As regards housing, the Contracting States, in so far as the matter is regulated by laws or regulations or is subject to the control of public authorities, shall accord to stateless persons lawfully staying in their territory treatment as favourable as possible and, in any event, not less favourable than that accorded to aliens generally in the same circumstances.

Article 22

Public Education

1. The Contracting States shall accord to stateless persons the same treatment as is accorded to nationals with respect to elementary education.

2. The Contracting States shall accord to stateless persons treatment as favourable as possible and, in any event, not less favourable than that accorded to aliens generally in the same circumstances, with respect to education other than elementary education and, in particular, as regards access to studies, the recognition of foreign school certificates, diplomas and degrees, the remission of fees and charges and the award of scholarships.

Article 23

Public Relief

The Contracting States shall accord to stateless persons lawfully staying in their territory the same treatment with respect to public relief and assistance as is accorded to their nationals.

Article 24

Labour Legislation and Social Security

1. The Contracting States shall accord to stateless persons lawfully staying in their territory the same treatment as is accorded to nationals in respect of the following matters:

a. In so far as such matters are governed by laws or regulations or are subject to the control of administrative authorities: remuneration, including family allowances where these form part of remuneration, hours of work, overtime arrangements, holidays with pay, restrictions on home work, minimum age of employment, apprenticeship and training, women's work and the work of young persons, and the enjoyment of the benefits of collective bargaining;

b. Social security (legal provisions in respect of employment injury, occupational diseases, maternity, sickness, disability, old age, death, unemployment, family responsibilities and any other contingency which, according to national laws or regulations, is covered by a social security scheme), subject to the following limitations:

i. There may be appropriate arrangements for the maintenance of acquired rights and rights in course of acquisition;

ii. National laws or regulations of the country of residence may prescribe special arrangements concnerning benefits or portions of benefits which are payable wholly out of public funds, and concerning allowances paid to persons who do not fulfil the contribution conditions prescribed for the award of a normal pension.

2. The right to compensation for the death of a stateless person resulting from employment injury or from occupational disease shall not be affected by the fact that the residence of the beneficiary is outside the territory of the Contracting State.

3. The Contracting States shall extend to stateless persons the benefits of agreements concluded between them, or which may be concluded between them in the future, concerning the maintenance of acquired rights and rights in the process of acquisition in regard to social security, subject only to the conditions which apply to nationals of the States signatory to the agreements in question.

4. The Contracting States will give sympathetic consideration to extending to stateless persons so far as possible the benefits of similar agreements which may at any time be in force between such Contracting States and non-contracting States.

CHAPTER V

ADMINISTRATIVE MEASURES

Article 25

Administrative Assistance

1. When the exercise of a right by a stateless person would normally require the assistance of authorities of a foreign country to whom he cannot have recourse, the Contracting State in whose territory he is residing shall arrange that such assistance be afforded to him by their own authorities.

2. The authority or authorities mentioned in paragraph 1 shall deliver or cause to be delivered under their supervision to stateless persons such documents or certifications as would normally be delivered to aliens by or through their national authorities.

3. Documents or certifications so delivered shall stand in the stead of the official instruments delivered to aliens by or through their national authorities and shall be given credence in the absence of proof to the contrary.

4. Subject to such exceptional treatment as may be granted to indigent persons, fees may be charged for the services mentioned herein, but such fees shall be moderate and commensurate with those charged to nationals for similar services.

5. The provisions of this article shall be without prejudice to articles 27 and 28.

Article 26

Freedom of Movement

Each Contracting State shall accord to stateless persons lawfully in its territory the right to choose their place of residence and to move freely within its territory, subject to any regulations applicable to aliens generally in the same circumstances.

Article 27

Identity Papers

The Contracting States shall issue identity papers to any stateless person in their territory who does not possess a valid travel document.

Article 28

Travel Documents

The Contracting States shall issue to stateless persons lawfully staying in their territory travel documents for the purpose of travel outside their territory, unless compelling reasons of national security or public order otherwise require, and the provisions of the Schedule to this Convention shall apply with respect to such documents. The Contracting States may issue such a travel document to any other stateless person in their territory; they shall in particular give sympathetic consideration to the issue of such a travel document to stateless persons in their territory who are unable to obtain a travel document from the country of their lawful residence.

Article 29

Fiscal Charges

1. The Contracting States shall not impose upon stateless persons duties, charges or taxes, of any description whatsoever, other or higher than those which are or may be levied on their nationals in similar situations.

2. Nothing in the above paragraph shall prevent the application to stateless persons of the laws and regulations concerning charges in respect of the issue to aliens of administrative documents including identity papers.

Article 30

Transfer of Assets

1. A Contracting State shall, in conformity with its laws and regulations, permit stateless persons to transfer assets which they have brought into its territory, to another country where they have been admitted for the purposes of resettlement.

2. A Contracting State shall give sympathetic consideration to the application of stateless persons for permission to transfer assets wherever they may be and which are necessary for their resettlement in another country to which they have been admitted.

Article 31

Expulsion

1. The Contracting States shall not expel a stateless person lawfully in their territory save on grounds of national security or public order.

2. The expulsion of such a stateless person shall be only in pursuance of a decision reached in accordance with due process of law. Except where compelling reasons of national security otherwise require, the stateless person shall be allowed to submit evidence to clear himself, and to appeal to and be represented for the purpose before competent authority or a person or persons specially designated by the competent authority.

3. The Contracting States shall allow such a stateless person a reasonable period within which to seek legal admission into another country. The Contracting States reserve the right to apply during that period such internal measures as they may deem necessary.

Article 32

Naturalization

The Contracting States shall as far as possible facilitate the assimilation and naturalization of stateless persons. They shall in particular make every effort to expedite naturalization prceedings and to reduce as far as possible the charges and costs of such proceedings.

CHAPTER VI

FINAL CLAUSES

Article 33

Information on National Legislation

The Contracting States shall communicate to the Secretary-General of the United Nations the laws and regulations which they may adopt to ensure the application of this Convention.

* * *

[For omitted procedural provision, Article 34, see below, Chapter IV.A.16.]

Article 35

Signature, Ratification and Accession

1. This Convention shall be open for signature at the Headquarters of the United Nations until 31 December 1955.

2. It shall be open for signature on behalf of:

a. Any State Member of the United Nations;

b. Any other State invited to attend the United Nations Conference on the Status of Stateless Persons; and

c. Any State to which an invitation to sign or to accede may be addressed by the General Assembly of the United Nations.

3. It shall be ratified and the instruments of ratification shall be deposited with the Secretary-General of the United Nations.

4. It shall be open for accession by the States referred to in paragraph 2 of this article. Accession shall be effected by the deposit of an instrument of accession with the Secretary-General of the United Nations.

Article 36

Territorial Application Clause

1. Any State may, at the time of signature, ratification or accession, declare that this Convention shall extend to all or any of the territories for the international relations of which it is responsible. Such a declaration shall take effect when the Convention enters into force for the State concerned.

2. At any time thereafter any such extension shall be made by notification addressed to the Secretary-General of the United Nations and shall take effect as from the ninetieth day after the day of receipt by the Secretary-General of the United Nations of this notification, or as from the date of entry into force of the Convention for the State concerned, whichever is the later.

3. With respect to those territories to which this Convention is not extended at the time of signature, ratification or accession, each State concerned shall consider the possibility of taking the necessary steps in order to extend the application of this Convention to such territories, subject, where necessary for constitutional reasons, to the consent of the Governments of such territories.

Article 37

Federal Clause

In the case of a Federal or non-unitary State, the following provisions shall apply:

    a. With respect to those articles of this Convention that come within the legislative jurisdiction of the federal legislative authority, the obligations of the Federal Government shall to this extent be the same as those of Parties which are not Federal States;

    b. With respect to those articles of this Convention that come within the legislative jurisdiction of constituent states, provinces or cantons which are not, under the constitutional system of the Federation, bound to take legislative action, the Federal Government shall bring such articles with a favourable recommendation to the notice of the appropriate authorities of states, provinces or cantons at the earliest possible moment.

    c. A Federal State Party to this Convention shall, at the request of any other Contracting State transmitted through the Secretary-General of the United Nations, supply a statement of the law and practice of the Federation and its constituent units in regard to any particular provision of the Convention showing the extent to which effect has been given to that provision by legislative or other action.

Article 38

Reservations

1. At the time of signature, ratification or accession, any State may make reservations to articles of the Convention other than to articles 1, 3, 4, 16 (1) and 33 to 42 inclusive.

2. Any State making a reservation in accordance with paragraph 1 of this

article may at any time withdraw the reservation by a communication to that effect addressed to the Secretary-General of the United Nations.

Article 39

Entry into Force

1. This Convention shall come into force on the ninetieth day following the day of deposit of the sixth instrument of ratification or accession.

2. For each State ratifying or acceding to the Convention after the deposit of the sixth instrument of ratification or accession, the Convention shall enter into force on the ninetieth day following the date of deposit by such State of its instrument of ratification or accession.

Article 40

Denunciation

1. Any Contracting State may denounce this Convention at any time by a notification addressed to the Secretary-General of the United Nations.

2. Such denunciation shall take effect for the Contracting State concerned one year from the date upon which it is received by the Secretary-General of the United Nations.

3. Any State which has made a declaration or notification under article 36 may, at any time thereafter, by a notification to the Secretary-General of the United Nations, declare that the Convention shall cease to extend to such territory one year after the date of receipt of the notification by the Secretary-General.

Article 41

Revision

1. Any Contracting State may request revision of this Convention at any time by a notification addressed to the Secretary-General of the United Nations.

2. The General Assembly of the United Nations shall recommend the steps, if any, to be taken in respect of such request.

Article 42

Notifications by the Secretary-General of the United Nations

The Secretary-General of the United Nations shall inform all Members of the United Nations and non-member States referred to in article 35:

a. Of signatures, ratifications and accessions in accordance with article 35;

b. Of declarations and notifications in accordance with article 36;

c. Of reservations and withdrawals in accordance with article 38;

d. Of the date on which this Convention will come into force in accordance with article 39;

e. Of denunciations and notifications in accordance with article 40;

f. Of requests for revision in accordance with article 41.

IN FAITH WHEREOF the undersigned, duly authorized, have signed this Convention on behalf of their respective Governments.

DONE at New York, this twenty-eighth day of September, one thousand nine hundred and fifty-four, in a single copy, of which the English, French and Spanish texts are equally authentic and which shall remain deposited in the archives of the United Nations, and certified true copies of which shall be delivered to all Members of the United Nations and to the non-member States referred to in article 35.

4. CONVENTION RELATING TO THE STATUS OF REFUGEES (1951)

Adopted on 28 July 1951, 189 U.N.T.S.150. In force 22 April 1954 in accordance with Article 43.

PREAMBLE

The High Contracting Parties,

Considering that the Charter of the United Nations and the Universal Declaration of Human Rights approved on 10 December 1948 by the General Assembly have affirmed the principle that human beings shall enjoy fundamental rights and freedoms without discrimination,

Considering that the United Nations has, on various occasions, manifested its profound concern for refugees and endeavoured to assure refugees the widest possible exercise of these fundamental rights and freedoms,

Considering that it is desirable to revise and consolidate previous international agreements relating to the status of refugees and to extend the scope of and the protection accorded by such instruments by means of a new agreement,

Considering that the grant of asylum may place unduly heavy burdens on certain countries, and that a satisfactory solution of a problem of which the United Nations has recognized the international scope and nature cannot therefore be achieved without international co-operation,

Expressing the wish that all States, recognizing the social and humanitarian nature of the problem of refugees, will do everything within their power to prevent this problem from becoming a cause of tension between States,

Noting that the United Nations High Commissioner for Refugees is charged with the task of supervising international conventions providing for the protection of refugees, and recognizing that the effective co-ordination of measures taken to deal with this problem will depend upon the co-operation of States with the High Commissioner,

Have agreed as follows:

CHAPTER I

GENERAL PROVISIONS

Article 1

Definition of the Term "Refugee"

A. For the purposes of the present Convention, the term "refugee" shall apply to any person who:

(1) Has been considered a refugee under the Arrangements of 12 May 1926 and 30 June 1928 or under the Conventions of 28 October 1933 and 10 February 1938, the Protocol of 14 September 1939 or the Constitution of the International Refugee Organization;

Decisions of non-eligibility taken by the International Refugee Organization during the period of its activities shall not prevent the status of refugee being accorded to persons who fulfil the conditions of paragraph 2 of this section;

(2) As a result of events occurring before 1 January 1951 and owing to well-founded fear of being persecuted for reasons of race, religion, nationality, membership of a particular social group or political opinion, is outside the country of his nationality and is unable, or owing to such fear, is unwilling to avail himself of the protection of that country; or who, not having a nationality and being outside the country of his former habitual residence as a result of such events, is unable or, owing to such fear, is unwilling to return to it.

In the case of a person who has more than one nationality, the term "the country of his nationality" shall mean each of the countries of which he is a national, and a person shall not be deemed to be lacking the protection of the country of his nationality if, without any valid reason based on well-founded fear, he has not availed himself of the protection of one of the countries of which he is a national.

B. (1) For the purposes of this Convention, the words "events occurring before 1 January 1951" in article 1, Section A, shall be understood to mean either

a. "events occurring in Europe before 1 January 1951"; or

b. "events occurring in Europe or elsewhere before 1 January 1951"; and each Contracting State shall make a declaration at the time of signature, ratification or accession, specifying which of these meanings it applies for the purpose of its obligations under this Convention.

(2) Any Contracting State which has adopted alternative

a. may at any time extend its obligations by adopting alternative

b. by means of a notification addressed to the Secretary-General of the United Nations.

C. This Convention shall cease to apply to any person falling under the terms of section A if:

1. He has voluntarily re-availed himself of the protection of the country of his nationality; or

2. Having lost his nationality, he has voluntarily reacquired it; or

3. He has acquired a new nationality, and enjoys the protection of the country of his new nationality; or

4. He has voluntarily re-established himself in the country which he left or outside which he remained owing to fear of persecution; or

5. He can no longer, because the circumstances in connexion with which he has been recognized as a refugee have ceased to exist, continue to refuse to avail himself of the protection of the country of his nationality;

Provided that this paragraph shall not apply to a refugee falling under section A (1) of this article who is able to invoke compelling reasons arising out of previous persecution for refusing to avail himself of the protection of the country of nationality;

6. Being a person who has no nationality he is, because the circumstances in connexion with which he has been recognized as a refugee have ceased to exist, able to return to the country of his former habitual residence;

Provided that this paragraph shall not apply to a refugee falling under section A (1) of this article who is able to invoke compelling reasons arising out of previous persecution for refusing to return to the country of his former habitual residence.

D. This Convention shall not apply to persons who are at present receiving from organs or agencies of the United Nations other than the United Nations High Commissioner for Refugees protection or assistance.

When such protection or assistance has ceased for any reason, without the position of such persons being definitively settled in accordance with the relevant resolutions adopted by the General Assembly of the United Nations, these persons shall *ipso facto* be entitled to the benefits of this Convention.

E. This Convention shall not apply to a person who is recognized by the competent authorities of the country in which he has taken residence as having the rights and obligations which are attached to the possession of the nationality of that country.

F. The provisions of this Convention shall not apply to any person with respect to whom there are serious reasons for considering that:

a. He has committed a crime against peace, a war crime, or crime against humanity, as defined in the international instruments drawn up to make provision in respect of such crimes;

b. He has committed a serious non-political crime outside the country of refuge prior to his admission to that country as a refugee;

c. He has been guilty of acts contrary to the purposes and principles of the United Nations.

Article 2

General Obligations

Every refugee has duties to the country in which he finds himself, which require in particular that he conform to its laws and regulations as well as to measures taken for the maintenance of public order.

Article 3

Non-Discrimination

The Contracting States shall apply the provisions of this Convention to refugees without discrimination as to race, religion or country of origin.

Article 4

Religion

The Contracting States shall accord to refugees within their territories treatment at least as favourable as that accorded to their nationals with respect to freedom to practice their religion and freedom as regards the religious education of their children.

Article 5

Rights Granted Apart from this Convention

Nothing in this Convention shall be deemed to impair any rights and benefits granted by a Contracting State to refugees apart from this Convention.

Article 6

The Term "In the Same Circumstances"

For the purpose of this Convention, the term "in the same circumstances" implies that any requirements (including requirements as to length and conditions of sojourn or residence) which the particular individual would have to fulfil for the enjoyment of the right in question, if he were not a refugee, must be fulfilled by him, with the exception of requirements which by their nature a refugee is incapable of fulfilling.

Article 7

Exemption from Reciprocity

1. Except where this Convention contains more favourable provisions, a Contracting State shall accord to refugees the same treatment as is accorded to aliens generally.

2. After a period of three years' residence, all refugees shall enjoy exemption from legislative reciprocity in the territory of the Contracting States.

3. Each Contracting State shall continue to accord to refugees the rights and benefits to which they were already entitled, in the absence of reciprocity, at the date of entry into force of this Convention for that State.

4. The Contracting States shall consider favourably the possibility of according to refugees, in the absence of reciprocity, rights and benefits beyond those to which they are entitled according to paragaphs 2 and 3, and to extending exemption from reciprocity to refugees who do not fulfil the conditions provided for in paragraphs 2 and 3.

5. The provisions of paragraphs 2 and 3 apply both to the rights and benefits referred to in articles 13, 18, 19, 21 and 22 of this Convention and to rights and benefits for which this Convention does not provide.

Article 8

Exemption from Exceptional Measures

With regard to exceptional measures which may be taken against the person, property or interests of nationals of a foreign State, the Contracting States shall not apply such measures to a refugee who is formally a national of the said State solely on account of such nationality. Contracting States which, under their legislation, are prevented from applying the general principle expressed in this article, shall, in appropriate cases, grant exemptions in favour of such refugees.

Article 9

Provisional Measures

Nothing in this Convention shall prevent a Contracting State, in time of war or other grave and exceptional circumstance, from taking provisionally measures which it considers to be essential to the national security in the case of a particular person, pending a determination by the Contracting State that that person is in fact a refugee and that the continuance of such measures is necessary in his case in the interests of national security.

Article 10

Continuity of Residence

1. Where a refugee has been forcibly displaced during the Second World War and removed to the territory of a Contracting State, and is resident there, the period of such enforced sojourn shall be considered to have been lawful residence within that territory.

2. Where a refugee has been forcibly displaced during the Second World War from the territory of a Contracting State and has, prior to the date of entry into force of this Convention, returned there for the purpose of taking up residence, the period of residence before and after such enforced displacement shall be regarded as one uninterrupted period for any purposes for which uninterrupted residence is required.

Article 11

Refugee Seamen

In the case of refugees regularly serving as crew members on board a ship flying the flag of a Contracting State, that State shall give sympathetic consideration to their estabishment on its territory and the issue of travel documents to them or their temporary admission to its territory particularly with a view to facilitating their establishment in another country.

CHAPTER II

JURIDICAL STATUS

Article 12

Personal Status

1. The personal status of a refugee shall be governed by the law of the country of his domicile or, if he has no domicile, by the law of the country of his residence.

2. Rights previously acquired by a refugee and dependent on personal status, more particularly rights attaching to marriage, shall be respected by a Contracting State, subject to compliance, if this be necessary, with the formal-

ities required by the law of that State, provided that the right in question is one which would have been recognized by the law of that State had he not become a refugee.

Article 13

Movable and Immovable Property

The Contracting States shall accord to a refugee treatment as favourable as possible and, in any event, not less favourable than that accorded to aliens generally in the same circumstances, as regards the acquisition of movable and immovable property and other rights pertaining thereto, and to leases and other contracts relating to movable and immovable property.

Article 14

Artistic Rights and Industrial Property

In respect of the protection of industrial property, such as inventions, designs or models, trade marks, trade names, and of rights in literary, artistic and scientific works, a refugee shall be accorded in the country in which he has his habitual residence the same protection as is accorded to nationals of that country. In the territory of any other Contracting State, he shall be accorded the same protection as is accorded in that territory to nationals of the country in which he has his habitual residence.

Article 15

Right of Association

As regards non-political and non-profit-making associations and trade unions the Contracting States shall accord to refugees lawfully staying in their territory the most favourable treatment accorded to nationals of a foreign country, in the same circumstances.

Article 16

Access to Courts

1. A refugee shall have free access to the courts of law on the territory of all Contracting States.

2. A refugee shall enjoy in the Contracting State in which he has his habitual residence the same treatment as a national in matters pertaining to access to the courts, including legal assistance and exemption from *cautio judicatum solvi*.

3. A refugee shall be accorded in the matters referred to in paragraph 2 in countries other than that in which he has his habitual residence the treatment granted to a national of the country of his habitual residence.

CHAPTER III

GAINFUL EMPLOYMENT

Article 17

Wage-Earning Employment

1. The Contracting States shall accord to refugees lawfully staying in their

territory the most favourable treatment accorded to nationals of a foreign country in the same circumstances, as regards the right to engage in wage-earning employment.

2. In any case, restrictive measures imposed on aliens or the employment of aliens for the protection of the national labour market shall not be applied to a refugee who was already exempt from them at the date of entry into force of this Convention for the Contracting State concerned, or who fulfils one of the following conditions:

　　a. He has completed three years' residence in the country;

　　b. He has a spouse possessing the nationality of the country of residence. A refugee may not invoke the benefit of this provision if he has abandoned his spouse;

　　c. He has one or more children possessing the nationality of the country of residence.

3. The Contracting States shall give sympathetic consideration to assimilating the rights of all refugees with regard to wage-earning employment to those of nationals, and in particular of those refugees who have entered their territory pursuant to programmes of labour recruitment or under immigration schemes.

Article 18

Self-Employment

　　The Contracting States shall accord to a refugee lawfully in their territory treatment as favourable as possible and, in any event, not less favourable than that accorded to aliens generally in the same circumstances, as regards the right to engage on his own account in agriculture, industry, handicrafts and commerce and to establish commercial and industrial companies.

Article 19

Liberal Professions

　　1. Each Contracting State shall accord to refugees lawfully staying in their territory who hold diplomas recognized by the competent authorities of that State, and who are desirous of practising a liberal profession, treatment as favourable as possible and, in any event, not less favourable than that accorded to aliens generally in the same circumstances.

　　2. The Contracting States shall use their best endeavours consistently with their laws and constitutions to secure the settlement of such refugees in the territories, other than the metropolitan territory, for whose international relations they are responsible.

CHAPTER IV

WELFARE

Article 20

Rationing

　　Where a rationing system exists, which applies to the population at large and regulates the general distribution of products in short supply, refugees shall be accorded the same treatment as nationals.

Article 21

Housing

As regards housing, the Contracting States, in so far as the matter is regulated by laws or regulations or is subject to the control of public authorities, shall accord to refugees lawfully staying in their territory treatment as favourable as possible and, in any event, not less favourable than that accorded to aliens generally in the same circumstances.

Article 22

Public Education

1. The Contracting States shall accord to refugees the same treatment as is accorded to nationals with respect to elementary education.

2. The Contracting States shall accord to refugees treatment as favourable as possible, and, in any event, not less favourable than that accorded to aliens generally in the same circumstances, with respect to education other than elementary education and, in particular, as regards access to studies, the recognition of foreign school certificates, diplomas and degrees, the remission of fees and charges and the award of scholarships.

Article 23

Public Relief

The Contracting States shall accord to refugees lawfully staying in their territory the same treatment with respect to public relief and assistance as is accorded to their nationals.

Article 24

Labour Legislation and Social Security

1. The Contracting States shall accord to refugees lawfully staying in their territory the same treatment as is accorded to nationals in respect of the following matters:

a. In so far as such matters are governed by laws or regulations or are subject to the control of administrative authorities: remuneration, including family allowances where these form part of remuneration, hours of work, overtime arrangements, holidays with pay, restrictions on home work, minimum age of employment, apprenticeship and training, women's work and the work of young persons, and the enjoyment of the benefits of collective bargaining;

b. Social security (legal provisions in respect of employment injury, occupational diseases, maternity, sickness, disability, old age, death, unemployment, family responsibilities and any other contingency which, according to national laws or regulations, is covered by a social security scheme), subject to the following limitations:

     i. There may be appropriate arrangements for the maintenance of acquired rights and rights in course of acquisition;

    ii. National laws or regulations of the country of residence may prescribe special arrangements concerning benefits or portions of benefits which are payable wholly out of public funds, and concerning allowances paid to persons who do not fulfil the contribution conditions prescribed for the award of a normal pension.

2. The right to compensation for the death of a refugee resulting from employment injury or from occupational disease shall not be affected by the fact that the residence of the beneficiary is outside the territory of the Contracting State.

3. The Contracting States shall extend to refugees the benefits of agreements concluded between them, or which may be concluded between them in the future, concerning the maintenance of acquired rights and rights in the process of acquisition in regard to social security, subject only to the conditions which apply to nationals of the States signatory to the agreements in question.

4. The Contracting States will give sympathetic consideration to extending to refugees so far as possible the benefits of similar agreements which may at any time be in force between such Contracting States and non-contracting States.

CHAPTER V

ADMINISTRATIVE MEASURES

Article 25

Administrative Assistance

1. When the exercise of a right by a refugee would normally require the assistance of authorities of a foreign country to whom he cannot have recourse, the Contracting States in whose territory he is residing shall arrange that such assistance be afforded to him by their own authorities or by an international authority.

2. The authority or authorities mentioned in paragraph 1 shall deliver or cause to be delivered under their supervision to refugees such documents or certifications as would normally be delivered to aliens by or through their national authorities.

3. Documents or certifications so delivered shall stand in the stead of the official instruments delivered to aliens by or through their national authorities, and shall be given credence in the absence of proof to the contrary.

4. Subject to such exceptional treatment as may be granted to indigent persons, fees may be charged for the services mentioned herein, but such fees shall be moderate and commensurate with those charged to nationals for similar services.

5. The provisions of this article shall be without prejudice to articles 27 and 28.

Article 26

Freedom of Movement

Each Contracting State shall accord to refugees lawfully in its territory the right to choose their place of residence and to move freely within its territory subject to any regulations applicable to aliens generally in the same circumstances.

Article 27

Identity Papers

The Contracting States shall issue identity papers to any refugee in their territory who does not possess a valid travel document.

Article 28

Travel Documents

1. The Contracting States shall issue to refugees lawfully staying in their territory travel documents for the purpose of travel outside their territory, unless compelling reasons of national security or public order otherwise require, and the provisions of the Schedule to this Convention shall apply with respect to such documents. The Contracting States may issue such a travel document to any other refugee in their territory; they shall in particular give sympathetic consideration to the issue of such a travel document to refugees in their territory who are unable to obtain a travel document from the country of their lawful residence.

2. Travel documents issued to refugees under previous international agreements by parties thereto shall be recognized and treated by the Contracting States in the same way as if they had been issued pursuant to this article.

Article 29

Fiscal Charges

1. The Contracting States shall not impose upon refugees duties, charges or taxes, of any description whatsoever, other or higher than those which are or may be levied on their nationals in similar situations.

2. Nothing in the above paragraph shall prevent the application to refugees of the laws and regulations concerning charges in respect of the issue to aliens of administrative documents including identity papers.

Article 30

Transfer of Assets

1. A Contracting State shall, in conformity with its laws and regulations, permit refugees to transfer assets which they have brought into its territory, to another country where they have been admitted for the purposes of resettlement.

2. A Contracting State shall give sympathetic consideration to the application of refugees for permission to transfer assets wherever they may be and which are necessary for their settlement in another country to which they have been admitted.

Article 31

Refugees Unlawfully in the Country of Refuge

1. The Contracting States shall not impose penalties, on account of their illegal entry or presence, on refugees who, coming directly from a territorywhere their life or freedom was threatened in the sense of article 1, enter or are present in their territory without authorization, provided they present themselves without delay to the authorities and show good cause for their illegal entry or presence.

2. The Contracting States shall not apply to the movements of such refugees restrictions other than those which are necessary and such restrictions shall only be applied until their status in the country is regularized or they obtain admission into another country. The Contracting States shall allow such refugees a reasonable period and all the necessary facilities to obtain admission into another country.

Article 32

Expulsion

1. The Contracting States shall not expel a refugee lawfully in their territory save on grounds of national security or public order.

2. The expulsion of such a refugee shall be only in pursuance of a decision reached in accordance with due process of law. Except where compelling reasons of national security otherwise require, the refugee shall be allowed to submit evidence to clear himself, and to appeal to and be represented for the purpose before competent authority or a person or persons specially designated by the competent authority.

3. The Contracting States shall allow such a refugee a reasonable period within which to seek legal admission into another country. The Contracting States reserve the right to apply during that period such internal measures as they may deem necessary.

Article 33

Prohibition of Expulsion or Return ("Refoulement")

1. No Contracting State shall expel or return ("refouler") a refugee in any manner whatsoever to the frontiers of territories where his life or freedom would be threatened on account of his race, religion, nationality, membership of a particular social group or political opinion.

2. The benefit of the present provision may not, however, be claimed by a refugee whom there are reasonable grounds for regarding as a danger to the security of the country in which he is, or who, having been convicted by a final judgment of a particularly serious crime, constitutes a danger to the community of that country.

Article 34

Naturalization

The Contracting States shall as far as possible facilitate the assimilation and naturalization of refugees. They shall in particular make every effort to expedite naturalization proceedings and to reduce as far as possible the charges and costs of such proceedings.

CHAPTER VI

EXECUTORY AND TRANSITORY PROVISIONS

Article 35

Co-operation of the National Authorities with the United Nations

1. The Contracting States undertake to co-operate with the Office of the United Nations High Commissioner for Refugees, or any other agency of the United Nations which may succeed it, in the exercise of its functions, and shall in particular facilitate its duty of supervising the application of the provisions of this Convention.

2. In order to enable the Office of the High Commissioner or any other agency of the United Nations which may succeed it, to make reports to the competent organs of the United Nations, the Contracting States undertake to provide them in the appropriate form with information and statistical data requested concerning:

a. The condition of refugees,

b. The implementation of this Convention, and

c. Laws, regulations and decrees which are, or may hereafter be, in force relating to refugees.

Article 36

Information on National Legislation

The Contracting States shall communicate to the Secretary-General of the United Nations the laws and regulations which they may adopt to ensure the application of this Convention.

Article 37

Relation to Previous Conventions

Without prejudice to article 28, paragraph 2, of this Convention, this Convention replaces, as between parties to it, the Arrangements of 5 July 1922, 31 May 1924, 12 May 1926, 30 June 1928 and 30 July 1935, the Conventions of 28 October 1933 and 10 February 1938, the Protocol of 14 September 1939 and the Agreement of 15 October 1946.

CHAPTER VII

FINAL CLAUSES

* * *

[For omitted procedural provision, Article 38, see below, Chapter IV.A.16.]

Article 39

Signature, Ratification and Accession

1. This Convention shall be opened for signature at Geneva on 28 July 1951 and shall thereafter be deposited with the Secretary-General of the United Nations. It shall be open for signature at the European Office of the United Nations from 28 July to 31 August 1951 and shall be re-opened for signature at the Headquarters of the United Nations from 17 September 1951 to 31 December 1952.

2. This Convention shall be open for signature on behalf of all States Members of the United Nations, and also on behalf of any other State invited to attend the Conference of Plenipotentiaries on the Status of Refugees and Stateless Persons or to which an invitation to sign will have been addressed by the General Assembly. It shall be ratified and the instruments of ratification shall be deposited with the Secretary-General of the United Nations.

3. This Convention shall be open from 28 July 1951 for accession by the States referred to in paragraph 2 of this article. Accession shall be effected by the deposit of an instrument of accession with the Secretary-General of the United Nations.

Article 40

Territorial Application Clause

1. Any State may, at the time of signature, ratification or accession, declare that this Convention shall extend to all or any of the territories for the international relations of which it is responsible. Such a declaration shall take effect when the Convention enters into force for the State concerned.

2. At any time thereafter any such extension shall be made by notification addressed to the Secretary-General of the United Nations and shall take effect as from the ninetieth day after the day of receipt by the Secretary-General of the United Nations of this notification, or as from the date of entry into force of the Convention for the State concerned, whichever is the later.

3. With respect to those territories to which this Convention is not extended at the time of signature, ratification or accession, each State concerned shall consider the possibility of taking the necessary steps in order to extend the application of this Convention to such territories, subject, where necessary for constitutional reasons, to the consent of the Governments of such territories.

Article 41

Federal Clause

In the case of a Federal or non-unitary State, the following provisions shall apply:

    a. With respect to those articles of this Convention that come within the legislative jurisdiction of the federal legislative authority, the obligations of the Federal Government shall to this extent be the same as those of Parties which are not Federal States;

    b. With respect to those articles of this Convention that come within the legislative jurisdiction of constituent states, provinces or cantons which are not, under the constitutional system of the Federation, bound to take legislative action, the Federal Government shall bring such articles with a favourable recommendation to the notice of the appropriate authorities of states, provinces or cantons at the earliest possible moment;

c. A Federal State Party to this Convention shall, at the request of any other Contracting State transmitted through the Secretary-General of the United Nations, supply a statement of the law and practice of the Federation and its constituent units in regard to any particular provision of the Convention showing the extent to which effect has been given to that provision by legislative or other action.

Article 42

Reservations

1. At the time of signature, ratification or accession, any State may make reservations to articles of the Convention other than to articles 1, 3, 4, 16 (1), 33, 36–46 inclusive.

2. Any State making a reservation in accordance with paragraph 1 of this article may at any time withdraw the reservation by a communication to that effect addressed to the Secretary-General of the United Nations.

Article 43

Entry into Force

1. This Convention shall come into force on the ninetieth day following the day of deposit of the sixth instrument of ratification or accession.

2. For each State ratifying or acceding to the Convention after the deposit of the sixth instrument of ratification or accession, the Convention shall enter into force on the ninetieth day following the date of deposit by such State of its instrument of ratification or accession.

Article 44

Denunciation

1. Any Contracting State may denounce this Convention at any time by a notification addressed to the Secretary-General of the United Nations.

2. Such denunciation shall take effect for the Contracting State concerned one year from the date upon which it is received by the Secretary-General of the United Nations.

3. Any State which has made a declaration or notification under article 40 may, at any time thereafter, by a notification to the Secretary-General of the United Nations, declare that the Convention shall cease to extend to such territory one year after the date of receipt of the notification by the Secretary-General.

Article 45

Revision

1. Any Contracting State may request revision of this Convention at any time by a notification addressed to the Secretary-General of the United Nations.

2. The General Assembly of the United Nations shall recommend the steps, if any, to be taken in respect of such request.

Article 46

Notifications by the Secretary-General of the United Nations

The Secretary-General of the United Nations shall inform all Members of the United Nations and non-member States referred to in article 39:

a. Of declarations and notifications in accordance with section B of article 1;

b. Of signatures, ratifications and accessions in accordance with article 39;

c. Of declarations and notifications in accordance with article 40;

d. Of reservations and withdrawals in accordance with article 42;

e. Of the date on which this Convention will come into force in accordance with article 43;

f. Of denunciations and notifications in accordance with article 44;

g. Of requests for revision in accordancd with article 45.

IN FAITH WHEREOF the undersigned, duly authorized, have signed this Convention on behalf of their respective Governments.

DONE at Geneva, this twenty-eighth day of July, one thousand nine hundred and fifty-one, in a single copy, of which the English and French texts are equally authentic and which shall remain deposited in the archives of the United Nations, and certified true copies of which shall be delivered to all members of the United Nations and to the non-member States referred to in article 39.

5. PROTOCOL RELATING TO THE STATUS OF REFUGEES (1967) G.A. Res. 2198 (XXI), 21 U.N. GAOR, Supp (No. 16) at 48, U.N. Doc. A/6316 (1966). Signed 21 January 1967. In force 4 October 1967 in accordance with Article VIII.

THE STATES PARTIES TO THE PRESENT PROTOCOL,

Considering that the Convention relating to the Status of Refugees done at Geneva on 28 July 1951 (hereinafter referred to as the Convention) covers only those persons who have become refugees as a result of events occurring before 1 January 1951,

Considering that new refugee situations have arisen since the Convention was adopted and that the refugees concerned may therefore not fall within the scope of the Convention,

Considering that it is desirable that equal status should be enjoyed by all refugees covered by the definition in the Convention irrespective of the dateline 1 January 1951,

Have agreed as follows:

Article I

General Provision

1. The States Parties to the present Protocol undertake to apply articles 2 to 34 inclusive of the Convention to refugees as hereinafter defined.

2. For the purpose of the present Protocol, the term "refugee" shall, except as regards the application of paragraph 3 of this article, mean any person within the definition of article 1 of the Convention as if the words "As a result of events occurring before 1 January 1951 and . . . " and the words " . . . as a result of such events," in article 1 A (2) were omitted.

3. The present Protocol shall be applied by the States Parties hereto without any geographic limitation, save that existing declarations made by States already Parties to the Convention in accordance with article 1 B (1) (*a*) of the Convention, shall, unless extended under article 1 B (2) thereof, apply also under the present Protocol.

Article II

Co-operation of the National Authorities with the United Nations

1. The States Parties to the present Protocol undertake to co-operate with the Office of the United Nations High Commissioner for Refugees, or any other agency of the United Nations which may succeed it, in the exercise of its functions, and shall in particular facilitate its duty of supervising the application of the provisions of the present Protocol.

2. In order to enable the Office of the High Commissioner or any other agency of the United Nations which may succeed it, to make reports to the competent organs of the United Nations, the States Parties to the present Protocol undertake to provide them with the information and statistical data requested, in the appropriate form, concerning:

    a. The condition of refugees;

    b. The implementation of the present Protocol;

    c. Laws, regulations and decrees which are, or may hereafter be, in force relating to refugees.

Article III

Information on National Legislation

The States Parties to the present Protocol shall communicate to the Secretary-General of the United Nations the laws and regulations which they may adopt to ensure the application of the present protocol.

* * *

[For omitted procedural provision, Article IV, see below, Chapter IV.A.16.]

Article V

Accession

The present Protocol shall be open for accession on behalf of all States Parties to the Convention and of any other State Member of the United Nations of member of any of the specialized agencies or to which an invitation to accede may have been addressed by the General Assembly of the United Nations. Accession shall be effected by the deposit of an instrument of accession with the Secretary-General of the United Nations.

Article VI

Federal Clause

In the case of a Federal or non-unitary State, the following provisions shall apply:

a. With respect to those articles of the Convention to be applied in accordance with article I, paragraph 1, of the present Protocol that come within the legislative jurisdiction of the federal legislative authority, the obligations of the Federal Government shall to this extent be the same as those of States Parties which are not Federal States;

b. With respect to those articles of the Convention to be applied in accordance with article I, paragraph 1, of the present Protocol that come within the legislative jurisdiction of constituent states, provinces or cantons which are not, under the constitutional system of the Federation, bound to take legislative action, the Federal Government shall bring such articles with a favourable recommendation to the notice of the appropriate authorities of states, provinces or cantons at the earliest possible moment;

c. A Federal State Party to the present Protocol shall, at the request of any other State Party hereto transmitted through the Secretary-General of the United Nations, supply a statement of the law and practice of the Federation and its constituent units in regard to any particular provision of the Convention to be applied in accordance with article I, paragraph 1, of the present Protocol, showing the extent to which effect has been given to that provision by legislative or other action.

Article VII

Reservations and Declarations

1. At the time of accession, any State may make reservations in respect of article IV of the present Protocol and in respect of the application in accordance with article I of the present Protocol of any provisions of the Convention other than those contained in articles 1, 3, 4, 16 (1) and 33 thereof, provided that in the case of a State Party to the Convention reservations made under this article shall not extend to refugees in respect of whom the Convention applies.

2. Reservations made by States Parties to the Convention in accordance with

article 42 thereof shall, unless withdrawn, be applicable in relation to their obligations under the present Protocol.

3. Any State making a reservation in accordance with paragraph 1 of this article may at any time withdraw such reservation by a communication to that effect addressed to the Secretary-General of the United Nations.

4. Declarations made under article 40, paragraphs 1 and 2, of the Convention by a State Party thereto which accedes to the present Protocol shall be deemed to apply in respect of the present Protocol, unless upon accession a notification to the contrary is addressed by the State Party concerned to the Secretary-General of the United Nations. The provisions of article 40, paragraphs 2 and 3, and of article 44, paragraph 3, of the Convention shall be deemed to apply *mutatis mutandis* to the present Protocol.

Article VIII

Entry into Force

1. The present Protocol shall come into force on the day of deposit of the sixth instrument of accession.

2. For each State acceding to the Protocol after the deposit of the sixth instrument of accession, the Protocol shall come into force on the date of deposit by such State of its instrument of accession.

Article IX

Denunciation

1. Any State Party hereto may denounce this Protocol at any time by a notification addressed to the Secretary-General of the United Nations.

2. Such denunciation shall take effect for the State Party concerned one year from the date on which it is received by the Secretary-General of the United Nations.

Article X

Notifications by the Secretary-General of the United Nations

The Secretary-General of the United Nations shall inform the States referred to in article V above of the date of entry into force, accessions, reservations and withdrawals of reservations to and denunciations of the present Protocol, and of declarations and notifications relating hereto.

Article XI

Deposit in the Archives of the Secretariat of the United Nations

A copy of the present Protocol, of which the Chinese, English, French, Russian and Spanish texts are equally authentic, signed by the President of the General Assembly and by the Secretary-General of the United Nations, shall be deposited in the archives of the Secretariat of the United Nations. The Secretary-General will transmit certified copies thereof to all States Members of the United Nations and to the other States referred to in article V above.

6. DECLARATION ON TERRITORIAL ASYLUM (1967)
G.A. Res. 2312 (XXII), 22 U.N. GAOR, Supp. (No. 16) at 81, U.N. Doc. A/6716 (1967).

THE GENERAL ASSEMBLY,

Recalling its resolutions 1839 (XVII) of 19 December 1962, 2100 (XX) of 20 December 1965 and 2203 (XXI) of 16 December 1966 concerning a declaration on the right of asylum,

Considering the work of codification to be undertaken by the International Law Commission in accordance with General Assembly resolution 1400 (XIV) of 21 November 1959,

Adopts the following Declaration:

DECLARATION ON TERRITORIAL ASYLUM

THE GENERAL ASSEMBLY,

Noting that the purposes proclaimed in the Charter of the United Nations are to maintain international peace and security, to develop friendly relations among all nations and to achieve international co-operation in solving international problems of an economic, social, cultural or humanitarian character and in promoting and encouraging respect for human rights and for fundamental freedoms for all without distinction as to race, sex, language or religion,

Mindful of the Universal Declaration of Human Rights, which declares in article 14 that:

"1. Everyone has the right to seek and to enjoy in other countries asylum from persecution."

"2. This right may not be invoked in the case of prosecutions genuinely arising from non-political crimes or from acts contrary to the purposes and principles of the United Nations,"

Recalling also article 13, paragraph 2, of the Universal Declaration of Human Rights, which states:

"Everyone has the right to leave any country, including his own, and to return to his country,"

Recognizing that the grant of asylum by a State to persons entitled to invoke article 14 of the Universal Declaration of Human Rights is a peaceful and humanitarian act and that, as such, it cannot be regarded as unfriendly by any other State,

Recommends that, without prejudice to existing instruments dealing with asylum and the status of refugees and stateless persons, States should base themselves in their practices relating to territorial asylum on the following principles:

Article 1

1. Asylum granted by a State, in the exercise of its sovereignty, to persons entitled to invoke article 14 of the Universal Declaration of Human Rights,

including persons struggling against colonialism, shall be respected by all other States.

2. The right to seek and to enjoy asylum may not be invoked by any person with respect to whom there are serious reasons for considering that he has committed a crime against peace, a war crime or a crime against humanity, as defined in the international instruments drawn up to make provision in respect of such crimes.

3. It shall rest with the State granting asylum to evaluate the grounds for the grant of asylum.

Article 2

1. The situation of persons referred to in article 1, paragraph 1, is, without prejudice to the sovereignty of States and the purposes and principles of the United Nations, of concern to the international community.

2. Where a State finds difficulty in granting or continuing to grant asylum, States individually or jointly or through the United Nations shall consider, in a spirit of international solidarity, appropriate measures to lighten the burden on that State.

Article 3

1. No person referred to in article 1, paragraph 1, shall be subjected to measures such as rejection at the frontier or, if he has already entered the territory in which he seeks asylum, expulsion or compulsory return to any State where he may be subjected to persecution.

2. Exception may be made to the foregoing principle only for overriding reasons of national security or in order to safeguard the population, as in the case of a mass influx of persons.

3. Should a State decide in any case that exception to the principle stated in paragraph 1 of this article would be justified, it shall consider the possibility of granting to the person concerned, under such conditions as it may deem appropriate, an opportunity, whether by way of provisional asylum or otherwise, of going to another State.

Article 4

States granting asylum shall not permit persons who have received asylum to engage in activities contrary to the purposes and principles of the United Nations.

I. FREEDOM OF INFORMATION

INTRODUCTION

In 1948, the UN convened in Geneva a Conference on Freedom of Information. Three proposed Conventions were detailed in the Final Act of the Conference:

1. on freedom of information,
2. on access to information and its transmission between countries,
3. on the right of correction.

Despite this promising start, it has proved extremely dificult to reconcile fundamentally divergent views on freedom of information, on the role of private enterprise and the state in this area and on the activities of the large (and mainly Western) news-gathering agencies. The proposed Convention on Freedom of Information, along with a Declaration on the same topic, have been on the General Assembly agenda since 1949, but there has been no substantive discussion in recent years. The proposed instruments are, indeed, seen as something of an embarrassing joke.

The General Assembly, in 1949, approved the text of a draft Convention of the International Transmission of News and the Right of Correction, incorporating two of the items of the 1948 Conference. The Assembly decided, however, that the Convention would not be opened for signature until definitive action had been taken on the draft Convention on Freedom of Information, which was seen as intimately related to it. Ultimately, in 1952, the Assembly agreed to open for signature a Convention on the International Right of Correction which reproduced the provisions relating to correction in the preamble and operative articles of the 1949 draft. The material on transmission of news is accordingly in limbo along with that on freedom of information generally. *See* A. Gaspard, "International Action to Preserve Press Freedom," in *The International Protection of Human Rights*, 183 (E. Luard ed. 1967).

For the related efforts of UNESCO in this area see Chapter III.

1. CONVENTION ON THE INTERNATIONAL RIGHT OF CORRECTION (1952)

G.A. Res. 630 (VII), 7 U.N. GAOR, Supp. (No. 20) at 27, U.N. Doc. A/2361 (1952). In force 24 August 1962 in accordance with Article VIII.

THE CONTRACTING STATES,

Desiring to implement the right of their peoples to be fully and reliably informed,

Desiring to improve understanding between their peoples through the free flow of information and opinion,

Desiring thereby to protect mankind from the scourge of war, to prevent the recurrence of aggression from any source, and to combat all propaganda which is either designed or likely to provoke or encourage any threat to the peace, breach of the peace, or act of aggression,

Considering the danger to the maintenance of friendly relations between peoples and to the preservation of peace, arising from the publication of inaccurate reports,

Considering that at its second regular session the General Assembly of the United Nations recommended the adoption of measures designed to combat the dissemination of false or distorted reports likely to injure friendly relations between States,

Considering, however, that it is not at present practicable to institute, on the international level, a procedure for verifying the accuracy of a report which might lead to the imposition of penalties for the publication of false or distorted reports,

Considering, moreover, that to prevent the publication of reports of this nature or to reduce their pernicious effects, it is above all necessary to promote a wide circulation of news and to heighten the sense of responsibility of those regularly engaged in the dissemination of news,

Considering that an effective means to these ends is to give States directly affected by a report, which they consider false or distorted and which is disseminated by an information agency, the possibility of securing commensurate publicity for their corrections,

Considering that the legislation of certain States does not provide for a right of correction of which foreign governments may avail themselves, and that it is therefore desirable to institute such a right on the international level, and

Having resolved to conclude a Convention for these purposes,

Have agreed as follows:

Article I

For the purposes of the present Convention:

1. "News dispatch" means news material transmitted in writing or by means of telecommunications, in the form customarily employed by information agencies in transmitting such news material, before publication, to newspapers, news periodicals and broadcasting organizations.

2. "Information agency" means a Press, broadcasting, film, television or facsimile organization, public or private, regularly engaged in the collection and dissemination of news material, created and organized under the laws and regulations of the Contracting State in which the central organization is domiciled and which, in each Contracting State where it operates, functions under the laws and regulations of that State.

3. "Correspondent" means a national of a Contracting State or an individual employed by an information agency of a Contracting State, who in either case is regularly engaged in the collection and the reporting of news material, and who when outside his State is identified as a correspondent by a valid passport or by a similar document internationally acceptable.

Article II

1. Recognizing that the professional responsibility of correspondents and

information agencies requires them to report facts without discrimination and in their proper context and thereby to promote respect for human rights and fundamental freedoms, to further international understanding and co-operation and to contribute to the maintenance of international peace and security,

Considering also that, as a matter of professional ethics, all correspondents and information agencies should, in the case of news dispatches transmitted or published by them and which have been demonstrated to be false or distorted, follow the customary practice of transmitting through the same channels, or of publishing corrections of such dispatches,

The Contracting States agree that in cases where a Contracting State contends that a news dispatch capable of injuring its relations with other States or its national prestige or dignity transmitted from one country to another by correspondents or information agencies of a Contracting or non-Contracting State and published or disseminated abroad is false or distorted, it may submit its version of the facts (hereinafter called "communiqué") to the Contracting States within whose territories such dispatch has been published or disseminated. A copy of the communiqué shall be forwarded at the same time to the correspondent or information agency concerned to enable that correspondent or information agency to correct the news dispatch in question.

2. A communiqué may be issued only with respect to news dispatches and must be without comment or expression of opinion. It should not be longer than is necessary to correct the alleged inaccuracy or distortion and must be accompanied by a verbatim text of the dispatch as published or disseminated, and by evidence that the dispatch has been transmitted from abroad by a correspondent or an information agency.

Article III

1. With the least possible delay and in any case not later than five clear days from the date of receiving a communiqué transmitted in accordance with provisions of article II, a Contracting State, whatever be its opinion concerning the facts in question, shall:

   a. Release the communiqué to the correspondents and information agencies operating in its territory through the channels customarily used for the release of news concerning international affairs for publication; and

   b. Transmit the communiqué to the headquarters of the information agency whose correspondent was responsible for originating the dispatch in question, if such headquarters are within its territory.

2. In the event that a Contracting State does not discharge its obligation under this article, with respect to the communiqué of another Contracting State, the latter may accord, on the basis of reciprocity, similar treatment to a communiqué thereafter submitted to it by the defaulting State.

Article IV

1. If any of the Contracting States to which a communiqué has been transmitted in accordance with article II fails to fulfil, within the prescribed time-limit, the obligations laid down in article III, the Contracting State exercis-

ing the right of correction may submit the said communiqué, together with a verbatim text of the dispatch as published or disseminated, to the Secretary-General of the United Nations and shall at the same time notify the State complained against that it is doing so. The latter State, may, within five clear days after receiving such notice, submit its comments to the Secretary-General, which shall relate only to the allegation that it has not discharged its obligations under article III.

2. The Secretary-General shall in any event, within ten clear days after receiving the communiqué, give appropriate publicity through the information channels at his disposal to the communiqué, together with the dispatch and the comments, if any, submitted to him by the State complained against.

* * *

[For omitted procedural provision, Article V, see below, Chapter IV.A.16.]

Article VI

1. The present Convention shall be open for signature to all States Members of the United Nations, to every State invited to the United Nations Conference on Freedom of Information held at Geneva in 1948, and to every other State which the General Assembly may, by resolution, declare to be eligible.

2. The present Convention shall be ratified by the States signatory hereto in conformity with their respective constitutional processes. The instruments of ratification shall be deposited with the Secretary-General of the United Nations.

Article VII

1. The present Convention shall be open for accession to the States referred to in article VI (1).

2. Accession shall be effected by the deposit of an instrument of accession with the Secretary-General of the United Nations.

Article VIII

When any six of the States referred to in article VI (1) have deposited their instruments of ratification or accession, the present Convention shall come into force among them on the thirtieth day after the date of the deposit of the sixth instrument of ratification or accession. It shall come into force for each State which ratifies or accedes after that date on the thirtieth day after the deposit of its instrument of ratification or accession.

Article IX

The provisions of the present Convention shall extend to or be applicable equally to a contracting metropolitan State and to all territories, be they Non-Self-Governing, Trust or Colonial Territories, which are being administered or governed by such metropolitan State.

Article X

Any Contracting State may denounce the present Convention by notification to the Secretary-General of the United Nations. Denunciation shall take effect six months after the date of receipt of the notification by the Secretary-General.

Article XI

The present Convention shall cease to be in force as from the date when the denunciation which reduces the number of parties to less than six becomes effective.

Article XII

1. A request for the revision of the present Convention may be made at any time by any Contracting State by means of a notification to the Secretary-General of the United Nations.

2. The General Assembly shall decide upon the steps, if any, to be taken in respect of such request.

Article XIII

The Secretary-General of the United Nations shall notify the States referred to in article VI (1) of the following:

a. Signatures, ratifications and accessions received in accordance with articles VI and VII;

b. The date upon which the present Convention comes into force in accordance with article VIII;

c. Denunciations received in accordance with article X;

d. Abrogation in accordance with article XI;

e. Notifications received in accordance with article XII.

Article XIV

1. The present Convention, of which the Chinese, English, French, Russian and Spanish texts shall be equally authentic, shall be deposited in the archives of the United Nations.

2. The Secretary-General of the United Nations shall transmit a certified copy to each State referred to in article VI (1).

3. The present Convention shall be registered with the Secretariat of the United Nations on the date of its coming into force.

J. MARRIAGE AND THE FAMILY, CHILDHOOD AND YOUTH

INTRODUCTION

The 1949 Convention for the Suppression of the Traffic in Persons and the Exploitation of the Prostitution of Others deals with prostitution and the traffic in women and children for the purposes of prostitution. It consolidates and updates a number of earlier treaties going back as far as 1904. In less semantically conscious days the topic was known as "The White Slave Trade" and the 1949 Convention is often collected along with the treaties on slavery (*supra*, this Chapter, Section 5). It seemed to us, however, that it fits more appropriately with the instruments preceding it which are also devoted to the dignity of women and children.

1. CONVENTION ON CONSENT TO MARRIAGE, MINIMUM AGE FOR MARRIAGE AND REGISTRATION OF MARRIAGES (1962) G.A. Res. 1763A (XVII), 17 U.N. GAOR, Supp. (No. 17) at 28, U.N. Doc. A/5217 (1962). In force 9 December 1964 in accordance with Article 6.

THE CONTRACTING STATES,

Desiring, in conformity with the Charter of the United Nations, to promote universal respect for, and observance of, human rights and fundamental freedoms for all, without distinction as to race, sex, language or religion,

Recalling that article 16 of the Universal Declaration of Human Rights states that:

"(1) Men and women of full age, without any limitation due to race, nationality or religion, have the right to marry and to found a family. They are entitled to equal rights as to marriage, during marriage and at its dissolution.

"(2) Marriage shall be entered into only with the free and full consent of the intending spouses.",

Recalling further that the General Assembly of the United Nations declared, by resolution 843 (IX) of 17 December 1954, that certain customs, ancient laws and practices relating to marriage and the family were inconsistent with the principles set forth in the Charter of the United Nations and in the Universal Declaration of Human Rights,

Reaffirming that all States, including those which have or assume responsibility for the administration of Non-Self-Governing and Trust Territories until their achievement of independence, should take all appropriate measures with a view to abolishing such customs, ancient laws and practices by ensuring, *inter alia*, complete freedom in the choice of a spouse, eliminating completely child marriages and the betrothal of young girls before the age of puberty, establishing appropriate penalties where necessary and establishing a civil or other register in which all marriages will be recorded,

Hereby agree as hereinafter provided:

Article 1

1. No marriage shall be legally entered into without the full and free consent of both parties, such consent to be expressed by them in person after due publicity and in the presence of the authority competent to solemnize the marriage and of witnesses, as prescribed by law.

2. Notwithstanding anything in paragraph 1 above, it shall not be necessary for one of the parties to be present when the competent authority is satisfied that the circumstances are exceptional and that the party has, before a competent authority and in such manner as may be prescribed by law, expressed and not withdrawn consent.

Article 2

States parties to the present Convention shall take legislative action to specify a minimum age for marriage. No marriage shall be legally entered into by any person under this age, except where a competent authority has granted a dispensation as to age, for serious reasons, in the interest of the intending spouses.

Article 3

All marriages shall be registered in an appropriate official register by the competent authority.

Article 4

1. The present Convention shall, until 31 December 1963, be open for signature on behalf of all States Members of the United Nations or members of any of the specialized agencies, and of any other State invited by the General Assembly of the United Nations to become a party to the Convention.

2. The present Convention is subject to ratification. The instruments of ratification shall be deposited with the Secretary-General of the United Nations.

Article 5

1. The present Convention shall be open for accession to all States referred to in article 4, paragraph 1.

2. Accession shall be effected by the deposit of an instrument of accession with the Secretary-General of the United Nations.

Article 6

1. The present Convention shall come into force on the ninetieth day following the date of deposit of the eighth instrument of ratification or accession.

2. For each State ratifying or acceding to the Convention after the deposit of

the eighth instrument of ratification or accession, the Convention shall enter into force on the ninetieth day after deposit by such State of its instrument of ratification or accession.

Article 7

1. Any Contracting State may denounce the present Convention by written notification to the Secretary-General of the United Nations. Denunciation shall take effect one year after the date of receipt of the notification by the Secretary-General.

2. The present Convention shall cease to be in force as from the date when the denunciation which reduces the number of parties to less than eight becomes effective.

* * *

[For omitted procedural provision, Article 8, see below, Chapter IV.B.16.]

Article 9

The Secretary-General of the United Nations shall notify all States Members of the United Nations and the non-member States contemplated in article 4, paragraph 1, of the present Convention of the following:

a. Signatures and instruments of ratification received in accordance with article 4;

b. Instruments of accession received in accordance with article 5;

c. The date upon which the Convention enters into force in accordance with article 6;

d. Notifications of denunciation received in accordance with article 7, paragraph 1;

e. Abrogation in accordance with article 7, paragraph 2.

Article 10

1. The present Convention, of which the Chinese, English, French, Russian, and Spanish texts shall be equally authentic, shall be deposited in the archives of the United Nations.

2. The Secretary-General of the United Nations shall transmit a certified copy of the Convention to all States Members of the United Nations and to the non-member States contemplated in article 4, paragraph 1.

2. DECLARATION OF THE RIGHTS OF THE CHILD
(1959) G.A. Res. 1386 (XIV), 14 U.N. GAOR Supp. (No. 16) at 19, U.N. Doc. A/4354 (1959).

PREAMBLE

Whereas the peoples of the United Nations have, in the Charter, reaffirmed their faith in fundamental human rights and in the dignity and worth of the human person, and have determined to promote social progress and better standards of life in larger freedom,

Whereas the United Nations has, in the Universal Declaration of Human Rights, proclaimed that everyone is entitled to all the rights and freedoms set forth therein, without distinction of any kind, such as race, colour, sex, language, religion, political or other opinion, national or social origin, property, birth or other status,

Whereas the child, by reason of his physical and mental immaturity, needs special safeguards and care, including appropriate legal protection, before as well as after birth,

Whereas the need for such special safeguards has been stated in the Geneva Declaration of the Rights of the Child of 1924, and recognized in the Universal Declaration of Human Rights and in the statutes of specialized agencies and international organizations concerned with the welfare of children,

Whereas mankind owes to the child the best it has to give,

Now therefore,

THE GENERAL ASSEMBLY

Proclaims this Declaration of the Rights of the Child to the end that he may have a happy childhood and enjoy for his own good and for the good of society the rights and freedoms herein set forth, and calls upon parents, upon men and women as individuals, and upon voluntary organizations, local authorities and national Governments to recognize these rights and strive for their observance by legislative and other measures progressively taken in accordance with the following principles:

Principle 1

The child shall enjoy all the rights set forth in this Declaration. Every child, without any exception whatsoever, shall be entitled to these rights, without distinction or discrimination on account of race, colour, sex, language, religion, political or other opinion, national or social origin, property, birth or other status, whether of himself or of his family.

Principle 2

The child shall enjoy special protection, and shall be given opportunities and facilities, by law and by other means, to enable him to develop physically, mentally, morally, spiritually and socially in a healthy and normal manner and in conditions of freedom and dignity. In the enactment of laws for this purpose, the best interests of the child shall be the paramount consideration.

Principle 3

The child shall be entitled from his birth to a name and a nationality.

Principle 4

The child shall enjoy the benefits of social security. He shall be entitled to grow and develop in health; to this end, special care and protection shall be provided both to him and to his mother, including adequate prenatal and post-natal care. The child shall have the right to adequate nutrition, housing, recreation and medical services.

Principle 5

The child who is physically, mentally or socially handicapped shall be given the special treatment, education and care required by his particular condition.

Principle 6

The child, for the full and harmonious development of his personality, needs love and understanding. He shall, wherever possible, grow up in the care and under the responsibility of his parents, and, in any case, in an atmosphere of affection and of moral and material security; a child of tender years shall not, save in exceptional circumstances, be separated from his mother. Society and the public authorities shall have the duty to extend particular care to children without a family and to those without adequate means of support. Payment of State and other assistance towards the maintenance of children of large families is desirable.

Principle 7

The child is entitled to receive education, which shall be free and compulsory, at least in the elementary stages. He shall be given an education which will promote his general culture and enable him, on a basis of equal opportunity, to develop his abilities, his individual judgment, and his sense of moral and social responsibility, and to become a useful member of society.

The best interests of the child shall be the guiding principle of those responsible for his education and guidance; that responsibility lies in the first place with his parents.

The child shall have full opportunity for play and recreation, which should be directed to the same purposes as education; society and the public authorities shall endeavour to promote the enjoyment of this right.

Principle 8

The child shall in all circumstances be among the first to receive protection and relief.

Principle 9

The child shall be protected against all forms of neglect, cruelty and exploitation. He shall not be the subject of traffic, in any form.

The child shall not be admitted to employment before an appropriate minimum age; he shall in no case be caused or permitted to engage in any occupation or employment which would prejudice his health or education, or interfere with his physical, mental or moral development.

Principle 10

The child shall be protected from practices which may foster racial, religious and any other form of discrimination. He shall be brought up in a spirit of understanding, tolerance, friendship among peoples, peace and universal brotherhood, and in full consciousness that his energy and talents should be devoted to the service of his fellow men.

3. DECLARATION ON THE PROTECTION OF WOMEN AND CHILDREN IN EMERGENCY AND ARMED CONFLICT (1974) G.A. Res. 3318 (XXIX), 29 U.N. GAOP Supp. (No. 31) at 146, U.N. Doc. A/9631 (1974).

THE GENERAL ASSEMBLY,

Having considered the recommendation of the Economic and Social Council contained in its resolution 1861 (LVI) of 16 May 1974,

Expressing its deep concern over the sufferings of women and children belonging to the civilian population who in periods of emergency and armed conflict in the struggle for peace, self-determination, national liberation and independence are too often the victims of inhuman acts and consequently suffer serious harm,

Aware of the suffering of women and children in many areas of the world, especially in those areas subject to suppression, aggression, colonialism, racism, alien domination and foreign subjugation,

Deeply concerned by the fact that, despite general and unequivocal condemnation, colonialism, racism and alien and foreign domination continue to subject many peoples under their yoke, cruelly suppressing the national liberation movements and inflicting heavy losses and incalculable sufferings on the populations under their domination, including women and children,

Deploring the fact that grave attacks are still being made on fundamental freedoms and the dignity of the human person and that colonial and racist foreign domination Powers continue to violate international humanitarian law,

Recalling the relevant provisions contained in the instruments of international humanitarian law relative to the protection of women and children in time of peace and war,

Recalling, among other important documents, its resolutions 2444 (XXIII) of 19 December 1968, 2597 (XXIV) of 16 December 1969 and 2674 (XXV) and 2675 (XXV) of 9 December 1970, on respect for human rights and on basic principles for the protection of civilian populations in armed conflicts, as well as Economic and Social Council resolution 1515 (XLVIII) of 28 May 1970 in which the Council requested the General Assembly to consider the possibility of drafting a declaration on the protection of women and children in emergency or wartime,

Conscious of its responsibility for the destiny of the rising generation and for the destiny of mothers, who play an important role in society, in the family and particularly in the upbringing of children,

Bearing in mind the need to provide special protection of women and children belonging to the civilian population,

Solemnly proclaims this Declaration on the Protection of Women and Children in Emergency and Armed Conflict and calls for the strict observance of the Declaration by all Member States:

1. Attacks and bombings on the civilian population, inflicting incalculable suffering, especially on women and children, who are the most vulnerable members of the population, shall be prohibited, and such acts shall be condemned.

2. The use of chemical and bacteriological weapons in the course of military operations constitutes one of the most flagrant violations of the Geneva Protocol of 1925, the Geneva Conventions of 1949 and the principles of international humanitarian law and inflicts heavy losses on civilian populations, including defenseless women and children, and shall be severely condemned.

3. All States shall abide fully by their obligations under the Geneva Protocol of 1925 and the Geneva Conventions of 1949, as well as other instruments of international law relative to respect for human rights in armed conflicts, which offer important guarantees for the protection of women and children.

4. All efforts shall be made by States involved in armed conflicts, military operations in foreign territories or military operations in territories still under colonial domination to spare women and children from the ravages of war. All the necessary steps shall be taken to ensure the prohibition of measures such as persecution, torture, punitive measures, degrading treatment and violence, particularly against that part of the civilian population that consists of women and children.

5. All forms of repression and cruel and inhuman treatment of women and children, including imprisonment, torture, shooting, mass arrests, collective punishment, destruction of dwellings and forcible eviction, committed by belligerents in the course of military operations or in occupied territories shall be considered criminal.

6. Women and children belonging to the civilian population and finding themselves in circumstances of emergency and armed conflict in the struggle for peace, self-determination, national liberation and independence, or who live in occupied territories, shall not be deprived of shelter, food, medical aid or other inalienable rights, in accordance with the provisions of the Universal Declaration of Human Rights, the International Covenant on Civil and Political Rights, the International Covenant on Economic, Social and Cultural Rights, the Declaration of the Rights of the Child or other instruments of international law.

4. DECLARATION ON THE PROMOTION AMONG YOUTH OF THE IDEALS OF PEACE, MUTUAL RESPECT AND UNDERSTANDING BETWEEN PEOPLES

(1965) G.A. Res. 2037 (XX), 20 U.N. GAOR Supp. (No. 14) at 40, U.N. Doc. A/6014 (1965).

THE GENERAL ASSEMBLY,

Recalling that under the terms of the Charter of the United Nations the peoples have declared themselves determined to save succeeding generations from the scourge of war,

Recalling further that in the Charter the United Nations has affirmed its faith in fundamental human rights, in the dignity of the human person and in the equal rights of men and nations,

Reaffirming the principles embodied in the Universal Declaration of Human Rights, the Declaration on the Granting of Independence to Colonial Countries and Peoples, the United Nations Declaration on the Elimination of All Forms of Racial Discrimination, General Assembly resolution 110 (II) of 3 November 1947 condemning all forms of propaganda designed or likely to provoke or encourage any threat to the peace, the Declaration of the Rights of the Child, and General Assembly resolution 1572 (XV) of 18 December 1960, which have a particular bearing upon the upbringing of young people in a spirit of peace, mutual respect and understanding among peoples,

Recalling that the purpose of the United Nations Educational, Scientific and Cultural Organization is to contribute to peace and security by promoting collaboration among nations through education, science and culture, and recognizing the role and contributions of that organization towards the education of young people in the spirit of international understanding, co-operation and peace,

Taking into consideration the fact that in the conflagrations which have afflicted mankind it is the young people who have had to suffer most and who have had the greatest number of victims,

Convinced that young people wish to have an assured future and that peace, freedom and justice are among the chief guarantees that their desire for happiness will be fulfilled,

Bearing in mind the important part being played by young people in every field of human endeavor and the fact that they are destined to guide the fortunes of mankind,

Bearing in mind furthermore that, in this age of great scientific, technological and cultural achievements, the energies, enthusiasm and creative abilities of the young should be devoted to the material and spiritual advancement of all peoples,

Convinced that the young should know, respect, and develop the cultural heritage of their own country and that of all mankind,

Convinced furthermore that the education of the young and exchanges of young people and of ideas in a spirit of peace, mutual respect and understanding between peoples can help to improve international relations and to strengthen peace and security,

Proclaims this Declaration on the Promotion among Youth of the Ideals of Peace, Mutual Respect and Understanding between Peoples and calls upon Governments, non-governmental organizations and youth movements to recognize the principles set forth therein and to ensure their observance by means of appropriate measures:

Principle I

Young people shall be brought up in the spirit of peace, justice, freedom, mutual respect and understanding in order to promote equal rights for all human beings and all nations, economic and social progress, disarmament and the maintenance of international peace and security.

Principle II

All means of education, including as of major importance the guidance given by parents or family, instruction and information intended for the young should foster among them the ideals of peace, humanity, liberty and international solidarity and all other ideals which help to bring peoples closer together, and acquaint them with the role entrusted to the United Nations as a means of preserving and maintaining peace and promoting international understanding and co-operation.

Principle III

Young people shall be brought up in the knowledge of the dignity and equality of all men, without distinction as to race, colour, ethnic origins or beliefs, and in respect for fundamental human rights and for the right of peoples to self-determination.

Principle IV

Exchanges, travel, tourism, meetings, the study of foreign languages, the twinning of towns and universities without discrimination and similar activities should be encouraged and facilitated among young people of all countries in order to bring them together in educational, cultural and sporting activities in the spirit of this Declaration.

Principle V

National and international associations of young people should be encouraged to promote the purposes of the United Nations, particularly international peace and security, friendly relations among nations based on respect for the equal sovereignty of States, the final abolition of colonialism and of racial discrimination and other violations of human rights.

Youth organizations in accordance with this Declaration should take all appropriate measures within their respective fields of activity in order to make their contribution without any discrimination to the work of educating the young generation in accordance with these ideals.

Such organizations, in conformity with the principle of freedom of association, should promote the free exchange of ideas in the spirit of the principles of this Declaration and of the purposes of the United Nations set forth in the Charter.

All youth organizations should conform to the principles set forth in this Declaration.

Principle VI

A major aim in educating the young shall be to develop all their faculties and to train them to acquire higher moral qualities, to be deeply attached to the noble ideals of peace, liberty, the dignity and equality of all men, and imbued with respect and love for humanity and its creative achievements. To this end the family has an important role to play.

Young people must become conscious of their responsibilities in the world they will be called upon to manage and should be inspired with confidence in a future of happiness for mankind.

5. CONVENTION FOR THE SUPPRESSION OF THE TRAFFIC IN PERSONS AND OF THE EXPLOITATION OF THE PROSTITUTION OF OTHERS (1949) G.A. Res. 317 (IV), 4 U.N. GAOR at 33, U.N. Doc. A/1251 (1949). In force 25 July 1951 in accordance with Article 24.

PREAMBLE

Whereas prostitution and the accompanying evil of the traffic in persons for the purpose of prostitution are incompatible with the dignity and worth of the human person and endanger the welfare of the individual, the family and the community,

Whereas, with respect to the suppression of the traffic in women and children, the following international instruments are in force:

1. International Agreement of 18 May 1904 for the Suppression of the White Slave Traffic, as amended by the Protocol approved by the General Assembly of the United Nations on 3 December 1948,

2. International Convention of 4 May 1910 for the Suppression of the White Slave Traffic, as amended by the above-mentioned Protocol,

3. International convention of 30 September 1921 for the Suppression of the Traffic in Women and Children, as amended by the Protocol approved by the General Assembly of the United Nations on 20 October 1947,

4. International Convention of 11 October 1933 for the Suppression of the Traffic in Women of Full Age, as amended by the aforesaid Protocol,

Whereas the League of Nations in 1937 prepared a draft Convention extending the scope of the above-mentioned instruments, and

Whereas developments since 1937 make feasible the conclusion of a convention consolidating the above-mentioned instruments and embodying the substance of the 1937 draft Convention as well as desirable alterations therein:

Now therefore
The Contracting Parties
Hereby agree as hereinafter provided:

Article 1

The Parties to the present Convention agree to punish any person who, to gratify the passions of another:

1. Procures, entices or leads away, for purposes of prostitution, another person, even with the consent of that person;

2. Exploits the prostitution of another person, even with the consent of that person.

Article 2

The Parties to the present Convention further agree to punish any person who:

1. Keeps or manages, or knowingly finances or takes part in the financing of a brothel;

2. Knowingly lets or rents a building or other place or any part thereof for the purpose of the prostitution of others.

Article 3

To the extent permitted by domestic law, attempts to commit any of the offences referred to in articles 1 and 2, and acts preparatory to the commission thereof, shall also be punished.

Article 4

To the extent permitted by domestic law, intentional participation in the acts referred to in articles 1 and 2 above shall also be punishable.

To the extent permitted by domestic law, acts of participation shall be treated as separate offences whenever this is necessary to prevent impunity.

Article 5

In cases where injured persons are entitled under domestic law to be parties to proceedings in respect of any of the offences referred to in the present Convention, aliens shall be so entitled upon the same terms as nationals.

Article 6

Each Party to the present Convention agrees to take all the necessary measures to repeal or abolish any existing law, regulation or administrative provision by virtue of which persons who engage in or are suspected of engaging in prostitution are subject either to special registration or to the possession of a special document or to any exceptional requirements for supervision or notification.

Article 7

Previous convictions pronounced in foreign States for offences referred to in the present Convention shall, to the extent permitted by domestic law, be taken into account for the purpose of:

1. Establishing recidivism;

2. Disqualifying the offender from the exercise of civil rights.

Article 8

The offences referred to in articles 1 and 2 of the present Convention shall be regarded as extraditable offences in any extradition treaty which has been or may hereafter be concluded between any of the Parties to this Convention.

The Parties to the present Convention which do not make extradition conditional on the existence of a treaty shall henceforward recognize the offences referred to in articles 1 and 2 of the present Convention as cases for extradition between themselves.

Extradition shall be granted in accordance with the law of the State to which the request is made.

Article 9

In States where the extradition of nationals is not permitted by law, nationals who have have returned to their own State after the commission abroad of any of the offences referred to in articles 1 and 2 of the present Convention shall be prosecuted in and punished by the courts of their own State.

This provision shall not apply if, in a similar case between the Parties to the present Convention, the extradition of an alien cannot be granted.

Article 10

The provisions of article 9 shall not apply when the person charged with the offence has been tried in a foreign State and, if convicted, has served his sentence or had it remitted or reduced in conformity with the laws of that foreign State.

Article 11

Nothing in the present Convention shall be interpreted as determining the attitude of a Party towards the general question of the limits of criminal jurisdiction under international law.

Article 12

The present Convention does not affect the principle that the offences to which it refers shall in each State be defined, prosecuted and punished in conformity with its domestic law.

Article 13

The Parties to the present Convention shall be bound to execute letters of request relating to offences referred to in the Convention in accordance with their domestic law and practice.

The transmission of letters of request shall be effected:

1. By direct communication between the judicial authorities; or

2. By direct communication between the Ministers of Justice of the two States, or by direct communication from another competent authority of the State making the request to the Minister of Justice of the State to which the request is made; or

3. Through the diplomatic or consular representative of the State making the request in the State to which the request is made; this representative shall send the letters of request direct to the competent judicial authority or to the authority indicated by the Government of the State to which the request is made, and shall receive direct from such authority the papers constituting the execution of the letters of request.

In cases 1 and 3 a copy of the letters of request shall always be sent to the superior authority of the State to which application is made.

Unless otherwise agreed, the letters of request shall be drawn up in the language of the authority making the request, provided always that the State to which the request is made may require a translation in its own language, certified correct by the authority making the request.

Each Party to the present Convention shall notify to each of the other Parties to the Convention the method or methods of transmission mentioned above which it will recognize for the letters of request of the latter State.

Until such notification is made by a State, its existing procedure in regard to letters of request shall remain in force.

Execution of letters of request shall not give rise to a claim for reimbursement of charges or expenses of any nature whatever other than expenses of experts.

Nothing in the present article shall be construed as an undertaking on the part of the Parties to the present Convention to adopt in criminal matters any form or methods of proof contrary to their own domestic laws.

Article 14

Each Party to the present Convention shall establish or maintain a service charged with the co-ordination and centralization of the results of the investigation of offences referred to in the present Convention.

Such services should compile all information calculated to facilitate the prevention and punishment of the offences referred to in the present Convention and should be in close contact with the corresponding services in other States.

Article 15

To the extent permitted by domestic law and to the extent to which the authorities responsible for the services referred to in article 14 may judge desirable, they shall furnish to the authorities responsible for the corresponding services in other States the following information:

1. Particulars of any offence referred to in the present Convention or any attempt to commit such offence;

2. Particulars of any search for and any prosecution, arrest, conviction, refusal of admission or expulsion of persons guilty of any of the offences referred to in the present Convention, the movements of such persons and any other useful information with regard to them.

The information so furnished shall include descriptions of the offenders, their fingerprints, photographs, methods of operation, police records and records of conviction.

Article 16

The Parties to the present Convention agree to take or to encourage, through their public and private educational, health, social, economic and other related services, measures for the prevention of prostitution and for the rehabilitation and social adjustment of the victims of prostitution and of the offences referred to in the present Convention.

Article 17

The Parties to the present Convention undertake, in connexion with immigration and emigration, to adopt or maintain such measures as are required, in terms of their obligations under the present Convention, to check the traffic in persons of either sex for the purpose of prostitution.

In particular they undertake:

1. To make such regulations as are necessary for the protection of immigrants or emigrants, and in particular, women and children, both at the place of arrival and departure and while *en route*;

2. To arrange for appropriate publicity warning the public of the dangers of the aforesaid traffic;

3. To take appropriate measures to ensure supervision of railway stations, airports, seaports and *en route*, and of other public places, in order to prevent international traffic in persons for the purpose of prostitution;

4. To take appropriate measures in order that the appropriate authorities be informed of the arrival of persons who appear, *prima facie*, to be the principals and accomplices in or victims of such traffic.

Article 18

The Parties to the present Convention undertake, in accordance with the conditions laid down by domestic law, to have declarations taken from aliens who are prostitutes, in order to establish their identity and civil status and to discover who has caused them to leave their State. The information obtained shall be communicated to the authorities of the State of origin of the said persons with a view to their eventual repatriation.

Article 19

The Parties to the present Convention undertake, in accordance with the conditions laid down by domestic law and without prejudice to prosecution or other action for violations thereunder and so far as possible:

1. Pending the completion of arrangements for the repatriation of destitute victims of international traffic in persons for the purpose of prostitution, to make suitable provisions for their temporary care and maintenance;

2. To repatriate persons referred to in article 18 who desire to be repatriated or who may be claimed by persons exercising authority over them or whose expulsion is ordered in conformity with the law. Repatriation shall take place only after agreement is reached with the State of destination as to identity and nationality as well as to the place and date of arrival at frontiers. Each Party to the present Convention shall facilitate the passage of such persons through its territory.

Where the persons referred to in the preceding paragraph cannot themselves repay the cost of repatriation and have neither spouse, relatives nor guardian to pay for them, the cost of repatriation as far as the nearest frontier or port of embarkation or airport in the direction of the State of origin shall be borne by the State where they are in residence, and the cost of the remainder of the journey shall be borne by the State of origin.

Article 20

The Parties to the present Convention shall, if they have not already done so, take the necessary measures for the supervision of employment agencies in order to prevent persons seeking employment, in particular women and children, from being exposed to the danger of prostitution.

Article 21

The Parties to the present Convention shall communicate to the Secretary-General of the United Nations such laws and regulations as have already been promulgated in their States, and thereafter annually such laws and regulations as may be promulgated, relating to the subjects of the present Convention, as well as all measures taken by them concerning the application of the Convention. The information received shall be published periodically by the Secretary-General and sent to all Members of the United Nations and to non-member States to which the present Convention is officially communicated in accordance with article 23.

* * *

[For omitted procedural provision, Article 22, see below, Chapter IV.A.16.]

Article 23

The present Convention shall be open for signature on behalf of any Member of the United Nations and also on behalf of any other State to which an invitation has been addressed by the Economic and Social Council.

The present Convention shall be ratified and the instruments of ratification shall be deposited with the Secretary-General of the United Nations.

The States mentioned in the first paragraph which have not signed the Convention may accede to it.

Accession shall be effected by deposit of an instrument of accession with the Secretary-General of the United Nations.

For the purposes of the present Convention the word "State" shall include all the colonies and Trust Territories of a State signatory or acceding to the Convention and all territories for which such State is internationally responsible.

Article 24

The present Convention shall come into force on the ninetieth day following the date of deposit of the second instrument of ratification or accession.

For each State ratifying or acceding to the Convention after the deposit of the second instrument of ratification or accession, the Convention shall enter into force ninety days after the deposit by such State of its instrument of ratification or accession.

Article 25

After the expiration of five years from the entry into force of the present

Convention, any Party to the Convention may denounce it by a written notification addressed to the Secretary-General of the United Nations.

Such denunciation shall take effect for the Party making it one year from the date upon which it is received by the Secretary-General of the United Nations.

Article 26

The Secretary-General of the United Nations shall inform all Members of the United Nations and non-member States referred to in article 23:

a. Of signatures, ratifications and accessions received in accordance with article 23;

b. Of the date on which the present Convention will come into force in accordance with article 24;

c. Of denunciations received in accordance with article 25.

Article 27

Each Party to the present Convention undertakes to adopt, in accordance with its Constitution, the legislative or other measures necessary to ensure the application of the Convention.

Article 28

The provisions of the present Convention shall supersede in the relations between the Parties thereto the provisions of the international instruments referred to in sub-paragraphs 1, 2, 3 and 4 of the second paragraph of the Preamble, each of which shall be deemed to be terminated when all the Parties thereto shall have become Parties to the present Convention.

FINAL PROTOCOL

Nothing in the present Convention shall be deemed to prejudice any legislation which ensures, for the enforcement of the provisions for securing the suppression of the traffic in persons and of the exploitation of others for purposes of prostitution, stricter conditions than those provided by the present Convention.

The provisions of articles 23 to 26 inclusive of the Convention shall apply to the present Protocol.

K. PERSONS HAVING SPECIAL NEEDS

INTRODUCTION

These documents need little explanation. The first two represent an acknowledgement that mentally retarded persons and disabled persons have the same rights to human dignity as other members of the community. In the exercise of this right, they are entitled, in particular, to assistance in the development of their personality and talents to the greatest possible extent. The third establishes a framework for promoting the interests of victims both of an ordinary crime and of abuse of power.

1. DECLARATION ON THE RIGHTS OF MENTALLY RETARDED PERSONS (1971) G.A. Res. 2856 (XXVI), 26 U.N. GAOR, Supp. (No. 29) at 93, U.N. Doc.A/8429 (1971).

THE GENERAL ASSEMBLY,

Mindful of the pledge of the States Members of the United Nations under the Charter to take joint and separate action in co-operation with the Organization to promote higher standards of living, full employment and conditions of economic and social progress and development,

Reaffirming faith in human rights and fundamental freedoms and in the principles of peace, of the dignity and worth of the human person and of social justice proclaimed in the Charter,

Recalling the principles of the Universal Declaration of Human Rights, the International Covenants on Human Rights, the Declaration of the Rights of the Child and the standards already set for social progress in the constitutions, conventions, recommendations and resolutions of the International Labour Organisation, the United Nations Educational, Scientific and Cultural Organization, the World Health Organization, the United Nations Children's Fund and other organizations concerned.

Emphasizing that the Declaration on Social Progress and Development has proclaimed the necessity of protecting the rights and assuring the welfare and rehabilitation of the physically and mentally disadvantaged,

Bearing in mind the necessity of assisting mentally retarded persons to develop their abilities in various fields of activities and of promoting their integration as far as possible in normal life,

Aware that certain countries, at their present stage of development, can devote only limited efforts to this end,

Proclaims this Declaration on the Rights of Mentally Retarded Persons and calls for national and international action to ensure that it will be used as a common basis and frame of reference for the protection of these rights:

1. The mentally retarded person has, to the maximum degree of feasibility, the same rights as other human beings.

2. The mentally retarded person has a right to proper medical care and physical therapy and to such education, training, rehabilitation and guidance as will enable him to develop his ability and maximum potential.

3. The mentally retarded person has a right to economic security and to a decent standard of living. He has a right to perform productive work or to engage in any other meaningful occupation to the fullest possible extent of his capabilities.

4. Whenever possible, the mentally retarded person should live with his own family or with foster parents and participate in different forms of community life. The family with which he lives should receive assistance. If care in an institution becomes necessary, it should be provided in surroundings and other circumstances as close as possible to those of normal life.

5. The mentally retarded person has a right to a qualified guardian when this is required to protect his personal well-being and interests.

6. The mentally retarded person has a right to protection from exploitation, abuse and degrading treatment. If prosecuted for any offence, he shall have a right to due process of law with full recognition being given to his degree of mental responsibility.

7. Whenever mentally retarded persons are unable, because of the severity of their handicap, to exercise all their rights in a meaningful way or it should become necessary to restrict or deny some or all of these rights, the procedure used for that restriction or denial of rights must contain proper legal safeguards against every form of abuse. This procedure must be based on an evaluation of the social capability of the mentally retarded person by qualified experts and must be subject to periodic review and to the right of appeal to higher authorities.

2. DECLARATION ON THE RIGHTS OF DISABLED PERSONS (1975) G.A. Res. 3447 (XXX), 30 U.N. GAOR, Supp. (No. 34) at 88, U.N. Doc.A/10034 (1975).

THE GENERAL ASSEMBLY,

Mindful of the pledge made by Member States, under the Charter of the United Nations; to take joint and separate action in co-operation with the Organization to promote higher standards of living, full employment and conditions of economic and social progress and development,

Reaffirming its faith in human rights and fundamental freedoms and in the principles of peace, of the dignity and worth of the human person and of social justice proclaimed in the Charter,

Recalling the principles of the Universal Declaration of Human Rights, the International Covenants on Human Rights, the Declaration of the Rights of the Child and the Declaration on the Rights of Mentally Retarded Persons, as well as the standards already set for social progress in the constitutions, conventions, recommendations and resolutions of the International Labour Organisation, the

United Nations Educational, Scientific and Cultural Organization, the World Health Organization, the United Nations Children's Fund and other organizations concerned,

Recalling also Economic and Social Council resolution 1921 (LVIII) of 6 May 1975 on the prevention of disability and the rehabilitation of disabled persons,

Emphasizing that the Declaration on Social Progress and Development has proclaimed the necessity of protecting the rights and assuring the welfare and rehabilitation of the physically and mentally disadvantaged,

Bearing in mind the necessity of preventing physical and mental disabilities and of assisting disabled persons to develop their abilities in the most varied fields of activities and of promoting their integration as far as possible in normal life,

Aware that certain countries, at their present stage of development, can devote only limited efforts to this end,

Proclaims this Declaration on the Rights of Disabled Persons and calls for national and international action to ensure that it will be used as a common basis and frame of reference for the protection of these rights:

1. The term "disabled person" means any person unable to ensure by himself or herself, wholly or partly, the necessities of a normal individual and/or social life, as a result of deficiency, either congenital or not, in his or her physical or mental capabilities.

2. Disabled persons shall enjoy all the rights set forth in this Declaration. These rights shall be granted to all disabled persons without any exception whatsoever and without distinction or discrimination on the basis of race, colour, sex, language, religion, political or other opinions, national or social origin, state of wealth, birth or any other situation applying either to the disabled person himself or herself or to his or her family.

3. Disabled persons have the inherent right to respect for their human dignity. Disabled persons, whatever the origin, nature and seriousness of their handicaps and disabilities, have the same fundamental rights as their fellow-citizens of the same age, which implies first and foremost the right to enjoy a decent life, as normal and full as possible.

4. Disabled persons have the same civil and political rights as other human beings; paragraph 7 of the Declaration on the Rights of Mentally Retarded Persons applies to any possible limitation or suppression of those rights for mentally disabled persons.

5. Disabled persons are entitled to the measures designed to enable them to become as self-reliant as possible.

6. Disabled persons have the right to medical, psychological and functional treatment, including prosthetic and orthetic appliances, to medical and social rehabilitation, education, vocational training and rehabilitation, aid, counselling, placement services and other services which will enable them to develop their capabilities and skills to the maximum and will hasten the process of their social integration or reintegration.

7. Disabled persons have the right to economic and social security and to a decent level of living. They have the right, according to their capabilities, to secure and retain employment or to engage in a useful, productive and remunerative occupation and to join trade unions.

8. Disabled persons are entitled to have their special needs taken into consideration at all stages of economic and social planning.

9. Disabled persons have the right to live with their families or with foster parents and to participate in all social, creative or recreational activities. No disabled person shall be subjected, as far as his or her residence is concerned, to differential treatment other than that required by his or her condition or by the improvement which he or she may derive therefrom. If the stay of a disabled person in a specialized establishment is indispensable, the environment and living conditions therein shall be as close as possible to those of the normal life of a person of his or her age.

10. Disabled persons shall be protected against all exploitation, all regulations and all treatment of a discriminatory, abusive or degrading nature.

11. Disabled persons shall be able to avail themselves of qualified legal aid when such aid proves indispensable for the protection of their persons and property. If judicial proceedings are instituted against them, the legal procedure applied shall take their physical and mental condition fully into account.

12. Organizations of disabled persons may be usefully consulted in all matters regarding the rights of disabled persons.

13. Disabled persons, their families and communities shall be fully informed, by all appropriate means, of the rights contained in this Declaration.

3. DECLARATION OF BASIC PRINCIPLES OF JUSTICE FOR VICTIMS OF CRIME AND ABUSE OF POWER (1985) G.A. Res. 40/34 (1985).

THE GENERAL ASSEMBLY,

Recalling that the Sixth United Nations Congress on the Prevention of Crime and the Treatment of Offenders recommended that the United Nations should continue its present work on the development of guidelines and standards regarding abuse of economic and political power,

Cognizant that millions of people throughout the world suffer harm as a result of crime and the abuse of power and that the rights of these victims have not been adequately recognized,

Recognizing that the victims of crime and the victims of abuse of power, and also frequently their families, witnesses and others who aid them, are unjustly subjected to loss, damage or injury and that they may, in addition, suffer hardship when assisting in the prosecution of offenders,

1. *Affirms* the necessity of adopting national and international measures in order to secure the universal and effective recognition of, and respect for, the rights of victims of crime and of abuse of power;

2. *Stresses* the need to promote progress by all States in their efforts to that end, without prejudice to the rights of suspects or offenders;

3. *Adopts* the Declaration of Basic Principles of Justice for Victims of Crime and Abuse of Power, annexed to the present resolution, which is designed to

assist Governments and the international community in their efforts to secure justice and assistance for victims of crime and victims of abuse of power;

4. *Calls upon* Member States to take the necessary steps to give effect to the provisions contained in the Declaration and, in order to curtail victimization as referred to hereinafter, endeavour:

    a. To implement social, health, including mental health, education, economic and specific crime prevention policies to reduce victimization and encourage assistance to victims in distress;

    b. To promote community efforts and public participation in crime prevention;

    c. To review periodically their existing legislation and practices in order to ensure responsiveness to changing circumstances, and to enact and enforce legislation proscribing acts that violate internationally recognized norms relating to human rights, corporate conduct and other abuses of power;

    d. To establish and strengthen the means of detecting, prosecuting and sentencing those guilty of crimes;

    e. To promote disclosure of relevant information to expose official and corporate conduct to public scrutiny, and other ways of increasing responsiveness to public concerns;

    f. To promote the observance of codes of conduct and ethical norms, in particular international standards, by public servants, including law enforcement, correctional, medical, social service and military personnel, as well as the staff of economic enterprises;

    g. To prohibit practices and procedures conducive to abuse, such as secret places of detention and incommunicado detention;

    h. To co-operate with other States, through mutual judicial and administrative assistance, in such matters as the detention and pursuit of offenders, their extradition and the seizure of their assets, to be used for restitution to the victims;

5. *Recommends* that, at the international and regional levels, all appropriate measures should be taken:

    a. To promote training activities designed to foster adherence to United Nations standards and norms and to curtail possible abuses;

    b. To sponsor collaborative action-research on ways in which victimization can be reduced and victims aided, and to promote information exchanges on the most effective means of so doing;

    c. To render direct aid to requesting Governments designed to help them curtail victimization and alleviate the plight of victims;

    d. To develop ways and means of providing recourse for victims where national channels may be insufficient;

6. *Requests* the Secretary-General to invite Member States to report periodically to the General Assembly on the implementation of the Declaration as well as on measures taken by them to this effect;

7. *Also requests* the Secretary-General to make use of the opportunities, which all relevant bodies and organizations within the United Nations system offer, to assist Member States, whenever necessary, in improving ways and

means of protecting victims both at the national level and through international co-operation;

8. *Further requests* the Secretary-General to promote the objectives of the Declaration, in particular by ensuring its widest possible dissemination;

9. *Urges* the specialized agencies and other entities and bodies of the United Nations system, other relevant intergovernmental and non-governmental organizations and the public to co-operate in the implementation of the provisions of the Declaration.

ANNEX

DECLARATION OF BASIC PRINCIPLES OF JUSTICE FOR VICTIMS OF CRIME AND ABUSE OF POWER

A. Victims of Crime

1. "Victims" means persons who, individually or collectively, have suffered harm, including physical or mental injury, emotional suffering, economic loss or substantial impairment of their fundamental rights, through acts or omissions that are in violation of criminal laws operative within Member States, including those laws proscribing criminal abuse of power.

2. A Person may be considered a victim, under this Declaration, regardless of whether the perpetrator is identified, apprehended, prosecuted or convicted and regardless of the familial relationship between the perpetrator and the victim. The term "victim" also includes, where appropriate, the immediate family or dependants of the direct victim and persons who have suffered harm in intervening to assist victims in distress or to prevent victimization.

3. The provisions contained herein shall be applicable to all, without distinction of any kind, such as race, colour, sex, age, language, religion, nationality, political or other opinion, cultural beliefs or practices, property, birth or family status, ethnic or social origin, and disability.

ACCESS TO JUSTICE AND FAIR TREATMENT

4. Victims should be treated with compassion and respect for their dignity. They are entitled to access to the mechanisms of justice and to prompt redress, as provided for by national legislation, for the harm that they have suffered.

5. Judicial and administrative mechanisms should be established and strengthened where necessary to enable victims to obtain redress through formal or informal procedures that are expeditious, fair, inexpensive and accessible. Victims should be informed of their rights in seeking redress through such mechanisms.

6. The responsiveness of judicial and administrative processes to the needs of victims should be facilitated by:

  a. Informing victims of their role and the scope, timing and progress of the proceedings and of the disposition of their cases, especially where serious crimes are involved and where they have requested such information;

b. Allowing the views and concerns of victims to be presented and considered at appropriate stages of the proceedings where their personal interests are affected, without prejudice to the accused and consistent with the relevant national criminal justice system;

c. Providing proper assistance to victims throughout the legal process;

d. Taking measures to minimize inconvenience to victims, protect their privacy, when necessary, and ensure their safety, as well as that of their families and witnesses on their behalf, from intimidation and retaliation;

e. Avoiding unnecessary delay in the disposition of cases and the execution of orders or decrees granting awards to victims.

7. Informal mechanisms for the resolution of disputes, including mediation, arbitration and customary justice or indigenous practices, should be utilized where appropriate to facilitate conciliation and redress for victims.

RESTITUTION

8. Offenders or third parties responsible for their behaviour should, where appropriate, make fair restitution to victims, their families or dependants. Such restitution should include the return of property or payment for the harm or loss suffered, reimbursement of expenses incurred as a result of the victimization, the provision of services and the restoration of rights.

9. Governments should review their practices, regulations and laws to consider restitution as an available sentencing option in criminal cases, in addition to other criminal sanctions.

10. In cases of substantial harm to the environment, restitution, if ordered, should include, as far as possible, restoration of the environment, reconstruction of the infrastructure, replacement of community facilities and reimbursement of the expenses of relocation, whenever such harm results in the dislocation of a community.

11. Where public officials or other agents acting in an official or quasi-official capacity have violated national criminal laws, the victims should receive restitution from the State whose officials or agents were responsible for the harm inflicted. In cases where the Government under whose authority the victimizing act or omission occurred is no longer in existence, the State or Government successor in title should provide restitution to the victims.

COMPENSATION

12. When compensation is not fully available from the offender or other sources, States should endeavour to provide financial compensation to:

a. Victims who have sustained significant bodily injury or impairment of physical or mental health as a result of serious crimes;

b. The family, in particular dependants of persons who have died or become physically or mentally incapacitated as a result of such victimization.

13. The establishment, strengthening and expansion of national funds for compensation to victims should be encouraged. Where appropriate, other funds may also be established for this purpose, including those cases where the State of which the victim is a national is not in a position to compensate the victim for the harm.

ASSISTANCE

14. Victims should receive the necessary material, medical, psychological and social assistance through governmental, voluntary, community-based and indigenous means.

15. Victims should be informed of the availability of health and social services and other relevant assistance and be readily afforded access to them.

16. Police, justice, health, social service and other personnel concerned should receive training to sensitize them to the needs of victims, and guidelines to ensure proper and prompt aid.

17. In providing services and assistance to victims, attention should be given to those who have special needs because of the nature of the harm inflicted or because of factors such as those mentioned in paragraph 3 above.

B. Victims of Abuse of Power

18. "Victims" means persons who, individually or collectively, have suffered harm, including physical or mental injury, emotional suffering, economic loss or substantial impairment of their fundamental rights, through acts or omissions that do not yet constitute violations of national criminal laws but of internationally recognized norms relating to human rights.

19. States should consider incorporating into the national law norms proscribing abuses of power and providing remedies to victims of such abuses. In particular, such remedies should include restitution and/or compensation, and necessary material, medical, psychological and social assistance and support.

20. States should consider negotiating multilateral international treaties relating to victims, as defined in paragraph 18.

21. States should periodically review existing legislation and practices to ensure their responsiveness to changing circumstances, should enact and enforce, if necessary, legislation proscribing acts that constitute serious abuses of political or economic power, as well as promoting policies and mechanisms for the prevention of such acts, and should develop and make readily available appropriate rights and remedies for victims of such acts.

L. SOCIAL WELFARE, PROGRESS, DEVELOPMENT AND THE NEW INTERNATIONAL ECONOMIC ORDER

INTRODUCTION

The documents in this section have a general thrust which is neatly encapsulated in the preambular paragraph of the Declaration on the Establishment of a New International Economic Order in which Members of the United Nations proclaim their "united determination to work urgently for THE ESTABLISHMENT OF A NEW INTERNATIONAL ECONOMIC ORDER based on equity, sovereign equality, interdependence, common interest and cooperation among all States, irrespective of their economic and social systems which shall correct inequities and redress existing injustices, make it possible to eliminate the widening gap between the developed and developing countries and ensure steadily accelerating economic and social development and peace and justice for present and future generations. . . . "

For the most part, these documents speak in generalities. However, one specific context in which the gap between developed and developing countries has been much debated is the governmental taking of foreign property. Debated in particular are the grounds upon which this may be done, whether and how much compensation must be paid and the procedures—national or international—by which disputes concerning takings and compensation are to be resolved. The first major statement on this topic in the United Nations was the 1962 Resolution entitled "Permanent Sovereignty over Natural Resources."[13] That Resolution was adopted by a vote of 87 for, 2 against (France, South Africa) and 12 abstentions (mainly the socialist States), an overwhelming show of support that suggests it might be viewed as a consensus crystallizing international customary law on this matter. The size of the vote, however concealed a chasm between the differing views that the Resolution arguably supports. It is far from clear whether the Resolution (i) represented an adoption of the basic Western, especially the United States, view that there should be prompt, adequate and effective compensation provided under international standards, or whether the Resolution (ii) constituted a new consensus that something much less was required, or whether (iii) it merely represented an undermining of any consensus there had been, without anything being provided in its place. The erosion of the Western position on this item continued through operative paragraph 4 of the Declaration on the Establishment of a New International Economic Order and Article 2 of the Charter of Economic Rights and Duties of States. As a practical matter, even developing countries normally pay *some* compensation by way of settlement following expropriations. After referring to "disturbing" efforts to undermine the "old" rule, one commentator remarks:

> The principal reassuring factor is the realization that in the great majority of expropriation cases, the host country ultimately has

granted compensation, thus implying existence of a duty to compensate at some level. The amount of compensation, and the terms and conditions under which it is granted, leave much to be desired, yet there appears to be a common disposition to pay something in the general area of book value. This is too little comfort, indeed, but the industrial nations of the world may draw some comfort from the fact that nations, in practice, generally appear to acknowledge some right to compensation.[14]

The NIEO Declaration and its accompanying Programme of Action were adopted in May of 1974 at a Special Session of the General Assembly. Unanimity was marred, however, by the fact that no fewer than 38 countries made supplementary statements or expressed reservations concerning the content of the Declaration, in particular the United States, West Germany, Japan, France and the United Kingdom.

The Charter of Economic Rights and Duties of States was completed at the Regular Session of the General Assembly later in 1974, as a follow up to the Declaration. It was adopted by a vote of 120 to 6 with 10 abstentions. While it is called a "Charter" (a term usually confined to especially important treaties), and while it contains much normative language (words like "declaring" and "rights"), it was adopted not as a treaty but as a General Assembly Resolution. Any status it might have as a manifestation of international customary law is seriously undercut by the identity of the dissenters and abstainers. As one writer points out:

> After the rejection of an application by the EEC states to continue the comparatively short-term negotiations of the working group until a universally acceptable formulation of the charter could be found, six OECD states (Belgium, Denmark, the Federal Republic of Germany, Great Britain, Luxembourg, and USA) voted against the adoption of the charter, while 10 market-economy industrial nations (Austria, Canada, France, Ireland, Israel, Italy, Japan, the Netherlands, Norway, Spain) abstained. This rejection of the charter by the OECD nations, whose business enterprises control more than 75% of the world market, has resulted in poor chances for the early realization of an NIEO in international economic relations, especially as the oil and currency crises have so far been successfully managed and the OECD states are therefore under less pressure to support reforms.[15]

From the large body of literature on the NIEO, we suggest in particular S. Schwebel, *"The Story of the U.N.'s Declaration on Permanent Sovereignty Over Natural Resources,"* 49 *Am. Bar Assoc. J.* 463 (1963); F. Bergsten, *Toward a New International Economic Order* (1975); D. Denoon ed., *The New International Economic Order: A U.S. Response* (1979); C. Okolie, *International Law Perspectives of the Developing Countries: The Relationship of Law and Economic Development to Basic Human Rights* (1978). There is a very thorough collection of documents in A. Mutharika, *The International Law of Development*, (4 vols) (1978).

1. PERMANENT SOVEREIGNTY OVER NATURAL RESOURCES (1962) G.A. Res. 1803 (XVII), 17 U.N. GAOR Supp. (No. 17) at 15, U.N. Doc. A/5217 (1962).

THE GENERAL ASSEMBLY,

Recalling its resolutions 523 (VI) of 12 January 1952 and 626 (VII) of 21 December 1952,

Bearing in mind its resolution 1314 (XIII) of 12 December 1958, by which it established the Commission on Permanent Sovereignty over Natural Resources and instructed it to conduct a full survey of the status of permanent sovereignty over natural wealth and resources as a basic constituent of the right to self-determination, with recommendations, where necessary, for its strengthening, and decided further that, in the conduct of the full survey of the status of the permanent sovereignty of peoples and nations over their natural wealth and resources, due regard should be paid to the rights and duties of States under international law and to the importance of encouraging international co-operation in the economic development of developing countries,

Bearing in mind its resolution 1515 (XV) of 15 December 1960, in which it recommended that the sovereign right of every State to dispose of its wealth and its natural resources should be respected,

Considering that any measure in this respect must be based on the recognition of the inalienable right of all States freely to dispose of their natural wealth and resources in accordance with their national interests, and on respect for the economic independence of States,

Considering that nothing in paragraph 4 below in any way prejudices the position of any Member State on any aspect of the question of the rights and obligations of successor States and Governments in respect of property acquired before the accession to complete sovereignty of countries formerly under colonial rule,

Noting that the subject of succession of States and Governments is being examined as a matter of priority by the International Law Commission,

Considering that it is desirable to promote international co-operation for the economic development of developing countries, and that economic and financial agreements between the developed and the developing countries must be based on the principles of equality and of the right of peoples and nations to self-determination,

Considering that the provision of economic and technical assistance, loans and increased foreign investment must not be subject to conditions which conflict with the interests of the recipient State,

Considering the benefits to be derived from exchanges of technical and scientific information likely to promote the development and use of such resources and wealth, and the important part which the United Nations and other international organizations are called upon to play in that connexion,

Attaching particular importance to the question of promoting the economic development of developing countries and securing their economic independence,

Noting that the creation and strengthening of the inalienable sovereignty of States over their natural wealth and resources reinforces their economic independence,

Desiring that there should be further consideration by the United Nations of the subject of permanent sovereignty over natural resources in the spirit of international co-operation in the field of economic development, particularly that of the developing countries,

I

Declares that:

1. The right of peoples and nations to permanent sovereignty over their natural wealth and resources must be exercised in the interest of their national development and of the well-being of the people of the State concerned.

2. The exploration, development and disposition of such resources, as well as the import of the foreign capital required for these purposes, should be in conformity with the rules and conditions which the peoples and nations freely consider to be necessary or desirable with regard to the authorization, restriction or prohibition of such activities.

3. In cases where authorization is granted, the capital imported and the earnings on that capital shall be governed by the terms thereof, by the national legislation in force, and by international law. The profits derived must be shared in the proportions freely agreed upon, in each case, between the investors and the recipient State, due care being taken to ensure that there is no impairment, for any reason, of that State's sovereignty over its natural wealth and resources.

4. Nationalization, expropriation or requisitioning shall be based on grounds or reasons of public utility, security or the national interest which are recognized as overriding purely individual or private interests, both domestic and foreign. In such cases the owner shall be paid appropriate compensation, in accordance with the rules in force in the State taking such measures in the exercise of its sovereignty and in accordance with international law. In any case where the question of compensation gives rise to a controversy, the national jurisdiction of the State taking such measures shall be exhausted. However, upon agreement by sovereign States and other parties concerned, settlement of the dispute should be made through arbitration or international adjudication.

5. The free and beneficial exercise of the sovereignty of peoples and nations over their natural resources must be furthered by the mutual respect of States based on their sovereign equality.

6. International co-operation for the economic development of developing countries, whether in the form of public or private capital investments, exchange of goods and services, technical assistance, or exchange of scientific information, shall be such as to further their independent national development and shall be based upon respect for their sovereignty over their natural wealth and resources.

7. Violation of the rights of peoples and nations to sovereignty over their natural wealth and resources is contrary to the spirit and principles of the Charter of the United Nations and hinders the development of international co-operation and the maintenance of peace.

8. Foreign investment agreements freely entered into by or between sovereign States shall be observed in good faith; States and international organizations shall strictly and conscientiously respect the sovereignty of peoples and nations over their natural wealth and resources in accordance with the Charter and the principles set forth in the present resolution.

* * *

[Material in the Resolution of a non-substantive nature has been omitted]

2. DECLARATION ON SOCIAL PROGRESS AND DEVELOPMENT (1969) G.A. Res. 2542 (XXIV), 24 U.N. GAOR Supp. (No. 30) at 49, U.N. Doc. A/7630 (1969)

THE GENERAL ASSEMBLY,

Mindful of the pledge of Members of the United Nations under the Charter to take joint and separate action in co-operation with the Organization to promote higher standards of living, full employment and conditions of economic and social progress and development,

Reaffirming faith in human rights and fundamental freedoms and in the principles of peace, of the dignity and worth of the human person, and of social justice proclaimed in the Charter,

Recalling the principles of the Universal Declaration of Human Rights, the International Covenants on Human Rights, the Declaration of the Rights of the Child, the Declaration on the Granting of Independence to Colonial Countries and Peoples, the International Convention on the Elimination of All Forms of Racial Discrimination, the United Nations Declaration on the Elimination of All Forms of Racial Discrimination, the Declaration on the Promotion among Youth of the Ideals of Peace, Mutual Respect and Understanding between Peoples, the Declaration on the Elimination of Discrimination against Women and the resolutions of the United Nations,

Bearing in mind the standards already set for social progress in the constitutions, conventions, recommendations and resolutions of the International Labour Organisation, the Food and Agriculture Organization of the United Nations, the United Nations Educational, Scientific and Cultural Organization, the World Health Organization, the United Nations Children's Fund and of other organizations concerned,

Convinced that man can achieve complete fulfilment of his aspirations only within a just social order and that it is consequently of cardinal importance to accelerate social and economic progress everywhere, thus contributing to international peace and solidarity,

Convinced that international peace and security on the one hand, and social progress and economic development on the other, are closely interdependent and influence each other,

Persuaded that social development can be promoted by peaceful coexistence, friendly relations and co-operation among States with different social, economic or political systems,

Emphasizing the interdependence of economic and social development in the wider process of growth and change, as well as the importance of a strategy of intergrated development which takes full account at all stages of its social aspects,

Regretting the inadequate progress achieved in the world social situation despite the efforts of States and the international community,

Recognizing that the primary responsibility for the development of the developing countries rests on those countries themselves and acknowledging the pressing need to narrow and eventually close the gap in the standards of living between economically more advanced and developing countries and, to that end, that Member States shall have the responsibility to pursue internal and external policies designed to promote social development throughout the world, and in particular to assist developing countries to accelerate their economic growth,

Recognizing the urgency of devoting to works of peace and social progress resources being expended on armaments and wasted on conflict and destruction,

Conscious of the contribution that science and technology can render towards meeting the needs common to all humanity,

Believing that the primary task of all States and international organizations is to eliminate from the life of society all evils and obstacles to social progress, particularly such evils as inequality, exploitation, war, colonialism and racism,

Desirous of promoting the progress of all mankind towards these goals and of overcoming all obstacles to their realization,

Solemnly proclaims this Declaration on Social Progress and Development and calls for national and international action for its use as a common basis for social development policies:

PART I

PRINCIPLES

Article 1

All peoples and all human beings, without distinction as to race, colour, sex, language, religion, nationality, ethnic origin, shall have the right to live in dignity and freedom and to enjoy the fruits of social progress and should, on their part, contribute to it.

Article 2

Social progress and development shall be founded on respect of the dignity and value of the human person and shall ensure the promotion of human rights and social justice, which requires:

(*a*) The immediate and final elimination of all forms of inequality, exploitation of peoples and individuals, colonialism and racism, including nazism and *apartheid*, and all other policies and ideologies opposed to the purposes and principles of the United Nations;

(*b*) The recognition and effective implementation of civil and political rights as well as of economic, social and cultural rights without any discrimination.

Article 3

The following are considered primary conditions of social progress and development:

(*a*) National independence based on the right of peoples to self-determination;

(*b*) The principle of non-interference in the internal affairs of States;

(*c*) Respect for the sovereignty and territorial integrity of States;

(*d*) Permanent sovereignty of each nation over its natural wealth and resources;

(*e*) The right and responsibility of each State and, as far as they are concerned, each nation and people to determine freely its own objectives of social development, to set its own priorities and to decide in conformity with the principles of the Charter of the United Nations the means and methods of their achievement without any external interference;

(*f*) Peaceful coexistence, peace, friendly relations and co-operation among States irrespective of differences in their social, economic or political systems.

Article 4

The family as a basic unit of society and the natural environment for the growth and well-being of all its members, particularly children and youth, should be assisted and protected so that it may fully assume its responsibilities within the community. Parents have the exclusive right to determine freely and responsibly the number and spacing of their children.

Article 5

Social progress and development require the full utilization of human resources, including, in particular:

(*a*) The encouragement of creative initiative under conditions of enlightened public opinion;

(*b*) The dissemination of national and international information for the purpose of making individuals aware of changes occurring in society as a whole;

(*c*) The active participation of all elements of society, individually or through associations, in defining and in achieving the common goals of development with full respect for the fundamental freedoms embodied in the Universal Declaration of Human Rights;

(*d*) The assurance to disadvantaged or marginal sectors of the population of equal opportunities for social and economic advancement in order to achieve an effectively integrated society.

Article 6

Social development requires the assurance to everyone of the right to work and the free choice of employment.

Social progress and development require the participation of all members of society in productive and socially useful labour and the establishment, in conformity with human rights and fundamental freedoms and with the principles of justice and the social function of property, of forms of ownership of land and of the means of production which preclude any kind of exploitation of man, ensure equal rights to property for all and create conditions leading to genuine equality among people.

Article 7

The rapid expansion of national income and wealth and their equitable distribution among all members of society are fundamental to all social progress, and they should therefore be in the forefront of the preoccupations of every State and Government.

The improvement in the position of the developing countries in international trade resulting among other things from the achievement of favourable terms of trade and of equitable and remunerative prices at which developing countries market their products is necessary in order to make it possible to increase national income and in order to advance social development.

Article 8

Each Government has the primary role and ultimate responsibility of ensuring the social progress and well-being of its people, of planning social development measures as part of comprehensive development plans, of encouraging and co-ordinating or integrating all national efforts towards this end and of introducing necessary changes in the social structure. In planning social development measures, the diversity of the needs of developing and developed areas, and of urban and rural areas, within each country, shall be taken into due account.

Article 9

Social progress and development are the common concerns of the international community, which shall supplement, by concerted international action, national efforts to raise the living standards of peoples.

Social progress and economic growth require recognition of the common interest of all nations in the exploration, conservation, use and exploitation, exclusively for peaceful purposes and in the interests of all mankind, of those areas of the environment such as outer space and the sea-bed and ocean floor and the subsoil thereof, beyond the limits of national jurisdiction, in accordance with the Purposes and Principles of the Charter of the United Nations.

PART II

OBJECTIVES

Social progress and development shall aim at the continuous raising of the material and spiritual standards of living of all members of society, with respect for and in compliance with human rights and fundamental freedoms, through the attainment of the following main goals:

Article 10

(a) The assurance at all levels of the right to work and the right of everyone to form trade unions and workers' associations and to bargain collectively; promotion of full productive employment and elimination of unemployment and under-employment; establishment of equitable and favourable conditions of work for all, including the improvement of health and safety conditions; assurance of just remuneration for labour without any discrimination as well as a sufficiently high minimum wage to ensure a decent standard of living; the protection of the consumer;

(b) The elimination of hunger and malnutrition and the guarantee of the right to proper nutrition;

(c) The elimination of poverty; the assurance of a steady improvement in levels of living and of a just and equitable distribution of income;

(d) The achievement of the highest standards of health and the provision of health protection for the entire population, if possible free of charge;

(e) The eradication of illiteracy and the assurance of the right to universal access to culture, to free compulsory education at the elementary level and to free education at all levels; the raising of the general level of life-long education;

(f) The provision of all, particularly persons in low income groups and large families, of adequate housing and community services.

Social progress and development shall aim equally at the progressive attainment of the following main goals:

Article 11

(a) The provision of comprehensive social security schemes and social welfare services; the establishment and improvement of social security and insurance schemes for all persons who, because of illness, disability or old age, are temporarily or permanently unable to earn a living, with a view to ensuring a proper standard of living for such persons and for their families and dependents;

(b) The protection of the rights of the mother and child; concern for the upbringing and health of children; the provision of measures to safeguard the health and welfare of women and particularly of working mothers during pregnancy and the infancy of their children, as well as of mothers whose earnings are the sole source of livelihood for the family; the granting to women of pregnancy and maternity leave and allowances without loss of employment or wages;

(c) The protection of the rights and the assuring of the welfare of children, the aged and the disabled; the provision of protection for the physically or mentally disadvantaged;

(d) The education of youth in, and promotion among them of, the ideals of justice and peace, mutual respect and understanding among peoples; the promotion of full participation of youth in the process of national development;

(*e*) The provision of social defence measures and the elimination of conditions leading to crime and delinquency, especially juvenile delinquency;

(*f*) The guarantee that all individuals, without discrimination of any kind, are made aware of their rights and obligations and receive the necessary aid in the exercise and safeguarding of their rights.

Social progress and development shall further aim at achieving the following main objectives:

Article 12

(*a*) The creation of conditions for rapid and sustained social and economic development, particularly in the developing countries; change in international economic relations; new and effective methods of international co-operation in which equality of opportunity should be as much a prerogative of nations as of individuals within a nation;

(*b*) The elimination of all forms of discrimination and exploitation and all other practices and ideologies contrary to the purposes and principles of the Charter of the United Nations;

(*c*) The elimination of all forms of foreign economic exploitation, particularly that practiced by international monopolies, in order to enable the people of every country to enjoy in full the benefits of their national resources.

Social progress and development shall finally aim at the attainment of the following main goals:

Article 13

(*a*) Equitable sharing of scientific and technological advances by developed and developing countries, and a steady increase in the use of science and technology for the benefit of the social development of society;

(*b*) The establishment of a harmonious balance between scientific, technological and material progress and the intellectual, spiritual, cultural and moral advancement of humanity;

(*c*) The protection and improvement of the human environment.

PART III

MEANS AND METHODS

On the basis of the principles set forth in this Declaration, the achievement of the objectives of social progress and development requires the mobilization of the necessary resources by national and international action, with particular attention to such means and methods as:

Article 14

(*a*) Planning for social progress and development, as an integrated part of balanced over-all development planning;

(*b*) The establishment, where necessary, of national systems for framing and carrying out social policies and programmes, and the promotion by the countries concerned of planned regional development, taking into account differing regional conditions and needs, particularly the development of regions which are less favoured or under-developed by comparison with the rest of the country;

(c) The promotion of basic and applied social research, particularly comparative international research applied to the planning and execution of social development programmes.

Article 15

(a) The adoption of measures to ensure the effective participation, as appropriate, of all the elements of society in the preparation and execution of national plans and programmes of economic and social development;

(b) The adoption of measures for an increasing rate of popular participation in the economic, social, cultural and political life of countries through national governmental bodies, non-governmental organizations, co-operatives, rural associations, workers' and employers' organizations and women's and youth organizations, by such methods as national and regional plans for social and economic progress and community development, with a view to achieving a fully integrated national society, accelerating the process of social mobility and consolidating the democratic system;

(c) Mobilization of public opinion, at both national and international levels, in support of the principles and objectives of social progress and development;

(d) The dissemination of social information, at the national and the international level, to make people aware of changing circumstances in society as a whole, and to educate the consumer.

Article 16

(a) Maximum mobilization of all national resources and their rational and efficient utilization; promotion of increased and accelerated productive investment in social and economic fields and of employment; orientation of society towards the development process;

(b) Progressively increasing provision of the necessary budgetary and other resources required for financing the social aspects of development;

(c) Achievement of equitable distribution of national income, utilizing, *inter alia*, the fiscal system and government spending as an instrument for the equitable distribution and redistribution of income in order to promote social progress;

(d) The adoption of measures aimed at prevention of such an outflow of capital from developing countries as would be detrimental to their economic and social development.

Article 17

(a) The adoption of measures to accelerate the process of industrialization, especially in developing countries, with due regard for its social aspects, in the interests of the entire population; development of an adequate organizational and legal framework conducive to an uninterrupted and diversified growth of the industrial sector; measures to overcome the adverse social effects which may result from urban development and industrialization, including automation; maintenance of a proper balance between rural and urban development, and in particular, measures designed to ensure healthier living conditions, especially in large industrial centres;

(*b*) Integrated planning to meet the problems of urbanization and urban development;

(*c*) Comprehensive rural development schemes to raise the levels of living of the rural populations and to facilitate such urban-rural relationships and population distribution as will promote balanced national development and social progress;

(*d*) Measures for appropriate supervision of the utilization of land in the interests of society.

The achievement of the objectives of social progress and development equally requires the implementation of the following means and methods:

Article 18

(*a*) The adoption of appropriate legislative, administrative and other measures ensuring to everyone not only political and civil rights, but also the full realization of economic, social and cultural rights without any discrimination;

(*b*) The promotion of democratically based social and institutional reforms and motivation for change basic to the elimination of all forms of discrimination and exploitation and conducive to high rates of economic and social progress, to include land reform, in which the ownership and use of land will be made to serve best the objectives of social justice and economic development;

(*c*) The adoption of measures to boost and diversify agricultural production through, *inter alia*, the implementation of democratic agrarian reforms, to ensure an adequate and well-balanced supply of food, its equitable distribution among the whole population and the improvement of nutritional standards;

(*d*) The adoption of measures to introduce, with the participation of the Government, low-cost housing programmes in both rural and urban areas;

(*e*) Development and expansion of the system of transportation and communications, particularly in developing countries.

Article 19

(*a*) The provision of free health services to the whole population and of adequate preventive and curative facilities and welfare medical services accessible to all;

(*b*) The enactment and establishment of legislative measures and administrative regulations with a view to the implementation of comprehensive programmes of social security schemes and social welfare services and to the improvement and co-ordination of existing services;

(*c*) The adoption of measures and the provision of social welfare services to migrant workers and their families, in conformity with the provisions of Convention No. 97 of the International Labour Organisation* and other international instruments relating to migrant workers;

---

*Convention concerning Migration for Employment (Revised 1949), International Labour Office, *Conventions and Recommendations, 1919–1966* (Geneva, 1966), p. 743.

(*d*) The institution of appropriate measures for the rehabilitation of mentally or physically disabled persons, especially children and youth, so as to enable them to the fullest possible extent to be useful members of society—these measures shall include the provision of treatment and technical appliances, education, vocational and social guidance, training and selective placement, and other assistance required—and the creation of social conditions in which the handicapped are not discriminated against because of their disabilities.

Article 20

(*a*) The provision of full democratic freedoms to trade unions; freedom of association for all workers, including the right to bargain collectively and to strike; recognition of the right to form other organizations of working people; the provision for the growing participation of trade unions in economic and social development; effective participation of all members of trade unions in the deciding of economic and social issues which affect their interest;

(*b*) The improvement of health and safety conditions for workers, by means of appropriate technological and legislative measures and the provision of the material prerequisites for the implementation of those measures, including the limitation of working hours;

(*c*) The adoption of appropriate measures for the development of harmonious industrial relations.

Article 21

(*a*) The training of national personnel and cadres, including administrative, executive, professional and technical personnel needed for social development and for over-all development plans and policies;

(*b*) The adoption of measures to accelerate the extension and improvement of general, vocational and technical education and of training and retraining, which should be provided free at all levels;

(*c*) Raising the general level of education; development and expansion of national information media, and their rational and full use towards continuing education of the whole population and towards encouraging its participation in social development activities; the constructive use of leisure, particularly that of children and adolescents;

(*d*) The formulation of national and international policies and measures to avoid the "brain drain" and obviate its adverse effects.

Article 22

(*a*) The development and co-ordination of policies and measures designed to strengthen the essential functions of the family as a basic unit of society;

(*b*) The formulation and establishment, as needed, of programmes in the field of population, within the framework of national demographic policies and as part of the welfare medical services, including education, training of personnel and the provision to families of the knowledge and means necessary to enable them to exercise their right to determine freely and responsibly the number and spacing of their children;

(*c*) The establishment of of appropriate child-care facilities in the interest of children and working parents.

The achievement of the objectives of social progress and development finally requires the implementation of the following means and methods:

Article 23

(*a*) The laying down of economic growth rate targets for the developing countries within the United Nations policy for development, high enough to lead to a substantial acceleration of their rates of growth;

(*b*) The provision of greater assistance on better terms; the implementation of the aid volume target of a minimum of 1 per cent of the gross national product at market prices of economically advanced countries; the general easing of the terms of lending to the developing countries through low interest rates on loans and long grace periods for the repayment of loans, and the assurance that the allocation of such loans will be based strictly on socio-economic criteria free of any political considerations.;

(*c*) The provision of technical, financial and material assistance, both bilateral and multilateral, to the fullest possible extent and on favourable terms, and improved co-ordination of international assistance for the achievement of the social objectives of national development plans;

(*d*) The provision to the developing countries of technical, financial and material assistance and of favourable conditions to facilitate the direct exploitation of their national resources and natural wealth by those countries with a view to enabling the peoples of those countries to benefit fully from their national resources;

(*e*) The expansion of international trade based on principles of equality and non-discrimination, the rectification of the position of developing countries in international trade by equitable terms of trade, a general non-reciprocal and non-discriminatory system of preferences for the exports of developing countries to the developed countries, the establishment and implementation of general and comprehensive commodity agreements, and the financing of reasonable buffer stocks by international institutions.

Article 24

(*a*) Intensification of international co-operation with a view to ensuring the international exchange of information, knowledge and experience concerning social progress and development;

(*b*) The broadest possible international technical, scientific and cultural co-operation and reciprocal utilization of the experience of countries with different economic and social systems and different levels of development, on the basis of mutual advantage and strict observance of and respect for national sovereignty;

(*c*) Increased utilization of science and technology for social and economic development; arrangements for the transfer and exchange of technology, including know-how and patents, to the developing countries.

Article 25

(*a*) The establishment of legal and administrative measures for the protection and improvement of the human environment, at both national and international level;

(*b*) The use and exploitation, in accordance with the appropriate international regimes, of the resources of areas of the environment such as outer space and the sea-bed and ocean floor and the subsoil thereof, beyond the limits of national jurisdiction, in order to supplement national resources available for the achievement of economic and social progress and development in every country, irrespective of its geographical location, special consideration being given to the interests and needs of the developing countries.

Article 26

Compensation for damages, be they social or economic in nature—including restitution and reparations—caused as a result of aggression and of illegal occupation of territory by the aggressor.

Article 27

(*a*) The achievement of general and complete disarmament and the channelling of the progressively released resources to be used for economic and social progress for the welfare of people everywhere and, in particular, for the benefit of developing countries;

(*b*) The adoption of measures contributing to disarmament, including, *inter alia*, the complete prohibition of tests of nuclear weapons, the prohibition of the development, production and stockpiling of chemical and bacteriological (biological) weapons and the prevention of the pollution of oceans and inland waters by nuclear wastes.

3. DECLARATION ON THE ESTABLISHMENT OF A NEW INTERNATIONAL ECONOMIC ORDER (1974)

G.A. Res. 3201 (S-VI), U.N. GAOR, Sixth Special Session, Supp. (No.1), U.N.Doc.A/9559 (1974).

THE GENERAL ASSEMBLY

Adopts the following Declaration:

DECLARATION ON THE ESTABLISHMENT OF A
NEW INTERNATIONAL ECONOMIC ORDER

We, the Members of the United Nations,

Having convened a special session of the General Assembly to study for the first time the problems of raw materials and development, devoted to the consideration of the most important economic problems facing the world community,

Bearing in mind the spirit, purpose and principles of the Charter of the United Nations to promote the economic advancement and social progress of all peoples,

Solemnly proclaim our united determination to work urgently for THE ESTABLISHMENT OF A NEW INTERNATIONAL ECONOMIC ORDER based on equity, sovereign equality, interdependence, common interest and co-operation among all States, irrespective of their economic and social systems which shall correct inequalities and redress existing injustices, make it possible to eliminate the widening gap between the developed and the developing countries and ensure steady accelerating economic and social development and peace and justice for present and future generations, and, to that end, declare:

1. The greatest and most significant achievement during the last decades has been the independence from colonial and alien domination of a large number of peoples and nations which has enabled them to become members of the community of free peoples. Technological progress has also been made in all spheres of economic activities in the last three decades, thus providing a solid potential for improving the well-being of all peoples. However, the remaining vestiges of alien and colonial domination, foreign occupation, racial discrimination, *apartheid* and neo-colonialism in all its forms continue to be among the greatest obstacles to the full emancipation and progress of the developing countries and all the peoples involved. The benefits of technological progress are not shared equitably by all members of the international community. The developing countries, which constitute 70 per cent of the world's population, account for only 30 per cent of the world's income. It has proved impossible to achieve an even and balanced development of the international community under the existing international economic order. The gap between the developed and the developing countries continues to widen in a system which was established at a time when most of the developing countries did not even exist as independent States and which perpetuates inequality.

2. The present international economic order is in direct conflict with current developments in international political and economic relations. Since 1970, the world economy has experienced a series of grave crises which have had severe repercussions, especially on the developing countries because of their generally greater vulnerability to external economic impulses. The developing world has become a powerful factor that makes its influence felt in all fields of international activity. These irreversible changes in the relationship of forces in the world necessitate the active, full and equal participation of the developing countries in the formulation and application of all decisions that concern the international community.

3. All these changes have thrust into prominence the reality of interdependence of all the members of the world community. Current events have brought into sharp focus the realization that the interests of the developed countries and those of the developing countries can no longer be isolated from each other, that there is a close interrelationship between the prosperity of the developed countries and the growth and development of the developing countries, and that the prosperity of the international community as a whole depends upon the prosperity of its constituent parts. International co-operation for development is

the shared goal and common duty of all countries. Thus the political, economic and social well-being of present and future generations depends more than ever on co-operation between all the members of the international community on the basis of sovereign equality and the removal of the disequilibrium that exists between them.

4. The new international economic order should be founded on full respect for the following principles:

a. Sovereign equality of States, self-determination of all peoples, inadmissibility of the acquisition of territories by force, territorial integrity and noninterference in the internal affairs of other States;

b. The broadest co-operation of all the States members of the international community, based on equity, whereby the prevailing disparities in the world may be banished and prosperity secured for all;

c. Full and effective participation on the basis of equality of all countries in the solving of world economic problems in the common interest of all countries, bearing in mind the necessity to ensure the accelerated development of all the developing countries, while devoting particular attention to the adoption of special measures in favour of the least developed, land-locked and island developing countries as well as those developing countries most seriously affected by economic crises and natural calamities, without losing sight of the interests of other developing countries;

d. The right of every country to adopt the economic and social system that it deems the most appropriate for its own development and not to be subjected to discrimination of any kind as a result;

e. Full permanent sovereignty of every State over its natural resources and all economic activities. In order to safeguard these resources, each State is entitled to exercise effective control over them and their exploitation with means suitable to its own situation, including the right to nationalization or transfer of ownership to its nationals, this right being an expression of the full permanent sovereignty of the State. No State may be subjected to economic, political or any other type of coercion to prevent the free and full exercise of this inalienable right;

f. The right of all States, territories and peoples under foreign occupation, alien and colonial domination or *apartheid* to restitution and full compensation for the exploitation and depletion of, and damages to, the natural resources and all other resources of those States, territories and peoples;

g. Regulation and supervision of the activities of transnational corporations by taking measures in the interest of the national economies of the countries where such transnational corporations operate on the basis of the full sovereignty of those countries;

h. The right of the developing countries and the peoples of territories under colonial and racial domination and foreign occupation to achieve their liberation and to regain effective control over their natural resources and economic activities;

i. The extending of assistance to developing countries, peoples and territories which are under colonial and alien domination, foreign occupation, racial discrimination or *apartheid* or are subjected to economic, political or any other type of coercive measures to obtain from them the subordination of the exercise of their sovereign rights and to secure from them advantages of any kind, and to neo-colonialism in all its forms, and which have established or are endeavouring to establish effective control over their natural resources and economic activities that have been or are still under foreign control;

j. Just and equitable relationship between the prices of raw materials, primary commodities, manufactured and semi-manufactured goods exported by developing countries and the prices of raw materials, primary commodities, manufactures, capital goods and equipment imported by them with the aim of bringing about sustained improvement in their unsatisfactory terms of trade and the expansion of the world economy;

k. Extension of active assistance to developing countries by the whole international community, free of any political or military conditions;

l. Ensuring that one of the main aims of the reformed international monetary system shall be the promotion of the development of the developing countries and the adequate flow of real resources to them;

m. Improving the competitiveness of natural materials facing competition from synthetic substitutes;

n. Preferential and non-reciprocal treatment for developing countries, wherever feasible, in all fields of international economic co-operation whenever possible;

o. Securing favourable conditions for the transfer of financial resources to developing countries;

p. Giving to the developing countries access to the achievements of modern science and technology, and promoting the transfer of technology and the creation of indigenous technology for the benefit of the developing countries in forms and in accordance with procedures which are suited to their economies;

q. The need for all States to put an end to the waste of natural resources, including food products;

r. The need for developing countries to concentrate all their resources for the cause of development;

s. The strengthening, through individual and collective actions, of mutual economic, trade, financial and technical co-operation among the developing countries, mainly on a preferential basis;

t. Facilitating the role which producers' associations may play within the framework of international co-operation and, in pursuance of their aims, *inter alia* assisting in the promotion of sustained growth of the world economy and accelerating the development of developing countries.

5. The unanimous adoption of the International Development Strategy for the Second United Nations Development Decade was an important step in the promotion of international economic co-operation on a just and equitable basis. The accelerated implementation of obligations and commitments assumed by

the international community within the framework of the Strategy, particularly those concerning imperative development needs of developing countries, would contribute significantly to the fulfilment of the aims and objectives of the present Declaration.

6. The United Nations as a universal organization should be capable of dealing with problems of international economic co-operation in a comprehensive manner and ensuring equally the interest of all countries. It must have an even greater role in the establishment of a new international economic order. The Charter of Economic Rights and Duties of States, for the preparation of which the present Declaration will provide an additional source of inspiration, will constitute a significant contribution in this respect. All the States Members of the United Nations are therefore called upon to exert maximum efforts with a view to securing the implementation of the present Declaration, which is one of the principal guarantees for the creation of better conditions for all peoples to reach a life worthy of human dignity.

7. The present Declaration on the Establishment of a New International Economic Order shall be one of the most important bases of economic relations between all peoples and all nations.

4. PROGRAMME OF ACTION ON THE ESTABLISHMENT OF A NEW INTERNATIONAL ECONOMIC ORDER (1974) G.A. Res. 3202 (S-VI), U.N. GAOR, Sixth Special Session, Supp. (No.1), U.N.Doc.A/9559 (1974).

THE GENERAL ASSEMBLY

Adopts the following Programme of Action:

PROGRAMME OF ACTION ON THE ESTABLISHMENT OF A NEW
INTERNATIONAL ECONOMIC ORDER

Contents

Section

Introduction

VIII. Assistance in the exercise of permanent sovereignty of States over natural resources

IX. Strengthening the role of the United Nations system in the field of international economic co-operation

X. Special Programme

Introduction

1. In view of the continuing severe economic imbalance in the relations between developed and developing countries, and in the context of the constant and continuing aggravation of the imbalance of the economies of the developing countries and the consequent need for the mitigation of their current economic difficulties, urgent and effective measures need to be taken by the international community to assist the developing countries, while devoting particular attention to the least developed, land-locked and island developing countries and those developing countries most seriously affected by economic crises and natural calamities leading to serious retardation of development processes.

2. With a view to ensuring the application of the Declaration on the Establishment of a New International Economic Order, it will be necessary to adopt and implement within a specified period a programme of action of unprecedented scope and to bring about maximum economic co-operation and understanding among all States, particularly between developed and developing countries, based on the principles of dignity and sovereign equality.

I. Fundamental Problems of Raw Materials and Primary Commodities as Related to Trade and Development

1. Raw materials

All efforts should be made:

(*a*) To put an end to all forms of foreign occupation, racial discrimination, *apartheid*, colonial, neo-colonial and alien domination and exploitation through the exercise of permanent sovereignty over natural resources;

(*b*) To take measures for the recovery, exploitation, development, marketing and distribution of natural resources, particularly of developing countries, to serve their national interests, to promote collective self-reliance among them and to strengthen mutually beneficial international economic co-operation with a view to bringing about the accelerated development of developing countries;

(*c*) To facilitate the functioning and to further the aims of producers' associations, including their joint marketing arrangements, orderly commodity trading, improvement in the export income of producing developing countries and in their terms of trade, and sustained growth of the world economy for the benefit of all;

(*d*) To evolve a just and equitable relationship between the prices of raw materials, primary commodities, manufactured and semi-manufactured goods exported by developing countries and the prices of raw materials, primary commodities, food, manufactured and semi-manufactured goods and capital equipment imported by them, and to work for a link between the prices of exports of developing countries and the prices of their imports from developed countries;

(*e*) To take measures to reverse the continued trend of stagnation or decline in the real price of several commodities exported by developing countries, despite a general rise in commodity prices, resulting in a decline in the export earnings of these developing countries;

(*f*) To take measures to expand the markets for natural products in relation to synthetics, taking into account the interests of the developing countries, and to utilize fully the ecological advantages of these products;

(*g*) To take measures to promote the processing of raw materials in the producer developing countries.

2. Food

All efforts should be made:

(*a*) To take full account of specific problems of developing countries, particularly in times of food shortages, in the international efforts connected with the food problem;

(*b*) To take into account that, owing to lack of means, some developing countries have vast potentialities of unexploited or underexploited land which, if reclaimed and put into practical use, would contribute considerably to the solution of the food crisis;

(*c*) By the international community to undertake concrete and speedy measures with a view to arresting desertification, salination and damage by locusts or any other similar phenomenon involving several developing countries, particularly in Africa, and gravely affecting the agricultural production capacity of these countries, and also to assist the developing countries affected by any such phenomenon to develop the affected zones with a view to contributing to the solution of their food problems;

(*d*) To refrain from damaging or deteriorating natural resources and food resources, especially those derived from the sea, by preventing pollution and taking appropriate steps to protect and reconstitute those resources;

(*e*) By developed countries, in evolving their policies relating to production, stocks, imports and exports of food, to take full account of the interests of:

    i. Developing importing countries which cannot afford high prices for their imports;

    ii. Developing exporting countries which need increased market opportunities for their exports;

(*f*) To ensure that developing countries can import the necessary quantity of food without undue strain on their foreign exchange resources and without unpredictable deterioration in their balance of payments, and, in this context, that special measures are taken in respect of the least developed, land-locked and island developing countries as well as those developing countries most seriously affected by economic crises and natural calamities;

(*g*) To ensure that concrete measures to increase food production and storage facilities in developing countries are introduced, *inter alia*, by ensuring an increase in all available essential inputs, including fertilizers, from developed countries on favourable terms;

(*h*) To promote exports of food products of developing countries through just and equitable arrangements, *inter alia*, by the progressive elimination of such protective and other measures as constitute unfair competition.

3. General trade

All efforts should be made:

(*a*) To take the following measures for the amelioration of terms of trade of developing countries and concrete steps to eliminate chronic trade deficits of developing countries:

    i. Fulfilment of relevant commitments already undertaken in the United Nations Conference on Trade and Development and in the International Development Strategy for the Second United Nations Development Decade;

    ii. Improved access to markets in developed countries through the progressive removal of tariff and non-tariff barriers and of restrictive business practices;

    iii. Expeditious formulation of commodity agreements where appropriate, in order to regulate as necessary and to stabilize the world markets for raw materials and primary commodities;

    iv. Preparation of an over-all integrated programme, setting out guidelines and taking into account the current work in this field, for a comprehensive range of commodities of export interest to developing countries;

    v. Where products of developing countries compete with the domestic production in developed countries, each developed country should facilitate the expansion of imports from developing countries and provide a fair and reasonable opportunity to the developing countries to share in the growth of the market;

    vi. When the importing developed countries derive receipts from customs duties, taxes and other protective measures applied to imports of these products, consideration should be given to the claim of the developing countries that these receipts should be reimbursed in full to the exporting developing countries or devoted to providing additional resources to meet their development needs;

    vii. Developed countries should make appropriate adjustments in their economies so as to facilitate the expansion and diversification of imports from developing countries and thereby permit a rational, just and equitable international division of labour;

    viii. Setting up general principles for pricing policy for exports of commodities of developing countries, with a view to rectifying and achieving satisfactory terms of trade for them;

    ix. Until satisfactory terms of trade are achieved for all developing countries, consideration should be given to alternative means, including improved compensatory financing schemes for meeting the development needs of the developing countries concerned;

x. Implementation, improvement and enlargement of the generalized system of preferences for exports of agricultural primary commodities, manufactures and semi-manufactures from developing to developed countries and consideration of its extension to commodities, including those which are processed or semi-processed; developing countries which are or will be sharing their existing tariff advantages in some developed countries as the result of the introduction and eventual enlargement of the generalized system of preferences should, as a matter of urgency, be granted new openings in the markets of other developed countries which should offer them export opportunities that at least compensate for the sharing of those advantages;

xi. The setting up of buffer stocks within the framework of commodity arrangements and their financing by international financial institutions, wherever necessary, by the developed countries and, when they are able to do so, by the developing countries, with the aim of favouring the producer developing and consumer developing countries and of contributing to the expansion of world trade as a whole;

xii. In cases where natural materials can satisfy the requirements of the market, new investment for the expansion of the capacity to produce synthetic materials and substitutes should not be made;

(b) To be guided by the principles of non-reciprocity and preferential treatment of developing countries in multilateral trade negotiations between developed and developing countries, and to seek sustained and additional benefits for the international trade of developing countries, so as to achieve a substantial increase in their foreign exchange earnings, diversification of their exports and acceleration of the rate of their economic growth.

4. Transportation and insurance

All efforts should be made:

(a) to promote an increasing and equitable participation of developing countries in the world shipping tonnage:

(b) To arrest and reduce the ever-increasing freight rates in order to reduce the costs of imports to, and exports from, the developing countries;

(c) To minimize the cost of insurance and re-insurance for developing countries and to assist the growth of domestic insurance and reinsurance markets in developing countries and the establishment to this end, where appropriate, of institutions in these countries or at the regional level;

(d) To ensure the early implementation of the code of conduct for liner conferences;

(e) To take urgent measures to increase the import and export capability of the least developed countries and to offset the disadvantages of the adverse geographic situation of land-locked countries, particularly with regard to their transportation and transit costs, as well as developing island countries in order to increase their trading ability;

(*f*) By the developed countries to refrain from imposing measures or implementing policies designed to prevent the importation, at equitable prices, of commodities from the developing countries or from frustrating the implementation of legitimate measures and policies adopted by the developing countries in order to improve prices and encourage the export of such commodities.

II. International Monetary System and Financing of the Development of Developing Countries

1. Objectives

All efforts should be made to reform the international monetary system with, *inter alia*, the following objectives:

(*a*) Measures to check the inflation already experienced by the developed countries, to prevent it from being transferred to developing countries and to study and devise possible arrangements within the International Monetary Fund to mitigate the effects of inflation in developed countries on the economies of developing countries;

(*b*) Measures to eliminate the instability of the international monetary system, in particular the uncertainty of the exchange rates, especially as it affects adversely the trade in commodities;

(*c*) Maintenance of the real value of the currency reserves of the developing countries by preventing their erosion from inflation and exchange rate depreciation of reserve currencies;

(*d*) Full and effective participation of developing countries in all phases of decision-making for the formulation of an equitable and durable monetary system and adequate participation of developing countries in all bodies entrusted with this reform and, particularly, in the proposed Council of Governors of the International Monetary Fund;

(*e*) Adequate and orderly creation of additional liquidity with particular regard to the needs of the developing countries through the additional allocation of special drawing rights based on the concept of world liquidity needs to be appropriately revised in the light of the new international environment; any creation of international liquidity should be made through international multilateral mechanisms;

(*f*) Early establishment of a link between special drawing rights and additional development financing in the interest of developing countries, consistent with the monetary characteristics of special drawing rights;

(*g*) Review by the International Monetary Fund of the relevant provisions in order to ensure effective participation by developing countries in the decision-making process;

(*h*) Arrangements to promote an increasing net transfer of real resources from the developed to the developing countries;

(*i*) Review of the methods of operation of the International Monetary Fund, in particular the terms for both credit repayments and "stand-by" arrangements, the system of compensatory financing, and the terms of the financing of commodity buffer stocks, so as to enable the developing countries to make more effective use of them.

2. Measures

All efforts should be made to take the following urgent measures to finance the development of developing countries of the time-bound programme, as already laid down in the International Development Strategy for the Second United Nations Development Decade, for the net amount of financial resource transfers to developing countries; increase in the official component of the net amount of financial resource transfers to developing countries so as to meet and even to exceed the target of the Strategy;

(*b*) International financing institutions should effectively play their role as development financing banks without discrimination on account of the political or economic system of any member country, assistance being untied;

(*c*) More effective participation by developing countries, whether recipients or contributors, in the decision-making process in the competent organs of the International Bank for Reconstruction and Development and the International Development Association, through the establishment of a more equitable pattern of voting rights;

(*d*) Exemption, wherever possible, of the developing countries from all import and capital outflow controls imposed by the developed countries;

(*e*) Promotion of foreign investment, both public and private, from developed to developing countries in accordance with the needs and requirements in sectors of their economies as determined by the recipient countries;

(*f*) Appropriate urgent measures, including international action, should be taken to mitigate adverse consequences for the current and future development of developing countries arising from the burden of external debt contracted on hard terms;

(*g*) Debt renegotiation on a case-by-case basis with a view to concluding agreements on debt cancellation, moratorium, rescheduling or interest subsidization;

(*h*) International financial institutions should take into account the special situation of each developing country in reorienting their lending policies to suit these urgent needs; there is also need for improvement in practices of international financial institutions in regard to, *inter alia*, development financing and international monetary problems;

(*i*) Appropriate steps should be taken to give priority to the least developed, land-locked and island developing countries and to the countries most seriously affected by economic crises and natural calamities, in the availability of loans for development purposes which should include more favourable terms and conditions.

III. Industrialization

All efforts should be made by the international community to take measures to encourage the industrialization of the developing countries, and to this end:

(*a*) The developed countries should respond favourably, within the framework of their official aid as well as international financial institutions, to the requests of developing countries for the financing of industrial projects;

(*b*) The developed countries should encourage investors to finance industrial production projects, particularly export-oriented production, in developing countries, in agreement with the latter and within the context of their laws and regulations;

(*c*) With a view to bringing about a new international economic structure which should increase the share of the developing countries in world industrial production, the developed countries and the agencies of the United Nations system, in co-operation with the developing countries, should contribute to setting up new industrial capacities including raw materials and commodity-transforming facilities as a matter of priority in the developing countries that produce those raw materials and commodities;

(*d*) The international community should continue and expand, with the aid of the developed countries and the international institutions, the operational and instruction-oriented technical assistance programmes, including vocational training and management development of national personnel of the developing countries, in the light of their special development requirements.

IV. Transfer of Technology

All efforts should be made:

(*a*) To formulate an international code of conduct for the transfer of technology corresponding to needs and conditions prevalent in developing countries;

(*b*) To give access on improved terms to modern technology and to adapt that technology, as appropriate, to specific economic, social and ecological conditions and varying stages of development in developing countries;

(*c*) To expand significantly the assistance from developed to developing countries in research and development programmes and in the creation of suitable indigenous technology;

(*d*) To adapt commercial practices governing transfer of technology to the requirements of the developing countries and to prevent abuse of the rights of sellers;

(*e*) To promote international co-operation in research and development in exploration and exploitation, conservation and the legitimate utilization of natural resources and all sources of energy.

In taking the above measures, the special needs of the least developed and land-locked countries should be borne in mind.

V. Regulation and Control Over the Activities of Transnational Corporations

All efforts should be made to formulate, adopt and implement an international code of conduct for transnational corporations:

(*a*) To prevent interference in the internal affairs of the countries where they operate and their collaboration with racist régimes and colonial administrations;

(*b*) To regulate their activities in host countries, to eliminate restrictive business practices and to conform to the national development plans and objectives of developing countries, and in this context facilitate, as necessary, the review and revision of previously concluded arrangements;

(*c*) To bring about assistance, transfer of technology and management skills to developing countries on equitable and favourable terms;

(*d*) To regulate the repatriation of the profits accruing from their operations, taking into account the legitimate interests of all parties concerned;

(*e*) To promote reinvestment of their profits in developing countries.

VI. Charter of Economic Rights and Duties of States

The Charter of Economic Rights and Duties of States, the draft of which is being prepared by a working group of the United Nations and which the General Assembly has already expressed the intention of adopting at its twenty-ninth regular session, shall constitute an effective instrument towards the establishment of a new system of international economic relations based on equity, sovereign equality, and interdependence of the interests of developed and developing countries. It is therefore of vital importance that the aforementioned Charter be adopted by the General Assembly at its twenty-ninth session.

VII. Promotion of Co-Operation Among Developing Countries

1. Collective self-reliance and growing co-operation among developing countries will further strengthen their role in the new international economic order. Developing countries, with a view to expanding co-operation at the regional, subregional and interregional levels, should take further steps, *inter alia*:

a. To support the establishment and/or improvement of an appropriate mechanism to defend the prices of their exportable commodities and to improve access to and stabilize markets for them. In this context the increasingly effective mobilization by the whole group of oil-exporting countries of their natural resources for the benefit of their economic development is to be welcomed. At the same time there is the paramount need for co-operation among the developing countries in evolving urgently and in a spirit of solidarity all possible means to assist developing countries to cope with the immediate problems resulting from this legitimate and perfectly justified action. The measures already taken in this regard are a positive indication of the evolving co-operation between developing countries;

b. To protect their inalienable right to permanent sovereignty over their natural resources;

c. To promote, establish or strengthen economic integration at the regional and subregional levels;

d. To increase considerably their imports from other developing countries;

e. To ensure that no developing country accords to imports from developed countries more favourable treatment than that accorded to imports from developing countries. Taking into account the existing international agreements, current limitations and possibilities and also their future evolution, preferential treatment should be given to the procurement of import requirements from other developing countries. Wherever possible, preferential treatment should be given to imports from developing countries and the exports of those countries;

f. To promote close co-operation in the fields of finance, credit relations and monetary issues, including the development of credit relations on a preferential basis and on favourable terms;

g. To strengthen efforts which are already being made by developing countries to utilize available financial resources for financing development in the developing countries through investment, financing of export-oriented and emergency projects and other long-term assistance;

h. To promote and establish effective instruments of co-operation in the fields of industry, science and technology, transport, shipping and mass communication media.

2. Developed countries should support initiatives in the regional, subregional and interregional co-operation of developing countries through the extension of financial and technical assistance by more effective and concrete actions, particularly in the field of commercial policy.

VIII. Assistance in the Exercise of Permanent Sovereignty of States Over Natural Resources

All efforts should be made:

(*a*) To defeat attempts to prevent the free and effective exercise of the rights of every State to full and permanent sovereignty over its natural resources;

(*b*) To ensure that competent agencies of the United Nations system meet requests for assistance from developing countries in connexion with the operation of nationalized means of production.

IX. Strengthening the Role of the United Nations System in the Field of International Economic Co-Operation

1. In furtherance of the objectives of the International Development Strategy for the Second United Nations Development Decade and in accordance with the aims and objectives of the Declaration on the Establishment of a New

International Economic Order, all Member States pledge to make full use of the United Nations system in the implementation of the present Programme of Action, jointly adopted by them, in working for the establishment of a new international economic order and thereby strengthening the role of the United Nations in the field of world-wide co-operation for economic and social development.

2. The General Assembly of the United Nations shall conduct an over-all review of the implementation of the Programme of Action as a priority item. All the activities of the United Nations system to be undertaken under the Programme of Action as well as those already planned, such as the World Population Conference, 1974, the World Food Conference, the Second General Conference of the United Nations Industrial Development Organization and the mid-term review and appraisal of the International Development Strategy for the Second United Nations Development Decade should be so directed as to enable the special session of the General Assembly on development, called for under Assembly resolution 3172 (XXVIII) of 17 December 1973, to make its full contribution to the establishment of the new international economic order. All Member States are urged, jointly and individually, to direct their efforts and policies towards the success of that special session.

3. The Economic and Social Council shall define the policy framework and co-ordinate the activities of all organizations, institutions and subsidiary bodies within the United Nations system which shall be entrusted with the task of implementing the present Programme of Action. In order to enable the Economic and Social Council to carry out its tasks effectively:

a. All organizations, institutions and subsidiary bodies concerned within the United Nations system shall submit to the Economic and Social Council progress reports on the implementation of the Programme of Action within their respective fields of competence as often as necessary, but not less than once a year;

b. The Economic and Social Council shall examine the progress reports as a matter of urgency, to which end it may be convened, as necessary, in special session or, if need be, may function continuously. It shall draw the attention of the General Assembly to the problems and difficulties arising in connexion with the implementation of the Programme of Action.

4. All organizations, institutions, subsidiary bodies and conferences of the United Nations system are entrusted with the implementation of the Programme of Action. The activities of the United Nations Conference on Trade and Development, as set forth in General Assembly resolution 1995 (XIX) of 30 December 1964, should be strengthened for the purpose of following in collaboration with other competent organizations the development of international trade in raw materials throughout the world.

5. Urgent and effective measures should be taken to review the lending policies of international financial institutions, taking into account the special situation of each developing country, to suit urgent needs, to improve the practices of these institutions in regard to *inter alia*, development financing and international monetary problems, and to ensure more effective participation by

developing countries—whether recipients or contributors—in the decision-making process through appropriate revision of the pattern of voting rights.

6. The developed countries and others in a position to do so should contribute substantially to the various organizations, programmes and funds established within the United Nations system for the purpose of accelerating economic and social development in developing countries.

7. The present Programme of Action complements and strengthens the goals and objectives embodied in the International Development Strategy for the Second United Nations Development Decade as well as the new measures formulated by the General Assembly at its twenty-eighth session to offset the shortfalls in achieving those goals and objectives.

8. The implementation of the Programme of Action should be taken into account at the time of the mid-term review and appraisal of the International Development Strategy for the Second United Nations Development Decade. New commitments, changes, additions and adaptations in the Strategy should be made, as appropriate, taking into account the Declaration on the Establishment of a New International Economic Order and the present Programme of Action.

X. Special Programme

The General Assembly adopts the following Special Programme, including particularly emergency measures to mitigate the difficulties of the developing countries most seriously affected by economic crisis, bearing in mind the particular problem of the least developed and land-locked countries:

THE GENERAL ASSEMBLY,

Taking into account the following considerations:

a. The sharp increase in the prices of their essential imports such as food, fertilizers, energy products, capital goods, equipment and services, including transportation and transit costs, has gravely exacerbated the increasingly adverse terms of trade of a number of developing countries, added to the burden of their foreign debt and cumulatively, created a situation which, if left untended, will make it impossible for them to finance their essential imports and development and result in a further deterioration in the levels and conditions of life in these countries. The present crisis is the outcome of all the problems that have accumulated over the years: in the field of trade, in monetary reform, the world-wide inflationary situation, inadequacy and delay in provision of financial assistance and many other similar problems in the economic and developmental fields. In facing the crisis, this complex situation must be borne in mind so as to ensure that the Special Programme adopted by the international community provides emergency relief and timely assistance to the most seriously affected countries. Simultaneously, steps are being taken to resolve these outstanding problems through a fundamental restructuring of the world economic system, in order to allow these countries while solving the present difficulties to reach an acceptable level of development.

b. The special measures adopted to assist the most seriously affected countries must encompass not only the relief which they require on an emergency basis to maintain their import requirements, but also, beyond that, steps to consciously promote the capacity of these countries to produce and earn more. Unless such a comprehensive approach is adopted, there is every likelihood that the difficulties of the most seriously affected countries may be perpetuated. Nevertheless, the first and most pressing task of the international community is to enable these countries to meet the shortfall in their balance-of-payments positions. But this must be simultaneously supplemented by additional development assistance to maintain and thereafter accelerate their rate of economic development.

c. The countries which have been most seriously affected are precisely those which are at the greatest disadvantage in the world economy: the least developed, the land-locked and other low-income developing countries as well as other developing countries whose economies have been seriously dislocated as a result of the present economic crisis, natural calamities, and foreign aggression and occupation. An indication of the countries thus affected, the level of the impact on their economies and the kind of relief and assistance they require can be assessed on the basis, *inter alia*, of the following criteria:

    i. Low *per capita* income as a reflection of relative poverty, low productivity, low level of technology and development;

    ii. Sharp increase in their import cost of essentials relative to export earnings;

    iii. High ratio of debt servicing to export earnings;

    iv. Insufficiency in export earnings, comparative inelasticity of export incomes and unavailability of exportable surplus;

    v. Low level of foreign exchange reserves or their inadequacy for requirements;

    vi. Adverse impact of higher transportation and transit costs;

    vii. Relative importance of foreign trade in the development process.

d. The assessment of the extent and nature of the impact on the economies of the most seriously affected countries must be made flexible, keeping in mind the present uncertainty in the world economy, the adjustment policies that may be adopted by the developed countries and the flow of capital and investment. Estimates of the payments situation and needs of these countries can be assessed and projected reliably only on the basis of their average performance over a number of years. Long-term projections, at this time, cannot but be uncertain.

e. It is important that, in the special measures to mitigate the difficulties of the most seriously affected countries, all the developed countries as well as the developing countries should contribute according to their level of development and the capacity and strength of their economics. It is notable that some developing countries, despite their own difficulties and development needs, have shown a willingness to play a concrete and helpful role in ameliorating the difficulties faced by the poorer developing countries. The various initiatives and measures taken recently by certain developing countries with adequate resources on a bilateral and multilateral basis to contribute to alleviating the difficulties of other developing countries are a reflection of their commitment to the principle of effective economic co-operation among developing countries.

f. The response of the developed countries which have by far the greater capacity to assist the affected countries in overcoming their present difficulties must be commensurate with their responsibilities. Their assistance should be in addition to the presently available levels of aid. They should fulfil and if possible exceed the targets of the International Development Strategy for the Second United Nations Development Decade on financial assistance to the developing countries, especially that relating to official development assistance. They should also give serious consideration to the cancellation of the external debts of the most seriously affected countries. This would provide the simplest and quickest relief to the affected countries. Favourable consideration should also be given to debt moratorium and rescheduling. The current situation should not lead the industrialized countries to adopt what will ultimately prove to be a self-defeating policy aggravating the present crisis.

Recalling the constructive proposals made by His Imperial Majesty the Shahanshah of Iran and His Excellency Mr. Houari Boumediène, President of the People's Democratic Republic of Algeria,

1. *Decides* to launch a Special Programme to provide emergency relief and development assistance to the developing countries most seriously affected, as a matter of urgency, and for the period of time necessary, at least until the end of the Second United Nations Development Decade, to help them overcome their present difficulties and to achieve self-sustaining economic development;

2. *Decides* as a first step in the Special Programme to request the Secretary-General to launch an emergency operation to provide timely relief to the most seriously affected developing countries, as defined in subparagraph (c) above, with the aim of maintaining unimpaired essential imports for the duration of the coming twelve months and to invite the industrialized countries and other potential contributors to announce their contributions for emergency assistance, or intimate their intention to do so, by 15 June 1974 to be provided through bilateral or multilateral channels, taking into account the commitments and measures of assistance announced or already taken by some countries, and further requests the Secretary-General to report the progress of the emergency operation to the General Assembly at its twenty-ninth session, through the Economic and Social Council at its fifty-seventh session;

3. *Calls upon* the industrialized countries and other potential contributors to extend to the most seriously affected countries immediate relief and assistance which must be of an order of magnitude that is commensurate with the needs of these countries. Such assistance should be in addition to the existing level of aid and provided at a very early date to the maximum possible extent on a great

basis and, where not possible, on soft terms. The disbursement and relevant operational procedures and terms must reflect this exceptional situation. The assistance could be provided either through bilateral or multilateral channels, including such new institutions and facilities that have been or are to be set up. The special measures may include the following:

a. Special arrangements on particularly favourable terms and conditions including possible subsidies for and assured supplies of essential commodities and goods;

b. Deferred payments for all or part of imports of essential commodities and goods;

c. Commodity assistance, including food aid, on a grant basis or deferred payments in local currencies, bearing in mind that this should not adversely affect the exports of developing countries;

d. Long-term suppliers' credits on easy terms;

e. Long-term financial assistance on concessionary terms;

f. Drawings from special International Monetary Fund facilities on concessional terms;

g. Establishment of a link between the creation of special drawing rights and development assistance, taking into account the additional financial requirements of the most seriously affected countries;

h. Subsidies, provided bilaterally or multilaterally, for interest on funds available on commercial terms borrowed by the most seriously affected countries;

i. Debt renegotiation on a case-by-case basis with a view to concluding agreements on debt cancellation, moratorium or rescheduling;

j. Provision on more favourable terms of capital goods and technical assistance to accelerate the industrialization of the affected countries;

k. Investment in industrial and development projects on favourable terms;

l. Subsidizing the additional transit and transport costs, especially of the land-locked countries;

4. *Appeals* to the developed countries to consider favourably the cancellation, moratorium or rescheduling of the debts of the most seriously affected developing countries, on their request, as an important contribution to mitigating the grave and urgent difficulties of these countries;

5. *Decides* to establish a Special Fund under the auspices of the United Nations, through voluntary contributions from industrialized countries and other potential contributors, as a part of the Special Programme, to provide emergency relief and development assistance, which will commence its operations at the latest by 1 January 1975;

6. *Establishes* an *Ad Hoc* Committee on the Special Programme, composed of thirty-six Member States appointed by the President of the General Assembly, after appropriate consultations, bearing in mind the purposes of the Special Fund and its terms of reference:

(a) To make recommendations, *inter alia*, on the scope, machinery and modes of operation of the Special Fund, taking into account the need for:

i. Equitable representation on its governing body;

ii. Equitable distribution of its resources;

iii. Full utilization of the services and facilities of existing international organizations;

iv. The possibility of merging the United Nations Capital Development Fund with the operations of the Special Fund;

v. A central monitoring body to oversee the various measures being taken both bilaterally and multilaterally;

and, to this end, bearing in mind the different ideas and proposals submitted at the sixth special session, including those put forward by Iran[10] and those made at the 2208th plenary meeting, and the comments thereon, and the possibility of utilizing the Special Fund to provided an alternative channel for normal development assistance after the emergency period;

(*b*) To monitor, pending commencement of the operations of the Special Fund, the various measures being taken both bilaterally and multilaterally to assist the most seriously affected countries;

(*c*) To prepare, on the basis of information provided by the countries concerned and by appropriate agencies of the United Nations system, a broad assessment of:

i. The magnitude of the difficulties facing the most seriously affected countries;

ii. The kind and quantities of the commodities and goods essentially required by them;

iii. Their need for financial assistance;

iv. Their technical assistance requirements, including especially access to technology;

7. *Requests* the Secretary-General of the United Nations, the Secretary-General of the United Nations Conference on Trade and Development, the President of the International Bank for Reconstruction and Development, the Managing Director of the International Monetary Fund, the Administrator of the United Nations Development Programme and the heads of the other competent international organizations to assist the *Ad Hoc* Committee on the Special Programme in performing the functions assigned to it under paragraph 6 above, and to help, as appropriate, in the operations of the Special Fund;

8. *Requests* the International Monetary Fund to expedite decisions on:

(*a*) The establishment of an extended special facility with a view to enabling the most seriously affected developing countries to participate in it on favourable terms;

(*b*) The creation of special drawing rights and the early establishment of the link between their allocation and development financing;

(*c*) The establishment and operation of the proposed new special facility to extend credits and subsidize interest charges on commercial funds borrowed by Member States, bearing in mind the interests of the developing countries and especially the additional financial requirements of the most seriously affected countries;

9. *Requests* the World Bank Group and the International Monetary fund to place their managerial, financial and technical services at the disposal of

Governments contributing to emergency financial relief so as to enable them to assist without delay in channelling funds to the recipients, making such institutional and procedural changes as may be required;

10. *Invites* the United Nations Development Programme to take the necessary steps, particularly at the country level, to respond on an emergency basis to requests for additional assistance which it may be called upon to render within the framework of the Special Programme;

11. *Requests* the *Ad Hoc* Committee on the Special Programme to submit its report and recommendations to the Economic and Social Council at its fifty-seventh session and invites the Council, on the basis of its consideration of that report, to submit suitable recommendations to the General Assembly at its twenty-ninth session;

12. *Decides* to consider as a matter of high priority at its twenty-ninth session, within the framework of a new international economic order, the question of special measures for the most seriously affected countries.

5. CHARTER OF ECONOMIC RIGHTS AND DUTIES OF STATES (1974) G.A. Res. 3281 (XXIX), 29 U.N. GAOR, Supp. (No.31) at 50, U.N.Doc.A/9631 (1974).

PREAMBLE

THE GENERAL ASSEMBLY,

Reaffirming the fundamental purposes of the United Nations, in particular, the maintenance of international peace and security, the development of friendly relations among nations and the achievement of international co-operation in solving international problems in the economic and social fields,

Affirming the need for strengthening international co-operation in these fields,

Reaffirming further the need for strengthening international co-operation for development,

Declaring that it is a fundamental purpose of this Charter to promote the establishment of the new international economic order, based on equity, sovereign equality, interdependence, common interest and co-operation among all States, irrespective of their economic and social systems,

Desirous of contributing to the creation of conditions for:

a. The attainment of wider prosperity among all countries and of higher standards of living for all peoples,

b. The promotion by the entire international community of economic and social progress of all countries, especially developing countries,

c. The encouragement of co-operation, on the basis of mutual advantage and equitable benefits for all peace-loving States which are willing to carry out the provisions of this Charter, in the economic, trade, scientific and technical fields, regardless of political, economic or social systems,

d. The overcoming of main obstacles in the way of the economic development of the developing countries,

e. The acceleration of the economic growth of developing countries with a view to bridging the economic gap between developing and developed countries,

f. The protection, preservation and enhancement of the environment,

Mindful of the need to establish and maintain a just and equitable economic and social order through:

a. The achievement of more rational and equitable international economic relations and the encouragement of structural changes in the world economy,

b. The creation of conditions which permit the further expansion of trade and intensification of economic co-operation among all nations,

c. The strengthening of the economic independence of developing countries,

d. The establishment and promotion of international economic relations, taking into account the agreed differences in development of the developing countries and their specific needs,

Determined to promote collective economic security for development particular of the developing countries, with strict respect for the sovereign equality of each State and through the co-operation of the entire international community,

Considering that genuine co-operation among States, based on joint consideration of and concerted action regarding international economic problems is essential for fulfilling the international community's common desire to achieve a just and rational development of all parts of the world,

Stressing the importance of ensuring appropriate conditions for the conduct of normal economic relations among all States, irrespective of differences of social and economic systems, and for the full respect for the rights of all peoples as well as the strengthening of instruments of international economic co-operation as means for the consolidation of peace for the benefit of all,

Convinced of the need to develop a system of international economic relations on the basis of sovereign equality, mutual and equitable benefit and a close interrelationship of the interests of all States,

Reiterating that the responsibility for the development of every country rests primarily upon itself but that concomitant and effective international co-operation is an essential factor for the full achievement of its own development goals,

Firmly convinced of the urgent need to evolve a substantially improved system of international economic relations,

Solemnly adopts the present Charter of Economic Rights and Duties of States

CHAPTER I

Fundamentals of international economic relations

Economic as well as political and other relations among States shall be governed, *inter alia*, by the following principles:

a. Sovereignty, territorial integrity and political independence of States;

b. Sovereign equality of all States;

c. Non aggression;

d. Non-intervention;

e. Mutual and equitable benefit;

f. Peaceful coexistence;

g. Equal rights and self-determination of peoples;

h. Peaceful settlement of disputes;

i. Remedying of injustices which have been brought about by force and which deprive a nation of the natural means necessary for its normal development;

j. Fulfilment in good faith of international obligations;

k. Respect for human rights and fundamental freedoms;

l. No attempt to seek hegemony and spheres of influence;

m. Promotion of international social justice;

n. International co-operation for development;

o. Free access to and from the sea by land-locked countries within the framework of the above principles.

CHAPTER II

Economic rights and duties of States

Article 1

Every State has the sovereign and inalienable right to choose its economic system as well as its political, social and cultural systems in accordance with the will of its people, without outside interference, coercion or threat in any form whatsoever.

Article 2

1. Every State has and shall freely exercise full permanent sovereignty, including possession, use and disposal, over all its wealth, natural resources and economic activities.

2. Each State has the right:

a. To regulate and exercise authority over foreign investment within its national jurisdiction in accordance with its laws and regulations and in conformity with its national objectives and priorities. No State shall be compelled to grant preferential treatment to foreign investment;

b. To regulate and supervise the activities of transnational corporations within its national jurisdiction and take measures to ensure that such activities comply with its laws, rules and regulations and conform with its economic and social policies. Transnational corporations shall not intervene in the internal affairs of a host State. Every State should, with full regard for its sovereign rights, co-operate with other States in the exercise of the right set forth in this subparagraph;

c. To nationalize, expropriate or transfer ownership of foreign property, in which case appropriate compensation should be paid by the State adopting such measures, taking into account its relevant laws and regulations and all circumstances that the State considers pertinent. In any case where the question of compensation gives rise to a controversy, it shall be settled under the domestic law of the nationalizing State and by its tribunals, unless it is freely and mutually agreed by all States concerned that other peaceful means be sought on the basis of the sovereign equality of States and in accordance with the principle of free choice of means.

Article 3

In the exploitation of natural resources shared by two or more countries, each State must co-operate on the basis of a system of information and prior consultations in order to achieve optimum use of such resources without causing damage to the legitimate interest of others.

Article 4

Every State has the right to engage in international trade and other forms of economic co-operation irrespective of any differences in political, economic and social systems. No State shall be subjected to discrimination of any kind based solely on such differences. In the pursuit of international trade and other forms of economic co-operation, every State is free to choose the forms of organization of its foreign economic relations and to enter into bilateral and multilateral arrangements consistent with its international obligations and with the needs of international economic co-operation.

Article 5

All States have the right to associate in organizations of primary commodity producers in order to develop their national economies to achieve stable financing for their development, and in pursuance of their aims, to assist in the promotion of sustained growth of the world economy, in particular accelerating the development of developing countries. Correspondingly all States have the duty to respect that right by refraining from applying economic and political measures that would limit it.

Article 6

It is the duty of States to contribute to the development of international trade of goods, particularly by means of arrangements and by the conclusion of long-term multilateral commodity agreements, where appropriate, and taking into account the interests of producers and consumers. All States share the responsibility to promote the regular flow and access of all commercial goods traded at stable, remunerative and equitable prices, thus contributing to the equitable development of the world economy, taking into account, in particular, the interests of developing countries.

Article 7

Every State has the primary responsibility to promote the economic, social and cultural development of its people. To this end, each State has the right and the responsibility to choose its means and goals of development, fully to mobilize and use its resources, to implement progressive economic and social reforms and to ensure the full participation of its people in the process and benefits of development. All States have the duty, individually and collectively, to co-operate in order to eliminate obstacles that hinder such mobilization and use.

Article 8

States should co-operate in facilitating more rational and equitable international economic relations and in encouraging structural changes in the context of a balanced world economy in harmony with the needs and interests of all countries, especially developing countries, and should take appropriate measures to this end.

Article 9

All States have the responsibility to co-operate in the economic, social, cultural, scientific and technological fields for the promotion of economic and social progress throughout the world, especially that of the developing countries.

Article 10

All States are juridically equal and, as equal members of the international community, have the right to participate fully and effectively in the international decision-making process in the solution of world economic, financial and monetary problems, *inter alia*, through the appropriate international organizations in accordance with their existing and evolving rules, and to share equitably in the benefits resulting therefrom.

Article 11

All States should co-operate to strengthen and continuously improve the efficiency of international organizations in implementing measures to stimulate the general economic progress of all countries, particularly of developing countries, and therefore should co-operate to adapt them, when appropriate, to the changing needs of international economic co-operation.

Article 12

1. States have the right, in agreement with the parties concerned, to participate in subregional, regional and interregional co-operation in the pursuit of their economic and social development. All States engaged in such co-operation have the duty to ensure that the policies of those groupings to which they belong correspond to the provisions of the Charter and are outward-looking, consistent with their international obligations and with the needs of international economic co-operation and have full regard for the legitimate interests of third countries, especially developing countries.

2. In the case of groupings to which the States concerned have transferred

or may transfer certain competences as regards matters that come within the scope of the present Charter, its provisions shall also apply to those groupings, in regard to such matters, consistent with the responsibilities of such States as members of such groupings. Those States shall co-operate in the observance by the groupings of the provisions of this Charter.

Article 13

1. Every State has the right to benefit from the advances and developments in science and technology for the acceleration of its economic and social development.

2. All States should promote international scientific and technological co-operation and the transfer of technology, with proper regard for all legitimate interests including, *inter alia*, the rights and duties of holders, suppliers and recipients of technology. In particular, all States should facilitate the access of developing countries to the achievements of modern science and technology, the transfer of technology and the creation of indigenous technology for the benefit of the developing countries in forms and in accordance with procedures which are suited to their economies and their needs.

3. Accordingly, developed countries should co-operate with the developing countries in the establishment, strengthening and development of their scientific and technological infrastructures and their scientific research and technological activities so as to help to expand and transform the economies of developing countries.

4. All States should co-operate in exploring with a view to evolving further internationally accepted guidelines or regulations for the transfer of technology, taking fully into account the interests of developing countries.

Article 14

Every State has the duty to co-operate in promoting a steady and increasing expansion and liberalization of world trade and an improvement in the welfare and living standards of all peoples, in particular those of developing countries. Accordingly, all States should co-operate, *inter alia*, towards the progressive dismantling of obstacles to trade and the improvement of the international framework for the conduct of world trade and, to these ends, co-ordinated efforts shall be made to solve in an equitable way the trade problems of all countries, taking into account the specific trade problems of the developing countries. In this connexion, States shall take measures aimed at securing additional benefits for the international trade of developing countries so as to achieve a substantial increase in their foreign exchange earnings, the diversification of their exports, the acceleration of the rate of growth of their trade, taking into account their development needs, an improvement in the possibilities for these countries to participate in the expansion of world trade and a balance more favourable to developing countries in the sharing of the advantages resulting from this expansion, through, in the the largest possible measure, a substantial improvement in the conditions of access for the products of interest to the developing countries and, wherever appropriate, measures designed to attain stable, equitable and remunerative prices for primary products.

Article 15

All States have the duty to promote the achievement of general and complete disarmament under effective international control and to utilize the resources freed by effective disarmament measures for the economic and social development of countries, allocating a substantial portion of such resources as additional means for the development needs of developing countries.

Article 16

1. It is the right and duty of all States, individually and collectively, to eliminate colonialism, *apartheid*, racial discrimination, neo-colonialism and all forms of foreign aggression, occupation and domination, and the economic and social consequences thereof, as a prerequisite for development. States which practice such coercive policies are economically responsible to the countries, territories and peoples affected for the restitution and full compensation for the exploitation and depletion of, and damages to, the natural and all other resources of those countries, territories and peoples. It is the duty of all States to extend assistance to them.

2. No State has the right to promote or encourage investments that may constitute an obstacle to the liberation of a territory occupied by force.

Article 17

International co-operation for development is the shared goal and common duty of all States. Every State should co-operate with the efforts of developing countries to accelerate their economic and social development by providing favourable external conditions and by extending active assistance to them, consistent with their development needs and objectives, with strict respect for the sovereign equality of States and free of any conditions derogating from their sovereignty.

Article 18

Developed countries should extend, improve and enlarge the system of generalized non-reciprocal and non-discriminatory tariff preferences to the developing countries consistent with the relevant agreed conclusions and relevant decisions as adopted on this subject, in the framework of the competent international organizations. Developed countries should also give serious consideration to the adoption of other differential measures, in areas where this is feasible and appropriate and in ways which will provide special and more favourable treatment, in order to meet the trade and development needs of the developing countries. In the conduct of international economic relations the developed countries should endeavour to avoid measures having a negative effect on the development of the national economies of the developing countries, as promoted by generalized tariff preferences and other generally agreed differential measures in their favour.

Article 19

With a view to accelerating the economic growth of developing countries and bridging the economic gap between developed and developing countries, developed countries should grant generalized preferential, non-reciprocal and non-discriminatory treatment to developing countries in those fields of international economic co-operation where it may be feasible.

Article 20

Developing countries should, in their efforts to increase their over-all trade, give due attention to the possibility of expanding their trade with socialist countries, by granting to these countries conditions for trade not inferior to those granted normally to the developed market economy countries.

Article 21

Developing countries should endeavour to promote the expansion of their mutual trade and to this end may, in accordance with the existing and evolving provisions and procedures of international agreements where applicable, grant trade preferences to other developing countries without being obliged to extend such preferences to developed countries, provided these arrangements do not constitute an impediment to general trade liberalization and expansion.

Article 22

1. All States should respond to the generally recognized or mutually agreed development needs and objectives of developing countries by promoting increased net flows of real resources to the developing countries from all sources, taking into account any obligations and commitments undertaken by the States concerned, in order to reinforce the efforts of developing countries to accelerate their economic and social development.

2. In this context, consistent with the aims and objectives mentioned above and taking into account any obligations and commitments undertaken in this regard, it should be their endeavour to increase the net amount of financial flows from official sources to developing countries and to improve the terms and conditions thereof.

3. The flow of development assistance resources should include economic and technical assistance.

Article 23

To enhance the effective mobilization of their own resources, the developing countries should strengthen their economic co-operation and expand their mutual trade so as to accelerate their economic and social development. All countries, especially developed countries, individually as well as through the competent international organizations of which they are members, should provide appropriate and effective support and co-operation.

Article 24

All States have the duty to conduct their mutual economic relations in a manner which takes into account the interests of other countries. In particular, all States should avoid prejudicing the interests of developing countries.

Article 25

In furtherance of world economic development, the international community, especially its developed members, shall pay special attention to the particular needs and problems of the least developed among the developing countries, of land-locked developing countries and also island developing countries, with a view to helping them to overcome their particular difficulties and thus contribute to their economic and social development.

Article 26

All States have the duty to coexist in tolerance and live together in peace, irrespective of differences in political, economic, social and cultural systems, and to facilitate trade between States having different economic and social systems. International trade should be conducted without prejudice to generalized non-discriminatory and non-reciprocal preferences in favour of developing countries, on the basis of mutual advantage, equitable benefits and the exchange of most-favoured-nation treatment.

Article 27

1. Every State has the right to enjoy fully the benefits of world invisible trade and to engage in the expansion of such trade.

2. World invisible trade, based on efficiency and mutual and equitable benefit, furthering the expansion of the world economy, is the common goal of all States. The role of developing countries in world invisible trade should be enhanced and strengthened consistent with the above objectives, particular attention being paid to the special needs of developing countries.

3. All States should co-operate with developing countries in their endeavours to increase their capacity to earn foreign exchange from invisible transactions, in accordance with the potential and needs of each developing country and consistent with the objectives mentioned above.

Article 28

All States have the duty to co-operate in achieving adjustments in the prices of exports of developing countries in relation to prices of their imports so as to promote just and equitable terms of trade for them, in a manner which is remunerative for producers and equitable for producers and consumers.

CHAPTER III

Common responsibilities towards the international community

Article 29

The sea-bed and ocean floor and the subsoil thereof, beyond the limits of national jurisdiction, as well as the resources of the area, are the common heritage of mankind. On the basis of the principles adopted by the General Assembly in resolution 2749 (XXV) of 17 December 1970, all States shall ensure that the exploration of the area and exploitation of its resources are carried out exclusively for peaceful purposes and that the benefits derived therefrom are shared equitably by all States, taking into account the particular interests and needs of developing countries; an international régime applying to the area and its resources and including appropriate international machinery to give effect to its provisions shall be established by an international treaty of a universal character, generally agreed upon.

Article 30

The protection, preservation and the enhancement of the environment for the present and future generations is the responsibility of all States. All States shall endeavour to establish their own environmental and developmental policies in conformity with such responsibility. The environmental policies of all States should enhance and not adversely affect the present and future development potential of developing countries. All States have the responsibility to ensure that activities within their jurisdiction or control do not cause damage to the environment of other States or of areas beyond the limits of national jurisdiction. All States should co-operate in evolving international norms and regulations in the field of the environment.

CHAPTER IV

Final provisions

Article 31

All States have the duty to contribute to the balanced expansion of the world economy, taking duly into account the close interrelationship between the well-being of the developed countries and the growth and development of the developing countries, and the fact that the prosperity of the international community as a whole depends upon the prosperity of its constituent parts.

Article 32

No State may use or encourage the use of economic, political or any other type of measures to coerce another State in order to obtain from it the subordination of the exercise of its sovereign rights.

Article 33

1. Nothing in the present Charter shall be construed as impairing or derogating from the provisions of the Charter of the United Nations or actions taken in pursuance thereof.

2. In their interpretation and application, the provisions of the present Charter are interrelated and each provision should be construed in the context of the other provisions.

Article 34

An item on the Charter of Economic Rights and Duties of States shall be inscribed in the agenda of the General Assembly at its thirtieth session, and thereafter on the agenda of every fifth session. In this way a systematic and comprehensive consideration of the implementation of the Charter, covering both progress achieved and any improvements and additions which might become necessary, would be carried out and appropriate measures recommended. Such consideration should take into account the evolution of all the economic, social, legal and other factors related to the principles upon which the present Charter is based and on its purpose.

6. UNIVERSAL DECLARATION ON THE ERADICATION OF HUNGER AND MALNUTRITION (1974)

Adopted on 16 November 1974 by the World Food Conference convened under General Assembly resolution 3180 (XXVIII) of 17 December 1973; and endorsed by the General Assembly in its resolution 3348 (XXIX) of 17 December 1974.

The World Food Conference,

Convened by the General Assembly of the United Nations and entrusted with developing ways and means whereby the international community, as a whole, could take specific action to resolve the world food problem within the broader context of development and international economic co-operation,
   Adopts the following Declaration:

UNIVERSAL DECLARATION ON THE ERADICATION OF HUNGER AND MALNUTRITION

Recognizing that:

(*a*) The grave food crisis that is afflicting the peoples of the developing countries where most of the world's hungry and ill-nourished live and where more than two thirds of the world's food—an imbalance which threatens to increase in the next 10 years—is not only fraught with grave economic and social implications, but also acutely jeopardizes the most fundamental principles and values associated with the right to life and human dignity as enshrined in the Universal Declaration of Human Rights;

(*b*) The elimination of hunger and malnutrition, included as one of the objectives in the United Nations Declaration on Social Progress and Development, and the elimination of the causes that determine this situation are the common objectives of all nations;

(*c*) The situation of the peoples afflicted by hunger and malnutrition arises from their historical circumstances, especially social inequalities, including in many cases alien and colonial domination, foreign occupation, racial discrimination, *apartheid* and neo-colonialism in all its forms, which continue to be among the greatest obstacles to the full emancipation and progress of the developing countries and all the peoples involved;

(*d*) This situation has been aggravated in recent years by a series of crises to which the world economy has been subjected, such as the deterioration in the international monetary system, the inflationary increase in import costs, the heavy burdens imposed by external debt on the balance of payments of many developing countries, a rising food demand partly due to demographic pressure, speculation, and a shortage of, and increased costs for, essential agricultural inputs;

(*e*) These phenomena should be considered within the framework of the on-going negotiations on the Charter of Economic Rights and Duties of States, and the General Assembly of the United Nations should be urged unanimously to agree upon, and to adopt, a Charter that will be an effective instrument for the establishment of new international economic relations based on principles of equity and justice;

(*f*) All countries, big or small, rich or poor, are equal. All countries have the full right to participate in the decisions on the food problem;

(*g*) The well-being of the peoples of the world largely depends on the adequate production and distribution of food as well as the establishment of a world food security system which would ensure adequate availability of, and reasonable prices for, food at all times, irrespective of periodic fluctuations and vagaries of weather and free of political and economic pressures, and should thus facilitate, amongst other things, the development process of developing countries;

(*h*) Peace and justice encompass an economic dimension helping the solution of the world economic problems, the liquidation of underdevelopment, offering a lasting and definitive solution of the food problem for all peoples and guaranteeing to all countries the right to implement freely and effectively their development programmes. To this effect, it is necessary to eliminate threats and resort to force and to promote peaceful co-operation between States to the fullest extent possible, to apply the principles of non-interference in the internal affairs of other States, full equality of rights and respect of national independence and sovereignty, as well as to encourage the peaceful co-operation between all States, irrespective of their political, social and economic systems. The further improvement of international relations will create better conditions for international co-operation in all fields which should make possible large financial and material resources to be used, *inter alia*, for developing agricultural production and substantially improving world food security;

(*i*) For a lasting solution of the food problem all efforts should be made to eliminate the widening gaps which today separate developed and developing countries and to bring about a new international economic order. It should be possible for all countries to participate actively and effectively in the new international economic relations by the establishment of suitable international systems, where appropriate, capable of producing adequate action in order to establish just and equitable relations in international economic co-operation;

(*j*) Developing countries reaffirm their belief that the primary responsibility for ensuring their own rapid development rests with themselves. They declare, therefore, their readiness to continue to intensify their individual and collective efforts with a view to expanding their mutual co-operation in the field of agricultural development and food production, including the eradication of hunger and malnutrition;

(k) Since, for various reasons, many developing countries are not yet always able to meet their own food needs, urgent and effective international actions should be taken to assist them, free of political pressures,

Consistent with the aims and objectives of the Declaration on the Establishment of a New International Economic Order and the Programme of Action adopted by the General Assembly at its sixth special session,

The Conference consequently solemnly proclaims:

1. Every man, woman and child has the inalienable right to be free from hunger and malnutrition in order to develop fully and maintain their physical and mental faculties. Society today already possesses sufficient resources, organizational ability and technology and hence the competence to achieve this objective. Accordingly, the eradication of hunger is a common objective of all the countries of the international community, especially of the developed countries and others in a position to help.

2. It is a fundamental responsibility of Governments to work together for higher food production and a more equitable and efficient distribution of food between countries and within countries. Governments should initiate immediately a greater concerted attack on chronic malnutrition and deficiency diseases among the vulnerable and lower income groups. In order to ensure adequate nutrition for all, Governments should formulate appropriate food and nutrition policies integrated in over-all socio-economic and agricultural development plans based on adequate knowledge of available as well as potential food resources. The importance of human milk in this connexion should be stressed on nutritional grounds.

3. Food problems must be tackled during the preparation and implementation of national plans and programmes for economic and social development, with emphasis on their humanitarian aspects.

4. It is a responsibility of each State concerned, in accordance with its sovereign judgement and internal legislation, to remove the obstacles to food production and to provide proper incentives to agricultural producers. Of prime importance for the attainment of these objectives are effective measures of socio-economic transformation by agrarian, tax, credit and investment policy reform and the reorganization of rural structures, such as the reform of the conditions of ownership, the encouragement of producer and consumer co-operatives, the mobilization of the full potential of human resources, both male and female, in the developing countries for an integrated rural development and the involvement of small farmers, fishermen and landless workers in attaining the required food production and employment targets. Moreover, it is necessary to recognize the key role of women in agricultural production and rural economy in many countries, and to ensure that appropriate education, extension programmes and financial facilities are made available to women on equal terms with men.

5. Marine and inland water resources are today becoming more important than ever as a source of food and economic prosperity. Accordingly, action should be taken to promote a rational exploitation of these resources, preferably

for direct human consumption, in order to contribute to meeting the food requirements of all peoples.

6. The efforts to increase food production should be complemented by every endeavour to prevent wastage of food in all its forms.

7. To give impetus to food production in developing countries and in particular in the least developed and most seriously affected among them, urgent and effective international actions should be taken, by the developed countries and other countries in a position to do so, to provide them with sustained additional technical and financial assistance on favourable terms and in a volume sufficient to their needs on the basis of bilateral and multilateral arrangements. This assistance must be free of conditions inconsistent with the sovereignty of the receiving States.

8. All countries, and primarily the highly industrialized countries, should promote the advancement of food production technology and should make all efforts to promote the transfer, adaptation and dissemination of appropriate food production technology for the benefit of the developing countries and, to that end, they should *inter alia* make all efforts to disseminate the results of their research work to Governments and scientific institutions of developing countries in order to enable them to promote a sustained agricultural development.

9. To assure the proper conservation of natural resources being utilized, or which might be utilized, for food production, all countries must collaborate in order to facilitate the preservation of the environment, including the marine environment.

10. All developed countries and others able to do so should collaborate technically and financially with the developing countries in their efforts to expand land and water resources for agricultural production and to assure a rapid increase in the availability, at fair costs, of agricultural inputs such as fertilizers and other chemicals, high-quality seeds, credit and technology. Co-operation among developing countries, in this connexion, is also important.

11. All States should strive to the utmost to readjust, where appropriate, their agricultural policies to give priority to food production, recognizing, in this connexion the interrelationship between the world food problem and international trade. In the determination of attitudes towards farm support programmes for domestic food production, developed countries should take into account, as far as possible, the interest of the food-exporting developing countries, in order to avoid detrimental effect on their exports. Moreover, all countries should co-operate to devise effective steps to deal with the problem of stabilizing world markets and promoting equitable and remunerative prices, where appropriate through international arrangements, to improve access to markets through reduction or elimination of tariff and non-tariff barriers on the products of interest to the developing countries, to substantially increase the export earnings of these countries, to contribute to the diversification of their exports, and apply to them, in the multilateral trade negotiations, the principles as agreed upon in the Tokyo Declaration, including the concept of non-reciprocity and more favourable treatment.

12. As it is the common responsibility of the entire international community to ensure the availability at all times of adequate world supplies of basic

food-stuffs by way of appropriate reserves, including emergency reserves, all countries should co-operate in the establishment of an effective system of world food security by:

Participating in and supporting the operation of the Global Information and Early Warning System on Food and Agriculture;

Adhering to the objectives, policies and guidelines of the proposed International Undertaking on World Food Security as endorsed by the World Food Conference;

Earmarking, where possible, stocks or funds for meeting international emergency food requirements as envisaged in the proposed International Undertaking on World Food Security and developing international guidelines to provide for the co-ordination and the utilization of such stocks;

Co-operating in the provision of food aid for meeting emergency and nutritional needs as well as for stimulating rural employment through development projects.

All donor countries should accept and implement the concept of forward planning of food aid and make all efforts to provide commodities and/or financial assistance that will ensure adequate quantities of grains and other food commodities.

Time is short. Urgent and sustained action is vital. The Conference, therefore, calls upon all peoples expressing their will as individuals, and through their Governments and non-governmental organizations, to work together to bring about the end of the age-old scourge of hunger.

The Conference affirms:

The determination of the participating States to make full use of the United Nations system in the implementation of this Declaration and the other decisions adopted by the Conference.

7. DECLARATION ON THE USE OF SCIENTIFIC AND TECHNOLOGICAL PROGRESS IN THE INTERESTS OF PEACE AND FOR THE BENEFIT OF MANKIND

(1975) G.A. Res. 3384 (XXX), 30 U.N. GAOR Supp. (No. 34) at 86, U.N. Doc. A/10034 (1975).

THE GENERAL ASSEMBLY,

Noting that scientific and technological progress has become one of the most important factors in the development of human society,

Taking into consideration that, while scientific and technological developments provide ever increasing opportunities to better the conditions of life of peoples and nations, in a number of instances they can give rise to social problems, as well as threaten the human rights and fundamental freedoms of the individual,

Noting with concern that scientific and technological achievements can be used to intensify the arms race, suppress national liberation movements and deprive individuals and peoples of their human rights and fundamental freedoms,

Also noting with concern that scientific and technological achievements can entail dangers for the civil and political rights of the individual or of the group and for human dignity,

Noting the urgent need to make full use of scientific and technological developments for the welfare of man and to neutralize the present and possible future harmful consequences of certain scientific and technological achievements,

Recognizing that scientific and technological progress is of great importance in accelerating the social and economic development of developing countries,

Aware that the transfer of science and technology is one of the principal ways of accelerating the economic development of developing countries,

Reaffirming the right of peoples to self-determination and the need to respect human rights and freedoms and the dignity of the human person in the conditions of scientific and technological progress,

Desiring to promote the realization of the principles which form the basis of the Charter of the United Nations, the Universal Declaration of Human Rights, the International Covenants on Human Rights, the Declaration on the Granting of Independence to Colonial Countries and Peoples, the Declaration on Principles of International Law concerning Friendly Relations and Co-operation among States in accordance with the Charter of the United Nations, the Declaration on Social Progress and Development, and the Charter of Economic Rights and Duties of States,

Solemnly proclaims that:

1. All States shall promote international co-operation to ensure that the results of scientific and technological developments are used in the interests of strengthening international peace and security, freedom and independence, and also for the purpose of the economic and social development of peoples and the realization of human rights and freedoms in accordance with the Charter of the United Nations.

2. All States shall take appropriate measures to prevent the use of scientific and technological developments, particularly by the State organs, to limit or interfere with the enjoyment of the human rights and fundamental freedoms of the individual as enshrined in the Universal Declaration of Human Rights, the International Covenants on Human Rights and other relevant international instruments.

3. All States shall take measures to ensure that scientific and technological achievements satisfy the material and spiritual needs of all sectors of the population.

4. All States shall refrain from any acts involving the use of scientific and technological achievements for the purpose of violating the sovereignty and

territorial integrity of other States, interfering in their internal affairs, waging aggressive wars, suppressing national liberation movements or pursuing a policy of racial discrimination. Such acts are not only a flagrant violation of the Charter of the United Nations and principles of international law, but constitute an inadmissible distortion of the purposes that should guide scientific and technological developments for the benefit of mankind.

5. All States shall co-operate in the establishment, strengthening and development of the scientific and technological capacity of developing countries with a view to accelerating the realization of the social and economic rights of the peoples of those countries.

6. All States shall take measures to extend the benefits of science and technology to all strata of the population and to protect them, both socially and materially, from possible harmful effects of the misuse of scientific and technological developments, including their misuse to infringe upon the rights of the individual or of the group, particularly with regard to respect for privacy and the protection of the human personality and its physical and intellectual integrity.

7. All States shall take the necessary measures, including legislative measures, to ensure that the utilization of scientific and technological achievements promotes the fullest realization of human rights and fundamental freedoms without any discrimination whatsoever on grounds of race, sex, language or religious beliefs.

8. All States shall take effective measures, including legislative measures, to prevent and preclude the utilization of scientific and technological achievements to the detriment of human rights and fundamental freedoms and the dignity of the human person.

9. All States shall, whenever necessary, take action to ensure compliance with legislation guaranteeing human rights and freedoms in the conditions of scientific and technological developments.

8. DECLARATION ON THE RIGHT OF PEOPLES TO PEACE (1984) G. A. Res. 39/11 (1984).

THE GENERAL ASSEMBLY,

Having considered the item entitled "Right of peoples to peace",

Convinced that a proclamation of the right of peoples to peace would contribute to the efforts aimed at the strengthening of international peace and security,

1. *Approves* the Declaration on the Right of Peoples to Peace, the text of which is annexed to the present resolution;

2. *Requests* the Secretary-General to ensure the widest dissemination of the Declaration to States, intergovernmental and non-governmental organizations as well as other appropriate organizations.

ANNEX

DECLARATION ON THE RIGHT OF PEOPLES TO PEACE

THE GENERAL ASSEMBLY,

Reaffirming that the principal aim of the United Nations is the maintenance of international peace and security,

Bearing in mind the fundamental principles of international law set forth in the Charter of the United Nations,

Expressing the will and the aspirations of all peoples to eradicate war from the life of mankind and above all, to avert a world-wide nuclear catastrophe,

Convinced that life without war serves as the primary international prerequisite for the material well-being, development and progress of countries, and for the full implementation of the rights and fundamental human freedoms proclaimed by the United Nations,

Aware that in the nuclear age the establishment of a lasting peace on Earth represents the primary condition for the preservation of human civilization and the survival of mankind,

Recognizing that the maintenance of a peaceful life for peoples is the sacred duty of each State,

1. *Solemnly proclaims* that the peoples of our planet have a sacred right to peace;

2. *Solemnly declares* that the preservation of the right of peoples to peace and the promotion of its implementation constitute a fundamental obligation of each State;

3. *Emphasizes* that ensuring the exercise of the right of peoples to peace demands that the policies of States be directed towards the elimination of the threat of war, particularly nuclear war, the renunciation of the use of force in international relations and the settlement of international disputes by peaceful means on the basis of the Charter of the United Nations;

4. *Appeals* to all States and international organizations to do their utmost to assist in implementing the right of peoples to peace through the adoption of appropriate measures at both the national and the international level.

M. REAFFIRMATION OF PRINCIPLES

INTRODUCTION

This document is presented here as a summary of the United Nations' concerns in the human rights area. It revisits many of the themes of the previous pages and captures the way in which they fit together in the work of the organization. It was adopted as the Final Act of the International Conference on Human Rights held under United Nations auspices in Teheran in 1968 and was later endorsed by the General Assembly as "an important and timely reaffirmation of the principles embodied in the Universal Declaration of Human Rights and in other international instruments in the field of human rights." G.A. Resolution 2442 (XXIII), 23 UN GAOR, Supp. No. 18 at 49–50, U.N.Doc. A/7218 (1968).

1. PROCLAMATION OF TEHERAN (1968) 23 U.N. GAOR, U.N. Doc. A/Conf. 32/41 (1968).

THE INTERNATIONAL CONFERENCE ON HUMAN RIGHTS,

Having met at Teheran from April 22 to May 13, 1968 to review the progress made in the twenty years since the adoption of the Universal Declaration of Human Rights and to formulate a programme for the future,

Having considered the problems relating to the activities of the United Nations for the promotion and encouragement of respect for human rights and fundamental freedoms,

Bearing in mind resolutions adopted by the Conference,

Noting that the observance of the International Year for Human Rights takes place at a time when the world is undergoing a process of unprecedented change,

Having regard to the new opportunities made available by the rapid progress of science and technology,

Believing that, in an age when conflict and violence prevail in many parts of the world, the fact of human interdependence and the need for human solidarity are more evident than ever before,

Recognizing that peace is the universal aspiration of mankind and that peace and justice are indispensable to the full realization of human rights and fundamental freedoms,

Solemnly proclaims that:

1. It is imperative that members of the international community fulfill their solemn obligations to promote and encourage respect for human rights and fundamental freedoms for all without distinctions of any kind such as race, colour, sex, language, religion, political or other opinions;

2. The Universal Declaration of Human Rights states a common under-

standing of the peoples of the world concerning the inalienable and inviolable rights of all members of the human family and constitutes an obligation for the members of the international community;

3. The International Covenant on Civil and Political Rights, the International Covenant on Economic, Social and Cultural Rights, the Declaration on the Granting of Independence to Colonial Countries and Peoples, the International Convention on the Elimination of All Forms of Racial Discrimination as well as other conventions and declarations in the field of human rights adopted under the auspices of the United Nations, the specialized agencies and the regional intergovernmental organizations, have created new standards and obligations to which States should conform;

4. Since the adoption of the Universal Declaration of Human Rights the United Nations has made substantial progress in defining standards for the enjoyment and protection of human rights and fundamental freedoms. During this period many important international instruments were adopted but much remains to be done in regard to the implementation of those rights and freedoms;

5. The primary aim of the United Nations in the sphere of human rights is the achievement by each individual of the maximum freedom and dignity. For the realization of this objective, the laws of every country should grant each individual, irrespective of race, language, religion or political belief, freedom of expression, of information, of conscience and of religion, as well as the right to participate in the political, economic, cultural and social life of his country;

6. States should reaffirm their determination effectively to enforce the principles enshrined in the Charter of the United Nations and in other international instruments that concern human rights and fundamental freedoms;

7. Gross denials of human rights under the repugnant policy of *apartheid* is a matter of the gravest concern to the international community. This policy of *apartheid*, condemned as a crime against humanity, continues seriously to disturb international peace and security. It is therefore imperative for the international community to use every possible means to eradicate this evil. The struggle against *apartheid* is recognized as legitimate;

8. The peoples of the world must be made fully aware of the evils of racial discrimination and must join in combating them. The implementation of this principle of non-discrimination, embodied in the Charter of the United Nations, the Universal Declaration of Human Rights, and other international instruments in the field of human rights, constitutes a most urgent task of mankind at the international as well as at the national level. All ideologies based on racial superiority and intolerance must be condemned and resisted;

9. Eight years after the General Assembly's Declaration on the Granting of Independence to Colonial Countries and Peoples the problems of colonialism continue to preoccupy the international community. It is a matter of urgency that all Member States should co-operate with the appropriate organs of the United Nations so that effective measures can be taken to ensure that the Declaration is fully implemented;

10. Massive denials of human rights, arising out of aggression or any armed

conflict with their tragic consequences, and resulting in untold human misery, engender reactions which could engulf the world in ever growing hostilities. It is the obligation of the international community to co-operate in eradicating such scourges;

11. Gross denials of human rights arising from discrimination on grounds of race, religion, belief or expressions of opinion outrage the conscience of mankind and endanger the foundations of freedom, justice and peace in the world;

12. The widening gap between the economically developed and developing countries impedes the realization of human rights in the international community. The failure of the Development Decade to reach its modest objectives makes it all the more imperative for every nation, according to its capacities, to make the maximum possible effort to close this gap;

13. Since human rights and fundamental freedoms are indivisible, the full realization of civil and political rights without the enjoyment of economic, social and cultural rights is impossible. The achievement of lasting progress in the implementation of human rights is dependent upon sound and effective national and international policies of economic and social development;

14. The existence of over seven hundred million illiterates throughout the world is an enormous obstacle to all efforts at realizing the aims and purposes of the Charter of the United Nations and the provisions of the Universal Declaration of Human Rights. International action aimed at eradicating illiteracy from the face of the earth and promoting education at all levels requires urgent attention;

15. The discrimination of which women are still victims in various regions of the world must be eliminated. An inferior status for women is contrary to the Charter of the United Nations as well as the provisions of the Universal Declaration of Human Rights. The full implementation of the Declaration on the Elimination of discrimination against Women is a necessity for the progress of mankind;

16. The protection of the family and of the child remains the concern of the international community. Parents have a basic human right to determine freely and responsibly the number and the spacing of their children;

17. The aspirations of the younger generation for a better world, in which human rights and fundamental freedoms are fully implemented, must be given the highest encouragement. It is imperative that youth participate in shaping the future of mankind;

18. While recent scientific discoveries and technological advances have opened vast prospects for economic, social and cultural progress, such developments may nevertheless endanger the rights and freedoms of individuals and will require continuing attention;

19. Disarmament would release immense human and material resources now devoted to military purposes. These resources should be used for the promotion of human rights and fundamental freedoms. General and complete disarmament is one of the highest aspirations of all peoples;

Therefore,

The International Conference on Human Rights,

1. *Affiriming* its faith in the principles of the Universal Declaration of Human Rights and other international instruments in this field,

2. *Urges* all peoples and governments to dedicate themselves to the principles enshrined in the Universal Declaration of Human Rights and to redouble their efforts to provide for all human beings a life consonant with freedom and dignity and conducive to physical, mental, social and spiritual welfare.

II. International Labour Organization (ILO) Documents

INTRODUCTION

The ILO was created in 1919 contemporaneously with the League of Nations. After the creation of the UN, it became one of the "specialized agencies" brought in to a relationship with that organization pursuant to Articles 57 and 63 of the UN Charter. It has made enormous contributions of both substance and procedure in the areas of economic rights, labor standards and freedom of association. Its procedural contributions are considered in Chapter *V infra*. In this chapter, we reproduce what we believe are the most significant parts of its constitutional documents and the most important of its many substantive instruments.

For further reading, *see* any of the numerous books on the Organization by C. Wilfred Jenks, a former Director-General of the International Labor Office, e.g., *Human Rights and International Labour Standards* (1960). We also recommend E. Haas, *Beyond the Nation-State* (1964); A. Alcock, *History of the International Labour Organization* (1971); and E. Phelan, *Yes and Albert Thomas* (1936), (a remarkable biography of the first Director-General by a close associate). The International Labour Office in Geneva periodically produces a very useful ILO Catalogue of Publications in Print.

1. INTERNATIONAL LABOUR ORGANIZATION CONSTITUTION (1919)

The original text of the Constitution, established in 1919, has been modified by the amendment of 1922 which entered into force on 4 June 1934; the Instrument of Amendment of 1945 which entered into force on 26 September 1946; the Instrument of Amendment of 1946 which entered into force on 20 April 1948; the Instrument of Amendment of 1953 which entered into force on 20 May 1954; the Instrument of Amendment of 1962 which entered into force on 22 May 1963; and the Instrument of Amendment of 1972 which entered into force on 1 November 1974.

PREAMBLE

Whereas universal and lasting peace can be established only if it is based upon social justice;

And whereas conditions of labour exist involving such injustice, hardship and privation to large numbers of people as to produce unrest so great that the peace and harmony of the world are imperilled; and an improvement of those conditions is urgently required: as, for example, by the regulation of the hours of work, including the establishment of a maximum working day and week, the regulation of the labour supply, the prevention of unemployment, the provision of an adequate living wage, the protection of the worker against sickness, disease and injury arising out of his employment, the protection of children, young persons and women, provision for old age and injury, protection of the interests of workers when employed in countries other than their own, recognition of the principle of equal remuneration for work of equal value, recognition of the principle of freedom of association, the organisation of vocational and technical education and other measures;

Whereas also the failure of any nation to adopt humane conditions of labour is an obstacle in the way of other nations which desire to improve the conditions in their own countries;

The High Contracting Parties, moved by sentiments of justice and humanity as well as by the desire to secure the permanent peace of the world, and with a view to attaining the objectives set forth in this Preamble, agree to the following Constitution of the International Labour Organisation:

CHAPTER I—ORGANIZATION

Article 1

1. A permanent organisation is hereby established for the promotion of the objects set forth in the Preamble to this Constitution and in the Declaration concerning the aims and purposes of the International Labour Organization adopted at Philadelphia on 10 May 1944 the text of which is annexed to this Constitution.

* * *

2. DECLARATION OF PHILADELPHIA (1944) DECLARATION CONCERNING THE AIMS AND PURPOSES OF THE INTERNATIONAL LABOUR ORGANIZATION

The General Conference of the International Labour Organization, meeting in its Twenty-sixth Session in Philadelphia, hereby adopts, this tenth day of May in the year nineteen hundred and forty-four, the present Declaration of the aims and purposes of the International Labour Organization and of the principles which should inspire the policy of its Members.

I

The Conference reaffirms the fundamental principles on which the Organization is based and, in particular, that—

a. labour is not a commodity;

b. freedom of expression and of association are essential to sustained progress;

c. poverty anywhere constitutes a danger to prosperity everywhere;

d. the war against want requires to be carried on with unrelenting vigour within each nation, and by continuous and concerted international effort in which the representatives of workers and employers, enjoying equal status with those of governments, join with them in free discussion and democratic decision with a view to the promotion of the common welfare.

II

Believing that experience has fully demonstrated the truth of the statement in the Constitution of the International Labour Organization that lasting peace can be established only if it is based on social justice, the Conference affirms that—

a. all human beings, irrespective of race, creed or sex, have the right to pursue both their material well-being and their spiritual development in conditions of freedom and dignity, of economic security and equal opportunity;

b. the attainment of the conditions in which this shall be possible must constitute the central aim of national and international policy;

c. all national and international policies and measures, in particular those of an economic and financial character, should be judged in this light and accepted only in so far as they may be held to promote and not to hinder the achievement of this fundamental objective;

d. it is a responsibility of the International Labour Organisation to examine and consider all international economic and financial policies and measures in the light of this fundamental objective;

e. in discharging the tasks entrusted to it the International Labour Organization, having considered all relevant economic and financial factors, may include in its decisions and recommendations any provisions which it considers appropriate.

III

The Conference recognises the solemn obligation of the International Labour Organization to further among the nations of the world programmes which will achieve:

a. full employment and the raising of standards of living;

b. the employment of workers in the occupations in which they can have the satisfaction of giving the fullest measure of their skill and attainments and make their greatest contribution to the common well-being;

c. the provision, as a means to the attainment of this end and under adequate guarantees for all concerned, of facilities for training and the transfer of labour, including migration for employment and settlement;

d. policies in regard to wages and earnings, hours and other conditions of work calculated to ensure a just share of the fruits of progress to all, and a minimum living wage to all employed and in need of such protection;

e. the effective recognition of the right of collective bargaining, the co-operation of management and labour in the continuous improvement of productive efficiency, and the collaboration of workers and employers in the preparation and application of social and economic measures;

f. the extension of social security measures to provide a basic income to all in need of such protection and comprehensive medical care;

g. adequate protection for the life and health of workers in all occupations;

h. provision for child welfare and maternity protection;

i. the provision of adequate nutrition, housing and facilities for recreation and culture;

j. the assurance of equality of educational and vocational opportunity.

IV

Confident that the fuller and broader utilisation of the world's productive resources necessary for the achievement of the objectives set forth in this Declaration can be secured by effective international and national action, including measures to expand production and consumption, to avoid severe economic fluctuations, to promote the economic and social advancement of the less developed regions of the world, to assure greater stability in world prices of primary products, and to promote a high and steady volume of international trade, the Conference pledges the full co-operation of the International Labour Organization with such international bodies as may be entrusted with a share of the responsibility for this great task and for the promotion of the health, education and well-being of all peoples.

V

The Conference affirms that the principles set forth in this Declaration are fully applicable to all peoples everywhere and that, while the manner of their application must be determined with due regard to the stage of social and economic development reached by each people, their progressive application to peoples who are still dependent, as well as to those who have already achieved self-government, is a matter of concern to the whole civilised world.

3. FORCED LABOUR CONVENTION (1930) Convention (No. 29) concerning Forced Labour 39 U.N.T.S.55. In force 1 May 1932 in accordance with Article 28.

THE GENERAL CONFERENCE OF THE INTERNATIONAL LABOUR ORGANIZATION,

Having been convened at Geneva by the Governing Body of the International Labour Office, and having met in its fourteenth session on 10 June 1930, and

Having decided upon the adoption of certain proposals with regard to forced or compulsory labour, which is included in the first item on the agenda of the session, and

Having determined that these proposals shall take the form of an international Convention,

Adopts this twenty-eighth day of June of the year one thousand nine hundred and thirty the following Convention, which may be cited as the Forced Labour Convention, 1930, for ratification by the Members of the International

Labour Organization in accordance with the provisions of the Constitution of the International Labour Organization:

Article 1

1. Each Member of the International Labour Organization which ratifies this Convention undertakes to suppress the use of forced or compulsory labour in all its forms within the shortest possible period.

2. With a view to this complete suppression, recourse to forced or compulsory labour may be had, during the transitional period, for pubic purposes only and as an exceptional measure, subject to the conditions and guarantees hereinafter provided.

3. At the expiration of a period of five years after the coming into force of this Convention, and when the Governing Body of the International Labour Office prepares the report provided for in article 31 below, the said Governing Body shall consider the possibility of the suppression of forced or compulsory labour in all its forms without a further transitional period and the desirability of placing this question on the agenda of the Conference.

Article 2

1. For the purposes of this Convention the term "forced or compulsory labour" shall mean all work or service which is exacted from any person under the menace of any penalty and for which the said person has not offered himself voluntarily.

2. Nevertheless, for the purposes of this Convention, the term "forced or compulsory labour" shall not include;

(*a*) Any work or service exacted in virtue of compulsory military service laws for work of a purely military character;

(*b*) Any work or service which forms part of the normal civic obligations of the citizens of a fully self-governing country;

(*c*) Any work or service exacted from any person as a consequence of a conviction in a court of law, provided that the said work or service is carried out under the supervision and control of a public authority and that the said person is not hired to or placed at the disposal of private individuals, companies or associations;

(*d*) Any work or service exacted in cases of emergency, that is to say, in the event of war or of a calamity or threatened calamity, such as fire, flood, famine, earthquake, violent epidemic or epizootic diseases, invasion by animal, insect or vegetable pests, and in general any circumstance that would endanger the existence or the well-being of the whole or part of the population;

(*e*) Minor communal services of a kind which, being performed by the members of the community in the direct interest of the said community, can therefore be considered as normal civic obligations incumbent upon the members of the community, provided that the members of the community or their direct representatives shall have the right to be consulted in regard to the need for such services.

Article 3

For the purposes of this Convention the term "competent authority" shall mean either an authority of the metropolitan country or the highest central authority in the territory concerned.

Article 4

1. The competent authority shall not impose or permit the imposition of forced or compulsory labour for the benefit of private individuals, companies or associations.

2. Where such forced or compulsory labour for the benefit of private individuals, companies or associations exists at the date on which a Member's ratification of this Convention is registered by the Director-General of the International Labour Office, the Member shall completely suppress such forced or compulsory labour from the date on which this Convention comes into force for that Member.

Article 5

1. No concession granted to private individuals, companies or associations shall involve any form of forced or compulsory labour for the production or the collection of products which such private individuals, companies or associations utilise or in which they trade.

2. Where concessions exist containing provisions involving such forced or compulsory labour, such provisions shall be rescinded as soon as possible, in order to comply with article 1 of this Convention.

Article 6

Officials of the administration, even when they have the duty of encouraging the populations under their charge to engage in some form of labour, shall not put constraint upon the said populations or upon any individual members thereof to work for private individuals, companies or associations.

Article 7

1. Chiefs who do not exercise administrative functions shall not have recourse to forced or compulsory labour.

2. Chiefs who exercise administrative functions may, with the express permission of the competent authority, have recourse to forced or compulsory labour, subject to the provisions of article 10 of this Convention.

3. Chiefs who are duly recognised and who do not receive adequate remuneration in other forms may have the enjoyment of personal services, subject to due regulation and provided that all necessary measures are taken to prevent abuses.

Article 8

1. The responsibility for every decision to have recourse to forced or compulsory labour shall rest with the highest civil authority in the territory concerned.

2. Nevertheless, that authority may delegate powers to the highest local authorities to exact forced or compulsory labour which does not involve the removal of the workers from their place of habitual residence. That authority may also delegate, for such periods and subject to such conditions as may be laid down in the regulations provided for in article 23 of this Convention, powers to the highest local authorities to exact forced or compulsory labour which involves the removal of the workers from their place of habitual residence for the purpose of facilitating the movement of officials of the administration, when on duty, and for the transport of Government stores.

Article 9

Except as otherwise provided for in Article 10 of this Convention, any authority competent to exact forced or compulsory labour shall, before deciding to have recourse to such labour, satisfy itself:

(*a*) That the work to be done or the service to be rendered is of important direct interest for the community called upon to do the work or render the service;

(*b*) That the work or service is of present or imminent necessity;

(*c*) That it has been impossible to obtain voluntary labour for carrying out the work or rendering the service by the offer of rates of wages and conditions of labour not less favourable than those prevailing in the area concerned for similar work or service; and

(*d*) That the work or service will not lay too heavy a burden upon the present population, having regard to the labour available and its capacity to undertake the work.

Article 10

1. Forced or compulsory labour exacted as a tax and forced or compulsory labour to which recourse is had for the execution of pubic works by chiefs who exercise administrative functions shall be progressively abolished.

2. Meanwhile, where forced or compulsory labour is exacted as a tax, and where recourse is had to forced or compulsory labour for the execution of public works by chiefs who exercise administrative functions, the authority concerned shall first satisfy itself:

a. That the work to be done or the service to be rendered is of important direct interest for the community called upon to do the work or render the service;

b. That the work or the service is of present or imminent necessity;

c. That the work or service will not lay too heavy a burden upon the present population, having regard to the labour available and its capacity to undertake the work;

d. That the work or service will not entail the removal of the workers from their place of habitual residence;

e. That the execution of the work or the rendering of the service will be directed in accordance with the exigencies of religion, social life and agriculture.

Article 11

1. Only adult able-bodied males who are of an apparent age of not less than 18 and not more than 45 years may be called upon for forced or compulsory labour. Except in respect of the kinds of labour provided for in Article 10 of this Convention, the following limitations and conditions shall apply:

a. Whenever possible prior determination by a medical officer appointed by the administration that the persons concerned are not suffering from any infectious or contagious disease and that they are physically fit for the work required and for the conditions under which it is to be carried out;

b. Exemption of school teachers and pupils and of officials of the administration in general;

c. The maintenance in each community of the number of adult able-bodied men indispensable for family and social life;

d. Respect for conjugal and family ties.

2. For the purposes of sub-paragraph (c) of the preceding paragraph, the regulations provided for in article 23 of this Convention shall fix the proportion of the resident adult able-bodied males who may be taken at any one time for forced or compulsory labour, provided always that this proportion shall in no case exceed 25 per cent. In fixing this proportion the competent authority shall take account of the density of the population, of its social and physical development, of the seasons, and of the work which must be done by the persons concerned on their own behalf in their locality, and, generally, shall have regard to the economic and social necessities of the normal life of the community concerned.

Article 12

1. The maximum period for which any person may be taken for forced or compulsory labour of all kinds in any one period of twelve months shall not exceed sixty days, including the time spent in going to and from the place of work.

2. Every person from whom forced or compulsory labour is exacted shall be furnished with a certificate indicating the periods of such labour which he has completed.

Article 13

1. The normal working hours of any person from whom forced or compulsory labour is exacted shall be the same as those prevailing in the case of voluntary labour, and the hours worked in excess of the normal working hours shall be remunerated at the rates prevailing in the case of overtime for voluntary labour.

2. A weekly day of rest shall be granted to all persons from whom forced or compulsory labour of any kind is exacted and this day shall coincide as far as possible with the day fixed by tradition or custom in the territories or regions concerned.

Article 14

1. With the exception of the forced or compulsory labour provided for in

article 10 of this Convention, forced or compulsory labour of all kinds shall be remunerated in cash at rates not less than those prevailing for similar kinds of work either in the district in which the labour is employed or in the district from which the labour is recruited, whichever may be the higher.

2. In the case of labour to which recourse is had be chiefs in the exercise of their administrative functions, payment of wages in accordance with the provisions of the preceding paragraph shall be introduced as soon as possible.

3. The wages shall be paid to each worker individually and not to his tribal chief or to any other authority.

4. For the purpose of payment of wages the days spent in travelling to and from the place of work shall be counted as working days.

5. Nothing in this article shall prevent ordinary rations being given as a part of wages, such rations to be at least equivalent in value to the money payment they are taken to represent, but deductions from wages shall not be made either for the payment of taxes or for special food, clothing or accommodation supplied to a worker for the purpose of maintaining him in a fit condition to carry on his work under the special conditions of any employment, or for the supply of tools.

Article 15

1. Any laws or regulations relating to workmen's compensation for accidents or sickness arising out of the employment of the worker and any laws or regulations providing compensation for the dependents of deceased or incapacitated workers which are or shall be in force in the territory concerned shall be equally applicable to persons from whom forced or compulsory labour is exacted and to voluntary workers.

2. In any case it shall be an obligation on any authority employing any worker on forced or compulsory labour to ensure the subsistence of any such worker who, by accident or sickness arising out of his employment, is rendered wholly or partially incapable of providing for himself, and to take measures to ensure the maintenance of any persons actually dependent upon such a worker in the event of his incapacity or decease arising out of his employment.

Article 16

1. Except in cases of special necessity, persons from whom forced or compulsory labour is exacted shall not be transferred to districts where the food and climate differ so considerably from those to which they have been accustomed as to endanger their health.

2. In no case shall the transfer of such workers be permitted unless all measures relating to hygiene and accommodation which are necessary to adapt such workers to the conditions and to safeguard their health can be strictly applied.

3. When such transfer cannot be avoided, measures of gradual habituation to the new conditions of diet and of climate shall be adopted on competent medical advice.

4. In cases where such workers are required to perform regular work to which they are not accustomed, measures shall be taken to ensure their habituation to it, especially as regards progressive training, the hours of work

and the provision of rest intervals, and any increase or amelioration of diet which may be necessary.

Article 17

Before permitting recourse to forced or compulsory labour for works of construction or maintenance which entail the workers remaining at the workplaces for considerable periods, the competent authority shall satisfy itself:

(1) That all necessary measures are taken to safeguard the health of the workers and to guarantee the necessary medical care, and, in particular, (*a*) that the workers are medically examined before commencing the work and at fixed intervals during the period of service, (*b*) that there is an adequate medical staff, provided with the dispensaries, infirmaries, hospitals and equipment necessary to meet all requirements, and (*c*) that the sanitary conditions of the workplaces, the supply of drinking water, food, fuel, and cooking utensils, and, where necessary, of housing and clothing, are satisfactory;

(2) That definite arrangements are made to ensure the subsistence of the families of the workers, in particular by facilitating the remittance, by a safe method, of part of the wages to the family, at the request or with the consent of the workers;

(3) That the journeys of the workers to and from the workplaces are made at the expense and under the responsibility of the administration, which shall facilitate such journeys by making the fullest use of all available means of transport;

(4) That, in case of illness or accident causing incapacity to work of a certain duration, the worker is repatriated at the expense of the administration;

(5) That any worker who may wish to remain as a voluntary worker at the end of his period of forced or compulsory labour is permitted to do so without, for a period of two years, losing his right to repatriation free of expense to himself.

Article 18

1. Forced or compulsory labour for the transport of persons or goods, such as the labour of porters or boatmen, shall be abolished within the shortest possible period. Meanwhile the competent authority shall promulgate regulations determining, *inter alia*, (*a*) that such labour shall only be employed for the purpose of facilitating the movement of officials of the administration, when on duty, or for the transport of Government stores, or, in cases of very urgent necessity, the transport of persons other than officials, (*b*) that the workers so employed shall be medically certified to be physically fit, where medical examination is possible, and that where such medical examination is not practicable the person employing such workers shall be held responsible for ensuring that they are physically fit and not suffering from any infectious or contagious disease, (*c*) the maximum load which these workers may carry, (*d*) the maximum distance from their homes to which they may be taken, (*e*) the maximum number of days per month or other period for which they may be taken, including the days spent in returning to their homes, and (*f*) the persons

entitled to demand this form of forced or compulsory labour and the extent to which they are entitled to demand it.

2. In fixing the maxima referred to under (c), (d) and (e) in the foregoing paragraph, the competent authority shall have regard to all relevant factors, including the physical development of the population from which the workers are recruited, the nature of the country through which they must travel and the climatic conditions.

3. The competent authority shall further provide that the normal daily journey of such workers shall not exceed a distance corresponding to an average working day of eight hours, it being understood that account shall be taken not only of the weight to be carried and the distance to be covered, but also of the nature of the road, the season and all other relevant factors, and that, where hours of journey in excess of the normal daily journey are exacted, they shall be remunerated at rates higher than the normal rates.

Article 19

1. The competent authority shall only authorise recourse to compulsory cultivation as a method of precaution against famine or a deficiency of food supplies and always under the condition that the food or produce shall remain the property of the individuals or the community producing it.

2. Nothing in this article shall be construed as abrogating the obligation on members of a community, where production is organised on a communal basis by virtue of law or custom and where the produce or any profit accruing from the sale thereof remain the property of the community, to perform the work demanded by the community by virtue of law or custom.

Article 20

Collective punishment laws under which a community may be punished for crimes committed by any of its members shall not contain provisions for forced or compulsory labour by the community as one of the methods of punishment.

Article 21

Forced or compulsory labour shall not be used for work underground in mines.

Article 22

The annual reports that Members which ratify this Convention agree to make to the International Labour Office, pursuant to the provisions of article 22 of the Constitution of the International Labour Organization, on the measures they have taken to give effect to the provisions of this Convention, shall contain as full information as possible, in respect of each territory concerned, regarding the extent to which recourse has been had to forced or compulsory labour in that territory, the purposes for which it has been employed, the sickness and death rates, hours of work, methods of payment of wages and rates of wages, and any other relevant information.

Article 23

1. To give effect to the provisions of this Convention the competent authority shall issue complete and precise regulations governing the use of forced or compulsory labour.

2. These regulations shall contain, *inter alia*, rules permitting any person from whom forced or compulsory labour is exacted to forward all complaints relative to the conditions of labour to the authorities and ensuring that such complaints will be examined and taken into consideration.

Article 24

Adequate measures shall in all cases be taken to ensure that the regulations governing the employment of forced or compulsory labour are strictly applied, either by extending the duties of any existing labour inspectorate which has been established for the inspection of voluntary labour to cover the inspection of forced or compulsory labour or in some other appropriate manner. Measures shall also be taken to ensure that the regulations are brought to the knowledge of persons from whom such labour is exacted.

Article 25

The illegal exaction of forced or compulsory labour shall be punishable as a penal offence, and it shall be an obligation on any Member ratifying this Convention to ensure that the penalties imposed by law are really adequate and are strictly enforced.

Article 26

1. Each Member of the International Labour Organization which ratifies this Convention undertakes to apply it to the territories placed under its sovereignty, jurisdiction, protection, suzerainty, tutelage or authority, so far as it has the right to accept obligations affecting matters of internal jurisdiction; provided that, if such Member may desire to take advantage of the provisions of article 35 of the Constitution of the International Labour Organization, it shall append to its ratification a declaration stating:

1. The territories to which it intends to apply the provisions of this Convention without modification;

2. The territories to which it intends to apply the provisions of this Convention with modifications, together with details of the said modifications;

3. The territories in respect of which it reserves its decision.

2. The aforesaid declaration shall be deemed to be an integral part of the ratification and shall have the force of ratification. It shall be open to any Member, by a subsequent declaration, to cancel in whole or in part the reservations made, in pursuance of the provisions of subparagraphs (2) and (3) of this article, in the original declaration.

Article 27

The formal ratifications of this Convention under the conditions set forth in

the Constitution of the International Labour Organization shall be communicated to the Director-General of the International Labour Office for registration.

Article 28

1. This Convention shall be binding only upon those Members whose
ratifications have been registered with the International Labour Office.

2. It shall come into force twelve months after the date on which the
ratifications of two Members of the International Labour Organization have
been registered with the Director-General.

3. Thereafter, this Convention shall come into force for any Member twelve
months after the date on which the ratification has been registered.

Article 29

As soon as the ratifications of two Members of the International Labour
Organization have been registered with the International Labour Office, the
Director-General of the International Labour Office shall so notify all the
Members of the International Labour Organization. He shall likewise notify
them of the registration of ratifications which may be communicated subse-
quently by other Members of the Organization.

Article 30

1. A Member which has ratified this Convention may denounce it after the
expiration of ten years from the date on which the Convention first comes into
force, by an act communicated to the Director-General of the International
Labour Office for registration. Such denunciation shall not take effect until one
year after the date on which it is registered with the International Labour Office.

2. Each Member which has ratified this Convention and which does not,
within the year following the expiration of the period of ten years mentioned in
the preceding paragraph, exercise the right of denunciation provided for in this
article, will be bound for another period of five years and, thereafter, may
denounce this Convention at the expiration of each period of five years under
the terms provided for in this article.

Article 31

At the expiration of each period of five years after the coming into force of
this Convention, the Governing Body of the International Labour Office shall
present to the General Conference a report on the working of this Convention
and shall consider the desirability of placing on the agenda of the Conference the
question of its revision in whole or in part.

Article 32

1. Should the Conference adopt a new Convention revising this Convention
in whole or in part, the ratification by a Member of the new revising Convention
shall *ipso jure* involve denunciation of this Convention without any requirement
of delay, notwithstanding the provisions of article 30 above, if and when the
new revising Convention shall have come into force.

2. As from the date of the coming into force of the new revising Convention, the present Convention shall cease to be open to ratification by the Members.

3. Nevertheless, this Convention shall remain in force in its actual form and content for those Members which have ratified it but have not ratified the revising Convention.

Article 33

The French and English texts of this Convention shall both be authentic.

4. ABOLITION OF FORCED LABOUR CONVENTION

(1957) Convention (No. 105) concerning the Abolition of Forced Labour, 320 U.N.T.S. 291. In force 17 January 1959 in accordance with Article 4.

THE GENERAL CONFERENCE OF THE INTERNATIONAL LABOUR ORGANIZATION,

Having been convened at Geneva by the Governing Body of the International Labour Office, and having met in its fortieth session on 5 June 1957, and

Having considered the question of forced labour, which is the fourth item on the agenda of the session, and

Having noted the provisions of the Forced Labour Convention, 1930, and

Having noted that the Slavery Convention, 1926, provides that all necessary measures shall be taken to prevent compulsory or forced labour from developing into conditions analogous to slavery and that the Supplementary Convention on the Abolition of Slavery, the Slave Trade, and Institutions and Practices Similar to Slavery, 1956, provides for the complete abolition of debt bondage and serfdom, and

Having noted that the Protection of Wages Convention, 1949, provides that wages shall be paid regularly and prohibits methods of payment which deprive the worker of a genuine possibility of terminating his employment, and

Having decided upon the adoption of further proposals with regard to the abolition of certain forms of forced or compulsory labour constituting a violation of the rights of man referred to in the Charter of the United Nations and enunciated by the Universal Declaration of Human Rights, and

Having determined that these proposals shall take the form of an international Convention,

Adopts this twenty-fifth day of June of the year one thousand nine hundred and fifty-seven the following Convention, which may be cited as the Abolition of Forced Labour Convention, 1957:

Article 1

Each Member of the International Labour Organization which ratifies this Convention undertakes to suppress and not to make use of any form of forced or compulsory labour:

　　a. As a means of political coercion or education or as a punishment

for holding or expressing political views or views ideologically opposed to the established political, social or economic system;

b. As a method of mobilising and using labour for purposes of
economic development;

c. As a means of labour discipline;

d. As a punishment for having participated in strikes;

e. As a means of racial, social, national or religious discrimination.

Article 2

Each Member of the International Labour Organization which ratifies this
Convention undertakes to take effective measures to secure the immediate and
complete abolition of forced or compulsory labour as specified in article 1 of this
Convention.

Article 3

The formal ratifications of this Convention shall be communicated to the
Director-General of the International Labour Office for registration.

Article 4

1. This Convention shall be binding only upon those Members of the
International Labour Organization whose ratifications have been registered with
the Director-General.

2. It shall come into force twelve months after the date on which the
ratifications of two Members have been registered with the Director-General.

3. Thereafter, this Convention shall come into force for any Member twelve
months after the date on which its ratification has been registered.

Article 5

1. A Member which has ratified this Convention may denounce it after the
expiration of ten years from the date on which the Convention first comes into
force, by an act communicated to the Director-General of the International
Labour Office for registration. Such denunciation shall not take effect until one
year after the date on which it is registered.

2. Each Member which has ratified this Convention and which does not,
within the year following the expiration of the period of ten years mentioned in
the preceding paragraph, exercise the right of denunciation provided for in this
article, will be bound for another period of ten years and, thereafter, may
denounce this Convention at the expiration of each period of ten years under the
terms provided for in this article.

Article 6

1. The Director-General of the International Labour Office shall notify all
Members of the International Labour Organization of the registration of all
ratifications and denunciations communicated to him by the Members of the
Organization.

2. When notifying the Members of the Organization of the registration of
the second ratification communicated to him, the Director-General shall draw

the attention of the Members of the Organization to the date upon which the Convention will come into force.

Article 7

The Director-General of the International Labour Office shall communicate to the Secretary-General of the United Nations for registration in accordance with Article 102 of the Charter of the Untied Nations full particulars of all ratifications and acts of denunciation registered by him in accordance with the provisions of the preceding articles.

Article 8

At such times as it may consider necessary the Governing Body of the International Labour Office shall present to the General Conference a report on the working of the Convention and shall examine the desirability of placing on the agenda of the Conference the question of its revision in whole or in part.

Article 9

1. Should the Conference adopt a new Convention revising this Convention in whole or in part, then, unless the new Convention otherwise provides:
(*a*) The ratification by a Member of the new revising Convention shall *ipso jure* involve the immediate denunciation of this Convention, notwithstanding the provisions of article 5 above, if and when the new revising Convention shall have come into force;
(*b*) As from the date when the new revising Convention comes into force this Convention shall cease to be open to ratification by the Members.
2. This Convention shall in any case remain in force in its actual form and content for those Members which have ratified it but have not ratified the revising Convention.

Article 10

The English and French versions of the text of this Convention are equally authoritative.

The foregoing is the authentic text of the Convention duly adopted by the General Conference of the International Labour Organization during its fortieth session which was held at Geneva and declared closed the twenty-seventh day of June 1957.

IN FAITH WHEREOF we have appended our signatures this fourth day of July 1957.

5. FREEDOM OF ASSOCIATION AND PROTECTION OF THE RIGHT TO ORGANIZE CONVENTION (1948)

Convention (No. 87) Concerning Freedom of Association and Protection of the Rights to Organize, 68 U.N.T.S. 17. In force 4 July 1950 in accordance with Article 15.

THE GENERAL CONFERENCE OF THE INTERNATIONAL LABOUR
ORGANIZATION,

Having been convened at San Francisco by the Governing Body of the International Labour Office, and having met in its thirty-first session on 17 June 1948,

Having decided to adopt, in the form of a Convention, certain proposals concerning freedom of association and protection of the right to organise which is the seventh item on the agenda of the session,

Considering that the Preamble to the Constitution of the International Labour Organization declares "recognition of the principle of freedom of association" to be a means of improving conditions of labour and of establishing peace,

Considering that the Declaration of Philadelphia reaffirms that "freedom of expression and of association are essential to sustained progress",

Considering that the International Labour Conference, at its thirtieth session, unanimously adopted the principles which should form the basis for international regulation,

Considering that the General Assembly of the United Nations, at its second session, endorsed these principles and requested the International Labour Organization to continue every effort in order that it may be possible to adopt one or several international Conventions,

Adopts this ninth day of July of the year one thousand nine hundred and forty-eight the following Convention, which may be cited as the Freedom of Association and Protection of the Right to Organize Convention, 1948:

PART I

FREEDOM OF ASSOCIATION

Article 1

Each Member of the International Labour Organization for which this Convention is in force undertakes to give effect to the following provisions.

Article 2

Workers and employers, without distinction whatsoever, shall have the right to establish and, subject, only to the rules of the organization concerned, to join organizations of their own choosing without previous authorisation.

Article 3

1. Workers' and employers' organizations shall have the right to draw up their constitutions and rules, to elect their representatives in full freedom, to organise their administration and activities and to formulate their programmes.

2. The public authorities shall refrain from any interference which would restrict this right or impede the lawful exercise thereof.

Article 4

Workers' and employers' organizations shall not be liable to be dissolved or suspended by administrative authority.

Article 5

Workers' and employers' organizations shall have the right to establish and join federations and confederations and any such organization, federation or confederation shall have the right to affiliate with international organisations of workers and employers.

Article 6

The provisions of articles 2, 3 and 4 hereof apply to federations and confederations of workers' and employers' organizations.

Article 7

The acquisition of legal personality by workers' and employers' organizations, federations and confederations shall not be made subject to conditions of such a character as to restrict the application of the provisions of articles 2, 3 and 4 hereof.

Article 8

1. In exercising the rights provided for in this Convention workers and employers and their respective organizations, like other persons or organised collectivities, shall respect the law of the land.
2. The law of the land shall not be such as to impair, nor shall it be so applied as to impair, the guarantees provided for in this Convention.

Article 9

1. The extent to which the guarantees provided for in this Convention shall apply to the armed forces and the police shall be determined by national laws or regulations.
2. In accordance with the principle set forth in paragraph 8 of article 19 of the Constitution of the International Labour Organization the ratification of this Convention by any Member shall not be deemed to affect any existing law, award, custom or agreement in virtue of which members of the armed forces or the police enjoy any right guaranteed by this Convention.

Article 10

In this Convention the term "organization" means any organization of workers or of employers for furthering and defending the interests of workers or of employers.

PART II

PROTECTION OF THE RIGHT TO ORGANIZE

Article 11

Each Member of the International Labour Organization for which this Convention is in force undertakes to take all necessary and appropriate measures to ensure that workers and employers may exercise freely the right to organize.

PART III

MISCELLANEOUS PROVISIONS

Article 12

1. In respect of the territories referred to in article 35 of the Constitution of the International Labour Organization as amended by the Constitution of the International Labour Organization Instrument of Amendment, 1946, other than the territories referred to in paragraphs 4 and 5 of the said article as so amended, each Member of the Organization which ratifies this Convention shall communicate to the Director-General of the International Labour Office with or as soon as possible after its ratification a declaration stating:

a. The territories in respect of which it undertakes that the provisions of the Convention shall be applied without modification;

b. The territories in respect of which it undertakes that the provisions of the Convention shall be applied subject to modifications, together with details of the said modifications;

c. The territories in respect of which the Convention is inapplicable and in such cases the grounds on which it is inapplicable;

d. The territories in respect of which it reserves its decision.

2. The undertakings referred to in subparagraphs (*a*) and (*b*) of paragraph 1 of this article shall be deemed to be an integral part of the ratification and shall have the force of ratification.

3. Any Member may at any time by a subsequent declaration cancel in whole or in part any reservations made in its original declaration in virtue of subparagraphs (*b*), (*c*) or (*d*) of paragraph 1 of this article.

4. Any Member may, at any time at which this Convention is subject to denunciation in accordance with the provisions of article 16, communicate to the Director-General a declaration modifying in any other respect the terms of any former declaration and stating the present position in respect of such territories as it may specify.

Article 13

1. Where the subject matter of this Convention is within the self-governing powers of any non-metropolitan territory, the Member responsible for the international relations of that territory may, in agreement with the government of the territory, communicate to the Director-General of the International Labour Office a declaration accepting on behalf of the territory the obligations of this Convention.

2. A declaration accepting the obligations of this Convention may be communicated to the Director-General of the International Labour Office:

a. By two or more Members of the Organization in respect of any territory which is under their joint authority; or

b. By any international authority responsible for the administration of any territory, in virtue of the Charter of the United Nations or otherwise, in respect of any such territory.

3. Declarations communicated to the Director-General of the International Labour Office in accordance with the preceding paragraphs of this article shall indicate whether the provisions of the Convention will be applied in the territory concerned without modification or subject to modifications; when the declaration indicates that the provisions of the Convention will be applied subject to modifications it shall give details of the said modifications.

4. The Member, Members or international authority concerned may at any time by a subsequent declaration renounce in whole or in part the right to have recourse to any modification indicated in any former declaration.

5. The Member, Members or international authority concerned may, at any time at which this Convention is subject to denunciation in accordance with the provisions of article 16, communicate to the Director-General of the International Labour Office a declaration modifying in any other respect the terms of any former declaration and stating the present position in respect of the application of the Convention.

PART IV

FINAL PROVISIONS

Article 14

The formal ratifications of this Convention shall be communicated to the Director-General of the International Labour Office for registration.

Article 15

1. This Convention shall be binding only upon those Members of the International Labour Organization whose ratifications have been registered with the Director-General.

2. It shall come into force twelve months after the date on which the ratifications of two Members have been registered with the Director-General.

3. Thereafter, this Convention shall come into force for any Member twelve months after the date on which its ratification has been registered.

Article 16

1. A Member which has ratified this Convention may denounce it after the expiration of ten years from the date on which the Convention first comes into force, by an act communicated to the Director-General of the International Labour Office for registration. Such denunciation shall not take effect until one year after the date on which it is registered.

2. Each Member which has ratified this Convention and which does not, within the year following the expiration of the period of ten years mentioned in the preceding paragraph, exercise the right of denunciation provided for in this article, will be bound for another period of ten years and, thereafter, may denounce this Convention at the expiration of each period of ten years under the terms provided for in this article.

Article 17

1. The Director-General of the International Labour Office shall notify all Members of the International Labour Organization of the registration of all ratifications, declarations and denunciations communicated to him by the Members of the Organization.

2. When notifying the Members of the Organization of the registration of the second ratification communicated to him, the Director-General shall draw the attention of the Members of the Organization to the date upon which the Convention will come into force.

Article 18

The Director-General of the International Labour Office shall communicate to the Secretary-General of the United Nations for registration in accordance with Article 102 of the Charter of the United Nations full particulars of all ratifications, declarations and acts of denunciation registered by him in accordance with the provisions of the preceding articles.

Article 19

At the expiration of each period of ten years after the coming into force of this Convention, the Governing body of the International Labour Office shall present to the General Conference a report on the working of this Convention and shall consider the desirability of placing on the agenda of the Conference the question of its revision in whole or in part.

Article 20

1. Should the Conference adopt a new Convention revising this Convention in whole or in part, then, unless the new Convention otherwise provides:

   a. The ratification by a Member of the new revising Convention shall _ipso jure_ involve the immediate denunciation of this Convention, notwithstanding the provisions of article 16 above, if and when the new revising Convention shall have come into force;

   b. As from the date when the new revising Convention comes into force this Convention shall cease to be open to ratification by the Members.

2. This Convention shall in any case remain in force in its actual form and content for those Members which have ratified it but have not ratified the revising Convention.

Article 21

The English and French versions of the text of this Convention are equally authoritative.

The foregoing is the authentic text of the Convention duly adopted by the General Conference of the International Labour Organization during its thirty-first session which was held at San Francisco and declared closed the tenth day of July 1948.

IN FAITH WHEREOF we have appended our signatures this thirty-first day of August 1948.

6. RIGHT TO ORGANIZE AND COLLECTIVE BARGAINING CONVENTION (1949) Convention (No. 98) concerning the Application of the Principles of the Right to Organize and to Bargain Collectively

96 U.N.T.S. 257. In force 18 July 1951 in accordance with Article 8.

THE GENERAL CONFERENCE OF THE INTERNATIONAL LABOUR ORGANIZATION,

Having been convened at Geneva by the Governing Body of the International Labour Office, and having met in its thirty-second session on 8 June 1949, and

Having decided upon the adoption of certain proposals concerning the application of the principles of the right to organize and to bargain collectively, which is the fourth item on the agenda of the session, and

Having determined that these proposals shall take the form of an international Convention,

Adopts this first day of July of the year one thousand nine hundred and forty-nine the following Convention, which may be cited as the Right to Organize and Collective Bargaining Convention 1949:

Article 1

1. Workers shall enjoy adequate protection against acts of anti-union discrimination in respect of their employment.

2. Such protection shall apply more particularly in respect of acts calculated to:

    a. Make the employment of a worker subject to the condition that he shall not join a union or shall relinquish trade union membership;

    b. Cause the dismissal of or otherwise prejudice a worker by reason of union membership or because of participation in union activities outside working hours or, with the consent of the employer, within working hours.

Article 2

1. Workers' and employers' organizations shall enjoy adequate protection against any acts of interference by each other or each other's agents or members in their establishment, functioning or administration.

2. In particular, acts which are designed to promote the establishment of workers' organizations under the domination of employers or employers' organizations, or to support workers' organizations by financial or other means, with the object of placing such organizations under the control of employers or employers' organizations, shall be deemed to constitute acts of interference within the meaning of this article.

Article 3

Machinery appropriate to national conditions shall be established, where necessary, for the purpose of ensuring respect for the right to organize as defined in the preceding articles.

Article 4

Measures appropriate to national conditions shall be taken, where necessary, to encourage and promote the full development and utilisation of machinery for voluntary negotiation between employers or employers' organizations and workers' organizations, with a view to the regulation of terms and conditions of employment by means of collective agreements.

Article 5

1. The extent to which the guarantees provided for in this Convention shall apply to the armed forces and the police shall be determined by national laws or regulations.

2. In accordance with the principle set fourth in paragraph 8 of article 19 of the Constitution of the International Labour Organization the ratification of this Convention by any Member shall not be deemed to affect any existing law, award, custom or agreement in virtue of which members of the armed forces or the police enjoy any right guaranteed by this Convention.

Article 6

This Convention does not deal with the position of public servants engaged in the administration of the State, nor shall it be construed as prejudicing their rights or status in any way.

Article 7

The formal ratifications of this Convention shall be communicated to the Director-General of the International Labour Office for registration.

Article 8

1. This Convention shall be binding only upon those Members of the International Labour Organization whose ratifications have been registered with the Director-General.

2. It shall come into force twelve months after the date on which the ratifications of two Members have been registered with the Director-General.

3. Thereafter, this Convention shall come into force for any Member twelve months after the date on which its ratification has been registered.

Article 9

1. Declarations communicated to the Director-General of the International Labour Office in accordance with paragraph 2 of article 35 of the Constitution of the International Labour Organization shall indicate:

a. The territories in respect of which the Member concerned undertakes that the provisions of the Convention shall be applied without modification;

b. The territories in respect of which it undertakes that the provisions of the Convention shall be applied subject to modifications, together with details of the said modifications;

c. The territories in respect of which the Convention is inapplicable and in such cases the grounds on which it is inapplicable;

d. The territories in respect of which it reserves its decision pending further consideration of the position.

2. The undertakings referred to in subparagraphs (*a*) and (*b*) of paragraph 1 of this article shall be deemed to be an integral part of the ratification and shall have the force of ratification.

3. Any Member may at any time by a subsequent declaration cancel in whole or in part any reservation made in its original declaration in virtue of subparagraphs (*b*), (*c*) or (*d*) of paragraph 1 of this article.

4. Any member may, at any time at which the Convention is subject to denunciation in accordance with the provisions of article 11, communicate to the Director-General a declaration modifying in any other respect the terms of any former declaration and stating the present position in respect of such territories as it may specify.

Article 10

1. Declarations communicated to the Director-General of the International Labour Office in accordance with paragraphs 4 or 5 of article 35 of the Constitution of the International Labour Organization shall indicate whether the provisions of the Convention will be applied in the territory concerned without modification or subject to modifications; when the declaration indicates that the provisions of the Convention will be applied subject to modifications, it shall give details of the said modifications.

2. The Member, Members or international authority concerned may at any time by a subsequent declaration renounce in whole or in part the right to have recourse to any modification indicated in any former declaration.

3. The Member, Members or international authority concerned may, at any time at which this Convention is subject to denunciation in accordance with the provisions of article 11, communicate to the Director-General a declaration modifying in any other respect the terms of any former declaration and stating the present position in respect of the application of the Convention.

Article 11

1. A Member which has ratified this Convention may denounce it after the expiration of ten years from the date on which the Convention first comes into force, by an act communicated to the Director-General of the International Labour Office for registration. Such denunciation shall not take effect until one year after the date on which it is registered.

2. Each Member which has ratified this Convention and which does not, within the year following the expiration of the period of ten years mentioned in the preceding paragraph, exercise the right of denunciation provided for in this

article, will be bound for another period of ten years and, thereafter, may denounce this Convention at the expiration of each period of ten years under the terms provided for in this article.

Article 12

1. The Director-General of the International Labour Office shall notify all Members of the International Labour Organization of the registration of all ratifications, declarations and denunciations communicated to him by the Members of the Organization.

2. When notifying the Members of the Organization of the registration of the second ratification communicated to him, the Director-General shall draw the attention of the Members of the Organization to the date upon which the Convention will come into force.

Article 13

The Director-General of the International Labour Office shall communicate to the Secretary-General of the United Nations for registration in accordance with Article 102 of the Charter of the United Nations full particulars of all ratifications, declarations and acts of denunciation registered by him in accordance with the provisions of the preceding articles.

Article 14

At the expiration of each period of ten years after the coming into force of this convention, the Governing Body of the International Labour Office shall present to the General Conference a report on the working of this Convention and shall consider the desirability of placing on the agenda of the Conference the question of its revision in whole or in part.

Article 15

1. Should the Conference adopt a new Convention revising this Convention in whole or in part, then, unless the new Convention otherwise provides:
   a. The ratification by a Member of the new revising Convention shall *ipso jure* involve the immediate denunciation of this Convention, notwithstanding the provisions of article 11 above, if and when the new revising Convention shall have come into force;
   b. As from the date when the new revising Convention comes into force this Convention shall cease to be open to ratification by the Members.

2. This Convention shall in any case remain in force in its actual form and content for those Members which have ratified it but have not ratified the revising Convention.

Article 16

The English and French versions of the text of this Convention are equally authoritative.

The foregoing is the authentic text of the Convention duly adopted by the General Conference of the International Labour Organization during its thirty-second session which was held at Geneva and declared closed the second day of July 1949.

IN FAITH WHEREOF we have appended our signatures this eighteenth day of August 1949.

7. WORKERS' REPRESENTATIVES CONVENTION

(1971) Convention (No. 135) concerning Protection and Facilities to be Afforded to Workers' Representatives in the Undertaking

International Labour Conference, 56th Sess., Record of Proceedings 780. In force 30 June 1973 in accordance with Article 8.

THE GENERAL CONFERENCE OF THE INTERNATIONAL LABOUR ORGANIZATION,

Having been convened at Geneva by the Governing Body of the International Labour Office, and having met in its fifty-sixth session on 2 June 1971, and

Noting the terms of the Right to Organize and Collective Bargaining Convention, 1949, which provides for protection of workers against acts of anti-union discrimination in respect of their employment, and

Considering that it is desirable to supplement these terms with respect to workers' representatives, and

Having decided upon the adoption of certain proposals with regard to protection and facilities afforded to workers' representatives in the undertaking, which is the fifth item on the agenda of the session, and

Having determined that these proposals shall take the form of an international Convention,

Adopts this twenty-third day of June of the year one thousand nine hundred and seventy-one the following Convention, which may be cited as the Workers' Representatives Convention, 1971:

Article 1

Workers' representatives in the undertaking shall enjoy effective protection against any act prejudicial to them, including dismissal, based on their status or activities as a workers' representative or on union membership or participation in union activities, in so far as they act in conformity with existing laws or collective agreements or other jointly agreed arrangements.

Article 2

1. Such facilities in the undertaking shall be afforded to workers' representatives as may be appropriate in order to enable them to carry out their functions promptly and efficiently.

2. In this connection account shall be taken of the characteristics of the industrial relations system of the country and the needs, size and capabilities of the undertaking concerned.

3. The granting of such facilities shall not impair the efficient operation of the undertaking concerned.

Article 3

For the purpose of this Convention the term "workers' representatives" means persons who are recognised as such under national law or practice, whether they are:

a. trade union representatives, namely, representatives designated or elected by trade unions or by the members of such unions; or

b. elected representatives, namely, representatives who are freely elected by the workers of the undertaking in accordance with provisions of national laws or regulations or of collective agreements and whose functions do not include activities which are recognised as the exclusive prerogative of trade union in the country concerned.

Article 4

National laws or regulations, collective agreements, arbitration awards or court decisions may determine the type or types of workers' representatives which shall be entitled to the protection and facilities provided for in this Convention.

Article 5

Where there exist in the same undertaking both trade union representatives and elected representatives, appropriate measures shall be taken, wherever necessary, to ensure that the existence of elected representatives is not used to undermine the position of the trade unions concerned or their representatives and to encourage co-operation on all relevant matters between the elected representatives and the trade unions concerned and their representatives.

Article 6

Effect may be given to this Convention through national laws or regulations or collective agreements, or in any other manner consistent with national practice.

Article 7

The formal ratifications of this Convention shall be communicated to the Director-General of the International Labour Office for registration.

Article 8

1. This Convention shall be binding only upon those Members of the International Labour Organization whose ratifications have been registered with the Director-General.

2. It shall come into force twelve months after the date on which the ratifications of two Members have been registered with the Director-General.

3. Thereafter, this Convention shall come into force for any Member twelve months after the date on which its ratification has been registered.

Article 9

1. A Member which has ratified this Convention may denounce it after the

expiration of ten years from the date on which the Convention first comes into force, by an act communicated to the Director-General of the International Labour Office for registration. Such denunciation shall not take effect until one year after the date on which it is registered.

2. Each Member which has ratified this Convention and which does not, within the year following the expiration of the period of ten years mentioned in the preceding paragraph, exercise the right of denunciation provided for in this article, will be bound for another period of ten years and, thereafter, may denounce this Convention at the expiration of each period of ten years under the terms provided for in this article.

Article 10

1. The Director-General of the International Labour Office shall notify all Members of the International Labour Organization of the registration of all ratifications and denunciations communicated to him by the Members of the Organization.

2. When notifying the Members of the Organization of the registration of the second ratification communicated to him, the Director-General shall draw the attention of the Members of the Organization to the date upon which the Convention will come into force.

Article 11

The Director-General of the International Labour Office shall communicate to the Secretary-General of the United Nations for registration in accordance with Article 102 of the Charter of the United Nations full particulars of all ratifications and acts of denunciation registered by him in accordance with the provisions of the preceding articles.

Article 12

At such times as it may consider necessary the Governing Body of the International Labour Office shall present to the General Conference a report on the working of this Convention and shall examine the desirability of placing on the agenda of the Conference the question of its revision in whole or in part.

Article 13

1. Should the Conference adopt a new Convention revising this Convention in whole or in part, then, unless the new Convention otherwise provides:
   a. The ratification by a Member of the new revising Convention shall *ipso jure* involve the immediate denunciation of this Convention, notwithstanding the provisions of article 9 above, if and when the new revising Convention shall have come into force;
   b. As from the date when the new revising Convention comes into force this Convention shall cease to be open to ratification by the Members.

2. This Convention shall in any case remain in force in its actual form and content for those Members which have ratified it but have not ratified the revising Convention.

Article 14

The English and French versions of the text of this Convention are equally authoritative.

The foregoing is the authentic text of the Convention duly adopted by the General Conference of the International Labour Organization during its fifty-sixth session which was held at Geneva and declared closed the twenty-third day of June 1971.

IN FAITH WHEREOF we have appended our signatures this thirtieth day of June 1971.

8. EQUAL REMUNERATION CONVENTION (1951)
Convention (No. 100) concerning Equal Remuneration for Men and Women Workers for Work of Equal Value
165 U.N.T.S. 303. In force 23 May 1953 in accordance with Article 6.

THE GENERAL CONFERENCE OF THE INTERNATIONAL LABOUR ORGANIZATION,

Having been convened at Geneva by the Governing Body of the International Labour Office, and having met in its thirty-fourth session on 6 June 1951, and

Having decided upon the adoption of certain proposals with regard to the principle of equal remuneration for men and women workers for work of equal value, which is the seventh item on the agenda of the session, and

Having determined that these proposals shall take the form of an international Convention,

Adopts this twenty-ninth day of June of the year one thousand nine hundred and fifty-one the following Convention, which may be cited as the Equal Remuneration Convention, 1951:

Article 1

For the purpose of this Convention:
a. The term "remuneration" includes the ordinary, basic or minimum wage or salary and any additional emoluments whatsoever payable directly or indirectly, whether in cash or in kind, by the employer to the worker and arising out of the worker's employment;
b. The term "equal remuneration for men and women workers for work of equal value" refers to rates of remuneration established without discrimination based on sex.

Article 2

1. Each Member shall, by means appropriate to the methods in operation for determining rates of remuneration, promote and, in so far as is consistent with such methods, ensure the application to all workers of the principle of equal remuneration for men and women workers for work of equal value.
2. This principle may be applied by means of:
a. National laws or regulations;

b. Legally established or recognized machinery for wage determination;

c. Collective agreements between employers and workers; or

d. A combination of these various means.

Article 3

1. Where such action will assist in giving effect to the provisions of this Convention, measures shall be taken to promote objective appraisal of jobs on the basis of the work to be performed.

2. The methods to be followed in this appraisal may be decided upon by the authorities responsible for the determination of rates of remuneration, or, where such rates are determined by collective agreements, by the parties thereto.

3. Differential rates between workers, which correspond, without regard to sex, to differences, as determined by such objective appraisal, in the work to be performed, shall not be considered as being contrary to the principle of equal remuneration for men and women workers for work of equal value.

Article 4

Each Member shall co-operate as appropriate with the employers' and workers' organizations concerned for the purpose of giving effect to the provisions of this Convention.

Article 5

The formal ratification of this Convention shall be communicated to the Director-General of the International Labour Office for registration.

Article 6

1. This Convention shall be binding only upon those Members of the International Labour Organization whose ratifications have been registered with the Director-General.

2. It shall come into force twelve months after the date on which the ratifications of two Members have been registered with the Director-General.

3. Thereafter, this Convention shall come into force for any Member twelve months after the date on which its ratification has been registered.

Article 7

1. Declarations communicated to the Director-General of the International Labour Office in accordance with paragraph 2 of article 35 of the Constitution of the International Labour Organization shall indicate:

a. The territories in respect of which the Member concerned undertakes that the provisions of the Convention shall be applied without modification;

b. The territories in respect of which it undertakes that the provisions of the Convention shall be applied subject to modifications, together with details of the said modifications;

c. The territories in respect of which the Convention is inapplicable and in such cases the grounds on which it is inapplicable;

d. The territories in respect of which it reserves its decisions pending further consideration of the position.

2. The undertakings referred to in subparagraphs (*a*) and (*b*) of paragraph 1 of this article shall be deemed to be an integral part of the ratification and shall have the force of ratification.

3. Any Member may at any time by a subsequent declaration cancel in whole or in part any reservation made in its original declaration by virtue of subparagraphs (*b*), (*c*) or (*d*) of paragraph 1 of this article.

4. Any Member may, at any time at which the Convention is subject to denunciation in accordance with the provisions of article 9, communicate to the Director-General a declaration modifying in any other respect the terms of any former declaration and stating the present position in respect of such territories as it may specify.

Article 8

1. Declarations communicated to the Director-General of the International Labour Office in accordance with paragraphs 4 or 5 of article 35 of the Constitution of the International Labour Organization shall indicate whether the provisions of the Convention will be applied in the territory concerned without modification or subject to modification; when the declaration indicates that the provisions of the Convention will be applied subject to modification, it shall give details of the said modifications.

2. The Member, Members or international authority concerned may at any time by a subsequent declaration renounce in whole or in part the right to have recourse to any modification indicated in any former declaration.

3. The Member, Members or international authority concerned may, at any time at which this Convention is subject to denunciation in accordance with the provisions of article 9, communicate to the Director-General a declaration modifying in any other respect the terms of any former declaration and stating the present position in respect of the application of the Convention.

Article 9

1. A Member which has ratified this Convention may denounce it after the expiration of ten years from the date on which the Convention first comes into force, by an act communicated to the Director-General of the International Labour Office for registration. Such denunciation shall not take effect until one year after the date on which it is registered.

2. Each Member which has ratified this Convention and which does not, within the year following the expiration of the period of ten years mentioned in the preceding paragraph, exercise the right of denunciation provided for in this article, will be bound for another period of ten years and, thereafter, may denounce this Convention at the expiration of each period of ten years under the terms provided for in this article.

Article 10

1. The Director-General of the International Labour Office shall notify all Members of the International Labour Organization of the registration of all

ratifications, declarations and denunciations communicated to him by the Members of the Organization.

2. When notifying the Members of the Organization of the registration of the second ratification communicated to him, the Director-General shall draw the attention of the Members of the Organization to the date upon which the Convention will come into force.

Article 11

The Director-General of the International Labour Office shall communicate to the Secretary-General of the United Nations for registration in accordance with Article 102 of the Charter of the United Nations full particulars of all ratifications, declarations and acts of denunciation registered by him in accordance with the provisions of the preceding articles.

Article 12

At such times as it may consider necessary, the Governing Body of the International Labour Office shall present to the General Conference a report on the working of this Convention and shall examine the desirability of placing on the agenda of the Conference the question of its revision in whole or in part.

Article 13

1. Should the Conference adopt a new Convention revising this Convention in whole or in part, then, unless the new Convention otherwise provides:

a. The ratification by a Member of the new revising Convention shall *ipso jure* involve the immediate denunciation of this Convention, notwithstanding the provisions of article 9 above, if and when the new revising Convention shall have come into force;

b. As from the date when the new revising Convention comes into force this Convention shall cease to be open to ratification by the Members.

2. This Convention shall in any case remain in force in its actual form and content for those Members which have ratified it but have not ratified the revising Convention.

9. DISCRIMINATION (EMPLOYMENT AND OCCUPATION) CONVENTION (1958) Convention (No. 111) concerning Discrimination in Respect of Employment and Occupation

362 U.N.T.S. 31. In force 15 June 1960 in accordance with Article 8.

THE GENERAL CONFERENCE OF THE INTERNATIONAL LABOUR ORGANIZATION,

Having been convened at Geneva by the Governing Body of the International Labour Office, and having met in its forty-second session on 4 June 1958, and *Having decided* upon the adoption of certain proposals with regard to discrimination in the field of employment and occupation, which is the fourth item on the agenda of the session, and

Having determined that these proposals shall take the form of an international Convention, and

Considering that the Declaration of Philadelphia affirms that all human beings, irrespective of race, creed or sex, have the right to pursue both their material well-being and their spiritual development in conditions of freedom and dignity, of economic security and equal opportunity, and

Considering further that discrimination constitutes a violation of rights enunciated by the Universal Declaration of Human Rights,

Adopts this twenty-fifth day of the year one thousand nine hundred and fifty-eight the following Convention, which may be cited as the Discrimination (Employment and Occupation) Convention, 1958:

Article 1

1. For the purpose of this Convention the term "discrimination" includes:
   a. Any distinction, exclusion or preference made on the basis of race, colour, sex, religion, political opinion, national extraction or social origin, which has the effect of nullifying or impairing equality of opportunity or treatment in employment or occupation;
   b. Such other distinction, exclusion or preference which has the effect of nullifying or impairing equality of opportunity or treatment in employment or occupation as may be determined by the Member concerned after consultation with representative employers' and workers' organizations, where such exist, and with other appropriate bodies.

2. Any distinction, exclusion or preference in respect of a particular job based on the inherent requirements thereof shall not be deemed to be discrimination.

3. For the purpose of this Convention the terms "employment" and "occupation" include access to vocational training, access to employment and to particular occupations, and terms and conditions of employment.

Article 2

Each Member for which this Convention is in force undertakes to declare and pursue a national policy designed to promote, by methods appropriate to national conditions and practice, equality of opportunity and treatment in respect of employment and occupation, with a view to eliminating any discrimination in respect thereof.

Article 3

Each Member for which this Convention is in force undertakes, by methods appropriate to national conditions and practice:
   a. To seek the co-operation of employers' and workers' organizations and other appropriate bodies in promoting the acceptance and observance of this policy;
   b. To enact such legislation and to promote such educational

programmes as may be calculated to secure the acceptance and observance of the policy;

c. To repeal any statutory provisions and modify any administrative instructions or practices which are inconsistent with the policy;

d. To pursue the policy in respect of employment under the direct control of a national authority;

e. To ensure observance of the policy in the activities of vocational guidance, vocational training and placement services under the direction of a national authority;

f. To indicate in its annual reports on the application of the Convention the action taken in pursuance of the policy and the results secured by such action.

Article 4

Any measures affecting an individual who is justifiably suspected of, or engaged in, activities prejudicial to the security of the State shall not be deemed to be discrimination, provided that the individual concerned shall have the right to appeal to a competent body established in accordance with national practice.

Article 5

1. Special measures of protection or assistance provided in other Conventions or Recommendations adopted by the International Labour Conference shall not be deemed to be discrimination.

2. Any Member may, after consultation with representative employers' and workers' organizations, where such exist, determine that other special measures designed to meet the particular requirements of persons who, for reasons such as sex, age, disablement, family responsibilities or social or cultural status, are generally recognised to require special protection or assistance, shall not be deemed to be discrimination.

Article 6

Each Member which ratifies this Convention undertakes to apply it to non-metropolitan territories in accordance with the provisions of the Constitution of the International Labour Organization.

Article 7

The formal ratifications of this Convention shall be communicated to the Director-General of the International Labour Office for registration.

Article 8

1. This Convention shall be binding only upon those Members of the International Labour Organization whose ratifications have been registered with the Director-General.

2. It shall come into force twelve months after the date on which the ratifications of two Members have been registered with the Director-General.

3. Thereafter, this Convention shall come into force for any Member twelve months after the date on which its ratification has been registered.

Article 9

1. A Member which has ratified this Convention may denounce it after the expiration of ten years from the date on which the Convention first comes into force, by an act communicated to the Director-General of the International Labour Office for registration. Such denunciation shall not take effect until one year after the date on which it is registered.

2. Each Member which has ratified this Convention and which does not, within the year following the expiration of the period of ten years mentioned in the preceding paragraph, exercise the right of denunciation provided for in this article, will be bound for another period of ten years and, thereafter, may denounce this Convention at the expiration of each period of ten years under the terms provided for in this article.

Article 10

1. The Director-General of the International Labour Office shall notify all Members of the International Labour Organization of the registration of all ratifications and denunciations communicated to him by the Members of the Organization.

2. When notifying the Members of the Organization of the registration of the second ratification communicated to him, the Director-General shall draw the attention of the Members of the Organization to the date upon which the Convention will come into force.

Article 11

The Director-General of the International Labour Office shall communicate to the Secretary-General of the United Nations for registration in accordance with Article 102 of the Charter of the United Nations full particulars of all ratifications and acts of denunciation registered by him in accordance with the provisions of the preceding articles.

Article 12

At such times as it may consider necessary the Governing Body of the International Labour Office shall present to the General Conference a report on the working of this Convention and shall examine the desirability of placing on the agenda of the Conference the question of its revision in whole or in part.

Article 13

1. Should the Conference adopt a new Convention revising this Convention in whole or in part, then, unless the new Convention otherwise provides:
    a. The ratification by a Member of the new revising Convention shall *ipso jure* involve the immediate denunciation of this Convention, notwithstanding the provisions of article 9 above, if and when the new revising Convention shall have come into force;
    b. As from the date when the new revising Convention comes into force this Convention shall cease to be open to ratification by the Members.

2. This Convention shall in any case remain in force in its actual form and content for those Members which have ratified it but have not ratified the revising Convention.

Article 14

The English and French versions of the text of this Convention are equally authoritative.

The foregoing is the authentic text of the Convention duly adopted by the General Conference of the International Labour Organization during its forty-second session which was held at Geneva and declared closed the twenty-sixth day of June 1958.

IN FAITH WHEREOF we have appended our signatures this fifth day of July 1958.

10. EMPLOYMENT POLICY CONVENTION (1964) Convention (No. 122) concerning Employment Policy
569 U.N.T.S. 65. In force 15 July 1966 in accordance with Article 5.

THE GENERAL CONFERENCE OF THE INTERNATIONAL LABOUR ORGANIZATION,

Having been convened at Geneva by the Governing Body of the International Labour Office, and having met in its forty-eighth session on 17 June 1964, and

Considering that the Declaration of Philadelphia recognises the solemn obligation of the International Labour Organization to further among the nations of the world programmes which will achieve full employment and the raising of standards of living, and that the Preamble to the Constitution of the International Labour Organization provides for the prevention of unemployment and the provision of an adequate living wage, and

Considering further that under the terms of the Declaration of Philadelphia it is the responsibility of the International Labour Organization to examine and consider the bearing of economic and financial policies upon employment policy in the light of the fundamental objective that "all human beings, irrespective of race, creed or sex, have the right to pursue both their material well-being and their spiritual development in conditions of freedom and dignity, of economic security and equal opportunity", and

Considering that the Universal Declaration of Human Rights provides that "everyone has the right to work, to free choice of employment, to just and favourable conditions of work and to protection against unemployment", and

Noting the terms of existing international labour Conventions and Recommendations of direct relevance to employment policy, and in particular of the Employment Service Convention and Recommendation, 1948, the Vocational Guidance Recommendation, 1949, the Vocational Training Recommendation, 1962, and the Discrimination (Employment and Occupation) Convention and Recommendation, 1958, and

Considering that these instruments should be placed in the wider framework of an international programme for economic expansion on the basis of full, productive and freely chosen employment, and

Having decided upon the adoption of certain proposals with regard to employment policy, which are included in the eighth item on the agenda of the session, and

Having determined that these proposals shall take the form of an international Convention,

Adopts this ninth day of July of the year one thousand nine hundred and sixty-four the following Convention, which may be cited as the Employment Policy Convention, 1964:

Article 1

1. With a view to stimulating economic growth and development, raising levels of living, meeting manpower requirements and overcoming unemployment and underemployment, each Member shall declare and pursue, as a major goal, an active policy designed to promote full, productive and freely chosen employment.

2. The said policy shall aim at ensuring that:
    a. There is work for all who are available for and seeking work;
    b. Such work is as productive as possible;
    c. There is freedom of choice of employment and the fullest possible opportunity for each worker to qualify for, and to use his skills and endowments in, a job for which he is well suited, irrespective of race, colour, sex, religion, political opinion, national extraction or social origin.

3. The said policy shall take due account of the stage and level of economic development and the mutual relationships between employment objectives and other economic and social objectives, and shall be pursued by methods that are appropriate to national conditions and practices.

Article 2

Each Member shall, by such methods and to such extent as may be appropriate under national conditions:
    a. Decide on and keep under review, within the framework of a co-ordinated economic and social policy, the measures to be adopted for attaining the objectives specified in article 1;
    b. Take such steps as may be needed, including when appropriate the establishment of programmes, for the application of these measures.

Article 3

In the application of this Convention, representatives of the persons affected by the measures to be taken, and in particular representatives of employers and workers, shall be consulted concerning employment policies, with a view to taking fully into account their experience and views and securing their full co-operation in formulating and enlisting support for such policies.

Article 4

The formal ratifications of this Convention shall be communicated to the Director-General of the International Labour Office for registration.

Article 5

1. This Convention shall be binding only upon those Members of the International Labour Organization whose ratifications have been registered with the Director-General.

2. It shall come into force twelve months after the date on which the ratifications of two Members have been registered with the Director-General.

3. Thereafter, this Convention shall come into force for any Member twelve months after the date on which its ratification has been registered.

Article 6

1. A Member which has ratified this Convention may denounce it after the expiration of ten years from the date on which the Convention first comes into force, by an act communicated to the Director-General of the International Labour Office for registration. Such denunciation shall not take effect until one year after the date on which it is registered.

2. Each Member which has ratified this Convention and which does not, within the year following the expiration of the period of ten years mentioned in the preceding paragraph, exercise the right of denunciation provided for in this article, will be bound for another period of ten years and, thereafter, may denounce this Convention at the expiration of each period of ten years under the terms provided for in this article.

Article 7

1. The Director-General of the International Labour Office shall notify all Members of the International Labour Organization of the registration of all ratifications and denunciations communicated to him by the Members of the Organization.

2. When notifying the Members of the Organization of the registration of the second ratification communicated to him, the Director-General shall draw the attention of the Members of the Organization to the date upon which the Convention will come into force.

Article 8

The Director-General of the International Labour Office shall communicate to the Secretary-General of the United Nations for registration in accordance with Article 102 of the Charter of the United Nations full particulars of all ratifications and acts of denunciation registered by him in accordance with the provisions of the preceding articles.

Article 9

At such times as it may consider necessary the Governing Body of the International Labour Office shall present to the General Conference a report on the working of this Convention and shall examine the desirability of placing on the agenda of the Conference the question of its revision in whole or in part.

Article 10

1. Should the Conference adopt a new Convention revising this Convention in whole or in part, then, unless the new Convention otherwise provides:
   a. The ratification by a Member of the new revising Convention shall *ipso jure* involve the immediate denunciation of this Convention, notwithstanding the provisions of article 6 above, if and when the new revising Convention shall have come into force;
   b. As from the date when the new revising Convention comes into force this Convention shall cease to be open to ratification by the Members.

2. This Convention shall in any case remain in force in its actual form and content for those Members which have ratified it but have not ratified the revising Convention.

Article 11

The English and French versions of the text of this Convention are equally authoritative.

III. United Nations Educational, Scientific and Cultural Organization (UNESCO) Documents

INTRODUCTION

The basic goal of UNESCO is to contribute to peace through promoting international cooperation in education, science and culture. It has been particularly concerned with fostering universal literacy through non-discriminatory educational systems, with promoting the exchange of scientists, artists and teachers, and with the role of the press. Not all of its activities have been free from controversy. This was particularly true of the drafting of the 1978 Declaration concerning the mass media and the related "McBride Report," International Commission for the Study of Communication Problems, *Many Voices, One World* (1980), which were viewed in some quarters as a frontal attack on Western views of freedom of the press. (For a balanced statement of Third World views on these matters, see N. Aggarwal, "Press Freedom: A Third World View," 4, *The Interdependant*, 1 (Jan. 1977).)

Like the International Labor Organization, UNESCO is a specialized agency of the United Nations.

The role of UNESCO in this area is well discussed in S. Marks, "UNESCO and Human Rights: The Implementation of Rights Relating to Education, Science, Culture and Communication," 13, *Texas Int'l L.J.35* (1977).

1. UNESCO CONSTITUTION (1945) (Preamble and Article 1)
4 U.N.T.S. 275, as amended 575 U.N.T.S. 264

The Governments of the States parties to this Constitution on behalf of their peoples declare:

That since wars begin in the minds of men, it is in the minds of men that the defences of peace must be constructed;

That ignorance of each other's ways and lives has been a common cause, throughout the history of mankind, of that suspicion and mistrust between the peoples of the world through which their differences have all too often broken into war;

That the great and terrible war which has now ended was a war made possible by the denial of the democratic principles of the dignity, equality and mutual respect of men, and by the propagation, in their place, through ignorance and prejudice, of the doctrine of the inequality of men and races;

That the wide diffusion of culture, and the education of humanity for justice and liberty and peace are indispensable to the dignity of man and constitute a sacred duty which all the nations must fulfil in a spirit of mutual assistance and concern;

That a peace based exclusively upon the political and economic arrangements of governments would not be a peace which could secure the unanimous, lasting and sincere support of the peoples of the world, and that the peace must therefore be founded, if it is not to fail, upon the intellectual and moral solidarity of mankind.

For these reasons, the States parties to this Constitution, believing in full and equal opportunities for education for all, in the unrestricted pursuit of objective truth, and in the free exchange of ideas and knowledge, are agreed and determined to develop and to increase the means of communication between their peoples and to employ these means for the purposes of mutual understanding and a truer and more perfect knowledge of each other's lives;

In consequence whereof they do hereby create the United Nations Educational, Scientific and Cultural Organization for the purpose of advancing, through the educational and scientific and cultural relations of the peoples of the world, the objectives of international peace and of the common welfare of mankind for which the United Nations Organization was established and which its Charter proclaims.

PURPOSES AND FUNCTIONS

Article 1

1. The purpose of the Organization is to contribute to peace and security by promoting collaboration among the nations through education, science and culture in order to further universal respect for justice, for the rule of law and for the human rights and fundamental freedoms which are affirmed for the peoples of the world, without distinction of race, sex, language or religion, by the Charter of the United Nations.

2. To realize this purpose the Organization will:

a. collaborate in the work of advancing the mutual knowledge and understanding of peoples, through all means of mass communication and to that end recommend such international agreements as may be necessary to promote the free flow of ideas by word and image;

b. give fresh impulse to popular education and to the spread of culture;

c. by collaborating with Members, at their request, in the development of educational activities;

by instituting collaboration among the nations to advance the ideal of equality of educational opportunity without regard to race, sex or any distinctions, economic or social;

by suggesting educational methods best suited to prepare the children of the world for the responsibilities of freedom;

d. maintain, increase and diffuse knowledge;

by assuring the conservation and protection of the world's inheritance of books, works of art and monuments of history and science, and recommending to the nations concerned the necessary international conventions;

by encouraging co-operation among the nations in all branches of intellectual activity, including the international exchange of persons active in the fields of education, science and culture and the exchange of publications, objects of artistic and scientific interest and other materials of information;

by initiating methods of international co-operation calculated to give the people of all countries access to the printed and published materials produced by any of them.

3. With a view to preserving the independence, integrity and fruitful diversity of the cultures and educational systems of the States Members of this Organization, the Organization is prohibited from intervening in matters which are essentially within their domestic jurisdiction.

2. CONVENTION AGAINST DISCRIMINATION IN EDUCATION (1960) 429 U.N.T.S. 93. In force 22 May 1962 in accordance with Article 14.

The General Conference of the United Nations Educational, Scientific and Cultural Organization, meeting in Paris from 14 November to 15 December 1960, at its eleventh session,

Recalling that the Universal Declaration of Human Rights asserts the principle of non-discrimination and proclaims that every person has the right to education,

Considering that discrimination in education is a violation of rights enunciated in that Declaration,

Considering that, under the terms of its Constitution, the United Nations Educational, Scientific and Cultural Organization has the purpose of instituting collaboration among the nations with a view to furthering for all universal respect for human rights and equality of educational opportunity.

Recognizing that, consequently, the United Nations Educational, Scientific and Cultural Organization, while respecting the diversity of national educational systems, has the duty not only to proscribe any form of discrimination in education but also to promote equality of opportunity and treatment for all in education,

Having before it proposals concerning the different aspects of discrimination in education, constituting item 17.1.4 of the agenda of the session,

Having decided at its tenth session that this question should be made the subject of an international convention as well as of recommendations to Member States.

Adopts this Convention on the fourteenth day of December 1960.

Article 1

1. For the purpose of this Convention, the term "discrimination" includes any distinction, exclusion, limitation or preference which, being based on race, colour, sex, language, religion, political or other opinion, national or social origin, economic condition or birth, has the purpose or effect of nullifying or impairing equality of treatment in education and in particular:

    a. Of depriving any person or group of persons of access to education of any type or at any level;

b. Of limiting any person or group of persons to education of an inferior standard;

c. Subject to the provisions of article 2 of this Convention, of establishing or maintaining separate educational systems or institutions for persons or groups of persons; or

d. Of inflicting on any person or group of persons conditions which are incompatible with the dignity of man.

2. For the purposes of this Convention, the term "education" refers to all types and levels of education, and includes access to education, the standard and quality of education, and the conditions under which it is given.

Article 2

When permitted in a State, the following situations shall not be deemed to constitute discrimination, within the meaning of article 1 of this Convention:

a. The establishment or maintenance of separate educational systems or institutions for pupils of the two sexes, if these systems or institutions offer equivalent access to education, provide a teaching staff with qualifications of the same standard as well as school premises and equipment of the same quality, and afford the opportunity to take the same or equivalent courses of study;

b. The establishment or maintenance, for religious or linguistic reasons, of separate educational systems or institutions offering an education which is in keeping with the wishes of the pupil's parents or legal guardians, if participation in such systems or attendance at such institutions is optional and if the education provided conforms to such standards as may be laid down or approved by the competent authorities, in particular for education of the same level;

c. The establishment or maintenance of private educational institutions, if the object of the institutions is not to secure the exclusion of any group but to provide educational facilities in addition to those provided by the public authorities, if the institutions are conducted in accordance with that object, and if the education provided conforms with such standards as may be laid down or approved by the competent authorities, in particular for education of the same level.

Article 3

In order to eliminate and prevent discrimination within the meaning of this Convention, the States Parties thereto undertake:

a. To abrogate any statutory provisions and any administrative instructions and to discontinue any administrative practices which involve discrimination in education;

b. To ensure, by legislation where necessary, that there is no discrimination in the admission of pupils to educational institutions;

c. Not to allow any differences of treatment by the public authorities between nationals, except on the basis of merit or need, in the matter of school fees and the grant of scholarships or other forms of assistance to pupils and necessary permits and facilities for the pursuit of studies in foreign countries;

d. Not to allow, in any form of assistance granted by the public authorities to educational institutions, any restrictions or preference based solely on the ground that pupils belong to a particular group;

e. To give foreign nationals resident within their territory the same access to education as that given to their own nationals.

Article 4

The States Parties to this Convention undertake furthermore to formulate, develop and apply a national policy which, by methods appropriate to the circumstances and to national usage, will tend to promote equality of opportunity and of treatment in the matter of education and in particular:

a. To make primary education free and compulsory; make secondary education in its different forms generally available and accessible to all; make higher education equally accessible to all on the basis of individual capacity; assure compliance by all with the obligation to attend school prescribed by law;

b. To ensure that the standards of education are equivalent in all public education institutions of the same level, and that the conditions relating to the quality of the education provided are also equivalent;

c. To encourage and intensify by appropriate methods the education of persons who have not received any primary education or who have not completed the entire primary education course and the continuation of their education on the basis of individual capacity;

d. To provide training for the teaching profession without discrimination.

Article 5

1. The States Parties to this Convention agree that:

a. Education shall be directed to the full development of the human personality and to the strengthening of respect for human rights and fundamental freedoms; it shall promote understanding, tolerance and friendship among all nations, racial or religious groups, and shall further the activities of the United Nations for the maintenance of peace;

b. It is essential to respect the liberty of parents and, where applicable, of legal guardians, firstly to choose for their children institutions other than those maintained by the public authorities but conforming to such minimum educational standards as may be laid down or approved by the competent authorities and, secondly, to ensure in a manner consistent with the procedures followed in the State for the application of its legislation, the religious and moral education of the children in conformity with their own convictions; and no person or group of persons should be compelled to receive religious instruction inconsistent with his or their conviction;

c. It is essential to recognize the right of members of national minorities to carry on their own educational activities, including the maintenance of schools and, depending on the educational policy of each State, the use or the teaching of their own language, provided however:

    i. That this right is not exercised in a manner which prevents the members of these minorities from understanding the culture and language of the community as a whole and from participating in its activities, or which prejudices national sovereignty;

    ii. That the standard of education is not lower than the general standard laid down or approved by the competent authorities; and

    iii. That attendance at such schools is optional.

2. The States Parties to this Convention undertake to take all necessary measures to ensure the application of the principles enunciated in paragraph 1 of this article.

Article 6

In the application of this Convention, the States Parties to it undertake to pay the greatest attention to any recommendations hereafter adopted by the General Conference of the United Nations Educational, Scientific and Cultural Organization defining the measures to be taken against the different forms of discrimination in education and for the purpose of ensuring equality of opportunity and treatment in education.

Article 7

The States Parties to this Convention shall in their periodic reports submitted to the General Conference of the United Nations Educational, Scientific and Cultural Organization on dates and in a manner to be determined by it, give information on the legislative and administrative provisions which they have adopted and other action which they have taken for the application of this Convention, including that taken for the formulation and the development of the national policy defined in article 4 as well as the results achieved and the obstacles encountered in the application of that policy.

Article 8

Any dispute which may arise between any two or more States Parties to this Convention concerning the interpretation or application of this Convention which is not settled by negotiations shall at the request of the parties to the dispute be referred, failing other means of settling the dispute, to the International Court of Justice for decision.

Article 9

Reservations to this Convention shall not be permitted.

Article 10

This Convention shall not have the effect of diminishing the rights which individuals or groups may enjoy by virtue of agreements concluded between two or more States, where such rights are not contrary to the letter or spirit of this Convention.

Article 11

This Convention is drawn up in English, French, Russian and Spanish, the four texts being equally authoritative.

Article 12

1. This Convention shall be subject to ratification or acceptance by States Members of the United Nations Educational, Scientific and Cultural Organization in accordance with their respective constitutional procedures.

2. The instruments of ratification or acceptance shall be deposited with the Director-General of the United Nations Educational, Scientific and Cultural Organization.

Article 13

1. This Convention shall be open to accession by all States not Members of the United Nations Educational, Scientific and Cultural Organization which are invited to do so by the Executive Board of the Organization.

2. Accession shall be effected by the deposit of an instrument of accession with the Director-General of the United Nations Educational, Scientific and Cultural Organization.

Article 14

This Convention shall enter into force three months after the date of the deposit of the third instrument of ratification, acceptance or accession, but only with respect to those States which have deposited their respective instruments on or before that date. It shall enter into force with respect to any other State three months after the deposit of its instrument of ratification, acceptance or accession.

Article 15

The States Parties to this Convention recognize that the Convention is applicable not only to their metropolitan territory but also to all non-self-governing, trust, colonial and other territories for the international relations of which they are responsible; they undertake to consult, if necessary, the governments or other competent authorities of these territories on or before ratification, acceptance or accession with a view to securing the application of the Convention to those territories, and to notify the Director-General of the United Nations Educational, Scientific and Cultural Organization of the territories to which it is accordingly applied, the notification to take effect three months after the date of its receipt.

Article 16

1. Each State Party to this Convention may denounce the Convention on its

own behalf or on behalf of any territory for whose international relations it is responsible.

2. The denunciation shall be notified by an instrument in writing, deposited with the Director-General of the United Nations Educational, Scientific and Cultural Organization.

3. The denunciation shall take effect twelve months after the receipt of the instrument of denunciation.

Article 17

The Director-General of the United Nations Educational, Scientific and Cultural Organization shall inform the States Members of the Organization, the States not members of the Organization which are referred to in article 13, as well as the United Nations, of the deposit of all the instruments of ratification, acceptance and accession provided for in articles 12 and 13, and of notifications and denunciations provided for in articles 15 and 16 respectively.

Article 18

1. This Convention may be revised by the General Conference of the United Nations Educational, Scientific and Cultural Organization. Any such revision shall, however, bind only the States which shall become Parties to the revising convention.

2. If the General Conference should adopt a new convention revising this Convention in whole or in part, then, unless the new convention otherwise provides, this Convention shall cease to be open to ratification, acceptance or accession as from the date on which the new revising convention enters into force.

Article 19

In conformity with Article 102 of the Charter of the United Nations, this Convention shall be registered with the Secretariat of the United Nations at the request of the Director-General of the United Nations Educational, Scientific and Cultural Organization.

DONE in Paris, this fifteenth day of December 1960, in two authentic copies bearing the signatures of the President of the eleventh session of the General Conference and of the Director-General of the United Nations Educational, Scientific and Cultural Organization, which shall be deposited in the archives of the United Nations Educational, Scientific and Cultural Organization, and certified true copies of which shall be delivered to all the States referred to in articles 12 and 13 as well as to the United Nations.

The foregoing is the authentic text of the Convention duly adopted by the General Conference of the United Nations Educational, Scientific and Cultural Organization during its eleventh session, which was held in Paris and declared closed the fifteenth day of December 1960.

IN FAITH WHEREOF we have appended our signatures this fifteenth day of December 1960.

3. DECLARATION OF THE PRINCIPLES OF INTER-NATIONAL CULTURAL COOPERATION (1966) Proclaimed by the General Conference of the United Nations Educational, Scientific and Cultural Organization at its fourteenth session, on 4 November 1966, UNESCO Doc. 14C/Resolutions at 86 (1967).

The General Conference of the United Nations Educational, Scientific and Cultural Organization, met in Paris for its fourteenth session, this fourth day of November 1966, being the twentieth anniversary of the foundation of the Organization,

Recalling that the Constitution of the Organization declares that "since wars begin in the minds of men, it is in the minds of men that the defences of peace must be constructed" and that the peace must be founded, if it is not to fail, upon the intellectual and moral solidarity of mankind,

Recalling that the Constitution also states that the wide diffusion of culture and the education of humanity for justice and liberty and peace are indispensable to the dignity of man and constitute a sacred duty which all the nations must fulfil in a spirit of mutual assistance and concern,

Considering that the Organization's Member States, believing in the pursuit of truth and the free exchange of ideas and knowledge, have agreed and determined to develop and to increase the means of communication between their peoples,

Considering that, despite the technical advances which facilitate the development and dissemination of knowledge and ideas, ignorance of the way of life and customs of peoples still presents an obstacle to friendship among the nations, to peaceful co-operation and to the progress of mankind,

Taking account of the Universal Declaration of Human Rights, the Declaration of the Rights of the Child, the Declaration on the Granting of Independence to Colonial Countries and Peoples, the United Nations Declaration on the Elimination of all Forms of Racial Discrimination, the Declaration on the Promotion among Youth of the Ideals of Peace, Mutual Respect and Understanding between Peoples, and the Declaration on the Inadmissibility of Intervention in the Domestic Affairs of States and the Protection of their Independence and Sovereignty, proclaimed successively by the General Assembly of the United Nations,

Convinced by the experience of the Organization's first twenty years that, if international cultural co-operation is to be strengthened, its principles require to be affirmed,

Proclaims this Declaration of the principles of international cultural co-operation, to the end that governments, authorities, organizations, associations and institutions responsible for cultural activities may constantly be guided by these principles; and for the purpose, as set out in the Constitution of the Organization, of advancing, through the educational, scientific and cultural relations of the peoples of the world, the objectives of peace and welfare that are defined in the Charter of the United Nations:

Article I

1. Each culture has a dignity and value which must be respected and preserved.

2. Every people has the right and the duty to develop its culture.

3. In their rich variety and diversity, and in the reciprocal influences they exert on one another, all cultures form part of the common heritage belonging to all mankind.

Article II

Nations shall endeavour to develop the various branches of culture side by side and, as far as possible, simultaneously, so as to establish a harmonious balance between technical progress and the intellectual and moral advancement of mankind.

Article III

International cultural co-operation shall cover all aspects of intellectual and creative activities relating to education, science and culture.

Article IV

The aims of international cultural co-operation in its various forms, bilateral or multilateral, regional or universal, shall be:

1. To spread knowledge, to stimulate talent and to enrich cultures;

2. To develop peaceful relations and friendship among the peoples and bring about a better understanding of each other's way of life;

3. To contribute to the application of the principles set out in the United Nations Declarations that are recalled in the Preamble to this Declaration;

4. To enable everyone to have access to knowledge, to enjoy the arts and literature of all peoples, to share in advances made in science in all parts of the world and in the resulting benefits, and to contribute to the enrichment of cultural life;

5. To raise the level of the spiritual and material life of man in all parts of the world.

Article V

Cultural co-operation is a right and a duty for all peoples and all nations, which should share with one another their knowledge and skills.

Article VI

International co-operation, while promoting the enrichment of all cultures through its beneficent action, shall respect the distinctive character of each.

Article VII

1. Broad dissemination of ideas and knowledge, based on the freest exchange and discussion, is essential to creative activity, the pursuit of truth and the development of the personality.

2. In cultural co-operation, stress shall be laid on ideas and values conducive

to the creation of a climate of friendship and peace. Any mark of hostility in attitudes and in expression of opinion shall be avoided. Every effort shall be made, in presenting and disseminating information, to ensure its authenticity.

Article VIII

Cultural co-operation shall be carried on for the mutual benefit of all the nations practising it. Exchanges to which it gives rise shall be arranged in a spirit of broad reciprocity.

Article IX

Cultural co-operation shall contribute to the establishment of stable, long-term relations between peoples, which should be subjected as little as possible to the strains which may arise in international life.

Article X

Cultural co-operation shall be specially concerned with the moral and intellectual education of young people in a spirit of friendship, international understanding and peace and shall foster awareness among States of the need to stimulate talent and promote the training of the rising generations in the most varied sectors.

Article XI

1. In their cultural relations, States shall bear in mind the principles of the United Nations. In seeking to achieve international co-operation, they shall respect the sovereign equality of States and shall refrain from intervention in matters which are essentially within the domestic jurisdiction of any State.

2. The principles of this Declaration shall be applied with due regard for human rights and fundamental freedoms.

4. DECLARATION ON FUNDAMENTAL PRINCIPLES CONCERNING THE CONTRIBUTION OF THE MASS MEDIA TO STRENGTHENING PEACE AND INTER-NATIONAL UNDERSTANDING, THE PROMOTION OF HUMAN RIGHTS AND TO COUNTERING RACIALISM, *APARTHEID* AND INCITEMENT TO WAR

(1978) Adopted by the General Conference of the United Nations Educational, Scientific and Cultural Organization on 22 November 1978.

PREAMBLE

The General Conference,

1. *Recalling* that by its Constitution the purpose of UNESCO is to "contribute to peace and security by promoting collaboration among the nations through education, science and culture in order to further universal respect for justice, for the rule of law and for the human rights and fundamental freedoms" (Art.

I, 1), and that to realize this purpose the Organization will strive "to promote the free flow of ideas by word and image" (Art. I, 2),

2. Further *recalling* that under the Constitution the Member States of UNESCO, "believing in full and equal opportunities for education for all, in the unrestricted pursuit of objective truth, and in the free exchange of ideas and knowledge, and agreed and determined to develop and to increase the means of communication between their peoples and to employ these means for the purposes of mutual understanding and a truer and more perfect knowledge of each other's lives" (sixth preambular paragraph),

3. *Recalling* the purposes and principles of the United Nations, as specified in the Charter,

4. *Recalling* the Universal Declaration of Human Rights, adopted by the General Assembly of the United Nations in 1948 and particularly Article 19 which provides that "everyone has the right to freedom of opinion and expression; this right includes freedom to hold opinions without interference and to seek, receive and impart information and ideas through any media and regardless of frontiers;" and the International Covenant on Civil and Political Rights, adopted by the General Assembly of the United Nations in 1966, Article 19 of which proclaims the same principles and Article 20 of which condemns incitement to war, the advocacy of national, racial or religious hatred and any form of discrimination, hostility or violence,

5. *Recalling* Article 4 of the International Convention on the Elimination of all Forms of Racial Discrimination adopted by the General Assembly of the United Nations in 1965, and the International Convention on the Suppression and Punishment of the Crime of *Apartheid* adopted by the General Assembly of the United Nations in 1973, whereby the States acceding to these Conventions undertook to adopt immediate and positive measures designed to eradicate all incitement to, or acts of, racial discrimination, and agreed to prevent any encouragement of the crime of *apartheid* and similar segregationist policies or their manifestations,

6. *Recalling* the Declaration on the Promotion among Youth of the Ideals of Peace, Mutual Respect and Understanding between Peoples, adopted by the General Assembly of the United Nations in 1965,

7. *Recalling* the declarations and resolutions adopted by the various organs of the United Nations concerning the establishment of a New International Economic Order and the role UNESCO is called upon to play in this respect,

8. *Recalling* the Declaration of the Principles of International Cultural Co-operation, adopted by the General Conference of UNESCO in 1966,

9. *Recalling* Resolution 59(I) of the General Assembly of the United Nations, adopted in 1946 and declaring

"Freedom of information is a fundamental human right and is the touchstone of all freedoms to which the United Nations is conse crated; Freedom of information requires as an indispensable element the willingness and capacity to employ its privileges without abuse. It requires as a basic discipline the moral obligation to seek the facts without prejudice and to spread knowledge without malicious intent;"

10. *Recalling* Resolution 110(II) of the General Assembly of the United Nations adopted in 1947 condemning all forms of propaganda which are designed or likely to provoke or encourage any threat to the peace, breach of the peace, or act of aggression,

11. *Recalling* Resolution 127(II), also adopted by the General Assembly in 1947, which invites Member States to take measures, within the limits of constitutional procedures, to combat the diffusion of false or distorted reports likely to injure friendly relations between States, as well as the other resolutions of the General Assembly concerning the mass media and their contribution to strengthening peace, thus contributing to the growth of trust and friendly relations among States,

12. *Recalling* Resolution 9.12 adopted by the General Conference of UNESCO in 1968 reiterating UNESCO's objective to help to eradicate colonialism and racialism, and Resolution 12.1 adopted by the General Conference of UNESCO in 1976 which proclaims that colonialism, neo-colonialism and racialism in all its forms and manifestations are incompatible with the fundamental aims of UNESCO,

13. *Recalling* Resolution 4.301 adopted in 1970 by the General Conference of UNESCO on the contribution of the information media to furthering international understanding and co-operation in the interests of peace and human welfare, and to countering propaganda on behalf of war, racialism *apartheid* and hatred among nations, and *aware* of the fundamental contribution that mass media can make to the realization of these objectives,

14. *Recalling* the Declaration on Race and Racial Prejudice adopted by the General Conference of UNESCO at its twentieth session,

15. *Conscious* of the complexity of the problems of information in modern society, of the diversity of solutions which have been offered to them, as evidenced in particular by consideration given to them within UNESCO as well as of the legitimate desire of all parties concerned that their aspirations, points of view and cultural identity be taken into due consideration,

16. *Conscious* of the aspirations of the developing countries for the establishment of a new, more just and more effective world information and communication order,

17. Proclaims on this twenty-second day of November 1978 this Declaration on Fundamental Principles concerning the Contribution of the Mass Media to Strengthening Peace and International Understanding, to the Promotion of Human Rights and to Countering Racialism, *Apartheid* and Incitement to War.

Article I

The Strengthening of peace and international understanding, the promotion of human rights and the countering of racialism, *apartheid* and incitement to war demand a free flow and a wider and better balanced dissemination of information. To this end, the mass media have a leading contribution to make. This contribution will be more effective to the extent that the information reflects the different aspects of the subject dealt with.

Article II

1. The exercise of freedom of opinion, expression and information, recog-

nized as an integral part of human rights and fundamental freedoms, is a vital factor in the strengthening of peace and international understanding.

2. Access by the public to information should be guaranteed by the diversity of the sources and means of information available to it, thus enabling each individual to check the accuracy of facts and to appraise events objectively. To this end, journalists must have freedom to report and the fullest possible facilities of access to information. Similarly, it is important that the mass media be responsive to concerns of peoples and individuals, thus promoting the participation of the public in the elaboration of information.

3. With a view to the strengthening of peace and international understanding, to promoting human rights and to countering racism, *apartheid* and incitement to war, the mass media throughout the world, by reason of their role, contribute effectively to promoting human rights, in particular by giving expression to oppressed peoples who struggle against colonialism, neo-colonialism, foreign occupation and all forms of racial discrimination and oppression and who are unable to make their voices heard within their own territories.

4. If the mass media are to be in a position to promote the principles of this Declaration in their activities, it is essential that journalists and other agents of the mass media, in their own country or abroad, be assured of protection guaranteeing them the best conditions for the exercise of their profession.

Article III

1. The mass media have an important contribution to make to the strengthening of peace and international understanding and in countering racism, *apartheid* and incitement to war.

2. In countering aggressive war, racism, *apartheid* and other violations of human rights which are *inter alia* spawned by prejudice and ignorance, the mass media, by disseminating information on the aims aspirations, cultures and needs of all people, contribute to eliminate ignorance and misunderstanding between peoples, to make nationals of a country sensitive to the needs and desires of others, to ensure the respect of the rights and dignity of all nations, all peoples and all individuals without distinction of race, sex, language, religion or nationality and to draw attention to the great evils which afflict humanity, such as poverty, malnutrition and diseases, thereby promoting the formulation by States of policies best able to promote the reduction of international tension and the peaceful and the equitable settlement of international disputes.

Article IV

The mass media have an essential part to play in the education of young people in a spirit of peace, justice, freedom, mutual respect and understanding, in order to promote human rights, equality of rights as between all human beings and all nations, and economic and social progress. Equally they have an important role to play in making known the views and aspirations of the younger generation.

Article V

In order to respect freedom of opinion, expression and information and in order that information may reflect all points of view, it is important that the points of view presented by those who consider that the information published or disseminated about them has seriously prejudiced their effort to strengthen peace and international understanding, to promote human rights or to counter racism, *apartheid* and incitement to war be disseminated.

Article VI

For the establishment of a new equilibrium and greater reciprocity in the flow of information, which will be conducive to the institution of a just and lasting peace and to the economic and political independence of the developing countries, it is necessary to correct the inequalities in the flow of information to and from developing countries, and between those countries. To this end, it is essential that their mass media should have conditions and resources enabling them to gain strength and expand, and to co-operate both among themselves and with the mass media in developed countries.

Article VII

By disseminating more widely all of the information concerning the objectives and principles universally accepted which are the bases of the resolutions adopted by the different organs of the United Nations, the mass media contribute effectively to the strengthening of peace and international understanding, to the promotion of human rights, as well as to the establishment of a more just and equitable international economic order.

Article VIII

Professional organizations, and people who participate in the professional training of journalists and other agents of the mass media and who assist them in performing their functions in a responsible manner should attach special importance to the principles of this Declaration when drawing up and ensuring application of their codes of ethics.

Article IX

In the spirit of this Declaration it is for the international community to contribute to the creation of the conditions for a free flow and wider and more balanced dissemination of information, and the conditions for the protection, in the exercise of their functions, of journalists and other agents of the mass media. UNESCO is well placed to make a valuable contribution in this respect.

Article X

1. With due respect for constitutional provisions designed to guarantee freedom of information and for the applicable international instruments and agreements, it is indispensable to create and maintain throughout the world the conditions which make it possible for the organizations and person professionally involved in the dissemination of information to achieve the objectives of this Declaration.

2. It is important that a free flow and wider and better balanced dissemination of information be encouraged.

3. To this end, it is necessary that States should facilitate the procurement, by the mass media in the developing countries, of adequate conditions and resources enabling them to gain strength and expand, and that they should support co-operation by the latter both among themselves and with the mass media in developed countries.

4. Similarly, on a basis of equality of rights, mutual advantage, and respect for the diversity of cultures which go to make up the common heritage of mankind, it is essential that bilateral and multilateral exchanges of information among all States, and in particular between those which have different economic and social systems be encouraged and developed.

Article XI

For this Declaration to be fully effective it is necessary, with due respect for the legislative and administrative provisions and the other obligations of Member States, to guarantee the existence of favourable conditions for the operation of the mass media, in conformity with the provisions of the Universal Declaration of Human Rights and with the corresponding principles proclaimed in the International Covenant on Civil and Political Rights adopted by the General Assembly of the United Nations in 1966.

5. DECLARATION ON RACE AND RACIAL PREJUDICE (1978) Adopted by the General Conference of the United Nations Educational, Scientific and Cultural Organization 1978

PREAMBLE

The General Conference of the United Nations Educational, Scientific and Cultural Organization, meeting at Paris at its twentieth session, from 24 October to 28 November 1978,

Whereas it is stated in the Preamble to the Constitution of Unesco, adopted on 16 November 1945, that "the great and terrible war which has now ended was a war made possible by the denial of the democratic principles of the dignity, equality and mutual respect of men, and by the propagation, in their place, through ignorance and prejudice, of the doctrine of the inequality of men and races," and whereas, according to Article I of the said Constitution, the purpose of Unesco "is to contribute to peace and security by promoting collaboration among the nations through education, science and culture in order to further universal respect for justice, for the rule of law and for the human rights and fundamental freedoms which are affirmed for the peoples of the world, without distinction of race, sex, language or religion, by the Charter of the United Nations,"

Recognizing that, more than three decades after the founding of Unesco, these principles are just as significant as they were when they were embodied in its Constitution,

Mindful of the process of decolonization and other historical changes which have led most of the peoples formerly under foreign rule to recover their sovereignty, making the international community a universal and diversified whole and creating new opportunities of eradicating the scourge of racism and of putting an end to its odious manifestations in all aspects of social and political life, both nationally and internationally,

Convinced that the essential unity of the human race and consequently the fundamental equality of all human beings and all peoples, recognized in the loftiest expressions of philosophy, morality and religion, reflect an ideal towards which ethics and science are converging today,

Convinced that all peoples and all human groups, whatever their composition or ethnic origin, contribute according to their own genius to the progress of the civilizations and cultures which, in their plurality and as a result of their interpenetration, constitute the common heritage of mankind,

Confirming its attachment to the principles proclaimed in the United Nations Charter and the Universal Declaration of Human Rights and its determination to promote the implementation of the International Covenants on Human Rights as well as the Declaration on the Establishment of a New International Economic Order,

Determined also to promote the implementation of the United Nations Declaration and the International Convention on the Elimination of all Forms of Racial Discrimination,

Noting the International Convention on the Prevention and Punishment of the Crime of Genocide, the International Convention on the Suppression and Punishment of the Crime of Apartheid and the Convention on the Non-Applicability of Statutory Limitations to War Crimes and Crimes against Humanity,

Recalling also the international instruments already adopted by Unesco, including in particular the Convention and Recommendation against Discrimination in Education, the Recommendation concerning the Status of Teachers, the Declaration of the Principles of International Cultural Co-operation, the Recommendation concerning Education for International Understanding, Co-operation and Peace and Education relating to Human Rights and Fundamental Freedoms, the Recommendation on the Status of Scientific Researchers, and the Recommendation on participation by the people at large in cultural life and their contribution to it,

Bearing in mind the four statements on the race question adopted by experts convened by Unesco,

Reaffirming its desire to play a vigorous and constructive part in the implementation of the programme of the Decade for Action to Combat Racism and Racial Discrimination, as defined by the General Assembly of the United Nations at its twenty-eighth session,

Noting with the gravest concern that racism, racial discrimination, colonialism and apartheid continue to afflict the world in everchanging forms, as a result both of the continuation of legislation provisions and government and administrative practices contrary to the principles of human rights and also of the continued existence of political and social structures, and of relationships and attitudes, characterized by injustice and contempt for human beings and leading to the exclusion, humiliation and exploitation, or to the forced assimilation, of the members of disadvantaged groups,

Expressing its indignation at these offences against human dignity, *deploring* the obstacles they place in the way of mutual understanding between peoples and *alarmed* at the danger of their seriously disturbing international peace and security,

Adopts and solemnly proclaims this Declaration on Race and Racial Prejudice:

Article 1

1. All human beings belong to a single species and are descended from a common stock. They are born equal in dignity and rights and all form an integral part of humanity.

2. All individuals and groups have the right to be different, to consider themselves as different and to be regarded as such. However, the diversity of life styles and the right to be different may not, in any circumstances, serve as a pretext for racial prejudice; they may not justify either in law or in fact any discriminatory practice whatsoever, nor provide a ground for the policy of apartheid, which is the extreme form of racism.

3. Identity of origin in no way affects the fact that human beings can and may live differently, nor does it preclude the existence of differences based on cultural, environmental and historical diversity nor the right to maintain cultural identity.

4. All peoples of the world possess equal faculties for attaining the highest level in intellectual, technical, social, economic, cultural and political development.

5. The differences between the achievements of the different peoples are entirely attributable to geographical, historical, political, economic, social and cultural factors. Such differences can in no case serve as a pretext for any rank-ordered classification of nations or peoples.

Article 2

1. Any theory which involves the claim that racial or ethnic groups are inherently superior or inferior, thus implying that some would be entitled to dominate or eliminate others, presumed to be inferior, or which bases value judgements on racial differentiation, has no scientific foundation and is contrary to the moral and ethical principles of humanity.

2. Racism includes racist ideologies, prejudiced attitudes, discriminatory behaviour, structural arrangements and institutionalized practices resulting in racial inequality as well as the fallacious notion that discriminatory relations between groups are morally and scientifically justifiable; it is reflected in discriminatory provisions in legislation or regulations and discriminatory practices as well as in anti-social beliefs and acts; it hinders the development of its victims, perverts those who practise it, divides nations internally, impedes international co-operation and gives rise to political tensions between peoples; it is contrary to the fundamental principles of international law and, consequently, seriously disturbs international peace and security.

3. Racial prejudice, historically linked with inequalities in power, reinforced by economic and social differences between individuals and groups, and still seeking today to justify such inequalities, is totally without justification.

Article 3

Any distinction, exclusion, restriction or preference based on race, colour, ethnic or national origin or religious intolerance motivated by racist consider-ations, which destroys or compromises the sovereign equality of States and the right of peoples to self-determination, or which limits in an arbitrary or discriminatory manner the right of every human being and group to full development is incompatible with the requirements of an international order which is just and guarantees respect for human rights; the right to full development implies equal access to the means of personal and collective advancement and fulfilment in a climate of respect for the values of civilizations and cultures, both national and world-wide.

Article 4

1. Any restriction on the complete self-fulfilment of human beings and free communication between them which is based on racial or ethnic considerations is contrary to the principle of equality in dignity and rights; it cannot be admitted.

2. One of the most serious violations of this principle is represented by apartheid, which, like genocide, is a crime against humanity, and gravely disturbs international peace and security.

3. Other policies and practices of racial segregation and discrimination constitute crimes against the conscience and dignity of mankind and may lead to political tensions and gravely endanger international peace and security.

Article 5

1. Culture, as a product of all human beings and a common heritage of mankind, and education in its broadest sense, offer men and women increas-ingly effective means of adaptation, enabling them not only to affirm that they are born equal in dignity and rights, but also to recognize that they should respect the right of all groups to their own cultural identity and the development of their distinctive cultural life within the national and international context, it being understood that it rests with each group to decide in complete freedom on the maintenance and, if appropriate, the adaptation or enrichment of the values which it regards as essential to its identity.

2. States, in accordance with their constitutional principles and procedures, as well as all other competent authorities and the entire teaching profession, have a responsibility to see that the educational resources of all countries are used to combat racism, more especially by ensuring that curricula and textbooks include scientific and ethical considerations concerning human unity and diversity and that no invidious distinctions are made with regard to any people; by training teachers to achieve these ends; by making the resources of the educational system available to all groups of the population without racial restriction or discrimination; and by taking appropriate steps to remedy the handicaps from which certain racial or ethnic groups suffer with regard to their level of education and standard of living and in particular to prevent such handicaps from being passed on to children.

3. The mass media and those who control or serve them, as well as all organized groups within national communities, are urged—with due regard to the principles embodied in the Universal Declaration of Human Rights, particularly the principle of freedom of expression—to promote understanding, tolerance and friendship among individuals and groups and to contribute to the eradication of racism, racial discrimination and racial prejudice, in particular by refraining from presenting a stereotyped, partial, unilateral or tendentious picture of individuals and of various human groups. Communication between racial and ethnic groups must be a reciprocal process, enabling them to express themselves and to be fully heard without let or hindrance. The mass media should therefore be freely receptive to ideas of individuals and groups which facilitate such communication.

Article 6

1. The State has prime responsibility for ensuring human rights and fundamental freedoms on an entirely equal footing in dignity and rights for all individuals and all groups.

2. So far as its competence extends and in accordance with its constitutional principles and procedures, the State should take all appropriate steps, *inter alia* by legislation, particularly in the spheres of education, culture and communication, to prevent, prohibit and eradicate racism, racist propaganda, racial segregation and apartheid and to encourage the dissemination of knowledge and the findings of appropriate research in natural and social sciences on the causes and prevention of racial prejudice and racist attitudes, with due regard to the principles embodied in the Universal Declaration of Human Rights and in the International Covenant on Civil and Political Rights.

3. Since laws proscribing racial discrimination are not in themselves sufficient, it is also incumbent on States to supplement them by administrative machinery for the systematic investigation of instances of racial discrimination, by a comprehensive framework of legal remedies against acts of racial discrimination, by broadly based education and research programmes designed to combat racial prejudice and racial discrimination and by programmes of positive political, social, educational and cultural measures calculated to promote genuine mutual respect among groups. Where circumstances warrant, special programmes should be undertaken to promote the advancement of disadvantaged groups and, in the case of nationals, to ensure their effective participation in the decision-making processes of the community.

Article 7

In addition to political, economic and social measures, law is one of the principal means of ensuring equality in dignity and rights among individuals, and of curbing any propaganda, any form of organization or any practice which is based on ideas or theories referring to the alleged superiority of racial or ethnic groups or which seeks to justify or encourage racial hatred and discrimination in any form. States should adopt such legislation as is appropriate to this end and see that it is given effect and applied by all their services, with due regard to the principles embodied in the Universal Declaration of Human Rights. Such legislation should form part of a political, economic and social framework conducive to its implementation. Individuals and other legal entities, both public and private, must conform with such legislation and use all appropriate means to help the population as a whole to understand and apply it.

Article 8

1. Individuals, being entitled to an economic, social, cultural and legal order, on the national and international planes, such as to allow them to exercise all their capabilities on a basis of entire equality of rights and opportunities, have corresponding duties towards their fellows, towards the society in which they live and towards the international community. They are accordingly under an obligation to promote harmony among the peoples, to combat racism and racial prejudice and to assist by every means available to them in eradicating racial discrimination in all its forms.

2. In the field of racial prejudice and racist attitudes and practices, specialists in natural and social sciences and cultural studies, as well as scientific organizations and associations, are called upon to undertake objective research on a wide interdisciplinary basis; all States should encourage them to this end.

3. It is, in particular, incumbent upon such specialists to ensure, by all means available to them, that their research findings are not misinterpreted, and also that they assist the public in understanding such findings.

Article 9

1. The principle of the equality in dignity and rights of all human beings and all peoples, irrespective of race, colour and origin, is a generally accepted and recognized principle of international law. Consequently any form of racial discrimination practised by a State constitutes a violation of international law giving rise to its international responsibility.

2. Special measures must be taken to ensure equality in dignity and rights for individuals and groups wherever necessary, while ensuring that they are not such as to appear racially discriminatory. In this respect, particular attention should be paid to racial or ethnic groups which are socially or economically disadvantaged, so as to afford them, on a completely equal footing and without discrimination or restriction, the protection of the laws and regulations and the advantages of the social measures in force, in particular in regard to housing, employment and health; to respect the authenticity of their culture and values; and to facilitate their social and occupational advancement, especially through education.

3. Population groups of foreign origin, particularly migrant workers and their families who contribute to the development of the host country, should benefit from appropriate measures designed to afford them security and respect for their dignity and cultural values and to facilitate their adaptation to the host environment and their professional advancement with a view to their subsequent reintegration in their country of origin and their contribution to its development; steps should be taken to make it possible for their children to be taught their mother tongue.

4. Existing desequilibria in international economic relations contribute to

the exacerbation of racism and racial prejudice; all States should consequently endeavour to contribute to the restructuring of the international economy on a more equitable basis.

Article 10

International organizations, whether universal or regional, governmental or non-governmental, are called upon to co-operate and assist, so far as their respective fields of competence and means allow, in the full and complete implementation of the principles set out in this Declaration, thus contributing to the legitimate struggle of all men, born equal in dignity and rights, against the tyranny and oppression of racism, racial segregation, apartheid and genocide, so that all the peoples of the world may be forever delivered from these scourges.

IV. United Nations and Specialized Agency Procedures

A. UNITED NATIONS PROCEDURES

INTRODUCTION

United Nations human rights treaties and practice include a surprising array of procedural techniques that virtually defy systematic analysis. The material in the following pages fits generally into the following categories[16]:

1. Reporting procedures.
2. Individual complaints procedures.
3. Standing procedures triggered primarily by complaints dealing with the general situation in a country rather than the redress of individual grievances.
4. State against state complaints procedures.
5. Visiting missions (including observation or supervision of elections).
6. *Ad hoc* fact-finding bodies.
7. Executive-style agencies of high status designed to deal with a specific problem through administrative and persuasive methods.
8. Procedures for the referral of disputes to the International Court of Justice.

Many of the procedures are discussed in the activists' "Bible" in this area, H. Hannum, ed., *Guide to International Human Rights Practice* (1984).

We turn to a brief discussion of each of these different types of procedure.[17]

1. Examples of reporting techniques may be found in the material on Trust and other Non-self-governing Territories, in the International Convention on the Elimination of All Forms of Racial Discrimination ("the Race Convention"), and both Covenants on Human Rights. Typical of reporting procedures is that states provide information on what they have been doing in respect of the area concerned and some kind of committee study takes place. This leads to comments of various degrees of specificity and perhaps to the mobilization of some kind of international pressure. Outside the decolonization area, none of the procedures yet approach in sophistication the ILO reporting procedure, *infra* Chapter V, on which they are largely modeled.

For a good discussion of reporting procedures in the context of the Covenants on Human Rights, *see* B. Ramcharan, "Implementing the International Covenants on Human Rights," in *Human Rights: Thirty Years After the Universal Declaration*, 159 (B. Ramcharan ed. 1979).

One of the great battles of the decolonization program was over the creation of procedures to deal with information from non-self-governing territories other than trust territories. The colonial powers, France in particular, took the view that if the Charter had envisioned procedures for dealing with such territories, it would have said so, as in the case of trust territories. Accordingly, it was argued that there was no power in the General Assembly to institute such procedures. Ultimately this argument did not prevail. By the time that the Special Committee on the Situation with regard to the Implementation of the Declaration on the Granting of Independence to Colonial Countries and Peoples was formed in 1961, it had already been accepted in practice that it was appropriate for the General Assembly to set up procedures for the examination of colonial information. The Special Committee took over the functions of an earlier Committee created for this task. Subsequently the Special Committee was to engage in other activities like those of the Trusteeship Council such as the hearing of petitioners, the sending of Visiting Missions and the observation of elections. *See* United Nations Department of Political Affairs, Trusteeship and Decolonization, "Fifteen Years of the United Nations Declaration on the Granting of Independence to Colonial Countries and Peoples," *Decolonization*, Vol. II, No. 6 (December 1975).

2. The only United Nations procedure aimed specifically at dealing with individual complaints that is currently operative is that under the Optional Protocol to the International Covenant on Civil and Political Rights. The similar procedure under the Race Convention has only recently received sufficient adherents to become operative. Complaints under the Optional Protocol are considered by the Human Rights Committee which is set up under the Covenant. It is hardly a judicial body with power to enforce judgments but it does have power to "forward its views" on a breach of the Covenant to a state accepting its jurisdiction. On the Protocol in general, *see* M. Tardu, *I Human Rights: The International Petition System*, Section 1A, 1–24 (1979).

3. The third category of standing complaints procedures dealing with the general condition in specific countries includes most of the petitions procedures in the decolonization area, the "gross violations" procedure under ECOSOC Resolution 1503 (XLVIII), and the more specialized procedures of the Commission on Human Rights dealing with the Disappeared and of the Sub-Commission on Prevention of Discrimination and Protection of Minorities dealing with slavery, indigenous populations and the human rights of persons detained or imprisoned.

The decolonization procedures are discussed in M. Tardu, *I Human Rights: The International Petition System*, Section 1B, 1–5 (Trusteeship Council), 6–8 (Special Committee on Decolonization).

* On the 1503 Procedures, *see* A. Cassese, "The Admissibility of Communications to the United Nations on Human Rights Violations," 5 *Human Rights Journal* 375 (1972–73); M. Tardu, *I Human Rights: The International Petition System*, Section 1A, 25–40.

For the Group of Experts on Slavery, *see* J. Lador-Lederer, "An International Human Rights Committee for Slavery," 3 *Israel L. Rev.*, 245 (1968); *The Anti-Slavery Reporter and Aborigines' Friend*, Vol. 12, No. 5 (November 1976) at 3–14.

The procedure on persons detained or imprisoned is discussed in K. Burke, "New United Nations Procedure to Protect Prisoners and Other Detainees," 64 *Calif. L. Rev.*, 201 (1976).

On the disappeared, *see* R. Clark and M. Berman, "State Terrorism: Disappearances," 13 *Rutgers L. J.*, 531 (1982).

4. State against state complaints have been little used in practice, mainly because states are reluctant to bring attention to the skeletons in the cupboards of other states for fear of retaliatory exposure of their own. Such procedures are, however, provided for in the Race Convention and the Covenant on Civil and Political Rights. Essentially, following an allegation by one state that another is

denying human rights, the procedures contemplate fact-finding and conciliation rather than judicial-type techniques.

5. Visiting missions to ascertain developments or watch elections or plebiscites are regular features of the decolonization area. "Periodic visits" were contemplated by the Charter, Article 87, in respect of Trust Territories. In 1965 the New Zealand Government agreed to the presence of a Mission under the auspices of the General Assembly and its Special Committee to observe elections in its territory, the Cook Islands, that led to a new associate relationship between New Zealand and the territory. Since that breakthrough, the Committee has sent numerous missions to other non-selfgoverning territories. *See* reference in Paragraph 1. *supra.*

6. From time to time the General Assembly and the Commission on Human Rights have created *ad hoc* bodies to examine the facts relating to human rights in particular countries, notably South Vietnam, southern Africa, Chile and the Israeli occupied territories. The rules of procedure followed by some of these bodies have been rudimentary and an effort was made to provide for some general standards that might be followed by such *ad hoc* bodies. Hence the Model Rules of Procedure for United Nations Bodies Dealing with Violations of Human Rights that were drafted by a Working Group of the Commission on Human Rights. The drafting effort was not a huge success—the standards that emerged were still vague.

On the need for such Rules to guarantee fairness, *see* S. Kaufman, "The Necessity for Rules of Procedure in Ad Hoc United Nations Investigations," 18 *American U.L.Rev.*, 739 (1968–69).

For some excellent material on fact-finding, *see* B. Ramcharan, ed., *International Fact-Finding in the Field of Human Rights* (1982).

7. Our example of the next kind of technique, an executive official of high status, is the High Commissioner for Refugees. The High Commissioner's Office was built on experience in the League of Nations, in particular the Nansen International Office for Refugees. It has played an enormously important role in the resettlement of refugees and in encouraging states to become parties to and abide by the treaties pertaining to refugees contained in Chapter I *supra. See* L. Holborn, *Refugees, A Problem of Our Time. The Work of the United Nations High Commissioner for Refugees*, 1951–1972 (1975). Proposals for a somewhat similar official, a High Commissioner for Human Rights, who would act as a kind of international ombudsman, have not yet emerged from the General Assembly. *See* R. Clark, *A United Nations High Commissioner for Human Rights* (1972).

8. Those of us schooled in Anglo-American ways of legal process tend to emphasize the role of judicial procedures. Clauses referring disputes to the International Court of Justice do appear in a significant number of the United Nations human rights treaties but none of these has ever resulted in the referral of a case to the court. We have placed the discussion of such provisions last in this introduction and in the collection of material that follows to symbolize the low priority given to judicial procedures by states.

The clauses in the treaties take somewhat different forms but they follow a pattern and it would be tedious to reproduce all examples.

(a) The most common type of clause is one which provides that any dispute between parties to the treaty relating to its interpretation or application which is not settled by negotiation shall be referred to the International Court at the request of any of the parties to the dispute. Provisions to this effect (with only minor differences in wording) appear in:

Supplementary Convention on the Abolition of Slavery, the Slave Trade, and Institutions and Practices Similar to Slavery (1956) Article 10 [Reproduced *infra* p. 401]

Convention on the Nationality of Married Women (1957) Article 10

Convention on the Reduction of Statelessness (1954) Article 14

Convention Relating to the Status of Refugees (1951) Article 38

Convention Relating to the Status of Stateless Persons (1954) Article 34

Convention for the Suppression of the Traffic in Persons and of the Exploitation of the Prostitution of Others (1949) Article 22

Protocol Relating to the Status of Refugees (1966) Article IV

A slight variant of this kind of provision appears in the Convention of the Prevention and Punishment of the Crime of Genocide (1948) Article IX [reproduced *infra* p. 401] which mentions disputes relating to the "fulfilment" of the Convention as well as to those concerning "interpretation or application." The Genocide provision proved in fact to be something of a watershed on States' attitudes towards such clauses when nineteen States made reservations upon ratifying the treaty, limiting the effect of Article IX to cases in which all parties to the dispute concur in referring it to the Court. Their power to make such reservations was essentially upheld by the International Court in its Advisory Opinion, Reservations to the Convention on Genocide [1951] I.C.J.15. Similar reservations have been made in respect of some of the other treaties containing this kind of clause.

Another variant of this group of provisions appears in Article 22 of the International Convention on the Elimination of All Forms of Racial Discrimination (1965) [reproduced *infra* p. 367] which provides for the referral to the Court of disputes that are not settled by means of negotiation or the elaborate special procedures in the Convention.

(b) A second group of provisions requires consent of all parties to a dispute before a reference may be made to the Court. Such a provision appears in Article 8 of the Convention on Consent to Marriage, Minimum Age for Marriage and Registration of Marriages (1961) [reproduced *infra* p. 401] and Article XII of the International Convention of the Suppression and Punishment of the Crime of Apartheid (1973) [reproduced *infra* p. 380]. Probably to the same effect are the more ambiguous provisions of Article 8 of the Slavery Convention (1926) as amended by the 1953 Protocol Amending the Slavery Convention and Article V of the Convention on the International Right of Correction (1952).

(c) Finally, the more recent Convention on the Elimination of All Forms of Discrimination Against Women (1979) Article 29 has a more flexible provision [reproduced *infra* p. 382] to the effect that: (i) Disputes must first be submitted to arbitration at the request of any of the parties to them; if the parties are unable to agree on the organization of the arbitration, any one of the disputants may refer the matter to the Court; (ii) On becoming party to the treaty, a State is expressly permitted to make a reservation declining to accept the whole dispute-settlement mechanism.

1. THE TRUSTEESHIP COUNCIL (UN CHARTER ARTICLES 86–91, RULES OF PROCEDURE OF THE TRUSTEESHIP COUNCIL ARTICLES 76–92) (1945, 1946)

UNITED NATIONS CHARTER

CHAPTER XIII. THE TRUSTEESHIP COUNCIL

Composition

Article 86

1. The Trusteeship Council shall consist of the following Members of the United Nations:
   a. those Members administering trust territories;
   b. such of those Members mentioned by name in Article 23 as are not administering trust territories; and
   c. as many other Members elected for three-year terms by the General Assembly as may be necessary to ensure that the total number of members of the Trusteeship Council is equally divided between those Members of the United Nations which administer trust territories and those which do not.
2. Each member of the Trusteeship Council shall designate one specially qualified person to represent it therein.

Functions and Powers

Article 87

The General Assembly and, under its authority, the Trusteeship Council, in carrying out their functions, may:
   a. consider reports submitted by the administering authority;
   b. accept petitions and examine them in consultation with the administering authority;
   c. provide for periodic visits to the respective trust territories at times agreed upon with the administering authority; and
   d. take these and other actions in conformity with the terms of the trusteeship agreements.

Article 88

The Trusteeship Council shall formulate a questionnaire on the political, economic, social, and educational advancement of the inhabitants of each trust territory, and the administering authority for each trust territory within the competence of the General Assembly shall make an annual report to the General Assembly upon the basis of such questionnaire.

Voting

Article 89

1. Each member of the Trusteeship Council shall have one vote.
2. Decisions of the Trusteeship Council shall be made by a majority of the members present and voting.

Procedure

Article 90

1. The Trusteeship Council shall adopt its own rules of procedure including the method of selecting its President.
2. The Trusteeship Council shall meet as required in accordance with its rules, which shall include provision for the convening of meetings on the request of a majority of its members.

Article 91

The Trusteeship Council shall, when appropriate, avail itself of the assistance of the Economic and Social Council and of the specialized agencies in regard to matters with which they are respectively concerned.

RULES OF PROCEDURE OF THE TRUSTEESHIP COUNCIL

1(1) U.N. TCOR, Supp. at 11, U.N. Doc. T/1/Rev. (originally issued in 1946; periodically re-issued with revisions).

XV. Petitions

Rule 76

Petitions may be accepted and examined by the Trusteeship Council if they concern the affairs of one or more Trust Territories or the operation of the International Trusteeship System as laid down in the Charter, except that with respect to petitions relating to a strategic area the functions of the Trusteeship Council shall be governed by Article 83 of the Charter and the terms of the relevant Trusteeship Agreements.

Rule 77

Petitioners may be inhabitants of Trust Territories, or other parties.

Rule 78

Petitions may be presented in writing in accordance with rules 79 to 86, or orally in accordance with rules 87 to 90.

Rule 79

A written petition may be in the form of a letter, telegram, memorandum or other document concerning the affairs of one or more Trust Territories or the operation of the International Trusteeship System as laid down in the Charter.

Rule 80

1. The Trusteeship Council may hear oral presentations in support or elaboration of a previously submitted written petition. Oral presentations shall be confined to the subject-matter of the petition as stated in writing by the petitioners. The Trusteeship Council, in exceptional cases, may also hear orally petitions which have not been previously submitted in writing, provided that the Trusteeship Council and the Administering Authority concerned have been previously informed with regard to their subject-matter.

2. The President of the Council shall be authorized between sessions of the Council, through the Secretary-General, to inform any petitioner who requests an opportunity for an oral presentation or petition under this rule, that the Council will grant him a hearing at such a time and place as the President may name. Before communicating such information to the petitioner, the President shall inquire of the Administering Authority or Authorities concerned as to whether there are substantial reasons why the matter should first be discussed in the Council. If the Administering Authority is of the opinion that such substantial reasons exist, the President shall defer action until the matter has been decided by the Council.

Rule 81

Normally, petitions shall be considered inadmissible if they are directed against judgements of competent courts of the Administering Authority or if they lay before the Council a dispute with which the courts have competence to deal. This rule shall not be interpreted so as to prevent consideration by the Trusteeship Council of petitions against legislation on the grounds of its incompatibility with the provisions of the Charter of the United Nations or of the Trusteeship Agreement, irrespective of whether decisions on cases arising under such legislation have previously been given by the courts of the Administering Authority.

Rule 82

Written petitions may be addressed directly to the Secretary-General or may be transmitted to him through the Administering Authority.

Rule 83

Written petitions submitted to the Administering Authority for transmission shall be communicated promptly to the Secretary-General, with or without comments by the Administering Authority, at its discretion, or with an indication that such comments will follow in due course.

Rule 84

1. Representatives of the Trusteeship Council engaged in periodic visits to Trust Territories or on other official missions authorized by the Council may accept written petitions, subject to such instructions as may have been received

from the Trusteeship Council. Petitions of this kind shall be transmitted promptly to the Secretary-General for circulation to the members of the Council. A copy of each such petition shall be communicated to the competent local authority. Any observations which the visiting representatives may wish to make on the petitions, after consultation with the local representative of the Administering Authority, shall be submitted to the Trusteeship Council.

2. The visiting mission shall decide which of the communications it receives are intended for its own information and which of these are petitions to be transmitted to the Secretary-General, pursuant to paragraph 1 of this rule, to be dealt with in accordance with rules 85 and 86.

Rule 85

1. The Secretary-General shall circulate promptly to the members of the Trusteeship Council all written petitions received by him which contain requests, complaints and grievances seeking action by the Trusteeship Council.

2. Petitions concerning general problems to which the attention of the Trusteeship Council has already been called and on which the Council has taken decisions or has made recommendations, as well as anonymous communications, shall be circulated by the Secretary-General in the manner provided for in rule 24.

3. In the case of lengthy petitions, the Secretary-General will first circulate a summary of the petition, the original petition being made available to the Trusteeship Council. The original petition, however, will be circulated if the President of the Trusteeship Council, during the recess of the Council, or the Council, if it is in session, so decides.

4. The Secretary-General shall not circulate petitions which are manifestly inconsequential, a list of which, with a summary of their contents, shall be communicated to the members of the Trusteeship Council.

5. With respect to petitions relating to a strategic area, the functions of the Trusteeship Council shall be governed by Article 83 of the Charter and the terms of the relevant Trusteeship Agreement.

Rule 86

1. Written petitions will normally be placed on the agenda of a regular session provided that they shall have been received by the Administering Authority concerned either directly or through the Secretary-General at least two months before the date of the next following regular session.

2. The date of receipt of a petition shall be considered as being:

a. In respect of a petition which is presented through the Administering Authority, the date on which the petition is received by the competent local authority in the Territory or the metropolitan government of the Administering Authority, as the case may be;

b. In respect of a petition received by a visiting mission, the date on which the copy of the petition is communicated to the local authority in accordance with rule 84;

c. In respect of a petition not presented through the Administering Authority, the date on which the petition is received by the Administering Authority through the Secretary-General. The Administering Authority concerned shall immediately notify the Secretary-General of the date of receipt of all such petitions.

3. In cases where the Administering Authority may be prepared to consider a written petition at shorter notice than is prescribed by the foregoing rules, or where, in exceptional cases, as a matter of urgency, it may be so decided by the Trusteeship Council in consultation with the Administering Authority concerned, such written petition may be placed on the agenda of a regular session notwithstanding that it has been presented after the due date, or it may be placed on the agenda of a special session.

4. Complete and precise written observations by the Administering Authority concerned on the petitions to which the established procedure is to be applied shall be transmitted within three months of the date of their receipt by the Administering Authority.

Rule 87

Requests to present petitions orally or to make oral presentations in support or elaboration of written petitions, in accordance with rule 80, may be addressed directly to the Secretary-General or may be transmitted to him through the Administering Authority. In the latter case the Administering Authority concerned shall communicate such requests promptly to the Secretary-General.

Rule 88

The Secretary-General shall promptly notify the members of the Trusteeship Council of all requests for oral petitions or oral presentations received by him, except for petitions relating to a strategic area with respect to which the functions of the Trusteeship Council shall be governed by Article 83 of the Charter and the terms of the relevant Trusteeship Agreement.

Rule 89

Representatives of the Trusteeship Council engaged in periodic visits to Trust Territories or on other official missions authorized by the Council may receive oral presentations or petitions, subject to such instructions as may have been received from the Trusteeship Council. Such oral presentations or petitions shall be recorded by the visiting mission, and the record shall be transmitted promptly to the Secretary-General for circulation to the members of the Council and to the Administering Authority for comment. A copy of each such record shall be communicated to the competent local authority. Any observations which the visiting representatives may wish to make on the oral presentations or petitions, after consultation with the local representative of the Administering Authority, shall be submitted to the Trusteeship Council.

Rule 90

The Trusteeship Council may designate one or more of its representatives to accept oral petitions the subject-matter of which has been previously communicated to the Trusteeship Council and to the Administering Authority concerned. Oral petitions and oral presentations may be examined either in public or in private, as may be determined, in accordance with rule 44.

Rule 91

In the examination of all petitions the Administering Authority concerned shall be entitled to designate and to have present a special representative who should be well informed on the Territory involved.

Rule 92

The Secretary-General shall inform the Administering Authorities and the petitioners concerned of the actions taken by the Trusteeship Council on each petition, and shall transmit to them the official records of the public meetings at which the petitions were examined.

2. THE SPECIAL COMMITTEE ON THE SITUATION WITH REGARD TO THE IMPLEMENTATION OF THE DECLARATION ON THE GRANTING OF INDEPENDENCE TO COLONIAL COUNTRIES AND PEOPLES (1961) General Assembly Resolution 1654 (XVI) adopted on 27 November 1961, 16 U.N. GAOR, Supp. (No. 17), U.N. Doc. A/5100 (1962).

THE GENERAL ASSEMBLY,

Recalling the Declaration on the granting of independence to colonial countries and peoples contained in its resolution 1514 (XV) of 14 December 1960,
Bearing in mind the purposes and principles of that Declaration,
Recalling in particular paragraph 5 of the Declaration providing that:

"Immediate steps shall be taken, in Trust and Non-Self-Governing Territories or all other territories which have not yet attained independence to transfer all powers to the peoples of those territories, without any conditions or reservations, in accordance with their freely expressed will and desire, without any distinction as to race, creed or colour, in order to enable them to enjoy complete independence and freedom,"

Noting with regret that, with a few exceptions, the provisions contained in the aforementioned paragraph of the Declaration have not been carried out,
Noting that, contrary to the provisions of paragraph 4 of the Declaration, armed action and repressive measures continue to be taken in certain areas with

increasing ruthlessness against dependent peoples, depriving them of their prerogative to exercise peacefully and freely their right to complete independence,

Deeply concerned that, contrary to the provisions of paragraph 6 of the Declaration, acts aimed at the partial or total disruption of national unity and territorial integrity are still being carried out in certain countries in the process of decolonization,

Convinced that further delay in the application of the Declaration is a continuing source of international conflict and disharmony, seriously impedes international co-operation, and is creating an increasingly dangerous situation in many parts of the world which may threaten international peace and security,

Emphasizing that inadequacy of political, economic, social or educational preparedness should never serve as a pretext for delaying independence,

1. *Solemnly reiterates and reaffirms* the objectives and principles enshrined in the Declaration on the granting of independence to colonial countries and peoples contained in its resolution 1514 (XV) of 14 December 1960;

2. *Calls upon* States concerned to take action without further delay with a view to the faithful application and implementation of the Declaration;

3. *Decides* to establish a Special Committee of seventeen members to be nominated by the President of the General Assembly at the present session;

4. *Requests* the Special Committee to examine the application of the Declaration, to make suggestions and recommendations on the progress and extent of the implementation of the Declaration, and to report to the General Assembly at its seventeenth session;

5. *Directs* the Special Committee to carry out its task by employment of all means which it will have at its disposal within the framework of the procedures and modalities which it shall adopt for the proper discharge of its functions;

6. *Authorizes* the Special Committee to meet elsewhere than at United Nations Headquarters, whenever and wherever such meetings may be required for the effective discharge of its functions, in consultation with the appropriate authorities;

7. *Invites* the authorities concerned to afford the Special Committee their fullest co-operation in carrying out its tasks;

8. *Requests* the Trusteeship Council, the Committee on Information from Non-Self-Governing Territories and the specialized agencies concerned to assist the Special Committee in its work within their respective fields;

9. *Requests* the Secretary-General to provide the Special Committee with all the facilities and the personnel necessary for the implementation of the present resolution.

EDITORS' NOTE:

The Special Committee subsequently took over the functions formerly exercised by the General Assembly's Special Committee for South West Africa and the committee in Information From Non-self-governing Territories. The membership was increased to 24 in 1962 and 25 in 1979 but returned to 24 after

Australia withdrew in 1985. Its functions were further expanded by resolution 1810 (XVII) of December 17, 1962, 17 U.N. GAOR, Supp. (No. 17), U.N. Doc. A/5217 (1963). The relevant provisions read:

THE GENERAL ASSEMBLY,

1. *Expresses its appreciation* to the Special Committee on the Situation with regard to the Implementation of the Declaration on the Granting of Independence to Colonial Countries and Peoples for the work it has accomplished;

2. *Takes note with approval* of the methods and procedures which the Special Committee has adopted for the discharge of its functions;

3. *Solemnly reiterates and reaffirms* the objectives and principles enshrined both in the Declaration contained in resolution 1514 (XV) and in resolution 1654 (XVI);

4. *Deplores* the refusal of certain administering Powers to co-operate in the implementation of the Declaration in territories under their administration;

5. *Calls upon* the administering Powers concerned to cease forthwith all armed action and repressive measures directed against peoples who have not yet attained independence, particularly against the political activities of their rightful leaders;

6. *Urges* all administering Powers to take immediate steps in order that all colonial territories and peoples may accede to independence without delay in accordance with the provisions of paragraph 5 of the Declaration;

7. *Decides* to enlarge the membership of the Special Committee established by resolution 1654 (XVI) by the addition of seven new members to be nominated by the President of the General Assembly;

8. *Invites* the enlarged Special Committee:

a. To continue to seek the most suitable ways and means for the speedy and total application of the Declaration to all territories which have not yet attained independence;

b. To propose specific measures for the complete application of the Declaration;

c. To submit to the General Assembly in due course, and not later than its eighteenth session, a full report containing its suggestions and recommendations on all the territories mentioned in paragraph 5 of the Declaration;

d. To apprise the Security Council of any developments in these territories which may threaten international peace and security;

9. *Requests* all Member States, especially the administering Powers, to afford the Special Committee their fullest co-operation;

10. *Requests* the Secretary-General to continue to provide the Special Committee with all the facilities and personnel necessary for the implementation of the present resolution.

EDITORS' NOTE:

In spite of the reference to "methods and procedures" in paragraph 2 of this

Resolution, the Committee has no formal procedural Rules like those of the Trusteeship Council. However, it tends to proceed in much the same way as the Council. The committee's role in the receipt of information concerning Non-Self-Governing Territories is governed by General Assembly res. 1970 (XVIII) of 16 December 1963, 18 U.N. GAOR, SUPP. (NO.15) 49, U.N. DOC A/5515 (1963).

THE GENERAL ASSEMBLY,

Recalling its resolution 1847 (XVII) of 19 December 1962 in which it decided to review at its eighteenth session the question of the further continuation of the Committee on Information from Non-Self-Governing Territories,

Considering that the Declaration regarding Non-Self-Governing Territories contained in Chapter XI of the Charter of the United Nations cannot be dissociated from the Declaration on the granting of independence to colonial countries and peoples contained in General Assembly resolution 1514 (XV) of 14 December 1960,

Considering that all United Nations activities concerning Non-Self-Governing Territories should now be co-ordinated and consolidated, with a view to the immediate ending of colonialism,

Recalling that, by resolutions 1654 (XVI) of 27 November 1961 and 1810 (XVII) of 17 December 1962, it established the Special Committee on the Situation with regard to the Implementation of the Declaration on the Granting of Independence to Colonial Countries and Peoples and that it has approved the Special Committee's methods and procedures,

Considering that the Special Committee, in view of the experience it has gained, is now in a position to take over the functions of the Committee on Information from Non-Self-Governing Territories,

Having regard to the views of the Secretary-General on this question,[16]

Considering that it is imperative to avoid any duplication of work or overlapping of responsibilities,

Having received the report of the Committee on Information from Non-Self-Governing Territories prepared at its fourteenth session, in 1963,[17]

1.*Takes note* of the report of the Committee on Information from Non-Self-Governing Territories on the work of its fourteenth session;

2. *Expresses its gratitude* to the Committee for its efforts and for its valuable contribution to the accomplishment of the purposes of the United Nations under Chapter XI of the Charter;

3. *Decides* to dissolve the Committee on Information from Non-Self-Governing Territories;

4. *Invites* Member States which have or which assume responsibilities for the administration of Territories whose peoples have not yet attained a full measure of self-government to transmit or continue to transmit to the Secretary-General information as prescribed under Article 73 e of the Charter, as well as the fullest possible information on political and constitutional development;

5. *Requests* the Special Committee to study this information and take it fully into account in examining the situation with regard to the implementation of the Declaration on the granting of independence to colonial countries and peoples in each of the Non-Self-Governing Territories, and to undertake any special study and prepare any special report it may consider necessary in addition to its activities under General Assembly resolutions 1654 (XVI) and 1810 (XVII);

6. *Requests* the Secretary-General to continue to provide the Special Committee with all the facilities and personnel necessary for the implementation of the present resolution.

3. INTERNATIONAL CONVENTION ON THE ELIMINATION OF ALL FORMS OF RACIAL DISCRIMINATION (ARTICLES 8–16, 22) (1965)

Article 8

1. There shall be established a Committee on the Elimination of Racial Discrimination (hereinafter referred to as the Committee) consisting of eighteen experts of high moral standing and acknowledged impartiality elected by States Parties from among their nationals, who shall serve in their personal capacity, consideration being given to equitable geographical distribution and to the representation of the different forms of civilization as well as of the principal legal systems.

2. The members of the Committee shall be elected by secret ballot from a list of persons nominated by the States Parties. Each State Party may nominate one person from among its own nationals.

3. The initial election shall be held six months after the date of the entry into force of this Convention. At least three months before the date of each election the Secretary-General of the United Nations shall address a letter to the States Parties inviting them to submit their nominations within two months. The Secretary-General shall prepare a list in alphabetical order of all persons thus nominated, indicating the States Parties which have nominated them, and shall submit it to the States Parties.

4. Elections of the members of the Committee shall be held at a meeting of States Parties convened by the Secretary-General at United Nations Headquarters. At that meeting, for which two thirds of the States Parties shall constitute a quorum, the persons elected to the Committee shall be those nominees who obtain the largest number of votes and an absolute majority of the votes of the representatives of States Parties present and voting.

5. (*a*) The members of the Committee shall be elected for a term of four years. However, the terms of nine of the members elected at the first election shall expire at the end of two years; immediately after the first election the names of these nine members shall be chosen by lot by the Chairman of the Committee.

(*b*) For the filling of casual vacancies, the State Party whose expert has ceased to function as a member of the Committee shall appoint another expert from among its nationals, subject to the approval of the Committee.

6. States Parties shall be responsible for the expenses of the members of the Committee while they are in performance of Committee duties.

Article 9

1. States Parties undertake to submit to the Secretary-General of the United Nations, for consideration by the Committee, a report on the legislative, judicial, administrative or other measures which they have adopted and which give effect to the provisions of this Convention: (*a*) within one year after the entry into force of the Convention for the State concerned; and (*b*) thereafter every two years and whenever the Committee so requests. The Committee may request further information from the States Parties.

2. The Committee shall report annually, through the Secretary-General, to the General Assembly of the United Nations on its activities and may make suggestions and general recommendations based on the examination of the reports and information received from the States Parties. Such suggestions and general recommendations shall be reported to the General Assembly together with comments, if any, from States Parties.

Article 10

1. The Committee shall adopt its own rules of procedure.

2. The Committee shall elect its officers for a term of two years.

3. The secretariat of the Committee shall be provided by the Secretary-General of the United Nations.

4. The meetings of the Committee shall normally be held at United Nations Headquarters.

Article 11

1. If a State Party considers that another State Party is not giving effect to the provisions of this convention, it may bring the matter to the attention of the Committee. The Committee shall then transmit the communication to the State Party concerned. Within three months, the receiving State shall submit to the Committee written explanations or statements clarifying the matter and the remedy, if any, that may have been taken by that State.

2. If the matter is not adjusted to the satisfaction of both parties, either by bilateral negotiations or by any other procedure open to them, within six months after the receipt by the receiving State of the initial communication, either State shall have the right to refer the matter again to the Committee by notifying the Committee and also the other State.

3. The Committee shall deal with a matter referred to it in accordance with paragraph 2 of this article after it has ascertained that all available domestic remedies have been invoked and exhausted in the case, in conformity with the generally recognized principles of international law. This shall not be the rule where the application of the remedies is unreasonably prolonged.

4. In any matter referred to it, the Committee may call upon the States Parties concerned to supply any other relevant information.

5. When any matter arising out of this article is being considered by the Committee, the States Parties concerned shall be entitled to send a representative to take part in the proceedings of the Committee, without voting rights, while the matter is under consideration.

Article 12

1. (*a*) After the committee has obtained and collated all the information it deems necessary, the Chairman shall appoint an *ad hoc* Conciliation Commission (hereinafter referred to as the Commission) comprising five persons who may or may not be members of the Committee. The members of the Commission shall be appointed with the unanimous consent of the parties to the dispute, and its good offices shall be made available to the States concerned with a view to an amicable solution of the matter on the basis of respect for this Convention.

(*b*) If the States parties to the dispute fail to reach agreement within three months on all or part of the composition of the Commission, the members of the Commission not agreed upon by the States parties to the dispute shall be elected by secret ballot by a two-thirds majority vote of the Committee from among its own members.

2. The members of the Commission shall serve in their personal capacity. They shall not be nationals of the States parties to the dispute or of a State not Party to this Convention.

3. The Commission shall elect its own Chairman and adopt its own rules of procedure.

4. The meetings of the Commission shall normally be held at United Nations Headquarters or at any other convenient place as determined by the Commission.

5. The secretariat provided in accordance with article 10, paragraph 3, of this convention shall also service the Commission whenever a dispute among States Parties brings the Commission into being.

6. The States parties to the dispute shall share equally all the expenses of the members of the Commission in accordance with estimates to be provided by the Secretary-General of the United Nations.

7. The Secretary-General shall be empowered to pay the expenses of the members of the Commission, if necessary, before reimbursement by the States parties to the dispute in accordance with paragraph 6 of this article.

8. The information obtained and collated by the Committee shall be made available to the Commission, and the Commission may call upon the States concerned to supply any other relevant information.

Article 13

1. When the Commission has fully considered the matter, it shall prepare and submit to the Chairman of the Committee a report embodying its findings on all questions of fact relevant to the issue between the parties and containing such recommendations as it may think proper for the amicable solution of the dispute.

2. The Chairman of the Committee shall communicate the report of the Commission to each of the States parties to the dispute. These States shall, within three months, inform the Chairman of the Committee whether or not they accept the recommendations contained in the report of the Commission.

3. After the period provided for in paragraph 2 of this article, the Chairman of the Committee shall communicate the report of the Commission and the declarations of the States Parties concerned to the other States Parties to this Convention.

Article 14

1. A State Party may at any time declare that it recognizes the competence of the committee to receive and consider communications from individuals or groups of individuals within its jurisdiction claiming to be victims of a violation by that State Party of any of the rights set forth in this Convention. No communication shall be received by the Committee if it concerns a State Party which has not made such a declaration.

2. Any State Party which makes a declaration as provided for in paragraph 1 of this article may establish or indicate a body within its national legal order which shall be competent to receive and consider petitions from individuals and groups of individuals within its jurisdiction who claim to be victims of a violation of any of the rights set forth in this Convention and who have exhausted other available local remedies.

3. A declaration made in accordance with paragraph 1 of this article and the name of any body established or indicated in accordance with paragraph 2 of this article shall be deposited by the State Party concerned with the Secretary-General of the United Nations, who shall transmit copies thereof to the other States Parties. A declaration may be withdrawn at any time by notification to the Secretary-General, but such a withdrawal shall not affect communications pending before the Committee.

4. A register of petitions shall be kept by the body established or indicated in accordance with paragraph 2 of this article, and certified copies of the register shall be filed annually through appropriate channels with the Secretary-General on the understanding that the contents shall not be publicly disclosed.

5. In the event of failure to obtain satisfaction from the body established or indicated in accordance with paragraph 2 of this article, the petitioner shall have the right to communicate the matter to the Committee within six months.

6. (*a*) The Committee shall confidentially bring any communication referred to it to the attention of the State Party alleged to be violating any provision of this Convention, but the identity of the individual or groups of individuals concerned shall not be revealed without his or their express consent. The Committee shall not receive anonymous communications.

(*b*) Within three months, the receiving State shall submit to the Committee written explanations or statements clarifying the matter and the remedy, if any, that may have been taken by that State.

7. (*a*) The committee shall consider communications in the light of all information made available to it by the State Party concerned and by the petitioner. The Committee shall not consider any communication from a

petitioner unless it has ascertained that the petitioner has exhausted all available domestic remedies. However, this shall not be the rule where the application of the remedies is unreasonably prolonged.

(*b*) The Committee shall forward its suggestions and recommendations, if any, to the State Party concerned and to the petitioner.

8. The Committee shall include in its annual report a summary of such communications and, where appropriate, a summary of the explanations and statements of the States Parties concerned and of its own suggestions and recommendations.

9. The Committee shall be competent to exercise the functions provided for in this article only when at least ten States Parties to this Convention are bound by declarations in accordance with paragraph 1 of this article.

Article 15

1. Pending the achievement of the objectives of the Declaration on the Granting of Independence to Colonial Countries and Peoples, contained in General Assembly resolution 1514 (XV) of 14 December 1960, the provisions of this Convention shall in no way limit the right of petition granted to these peoples by other international instruments or by the United Nations and its specialized agencies.

2. (*a*) The Committee established under article 8, paragraph 1, of this Convention shall receive copies of the petitions from, and submit expressions of opinion and recommendations on these petitions to, the bodies of the United Nations which deal with matters directly related to the principles and objectives of this Convention in their consideration of petitions from the inhabitants of Trust and Non-Self-Governing Territories and all other territories to which General Assembly resolution 1514 (XV) applies, relating to matters covered by this Convention which are before these bodies.

(*b*) The Committee shall receive from the competent bodies of the United Nations copies of the reports concerning the legislative, judicial, administrative or other measures directly related to the principles and objectives of this Convention applied by the administering Powers within the Territories mentioned in subparagraph (*a*) of this paragraph, and shall express opinions and make recommendations to these bodies.

3. The Committee shall include in its report to the General Assembly a summary of the petitions and reports it has received from United Nations bodies, and the expressions of opinion and recommendations of the Committee relating to the said petitions and reports.

4. The Committee shall request from the Secretary-General of the United Nations all information relevant to the objectives of this Convention and available to him regarding the Territories mentioned in paragraph 2 (*a*) of this article.

Article 16

The provisions of this Convention concerning the settlement of disputes or complaints shall be applied without prejudice to other procedures for settling disputes or complaints in the field of discrimination laid down in the constituent instruments of, or in conventions adopted by, the United Nations and its specialized agencies, and shall not prevent the States Parties from having recourse to other procedures for settling a dispute in accordance with general or special international agreements in force between them.

Article 22

Any dispute between two or more States Parties with respect to the interpretation or application of this Convention, which is not settled by negotiation or by the procedures expressly provided for in this Convention, shall, at the request of any of the parties to the dispute, be referred to the International Court of Justice for decision, unless the disputants agree to another mode of settlement.

4. INTERNATIONAL COVENANT ON ECONOMIC, SOCIAL AND CULTURAL RIGHTS (ARTICLES 16–24) (1966)

PART IV

Article 16

1. The States Parties to the present Covenant undertake to submit in conformity with this part of the Covenant reports on the measures which they have adopted and the progress made in achieving the observance of the rights recognized herein.

2. (*a*) All reports shall be submitted to the Secretary-General of the United Nations, who shall transmit copies to the Economic and Social Council for consideration in accordance with the provisions of the present Covenant;

(*b*) The Secretary-General of the United Nations shall also transmit to the specialized agencies copies of the reports, or any relevant parts therefrom, from States Parties to the present Covenant which are also members of these specialized agencies in so far as these reports, or parts therefrom, relate to any matters which fall within the responsibilities of the said agencies in accordance with their constitutional instruments.

Article 17

1. The States Parties to the present Covenant shall furnish their reports in stages, in accordance with a programme to be established by the Economic and Social Council within one year of the entry into force of the present Covenant after consultation with the States Parties and the specialized agencies concerned.

2. Reports may indicate factors and difficulties affecting the degree of fulfilment of obligations under the present Covenant.

3. Where relevant information has previously been furnished to the United Nations or to any specialized agency by any State Party to the present Covenant, it will not be necessary to reproduce that information, but a precise reference to the information so furnished will suffice.

Article 18

Pursuant to its responsibilities under the Charter of the United Nations in the field of human rights and fundamental freedoms, the Economic and Social Council may make arrangements with the specialized agencies in respect of their reporting to it on the progress made in achieving the observance of the provisions of the present Covenant falling within the scope of their activities. These reports may include particulars of decisions and recommendations on such implementation adopted by their competent organs.

Article 19

The Economic and Social Council may transmit to the Commission on Human Rights for study and general recommendation or, as appropriate, for information the reports concerning human rights submitted by States in accordance with articles 16 and 17, and those concerning human rights submitted by the specialized agencies in accordance with article 18.

Article 20

The States Parties to the present Covenant and the specialized agencies concerned may submit comments to the Economic and Social Council on any general recommendation under article 19 or reference to such general recommendation in any report of the Commission on Human Rights or any documentation referred to therein.

Article 21

The Economic and Social Council may submit from time to time to the General Assembly reports with recommendations of a general nature and a summary of the information received from the States Parties to the present Covenant and the specialized agencies on the measures taken and the progress made in achieving general observance of the rights recognized in the present Covenant.

Article 22

The Economic and Social Council may bring to the attention of other organs of the United Nations, their subsidiary organs and specialized agencies concerned with furnishing technical assistance any matters arising out of the reports referred to in this part of the present Covenant which may assist such bodies in deciding, each within its field of competence, on the advisability of international measures likely to contribute to the effective progressive implementation of the present Covenant.

Article 23

The States Parties to the present Covenant agree that international action for the achievement of the rights recognized in the present Covenant includes such methods as the conclusion of conventions, the adoption of recommendations, the furnishing of technical assistance and the holding of regional meetings and technical meetings for the purpose of consultation and study organized in conjunction with the Governments concerned.

Article 24

Nothing in the present Covenant shall be interpreted as impairing the provisions of the Charter of the United Nations and of the constitutions of the specialized agencies which define the respective responsibilities of the various organs of the United Nations and of the specialized agencies in regard to the matters dealt with in the present Covenant.

5. INTERNATIONAL COVENANT ON CIVIL AND POLITICAL RIGHTS (ARTICLES 28–45) (1966)

PART IV

Article 28

1. There shall be established a Human Rights Committee (hereafter referred to in the present Covenant as the Committee). It shall consist of eighteen members and shall carry out the functions hereinafter provided.
2. The Committee shall be composed of nationals of the States Parties to the present Covenant who shall be persons of high moral character and recognized competence in the field of human rights, consideration being given to the usefulness of the participation of some persons having legal experience.
3. The members of the Committee shall be elected and shall serve in their personal capacity.

Article 29

1. The members of the Committee shall be elected by secret ballot from a list of persons possessing the qualifications prescribed in article 28 and nominated for the purpose by the States Parties to the present Covenant.
2. Each State Party to the present Covenant may nominate not more than two persons. These persons shall be nationals of the nominating State.
3. A person shall be eligible for renomination.

Article 30

1. The initial election shall be held no later than six months after the date of the entry into force of the present Covenant.
2. At least four months before the date of each election to the Committee, other than an election to fill a vacancy declared in accordance with article 34, the Secretary-General of the United Nations shall address a written invitation to the States Parties to the present Covenant to submit their nominations for membership of the Committee within three months.
3. The Secretary-General of the United Nations shall prepare a list in alphabetical order of all the persons thus nominated, with an indication of the States

Parties which have nominated them, and shall submit it to the States Parties to the present Covenant no later than one month before the date of each election.

4. Elections of the members of the Committee shall be held at a meeting of the States Parties to the present Covenant convened by the Secretary-General of the United Nations at the Headquarters of the United Nations. At that meeting, for which two thirds of the States Parties to the present Covenant shall constitute a quorum, the persons elected to the Committee shall be those nominees who obtain the largest number of votes and an absolute majority of the votes of the representatives of States Parties present and voting.

Article 31

1. The Committee may not include more than one national of the same State.

2. In the election of the Committee, consideration shall be given to equitable geographical distribution of membership and to the representation of the different forms of civilization and of the principal legal systems.

Article 32

1. The members of the Committee shall be elected for a term of four years. They shall be eligible for re-election if renominated. However, the terms of nine of the members elected at the first election shall expire at the end of two years; immediately after the first election, the names of these nine members shall be chosen by lot by the Chairman of the meeting referred to in article 30, paragraph 4.

2. Elections at the expiry of office shall be held in accordance with the preceding articles of this part of the present Covenant.

Article 33

1. If, in the unanimous opinion of the other members, a member of the Committee has ceased to carry out his functions for any cause other than absence of a temporary character, the Chairman of the Committee shall notify the Secretary-General of the United Nations, who shall then declare the seat of that member to be vacant.

2. In the event of the death or the resignation of a member of the Committee, the Chairman shall immediately notify the Secretary-General of the United Nations, who shall declare the seat vacant from the date of death or the date on which the resignation takes effect.

Article 34

1. When a vacancy is declared in accordance with article 33 and if the term of office of the member to be replaced does not expire within six months of the declaration of the vacancy, the Secretary-General of the United Nations shall notify each of the States Parties to the present Covenant, which may within two months submit nominations in accordance with article 29 for the purpose of filling the vacancy.

2. The Secretary-General of the United Nations shall prepare a list in alphabetical order of the persons thus nominated and shall submit it to the States Parties to the present Covenant. The election to fill the vacancy shall then

take place in accordance with the relevant provisions of this part of the present Covenant.

3. A member of the Committee elected to fill a vacancy declared in accordance with article 33 shall hold office for the remainder of the term of the member who vacated the seat on the Committee under the provisions of that article.

Article 35

The members of the Committee shall, with the approval of the General Assembly of the United Nations, receive emoluments from United Nations resources on such terms and conditions as the General Assembly may decide, having regard to the importance of the Committee's responsibilities.

Article 36

The Secretary-General of the United Nations shall provide the necessary staff and facilities for the effective performance of the functions of the Committee under the present Covenant.

Article 37

1. The Secretary-General of the United Nations shall convene the initial meeting of the Committee at the Headquarters of the United Nations.

2. After its initial meeting, the Committee shall meet at such times as shall be provided in its rules of procedure.

3. The Committee shall normally meet at the Headquarters of the United Nations or at the United Nations Office at Geneva.

Article 38

Every member of the Committee shall, before taking up his duties, make a solemn declaration in open committee that he will perform his functions impartially and conscientiously.

Article 39

1. The Committee shall elect its officers for a term of two years. They may be re-elected.

2. The Committee shall establish its own rules of procedure, but these rules shall provide, *inter alia*, that:

　　a. Twelve members shall constitute a quorum;

　　b. Decision of the Committee shall be made by a majority vote of the members present.

Article 40

1. The States Parties to the present Covenant undertake to submit reports on the measures they have adopted which give effect to the rights recognized herein and on the progress made in the enjoyment of those rights:

　　a. Within one year of the entry into force of the present Covenant for the States Parties concerned;

　　b. Thereafter whenever the Committee so requests.

2. All reports shall be submitted to the Secretary-General of the United

Nations, who shall transmit them to the Committee for consideration. Reports shall indicate the factors and difficulties, if any, affecting the implementation of the present Covenant.

3. The Secretary-General of the United Nations may, after consultation with the Committee, transmit to the specialized agencies concerned copies of such parts of the reports as may fall within their field of competence.

4. The Committee shall study the reports submitted by the States Parties to the present Covenant. It shall transmit its reports, and such general comments as it may consider appropriate, to the States Parties. The Committee may also transmit to the Economic and Social Council these comments along with the copies of the reports it has received from States Parties to the present Covenant.

5. The States Parties to the present Covenant may submit to the Committee observations on any comments that may be made in accordance with paragraph 4 of this article.

Article 41

1. A State Party to the present Covenant may at any time declare under this article that it recognizes the competence of the Committee to receive and consider communications to the effect that a State Party claims that another State Party is not fulfilling its obligations under the present Covenant. Communications under this article may be received and considered only if submitted by a State Party which has made a declaration recognizing in regard to itself the competence of the Committee. No communication shall be received by the Committee if it concerns a State Party which has not made such a declaration. Communications received under this article shall be dealt with in accordance with the following procedure:

a. If a State Party to the present Covenant considers that another State Party is not giving effect to the provisions of the present Covenant, it may, by written communication, bring the matter to the attention of that State Party. Within three months after the receipt of the communication the receiving State shall afford the State which sent the communication an explanation, or any other statement in writing clarifying the matter which should include, to the extent possible and pertinent, reference to domestic procedures and remedies taken, pending, or available in the matter.

b. If the matter is not adjusted to the satisfaction of both States Parties concerned within six months after the receipt by the receiving State of the initial communication, either State shall have the right to refer the matter to the Committee, by notice given to the Committee and to the other State.

c. The Committee shall deal with a matter referred to it only after it has ascertained that all available domestic remedies have been invoked and exhausted in the matter, in conformity with the generally recognized principles of international law. This shall not be the rule where the application of the remedies is unreasonably prolonged.

d. The Committee shall hold closed meetings when examining communications under this article.

e. Subject to the provisions of sub-paragraph (*c*), the Committee shall make available its good offices to the States Parties concerned with a view to a friendly solution of the matter on the basis of respect for human rights and fundamental freedoms as recognized in the present Covenant.

f. In any matter referred to it, the Committee may call upon the States Parties concerned, referred to in sub-paragraph (*b*), to supply any relevant information.

g. The States Parties concerned, referred to in sub-paragraph (*b*), shall have the right to be represented when the matter is being considered in the Committee and to make submissions orally and/or in writing.

h. The Committee shall, within twelve months after the date of receipt of notice under sub-paragraph (*b*), submit a report:

i. If a solution within the terms of sub-paragraph (*e*) is reached, the Committee shall confine its report to a brief statement of the facts and of the solution reached;

ii. If a solution within the terms of sub-paragraph (*e*) is not reached, the Committee shall confine its report to a brief statement of the facts; the written submissions and record of the oral submissions made by the States Parties concerned shall be attached to the report.

In every matter, the report shall be communicated to the States Parties concerned.

2. The provisions of this article shall come into force when ten States Parties to the present Covenant have made declarations under paragraph 1 of this article. Such declarations shall be deposited by the States Parties with the Secretary-General of the United Nations, who shall transmit copies thereof to the other States Parties. A declaration may be withdrawn at any time by notification to the Secretary-General. Such a withdrawal shall not prejudice the consideration of any matter which is the subject of a communication already transmitted under this article; no further communication by any State Party shall be received after the notification of withdrawal of the declaration has been received by the Secretary-General, unless the State Party concerned has made a new declaration.

Article 42

1. (*a*) If a matter referred to the Committee in accordance with article 41 is not resolved to the satisfaction of the States Parties concerned, the Committee may, with the prior consent of the States Parties concerned, appoint an *ad hoc* Conciliation Commission (hereinafter referred to as the Commission). The good offices of the Commission shall be made available to the States Parties concerned with a view to an amicable solution of the matter on the basis of respect for the present Covenant;

(*b*) The Commission shall consist of five persons acceptable to the States

Parties concerned. If the States Parties concerned fail to reach agreement within three months on all or part of the composition of the Commission, the members of the Commission concerning whom no agreement has been reached shall be elected by secret ballot by a two thirds majority vote of the Committee from among its members.

2. The members of the Commission shall serve in their personal capacity. They shall not be nationals of the States Parties concerned, or of a State not party to the present Covenant, or of a State Party which has not made a declaration under article 41.

3. The Commission shall elect its own Chairman and adopt its own rules of procedure.

4. The meetings of the Commission shall normally be held at the Headquarters of the United Nations or at the United Nations Office at Geneva. However, they may be held at such other convenient places as the Commission may determine in consultation with the Secretary-General of the United Nations and the States Parties concerned.

5. The secretariat provided in accordance with article 36 shall also service the commissions appointed under this article.

6. The information received and collated by the Committee shall be made available to the Commission and the Commission may call upon the States Parties concerned to supply any other relevant information.

7. When the Commission has fully considered the matter, but in any event not later than twelve months after having been seized of the matter, it shall submit to the Chairman of the Committee a report for communication to the States Parties concerned:

 a. If the Commission is unable to complete its consideration of the matter within twelve months, it shall confine its report to a brief statement of the status of its consideration of the matter;

 b. If an amicable solution to the matter on the basis of respect for human rights as recognized in the present Covenant is reached, the Commission shall confine its report to a brief statement of the facts and of the solution reached;

 c. If a solution within the terms of sub-paragraph (*b*) is not reached, the Commission's report shall embody its findings on all questions of fact relevant to the issues between the States Parties concerned, and its views on the possibilities of an amicable solution of the matter. This report shall also contain the written submissions and a record of the oral submissions made by the States Parties concerned;

 d. If the Commission's report is submitted under sub-paragraph (*c*), the States Parties concerned shall, within three months of the receipt of the report, notify the Chairman of the Committee whether or not they accept the contents of the report of the Commission.

8. The provisions of this article are without prejudice to the responsibilities of the Committee under article 41.

9. The States Parties concerned shall share equally all the expenses of the members of the Commission in accordance with estimates to be provided by the Secretary-General of the United Nations.

10. The Secretary-General of the United Nations shall be empowered to pay the expenses of the members of the Commission, if necessary, before reimbursement by the States Parties concerned, in accordance with paragraph 9 of this article.

Article 43

The members of the Committee, and of the *ad hoc* conciliation commissions which may be appointed under article 42, shall be entitled to the facilities, privileges and immunities of experts on mission for the United Nations as laid down in the relevant sections of the Convention on the Privileges and Immunities of the United Nations.

Article 44

The provisions for the implementation of the present Covenant shall apply without prejudice to the procedures prescribed in the field of human rights by or under the constituent instruments and the conventions of the United Nations and of the specialized agencies and shall not prevent the States Parties to the present Covenant from having recourse to other procedures for settling a dispute in accordance with general or special international agreements in force between them.

Article 45

The Committee shall submit to the General Assembly of the United Nations, through the Economic and Social Council, an annual report on its activities.

6. OPTIONAL PROTOCOL TO THE INTERNATIONAL COVENANT ON CIVIL AND POLITICAL RIGHTS (1966) G.A. Res. 2200A (XXI), 21 U.N. GAOR, Supp. (No. 16) at 59, U.N. Doc.A/6316 (1966). In force 23 March 1976 in accordance with Article 9.

THE STATES PARTIES TO THE PRESENT PROTOCOL,

Considering that in order further to achieve the purposes of the Covenant on Civil and Political Rights (hereinafter referred to as the Covenant) and the implementation of its provisions it would be appropriate to enable the Human Rights Committee set up in part IV of the Covenant (hereinafter referred to as the Committee) to receive and consider, as provided in the present Protocol, communications from individuals claiming to be victims of violations of any of the rights set forth in the Covenant.

Have agreed as follows:

Article 1

A State Party to the Covenant that becomes a party to the present Protocol recognizes the competence of the Committee to receive and consider communications from individuals subject to its jurisdiction who claim to be victims of a violation by that State Party of any of the rights set forth in the Covenant. No communication shall be received by the Committee if it concerns a State Party to the Covenant which is not a party to the present Protocol.

Article 2

Subject to the provisions of article 1, individuals who claim that any of their rights enumerated in the Covenant have been violated and who have exhausted all available domestic remedies may submit a written communication to the Committee for consideration.

Article 3

The Committee shall consider inadmissible any communication under the present Protocol which is anonymous, or which it considers to be an abuse of the right of submission of such communications or to be incompatible with the provisions of the Covenant.

Article 4

1. Subject to the provisions of article 3, the Committee shall bring any communications submitted to it under the present Protocol to the attention of the State Party to the present Protocol alleged to be violating any provision of the Covenant.

2. Within six months, the receiving State shall submit to the Committee written explanations or statements clarifying the matter and the remedy, if any, that may have been taken by that State.

Article 5

1. The committee shall consider communications received under the present Protocol in the light of all written information made available to it by the individual and by the State Party concerned.

2. The Committee shall not consider any communication from an individual unless it has ascertained that

a. The same matter is not being examined under another procedure of international investigation or settlement;

b. The individual has exhausted all available domestic remedies. This shall not be the rule where the application of the remedies is unreasonably prolonged.

3. The Committee shall hold closed meetings when examining communications under the present Protocol.

4. The Committee shall forward its views to the State Party concerned and to the individual.

Article 6

The Committee shall include in its annual report under article 45 of the Covenant a summary of its activities under the present Protocol.

Article 7

Pending the achievement of the objectives of resolution 1514 (XV) adopted by the General Assembly of the United Nations on 14 December 1960 concerning the Declaration on the Granting of Independence to Colonial Countries and Peoples, the provisions of the present Protocol shall in no way limit the right of petition granted to these peoples by the Charter of the United Nations and other international conventions and instruments under the United Nations and its specialized agencies.

Article 8

1. The present Protocol is open for signature by any State which has signed the Covenant.
2. The present Protocol is subject to ratification by any State which has ratified or acceded to the Covenant. Instruments of ratification shall be deposited with the Secretary-General of the United Nations.
3. The present Protocol shall be open to accession by any State which has ratified or acceded to the Covenant.
4. Accession shall be effected by the deposit of an instrument of accession with the Secretary-General of the United Nations.
5. The Secretary-General of the United Nations shall inform all States which have signed the present Protocol or acceded to it of the deposit of each instrument of ratification or accession.

Article 9

1. Subject to the entry into force of the Covenant, the present Protocol shall enter into force three months after the date of the deposit with the Secretary-General of the United Nations of the tenth instrument of ratification or instrument of accession.
2. For each State ratifying the present Protocol or acceding to it after the deposit of the tenth instrument of ratification or instrument of accession, the present Protocol shall enter into force three months after the date of the deposit of its own instrument of ratification or instrument of accession.

Article 10

The provisions of the present Protocol shall extend to all parts of federal States without any limitations or exceptions.

Article 11

1. Any State Party to the present Protocol may propose an amendment and file it with the Secretary-General of the United Nations. The Secretary-General shall thereupon communicate any proposed amendments to the States Parties to the present Protocol with a request that they notify him whether they favour a conference of States Parties for the purpose of considering and voting upon the proposal. In the event that at least one third of the States Parties favours such a conference, the Secretary-General shall convene the conference under the auspices of the United Nations. Any amendment adopted by a majority of the

States Parties present and voting at the conference shall be submitted to the General Assembly of the United Nations for approval.

2. Amendments shall come into force when they have been approved by the General Assembly of the United Nations and accepted by a two-thirds majority of the States Parties to the present Protocol in accordance with their respective constitutional processes.

3. When amendments come into force, they shall be binding on those States Parties which have accepted them, other States Parties still being bound by the provisions of the present Protocol and any earlier amendment which they have accepted.

Article 12

1. Any State Party may denounce the present Protocol at any time by written notification addressed to the Secretary-General of the United Nations. Denunciation shall take effect three months after the date of receipt of the notification by the Secretary-General.

2. Denunciation shall be without prejudice to the continued application of the provisions of the present Protocol to any communication submitted under article 2 before the effective date of denunciation.

Article 13

Irrespective of the notifications made under article 8, paragraph 5, of the present Protocol, the Secretary-General of the United Nations shall inform all States referred to in article 48, paragraph 1, of the Covenant of the following particulars:

    a. Signatures, ratifications and accessions under article 8;

    b. The date of the entry into force of the present Protocol under article 9 and the date of the entry into force of any amendments under article 11;

    c. Denunciations under article 12.

Article 14

1. The present Protocol, of which the Chinese, English, French, Russian and Spanish texts are equally authentic, shall be deposited in the archives of the United Nations.

2. The Secretary-General of the United Nations shall transmit certified copies of the present Protocol to all States referred to in article 48 of the Covenant.

7. INTERNATIONAL CONVENTION ON THE SUPPRESSION AND PUNISHMENT OF THE CRIME OF APARTHEID (ARTICLES VII–XII) (1973)

Article VII

1. The States Parties to the present Convention undertake to submit

periodic reports to the group established under article IX on the legislative, judicial, administrative or other measures that they have adopted and that give effect to the provisions of the Convention.

2. Copies of the reports shall be transmitted through the Secretary-General of the United Nations to the Special Committee on *Apartheid*.

Article VIII

Any State Party to the present Convention may call upon any competent organ of the United Nations to take such action under the Charter of the United Nations as it considers appropriate for the prevention and suppression of the crime of *apartheid*.

Article IX

1. The Chairman of the Commission on Human Rights shall appoint a group consisting of three members of the Commission on Human Rights, who are also representatives of States Parties to the present Convention, to consider reports submitted by States Parties in accordance with article VII.

2. If, among the members of the Commission on Human Rights, there are no representatives of States Parties to the present Convention or if there are fewer than three such representatives, the Secretary-General of the United Nations shall, after consulting all States Parties to the Convention, designate a representative of the State Party or representatives of the States Parties which are not members of the Commission on Human Rights to take part in the work of the group established in accordance with paragraph 1 of this article, until such time as representatives of the States Parties to the Convention are elected to the Commission on Human Rights.

3. The group may meet for a period of not more than five days, either before the opening or after the closing of the session of the Commission on Human Rights, to consider the reports submitted in accordance with article VII.

Article X

1. The States Parties to the present Convention empower the commission on Human Rights:

a. To request United Nations organs, when transmitting copies of petitions under article 15 of the International Convention on the Elimination of All Forms of Racial Discrimination, to draw its attention to complaints concerning acts which are enumerated in article II of the present Convention;

b. To prepare, on the basis of reports from competent organs of the United Nations and periodic reports from States Parties to the present Convention, a list of individuals, organizations, institutions and representatives of States which are alleged to be responsible for the crimes enumerated in article II of the Convention, as well as those against whom legal proceedings have been undertaken by States Parties to the Convention;

c. To request information from the competent United Nations organs concerning measures taken by the authorities responsible for the administration of Trust and Non-Self-Governing Territories, and all other Territories to which General Assembly resolution 1514 (XV) of 14 December 1960 applies, with regard to such individuals alleged to be responsible for crimes under article II of the Convention who are believed to be under their territorial and administrative jurisdiction.

2. Pending the achievement of the objectives of the Declaration on the Granting of Independence to Colonial Countries and Peoples, contained in General Assembly resolution 1514 (XV), the provisions of the present Convention shall in no way limit the right of petition granted to those peoples by other international instruments or by the United Nations and its specialized agencies.

Article XI

1. Acts enumerated in article II of the present Convention shall not be considered political crimes for the purpose of extradition.

2. The States Parties to the present Convention undertake in such cases to grant extradition in accordance with their legislation and with the treaties in force.

Article XII

Disputes between States Parties arising out of the interpretation, application or implementation of the present Convention which have not been settled by negotiation shall, at the request of the States Parties to the dispute, be brought before the International Court of Justice, save where the parties to the dispute have agreed on some other form of settlement.

8. CONVENTION ON THE ELIMINATION OF ALL FORMS OF DISCRIMINATION AGAINST WOMEN (ARTICLES 17–22, 29) (1979)

PART V

Article 17

1. For the purpose of considering the progress made in the implementation of the present Convention, there shall be established a Committee on the Elimination of Discrimination against Women (hereinafter referred to as the Committee) consisting, at the time of entry into force of the Convention, of eighteen and, after ratification of or accession to the Convention by the thirty-fifth State Party, of twenty-three experts of high moral standing and competence in the field covered by the Convention. The experts shall be elected by States Parties from among their nationals and shall serve in their personal capacity, consideration being given to equitable geographical distribution and to the representation of the different forms of civilization as well as the principal legal systems.

2. The members of the Committee shall be elected by secret ballot from a list of persons nominated by States Parties. Each State Party may nominate one person from among its own nationals.

3. The initial election shall be held six months after the date of the entry into force of the present Convention. At least three months before the date of each election the Secretary-General of the United Nations shall address a letter to the States Parties inviting them to submit their nominations within two months. The Secretary-General shall prepare a list in alphabetical order of all persons thus nominated, indicating the States Parties which have nominated them, and shall submit it to the States Parties.

4. Elections of the members of the Committee shall be held at a meeting of States Parties convened by the Secretary-General at United Nations Headquarters. At that meeting, for which two thirds of the States Parties shall constitute a quorum, the persons elected to the Committee shall be those nominees who obtain the largest number of votes and an absolute majority of the votes of the representatives of States Parties present and voting.

5. The members of the Committee shall be elected for a term of four years. However, the terms of nine of the members elected at the first election shall expire at the end of two years; immediately after the first election the names of these nine members shall be chosen by lot by the Chairman of the Committee.

6. The election of the five additional members of the Committee shall be held in accordance with the provisions of paragraphs 2, 3 and 4 of this article, following the thirty-fifth ratification or accession. The terms of two of the additional members elected on this occasion shall expire at the end of two years, the names of these two members having been chosen by lot by the Chairman of the Committee.

7. For the filling of casual vacancies, the State Party whose expert has ceased to function as a member of the Committee shall appoint another expert from among its nationals, subject to the approval of the Committee.

8. The members of the Committee shall, with the approval of the General Assembly, receive emoluments from United Nations resources on such terms and conditions as the Assembly may decide, having regard to the importance of the Committee's responsibilities.

9. The Secretary-General of the United Nations shall provide the necessary staff and facilities for the effective performance of the functions of the Committee under the present Convention.

Article 18

1. States Parties undertake to submit to the Secretary-General of the United Nations, for consideration by the Committee, a report on the legislative, judicial, administrative or other measures which they have adopted to give effect to the provisions of the present Convention and on the progress made in this respect:

a. Within one year after the entry into force for the State concerned; and

b. Thereafter at least every four years and further whenever the Committee so requests.

2. Reports may indicate factors and difficulties affecting the degree of fulfilment of obligations under the present Convention.

Article 19

1. The Committee shall adopt its own rules of procedure.
2. The Committee shall elect its officers for a term of two years.

Article 20

1. The Committee shall normally meet for a period of not more than two weeks annually in order to consider the reports submitted in accordance with article 18 of the present Convention.
2. The meetings of the Committee shall normally be held at United Nations Headquarters or at any other convenient place as determined by the Committee.

Article 21

1. The Committee shall, through the Economic and Social Council, report annually to the General Assembly of the United Nations on its activities and may make suggestions and general recommendations based on the examination of reports and information received from the States Parties. Such suggestions and general recommendations shall be included in the report of the Committee together with comments, if any, from States Parties.
2. The Secretary-General shall transmit the reports of the Committee to the Commission on the Status of Women for its information.

Article 22

The specialized agencies shall be entitled to be represented at the consideration of the implementation of such provisions of the present Convention as fall within the scope of their activities. The Committee may invite the specialized agencies to submit reports on the implementation of the Convention in areas falling within the scope of their activities.

Article 29

1. Any dispute between two or more States Parties concerning the interpretation or application of the present Convention which is not settled by negotiation shall, at the request of one of them, be submitted to arbitration. If within six months from the date of the request for arbitration the parties are unable to agree on the organization of the arbitration, any one of those parties may refer the dispute to the International Court of Justice by request in conformity with the Statute of the Court.
2. Each State Party may at the time of signature or ratification of this Convention or accession thereto declare that it does not consider itself bound by paragraph 1 of this article. The other States Parties shall not be bound by that paragraph with respect to any State Party which has made such a reservation.
3. Any State Party which has made a reservation in accordance with paragraph 2 of this article may at any time withdraw that reservation by notification to the Secretary-General of the United Nations.

9. THE COMMISSION ON HUMAN RIGHTS "GROSS VIOLATIONS" PROCEDURES (1970) Res. 1503 (XLVIII), 48 U.N. ESCOR, Supp. (No. 1A) at 8, U.N. Doc.E/4832/Add. 1 (1970).

THE ECONOMIC AND SOCIAL COUNCIL,

Noting resolutions 7 (XXVI) and 17 (XXV) of the Commission on Human Rights and resolution 2 (XXI) of the Sub-Commission on Prevention of Discrimination and Protection of Minorities,

1. *Authorizes* the Sub-Commission on Prevention of Discrimination and Protection of Minorities to appoint a working group consisting of not more than five of its members, with due regard to geographical distribution, to meet once a year in private meetings for a period not exceeding ten days immediately before the sessions of the Sub-Commission to consider all communications, including replies of Governments thereon, received by the Secretary-General under Council resolution 728 F (XXVIII) of 30 July 1959 with a view to bringing to the attention of the Sub-Commission those communications, together with replies of Governments, if any, which appear to reveal a consistent pattern of gross and reliably attested violations of human rights and fundamental freedoms within the terms of reference of the Sub-Commission;

2. *Decides* that the Sub-Commission on Prevention of Discrimination and Protection of Minorities should, as the first stage in the implementation of the present resolution, devise at its twenty-third session appropriate procedures for dealing with the question of admissibility of communications received by the Secretary-General under Council resolution 728 F (XXVIII) and in accordance with Council resolution 1235 (XLII) of 6 June 1967;

3. *Requests* the Secretary-General to prepare a document on the question of admissibility of communications for the Sub-Commission's consideration at its twenty-third session;

4. *Further requests* the Secretary-General:

a. To furnish to the members of the Sub-Commission every month a list of communications prepared by him in accordance with Council resolution 728 F (XXVIII) and a brief description of them, together with the text of any replies received from Governments;

b. To make available to the members of the working group at their meetings the originals of such communications listed as they may request, having due regard to the provisions of paragraph 2 (*b*) of Council resolution 728 F (XXVIII) concerning the divulging of the identity of the authors of communications;

c. To circulate to the members of the Sub-Commission, in the working languages, the originals of such communications as are referred to the Sub-Commission by the working group;

5. *Requests* the Sub-Commission on Prevention of Discrimination and Protection of Minorities to consider in private meetings, in accordance with paragraph 1 above, the communications brought before it in accordance with the decision of a majority of the members of the working group and any replies of Governments relating thereto and other relevant information, with a view to

determining whether to refer to the Commission on Human Rights particular situations which appear to reveal a consistent pattern of gross and reliably attested violations of human rights requiring consideration by the Commission;

6. *Requests* the Commission on Human Rights after it has examined any situation referred to it by the Sub-Commission to determine:

a. Whether it requires a thorough study by the Commission and a report and recommendations thereon to the Council in accordance with paragraph 3 of Council resolution 1235 (XLII);

b. Whether it may be a subject of an investigation by an *ad hoc* committee to be appointed by the Commission which shall be undertaken only with the express consent of the State concerned and shall be conducted in constant co-operation with that State and under conditions determined by agreement with it. In any event, the investigation may be undertaken only if:

    i. All available means at the national level have been resorted to and exhausted;

    ii. The situation does not relate to a matter which is being dealt with under other procedures prescribed in the constituent instruments of, or conventions adopted by, the United Nations and the specialized agencies, or in regional conventions, or which the State concerned wishes to submit to other procedures in accordance with general or special international agreements to which it is a party.

7. *Decides* that if the Commission on Human Rights appoints an *ad hoc* committee to carry on an investigation with the consent of the State concerned:

a. The composition of the committee shall be determined by the Commission. The members of the committee shall be independent persons whose competence and impartiality is beyond question. Their appointment shall be subject to the consent of the Government concerned;

b. The committee shall establish its own rules of procedure. It shall be subject to the quorum rule. It shall have authority to receive communications and hear witnesses, as necessary. The investigation shall be conducted in co-operation with the Government concerned;

c. The committee's procedure shall be confidential, its proceedings shall be conducted in private meetings and its communications shall not be publicized in any way;

d. The committee shall strive for friendly solutions before, during and even after the investigation;

e. The committee shall report to the Commission on Human Rights with such observations and suggestions as it may deem appropriate;

8. *Decides* that all actions envisaged in the implementation of the present resolution by the Sub-Commission on Prevention of Discrimination and Protection of Minorities or the Commission on Human Rights shall remain confidential until such time as the Commission may decide to make recommendations to the Economic and Social Council;

9. *Decides* to authorize the Secretary-General to provide all facilities which may be required to carry out the present resolution, making use of the existing staff of the Division of Human Rights of the United Nations Secretariat;

10. *Decides* that the procedure set out in the present resolution for dealing with communications relating to violations of human rights and fundamental freedoms should be reviewed if any new organ entitled to deal with such communications should be established within the United Nations or by international agreement.

RESOLUTION 1 (XXIV) ADOPTED BY THE SUB-COMMISSION ON PREVENTION OF DISCRIMINATION AND PROTECTION OF MINORITIES ON 13 AUGUST 1971 IN IMPLEMENTATION OF ECOSOC RES. 1503, U.N. Doc.E/CN.4 /1070 (1971).

THE SUB-COMMISSION ON PREVENTION OF DISCRIMINATION AND PROTECTION OF MINORITIES,

Considering that the Economic and Social Council, by its resolution 1503 (XLVIII), decided that the Sub-Commission should devise appropriate procedures for dealing with the question of admissibility of communications received by the Secretary-General under Council resolution 728 F (XXVIII) of 30 July 1959 and in accordance with Council resolution 1235 (XLII) of 6 June 1967,

Adopts the following provisional procedures for dealing with the question of admissibility of communications referred to above:

(1) *Standards and criteria*

a. The object of the communication must not be inconsistent with the relevant principles of the Charter, of the Universal Declaration of Human Rights and of the other applicable instruments in the field of human rights.

b. Communications shall be admissible only if, after consideration thereof, together with the replies if any of the Governments concerned, there are reasonable grounds to believe that they may reveal a consistent pattern of gross and reliably attested violations of human rights and fundamental freedoms, including policies of racial discrimination and segregation and of *apartheid*, in any country, including colonial and other dependent countries and peoples.

(2) *Source of communications*

a. Admissible communications may originate from a person or group of persons who, it can be reasonably presumed, are victims of the violations referred to in subparagraph (1) (b) above, any person or group of persons who have direct and reliable knowledge of those violations, or non-governmental organizations acting in good faith in accordance with recognized principles of human rights, not resorting to politically motivated stands contrary to the provisions of the Charter of the United Nations and having direct and reliable knowledge of such violations.

b. Anonymous communications shall be inadmissible; subject to the requirements of subparagraph 2(b) of resolution 728 F (XXVIII) of the

Economic and Social Council, the author of a communication, whether an individual, a group of individuals or an organization, must be clearly identified.

c. Communications shall not be inadmissible solely because the knowledge of the individual authors is second-hand, provided that they are accompanied by clear evidence.

(3) *Contents of communications and nature of allegations*

a. The communication must contain a description of the facts and must indicate the purpose of the petition and the rights that have been violated.

b. Communications shall be inadmissible if their language is essentially abusive and in particular if they contain insulting references to the State against which the complaint is directed. Such communications may be considered if they meet the other criteria for admissibility after deletion of the abusive language.

c. A communication shall be inadmissible if it has manifestly political motivations and its subject is contrary to the provisions of the Charter of the United Nations.

d. A communication shall be inadmissible if it appears that it is based exclusively on reports disseminated by mass media:

(4) *Existence of other remedies*

a. Communications shall be inadmissible if their admission would prejudice the functions of the specialized agencies of the United Nations system.

b. Communications shall be inadmissible if domestic remedies have not been exhausted, unless it appears that such remedies would be ineffective or unreasonably prolonged. Any failure to exhaust remedies should be satisfactorily established.

c. Communications relating to cases which have been settled by the State concerned in accordance with the principles set forth in the Universal Declaration of Human Rights and other applicable documents in the field of human rights will not be considered.

(5) *Timeliness*

A communication shall be inadmissible if it is not submitted to the United Nations within a reasonable time after the exhaustion of the domestic remedies as provided above.

10. STATUTE OF THE HIGH COMMISSIONER FOR REFUGEES (1950) G.A. Res. 428 (V), 5 U.N. GAOR, Supp. (No.20) at 46, U.N. Doc.A/1775 (1950).

CHAPTER I

GENERAL PROVISIONS

1. The United Nations High Commissioner for Refugees, acting under the authority of the General Assembly, shall assume the function of providing international protection, under the auspices of the Untied Nations, to refugees

who fall within the scope of the present Statute and of seeking permanent solutions for the problem of refugees by assisting governments and, subject to the approval of the governments concerned, private organizations to facilitate the voluntary repatriation of such refugees, or their assimilation within new national communities.

In the exercise of his functions, more particularly when difficulties arise, and for instance with regard to any controversy concerning the international status of these persons, the High Commissioner shall request the opinion of an advisory committee on refugees if it is created.

2. The work of the High Commissioner shall be of an entirely non-political character; it shall be humanitarian and social and shall relate, as a rule, to groups and categories of refugees.

3. The High Commissioner shall follow policy directives given him by the General Assembly or the Economic and Social Council.

4. The Economic and Social Council may decide, after hearing the views of the High Commissioner on the subject, to establish an advisory committee on refugees, which shall consist of representatives of States Members and States non-members of the United Nations, to be selected by the Council on the basis of their demonstrated interest in and devotion to the solution of the refugee problem.

5. The General Assembly shall review, not later than at its eighth regular session, the arrangements for the Office of the High Commissioner with a view to determining whether the Office should be continued beyond 31 December 1953*.

CHAPTER II

FUNCTIONS OF THE HIGH COMMISSIONER

6. The competence of the High Commissioner shall extend to:

A. i. Any person who has been considered a refugee under the Arrangements of 12 May 1926 and 30 June 1928 or under the Conventions of 28 October 1933 and 10 February 1938, the Protocol of 14 September 1939 or the Constitution of the International Refugee Organization;

ii. Any person who, as a result of events occurring before 1 January 1951 and owing to well-founded fear of being persecuted for reasons of race, religion, nationality or political opinion, is outside the country of his nationality and is unable or, owing to such fear or for reasons other than personal convenience, is unwilling to avail himself of the protection of that country; or who, not having a nationality and being outside the country of his former habitual residence, is unable or, owing to such fear or for reasons other than personal convenience, is unwilling to return to it.

Decisions as to eligibility taken by the International Refugee

---

*The Office has from time to time been prolonged for further periods.

Organization during the period of its activities shall not prevent the status of refugee being accorded to persons who fulfil the conditions of the present paragraph;

The competence of the High Commissioner shall cease to apply to any person defined in section A above if:

a. He has voluntarily re-availed himself of the protection of the country of his nationality; or

b. Having lost his nationality, he has voluntarily re-acquired it; or

c. He has acquired a new nationality, and enjoys the protection of the country of his new nationality; or

d. He has voluntarily re-established himself in the country which he left or outside which he remained owing to fear of persecution; or

e. He can no longer, because the circumstances in connexion with which he has been recognized as a refugee have ceased to exist, claim grounds other than those of personal convenience, for continuing to refuse to avail himself of the protection of the country of his nationality. Reasons of a purely economic character may not be invoked; or

f. Being a person who has no nationality, he can no longer, because the circumstances in connexion with which he has been recognized as a refugee have ceased to exist and he is able to return to the country of his former habitual residence, claim grounds other than those of personal convenience for continuing to refuse to return to that country;

B. Any other person who is outside the country of his nationality or, if he has no nationality, the country of his former habitual residence, because he has or had well-founded fear of persecution by reason of his race, religion, nationality or political opinion and is unable or, because of such fear, is unwilling to avail himself of the protection of the government of the country of his nationality, or, if he has no nationality, to return to the country of his former habitual residence.

7. Provided that the competence of the High Commissioner as defined in paragraph 6 above shall not extend to a person:

a. Who is a national of more than one country unless he satisfies the provisions of the preceding paragraph in relation to each of the countries of which he is a national; or

b. Who is recognized by the competent authorities of the country in which he has taken residence as having the rights and obligations which are attached to the possession of the nationality of that country; or

c. Who continues to receive from other organs or agencies of the United Nations protection or assistance; or

d. In respect of whom there are serious reasons for considering that he has committed a crime covered by the provisions of treaties of extradition or a crime mentioned in article VI of the London Charter of the International Military Tribunal or by the provisions of article 14, paragraph 2, of the Universal Declaration of Human Rights.

8. The High Commissioner shall provide for the protection of refugees falling under the competence of his Office by:

a. Promoting the conclusion and ratification of international conventions for the protection of refugees, supervising their application and proposing amendments thereto;

b. Promoting through special agreements with governments the execution of any measures calculated to improve the situation of refugees and to reduce the number requiring protection;

c. Assisting governmental and private efforts to promote voluntary repatriation or assimilation within new national communities;

d. Promoting the admission of refugees, not excluding those in the most destitute categories, to the territories of States;

e. Endeavouring to obtain permission for refugees to transfer their assets and especially those necessary for their resettlement;

f. Obtaining from governments information concerning the number and conditions of refugees in their territories and the laws and regulations concerning them;

g. Keeping in close touch with the governments and inter-governmental organizations concerned;

h. Establishing contact in such manner as he may think best with private organizations dealing with refugee questions;

i. Facilitating the co-ordination of the efforts of private organizations concerned with the welfare of refugees.

9. The High Commissioner shall engage in such additional activities, including repatriation and resettlement, as the General Assembly may determine, within the limits of the resources placed at his disposal.

10. The High Commissioner shall administer any funds, public or private, which he receives for assistance to refugees, and shall distribute them among the private and, as appropriate, public agencies which he deems best qualified to administer such assistance.

The High Commissioner may reject any offers which he does not consider appropriate or which cannot be utilized.

The High Commissioner shall not appeal to governments for funds or make a general appeal, without the prior approval of the General Assembly.

The High Commissioner shall include in his annual report a statement of his activities in this field.

11. The High Commissioner shall be entitled to present his views before the General Assembly, the Economic and Social Council and their subsidiary bodies.

The High Commissioner shall report annually to the General Assembly through the Economic and Social Council; his report shall be considered as a separate item on the agenda of the General Assembly.

12. The High Commissioner may invite the co-operation of the various specialized agencies.

CHAPTER III

ORGANIZATION AND FINANCES

13. The High Commissioner shall be elected by the General Assembly on the nomination of the Secretary-General. The terms of appointment of the High Commissioner shall be proposed by the Secretary-General and approved by the General Assembly. The High Commissioner shall be elected for a term of three years, from 1 January 1951.

14. The High Commissioner shall appoint, for the same term, a Deputy High Commissioner of a nationality other than his own.

15. (*a*) Within the limits of the budgetary appropriations provided, the staff of the Office of the High Commissioner shall be appointed by the High Commissioner and shall be responsible to him in the exercise of their functions.

(*b*) Such staff shall be chosen from persons devoted to the purposes of the Office of the High Commissioner.

(*c*) Their conditions of employment shall be those provided under the staff regulations adopted by the General Assembly and the rules promulgated thereunder by the Secretary-General.

(*d*) Provision may also be made to permit the employment of personnel without compensation.

16. The High Commissioner shall consult the governments of the countries of residence of refugees as to the need for appointing representatives therein. In any country recognizing such need, there may be appointed a representative approved by the government of that country. Subject to the foregoing, the same representative may serve in more than one country.

17. The High Commissioner and the Secretary-General shall make appropriate arrangements for liaison and consultation on matters of mutual interest.

18. The Secretary-General shall provide the High Commissioner with all necessary facilities within budgetary limitations.

19. The Office of the High Commissioner shall be located in Geneva, Switzerland.

20. The Office of the High Commissioner shall be financed under the budget of the United Nations. Unless the General Assembly subsequently decides otherwise, no expenditure, other than administrative expenditures relating to the functioning of the Office of the High Commissioner, shall be borne on the budget of the United Nations, and all other expenditures relating to the activities of the High Commissioner shall be financed by voluntary contributions.

21. The administration of the Office of the High Commissioner shall be subject to the Financial Regulations of the United Nations and to the financial rules promulgated thereunder by the Secretary-General.

22. Transactions relating to the High Commissioner's funds shall be subject to audit by the United Nations Board of Auditors, provided that the Board may accept audited accounts from the agencies to which funds have been allocated. Administrative arrangements for the custody of such funds and their allocation shall be agreed between the High Commissioner and the Secretary-General in accordance with the Financial Regulations of the United Nations and rules promulgated thereunder by the Secretary-General.

11. GROUP OF EXPERTS ON SLAVERY (1974)

Resolution adopted by the Sub-Commission on Prevention of Discrimination and Protection of Minorities, 21 August 1974 Res. 11 (XXVII), U.N. Doc.E/CN./1160,ECN,4/Sub.2/354 at 57–58 (1974).

11 (XXVII) Question of Slavery and the Slave Trade in all their Practices and Manifestations including the Slavery-like Practices of Colonialism and *Apartheid*

THE SUB-COMMISSION ON PREVENTION OF DISCRIMINATION AND PROTECTION OF MINORITIES,

Noting that the Economic and Social Council, on 17 May 1974 authorized the Sub-Commission to appoint a group of 5 of its members to meet for not more than 3 working days, prior to each session of the Sub-Commission, to review developments in the field of slavery and the Slave Trade in all their Practices and Manifestations including the Slavery-like Practices of Colonialism and *Apartheid*, the traffic in persons and the exploitation of the prostitution of others as they are defined in the Slavery Convention of 1926, the Supplementary Convention on the Abolition of Slavery, the Slave Trade and Institutions and Practices Similar to Slavery of 1956, and the Convention for the Suppression of the Traffic in Persons and the Exploitation of the Prostitution of Others of 1949,

1. *Establishes* that group, whose members will be appointed by the chairman of the Sub-Commission pursuant to decision 17 (LVI) of the Economic and Social Council of 17 May 1974;

2. *Decides* that the Working Group shall be constituted as follows:

(a) the names of the 5 members shall be selected by the Chairman of the Sub-Commission, in consultation with the members from each geographical area, to constitute the Working Group for the next session, one from each of the following geographical areas, namely (i) African (ii) Asian (iii) East European (iv) Western European and Other States (v) Latin American, taking into account decision D of the Economic and Social Council of 17 May 1974;

(b) if necessary, the chairman or outgoing Chairman may at any time, in order to fill a vacancy, designate a member from among the names of the Sub-Commission members of the same geographical area;

3. *Requests* the Working Group at its meetings in 1975, to prepare a report to the Sub-Commission, for consideration at its 28th Session, pursuant to Sub-Commission res. 7(XXVI), including proposals for the future method of work of the Working Group and the Sub-Commission in their examination of the question;

4. *Requests* Governments, specialized agencies, regional intergovernmental organizations, the non-governmental organizations and consultative status concerned and individuals to submit to the Secretary-General for transmission to the Working Group of the Sub-Commission such reliable information on slavery and the slave trade in all their practices and manifestations, the traffic in persons and the exploitation of the prostitution of others as they may be available to them;

5. *Decides* to review this decision when the International Covenant on Civil and Political Rights comes into force.

[The Working Group has been kept in existence notwithstanding the coming into force of the Covenant on Civil and Political Rights.]

12. HUMAN RIGHTS OF PERSONS DETAINED OR IMPRISONED (1974) Resolution Adopted by the Sub-Commission on Prevention of Discrimination and Protection of Minorities on 20 August 1974 U.N. Doc.E/CN.4/1160,E/CN.4/Sub.2/354 at 52–53 (1974).

7 (XXVII) The Question of the Human Rights of Persons Subjected to Any Form of Detention or Imprisonment

The Sub-Commission on Prevention of Discrimination and Protection of Minorities,
Gravely concerned at numerous reports that violations of the basic human rights of persons detained or imprisoned persist in various parts of the world,
Believing that persons subjected to any form of detention or imprisonment for any reason whatsoever should enjoy at least the following basic human rights: the right not to be subjected to arrest or detention arbitrarily, the right not to be subjected to torture or to cruel, inhuman or degrading treatment or punishment; the right to be treated with humanity and with respect for the inherent dignity of the human person; the right to equal protection of the law, without any discrimination; the right to be informed of the reasons or grounds of the arrest or detention; the right to be brought promptly before a court and to have a trial within a reasonable time; the right to communicate with legal counsel; the right to be tried in his presence, and to defend himself in person or through legal assistance of his own choosing; the right to examine, or have examined, the witnesses against him and to obtain the attendance and examination of witnesses on his behalf under the same conditions as witnesses against him; the right to have free assistance of an interpreter if he cannot understand or speak the language used in court; the right not to be compelled to testify against himself or to confess his guilt; the right to a fair and public hearing by an independent and impartial tribunal; the right to be presumed innocent until proved guilty according to law; and the right not to be held guilty of any criminal offence on account of any act or omission which did not constitute a criminal offence, under national or international law at the time when it was committed, nor to get a heavier penalty than the one that was applicable at the time when the criminal offence was committed,
Considering that although States may, in time of public emergency which threatens the life of the nation, take measures derogating from certain rights under certain conditions, article 4, paragraph 2, of the International Covenant on Civil and Political Rights nevertheless prohibits derogation of the right not to be subjected to torture or to cruel, inhuman or degrading treatment or punishment,
Noting that torture and other forms of cruel, inhuman or degrading treatment and punishment are flagrant violations of human rights that continue to occur notwithstanding their rejection by the General Assembly in resolution 3059 (XXVIII), and that all available information suggests that in several countries there may be a consistent pattern of such violations,
1. *Decides* to review annually developments in the field and for this purpose to retain the item on its agenda. In reviewing those developments the Sub-Commission will take into account any reliably attested information from Governments, the specialized agencies, the regional intergovernmental organi-

zations and the non-governmental organizations in consultative status with the Economic and Social Council concerned, provided that such non-governmental organizations act in good faith and that their information is not politically motivated, contrary to the principles of the Charter of the United Nations;

2. *Requests* the Secretary-General to transmit to the Sub-Commission the information referred to in paragraph 1 above.

13. WORKING GROUP ON DISAPPEARANCES (1980)
Constituted by Commission on Human Rights Res. 20 (XXXVI), 1980 U.N. ESCOR, Supp. (No. 3) at 180, U.N. Doc.E/1980/13 (1980).

QUESTION OF MISSING AND DISAPPEARED PERSONS

THE COMMISSION ON HUMAN RIGHTS,

Bearing in mind General Assembly resolution 33/173 of 20 December 1978, which requested the Commission on Human Rights to consider the question of missing or disappeared persons with a view to making appropriate recommendations,

Taking into account resolution 1979/38 of 10 May 1979 of the Economic and Social Council, which requested the Commission to consider the question as a matter of priority, and resolution 5 B (XXXII) of the Sub-Commission on Prevention of Discrimination and Protection of Minorities,

Convinced of the need to take appropriate action, in consultation with the Governments concerned, to promote the implementation of the provisions of General Assembly resolution 33/173 and other United Nations resolutions relevant to the plight of missing and disappeared persons,

1. *Decides* to establish for a period of one year a working group consisting of five of its members, to serve as experts in their individual capacities, to examine questions relevant to enforced or involuntary disappearances of persons.

2. *Requests* the Chairman of the Commission to appoint the members of the group,

3. *Decides* that the working group, in carrying out its mandate, shall seek and receive information from Governments, intergovernmental organizations, humanitarian organizations and other reliable sources,

4. *Requests* the Secretary-General to appeal to all Governments to co-operate with and assist the working group in the performance of its tasks and to furnish all information required,

5. *Further requests* the Secretary-General to provide the working group with all necessary assistance, in particular staff and resources they require in order to perform their functions in an effective and expeditious manner;

6. *Invites* the working group, in establishing its working methods, to bear in mind the need to be able to respond effectively to information that comes before it and to carry out its work with discretion,

7. *Requests* the working group to submit to the Commission at its thirty-seventh session a report on its activities, together with its conclusions and recommendations,

8. *Further requests* the Sub-Commission on Prevention of Discrimination and Protection of Minorities to continue studying the most effective means for eliminating enforced or involuntary disappearances of persons, with a view to making general recommendations to the Commission at its thirty-seventh session,

9. *Decides* to consider this question again at its thirty-seventh session under a subitem entitled "Question of Missing and Disappeared Persons."

[The mandate of the Working Group has been extended since 1981.]

14. WORKING GROUP ON INDIGENOUS POPULATIONS (1982) ECOSOC Res. 1982/34, 1982 U.N. ESCOR, Supp. (No.1) at 26, U.N. Doc.E/1982/82 (1982).

1982/34. STUDY OF THE PROBLEM OF DISCRIMINATION AGAINST INDIGENOUS POPULATIONS

THE ECONOMIC AND SOCIAL COUNCIL,

Recalling its resolution 1589 (L) of 21 May 1971, resolutions 22 (XXXVII) of 10 March 1981 and 1982/19 of 10 March 1982 of the Commission on Human Rights and resolutions 8 (XXIV) of 18 August 1971, 5 (XXXIII) of 10 September 1980 and 2 (XXXIV) of 8 September 1981 of the Sub-Commission on Prevention of Discrimination and Protection of Minorities.

Recognizing the urgent need to promote and to protect the human rights and fundamental freedoms of indigenous populations,

Bearing in mind the concerns expressed in this regard at the World Conference to Combat Racism and Racial Discrimination in 1978.

Believing that special attention should be given to appropriate avenues of recourse at the national, regional and international levels in order to advance the promotion and protection of the human rights and fundamental freedoms of indigenous populations.

Mindful of the conclusions of the Sub-Commission on Prevention of Discrimination and Protection of Minorities and of the Commission on Human Rights that the plight of indigenous peoples is of a serious and pressing nature and that special measures are urgently needed to promote and protect the human rights and fundamental freedoms of indigenous populations.

1. *Authorizes* the Sub-Commission on Prevention of Discrimination and Protection of Minorities to establish annually a working group on indigenous populations which shall meet for up to five working days before the annual sessions of the Sub-Commission in order to review developments pertaining to the promotion and protection of the human rights and fundamental freedoms of indigenous populations, including information requested by the Secretary-

General annually from Governments, specialized agencies, regional intergovernmental organizations and non-governmental organizations in consultative status, particularly those of indigenous peoples, to analyse such materials, and to submit its conclusions to the Sub-Commission bearing in mind the report of the Special Rapporteur of the Sub-Commission;

2. *Decides* that the Working Group shall give special attention to the evolution of standards concerning the rights of indigenous populations, taking account of both the similarities and the differences in the situations and aspirations of indigenous populations throughout the world;

3. *Requests* the Secretary-General to assist the working group on indigenous populations and make all necessary arrangements to enable it to carry out its functions.

15. MODEL RULES OF PROCEDURE FOR UNITED NATIONS BODIES DEALING WITH VIOLATIONS OF HUMAN RIGHTS (1972, 1974)

These Rules were drafted by a Working Group of the Commission on Human Rights in 1972 and 1974. See the Group's Reports U.N. Doc.E/CN.4/1086 (1972) and E/CN.4/1134 (1974). The Economic and Social Council took note of the Reports and drew them to the attention of all organs and bodies within the Untied Nations system dealing with questions of human rights and fundamental freedoms. ECOSOC Res. 1870(LVI), 56 U.N. ESCOR, Supp. No.1 at 23, U.N. Doc.E/5544 (1974). [Words in brackets indicate a lack of unanimity in the Working Group.]

SECTION I: APPLICABILITY

Rule 1

[These model rules shall be applicable upon the decision of the competent organ to *ad hoc* bodies of the United Nations entrusted with studies of particular situations where reliable evidence exists of a consistent pattern of gross [and massive] violations of fundamental human rights and freedoms, including policies of racial discrimination and segregation, and of *apartheid*, in all countries, with particular reference to colonial and other dependent countries and territories.]

Rule 2

Only the organ which establishes the *ad hoc* body may, on its own initiative or on the proposal of the *ad hoc* body, make modifications to the present rules or add to them such further provisions as it deems necessary for the *ad hoc* body to perform its functions, taking into account in particular the provisions of rule 10.

SECTION II: CONSTITUTION OF THE AD HOC BODY

STATUS OF THE AD HOC BODY AND TERMS OF REFERENCE

Rule 3

The *ad hoc* body shall be considered as a subsidiary organ of the United Nations organ which established it and its terms of reference shall be those determined by the resolution or other decision of the organ which established it or any competent principal organ of the United Nations.

MEMBERSHIP

Rule 4

(a) Where the membership of the *ad hoc* body consists of States, each State shall be represented by an accredited representative who may be accompanied by such alternate representatives and advisers as may be required by the accredited representative or as the *ad hoc* body may determine.

(b) Where the membership of the *ad hoc* body consists of individuals, the members shall be those designated in the manner decided upon by the organ establishing the *ad hoc* body.

CREDENTIALS

Rule 5

[Only for *ad hoc* bodies consisting of representatives of Governments.]

The credentials of the representatives of Governments members of the *ad hoc* body and the names of any of their alternates or advisers shall be submitted to the Secretary-General, if possible, not later than one week before the date fixed for the first meeting of the *ad hoc* body.

SOLEMN DECLARATION BY MEMBERS

Rule 6

Upon assuming his duties, each member of the *ad hoc* body acting in his individual capacity shall make the following solemn declaration in open meeting:

"I solemnly declare that I will perform my duties and exercise my powers as a member of the *ad hoc* body honourably, faithfully, impartially and conscientiously."

MEETINGS

Rule 7

(a) The Secretary-General shall notify the members of the *ad hoc* body of the date and place of the first meeting at least 30 days in advance of the meeting and, in case of urgency, at least two weeks in advance of the meeting.

(b) Further meetings of the *ad hoc* body shall be held, as circumstances may require, by decision of the *ad hoc* body or its Chairman, or at the request of the majority of the members of the *ad hoc* body, upon such dates as may be fixed by the Chairman after consultation with the Secretary-General and, when possible, with the other members of the *ad hoc* body.

(c) Meetings shall normally be held at United Nations Headquarters. Another place for a meeting may be designated by the *ad hoc* body in consultation with the Secretary-General, who shall furnish services and facilities within the limits of his administrative possibilities and in accordance with the regulations, rules, decisions and practices applicable to United Nations organs.

QUORUM

Rule 8

The majority of the members who compose the *ad hoc* body shall constitute a quorum.

PUBLICITY OF MEETINGS

Rule 9

Unless the organ which establishes the *ad hoc* body has decided on the public or private character of the meetings of the *ad hoc* body, the latter may decide this question. At the close of each private meeting, the *ad hoc* body may issue a communiqué through the Secretary-General.

EXPENDITURE OF FUNDS

Rule 10

(a) No decision involving expenditure shall be made by the *ad hoc* body until the Secretary-General has prepared and circulated to its members a statement on the financial and administrative implications thereof. It shall be the duty of the Chairman to draw the attention of members to the statement and to invite discussions on it.

(b) The Secretary-General shall meet the expenses to be incurred in respect of the *ad hoc* body and furnish the services and facilities requested by it within the limits of his administrative and budgetary resources and in accordance with the regulations, rules, decisions and practices applicable to United Nations organs and bodies.

SECTION III: AGENDA OF MEETINGS

Rule 11

(a) The provisional agenda for the first meeting shall be drawn up by the Secretary-General in conformity with the relevant decisions of the competent organ which has established the *ad hoc* body.

(b) The provisional agenda for subsequent meetings shall be prepared by the Secretary-General in consultation with the Chairman of the *ad hoc* body in conformity with the terms of reference of the body and shall include:

    i. any matter which the *ad hoc* body has decided to include at its previous session;

    ii. any item proposed by the Chairman of the *ad hoc* body;

    iii. any item proposed by the majority of the *members* of the *ad hoc* body;

    iv. any item proposed by the Secretary-General.

(c) The provisional agenda for the meetings shall be communicated to the members of the *ad hoc* body as early as possible and, whenever practicable, simultaneously with the notification of the meeting under rule 7.

(d) The first item on the provisional agenda after the election of the officers, when required, shall be the adoption of the agenda.

SECTION IV: OFFICERS

Rule 12

(a) The *ad hoc* body shall elect by secret ballot from among its members a Chairman, one or more Vice-Chairmen and a Rapporteur. If only one candidate is presented for any office, the *ad hoc* body may decide to dispense with the secret ballot and the candidate shall be declared to be elected unanimously.

(b) The Chairman shall declare the opening and closing of each meeting of the *ad hoc* body, direct its discussions, ensure observance of the rules of procedure, accord the right to speak, put questions and announce decisions. The Chairman, subject to the rules of procedure, shall have control of the proceedings of the *ad hoc* body and over the maintenance of order at its meetings. He shall rule on points of order. Discussion shall be confined to the question before the *ad hoc* body, and the Chairman may call a speaker to order if his remarks are not relevant to the subject under discussion.

(c) The Chairman, in the exercise of his functions, shall remain under the authority of the *ad hoc* body.

(d) If the Chairman is unable to be present at a meeting or any part thereof, he shall designate a Vice-Chairman to act in his place.

(e) A Vice-Chairman acting as Chairman shall have the same powers and duties as the Chairman.

(f) If any of the officers of the *ad hoc* body ceases or, for any reason, is no longer able to act as an officer of the *ad hoc* body, a new officer shall be elected for the unexpired term of his predecessor, from among the membership of the *ad hoc* body.

SECTION V: SECRETARIAT

Rule 13

(a) The secretariat of the *ad hoc* body shall be provided by the Secretary-General.

(b) The Secretary-General or his representative will be present at the meetings of the *ad hoc* body. He or his representative may make either oral or written statements to the meetings of the *ad hoc* body.

(c) The Secretary-General shall be responsible for keeping the members of the *ad hoc* body informed on any questions which may be brought before it for consideration.

(d) The Secretary-General shall be responsible for all necessary arrangements regarding the organization of the meetings of the *ad hoc* body.

SECTION VI: LANGUAGES

Rule 14

(a) The working languages of the *ad hoc* body shall be determined by the *ad hoc* body or the organ which established it from among the working languages of the latter organ.

(b) Speeches made in any of the working languages shall be interpreted into the other working languages.

(c) Any member of the *ad hoc* body, or a person appearing before the *ad hoc* body, may make a statement in a language other than the working languages. In this case, he shall himself provide for interpretation into one of the working languages. Exceptionally, when a person appearing before the *ad hoc* body is unable to employ any of the working languages, the *ad hoc* body may agree, when budgetary provisions permit, and in the light of practical possibilities, to use an *ad hoc* interpreter. Interpretation into the other working languages shall be based on the interpretation into the first working language.

(d) An *ad hoc* interpreter who is not bound by an oath of office to the United Nations shall be required to swear or declare solemnly that he will interpret honestly, faithfully and accurately the statements made at the meeting.

SECTION VII: VOTING AND CONDUCT OF BUSINESS

VOTING

Rule 15

(a) Each member of the *ad hoc* body shall have one vote.

(b) Except as otherwise provided in the terms of reference of the *ad hoc* body, decisions of the *ad hoc* body shall be made by a majority of the members present and voting. For the purpose of these rules, "members present and voting" means members casting an affirmative or negative vote. Members who abstain from voting shall be considered as not voting.

(c) Subject to rule 12 (a), the *ad hoc* body normally shall vote by show of hands, except that any member may request a roll-call vote, which shall be taken in the English alphabetical order of the names of the members of the *ad hoc* body, it being understood that the Chairman will vote last. The vote of each member participating in any roll-call vote shall be inserted in the report.

(d) If the vote is equally divided, the proposal shall be regarded as rejected.

CONDUCT OF BUSINESS

Rule 16

Any procedural matter arising out of the voting and the conduct of business of meetings of the *ad hoc* body and not covered by the present rules shall be dealt with by the Chairman in the light of the rules of procedure of the competent organ which established the *ad hoc* body or of the General Assembly.

SECTION VIII: CO-OPERATION WITH STATES

Rule 17

(a) The organ which establishes the *ad hoc* body may invite any State, through the Secretary-General, to extend co-operation and such assistance to the *ad hoc* body as the State considers may be useful and helpful in the proper performance of the *ad hoc* body's functions.

[(b) Subject to the request made by the organ establishing the *ad hoc* body for co-operation and assistance and in accordance with the terms of reference of the *ad hoc* body, the *ad hoc* body may request the State directly concerned with the subject of the study or investigation to render to the *ad hoc* body such co-operation and assistance as that State may consider useful for the purposes of the study or investigation. That State shall also be entitled to render on its own initiative such co-operation and assistance.]

SECTION IX: [SOURCES OF INFORMATION]

Rule 18

[Rules concerning sources of information as well as methods of work of the *ad hoc* body regarding the gathering of other evidence, including matters of form, content, relevance and admissibility of such evidence shall be determined by the organs establishing the *ad hoc* body in the terms of reference of the *ad hoc* body unless the *ad hoc* body itself is explicitly authorized to draw up rules on such matters.]

SECTION X: RECORDS

Rule 19

The form of records of the *ad hoc* body, their distribution and publication, shall be determined by the organ which establishes it, subject to the provisions in force in the United Nations in this respect and the budgetary appropriations for the *ad hoc* body.

SECTION XI: REPORTS

Rule 20

(a) At the conclusion of its work, the *ad hoc* body shall draw up its report in private in accordance with its terms of reference and submit it to the organ establishing it, which shall decide whether or not it shall be published.

(b) If a member abstains from voting on the report or dissents from the whole or any part of the report, the fact shall be recorded and any member may, if he so wishes, have included in the report a statement of his separate position.

(c) After publication of the report, the State directly concerned by the subject of the study or investigation may present any observations and comments on the report to the organ to which the report is submitted.

16. REFERENCE OF DISPUTES TO THE INTERNA-TIONAL COURT OF JUSTICE (1948, 1956, 1962, 1965, 1973, 1979)

(i) SUPPLEMENTARY CONVENTION ON THE ABOLITION OF SLAVERY, THE SLAVE TRADE, AND INSTITUTIONS AND PRACTICES SIMILAR TO SLAVERY (1956). SEE ABOVE, CHAPTER I.D.3. ARTICLE 10.

Article 10

Any dispute between States Parties to this Convention relating to its interpretation or application, which is not settled by negotiation, shall be referred to the International Court of Justice at the request of any one of the parties to the dispute, unless the parties concerned agree on another mode of settlement.

(ii) GENOCIDE CONVENTION (1948). SEE ABOVE, CHAPTER I.F.1. AR-TICLE IX.

Article IX

Disputes between the Contracting Parties relating to the interpretation, application or fulfilment of the present Convention, including those relating to the responsibility of a State for genocide or for any of the other acts enumerated in article III, shall be submitted to the International Court of Justice at the request of any of the parties to the dispute.

(iii) CONVENTION ON CONSENT TO MARRIAGE, MINIMUM AGE FOR MARRIAGE AND REGISTRATION OF MARRIAGES (1962). SEE ABOVE, CHAPTER I.J.1. ARTICLE 8.

Article 8

Any dispute which may arise between any two or more Contracting States concerning the interpretation or application of the present Convention which is not settled by negotiation shall, at the request of all the parties to the dispute, be referred to the International Court of Justice for decision, unless the parties agree to another mode of settlement.

See also: International Convention on the Elimination of All Forms of Racial Discrimination (1965) Article 22, p. 367 above.

International Convention on the Suppression and Punishment of the Crime of Apartheid (1973) Article XII, p. 380 above.

Convention on the Elimination of All Forms of Discrimination Against Women (1979) Article 29, p. 382 above.

B. INTERNATIONAL LABOUR ORGANIZATION PROCEDURES

INTRODUCTION

The documents that follow deal with the work of bodies operating in three distinct areas. The first area, that of examination of reports from member states (or "supervision") is the work of the Committee of Experts on the Application of Conventions and Recommendations and the Conference Committee on the same topic.

The second area, Representations under Articles 24 and 25 of the ILO Constitution and Complaints under Articles 26–34 of the Constitution, relates to allegations that member states are not fulfilling their treaty obligations.

The third area, involving the work of the Fact-Finding and Conciliation Commission on Freedom of Association and the Committee on Freedom of Association deals exclusively with trade union rights.

The set of procedures of the two Committees examining reports, which is usually regarded as the most sophisticated of its kind, flows from the provisions of Articles 19 and 22 of the ILO Constitution which require reporting on the domestic effect given by members of the Organization to ILO Conventions (whether ratified or not by the state concerned) and Recommendations. The two different Committees represent different methods of dealing with the matter, one of them an "expert" body and the other a frankly political body which nevertheless has a great deal of expertise on labor questions. The procedure for the examination of reports, first by the experts and later by the political body, operates by the increasing use of publicity for the "mobilization of shame" to the point where the Report of the Conference Committee is presented to the annual Conference of the Organization for adoption. The Report may be sharply critical of the shortcomings of various governments.

The terms of reference of the Committee of Experts were last revised in 1947. They are in very general terms. Accordingly, we have included in addition to the relevant provisions of the Constitution an extract from the Committee's 1977 Report which includes not only the formal terms of reference but also a statement of its principles and working methods. Also included in this extract are the principles concerning "direct contacts" with states (an important 1967 innovation aimed at increasing compliance) and the rules adopted by the Governing Body of the ILO in 1976 regarding supply of reports by Governments on the application of ratified Conventions.

The terms of reference of the Conference Committee are also defined in general terms (Article 7 of the Standing Orders of the International Labor Conference). To fill in the detail in this case, we have reproduced an extremely helpful paper on the work of the Committee which was prepared by the International Labor Office for the Committee's guidance at the 1979 Conference.

The procedures for Representations and Complaints have been little used but they have great potential and their existence as a last resort has probably contributed to the effectiveness of the reporting procedure. *See* M. Tardu, *I Human Rights: The International Petition System*, Section IIA, 5, 8–10 (1979).

The Fact-Finding and Conciliation Commission on Freedom of Association was set up in 1950 by arrangement between the ILO and the Economic and Social Council of the UN. It has jurisdiction to examine complaints of infringement of trade union rights referred to it by the Governing Body of ILO in respect both of countries that have ratified the ILO's freedom of association Conventions, and those that have not. In the latter event, the consent of the State is required. No procedure is laid down in the constitutive documents. The procedures followed in practice have been similar to those for a Commission of Inquiry established pursuant to Article 25 of the ILO Constitution.

The Fact Finding and Conciliation Commission on Freedom of Association deals with few complaints because of the failure of most States concerned to consent to its jurisdiction. Another more informal body, which does not need State consent, has a much larger case-load. This is the Governing Body's Committee on Freedom of Association. It examines complaints (mainly from workers' organizations) to see whether there is sufficient justification for their referral to the Fact-Finding Commission. In the course of doing so it often makes comments on the merits, even where no further ILO action is recommended.

The procedures of these two bodies have developed by accretion over a period of years. In order to capture them as best we can, we include an outline of existing procedures prepared by the International Labor Office in 1977 on the basis of decisions taken until then as well as the 193rd Report of the Committee containing recommendations for further development of its procedures which were approved by the Governing Body at its 210th Session (May–June 1979).[18]

On the ILO procedures in general see E. Landy, *The Effectiveness of International Supervision: Thirty Years of I.L.O. Experience* (1966); N. Valticos, "The International Labor Organization," in *The Effectiveness of International Decisions*, 134 (S. Schwebel ed. 1971); N. Valticos, "The Role of the ILO: Present Action and Future Perspectives," in *Human Rights: Thirty Years After the Universal Declarations*, 211, 216–231 (B. Ramcharan ed. 1979).

On freedom of association, see E. Haas, *Human Rights and International Action: the Case of Freedom of Association* (1970).

1. THE COMMITTEE OF EXPERTS ON THE APPLICATION OF CONVENTIONS AND RECOMMENDATIONS (1977)

II. FIFTIETH ANNIVERSARY OF THE COMMITTEE

10. Fifty years have now elapsed since the Committee held its first session in May 1927. At that first session, the Committee was composed of eight members and met for three days. It had to examine 180 reports on the application of ratified Conventions from 26 States. The International Labour Organisation was composed of 55 member States, the Conference had adopted

23 Conventions and 28 Recommendations, and the number of ratifications of Conventions was 229. Since then, the number of States Members of the International Labour Organisation has grown to 133, the number of Conventions adopted to 147, of Recommendations to 155, and the number of ratifications to 4,345, and the number of declarations of application of Conventions to non-metropolitan territories has reached 1,332 of which 1,226 are without modifications. Consequently, this year the Committee was called on to examine almost 2,500 reports on the application of ratified Conventions.

11. The Conference resolution of 1926 which led to the establishment of the Committee described its purpose as "making the best and fullest use" of the reports on ratified Conventions and as "securing such additional data as may be provided for in the forms approved by the Governing Body and found desirable to supplement that already available." The findings of the Committee were to be placed before the Conference through the Governing Body. Subsequently, when the constitutional amendments of 1946 broadened the scope of reporting to include information on the submission of newly adopted Conventions and Recommendations to the competent national authorities, on the effect given to unratified Conventions and to Recommendations and on the application of ratified Conventions in non-metropolitan territories, the Governing Body extended the terms of reference of the Committee of Experts to cover these additional questions.

12. The report of the Conference Committee which proposed the establishment of a committee of experts in 1926 endorsed a suggestion that the members of this body "should be persons of independent standing." Since making the original appointments, the Governing Body has followed the principle that the experts "should be chosen on the ground of their technical competence alone, that they should be completely impartial and that they should be in no sense considered as representatives of governments."

13. Since the original Committee of eight members was set up in 1927, the task of supervision has grown steadily along with the expansion of the ILO's standard-setting activities and the extension of the Committee's terms of reference. As more and more States have joined the Organisation and as the number of instruments has increased, the total of ratifications has risen steadily. In addition to examining the reports thus received on ratified Conventions, the Committee is now also called upon, as indicated above, to consider the information due from governments on the submission of newly adopted instruments to the competent authorities and on the effect given to unratified Conventions and to Recommendations, as well as to exercise certain functions in relation to instruments adopted under the auspices of other international organisations. To cope with these ever-expanding tasks the Committee's membership was gradually increased. At present, it has 18 members. Along with this increase in size the geographical composition of the Committee has come to reflect the ILO's expanding membership. The Governing Body's practice is to include on the Committee persons from every part of the world with first-hand experience of different legal, economic and social systems. The Committee is now composed of five members from Western Europe; three from Eastern Europe; three from Africa; three from South America and the Caribbean; one from North America;

and three from Asia. While initial appointments of members are for three years, the Governing Body generally extends the appointments for successive terms so as to draw on the cumulative experience of the Committee's members and ensure a maximum of continuity and uniformity in assessing the extent to which member States comply with their international obligations.

14. Within the framework of the terms of reference laid down by the Governing Body, it is for the Committee of Experts to decide on the practical methods to be followed in discharging its tasks. The Committee has thus gradually evolved a number of specific procedures designed to enable it to cope with its various functions despite its greatly increased workload. The Committee's present methods of work are described in paragraph 38 below under the heading "Organisation of the work of the Committee." Before setting them out, however, it seems appropriate to describe briefly the manner in which they have evolved over the years.

15. Thus, in 1949 the Committee originated the practice of giving special and searching attention to the first reports received after ratification (which now number between 150 and 200 every year) and asked the Office to prepare a careful comparative analysis of the national position.

16. Since 1950, the Committee has been called on to examine reports requested from member States by the Governing Body on the application of certain unratified Conventions or of Recommendations. Its practice is to make a general survey of the situation in the reporting countries with respect to the instruments selected. Since 1956, with a view to giving a more complete account of the effect of these standards, the Committee's surveys have been based, in the case of Conventions, both on the reports from ratifying States under article 22 of the Constitution and on the reports from non-ratifying States requested pursuant to article 19.

17. In 1957 the Committee decided to adopt a simplified procedure in the case of requests for supplementary information or of comments on minor points: instead of including these in its report, they are communicated directly to the governments concerned, and cases of this kind are merely listed in the Committee's report.

18. In 1959 the Committee put forward the idea that detailed reporting be placed on a two-yearly basis, subject to the safeguards required in certain cases. This system was approved by the Governing Body and the Conference Committee and has been in operation until this year, when it is to be replaced by the new system of detailed reporting mentioned in paragraph 22 below.

19. In 1963, the Committee undertook a close review of the practical application of ratified Conventions, dealing in particular with the incorporation of these standards in internal law and with the data available for assessing their effective implementation. Since then the Committee has pursued this matter and has drawn attention to cases where governments have failed to supply the statistical and other information on practical application called for in the forms of report.

20. On the occasion of its fortieth anniversary in 1967, the Committee put forward a suggestion which led to the introduction in 1968 of the procedure of direct contacts which has now become firmly established. Under this procedure

a representative of the Director-General, with the consent of the government, visits the country concerned in order to discuss the problems at issue with the competent national services. Originally introduced to deal with problems relating to the application of ratified Conventions, the direct contacts procedure was extended in 1973 to cover difficulties in fulfilling the constitutional obligations to submit Conventions and Recommendations to the competent national authorities and to submit reports and information under articles 19 and 22 of the Constitution, and to possible obstacles to the ratification of a given Convention. This procedure has also been used in recent years within the framework of the special ILO machinery for examining allegations of violations of trade union rights.

21. In 1972, the Committee undertook a review of the various aspects of the role which employers and workers and their organisations are called upon to play in giving effect to the instruments adopted by the Conference, and made a number of suggestions designed to promote a fuller participation by employers' and workers' organisations in the supervisory procedures, in particular by making observations on the reports and information supplied by their governments to the ILO under articles 19 and 22 of the ILO Constitution. The Committee has continued to follow this matter closely since then, as has also the Conference Committee which has shown a growing interest in encouraging contributions from employers' and workers' organisations. As a result of the various measures taken to facilitate their task, the observations received from employers' and workers' organisations have increased very substantially in recent years.

22. By 1976, the workload of the Committee, as well as that of many government services responsible for preparing reports, had grown to such an extent since the system of two-yearly detailed reporting was introduced in 1959 that the Governing Body decided, after consulting the Committee and the Conference Committee, to introduce a new and more flexible system of reporting on ratified Conventions, under which detailed reports may be requested at yearly, two-yearly or four-yearly intervals. The details of the new system are set out in paragraph 38 below, under the heading "Rules for the supply of reports on ratified Conventions."

23. Also in 1976, the Committee was entrusted by the Governing Body with responsibility for examining those parts of reports from States Parties to the International Covenant on Economic, Social and Cultural Rights which relate to matters falling within the responsibilities of the ILO, and for reporting on the progress made by States Parties in achieving the observance of the provisions of the Covenant falling within the scope of ILO activities. Particulars of this new responsibility, which the Committee will first be called upon to undertake in 1978, are set out in paragraphs 46 to 49 below.

24. It was in 1969 that the Committee was first called upon to exercise functions in relation to an instrument adopted under the auspices of another organisation, namely the European Code of Social Security, adopted by a regional organisation, the Council of Europe. Since then the Committee has each year had to examine reports from States which have ratified the Code and to draw up conclusions on the extent to which they give effect to its terms. Particulars of this responsibility are set out in paragraphs 50 to 52 below.

25. Without attempting to make an over-all assessment of the impact of its work, the Committee has since 1964 adopted the practice of listing the cases where governments, in response to its earlier comments, have introduced changes in their law and practice in order to give fuller effect to ratified Conventions. During the past 14 years, over 1,100 such instances of progress have come to the Committee's attention. These cases of progress have touched on all the subject areas covered by Conventions and have come from countries in all regions of the world.

26. The Committee is also aware that these examples of action taken in response to its comments represent only a limited proportion of the cases where international labour standards and the procedures to promote their implementation are able, in various ways, to exert a positive influence. There are many "invisible" or less apparent cases in which progress can be attributed to these standards and procedures. One such instance is when legislative or other measures are taken as a result of a government's decision to ratify a Convention. Other cases of "invisible" progress occur when measures are taken in relation with the submission of instruments to the competent authority, even if the instrument is not ratified; or where steps taken with a view to giving effect to the minimum standards of a ratified Convention act as a catalyst for further measures going beyond the requirements of the Convention; or, again, when the request for a report on an unratified Convention or a Recommendation leads to action resulting in the ratification of the Convention or to fuller implementation even in the absence of ratification. The Committee noted with interest the recent publication by the International Labour Office of a book on "The Impact of International Labour Conventions and Recommendations" which provides illustrations of cases of influence of these various kinds.

27. It seems appropriate to conclude this brief review of the development of the Committee's work by placing its action in the more general framework of ILO supervisory procedures as a whole. Regular supervision is the centre-piece of the arrangements by which the ILO seeks to follow up and supervise the implementation of its standards, but recourse may also be had, under the terms of the ILO Constitution to procedures of complaint and representation, which may be initiated by member States and organisations of employers and workers, or by the Governing Body, in order to investigate allegations of non-observance of a ratified Convention. In addition, there has been a progressive development over the years of other procedures, particularly the standing machinery for dealing with complaints in the field of freedom of association, but also at times ad hoc commissions or investigations. The growing utilisation of these procedures has placed at the disposal of the Organisation a widening range of means through which to bring to bear its influence on the resolution of problems and the adoption of social reforms on the basis of internationally agreed principles and standards.

28. There has also been a continual concern to co-ordinate the operation of the various supervisory procedures so that they will be complementary and mutually reinforcing. Thus regular supervision has been supplemented by the investigation, under the special procedures, of particularly complex issues, and special investigations have found a continuing echo through the work of the

standing supervisory bodies in following up the measures taken to implement the recommendations made within the framework of the special procedures.

FUNDAMENTAL PRINCIPLES, MANDATE AND METHODS OF WORK OF THE COMMITTEE

29. The preceding indications show how, during the 50 years since the Committee's first meeting in 1927, its tasks have increased as a result of the extension of the ILO's standard-setting activities, the very considerable increase in the membership of the Organisation, and new responsibilities arising from constitutional amendments and decisions of the Governing Body, and how the Committee's size, composition and procedures have undergone considerable development in response to those changes. The Committee's basic purposes and principles have, however, remained essentially the same throughout this period. Above all, the Committee remains conscious of the fact that its work can have value only to the extent that it remains true to its tradition of independence, objectivity and impartiality.

30. As it has done from time to time in the past, the Committee decided to undertake a fresh review of its methods of work this year, on the basis of a preliminary examination of the matter by a working party of four of its members. This review appeared particularly appropriate in the light of the new system for reporting on ratified Conventions approved by the Governing Body at its 201st Session (November 1976).

31. The Committee discussed the approach to be adopted in evaluating national law and practice against the requirements of international labour Conventions. It reaffirms that its function is to determine whether the requirements of a given Convention are being set, whatever the economic and social conditions existing in a given country. Subject only to any derogations which are expressly permitted by the Convention itself, these requirements remain constant and uniform for all countries. In carrying out this work the Committee is guided by the standards laid down in the Convention alone, mindful, however, of the fact that the modes of their implementation may be different in different States. These are international standards, and the manner in which their implementation is evaluated must be uniform and must not be affected by concepts derived from any particular social or economic system.

32. The Committee's terms of reference do not require it to give interpretations of Conventions, competence to do so being vested in the International Court of Justice by article 37 of the Constitution. Nevertheless, in order to carry out its function of evaluating the implementation of conventions, the Committee has to consider and express its views on the meaning of certain provisions of Conventions.

33. The Committee considered that its methods of work, as adapted and improved from time to time, enable it adequately to discharge its functions. It has nevertheless agreed upon certain innovations. In particular, it has decided that, while the preliminary examination of particular Conventions or subjects will continue to be entrusted to individual members of the Committee, opportunities should be provided for optional consultations among the members at

the preliminary stage of examination of reports. Thus, any member of the Committee may ask to be consulted by the expert responsible for a given Convention or subject before draft findings are finalised, and the responsible expert may himself consult other members in cases where he considers this desirable. However, the final wording of the drafts to be submitted to the Committee will remain the sole responsibility of the expert entrusted with the examination of the reports or information concerned. All members will, of course, remain free to present their observations on the drafts when these are considered by the Committee in plenary sitting.

34. The Committee noted that the new system for spacing out of reports on ratified Conventions adopted by the Governing Body will introduce greater flexibility into the periodicity of reporting, with a series of safeguards to ensure that regular and rapid attention be given to important matters and serious situations. In such cases, as a result of these various safeguards, detailed reports will be requested at two-yearly or even yearly intervals, instead of on a four-yearly basis. The Committee noted that, as hitherto, each country will also be required to supply a general report each year on ratified Conventions for which detailed reports are not due. Where such general reports indicate substantial changes in legislation or practice affecting the application of particular Conventions, these will be examined without awaiting the next detailed report on the Conventions concerned. Having regard to the fact that more rapid attention is also to be given to cases in which the application of ratified Conventions has been the subject of comments by employers' or workers' organisations, the Committee considers it important that the above-mentioned general report should include particulars of any comments received from such organisations in respect of the standards concerned.

35. With the greater spacing out of detailed reporting, the Committee is concerned to examine as closely as possible the manner in which Conventions are applied in practice. It therefore once again emphasises the importance of governments supplying full information in reply to the questions in the report forms concerning this aspect, including any necessary statistical data and information on the results of labour inspection, extracts from the reports of inspection services, and decisions of courts of law or other tribunals involving questions of principle relating to the application of the Convention.

36. A particularly valuable source of information on practical application is constituted by observations received from employers' and workers' organisations on the application of ratified Conventions by their governments. The Committee has already in previous reports welcomed the fact that the action taken in recent years by the Office to make fuller information available to these organisations—which last year, following a request from the Workers' members of the Conference Committee, for the first time included copies of the Committee's observations and direct requests to their government—has resulted in a marked increase in the interest taken by these organisations (further details of which are given in section V of this report). The Committee considers it likely that a further impetus to this trend will be given by the adoption by the Conference in 1976 of the Tripartite Consultation (International Labour Standards) Convention, 1976 (No. 144)—which has already received its first ratifica-

tion—and the Tripartite Consultation (Activities of the International Labour Organisation) Recommendation, 1976 (No. 152). The systematic consultations with employers' and workers' organisations on matters relating to international labour standards foreseen by these instruments should not only enhance and generalise the impact of ILO standards at the national level, but should also make available to the Committee more ample information on the way in which Conventions are actually applied.

37. The Committee intends, at its next session, to undertake once again a general examination of the means available to it to assess the extent to which ratified Conventions are made effective in actual practice, and ways in which the flow of information on this aspect of the implementation of ILO standards could be further improved.

38. Following the changes in the reporting system adopted by the Governing Body and the review by the Committee of its working methods in the light of those changes, the committee considers it appropriate to restate below, as its has done on various previous occasions, its terms of reference, composition, fundamental principles, and organisation of work. It also sets out again the principles governing the procedure of direct contacts, as last restated in the Committee's report of 1973. For the sake of completeness, the Committee is also reproducing the rules for presentation of reports on ratified conventions approved by the Governing Body in November 1976.

TERMS OF REFERENCE IN REGARD TO OBLIGATIONS UNDER THE ILO CONSTITUTION AND ILO CONVENTIONS

(a) In pursuance of its terms of reference as revised by the Governing Body at its 103rd Session (Geneva, 1947), the Committee is called upon "to examine:
  i. the annual reports under article 22 of the Constitution on the measures taken by Members to give effect to the provisions of Conventions to which they are parties, and the information furnished by Members concerning the results of inspection;
  ii. the information and reports concerning Conventions and Recommendations communicated by Members in accordance with article 19 of the Constitution;
  iii. information and reports on the measures taken by Members in accordance with Article 35 of the Constitution."

COMPOSITION OF THE COMMITTEE

(b) The members of the Committee are appointed by the Governing Body in their personal capacity, on the proposal of the Director-General, for a period of three years. Their term of office is renewable for successive periods of three years. According to the principles adopted by the Governing Body when making the initial appointments to the Committee, its members are chosen as persons of independent standing, completely impartial and on the ground of their competence. They are drawn from all parts of the world so as to possess first-hand experience of different legal, economic and social systems.

FUNDAMENTAL PRINCIPLES

(c) The Committee's fundamental principles as voiced on a number of occasions, call for impartiality and objectivity in pointing out the extent to which it appears that the position in each State is in conformity with the terms of the Conventions and the obligations which that State has undertaken by virtue of the constitution of the ILO. The members of the Committee must accomplish their task in complete independence as regards all member States.

ORGANISATION OF THE WORK OF THE COMMITTEE

(d) The Committee holds its annual session at a date and for a period determined by the Governing Body.

(e) At the opening sitting, the Committee elects its Chairman and Reporter for the session.

(f) The sittings of the Committee are held in private. Its documents and deliberations are confidential.

(g) The United Nations is invited to designate a representative to attend the sessions of the Committee.

(h) When the committee deals with instruments or matters falling within the sphere of competence of other specialised agencies of the United Nations family, representatives of these agencies are invited to participate in the sittings of the Committee.

(i) The Committee assigns to each of its members the initial responsibility for a group of Conventions or for a given subject. Reports and information received by the Office in sufficient time are circulated to the members concerned in advance of the session. Each member of the Committee responsible for a group of Conventions or for a given subject prepares for submission to the Committee preliminary findings, in the form of draft observations or direct requests on the instruments or subject concerned. Any other member may ask to be consulted by the expert responsible for a given Convention or subject before draft findings are finalised, and the responsible expert may himself consult other members in cases where he considers this desirable. However, the final wording of the drafts to be submitted to the Committee remains the sole responsibility of the expert entrusted with the examination of the reports or information concerned. All draft findings are considered and approved by the Committee in plenary sittings.

(j) The Committee appoints small working parties to deal with questions of principle or of special complexity. This is the case, in particular, as regards the comprehensive surveys of reports, under articles 19 and 22 of the Constitution, on certain subjects selected by the Governing Body or the study of certain questions selected by the Committee. These working parties generally meet for a few days before the Committee session. Having regard to the nature and extent of all the work involved they sometimes also meet during the session. Apart from this, certain questions may arise during the Committee's sessions which it is deemed appropriate to refer to a specially appointed working party. The working parties are composed so as to include members with a knowledge of different legal, economic and social systems. Their findings are subsequently submitted to the whole Committee.

(k) The documentation available to the Committee includes the information supplied by governments in their reports or in the Conference Committee on the Application of Conventions and Recommendations, the texts of legislation, collective agreements or court decisions directly relevant to the implementation of standards, the information on the results of inspections furnished by States Members, comments made by employers' and workers' organisations, conclusions of other ILO bodies (such as commissions of inquiry and the Freedom of Association Committee of the Governing Body) and the results of technical co-operation.

(l) The Committee asks the Office to prepare, in the case of first reports received from the Governments after ratification of a Convention, a comparative analysis of the position in the country concerned, for consideration by the member of the Committee responsible for the Convention. The Committee also asks the Office, upon receipt of a report, to ascertain whether it takes account of previous observations or direct requests by the Committee or the Conference Committee; if not, the Office is requested, without entering into the substance of the matter, to draw the government's attention to the need for a reply. The Office is also requested, where reports are not accompanied by copies of relevant legislation, statistical data or other documentation necessary for their full examination and this material is not otherwise available, to write to the governments concerned to request them to supply the documents in question.

(m) The findings of the Committee take the form of observations, comments and surveys included in its report or of requests communicated directly to governments by the Director-General on behalf of the Committee.

(n) Although the conclusions of the Committee have represented traditionally unanimous agreement amongst all its members, decisions can be taken by a majority. In such a case it is the established practice of the Committee to include in its report also the opinion of the dissenting members, if they so request, together with any response which the Committee may deem appropriate.

(o) The report of the Committee is submitted to the Governing Body, and it is published as Report III (Part 4) to the next General Session of the Conference.

(p) A special element in the working methods of the Committee consists in the establishment of direct contacts with governments encountering special difficulties in applying ratified Conventions or in fulfilling various constitutional obligations relating to Conventions and Recommendations. The principles governing this procedure are set out below.

SECRETARIAT OF THE COMMITTEE

(q) It is a necessity for the work of the Committee that it have at its disposal a qualified secretariat. This is placed at its disposal by the Director-General of the ILO.

* * *

PRINCIPLES GOVERNING THE PROCEDURE OF DIRECT CONTACTS

(a) The discrepancies noted and the practical or legal difficulties encountered in the application of a ratified Convention, as well as the difficulties set with in matters connected with international standards, including more particularly difficulties in fulfilling various constitutional obligations (article 19 and 22 of the Constitution) and possible obstacles to the ratification of a given Convention, should be sufficiently important to warrant such contacts.

(b) The Committee of Experts may suggest the possibility of having recourse to direct contacts, whereupon the Director-General will explore the matter with the government concerned: the Conference Committee may also make such a suggestion, following its discussion of a case; the government concerned may itself take the initiative.

(c) The contacts should in all cases take place with the full consent of the government concerned.

(d) The points to be dealt with should be clearly specified in advance.

(e) While these contacts are taking place, the supervisory bodies will suspend their examination of cases for a period which will normally not exceed one year, so as to be able to take account of the outcome of these contacts.

(f) The form which the contacts will take should be determined in the light of their purpose, which is to enable the government to explain all the elements of the case, so as to permit the Committee to assess fully all the facts involved.

(g) The contacts should bring together persons thoroughly acquainted with all aspects of the case, including government representatives with sufficient responsibility and experience to speak with authority about the position in their country and about their own government's attitudes and intentions in the matter.

(h) It will be for the Director-General to designate the representative on behalf of the International Labour Organisation, who will be either an independent person or an ILO official fully conversant with the case; normally, it would not appear appropriate that this representative be a member of the Committee of Experts, but this possibility might be left open in certain special cases.

(i) The representative of the Director-General may, in agreement with the government concerned, visit the country to hold discussion on the matter with government representatives, in order to explain the point of view of the supervisory bodies, acquaint himself in detail with the government's position and the exact nature of the difficulties in question, and make available to the Committee of Experts any relevant information supplied to him by the government.

(j) The representative of the Director-General should, in the course of his assignment, make contact with the organisations of employers and workers so as to keep them informed of the topics discussed and elicit their points of view.

(k) The scope of the direct contacts and the mandate given to the persons selected for the purpose by the Director-General should not in any way be construed as limiting the functions and responsibilities of the Committee of Experts and the Conference Committee for examining the extent to which national law and practice conform to Conventions that have been ratified.

RULES FOR THE SUPPLY OF REPORTS ON RATIFIED CONVENTIONS
(APPROVED BY THE GOVERNING BODY AT ITS 201st SESSION—
NOVEMBER 1976)

(a) First reports

First reports should continue to be requested immediately after the entry into force of a Convention for a country.

(b) Subsequent reports: Conventions for which reports should normally be requested at two-yearly intervals

Reports subsequent to the first report should normally be requested at two-yearly intervals for the following Conventions:

Freedom of Association	Nos. 11, 84, 87, 98, 135, 141.
Forced Labour	Nos. 29, 105.
Discrimination	Nos. 100, 111.
Employment Policy	No. 122.
Migrant Workers	Nos. 97, 143.
Labour Inspection	Nos. 81, 85, 129.
Tripartite Consultation	No. 144.

When a new Convention enters into force the Governing Body will decide, when approving the report form for the Convention, whether it should be included in the list of Conventions for which reports should normally be requested at two-yearly intervals. The Governing Body may periodically review the list of Conventions for which reports should normally be requested at two-yearly intervals.

(c) Subsequent reports: other Conventions

The two reports following the first report should normally be requested at two-yearly intervals. Thereafter, reports should normally be requested at four-yearly intervals.

(d) General reports

As hitherto, each country will be requested to supply a general report each year on those Conventions for which detailed reports are not due. Where this general report indicates substantial changes in legislation or practice affecting the application of particular Conventions, these should be examined without awaiting the next detailed report on the Conventions concerned.

(e) Cases in which more frequent reporting is to be requested

(i) *Failure to report or to reply to comments by supervisory bodies*
When a detailed report is not sent in the year for which it is due, or when the report does not reply to the comments made by the supervisory bodies, a detailed report will be due the following year.

(ii) *Serious problems of application*
In cases in which there are serious problems of application the Committee

of Experts on the Application of Conventions and Recommendations or the Conference Committee on the Application of Conventions and Recommendations should, as hitherto, be able to request that a detailed report be supplied earlier than the year in which it would normally be due.

(iii) *Observations by workers' or employers' organisations*

When observations on the application of a ratified Convention are made by a national or international organisation of workers or employers, the Committee of Experts on the Application of Conventions and Recommendations or the Conference Committee on the Application of Conventions and Recommendations should be able to request, in the light of any explanations given by the government in reply to the observations, that a detailed report be supplied earlier than the year in which it would normally be due. Where these observations are sent directly to the Office, they should be communicated to the government concerned to enable it to make any comments it thinks fit.

(iv) *Governing Body decisions*

The Governing Body will be free to decide that detailed reports should be requested at shorter intervals if it considers this necessary owing to current developments, relevance to the objectives of the long-term plan or any other reason.

2. THE CONFERENCE COMMITTEE ON THE APPLICATION OF CONVENTIONS AND RECOMMENDATIONS (1979)

STANDING ORDERS OF THE INTERNATIONAL LABOUR CONFERENCE

Article 7

Committee on the Application of Conventions and Recommendations

1. The Conference shall, as soon as possible, appoint a Committee to consider

   a. the measures taken by Members to give effect to the provisions of Conventions to which they are parties and the information furnished by Members concerning the results of inspections;

   b. the information and reports concerning Conventions and Recommendations communicated by Members in accordance with article 19 of the Constitution;

   c. the measures taken by Members in accordance with article 35 of the Constitution.

2. The Committee shall submit a report to the Conference.

WORK OF THE COMMITTEE (PAPER PREPARED FOR THE COMMITTEE'S GUIDANCE AT ITS 1979 SESSION)

I. INTRODUCTION

The object of this note is to indicate briefly the manner in which the work of the Committee is usually carried out.

II. TERMS OF REFERENCE OF THE COMMITTEE

The terms of reference of the Committee are defined in article 7 of the Standing Orders of the Conference. By virtue of this article the Committee is called upon to consider:

a. the measures taken by Members to give effect to the provisions of Conventions to which they are parties and the information furnished by Members concerning the results of inspections;

b. the information and reports concerning Conventions and Recommendations communicated by Members in accordance with article 19 of the Constitution;

c. the measures taken by Members in accordance with article 35 of the Constitution.

III. WORKING DOCUMENTS

Report of the Committee of Experts. The basic working document of the Committee is the report of the Committee of Experts on the Application of Conventions and Recommendations (Report III, Part 4A and B), printed in two volumes.

Volume A of this report contains, in Part One, the General Report of the Committee (pages 3–39 of the report), and in Part Two, the observations of the Committee concerning the application of ratified Conventions and concerning the submission of Conventions and Recommendations to the competent authorities in member States (pages 43–258). An index to these observations will be found at the beginning of the report, pages VII–XV.

It will be recalled that, as regards ratified Conventions, the work of the Committee of Experts is based on reports by governments. In accordance with the new procedure for detailed reporting approved by the Governing Body in November 1976, detailed reports may be requested at yearly, two-yearly or four-yearly intervals.[19]

With reference to the footnotes to certain observations, asking the government concerned to report in detail earlier than the year in which a report on the Convention in question would normally be due, and/or to supply full particulars to the Conference (see paragraph 116 of the General Report of the Committee of Experts), the Committee of Experts has emphasised that such footnotes are not intended in any way to imply that the Conference will not wish, in accordance with its usual practice, to receive information from the governments on the other observations which the Committee has made.

In addition to the observations contained in its report, the Committee of Experts has, as in previous years, made direct requests which are communicated to governments by the Office on the Committee's behalf (see paragraph 115 of the General Report of the Committee of Experts). A list of these direct requests will be found at the beginning of Volume A, pages VII to XV.

Volume B of the report contains a general survey by the Committee of Experts of the reports relating to the Forced Labour Convention, 1930 (No. 29) and the Abolition of Forced Labour Convention, 1957 (No. 105).

Summaries. The information and reports on which the work of the Committee of Experts was based are summarised in the following documents, which are submitted to the Conference:

    i. summary of reports supplied by governments on ratified Conventions (articles 22 and 35 of the Constitution) *(Report III, Part 1);*

    ii. summary of reports supplied by governments on Conventions Nos. 29 and 105 (article 19 of the Constitution) *(Report III, Part 2);*

    iii. summary of information supplied by governments on the submission to the competent authorities of Conventions and Recommendations adopted by the Conference (article 19 of the Constitution) *(Report III, Part 3).*

Other information. In addition, as and when relevant information is received by the Secretariat, documents are prepared and distributed containing the substance of:

    i. written replies of governments to the observations made by the Committee of Experts;

    ii. supplementary information which reached the International Labour Office after the meeting of the Committee of Experts.

IV. COMPOSITION OF THE COMMITTEE AND VOTING PROCEDURE

A. *Composition of the committee*

The Committee of the 65th Session of the Conference consists of 000 members, that is:

— 91 titular Government members;
— 31 titular Employers' members;
— 56 titular Workers' members.

B. *Voting procedure*

Only titular members have the right to vote. In order to ensure equality of voting between the three groups:

— each Government member has 248 votes;
— each Employers' member has 728 votes;
— each Workers' member has 403 votes.

C. *Discussion of observations*

In Part Two of its report, the Committee of Experts makes observations on the manner in which various governments are fulfilling their obligations. The governments concerned can reply in writing or orally.

In order to expedite the work of the Committee, it is customary for the officers of the Committee to select those observations regarding which Government delegates might be invited to supply information to the Committee. The draft list of observations so selected by the officers is submitted to the Committee for approval, and members are then able to propose that other cases be added to the list.

1. *Written replies*. The written replies of governments are reproduced in the documents which are distributed to the Committee (see above, under III). When a sufficient period—at least 24 hours—has elapsed after the distribution of each document, members of the Committee wishing to comment on the information contained in the document may so inform the Chairman and the representative of the government concerned will then have the possibility of supplying the relevant information (see below, oral replies).

2. *Oral replies*. According to the procedure customarily followed, representatives of governments *which are not members* of the Committee are kept informed of the agenda of the Committee and of the date on which they may be heard:

(a) through the *Daily Bulletin*;

(b) by means of letters sent to them individually by the Chairman of the Committee.

In order to avoid any loss of time the representatives of governments *which are not members* of the Committee are customarily given priority to speak at the beginning of each sitting.

When a Government representative makes oral statements, the members of the Committee are free to comment once the Government representative in question has finished his statement on a given Convention or question.

D. *Reports received too late for examination by the Committee of Experts*

In accordance with established practice, such reports will be referred to the Committee of Experts for examination at its next meeting.

V. SCHEDULE OF WORK

A. *General discussion*

1. *General questions*. Each year the Committee holds a general discussion which is primarily based on the General Report of the Committee of Experts *(Report III, Part 4A, pages 3–39)*.

2. *General survey*. In accordance with its usual practice, the Committee will also wish to discuss the general survey by the Committee of Experts on forced labour.

B. *Special list and special paragraphs*

In past years, the committee has included in its report a separate section in which it has drawn the attention of the Conference to cases where governments have apparently encountered serious difficulties in discharging their obligations. In recent years, the following criteria were applied by the Committee in deciding which cases were to be included:

Supply of information

(1) None of the reports on ratified Conventions have been supplied during the past two years.

(2) First reports on ratified Conventions have not been supplied for at least two years.

(3) None of the reports on unratified Conventions and on Recommendations requested under article 19, paragraphs 5, 6 and 7 of the Constitution have been supplied during the past five years.

(4) No indication is available that steps have been taken to submit the Conventions and Recommendations adopted during the *last seven* sessions of the Conference[20] to the competent authorities, in accordance with article 19 of the Constitution.

(5) No information has been received as regards all or most of the observations and direct requests of the Committee of Experts to which a reply was requested for the period ending 30 June 1978.

(6) The government has failed, despite repeated invitations by the Conference Committee, to take part in the discussion concerning its country.

Application of ratified Conventions

(7) The Committee examined the application of certain Conventions in various countries and noted with grave concern that in some of them there was continued failure to implement fully the Conventions concerned and that full information should therefore be supplied on the measures taken to ensure such compliance. The Committee draws particular attention in this connection to the following cases.

The Committee has also drawn the attention of the Conference to its discussions regarding certain cases by means of special paragraphs in its report.

In 1978, following discussion, the Committee concluded that it seemed appropriate to examine what changes might be made in its working methods as regards the special list and the special paragraphs, and suggested that for this purpose a tripartite working party be appointed at the 65th Session of the Conference. The Committee may therefore wish, at the outset of its work, to consider the establishment of such a working party. The meetings of the committee and of the working party—which should not take place at the same time—could be arranged in such a way that the Committee's general discussion on matters other than the special list and special paragraphs could be pursued.

3. REPRESENTATIONS (ARTICLES 24 AND 25 OF THE ILO CONSTITUTION, STANDING ORDERS CONCERNING THE PROCEDURE FOR THE DISCUSSION OF REPRESENTATIONS) (1919, 1932, 1938)

ILO Constitution (1919)

REPRESENTATIONS OF NON-OBSERVANCE OF CONVENTIONS

Article 24

In the event of any representation being made to the International labour Office by an industrial association of employers or of workers that any of the Members has failed to secure in any respect the effective observance within its jurisdiction of any Convention to which it is a party, the Governing Body may communicate this representation to the government against which it is made, and may invite that government to make such statement on the subject as it may think fit.

PUBLICATION OF REPRESENTATION

Article 25

If no statement is received within a reasonable time from the government in question, or if the statement when received is not deemed to be satisfactory by the Governing Body, the latter shall have the right to publish the representation and the statement, if any, made in reply to it.

ILO Standing Orders Concerning the Procedure for the Discussion on Representations (Adopted by the Governing Body on 8 April 1932. Amended by the Governing Body on 5 February 1938).

GENERAL PROVISIONS

Article 1

1. All the steps in the procedure concerning a representation received by the Office in accordance with Article 24 of the Constitution of the Organisation shall be confidential until such time as the matter is finally disposed of by the Governing Body.

2. The meetings of the Governing Body at which these steps are discussed shall be held in private.

Article 2

1. When a representation is made to the Director-General of the International Labour Office within the meaning of Article 24 of the Constitution of the Organisation, he shall acknowledge its receipt and then communicate it immediately to all members of the Governing Body for consideration at its next session.

2. Before that session the Director-General of the International Labour Office shall communicate to the Governing Body all the information in his possession as regards the receivability of the representation without proceeding for that purpose to put any part of the procedure into operation.

3. When a representation is submitted to the Governing Body, the latter shall set up a committee composed of three of its members chosen respectively from the Government, Employers' and Workers' groups which shall, before any decision is reached, lay before the Governing Body proposals concerning the steps to be taken at each of the stages of the procedure referred to below. No representative or national of the State against which the representation has been made and no person occupying an official position in the association of employers or workers which has made the representation may be a member of this committee.

RECEIVABILITY OF THE REPRESENTATION AS REGARDS FORM

Article 3

1. The Governing Body shall, during the session at which the question is submitted to it and after hearing the views of the committee provided for in paragraph 3 of Article 2 above, examine the receivability of the representation as regards form.

2. The receivability of a representation as regards form is subject to the following conditions:

    a. it must be communicated to the International Labour Office in writing;

    b. it must emanate from an industrial association of employers or workers;

    c. it must make specific reference to Article 24 of the Constitution of the Organisation;

    d. it must concern a Member of the International Labour Organisation;

    e. it must refer to a Convention ratified by the Member against which it is made; and

    f. it must allege that the Member against which it is made has failed to secure in some respect the effective observance within its jurisdiction of the said Convention.

EXAMINATION OF THE SUBSTANCE OF THE REPRESENTATION

Article 4

1. If it is declared to be receivable as regards form, the Governing Body shall, after hearing the views of the Committee provided for in paragraph 3 of Article 2 above, make a preliminary examination of the representation as regards substance.

2. During that examination the Governing Body shall decide—

    a. to declare that the representation is not well founded; or

    b. to communicate the representation to the Government against which it is made without inviting that Government to make any statement in reply; or

    c. to obtain further information; or

    d. to communicate the representation to the Government against which it made and to invite the latter to make such statement on the subject as it may think fit.

3. In any case the International Labour Office shall inform the industrial association of employers or workers who made the representation of the decision taken.

4. In cases (a) and (b) the procedure shall be declared closed.

5. In case (c) the decision shall be postponed until such further information shall have been received.

Article 5

1. If the Governing Body decides to communicate the representation to the Government against which it is made and to invite that Government to make the statement provided for in Article 24 of the Constitution, it shall fix a reasonable time limit within the meaning of Article 25.

2. If the Government against which the representation is made has any observations to make on the subject of the length of the time, it may ask to

appoint a representative who shall be heard by the Governing Body on the particular point in question at the earliest possible moment.

Article 6

If at the end of the time limit the Governing Body has received no reply, it may, after hearing the views of the Committee provided for in paragraph 3 of Article 2 above—

    a. prolong the time limit; or

    b. decide to open the discussion on the application of Article 25 of the Constitution.

Article 7

1. If the Governing Body receives a statement which, after considering the report of the Committee provided for in paragraph 3 of Article 2 above, it considers to be satisfactory it shall declare the whole procedure closed.

2. The International Labour Office shall, in writing, inform the Government against which the representation was made and the industrial association which made the representation of the decision taken.

Article 8

If the Governing Body receives a statement which, after considering the report of the Committee provided for in paragraph 3 of Article 2 above, it does not consider satisfactory it may—

    a. ask for further information, in which case the decision shall be adjourned until such information shall be received; or

    b. decide to open the discussion on the application of Article 25 of the Constitution.

Article 9

1. When the Governing Body, in accordance with Articles 6 and 8 above, decides to open the discussion on the application of Article 25 of the Constitution, it shall in the first instance fix the date at which the proceedings on this question shall take place.

2. It may then, if necessary, and in accordance with the terms of paragraph 5 of Article 26 of the Constitution, invite the Government against which the representation has been made to send a representative to take part in these proceedings.

3. Such representative may speak under the same conditions as the members of the Governing Body, but he shall not have the right to vote.

Article 10

If the Government against which the representation has been made appoints no representative to take part in the proceedings of the Governing Body relative to the representation which concerns it, that Government shall be considered to have renounced the rights to which it is entitled under paragraph 5 of Article 26 of the Constitution.

Article 11

1. When the Governing Body has discussed the question in the light of the report of the Committee provided for in paragraph 3 of Article 2 above, it may—
   a. declare the whole procedure to be closed; or
   b. ask for further information, in which case a final decision shall be adjourned until such information shall have been received; or
   c. declare that the representation is well founded and decide to publish it as well as the statement, if any, made in reply to it.
2. In any event the International Labour Office shall, in writing, inform the Government against which the representation has been made and the industrial association which made the representation, of the decision taken.

DECISIONS

Article 12

1. In the event of the Governing Body deciding to publish the representation and the statement, if any, made in reply to it, it shall decide the form and date of publication.
2. The International Labour Office shall, in writing, inform the Government against which the representation is made and the industrial association which made the representation, of the decisions taken by the Governing Body in this connection.

Article 13

When a representation within the meaning of Article 24 of the Constitution of the Organisation is communicated to the Governing Body, the latter may at any time in accordance with paragraph 4 of Article 26 of the Constitution adopt against the Government against which the representation is made and concerning the Convention the effective observance of which is contested, the procedure of complaint provided for in Articles 26 and the following articles.

4. COMPLAINTS BY MEMBER STATES (ARTICLES 26–34 OF THE ILO CONSTITUTION) (1919)

COMPLAINTS OF NON-OBSERVANCE

Article 26

1. Any of the Members shall have the right to file a complaint with the International Labour Office if it is not satisfied that any other Member is securing the effective observance of any Convention which both have ratified in accordance with the foregoing articles.
2. The Governing Body may, if it thinks fit, before referring such a complaint to a Commission of Inquiry, as hereinafter provided for, communicate with the government in question in the manner described in article 24.
3. If the Governing Body does not think it necessary to communicate the

complaint to the government in question, or if, when it has made such communication, no statement in reply has been received within a reasonable time which the Governing Body considers to be satisfactory, the Governing Body may appoint a Commission of Inquiry to consider the complaint and to report thereon.

4. The Governing Body may adopt the same procedure either of its own motion or on receipt of a complaint from a delegate to the Conference.

5. When any matter arising out of article 25 or 26 is being considered by the Governing Body, the government in question shall, if not already represented thereon, be entitled to send a representative to take part in the proceedings of the Governing Body while the matter is under consideration. Adequate notice of the date on which the matter will be considered shall be given to the government in question.

CO-OPERATION WITH COMMISSION OF INQUIRY

Article 27

The Members agree that, in the event of the reference of a complaint to a Commission of Inquiry under article 26, they will each, whether directly concerned in the complaint or not, place at the disposal of the Commission all the information in their possession which bears upon the subject-matter of the complaint.

REPORT OF COMMISSION OF INQUIRY

Article 28

When the Commission of Inquiry has fully considered the complaint, it shall prepare a report embodying its findings on all questions of fact relevant to determining the issue between the parties and containing such recommendations as it may think proper as to the steps which should be taken to meet the complaint and the time within which they should be taken.

ACTION ON REPORT OF COMMISSION OF INQUIRY

Article 29

1. The Director-General of the International Labour Office shall communicate the report of the Commission of Inquiry to the Governing Body and to each of the governments concerned in the complaint, and shall cause it to be published.

2. Each of these governments shall within three months inform the Director-General of the International Labour Office whether or not it accepts the recommendations contained in the report of the Commission; and if not, whether it proposes to refer the complaint to the International Court of Justice.

FAILURE TO SUBMIT CONVENTIONS OR RECOMMENDATIONS TO COMPETENT AUTHORITIES

Article 30

In the event of any Member failing to take the action required by paragraphs

5 (*b*), 6 (*b*) or 7 (*b*) (i) of article 19 with regard to a Convention or Recommendation, any other Member shall be entitled to refer the matter to the Governing Body. In the event of the Governing Body finding that there has been such a failure, it shall report the matter to the Conference.

DECISIONS OF INTERNATIONAL COURT OF JUSTICE

Article 31

The decision of the International Court of Justice in regard to a complaint or matter which has been referred to it in pursuance of article 29 shall be final.

Article 32

The International Court of Justice may affirm, vary or reverse any of the findings or recommendations of the Commission of Inquiry, if any.

FAILURE TO CARRY OUT RECOMMENDATIONS OF COMMISSION OF INQUIRY OR ICJ

Article 33

In the event of any Member failing to carry out within the time specified the recommendations, if any, contained in the report of the Commission of Inquiry, or in the decision of the International Court of Justice, as the case may be, the Governing Body may recommend to the Conference such action as it may deem wise and expedient to secure compliance therewith.

COMPLIANCE WITH RECOMMENDATIONS OF COMMISSION OF INQUIRY OR ICJ

Article 34

The defaulting government may at any time inform the Governing Body that it has taken the steps necessary to comply with the recommendations of the Commission of Inquiry or with those in the decision of the International Court of Justice, as the case may be, and may request it to constitute a Commission of Inquiry to verify its contention. In this case the provisions of articles 27, 28, 29, 31 and 32 shall apply, and if the report of the Commission of Inquiry or the decision of the International Court of Justice is in favour of the defaulting government, the Governing Body shall forthwith recommend the discontinuance of any action taken in pursuance of article 33.

5. THE FACT-FINDING AND CONCILIATION COMMISSION ON FREEDOM OF ASSOCIATION (1949, 1950)

This Commission was formed by agreement between the ILO and the Economic and Social Council of the United Nations.

Decision of the Governing Body of the ILO of 6 January 1950,

[1949] U.N.Y.B. on Human Rights 293, later approved by ECOSOC, [1950] U.N.Y.B. on Human Rights 498–499.

1. . . . The Governing Body of the International Labour Office, in the course of its 110th Session held in Mysore, examined the proposals relating to the establishment of a Fact-Finding and Conciliation Commission on Freedom of Association and the comments on these proposals . . .

2. . . . The Governing Body decided, on 6 January 1950, to establish the Fact-Finding and Conciliation Commission on Freedom of Association referred to in the resolution adopted by the Governing Body on 20 June 1949 and communicated to the Economic and Social Council at its Ninth Session, and also agreed, in accordance with the request made by the Economic and Social Council in its resolution of 2 August 1949, to establish this Commission on behalf of the United Nations in accordance with the relationship agreement between the two organizations.

3. The Governing Body decided that the Commission will consist of nine persons appointed by the Governing Body. These persons will be chosen for their personal qualifications and will be expected to discharge their duties with complete independence. The Commission will be authorized to arrange for its work to be done when appropriate by panels of not less than three nor more than five members.

4. The Governing Body confirmed the terms of reference of the Commission envisaged by the proposals approved by it on 22 June 1949. These terms of reference are as follows:

"It would be open to the Governing Body to refer to the Commission for impartial examination any allegations or infringements of trade union rights which the Governing Body, or the Conference acting on the report of the Credentials Committee, considers it appropriate to refer to the Commission for investigation. It would also be open to any Government against which an allegation of the infringement of trade union rights is made to refer such an allegation to the Commission for investigation. The Commission would be essentially a fact-finding body, but would be authorized to discuss situations referred to it for investigation with the Government concerned with a view to securing the adjustment of difficulties by agreement."

5. The Governing Body approved the following arrangements for the working of the Commission:

    i. With the exception of cases covered by Article 26 of the ILO Constitution, no complaint will be referred to the Commission without the consent of the Government concerned. If the Governing Body is of the opinion that a complaint should be investigated it will first seek the consent of the Government concerned. If such consent is not forthcoming, the Governing Body will give consideration to such refusal with a view to taking any appropriate alternative action designed to safeguard the rights relating the freedom of association involved in the case, including measures to give full publicity to the charges made, together with any comments by the Government concerned, and to that Government's refusal to co-operate in ascertaining the facts and in measures of conciliation. It was contemplated that the consent of any Government might be given either in an individual case or more generally in advance for certain categories of case or for any case which might arise.

ii. Any communication proposing reference of matters to the Commission which may be received by the International Labour Office from Governments or from trade union or employers' organizations (other than formal requests from the General Assembly or the Economic and Social Council) will be examined in the first instance by the Officers of the Governing Body. If the Officers of the Governing Body consider that such communications warrant circulation to the members of the Governing Body as a whole, they will then be so circulated, and it will be open to any member of the Governing Body to take the matter up and suggest the reference of the case to the Commission. The Governing Body decided that communications from sources other than those mentioned above should not be receivable.

iii. The Commission will report to the Governing Body and it will be for the Governing Body to consider in the first instance what further action shall be taken on the basis of the report. Subject to the above arrangements and understandings the Commission will work out its own rules of procedure.

6. The reference to article 26 of the ILO Constitution contained in paragraph 5 (i) above is designed to make it clear that the arrangements approved by the Governing Body at Mysore do not in any way replace the existing provisions of articles 24 to 34 of the Constitution of the International Labour Organisation. In virtue of articles 24 and 25 of the Constitution any industrial association of employers or workers may make a representation that a State for which any Convention, including the Freedom of Association and Protection of the Right to Organize Convention, 1948, or the Right to Organize and Collective Bargaining Convention, 1949, is in force is failing to secure the effective observance within its territories of the provisions of the Convention or Conventions to which it is a party, and the Governing Body may publish the representation and any statement made in reply to it. In virtue of articles 26 to 34, any Member may file a complaint that another Member which is a party to one of these Conventions is failing to give effect thereto and the Governing Body may refer such a complaint to a commission of enquiry. The Governing Body may also adopt the same procedure on its own motion or on receipt of a complaint from a delegate to the Conference. When the commission of enquiry has fully considered the complaint, it has to prepare a report embodying its findings on all questions of fact relevant to determining the issue between the parties and containing such recommendations as it may think appropriate as to the steps which should be taken to meet the complaint and the time within which they should be taken. Any Government concerned in a complaint which does not accept the recom-

mendations contained in the report of the commission of enquiry may refer the complaint to the International Court of Justice. In the event of any Member failing to carry out within the time specified the recommendations, if any, contained in the report of the Commission of Enquiry or in the decision of the International Court of Justice, as the case may be, the Governing Body may recommend to the Conference such action as it may deem wise and expedient to secure compliance therewith. These procedures provided for in the Constitution are applicable irrespective of the consent of the State concerned, subject only to that State having ratified the Convention non-observance of which is alleged. The arrangements approved by the Governing Body at Mysore do not impair or qualify these provisions of the Constitution in any way.

7. The Governing Body also decided to communicate to the Economic and Social Council for its consideration the following suggestions concerning the manner in which the services of the Commission might be made available to the appropriate organs of the United Nations.

    i. It should be open to the Economic and Social Council and to the General Assembly to refer allegations of infringements of trade union rights to the Commission.

    ii. All allegations against ILO Member States presented by the General Assembly or the Economic and Social Council should be forwarded to the Governing Body for its consideration as to referral to the Commission.

    iii. All allegations against non-ILO Member States presented by the General Assembly or the Economic and Social Council should be transmitted to the Commission through the Governing Body.

    iv. Before the Governing Body refers to the Commission an allegation which it has received against a non-ILO State by a Member of the United Nations, the allegation should be referred to the Economic and Social Council for its consideration.

    v. The Commission's reports should be addressed to the requesting body, whether the General Assembly, the Economic and Social Council, the International Labour Organisation or the Governing Body. Such reports addressed to the General Assembly or the Economic and Social Council would be transmitted through the Governing Body.

    vi. A general account of the work of the Commission would be contained in the annual report of the International Labour Organisation to the United Nations.

    vii. In any case in which it appeared to the Governing Body, when examining the Commission's report, that questions involving human rights in general were involved, the Governing Body would draw the matter specifically to the attention of the Economic and Social Council.

    viii. The Secretary-General of the United Nations would communicate to the Director-General of the International Labour Office communications relating to trade union rights received by him in accordance with the procedure laid down by the Economic and

Social Council for the examination of communications concerning human rights and such communications would be dealt with by the International Labour Organisation in accordance with the procedure indicated in paragraph 5 (ii) above . . .

6. THE COMMITTEE ON FREEDOM OF ASSOCIATION (1977, 1979)

(i) Extract from ILO Document GB/LS/March 1977, Outline of Existing Procedures for the Examination of Complaints Alleging Infringements of Trade Union Rights.

PRELIMINARY EXAMINATION OF COMPLAINTS BY THE COMMITTEE ON FREEDOM OF ASSOCIATION

COMPOSITION AND FUNCTIONING OF THE COMMITTEE

36. The Committee consists of nine regular and nine substitute members, chosen from among the Government group, the Employers' group and the Workers' group of the Governing Body, three regular and three substitute members from each group. Each member sits in a personal capacity.

37. No representative or national of the State against which a representation has been made or person occupying an official position in the national association of employers or workers which has made the representation may participate in the Committee's deliberations or even be present in the room during the hearing of the complaint in question.[21]

38. Substitute members—Government, Employer and Worker—who are present and who so request may participate in the discussion of the cases before the Committee, irrespective of whether all the regular members are present or not; it has, however, not been usual for substitute members to participate in discussions except when replacing a regular member for the purposes of the particular case. Substitute members are bound, in the same manner as regular members, by the rule laid down by the Governing Body and referred to in paragraph 37 above.[22]

39. The Committee always endeavours to reach unanimous decisions. In the event of a vote, substitutes do not vote when all the regular members for the group are voting. In the event of a regular Government member being absent or disqualified in respect of a particular case under consideration (see paragraph 37 above), the Government member appointed by the Governing Body as the particular substitute for that regular member replaces him. The right to record an abstention may be exercised on the same conditions as the right to record an affirmative or negative vote.[23]

40. If both a regular Government member and his appointed substitute are not available when the Committee is considering a particular case, the Committee calls upon one of the remaining substitute members to complete the quorum

of three; in selecting such substitute member, the committee has regard to seniority and also to the rule referred to in paragraph 37 above.[24]

HEARING OF THE PARTIES

41. The Committee may request and obtain from the Governing Body authorisation to hear the representatives of governments concerned before it submits its final recommendations to the Governing Body.[25]

MANDATE AND RESPONSIBILITY OF THE COMMITTEE

42. The responsibilities of the Committee are essentially to consider for recommendation to the Governing Body whether cases are worthy of examination by the Governing Body.

43. The Committee (after preliminary examination, including the consideration of any observations made by the governments concerned, if received within a reasonable period of time) reports to the next session of the Governing Body that a case does not call for further examination if it finds, for example, that the alleged facts, if proved, would not constitute an infringement of the exercise of trade union rights, or that the allegations made are so purely political in character that it is undesirable to pursue the matter further, or that the allegations made are too vague to permit a consideration of the case on its merits, or that the complainant has not offered sufficient evidence to justify reference of the matter to the Fact-Finding and Conciliation Commission.[26]

44. The Committee may recommend the Governing Body to communicate the conclusions of the Committee to the governments concerned, drawing their attention to the anomalies which it has observed and inviting them to take appropriate measures to remedy the situation.

45. In all cases where it suggests that the Governing Body should make recommendations to a government, the Committee adds to its conclusions on such cases a paragraph proposing that the government concerned be invited to state, after a reasonable period has elapsed and taking account of the circumstances of the case, what action it has been able to take on the recommendations made to it.[27]

46. A certain distinction is made between countries which have ratified one or more Conventions on freedom of association and those which have not.

47. In the first case (ratified Conventions) examination of the action taken on the recommendations of the Governing Body is normally entrusted to the Committee of Experts on the Application of Conventions and Recommendations, whose attention is specifically drawn in the concluding paragraph of the Committee's reports to discrepancies between national laws and practice and the terms of the Conventions, or to the incompatibility of a given situation with the provisions of these instruments. Clearly, this possibility is not such as to hinder the Committee from examining, through the procedure outlined below, the effect given to certain recommendations made by it, this can be of use taking into account the nature or urgency of certain questions.[28]

48. In the second case (non-ratified Conventions), if there is no reply, or if

the reply given is partly or entirely unsatisfactory, the matter may be followed up periodically, the Committee instructing the Director-General at suitable intervals according to the nature of each case, to remind the government concerned of the matter and to request it to supply information as to the action taken on the recommendations approved by the Governing Body. The Committee itself, from time to time, reports on the situation.[29]

49. The Committee may recommend the Governing Body to attempt to secure the consent of the government concerned to the reference of the case to the Fact-Finding and Conciliation Commission. The Committee submits to each session of the Governing Body a progress report on all cases which the Governing Body has determined warrant further examination. In every case in which the government against which the complaint is made has refused to consent to referral to the Fact-Finding and Conciliation Commission or has not within four months replied to a request for such consent, the Committee may include in its report to the Governing Body recommendations as to the "appropriate alternative action" which the Committee may believe the Governing Body might take.[30] In certain cases, the Governing Body itself has discussed the measures to be taken where a government has not consented to a referral to the Fact-Finding and Conciliation Commission.

(ii) Extract from the One Hundred and Ninety-Third Report of the Committee on Freedom of Association Containing Recommendations for Further Development of the Procedures Which Were Approved by the Governing Body at its 210th Session (May–June 1979).

I. INTRODUCTION

1. The Committee on Freedom of Association, set up by the Governing Body at its 117th Session (November 1951), set at the International Labour Office, Geneva, on 12 and 13 February 1979, under the chairmanship of Mr. Roberto Ago, former Chairman of the Governing Body.

2. The Committee has examined certain procedural questions submitted to it by the Governing Body. It submits for the Governing Body's approval a report on this subject. The Committee recommends that the Governing Body examine this report at its 209th Session.

II. QUESTIONS OF PROCEDURE

3. The International Labour Conference adopted at its 63rd Session (June 1977) a resolution concerning the promotion, protection and strengthening of freedom of association, trade union and other human rights in which it requested the Governing Body, inter alia, "to improve the application of existing procedures so as to ensure speedy and effective action in cases in which freedom of association is impaired, particularly when human life is in jeopardy" (paragraph 3(b)).

4. In view of this request, the Governing Body decided at its 204th Session

(November 1977) to refer paragraph 3(b) of the above-mentioned resolution to its Committee on Freedom of Association for consideration.

5. It should be recalled that the Committee has frequently reviewed its procedure—the basic rules of which were adopted in 1951—for the purpose of introducing improvements, expediting the examination of cases and ensuring the follow-up of its recommendations. Over the years a number of measures have been adopted by the Committee, and approved by the Governing Body, in order to achieve this purpose. Only recently, at its sessions in February and May 1978, the Committee examined various aspects of its procedure with a view to improving it further.

6. Also at its meeting in May 1978 the Committee considered certain suggestions that had been put forward and discussed during the 205th Session of the Governing Body (February–March 1978). These suggestions concerned additional measures which could be envisaged in cases where governments had displayed an unwillingness to co-operate with the established procedure for the examination of complaints, more especially by not replying to allegations of infringements of trade union rights made against them, or in cases where the violations of trade union rights were of a particularly serious nature. The Governing Body decided to refer these questions to the Committee for consideration.

7. In the present report, the Committee proposes to review certain aspects of its procedure, examining in each case the improvements made in the past and the new measures proposed with a view to speeding up the Committee's work and increasing its efficiency. After dealing with these questions of procedure in the strict sense of the term, the Committee will also examine certain special measures suggested in the Governing Body during its session in February–March 1978.

8. First of all, the Committee wishes to recall that the influence which it can have is above all a moral one. It derives from the objectiveness of the procedures which the Committee follows and the persuasive effect and the authority of the conclusions unanimously reached on the basis of established principles by such a body as the Committee, which is composed of Government, Employers' and Workers' members. Finally, this influence derives to some extent from the publicity which the conclusions of an international body entail. One of the main achievements of the Committee is to have succeeded in gaining wider recognition for the international value of the principles of freedom of association. In its endeavour the co-operation of the governments concerned and the weight of public opinion are the most important elements for the carrying out of the Committee's task.

9. For example, among the numerous cases examined by the Committee, a substantial proportion have raised issues relating to fundamental human rights, particularly in connection with the arrest, detention or exile of trade unionists. To questions of such gravity, the Governing Body, and public opinion in general, have rightly paid special attention. In many of these cases—including, in particular, cases where such measures had not been taken within the context of judicial proceedings—the governments concerned finally released the persons in question or allowed their return from exile. While there is no doubt that,

in a large number of cases, the positive results achieved can be directly linked to the action of the Committee, it can also be said that in other cases of achievement, the Committee's efforts, coupled with other factors which prevailed, have contributed to a large extent in obtaining the desired results from governments.

10. Thus, since the beginning of 1976 the Committee, in the course of its examination of certain cases involving the arrest, detention or exile of trade unionists, has been informed of the release of over 250 trade unionists,[31] and in one case[32] the Committee was informed of the granting of a general amnesty which enabled large numbers of trade unionists to be released from detention or to return from exile.

A. Aspects of the Procedure Where There is Room for Improvement

(1) RULES CONCERNING RELATIONS WITH COMPLAINANTS

(i) IMPROVEMENTS MADE IN THE PAST

11. Difficulties sometimes arise in cases where the statements contained in a complaint and the observations furnished by the government concerned contradict one another without containing any convincing evidence, thereby making it impossible for the Committee to reach an informed opinion. It was therefore decided that in such cases, the Committee, without disclosing the government's replies, should seek further information in writing from the complainant in regard to questions concerning the terms of the complaint requiring further elucidation.[33]

12. More generally, in order to give complainants the opportunity to acquaint themselves with the observations furnished by the governments concerned on complaints made against them, the Committee decided at its February 1969 session to use more often the possibility of asking the complainants for additional comments or details, in the light of the observations of the governments. To avoid slowing down the procedure, it was decided that this method should not be followed automatically in all cases but only where it appeared that such a request to the complainants for comments would be helpful in establishing facts.[34]

13. At its November 1971 Session the Committee decided to take a further step by informing the complainants, in appropriate cases, of the substance of the governments' observations and by inviting the complainants to submit their comments thereon within a given period of time.[35]

(ii) NEW PROPOSAL

14. There are cases where there is a lapse of several months between the receipt of the government's observations and the next meeting of the committee at which such information or comments can be requested from the complainants. In order to expedite the procedure, the Committee considers that it would

be useful if the Director-General were to ascertain whether in the light of the observations sent by the government concerned further information or comments from the complainants were necessary on matters relating to the complaint and, if so, to write directly to the complainants, in the name of the Committee and without waiting for its next session, requesting the desired information or the comments on the government's observations by a given date, it being understood that the government, as defendant, would have an opportunity to reply to any new information or comments submitted by the complainants.

(2) RULES CONCERNING RELATIONS WITH GOVERNMENTS

(i) IMPROVEMENTS MADE IN THE PAST

15. In order to make the procedure more expeditious, the Director-General was empowered to ascertain whether the observations of governments on the subject matter of a complaint or the governments' replies to requests for further information were sufficient to permit the committee to examine the complaint and, if not, to write directly to the government concerned, in the name of the Committee and without waiting for its next session, to inform it that it would be desirable if the government were to furnish more precise information on the points raised by the Committee or the complainant.[36]

16. In cases where governments delay in forwarding their observations or the information requested from them, the Committee decided to mention them in a special paragraph of its reports and to address a pressing appeal to the governments concerned. The Committee also decided that if certain governments still failed to reply, they would be warned that at its following session the Committee might submit a report on the substance of the matter, even if the information awaited from the governments in question had still not been received. Where the governments were obviously unwilling to co-operate, the Committee decided that it might recommend, as an exceptional measure, that wider publicity be given to the allegations, the recommendations of the Governing Body and the obstructive attitude of the governments concerned. The Committee considered that the ILO regional offices might, in such cases of delay, be called upon to approach these governments and point out to them the importance that should be attached to the communication of the information or observations requested.[37]

17. In February 1977, the Committee introduced an additional measure aimed at obtaining long outstanding replies from governments. This measure consists in informing, the governments concerned, immediately after the May session of the committee, that the Chairman of the Committee will make contact with their representatives attending the session of the International Labour Conference, in order to draw their attention to the particular cases involved and to discuss with them the reasons for the delay in transmitting their observations. The Chairman then reports to the Committee on the results of such contacts.[38] This procedure has already been followed twice, at the 1977 and 1978 sessions of the International Labour Conference.

18. Another aspect of the procedure concerning relations with governments relates to the follow-up action taken by governments on the recommendations addressed to them. In the case of countries having ratified the freedom of association Conventions, examination of the action taken is normally entrusted to the Committee of Experts on the Application of Conventions and Recommendations, whose attention is specifically drawn by the Committee to discrepancies noted between national laws and practice and the terms of the Conventions. This does not prevent the Committee on Freedom of Association from examining the effect given to certain recommendations made by it, especially taking into account the nature or urgency of certain questions.

19. Where a country has not ratified the Convention involved, the Committee in some cases invites the government concerned to state, after a reasonable period has elapsed, what action it has been able to take on the recommendations made to it. If there is no reply, or if the reply given is partly or entirely unsatisfactory, the matter may be followed up periodically, and the Committee from time to time reports on the situation.[39]

20. In cases where the governments are late in forwarding their observations or requested information, the Committee is of the opinion that it ought to use more systematically the possibility of presenting a report on the substance of the case, even if there are no observations or information from the government (see paragraph 16). The Committee will then have recourse to this procedure particularly in cases considered to be urgent.

(ii) NEW PROPOSAL

21. The Committee considers that it would be useful in appropriate cases to develop approaches by ILO external offices to governments in order to elicit the information requested of them, either during the examination of the case or in connection with the action to be taken on the Committee's recommendations, approved by the Governing Body. With this end in view the ILO external offices should be sent more detailed information with regard to complaints concerning their particular area. They should also be required more frequently, within the context of their contacts with governments, to approach governments which delay in transmitting their replies, in order to draw their attention to the importance of supply the observations or information requested of them.

(3) URGENT AND NON-URGENT REPORTS

(i) IMPROVEMENTS MADE IN THE PAST

22. In order to expedite the procedure, the Committee, at its session in November 1958, decided to introduce a distinction between urgent and less urgent cases. Matters involving human life or personal freedom, or new or changing conditions affecting the freedom of action of a trade union movement as a whole, cases arising out of a continuing state of emergency and cases involving the dissolution of an organisation are treated as cases of urgency.

23. In dealing with urgent cases certain special provisions are applicable; the attention of the government is called, when the complaint is communicated to

it, to the fact that it is an urgent case and the government is requested to supply a particularly speedy reply; cases of urgency are dealt with on a priority basis by the Committee; while the case remains under consideration, the Committee is authorised to make appropriate recommendations for the protection of the parties concerned; the report of the Committee on urgent cases is submitted immediately to the Governing Body. Reports on less urgent cases are postponed until the following session of the Governing Body.[40]

24. Priority of treatment was subsequently also given to cases on which a report had already been submitted to the Governing Body.[41]

(ii) NEW PROPOSAL

25. For more than one year now the Committee has been testing a new system whereby the examination of the Committee's reports on less urgent cases is no longer postponed until the following session of the Governing Body. This new system has involoved the inclusion of all cases examined—whether or not they fall within the category of "urgent" or "less urgent"—in its report which is submitted immediately to the Governing Body. This was found possible because most cases were of an urgent nature and the Committee considered that examination of the few remaining less urgent cases would not prevent immediate consideration of those cases before the Governing Body that were urgent in character. The Committee considers that it would be useful to adopt this procedure definitely and that in order to deal rapidly with all cases, consideration of less urgent cases examined by the Committee should no longer be adjourned as a matter of course until the following session of the Governing Body.

(4) MISSIONS ON THE SPOT

(i) IMPROVEMENTS MADE IN THE PAST

26. "Direct contacts" missions are an important aspect of the Committee's procedure whereby a representative of the Director-General of the ILO—who can be an independent person or an official of the ILO—is sent to the country concerned in order to ascertain the facts relating to a case and to seek possible solutions to the difficulties encountered, either during the examination of the case or at the stage of the action to be taken on the recommendations of the Governing Body. The Committee and the Governing Body remain fully competent to appraise the situation at the outcome of these direct contacts. This procedure can only be established at the invitation of the governments concerned or at least with their consent.[42]

27. Again for the purpose of expediting the procedure, further improvements were made recently. At its February 1977 Session the Committee stated its intention to make wider use of direct contacts, particularly where serious allegations are involved or where difficulty is experienced in obtaining sufficiently precise information. In addition, the Committee decided that, in cases where a complaint of a particularly urgent or serious nature had been presented between two sessions of the Committee, the Director-General may, having

received the prior approval of the Chairman of the Committee, propose to the government concerned that the direct contacts procedure be engaged with a view to placing before the Committee a report on the situation as soon as possible.[43] At its session in February–March 1978 the Governing Body, in approving the report of its Committee on Standing Orders and on the Application of Conventions and Recommendations, stressed the importance of direct contacts and invited the Director-General, the supervisory bodies and the governments concerned to have recourse to the procedure of direct contacts whenever it might contribute to a better understanding of situations and the useful examination of solutions to problems.

(ii) NEW PROPOSAL

28. In most cases direct contacts have not taken place until some time after the events under consideration have occurred. A speedier mission by an ILO representative in the country concerned in certain cases where complaints have been received would appear desirable for a variety of purposes: to transmit to the competent authorities in the country the concern to which the events described in the complaint have given rise; to explain to these authorities the principles of freedom of association involved; to obtain from the authorities their initial reaction, as well as any comments and information with regard to the matters raised in the complaint; to explain to the authorities the special procedure in cases of alleged infringements of trade union rights, and in particular the direct contacts method which may subsequently be requested by the government in order to facilitate a full appraisal of the situation by the Committee and the Governing Body; to request and encourage the authorities to communicate as soon as possible a detailed reply containing the observations of the government on the complaint. A procedure of this kind has been used in recent cases.[44]

29. The Committee accordingly considers that it would be useful to adopt a new procedure under which the Director-General, upon receipt of a complaint containing allegations of a particularly serious nature, and after having received the prior approval of the Chairman of the Committee, may appoint a representative whose mandate would be to carry out the preliminary contacts described above. The report of the representative of the Director-General would be submitted to the Committee at its next meeting for consideration together with all the other information made available.

(5) HEARING OF THE PARTIES

(i) USE OF THIS METHOD IN THE PAST

30. In two of the early cases of alleged infringements of trade union rights, the Governing Body accepted the suggestion made by the Committee to afford an opportunity to the governments concerned to discuss with the Committee the matters at issue, before the Committee submitted its recommendations to the Governing Body.[45] More recently the Governing Body, on the recommendation of the Committee, has invited the Minister of Labour of one country to

present oral information as regards the questions raised in one case. This invitation was also extended to the principal complainant organisations involved in the case.[46]

(ii) NEW PROPOSALS

31. For various reasons, which are mentioned below, the Committee considers that it would be useful for hearings of the parties to be held on a more frequent basis. There are a number of circumstances in which such a procedure would enable the Committee to examine more thoroughly the questions involved, as a result of which its conclusions would be based on a fuller understanding of the questions at issue as well as the different points of view of the parties concerned and its recommendations to the Governing Body would carry increased weight and have better chances of general acceptance and effective implementation.

32. In accordance with the preceding paragraph, the Committee will decide, in the appropriate instances and taking into account all the circumstances of the case, whether it should hear the parties, or one of them, during its sessions so as to obtain more complete information on the matter. It would be able to do this notably in the following cases: (a) in appropriate cases where the complainants and the governments have submitted contradictory statements on the substance of the matters at issue, and where the Committee might consider it useful for the representatives of the parties to furnish orally more detailed information as requested by the Committee; (b) in cases in which the Committee might consider it useful to have an exchange of views with the governments in question, on the one hand, and with the complainants, on the other, on certain important matters in order to appreciate more fully the factual situation and the eventual developments in the situation which might lead to a solution of the problems involved, and to seek to conciliate on the basis of the principles of freedom of association; (c) in other cases where particular difficulties have arisen in the examination of the questions involved or in the implementation of its recommendations, and where the Committee might consider it appropriate to discuss the matters with the representative of the government concerned.

B. Special Measures Suggested in the Governing Body

33. During the 205th Session of the Governing Body (February–March 1978) the Workers' members, in particular, expressed deep concern about the large number of serious cases of infringements of trade union rights that were before the Committee. They considered that, in the circumstances, it would be necessary to have recourse to special measures which should act as a "moral constraint" on the governments involved in these cases. Two types of situation were mentioned in this respect. First, certain governments delay in forwarding the observations or the information requested from them, thereby preventing the committee from examining the substance of a case in full knowledge of the facts. Secondly, certain governments do not take steps to implement the

recommendations made by the Committee and the Governing Body, and despite a long lapse of time no changes are made in a situation where trade union rights have been severely restricted. Regarding the first situation, it was proposed that the Committee should prepare a special list of countries whose governments refused to co-operate with the procedure and that the ILO should give publicity to such a list. In the second situation, it was proposed that the ILO should have recourse to new and more severe measures in order to ensure the more effective implementation of its recommendations. Such measures would include, in particular, the withholding of technical co-operation, the refusal to hold meetings and the closure of ILO field offices in the countries where freedom of association was seriously violated.

34. Other members of the Governing Body expressed certain doubts about these proposals. They considered that the effectiveness of the procedure concerning freedom of association depended essentially on the co-operation of governments. It was not the procedure of the Committee that should be questioned, but the effectiveness of the whole action of the ILO as regards certain governments which had displayed an unwillingness to co-operate. A change in the methods or procedures would not improve the trade union situation in the world. Patience, endurance and perseverance were still the best ways to achieve results. With regard, in particular, to the establishment of a special list of countries whose governments did not co-operate, the question was raised as to whether this method might not aggravate the lack of co-operation and make the work of the Committee more difficult. Furthermore, this list would have to be drawn upon the basis of countries against which a complaint had been lodged. There were other countries where the trade union situation was the cause of concern but which had not been the subject of a complaint. It was possible, therefore, that the proposed list would not reflect in an objective manner the position with regard to freedom of association. As regards the other measures which had been proposed for certain cases where no further progress could be expected, these measures could be effective depending on the circumstances. In some cases, however, the withholding of technical co-operation would only affect the lot of the workers concerned and would not facilitate any positive development of the situation.

35. In considering these views, it should first be pointed out that the Committee performs functions of a quasi-judicial nature and that its primary objective is to give guidance in order to redress situations which need to be brought into line with the commonly accepted principles relating to freedom of association. The effect of the committee's recommendations should not only be appraised in the light of the action taken by governments as directly related with these recommendations. Account should also be taken of the possible preventive effect on governments of the very existence of the procedure. Moreover, the Committee's recommendations do not always call for immediate action by governments but sometimes consist in the preparation of the ground for the adoption of positive measures in the more distant future. Objectivity, perseverance and the weight of public opinion are the most valuable means at its disposal.

36. In order to carry out its activities the Committee needs the co-operation

of governments and it is only by a strong measure of government support that the persuasive and moral influence of the Committee can lead to practical results being obtained. Its procedure accordingly consists, to a large extent, of a dialogue which cannot be successful without obtaining such co-operation. It is vital that the procedure should command the confidence and respect both of governments and of workers' and employers' organisations, and this it can only do if it is clear that it plays a constructive role in securing the fuller observance of trade union rights.

37. Experience showed that the dragging out of the procedure is often due to excessive dilatoriness on the part of some governments in sending all the information necessary for the examination of cases in which they are involved. In this connection, the Committee itself pointed out in its first report that the purpose of the whole procedure was to promote respect for trade union rights in law and in fact, and that if it protected governments against unreasonable accusations, governments on their side should recognise the importance for the protection of their good name of formulating for objective examination detailed factual replies to such factual charges as might be put forward.

38. The Committee has noted in paragraph 20 the procedures that it proposes to use more systematically when a government delays in forwarding the observations or information requested from it. The Committee will, in any case, continue to stress these cases in appropriate paragraphs in the introduction of its report.

39. With regard to the other type of measures referred to in the preceding paragraphs (withholding of technical co-operation, refusal to hold meetings, closure of ILO offices), the Committee notes that the Director-General has, in certain very exceptional cases, withheld technical co-operation in the field of workers' education in respect of countries where there had been very serious infringements of trade union rights. One or the other of the special measures which have been proposed ould be appropriate in cases where no progress is made towards the improvement of situations in which the principles of freedom of association have been seriously violated and where governments are manifestly reluctant to co-operate. However, the effectiveness of such measures would depend on the circumstances surrounding each particular case. Whatever the situation, the Committee—which has quasi-judicial functions—does not consider itself competent to examine or propose any of these measures when formulating its recommendations to the Governing Body. Decisions on such matters would lie with other bodies, in particular the Governing Body. The information provided by the Committee as to the seriousness of the infringements of freedom of association in the case under examination might constitute one of the factors essential to the taking of such decisions, on the understanding that the Governing Body would also take into account other factors which it considered useful, such as the consequences which the measures proposed could have on the workers in the country concerned or on the relations between the ILO and that country.

C. UNESCO PROCEDURES

INTRODUCTION

UNESCO has established two significant procedures. The first is in the 1962 Protocol to the Convention Against Discrimination in Education (see above, Chapter III.2).[47] It is substantially similar to the State against State procedures in the Race Convention (see above Chapter IV.A.16) and the International Covenant on Civil and Political Rights (above Chapter IV.A.16). The second procedure was created in 1978 to deal with cases and questions that may be submitted to UNESCO concerning the exercise of human rights within its sphere of competence, such as the right to education, the right to share in scientific advancement, the right to participate fully in cultural life, and the right to information, including freedom of opinion and expression. This procedure was inspired in part by the procedure contained in the Optional Protocol to the International Covenant on Civil and Political Rights and in part by the procedures contained in ECOSOC Resolution 1503, both of which were reproduced in Chapter IV.A. The UNESCO procedure combines features of both these models in dealing with the examination of individual cases and with questions of massive, systematic or flagrant violations of human rights which result either from a policy contrary to human rights applied *de jure* or *de facto* by a state or from an accumulation of individual cases forming a consistent pattern.

1. PROTOCOL INSTITUTING A CONCILIATION AND GOOD OFFICES COMMISSION TO BE RESPONSIBLE FOR SEEKING THE SETTLEMENT OF ANY DISPUTES WHICH MAY ARISE BETWEEN STATES PARTIES TO THE CONVENTION AGAINST DISCRIMINATION IN EDUCATION (1962)

Adopted by the General Conference of the United Nations Educational, Scientific and Cultural Organization on 10 December 1962 entry into force: 24 October 1968, in Accordance with Article 24.

The General Conference of the United Nations Educational, Scientific and Cultural Organization, meeting in Paris from 9 November to 12 December 1962, at its twelfth session,

Having adopted, at its eleventh session, the Convention against Discrimination in Education,

Desirous of facilitating the implementation of that Convention, and

Considering that it is important, for this purpose, to institute a Conciliation and Good Offices Commission to be responsible for seeking the amicable settlement of any disputes which may arise between States Parties to the Convention, concerning its application or interpretation.

Adopts this Protocol on the tenth day of December 1962.

Article 1

There shall be established under the auspices of the United Nations Educational, Scientific and Cultural Organization a Conciliation and Good Offices Commission, hereinafter referred to as the Commission, to be responsible for seeking the amicable settlement of disputes between States Parties to the Convention against Discrimination in Education, hereinafter referred to as the Convention, concerning the application or interpretation of the Convention.

Article 2

1. The Commission shall consist of eleven members who shall be persons of high moral standing and acknowledged impartiality and shall be elected by the General Conference of the United Nations Educational, Scientific and Cultural Organization, hereinafter referred to as the General Conference.

2. The members of the Commission shall serve in their personal capacity.

Article 3

1. The members of the Commission shall be elected from a list of persons nominated for the purpose by the States Parties to this Protocol. Each State shall, after consulting its National Commission for UNESCO, nominate not more than four persons. These persons must be nationals of States Parties to this Protocol.

2. At least four months before the date of each election to the Commission, the Director-General of the United Nations Educational, Scientific and Cultural Organization, hereinafter referred to as the Director-General, shall invite the States Parties to the present Protocol to send within two months, their nominations of the persons referred to in paragraph 1 of this article. He shall prepare a list in alphabetical order of the persons thus nominated and shall submit it, at least one month before the election, to the Executive Board of the United Nations Educational, Scientific and Cultural Organization, hereinafter referred to as the Executive Board, and to the States Parties to the Convention. The Executive Board shall transmit the aforementioned list, with such suggestions as it may consider useful, to the General Conference, which shall carry out the election of members of the Commission in conformity with the procedure it normally follows in elections of two or more persons.

Article 4

1. The Commission may not include more than one national of the same State.

2. In the election of members of the Commission, the General Conference shall endeavour to include persons of recognized competence in the field of education and persons having judicial experience or legal experience particularly of an international character. It shall also give consideration to equitable geographical distribution of membership and to the representation of the different forms of civilization as well as of the principal legal systems.

Article 5

The members of the Commission shall be elected for a term of six years. They shall be eligible for re-election if renominated. The terms of four of the members elected at the first election shall, however, expire at the end of two years, and the terms of three other members at the end of four years. Immediately after the first election, the names of these members shall be chosen by lot by the President of the General Conference.

Article 6

1. In the event of the death or resignation of a member of the Commission, the Chairman shall immediately notify the Director-General, who shall declare the seat vacant from the date of death or the date on which the resignation takes effect.

2. If, in the unanimous opinion of the other members, a member of the Commission has ceased to carry out his functions for any cause other than absence of a temporary character or is unable to continue the discharge of his duties, the Chairman of the Commission shall notify the Director-General and shall thereupon declare the seat of such member to be vacant.

3. The Director-General shall inform the Member States of the United Nations Educational, Scientific and Cultural Organization, and any States not members of the Organization which have become Parties to this Protocol under the provisions of article 23, of any vacancies which have occurred in accordance with paragraphs 1 and 2 of this article.

4. In each of the cases provided for by paragraphs 1 and 2 of this article, the General Conference shall arrange for the replacement of the member whose seat has fallen vacant, for the unexpired portion of his term of office.

Article 7

Subject to the provisions of article 6, a member of the Commission shall remain in office until his successor takes up his duties.

Article 8

1. If the Commission does not include a member of the nationality of a State which is party to a dispute referred to it under the provisions of article 12 or article 13, that State, or if there is more than one, each of those States, may choose a person to sit on the commission as a member *ad hoc*.

2. The States thus choosing a member *ad hoc* shall have regard to the qualities required of members of the Commission by virtue of article 2, paragraph 1, and article 4, paragraphs 1 and 2. Any member *ad hoc* thus chosen shall be of the nationality of the State which chooses him or of a State Party to the Protocol, and shall serve in a personal capacity.

3. Should there be several States Parties to the dispute having the same interest they shall, for the purpose of choosing members *ad hoc*, be reckoned as one party only. The manner in which this provision shall be applied shall be determined by the Rules of Procedure of the Commission referred to in article 11.

Article 9

Members of the Commission and members *ad hoc* chosen under the provisions of article 8 shall receive travel and *per diem* allowances in respect of the periods during which they are engaged on the work of the Commission from the resources of the United Nations Educational, Scientific and Cultural Organization on terms laid down by the Executive Board.

Article 10

The Secretariat of the Commission shall be provided by the Director-General.

Article 11

1. The Commission shall elect its Chairman and Vice-Chairman for a period of two years. They may be re-elected.

2. The Commission shall establish its own Rules of Procedure, but these rules shall provide, *inter alia*, that:

    a. Two-thirds of the members, including the members *ad hoc*, if any, shall constitute a quorum.

    b. Decisions of the Commission shall be made by a majority vote of the members and members *ad hoc* present; if the votes are equally divided, the Chairman shall have a casting vote.

    c. If a State refers a matter to the Commission under article 12 or article 13:

        i. Such State, the State complained against, and any State Party to this Protocol whose national is concerned in such matter may make submissions in writing to the Commission;

        ii. Such State and the State complained against shall have the right to be represented at the hearings of the matter and to make submissions orally.

3. The Commission, on the occasion when it first proposes to establish its Rules of Procedure, shall send them in draft form to the States then Parties to the Protocol who may communicate any observation and suggestion they may wish to make within three months. The Commission shall re-examine its Rules of Procedure if at any time so requested by any State Party to the Protocol.

Article 12

1. If a State Party to this Protocol considers that another State Party is not giving effect to a provision of the Convention, it may, by written communication, bring the matter to the attention of that State. Within three months after the receipt of the communication, the receiving State shall afford the complaining State an explanation or statement in writing concerning the matter, which should include, to the extent possible and pertinent, references to procedures and remedies taken, or pending, or available in the matter.

2. If the matter is not adjusted to the satisfaction of both parties, either by bilateral negotiations or by any other procedure open to them, within six months after the receipt by the receiving State of the initial communication, either State

shall have the right to refer the matter to the Commission, by notice given to the Director-General and to the other State.

3. The provisions of the preceding paragraphs shall not affect the rights of States Parties to have recourse, in accordance with general or special international agreements in force between them, to other procedures for settling disputes including that of referring disputes by mutual consent to the Permanent Court of Arbitration at The Hague.

Article 13

From the beginning of the sixth year after the entry into force of this Protocol, the Commission may also be made responsible for seeking the settlement of any dispute concerning the application or interpretation of the Convention arising between States which are Parties to the Convention but are not, or are not all, Parties to this Protocol, if the said States agree to submit such dispute to the Commission. The conditions to be fulfilled by the said States in reaching agreement shall be laid down by the Commission's Rules of Procedure.

Article 14

The Commission shall deal with a matter referred to it under article 12 or article 13 of this Protocol only after it has ascertained that all available domestic remedies have been invoked and exhausted in the case, in conformity with the generally recognized principles of international law.

Article 15

Except in cases where new elements have been submitted to it, the Commission shall not consider matters it has already dealt with.

Article 16

In any matter referred to it, the Commission may call upon the States concerned to supply any relevant information.

Article 17

1. Subject to the provisions of article 14, the Commission, after obtaining all the information it thinks necessary, shall ascertain the facts, and make available its good offices to the States concerned with a view to an amicable solution of the matter on the basis of respect for the Convention.

2. The Commission shall in every case, and in no event later than eighteen months after the date of receipt by the Director-General of the notice under article 12, paragraph 2, draw up a report in accordance with the provisions of paragraph 3 below which will be sent to the States concerned and then communicated to the Director-General for publication. When an advisory opinion is requested of the International Court of Justice, in accordance with article 18, the time-limit shall be extended appropriately.

3. If a solution within the terms of paragraph 1 of this article is reached, the Commission shall confine its report to a brief statement of the facts and of the solution reached. If such a solution is not reached, the Commission shall draw up a report on the facts and indicate the recommendations which it made with

a view to conciliation. If the report does not represent in whole or in part the unanimous opinion of the members of the Commission, any member of the Commission shall be entitled to attach to it a separate opinion. The written and oral submissions made by the parties to the case in accordance with article 11, paragraph 2 (*c*), shall be attached to the report.

Article 18

The Commission may recommend to the Executive Board, or to the General Conference if the recommendation is made within two months before the opening of one of its sessions, that the International Court of Justice be requested to give an advisory opinion on any legal question connected with a matter laid before the Commission.

Article 19

The Commission shall submit to the General Conference at each of its regular sessions a report on its activities, which shall be transmitted to the General Conference by the Executive Board.

Article 20

1. The Director-General shall convene the first meeting of the Commission at the Headquarters of the United Nations Educational, Scientific and Cultural Organization within three months after its nomination by the General Conference.

2. Subsequent meetings of the Commission shall be convened when necessary by the Chairman of the Commission to whom, as well as to all other members of the Commission, the Director-General shall transmit all matters referred to the Commission in accordance with the provisions of this Protocol.

3. Notwithstanding paragraph 2 of this article, when at least one-third of the members of the Commission consider that the Commission should examine a matter in accordance with the provisions of this Protocol, the Chairman shall on their so requiring convene a meeting of the Commission for that purpose.

Article 21

The present Protocol is drawn up in English, French, Russian and Spanish, all four texts being equally authentic.

Article 22

1. This Protocol shall be subject to ratification or acceptance by States Members of the United Nations Educational, Scientific and Cultural Organization which are Parties to the Convention.

2. The instruments of ratification or acceptance shall be deposited with the Director-General.

Article 23

1. This Protocol shall be open to accession by all States not Members of the United Nations Educational, Scientific and Cultural Organization which are Parties to the Convention.

2. Accession shall be effected by the deposit of an instrument of accession with the Director-General.

Article 24

This Protocol shall enter into force three months after the date of the deposit of the fifteenth instrument of ratification, acceptance or accession, but only with respect to those States which have deposited their respective instruments on or before that date. It shall enter into force with respect to any other State three months after the deposit of its instrument of ratification, acceptance or accession.

Article 25

Any State may, at the time of ratification, acceptance or accession or at any subsequent date, declare, by notification to the Director General, that it agrees, with respect to any other State assuming the same obligation, to refer to the International Court of Justice, after the drafting of the report provided for in article 17, paragraph 3, any dispute covered by this Protocol on which no amicable solution has been reached in accordance with article 17, paragraph 1.

Article 26

1. Each State Party to this Protocol may denounce it.
2. The denunciation shall be notified by an instrument in writing, deposited with the Director-General.
3. Denunciation of the Convention shall automatically entail denunciation of this Protocol.
4. The denunciation shall take effect twelve months after the receipt of the instrument of denunciation. The State denouncing the Protocol shall, however, remain bound by its provisions in respect of any cases concerning it which have been referred to the Commission before the end of the time-limit stipulated in this paragraph.

Article 27

The Director-General shall inform the States Members of the United Nations Educational, Scientific and Cultural Organization, the States not Members of the Organization which are referred to in article 23, as well as the United Nations, of the deposit of all the instruments of ratification, acceptance and accession provided for in articles 22 and 23, and of the notifications and denunciations provided for in articles 25 and 26 respectively.

2. PROCEDURES FOR THE EXAMINATION OF COMMUNICATIONS (1978)

Study of the procedures which should be followed in the examination of cases and questions which might be submitted to Unesco concerning the exercise of human rights in the spheres of its competence, in order to make its action more effective: Report of the Working Party of the Executive Board (104 EX/3) (1978)

THE EXECUTIVE BOARD,

1. *Mindful* that the competence and role of Unesco in the field of human rights derive primarily from Article I.1 of the Constitution of Unesco, which states: "The purpose of the Organization is to contribute to peace and security by promoting collaboration among the nations through education, science and culture in order to further universal respect for justice, for the rule of law and for the human rights and fundamental freedoms which are affirmed for the peoples of the world, without distinction of race, sex, language or religion, by the Charter of the United Nations," and from the Charter of the United Nations,

2. *Recalling* the Universal Declaration of Human Rights, the international covenants on human rights and the various conventions and recommendations adopted by Unesco,

3. *Recalling* 19 C/Resolution 6.113 concerning Unesco's responsibilities in the field of human rights,

4. *Recalling* also 19 C/Resolution 12.1: "Unesco's contribution to peace and its tasks with respect to the promotion of human rights and the elimination of colonialism and racialism—long-term programme of measures whereby Unesco can contribute to the strengthening of peace;" and in particular paragraph 10 of the resolution, which invites the Executive Board and the Director-General:

"a. to examine with particular attention the general situation with regard to respect for human rights throughout the world in Unesco's fields of competence,

b. to study the procedures which should be followed in the examination of cases and questions which might be submitted to Unesco concerning the exercise of human rights in the spheres to which its competence extends, in order to make its action more effective,

c. to continue to establish, with a view to the implementation of subparagraphs (a) and (b), close co-operation and co-ordination with the relevant United Nations organs so as to take advantage of their work and the lessons that can be learned from them in this field,"

5. *Having considered* the report of a working group of the Board set up by virtue of 102 EX/Decision 5.6.2 to carry out an in-depth study of document 102 EX/19, the analytical summary of discussions that took place at the 102nd session of the Board, and additional written comments provided by members of the Board,

6. *Mindful* of Article I.3 of the Constitution of Unesco, which states: "With a view to preserving the independence, integrity and fruitful diversity of the cultures and educational systems of the States members of the Organization, the Organization is prohibited from intervening in matters which are essentially within their domestic jurisdiction,"

7. *Considering* that, in matters concerning human rights within its fields of competence, Unesco, basing its efforts on moral considerations and its specific competence, should act in a spirit of international co-operation, conciliation and mutual understanding; and *recalling* that Unesco should not play the role of an international judicial body,

8. *Recognizing* the important role of the Director-General, in:

a. seeking, continually to strengthen the action of Unesco in the promotion of human rights, both through the settlement of cases and the elimination of massive, systematic or flagrant violations of human rights and fundamental freedoms, and

b. initiating consultations, in conditions of mutual respect, confidence and confidentiality, to help reach solutions to particular problems concerning human rights,

9. *Invites* the Director-General to pursue this role;

10. *Considering* that, in the exercise of its competence in the field of human rights, Unesco is called upon to examine:

a. cases concerning violations of human rights which are individual and specific,

b. questions of massive, systematic or flagrant violations of human rights which result either from a policy contrary to human rights applied *de jure* or *de facto* by a State or from an accumulation of individual cases forming a consistent pattern,

11. *Considering* the terms of reference of the Committee on Conventions and Recommendations in Education,

12. *Taking into account* the tasks already entrusted to the Committee concerning human rights matters within the Organization's fields of competence,

13. *Decides* that the Committee will henceforth be designated "the Committee on Conventions and Recommendations;"

14. *Decides* that the Committee will continue to carry out its functions with respect to conventions and recommendations and will consider communications received by the Organization concerning cases and questions of violations of human rights within Unesco's fields of competence in accordance with the following conditions and procedures:

CONDITIONS

(a) Communications shall be deemed admissible if they meet the following conditions:

    i. the communication must not be anonymous;

    ii. the communication must originate from a person or a group of persons who, it can be reasonably presumed, are victims of an alleged violation of any of the human rights referred to in paragraph (iii) below. It may also originate from any person, group of persons or non-governmental organization having reliable knowledge of those violations;

    iii. the communication must concern violations of human rights falling within Unesco's competence in the fields of education, science, culture and information and must not be motivated exclusively by other considerations;

    iv. the communication must be compatible with the principles of the Organization, the Charter of the United Nations, the Universal Declaration of Human Rights, the international covenants on human rights and other international instruments in the field of human rights;

v. the communication must not be manifestly ill-founded and must appear to contain relevant evidence;

vi. the communication must be neither offensive nor an abuse of the right to submit communications. However, such a communication may be considered if it meets all other criteria or admissibility, after the exclusion of the offensive or abusive parts;

vii. the communication must not be based exclusively on information disseminated through the mass media;

viii. the communication must be submitted within a reasonable time-limit following the facts which constitute its subject-matter or within a reasonable time-limit after the facts have become known;

ix. the communication must indicate whether an attempt has been made to exhaust available domestic remedies with regard to the facts which constitute the subject-matter of the communication and the result of such an attempt, if any;

x. communications relating to matters already settled by the States concerned in accordance with the human rights principles set forth in the Universal Declaration of Human Rights and the international covenants on human rights shall not be considered;

PROCEDURES

(b) The Director-General shall:

i. acknowledge receipt of communications and inform the authors thereof of the above-mentioned conditions governing admissibility;

ii. ascertain that the author of the communication has no objection to his communication, after having been communicated to the government concerned, being brought to the notice of the Committee and to his name being divulged;

iii. upon receipt of an affirmative answer from the author of the communication, transmit the communication to the government concerned, informing it that the communication will be brought to the notice of the Committee, together with any reply the government may wish to make;

iv. transmit the communication to the Committee, together with the reply, if any, of the government concerned and additional relevant information from the author, taking into account the need to proceed without undue delay;

(c) the Committee shall examine in private session the communications transmitted to it by the Director-General;

(d) the Committee shall decide on the admissibility of communications in accordance with the above-mentioned conditions;

(e) representatives of the governments concerned may attend meetings of the Committee in order to provide additional information or to answer questions from members of the Committee on either admissibility or the merits of the communication;

(f) the Committee may avail itself of the relevant information at the disposal of the Director-General;

(g) in consideration of a communication, the Committee may, in exceptional circumstances, request the Executive Board to authorize it under Rule 29 of the Rules of Procedure to take appropriate action;

(h) the Committee may keep a communication submitted to it on its agenda while seeking additional information it may consider necessary for the disposition of the matter;

(i) the Director-General shall notify the author of the communication and the government concerned of the Committee's decision on the admissibility of the communication;

(j) the Committee shall dismiss any communication which, having been found admissible, does not, upon examination of the merits, appear to warrant further action. The author of the communication and the government concerned shall be notified accordingly;

(k) communications which warrant further consideration shall be acted upon by the Committee with a view to helping to bring about a friendly solution designed to advance the promotion of the human rights falling within Unesco's fields of competence;

15. *Decides further* that the Committee shall submit confidential reports to the Executive Board at each session on the carrying out of its mandate under the present decision. These reports shall contain appropriate information arising from its examination of the communications which the Committee considers it useful to bring to the notice of the Executive Board. The reports shall also contain recommendations which the Committee may wish to make either generally or regarding the disposition of a communication under consideration;

16. *Decides* to consider confidential reports of the Committee in private session and to take further action as necessary in accordance with Rule 28 of the Rules of Procedure;

17. *Decides also* that communications transmitted to it by the Committee which testify to the existence of a question shall be dealt with in accordance with paragraph 18 below;

18. *Considers* that questions of massive, systematic or flagrant violations of human rights and fundamental freedoms—including, for example, those perpetrated as a result of policies of aggression, interference in the internal affairs of States, occupation of foreign territory and implementation of a policy of colonialism, genocide, apartheid, racialism, or national and social oppression—falling within Unesco's fields of competence should be considered by the Executive Board and the General Conference in public meetings;

19. *Decides* to consider at its 105th session the report to be made by the Executive Board and the Director-General to the General Conference, at its twentieth session, on the implementation of Part II of 19 C/Resolution 12.1.

GUIDELINES FOR PERSONS WISHING TO CALL THE ATTENTION OF UNESCO TO CASES AND QUESTIONS CONCERNING HUMAN RIGHTS

[ISSUED BY UNESCO, 1978]

I. UNESCO'S COMPETENCE IN THE FIELD OF HUMAN RIGHTS

1. According to its Constitution, adopted on 16 November 1945, the purpose of Unesco is "to contribute to peace and security by promoting collaboration among the nations through education, science and culture in order to further universal respect for justice, for the rule of law and for the human rights and fundamental freedoms which are affirmed for the peoples of the world, without distinction of race, sex, language or religion, by the Charter of the United Nations." Unesco's activities as a whole are aimed therefore at contributing to respect for human rights.

2. While Unesco endeavours to spread knowledge about *all human rights*, particularly by promoting their inclusion in educational courses, it can only act upon communications alleging violations of human rights in so far as the rights concerned fall within its fields of competence, namely, education, science, culture and information. It must be stressed that in no case is Unesco an international court nor can it become one. The rights falling within Unesco's spheres of competence are essentially the following:

— the right to education (Article 26 of the Universal Declaration of human rights);

— the right to share in scientific advancement (Article 27);

— the right to participate freely in cultural life (Article 27);

— the right to information, including freedom of opinion and expression (Article 19).

These rights imply the exercise of others, the most noteworthy of which are set out below:

— the right to freedom of thought, conscience and religion (Article 18);

— the right to seek, receive and impart information and ideas through any media and regardless of frontiers (Article 19);

— the right to the protection of the moral and material interests resulting from any scientific, literary or artistic production (Article 27);

— the right to freedom of assembly and association (Article 20) for the purposes of activities connected with education, science, culture and information.

3. Many conventions and recommendations adopted by Unesco concern human rights, and a list of them can be supplied on request. No procedure for individual complaints is provided for in these instruments. On the other hand, Unesco's Executive Board, which is responsible for implementing the Organization's programme under the authority of the General Conference, has drawn up procedures for the examination of individual communications alleging violations of those human rights which lie within Unesco's competence.

II. PROCEDURES FOR THE EXAMINATION OF INDIVIDUAL COMMUNICATIONS SUBMITTED TO UNESCO

4. In accordance with Decision 104 EX/3.3 of the Executive Board of Unesco, adopted at its 104th session in 1978, persons, groups of persons and non-governmental organizations may submit communications to Unesco concerning alleged violations of those human rights which fall within Unesco's fields of competence. The Executive Board decision instituting these procedures is annexed to these guidelines.

5. Communications submitted to Unesco must concern:
— *cases* concerning violations of human rights which are *individual and specific*;
— *questions* of *massive, systematic or flagrant violations* of human rights which result either from a policy contrary to human rights applied *de jure* or *de facto* by a State or from an accumulation of individual cases forming a consistent pattern.

Communications concerning *cases* are considered, as a rule, in *private meetings*; communications concerning *questions* are considered by the Executive Board and by the General Conference in *public meetings*.

6. The Executive Board's Committee on Conventions and Recommendations, which is the main body responsible for examining the communications, first decides in private session on the admissibility of communications. There are ten conditions governing admissibility; if any one of them is not met, no further action is taken on the communication. These conditions are listed in paragraph 14(a) of the decision reproduced in the annex. It rests with the authors of communications to show that these conditions have been fulfilled.

III. HOW TO SUBMIT A COMMUNICATION TO UNESCO

7. If a person, group of persons or non-governmental organization considers itself to be the victim of a violation of human rights falling within Unesco's fields of competence, or has reliable knowledge of such a violation, it can write to the *Director-General* of Unesco (Place de Fontenoy, 75700 Paris). The letter must be signed and should be written in one of the official languages of Unesco (English, French, Arabic, Russian, Spanish) but preferably in English or French; if it is written in another language, examination of the communication may be delayed owing to the time required for translation. The letter should be typed, if possible, or written very legibly.

8. Before writing to Unesco the author should be familiar with the Universal Declaration of Human Rights and the first part of these guidelines.

9. The allegations should be set out in a concise statement, specifying which of the human rights is/are considered to have been violated and which of Unesco's fields of competence is/are concerned. The date of the decisions complained of and the authority which took them should be clearly indicated, including, in particular, whatever legal remedies have been used (for instance, recourse to the courts in the country concerned) and the results of such action. There should also be an indication as to whether another international proce-

dure has been used and, if so, before what body, the date on which the matter was referred to it and any results of this procedure.

10. The Division of Human Rights and Peace will acknowledge receipt of the communication on behalf of the Director-General. It will inform the author of the conditions mentioned in paragraph 6 above and will first ask him whether he has any objection to his name being divulged and to his communication being brought to the notice of the Committee on Conventions and Recommendations after it has been transmitted to the government concerned.

11. Upon receipt of an affirmative answer on this point, the Director-General will transmit the communication to the government concerned, informing it that the communication will be brought to the notice of the Committee, together with any reply the government may wish to make. Until the Secretariat has received an affirmative answer, no further action can be taken on the communication.

12. The government concerned may participate in the examination of the communication by the Committee in order to provide additional information or to answer questions from members of the Committee. Should the Committee decide, having regard to exceptional circumstances, that it would be desirable to give the author a hearing, it will seek the Executive Board's authorization to do so. There is accordingly no need for the author of the communication to come to Unesco headquarters on his own initiative at any stage of the procedure.

IV. ACTION TAKEN ON THE COMMUNICATION AFTER IT HAS BEEN EXAMINED BY THE COMMITTEE

13. The Committee will decide whether the conditions governing admissibility (see paragraph 6 above) have been met. The author of the communication will be notified of its decision.

14. If the communication is found admissible, the Committee will proceed to examine it upon its merits and it may then come to the conclusion that it warrants follow-up action in conformity with respect for human rights. It should be noted once again that Unesco is not an international court and that it will therefore first endeavour to solve the problem in a spirit of international cooperation, conciliation and mutual understanding.

15. Whether such a solution is found or not, the Committee will report to the Executive Board of Unesco. The reports of the Committee are confidential and its meetings, like those of the Executive Board, are private. It is only when the report deals with "questions of massive, systematic or flagrant violations" that the Executive Board, and possibly the General Conference, may discuss it in a public meeting.

V. REGIONAL CONVENTIONS

A. COUNCIL OF EUROPE

INTRODUCTION

The 21 Western European democracies and "near" democracies comprising the Council of Europe became the first regional association of nations to sign a treaty collectively declaring and enforcing human rights.

And in doing so, they expanded upon the United Nations Declaration of Human Rights to produce a document which now provides a principal human rights guidepost in all new constitution-making throughout the world.

Entered into on November 4, 1950, and effective September 3, 1953, the European Convention for the Protection of Human Rights and Fundamental Freedoms consists of a basic Convention text and eight Protocols. Two of the Protocols—Nos. 3 and 5—modify and are incorporated into the text. Protocols 1, 2, 4, 6, 7 and 8 are published separately and have been separately ratified by most member states.

Principles of human rights had previously been promulgated on a collective basis in the regional association of nations which had proclaimed the famous Four Freedoms and the right of self-determination as expounded in the Atlantic Charter of August, 1941. They were then reaffirmed in the 1942 Declaration of the twenty-six United Nations and incorporated into the United Nations Charter in 1945. But these documents were just declarations of a general intention without the organization or power to enforce the guarantee of human rights.

Mindful of then recent Nazi experience and the existing denials of freedom in Soviet-dominated Europe, the signatories sought first to provide for rights of individuals free from illegitimate state interference. Second, they sought to establish an international guarantee of enforceable fundamental rights which would be supplemental to existing national guarantees in the Western democracies which were member states of the Council of Europe.

The 1950 Convention sets forth the twelve most commonly recognized human rights, such as the right to life, liberty, expression, due process, etc. The First Protocol on March 20, 1952, added three further rights: the right to property, parental rights and the right to free elections. The Second Protocol conferred on the European Court of Human Rights competence to give advisory opinions. The Fourth added freedom from imprisonment for debt and aspects of freedom of movement. And the Sixth Protocol, ratified on April 2, 1983, abolished the death penalty in peacetime. "The Sixth Protocol," as explained by the Council, "is the first instrument in international law to make abolition of the death penalty into a legal obligation for the Contracting Parties. So far the death penalty had only been referred to in the texts of a few international instruments, such as the International Covenant on Civil and Political Rights adopted by the United Nations General Assembly in 1966 and the 1969 American Human Rights Convention."

Protocol No. 7 was prepared by a Committee of Experts for the Extension of Rights thus far embodied in the European Convention, a body acting on behalf of the Council of Europe. This Committee was instructed to insert into the new

Protocol as many of the substantive provisions of the United Nations Convenant on Civil and Political Rights as possible. Beginning its work in 1976, the Committee eventually produced a Draft Protocol which was adopted by the Committee of Ministers of the Council of Europe on November 22, 1984.

However, Protocol No. 7 differs in coverage from the Covenant on Civil and Political Rights. For example, unlike the United Nations Covenant, Article 1 of Protocol No. 7 spells out the circumstances under which aliens may be expelled from their country of residence before being allowed to exercise their rights. The Protocol permits expulsion before the exercise of rights when necessary in the interest of public order or . . . [for] reasons of national security.

In general, Protocol No. 7 provides minimum guarantees for aliens, but it provides a host of new protections for citizens of member states. Article 2 establishes a right of review of convictions or sentences. Article 4 provides a limited form of double jeopardy protection. Article 3 creates an unusual right of compensation for those who have been convicted of criminal offenses and are subsequently pardoned or have their convictions reversed. Article 5 establishes equality of spousal rights and responsibilities at private law.

Protocol 8 is procedural rather than substantive. It does not add to the catalog of human rights to be presented. Rather, it amends the 1950 Convention to improve and expedite the procedures of both the Commission and Court of Human Rights. Adopted on January 25, 1985, it was opened for signature on March 19, 1985.

As a treaty among sovereign states, the European convention has a legally binding character, unlike the U.N.'s Universal Declaration which is hortatory in nature and is an appeal to the international conscience. The enforcement machinery consists of both a European Commission and a European Court of Human Rights which have been given wide authority. They are empowered to hear and adjudicate disputes (on both individual and interstate bases) arising out of alleged violations of rights protected by the treaty. Significantly, jurisdiction of the Commission or Court cannot be invoked until all domestic remedies have been exhausted, providing such remedies are available and are not being withheld or unreasonably delayed.

The main mission of the European Commission is carried out through inquiry and concililation. A failure to reach a friendly settlement may result in a formal legal opinion or the Commission may refer the matter to the European Court of Human Rights. The European Court of Human Rights then may determine whether a violation of the Convention has been committed and/or award just satisfaction—providing that the laws of the violating country do not provide for such remedy under Art. 50. Generally, the European Court will not act upon individual claims of rights deprivation unless such claims are referred to it by the Commission or by a member state of the European Convention.

The specific rights conferred by the European Convention, plus the powers and duties of its Commission and Court should be compared with the American Convention on Human Rights of 1969 (promulgated nearly twenty years later) and its comparable enforcement agencies.

The best general works on the European Convention are by A. H. Robertson, based in part upon his experience as Head of the Directorate of

Human Rights of the Council of Europe. These are *Human Rights in National and International Law*, Manchester, 1968; and *Human Rights in Europe*, 2d ed., Manchester, 1977. Also significant is *Human Rights under the European Convention* by Zaim N. Nedjati, North-Holland, 1978. *See* also S. Castberg, *The European Convention on Human Rights*, Leyden, 1974; J. E. S. Fawcett, *The Application of the European Convention on Human Rights*, Oxford, 1969; and G. L. Weil, *The European Convention on Human Rights*, Leyden, 1963.

For additional backgrounds, *see* the Council of Europe's *Yearbook of the European Convention on Human Rights*. See particularly the section devoted to a "Selective Bibliography."

1. EUROPEAN CONVENTION ON HUMAN RIGHTS (1950) (Protocols 1–8 (1952–1985))

CONVENTION FOR THE PROTECTION OF HUMAN RIGHTS AND FUNDAMENTAL FREEDOMS Signed at Rome, 4 November 1950; entered into force on 3 September 1953. Council of Europe, European Convention on Human Rights: Collected Texts, Section 1, Doc. 1 (7th ed., Strasbourg, 1971).

The Governments signatory hereto, being Members of the Council of Europe,

Considering the Universal Declaration of Human Rights proclaimed by the General Assembly of the United Nations on 10 December 1948;

Considering that this Declaration aims at securing the universal and effective recognition and observance of the Rights therein declared;

Considering that the aim of the Council of Europe is the achievement of greater unity between its Members and that one of the methods by which that aim is to be pursued is the maintenance and further realisation of Human Rights and Fundamental Freedoms;

Reaffirming their profound belief in those Fundamental Freedoms which are the foundation of justice and peace in the world and are best maintained on the one hand by an effective political democracy and on the other by a common understanding and observance of the Human Rights upon which they depend;

Being resolved, as the Governments of European countries which are likeminded and have a common heritage of political traditions, ideals, freedom and the rule of law to take the first steps for the collective enforcement of certain of the Rights stated in the Universal Declaration,

Have agreed as follows:

Article 1

The High Contracting Parties shall secure to everyone within their jurisdiction the rights and freedoms defined in Section I of this Convention.

SECTION I

Article 2

1. Everyone's right to life shall be protected by law. No one shall be

deprived of his life intentionally save in the execution of a sentence of a court following his conviction of a crime for which this penalty is provided by law.

2. Deprivation of life shall not be regarded as inflicted in contravention of this Article when it results from the use of force which is no more than absolutely necessary:

a. in defence of any person from unlawful violence;

b. in order to effect a lawful arrest or to prevent the escape of a person lawfully detained;

c. in action lawfully taken for the purpose of quelling a riot or insurrection.

Article 3

No one shall be subjected to torture or to inhuman or degrading treatment or punishment.

Article 4

1. No one shall be held in slavery or servitude.

2. No one shall be required to perform forced or compulsory labour.

3. For the purpose of this Article the term 'forced or compulsory labour' shall not include:

a. any work required to be done in the ordinary course of detention imposed according to the provisions of Article 5 of this Convention or during conditional release from such detention;

b. any service of a military character or, in case of conscientious objectors in countries where they are recognised, service exacted instead of compulsory military service;

c. any service exacted in case of an emergency or calamity threatening the life or well-being of the community;

d. any work or service which forms part of normal civic obligations.

Article 5

1. Everyone has the right to liberty and security of person.

No one shall be deprived of his liberty save in the following cases and in accordance with a procedure prescribed by law;

a. the lawful detention of a person after conviction by a competent court;

b. the lawful arrest or detention of a person for non-compliance with the lawful order of a court or in order to secure the fulfilment of any obligation prescribed by law;

c. the lawful arrest or detention of a person effected for the purpose of bringing him before the competent legal authority on reasonable suspicion of having committed an offence or when it is reasonably considered necessary to prevent his committing an offence or fleeing after having done so;

d. the detention of a minor by lawful order for the purpose of educational supervision or his lawful detention for the purpose of bringing him before the competent legal authority;

e. the lawful detention of persons for the prevention of the spreading of infectious diseases, of persons of unsound mind, alcoholics or drug addicts or vagrants;

f. the unlawful arrest or detention of a person to prevent his effecting an unauthorised entry into the country or of a person against whom action is being taken with a view to deportation or extradition.

2. Everyone who is arrested shall be informed promptly, in a language which he understands, of the reasons for his arrest and of any charge against him.

3. Everyone arrested or detained in accordance with the provisions of paragraph 1(c) of this Article shall be brought promptly before a judge or other officer authorised by law to exercise judicial power and shall be entitled to trial within a reasonable time or to release pending trial. Release may be conditioned by guarantees to appear for trial.

4. Everyone who is deprived of his liberty by arrest or detention shall be entitled to take proceedings by which the lawfulness of his detention shall be decided speedily by a court and his release ordered if the detention is not lawful.

5. Everyone who has been the victim of arrest or detention in contravention of the provisions of this Article shall have an enforceable right to compensation.

Article 6

1. In the determination of his civil rights and obligations or of any criminal charge against him, everyone is entitled to a fair and public hearing within a reasonable time by an independent and impartial tribunal established by law. Judgment shall be pronounced publicly but the press and public may be excluded from all or part of the trial in the interest of morals, public order or national security in a democratic society, where the interests of junveniles or the protection of the private life of the parties so require, or to the extent strictly necessary in the opinion of the court in special circumstances where publicity would prejudice the interests of justice.

2. Everyone charged with a criminal offence shall be presumed innocent until proved guilty according to law.

3. Everyone charged with a criminal offence has the following minimum rights:

a. to be informed promptly, in a language which he understands and in detail, of the nature and cause of the accusation against him;

b. to have adequate time and facilities for the preparation of his defence;

c. to defend himself in person or through legal assistance of his own choosing or, if he has not sufficient means to pay for legal assistance, to be given it free when the interests of justice so require;

d. to examine or have examined witnesses against him and to obtain the attendance and examination of witnesses on his behalf under the same conditions as witnesses against him;

e. to have the free assistance of an interpreter if he cannot understand or speak the language used in court.

Article 7

1. No one shall be held guilty of any criminal offence on account of any act or omission which did not constitute a criminal offence under national or international law at the time when it was committed. Nor shall a heavier penalty be imposed than the one that was applicable at the time the criminal offence was committed.

2. This Article shall not prejudice the trial and punishment of any person for any act or omission which, at the time when it was committed, was criminal according to the general principles of law recognised by civilised nations.

Article 8

1. Everyone has the right to respect for his private and family life, his home and his correspondence.

2. There shall be no interference by a public authority with the exercise of this right except such as in accordance with the law and is necessary in a democratic society in the interests of national security, public safety or the economic well-being of the country, for the prevention of disorder or crime, for the protection of health or morals, or for the protection of the rights and freedoms of others.

Article 9

1. Everyone has the right to freedom of thought, conscience and religion; this right includes freedom to change his religion or belief and freedom, either alone or in community with others and in public or private, to manifest his religion or belief, in worship, teaching, practice and observance.

2. Freedom to manifest one's religion or beliefs shall be subject only to such limitations as are prescribed by law and are necessary in a democratic society in the interests of public safety, for the protection of public order, health or morals, or for the protection of the rights and freedoms of others.

Article 10

1. Everyone has the right to freedom of expression. This right shall include freedom to hold opinions and to receive and impart information and ideas without interference by public authority and regardless of frontiers. This Article shall not prevent States from requiring the licensing of broadcasting, television or cinema enterprises.

2. The exercise of these freedoms, since it carries with it duties and responsibilities, may be subject to such formalities, conditions, restrictions or penalties as are prescribed by law and are necessary in a democratic society, in the interests of national security, territorial integrity or public safety, for the prevention of disorder or crime, for the protection of health or morals, for the protection of the reputation or rights of others, for preventing the disclosure of information received in confidence, or for maintaining the authority and impartiality of the judiciary.

Article 11

1. Everyone has the right to freedom of peaceful assembly and to freedom of association with others, including the right to form and to join trade unions for the protection of his interests.

2. No restrictions shall be placed on the exercise of these rights other than such as are prescribed by law and are necessary in a democratic society in the interests of national security or public safety, for the prevention of disorder or crime, for the protection of health or morals or for the protection of the rights and freedoms of others. This Article shall not prevent the imposition of lawful restrictions on the exercise of these rights by members of the armed forces, of the police or of the administration of the State.

Article 12

Men and women of marriageable age have the right to marry and to found a family, according to the national laws governing the exercise of this right.

Article 13

Everyone whose rights and freedoms as set forth in this Convention are violated shall have an effective remedy before a national authority notwithstanding that the violation has been committed by persons acting in an official capacity.

Article 14

The enjoyment of the rights and freedoms set forth in this Convention shall be secured without discrimination on any ground such as sex, race, colour, language, religion, political or other opinion, national or social origin, association with a national minority, property, birth or other status.

Article 15

1. In time of war or other public emergency threatening the life of the nation any High Contracting Party may take measures derogating from its obligations under this Convention to the extent strictly required by the exigencies of the situation, provided that such measures are not inconsistent with its other obligations under international law.

2. No derogation from Article 2, except in respect of deaths resulting from lawful acts of war, or from Articles 3, 4 (paragraph 1) and 7 shall be made under this provision.

3. Any High Contracting Party availing itself of this right of derogation shall keep the Secretary General of the Council of Europe fully informed of the measures which it has taken and the reasons therefor. It shall also inform the Secretary General of the Council of Europe when such measures have ceased to operate and the provisions of the Convention are again being fully executed.

Article 16

Nothing in Articles 10, 11 and 14 shall be regarded as preventing the High Contracting Parties from imposing restrictions on the poltical activity of aliens.

Article 17

Nothing in this Convention may be interpreted as implying for any State, group or person any right to engage in any activity or perform any act aimed at the destruction of any of the rights and freedoms set forth herein or at their limitation to a greater extent than is provided for in the Convention.

Article 18

The restrictions permitted under this Convention to the said rights and freedoms shall not be applied for any purpose other than those for which they have been prescribed.

SECTION II

Article 19[48]

To ensure the observance of the engagements undertaken by the High Contracting Parties in the present Convention, there shall be set up:

1. A European Commission of Human Rights hereinafter referred to as 'the Commission;'

2. A European Court of Human Rights, hereinafter referred to as 'the Court.'

SECTION III

Article 20

The Commission shall consist of a number of members equal to that of the High Contracting Parties. No two members of the commission may be nationals of the same State.

Article 21

1. The members of the Commission shall be elected by the Committee of Ministers by an absolute majority of votes, from a list of names drawn up by the Bureau of the Consultative Assembly; each group of the Representatives of the High Contracting Parties in the Consultative Assembly shall put forward three candidates, of whom two at least shall be its nationals.

2. As far as applicable, the same procedure shall be followed to complete the Commission in the event of other States subsequently becoming Parties to this Convention, and in filling casual vacancies.

Article 22[49]

1. The members of the Commission shall be elected for a period of six years. They may be re-elected. However, of the members elected at the first election, the terms of seven members shall expire at the end of three years.

2. The members whose terms are to expire at the end of the initial period of three years shall be chosen by lot by the Secretary General of the Council of Europe immediately after the first election has been completed.

3. In order to ensure that, as far as possible, one half of the membership of

the Commission shall be renewed every three years, the Committee of Ministers may decide, before proceeding to any subsequent election, that the term or terms of office of one or more members to be elected shall be for a period other than six years but not more than nine and not less than three years.

4. In cases where more than one term of office is involved and the Committee of Ministers applies the preceding paragraph, the allocation of the terms of office shall be effected by the drawing of lots by the Secretary General, immediately after the election.

5. A member of the Commission elected to replace a member whose term of office has not expired shall hold office for the remainder of his predecessor's term.

6. The members of the Commission shall hold office until replaced. After having been replaced, they shall continue to deal with such cases as they already have under consideration.

Article 23

The members of the Commission shall sit on the Commission in their individual capacity.

Article 24

Any High Contracting Party may refer to the Commission, through the Secretary General of the Council of Europe, any alleged breach of the provisions of the Convention by another High Contracting Party.

Article 25

1. The Commission may receive petitions addressed to the Secretary General of the Council of Europe from any person, non-governmental organisation or group of individuals claiming to be the victim of a violation by one of the High Contracting Parties of the rights set forth in this Convention, provided that the High Contracting Party against which the complaint has been lodged has declared that it recognises the competence of the Commission to receive such petitions. Those of the High Contracting Parties who have made such a declaration undertake not to hinder in any way the effective exercise of this right.

2. Such declarations may be made for a specific period.

3. The declarations shall be deposited with the Secretary General of the Council of Europe who shall transmit copies thereof to the High Contracting Parties and publish them.

4. The Commission shall only exercise the powers provided for in this Article when at least six High Contracting Parties are bound by declarations made in accordance with the preceding paragraphs.

Article 26

The Commission may only deal with the matter after all domestic remedies have been exhausted, according to the generally recognised rules of international law, and within a period of six months from the date on which the final decision was taken.

Article 27

1. The Commission shall not deal with any petition submitted under Article 25 which
    a. is anonymous, or
    b. is substantially the same as a matter which has already been examined by the Commission or has already been submitted to another procedure of international investigation or settlement and if it contains no relevant new information.

2. The Commission shall consider inadmissible any petition submitted under Article 25 which it considers incompatible with the provisions of the present Convention, manifestly ill-founded, or an abuse of the right of petition.

3. The Commission shall reject any petition referred to it which it considers inadmissible under Article 26.

Article 28

In the event of the Commission accepting a petition referred to it:

(*a*) it shall, with a view to ascertaining the facts, undertake together with the representatives of the parties an examination of the petition and, if need be, an investigation, for the effective conduct of which the States concerned shall furnish all necessary facilities, after an exchange of views with the Commission;

(*b*) it shall place itself at the disposal of the parties concerned with a view to securing a friendly settlement of the matter on the basis of respect for Human Rights as defined in this Convention.

Article 29[50]

After it has accepted a petition submitted under Article 25, the Commission may nevertheless decide unanimously to reject the petition if, in the course of its examination, it finds that the existence of one of the grounds for non-acceptance provided for in Article 27 has been established.

In such a case, the decision shall be communicated to the parties.

Article 30[51]

If the Commission succeeds in effecting a friendly settlement in accordance with Article 28, it shall draw up a Report which shall be sent to the States concerned, to the Committee of Ministers and to the Secretary General of the Council of Europe for publication. This Report shall be confined to a brief statement of the facts and of the solution reached.

Article 31

1. If a solution is not reached, the Commission shall draw up a Report on the facts and state its opinion as to whether the facts found disclose a breach by the State concerned of its obligations under the Convention. The opinions of all the members of the Commission on this point may be stated in the Report.

2. The Report shall be transmitted to the Committee of Ministers. It shall also be transmitted to the States concerned, who shall not be at liberty to publish it.

3. In transmitting the Report to the Committee of Ministers the Commission may make such proposals as it thinks fit.

Article 32

1. If the question is not referred to the Court in accordance with Article 48 of this Convention within a period of three months from the date of the transmission of the Report to the Committee of Ministers, the Committee of Ministers shall decide by a majority of two-thirds of the members entitled to sit on the Committee whether there has been a violation of the Convention.

2. In the affirmative case the Committee of Ministers shall prescribe a period during which the Contracting Party concerned must take the measures required by the decision of the Committee of Ministers.

3. If the High Contracting Party concerned has not taken satisfactory measures within the prescribed period, the Committee of Ministers shall decide by the majority provided for in paragraph 1 above what effect shall be given to its original decision and shall publish the Report.

4. The High Contracting Parties undertake to regard as binding on them any decision which the Committee of Ministers may take in application of the preceding paragraphs.

Article 33

The Commission shall meet *in camera*.

Article 34 [52]

Subject to the provisions of Article 29, the Commission shall take its decisions by a majority of the members present and voting.

Article 35

The Commission shall meet as the circumstances require. The meetings shall be convened by the Secretary General of the Council of Europe.

Article 36

The Commission shall draw up its own rules of procedure.

Article 37

The secretariat of the Commission shall be provided by the Secretary General of the Council of Europe.

SECTION IV

Article 38

The European Court of Human Rights shall consist of a number of judges equal to that of the Members of the Council of Europe. No two judges may be nationals of the same State.

Article 39

1. The members of the Court shall be elected by the Consultative Assembly by a majority of the votes cast from a list of persons nominated by the Members of the Council of Europe; each Member shall nominate three candidates, of whom two at least shall be its nationals.

2. As far as applicable, the same procedure shall be followed to complete the Court in the event of the admission of new Members of the Council of Europe, and in filling casual vacancies.

3. The candidates shall be of high moral character and must either possess the qualifications required for appointment to high judicial office or be jurisconsults of recognised competence.

Article 40 [53]

1. The members of the Court shall be elected for a period of nine years. They may be re-elected. However, of the members elected at the first election the terms of four members shall expire at the end of three years, and the terms of four more members shall expire at the end of six years.

2. The members whose terms are to expire at the end of the initial periods of three and six years shall be chosen by lot by the Secretary General immediately after the first election has been completed.

3. In order to ensure that, as far as possible, one third of the membership of the Court shall be renewed every three years, the Consultative Assembly may decide, before proceeding to any subsequent election, that the term or terms of office of one or more members to be elected shall be for a period other than nine years but not more than twelve and not less than six years.

4. In cases where more than one term of office is involved and the Consultative Assembly applies the preceding paragraph, the allocation of the terms of office shall be effected by the drawing of lots by the Secretary General immediately after the election.

5. A member of the Court elected to replace a member whose term of office has not expired shall hold office for the remainder of his predecessor's term.

6. The members of the Court shall hold office until replaced. After having been replaced, they shall continue to deal with such cases as they already have under consideration.

Article 41

The Court shall elect its President and Vice-President for a period of three years. They may be re-elected.

Article 42

The members of the Court shall receive for each day of duty a compensation to be determined by the Committee of Ministers.

Article 43

For a consideration of each case brought before it the Court shall consist of a Chamber composed of seven judges. There shall sit as an *ex officio* member of the Chamber the judge who is a national of any State party concerned, or, if there is none, a person of its choice who shall sit in the capacity of judge; the names of the other judges shall be chosen by lot by the President before the opening of the case.

Article 44

Only the High Contracting Parties and the Commission shall have the right to bring a case before the Court.

Article 45

The jurisdiction of the Court shall extend to all cases concerning the interpretation and application of the present Convention which the High Contracting Parties or the Commission shall refer to it in accordance with Article 48.

Article 46

1. Any of the High Contracting Parties may at any time declare that it recognises as compulsory *ipso facto* and without special agreement the jurisdiction of the Court in all matters concerning the interpretation and application of the present Convention.

2. The declarations referred to above may be made unconditionally or on condition of reciprocity on the part of several or certain other High Contracting Parties or for a specified period.

3. These declarations shall be deposited with the Secretary-General of the Council of Europe who shall transmit copies thereof to the High Contracting Parties.

Article 47

The Court may only deal with a case after the Commission has acknowledged the failure of efforts for a friendly settlement and within the period of three months provided for in Article 32.

Article 48

The following may bring a case before the Court, provided that the High Contracting Party concerned, if there is only one, or the High Contracting Parties concerned, if there is more than one, are subject to the compulsory jurisdiction of the Court or, failing that, with the consent of the High Contracting Party concerned, if there is only one, or of the High Contracting Parties concerned if there is more than one:

a. the Commission;

b. a High Contracting Party whose national is alleged to be a victim;

c. a High Contracting Party which referred the case to the Commission;

d. a High Contracting Party against which the complaint has been lodged.

Article 49

In the event of dispute as to whether the Court has jurisdiction, the matter shall be settled by the decision of the Court.

Article 50

If the Court finds that a decision or a measure taken by a legal authority or any other authority of a High Contracting Party is completely or partially in conflict with the obligations arising from the present Convention, and if the internal law of the said Party allows only partial reparation to be made for the consequences of this decision or measure, the decision of the Court shall, if necessary, afford just satisfaction to the injured party.

Article 51

1. Reasons shall be given for the judgment of the Court.
2. If the judgment does not represent in whole or in part the unanimous opinion of the judges, any judge shall be entitled to deliver a separate opinion.

Article 52

The judgment of the Court shall be final.

Article 53

The High Contracting Parties undertake to abide by the decision of the Court in any case to which they are parties.

Article 54

The judgment of the Court shall be transmitted to the Committee of Ministers which shall supervise its execution.

Article 55

The Court shall draw up its own rules and shall determine its own procedure.

Article 56

1. The first election of the members of the Court shall take place after the declarations by the High Contracting Parties mentioned in Article 46 have reached a total of eight.
2. No case can be brought before the Court before this election.

SECTION V

Article 57

On receipt of a request from the Secretary General of the Council of Europe any High Contracting Party shall furnish an explanation of the manner in which its internal law ensures the effective implementation of any of the provisions of this Convention.

Article 58

The expenses of the Commission and the Court shall be borne by the Council of Europe.

Article 59

The members of the Commission and of the Court shall be entitled, during the discharge of their functions, to the privileges and immunities provided for in Article 40 of the Statute of the Council of Europe and in the agreements made thereunder.

Article 60

Nothing in this Convention shall be construed as limiting or derogating from any of the human rights and fundamental freedoms which may be ensured under the laws of any High Contracting Party or under any other agreement to which it is a Party.

Article 61

Nothing in this Convention shall prejudice the powers conferred on the Committee of Ministers by the Statute of the Council of Europe.

Article 62

The High Contracting Parties agree that, except by special agreement, they will not avail themselves of treaties, conventions or declarations in force between them for the purpose of submitting, by way of petition, a dispute arising out of the interpretation or application of this Convention to a means of settlement other than those provided for in this Convention.

Article 63

1. Any State may at the time of its ratification or at any time thereafter declare by notification addressed to the Secretary General of the Council of Europe that the present Convention shall extend to all or any of the territories for whose international relations it is responsible.

2. The Convention shall extend to the territory or territories named in the notification as from the thirtieth day after the receipt of this notification by the Secretary General of the Council of Europe.

3. The provisions of this Convention shall be applied in such territories with due regard, however, to local requirements.

4. Any State which has made a declaration in accordance with paragraph 1 of this Article may at any time thereafter declare on behalf of one or more of the territories to which the declaration relates that it accepts the competence of the Commission to receive petitions from individuals, non-governmental organisations or groups of individuals in accordance with Article 25 of the present Convention.

Article 64

1. Any State may, when signing this Convention or when depositing its instrument of ratification, make a reservation in respect of any particular provision of the Convention to the extent that any law then in force in its territory is not in conformity with the provision. Reservations of a general character shall not be permitted under this Article.

2. Any reservation made under this Article shall contain a brief statement of the law concerned.

Article 65

1. A High Contracting Party may denounce the present Convention only after the expiry of five years from the date on which it became a Party to it and after six months' notice contained in a notification addressed to the Secretary General of the Council of Europe, who shall inform the other High Contracting Parties.

2. Such a denunciation shall not have the effect of releasing the High Contracting Party concerned from its obligations under this Convention in respect of any act which, being capable of constituting a violation of such obligations, may have been performed by it before the date at which the denunciation became effective.

3. Any High Contracting Party which shall cease to be a Member of the Council of Europe shall cease to be a Party to this Convention under the same conditions.

4. The Convention may be denounced in accordance with the provisions of the preceding paragraphs in respect of any territory to which it has been declared to extend under the terms of Article 63.

Article 66

1. This convention shall be open to the signature of the Members of the Council of Europe. It shall be ratified. Ratifications shall be deposited with the Secretary General of the Council of Europe.

2. The present Convention shall come into force after the deposit of ten instruments of ratification.

3. As regards any signatory ratifying subsequently, the Convention shall come into force at the date of the deposit of its instrument of ratification.

4. The Secretary General of the Council of Europe shall notify all the Members of the Council of Europe of the entry into force of the Convention, the names of the High Contracting Parties who have ratified it, and the deposit of all instruments of ratification which may be effected subsequently.

Done at Rome this 4th day of November 1950, in English and French, both texts being equally authentic, in a single copy which shall remain deposited in the archives of the Council of Europe. The Secretary General shall transmit certified copies to each of the signatories.

* * *

Note that Protocols 3 and 5 modify the text of the Convention and are incorporated into the text. Thus they are not separately set forth as are the other Protocols.

FIRST PROTOCOL TO THE CONVENTION

The Governments signatory hereto, being Members of the Council of Europe,
Being resolved to take steps to ensure the collective enforcement of certain rights and

freedoms other than those already included in Section I of the Convention for the Protection of Human Rights and Fundamental Freedoms signed at Rome on 4 November 1950 (hereinafter referred to as 'the Convention'),
  Have agreed as follows:

Article 1

Every natural or legal person is entitled to the peaceful enjoyment of his possessions. No one shall be deprived of his possessions except in the public interest and subject to the conditions provided for by law and by the general principles of international law.

The preceding provisions shall not, however, in any way impair the right of a State to enforce such laws as it deems necessary to control the use of property in accordance with the general interest or to secure the payment of taxes or other contributions or penalties.

Article 2

No person shall be denied the right to education. In the exercise of any functions which it assumes in relation to education and to teaching, the State shall respect the right of parents to ensure such education and teaching in conformity with their own religious and philosophical convictions.

Article 3

The High Contracting Parties undertake to hold free elections at reasonable intervals by secret ballot, under conditions which will ensure the free expression of the opinion of the people in the choice of the legislature.

Article 4

Any High Contracting Party may at the time of signature or ratification or at any time thereafter communicate to the Secretary General of the Council of Europe a declaration stating the extent to which it undertakes that the provisions of the present Protocol shall apply to such of the territories for the international relations of which it is responsible as are named therein.

Any High Contracting Party which has communicated a declaration in virtue of the preceding paragraph may from time to time communicate a further declaration modifying the terms of any former declaration or terminating the application of the provisions of this Protocol in respect of any territory.

A declaration made in accordance with this Article shall be deemed to have been made in accordance with Paragraph (1) of Article 63 of the Convention.

Article 5

As between the High Contracting Parties the provisions of Articles 1, 2, 3 and 4 of this Protocol shall be regarded as additional Articles to the Convention and all the provisions of the Convention shall apply accordingly.

Article 6

This Protocol shall be open for signature by the Members of the Council of Europe, who are the signatories of the Convention; it shall be ratified at the same time as or after the ratification of the Convention. It shall enter into force after the deposit of ten instruments of ratification. As regards any signatory ratifying subsequently, the Protocol shall enter into force at the date of the deposit of ten instruments of ratification.

The instruments of ratification shall be deposited with the Secretary General of the Council of Europe, who will notify all Members of the names of those who have ratified.

Done at Paris on the 20th day of March 1952, in English and French, both texts being equally authentic, in a single copy which shall remain deposited in the archives of the Council of Europe. The Secretary General shall transmit certified copies to each of the signatory Governments.

SECOND PROTOCOL CONFERRING UPON THE EUROPEAN COURT OF HUMAN RIGHTS COMPETENCE TO GIVE ADVISORY OPINIONS

The member States of the Council of Europe signatory hereto:

Having regard to the provisions of the Convention for the Protection of Human Rights and Fundamental Freedoms signed at Rome on 4 November 1950 (hereinafter referred to as 'the Convention') and, in particular, Article 19 instituting, among other bodies, a European Court of Human Rights (hereinafter referred to as 'the Court');

Considering that it is expedient to confer upon the Court competence to give advisory opinions subject to certain conditions,

Have agreed as follows:

Article 1

1. The Court may, at the request of the Committee of Ministers, give advisory opinions on legal questions concerning the interpretation of the Convention and the Protocols thereto.

2. Such opinions shall not deal with any question relating to the content or scope of the rights or freedoms defined in Section I of the Convention and in the Protocols thereto, or with any other question which the Commission, the Court or the Committee of Ministers might have to consider in consequence of any such proceedings as could be instituted in accordance with the Convention.

3. Decisions of the Committee of Ministers to request an advisory opinion of the Court shall require a two-thirds majority vote of the representatives entitled to sit on the Committee.

Article 2

The Court shall decide whether a request for an advisory opinion submitted by the Committee of Ministers is within its consultative competence as defined in Article 1 of this Protocol.

Article 3

1. For the consideration of requests for an advisory opinion, the Court shall sit in plenary session.

2. Reasons shall be given for advisory opinions of the Court.

3. If the advisory opinion does not represent in whole or in part the unanimous opinion of the judges, any judge shall be entitled to deliver a separate opinion.

4. Advisory opinions of the Court shall be communicated to the Committee of Ministers.

Article 4

The powers of the Court under Article 55 of the Convention shall extend to the drawing up of such rules and the determination of such procedure as the Court may think necessary for the purposes of this Protocol.

Article 5

1. This Protocol shall be open to signature by member States of the Council of Europe, signatories to the Convention, who may become Parties to it by:

    a. signature without reservation in respect of ratification or acceptance;

    b. signature with reservation in respect of ratification or acceptance, followed by ratification or acceptance.

Instruments of ratification or acceptance shall be deposited with the Secretary General of the Council of Europe.

2. This Protocol shall enter into force as soon as all States Parties to the Convention shall become Parties to the Protocol, in accordance with the provisions of paragraph 1 of this Article.

3. From the date of entry into force of this Protocol, Articles 1 to 4 shall be considered an integral part of the Convention.

4. The Secretary General of the Council of Europe shall notify the member States of the Council of:

    a. any signature without reservation in respect of ratification or acceptance;

    b. any signature with reservation in respect of ratification or acceptance;

    c. the deposit of any instrument of ratification or acceptance;

    d. the date of entry into force of this Protocol in accordance with paragraph 2 of this Article.

In witness whereof, the undersigned, being duly authorised thereto, have signed this Protocol.

Done at Strasbourg, this 6th day of May 1963, in English and in French, both texts being equally authoritative, in a single copy which shall remain deposited in the archives of the Council of Europe. The Secretary General shall transmit certified copies to each of the signatory States.

FOURTH PROTOCOL SECURING CERTAIN RIGHTS AND FREEDOMS OTHER THAN THOSE ALREADY INCLUDED IN THE CONVENTION AND IN THE FIRST PROTOCOL THERETO

The Governments signatory hereto, being Members of the Council of Europe;

Being resolved to take steps to ensure the collective enforcement of certain rights and freedoms other than those already included in Section I of the Convention for the Protection of Human Rights and Fundamental Freedoms signed at Rome on 4 November 1950 (hereinafter referred to as 'the Convention') and in Articles 1 to 3 of the First Protocol to the Convention, signed at Paris on 20 March 1952,

Have agreed as follows:

Article 1

No one shall be deprived of his liberty merely on the ground of inability to fulfil a contractual obligation.

Article 2

1. Everyone lawfully within the territory of a State shall, within that territory, have the right to liberty of movement and freedom to choose his residence.

2. Everyone shall be free to leave any country, including his own.

3. No restrictions shall be placed on the exercise of these rights other than such as are in accordance with law and are necessary in a democratic society in the interests of national security or public safety, for the maintenance of *ordre public*, for the prevention of crime, for the protection of health or morals, or for the protection of the rights and freedoms of others.

4. The rights set forth in paragraph 1 may also be subject, in particular areas, to restrictions imposed in accordance with law and justified by the public interest in a democratic society.

Article 3

1. No one shall be expelled, by means either of an individual or of a collective measure, from the territory of the State of which he is a national.

2. No one shall be deprived of the right to enter the territory of the State of which he is a national.

Article 4

Collective expulsion of aliens is prohibited.

Article 5

1. Any High Contracting Party may, at the time of signature or ratification of this Protocol, or at any time thereafter, communicate to the Secretary General of the Council of Europe a declaration stating the extent to which it undertakes that the provisions of this Protocol shall apply to such of the territories for the international relations of which it is responsible as are named therein.

2. Any High Contracting Party which has communicated a declaration in virtue of the preceding paragraph may, from time to time, communicate a further declaration modifying the terms of any former declaration or terminating the application of the provisions of this Protocol in respect of any territory.

3. A declaration made in accordance with this Article shall be deemed to have been made in accordance with paragraph 1 of Article 63 of the Convention.

4. The territory of any State to which this Protocol applies by virtue of ratification or acceptance by that State, and each territory to which this Protocol

is applied by virtue of a declaration by that State under this Article, shall be treated as separate territories for the purpose of the references in Articles 2 and 3 to the territory of a State.

Article 6

1. As between the High Contracting Parties the provisions of Articles 1 to 5 of this Protocol shall be regarded as additional Articles to the Convention, and all the provisions of the Convention shall apply accordingly.

2. Nevertheless, the right of individual recourse recognised by a declaration made under Article 25 of the Convention, or the acceptance of the compulsory jurisdiction of the Court by a declaration made under Article 46 of the Convention, shall not be effective in relation to this Protocol unless the High Contracting Party concerned has made a statement recognising such right, or accepting such jurisdiction, in respect of all or any of Articles 1 to 4 of the Protocol.

Article 7

1. This Protocol shall be open for signature by the Members of the Council of Europe who are the signatories of the Convention; it shall be ratified at the same time as or after the ratification of the Convention. It shall enter into force after the deposit of five instruments of ratification. As regards any signatory ratifying subsequently, the Protocol shall enter into force at the date of the deposit of its instrument of ratification.

2. The instruments of ratification shall be deposited with the Secretary General of the Council of Europe, who will notify all Members of the names of those who have ratified.

In witness whereof, the undersigned, being duly authorised thereto, have signed this Protocol.

Done at Strasbourg, this 16th day of September 1963, in English and in French, both texts being equally authoritative, in a single copy which shall remain deposited in the archives of the Council of Europe. The Secretary General shall transmit certified copies to each of the signatory States.

SIXTH PROTOCOL TO THE CONVENTION FOR THE PROTECTION OF HUMAN RIGHTS AND FUNDAMENTAL FREEDOMS CONCERNING THE ABOLITION OF THE DEATH PENALTY

The member States of the Council of Europe, signatory to this Protocol to the Convention for the Protection of Human Rights and Fundamental Freedoms, signed at Rome on 4 November 1950 (hereinafter referred to as "the Convention"),

Considering that the evolution that has occurred in several member States of the Council of Europe expresses a general tendency in favour of abolition of the death penalty,

Have agreed as follows:

Article 1

The death penalty shall be abolished. No one shall be condemned to such penalty or executed.

Article 2

A State may make provision in its law for the death penalty in respect of acts committed in time of war or of imminent threat of war; such penalty shall be applied only in the instances laid down in the law and in accordance with its provisions. The State shall communicate to the Secretary General of the Council of Europe the relevant provisions of that law.

Article 3

No derogation from the provisions of this Protocol shall be made under Article 15 of the Convention.

Article 4

No reservation may be made under Article 64 of the Convention in respect of the provisions of this Protocol.

Article 5

1. Any State may at the time of signature or when depositing its instrument of ratification, acceptance or approval, specify the territory or territories to which this Protocol shall apply.

2. Any State may at any later date, by a declaration addressed to the Secretary General of the Council of Europe, extend the application of this Protocol to any other territory specified in the declaration. In respect of such territory the Protocol shall enter into force on the first day of the month following the date of receipt of such a declaration by the Secretary General.

3. Any declaration made under the two preceding paragraphs may, in respect of any territory specified in such declaration, be withdrawn by a notification addressed to the Secretary General. The withdrawal shall become effective on the first day of the month following the date of receipt of such notification by the Secretary General.

Article 6

As between the States Parties the provisions of Articles 1 to 5 of this Protocol shall be regarded as additional articles to the Convention and all the provisions of the Convention shall apply accordingly.

Article 7

This Protocol shall be open for signature by the member States of the Council of Europe, signatories to the Convention. It shall be subject to ratification, acceptance or approval. A member State of the Council of Europe may not ratify, accept or approve this Protocol unless it has, simultaneously or previously, ratified the Convention. Instruments of ratification, acceptance or approval shall be deposited with the Secretary General of the Council of Europe.

Article 8

1. This Protocol shall enter into force on the first day of the month following the date on which five member States of the Council of Europe have expressed

their consent to be bound by the Protocol in accordance with the provisions of Article 7.

2. In respect of any member State which subsequently expresses its consent to be bound by it, the Protocol shall enter into force on the first day of the month following the date of the deposit of the instrument of ratification, acceptance or approval.

Article 9

The Secretary General of the Council of Europe shall notify the member States of the Council of:

a. any signature;

b. the deposit of any instrument of ratification, acceptance or approval;

c. any date of entry into force of this Protocol in accordance with Articles 5 and 8;

d. any other act, notification or communication relating to this Protocol.

IN WITNESS WHEREOF the undersigned, being duly authorised thereto, have signed this Protocol.

DONE at Strasbourg, the twenty-eighth day of April one thousand nine hundred and eighty-three, in English and French, both texts being equally authentic, in a single copy which shall be deposited in the archives of the Council of Europe. The Secretary General of the Council of Europe shall transmit certified copies to each member State of the Council of Europe.

SEVENTH PROTOCOL TO THE CONVENTION FOR THE PROTECTION OF HUMAN RIGHTS AND FUNDAMENTAL FREEDOMS

The member States of the Council of Europe signatory hereto,

Being resolved to take further steps to ensure the collective enforcement of certain rights and freedoms by means of the Convention for the Protection of Human Rights and Fundamental Freedoms signed at Rome on 4 November 1950 (hereinafter referred to as "the Convention");

Have agreed as follows:

Article 1

1. An alien lawfully resident in the territory of a State shall not be expelled therefrom except in pursuance of a decision reached in accordance with law and shall be allowed:

a. to submit reasons against his expulsion,

b. to have his case reviewed, and

c. to be represented for these purposes before the competent authority or a person or persons designated by that authority.

2. An alien may be expelled before the exercise of his rights under paragraph 1(a), (b) and (c) of this Article, when such expulsion is necessary in the interests of public order or is grounded on reasons of national security.

Article 2

1. Everyone convicted of a criminal offence by a tribunal shall have the right to have conviction or sentence reviewed by a higher tribunal. The exercise of this right, including the grounds on which it may be exercised, shall be governed by law.

2. This right may be subject to exceptions in regard to offences of a minor character, as prescribed by law, or in cases in which the person concerned was tried in the first instance by the highest tribunal or was convicted following an appeal against acquittal.

Article 3

When a person has by a final decision been convicted of a criminal offence and when subsequently his conviction has been reversed, or he has been pardoned, on the ground that a new or newly discovered fact shows conclusively that there has been a miscarriage of justice, the person who has suffered punishment as a result of such conviction shall be compensated according to the law or the practice of the State concerned, unless it is proved that the non-disclosure of the unkown fact in time is wholly or partly attributable to him.

Article 4

1. No one shall be liable to be tried or punished again in criminal proceedings under the jurisdiction of the same State for an offence for which he has already been finally acquitted or convicted in accordance with the law and penal procedure of that State.

2. The provisions of the preceding paragraph shall not prevent the re-opening of the case in accordance with the law and penal procedure of the State concerned, if there is evidence of new or newly discovered facts, or if there has been a fundamental defect in the previous proceedings, which could affect the outcome of the case.

3. No derogation from this Article shall be made under Article 15 of the Convention.

Article 5

1. Spouses shall enjoy equality of rights and responsibilities of a private law character between them, and in their relations with their children, as to marriage, during marriage and in the event of its dissolution. This Article shall not prevent States from taking such measures as are necessary in the interests of the children.

Article 6

1. Any State may at the time of signature or when depositing its instrument of ratification, acceptance or approval, specify the territory or territories to which this Protocol shall apply and state the extent to which it undertakes that the provisions of this Protocol shall apply to this or these territories.

2. Any State may at any later date, by a declaration addressed to the Secretary General of the Council of Europe, extend the application of this

Protocol to any other territory specified in the declaration. In respect of such territory the Protocol shall enter into force on the first day of the month following the expiration of a period of two months after the date of receipt by the Secretary General of such declaration.

3. Any declaration made under the two preceding paragraphs may, in respect of any territory specified in such declaration, be withdrawn or modified by a notification addressed to the Secretary General. The withdrawal or modification shall become effective on the first day of the month following the expiration of a period of two months after the date of receipt of such notification by the Secretary General.

4. A declaration made in accordance with this Article shall be deemed to have been made in accordance with paragraph 1 of Article 63 of the Convention.

5. The territory of any State to which this Protocol applies by virtue of ratification, acceptance or approval by that State, and each territory to which this Protocol is applied by virtue of a declaration by that State under this Article, may be treated as separate territories for the purpose of the reference in Article 1 to the territory of a State.

Article 7

1. As between the States Parties, the provisions of Articles 1 to 6 of this Protocol shall be regarded as additional Articles to the Convention, and all the provisions of the Convention shall apply accordingly.

2. Nevertheless, the right of individual recourse recognised by a declaration made under Article 25 of the Convention, or the acceptance of the compulsory jurisdiction of the Court by a declaration made under Article 46 of the Convention, shall not be effective in relation to this Protocol unless the State concerned has made a statement recognising such right, or accepting such jurisdiction in respect of Articles 1 to 5 of this Protocol.

Article 8

This Protocol shall be open for signature by member States of the Council of Europe which have signed the Convention. It is subject to ratification, acceptance or approval. A member State of the Council of Europe may not ratify, accept or approve this Protocol without previously or simultaneously ratifying the Convention. Instruments of ratification, acceptance or approval shall be deposited with the Secretary General of the Council of Europe.

Article 9

1. This Protocol shall enter into force on the first day of the month following the expiration of a period of two months after the date on which seven member States of the Council of Europe have expressed their consent to be bound by the Protocol in accordance with the provisions of Article 8.

2. In respect of any member State which subsequently expresses its consent to be bound by it, the Protocol shall enter into force on the first day of the month following the expiration of a period of two months after the date of the deposit of the instrument of ratification, acceptance or approval.

Article 10

The Secretary General of the Council of Europe shall notify all the member States of the Council of:

a. any signature;

b. the deposit of any instrument of ratification, acceptance or approval;

c. any date of entry into force of this Protocol in accordance with Articles 6 and 9;

d. any other act, notification or declaration relating to this Protocol.

IN WITNESS WHEREOF the undersigned, being duly authorised thereto, have signed this Protocol.

DONE at Strasbourg, the twenty-second of November one thousand nine hundred and eighty four, in English and French, both texts being equally authentic, in a single copy which shall be deposited in the archives of the Council of Europe shall transmit certified copies to each member State of the Council.

PROTOCOL NO. 8 TO THE CONVENTION FOR THE PROTECTION OF HUMAN RIGHTS AND FUNDAMENTAL FREEDOMS

(adopted by the Committee of Ministers on 25 January 1985 at the 379th meeting of the Ministers' Deputies)

The member States of the Council of Europe, signatories to this Protocol to the Convention for the Protection of Human Rights and Fundamental Freedoms, signed at Rome on 4 November 1950 (hereinafter referred to as "the Convention"),

Considering that it is desirable to amend certain provisions of the Convention with a view to improving and in particular to expediting the procedure of the European Commission of Human Rights,

Considering that it is also advisable to amend certain provisions of the Convention concerning the procedure of the European Court of Human Rights,

Have agreed as follows:

Article 1

The existing text of Article 20 of the Convention shall become paragraph 1 of that Article and shall be supplemented by the following four paragraphs:

"2. The Commission shall sit in plenary session. It may, however, set up Chambers, each composed of at least seven members. The Chambers may examine petitions submitted under Article 25 of this Convention which can be dealt with on the basis of established case law or which raise no serious question affecting the interpretation or application of the Convention. Subject to this restriction and to the provisions of paragraph 5 of this Article, the Chambers shall exercise all the powers conferred on the Commission by the Convention.

The member of the Commission elected in respect of a High Contracting Party against which a petition has been lodged shall have the right to sit on a Chamber to which that petition has been referred.

3. The Commission may set up committees, each composed of at least three members, with the power, exercisable by a unanimous vote, to declare inadmissible or strike from its list of cases a petition submitted under Article 25, when such a decision can be taken without further examination.

4. A Chamber or committee may at any time relinquish jurisdiction in favour of the plenary Commission, which may also order a transfer of any petition referred to a Chamber or committee.

5. Only the plenary Commission can exercise the following powers:

    a. the examination of applications submitted under Article 24;

    b. the bringing of a case before the Court in accordance with Article 48(a);

    c. the drawing up of Rules of Procedure in accordance with Article 36.''

Article 2

Article 21 of the Convention shall be supplemented by the following third paragraph:

"3. The candidates shall be of high moral character and must either possess the qualifications required for appointment to high judicial office or be persons of recognised competence in national or international law."

Article 3

Article 23 of the Convention shall be supplemented by the following sentence:

"During their term of office they shall not hold any position which is incompatible with their independence and impartiality as members of the Commission or the demands of this office."

Article 4

The text, with modifications, of Article 28 of the Convention shall become paragraph 1 of that Article and the text, with modifications, of Article 30 shall become paragraph 2. The new text of Article 28 shall read as follows:

"Article 28

1. In the event of the Commission accepting a petition referred to it:

    a. it shall, with a view to ascertaining the facts, undertake together with the representatives of the parties an examination of the petition and, if need be, an investigation, for the effective conduct of which the States concerned shall furnish all necessary facilities, after an exchange of views with the Commission;

    b. it shall at the same time place itself at the disposal of the parties concerned with a view to securing a friendly settlement of the matter on the basis of respect for Human Rights as defined in this Convention.

2. If the Commission succeeds in effecting a friendly settlement, it shall draw up a Report which shall be sent to the States concerned, to the Committee of Ministers and to the Secretary General of the Council of Europe for

Publication. This Report shall be confined to a brief statement of the facts and of the solutions reached."

Article 5

In the first paragraph of Article 29 of the Convention, the word "unanimously" shall be replaced by the words "by a majority of two-thirds of its members."

Article 6

The following provision shall be inserted in the Convention:

"*Article 30*

1. The Commission may at any stage of the proceedings decide to strike a petition out of its list of cases where the circumstances lead to the conclusion that:

    a. the applicant does not intend to pursue his petition, or

    b. the matter has been resolved, or

    c. for any other reason established by the Commission, it is no longer justified to continue the examination of the petition.

However, the Commission shall continue the examination of a petition if respect for Human Rights as defined in this Convention so requires.

2. Where the Commission decides to strike a petition out of its list after having accepted it, shall draw up a Report which shall contain a statement of the facts and the decision striking out the petition together with the reasons therefore. The report shall be transmitted to the parties, as well as to the Committee of Ministers for information. The Commission may publish it.

3. The Commission may decide to restore a petition to its list of cases if it considers that the circumstances justify such a course."

Article 7

In Article 31 of the Convention, paragraph 1 shall read as follows:

"1. If the examination of a petition has not been completed in accordance with Article 28 (paragraph 2), 29 or 30, the Commission shall draw up a Report on the facts and state its opinion as to whether the facts found disclose a breach by the State concerned of its obligations under the Convention. The individual opinions of members of the Commission on this point may be stated in the Report."

Article 8

Article 34 of the Convention shall read as follows:

"Subject to the provisions of Articles 20 (paragraph 3) and 29, the Commission shall take its decisions by a majority of the members present and voting."

Article 9

Article 40 of the Convention shall be supplemented by the following seventh paragraph:

"7. The members of the Court shall sit on the Court in their individual capacity. During their term of office they shall not hold any position which is incompatible with their independence and impartiality as members of the Court or the demands of this office."

Article 10

Article 41 of the Convention shall read as follows:
"The Court shall elect its President and one or two Vice-Presidents for a period of three years. They may be re-elected."

Article 11

In the first sentence of Article 43 of the Convention, the word "seven" shall be replaced by the word "nine".

Article 12

1. This Protocol shall be open for signature by member States of the Council of Europe signatories to the Convention, which may express their consent to be bound by:
   a. signature without reservation as to ratification, acceptance or approval, or
   b. signature subject to ratification, acceptance or approval, followed by ratification, acceptance or approval.
2. Instruments of ratification, acceptance or approval shall be deposited with the Secretary General of the Council of Europe.

Article 13

This Protocol shall enter into force on the first day of the month following the expiration of a period of three months after the date on which all Parties to the Convention have expressed their consent to be bound by the Protocol in accordance with the provisions of Article 12.

Article 14

The Secretary General of the Council of Europe shall notify the member States of the Council of:
   a. any signature;
   b. the deposit of any instrument of ratification, acceptance or approval;
   c. the date of entry into force of this Protocol in accordance with Article 13;
   d. any other act, notification or communication relating to this Protocol.

IN WITNESS WHEREOF the undersigned, being duly authorised thereto, have signed this Protocol.

DONE at ...., the ...., in English and French, both texts being equally authentic, in a single copy which shall be deposited in the archives of the Council of Europe. The Secretary General shall transmit certified copies to each member State of the Council of Europe.

2. EUROPEAN COMMISSION OF HUMAN RIGHTS: RULES OF PROCEDURE (1971)

Adopted by the Commission, 2 April 1955; with amendments to 18 December 1970. Council of Europe, European Convention on Human Rights: Collected Texts, Section 2 (7th ed., Strasbourg, 1971).

The Commission,
Having regard to the Convention for the Protection of Human Rights and Fundamental Freedoms and Protocols, hereinafter called the Convention;
Pursuant to Article 36 of the Convention;
Adopts the present Rules:

TITLE I. ORGANISATION AND WORKING OF THE COMMISSION

CHAPTER I. MEMBERS OF THE COMMISSION

Rule 1

1. The duration of the term of office of members of the Commission elected on 18th May 1954 shall be calculated as from this date. Similarly, the duration of the term of office of any member elected as a consequence of a State becoming a party to the Convention after 18th May 1954 shall be calculated as from his election.

2. However, when a member is re-elected on the expiry of his term of office or is elected to replace a member whose term of office has expired or is about to expire, the duration of his term of office shall, in either case, be calculated as from the date of such expiry.

3. In accordance with Article 22, paragraph (3), of the Convention, a member elected to replace a member whose term of office has not expired shall hold office for the remainder of his predecessor's term.

4. In accordance with Article 22, paragraph (4), of the Convention, members shall hold office until replaced. After having been replaced, they shall continue to deal with such cases as they already have under consideration.

Rule 2

Before taking up his duties, each member of the Commission shall, at the first meeting of the Commission at which he is present after his election, make the following oath or solemn declaration:

"I swear," or "I solemnly declare"—"that I will exercise all my powers and duties honourably and faithfully, impartially and conscientiously and that I will keep secret all deliberations."

Rule 3

1. Members of the Commission shall take precedence after the President and Vice-President according to the length of time they have been in office.

2. Members having the same length of time in office shall take precedence according to age.

3. Re-elected members shall take precedence having regard to the duration of their previous terms of office.

Rule 4

Resignation of a member shall be notified to the President who shall transmit it to the Secretary-General of the Council of Europe. Subject to the provisions of Rule 1, paragraph (4), it shall constitute vacation of office.

CHAPTER II. PRESIDENCY OF THE COMMISSION

Rule 5

1. The Commission shall elect the President and Vice-President during the month following the date of the entry into office of members elected at periodical elections of part of the Commission in accordance with paragraph (1) of Article 22 of the Convention.

2. If the President or Vice-President, before the normal expiry of his term of office as President or Vice-President, ceases to be a member of the Commission or resigns his office, the Commission shall elect a successor to hold office for the remainder of the said term.

3. The elections referred to in this Rule shall be by secret ballot; only the members present shall take part. Election shall be by an absolute majority of votes.

If no member receives an absolute majority, a second ballot shall take place. The member receiving the most votes shall then be elected. In the case of equal voting the member having precedence under Rule 3 shall be elected.

Rule 6

The President shall direct the work and preside at the meetings of the Commission.

Rule 7

The Vice-President shall take the place of the President if the latter is unable to carry out his duties or if the office of President is vacant.

Rule 8

If the President and Vice-President are at the same time unable to carry out their duties or if their offices are at the same time vacant, the duties of President shall be carried out by another member according to the order of precedence laid down in Rule 3.

Rule 9

If the President is a national of a High Contracting Party which is party to a case brought before the Commission, he shall relinquish the office of President in respect of that case.

Rule 10

If the President of the Commission for some special reason considers that he should relinquish the office of President in a particular case, he shall so inform the Vice-President or the member acting in his place.

CHAPTER III. SECRETARIAT OF THE COMMISSION

Rule 11

1. Pursuant to Article 37 of the Convention, the Secretariat of the Commission shall be provided by the Secretary-General of the Council of Europe.
2. The Secretary-General shall appoint the Secretary of the Commission.

Rule 12

The Secretary
   a. shall assist the Commission and its members in the fulfilment of their duties;
   b. shall be the channel for all communications concerning the Commission;
   c. shall have custody of the seals, stamps and archives of the Commission.

Rule 13

1. A special register shall be kept at the Secretariat in which all cases, relevant pleadings and exhibits shall be entered in the order of their submission and without intervening spaces or deletions. Nothing shall be written in the register in abbreviated form.
2. A note of the entry in the register shall be endorsed by the Secretary of the Commission on the original documents and, at the request of the parties, on copies presented by them for that purpose.
3. Entries in the register and the notes of entries provided for in paragraph (2) of this Rule shall have effect as certified matters of record.
4. The manner of keeping the register shall be laid down by the President in agreement with the Secretary.

Rule 14

The duties of the Secretariat shall be laid down by the President in agreement with the Secretary-General of the Council of Europe.

Rules 15 to 21 (deleted)

CHAPTER IV. THE WORKING OF THE COMMISSION

Rule 22

The seat of the Commission shall be at the seat of the Council of Europe at Strasbourg. The Commission or any of its organs may, however, if they think fit, carry out their duties elsewhere.

Rule 23

1. The Commission shall meet at the decision of the President when the latter considers that circumstances so require. It shall also meet if at least one third of its members so request.

2. Pursuant to Article 35 of the Convention, the Commission shall be convened by the Secretary-General of the Council of Europe.

Rule 24

The date and time of meetings shall be laid down by the President of the Commission.

Rule 25

A quorum of the Commission shall be nine members. However, seven members shall constitute a quorum when the Commission considers the admissibility of an applicaton submitted under Article 25 of the Convention and provided that the group of three members referred to in Rule 34 has unanimously reported that the application appears to be inadmissible.

Rule 26

Sessions of the Commission shall be held in camera.

Rule 27

1. The Commission shall deliberate in private. Its deliberations shall be and shall remain secret.

2. Only the members of the Commission shall take part in the deliberations of the Commission.

3. The Secretary shall as a rule be present at the deliberations. No other person may be admitted except by decision of the Commission.

Rule 28

Every member present at the deliberations shall state his opinion and the reasons therefor. The junior member according to the order of precedence laid down in Rule 3 shall speak first.

Rule 29

1. Subject to the provisions of Article 29 of the Convention, decisions of the Commission shall be taken by a majority of members present and voting.

2. The votes shall be cast in the inverse order to the order of precedence laid down in Rule 3.

3. If the voting is equal, the President shall have a casting vote.

Rule 30

The minutes of deliberations shall be secret; they shall be limited to a record of the subject of the discussions, the votes taken, the names of those voting for and against a motion and any statements expressly made for insertion in the minutes.

Rule 31

1. Members who are prevented by illness or other serious reason from taking part in the meetings shall, as soon as possible, give notice thereof to the Secretary of the Commission who shall inform the President.

2. If the President and a member who has been prevented from being present at the hearing of oral explanations by the parties, or the hearing of experts or witnesses, cannot reach a conclusion on the question whether or not that member shall take part in the deliberations or decision of the Commission subsequent to such hearing, the President shall refer the question for a decision by the Commission.

Rule 32

1. If a member for some special reason considers that he should not take part in the examination of a particular case, the President and the member concerned shall consult together. In the event of disagreement, the Commission shall decide.

2. If the President considers that a member should not, for some special reason, take part in the examination of a particular case, he shall so notify the member concerned and refer the question for a decision by the Commission.

Rule 33

Members of the Commission may not take part in the examination of any case in which they have previously acted as the agents, advisers or legal representatives of one of the parties or concerning which they have been required to state an opinion as members of a tribunal, commission of enquiry, or in any other capacity. In the event of doubt or dispute, the Commission shall decide.

Rule 34

1. The Commission shall, as circumstances require, constitute one or more groups, each consisting of three of its members, to carry out the duties laid down in Rule 45. It shall also appoint two substitute members for each group.

2. During the interval between sessions of the Commission, the President may, if necessary, either constitute a group or replace any member who is unable to take part in the work of a group already constitued.

3. The President of each group shall be the member of that group who has precedence under Rule 3.

TITLE II. PROCEDURE

CHAPTER I. GENERAL RULES

Rule 35

1. The official languages of the Commission shall be French and English.

2. The President may authorise a member to speak in another language.

Rule 36

1. The High Contracting Parties shall be represented before the Commission by their agents who may have the assistance of counsel or advocates.

2. The persons, non-governmental organisations and groups of individuals referred to in Article 25 of the Convention may represent their case in person before the Commission. They may be assisted or represented by a member of the Bar, by a solicitor or by a professor of law, or by any other lawyer approved by the Commission.

Rule 37

The Commission may, at the request of a party or of a person representing or assisting that party, permit the use by such party or person of a language other than English or French.

Rule 38

1. The Commission shall deal with cases in the order in which they become ready for hearing. It may, however, decide to give precedence to a particular case.

2. The Commission or, if it is not in session, its President may at the request of a party or *ex officio* order a case to be adjourned.

Rule 39

The Commission may, if it considers necessary, order the joinder of two or more cases.

CHAPTER II. INSTITUTION OF PROCEEDINGS

Rule 40

1. Any claims submitted under Article 24 or 25 of the Convention shall be submitted in the form of an application in writing and shall be signed by the applicant or his representative.

2. Where an application is submitted by a non-governmental organisation or by a group of individuals, it shall be signed by those persons competent to represent such organisation or group, if such organisation or group is properly constituted according to the laws of the State to which it is subject. The application shall in all other cases be signed by the persons composing the group submitting the application.

Rule 41

1. The application shall mention:
   a. the name of the applicant;
   b. the name of the High Contracting Party against which the claim is made;
   c. the object of the claim;
   d. as far as possible the provision of the Convention alleged to have been violated;

e. a statement of the facts and argument;

f. any attached documents.

2. The applicant shall provide information enabling it to be shown that the conditions laid down in Article 26 of the Convention have been satisifed.

Rule 42

Where the applicant intends to claim damages for an alleged injury, the amount of damages claimed may be stated in the application.

Rule 43

The Secretary-General of the Council of Europe shall transmit the application and any relevant documents to the President of the Commission.

Rule 44

Where, pursuant to Article 24 of the Convention, an application is brought before the Commission by a High Contracting Party, the President of the Commission shall through the Secretary-General of the Council of Europe give notice of such application to the High Contracting Party against which the claim is made and shall invite it to submit to the Commission its observations in writing on the admissibility of such application.

Rule 45

1. Any application submitted pursuant to Article 25 of the Convention shall be referred by the President of the Commission to the group of three members mentioned in Rule 34, which shall make a preliminary examination as to its admissibility. The group of three members shall then submit to the Commission a Report on such preliminary examination.

2. If the group of three members unanimously reports that the application appears to be admissible, the President of the Commission shall through the Secretary-General of the Council of Europe give notice of such application to the High Contracting Party against which the claim is made and shall invite it to submit to the Commission its observations in writing on the admissibility of such application.

3. If the group of three members does not unanimously report that the application appears to be admissible, the Commission shall consider the application and may

a. either, declare at once that the application is inadmissible,

b. or, through the Secretary-General of the Council of Europe give notice of such application to the High Contracting Party against which the claim is made and invite it to submit to the Commission its observations in writing on the admissibility of such application.

Rule 46

1. Except for the case provided for in Rule 45, paragraph (3) (a), the Commission, before it decides as to the admissibility of an application, may, if it thinks fit, invite the parties to submit to it their further comments in writing. It may also invite the parties to make oral explanations.

2. During the interval between sessions of the Commission, the President may, if he thinks fit, exercise the powers mentioned in paragraph (1) of this Rule.

3. The decision of the Commission in regard to the admissibility of the application shall be accompanied by reasons. The Secretary of the Commission shall communicate such decision to the applicant and, except for the case provided for in Rule 45, paragraph 3 (*a*), to the respondent party.

CHAPTER III. PROCEDURE AFTER THE ACCEPTANCE OF AN APPLICATION

Rule 47

When the Commission accepts an application, the President shall lay down the time-limits within which the parties shall file their submissions and evidence.

Rule 48

1. Each pleading shall be signed in the original by the party or its representative.

2. Each pleading shall be dated. For the purpose of determining any time-limits, the date of the filing of the pleading with the Secretariat-General of the Council of Europe shall alone be taken into consideration.

3. Any document submitted as an appendix and written in a language other than the official languages shall, unless the President otherwise decides, be accompanied by translation into one of the official languages. Translations of extracts may be submitted, however, in the case of lengthy documents. The Commission may at any time require a more complete translation or a certified translation to be submitted.

Rule 49 (deleted)

Rule 50

1. The Commission may take any measure which it considers expedient in order to carry out the duties laid down in Article 28 of the Convention.

2. The Commission shall take formal note of the refusal of a party to comply with such measures.

Rule 51

1. The Commission may charge one or more of its members to carry out an enquiry or any other form of investigation or to perform any other task necessary for the proper execution of its functions under Article 28 of the Convention. Such member or members shall duly report to the Commission.

2. The Commission may also appoint one of its members as rapporteur.

Rule 52 (deleted)

Rule 53

1. The Commission may put questions to the parties and request them to give explanations.

2. Each member of the Commission shall have the same right and shall give notice to the President if he wishes to exercise it.

Rule 54

1. The Commission may, at the request of a party of *proprio motu*, decide to hear as a witness or expert or in any other capacity any person whose evidence or statements seem likely to assist it in the carrying out of its task.

2. Any witness, expert or other person whom the Commission decides to hear shall be summoned by the Secretary. The summons shall indicate:

— the names, first names, occupation and domicile of the parties in the case;

— the facts or points regarding which the person concerned will be heard;

— the arrangements made, in accordance with paragraph 3, paragraph 4 or paragraph 5 of this Rule, to reimburse the person concerned for any expenses incurred by him.

3. The expenses incurred by any witness, expert or other person whom the Commission decides to hear at the request of a High Contracting Party shall be borne by that Party.

4. The expenses incurred by any witness, expert or other person whom the Commission decides to hear at the request of a person, non-governmental organisation or group of individuals which has referred a matter to the Commission under Article 25 of the Convention, shall be borne either by the applicant or by the Council of Europe as the Commission may decide. In the latter case they shall be fixed by the President.

5. The expenses incurred by any witness, expert or other person whom the Commission *proprio motu* decides to hear shall be fixed by the President and be borne by the Council of Europe.

6. Any witness, expert or other person whom the Commission decides to hear may, if he has not sufficient knowledge of English or French, be authorised by the President to speak in another language.

Rule 55

1. After establishing the identity of the witnesses or experts, the President or the member or members mentioned in Rule 51, paragraph 1, shall request them to take the following oath:

a. for witnesses: "I swear that I will speak the truth, the whole truth and nothing but the truth."

b. for experts: "I swear that my statement will be in accordance with my sincere belief."

2. Instead of taking the oath in the terms set out in paragraph (1) of this Rule, the witnesses or experts may make the following declaration:

a. for witnesses: "I solemnly declare upon my honour and conscience that I will speak the truth, the whole truth and nothing but the truth."

b. for experts: "I solemnly declare upon my honour and conscience that my statement will be in accordance with my sincere belief."

Rule 56

Questions may be put to the witnesses, experts or other persons mentioned in Rule 54, paragraph (1):
    a. by the President or any member of the Commission;
    b. by a party, with the permission of the President or of the member or members mentioned in Rule 51, paragraph 1.

Rule 57

Where, without good reason, a witness, expert or other person who has been duly required to appear, fails to appear or refuses to give evidence, the Secretary-General of the Council of Europe shall, at the request of the President, so inform that High Contracting Party to whose jurisdiction the person concerned is subject. The same provisions shall apply where a witness or expert has, in the opinion of the Commission, violated the oath or solemn declaration mentioned in Rule 55.

Rule 58

If the Commission considers that it is expedient to examine a case in a place other than the seat of the Council of Europe, it shall, through the Secretary-General of the Council of Europe, request any High Contracting Party concerned to grant it all necessary facilities, as mentioned in paragraph (*a*) of Article 28 of the Convention, in order that it may carry out its task.

Rule 59

The Secretariat shall draw up the minutes of the hearings. The minutes shall be signed by the President and by the Secretary. They shall constitute certified matters of record.

Rule 59a

Where the Commission decides to reject an application under Article 29 of the Convention, its decision shall be accompanied by reasons. The Secretary shall communicate the Commission's decision to the parties.

CHAPTER IV. THE REPORT OF THE COMMISSION

Rule 60

The Report provided for in Article 30 of the Convention shall contain:
    — the date on which it was drawn up;
    — the names of the President and members of the Commission;
    — a description of the parties;
    — the names of the representatives and counsel of the parties;
    — a statement of the facts;
    — the terms of the solution reached.

Rule 61

The Report referred to in Rule 60 shall be signed by the President and by the

Secretary. It shall be sent to the High Contracting Parties concerned, to the Committee of Ministers and to the Secretary-General of the Council of Europe for publication.

Rules 62 to 64 (deleted)

Rule 65

The Report provided for in Article 31 of the Convention shall be drawn up after deliberation by the Commission in plenary session.

Rule 66

The Report shall contain:
— the date on which it was drawn up;
— the names of the President and members who took part in the deliberation mentioned in Rule 65;
— a description of the parties;
— the names of the representatives and counsel of the parties;
— a statement of the proceedings;
— a statement of the facts;
— the opinion of the Commission as to whether the facts found disclose a breach by the High Contracting Party concerned of its obligations under the Convention;
— the reasons on which that opinion is based;
— a statement of the number of members forming the majority;
— any proposal which the Commission may consider appropriate.

Rule 67

Each member may, in accordance with paragraph (1) of Article 31 of the Convention, include in the Report a statement of his opinion.

Rule 68

Where the Commission decides to make proposals concerning damages as envisaged in Rule 42, it shall make them in pursuance of paragraph (3) of Article 31 of the Convention.

Rule 69

The Report and any proposals shall be signed by the President and by the Secretary. They shall be sent through the Secretary-General of the Council of Europe to the Committee of Ministers and only to those High Contracting Parties which are concerned.

Rule 70

During the period of three months following the transmission of the Report of the Committee of Ministers, the Commission shall consider at a plenary session whether or not to bring the case before the European Court of Human Rights in pursuance of Article 48, paragraph (a), of the Convention.

TITLE III. RELATIONS OF THE COMMISSION WITH THE COURT

Rule 71

The Commission shall assist the European Court of Human Rights in any case brought before the Court. For this purpose and in accordance with Rule 29, paragraph (1) of the Rules of Court, the Commission shall as soon as possible appoint, at a plenary session, one or more of its members to take part, as a delegate, in the consideration of the case before the Court. These delegates may be assisted by any person appointed by the Commission. In discharging their functions they shall act in accordance with such directives as they may receive from the Commission.

Rule 72

1. When, in pursuance of Article 48, paragraph (a) of the Convention, the Commission decides to bring a case before the Court, it shall, in accordance with Rule 31, paragraph (2) of the Rules of Court, draw up a request indicating in particular:
   a. the parties to the proceedings before the Commission;
   b. the date on which the Commission adopted its Report;
   c. the date on which, as certified by the Secretary of the Commission in a document attached to the request, the Report was transmitted to the Committee of Ministers;
   d. the names and addresses of its delegates.
2. The Secretary of the Commission shall transmit to the Registry of the Court thirty copies of the request referred to in paragraph (1) of this Rule.

Rule 73

When, in pursuance of Article 48, paragraph (b), (c) or (d) of the Convention, a High Contracting Party brings a case before the Court, the Secretary of the Commission shall communicate to the Registry of the Court as soon as possible:
   a. the names and addresses of the Commission's delegates;
   b. any other information which the Commission may consider appropriate.

Rule 74

The Secretary of the Commission shall, as soon as he has transmitted the request referred to in Rule 72, paragraph (2) above, or has received the communication mentioned in Rule 32, paragraph (1) (c) of the Rules of Court, file with the Registry of the Court an adequate number of copies of the Commission's Report.

Rule 75

The Commission shall communicate to the Court, at its request, any memorial, evidence, document or information concerning the case, with the exception of documents relating to the attempt to secure a friendly settlement in accordance with Article 28, paragraph (b) of the Convention. The communicaton of those documents shall be subject in each case to a decision of the Commission.

Rule 76

When a case brought before the Commission in pursuance of Article 25 of the Convention is subsequently referred to the Court, the Secretary of the Commission shall immediately notify the applicant. Unless the Commission shall otherwise decide, the Secretary shall also in due course communicate to him the Commission's Report, informing him that he may, within a time-limit fixed by the President, submit to the Commission his written observatons on the said Report. The Commission shall decide what action, if any, shall be taken in respect of those observations.

ADDENDUM TO RULES OF PROCEDURE

LEGAL AID

Rule 1

The Commission may, either at the request of an applicant lodging an application under Article 25 of the Convention or *proprio motu*, grant free legal aid to that applicant for the representation of his case before the Commission:

(*a*) where observations in writing on the admissibility of that application have been received from the respondent Government in pursuance of Rule 45, paragraphs 2 or 3 (*b*), or where the time-limit for their submission has expired, or

(*b*) where the application has been declared admissible.

Rule 2

Free legal aid shall only be granted where the Commission is satisfied:

(*a*) that it is essential for the proper discharge of the Commission's duties;

(*b*) that the applicant has not sufficient means to meet all or part of the costs involved.

Rule 3

(*a*) In order to determine whether or not the applicant has sufficient means to meet all or part of the costs involved, the Commission shall require him to complete a form of declaration stating his income, capital assets and any financial commitments in respect of dependents, or any other financial obligations. Such declaration shall be certified by the appropriate domestic authority or authorities.

(*b*) Before making a grant of free legal aid, the Commission shall request the respondent Government to submit its comments in writing.

(*c*) The Commission shall, after receiving the information mentioned in paragraphs (*a*) and (*b*), decide whether or not to grant free legal aid and shall inform the parties accordingly.

(*d*) The President shall fix the time-limits within which the parties shall be requested to supply the information referred to in this Rule.

Rule 4

(*a*) Fees shall by payable only to a barrister-at-law, solicitor or professionally qualified person of similar status. Fees may, where appropriate, be paid to more than one such lawyer as defined above.

(*b*) Legal aid may be granted to cover not only lawyers' fees but also travelling and subsistence expenses and other necessary out-of-pocket expenses incurred by the applicant or appointed lawyer.

Rule 5

(*a*) On the Commission deciding to grant legal aid, the Secretary shall, by agreement with the appointed lawyer, fix the rate of fees to be paid to him.

(*b*) The Secretary shall as soon as possible notify the Secretary-General of the Council of Europe of the rate of fees so agreed.

Rule 6

The Commission may, at any time, if it finds that the conditions set out in Rule 2 are no longer satisfied, revoke its grant of free legal aid to an applicant, in whole or in part, and shall at once notify the parties thereof.

3. EUROPEAN COURT OF HUMAN RIGHTS: RULES OF PROCEDURE (1982)

REVISED RULES OF COURT (ADOPTED ON 24 NOVEMBER 1982)

CONTENTS

Chapter III (The registry)

Rule 11 (Election of the Registrar)
Rule 12 (Election of the Deputy Registrar)
Rule 13 (Other staff, equipment and facilities)
Rule 14 (Functions of the Registrar)

Chapter IV (The working of the Court)

Rule 15 (Seat of the Court)
Rule 16 (Sessions of the plenary Court)
Rule 17 (Quorum)
Rule 18 (Public character of the hearings)
Rule 19 (Deliberations)
Rule 20 (Votes)

Chapter V (The Chambers)

Rule 21 (Composition of the Court when constituted in a Chamber)
Rule 22 (Substitute judges)
Rule 23 (*Ad hoc* judges)
Rule 24 (Inability to sit, withdrawal or exemption)
Rule 25 (Common interest)

Title II—(Procedure)

Chapter I (General rules)

Rule 26 (Possibility of particular derogations)
Rule 27 (Official languages)
Rule 28 (Representation of the Parties)
Rule 29 (Relations between the Court and the Commission and release of the report of the Commission)
Rule 30 (Representation)
Rule 31 (Communications, notifications and summonses addressed to persons other than the agents of the Parties or the Delegates of the Commission)

Chapter II (Institution of proceedings)

Rule 32 (Filing of the application or request)
Rule 33 (Communication of the application or request)
Rule 34 (Question whether a Contracting Party has the right to bring a case before the Court)
Rule 35 (Notice of composition of the Chamber)
Rule 36 (Interim measures)

Chapter III (Examination of cases)

Rule 37 (Written procedure)
Rule 38 (Fixing of the date of the opening of the oral proceedings)
Rule 39 (Conduct of the hearings)
Rule 40 (Measures for taking evidence)

The European Court of Human Rights,

Having regard to the Convention for the Protection of Human Rights and Fundamental Freedoms and the Protocols thereto;

Makes the present Rules:

Rule 1

(Definitions)

For the purposes of these Rules unless the context otherwise requires:

(a) the term "Convention" means the Convention for the Protection of Human Rights and Fundamental Freedoms and the Protocols thereto;

(b) the expression "Protocol No. 2" means Protocol No. 2 to the Convention conferring upon the European Court of Human Rights competence to give advisory opinions;

(c) the expression "plenary Court" means the European Court of Human Rights sitting in plenary session;

(d) the term "Chamber" means any Chamber constituted in pursuance of Article 43 of the Convention;

(e) the term "Court" means either the plenary Court or the Chambers;

(f) the expression "*ad hoc* judge" means any person, other than an elected judge, chosen by a Contracting Party in pursuance of Article 43 of the Convention to sit as a member of a Chamber;

(g) the term "judge" or "judges" means the judges elected by the Consultative Assembly of the Council of Europe or *ad hoc* judges;

(h) the term "Parties" means those Contracting Parties which are the Applicant and Respondent Parties;

(i) the term "Commission" means the European Commission of Human Rights;

(j) the expression "Delegates of the Commission" means the member or members of the Commission delegated by it to take part in the consideration of a case before the Court;

(k) the term "applicant" means:

—Title I and in Rules 49 and 52 of the present Rules, the person, non-governmental organisation or group of individuals who lodged a complaint with the Commission under Article 25 of the Convention;

—in Title II with the exception of Rules 49 and 52, such a person, organisation or group when he or it expressed the desire, in accordance with Rules 33, to take part in the proceedings pending before the Court.

(l) the expression "report of the Commission" means the report provided for in Article 31 of the Convention;

(m) the expression "Committee of Ministers" means the Committee of Ministers of the Council of Europe.

TITLE I

ORGANISATION AND WORKING OF THE COURT

CHAPTER 1

Judges

Rule 2

(Calculation of term of office)

1. The duration of the term of office of an elected judge shall be calculated as from his election. However, when a judge is re-elected on the expiry of his

term of office or is elected to replace a judge whose term of office has expired or is about to expire, the duration of his term of office shall, in either case, be calculated as from the date of such expiry.

2. In accordance with Article 40 § 5 of the Convention, a judge elected to replace a judge whose term of office has not expired shall hold office for the remainder of his predecessor's term.

3. In accordance with Article 40 § 6 of the Convention, an elected judge shall hold office until his successor has taken the oath or made the declaration provided for in Rule 3. Thereafter he shall continue to deal with any case in connection with which hearings or, failing that, deliberations have begun before him.

Rule 3

(Oath or solemn declaration)

1. Before taking up his duties, each elected judge shall, at the first sitting of the plenary Court at which he is present after his election or, in case of need, before the President, take the following oath or make the following solemn declaration:

"I swear"—or "I solemnly declare"—"that I will exercise my functions as a judge honourably, independently and impartially and that I will keep secret all deliberations."

2. This act shall be recorded in minutes.

Rule 4

(Obstacle to the exercise of the functions of judge)

A judge may not exercise his functions while he is a member of a Government or while he holds a post or exercises a profession which is incompatible with his independence and impartiality. In case of need the plenary Court shall decide.

Rule 5

(Precedence)

1. Elected judges shall take precedence after the President and the Vice-President according to the date of their election; in the event of re-election, even if it is not an immediate re-election, the length of time during which the judge concerned previously exercised his functions as a judge shall be taken into account.

2. Judges elected on the same date shall take precedence according to age.

3. *Ad hoc* judges shall take precedence after the elected judges according to age.

Rule 6

(Resignation)

Resignation of a judge shall be notified to the President who shall transmit it to the Secretary General of the Council of Europe. Subject to the provisions of Rules 2 § 3, resignation shall constitute vacation of office.

CHAPTER II

Presidency of the Court

Rule 7

(Election of the President and Vice-President)

1. The Court shall elect its President and Vice-President for a period of three years, provided that such period shall not exceed the duration of their term of office as judges. They may be re-elected.

2. The President and Vice-President shall continue to exercise their functions until the election of their respective successors.

3. If the President or Vice-President ceases to be a member of the Court or resigns his office before its normal expiry, the plenary Court shall elect a successor for the remainder of the term of that office.

4. The elections referred to in this Rules shall be by secret ballot; only the elected judges who are present shall take part. If no judge receives an absolute majority of the elected judges present, a ballot shall take place between the two judges who have received most votes. In the case of equal voting, preference shall be given to the judge having precedence in accordance with Rule 5.

Rule 8

(Functions of the President)

The President shall direct the work and administration of the Court and shall preside at its sessions. He shall represent the Court and, in particular, be responsible for its relations with the authorities of the Council of Europe.

Rule 9

(Functions of the Vice-President)

The Vice-President shall take the place of the President if the latter is unable to carry out his functions or if the office of President is vacant.

Rule 10

(Replacement of the President and Vice-President)

If the President and Vice-President are at the same time unable to carry out their functions or if their offices are at the same time vacant, the office of President shall be assumed by another elected judge in accordance with the order of precedence provided for in Rule 5.

CHAPTER III

The registry

Rule 11

(Election of the Registrar)

1. The plenary Court shall elect its Registrar after the President has in this respect consulted the Secretary General of the Council of Europe. The candi-

dates must possess the legal knowledge and the experience necessary to carry out the functions attaching to the post and must have an adequate working knowledge of the two official languages of the Court.

2. The Registrar shall be elected for a term of seven years. He may be re-elected.

3. The elections referred to in this Rule shall be by secret ballot; only the elected judges who are present shall take part. If no candidate receives an absolute majority of the elected judges present, a ballot shall take place between the two candidates who have received most votes. In the case of equal voting, preference shall be given to the older candidate.

4. Before taking up his functions, the Registrar shall take the following oath or make the following solemn declaration before the plenary Court or, if it is not in session, before the President:

"I swear"—or "I solemnly declare"—"that I will exercise loyally, discreetly and conscientiously the functions conferred upon me as Registrar of the European Court of Human Rights."

This act shall be recorded in minutes.

Rule 12

(Election of the Deputy Registrar)

1. The plenary Court shall also elect a Deputy Registrar according to the conditions and in the manner and for the term prescribed in Rule 11. It shall first consult the Registrar.

2. Before taking up his functions, the Deputy Registrar shall take an oath or make a solemn declaration before the plenary Court, or, if it is not in session, before the President, in similar terms to those prescribed in respect of the Registrar. This act shall be recorded in minutes.

Rule 13

(Other staff, equipment and facilities)

The President, or the Registrar on his behalf, shall request the Secretary General of the Council of Europe to provide the Registrar with the staff, permanent or temporary, equipment and facilities necessary for the Court.

The officials of the registry, other than the Registrar and the Deputy Registrar, shall be appointed by the Secretary General, with the agreement of the President or of the Registrar acting on the President's instructions.

Rule 14

(Functions of the Registrar)

1. The Registrar shall assist the Court in the performance of its functions. He shall be responsible for the organisation and activities of the registry under the authority of the President.

2. The Registrar shall have the custody of the archives of the Court and shall

be the channel for all communications and notifications made by, or addressed to, the Court in connection with the cases brought or to be brought before it.

3. The Registrar shall ensure that the dates of despatch and receipt of any communciation or notification relating to the above-mentioned cases may be easily verified. Communications or notifications addressed to the Agents of the Parties, to the Delegates of the Commission or to the representative, if any, of the applicant shall be considered as having been addressed to the Parties, to the Commission or to the applicant, as the case may be. The date of receipt shall be noted on each document received by the Registrar who shall transmit to the sender a receipt bearing this date and the number under which the document has been registered.

4. The Registrar shall, subject to the discretion attaching to his functions, reply to requests for information concerning the work of the Court, in particular from the press. He shall announce the date and time fixed for the hearings in open Court and shall be responsible for making immediately available to the public all judgments delivered by the Court.

5. General instructions drawn up by the Registrar and sanctioned by the President shall provide for the working of the registry.

CHAPTER IV

The Working of the Court

Rule 15

(Seat of the Court)

The seat of the European Court of Human Rights shall be at the seat of the Council of Europe at Strasbourg. The Court may, however, if it considers it expedient, exercise its functions elsewhere in the territories of the member States of the Council of Europe.

Rule 16

(Sessions of the plenary Court)

The plenary sessions of the Court shall be convened by the President whenever the exercise of its functions under the Convention and under these Rules so requires. The President shall convene a plenary session if at least one third of the members of the Court so request, and in any event once a year to consider administrative matters.

Rule 17

(Quorum)

1. The quorum of the plenary Court shall be twelve judges.
2. If there is no quorum, the President shall adjourn the sitting.

Rule 18

(Public character of the hearings)

The hearings shall be public, unless the Court shall in exceptional circumstances decide otherwise.

Rule 19

(Deliberations)

1. The Court shall deliberate in private. Its deliberations shall remain secret.

2. Only the judges shall take part in the deliberations. The Registrar or his substitute, as well as such other officials of the registry and interpreters whose assistance is deemed necessary, shall be present. No other person may be admitted except by special decision of the Court.

3. Each judge present at such deliberations shall state his opinion and the reasons therefor.

4. Any question which is to be voted upon shall be formulated in precise terms in the two official languages and the text shall, if a judge so requests, be distributed before the vote is taken.

5. The minutes of the private sittings of the Court for deliberations shall remain secret; they shall be limited to a record of the subject of the discussions, the votes taken, the names of those voting for and against a motion and any statements expressly made for insertion in the minutes.

Rule 20

(Votes)

1. The decisions of the Court shall be taken by the majority of judges present.

2. The votes shall be cast in the inverse order to the order of precedence provided for in Rule 5.

3. If the voting is equal, the President shall have a second and casting vote.

CHAPTER V

The Chambers

Rule 21

(Composition of the Court when constituted in a Chamber)

1. When a case is brought before the Court either by the Commission or by a Contracting State having the right to do so under Article 48 of the Convention, the Court shall be constituted in a Chamber of seven jduges.

2. On the reference of a case to the Court, the Registrar shall notify all the judges, including the newly-elected judges, that such a Chamber is to be constituted. If any judge, upon receiving such notification, believes that for one of the reasons set out in Rule 24 he will be unable to sit, he shall so inform the Registrar. The President shall then draw up the list of judges available to constitute the Chamber.

3. There shall sit as members *ex officio* of the Chamber:

(a) in accordance with Article 43 of the Convention, every judge who has the nationality of a Party;

(b) the President of the Court or, failing him, the Vice-President, provided that they do not sit by virtue of the preceding sub-paragraph.

4. The other judges named on the list provided for in paragraph 2 shall be called upon to complete the Chamber, as members or as substitutes, in the order determined by a drawing of lots effected by the President of the Court in the presence of the Registrar.

5. The President of the Chamber shall be the judge sitting by virtue of paragraph 3 (b) or, failing one, a judge appointed under paragraph 4 as a member of the Chamber, in accordance with the order of precedence provided for in Rule 5.

If the President of the Chamber is unable to sit or withdraws, he shall be replaced by the Vice-President or, if the same applies to him, by a judge appointed under paragraph 4 as a member of the Chamber, in accordance with the said order of precedence. However, where he is unable to sit or withdraws less than 24 hours before the opening of, or during or after, the hearings, his place shall be taken, in accordance with the said order of precedence, by one of the judges called upon to be present or present at the hearings.

6. If the President of the Court finds that two cases concern the same Party or Parties and raise similar issues, he may refer the second case to the Chamber already constituted, or in the course of constitution, for the consideration of the first case or, if there is none, proceed to the constitution of one Chamber to consider both cases.

Rule 22

(Substitute judges)

1. The substitute judges shall be called upon, in the order determined by the drawing of lots, to replace the judges appointed as members of the Chamber by virtue of Rule 21 § 4.

2. Judges who have been so replaced shall cease to be members of the Chamber.

3. The substitute judges shall be supplied with the documents relating to the proceedings. The President may convoke one or more of them, according to the above order of precedence, to attend the hearings and deliberations.

Rule 23

(Ad hoc *judges*)

1. If the Court does not include an elected judge having the nationality of a Party or if the judge called upon to sit in that capacity is unable to sit or withdraws, the President of the Court shall invite that Party to inform him within thirty days whether it wishes to appoint to sit as judge either another elected judge or, as an *ad hoc* judge, any other person possessing the qualifications required under Article 39 § 3 of the Convention and, if so, to state at the same time the name of the person so appointed. The same rule shall apply if the person so appointed is unable to sit or withdraws.

2. The Party concerned shall be presumed to have waived such right of appointment if it does not reply within thirty days.

3. An *ad hoc* judge shall, at the opening of the first sitting fixed for the

consideration of the case after he has been appointed, take the oath or make the solemn declaration provided for in Rule 3. This act shall be recorded in minutes.

Rule 24

(Inability to sit, withdrawal or exemption)

1. Any judge who is prevented from taking in sittings for which he has been convoked shall, as soon as possible, give notice thereof to the President of the Chamber or to the Registrar.

2. A judge may not take part in the consideration of any case in which he has a personal interest or has previously acted either as the agent, advocate or adviser of a Party or of a person having an interest in the case, or as member of a tribunal or commission of enquiry, or in any other capacity.

3. If a judge withdraws for one of the said reasons, or for some special reason, he shall inform the President who shall exempt him from sitting.

4. If the President considers that a reason exists for a judge to withdraw, he shall consult with the judge concerned; in the event of disagreement, the Court shall decide.

5. Any judge who has been called upon to sit on one or more recent cases may, at his own request, be exempted by the President from sitting on a new case.

Rule 25

(Common interest)

1. If several Parties have a common interest, they shall for the purposes of the provisions of this Chapter, be deemed to be one Party. The President of the Court shall invite them to agree to appoint a single elected judge or *ad hoc* judge in accordance with Article 43 of the Convention. If the parties are unable to agree, the President shall choose by lot, from among the persons proposed as judges by these Parties, the judge called upon to sit *ex officio*. The names of the other judges and substitute judges shall then be chosen by lot by the President from among the elected judges who are not nationals of any of these Parties.

2. In the event of dispute as to the existence of a common interest, the plenary Court shall decide.

TITLE II

PROCEDURE

CHAPTER I

General Rules

Rule 26

(Possibility of particular derogations)

The provisions of this Title shall not prevent the Court from derogating from the consideration of a particular case with the agreement of the Party or Parties and after having consulted the Delegates of the Commission and the applicant.

Rule 27

(Official languages)

1. The official languages of the Court shall be English and French.

2. A Party may, not later than the consultation provided for in Rule 38, apply to the President for leave to use another language at the oral hearings. If such leave is granted by the President, the Party concerned shall be responsible for the interpretation into English or French of the oral arguments or statements made by its Agent, advocates or advisers and shall, to the extent which the President may determine in each case, bear the other extra expenses involved in the use of a non-official language.

3. The President may grant the applicant, as well as any person assisting the Delegates under Rule 29 § 1, leave to use a non-official language. In that event, the Registrar shall make the necessary arrangements for the translation or interpretation into English and French of their comments or statements.

4. Any witness, expert or other person appearing before the Court may use his own language if he does not have sufficient knowledge of either of the two official languages. The Registrar shall, in that event, make the necessary arrangements for the interpretation into English and French of the statements of the witness, expert or other person concerned.

5. All judgments shall be given in English and in French; unless the Court decides otherwise, both texts shall be authentic.

Rule 28

(Representation of the Parties)

The Parties shall be represented by Agents who may have the assistance of advocates or advisers.

Rule 29

(Relations between the Court and the Commission and release of the report of the Commission)

1. The Commission shall delegate one or more of its membes to take part in the consideration of a case before the Court. The Delegates may be assisted by other persons.

2. The Court shall, whether a case is referred to it by a Contracting Party or by the Commission, take into consideration the report of the latter.

3. Unless the President decides otherwise, the said report shall be made available to the public through the Registrar as soon as possible after the case has been brought before the Court.

Rule 30

(Representation of the applicant)

1. The applicant shall be represented by an advocate authorised to practise in any of the Contracting States and resident in the territory of one of them, or by any other person approved by the President. The President may, however,

give leave to the applicant to present his own case, subject, if need be, to his being assisted by an advocate or other person as aforesaid.

2. Unless the President decides otherwise, the advocate or other person representing or assisting the applicant, or the applicant himself if he seeks leave to present his own case, must have an adequate knowledge of one of the Court's official languages.

Rule 31

(Communications, notifications and summonses addressed to persons other than the Agents of the Parties or the Delegates of the Commission)

1. If, for any communication, notification or summons addressed to persons other than the Agents of the Parties or the Delegates of the Commission, the Court considers it necessary to have the assistance of the Government of the State on whose territory such communication, notification or summons is to have effect, the President shall apply directly to that Government in order to obtain the necessary facilities.

2. The same rule shall apply when the Court desires to make or arrange for the making of an investigation on the spot in order to establish the facts or to procure evidence or when it orders the appearance of a person resident in, or having to cross, that territory.

CHAPTER II

Institution of proceedings

Rule 32

(Filing of the application or request)

1. Any Contracting Party which intends to bring a case before the Court under Article 48 of the Convention shall file with the registry an application, in forty copies, indicating
   a. the parties to the proceedings before the Commission,
   b. the date on which the Commission adopted its report,
   c. the date on which the report was transmitted to the Committee of Ministers,
   d. the object of the application,
   e. the name and address of the person appointed as Agent.

2. If the Commission intends to bring a case before the Cuort under Article 48 of the Convention, it shall file with the registry a request, in forty copies, signed by its President and containing the particulars indicated in sub-paragraphs (a), (b), (c) and (d) of paragraph 1 of this Rule together with the names and addresses of the Delegates of the Commission.

Rule 33

(Communication of the application or request)

1. On receipt of an application or request, the Registrar shall transmit a copy thereof:

a. to the President, Vice-President and judges, and also, as the case may be,

b. to any Contracting Party mentioned in Article 48 of the Convention,

c. to the Commission,

d. to the person, non-governmental organisation or group of individuals who lodged the complaint with the Commission under Article 25 of the Convention.

He shall also inform the Committee of Ministers, through the Secretary General of the Council of Europe, of the filing of the application or request.

2. The communications provided for in sub-paragraphs (a), (b) and (d) of paragraph 1 shall include a copy of the report of the Commission.

3. When making the communications provided for in sub-paragraph (b), (c) and (d) of paragraph 1, the Registrar shall invite;

a. the Contracting Party against which the complaint has been lodged before the Commission to notify him within two weeks of the name and address of its Agent;

b. any other Contracting Party which appears to have the right, under Article 48 of the Convention, to bring a case before the Court and which has not availed itself of that right, to inform him within four weeks whether it wishes to take part in the proceedings and, if so, to notify him at the same time of the name and address of its Agent;

c. the Commission to notify him as soon as possible of the names and addresses of its Delegates;

d. the person, non-governmental organisation or group of individuals who lodged the complaint with the Commission under Article 25 of the Convention to notify him within two weeks

— whether he or it wishes to take part in the proceedings pending before the Court;

— if so, of the name and address of the person appointed by him or it in accordance with Rule 30.

Rule 34

(Question whether a Contracting Party has the right to bring a case before the Court)

In the event of doubt or dispute as to whether a Contracting Party has the right under Article 48 of the Convention to bring a case before the Court, the President shall submit that question to the plenary Court for decision.

Rule 35

(Notice of composition of the Chamber)

As soon as a Chamber has been constituted for the consideration of a case, the Registrar shall communicate its composition to the judges, to the Agents of the Parties, to the Commission and to the applicant.

Rule 36

(Interim measures)

1. Before the constitution of a Chamber, the President of the Court may, at

the request of a Party, of the Commission, of the applicant or of any other person concerned, or *proprio motu*, indicate to the Parties any interim measure which it is advisable for them to adopt. The Chamber when constituted or, if the Chamber is not in session, its President shall have the same power.

2. Notice of these measures shall be immediately given to the Committee of Ministers.

CHAPTER III

Examination of cases

Rule 37

(Written procedure)

1. The President of the Chamber shall consult the Agents of the Parties, the Delegates of the Commission, or, if the latter have not yet been appointed, the President of the Commission, and the applicant on whether they each consider a written procedure to be necessary. If they so consider, he shall lay down the time-limits for the filing of the memorial or memorials or other documents.

2. The President may, in the interest of the proper administration of justice, invite or grant leave to any Contracting State which is not a party to the proceedings to submit written comments within a time-limit and on issues which he shall specify. He may extend such an invitation or grant such leave to any person concerned other than the applicant.

3. Where two cases have been referred to the same Chamber under Rule 21 § 6, the President of the Chamber may, in the interest of the proper administration of justice and after consulting the Agents of the Parties, the Delegates of the Commission and the applicants, order that the proceedings in both cases be conducted simultaneously, without prejudice to the decision of the Chamber on the joinder of the cases.

4. Memorials, comments and documents annexed thereto shall be filed with the registry; they shall be filed in forty copies when they are submitted by a Party, by another State or by the Commission. The Registrar shall transmit copies thereof to the judges, to the Agents of the Parties, to the Delegates of the Commission and to the applicant, as the case may be.

Rule 38

(Fixing of the date of the opening of the oral proceedings)

The President of the Chamber shall, after consulting the Agents of the Parties, the Delegates of the Commission and the applicant, fix the date of the opening of the oral proceedings. The Registrar shall notify them of the decision taken in this respect.

Rule 39

(Conduct of the hearings)

The President of the Chamber shall direct the hearings. He shall prescribe the order in which the Agents, advocates or advisers of the Parties, the Delegates of the Commission, any person assisting the Delegates in accordance with Rule 29 § 1 and the applicant shall be called upon to speak.

Rule 40

(Measures for taking evidence)

1. The Chamber may, at the request of a Party, of the Delegates of the Commission, of the applicant or of a third party invited or granted leave to submit written comments under Rule 37 § 2, or *proprio motu*, obtain any evidence which it considers capable of providing clarification on the facts of the case. The Chamber may, *inter alia*, decide to hear as a witness or expert or in any other capacity any person whose evidence or statements seem likely to assist it in the carrying out of its task.

When the Chamber is not in session, the President of the Chamber may exercise, by way of preparatory measure, the powers set forth in the immediately foregoing sub-paragraph, without prejudice to the decision of the Chamber on the relevance of the evidence so taken or sought.

2. The Chamber may ask any person or institution of its choice to obtain information, express an opinion or make a report, upon any specific point.

3. Where a report drawn up in accordance with the preceding paragraphs has been prepared at the request of a Party, the costs relating thereto shall be borne by that Party unless the Chamber decides otherwise. In other cases, the Chamber shall decide whether such costs are to be borne by the Council of Europe, or awarded against an applicant, or a third party, at whose request the report was prepared. In all cases, the cost shall be taxed by the President.

4. The Chamber may, at any time during the proceedings, depute one or more of its members to conduct an enquiry, carry out an investigation on the spot or take evidence in some other manner.

Rule 41

(Convocation of witnesses, experts and other persons; costs of their appearance)

1. Witnesses, experts or other persons whom the Chamber or the President of the Chamber decides to hear shall be summoned by the Registrar. If they appear at the request of a Party, the costs of their appearance shall be borne by that Party unless the Chamber decides otherwise. In other cases, the Chamber shall decide whether such costs are to be borne by the Council of Europe or awarded against an applicant, or a third party within the meaning of Rule 40 § 1, at whose request the person summoned appeared. In all cases, the costs shall, if need be, be taxed by the President.

2. The summons shall indicate:

— the case in connection with which it has been issued;

— the object of the enquiry, expert opinion or other measure ordered by the Chamber or the President of the Chamber;

— any provisions for the payment of the sum due to the person summoned.

Rule 42

(Oath or solemn declaration by witnesses and experts)

1. After the establishment of his identity and before giving evidence, every witness shall take the following oath or make the following solemn declaration:

"I swear"—or "I solemnly declare upon my honour and con-science"—"that I will speak the truth, the whole truth and nothing but the truth."

This act shall be recorded in minutes.

2. After the estabilshment of his identity and before carrying out his task, every expert shall take the following oath or make the following solemn declaration:

"I swear"—or "I solemnly declare"—"that I will discharge my duty as expert honourably and conscientiously."

This act shall be recorded in minutes.

This oath may be taken or this declaration made before the President of the Chamber, or before a judge or any public authority nominated by the President.

Rule 43

(Objection to a witness or expert; hearing of a person for purpose of information)

The Chamber shall decide in the event of any dispute arising from an objection to a witness or expert. It may hear for the purpose of information a person who cannot be heard as a witness

Rule 44

(Questions put during the hearings)

1. The President or any judge may put questions to the Agents, advocates or advisers of the Parties, to the witnesses and experts, to the Delegates of the Commission, to the applicant and to any other persons appearing before the Chamber.

2. The witnesses, experts and other persons referred to in Rule 40 § 1 may, subject to the control of the President, be examined by the Agents, advocates or advisers of the Parties, by the Delegates of the Commission, by any person assisting the Delegates in accordance with Rule 29 § 1 and by the applicant. In the event of an objection as the the relevance of a question put, the Chamber shall decide.

Rule 45

(Failure to appear or false evidence)

When, without good reason, a witness or any other person who has been duly summoned fails to appear or refuses to give evidence, the Registrar shall, on being so required by the President, inform that Contracting Party to whose jurisdiction such witness or other person is subject. The same provisions shall apply when a witness or expert has, in the opinion of the Chamber, violated the oath or solemn declaration provided for in Rule 42.

Rule 46

(Shorthand verbatim record of hearings)

1. The Registrar shall be responsible for the making of a shorthand verbatim record of each hearing. The verbatim record shall include:
   a. the composition of the Chamber at the hearing;
   b. a list of those appearing before the Court, that is to say, Agents, advocates and advisers of the Parties, Delegates of the Commission and persons assisting them, applicants, Contracting States and other persons referred to in Rule 37 § 2;
   c. the surnames, forenames, description and residence of each witness, expert or other person heard;
   d. the text of statements made, questions put and replies given;
   e. the text of any decision delivered by the Chamber during the hearing.
2. The Agents, advocates and advisers of the parties, the Delegates of the Commission, the applicant and the witnesses, experts and other persons mentioned in Rules 29 § 1 and 40 § 1 shall receive the verbatim record of their arguments, statements or evidence, in order that they may, subject to the control of the Registrar or the President of the Chamber, make corrections, but in no case may such corrections affect the sense and bearing of what was said. The Registrar, in accordance with the instructions of the President, shall fix the time-limits granted for this purpose.
3. The verbatim record, once so corrected, shall constitute certified matters of record.

Rule 47

(Preliminary objections)

1. A Party wishing to raise a preliminary objection must file a statement setting out the objection and the grounds therefor not later than the time when that Party informs the President of its intention not to submit a memorial or, alternatively, not later than the expiry of the time-limit laid down under Rule 37 § 1 for the filing of its first memorial.
2. Unless the Chamber decides otherwise, the filing of a preliminary objection shall not have the effect of suspending the proceedings on the merits. In all cases, the Chamber shall, after following the procedure provided for under Chapter III herein, give its decision on the objection or join the objection to the merits.

Rule 48

(Striking out of the list)

1. When the Party which has brought the case before the Court notifies the

Registrar of its intention not to proceed with the case and when the other Parties agree to such discontinuance, the Chamber shall, after consulting the Commission and the applicant, decide whether or not it is appropriate to approve the discontinuance and accordingly to strike the case out of its list.

2. When the Chamber is informed of a friendly settlement, arrangement or other fact of a kind to provide a solution of the matter, it may, after consulting, if necessary, the Parties, the Delegates of the Commission and the applicant, strike the case out of the list.

3. The striking out of a case shall be effected by means of a judgment which the President shall forward to the Committee of Ministers in order to allow them to supervise, in accordance with Article 54 of the Convention, the execution of any undertakings which may have been attached to the discontinuance or solution of the matter.

4. The Chamber may, having regard to the responsibilities of the Court under Article 19 of the Convention, decide that, notwithstanding the notice of discontinuance, friendly settlement, arrangement or other fact referred to in paragraphs 1 and 2 of this Rule, it should proceed with the consideration of the case.

Rule 49

(Question of the application of Article 50 of the Convention)

1. If proposals or comments on the application of Article 50 of the Convention have not been submitted to the Court in the document instituting proceedings, they may be submitted by a Party, by the Commission or by the applicant at any stage of the written or oral procedure.

2. The Chamber may, at any time during the proceedings, invite any party, the Commission and the applicant to submit comments on this question.

Rule 50

(Relinquishment of jurisdiction by the Chamber in favour of the plenary Court)

1. Where a case pending before a Chamber raises one or more serious questions affecting the interpretation of the Convention, the Chamber may, at any time during the proceedings, relinquish jurisdiction in favour of the plenary Court. The relinquishment of jurisdiction shall be obligatory where the resolution of such question or questions might have a result inconsistent with a judgment previously delivered by a Chamber or the plenary Court. Reasons need not be given for the decision to relinquish jurisdiction.

2. The plenary Court, when the case has been referred to it, may either retain jurisdiction over the whole case or may, after deciding the said question or questions, order that the case be referred back to the Chamber which shall, in regard to the remaining part of the case, recover its original jurisdiction.

3. Any provisions governing the Chambers shall apply, *mutatis mutandis*, to proceedings before the plenary Court.

4. When a case pending before a Chamber is referred to the plenary Court under paragraph 1 above, any *ad hoc* judge who is a member of that Chamber shall sit as a judge on the plenary Court.

CHAPTER IV

Judgments

Rule 51

(Procedure by default)

Where a party fails to appear or to present its case, the Chamber shall, subject to the provisions of Rule 48, give a decision in the case.

Rule 52

(Contents of the judgment)

1. The judgment shall contain:

a. the names of the President and the judges constituting the Chamber, and also the names of the Registrar and, where appropriate, the Deputy Registrar;

b. the dates on which it was adopted and delivered;

c. a description of the Party or Parties;

d. the names of the Agents, advocates or advisers of the Party or Parties;

e. the names of the Delegates of the Commission and of the persons assisting them;

f. the name of the applicant;

g. an account of the procedure followed;

h. the final submissions of the Party or Parties and, if any, of the Delegates of the Commission and of the applicant;

i. the facts of the case;

j. the reasons in point of law;

k. the operative provisions of the judgment;

l. the decision, if any, in respect of costs;

m. the number of judges constituting the majority;

n. where appropriate, a statement as to which of the two texts, English or French, is authentic.

2. Any judge who has taken part in the consideration of the case shall be entitled to annex to the judgment either a separate opinion, concurring with or dissenting from that judgment, or a bare statement of dissent.

Rule 53

(Judgment on the application of Article 50 of the Convention)

1. Where the Chamber finds that there is a breach of the Convention, it shall give in the same judgment a decision on the application of Article 50 of the Convention if that question, after being raised under Rule 49, ready for decision, if the question is not ready for decision, the Chamber shall reserve it in whole or in part and shall fix the further procedure. If, on the other hand, this question has not been raised under Rule 49, the Chamber shall lay down a time-limit within which it may be raised by any Party, by the Commission or by the applicant.

2. For the purposes of ruling on the application of Article 50 of the Convention, the Chamber shall, as far as possible, be composed of those judges who sat to consider the merits of the case. Those judges who have ceased to be members of the Court shall be recalled in order to deal with the question in accordance with Article 40 § 6 of the Convention; however, in the event of death, inability to sit, withdrawal or exemption from sitting, the judge concerned shall be replaced in the same manner as was applied for his appointment to the Chamber.

3. When the judgment finding a breach has been delivered under Rule 50 and does not contain a ruling on the application of Article 50 of the Convention, the plenary Court may decide, without prejudice to the provisions of paragraph 1 above, to refer the question back to the Chamber.

4. If the Court is informed that an agreement has been reached between the injured Party and the Party liable, it shall verify the equitable nature of such agreement and, where it finds the agreement to be equitable, strike the case out of the list by means of a judgment. Rule 48 § 3 shall apply in such circumstances.

Rule 54

(Signature, delivery and notification of the judgment)

1. The judgment shall be signed by the President and by the Registrar.

2. The judgment shall be read out by the President, or by another judge delegated by him, at a public hearing in one of the two official languages. It shall not be necessary for the other judges to be present. The Agents of the Parties, the Delegates of the Commission and the applicant shall be informed in due time of the date and time of delivery of the judgment.

However, in respect of a judgment striking a case out of the list or relating to the application of Article 50 of the Convention, the President may direct that the notification provided for under paragraph 4 of this Rule shall count as delivery.

3. The judgment shall be transmitted by the President to the Committee of Ministers.

4. The original copy, duly signed and sealed, shall be placed in the archives of the Court. The Registrar shall send certified copies to the Party or Parties, to the Commission, to the applicant, to the Secretary General of the Council of Europe, to the Contracting States and persons referred to in Rule 37 § 2 and to any other person directly concerned.

Rule 55

(Publication of judgments and other documents)

1. The Registrar shall be responsible for the publication of:
   — judgments of the Court;
   — documents relating to the proceedings, including the report of the Commission but excluding any document which the President considers unnecessary to publish;
   — verbatim records of public hearings;
   — any document which the President considers useful to publish.

Publications shall take place in the two official languages in the case of judgments, applications or requests instituting proceedings and the Commission's reports; the other documents shall be published in the official language in which they occur in the proceedings.

2. Documents deposited with the Registrar and not published shall be accessible to the public unless decided by the President either on his own initiative or at the request of a Party, of the Commission, of the applicant or of any other person concerned.

Rule 56

(Request for interpretation of a judgment)

1. A Party of the Commission may request the interpretation of a judgment within a period of three years following the delivery of that judgment.

2. The request shall state precisely the point or points in the operative provisions of the judgment on which interpretation is required. It shall be filed with the registry in forty copies.

3. The Registrar shall communicate the request, as appropriate, to any other Party, to the Commission and to the applicant, and shall invite them to submit any written comments within a time-limit laid down by the President of the Chamber. The President of the Chamber shall also fix the date of the hearing should the Chamber decide to hold one.

Written comments shall be filed with the registry, they shall be filed in forty copies when they are submitted by a Party or by the Commission.

4. The request for interpretation shall be considered by the Chamber which gave the judgment and which shall, as far as possible, be composed of the same judges. Those judges who have ceased to be members of the Court shall be recalled in order to deal with the case in accordance with Article 40 § 6 of the Convention; however, in the event of death, inability to sit, withdrawal or exemption from sitting, the judge concerned shall be replaced in the same manner as was applied for his appointment to the Chamber.

5. The Chamber shall decide by means of a judgment.

Rule 57

(Request for revision of a judgment)

1. A Party or the Commission may, in the event of the discovery of a fact which might by its nature have a decisive influence and which, when a judgment was delivered, was unknown both to the Court and to that Party or the Commission, request the Court, within a period of six months after that Party or the Commission, as the case may be, acquired knowledge of such fact, to revise that judgment.

2. The request shall mention the judgment of which the revision is requested and shall contain the information necessary to show that the conditions laid down in paragraph 1 have been complied with. It shall be accompanied by the original or a copy of all supporting documents. The request and supporting documents shall be filed with the registry in forty copies.

3. The Registrar shall communicate the request, as appropriate, to any other

Party, to the Commission and to the applicant, and shall invite them to submit any written comments within a time-limit laid down by the President. The President shall also fix the date of the hearing should the Chamber decide to hold one.

Written comments shall be filed with the registry; they shall be filed in forty copies if they are submitted by a Party or by the Commission.

4. The request for revision shall be considered by a Chamber constituted in accordance with Article 43 of the Convention, which shall decide whether the request is admissible or not under paragraph 1 of this Rule. In the affirmative, the Chamber shall refer the request to the Chamber which gave the original judgment or, if in the circumstances that is not reasonably possible, it shall retain the request and examine the merits thereof.

5. The Chamber decide by means of a judgment.

CHAPTER V

Advisory opinions

Rule 58

In proceedings in regard to advisory opinions the Court shall, in addition to the provisions of Protocol No. 2, apply the provisions which follow. It shall also apply the other provisions of these Rules to the extent to which it considers this to be appropriate.

Rule 59

The request for an advisory opinion shall be filed with the registry in forty copies. It shall state fully and precisely the question on which the opinion of the Court is sought, and also

a. the date on which the Committee of Ministers adopted the decision referred to in Article 1 § 3 of Protocol No. 2;

b. the names and addresses of the person or persons appointed by the Committee of Ministers to give the Court any explanations which it may require.

The request shall be accompanied by all documents likely to elucidate the question.

Rule 60

1. On receipt of a request, the Registrar shall transmit a copy thereof to the President, Vice-President and judges, as well as to the Commission.

2. He shall inform the Contracting Parties that the Court is prepared to receive their written comments. The President may decide that, by reason of the nature of the question, a similar invitation is to be sent to the Commission.

Rule 61

1. The President shall lay down the time-limits for the filing of written comments or other documents.

2. Written comments or other documents shall be filed with the registry in

sixty copies. The Registrar shall transmit copies thereof to the President, Vice-President and judges, to the Committee of Ministers, to each of the Contracting Parties and to the Commission.

Rule 62

After the closure of the written procedure, the President shall decide whether the Contracting Parties or the Commission which have submitted written comments are to be given an opportunity to develop them at an oral hearing held for the purpose.

Rule 63

If the Court considers that the request for an advisory opinion is not within its consultative competence as defined in Article 1 of Protocol No. 2 it shall so declare in a reasoned decision.

Rule 64

1. Advisory opinions shall be given by majority vote of the plenary Court. They shall mention the number of judges constituting the majority.

2. Any judge may, if he so desires, attach to the opinion of the Court either a separate opinion, concurring with or dissenting from the advisory opinion, or a bare statement of dissent.

Rule 65

The advisory opinion shall be read out by the President, or by another judge delegated by him, at a public hearing in one of the two official languages, prior notice having been given to the Committee of Ministers, to each of the Contracting Parties and to the Commission.

Rule 66

The opinion, as well as any decision given under Rule 63, shall be signed by the President and by the Registrar. The original copy, duly signed and sealed, shall be placed in the archives of the Court. The Registrar shall send certified copies to the Committee of Ministers, to the Contracting Parties, to the Commission and to the Secretary General of the Council of Europe.

Rule 67

(Final clause)

The present Rules shall enter into force on 1 January 1983. They shall, however, apply only to cases brought before the Court after that date.

ADDENDUM

Rules on Legal Aid to Applicants

The European Court of Human Rights,

Having regard to the Convention for the Protection of Human Rights and Fundamental Freedoms and the Protocols thereto,

Having regard to the Rules of Court,
Adopts the present Addendum to the Rules of Court.

Rule 1

(Definitions)

1. For the purposes of the present addendum
   a. the term "applicant" is to be understood as meaning the person, non-governmental organisation or group of individuals who, after lodging a complaint with the Commission under Article 25 of the Convention, has expressed the desire, in accordance with Rule 33 of the Rules of Court, to take part in the proceedings before the Court;
   b. the term "President" is to be understood as meaning the President of the Court until the constitution of the Chamber or in the event of relinquishment of jurisdiction under Rule 50 of the Rules of Court, and the President of the Chamber in all other instances.
2. Subject to the foregoing, the terms used herein shall, unless the context otherwise requires, have the same meaning as they have in the Rules of Court.

Rule 2

(Requests for information regarding legal aid before the Commission)

1. Unless the information is already available to him, the Registrar shall enquire whether or not the applicant applied for, and, if so, whether or not he was granted legal aid in connection with the representation of his case before the Commission pursuant to the addendum to the Rules of Procedure of the Commission.
2. At the same time the Registrar may, on the instructions of the President, ask the Commission to produce to the Court the file relating to the grant or refusal, if any, of legal aid to the applicant.

Rule 3

(Continuation in force of a grant made by the Commission)

1. Subject to the provisions of Rule 5 herein, where the applicant has been granted legal aid in connection with the representation of his case before the Commission, that grant shall continue in force for the purposes of his representation before the Court.
2. The President may, however, instruct the Registrar to obtain from the applicant information evidencing that the conditions laid down in Rule 4 § 2 herein are fulfilled. The Registrar shall bring any information so obtained to the attention of the Agents of the Parties and the Delegates of the Commission, in order to give them the opportunity to verify its correctness.

Rule 4

(Grant of legal aid by the President)

1. Where the applicant did not receive a grant of legal aid in connection with the representation of his case before the Commission or had such a grant

revoked, the President may at any time, at the request of the applicant, grant free legal aid to the applicant for the purposes of his representation before the Court.

2. Legal aid may be so granted only where the President is satisfied that

a. the applicant lacks sufficient means to meet all or part of the costs involved; and

b. such a course is necessary for the proper conduct of the case before the Court.

3. In order to determine whether or not the applicant lacks the sufficient means, the Registrar shall ask him to complete a form of declaration stating his income, capital assets and any financial commitments in respect of dependants, or any other financial obligations. Such declaration shall be certified by the appropriate domestic authority or authorities. This certified declaration may be replaced by a certificate of indigence delivered by the appropriate domestic authority or authorities as listed in the appendix to this addendum.

4. Before the President makes a grant of legal aid, the Registrar shall request the Agents of the Parties and the Delegates of the Commission to submit their comments in writing.

5. After receiving the information mentioned in paragraphs 3 and 4 and, if appropriate, Rule 2 § 2 above, the President shall decide whether or not legal aid is to be granted and to what extent. The Registrar shall notify the applicant, the Agents of the Parties and the Delegates of the Commission accordingly.

6. The Registrar, on the instructions of the President, shall fix the time-limits within which the information referred to in this Rule is to be supplied.

Rule 5

(Revocation or variation of a grant)

The President may, if he is satisfied that the conditions stated in Rule 4 § 2 are no longer fulfilled, at any time revoke or vary, in whole or in part, a grant of legal aid made or continued in force under the present addendum. The Registrar shall at once notify the applicant, the Agents of the Parties and the Delegates of the Commission accordingly.

Rule 6

(Fees and expenses payable)

1. Fees shall be payable only to the advocates or other persons appointed in accordance with Rule 30 of the Rules of Court.

2. Legal aid may be granted to cover not only fees for representation but also travelling and subsistence expenses and other necessary out-of-pocket expenses incurred by the applicants or by their representatives.

3. After consulting the representatives, the Registrar shall, on the instructions of the President, fix the amount of fees to be paid. The Registrar shall also in each case decide what particular expenses referred to above at paragraph 2 are to be covered by the grant of legal aid.

Rule 7

(Derogation from procedural requirements)

In case of urgency, the President may sanction a derogation from the procedural requirements of this addendum provided that the derogation in question is essential for the proper conduct of the case before the Court.

Rule 8

(Entry into force and transitional arrangements)

This addendum shall come into force at a date to be fixed by the President of the Court. Pending such entry into force, the grant of legal aid to an application in connection with the representation of his case before the Court shall continue to be governed by the addendum to the Rules of Procedure of the Commission.

4. EUROPEAN SOCIAL CHARTER (1961)

INTRODUCTION

The European Social Charter was signed on October 18, 1961 and came into effect in February, 1965. Providing for social and economic rights, the Charter was designed to supplement and complement the European Convention on Human Rights which was primarily concerned with political and civil rights.

The nineteen rights promulgated by the European Social Charter include:

Art. 1.	Right to work
Art. 2.	Right to just working conditions
Art. 3.	Right to safe and healthy working conditions
Art. 4.	Right to fair remuneration
Art. 5.	Right to establish labor organizations
Art. 6.	Right to bargain collectively
Art. 7.	Special rights for children and young persons
Art. 8.	Special rights for employed women
Art. 9.	Vocational guidance rights
Art. 10.	Vocational training rights
Art. 11.	Right to health protection
Art. 12.	Social security rights
Art. 13.	Right to social and medical assistance
Art. 14.	Right to benefit from social welfare services

Art. 15.   Special rights for the physically or mentally disabled

Art. 16.   Right of the family to social, legal and economic protection

Art. 17.   Special rights for mothers and children

Art. 18.   Right to engage in a gainful occupation in the territories of other contracting parties

Art. 19.   Rights of migrant workers

These nineteen rights constitute the social policies of the Charter, but all are not necessarily binding. Each Contracting Party is considered bound by not less than ten articles or 45 numbered paragraphs of Part II which must include at least five of seven key articles of the Charter: Articles 1, 5, 6, 12, 13, 16 and 19.

Securing these rights involves a complex system of supervision and administration based on the submission and evaluation of biennial reports. Each Contracting Party must submit a report covering the scope of the provisions to which it adheres. Copies of such reports are then sent to various national employers' and workers' organizations for comment and criticism. These organizations in turn may request that such reports be forwarded to the Secretary General of the Council of Europe. Independent experts also examine these reports and send their evaluations to the Governmental Committee which then transmits its report to the Parliamentary Assembly. An Assembly opinion is then given to the Committee of Ministers suggesting measures which could be taken by the nation involved to ensure proper application. Article 29 authorizes two-thirds of the Committee of Ministers to make any necessary recommendations.

European Treaty Series, No 48; 12 European Yearbook 397.

The Governments signatory hereto, being Members of the Council of Europe,

Considering that the aim of the Council of Europe is the achievement of greater unity between its Members for the purpose of safeguarding and realizing the ideals and principles which are their common heritage and of facilitating their economic and social progress, in particular by the maintenance and further realization of human rights and fundamental freedoms;

Considering that in the European Convention for the Protection of Human Rights and Fundamental Freedoms signed at Rome on 4th November 1950, and the Protocol thereto signed at Paris on 20th March 1952, the member States of the Council of Europe agreed to secure to their populations the civil and political rights and freedoms therein specified;

Considering that the enjoyment of social rights should be secured without discrimination on grounds of race, colour, sex, religion, political opinion, national extraction or social origin;

Being resolved to make every effort in common to improve the standard of living and to promote the social well-being of both their urban and rural populations by means of appropriate institutions and action,

Have agreed as follows:

PART I

The Contracting Parties accept as the aim of their policy, to be pursued by all approriate means, both national and international in character, the attainment of conditions in which the following rights and principles may be effectively realized:

(1) Everyone shall have the opportunity to earn his living in an occupation freely entered upon.

(2) All workers have the right to just conditions of work.

(3) All workers have the right to safe and healthy working conditions.

(4) All workers have the right to a fair remuneration sufficient for a decent standard of living for themselves and their families.

(5) All workers and employers have the right to freedom of association in national or international organizations for the protection of their economic and social interests.

(6) All workers and employers have the right to bargain collectively.

(7) Children and young persons have the right to a special protection against the physical and moral hazards to which they are exposed.

(8) Employed women, in case of maternity, and other employed women as appropriate, have the right to a special protection in their work.

(9) Everyone has the right to appropriate facilities for vocational guidance with a view to helping him choose an occupation suited to his personal aptitude and interests.

(10) Everyone has the right to appropriate facilities for vocational training.

(11) Everyone has the right to benefit from any measures enabling him to enjoy the highest possible standard of health attainable.

(12) All workers and their dependents have the right to social security.

(13) Anyone without adequate resources has the right to social and medical assistance.

(14) Everyone has the right to benefit from social welfare services.

(15) Disabled persons have the right to vocational training, rehabilitation and resettlement, whatever the origin and nature of their disability.

(16) The family as a fundamental unit of society has the right to appropriate social, legal and economic protection to ensure its full development.

(17) Mothers and children, irrespective of marital status and family relations, have the right to appropriate social and economic protection.

(18) The nationals of any one of the Contracting Parties have the right to engage in any gainful occupation in the territory of any one of the others on a footing of equality with the nationals of the latter, subject to restrictions based on cogent economic or social reasons.

(19) Migrant workers who are nationals of a Contracting Party and their families have the right to protection and assistance in the territory of any other Contracting Party.

PART II

The Contracting Parties undertake, as provided for in Part III, to consider themselves bound by the obligations laid down in the following articles and paragraphs.

The Right to Work

Article 1

With a view to ensuring the effective exercise of the right to work, the Contracting Parties undertake:

(1) to accept as one of their primary aims and responsibilities the achievement and maintenance of as high and stable a level of employment as possible, with a view to the attainment of full employment;

(2) to protect effectively the right of the worker to earn his living in an occpuation freely entered upon;

(3) to establish or maintain free employment services for all workers;

(4) to provide or promote appropriate vocational guidance, training and rehabilitation.

The Right to Just Conditions of Work

Article 2

With a view to ensuring the effective exercise of the right to just conditions of work, the Contracting Parties undertake:

(1) to provide for reasonable daily and weekly working hours, the working week to be progressively reduced to the extent that the increase of productivity and other relevant factors permit;

(2) to provide for public holidays with pay;

(3) to provide for a minimum of two weeks annual holiday with pay;

(4) to provide for additional paid holidays or reduced working hours for workers engaged in dangerous or unhealthy occupations as prescribed;

(5) to ensure a weekly rest period which shall, as far as possible, coincide with the day recognized by tradition or custom in the country or region concerned as a day of rest.

The Right to Safe and Healthy Working Conditions

Article 3

With a view to ensuring the effective exercise of the right to safe and healthy working conditions, the Contracting Parties undertake:

(1) to issue safety and health regulations;

(2) to provide for the enforcement of such regulations by measures of supervision;

(3) to consult, as appropriate, employers' and workers' organizations on measures intended to improve industrial safety and health.

The Right to a Fair Remuneration

Article 4

With a view to ensuring the effective exercise of the right to a fair remuneration, the Contracting Parties undertake:

(1) to recognize the right of workers to a remuneration such as will give them and their families a decent standard of living;

(2) to recognize the right of workers to an increased rate of remuneration for overtime work subject to exceptions in particular cases;

(3) to recognize the right of men and women workers to equal pay for work of equal value;

(4) to recognize the right of all workers to a reasonable period of notice for termination of employment;

(5) to permit deductions from wages only under conditions and to the extent prescribed by national laws or regulations or fixed by collective agreements or arbitration awards.

The exercise of these rights shall be achieved by freely concluded collective agreements, by statutory wave-fixing machinery, or by other means appropriate to national conditions.

The Right to Organize

Article 5

With a view to ensuring or promoting the freedom of workers and employers to form local, national or international organizations for the protection of their economic and social interests and to join those organizations, the Contracting Parties undertake that national law shall not be such as to impair, nor shall it be so applied as to impair, this freedom. The extent to which the guarantees provided for in this article shall apply to the police shall be determined by national laws or regulations. The principle governing the application to the members of the armed forces of these guarantees and the extent to which they shall apply to persons in this category shall equally be determined by national laws or regulations.

The Right to Bargain Collectively

Article 6

With a view to ensuring the effective exercise of the right to bargain collectively, the Contracting Parties undertake:

(1) to promote joint consultation between workers and employers;

(2) to promote, where necessary and appropriate, machinery for voluntary negotiations between employers or employers' organizations and workers' organizations, with a view to the regulation of terms and conditions of employment by means of collective agreements;

(3) to promote the establishment and use of appropriate machinery for conciliation and voluntary arbitration for the settlement of labour disputes;

and recognize:

(4) the right to workers and employers to collective action in cases of conflicts of interest, including the right to strike, subject to obligations that might arise out of collective agreements previously entered into.

The Right of Children and Young Persons to Protection

Article 7

With a view to ensuring the effective exercise of the right of children and young persons to protection, the Contracting Parties undertake:

(1) to provide that the minimum age of admission to employment shall be 15 years, subject to exceptions for children employed in prescribed light work without harm to their health, morals or education;

(2) to provide that a higher minimum age of admission to employment shall be fixed with respect to prescribed occupations regarded as dangerous or unhealthy;

(3) to provide that persons who are still subject to compulsory education shall not be employed in such work as would deprive them of the full benefits of their education;

(4) to provide that the working hours of persons under 16 years of age shall be limited in accordance with the needs of their development, and particuarly with their need for vocational training;

(5) to recognize the right of young workers and apprentices to a fair wage or other appropriate allowances;

(6) to provide that the time spent by young persons in vocational training during the normal working hours with the consent of the employer shall be treated as forming part of the working day;

(7) to provide that employed persons of under 18 years of age shall be entitled to not less than three weeks' annual holiday with pay;

(8) to provide that persons under 18 years of age shall not be employed in night work with the exception of certain occupations provided for by national laws or regulations;

(9) to provide that persons under 18 years of age employed in occupations prescribed by national laws or regulations shall be subject to regular medical control;

(10) to ensure special protection against physical and moral dangers to which children and young persons are exposed, and particularly against those resulting directly or indirectly from their work.

The Right of Employed Women to Protection

Article 8

With a view to ensuring the effective exercise of the right of employed women to protection, the Contracting Parties undertake:

(1) to provide either by paid leave, by adequate social security benefits or by benefits from public funds for women to take leave before and after childbirth up to a total of at least 12 weeks;

(2) to consider it as unlawful for an employer to give a woman notice of dismissal during her absence on maternity leave or to give her notice of dismissal at such a time that the notice would expire during such absence;

(3) to provide that mothers who are nursing their infants shall be entitled to sufficient time off for this purpose;

(4) (*a*) to regulate the employment of women workers on night work in industrial employment;

(*b*) to prohibit the employment of women workers in underground mining, and, as appropriate, on all other work which is unsuitable for them by reason of its dangerous, unhealthy, or arduous nature.

The Right to Vocational Guidance

Article 9

With a view to ensuring the effective exercise of the right to vocational guidance, the Contracting Parties undertake to provide or promote, as necessary, a service which will assist all persons, including the handicapped, to solve problems related to occupational choice and progress, with due regard to the individual's characteristics and their relation to occupational opportunity; this assistance should be available free of charge, both to young persons, including school children, and to adults.

The Right to Vocational Training

Article 10

With a view to ensuring the effective exercise of the right to vocational training, the Contracting Parties undertake:

(1) to provide or promote, as necessary, the technical and vocational training of all persons, including the handicapped, in consultation with employers' and workers' organizations, and to grant facilities for access to higher technical and university education, based solely on individual aptitude;

(2) to provide or promote a system of apprenticeship and other systematic arrangements for training young boys and girls in their various employments:

(3) to provide or promote, as necessary:

    a. adequate and readily available training facilities for adult workers;

    b. special facilities for the re-training of adult workers needed as a result of technological development or new trends in employment;

(4) to encourage the full utilization of the facilities provided by appropriate measures such as:

    a. reducing or abolishing any fees or charges;

    b. granting financial assistance in appropriate cases;

    c. including in the normal working hours time spent on supplementary training taken by the worker, at the request of his employer, during employment;

    d. ensuring, through adequate supervision, in consultation with the employers' and workers' organizations, the efficiency of apprenticeship and other training arrangements for young workers, and the adequate protection of young workers generally.

The Right to Protection of Health

Article 11

With a view to ensuring the effective exercise of the right to protection of health, the Contracting Parties undertake, either directly or in co-operation with public or private organizations, to take appropriate measures designed *inter alia*:

(1) to remove as far as possible the cases of ill-health;

(2) to provide advisory and educational facilities for the promotion of health and the encouragement of individual responsibility in matters of health;

(3) to prevent as far as possible epidemic, endemic and other dieseases.

The Right to Social Security

Article 12

With a view to ensuring the effective exercise of the right to social security, the Contracting Parties undertake:

(1) to establish or maintain a system of social security;

(2) to maintain the social security system at a satisfactory level at least equal to that required for ratification of International Labour Convention (No. 102) Concerning Minimum Standards of Social Security;

(3) to endeavour to raise progressively the system of social security to a higher level;

(4) to take steps, by the conclusion of appropriate bilateral and multilateral agreements, or by other means, and subject to the conditions laid down in such agreements, in order to ensure:

(*a*) equal treatment with their own nationals of the nationals of other Contracting Parties in respect of social security rights, including the retention of benefits arising out of social security legislation, whatever movements the persons protected may undertake between the territories of the Contracting Parties.

(*b*) the granting, maintenance and resumption of social security rights by such means as the accumulation of insurance or employment periods completed under the legislation of each of the Contracting Parties.

The Right to Social and Medical Assistance

Article 13

With a view to ensuring the effective exercise of the right to social and medical assistance, the Contracting Parties undertake:

(1) to ensure that any person who is without adequate resources and who is unable to secure such resources either by his own efforts or from other sources, in particular by benefits under a social security scheme, be granted adequate assistance, and, in case of sickness, the care necessitated by his condition;

(2) to ensure that persons receiving such assistance shall not, for that reason, suffer from a diminution of their political or social rights;

(3) to provide that everyone may receive by appropriate public or private services such advice and personal help as may be required to prevent, to remove, or to alleviate personal or family want:

(4) to apply the provisions referred to in paragraphs 1, 2 and 3 of this article on an equal footing with their nationals to nationals of other Contracting Parties lawfully within their territories, in accordance with their obligations under the European Convention on Social and Medical Assistance, signed at Paris on 11th December 1953.[54]

The Right to Benefit from Social Welfare Services

Article 14

With a view to ensuring the effective exercise of the right to benefit from social welfare services, the Contracting Parties undertake:

(1) to promote or provide services which, by using methods of social work, would contribute to the welfare and development of both individuals and groups in the community, and to their adjustment to the social environment;

(2) to encourage the participation of individuals and voluntary or other organizations in the establishment and maintenance of such services.

The Right of Physically or Mentally Disabled Persons to Vocational Training, Rehabilitation and Social Resettlement

Article 15

With a view to ensuring the effective exercise of the right of the physically or mentally disabled to vocational training, rehabilitation and resettlement, the Contracting Parties undertake:

(1) to take adequate measures for the provision of training facilities, including, where necessary, specialized institutions, public or private;

(2) to take adequate measures for the placing of disabled persons in employment, such as specialized placing services, facilities for sheltered employment and measures to encourage employers to admit disabled persons to employment.

The Right of the Family to Social, Legal and Economic Protection

Article 16

With a view to ensuring the necessary conditions for the full development of the family, which is a fundamental unit of society, the Contracting Parties undertake to promote the economic, legal and social protection of family life by such means as social and family benefits, fiscal arrangements, provision of family housing, benefits for the newly married, and other appropriate means.

The Right of Mothers and Children to Social and Economic Protection

Article 17

With a view to ensuring the effective exercise of the right of mothers and children to social and economic protection, the Contracting Parties will take all appropriate and necessary measures to that end, including the establishment or maintenance of appropriate institutions or services.

The Right to Engage in a Gainful Occupation in the Territory of Other Contracting Parties

Article 18

With a view to ensuring the effective exercise of the right to engage in a gainful occupation in the territory of any other Contracting Party, the Contracting Parties undertake:

(1) to apply existing regulations in a spirit of liberality;

(2) to simplify existing formalities and to reduce or abolish chancery dues and other charges payable by foreign workers or their employers;

(3) to liberalize, individually or collectively, regulations governing the employment of foreign workers;

and recognize:

(4) the right of their nationals to leave the country to engage in a gainful occupation in the territories of the other Contracting Parties.

The Right of Migrant Workers and their Families to Protection and Assistance

Article 19

With a view to ensuring the effective exercise of the right of migrant workers and their families to protection and assistance in the territory of any other Contracting Party, the Contracting Parties undertake:

(1) to maintain or to satisfy themselves that there are maintained adequate and free services to assist such workers, particularly in obtaining accurate information, and to take all appropriate steps, so far as national laws and regulations permit, against misleading propaganda relating to emigration and immigration;

(2) to adopt appropriate measures within their own jurisdiction to facilitate the departure, journey and reception of such workers and their families, and to provide within their own jurisdiction, appropriate services for health, medical attention and good hygienic conditions during the journey;

(3) to promote co-operation, as appropriate, between social services, public and private, in emigration and immigration countries;

(4) to secure for such workers lawfully within their territories, in so far as such matters are regulated by law or regulations or are subject to the control of administrative authorities, treatment not less favourable than that of their own nationals in respect of the following matters:

    a. remuneration and other employment and working conditions;

    b. membership of trade unions and enjoyment of the benefits of collective bargaining;

    c. accommodation;

(5) to secure for such workers lawfully within their territories treatment not less favourable than that of their own nationals with regard to employment taxes, dues or contributions payable in respect of employed persons;

(6) to facilitate as far as possible the reunion of the family of a foreign worker permitted to establish himself in the territory;

(7) to secure for such workers lawfully within their territories treatment not less favourable than that of their own nationals in respect of legal proceedings relating to matters referred to in this article;

(8) to secure that such workers lawfully residing within their territories are not expelled unless they endanger national security or offend against public interest or morality;

(9) to permit, within legal limits, the transfer of such parts of the earnings and savings of such workers as they may desire;

(10) to extend the protection and assistance provided for in this article to self-employed migrants in so far as such measures apply.

PART III

Undertakings

Article 20

1. Each of the Contracting Parties undertakes:

a. to consider Part I of this Charter as a declaration of the aims which it will pursue by all appropriate means, as stated in the introductory paragraph of that Part;

b. to consider itself bound by at least five of the following articles of Part II of this Charter: Articles 1, 5, 6, 12, 13, 16 and 19;

c. in addition to the articles selected by it in accordance with the preceeding sub-paragraphs, to consider itself bound by such a number of articles or numbered paragraphs of Part II of the Charter as it may select, provided that the total number of articles or numbered paragraphs by which it is bound is not less than 10 articles or 45 numbered paragraphs.

2. The articles or paragraphs selected in accordance with sub-paragraphs (*b*) and (*c*) of paragraph 1 of this article shall be notified to the Secretary-General of the Council of Europe at the time when the instrument of ratification or approval of the Contracting Party concerned is deposited.

3. Any Contracting Party may, at a later date, declare by notification to the Secretary-General that it considers itself bound by any articles or any numbered paragraphs of Part II of the Charter which it has not already accepted under the terms of paragraph 1 of this article. Such undertakings subsequently given shall be deemed to be an integral part of the ratification or approval, and shall have the same effect as from the thirtieth day after the date of the notification.

4. The Secretary-General shall communicate to all the signatory Governments and to the Director-General of the International Labour Office any notification which he shall have received pursuant to this Part of the Charter.

5. Each Contracting Party shall maintain a system of labour inspection appropriate to national conditions.

PART IV

Reports concerning Accepted Provisions

Article 21

The Contracting Parties shall send to the Secretary-General of the Council of Europe a report at two-yearly intervals, in a form to be determined by the Committee of Ministers, concerning the application of such provisions of Part II of the Charter as they have accepted.

Reports concerning Provisions which are not accepted

Article 22

The Contracting Parties shall send to the Secretary-General, at appropriate intervals as requested by the Committee of Ministers, reports relating to the provisions of Part II of the Charter which they did not accept at the time of their ratification or approval or in a subsequent notification. The Committee of Ministers shall determine from time to time in respect of which provisions such reports shall be requested and the form of the reports to be provided.

Communication of Copies

Article 23

1. Each Contracting Party shall communicate copies of its reports referred to

in Articles 21 and 22 to such of its national organizations as are members of the international organizations of employers and trade unions to be invited under Article 27, paragraph 2, to be represented at meetings of the Sub-committee of the Governmental Social Committee.

2. The Contracting Parties shall forward to the Secretary-General any comments on the said reports received from these national organizations, if so requested by them.

Examination of the Reports

Article 24

The reports sent to the Secretary-General in accordance with Articles 21 and 22 shall be examined by a Committee of Experts, who shall have also before them any comments forwarded to the Secretary-General in accordance with paragraph 2 of Article 23.

Committee of Experts

Article 25

1. The Committee of Experts shall consist of not more than seven members appointed by the Committee of Ministers from a list of independent experts of the highest integrity and of recognized competence in international social questions, nominated by the Contracting Parties.

2. The members of the Committee shall be appointed for a period for six years. They may be reappointed. However, of the members first appointed, the terms of office of two members shall expire at the end of four years.

3. The members whose terms of office are to expire at the end of the intiial period of four years shall be chosen by lot by the Committee of Ministers immediately after the first appointment has been made.

4. A member of the Committee of Experts appointed to replace a member whose term of office has not expired shall hold office for the remainder of his predecessor's term.

Participation of the International Labour Organization

Article 26

The International Labour Organization shall be invited to nominate a representative to participate in a consultative capacity in the deliberations of the Committee of Experts.

Sub-Committee of the Governmental Social Committee

Article 27

1. The reports of the Contracting Parties and the conclusions of the Committee of Experts shall be submitted for examination to a Sub-committee of the Governmental Social Committee of the Council of Europe.

2. The Sub-committee shall be composed of one representative of each of the Contracting Parties. It shall invite no more than two international organiza-

tions of employers and no more than two international trade union organizations as it may designate to be represented as observers in a consultative capacity at its meetings. Moreover, it may consult no more than two representatives of international non-governmental organizations having consultative status with the Council of Europe, in respect of questions with which the organizations are particularly qualified to deal, such as social welfare, and the economic and social protection of the family.

3. The Sub-committee shall present to the Committee of Ministers a report containing its conclusions and append the report of the Committee of Experts.

Consultative Assembly

Article 28

The Secretary-General of the Council of Europe shall transmit to the Consultative Assembly the conclusions of the Committee of Experts. The Consultative Assembly shall communicate its views on these Conclusions to the Committee of Ministers.

Committee of Ministers

Article 29

By a majority of two-thirds of the members entitled to sit on the Committee, the Committee of Ministers may, on the basis of the report of the Sub-committee, and after consultation with the Consultative Assembly, make to each Contracting Party any necessary recommendations.

PART V

Derogations in Time of War or Public Emergency

Article 30

1. In time of war or other public emergency threatening the life of the nation any Contracting Party may take measures derogating from its obligations under this Charter to the extent strictly required by the exigencies of the situation, provided that such measures are not inconsistent with its other obligations under international law.

2. Any Contracting Party which has availed itself of this right of derogation shall, within a reasonable lapse of time, keep the Secretary-General of the Council of Europe fully informed of the measures taken and of the reasons therefor. It shall likewise inform the Secretary-General when such measures have ceased to operate and the provisions of the Charter which it has accepted are again being fully executed.

3. The Secretary-General shall in turn inform other Contracting Parties and the Director-General of the International Labour Office of all communications received in accordance with paragraph 2 of this article.

Restrictions

Article 31

1. The rights and principles set forth in Part I when effectively realized, and

their effective exercise as provided for in Part II, shall not be subject to any restrictions or limitations not specified in those Parts, except such as are prescribed by law and are necessary in a democratic society for the protection of the rights and freedoms of others or for the protection of public interest, national security, public health, or morals.

2. The restrictions permitted under this Charter to the rights and obligations set forth herein shall not be applied for any purpose other than that for which they have been prescribed.

Relations between the Charter and Domestic Law or International Agreements

Article 32

The provisions of this Charter shall not prejudice the provisions of domestic law or of any bilateral or multilateral treaties, conventions or agreements which are already in force, or may come into force, under which more favourable treatment would be accorded to the persons protected.

Implementation by Collective Agreements

Article 33

1. In member States where the provisions of paragraphs 1, 2, 3, 4 and 5 of Article 2, paragraphs 4, 6 and 7 of Article 7 and paragraphs 1, 2, 3, and 4 of Article 10 of Part II of this Charter are matters normally left to agreements between employers or employers' organizations and workers' organizations, or are normally carried out otherwise than by law, the undertakings of those paragraphs may be given and compliance with them shall be treated as effective if their provisions are applied through such agreements or other means to the great majority of the workers concerned.

2. In member States where these provisions are normally the subject of legislation, the undertakings concerned may likewise be given, and compliance with them shall be regarded as effective if the provisions are applied by law to the great majority of the workers concerned.

Territorial Application

Article 34

1. This Charter shall apply to the metropolitan territory of each Contracting Party. Each signatory Government may, at the time of signature or of the deposit of its instrument of ratification or approval, specify, by declaration addressed to the Secretary-General of the Council of Europe, the territory which shall be considered to be its metropolitan territory for this purpose.

2. Any Contracting Party may, at the time of ratification or approval of this Charter or at any time thereafter, declare by notification addressed to the Secretary-General of the Council of Europe, that the Charter shall extend in whole or in part to a non-metropolitan territory or territories specified in the said declaration for whose international relations it is responsible or for which it assumes international responsibility. It shall specify in the declaration the

Articles or paragraphs of Part II of the Charter which it accepts as binding in respect of the territories named in the declaration.

3. The Charter shall extend to the territory or territories named in the aforesaid declarations as from the thirtieth day after the date on which the Secretary-General shall have received notification of such declaration.

4. Any Contracting Party may declare at a later date by notification addressed to the Secretary-General of the Council of Europe, that, in respect of one or more of the territories to which the Charter has been extended in accordance with paragraph 2 of this article, it accepts as binding any articles or any numbered paragraphs which it has not already accepted in respect of that territory or territories. Such undertakings subsequently given shall be deemed to be an integral part of the original declaration in respect of the territory concerned, and shall have the same effect as from the thirtieth day after the date of the notification.

5. The Secretary-General shall communicate to the other signatory Governments and to the Director-General of the International Labour Office any notification transmitted to him in accordance with this article.

Signature, Ratification and Entry into Force

Article 35

1. This Charter shall be open for signature by the Members of the Council of Europe. It shall be ratified or approved. Instruments of ratification or approval shall be deposited with the Secretary-General of the Council of Europe.

2. This Charter shall come into force as from the thirtieth day after the date of deposit of the fifth instrument of ratification or approval.

3. In respect of any signatory Government ratifying subsequently, the Charter shall come into force as from the thirtieth day after the date of deposit of its instrument of ratification or approval.

4. The Secretary-General shall notify all the Members of the Council of Europe and the Director-General of the International Labour Office, of the entry into force of the Charter, the names of the Contracting Parties which have ratified or approved it and the subsequent deposit of any instruments of ratification or approval.

Amendments

Article 36

Any Member of the Council of Europe may propose amendments to this Charter in a communication addressed to the Secretary-General of the Council of Europe. The Secretary-General shall transmit to the other Members of the Council of Europe any amendments so proposed, which shall then be considered by the Committee of Ministers and submitted to the Consultative Assembly for opinion. Any amendments approved by the Committee of Ministers shall enter into force as from the thirtieth day after all the Contracting Parties have informed the Secretary-General of their acceptance. The Secretary-General shall notify all the Members of the Council of Europe and the Director-General of the International Labour Office of the entry into force of such amendments.

Denunciation

Article 37

1. Any Contracting Party may denounce this Charter only at the end of a period of five years from the date on which the Charter entered into force for it, or at the end of any successive period of two years, and, in each case, after giving six months notice to the Secretary-General of the Council of Europe, who shall inform the other Parties and the Director-General of the International Labour Office accordingly. Such denunciation shall not affect the validity of the Charter in respect of the other Contracting Parties provided that at all times there are not less than five such Contracting Parties.

2. Any Contracting Party may, in accordance with the provisions set out in the preceding paragraph, denounce any article or paragraph of Part II of the Charter accepted by it provided that the number of articles or paragraphs by which this Contracting Party is bound shall never be less than 10 in the former case and 45 in the latter and that this number of articles or paragraphs shall continue to include the articles selected by the Contracting Party among those to which special reference is made in Article 20, paragraph 1, sub-paragraph (*b*).

3. Any Contracting Party may denounce the present Charter or any of the articles or paragraphs of Part II of the Charter, under the conditions specified in paragraph 1 of this article in respect of any territory to which the said Charter is applicable by virtue of a declaration made in accordance with paragraph 2 of Article 34.

Appendix

Article 38

The Appendix to this Charter shall form an integral part of it.

IN WITNESS WHEREOF, the undersigned, being duly authorized thereto, have signed this Charter.

DONE at Turin, this 18th day of October 1961, in English and French, both texts being equally authoritative, in a single copy which shall be deposited within the archives of the Council of Europe. The Secretary-General shall transmit certified copies to each of the Signatories.

APPENDIX TO THE SOCIAL CHARTER

Scope of the Social Charter in Terms of Persons Protected:

1. Without prejudice to Article 12, paragraph 4 and Article 13, paragraph 4, the persons covered by Articles 1 to 17 include foreigners only in so far as they are nationals of other Contracting Parties lawfully resident or working regularly within the territory of the Contracting Party concerned, subject to the understanding that these articles are to be interpreted in the light of the provisions of Articles 18 and 19.

This interpretation would not prejudice the extension of similar facilities to other persons by any of the Contracting Parties.

2. Each Contracting party will grant to refugees as defined in the Conven-

tion relating to the Status of Refugees, signed at Geneva on 28th July, 1951,[55] and lawfully staying in its territory, treatment as favourable as possible, and in any case not less favourable than under the obligations accepted by the Contracting Party under the said Convention and under any other existing international instruments applicable to those refugees.

<table>
<tr><td align="center">*PART I*
Paragraph 18</td><td align="center">and</td><td align="center">*PART II*
Article 18, paragraph 1</td></tr>
</table>

It is understood that these provisions are not concerned with the question of entry into the territories of the Contracting Parties and do not prejudice the provisions of the European Convention on Establishment, signed at Paris on 13th December, 1955.[56]

PART II

Article 1, paragraph 2

This provision shall not be interpreted as prohibiting or authorizing any union security clause or practice.

Article 4, paragraph 4

This provision shall be so understood as not to prohibit immediate dismissal for any serious offence.

Article 4, paragraph 5

It is understood that a Contracting Party may give the undertaking required in this paragraph if the great majority of workers are not permitted to suffer deductions from wages either by law or through collective agreements or arbitration awards, the exceptions being those persons not so covered.

Article 6, paragraph 4

It is understood that each Contracting Party may, in so far as it is concerned, regulate the exercise of the right to strike by law, provided that any further restriction that this might place on the right can be justified under the terms of Article 31.

Article 7, paragraph 8

It is understood that a Contracting Party may give the undertaking required in this paragraph if it fulfils the spirit of the undertaking by providing by law that the great majority of persons under 18 years of age shall not be employed in night work.

Article 12, paragraph 4

The words 'and subject to the conditions laid down in such agreements' in the introduction to this paragraph are taken to imply *inter alia* that with regard to benefits which are available independently of any insurance contribution a

Contracting Party may require the completion of a prescribed period of residence before granting such benefits to nationals of other Contracting Parties.

Article 13, paragraph 4

Governments not Parties to the European Convention on Social and Medical Assistance may ratify the Social Charter in respect of this paragraph provided that they grant to nationals of other Contracting Parties a treatment which is in conformity with the provisions of the said Convention.

Article 19, paragraph 6

For the purpose of this provision, the term 'family of a foreign worker' is understood to mean at least his wife and dependent children under the age of 21 years.

PART III

It is understood that the Charter contains legal obligations of an international character, the application of which is submitted solely to the supervision provided for in Part IV thereof.

Article 20, paragraph 1

It is understood that the 'numbered paragraphs' may include articles consisting of only one paragraph.

PART V

Article 30

The term 'in time of war or other public emergency' shall be so understood as to cover also the *threat* of war.

B. ORGANIZATION OF AMERICAN STATES

INTRODUCTION

The Organization of American States (OAS) is an international organization created by the American nation-states. It is a regional organization within the United Nations.

Inter-American activity in advancing human rights—co-ordinated by the Organization of American States (OAS)—dates back to the *Convention Relative to the Rights of Aliens*, signed in Mexico City in 1902. Important also (to name a few) were the *Convention on Asylum*, signed in Havana, Cuba, in 1928; the *Convention on Extradition*, signed in Montevideo, Uruguay, in 1933; the resolution on *Freedom of Association and Freedom of Expression for Workers*, adopted in Lima, Peru, in 1938; and the resolution on *Humanization of War*, adopted in Rio de Janeiro, Brazil, in 1942.

During the Inter-American Conference on Problems of War and Peace in 1945, "the American states expressed support for the first time for an international system of protection for human rights by proclaiming their adherence to the principles established in international law for safeguarding the essential rights of man, charging the Inter-American Juridical Committee with the preparation of a draft Declaration of International Rights and Duties of Man in order that it might be adopted by the American republics as a convention."[57]

Adopted on May 2, 1948, in Bogota, Colombia, as the final Act of the Ninth International Congress of American States, the American Declaration of the Rights and Duties of Man preceded the adoption of the United Nations Universal Declaration of Human Rights by seven months. But the American Declaration was not binding in law; it was formulated only as a statement of principles.

It was at the Fifth Meeting of Consultation of Ministers of Foreign Affairs, held in Santiago, Chile, in 1959, that action was taken to implement the 1948 Declaration. The ministers adopted the Declaration of Santiago (Resolution III), entrusting to the Inter-American Council of Jurists the study of the possible juridical relationship between respect for human rights and the effective exercise of representative democracy, and the right to set in motion the machinery of American international law. Resolution VIII was then adopted, charging the Council of Jurists with the preparation of a draft Convention on Human Rights. The meeting also called for the establishment of the Inter-American Commission on Human rights which was to be organized by the Council of the OAS.

The Inter-American Commission consists of seven members elected by the General Assembly of the OAS to represent all of the member states. This Commission is governed by the OAS Charter provisions and the American Declaration of the Rights and Duties of Man. It functions in accordance with the provisions of both the Statute and the Regulations of the Commission.

The powers of the Commissioners include authority to examine into the condition of human rights in OAS member states where flagrant and repeated abuses are reported. This includes authority to hear individual complaints, to request information, to request consent to pursue the investigations within the territory of the alleged violations, to make recommendations and to publish reports.

Organizational changes were made to amend the OAS Charter at the Third Special Inter-American Conference held in February, 1967. Originally created by a simple resolution, the Inter-American Commission now became a statutory organ with the principal function of promoting the observance and protection of human rights and serving as a consultative organ of the Organization in such matters.

It thus became the responsibility of the Commission to forward the final draft of the proposed American Convention. The Commission also would now be the administrative body enforcing the Convention. The Council of the OAS then, on October 2, 1968, submitted the revised draft Convention prepared by the Inter-American Commission on Human Rights, inviting recommendations and criticism.

The American Convention on Human Rights was signed on November 22, 1979, at the end of the Inter-American Specialized Conference on Human Rights, held in San Jose, Costa Rica. It has been known in international law as the Pact of San Jose. It came into force on July 11, 1978.

Because the American Convention did not create a new body but rather conferred new duties and powers on the already mandated Inter-American Commission on Human Rights, a dual mandate was established. Those states which ratified the Convention would be governed by that document, while those states which had not ratified the document would still be governed under the already existing powers of the Commission.

Because both groups of OAS countries are governed by the same Commission, an overlapping of functions is apparent. Member states which had not ratified the Convention are nevertheless eligible for many of the services offered to Convention member countries, such as advisory opinions and authoritative studies. In this way, non-Convention OAS states are encouraged to meet the minimum standards of the Convention and perhaps someday ratify the Convention themselves. This is considered a major step in the progression of human rights since the American Convention on Human Rights is thought by many to be the premier document on the rights of man.

While the Pact of San Jose generally resembles the European Convention on Human Rights, it has been described by the International Commission of Jurists as "perhaps the most complete of the human rights conventions at the regional or United Nations level."[58] The ratifying states, as pointed out by the International Commission of Jurists, are "legally bound, when necessary, to adopt their laws and norms of international law to the provisions of the Convention, and to respect the rights and freedoms expressed therein and to ensure to all persons subject to their jurisdiction the free and full exercise of those rights and freedoms without discrimination for any reason.[59]

The major contribution of the American Convention on Human Rights is to make the hearing of individual petitions mandatory rather than optional. Under

Article 44 acceptance of such procedure follows automatically upon ratification of the Convention by a Contracting Party.

In addition, the American Convention establishes an expanded range of powers. The Commission may conduct on-the-spot investigations in which the State involved "shall furnish to it, all necessary facilities." (Art. 48, 1d, 2). In the case of a violation, the Inter-American court of Human Rights may order that the injured party be "ensured the enjoyment of his right or freedom that was violated" and that the consequences of the violation be "remedied and that fair compensation be paid to the injured party." (Art. 63). Such order is than directly enforcible in accordance with local law in the state concerned. (Art. 68).

Background material on the Declaration and the Convention is found in two publications of the General Secretariat of the OAS: *The Organization of American States and Human Rights: Activity of the Inter-American Commission on Human Rights*, 1960–1967, published in 1972; and the *Inter-American Yearbook on Human Rights*, 1969–1970, published in 1976.

To understand the actual workings of the OAS in the field of human rights, four additional documents must be considered: (1) Statute of the Inter-American Commission on Human Rights, November, 1979; (2) Regulations of the Inter-American Commission on Human Rights, April, 1980; (3) Statute of the Inter-American Court of Human Rights, November, 1979; and (4) Rules of Procedure of the Inter-American Court of Human Rights, August, 1980. These are all incorporated in the 1981 (and subsequent issues of the) *OAS Handbook of Existing Rules Pertaining to Human Rights*. With regard to procedure, the 1979 Statute leaves it up to Regulations to determine how petitions and communications are to be handled, but the Regulations must adhere to Articles 44 through 51 of the American Convention on Human Rights.

1. AMERICAN DECLARATION OF THE RIGHTS AND DUTIES OF MAN (1948) Approved by the Ninth International Conference of American States, Bogotá, Colombia, March 30 to May 2, 1948. Resolution XXX, Pan American Union, Final Act of the Ninth Conference, 38–45, Washington, D.C., 1948

WHEREAS:

The American peoples have acknowledged the dignity of the individual, and their national constitutions recognize that juridical and political institutions, which regulate life in human society, have as their principal aim the protection of the essential rights of man and the creation of circumstances that will permit him to achieve spiritual and material progress and attain happiness;

The American states have on repeated occasions recognized that the essential rights of man are not derived from the fact that he is a national of a certain state, but are based upon attributes of his human personality;

The international protection of the rights of man should be the principal guide of an evolving American law;

The affirmation of essential human rights by the American States together with the guarantees given by the internal regimes of the states establish the initial system of protection considered by the American States as being suited to the present social and juridical conditions, not without a recognition on their part that they would increasingly strengthen that system in the international field as conditions become more favorable,

The Ninth International Conference of American States

AGREES:

To adopt the following

AMERICAN DECLARATION OF THE RIGHTS AND DUTIES OF MAN

Preamble

All men are born free and equal, in dignity and in rights, and, being endowed by nature with reason and conscience, they should conduct themselves as brothers one to another.

The fulfillment of duty by each individual is a prerequisite to the rights of all. Rights and duties are interrelated in every social and political activity of man. While rights exalt individual liberty, duties express the dignity of that liberty.

Duties of a juridical nature presuppose others of a moral nature which support them in principle and constitute their basis.

Inasmuch as spiritual development is the supreme end of human existence and the highest expression thereof, it is the duty of man to serve that end with all his strength and resources.

Since culture is the highest social and historical expression of that spiritual development, it is the duty of man to preserve, practice and foster culture by every means within his power.

And, since moral conduct constitutes the noblest flowering of culture, it is the duty of every man always to hold it in high respect.

CHAPTER ONE

RIGHTS

Article I. Every human being has the right to life, liberty and the security of his person. Right to life, liberty and personal security.

Article II. All persons are equal before the law and have the rights and duties established in this Declaration, without distinction as to race, sex, language, creed or any other factor. Right to equality before the law.

Article III. Every person has the right freely to profess a religious faith, and to manifest and practice it both in public and in private. Right to religious freedom and worship.

Article IV. Every person has the right to freedom of investigation, of opinion, and of the expression and dissemination of ideas, by any medium whatsoever. Right to freedom of investigation, opinion, expression and dissemination.

Article V. Every person has the right to the protection of the law against abusive attacks upon his honor, his reputation, and his private and family life.

Right to protection of honor, personal reputation and private and family life.

Article VI. Every person has the right to establish a family, the basic element of society, and to receive protection therefor.

Rights to a family and to the protection thereof.

Article VII. All women, during pregnancy and the nursing period, and all children have the right to special protection, care and aid.

Right to protection for mothers and children.

Article VIII. Every person has the right to fix his residence within the territory of the state of which he is a national, to move about freely within such territory, and not to leave it except by his own will.

Right to residence and movement.

Article IX. Every person has the right to the inviolability of his home.

Right to inviolability of the home.

Article X. Every person has the right to the inviolability and transmission of his correspondence.

Right to the inviolability and transmission of correspondence.

Article XI. Every person has the right to the preservation of his health through sanitary and social measures relating to food, clothing, housing and medical care, to the extent permitted by public and community resources.

Right to the preservation of health and to well-being.

Article XII. Every person has the right to an education, which should be based on the principles of liberty, morality and human solidarity.

Right to education.

Likewise every person has the right to an education that will prepare him to attain a decent life, to raise his standard of living, and to be a useful member of society.

The right to an education includes the right to equality of opportunity in every case, in accordance with natural talents, merit and the desire to utilize the resources that the state or the community is in a position to provide.

Every person has the right to receive, free, at least a primary education.

Article XIII. Every person has the right to take part in the cultural life of the community, to enjoy the arts, and to participate in the benefits that result from intellectual progress, especially scientific discoveries.

Right to the benefits of culture.

He likewise has the right to the protection of his moral and material interests as regards his inventions or any literary, scientific or artistic works of which he is the author.

Article XIV. Every person has the right to work, under proper conditions, and to follow his vocation freely, in so far as existing conditions of employment permit.

Right to work and to fair remuneration.

Every person who works has the right to receive such remuneration as will, in proportion to his capacity and skill, assure him a standard of living suitable for himself and for his family.

Article XV. Every person has the right to leisure time, to wholesome recreation and to the opportunity for advantageous use of his free time to his spiritual, cultural and physical benefit.

Right to leisure time and to the use thereof.

Article XVI. Every person has the right to social security which will protect him from the consequences of unemployment, old age, and any disabilities arising from causes beyond his control that make it physically or mentally impossible for him to earn a living.

Right to social security.

Article XVII. Every person has the right to be recognized everywhere as a person having rights and obligations, and to enjoy the basic civil rights.

Right to recognition of juridical personality and of civil rights.

Article XVIII. Every person may resort to the courts to ensure respect of his legal rights. There should likewise be available to him a simple, brief procedure whereby the courts will protect him from acts of authority that, to his prejudice, violate any fundamental constitutional rights.

Right to a fair trial.

Article XIX. Every person has the right to the nationality to which he is entitled by law and to change it, if he so wishes, for the nationality of any other country that is willing to grant it to him.

Right to nationality.

Article XX. Every person having legal capacity is entitled to participate in the government of his country, directly or through his representatives, and to take part in popular elections, which shall be by secret ballot, and shall be honest, periodic and free.

Right to vote and to participate in government.

Article XXI. Every person has the right to assemble peaceably with others in a formal public meeting or an informal gathering, in connection with matters of common interest of any nature.

Right of assembly.

Article XXII. Every person has the right to associate with others to promote, exercise and protect his legitimate interests of a political, economic, religious, social, cultural, professional, labor union or other nature.

Right of association.

Article XXIII. Every person has a right to own such private property as meets the essential needs of decent living and helps to maintain the dignity of the individual and of the home.

Right to property.

Article XXIV. Every person has the right to submit respectful petitions to any competent authority, for reasons of either general or private interest, and the right to obtain a prompt decision thereon.

Right of petition.

Article XXV. No person may be deprived of his liberty except in the cases and according to the procedures established by preexisting law.

No person may be deprived of liberty for nonfulfillment of obligations of a purely civil character.

Every individual who has been deprived of his liberty has the right to have the legality of his detention ascertained without delay by a court, and the right to be tried without undue delay or, otherwise, to be released. He also has the right to humane treatment during the time he is in custody.

Right of protection from arbitrary arrest.

Article XXVI. Every accused person is presumed to be innocent until proved guilty.

Every person accused of an offense has the right to be given an impartial and public hearing, and to be tried by courts previously established in accordance with pre-existing laws, and not to receive cruel, infamous or unusual punishment.

Right to due process of law.

Article XXVII. Every person has the right, in case of pursuit not resulting from ordinary crimes, to seek and receive asylum in foreign territory, in accordance with the laws of each country and with international agreements.

Right of asylum.

Article XXVIII. The rights of man are limited by the rights of others, by the security of all, and by the just demands of the general welfare and the advancement of democracy.

Scope of the rights of man.

CHAPTER TWO

DUTIES

Article XXIX. It is the duty of the individual so to conduct himself in relation to others that each and every one may fully form and develop his personality.

Duties to society.

Article XXX. It is the duty of every person to aid, support, educate and protect his minor children, and it is the duty of children to honor their parents always and to aid, support and protect them when they need it.

Duties toward children and parents.

Article XXXI. It is the duty of every person to acquire at least an elementary education.

Duty to receive instruction.

Article XXXII. It is the duty of every person to vote in the popular elections of the country of which he is a national, when he is legally capable of doing so.

Duty to vote.

Article XXXIII. It is the duty of every person to obey the law and other legitimate commands of the authorities of his country and those of the country in which he may be.

Duty to obey the law.

Article XXIV. It is the duty of every able-bodied person to render whatever civil and military service his country may require for its defense and preservation, and, in case of public disaster, to render such services as may be in his power.

It is likewise his duty to hold any public office to which he may be elected by popular vote in the state of which he is a national.

Duty to serve the community and the nation.

Article XXXV. It is the duty of every person to cooperate with the state and the community with respect to social security and welfare, in accordance with his ability and with existing circumstances.

Duties with respect to social security and welfare.

Article XXXVI. It is the duty of every person to pay the taxes established by law for the support of public services.

Duty to pay taxes.

Article XXXVII. It is the duty of every person to work, as far as his capacity and possibilities permit, in order to obtain the means of livelihood or to benefit his community.

Duty to work.

Article XXXVIII. It is the duty of every person to refrain from taking part in political activities that, according to law, are reserved exclusively to the citizens of the state in which he is an alien.

Duty to refrain from political activites in a foreign country.

2. AMERICAN CONVENTION ON HUMAN RIGHTS (1969)

Signed at the Inter-American Specialized Conference on Human Rights, San José, Costa Rica, November 7–22, 1969.

Organization of American States Treaty Series No. 36, at 1–21. OAS Official Records, OAS/Ser.A/16.

Preamble

The American states signatory to the present Convention.

Reaffirming their intention to consolidate in this hemisphere, within the framework of democratic institutions, a system of personal liberty and social justice based on respect for the essential rights of man;

Recognizing that the essential rights of man are not derived from one's being a national of a certain state, but are based upon attributes of the human personality, and that they therefore justify international protection in the form of a convention reinforcing or complementing the protection provided by the domestic law of the American states;

Considering that these principles have been set forth in the Charter of the Organization of American States, in the American Declaration of the Rights and Duties of Man, and in the Universal Declaration of Human Rights, and that they have been reaffirmed and refined in other international instruments, worldwide as well as regional in scope;

Reiterating that, in accordance with the Universal Declaration of Human Rights, the ideal of free men enjoying freedom from fear and want can be achieved only if conditions are created whereby everyone may enjoy his economic, social, and cultural rights, as well as his civil and political rights; and

Considering that the Third Special Inter-American Conference (Buenos Aires, 1967) approved the incorporation into the Charter of the Organization itself of broader standards with respect to economic, social, and educational rights and resolved that an inter-American convention on human rights should determine the structure, competence, and procedure of the organs responsible for these matters,

Have agreed upon the following:

PART I—STATE OBLIGATIONS AND RIGHTS PROTECTED

CHAPTER I—GENERAL OBLIGATIONS

Article 1. Obligation to Respect Rights

1. The States Parties to this Convention undertake to respect the rights and freedoms recognized herein and to ensure to all persons subject to their jurisdiction the free and full exercise of those rights and freedoms, without any discrimination for reasons of race, color, sex, language, religion, political or other opinion, national or social origin, economic status, birth, or any other social condition.

2. For the purposes of this Convention, "person" means every human being.

Article 2. Domestic Legal Effects

Where the exercise of any of the rights or freedoms referred to in Article 1 is not already ensured by legislative or other provisions, the States Parties undertake to adopt, in accordance with their constitutional processes and the provisions of this Convention, such legislative or other measures as may be necessary to give effect to those rights or freedoms.

CHAPTER II—CIVIL AND POLITICAL RIGHTS

Article 3. Right to Juridical Personality

Every person has the right to recognition as a person before the law.

Article 4. Right to Life

1. Every person has the right to have his life respected. This right shall be protected by law and, in general, from the moment of conception. No one shall be arbitrarily deprived of his life.

2. In countries that have not abolished the death penalty, it may be imposed only for the most serious crimes and pursuant to a final judgment rendered by a competent court and in accordance with a law establishing such punishment, enacted prior to the commission of the crime. The application of such punishment shall not be extended to crimes to which it does not presently apply.

3. The death penalty shall not be reestablished in states that have abolished it.

4. In no case shall capital punishment be inflicted for political offenses or related common crimes.

5. Capital punishment shall not be imposed upon persons who, at the time the crime was committed, were under 18 years of age or over 70 years of age; nor shall it be applied to pregnant women.

6. Every person condemned to death shall have the right to apply for amnesty, pardon, or commutation of sentence, which may be granted in all cases. Capital punishment shall not be imposed while such a petition is pending decision by the competent authority.

Article 5. Right to Humane Treatment

1. Every person has the right to have his physical, mental, and moral integrity respected.

2. No one shall be subjected to torture or to cruel, inhuman, or degrading punishment or treatment. All persons deprived of their liberty shall be treated with respect for the inherent dignity of the human person.

3. Punishment shall not be extended to any person other than the criminal.

4. Accused persons shall, save in exceptional circumstances, be segregated from convicted persons, and shall be subject to separate treatment appropriate to their status as unconvicted persons.

5. Minors while subject to criminal proceedings shall be separated from adults and brought before specialized tribunals, as speedily as possible, so that they may be treated in accordance with their status as minors.

6. Punishments consisting of deprivation of liberty shall have as an essential aim the reform and social readaptation of the prisoners.

Article 6. Freedom from Slavery

1. No one shall be subject to slavery or to involuntary servitude, which are prohibited in all their forms, as are the slave trade and traffic in women.

2. No one shall be required to perform forced or compulsory labor. This provision shall not be interpreted to mean that, in those countries in which the penalty established for certain crimes is deprivation of liberty at forced labor, the carrying out of such a sentence imposed by a competent court is prohibited. Forced labor shall not adversely affect the dignity or the physical or intellectual capacity of the prisoner.

3. For the purposes of this article, the following do not constitute forced or compulsory labor:

a. work or service normally required of a person imprisoned in executive of a sentence or formal decision passed by the competent judicial authority. Such work or service shall be carried out under the supervision and control of public authorities, and any persons performing such work or service shall not be placed at the disposal of any private party, company, or juridical person;

b. military service and, in countries in which conscientious objectors are recognized, national service that the law may provide for in lieu of military service;

c. service exacted in time of danger or calamity that threatens the existence or the well-being of the community; or

d. work or service that forms part of normal civic obligations.

Article 7. Right to Personal Liberty

1. Every person has the right to personal liberty and security.

2. No one shall be deprived of his physical liberty except for the reasons and under the conditions established beforehand by the constitution of the State Party concerned or by a law established pursuant thereto.

3. No one shall be subject to arbitrary arrest or imprisonment.

4. Anyone who is detained shall be informed of the reasons for his detention and shall be promptly notified of the charge or charges against him.

5. Any person detained shall be brought promptly before a judge or other officer authorized by law to exercise judicial power and shall be entitled to trial within a reasonable time or to be released without prejudice to the continuation of the proceedings. His release may be subject to guarantees to assure his appearance for trial.

6. Anyone who is deprived of his liberty shall be entitled to recourse to a competent court, in order that the court may decide without delay on the lawfulness of his arrest or detention and order his release if the arrest or

detention is unlawful. In State Parties whose laws provide that anyone who believes himself to be threatened with deprivation of his liberty is entitled to recourse to a competent court in order that it may decide on the lawfulness of such threat, this remedy may not be restricted or abolished. The interested party or another person in his behalf is entitled to seek these remedies.

7. No one shall be detained for debt. This principle shall not limit the orders of a competent judicial authority issued for nonfulfillment of duties of support.

Aritlce 8. *Right to a Fair Trial*

1. Every person has the right to a hearing, with due guarantees and within a reasonable time, by a competent, independent, and impartial tribunal, previously established by law, in the substantiation of any accusation of a criminal nature made against him or for the determination of his rights and obligations of a civil, labor, fiscal, or any other nature.

2. Every person accused of a criminal offense has the right to be presumed innocent so long as his guilt has not been proven according to law. During the proceedings, every person is entitled, with full equality, to the following minimum guarantees:

    a. the right of the accused to be assisted without charge by a translator or interpreter, if he does not understand or does not speak the language of the tribunal or court;

    b. prior notification in detail to the accused of the charges against him;

    c. adequate time and means for the preparation of his defense;

    d. the right of the accused to defend himself personally or to be assisted by legal counsel of his own choosing, and to communicate freely and privately with his counsel;

    e. the inalienable right to be assisted by counsel provided by the state, paid or not as the domestic law provides, if the accused does not defend himself personally or engage his own counsel within the time period established by law;

    f. the right of the defense to examine witnesses present in the court and to obtain the appearance, as witnesses, of experts or other persons who may throw light on the facts;

    g. the right not to be compelled to be a witness himself or to plead guilty; and

    h. the right to appeal the judgment to a higher court.

3. A confession of guilt by the accused shall be valid only if it is made without coercion of any kind.

4. An accused person acquitted by a nonappealable judgment shall not be subjected to a new trial for the same cause.

5. Criminal proceedings shall be public, except insofar as may be necessary to protect the interests of justice.

Article 9. *Freedom from Ex Post Facto Laws*

No one shall be convicted of any act or omission that did not constitute a criminal offense, under the applicable law, at the time it was committed. A heavier penalty shall not be imposed than the one that was applicable at the time the criminal offense was committed. If subsequent to the commission of the offense the law provides for the imposition of a lighter punishment, the guilty person shall benefit therefrom.

Article 10. Right to Compensation

Every person has the right to be compensated in accordance with the law in the event he has been sentenced by a final judgment through a miscarriage of justice.

Article 11. Right to Privacy

1. Everyone has the right to have his honor respected and his dignity recognized.

2. No one may be the object of arbitrary or abusive interference with his private life, his family, his home, or his correspondence, or of unlawful attacks on his honor or reputation.

3. Everyone has the right to the protection of the law against such interference or attacks.

Article 12. Freedom of Conscience and Religion

1. Everyone has the right to freedom of conscience and of religion. This right includes freedom to maintain or to change one's religion or beliefs, and freedom to profess or disseminate one's religion or beliefs, either individually or together with others, in public or in private.

2. No one shall be subject to restrictions that might impair his freedom to maintain or to change his religion or beliefs.

3. Freedom to manifest one's religion and beliefs may be subject only to the limitations prescribed by law that are necessary to protect public safety, order, health, or morals, or the rights or freedoms of others.

4. Parents or guardians, as the case may be, have the right to provide for the religious and moral education of their children or wards that is in accord with their own convictions.

Article 13. Freedom of Thought and Expression

1. Everyone has the right to freedom of thought and expression. This right includes freedom to seek, receive, and impart information and ideas of all kinds, regardless of frontiers, either orally, in writing, in print, in the form of art, or through any other medium of one's choice.

2. The exercise of the right provided for in the foregoing paragraph shall not be subject to prior censorship but shall be subject to subsequent imposition of liability, which shall be expressly established by law to the extent necessary to ensure:

    a. respect for the rights or reputations of others; or

    b. the protection of national security, public order, or public health or morals.

3. The right of expression may not be restricted by indirect methods or means, such as the abuse of government or private controls over newsprint,

radio broadcasting frequencies, or equipment used in the dissemination of information, or by any other means tending to impeded the communication and circulation of ideas and opinions.

4. Notwithstanding the provisions of paragraph 2 above, public entertainments may be subject by law to prior censorship for the sole purpose of regulating access to them for the moral protecton of childhood and adolescence.

5. Any propaganda for war and any advocacy of national, racial, or religious hatred that constitute incitements to lawless violence or to any other similar illegal action against any person or group of persons on any grounds including those of race, color, religion, language, or national origin shall be considered as offenses punishable by law.

Article 14. Right of Reply

1. Anyone injured by inaccurate or offensive statements or ideas disseminated to the public in general by a legally regulated medium of communication has the right to reply or to make a correction using the same communications outlet, under such conditions as the law may establish.

2. The correction or reply shall not in any case remit other legal liabilities that may have been incurred.

3. For the effective protection of honor and reputation, every publisher, and every newspaper, motion picture, radio, and television company, shall have a person responsible who is not protected by immunities or special privileges.

Article 15. Right of Assembly

The right of peaceful assembly, without arms, is recognized. No restrictions may be placed on the exercise of this right other than those imposed in conformity with the law necessary in a democratic society in the interest of national security, public safety or public order, or to protect public health or morals or the rights or freedoms of others.

Article 16. Freedom of Association

1. Everyone has the right to associate freely for ideological, religious, political, economic, labor, social, cultural, sports, or other purposes.

2. The exercise of this right shall be subject only to such restrictions established by law as may be necessay in a democratic society, in the interest of national security, public safety or public order, or to protect public health or morals or the rights and freedoms of others.

3. The provisions of this article do not bar the imposition of legal restrictions, including even deprivation of the exercise of the right of association, on members of the armed forces and the police.

Article 17. Rights of the Family

1. The family is the natural and fundamental group unit of society and is entitled to protection by society and the state.

2. The right of men and women of marriageable age to marry and to raise a family shall be recognized, if they meet the conditions required by domestic

laws, insofar as such conditions do not affect the principle of nondiscrimination established in this Convention.

3. No marriage shall be entered into without the free and full consent of the intending spouses.

4. The States Parties shall take appropriate steps to ensure the equality of rights and the adequate balancing of responsibilities of the spouses as to marriage, during marriage, and in the event of its dissolution. In case of dissolution, provision shall be made for the necessary protection of any children solely on the basis of their own best interests.

5. The law shall recognize equal rights for children born out of wedlock and those born in wedlock.

Article 18. Right to a Name

Every person has the right to a given name and to the surnames of his parents or that of one of them. The law shall regulate the manner in which this right shall be ensured for all, by the use of assumed names if necessary.

Article 19. Rights of the Child

Every minor child has the right to the measures of protection required by his condition as a minor on the part of his family, society, and the state.

Article 20. Right to Nationality

1. Every person has the right to a nationality.

2. Every person has the right to the nationality of the state in whose territory he was born if he does not have the right to any other nationality.

3. No one shall be arbitrarily deprived of his nationality or of the right to change it.

Article 21. Right to Property

1. Everyone has the right to the use and enjoyment of his property. The law may subordinate such use and enjoyment to the interest of society.

2. No one shall be deprived of his property except upon payment of just compensation, for reasons of public utility or social interest, and in the cases and according to the forms established by law.

3. Usury and any form of exploitation of man by man shall be prohibited by law.

Article 22. Freedom of Movement and Residence

1. Every person lawfully in the territory of a State Party has the right to move about in it, and to reside in it subject to the provisions of the law.

2. Every person has the right to leave any country freely, including his own.

3. The exercise of the foregoing rights may be restricted only pursuant to a law to the extent necessary in a democratic society to prevent crime or to protect national security, public safety, public order, public morals, public health, or the rights or freedoms of others.

4. The exercise of the rights recognized in paragraph 1 may also be restricted by law in designated zones for reasons of public interest.

5. No one can be expelled from the territory of the state of which he is a national or be deprived of the right to enter it.

6. An alien lawfully in the territory of a State party to this Convention may be expelled from it only pursuant to a decision reached in accordance with law.

7. Every person has the right to seek and be granted asylum in a foreign territory, in accordance with the legislation of the state and international conventions, in the event he is being pursued for political offenses or related common crimes.

8. In no case may an alien be deported or returned to a country, regardless of whether or not it is his country of origin, if in that country his right to life or personal freedom is in danger of being violated because of his race, nationality, religion, social status, or political opinions.

9. The collective expulsion of aliens is prohibited.

Article 23. Right to Participate in Government

1. Every citizen shall enjoy the follwing rights and opportunities:

a. to take part in the conduct of public affairs, directly or through freely chosen representatives;

b. to vote and to be elected in genuine periodic elections, which shall be by universal and equal suffrage and by secret ballot that guarantees the free expression of the will of the voters; and

c. to have access, under general conditions of equality, to the public service of his country.

2. The law may regulate the exercise of the rights and opportunities referred to in the preceding paragraph only on the basis of age, nationality, residence, language, education, civil and mental capacity, or sentencing by a competent court in criminal proceedings.

Article 24. Right to Equal Protection

All persons are equal before the law. Consequently, they are entitled, without discrimination, to equal protection of the law.

Article 25. Right to Judicial Protection

1. Everyone has the right to simple and prompt recourse, or any other effective recourse, to a competent court or tribunal for protection against acts that violate his fundamental rights recognized by the constitution or laws of the state concerned or by this Convention, even though such violation may have been committed by persons acting in the course of their official duties.

2. The States Parties undertake:

a. to ensure that any person claiming such remedy shall have his rights determined by the competent authority provided for by the legal system of the state;

b. to develop the possibilities of judicial remedy; and

c. to ensure that the competent authorities shall enforce such remedies when granted.

CHAPTER III—ECONOMIC, SOCIAL, AND CULTURAL RIGHTS

Article 26. Progressive Development

The States Parties undertake to adopt measures, both internally and through international cooperation, especially those of an economic and technical nature, with a view to achieving progressively, by legislation or other appropriate means, the full realization of the rights implicit in the economic, social, educational, scientific, and cultural standards set forth in the Charter of the Organization of American States as amended by the protocol of Buenos Aires.

CHAPTER IV—SUSPENSION OF GUARANTEES, INTERPRETATION, AND APPLICATION

Article 27. Suspension of Guarantees

1. In time of war, public danger, or other emergency that threatens the independence or security of a State Party, it may take measures derogating from its obligations under the present Convention to the extent and for the period of time strictly required by the exigencies of the situation, provided that such measures are not inconsistent with its other obligations under international law and do not involve discrimination on the ground of race, color, sex, language, religion, or social origin.

2. The foregoing provision does not authorize any suspension of the following articles: Article 3 (Right to Juridical Personality), Article 4 (Right to Life), Article 5 (Right to Humane Treatment), Article 6 (Freedom from Slavery), Article 9 (Freedom from *Ex Post Facto* Laws), Article 12 (Freedom of Conscience and Religion), Article 17 (Rights of the Family), Article 18 (Right to a Name), Article 19 (Rights of the Child), Article 20 (Right to Nationality), and Article 23 (Right to Participate in Government), or of the judicial guarantees essential for the protection of such rights.

3. Any State Party availing itself of the right of suspension shall immediately inform the other States Parties, through the Secretary General of the organization of American States, of the provisions the application of which it has suspended, the reasons that gave rise to the suspension, and the date set for the termination of such suspension.

Article 28. Federal Clause

1. Where a State Party is constituted as a federal state, the national government of such State Party shall implement all the provisions of the Convention over whose subject matter it exercises legislative and judicial jurisdiction.

2. With respect to the provisions over whose subject matter the constituent units of the federal state have jurisdiction, the national government shall immediately take suitable measures, in accordance with its constitution and its laws, to the end that the competent authorities of the constituent units may adopt appropriate provisions for the fulfillment of this Convention.

3. Whenever two or more States Parties agree to form a federation or other

type of association, they shall take care that the resulting federal or other compact contains the provisions necessary for continuing and rendering effective the standards of this Convention in the new state that is organized.

Article 29. Restrictions Regarding Interpretation

No provision of this Convention shall be interpreted as:

a. permitting any State Party, group, or person to suppress the enjoyment or exercise of the rights and freedoms recognized in this Convention or to restrict them to a greater extent than is provided for herein;

b. restricting the enjoyment or exercise of any right or freedom recognized by virtue of the laws of any State party or by virtue of another convention to which one of the said states is a party;

c. precluding other rights or guarantees that are inherent in the human personality or derived from representative democracy as a form of government; or

d. excluding or limiting the effect that the American Declaration of the Rights and Duties of Man and other international acts of the same nature may have.

Article 30. Scope of Restrictions

The restrictions that, pursuant to this Convention, may be placed on the enjoyment or exercise of the rights or freedoms recognized herein may not be applied except in accordance with laws enacted for reasons of general interest and in accordance with the purpose for which such restrictions have been established.

Article 31. Recognition of Other Rights

Other rights and freedoms recognized in accordance with the procedures established in Articles 76 and 77 may be included in the system of protection of this Convention.

CHAPTER V—PERSONAL RESPONSIBILITIES

Article 32. Relationship between Duties and Rights

1. Every person has responsibilities to his family, his community, and mankind.

2. The rights of each person are limited by the rights of others, by the security of all, and by the just demands of the general welfare, in a democratic society.

PART II—MEANS OF PROTECTION

CHAPTER VI—COMPETENT ORGANS

Article 33

The following organs shall have competence with respect to matters relating to the fulfillment of the commitments made by the States Parties to this Convention:

a. the Inter-American Commission on Human Rights, referred to as "The Commission"; and

b. the Inter-American Court of Human Rights, referred to as "The Court."

CHAPTER VII—INTER-AMERICAN COMMISSION ON HUMAN RIGHTS

Section 1. Organization

Article 34

The Inter-American Commission on Human Rights shall be composed of seven members, who shall be persons of high moral character and recognized competence in the field of human rights.

Article 35

The Commission shall represent all the member countries of the Organization of American States.

Article 36

1. The members of the Commission shall be elected in a personal capacity by the General Assembly of the Organization from a list of candidates proposed by the governments of the member states.

2. Each of those governments may propose up to three candidates, who may be nationals of the states proposing them or of any other member state of the Organization of American States. When a slate of three is proposed, at least one of the candidates shall be a national of a state other than the one proposing the slate.

Article 37

1. The members of the Commission shall be elected for a term of four years and may be reelected only once, but the terms of three of the members chosen in the first election shall expire at the end of two years. Immediately following that election the General Assembly shall determine the names of those three members by lot.

2. No two nationals of the same state may be members of the Commission.

Article 38

Vacancies that may occur on the Commission for reasons other than the normal expiration of a term shall be filled by the Permanent Council of the Organization in accordance with the provisions of the Statute of the Commission.

Article 39

The Commission shall prepare its Statute, which it shall submit to the General Assembly for approval. It shall establish its own Regulations.

Article 40

Secretariat services for the Commission shall be furnished by the appropriate specialized unit of the General Secretariat of the Organization. This unit shall be provided with the resources required to accomplish the tasks assigned to it by the Commission.

Section 2. Functions

Article 41

The main function of the Commission shall be to promote respect for and defense of human rights. In the exercise of its mandate, it shall have the following functions and powers:

a. to develop an awareness of human rights among the peoples of America;

b. to make recommendations to the governments of the member states, when it considers such action advisable, for the adoption of progressive measures in favor of human rights within the framework of their domestic law and constitutional provisions as well as appropriate measures to further the observance of those rights;

c. to prepare such studies or reports as it considers advisable in the performance of its duties;

d. to request the governments of the member states to supply it with information on the measures adopted by them in matters of human rights;

e. to respond, through the General Secretariat of the Organization of American States, to inquiries made by the member states on matters related to human rights and, within the limits of its possibilities, to provide those states with the advisory services they request;

f. to take action on petitions and other communications pursuant to its authority under the provisions of Articles 44 through 51 of this Convention; and

g. to submit an annual report to the General Assembly of the Organization of American States.

Article 42

The States Parties shall transmit to the Commission a copy of each of the reports and studies that they submit annually to the Executive Committees of the Inter-American Economic and Social Council and the Inter-American Council for Education, Science, and Culture, in their respective fields, so that the Commission may watch over the promotion of the rights implicit in the economic, social, educational, scientific, and cultural standards set forth in the Charter of the Organization of American States as amended by the Protocol of Buenos Aires.

Article 43

The States Parties undertake to provide the Commission with such information as it may request of them as to the manner in which their domestic law ensures the effective application of any provisions of this Convention.

Section 3. Competence

Article 44

Any person or group of persons, or any nongovernmental entity legally recognized in one or more member states of the organization, may lodge petitions with the Commission containing denunciations or complaints of violation of this Convention by a State Party.

Article 45

1. Any State Party may, when it deposits its instrument of ratification of or adherence to this Convention, or at any later time, declare that it recognizes the competence of the Commission to receive and examine communications in which a State Party alleges that another State Party has committed a violation of a human right set forth in this Convention.

2. Communciations presented by virtue of this article may be admitted and examined only if they are presented by a State Party that has made a declaration recognizing the aforementioned competence of the Commission. The Commission shall not admit any communication against a State Party that has not made such a declaration.

3. A declaration concerning recognition of competence may be made to be valid for an indefinite time, for a specified period, or for a specific case.

4. Declarations shall be deposited with the General Secretariat of the Organization of American States, which shall transmit copies thereof to the member states of that Organization.

Article 46

1. Admission by the Commission of a petition or communication lodged in accordance with Articles 44 or 45 shall be subject to the following requirements:

    a. that the remedies under domestic law have been pursued and exhausted in accordance with generally recognized principles of international law;

    b. that the petition or communication is lodged within a period of six months from the date on which the party alleging violation of his rights was notified of the final judgment;

    c. that the subject of the petition or communication is not pending in another international proceeding for settlement; and

    d. that, in the case of Article 44, the petition contains the name, nationality, profession, domicile, and signature of the person or persons or of the legal representative of the entity lodging the petition.

2. The provisions of paragraphs 1.a and 1.b of this article shall not be applicable when:

    a. the domestic legislation of the state concerned does not afford due process of law for the protection of the right or rights that have allegedly been violated;

b. the party alleging violation of his rights has been denied access to the remedies under domestic law or has been prevented from exhausting them; or

c. there has been unwarranted delay in rendering a final judgment under the aforementioned remedies.

Article 47

The Commission shall consider inadmissible any petition or communication submitted under Articles 44 or 45 if:

a. any of the requirements indicated in Article 46 has not been met;

b. the petition or communication does not state facts that tend to establish a violation of the rights guaranteed by this Convention;

c. the statements of the petitioner or of the state indicate that the petition or communication is manifestly groundless or obviously out of order; or

d. the petition or communication is substantially the same as one previously studied by the Commission or by another international organization.

Section 4. Procedure

Article 48

1. When the Commission receives a petition or communication alleging violation of any of the rights protected by this Convention, it shall proceed as follows:

a. If it considers the petition or communication admissible, it shall request information from the government of the state indicated as being responsible for the alleged violations and shall furnish that government a transcript of the pertinent portions of the petition or communication. This information shall be submitted within a reasonable period to be determined by the Commission in accordance with the circumstances of each case.

b. After the information has been received, or after the period established has elapsed and the information has not been received, the Commission shall ascertain whether the grounds for the petition or communication still exist. If they do not, the Commission shall order the record to be closed.

c. The Commission may also declare the petition or communication inadmissible or out of order on the basis of information or evidence subsequently received.

d. If the record has not been closed, the Commission shall, with the knowledge of the parties, examine the matter set forth in the petition or communication in order to verify the facts. If necessary and advisable, the Commission shall carry out an investigation, for the effective conduct of which it shall request, and the states concerned shall furnish to it, all necessary facilities.

e. The Commission may request the states concerned to furnish any pertinent information and, if so requested, shall hear oral statements or receive written statements from the parties concerned.

f. The Commission shall place itself at the disposal of the parties concerned with a view to reaching a friendly settlement of the matter on the basis of respect for the human rights recognized in this Convention.

2. However, in serious and urgent cases, only the presentation of a petition or communication that fulfills all the formal requirements of admissibility shall be necessary in order for the Commission to conduct an investigation with the prior consent of the state in whose territory a violation has allegedly been committed.

Article 49

If a friendly settlement has been reached in accordance with paragraph 1.f of Article 48, the Commission shall draw up a report, which shall be transmitted to the petitioner and to the States Parties to this Convention, and shall then be communicated to the Secretary General of the Organization of American States for publication. This report shall contain a brief statement of the facts and of the solution reached. If any party in the case so requests, the fullest possible information shall be provided to it.

Article 50

1. If a settlement is not reached, the Commission shall, within the time limit established by its Statute, draw up a report setting forth the facts and stating its conclusions. If the report, in whole or in part, does not represent the unanimous agreement of the members of the Commission, any member may attach to it a separate opinion. The written and oral statements made by the parties in accordance with paragraph 1.e of Article 48 shall also be attached to the report.

2. The report shall be transmitted to the states concerned, which shall not be at liberty to publish it.

3. In transmitting the report, the Commission may make such proposals and recommendations as it sees fit.

Article 51

1. If, within a period of three months from the date of the transmittal of the report of the Commission to the states concerned, the matter has not either been settled or submitted by the Commission or by the state concerned to the Court and its jurisdiction accepted, the Commission may, by the vote of an absolute majority of its members, set forth its opinion and conclusions concerning the question submitted for its consideration.

2. Where appropriate, the Commission shall make pertinent recommendations and shall prescribe a period within which the state is to take the measures that are incumbent upon it to remedy the situation examined.

3. When the prescribed period has expired, the Commission shall decide by the vote of an absolute majority of its members whether the state has taken adequate measures and whether to publish its report.

CHAPTER VIII—INTER-AMERICAN COURT OF HUMAN RIGHTS

Section 1. Organization

Article 52

1. The Court shall consist of seven judges, nationals of the member states of the Organization, elected in an individual capacity from among jurists of the highest moral authority and of recognized competence in the field of human rights, who possess the qualifications required for the exercise of the highest judicial functions in conformity with the law of the state of which they are nationals or of the state that proposes them as candidates.

2. No two judges may be nationals of the same state.

Article 53

1. The judges of the Court shall be elected by secret ballot by an absolute majority vote of the States Parties to the Convention, in the General Assembly of the Organization, from a panel of candidates proposed by those states.

2. Each of the States Parties may propose up to three candidates, nationals of the state that proposes them or of any other member state of the Organization of American States. When a slate of three is proposed, at least one of the candidates shall be a national of a state other than the one proposing the slate.

Article 54

1. The judges of the Court shall be elected for a term of six years and may be reelected only once. The term of three of the judges chosen in the first election shall expire at the end of three years. Immediately after the election, the names of the three judges shall be determined by lot in the General Assembly.

2. A judge elected to replace a judge whose term has not expired shall complete the term of the latter.

3. The judges shall continue in office until the expiration of their term. However, they shall continue to serve with regard to cases that they have begun to hear and that are still pending, for which purposes they shall not be replaced by the newly elected judges.

Article 55

1. If a judge is a national of any of the States Parties to a case submitted to the Court, he shall retain his right to hear that case.

2. If one of the judges called upon to hear a case should be a national of one of the States Parties to the case, any other State Party in the case may appoint a person of its choice to serve on the Court as an *ad hoc* judge.

3. If among the judges called upon to hear a case none is a national of any of the States Parties to the case, each of the latter may appoint an *ad hoc* judge.

4. An *ad hoc* judge shall possess the qualifications indicated in Article 52.

5. If several States Parties to the Convention should have the same interest in a case, they shall be considered as a single party for purposes of the above provisions. In case of doubt, the Court shall decide.

Article 56

Five judges shall constitute a quorum for the transaction of business by the Court.

Article 57

The Commission shall appear in all cases before the Court.

Article 58

1. The Court shall have its seat at the place determined by the States Parties to the Convention in the General Assembly of the Organization; however, it may convene in the territory of any member state of the Organization of American States when a majority of the Court consider it desirable, and with the prior consent of the state concerned. The seat of the Court may be changed by the States Parties to the Convention in the General Assembly by a two-thirds vote.

2. The Court shall appoint its own Secretary.

3. The Secretary shall have his office at the place where the Court has its seat and shall attend the meetings that the Court may hold away from its seat.

Article 59

The Court shall establish its Secretariat, which shall function under the direction of the Secretary of the Court, in accordance with the administrative standards of the General Secretariat of the Organization in all respect not incompatible with the independence of the Court. The staff of the Court's Secretariat shall be appointed by the Secretary General of the Organization, in consultation with the Secretary of the Court.

Article 60

The Court shall draw up its Statute which it shall submit to the General Assembly for approval. It shall adopt its own Rules of Procedure.

Section 2. Jurisdiction and Functions

Article 61

1. Only the States Parties and the Commission shall have the right to submit a case to the Court.

2. In order for the Court to hear a case, it is necessary that the procedures set forth in Articles 48 to 50 shall have been completed.

Article 62

1. A State Party may, upon depositing its instrument of ratification or adherence to this Convention, or at any subsequent time, declare that it recognizes as binding, *ipso facto*, and not requiring special agreement, the jurisdiction of the Court on all matters relating to the interpretation or application of this Convention.

2. Such declaration may be made unconditionally, on the condition of reciprocity, for a specified period, or for specific cases. It shall be presented to

the Secretary General of the Organization, who shall transmit copies thereof to the other member states of the Organization and to the Secretary of the Court.

3. The jurisdiction of the Court shall comprise all cases concerning the interpretation and application of the provisions of this Convention that are submitted to it, provided that the States Parties to the case recognize or have recognized such jurisdiction, whether by special declaration pursuant to the preceding paragraphs, or by a special agreement.

Article 63

1. If the Court finds that there has been a violation of a right or freedom protected by this Convention, the Court shall rule that the injured party be ensured the enjoyment of his right or freedom that was violated. It shall also rule, if appropriate, that the consequences of the measure or situation that constituted the breach of such right or freedom be remedied and that fair compensation be paid to the injured party.

2. In cases of extreme gravity and urgency, and when necessary to avoid irreparable damage to persons, the Court shall adopt such provisional measures as it deems pertinent in matters it has under consideration. With respect to a case not yet submitted to the Court, it may act at the request of the Commission.

Article 64

1. The member states of the Organization may consult the Court regarding the interpretation of this Convention or of other treaties concerning the protection of human rights in the American states. Within their spheres of competence, the organs listed in Chapter X of the Charter of the Organization of American States, as amended by the Protocol of Buenos Aires, may in like manner consult the Court.

2. The Court, at the request of a member state of the Organization, may provide that state with opinions regarding the compatibility of any of its domestic laws with the aforesaid international instruments.

Article 65

To each regular session of the General Assembly of the Organization of American States the Court shall submit, for the Assembly's consideration, a report on its work during the previous year. It shall specify, in particular, the cases in which a state has not complied with its judgments, making any pertinent recommendations.

Section 3. Procedure

Article 66

1. Reasons shall be given for the judgment of the Court.

2. If the judgment does not represent in whole or in part the unanimous opinion of the judges, any judge shall be entitled to have his dissenting or separate opinion attached to the judgment.

Article 67

The judgment of the Court shall be final and not subject to appeal. In case of disagreement as to the meaning or scope of the judgment, the Court shall interpret it at the request of any of the parties, provided the request is made within ninety days from the date of notification of the judgment.

Article 68

1. The States Parties to the Convention undertake to comply with the judgment of the Court in any case to which they are parties.

2. That part of a judgment that stipulates compensatory damages may be executed in the country concerned in accordance with domestic procedure governing the execution of judgments against the state.

Article 69

The parties to the case shall be notified of the judgment of the Court and it shall be transmitted to the States Parties to the Convention.

CHAPTER IX—COMMON PROVISIONS

Article 70

1. The judges of the Court and the members of the Commission shall enjoy, from the moment of their election and throughout their term of office, the immunities extended to diplomatic agents in accordance with international law. During the exercise of their official function they shall, in addition, enjoy the diplomatic privileges necessary for the performance of their duties.

2. At no time shall the judges of the Court or the members of the Commission be held liable for any decisions or opinions issued in the exercise of their functions.

Article 71

The position of judge of the Court or member of the Commission is incompatible with any other activity that might affect the independence or impartiality of such judge or member, as determined in the resepctive statutes.

Article 72

The judges of the Court and the members of the Commission shall receive emoluments and travel allowances in the form and under the conditions set forth in their statutes, with due regard for the importance and independence of their office. Such emoluments and travel allowances shall be determined in the budget of the Organization of American States, which shall also include the expenses of the Court and its Secretariat. To this end, the Court shall draw up its own budget and submit it for approval to the General Assembly through the General Secretariat. The latter may not introduce any changes in it.

Article 73

The General Assembly may, only at the request of the Commission or the Court, as the case may be, determine sanctions to be applied against members of the Commission or judges of the Court when there are justifiable grounds for such action as set forth in the respective statutes. A vote of a two-thirds majority of the member states of the Organization shall be required for a decision in the case of members of the Commission and, in the case of judges of the Court, a two-thirds majority vote of the States Parties to the Convention shall also be required.

PART III—GENERAL AND TRANSITORY PROVISIONS

CHAPTER X—SIGNATURE, RATIFICATION, RESERVATIONS, AMENDMENTS, PROTOCOLS, AND DENUNCIATION

Article 74

1. The Convention shall be open for signature and ratification by or adherence of any member state of the Organization of American States.

2. Ratification of or adherence to this Convention shall be made by the deposit of an instrument of ratification or adherence with the General Secretariat of the Organization of American States. As soon as eleven states have deposited their instruments of ratification or adherence, the Convention shall enter into force. With respect to any state that ratifies or adheres thereafter, the Convention shall enter into force on the date of the deposit of its instrument of ratification or adherence.

3. The Secretary General shall inform all member states of the Organization of the entry into force of the Convention.

Article 75

This Convention shall be subject to reservations only in conformity with the provisions of the Vienna Convention on the Law of Treaties signed on May 23, 1969.

Article 76

1. Proposals to amend this Convention may be submitted to the General Assembly for the action it deems appropriate by any State Party directly, and by the Commission or the Court through the Secretary General.

2. Amendments shall enter into force for the states ratifying them on the date when two-thirds of the States Parties to this Convention have deposited their respective instruments of ratification. With respect to the other States Parties, the amendments shall enter into force on the dates on which they deposit their respective instruments of ratification.

Article 77

1. In accordance with Article 31, any State Party and the Commission may submit proposed protocols to this Convention for consideration by the States Parties at the General Assembly with a view to gradually including other rights and freedoms within its system of protection.

2. Each protocol shall determine the manner of its entry into force and shall be applied only among the States Parties to it.

Article 78

1. The States Parties may denounce this Convention at the expiration of a five-year period starting from the date of its entry into force and by means of notice given one year in advance. Notice of the denunciation shall be addressed to the Secretary General of the Organization, who shall inform the other States Parties.

2. Such a denunciation shall not have the effect of releasing the State Party concerned from the obligations contained in this Convention with respect to any act that may constitute a violation of those obligations and that has been taken by that state prior to the effective date of denunciation.

CHAPTER XI—TRANSITORY PROVISIONS

Section I. Inter-American Commission on Human Rights

Article 79

Upon the entry into force of this Convention, the Secretary General shall, in writing, request each member state of the Organization to present, within ninety days, its candidates for membership on the Inter-American Commission on Human Rights. The Secretary General shall prepare a list in alphabetical order of the candidates presented, and transmit it to the member states of the Organization at least thirty days prior to the next session of the General Assembly.

Article 80

The members of the Commission shall be elected by secret ballot of the General Assembly from the list of the candidates referred to in Article 79. The candidates who obtain the largest number of votes and an absolute majority of the votes of the representatives of the member states shall be declared elected. Should it become necessary to have several ballots in order to elect all the members of the Commission, the candidates who receive the smallest number of votes shall be eliminated successively, in the manner determined by the General Assembly.

Section 2. Inter-American Court of Human Rights

Article 81

Upon the entry into force of this Convention, the Secretary General shall, in writing, request each State Party to present, within ninety days, its candidates for membership on the Inter-American Court of Human Rights. The Secretary General shall prepare a list in alphabetical order of the candidates presented and transmit it to the States Parties at least thirty days prior to the next session of the General Assembly.

Article 82

The judges of the Court shall be elected from the list of candidates referred to in Article 81, by secret ballot of the States Parties to the Convention in the General Assembly. The candidates who obtain the largest number of votes and an absolute majority of the votes of the representatives of the States Parties shall be declared elected. Should it become necessary to have several ballots in order to elect all the judges of the Court, the candidates who receive the smallest number of votes shall be eliminated successively, in the manner determined by the States Parties.

STATEMENTS AND RESERVATIONS (Omitted)

3. DRAFT PROTOCOL ADDITIONAL TO THE AMERICAN CONVENTION ON HUMAN RIGHTS (1986)

In its annual report of 1985–86, the Inter-American Commission on Human Rights set forth its views on "areas in which steps need to be taken towards full observance of the human rights set forth in the American Declaration of the Rights and Duties of Man and the American Convention on Human Rights." These were codified into a Draft Protocol Additional to the 1969 Convention— the Pact of San Jose de Costa Rica.

This Draft Additional was prepared pursuant to AG/RES. 619 (XII-0/82) of November, 1982, in which the General Assembly of the OAS instructed the General Secretariat to prepare such a Protocol to define economic, social and cultural rights.

In setting forth this additional category of "rights", the Commission took as its point of departure a nucleus comprised of labor, health and education rights. To these were added, according to the Report, "related rights or rights directly linked to them or to measures that aim at achieving them in practice."

The core of the Additional Protocol lies in the institutional means that have been proposed for the protection and promotion of such rights. Thus the special significance of Article 21 which has been proposed as a "realistic, flexible and effective system" of enforcement.

DRAFT PROTOCOL ADDITIONAL TO THE AMERICAN CONVENTION ON HUMAN RIGHTS (PACT OF SAN JOSE DE COSTA RICA, 1969) (1986)

Preamble

The States Parties to this Protocol Additional to the American Convention on Human Rights,

Reaffirming their intention to consolidate in this hemisphere, within the framework of democratic institutions, a system of personal liberty and social justice based on respect for the essential rights of man;

Recognizing that the essential rights of man are not derived from one's being a national of a certain State, but are based upon attributes of the human person, for which reason they merit international protection in the form of a convention reinforcing or complementing the protection provided by the domestic law of the American States;

Considering the close relationship that exists between economic, social, and cultural rights and civil and political rights, in that the two categories of rights constitute an indivisible whole based on the recognition of the dignity of the human person for which reason both requiere permanent protection and promotion if they are to be fully realized, although the violation of one group of rights in favor of the realization of the other group can never be justified;

Recognizing that, in accordance with the Universal Declaration of Human Rights and the American Convention on Human Rights, the ideal of free human beings enjoying freedom from fear and want can only be achieved if conditions are created whereby everyone may enjoy his economic, social and cultural rights as well as his civil and political rights;

Bearing in mind that, although fundamental economic, social and cultural rights have been embodied in earlier international instruments of both world and regional scope, it is essential that those rights be reaffirmed, developed and perfected in order to consolidate in America, on the basis of full respect for the rights of the individual, the democratic representative form of government as well as the right of its peoples to development, self-determination, and the free disposal, in accordance with international law, of their wealth and natural resources; and

Considering that the General Assembly of the Organization has repeatedly expressed its wish to draw up a protocol additional to the American Convention on Human Rights for the purpose of defining the economic, social, and cultural rights to be protected and to establish institutional arrangements for ensuring the appropriate protection of such rights; and

Considering that the American Convention on Human Rights provides that draft protocols additional to that Convention may be submitted for consideration to the States Parties, meeting together on the occasion of the General Assembly of the Organization of American States, for the purpose of gradually incorporating other rights and freedoms into the system for the protection thereof;

Have agreed upon the following Protocol Additional to the American Convention on Human Rights:

Article 1

Obligation to Adopt Measures

The States Parties to this Protocol Additional to the American Convention on Human Rights (Pact of San José, Costa Rica, 1969) undertake to adopt all the necessary measures within the extent of the resources available to them, to achieve the progressive realization of the rights recognized in this Protocol.

Article 2

Obligation of Non-discrimination

1. The States Parties to this Protocol undertake to guarantee the exercise of the rights set forth herein without discrimination of any kind.

2. The States Parties to this Protocol undertake to invest men and women with equal title to the enjoyment of all the economic, social and cultural rights set forth in this Protocol.

Article 3

Obligation to Enact Domestic Legislation

If the exercise of the rights set forth in this Protocol is not already guaranteed by legislative or other provisions, the States Parties undertake to adopt, in accordance with their constitutional processes and the provisions of this Protocol, such legislative or other measures as may be necessary for making those rights a reality.

Article 4

Inadmissibility of Restrictions

Prohibited if any restriction or diminution of a right recognized or guaranteed in a state's internal legislation or by means of international treaties, on the pretext that the present Protocol does not recognize the right or recognizes it to a lesser degree.

Article 5

Scope of Restrictions and Limitations

The State Parties may only establish restrictions and limitations on the enjoyment and exercise of the rights established in the present Protocol by means of laws promulgated with the purpose of preserving the general welfare in a democratic society, to the extent that they are compatible with these rights, public health and morality.

Article 6

Right to Work

Everyone shall have the right to work, which includes the right of opportunity to lead a descent life by carrying out an activity which one freely chooses or accepts.

Article 7

Just and Satisfactory Conditions of Work

The right to work defined in the foregoing article presupposes that the same is carried out in just and satisfactory conditions, which the State Parties to the Present Protocol undertake to guarantee in their internal legislation:

a. Remuneration which guarantees, at a minimum, to all workers decent living conditions for them and their families and just and equal wages for work of equal value, without distinction. Women must be guaranteed working conditions equal to those of men.

b. Freedom to change employment, opportunities of promotion and mobility, work stability and the corresponding indemnization in the case of unjustified dismissal.

c. Safety and hygiene at work.

d. The prohibition of night work or unhealthy or dangerous working conditions for persons under the age of 18 and, in general, all work which could place in danger the youth's health, safety or morals. As regards minors under the age of 16, the work day will be subordinated to the provisions regarding compulsory education and in no case will it constitute an excused absence from classes or a limitation on benefitting from education received.

e. The limitation on the hours of work, both daily and weekly. The days will be of shorter duration if the work is dangerous or unhealthy.

f. Rest, leisure, reasonable limitation of working hours and paid vacations as well as remuneration for public holidays.

Article 8

Trade Union Rights

1. The State Parties undertake to ensure the right of everyone to form trade unions and to join the trade union of his choice for the promotion and protection of his economic and social interests. As an extension of that right, the State Parties shall permit trade unions to establish national federations or confederations, or to join those that already exist, as well as to form international trade union organizations and to join that of their choice. The States Parties shall also permit trade unions, federations and confederations to function freely.

2. The exercise of the rights set forth above may be subject only to the restrictions stipulated by the law, provided that they are characteristic of a democratic society and necessary for safeguarding public order and protecting public health or morals and the rights and freedoms of other persons.

Article 9

Right to Strike

1. The States Parties to the present Protocol recognize the right to strike of trade union organizations.

2. The right to strike recognized in the present Protocol must be exercised in conformity with the laws of the corresponding State.

3. The provision of the present article shall not prevent States from imposing legal restrictions on the right to strike as regards members of the armed forces, the police or other public service agents of the State.

Article 10

Right to Social Security

1. Everyone shall have the right to social security that protects him against the consequences of unemployment, old age, and disability which, being the result of causes beyond his control, prevent him physically or mentally from earning the means for a decent living.

2. In the case of persons who are employed, the right to social security shall cover at least medical care and an allowance or retirement benefit in the case of occupational accidents or occupational disease and, in the case of women, paid maternity leave before and after childbirth.

Article 11

Right to Health

1. Everyone shall have the right to health, which is understood to mean the enjoyment of the highest degree of physical, mental and social wellbeing.
2. To that end, the State Parties undertake to recognize health as a public good and in particular to guarantee this right by means of the following:

a. Primary health care, that is, essential health care made available to all individuals and families in the community;

b. To extend the benefits of health services to all individuals subject to the State's jurisdiction;

c. Universal immunization against the principal infectioius diseases;

d. The prevention and treatment of endemic diseases;

e. The education of the population concerning the prevention and treatment of health problems;

f. The satisfaction of health needs of the highest risk groups, who because of their poverty are the most vulnerable.

Article 12

Right to a Health Environment

Everyone shall have the right to live in an environment free of pollution and to have access to basic urban services, especially a safe water supply and sewerage services.

Article 13

Right to Food

Everyone has the right to adequate nutrition which guarantees the possibility of enjoying the highest level of physical, emotional and intellectual development.

Article 14

Right to Education

1. Everyone has the right to education.
2. The State Parties to the present Protocol agree that, in general, education should be directed towards the full development of the human personality and human dignity, and ought to strengthen respect for human rights, fundamental freedoms and peace. They agree, also, that education ought to equip all persons in the task of achieving a decent existence and enabling one to participate effectively in a democratic society.
3. The States Parties to the present Protocol recognize that, in order to achieve the complete exercise of the right to education:

a. Primary education shall be compulsory and accesible to all without cost;

b. Secondary education in its different forms, including technical and professional secondary education, shall be made generally available and accessible to all by every appropriate means, and in particular, by the progressive introduction of free education;

c. Higher education shall be made equally accessible to all, on the basis of capacity, by every appropriate means, and in particular, by the progressive introduction of free education;

d. Basic education shall be encouraged or intensified as far as possible for those persons who have not received or completed the whole cycle of primary instruction;

e. Programs of special education shall be established for the handicapped, so as to provide special instruction and training for persons with physical disabilities or mental deficiencies.

Article 15

Right to Freedom of Education

1. The State Parties to this Protocol undertake to respect the liberty of parents and, where applicable, legal guardians to choose for their children schools other than those established by the public authorities, provided they conform to such minimum educational standards as which may be laid down or approved by the State, and to ensure the religious and moral education of their children in conformity with their own convictions.

2. No provision of this Article shall be construed so as to interfere with the freedom of individuals and organizations from establishing and directing educational institutions, subject to the observance of the principles set forth above and to the requirement that the education given in such institutions shall conform to such minimum standards as may be laid down by the State.

Article 16

Rights to the Benefits of Culture

1. The States Parties to this Protocol recognize the right of everyone:
   a. To take part in the cultural and artistic life of the community.
   b. To enjoy the benefits of scientific progress and its applications.

2. The steps to be taken by the States Parties to this Protocol to ensure the full exercise of this right shall include those necessary for the conservation, the development and the diffusion of science, culture and art.

3. The States Parties to the present Protocol undertake to respect the freedom indispensable for scientific research and creative activity.

4. The States Parties to this Protocol recognize the benefits to be derived from the encouragement and development of international contacts and cooperation in the scientific and cultural fields.

Article 17

Right to the Founding and the Protection of Families

1. The family is the natural and fundamental element of society and ought to be protected by the society and the State.
2. Everyone shall have the right to found a family, which he shall exercise in accordance with the provisions of the pertinent domestic legislation.
3. Without prejudice to the provisions of article 17 of the American Convention on Human Rights, the States Parties undertake, pursuant to the present Protocol, to accord special protection to the family group and in particular:

   a. To accord special attention and assistance to mothers during a reasonable period before and after childbirth.

   b. To guarantee children adequate nutrition both during nursing and while attending school.

   c. To adopt special measures for the protection of adolescents in order to guarantee the full development of their physical, intellectual and moral capacities.

   d. To undertake special programs of family training so as to help create a stable and positive environment in which children will receive and develop the values of understanding, solidarity, respect and responsibility.

Article 18

Rights of the Child

Every child has the right to the protection which the conditions of childhood requires as regards the family, society and the State. Every child has the right to grow under the protection and responsibility of its parents; except in exceptional circumstances, as defined by the courts, a child of young age ought not to be separated from its mother. Every child has the right to free and compulsory education, at least in its basic phase, and to continue at higher levels of the educational system.

Article 19

Protection of the Aged

Everyone shall have the right to special protection during his old age. To that end, the States Parties undertake to adopt the necessary measures for ensuring the realization of this right, and, in particular:

   a. To provide appropriate facilities, such as specialized food and medical attention for persons of an advanced age who lack it and are unable to provide for themselves.

   b. To undertake specific employment programs for providing the aged with an opportunity to engage in a productive activity appropriate to their ability and respectful of their vocation or wishes.

   c. To promote the formation of social organizations designed to improve the quality of life of the aged.

Article 20

Protection of Disabled Persons

Everyone affected by a reduction in physical or mental capabilities shall have the right to receive special care to enable them to fully develop of their personality. To that end, the States Parties undertake to adopt such measures as may be necessary for that purpose, and, in particular:

a. To undertake specific programs for providing disabled persons with the resources and necessary environment for achieving that objective, including employment programs adequate to their possibilities and which they shall be free to accept.

b. To include in urban development guidelines consideration of ways of solving the specific requirements generated by the necessities of this special group.

c. To promote the formation of social organizations in which disabled persons can develop a full life.

Article 21

Means of Protection

1. The Inter-American Commission on Human Rights will monitor the observance of the economic, social and cultural rights set forth in the present Protocol by means of the preparation of special reports. The Commission's Regulations shall determine the nature of these reports.

2. The Commission shall take into consideration the progressive nature of the observance of the rights subject to protection by this Protocol.

3. The States Parties to the present Protocol undertake to supply the Inter-American Commission on Human Rights, at its request, with information on the measures which they have adopted at their own initiative or at the request of the latter and on the progress achieved as regards the goal of ensuring the observance of the rights recognized in this Protocol.

4. In the exercise of the function set forth in the above paragraphs, the Commission shall be able to count on the advice of experts and to establish the relations it considers appropriate with the organs and agencies of the inter-american and the UN Systems.

5. Without prejudice to the above, in the case of the rights set forth in Articles 8, 9 and 15 of this Protocol, in the case of a violation of these rights directly imputable to a State Party to this Protocol, such a situation shall give rise to the application of the individual petition procedure set forth in Articles 44 to 51 and 61 to 69 of the American Convention on Human Rights and the corresponding involvement of the Commission and where applicable, the Inter-American Court of Human Rights.

Article 22

Signature and Ratification or Accession Entry into Force

1. This Protocol shall be open for signature and ratification or accession by any State Party to the American Convention on Human Rights.

2. Ratification or accession to this Protocol shall be effected through the deposit of an instrument of ratification or accession with the General Secretariat of the Organization of American States.

3. As soon as seven States have deposited their instruments of ratification or accession, the Protocol shall enter into force.

4. The Secretary General shall inform all the member States of the Organization of the entry into force of the Protocol.

4. STATUTE OF THE INTER-AMERICAN COMMISSION ON HUMAN RIGHTS (1979) Approved by Resolution No. 447 taken by the General Assembly of the OAS at its Ninth Regular Session, held in La Paz, Bolivia, October, 1979

STATUTE OF THE INTER-AMERICAN COMMISSION ON HUMAN RIGHTS

CHAPTER I

Nature and Purposes

Article 1

1. The Inter-American Commission on Human Rights is an organ of the Organization of the American States, created to promote the observance and defense of human rights and to serve as consultative organ of the Organization in this matter.

2. For the purpose of the present Statute, human rights are understood to be:

a. The rights set forth in the American Convention on Human Rights, in relation to the States parties thereto;

b. The rights set forth in the American Declaration of the Rights and Duties of Man, in relation to the other member states.

CHAPTER II

Membership and Structure

Article 2

1. The Inter-American Commission on Human Rights shall be composed of seven members, who shall be persons of high moral character and recognized competence in the field of human rights.

2. The Commission shall represent all the member states of the Organization.

Article 3

1. The members of the Commission shall be elected in a personal capacity by

the General Assembly of the Organization from a list of candidates proposed by the governments of the member states.

2. Each government may propose up to three candidates, who may be nationals of the state proposing them or of any other member state of the Organization. When a slate of three is proposed, at least one of the candidates shall be a national of a state other than the proposing state.

Article 4

1. At least six months prior to completion of the terms of office for which the members of the Commission were elected, the Secretary General shall request, in writing, each member state of the Organization to present its candidates within 90 days.

2. The Secretary General shall prepare a list in alphabetical order of the candidates nominated, and shall transmit it to the member states of the Organization at least thirty days prior to the next General Assembly,

Article 5

The members of the Commission shall be elected by secret ballot of the General Assembly from the list of candidates referred to in Article 3 (2). The candidates who obtain the largest number of votes and an absolute majority of the votes of the member states shall be declared elected. Should it become necessary to have several ballots to elect all the members of the Commission, the candidates who receive the smallest number of votes shall be eliminated successively, in the manner determined by the General Assembly.

Article 6

The members of the Commission shall be elected for a term of four years and may be re-elected only once.

Article 7

No two nationals of the same state may be members of the Commission.

Article 8

Membership of the Inter-American Commission on Human Rights is incompatible with engaging in other activities that might affect the independence or impartiality of the member.

Article 9

The duties of the members of the Commission are:

1. Except when justifiably prevented, to attend the regular and special meetings the Commission holds at its permanent headquarters or in any other place to which it may have decided to move temporarily.

2. To serve, except when justifiably prevented, on the special committees which the Commission may form to conduct on-site observations, or to perform any other duties within their ambit.

3. To maintain absolute secrecy about all matters which the Commission deems confidential.

4. To conduct themselves in their public and private life as befits the high moral authority of the office and the importance of the mission entrusted to the Commission.

Article 10

1. If a member commits a serious violation of any of the duties referred to in Article 9, the Commission, on the affirmative vote of five of its members, shall submit the case to the General Assembly of the Organization, which shall decide whether he should be removed from office.

2. The Commission shall hear the member in question before taking its decision.

Article 11

1. When a vacancy occurs for reasons other than the normal completion of a member's term of office, the Chairman of the Commission shall immediately notify the Secretary General of the Organization, who shall in turn inform the member states of the Organization.

2. In order to fill vacancies, each government may propose a candidate within a period of 30 days from the date of receipt of the Secretary General's communication that a vacancy has occurred.

3. The Secretary General shall prepare an alphabetical list of the candidates and shall transmit it to the Permanent Council of the Organization, which shall fill the vacancy.

4. When the term of office is due to expire within six months following the date on which a vacancy occurs, the vacancy shall not be filled.

Article 12

1. In those member states of the Organization that are Parties to the American Convention on Human Rights, the members of the Commission shall enjoy, from the time of their election and throughout their term of office, such immunities as are granted to diplomatic agents under international law. While in office, they shall also enjoy the diplomatic privileges required for the performance of their duties.

2. In those member states of the Organization that are not Parties to the American Convention on Human Rights, the members of the Commission shall enjoy the privileges and immunities pertaining to their posts that are required for them to perform their duties with independence.

3. The system of privileges and immunities of the members of the Commission may be regulated or supplemented by multilateral or bilateral agreements between the Organization and the member states.

Article 13

The members of the Commission shall receive travel allowances and per diem and fees, as appropriate, for their participation in the meetings of the Commission or in other functions which the Commission, in accordance with its Regulations, entrusts to them, individually or collectively. Such travel and per diem allowances and fees shall be included in the budget of the Organization, and their amounts and conditions shall be determined by the General Assembly.

Article 14

1. The Commission shall have a Chairman, a First-Vice Chairman and a Second Vice-Chairman, who shall be elected by an absolute majority of its members for a period of one year; they may be re-elected only once in each four-year period.
2. The Chairman and the two Vice-Chairmen shall be the officers of the Commission, and their functions shall be set forth in the Regulations.

Article 15

The Chairman of the Commission may go to the Commission's headquarters and remain there for such time as may be necessary for the performance of his duties.

CHAPTER III

Headquarters and Meetings

Article 16

1. The headquarters of the Commission shall be in Washington, D.C.
2. The Commission may move to and meet in the territory of any American state when it so decides by an absolute majority of votes, and with the consent, or at the invitation of the government concerned.
3. The Commission shall meet in regular and special sessions, in conformity with the provisions of the Regulations.

Article 17

1. An absolute majority of the members of the Commission shall constitute a quorum.
2. In regard to those states that are Parties to the Convention, decisions shall be taken by an absolute majority vote of the members of the Commission in those cases established by the American Convention on Human Rights and the present Statute. In other cases, an absolute majority of the members present shall be required.
3. In regard to those states that are not Parties to the Convention, decisions shall be taken by an absolute majority vote of the members of the Commission, except in matters of procedure, in which case, the decisions shall be taken by simple majority.

CHAPTER IV

Functions and Powers

Article 18

The Commission shall have the following powers with respect to the member states of the Organization of American States:

a. to develop an awareness of human rights among the peoples of the Americas;

b. to make recommendations to the governments of the states on the adoption of progressive measures in favor of human rights in the framework of their legislation, constitutional provisions and international commitments, as well as appropriate measures to further observance of those rights;

c. to prepare such studies or reports as it considers advisable for the performance of its duties;

d. to request that the governments of the states provide it with reports on measures they adopt in matters of human rights;

e. to respond to inquiries made by any member state through the General Secretariat of the Organization on matters related to human rights in the state and, within its possibilities, to provide those states with the advisory services they request;

f. to submit an annual report to the General Assembly of the Organization, in which due account shall be taken of the legal regime applicable to those States Parties to the American Convention on Human Rights and of that system applicable to those that are not Parties;

g. to conduct on-site observations in a state, with the consent or at the invitation of the government in question; and

h. to submit the program-budget of the Commission to the Secretary General, so that he may present it to the General Assembly.

Article 19

With respect to the States Parties to the American Convention on Human Rights, the Commission shall discharge its duties in conformity with the powers granted under the Convention and in the present Statute, and shall have the following powers in addition to those designated in Article 18:

a. to act on petitions and other communications, pursuant to the provisions of Articles 44 to 51 of the Convention;

b. to appear before the Inter-American Court of Human Rights in cases provided for in the Convention;

c. to request the Inter-American Court of Human Rights to take such provisional measures at it considers appropriate in serious and urgent cases which have not yet been submitted to it for consideration, whenever this becomes necessary to prevent irreparable injury to persons;

d. to consult the Court on the interpretation of the American Convention on Human Rights or of other treaties concerning the protection of human rights in the American states;

e. to submit additional draft protocols to the American Convention on Human Rights to the General Assembly, in order progressively to include other rights and freedoms under the system of protection of the Convention, and

f. to submit to the General Assembly, through the Secretary General, proposed amendments to the American Convention on Human Rights, for such action as the General Assembly deems appropriate.

Article 20

In relation to those member states of the Organization that are not Parties to the American Convention on Human Rights, the Commission shall have the following powers, in addition to those designated in Article 18:

a. to pay particular attention to the observance of the human rights referred to in Articles I, II, III, IV, XVIII, XXV, and XXVI of the American Declaration of the Rights and Duties of Man;

b. to examine communications submitted to it and any other available information, to address the government of any member state not a Party to the Convention for information deemed pertinent by this Commission, and to make recommendations to it, when it finds this appropriate, in order to bring about more effective observance of fundamental human rights; and

c. to verify, as a prior condition to the exercise of the powers granted under subparagraph b. above, whether the domestic legal procedures and remedies of each member state not a Party to the Convention have been duly applied and exhausted.

CHAPTER V

Secretariat

Article 21

1. The secretariat services of the Commission shall be provided by a specialized administrative unit under the direction of an Executive Secretary. This unit shall be provided with the resources and staff required to accomplish the tasks the Commission may assign to it.

2. The Executive Secretary, who shall be a person of high moral character and recognized competence in the field of human rights, shall be responsible for the work of the Secretariat and shall assist the Commission in the performance of its duties in accordance with the Regulations.

3. The Executive Secretary shall be appointed by the Secretary General of the Organization, in consulation with the Commission. Furthermore, for the Secretary General to be able to remove the Executive Secretary, he shall consult with the Commission and inform its members of the reasons for his decision.

CHAPTER VI

Statute and Regulations

Article 22

1. The present Statute may be amended by the General Assembly.

2. The Commission shall prepare and adopt its own Regulations, in accordance with the present Statute.

Article 23

1. In accordance with the provisions of Articles 44 to 51 of the American Convention on Human Rights, the Regulations of the Commission shall

determine the procedure to be followed in cases of petitions or communications alleging violation of any of the rights guaranteed by the Convention, and imputing such violation to any State Party to the Convention.

2. If the friendly settlement referred to in Articles 44–51 of the Convention is not reached, the Commission shall draft, within 180 days, the report required by Article 50 of the Convention.

Article 24

1. The Regulations shall establish the procedure to be followed in cases of communications containing accusations or complaints of violations of human rights imputable to states that are not Parties to the American Convention on Human Rights.

2. The Regulations shall contain, for this purpose, the pertinent rules established in the Statute of the Commission approved by the Council of the Organization in resolutions adopted on May 25 and June 8, 1960, with the modifications and amendments introduced by resolution XXII of the Second Special Inter-American Conference, and by the Council of the Organization at its meeting held on April 24, 1968, taking into account resolutions CP/RES. 253 (343/78), "Transition from the present Inter-American Commission on Human Rights to the Commission provided for in the American Convention on Human Rights," adopted by the Permanent Council of the Organization on September 20, 1979.

CHAPTER VII

Transitory Provisions

Article 25

Until the Commission adopts its new Regulations, the current Regulations (OEA/Ser.L/VII. 17, doc. 26) shall apply to all the member states of the Organization.

Article 26

1. The present Statute shall enter into effect 30 days after its approval by the General Assembly.

2. The Secretary General shall order immediate publication of the Statute, and shall give it the widest possible distribution.

5. REGULATIONS OF THE INTER-AMERICAN COMMISSION ON HUMAN RIGHTS (1980) Approved by the Commission at its 660th Meeting, 49th Session, held on April 8, 1980

TITLE I—ORGANIZATION OF THE COMMISSION

CHAPTER I
NATURE AND COMPOSITION

Article 1. Nature and Composition

1. The Inter-American Commission on Human Rights is an autonomous entity of the Organization of American States whose principal function is to promote the observance and defense of human rights and to serve as an advisory body to the Organization in this area.

2. The Commission represents all the member states of the Organization.

3. The Commission is composed of seven members elected in their individual capacity by the General Assembly of the Organization who shall be persons of high moral standing and recognized competence in the field of human rights.

CHAPTER II
MEMBERSHIP

Article 2. Duration of the Term of Office

1. The members of the Commission shall be elected for four years and may be re-elected only once.

2. In the event that new members of the Commission are not elected to replace those completing their term of office, the latter shall continue to serve until the new members are elected.

Article 3. Precedence

The members of the Commission shall follow the Chairman and Vice-Chairmen in order of precedence according to their length of service. When there are two or more members with equal seniority, precedence shall be determined according to age.

Article 4. Resignation

In the event that a member resigns, his resignation shall be presented to the Chairman of the Commission who shall notify the Secretary General of the Organization for the appropriate purposes.

CHAPTER III
OFFICERS

Article 5. Composition and functions

The Commission shall have as its officers a chairman, a first vice-chairman, and a second vice-chairman, who shall perform the functions set forth in these regulations.

Article 6. Election

1. In the election for each of the posts referred to in the preceding article, only members present shall participate.

2. Elections shall be by secret ballot. However, with the unanimous consent of the members present, the Commission may decide on another procedure.

3. The vote of an absolute majority of the members of the Commission shall be required for election to any of the posts referred to in Article 5.

4. Should it be necessary to take more than one ballot for election to any of these posts, the names receiving the lowest number of votes shall be eliminated successively.

Article 7. Resignation, Vacancy and Replacements

1. If the Chairman resigns from his post or ceases to be a member of the Commission, the Commission shall elect a successor to fill the post for the remainder of the term of office at the first meeting held after the date on which it is notified of the resignation or vacancy.

2. The same procedure shall be applied in the event of the resignation of either of the vice-chairmen, or if a vacancy occurs.

3. The First-Chairman shall serve as chairman until the Commission elects a new chairman under the provisions of paragraph 1 of this article.

4. The First Vice-Chairman shall also replace the Chairman if the latter is temporarily unable to perform his duties. The Second Vice-Chairman shall replace the chairman in the event of the absence or disability of the First Vice-Chairman, or if that post is vacant.

Article 8. Functions of the Chairman

The Duties of the Chairman shall be:

a. to represent the Commission before all the other organs of the Organization and other institutions;

b. to convoke regular and special meetings of the Commission in accordance with the statute and these regulations;

c. to preside over the sessions of the Commission and submit to it, for consideration, all matters appearing on the agenda of the work schedule approved for the corresponding session;

d. to give the floor to the members in the order in which they have requested it;

e. to rule on points of order that may arise during the discussions of the Commission. If any member so requests, the Chairman's ruling shall be submitted to the Commission for its decision;

f. to submit to a vote matters within his competence, in accordance with the pertinent provisions of these Regulations;

g. to promote the work of the Commission and see to compliance with its program-budget;

h. to present a written report to the Commission at the beginning of its regular or special sessions on what he has done during its recesses to carry out the functions assigned to him by the Statute and by these Regulations;

i. to see to compliance with the decisions of the Commission;

j. to attend the meetings of the General Assembly of the Organization and, as an observer, those of the United Nations Commission on

Human Rights; further, he may participate in the activities of other entities concerned with protecting and promoting respect for human rights;

k. to go to the headquarters of the Commission and remain there for as long as he considers necessary to carry out his functions;

l. to designate special committees, *ad hoc* committees, and subcommittees composed of several members, to carry out any mandate within his area of competence;

m. to perform any other functions that may be conferred upon him in these Regulations.

Article 9. Delegation of Functions

The Chairman may delegate to one of the vice-chairmen or to another member of the Commission the functions specified in Article 8a., j, and m.

CHAPTER IV
SECRETARIAT

Article 10. Composition

The Secretariat of the Commission shall be composed of an Executive Secretary, an Assistant Executive Secretary, and the professional, technical, and administrative staff needed to carry out its activities.

Article 11. Functions of the Executive Secretary

1. The functions of the Executive Secretary shall be:

a. to direct, plan, and coordinate the work of the Secretariat;

b. to prepare the draft work schedule for each session in consultation with the Chairman;

c. to provide advisory services to the Chairman and members of the Commission in the performance of their duties;

d. to present a written report to the Commission at the beginning of each session, on the activities of the Secretariat since the preceding session, and on any general matters that may be of interest to the Commission;

e. to implement the decisions entrusted to him by the Commission or by the Chairman.

2. The Assistant Executive Secretary shall replace the Executive Secretary in the event of his absence or disability.

3. The Executive Secretary, the Assistant Executive Secretary and the staff of the Secretariat must observe strict discretion in all matters that the Commission considers confidential.

Article 12. Functions of the Secretariat

1. The Secretariat shall prepare the draft reports, resolutions, studies and any other papers entrusted to it by the Commission or by the Chairman, and

shall see that the summary minutes of the sessions of the Commission and any documents considered by it are distributed among its members.

2. The Secretariat shall receive petitions addressed to the Commission and, when appropriate, shall request the necessary information from the governments concerned and, in general, it shall make the necessary arrangements to initiate any proceedings to which such petitions may give rise.

CHAPTER V
FUNCTIONING OF THE COMMISSION

Article 13. Sessions

1. The Commission shall meet for a period not to exceed a total of eight weeks a year, divided into however many regular meetings the Commission may decide, without prejudice to the fact that it may convoke special sessions at the decision of its Chairman, or at the request of an absolute majority of its members.

2. The sessions of the Commission shall be held at its headquarters. However, by an absolute majority vote of its members, the Commission may decide to meet elsewhere, with the consent or at the invitation of the government concerned.

3. Any member who because of illness or for any other serious reason is unable to attend all or part of any session or meeting of the Commission, or to fulfill any other functions, must notify the Executive Secretary to this effect as soon as possible, and he shall so inform the Chairman.

Article 14. Meetings

1. During the sessions, the Commission shall hold as many meetings as necessary to carry out its activities.

2. The length of the meetings shall be determined by the Commission subject to any changes that, for justifiable reasons, are decided on by the Chairman after consulting with the members of the Commission.

3. The meetings shall be closed unless the Commission decides otherwise.

4. The date and time for the next meeting shall be set at each meeting.

Article 15. Quorum for Meetings

The presence of an absolute majority of the members of the Commission shall be necessary to constitute a quorum.

Article 16. Discussion and Voting

1. The meetings shall conform primarily to the regulations and secondarily, to the pertinent provisions of the Regulations of the Permanent Council of the Organization of American States.

2. Members may not participate in the discussion and deliberation of a matter submitted to the Commission for consideration in the following cases:

    a. if they have a personal interest in it; or

    b. if previously they have participated in any capacity in a decision concerning the same facts on which the matter is based or have acted as an adviser to or representative of any of the parties involved in the decision.

3. In the event of doubt with respect to the provision in the preceding paragraph, the Commission shall decide.

4. When any member feels that he should abstain from participating in the study or decision of a matter, he shall so inform the Chairman, and if the latter does not agree, the Commission shall decide.

5. During the discussion of a given subject, any member may raise a point of order, which shall be ruled upon immediately by the Chairman or, when appropriate, by the majority of the members present. The discussion may be ended at any time, as long as the members have had the opportunity to express their opinion.

6. Once the discussion has been terminated, and if there is no consensus on the subject submitted to the Commission for deliberation, the Chairman shall put the matter to a vote in the reverse order of precedence among the members.

7. The Chairman shall announce the results of the vote and shall declare (as approved) the proposal that has the majority of votes. In the case of a tie, the Chairman shall decide.

Article 17. Special Quorum to take Decisions

1. Decisions shall be taken by an absolute majority vote of the members of the Commission in the following cases:

a. to elect the executive officers of the Commission;

b. for matters where such a majority is required under the provisions of the Convention, the Statutes or these Regulations;

c. to adopt a report on the situation of human rights in a specific state;

d. for any amendment or interpretation on the application of these Regulations.

2. To take decisions regarding other matters, a majority vote of members present shall be sufficient.

Article 18. Explanation of Vote

1. Whether or not members agree with the decisions of the majority, they shall be entitled to present a written explanation of their vote, which shall be included following that decision.

2. If the decision concerns the approval of a report or draft, the explanation of the vote shall be included after that report or draft.

3. When the decision does not appear in a separate document, the explanation of the vote shall be included in the minutes of the meeting, following the decision in question.

Article 19. Minutes of the Meetings

1. Summary minutes shall be taken of each meeting. They shall state the day and time at which it was held, the names of the members present, the matters dealt with, the decisions taken, the names of those voting for and against each

decision, and any statement made by a member especially for inclusion in the minutes.

2. The Secretariat shall distribute copies of the summary minutes of each meeting to the members of the Commission, who may present their observations to the Secretariat prior to the meeting at which they are to be approved.

Article 20. Compensation for Special Services

The Commission may assign any of its members, with the approval of an absolute majority, the preparation of a special study or other specific papers to be carried out individually outside the sessions. Such work shall be compensated in accordance with funds available in the budget. The amount of the fees shall be set on the basis of the number of days required for preparation and drafting of the paper.

Article 21. Program-budget

1. The proposed program-budget of the Commission shall be prepared by its Secretariat in consultation with the Chairman and shall be governed by the Organization's current budgetary standards.

2. The proposed program-budget shall provide at least the necessary items for:

a. the normal functioning of the Commission and its permanent services;

b. the holding of regular and special sessions of its headquarters or elsewhere, as decided in due course by the Commission;

c. on-site inspections, observations, seminars and other activities of the Commission;

d. participation by the Chairman in the work of the General Assembly of the Organization and in one of the annual meetings of the United Nations Commission on Human Rights;

e. the travel and stay of the Chairman at the headquarters of the Commission for the time necessary to perform his functions outside the sessions;

f. preparation of special studies or other specific work related to the promotion or protection of human rights;

g. the publication of documents, studies, reports, annual publications and other work related to the promotion or protection of human rights;

h. the provision of auxiliary services, fellowships, prizes and other means of promoting the teaching and investigation of such rights;

i. maintaining a documentation center and a specialized library;

j. the accomplishment of any other activity related to its functions and duties.

3. Once the Commission has approved the proposed program-budget, it shall present it to the Secretary General for him to submit it to the General Assembly for consideration in accordance with the provisions of the Statutes.

4. The Commission shall determine the priority for and how best to

administer each of the items in its program-budget after it has been approved by the Assembly.

TITLE II—PROCEDURES

CHAPTER I
GENERAL PROVISIONS

Article 22. Official Languages

1. The official languages of the Commission shall be Spanish, French, English and Portuguese. The working languages shall be those decided on by the Commission every two years, in accordance with the languages spoken by its members.

2. A member of the Commission may allow omission of the interpretation of debates and the preparation of documents in his language.

Article 23. Presentation of Petitions

1. Any person or group of persons or nongovernmental entity legally recognized in one or more of the member states of the Organization may submit petitions to the Commission, in accordance with these Regulations, on his own behalf or on behalf of third persons, with regard to alleged violations of a human rights recognized, as the case may be, in the American Convention on Human Rights or in the American Declaration of the Rights and Duties of Man.

2. The Commission may also, *motu propio*, take into consideration any available information that it considers pertinent and which might include the necessary factors to begin processing a case which in its opinion fulfills the requirements for the purpose.

Article 24. Form

1. The petition shall be lodged in writing.

2. The petitioner may appoint in the petition itself, or in another written petition, an attorney or other person to represent him before the Commission.

Article 25. Special Missions

The Commission may designate one or more of its members or staff members of the Secretariat to take specific measures, investigate facts or make the necessary arrangements for the Commission to perform its functions.

Article 26. Precautionary Measures

1. The Commission may, at its own initiative, or at the request of a party, take any action it considers necessary for the discharge of its functions.

2. In urgent cases when it becomes necessary to avoid irreparable damage to persons, the Commission may request that provisional measures be taken to avoid irreparable damage in cases where the denounced facts are true.

3. If the Commission is not in session, the Chairman, or in his absence, one of the Vice-Chairmen, shall consult with the other members through the Secretariat, on implementation of the provisions of paragraphs 1 and 2 above. If

it is not possible to consult within a reasonable time, the Chairman shall take the decision on behalf of the Commission and shall so inform its members immediately.

4. The request for such measures and their adoption shall not prejudice the final decision.

Article 27. Initial Processing

1. The Secretariat of the Commission shall be responsible for the study and initial processing of petitions lodged before the Commission and that fulfill all the requirements set forth in the Statutes and in these Regulations.

2. If a petition of the communication does not meet the requirements called for in these Regulations, the Secretariat of the Commission may request the petitioner or his representative to complete it.

3. If the Secretariat has any doubt as to the admissibility of a petition, he shall submit it for consideration to the Commission or to the Chairman during recesses of the Commission.

CHAPTER II
PETITIONS AND COMMUNICATIONS REGARDING STATES PARTIES TO THE AMERICAN CONVENTION ON HUMAN RIGHTS

Article 28. Condition for Considering the Petition

The Commission shall take into account petitions regarding alleged violations by a state party of human rights defined in the American Convention on Human Rights, only when they fulfill the requirements set forth in that Convention, in the Statute and in these Regulations.

Article 29. Requirements for the Petitions

Petitions addressed to the Commission shall include:

a. the name, nationality, profession or occupation, postal address, or domicile and signature of the person or persons making the denunciation; or in cases where the petitioner is a nongovernmental entity, its legal domicile or postal address, and the name and signature of its legal representative or representatives;

b. an account of the act or situation that is denounced, specifying the place and date of the alleged violations and, if possible, the name of the victims of such violations as well as that of any official that might have been apprised of the act or situation that was denounced.

c. an indication of the state in question which the petitioner considers responsible, by commission or omission, for the violation of a human right recognized in the American Convention on Human Rights in the case of states parties thereto, even if no specific reference is made to the article alleged to have been violated;

d. information on whether the remedies under domestic law have been exhausted or whether it has been impossible to do so.

Article 30. Omission of Requirements

Without prejudice to the provisions of Article 26, if the Commission considers that the petition is inadmissible or incomplete, it shall notify the petitioner and ask him to complete the requirements omitted in the petition.

Article 31. Initial Processing

1. The Commission, acting initially through its Secretariat, shall receive and process petitions lodged with it in accordance with the standards set forth below:

a. it shall enter the petition in a register specially prepared for that purpose, and the date on which it was received shall be marked on the petition or communication itself;

b. it shall acknowledge receipt of the petition to the petitioner, indicating that it will be considered in accordance with the Regulations;

c. if it accepts, in principle, the admissibility of the petition, it shall request information from the government of the state in question and include the pertinent parts of the petitions.

2. In serious or urgent cases when it is believed that the life, personal integrity or health of a person is in danger, the Commission shall request the promptest reply from the government, using for this purpose the means it considers most expeditious.

3. The request for information shall not constitute a prejudgment with regard to the decision the Commission may finally adopt on the admissibility of the petition.

4. In transmitting the pertinent parts of a communication to the government of the state in question, the identity of the petitioner shall be withheld, as shall any other information that could identify him, except when the petitioner expressly authorizes in writing the disclosure of his identity.

5. The information requested must be provided as quickly as possible, within 120 days after the date on which the request is sent.

6. The government of the state in question may, with justifiable cause, request a 30 day extension, but in no case shall extensions be granted for more than 180 days after the date on which the first communication is sent to to government of the State concerned.

7. The pertinent parts of the reply and the documents provided by the government shall be made known to the petitioner or to his representative, who shall be asked to submit his observations and any available evidence to the contrary within 30 days.

8. On receipt of the information or documents requested, the pertinent parts shall be transmitted to the government, which shall be allowed to submit its final observations within 30 days.

Article 32. Preliminary Questions

The Commission shall proceed to examine the case and decide on the following matters:

a. whether the remedies under domestic law have been exhausted, and it may determine any measures it considers necessary to clarify any remaining doubts;

b. other questions relating to the admissibility of the petition or its manifest inadmissibility based upon the record or submission of the parties;

c. whether grounds for the petition exist or subsist, and if not, to order the file closed.

Article 33. Examination by the Commission

The record shall be submitted by the Secretariat to the Commission for consideration at the first session held after the period referred to in Article 31, paragraph 5, if the government has not provided the information on that occasion, or after the periods indicated in paragraph 7 and 8 have elapsed if the petitioner has not replied or if the government has not submitted its final observations.

Article 34. Exhausting Domestic Remedies

1. For a petition to be admitted by the Commission, the remedies under domestic jurisdiction must have been invoked and exhausted in accordance with the general principles of international law.

2. The provisions of the preceding paragraph shall not be applicable when:

a. the domestic legislation of the state concerned does not afford due process of law for protection of the right or rights that have allegedly been violated;

b. the party alleging violation of his rights has been denied access to the remedies under domestic law or has been prevented from exhausting them;

c. there has been unwarranted delay in rendering a final judgment under the aforementioned remedies.

3. When the petitioner contends that he is unable to prove exhaustion as indicated in the article, it shall be up to the government against which the petition has been lodged to demonstrate to the Commission that the remedies under domestic law have not previously been exhausted, unless it is clearly evident from background information contained in the petition.

Article 35. Deadline for the Presentation of Petitions

1. The Commission shall refrain from taking up those petitions that are lodged after the six-month period following the date on which the party whose rights have allegedly been violated has been notified of the final ruling in cases where the remedies under domestic law have been exhausted.

2. In the circumstances set for the Article 34 paragraph (2) of these Regulations, the deadline for presentation of a petition to the Commission shall be within a reasonable period of time, in the Commission's judgment, as from the date on which the alleged violation of rights has occurred, considering the circumstances of each specific case.

Article 36. Duplication of Procedures

1. The Commission shall not consider a petition in cases where the subject of the petition:
a. is pending settlement in another procedure under an international governmental organization of which the state concerned is a member;
b. essentially duplicates a petition pending or already examined and settled by the Commission or by another international government organization of which the state concerned is a member.
2. The Commission shall not refrain from taking up and examining a petition in cases provided for in paragraph 1 when:
a. the procedure followed before the other organization or agency is one limited to an examination of the general situation on human rights in the state in question and there has been no decision on specific facts that are the subject of the petition submitted to the Commission, or is one that will not lead to an effective settlement of the violation denounced;
b. the petitioner before the Commission or a family member is the alleged victim of the violation denounced and the petitioner before the organizations in reference is a third party or a nongovernmental entity having no mandate from the former.

Article 37. Separation and Combination of Cases

1. Any petition that states different facts that concern more than one person, and that could constitute various violations that are unrelated in time and place shall be separated and processed as separate cases, provided the requirements set forth in Article 29 are met.
2. When two petitions deal with the same facts and persons, they shall be combined and processed in a single file.

Article 38. Declaration of Inadmissibility

The Commission shall declare inadmissible any petition when:
a. any of the requirements set forth in Article 29 of these Regulations has not been met;
b. when the petition does not state facts that constitute a violation of rights referred to in Article 28 of these Regulations in the case of States Parties to the American Convention on Human Rights;
c. the petition is manifestly groundless or inadmissible on the basis of the statement by the petitioner himself or the government.

Article 39. Presumption

The facts reported in the petition whose pertinent parts have been transmitted to the government of the state in reference shall be presumed to be true if, during the maximum period set by the Commission under the provisions of Article 31 paragraph 5, the government has not provided the pertinent information, as long as other evidence does not lead to a different conclusion.

Article 40. Hearing

1. If the file has not been closed and in order to verify the facts, the Commission may conduct a hearing following a summons to the parties and proceed to examine the matter set forth in the petition.

2. At that hearing, the Commission may request any pertinent information from the representative of the state in question and shall receive, if so requested, oral or written statements presented by the parties concerned.

Article 41. On-site Investigation

1. If necessary and advisable, the Commission shall carry out an on-site investigation, for the effective conduct of which it shall request, and the states concerned shall furnish to it, all necessary facilities.

2. However, in serious and urgent cases, only the presentation of a petition or communication that fulfills all the formal requirements of admissibility shall be necessary in order for the Commission to conduct an on-site investigation with the prior consent of the state in whose territory a violation has allegedly been committed.

3. Once the investigatory stage has been completed, the case shall be brought for consideration before the Commission, which shall prepare its decision in a period of 180 days.

Article 42. Friendly Settlement

1. At the request of any of the parties, or on its own initiative, the Commission shall place itself at the disposal of the parties concerned, at any stage of the examination of a petition, with a view to reaching a friendly settlement of the matter on the basis of respect for the human rights recognized in the American Convention on Human Rights.

2. If a friendly settlement is reached, the Commission shall prepare a report which shall be transmitted to the parties concerned and referred to the Secretary General of the Organization of American States for publication. This report shall contain a brief statement of the facts and of the solution reached. If any party in the case so requests, it shall be provided with the fullest possible information.

Article 43. Preparation of the Report

1. If a friendly settlement is not reached, the Commission shall examine the evidence provided by the government in question and the petitioner, evidence taken from witnesses to the facts or that obtained from documents, records, official publications, or through an on-site investigation.

2. After the evidence has been examined, the Commission shall prepare a report stating the facts and conclusions regarding the case submitted to it for its study.

Article 44. Proposals and Recommendations

1. In transmitting the report, the Commission may make such proposals and recommendations as it sees fit.

2. If, within a period of three months from the date of the transmittal of the

report of the Commission to the states concerned, the matter has not been settled or submitted by the Commission or by the state concerned to the Court and its jurisdiction accepted, the Commission may, by the vote of an absolute majority of its members, set forth its opinion and conclusions concerning the question submitted for its consideration.

3. The Commission may make the pertinent recommendations and prescribe a period within which the government in question must take the measures that are incumbent upon it to remedy the situation examined.

4. If the report does not represent in its entirety or in part the unanimous opinion of the members of the Commission, any member may add his opinion separately to that report.

5. Any verbal or written statement made by the parties shall also be included in the report.

6. The report shall be transmitted to the parties concerned, who shall not be authorized to publish it.

Article 45. Publication of the Report

1. When the prescribed period has expired, the Commission shall decide by the vote of an absolute majority of its members whether the state has taken suitable measures and whether to publish its report.

2. That report may be published by including it in the annual report to be presented by the Commission to the General Assembly of the Organization or in any other way the Commission may consider suitable.

Article 46. Communications from a Government

1. Communications presented by the government of a state party to the American Convention on Human Rights that has accepted the competence of the Commission to receive and examine such communications against other states parties shall be transmitted to the state party in question whether or not it has accepted the competence of the Commission. When it has not accepted such competence, the communication shall be transmitted so that the state can exercise its opinion under the provisions of Article 45 (3) of the Convention to recognize that competence in the specific case that is the subject of the communication.

2. Once the state in question has accepted the competence of the Commission to take up the communication of the other state party, the corresponding procedure shall be governed by the provisions of Chapter II insofar as they may be applicable.

Article 47. Referral of the Case to the Court

1. If a state party to the Convention has accepted the Court's jurisdiction in accordance with Article 62 of the Convention, the Commission may refer the case to the Court subsequent to transmittal to the government of the State in question of the report referred to in Article 43 of these Regulations.

2. When it is ruled that the case is to be referred to the Court, the Executive Secretary of the Commission shall immediately notify the Court, the petitioner and the government of the state in question.

3. If the state party has not accepted the Court's jurisdiction, the Commission may call upon that state to make use of the option referred to in Article 62, paragraph 2 of the Convention to recognize the Court's jurisdiction in the specific case that is the subject of the report.

CHAPTER III
PETITIONS CONCERNING STATES THAT ARE NOT PARTIES TO THE AMERICAN CONVENTION ON HUMAN RIGHTS

Article 48. Receipt of the Petitions

The Commission shall receive and examine any petition that contains a denunciation of alleged violations of human rights recognized in the American Declaration on the Rights and Duties of Man, concerning the member states of the Organization that are not parties to the American Convention on Human Rights.

Article 49. Applicable Procedure

The procedure applicable to petitions concerning member states of the Organization that are not parties to the American Convention on Human Rights shall be that provided for in the General Provisions included in Chapter I of Title II, in Articles 29 to 40 of these Regulations, and in the articles indicated below.

Article 50. Final Decision

1. In addition to the facts and conclusions, the Commission's final decision shall include any recommendations the Commission deems advisable and a deadline for their implementation.

2. That decision shall be transmitted to the petitioner and to the state in question.

3. When the state in question, prior to expiration of the deadline set forth in paragraph 1, requests reconsideration of the conclusions or recommendations in the Commission's report on the basis of new facts or arguments, the Commission, after hearing the petitioner, shall decide to stand by or amend its decision setting a new deadline for its implementation if appropriate.

4. If the state does not adopt the measures recommended by the Commission within the deadline referred to in paragraph 1 or 3, the Commission may publish its decision.

5. The decision referred to in the preceding paragraph may be published in the Annual Report to be presented by the Commission to the General Assembly of the Organization or in any other manner the Commission may see fit.

CHAPTER IV
ON-SITE OBSERVATIONS

Article 51. Designation of the Special Commission

On-site observations shall be carried out in each case by a special commission named for that purpose. The number of members of the Special Commission and the designation of its chairman shall be determined by the Commission. In cases of great urgency, such decisions may be made by the chairman subject to the approval of the Commission.

Article 52. Disqualification

A member of the Commission who is a national of or who resides in the territory of the state in which the on-site observation is to be carried out shall be disqualified from participating therein.

Article 53. Schedule of Activities

The Special Commission shall organize its own activities. To that end, it may appoint its own members and, after hearing the Executive Secretary, any staff members of the Secretariat or personnel necessary to carry out any activities related to its mission.

Article 54. Necessary Facilities

In extending an invitation for an on-site observation or in giving its consent, the government shall furnish to the Special Commission all necessary facilities for carrying out its mission. In particular, it shall bind itself not to take any reprisals of any kind against any persons or entities cooperating with the Special Commission or providing information or testimony.

Article 55. Other Applicable Standards

Without prejudice to the provisions in the preceding article, any on-site observation agreed upon by the Commission shall be carried out in accordance with the following standards:

a. the Special Commission or any of its members shall be able to interview freely and in private, any persons, groups, entities or institutions, and the government shall grant the pertinent guarantees to all those who provide the Commission with information, testimony or evidence of any kind;

b. the members of the Special Commission shall be able to travel freely throughout the territory of the country, for which purpose the government shall extend all the corresponding facilities, including the necessary documentation;

c. the government shall ensure the availability of local means of transportation;

d. the members of the Special Commission shall have access to the jails and all other detention and interrogation centers and shall be able to interview in private those persons imprisoned or detained;

e. the government shall provide the Special Commission with any document related to the observance of human rights that it may consider necessary for the presentation of its reports;

f. the Special Commission shall be able to use any method appropriate for collecting, recording or reproducing the information it considers useful;

g. the government shall adopt the security measures necessary to protect the Special Commission;

h. the government shall ensure the availability of appropriate lodging for the members of the Special Commission;

i. the same guarantees and facilities that are set forth here for the members of the Special Commission shall also be extended to the Secretariat staff;

j. any expenses incurred by the special committee, any of its members and the Secretariat staff shall be borne by the Organization, subject to the pertinent provisions.

CHAPTER V
GENERAL AND SPECIAL REPORTS

Article 56. Preparation of Draft Report

The Commission shall prepare the general or special draft reports that it considers necessary.

Article 57. Processing and Publication

1. The reports prepared by the Commission shall be transmitted as soon as possible through the General Secretariat of the Organization to the government or pertinent organs of the Organization.

2. Upon adoption of a report by the Commission, the Secretariat shall publish it in the manner determined by the Commission in each instance, except as provided for in Article 44, paragraph 6, of these Regulations.

Article 58. Report on Human Rights in a State

The preparation of reports on the status of human rights in a specific state shall meet the following standards:

a. after the draft report has been approved by the Commission, it shall be transmitted to the government of the member state in question so that it may make any observation it deems pertinent;

b. the Commission shall indicate to that government the deadline for presentation of its observations;

c. when the commission receives the observations from the government, it shall study them and, in light thereof, may uphold its report or change it and decide how it is to be published;

d. if no observation has been submitted on expiration of the deadline by the government, the Commission shall publish the report in the manner it deems suitable.

Article 59. Annual Report

The Annual Report presented by the Commission to the General Assembly of the Organization shall include the following:

a. a brief account of the origin, legal basis, structure and purposes of the Commission as well as the status of the American Convention;

b. a summary of the mandates and recommendation conferred upon the Commission by the General Assembly and the other competent organs, and of the status of implementation of such mandates and recommendations;

c. a list of the meetings held during the period covered by the report and of other activities carried out by the Commission to achieve its purposes, objectives, and mandates;

d. a summary of the activities of the Commission carried out in cooperation with other organs of the Organization and with regional or world organizations of the same type, and the results achieved through these activities;

e. a statement on the progress made in attaining the objectives set forth in the American Declaration of the Rights and Duties of Man and the American Convention on Human Rights;

f. a report on the areas in which measures should be taken to improve observance of human rights in accordance with the aforementioned Declaration and Convention;

g. any observations that the Commission considers pertinent with respect to petitions it has received, including those processed in accordance which the Commission decides to publish as reports, resolutions, or recommendations;

h. any general or special report that the Commission considers necessary with regard to the situation of human rights in the member states, noting in such reports the progress achieved and difficulties that have arisen in the effective observance of human rights;

i. any other information, observation, or recommendation that the Commission considers advisable to submit to the General Assembly and any new program that implies additional expense.

Article 60. Economic, Social and Cultural Rights

1. The states parties shall forward to the Commission copies of the reports and studies referred to in Article 42 of the American Convention on Human Rights on the same date on which they submit them to the pertinent organs.

2. The Commission may request annual reports from the other member states regarding the economic, social, and cultural rights recognized in the American Declaration of the Rights and Duties of Man.

3. Any person, group of persons, or organization may present reports, studies or other information to the Commission on the situation of such rights in all or any of the member states.

4. If the Commission does not receive the information referred to in the preceding paragraphs or considers it inadequate, it may send questionnaires to all or any of the members states, setting a deadline for the reply or it may turn to other available sources of information.

5. Periodically, the Commission may entrust to experts or specialized entities studies on the situation of one or more of the aforementioned rights in a specific country or group of countries.

6. The Commission shall make the pertinent observations and recommendations on the situation of such rights in all or any of the member states and shall include them in the Annual Report to the General Assembly or in a Special Report, as it considers most appropriate.

7. The recommendations may include the need for economic aid or some other form of cooperation to be provided among the member states, as called for in the Charter of the Organization and in other agreements of the inter-American system.

CHAPTER VI
HEARING BEFORE THE COMMISSION

Article 61. Decision to Hold Hearing

On its own initiative, or at the request of the person concerned, the Commission may decide to hold hearings on matters defined by the statute as within its jurisdiction.

Article 62. Conduct of the Hearing

1. The Chairman or the member of the Commission designated by him shall preside over the hearing and interrogation of persons appearing before it. Any member may take part in the questioning or make observations, with the authorization of the presiding officer.

2. At a hearing on a petition, parties appearing may also question persons who have been summoned.

Article 63. Attendance at the Hearing

1. Hearings convoked with the specific purpose of examining a petition shall be held in private, in the presence of the parties and their representatives if they are present, unless they agree that the hearing should be public.

2. In other cases, the Commission shall decide on the presence of other interested parties and of the general public.

TITLE III—RELATIONS WITH THE INTER-AMERICAN COURT OF HUMAN RIGHTS

CHAPTER I
DELEGATES, ADVISERS, WITNESSES, AND EXPERTS

Article 64. Delegates and Assistants

1. The Commission shall delegate one or more of its members to represent it and participate as delegates in the consideration of any matter before the Inter-American Court of Human Rights.

2. In appointing such delegates, the Commission shall issue any instructions it considers necessary to guide them in the court proceedings.

3. When it designates more than one delegate, the Commission shall assign to one of them the responsibility of settling situations that are not foreseen in the instructions, or of clarifying any doubts raised by a delegate.

4. The delegates may be assisted by any person designated by the Commission. In the discharge of their functions, the adviser shall act in accordance with the instructions of the delegates.

Article 64. Witnesses and Experts

1. The Commission may also request the Court to summon other persons as witnesses or experts.

2. The summoning of such witnesses or experts shall be in accordance with the regulations of the Court.

CHAPTER II
PROCEDURE BEFORE THE COURT

Article 66. Presentation of the Case

1. When, in accordance with Article 61 of the American Convention on Human Rights, the Commission decides to bring a case before the Court, it shall submit a request in accordance with the provisions of the statutes and the rules of the Court, and specifying:
    a. the parties who will be intervening in the proceedings before the Court;
    b. the date on which the Commission approved its report;
    c. the names and addresses of its delegates;
    d. a summary of the case;
    e. the grounds for requesting a ruling by the Court.
2. The Commission's request shall be accompanied by certified copies of the items in the file that the Commission or its delegate considers pertinent.

Article 67. Transmittal of other Elements

The Commission shall transmit to the Court, at its request, any other petition, evidence, document, or information concerning the case, with the exception of documents concerning the futile attempts to reach a friendly settlement. The transmittal of documents shall in each case be subject to the decision of the Commission, which shall withhold the name and identity of the petitioner.

Article 68. Notification of the Petitioner

When the Commission decides to refer a case to the Court, the Executive Secretary shall immediately notify the petitioner and alleged victim of the Commission's decision and offer him the opportunity of making observations in writing on the request submitted to the Court. The Commission shall decide on the action to be taken with respect to these observations.

Article 69. Provisional Measures

1. In cases of extreme gravity and urgency, and when it becomes necessary to avoid irreparable damage to persons in a matter that has not yet been submitted to the Court for consideration, the Commission may request it to adopt any provisional measures it deems pertinent.
2. When the Commission is not in session, that request may be made by the Chairman, or in his absence by one of his Vice-Chairmen, in order of precedence.

TITLE IV
FINAL PROVISIONS

Article 70. Interpretation

Any doubt that might arise with respect to the interpretation of these Regulations shall be resolved by an absolute majority of the members of the Commission.

Article 71. Amendment of the Regulations

The Regulations may be amended by an absolute majority of the members of the Commission.

6. STATUTE OF THE INTER-AMERICAN COURT OF HUMAN RIGHTS (1979) Adopted by the General Assembly of the OAS at its Ninth Regular Session, held in La Paz Bolivia, October 1979 (Resolution No. 448)

STATUTE OF THE INTER-AMERICAN COURT OF HUMAN RIGHTS

CHAPTER I

General Provisions

Article 1. Nature and Legal Organization

The Inter-American Court of Human Rights is an autonomous judicial institution whose purpose is the application and interpretation of the American Convention on Human Rights. The Court exercises its functions in accordance with the provisions of the aforementioned Convention and the present Statute.

Article 2. Jurisdiction

The Court shall exercise adjudicatory and advisory jurisdiction:

1. Its adjudicatory jurisdiction shall be governed by the Provisions of Article 61, 62 and 63 of the Convention, and

2. Its advisory jurisdiction shall be governed by the provisions of Article 64 of the Convention.

Article 3. Seat

1. The seat of the Court shall be San José, Costa Rica; however, the Court may convene in any member state of the Organization of American States (OAS) when a majority of the Court considers it desirable, and with the prior consent of the state concerned.

2. The seat of the Court may be changed by a vote of two-thirds of the States Parties of the Convention, in the OAS General Assembly.

CHAPTER II

Composition of the Court

Article 4. Composition

1. The Court shall consist of seven judges, nationals of the member states of the OAS, elected in an individual capacity from among jurists of the highest moral authority and of recognized competence in the field of human rights, who possess the qualifications required for the exercise of the highest judicial

functions under the law of the state of which they are nationals or of the state that proposes them as candidates.

2. No two judges may be nationals of the same state.

Article 5. Judicial Terms

1. The judges of the Court shall be elected for a term of six years and may be re-elected only once. A judge elected to replace a judge whose term has not expired shall complete that term.

2. The terms of office of the judges shall run from January 1 of the year following that of their election to December 31 of the year in which their terms expire.[60]

3. The judges shall serve until the end of their terms. Nevertheless, they shall continue to hear the cases they have begun to hear and that are still pending, and shall not be replaced by the newly elected judges in the handling of those cases.[61]

Article 6. Election of the Judges—Date

1. Election of judges shall take place, insofar as possible, during the session of the OAS General Assembly immediately prior to the expiration of the term of the outgoing judges.

2. Vacancies on the Court caused by death, permanent disability, resignation or dismissal of judges shall, insofar as possible, be filled at the next session of the OAS General Assembly. However, an election shall not be necessary when a vacancy occurs within six months of the expiration of a term.

3. If necessary in order to preserve a quorum of the Court, the States Parties to the Convention, at a meeting of the OAS Permanent Council, and at the request of the President of the Court, shall appoint one or more interim judges who shall serve until such time as they are replaced by elected judges.

Article 7. Candidates

1. Judges shall be elected by the States Parties to the Convention, at the OAS General Assembly, from a list of candidates nominated by those states.

2. Each State Party may nominate up to three candidates, nationals of the state that proposes them or of any other member state of the OAS.

3. When a slate of three is proposed, at least one of the candidates must be a national of a state other than the nominating state.

Article 8. Election—Preliminary Procedures

1. Six months prior to expiration of the terms to which the judges of the Court were elected, the Secretary General of the OAS shall address a written request to each State Party to the Convention that it nominate its candidates within the next ninety days.

2. The Secretary General of the OAS shall draw up an alphabetical list of the candidates nominated, and shall forward it to the States Parties, if possible, at least thirty days before the next session of the OAS General Assembly.

3. In the case of vacancies on the Court, as well as in the case of the death

or permanent disability of a candidate, the aforementioned time periods shall be shortened to a period that the Secretary General of the OAS deems reasonable.

Article 9. Voting

1. The judges shall be elected by secret ballot and by an absolute majority of the States Parties to the Convention, from among the candidates referred to in Article 7 of the present Statute.

2. The candidates who obtain the largest number of votes and an absolute majority shall be declared elected. Should several ballots be necessary, those candidates who receive the smallest number of votes shall be eliminated successively, in the manner determined by the States Parties.

Article 10. Ad Hoc Judges

1. If a judge is a national of any of the States Parties to a case submitted to the Court, he shall retain his right to hear that case.

2. If one of the judges called upon to hear a case is a national of one of the States Parties to the case, any other State Party to the case may appoint a person to serve on the Court as an *ad hoc* judge.

3. If among the judges called upon to hear a case, none is a national of the States Parties to the case, each of the latter may appoint an *ad hoc* judge. Should several states have the same interest in the case, they shall be regarded as a single party for purposes of the above provisions. In case of doubt, the Court shall decide.

4. The right of any state to appoint an *ad hoc* judge shall be considered relinquished if the state should fail to do so within thirty days following the written request from the President of the Court.

5. The provisions of Article 4, 11, 15, 16, 18, 19 and 20 of the present Statute shall apply to ad hoc judges.

Article 11. Oath

1. Upon assuming office, each judge shall take the following oath or make the following solemn declaration: "I swear"—or "I solemnly declare"—"that I shall exercise my functions as a judge honorably, independently and impartially and that I shall keep secret all deliberations."

2. The oath shall be administered by the President of the Court, and, if possible, in the presence of the other judges.

CHAPTER III

Structure of the Court

Article 12. Presidency

1. The Court shall elect from among its members a President and Vice-President who shall serve for a period of two years; they may be re-elected.

2. The President shall direct the work of the Court, represent it, regulate the disposition of matters brought before the Court, and preside over its sessions.

3. The Vice-President shall take the place of the President in the latter's temporary absence, or if the office of the President becomes vacant. In the latter

case, the Court shall elect a new Vice-President to serve out the term of the previous Vice-President.

4. In the absence of the President and the Vice-President, their duties shall be assumed by other judges, following the order of precedence established in Article 13 of the present Statute.

Article 13. Precedence

1. Elected judges shall take precedence after the President and Vice-President according to their seniority in office.

2. Judges having the same seniority in office shall take precedence according to age.

3. *Ad hoc* and interim judges shall take precedence after the elected judges, according to age. However, if an *ad hoc* or interim judge has previously served as an elected judge, he shall have precedence over any other *ad hoc* or interim judges.

Article 14. Secretariat

1. The Secretariat of the Court shall function under the immediate authority of the Secretary, in accordance with the administrative standards of the OAS General Secretariat, in all matters that are not incompatible with the independence of the Court.

2. The Secretary shall be appointed by the Court. He shall be a full-time employee serving in a position of trust to the Court, shall have his office at the seat of the Court and shall attend any meetings that the Court holds away from its seat.

3. There shall be an Assistant Secretary who shall assist the Secretary in his duties and shall replace him in his temporary absence.

4. The Staff of the Secretariat shall be appointed by the Secretary General of the OAS, in consultation with the Secretary of the Court.

CHAPTER IV

Rights, Duties and Responsibilities

Article 15. Privileges and Immunities

1. The judges of the Court shall enjoy, from the moment of their election and throughout their term of office, the immunities extended to diplomatic agents under international law. During the exercise of their functions, they shall, in addition, enjoy the diplomatic privileges necessary for the performance of their duties.

2. At no time shall the judges of the Court be held liable for any decisions or opinions issued in the exercise of their functions.

3. The Court itself and its staff shall enjoy the privileges and immunities provided for in the Agreement on Privileges and Immunities of the Organization of American States, of May 15, 1949, *mutatis mutandis*, taking into account the importance and independence of the Court.

4. The provision of paragraphs 1, 2 and 3 of this article shall apply to the

States Parties to the Convention. They shall also apply to such other member states of the OAS as expressly accept them, either in general or for specific cases.

5. The system of privileges and immunities of the judges of the Court and of its staff may be regulated or supplemented by multilateral or bilateral agreements between the Court, the OAS and its member states.

Article 16. Service

1. The judges shall remain at the disposal of the Court, and shall travel to the seat of the Court or to the place where the Court is holding its sessions as often and for as long a time as may be necessary, as established in the Regulations.

2. The President shall render his service on a permanent basis.

Article 17. Emoluments

1. The emoluments of the President and the judges of the Court shall be set in accordance with the obligations and incompatibilities imposed on them by Articles 16 and 18, and bearing in mind the importance and independence of their functions.

2. The ad hoc judges shall receive the emoluments established by regulation, within the limits of the Court's budget.

3. The judges shall also receive per diem and travel allowances, when appropriate.

Article 18. Incompatibilities

1. The position of judge of the Inter-American Court of Human Rights is incompatible with the following positions and activities.

    a. Members or high-ranking officials of the executive branch of government, except for those who hold positions that do not place them under the direct control of the executive branch and those of diplomatic agents who are not Chiefs of Missions to the OAS or to any of its member states;

    b. Officials of international organizations;

    c. Any others that might prevent the judges from discharging their duties, or that might affect their independence or impartiality, or the dignity and prestige of the office.

2. In case of doubt as to the incompatibility, the Court shall decide. If the incompatibility is not resolved, the provisions for Article 73 of the Convention and Article 20.2 of the present Statute shall apply.

3. Incompatibilities may lead only to dismissal of the judge and the imposition of applicable liabilities, but shall not invalidate the acts and decisions in which the judge in question participated.

Article 19. Disqualification

1. Judges may not take part in matters which, in the opinion of the Court, they or members of their family have a direct interest or in which they have previously taken part as agents, counsel or advocates, or as members of a national or international court or an investigatory committee, or in any other capacity.

2. If a judge is disqualified from hearing a case or for some other appropriate reason considers that he should not take part in a specific matter, he shall advise the President of his disqualification. Should the latter disagree, the Court shall decide.

3. If the President considers that a judge has cause for disqualification or for some other pertinent reason should not take part in a given matter, he shall advise him to that effect. Should the judge in question disagree, the Court shall decide.

4. When one or more judges are disqualified pursuant to this article, the President may request the States Parties to the Convention, in a meeting of the OAS Permanent Council, to appoint interim judges to replace them.

Article 20. Disciplinary Regime

1. In the performance of their duties and at all other times, the judges and staff of the Court shall conduct themselves in a manner that is in keeping with the office of those who perform an international judicial function. They shall be answerable to the Court for their conduct, as well as for any violation, act of negligence or omission committed in the exercise of their functions.

2. The OAS General Assembly shall have disciplinary authority over the judges, but may exercise that authority only at the request of the Court itself, composed for this purpose of the remaining judges. The Court shall inform the General Assembly of the reasons for its request.

3. Disciplinary authority over the Secretary shall lie with the Court, and over the rest of the staff, with the Secretary, who shall exercise that authority with the approval of the President.

4. The Court shall issue disciplinary rules, subject to the administrative regulations of the OAS General Secretariat insofar as they may be applicable in accordance with Article 59 of the Convention.

Article 21. Resignation—Incapacity

1. Any resignation from the Court shall be submitted in writing to the President of the Court. The resignation shall not become effective until the Court has accepted it.

2. The Court shall decide whether a judge is incapable of performing his functions.

3. The President of the Court shall notify the Secretary General of the OAS of the acceptance of a resignation or a determination of incapacity, for appropriate action.

CHAPTER V

The Workings of the Court

Article 22. Sessions

1. The Court shall hold regular and special sessions.

2. Regular sessions shall be held as determined by the Regulations of the Court.

3. Special sessions shall be convoked by the President or at the request of a majority of the judges.

Article 23. Quorum

1. The quorum for deliberations by the Court shall be five judges.
2. Decisions of the Court shall be taken by a majority vote of the judges present.
3. In the event of a tie, the President shall cast the deciding vote.

Article 24. Hearings, Deliberations, Decisions

1. The hearings shall be public, unless the Court, in exceptional circumstances, decides otherwise.
2. The Court shall deliberate in private. Its deliberations shall remain secret, unless the Court decides otherwise.
3. The decisions, judgments and opinions of the Court shall be delivered in public session, and the parties shall be given written notification thereof. In addition, the decisions, judgments and opinions shall be published, along with judges' individual votes and opinions and with such other data or background information that the Court may deem appropriate.

Article 25. Rules and Regulations

1. The Court shall draw up its Rules of Procedure.
2. The Rules of Procedure may delegate to the President or to Committees of the Court authority to carry out certain parts of the legal proceedings, with the exception of issuing final rulings or advisory opinions. Rulings or decisions issued by the President or the Committees of the Court that are not purely procedural in nature may be appealed before the full Court.
3. The Court shall also draw up its own Regulations.

Article 26. Budget, Financial System

1. The Court shall draw up its own budget and shall submit it for approval to the General Assembly of the OAS, through the General Secretariat. The latter may not introduce any changes in it.
2. The Court shall administer its own budget.

CHAPTER VI

Relations with Governments and Organizations

Article 27. Relations with the Host Country, Governments and Organizations

1. The relations of the Court with the host country shall be governed through a headquarters agreement. The seat of the Court shall be international in nature.
2. The relations of the Court with governments, with the OAS and its organs, agencies and entities and with other international governmental organizations involved in promoting and defending human rights shall be governed through special agreements.

Article 28. Relations with the Inter-American Commission on Human Rights

The Inter-American Commission on Human Rights shall appear as a party before the Court in all cases within the adjudicatory jurisdiction of the Court, pursuant to Article 2.1 of the present Statute.

Article 29. Agreements of Cooperation

1. The Court may enter into agreements of cooperation with such nonprofit institutions and law schools, bar associations, courts, academies and educational or research institutions dealing with related disciplines in order to obtain their cooperation and to strengthen and promote the juridical and institutional principles of the Convention in general and of the Court in particular.

2. The Court shall include an account of such agreements and their results in its annual report to the OAS General Assembly.

Article 30. Report to the OAS General Assembly

The Court shall submit a report on its work of the previous year to each regular session of the OAS General Assembly. It shall indicate those cases in which a state has failed to comply with the Court's ruling. It may also submit to the OAS General Assembly proposals or recommendations on ways to improve the inter-American system of human rights, insofar as they concern the work of the Court.

CHAPTER VII

Final Provisions

Article 31. Amendments to the Statute

The present Statute may be amended by the OAS General Assembly, at the initiative of any member or of the Court itself.

Article 32. Entry into Force

The present Statute shall enter into force on January 1, 1980.

7. RULES OF PROCEDURE OF THE INTER-AMERICAN COURT OF HUMAN RIGHTS (1980) Approved by the Court at its Third Regular Meeting, held July 30–August 9, 1980

RULES OF PROCEDURE ON THE INTER-AMERICAN COURT ON HUMAN RIGHTS

Article 1

1. The purpose of these Rules is to regulate the organization and establish the procedures of the Court.

2. The Court may adopt such other Rules as are necessary to carry out its functions.

3. In the absence of a provision in these Rules, or in the case of doubt as to their interpretation, the Court shall decide.

Article 2 Definitions

For the purposes of these Rules:

a. the term "Convention" means the American Convention on Human Rights (Pact of San José, Costa Rica);

b. the term "Statute" means the Statute of the Inter-American Court of Human Rights;

c. the term "Court" means the Inter-American Court of Human Rights;

d. the expression "Permanent Commission" means the commission composed of the President, Vice-President and third Judge;

e. the expression "Titular Judge" means any Judge elected in pursuance of Article 53 and 54 of the Convention;

f. the expression "*Ad Hoc* Judge" means any Judge appointed in pursuance of Article 55 of the Convention;

g. the expression "Interim Judge" means any Judge appointed in pursuance of Articles 6.3 and 19.4 of the Statute;

h. the expression "States Parties" means the States which have ratified or adhered to the Convention;

i. the expression "Member States" means the Member States of the Organization of American States;

j. the expression "Parties to the case" means the parties in a case before the Court;

k. the term "Commission" means the Inter-American Commission on Human Rights;

l. the expression "Delegates of the Commission" means the persons designated by the Commission to represent it in proceedings before the Court;

m. the expression "Report of the Commission" means the report provided for in Article 50 of the Convention;

n. the expression "General Assembly" means the General Assembly of the Organization of American States;

o. the expression "Permanent Council" means the Permanent Council of the Organization of American States;

p. the term "Secretary" means the Secretary of the Court;

q. the term "Deputy Secretary" means the Deputy Secretary of the Court.

TITLE I—ORGANIZATION AND FUNCTIONING OF THE COURT

CHAPTER I

The Presidency

Article 3. Election of the President and Vice-President

1. The President and Vice-President are elected for a period of two years.

Their terms begin on July 1 of the corresponding year. The election shall be held on July 1 or as soon as possible thereafter.

2. The election referred to in this Article shall be by secret ballot of the titular Judges who are present. If no Judge receives an absolute majority, a ballot shall take place between the two Judges who have received the most votes. In the case of a tie vote, the Judge having precedence in accordance with Article 13 of the Statute shall be deemed elected.

Article 4. Functions of the President

1. The functions of the President are;
    a. to represent the Court legally and officially;
    b. to preside over the meetings of the Court and to submit for its consideration the topics of the agenda;
    c. to rule on points of order that may arise during the discussions of the Court. If any Judge so requests, the point of order shall be submitted to a majority vote;
    d. to direct and promote the work of the Court;
    e. to present, at the beginning of each regular or special session, a report on the manner in which, during the recess between sessions, he has discharged the functions conferred upon him by these Rules;
    f. to exercise such other functions as are conferred upon him by the Statute, these Rules or the Court.

2. The President may delegate, in specific cases, the official or legal representation of the Court to the Vice-President or any of the judges or, if necessary, to the Secretary or Deputy Secretary.[62]

Article 5. The Vice-President

1. The Vice-President shall take the place of the President in the latter's temporary absence or if the office of President becomes vacant. In the latter case, the Court shall elect a new Vice-President to serve out the term of the previous Vice-President. The same procedure shall be followed if the Vice-President is no longer a member of the Court or if he resigns before the end of his term.

2. In the absence of the President and the Vice-President, their functions shall be assumed by the other Judges in the order of precedence established in Article 13 of the Statute.

3. The President shall not preside in proceedings before the Court when he is a national of one of the parties or in special situations in which he considers it appropriate. The same rule shall apply to the Vice-President or any Judge who is called upon to exercise the presidency.

Article 6. Commissions

1. The Permanent Commission is composed of the President, Vice-President and a third Judge named by the President. The Permanent Commission assists and advises the President in the exercise of his functions.

2. The Court may appoint other commissions for special matters. In urgent cases, they may be appointed by the President.

3. In performing their functions, the commissions shall be governed, wherever relevant, by the provisions of these Rules.

CHAPTER II
THE SECRETARIAT

Article 7. Election of the Secretary

1. The Court shall elect its Secretary. The candidates must possess the legal knowledge and the experience necessary to carry out the functions of the position and must have a knowledge of the working language of the Court.

2. The Secretary shall be elected for a period of five years and may be reelected. He may be freely removed at any time by the vote of no less than four Judges. The vote shall be by secret ballot.

3. The Secretary shall be elected in the manner provided for in Article 3.2 of these Rules.

Article 8. Deputy Secretary

1. The Deputy Secretary shall be appointed at the proposal of the Secretary in the manner provided for in the Statute. He shall assist the Secretary in the performance of his functions and substitute for him in his temporary absence.

2. If the Secretary and the Deputy Secretary are absent, the President may appoint an Acting Secretary.

Article 9. Oath of the Secretary and Deputy Secretary

The Secretary and the Deputy Secretary shall take an oath before the President of the Court.

Article 10. Functions of the Secretary

The functions of the Secretary are:

a. to communicate the decisions, advisory opinions, resolutions and other rulings and announce the times fixed for the hearings of the Court;

b. to deal with the correspondence of the Court;

c. to act as administrative head of the Court, under the authority of the President;

d. to plan, direct and coordinate the work of the staff of the Court;

e. to prepare, under the authority of the President, the draft programs, regulations, and budgets of the Court;

f. to attend all meetings of the Court held at the seat or away from it;

g. to carry out the decisions assigned to him by the Court or the President;

h. to ensure that minutes are taken of all meetings of the Court;

i. to perform any other duties established by the Statute, these Rules, the Court, or the President.

CHAPTER III
INTERNAL FUNCTIONING OF THE COURT

Article 11. Regular Sessions

The Court shall meet in two regular sessions each year, one at the beginning of each semester, on the dates decided upon by the Court at the immediately preceding session. In exceptional circumstances, the President may change the dates of the meeting.

Article 12. Special Sessions

1. Special sessions may be convoked by the President or at the request of a majority of the Judges.

2. In the cases mentioned in Article 63.2 of the Convention, any Judge may request that the Court be convened in the manner specified in the preceding paragraph.

Article 13. Quorum

The quorum for the deliberations of the Court is five Judges.

Article 14. Hearings, Deliberations and Decisions

1. The hearings shall be public, unless the Court shall in exceptional circumstances decide otherwise.

2. The Court shall deliberate in private. Its deliberations shall remain secret, unless the Court decides otherwise. Only the Judges shall take part in the deliberations. The Secretary or his substitute may be present. No other person may be admitted except by special decision of the Court and after having taken an oath.

3. Any question which is to be voted upon shall be formulated in precise terms in the working languages. If a Judge so requests, the text shall be distributed before the vote is taken.

4. The minutes of the deliberations of the Court shall be limited to a record of the subject of the discussion and the decisions taken. They shall also record the dissenting votes, if any, as well as the declarations made for the record that do not refer to the basis of the vote.

Article 15. Decisions of the Court—Voting

1. The President shall present, point by point, matters for discussion and for a vote. Each Judge shall vote either in the affirmative or the negative; abstentions shall not be permitted.

2. The votes shall be cast in the inverse order to the order of precedence established in Article 13 of the Statute.

3. The decisions of the Court shall be made by a majority of the Judges present.

4. If there is a tie vote, the President shall have a second and casting vote.

Article 16. Interim Judges

Interim Judges, appointed in pursuance of Article 6.3 and 19.4 of the

Statute, shall, during the period of their appointment, enjoy the same rights and functions as titular Judges, except for the limitations expressly established.

Article 17. Ad Hoc Judges

1. In a case arising under Article 10.2 or 10.3 of the Statute the President shall invite the States mentioned in that Article to appoint an *ad hoc* Judge within the thirty-day period specified in the Statue. He shall also inform them of the provisions relating thereto.

2. When it appears that two or more States have a common interest, the President shall invite them to appoint a single *ad hoc* Judge in conformity with Article 10 of the Statute. If within the thirty-day period specified in Article 10.4 of the Statute no agreement has been communicated to the Court, each State may submit a candidate within the next fifteen days. When this period has elapsed, the President shall choose by lot the *ad hoc* Judge to represent those States and he shall communicate the result to the interested parties.

3. A State which fails to exercise its rights within the period provided for shall be deemed to have waived them.

4. The Secretary shall communicate the appointment of the *ad hoc* Judges to the parties.

5. *Ad hoc* Judges shall take an oath at the opening of the first meeting devoted to the consideration of the case for which they have been appointed.

Article 18. Disqualifications

Disqualifications of the Judges and related matters shall be governed by the provisions of Article 19 of the Statute.

TITLE II
PROCEDURE

CHAPTER I

General Rules

Article 19. Official Languages

1. The official languages of the Court are those of the Organization of American States.

2. The working languages are those of the nationalities of the Judges and, whenever required, those of the parties as long as they are the official languages.

3. The working languages shall be determined at the beginning of the proceedings in each case.

4. The Court may authorize any party, agent, advocate, advisor, witness, expert, or other person who appears before it to use his own language if he does not have sufficient knowledge of an official language. The Court shall, in that event, make the necessary arrangements for the interpretation of the statements of such persons into the working language mentioned in the preceding paragraph.

5. In all cases the authentic text shall be designated accordingly.

Article 20. Representation of the Parties

The parties shall be represented by agents who may have the assistance of advocates, advisers, or any other person of their choice.

Article 21. Representation of the Commission

The Commission shall be represented by the delegates whom it designates. These delegates may, if they so wish, have the assistance of any person of their choice.

Article 22. Communications, Notifications and Summonses Addressed to Persons other than the Agents of the Parties or Delegates of the Commission

1. If, for any communication, notification or summons addressed to persons other than the agents of the parties or delegates of the Commission, the Court considers it necessary to have the assistance of the government of the State on whose territory such communication, notification or summons is to have effect, the President shall address an appropriate request to that government to obtain the same.

2. The same procedure shall apply when the Court wishes to undertake or arrange for an investigation in the territory of a State for the purpose of establishing the facts of procuring evidence, or when it orders the appearance of a person resident in, or having to cross, that territory.

Article 23. Interim Measures

1. At any stage of the proceedings involving cases of extreme gravity and urgency and when necessary to avoid irreparable damage to persons, the Court may, in matters it has under consideration, adopt whatever provisional measures, based on the provisions of Article 63.2 of the Convention, it deems appropriate.

2. With respect to matters not yet submitted to it, the Court may act at the request of the Commission.

3. Such request may be presented to the President or any Judge of the Court by any means of communication.

4. If the Court is not sitting, the President shall convoke it immediately. Pending the meeting of the Court, the President, in consultation with the Permanent Commission or with the Judges, if possible, shall call upon the parties, whenever necessary, to act so as to permit any decision of the Court regarding the request for provisional measures to have its appropriate effect.

5. The Court may at any time determine, *proprio motu* or at the request of one of the parties, whether the circumstances of the case require the adoption of provisional measures.

Article 24. Procedure by Default

1. When a party fails to appear in or to continue with a case, the Court shall, *proprio motu*, subject to the provisions of Article 42 of these Rules, take whatever measures are necessary to complete consideration of the case.

2. When a party, having the right to enter a case, does so at a later stage, it shall take the proceedings at that stage.

CHAPTER II
INSTITUTION OF THE PROCEEDINGS

Article 25. Filing of the Application

1. A State Party which intends to bring a case before the Court in accordance with the provisions of Article 61 of the Convention shall file with the Secretary an application, in twenty copies, indicating the object of the application, the human rights involved, and the name and address of its agent, including, if pertinent, its objections to the opinion of the Commission. On receipt of the application, the Secretary shall immediately request the report of the Commission.

2. If the Commission intends to bring a case before the Court in accordance with the provisions of Article 61 of the Convention, it shall file with the Secretary, together with its report, in twenty copies, its duly signed application which shall indicate the object of the application, the human rights involved, and the names of its delegates.

Article 26. Communication of the Application

1. On receipt of the application provided for in Article 25 of these Rules, the Secretary shall notify the Commission whenever the application is submitted under Article 25.1 as well as the States concerned in the case, transmitting copies thereof to them.

2. The Secretary shall inform the other States Parties and the Secretary General of the OAS of the receipt of the application.

3. When giving the notice provided for in paragraph 1, the Secretary shall request the State concerned to designate, within a period of two weeks, an agent who shall have an address for service at the seat of the Court to which all communications concerning the case shall be sent. If the State does not do so, a decision shall be deemed to have been notified twenty-four hours after it was rendered.

Article 27. Preliminary Objections

1. A preliminary objection must be filed, in twenty copies, no later than the expiration of the time fixed for the beginning of the written proceedings with respect to the party making the objection.

2. The preliminary objection shall set out the facts and the law on which the objection is based, the submissions and a list of the documents on support; it shall mention any evidence which the party may wish to produce. Copies of the supporting documents shall be attached.

3. The receipt by the Secretary of a preliminary objection shall not cause the suspension of the proceedings on the merits. The Court, or the President if the

Court is not sitting, shall fix the time-limit within which the other party may present a written statement of its observations and submissions.

4. The Court shall, after having received the replies or comments of every other party and of the delegates of the Commission, give its decision on the objection or join the objection to the merits.

CHAPTER III
EXAMINATION OF THE CASES

Article 28. Stages of the Proceedings

The proceedings before the Court shall consist of a written and an oral part.

Article 29. Fixing of Time-Limits

Before the Court meets, the President shall ascertain the views of the agents of the parties and the delegates of the Commission or, if they have not yet been appointed, the Chairman of the Commission, regarding the procedure to be followed. He shall then direct in what order and within what time-limits memorials, counter-memorials and other documents are to be filed.

Article 30. Written Proceeding

1. The written part of the proceedings in a case shall consist of a Memorial and Counter-Memorial.

2. The Court may, in special circumstances, authorize additional written submissions consisting of a Reply and a Rejoinder.

3. A Memorial shall contain a statement of the relevant facts, a statement of law, and the submissions.

4. A Counter-Memorial shall contain an admission or denial of the facts stated in the Memorial; any additional facts, if necessary; observations concerning the statement of law in the Memorial; a statement of law in answer thereto; and the submissions.

5. The Reply and Rejoinder, whenever authorized by the Court, shall not merely repeat the contentions of the parties, but shall be directed to bringing out the issues that still divide them.

6. The Memorials, Counter-Memorials, and accompanying documents shall be deposited with the Secretary in twenty copies. The Secretary shall send copies of this documentation to the agents of the parties and the delegates of the Commission.

Article 31. Joinder of Cases

1. In the event that two cases are presented which have common elements, the Court shall decide whether to join the cases.

2. The Court may at any time direct that the proceedings in two or more cases be joined.

Article 32. Oral Proceedings

When the case is ready for hearing, the President shall, after consulting the agents of the parties and the delegates of the Commission, fix the date for the opening of the oral proceedings.

Article 33. Conduct of the Hearings

The President shall direct the hearings. He shall prescribe the order in which the agents, the advocates or advisers of the parties, and the delegates of the Commission, as well as any other person appointed by them in accordance with Article 21, shall be called upon to speak.

Article 34. Inquiry, Expert Opinion and other Measures for Obtaining Information

1. The Court may, at the request of a party or the delegates of the Commission, or *proprio motu*, decide to hear as a witness, expert, or in any other capacity, any person whose testimony or statements seem likely to assist it in carrying out its functions.

2. The Court may, in consultation with the parties, entrust any body, office, commission, or authority of its choice with the task of obtaining information, expressing an opinion, or making a report upon any specific point.

3. Any report prepared in accordance with the preceding paragraph shall be sent to the Secretary and shall not be published until so authorized by the Court.

Article 35. Convocation of Witnesses, Experts and other Persons

1. Witnesses, experts, or other persons whom the Court decides to hear, shall be summoned by the Secretary. If they are called by a party, the expenses of their appearance shall be fixed by the President and borne by that party. In other cases, such expenses shall be fixed by the President and borne by the Court.

2. The summons shall indicate:

    a. the name of the party or parties;

    b. the object of the inquiry, expert opinion, or any other measure for obtaining information ordered by the Court;

    c. any provision for the payment of the sum due to the person summoned.

Article 36. Oath or Solemn Declaration by Witness and Experts

1. After the establishment of his identity and before giving evidence, every witness shall take the following oath or make the following solemn declaration:

> "I swear"—or "I solemnly declare upon my honor and conscience"—"that I will speak the truth, the whole truth and nothing but the truth."

2. After the establishment of his identity and before carrying out his task, every expert shall take the following oath or make the following solemn declaration:

> "I swear"—"I solemnly declare"—"that I will discharge my duty as an expert honorably and conscientiously."

3. This oath shall be taken or this declaration made before the Court or before any of its Judges who have been so delegated by the Court.

Article 37. Objection to a Witness or Expert; Hearing of a Person for Purpose of Information

The Court shall decide any dispute arising from an objection to a witness or expert. If the Court considers it necessary, it may nevertheless hear, for purposes of information, a person who cannot be heard as a witness.

Article 38. Questions Put During the Hearing

1. Any Judge may put questions to the agents, advocates, or advisers of the parties, to the witnesses and experts, to the delegates of the Commission, and to any other person appearing before the Court.
2. Subject to the control of the President, who has the power to decide as to the relevance of the questions put, the witnesses, experts, and other persons referred to in Article 34, may be examined by the agents, advocates or advisers of the parties, by the delegates of the Commission, and by any person appointed by them in accordance with Article 21.

Article 39. Failure to Appear or False Evidence

1. When without good reason, a witness or any other person who has been duly summoned, fails to appear or refuses to give evidence, the Secretary shall, on being so required by the President, inform the State to whose jurisdiction such witness or other person is subject. The same provision shall apply when a witness or expert has, in the opinion of the Court, violated the oath or solemn declaration mentioned in Article 36.
2. The State may not try any person on account of their testimony before the Court. The Court may, however, request the States to take the measures provided for in their domestic legislation against those who, in the opinion of the Court, have violated the oath or solemn declaration.

Article 40. Minutes of Hearings

1. Minutes shall be made of each hearing; they shall be signed by the President and the Secretary.
2. These minutes shall include:
    a. the names of the Judges present;
    b. the names of the agents, advocates, advisers, and delegates of the Commission present;
    c. the names, description and residence of the witnesses; experts, or other persons heard;
    d. the declaration expressly made for insertion in the minutes on behalf of the parties or the Commission;
    e. a summary record of the questions put by the Judges and the responses thereto;
    f. any decision by the Court delivered during the hearing.
3. Copies of the minutes shall be given to the agents of the parties and the delegates of the Commission.

4. The minutes shall be deemed to constitute the certified record.

Article 41. Transcript of the Hearings

1. The Secretary shall ensure that a transcript of the hearings be made.

2. The agents, advocates, and advisers of the parties, the delegates of the Commission and witnesses, experts, and other persons mentioned in Article 21 and 34, shall receive the transcript of their arguments, statements or evidence, to enable them, subject to the control of the Secretary, to make corrections within the time-limits fixed by the President.

Article 42. Discontinuance

1. When the party which has brought the case before the Court notifies the Secretary of its intention not to proceed with the case and when the other parties agree to such discontinuance, the Court shall, after having obtained the opinion of the Commission, decide whether it is appropriate to approve the discontinuance and, accordingly, to strike the case off its list.

2. When, in a case brought before the Court by the Commission, the Court is informed of a friendly settlement, arrangement or other fact of a kind to provide a solution of the matter, it may, after having obtained the opinion, if necessary, of the delegates of the Commission, strike the case off its list.

3. The Court may, having regard to its responsibilities, decide that it should proceed with the consideration of the case, notwithstanding the notice of discontinuance, friendly settlement, arrangement or other fact referred to in the two preceding paragraphs.

Article 43. Question of the Application of Article 63.1 of the Convention

If proposals or observations on the question of the application of Article 63.1 of the Convention have not been presented to the Court in the document instituting the proceedings, they may be presented by a party or by the Commission at any stage of the written or oral proceedings.

Article 44. Decisions

1. The judgments, advisory opinions, and the interlocutory decisions that put an end to a case or proceedings, shall be decided by the Court.

2. The other decisions shall be taken by the Court, if it is sitting or, if not, by the President, pursuant to the instructions of the Court.

CHAPTER IV

Judgments

Article 45. Contents of the Judgment

1. A judgment shall contain:
   a. the names of the Judges and the Secretary;
   b. the date on which it was delivered at a hearing in public;
   c. a description of the party or parties;
   d. the names of agents, advocates or advisers of the party or parties;

    e. the names of the delegates of the Commission;

    f. the statement of the proceedings;

    g. the submission of the party or parties and, if any, of the delegates of the Commission;

    h. the facts of the case;

    i. the legal arguments;

    j. the operative provisions of the judgment;

    k. the allocation, if any, of compensation;

    l. the decision, if any, in regard to costs;

    m. the number of Judges constituting the majority;

    n. a statement as to which text is authentic.

2. Where the Court finds that there is a breach of the Convention, it shall give in the same judgment a decision on the application of Article 63.1 of the Convention if that question, after being raised under Article 43 of these Rules, is ready for decision; if the question is not ready for decision, the Court shall decide on the procedure to follow. If, on the other hand, the matter has not been raised under Article 43, the Court shall determine the period within which it may be presented by a party or by the Commission.

3. If the Court is informed that an agreement has been reached between the victim of the violation and the State Party concerned, it shall verify the equitable nature of such agreement.

Article 46. Delivery and Communication of the Judgment

1. When the case is ready for a decision, the Court shall meet in private, take a preliminary vote, name one or more rappporteurs among the Judges of the respective majority and minority, and fix the date of the deliberation and final vote.

2. In the final deliberation, the Court shall take a final vote, approve the wording of the judgment, and fix the date of the public hearing at which it shall be communicated to the parties.

3. Until the aforementioned communication, the votes and details thereof, the texts, and the legal arguments shall remain secret.

4. The judgments shall be signed by all of the Judges who participated in the voting and the dissents and concurring opinions shall be signed by the Judges supporting them. A judgment shall, however, be valid if signed by a majority of the Judges.

5. An order of communication and execution, sealed and signed by the President and the Secretary, shall appear at the end of the judgment.

6. The originals of the decisions shall be placed in the archives of the Court. The Secretary shall send certified copies to the party or parties, the Commission, the Chairman of the Permanent Council, the Secretary General, and any other person directly concerned.

7. The Secretary shall transmit the judgment to all the States Parties.

Article 47. Publication of Judgments, Decisions and Other Documents

1. The Secretary shall be responsible for the publication of:

    a. judgments and other decisions of the Court;

    b. documents relating to the proceedings, including the report of the Commission, but excluding any particulars relating to the attempt to reach a friendly settlement;

    c. the transcripts of the public hearings;

    d. any other document whose publication the President considers useful.

2. Documents deposited with the Secretary and not published shall be accessible to the public unless otherwise decided by the President, either on his own initiative, at the request of a party, the Commission, or any other person concerned.

Article 48. Request for an Interpretation of a Judgment

1. Requests for an interpretation allowed under the terms of Article 67 of the Convention shall be presented in twenty copies and shall indicate precisely the points in the operative provision of the judgment on which interpretation is requested. It shall be filed with the Secretary.

2. The Secretary shall communicate the request to any other party and, where appropriate, to the Commission, and shall invite them to submit, in twenty copies, any written comments within a period fixed by the President.

3. The nature of the proceedings shall be determined by the Court.

4. A request for interpretation shall not suspend the effect of the judgment.

CHAPTER V

Advisory Opinions

Article 49. Interpretation of the Convention

1. The request for an advisory opinion provided for in Article 64.1 of the Convention shall be instituted by means of an application that shall state the specific questions on which the opinion of the Court is sought.

2. If an interpretation of the Convention is requested by;

    a. A Member State—the application shall indicate the provisions to be interpreted, the considerations giving rise to the consultation, and the name and address of the agent of the applicant;

    b. an OAS organ—the application shall indicate the provisions to be interpreted, how the consultation relates to its sphere of competence, the considerations giving rise to the consultation, and the names and address of its delegates.

Article 50. Interpretation of Other Treaties

1. If an interpretation is requested of other treaties concerning the protection of human rights in the American states, as provided for in Article 64.1 of the Convention, the application shall indicate the name of, and parties to, the treaty, the specific questions on which the opinion of the Court is sought, and the considerations giving rise to the consultation.

2. In case of an application submitted by one of the OAS Organs referred to

in Article 64.1 of the Convention, the provisions of Article 49.2 (b) of these rules shall apply, *mutatis mutandis.*

Article 51. Interpretation Relating to Domestic Laws

1. The request for an advisory opinion, provided for in Article 64.2 of the Convention, shall be instituted by means of an application that shall identify:

    a. the domestic laws, the provisions of the Convention and/or international treaties forming the subject of the consultation;

    b. the specific questions on which the opinion of the Court is sought;

    c. the name and address of the applicant's agent.

2. Ten copies of the domestic laws referred to in the preceding paragraph shall accompany the application.

Article 52

1. Upon receipt of the request for an advisory opinion, under Article 49 and 50 of these Rules, the Secretary shall transmit copies thereof to any State which might be concerned in this matter, as well as to the Secretary General of the OAS for transmission to the organs mentioned in Article 64.1 of the Convention. He shall likewise inform the aforementioned and the Commission that the Court is prepared to receive within the time-limit fixed by the President their written observations. These observations or other relevant documents shall be filed with the Secretariat in forty copies and shall be transmitted to the Commission, to the States and to the other bodies mentioned in Article 64.1 of the Convention.

2. At the conclusion of the written proceedings, the Court shall decide upon the format of the oral proceedings, and fix the order of presentation and time-limits for the hearing.

Article 53

When the circumstances require, the Court may apply any of the rules governing contentious proceedings to advisory proceedings.

Article 54

1. The hearings and advisory opinions shall be public.

2. When the court has completed its deliberations and adopted its advisory opinion, it shall be read in public and shall contain:

    a. a statement of the questions submitted to the Court;

    b. the date on which it is delivered;

    c. the names of the Judges;

    d. a summary of the proceedings;

    e. a summary of the considerations giving rise to the request;

    f. the conclusions of the Court;

    g. the legal arguments;

    h. a statement indicating which text of the opinion shall be deemed authoritative.

3. A Judge may, if he so wishes, attach his individual opinion to the

advisory opinion of the Court, whether he dissents from the majority or not, and may record his concurrence or dissent.

FINAL TITLE

CHAPTER VI

Article 55

These Rules may be amended or supplemented by the vote of an absolute majority of the titular Judges of the Court.

(These Rules are a corrected version of the Provisional Rules of Procedure which appear in the English version of OAS document OES/Ser.G/CP/doc. 1113/80 of October 15, 1980.)

8. COMPLAINT FORM

I. *EXPLANATORY NOTE:*

   a. The complainant should fill out this form carefully so that the IACHR can examine the case according to its Regulations.

   b. The form should be used only for an *individual complaint* on a specific case. However, if the complaint involves members of the same family and the alleged violation of human rights was commited *on the same date*, a single form may be used.

   c. Fill out the form legibly and be specific. This will make analysis and processing by the IACHR easier. The interested party must sign, and date this form.

II. *NAME OF THE COMPLAINANT:* _____

   Personal indentification document: _____

   Date and place of issue: _____

III. a. NAME(s) OF THE VICTIM(s) TO WHOM THIS COMPLAINT REFERS:

   _____

   _____

   b. DATE ON WHICH THE ALLEGED VIOLATION WAS COMMITTED AND SPECIFIC PLACE:_____

   _____

   c. NATURE OF THE ALLEGED VIOLATION AND IDENTIFICATION OF THE PERSONS ALLEGED TO BE RESPONSIBLE: _____

   _____

IV. ADDITIONAL INFORMATION: List any additional information about the complaint referred to in items III.a, b, and c of this form: for example, information about the victim received after the alleged violation, location and name of the place or places of detention, etc.

   _____

   _____

   _____

V. *HABEAS CORPUS:* specify clearly the following information:

   a. Indicate whether a writ of *habeas corpus* was filed with regard to the stated complaint:

   YES _____   NO_____

   b. Judicial body to which the writ of *habeas corpus* was presented and date of filing:

   Judicial   body   or
   bodies: _____

   _____

   _____

   Date(s):_____

c. Result of the writ of habeas corpus: _____

VI. *OTHER ACTIONS*: List other actions that have been taken *with government agencies* in relation to the complaint: _____

VII. *INFORMATION ON FILING OF THE COMPLAINT*:

   a. Indicate whether the complaint being filed on the present form has previously been lodged with the Inter-American Commission on Human Rights and, if so, on what date?

   YES_____   NO_____   DATE_____

   b. If the Inter-American commission on Human Rights has opened a case on this complaint, indicate the case number: _____

VIII. *ADDITIONAL DOCUMENTATION*: If available, attach to this form a photocopy of documents concerning the complaint that are of interest with regard to actions taken before government authorities: for example, copies of any writ of *habeas corpus* filed.

IX. *IDENTIFICATION*: Please indicate whether you wish your identity to remain confidential:

   YES_____   NO_____

I hereby declare that the above information is true and correct to the best of my knowledge.

SIGNATURE OF COMPLAINANT: _____

_____   _____
DATE   PLACE

FULL ADDRESS OF COMPLAINANT:

P.O. BOX: _____   ADDRESS: _____
CITY: _____   STATE OR PROVINCE _____
COUNTRY: _____
ZIP CODE _____   TELEPHONE: _____

C. ORGANIZATION OF AFRICAN UNITY

INTRODUCTION

Proposals that the Organization of African Unity, like the Council of Europe and the Organization of American States, should have its own human rights charter moved ahead in June, 1981, when the OAU, at its Eighteenth Assembly in Nairobi, Kenya, adopted the Banjul Charter on Human and People's Rights. The Charter went into effect on October 21, 1986.

In July, 1979, the Sixteenth Assembly of Heads of State and Government, in Monrovia, Liberia, passed the momentous Decision 115. This called for the preparation of a preliminary draft of the African Charter "to make provision for the establishment of organs and for the promotion and protection of human and peoples' rights."[63]

Senegal's President, Leopold S. Senghor, the principal proponent of an African Human rights charter, then played host to a so-called "meeting of experts" in Dakar from November 28th to December 8th, 1979, to formulate such a document. The objective of the experts was to create a charter that would be specifically responsive to African needs and which would reflect traditional African philosophy.

This approach had been made clear in a prior seminar on the subject sponsored by the United Nations together with the government of the United Arab Republic. At that time, Emmanuel M. Mwambe of Zambia asserted in his introductory statement that many Africans viewed documents such as the Universal Declaration of Human Rights as a "white" document and not properly reflective of African concerns.

The 65-article Dakar draft prepared by these "experts" (largely African jurists and lawyers) was then submitted to the OAU Ministerial Conference on Human and People's Right in Banjul, The Gambia, meeting from June 9th to 15th, 1980. That conference was charged with resolving all controversies arising out of the "experts" draft and submitting a final charter for the approval of the OAU summit conference in Freetown, Sierra Leone, scheduled from July 1st to 4th, 1980.

But the final charter could not be completed in time; the July, 1980, Banjul sessions failed to achieve a consensus. Agreement was reached only on the Preamble and the first eleven articles. A second Ministerial Conference had to be held in Banjul in January, 1981, when the draftsmen completed their task.

The final step in the adoption process occured during the Annual Summit meeting of the OAU in Nairobi, Kenya, in June, 1981. Edem Kodjo, the Secretary-General on the African Charter on Human and Peoples' Rights to the Plenary of the Council of Ministers on June 10.[64]

Despite early positive reaction to the Charter, some delegates still expressed doubts. They had four objections: (1) The Draft Charter left room for misinterpretation and could give rise to the possibility of conflict with constitutions and laws of member states;[65] (2) Article 45 of the Charter, which established the African Commission on Human and Peoples' Rights ("African Commission" or

"Commission"), did not make it clear that the Commission did not have the authority to interfere into the internal affairs of OAU member states;[66] (3) The Charter did not assert certain rights, such as the right of all peoples to independence and the special rights of women and wives; nor did it sufficiently enumerate certain duties such as the respect due to the constitution, the laws and attributes of a state;[67] (4) The Charter did not make it clear that the sole right of interpretation should be invested entirely with the Assembly of Heads of State and Government.[68]

The Council of Ministers made its official recommendations to the Assembly of Heads of State and Government, and on June 27, 1981 the Assembly adopted the Charter without amendment. The only change was cosmetic—a change of name. It was concluded that the title "African Charter on Human and Peoples' Rights" was too easily confused with the "Charter of the Organization of African Unity." The name "Banjul" replaced "African" in honor of the city in which the Charter was drafted.

The Banjul Charter is divided into three parts. Part I sets forth rights and duties, Part II elaborates the measures to safeguard the rights articulated in Part I, and Part III establishes general provisions concerning the African Commission.

The African Commission will be activated three months after the ratification of the Charter by a simple majority of the OAU member states. Banjul Charter, Article 63(3). Since there are fifty OAU members, a simple majority would require twenty-six ratifications.

1. BANJUL CHARTER ON HUMAN AND PEOPLES' RIGHTS (1981)
Adopted by the Organization of African Unity on June 27, 1981 at Nairobi, Kenya. (Organization of African Unity Document)

The African States members of the Organization of African Unity, parties to the present convention entitled "Banjul Charter on Human and Peoples' Rights,"

RECALLING Decision 115 (XVI) of the Assembly of Heads of State and Government at its Sixteenth Ordinary Session held in Monrovia, Liberia, from 17 to 20 July 1979 on the preparation of "a preliminary draft on an African Charter on Human and Peoples' Rights providing *inter alia* for the establishment of bodies to promote and protect human and peoples' rights;"

CONSIDERING the Charter of the Organization of African Unity, which stipulates that "freedom, equality, justice and dignity are essential objectives for the achievement of the legitimate aspirations of the African peoples;"

REAFFIRMING the pledge they solemnly made in Article 2 of the said Charter to eradicate all forms of colonialism from Africa, to coordinate and intensify their cooperation and efforts to achieve a better life for the peoples of Africa and to promote international cooperation having due regard to the Charter of the United Nations and the Universal Declaration of Human Rights;

TAKING INTO CONSIDERATION the virtues of their historical tradition and the values of African civilization which should inspire and characterize their reflection on the concept of human and peoples' rights;

RECOGNIZING on the one hand, that fundamental human rights stem from the attributes of human beings, which justifies their international protection and on the other hand that the reality and respect of peoples' rights should necessarily guarantee human rights;

CONSIDERING that the enjoyment of rights and freedom also implies the performance of duties on the part of everyone;

CONVINCED that it is henceforth essential to pay particular attention to the right to development and that civil and political rights cannot be dissociated from economic, social and cultural rights in their conception as well as universality and that the satisfaction of economic, social and cultural rights is a guarantee for the enjoyment of civil and political rights;

CONSCIOUS of their duty to achieve the total liberation of Africa, the peoples of which are still struggling for their dignity and genuine independence, and undertaking to eliminate colonialism, neo-colonialism, apartheid, zionism and to dismantle aggressive foreign military bases and all forms of discrimination, particularly those based on race, ethnic group, colour, sex, language, religion or political opinion;

REAFFIRMING their adherence to the principles of human and peoples' rights and freedoms contained in the declarations, conventions and other instruments adopted by the Organization of African Unity, the Movement of Non-Aligned Countries and the United Nations;

FIRMLY CONVINCED of their duty to promote and protect human and peoples' rights and freedoms taking into account the importance traditionally attached to these rights and freedoms in Africa;

HAVE AGREED AS FOLLOWS:

PART I: RIGHTS AND DUTIES

CHAPTER I

Human and Peoples' Rights

Article 1

The Member States of the Organization of African Unity parties to the present Charter shall recognize the rights, duties and freedoms enshrined in this Charter and shall undertake to adopt legislative or other measures to give effect to them.

Article 2

Every individual shall be entitled to the enjoyment of the rights and freedoms recognized and guaranteed in the present Charter without distinction of any kind such as race, ethnic group, colour, sex, language, religion, political or any other opinion, national and social origin, fortune, birth or other status.

Article 3

1. Every individual shall be equal before the law.

2. Every individual shall be entitled to equal protection of the law.

Article 4

Human beings are inviolable. Every human being shall be entitled to respect for his life and the integrity of his person. No one may be arbitrarily deprived of this right.

Article 5

Every individual shall have the right to the respect of the dignity inherent in a human being and to the recognition of his legal status. All forms of exploitation and degradation of man particularly slavery, slave trade, torture, cruel, inhuman or degrading punishment and treatment shall be prohibited.

Article 6

Every individual shall have the right to liberty and to the security of his person. No one may be deprived of his freedom except for reasons and conditions previously laid down by law. In particular, no one may be arbitrarily arrested or detained.

Article 7

1. Every individual shall have the right to have his cause heard. This comprises:
   a. The right to an appeal to competent national organs against acts violating his fundamental rights as recognized and guaranteed by conventions, laws, regulations and customs in force;
   b. the right to be presumed innocent until proved guilty by a competent court or tribunal;
   c. the right to defence, including the right to be defended by counsel of his choice;
   d. the right to be tried within a reasonable time by an impartial court or tribunal.
2. No one may be condemned for an act or omission which did not constitute a legally punishable offence at the time it was committed. No penalty may be inflicted for an offence for which no provision was made at the time it was committed. Punishment is personal and can be imposed only on the offender.

Article 8

Freedom of conscience, the profession and free practice of religion shall be guaranteed. No one may, subject to law and order, be submitted to measures restricting the exercise of these freedoms.

Article 9

1. Every individual shall have the right to receive information.
2. Every individual shall have the right to express and disseminate his opinions within the law.

Article 10

1. Every individual shall have the right to free association provided that he abides by the law.

2. Subject to the obligation of solidarity provided for in Article 29 no one may be compelled to join an association.

Article 11

Every individual shall have the right to assemble freely with others. The exercise of this right shall be subject only to necessary restrictions provided for by law in particular those enacted in the interest of national security, the safety, health, ethics and rights and freedoms of others.

Article 12

1. Every individual shall have the right to freedom of movement and residence within the borders of a State provided he abides by the law.

2. Every individual shall have the right to leave any country including his own, and to return to his country. This right may only be subject to restrictions, provided for by law for the protection of national security, law and order, public health or morality.

3. Every individual shall have the right, when persecuted, to seek and obtain asylum in other countries in accordance with the laws of those countries and international conventions.

4. A non-national legally admitted in a territory of a State Party to the present Charter, may only be expelled from it by virtue of a decision taken in accordance with the law.

5. The mass expulsion of non-nationals shall be prohibited. Mass expulsion shall be that which is aimed at national, racial, ethnic or religious groups.

Article 13

1. Every citizen shall have the right to participate freely in the government of his country, either directly or through freely chosen representatives in accordance with the provisions of the law.

2. Every citizen shall have the right of equal access to the public service of his country.

3. Every individual shall have the right of access to public property and services in strict equality of all persons before the law.

Article 14

The right to property shall be guaranteed. It may only be encroached upon in the interest of public need or in the general interest of the community and in accordance with the provisions of appropriate laws.

Article 15

Every individual shall have the right to work under equitable and satisfactory conditions and shall receive equal pay for equal work.

Article 16

1. Every individual shall have the right to enjoy the best attainable state of physical and mental health.

2. States Parties to the present Charter shall take the necessary measures to protect the health of their people and to ensure that they receive medical attention when they are sick.

Article 17

1. Every individual shall have the right to education.

2. Every individual may freely, take part in the cultural life of his community.

3. The promotion and protection of morals and traditional values recognized by the community shall be the duty of the State.

Article 18

1. The family shall be the natural unit and basis of society. It shall be protected by the State which shall take care of its physical health and moral [sic].

2. The State shall have the duty to assist the family which is the custodian of morals and traditional values recognized by the community.

3. The State shall ensure the elimination of every discrimination against women and also ensure the protection of the rights of the woman and the child as stipulated in international declarations and conventions.

4. The aged and disabled shall also have the right to special measures of protection in keeping with their physical or moral needs.

Article 19

All peoples shall be equal; they shall enjoy the same respect and shall have the same rights. Nothing shall justify the domination of a people by another.

Article 20

1. All peoples shall have right to existence. They shall have the unquestionable and inalienable right to self-determination. They shall freely determine their political status and shall pursue their economic and social development according to the policy they have freely chosen.

2. Colonized or oppressed peoples shall have the right to free themselves from the bonds of domination by resorting to any means recognized by the international community.

3. All peoples shall have the right to the assistance of the States Parties to the present Charter in their liberation struggle against foreign domination, be it political, economic or cultural.

Article 21

1. All peoples shall freely dispose of their wealth and natural resources. This right shall be exercise (sic) in the exclusive interest of the people. In no case shall a people be deprived of it.

2. In case of spoliation the dispossessed people shall have the right to the lawful recovery of its property as well as to an adequate compensation.

3. The free disposal of wealth and natural resources shall be exercised without prejudice to the obligation of promoting international economic cooperation based on mutual respect, equitable exchange and the principles of international law.

4. States parties to the present Charter shall individually and collectively exercise the right to free disposal of their wealth and natural resources with a view to strengthening African unity and solidarity.

5. States Parties to the present Charter shall undertake to eliminate all forms of foreign economic exploitation particularly that practised by international monopolies so as to enable their peoples to fully benefit from the advantages derived from their national resources.

Article 22

1. All peoples shall have the right to their economic, social and cultural development with due regard to their freedom and identity and in the equal enjoyment of the common heritage of mankind.

2. States shall have the duty, individually or collectively, to ensure the exercise of the right to development.

Article 23

1. All peoples shall have the right to national and international peace and security. The principles of solidarity and friendly relations implicitly affirmed by the Charter of the United Nations and reaffirmed by that of the Organization of African Unity shall govern relations between States.

2. For the purpose of strengthening peace, solidarity and friendly relations, States Parties to the present Charter shall ensure that:

a. any individual enjoying the right of asylum under Article 12 of the present Charter shall not engage in subversive activities against his country of origin or any other State party to the present Charter;

b. their territories shall not be used as bases for subversive or terrorist activities against the people of any other State party to the present Charter.

Article 24

All peoples have the right to a general satisfactory environment favourable to their development.

Article 25

States Parties to the present Charter shall have the duty to promote and ensure through teaching, education and publication, the respect of the rights and freedoms contained in the present Charter and to see to it that these freedoms and rights as well as corresponding obligations and duties are understood.

Article 26

States Parties to the present Charter shall have the duty to guarantee the independence of the Courts and shall allow the establishment and improvement of appropriate national institutions entrusted with the promotion and protection of the rights and freedoms guaranteed by the present Charter.

CHAPTER II

Duties

Article 27

1. Every individual shall have duties towards his family and society, the State and other legally recognized communities and the international community.

2. The rights and freedoms of each individual shall be exercised with due regard to the rights of others, collective security, morality and common interest.

Article 28

Every individual shall have the duty to respect and consider his fellow beings without discrimination, and to maintain relations aimed at promoting, safeguarding and reinforcing mutual respect and tolerance.

Article 29

The individual shall also have the duty:

1. To preserve the harmonious development of the family and to work for the cohesion and respect of the family, to respect, his parents at all times, to maintain them in case of need;

2. To serve his national community by placing his physical and intellectual abilities at its service;

3. Not to compromise the security of the State whose national or resident he is;

4. To preserve and strengthen social and national solidarity, particularly when the latter is threatened;

5. To preserve and strengthen the national independence and the territorial integrity of his country and to contribute to its defence in accordance with the law;

6. To work to the best of his abilities and competence, and to pay taxes imposed by law in the interest of the society;

7. To preserve and strengthen positive African cultural values in his relations with other members of the society, in the spirit of tolerance, dialogue and consultation and, in general, to contribute to the promotion of the moral well being of society;

8. To contribute to the best of his abilities, at all times and at all levels, to the promotion and achievement of African unity.

PART II—MEASURES OF SAFEGUARD

CHAPTER I

Establishment and Organization of the African Commission on Human and Peoples' Rights

Article 30

An African Commission on Human and Peoples' Rights, hereinafter called "the Commission," shall be established within the Organization of African Unity to promote human and peoples' rights and ensure their protection in Africa.

Article 31

1. The Commission shall consist of eleven members chosen from amongst African personalities of the highest reputation, known for their high morality, integrity, impartiality and competence in matters of human and peoples' rights; particular consideration being given to persons having legal experience.
2. The members of the Commission shall serve in their personal capacity.

Article 32

The Commission shall not include more than one national of the same State.

Article 33

The members of the Commission shall be elected by secret ballot by the Assembly of Heads of State and Government, from a list of persons nominated by the States parties to the present Charter.

Article 34

Each State Party to the present Charter may not nominate more than two candidates. The candidates must have the nationality of one of the States Parties to the present Charter. When two candidates are nominated by a State, one of them may not be a national of that State.

Article 35

1. The Secretary General of the Organization of African Unity shall invite States parties to the present Charter at least four months before the elections to nominate candidates;
2. The Secretary General of the Organization of African Unity shall make an alphabetical list of the persons thus nominated and communicate it to the Heads of State and Government at least one month before the elections.

Article 36

The members of the Commission shall be elected for a six year period and shall be eligible for re-election. However, the term of office of four of the members elected at the first election shall terminate after two years and the term of office of three others, at the end of four years.

Article 37

Immediately after the first election, the Chairman of the Assembly of Heads of State and Government of the Organization of African Unity shall draw lots to decide the names of those members referred to in Article 36.

Article 38

After their election, the members of the Commission shall make a solemn declaration to discharge their duties impartially and faithfully.

Article 39

1. In case of death or resignation of a member of the Commission, the Chairman of the Commission shall immediately inform the Secretary General of the Organization of African Unity, who shall declare the seat vacant from the date of death or from the date on which the resignation takes effect.

2. If, in the unanimous opinion of other members of the Commission, a member has stopped discharging his duties for any reason other than a temporary absence, the Chairman of the Commission shall inform the Secretary General of the Organization of African Unity, who shall then declare the seat vacant.

3. In each of the cases anticipated above, the Assembly of Heads of State and Government shall replace the member whose seat became vacant for the remaining period of his term unless the period is less than six months.

Article 40

Every member of the Commission shall be in office until the date his successor assumes office.

Article 41

The Secretary General of the Organization of African Unity shall appoint the Secretary of the Commission. He shall also provide the staff and services necessary for the effective discharge of the duties of the Commission. The Organization of African Unity shall bear the cost of the staff and services.

Article 42

1. The Commission shall elect its Chairman and Vice Chairman for a two-year period. They shall be eligible for re-election.

2. The Commission shall lay down its rules of procedure.

3. Seven members shall form the quorum.

4. In case of an equality of votes, the Chairman shall have a casting vote.

5. The Secretary-General may attend the meetings of the Commission. He shall neither participate in deliberations nor shall he be entitled to vote. The Chairman of the Commission may, however, invite him to speak.

Article 43

In discharging their duties, members of the Commission shall enjoy diplomatic privileges and immunities provided for in the General Convention on the Privileges and Immunities of the Organization of African Unity.

Article 44

Provision shall be made for the emoluments and allowances of the members of the Commission in the Regular Budget of the Organization of African Unity.

CHAPTER II

Mandate of the Commission

Article 45

The functions of the Commission shall be:
1. To promote Human and Peoples' Rights and in particular:
a. To collect documents, undertake studies and researches on African problems in the field of human and peoples' rights, organize seminars, symposia and conferences, disseminate information, encourage national and local institutions concerned with human and peoples' rights, and should the case arise, give its views or make recommendations to Governments.
b. to formulate and lay down, principles and rules aimed at solving legal problems relating to human and peoples' rights and fundamental freedoms upon which African Governments may base their legislation.
c. co-operate with other African and international institutions concerned with the promotion and protection of human and peoples' rights.
2. Ensure the protection of human and peoples' rights under conditions laid down by the present Charter.
3. Interpret all the provisions of the present Charter at the request of a State Party, an institution of the OAU or an African organization recognized by the OAU.
4. Perform any other tasks which may be entrusted to it by the Assembly of Heads of State and Government.

CHAPTER III

Procedure of the Commission

Article 46

The Commission may resort to any appropriate method of investigation; it may hear from the Secretary-General of the Organization of African Unity or any other person capable of enlightening it.

Communication From States

Article 47

If a State party to the present Charter has good reasons to believe that another State party to this Charter has violated the provisions of the Charter, it may draw, by written communication, the attention of that State to the matter. This communication shall also be addressed to the Secretary-General of the OAU and to the Chairman of the Commission. Within three months of the receipt of the communication, the State to which the communication is addressed shall give the enquiring State, written explanation or statement elucidating the matter. This should include as much as possible relevant information relating to the laws and rules of procedure applied and applicable and the redress already given or course of action available.

Article 48

If within three months from the date on which the original communication is received by the State to which it is addressed, the issue is not settled to the satisfaction of the two States involved through bilateral negotiation or by any other peaceful procedure, either State shall have the right to submit the matter to the Commission through the Chairman and shall notify the other States involved.

Article 49

Notwithstanding the provisions of Article 47, if a State party to the present Charter considers that another State party has violated the provisions of the Charter, it may refer the matter directly to the Commission by addressing a communication to the Chairman, to the Secretary-General of the Organization of African Unity and the State concerned.

Article 50

The Commission can only deal with a matter submitted to it after making sure that all local remedies, if they exist, have been exhausted, unless it is obvious to the Commission that the procedure of achieving these remedies would be unduly prolonged.

Article 51

1. The Commission may ask the States concerned to provide it with all relevant information.
2. When the Commission is considering the matter, States concerned may be represented before it and submit written or oral representations.

Article 52

After having obtained from the States concerned and from other sources all the information it deems necessary and after having tried all appropriate means to reach an amicable solution based on the respect of Human and Peoples' Rights, the Commission shall prepare, within a reasonable period of time from the notification referred to in Article 48, a report stating the facts and its findings. This report shall be sent to the States concerned and communicated to the Assembly of Heads of State and Government.

Article 53

While transmitting its report, the Commission may make to the Assembly of Heads of State and Government such recommendations as it deems useful.

Article 54

The Commission shall submit to each Ordinary Session of the Assembly of Heads of State and Government a report on its activities.

Other Communications

Article 55

1. Before each Session, the Secretary of the Commission shall make a list of the communications other than those of States parties to the present Charter and transmit them to the Members of the Commission, who shall indicate which communications should be considered by the Commission.

2. A communication shall be considered by the Commission if a simple majority of its members so decide.

Article 56

Communications relating to human and peoples' rights referred to in Article 55 received by the Commission, shall be considered if they:

1. indicate their authors even if the latter request anonymity,

2. are compatible with the Charter of the Organization of African Unity or with the present Charter,

3. are not written in disparaging or insulting language directed against the State concerned and its institutions or to the Organization of African Unity,

4. are not based exclusively on news disseminated through the mass media,

5. are sent after exhausting local remedies, if any, unless it is obvious that this procedure is unduly prolonged,

6. are submitted within a reasonable period from the time local remedies are exhausted or from the date the Commission is seized of the matter, and

7. do not deal with cases which have been settled by these States involved in accordance with the principles of the Charter of the United Nations, or the Charter of the Organization of African Unity or the provisions of the present Charter.

Article 57

Prior to any substantive consideration, all communications shall be brought to the knowledge of the State concerned by the Chairman of the Commission.

Article 58

1. When it appears after deliberations of the Commission that one or more communications apparently relate to special cases which reveal the existence of a series of serious or massive violations of human and peoples' rights, the Commission shall draw the attention of the Assembly of Heads of State and Government to these special cases.

2. The Assembly of Heads of State and Government may then request the Commission to undertake an in-depth study of these situations and make a factual report, accompanied by its finding (sic) and recommendations.

3. A case of emergency duly noticed by the Commission shall be submitted by the latter to the Chairman of the Assembly of Heads of State and Government who may request an in-depth study.

Article 59

1. All measures taken within the provisions of the present Chapter shall

remain confidential until such a time as the Assembly of Heads of State and Government shall otherwise decide.

2. However, the report shall be published by the Chairman of the Commission upon the decision of the Assembly of Heads of State and Government.

3. The report on the activities of the Commission shall be published by its Chairman after it has been considered by the Assembly of Heads of State and Government.

CHAPTER IV

APPLICABLE PRINCIPLES

Article 60

The Commission shall draw inspiration from international law on human and peoples' rights, particularly from the provisions of various African instruments on human and peoples' rights, the Charter of the United Nations, the Charter of the Organization of African Unity, the Universal Declaration of Human Rights, other instruments adopted by the United Nations and by African countries in the field of human and peoples' rights as well as from the provisions of various instruments adopted within the Specialised Agencies of the United Nations of which the parties to the present Charter are members.

Article 61

The Commission shall also take into consideration, as subsidiary measures to determine the principles of law, other general or special international conventions, laying down rules expressly recognized by member states of the Organization of African Unity, African practices consistent with international norms on human and peoples' rights, customs generally accepted as law, general principles of law recognized by African states as well as legal precedents and doctrine.

Article 62

Each State party shall undertake to submit every two years, from the date the present Charter comes into force, a report on the legislative or other measures taken with a view to giving effect to the rights and freedoms recognized and guaranteed by the present Charter.

Article 63

1. The present Charter shall be open to signature, ratification or adherence of the member states of the Organization of African Unity.

2. The instruments of ratification or adherence to the present Charter shall be deposited with the Secretary General of the Organization of African Unity.

3. The present Charter shall come into force three months after the reception by the Secretary General of the instruments of ratification or adherence of a simple majority of the member states of the Organization of African Unity.

PART III—GENERAL PROVISIONS

Article 64

1. After the coming into force of the present Charter, members of the Commission shall be elected in accordance with the relevant Articles of the present Charter.

2. The Secretary General of the Organization of African Unity shall convene the first meeting of the Commission at the Headquarters of the Organization within three months of the constitution of the Commission. Thereafter, the Commission shall be convened by its Chairman whenever necessary but at least once a year.

Article 65

For each of the States that will ratify or adhere to the present Charter after its coming into force, the Charter shall take effect three months after the date of the deposit by that State of its instrument of ratification or adherence.

Article 66

Special protocols or agreements may, if necessary, supplement the provisions of the present Charter.

Article 67

The Secretary General of the Organization of African Unity shall inform member states of the Organization of the deposit of each instrument of ratification or adherence.

Article 68

The present Charter may be amended if a State party makes a written request to that effect to the Secretary General of the Organization of African Unity. The Assembly of Heads of State and Government may only consider the draft amendment after all the States parties have been duly informed of it and the Commission has given its opinion on it at the request of the sponsoring State. The amendment shall be approved by a simple majority of the States parties. It shall come into force for each State which has accepted it in accordance with its constitutional procedure three months after the Secretary General has received notice of the acceptance.

D. REGIONAL COUNCIL ON HUMAN RIGHTS IN ASIA

INTRODUCTION

For more than two decades, the question of a regional convention on human rights has been on the agenda of human rights activists throughout the Continent of Asia. And for more than two decades they have despaired of framing a document which would satisfy the diverse peoples and diverse needs of the world's largest land mass. The most significant breakthrough in reaching that elusive goal has been the 1983 *Declaration of the Basic Duties of ASEAN Peoples and Governments,* which now binds the six-nation ASEAN bloc.

On August 8, 1967, the five nations of Indonesia, Malaysia, the Philippines, Singapore and Thailand formed the Association of Southeast Asian Nations (ASEAN), agreeing to work together for their common security and prosperity. They were joined in January, 1984, by the then newly independent state of Brunei Darussalem.

The *Declaration of the Basic Duties of Asean Peoples and Governments* was unanimously adopted by the First General Assembly of the Regional Council on Human Rights in Asia on December 9, 1983, at Jakarta, Indonesia, and presented to the ASEAN Secretariat on the same day. The Regional Council is a non-governmental organization largely composed of jurists who have been joined by other Asean citizens interested in human rights.

It is unique in the field of human rights in that its principles are couched in terms of "duties" rather than "rights". More than half of the provisions of the ASEAN Declaration begin with the words, "It is the duty of government." And other provisions dictate the duties of "individuals" and "peoples".

The Declaration reveals the intent of its framers to spread this human rights message throughout the continent. Article II (2) prescribes the "duty of governments to transform Asia into a region of peace and neutrality."

1. DECLARATION OF THE BASIC DUTIES OF ASEAN PEOPLES AND GOVERNMENTS

Inspired by Asian reverence for human life and dignity which recognizes in all persons basic individual and collective rights, rights that it is the duty of other persons and of governments to respect;

Moved by the wretchedness, the hunger, the pain, the suffering and the despair which engulf untold millions of Asians;

Aware that these inhuman conditions are neither predestined, inevitable nor irremediable, but are mainly caused by the failure to recognize, or the refusal to respect, the individual and collective rights of Asian peoples;

Convinced that these conditions prevent or retard the transformation of social, cultural, economic and political institutions that denigrate human life and dignity, and retard the development of Asian peoples; and

Deploring the failure of most Asian governments to ratify the International Covenants on Human Rights and their protocols, and to provide effective machinery for their implementation;

The *Regional Council on Human Rights in Asia* adopts this Declaration of the Basic Duties of ASEAN Peoples and Governments, and urges all governments and peoples of the region to incorporate these duties in their national constitutions and laws, and to faithfully implement and enforce them forthwith.

Article I.

Basic Principles

1. It is the duty of every government to insure and protect the basic rights of all persons to life, a decent standard of living, security, dignity, identity, freedom, truth, due process of law, and justice; and of its people to existence, sovereignty, independence, self-determination, and autonomous cultural, social, economic and political development.

2. In particular, it is the duty of every government to respect, implement, enforce, guarantee, preserve and protect, at all times, the following fundamental liberties and rights of the people and ensure that such rights and liberties are incorporated in its national constitution beyond impairment or abridgement by statute or executive action:

2.01. The right to life, liberty and security of person;

2.02. The right to freedom from torture, cruel, inhuman and degrading treatment or punishment;

2.03. The right to equal protection before the law, equality before the law, and to an independent and impartial judiciary;

2.04. The right to freedom from arbitrary arrest, detention, exile, search or seizure;

2.05. The right to freedom of movement and residence;

2.06. The right to freedom of thought, conscience and religion;

2.07. The right to freedom of opinion and expression;

2.08. The right to freedom of assembly and association; and the other rights and freedoms of individuals and of peoples set forth in:

— The Universal Declaration of Human Rights, International Covenant on Civil and Political Rights, and the International Covenant on Social, Economic and Cultural Rights;

— All Declarations of the General Assembly of the United Nations on particular human rights, such as, for example, the right of peoples to self-determination, the rights of women, of children, of the disabled, and of refugees, freedom from genocide, freedom from racial discrimination, and freedom from torture;

— The Declaration and Action Program for the Establishment of a

New International Economic Order and the Charter of Economic Rights and Duties of States;

— International humanitarian law, including the protocols to the Geneva Conventions of 1949;

— ILO Conventions, particularly those on the rights of workers to self organization and collective bargaining;

— The bill of rights of its own national constitution and laws, including customary law, when said rights are broader in scope than the basic rights recognized in international instruments; and

— This Declaration.

It is likewise the duty of every government to ratify the International Covenant on Human Rights and their protocols, of the United Nations.

3. It is the duty of all individuals and peoples to exercise their rights and freedoms in the spirit of human solidarity, respecting and defending the rights and freedoms of others. It is likewise the duty of all individuals and peoples to assert, defend and protect their sovereignty, to preserve and enhance their culture and identity, to develop and use their native talents, abilities and resources for the betterment of society, to respect and obey the laws which accord with this Declaration, and to denounce and resist persistent violations of their basic rights and freedoms.

4. The specification of a duty in this Declaration does not preclude the existence of other duties.

Article 2.

Peace

1. It is the duty of all governments and all peoples to strive actively and continuously for peace. Since social injustices frequently lead to breaches of peace, internally and externally, it is the duty of governments to promote and enhance social justice both within their countries and internationally. While recognizing that, given present conditions, every country has the right to equip itself for defense against aggression, it is nonetheless the duty of government to refrain from excessive military spending. In times of peace, military expenditures shall not exceed the expenditures for education or health.

2. It is the duty of governments to transform Asia into a region of peace and neutrality. In particular, it is their duty to abstain from alignment with any power bloc, to eliminate military entanglements with foreign powers, to abstain from military adventures, to ban foreign military bases and troops from their land, to refrain from developing, storing or using nuclear, biological or chemical weapons, and to bar the use of their oceans and sea lanes to armed vessels of foreign powers.

3. It is likewise the duty of all governments and of all peoples to strive towards general and complete disarmament.

Article 3.

Independent Development

1. It is the duty of government to insure the autonomous political,

economic, social and cultural development of its people. In particular, it is the duty of government, by the appropriate use and development of indigenous or foreign technology, to achieve the optimum and just use of domestic resources in order to meet the basic needs of the people and to ensure an improvement in their quality of life, in accordance with goals and processes freely chosen or approved by the people themselves.

2. It is the duty of government to eliminate all forms and consequences of foreign control or domination in the political, economic, social and cultural life of the nation. It is likewise the duty of government to eliminate the domination of the economy or any sector thereof by domestic monopolies or conglomerates, whether private or state owned. In particular, it is the duty of government:

(*a*) To control the activities of transnational corporations and other foreign and domestic investors to prevent exploitation of the people and to ensure that such activities contribute to the development of the nation and the equitable distribution of wealth and income among the different social classes;

(*b*) To reject all forms of aid or loans that impair national sovereignty, foster dependence on foreign capital, or create or aggravate social inequality; and

(*c*) To place under social control strategic industries or economic activities vital to the attainment of national development plans and goals chosen or approved by the people, such as energy production, telecommunications and public transport.

3. It is the duty of government and of the people to judiciously manage and use the nation's natural resources to preserve them for future generations, to prevent environmental and atmospheric degradation, to prevent monopolies of genetic pools of plants and animals, and to preserve and foster indigenous species.

4. It is the duty of government to eradicate nepotism, favoritism, corruption, and waste in public life. It is the duty of government officials to lead a simple and modest life, and to set an example of impartiality, integrity and service to the people.

5. It is the duty of all persons to refrain from wasteful or conspicuous consumption and ostentatious displays of wealth and power.

Article 4.

People's Participation

1. It is the duty of government to respect and promote the right of the people freely to participate directly at all levels of social, political and economic decision-making, to ensure that the people are provided with the information needed to make informed decisions, and to encourage the formation, and respect the autonomy, of authentic popular or grassroots organizations or movements at local, regional and national levels, rather than creating or supporting its own organizations. Government may not, directly or indirectly, compel the people to join any organization.

2. While the people should make all endeavors to fully participate in social, economic and political decision-making and in the formulation and implementation of local, regional and national priorities, plans, programs and projects,

such participation must be voluntary and not subject to any sanction or threats on the part of the authorities.

Article 5.

Social Justice

1. It is the duty of government to ensure a minimum decent standard of living for all the people, reduce the gap in access to goods and services by different economic and social sectors, and equalize wealth, power and opportunities without distinctions based on race, sex, language, religious belief, political conviction, economic or social status, or ethnic origin.

2. It is the duty of government to provide adequate support to families who have lost their breadwinners by death, disability, detention, imprisonment or the like, or whose head is unsuccessful in finding employment despite his efforts.

3. It is the duty of government to adopt policies to eliminate disparities between rural and urban areas and between geographic regions. In particular, such policies should insure, throughout the nation, basic social services, adequate food and nutrition, safe drinking water, clean air, and health care, free and compulsory education to at least the secondary level, and adult education in health, hygiene, voluntary family planning and vocational training, adequate housing, access roads and public transport, and proper technology.

4. In agriculture, it is the duty of government, with the participation of the people, to establish and enforce appropriate and equitable land use and land conservation measures, prevent depletion of land productivity, prevent the manufacture, importation and sale of agricultural inputs known to be biologically or environmentally harmful, subsidize the equitable distribution of land to tillers or cooperatives of tillers, prevent concentration of control or ownership of land, prevent landgrabbing, enforce floor prices on agricultural products and ceiling prices on agricultural inputs, provide technical assistance to farmers free or at a nominal cost, provide and maintain an effective marketing system for agricultural products, and foster the voluntary organization of independent associations or institutions that will enable farmers, by their organized cooperative efforts, to derive an adequate income from the land they till.

5. It is likewise the duty of government to ensure that lands of public domain, particularly those that are settled, are not placed under the beneficial use or control of foreign corporations or investors or of domestic monopolies or conglomerates, whether private or state owned, and to distribute idle lands of public domain to landless peasants, small farmers or cooperatives of such peasants and farmers.

6. (*a*) It is the duty of the people to respect the dignity of all kinds of labor and services rendered by workers and employees, both in the public and private sectors. It is also the duty of government to ensure that dignity and promote the well being of all such workers and employees by providing opportunities for workers and employees to upgrade their skills, guaranteeing rank and file workers' and employees' participation in the management of enterprises they are employed in, and in labor boards, commissions, tribunals, and arbitration

bodies, and providing them with compensation for work-related injuries or disabilities, unemployment and retirement benefits, and old age pensions.

(b) It is the duty of government to respect the rights of all workers and employees, under any and all circumstances, to free association and collective bargaining and to engage in concerted activities for their mutual aid and protection.

(c) It is the duty of government to foster the formation of genuine, voluntary and democratic trade unions, to recognize the right of such trade unions to affiliate with international trade union bodies, to respect the right of workers to engage in industrial agitation, including the right to strike, and to provide full protection to labor leaders, union members, organizers and persons engaged in labor activities, against harassment, threats, violence, or any form of arbitrary arrest or indefinite or prolonged detention.

(d) It is the duty of government to enact and enforce special legislation for the benefit of household and domestic workers to ensure that they receive and enjoy the same benefits and rights (particularly as regards wages, security of employment, working hours, social security benefits and maternity leave, etc.) as industrial workers. Particular protection must be afforded to female workers of this sector to ensure that they are not sexually harassed.

7. It is the duty of government to establish and maintain an effective health care delivery system, which incorporates useful indigenous or traditional health systems, with emphasis on primary health care, maintain an effective food and drug monitoring body, eliminate the importation and use of dangerous or useless drugs, keep the cost of medical and hospital care within the reach of average citizens, eliminate or prevent control by foreigners or by domestic monopolies or conglomerates of the nation's food and drug industry, guard against the homogenization of food culture and discourage the importation or production and sale of foods without or with low nutritive value, maintain and effectively supervise a health manpower development and distribution program, and promote appropriate research into the most pressing health problems of the nation.

8. It is the duty of government to adopt and implement development plans and programs that provide opportunities for income, employment and amenities of life in rural areas equal to those in urban areas, so as to discourage the excessive concentration of populations in cities and the continued migration from the countryside to urban centers. With reference to communities of urban and rural poor, it is the duty of government to recognize and respect their right to freely organize themselves to resist unjust eviction. In particular, it is the duty of government not to displace them or demolish their homes solely or principally for purposes of beautifying the site, providing facilities or structures for tourists, multinational corporations or domestic monopolies, or implementing a plan or project that enhances the advantages of the rich and the better-off. Where displacement of poor communities is to be undertaken for a justifiable cause, it is the duty of government to first consult with the community to be displaced, informing them of the reason for the displacement, considering in good faith any alternative plan they may propose, and involving them in the planning and scheduling of the relocation. In all cases of justified relocation, it

is the duty of government to provide relocation sites that provide income and employment opportunities and social services such as water, food, schools, power and transportation at least equal in quality, quantity and price to those available at the site from which the community is to be displaced.

9. It is the duty of government to safeguard the dignity, personality and nationality of women, single or married, prevent their exploitation, particularly as sex objects, and ensure that they receive a share in the fruits of development equal to men. In particular, it is the duty of government to ensure that women enjoy the same rights of inheritance as men, prevent discrimination against them in the exercise of their civil and political rights, in the practice of their profession, and in conditions of employment and opportunities for promotion, and provide maternity leave and other forms of protection for working mothers and adequate child care centers for their children.

10. It is the duty of government to give legal protection to children, incorporating special safeguards and care, before as well as after birth, to insure the right of all children, particularly orphans and the children of broken homes or of the poor and disadvantaged, to develop their native talents in freedom, and grow into responsible, mature citizens of their country and the world, conscious as well of their duties as of their rights. It is further the duty of government to recognize the primary right and duty of parents to guide and educate their children; but it is likewise the duty of government to protect children against all forms of neglect, cruelty and exploitation, particularly in employment harmful to their physical, mental or moral health.

11. It is the duty of government to assist physically and mentally disabled persons to lead as normal a life as possible, consistent with their disability, as integrated members of their family and community, to provide them with the best possible therapeutic and medical treatment within its means, to make special provisions to meet their needs, to prevent all forms of neglect, cruelty or exploitation of disabled persons, and to consult with organizations of disabled persons on all matters of direct concern to them.

12. It is the duty of government to assist the aged to lead as normal a life as possible, consistent with their age, as integrated members of their family and community, to provide them with all possible facilities, care and requirements, including old age pensions and security, within its means, and to prevent all forms of neglect, cruelty or exploitation of the aged.

Article 6.

Education

1. It is the duty of government to establish an educational system that provides equal education for all citizens of the highest quality within its means, responds to the needs of society, encourages critical thinking and creativity, promotes a scientific culture, inculcates respect for human rights, fosters loyalty to people and country, respects national traditions, and contributes to national development and the common good.

2. It is further the duty of government to refrain from using education as an instrument of propaganda, and to insure that the faculty and the student body

of all institutions of higher learning enjoy full autonomy and academic freedom, free from all police or military surveillance or harassment, with participation in management and educational policy making, and full access to information about institutional and public affairs.

3. It is likewise the duty of government to prevent foreign management, control or domination of the educational system and of research.

4. It is the duty of the people to avail themselves of the national educational system to the fullest extent possible in order to discover and develop their native talents, to continue educating themselves after formal schooling ends, and to participate in the social, economic, cultural and political life of their communities and of the country, using their skills, talents and critical and creative faculties for the promotion and enhancement of the rights of all and for the welfare of the nation.

Article 7.

Mass Communications Media

1. It is the duty of government to ensure the freedom of newspapers, radio and television stations and other mass communications media to gather and publish news of public interest as well as views and opinions thereon, and to prevent control over any media by foreign interests or a monopoly of such media by any private person or political interest group.

2. In particular, it is the duty of government to enforce the rights of authors, artists, journalists and writers:

(a) To freedom from imprisonment or other forms of harassment for exercising their right of expression;

(b) To freedom of movement;

(c) To access to information;

(d) To protect their sources of information;

(e) To participate in the management and the making of editorial policy of the medium they are employed in; and

(f) Where government owns any medium of mass communications, to insure its independence by creating an autonomous impartial governing board therefor composed of respected, independent-minded persons representing different social sectors or organizations, including opposition political parties.

3. It is also the duty of government to protect the public from misleading, harmful or deceptive advertising or labelling.

4. It is the duty of authors, artists, journalists and writers to use their rights and freedoms responsibly, respect the right to privacy of all persons, refrain from injuring reputations unless necessary in the public interest, and abstain from all propaganda for, advocacy of, or incitement to war or national, racial or religious discrimination, hatred, hostility or violence.

5. Whenever information sought is withheld or its publication prohibited on the ground that such disclosure would injure the safety and security of the nation, it is the right of the aggrieved party to raise the question in court. In such cases, the burden of proof shall be on government.

Article 8.

Cultural Communities

1. It is the duty of government to recognize that members of cultural communities have the same rights as other citizens including the right to participate on an equal basis in public life, and to take affirmative action to ensure such equality. Where equality has been denied in the past, it is the duty of government to provide special representation of cultural communities in order to obtain true equality. It is moreover the duty of government to enforce respect for the right of such peoples to preserve their identity, traditions, language, cultural heritage and customary laws, and enforce protection of their ancestral domains, providing them, if they so desire, with all care and facilities to develop, but respecting their right to determine for themselves the manner and extent of their relationship with the larger society. It is the duty of cultural communities, in turn, to exercise their rights with due respect for the legitimate interests of the nation as a whole, respecting the territorial integrity and political unity of the nation.

2. It is further the duty of government to review its land policies with a view to restoring all ancestral lands belonging to cultural communities to the tribe, bearing in mind the changes that have taken or are taking place in those communities.

Article 9.

The Military

1. It is the duty of the military to remain loyal at all times and in all places to the people, obey the laws, and submit itself to civilian supremacy.

2. Over and above its duty to obey superior orders, it is the duty of the military to defend and to preserve the sovereignty, the safety and the welfare of the people.

3. Consequently, it is the duty of the military (a) to respect the rights of all persons and peoples in accordance with this Declaration, without discrimination based on race, sex, language, culture, religion, political conviction, economic or social status, or ethnic origin; and (b) to accept the popular will on questions of national policy, refraining from imposing its own views and opinions on the people.

4. It is the duty of all governments and civilian leaders to strictly limit the activities and influence of military and para-military personnel to the functions required by an efficient defense against aggression, and to ban such personnel from discharging public functions which are civilian in nature.

Article 10.

Torture and Similar Practices

1. It is the duty of government, under any and all circumstances, to refrain from engaging in or authorizing torture, other cruel and degrading treatment or punishment, unexplained disappearances and extra-legal executions, and to take steps to eliminate such practices by others.

2. In particular, it is the duty of government to remove opportunities and motives to perpetrate these practices by adopting such measures as:

(*a*) Retaining unimpaired the right of access to civil courts by or on behalf of the person arrested, to question the legality of the arrest and detention.

(*b*) Banning secret arrests, secret detention places, and incommunicado detentions, requiring all arrests to be reported promptly to judicial authority and to the family of the person arrested, and making information thereon available to all persons interested. Reports shall include at least the date, time, place and cause of the arrest, the identity of the arresting officer, his official station and authority to effect the arrest, the place where the person arrested is detained, and the name of the officer in charge thereof.

(*c*) Permitting the family of persons arrested, lawyers, medical doctors and religious advisers of their choice, to visit, examine, treat and advise persons detained, without delay or hindrance.

(*d*) Advising persons under arrest or investigation of the right to remain silent and to counsel, and respecting that right; conducting no interrogations, formal or informal, except in the presence of their lawyer of choice; when they cannot afford to pay for the services of counsel, providing a competent, independent lawyer, and when no lawyers are available, some other adviser freely chosen by the detained persons; and accepting no waiver of such rights except in the presence and under advice of such lawyer or adviser.

(*e*) Conducting speedy investigations of persons detained and banning indefinite detentions or those in excess of the applicable penalty provided for by law.

(*f*) Allowing inspection of detention centers and interviews of persons under detention by impartial and independent national and international governmental or non-governmental organizations, with a view to determining whether treatment and conditions of detention comply with international minimum standards and recommending remedial and preventive measures.

(*g*) Suspending from office those charged with perpetrating torture or similar acts and disqualifying them from promotion, automatic or otherwise, while charges are pending.

(*h*) Disciplining immediate superiors of officers who are found guilty of perpetrating such acts, unless said immediate superiors show they have taken every reasonable precaution to prevent the acts.

(*i*) Continuously educating and training police, para-military, military and other investigative personnel to inculcate knowledge of and respect for human rights, and to improve methods of investigation, detection, and other aspects of law enforcement.

(*j*) Making violations of any of the above preventive measures a crime, whether or not torture or similar practices resulted therefrom, and conscientiously prosecuting and punishing those guilty thereof.

3. It is the duty of government to compensate victims of torture or similar practices and their families for the physical and psychological injuries inflicted upon them, without prejudice to reimbursing itself from those guilty of such practices.

4. Torture, cruel and degrading treatment or punishment, unexplained

disappearances and extra-legal executions are crimes against humanity. Consequently, it is the duty of government to recognize the rights of victims of such practices and their families to enforce their claims against those who have perpetrated such acts without limitations in space or time.

Article 11.

Public Emergencies

1. States of emergency are abnormal situations that threaten the basic rights of the people. Therefore, it is the duty of government:

(*a*) Not to declare a state of emergency except when a real danger exists to the very existence of the nation, threatening the organized life of the community, of such magnitude that normal measures and restrictions are clearly insufficient to meet it;

(*b*) To specify the grounds for and the duration of the state of emergency and to limit its effectivity to the existence of the conditions which gave rise to it;

(*c*) To subject the declaration of a state of emergency to approval by the legislative body and not to dissolve, suspend or adjourn that legislative body during the emergency;

(*d*) Not to exercise any kind of emergency power unless there is a prior formal, valid declaration of a state of emergency.

2. It is the duty of government, under a state of emergency validly declared, to take only such measures restrictive of human rights as are strictly required by the exigencies of the situation, so that no less stringent measures would suffice, and to enforce such measures without discrimination based on race, sex, language, religious belief, political conviction, economic or social status, or ethnic origin.

3. Even under a validly declared emergency, government may not deny or derogate from the following rights and freedoms: the right to recognition of personal dignity and legal personality, freedom of conscience and of religion, freedom from retroactive penal measures and from cruel and unusual punishments, the right to nationality and to leave from and return to one's country, the rights of workers, the right to habeas corpus, the right of access to civil courts and to fair, public and speedy trial, freedom from imprisonment for civil debt, and the right to participate in public life.

4. Government shall not, under any circumstances, resort to or authorize:

(*a*) Violence to life, health and physical or mental well-being of persons who are not or are no longer combatants in armed conflict, in particular, murder, political assassination or extra-legal executions, kidnapping or unexplained disappearances, torture, mutilation or any form of corporal punishment, use of so-called truth serums and other drugs, and slavery or other forms of involuntary servitude.

(*b*) Outrages upon personal dignity, in particular humiliating and degrading treatment, rape and enforced prostitution or any form of indecent assault.

(*c*) Arbitrary arrests and detention, that is, those made without probable cause previously determined by a civil court.

(*d*) Taking of hostages, collective punishments, pillage, and acts of terrorism.

(*e*) Individual or mass evacuations or forcible transfers, unless imperatively required by the security of the population concerned or by military reasons. Such transfers must be effected only after proper accommodation is provided, under satisfactory conditions of hygiene, health, safety and nutrition; and members of the same family must not be separated. Persons evacuated shall be returned to their homes at government expense as soon as the reasons for their evacuation cease.

(*f*) The passing and execution of sentences upon civilians by military courts or by any civil court which does not afford the judicial guarantees necessary for an adequate defence.

(*g*) The requisition or seizure of property or the compelling of individuals to perform services, without full and speedy compensation. Compensation shall include indemnity for death or disability resulting from compelled or required services.

(*h*) Threats to commit any of the foregoing acts.

5. The existence, grounds and legality of the declaration of emergency, its duration, and the measures taken under it, shall be subject to judicial review. In all such cases, the burden of proof shall be on government.

6. It is the duty of government to afford redress, including compensation for damages, to any person aggrieved by acts done during a state of emergency. No grant of amnesty, pardon or immunity shall exempt any government official from responsibility for reparation in damages to any person whom he shall have injured in violation of paragraphs 3 and 4 of this Article.

7. All measures taken during a state of emergency shall, upon its termination, automatically cease to have any further force or effect.

VI. OTHER INTERNATIONAL CONVENTIONS

1. LAWS OF WAR (1863, 1907–1977)

INTRODUCTION

Since that day in 1861 when Henri Dunant walked through the aftermath of the Battle of Solferino, there has been a concerted effort by nations to codify the Laws of War. Through such laws, human suffering and indignity, on and off the battlefield would be minimized. And now, rules and norms governing the act of war (i.e. the conduct of soldiers on the field, the treatment of prisoners of war, the occupation of foreign territories, etc.) have been laid down through such laws.

Long before the excesses of the Third Reich directed world wide attention to the evils of aggressive warfare, humanitarian spokesmen were well aware that war was destructive of fundamental human rights. Dunant, founder of the International Committee of the Red Cross, sought through international agreements to protect those rights—and this regime of law is the existing expression of that search. It recognizes that armed conflict is a reality of society and that armed conflict must of necessity and nature destroy the rights of some, limit the rights of others, and endanger the rights of all.

The human rights provisions here have been taken from the eleven recognized convenants on the laws of war. (All eleven are listed, together with code numbers to facilitate reference.) Such human rights provisions are divided into the twenty-one categories noted in this introduction—and then set forth by number in the documentary section which follows. The twenty-one categories are marked (1) (2) (3), etc.

Addressing a problem which is inherently paradoxical, the laws of war recognize the right to wage hostilities and at the same time seek to maintain the minimum precepts of human rights. Such regime of law is designed to protect fundamental human rights in balance with the rights and needs of states and other groups to use armed force in their own interests. The German *Kreigsraison* theory that any method of warfare is permissible if necessary for success, regardless of laws to the contrary, was rejected and punished at the war crimes trials following World War II. On the other hand, it is generally accepted that any method of warfare is permissible (if not specifically prohibited by law) if such method is indispensable for securing submission of the enemy. This balance is generally expressed as the concept of military necessity.

Terminology used in all of the legal documents address the horrors of armed conflict and the need to reduce or control such horrors. The preamble to the Hague Convention IV (HIV) of 1907 is an excellent example as well as one of the earliest pronouncements of this position (1).

The legal task is to identify those rights considered fundamental to humanity and to restrict actions that jeopardize the continued viability of those rights. This approach is widely recognized (2). Restrictions can be prohibitory (3) or limiting in nature (4) or merely encouragement to attain an improved condition (5).

Perhaps the most universal human rights statements deal with restricting the conduct of soldiers for the protection of women (6). The conduct of soldiers with respect to pillage and reprisals is also common. This prohibition—which can be traced back to the orders of Alexander the Great, was followed consistently in Caesar's Empire, in the Middle Ages and in the European wars of the 18th and 19th centuries. It was one of the first rules incorporated into the codification of the laws of war and can be considered the basis of the Fourth Geneva Convention of 1949 Relative to the Protection of Civilian Persons in Time of War (GCIV) (7).

While human rights have been the object of both destruction and protection throughout the history of war, the effort to establish a law on the subject is barely a century old. In 1864, Henri Dunant was instrumental in the preparation of the Red Cross Convention at Geneva, the first international document restricting conduct in the waging of war. It was followed by the Hague Conventions of 1899, 1907 and 1954; the Geneva Conventions of 1902, 1929 and 1949; and the Geneva Protocols of 1925 and 1977. The Hague Conventions were concerned primarily with methods of warfare, while the Geneva documents dealt with the persons involved in warfare.

The law dealing with methods is primarily encompassed in the Hague Convention No. IV of 1907, Respecting the Laws and Customs of War on Land (HIV); the Geneva Protocol of 1925 for the Prohibition of the Use in War of Asphyxiating, Poisonous or Other Gases and of Bacteriological Methods of Warfare (not noted here); and the Hague Convention of 1954 (H54) for the Protection of Cultural Property. The law of persons encompasses the four Geneva Conventions of 1949 for the Wounded and Sick in the Field (GCI), the Wounded and Sick at Sea (GCII), Prisoners of War (GCIII), and the Protection of Civilian Persons in Time of War (GCIV), plus the 1977 Geneva Protocols Additional to the Geneva Conventions of August 12, 1949 (GPI and GPII).

United Nations General Assembly Resolution 217A, of December 10, 1948, if often considered the basic law of human rights. For it purports to provide an exhaustive compendium of inalienable rights inherent in the maintenance of the dignity of man. Thus, its title as the Universal Declaration of Human Rights. The concepts of the Declaration, however, were expressed in formal treaty forty years before, predating both world wars. The Hague Conventions of 1907 (HIV and HV), in the preamble and its regulations, was such a prior codification of the rights of humanity. These Conventions were to be followed by other treaties, culminating in the United Nations Charter, the Universal Declaration of Human Rights and the 1949 Geneva Conventions (8).

Henri Dunant, as noted, is rightfully considered the father of human rights during time of war since his efforts established the International Red Cross, led to the first ultra-national document on human rights and provided the model for subsequent international treaties. It was, however, the United States that first formally declared the protection of human rights in warfare. General Orders 100 (GO100), prepared in the midst of the United States Civil War, by Dr. Francis Lieber, set forth many of the rights of humanity, later incorporated in both treaties dealing with the law of war and the various declarations of the United Nations (9).

The detailed regime of the laws of war as it relates to persons and set out in the four 1949 Geneva Conventions contain statements on fundamental human rights. There is a continued effort to define and to preserve in times of armed conflict the inalienable rights of humanity. Protection is the primary goal of this regime of law, for it is not enough that rights be identified and defined, discussed and enumerated. Without protective sanctions, the rights exist in the mind of man only, not implemented for lack of a remedy. The laws of war do provide sanctions. Grave breaches are defined, violators are to be sought out and punished and national courts are recognized as appropriate tribunals for the trial of violations of the law. Procedures have also been established for a third nation or international organization to act in protection of designated rights during ongoing conflict.

Rights recognized as fundamental closely parallel the rights of man spelled out in the Universal Declaration of the United Nations. Protections start with the individual, prohibiting torture and coercion (10). In addition, food and clothing appropriate to conditions are required (11). And if a person is sick or wounded, prompt medical care must be provided (12). The right of private property is recognized and protected (13). Special consideration is given to maintaining family integrity and protecting the children of the family (14). Limited provisions covering the right to work and conditions of labor are made (15). Nor do the laws of war overlook the spiritual needs of those involved in or affected by the disruptions of armed conflict (16).

During warfare many social agencies are not able or permitted to operate. This has caused great concern to the community of nations for protection of persons accused of crime. World War II provided too many examples of the abuse of court systems by political authority or the total disestablishment of any judicial system. This problem is extensively addressed by the laws of war, requiring not only judicial process before punishment, but also establishing the prerequisites of fairness and justice in the process itself (17).

Following the lead of rulers/conquerors such as Alexander and Caesar, the Hague Conventions of 1907 (HIV and HV) accepted and protected the nationhood of people. Subsequent treaties continue to recognize the value and contribution of all cultures to the community of nations. Individual rules have been adopted to preserve the cultural heritage of all peoples from the ravages of warfare (18).

Death is an inevitable result of war. The conditions and circumstances of combat create difficult and sometimes intolerable situations for appropriate recovery and burial of the dead. This problem is met head on, requiring the best effort to respect the dead and to provide burial consistent with culture, heritage, religion and the exigencies of warfare (19).

Underlying the concept of human rights is the principle that all persons are free and equal in dignity and in rights. The arch enemy of equality is the unreasoned discrimination practiced by tyrants and democracies alike. Armed conflict by its very nature encourages discrimination. The noncombatant must be separated from the soldier. Inability to carry on the fight must create distinctions among the wounded and potential prisoners. Recognition of enemy and non-enemy is crucial to battlefield survival. Yet if unreasoned discrimination controls the battlefield, each side resorts to extremes which savage the human spirit. Warfare becomes sanguinary, wasting and evermore destructive.[69] Denial of rights, degradation of human dignity, are forbidden in warfare. Specific prohibitions of discrimination are thus part of the laws controlling armed conflict. Difficulties of combat are subordinated to the principle of humanity (20).

A major issue in the international law of war is the scope of its application. The laws of wars are not exempt from questions of domestic versus community affairs, of national versus international jurisdiction. The laws of war accept this dichotomy but pursue the preservation of human dignity and rights. Article 3 in each of the four Geneva Conventions of 1949 is a brief statement protective of the very nature of humanity. It is designed to apply to that grey area between national and international concerns. The Second Protocol of 1977 to the Geneva Conventions (CPII) further amplified the fundamental rights of mankind while narrowing the gap of doubt (21).

Critical to any regime of law is the need for people to know the rules and regulations. In the crisis of warfare, people must know that there is such a regime of law, a consensus of the community of nations that human rights can and must be preserved under even the most trying of human conditions (22).

DOCUMENTS

(GO100) INSTRUMENTS FOR THE GOVERNMENT OF ARMIES OF THE UNITED STATES IN THE FIELD, General Orders, No. 100, April 24, 1863. (War of the Rebellion, Official Records, Series 3, III, 162)

(HIV) HAGUE CONVENTION NO. IV, *Respecting the Laws and Customs of War on Land*. Annex to the Convention, Regulations Respecting the Laws and Customs of War on Land, 18 October 1907. (36 Stat. 2277; Treaty Series No. 539; Malloy Treaties, Vol. II, p. 2269)

(HV) HAGUE CONVENTION NO. V, *Respecting the Rights and Duties of Neutral Powers and Persons in Case of War on Land*, 18 October 1907. (36 Stat. 2310; Treaty Series No. 540; Malloy, Treaties, Vol. II, p. 2290)

(GCI) GENEVA CONVENTION, *for the Amelioration of the Condition of the Wounded and Sick in Armed Forces in the Field*, 12 August 1949. (Treaties and Other International Acts Series 3362)

(GCII) GENEVA CONVENTION, *for the Amelioration of the Condition of Wounded, Sick and Shipwrecked Members of Armed Forces at Sea*, 12 August 1949. (Treaties and Other International Acts Series 3363)

(GCIII) GENEVA CONVENTION, *Relative to the Treatment of Prisoners of War*, 12 August 1949. (Treaties and Other International Acts Series 3364)

(GCIV) GENEVA CONVENTION, *Relative to the Protection of Civilian Persons in Time of War*, 12 August 1949. (Treaties and Other International Acts Series 3365)

(H54) HAGUE CONVENTION, *for the Protection of Cultural Property in the Event of Armed Conflict*, 1954.

(GPI)   PROTOCOL I, *Protocol Additional to the Geneva Conventions of 12 August 1949*, and Relating to the Protection of Victims of International Armed Conflicts (Protocol I), 1977.

(GPII)   PROTOCOL II, *Protocol Additional to the Geneva Conventions of 12 August 1949*, and Relating to the Protection of Victims of Non-International Armed Conflicts (Protocol II), 1977.

1. ON HORRORS OF WAR

(HIV)

Considering that, while seeking means to preserve peace and prevent armed conflicts between nations, it is likewise necessary to bear in mind the case where an appeal to arms may be brought about by events which their solicitude could not avert;

Animated by the desire to serve, even in this extreme case, the interests of humanity and the ever progressive needs of civilization;

Thinking it important, with this object, to revise the general laws and customs of war, either with a view to defining them with greater precision or to confining them within such limits as would mitigate their severity as far as possible; . . .

2. RECOGNITION OF HUMAN RIGHTS ISSUES

(HIV)

According to the views of the High Contracting Parties, these provisions, the wording of which has been inspired by the desire to diminish the evils of war, so far as military requirements permit, are intended to serve as a general rule of conduct for the belligerents in their mutual relations and in their relations with the inhabitants . . .

Until a more complete code of the laws of war has been issued, the High Contracting Parties deem it expedient to declare that, in cases not included in the Regulations adopted by them, the inhabitants and the belligerents remain under the protection and the rule of the principles of the law of nations, as they result from the usages established among civilized peoples, from the laws of humanity, and from the dictates of the public conscience.

(H54)

THE HIGH CONTRACTING PARTIES,

Recognizing that cultural property has suffered grave damage during recent armed conflicts and that, by reason of the developments in the technique of warfare, it is in increasing danger of destruction;

Being convinced that damage to cultural property belonging to any people whatsoever means damage to the cultural heritage of all mankind, since each people makes its contribution to the culture of the world;

Considering that the preservation of the cultural heritage is of great importance for all peoples of the world and that it is important that this heritage should receive international protection;

Guided by the principles concerning the protection of cultural property during armed conflict, as established in the Conventions of The Hague of 1899 and 1907 and in the Washington Pact of 15 April 1935; . . .

(GPI)

Article 1.

2. In cases not covered by this Protocol or by other international agreements, civilians and combatants remain under the protection and authority of the principles of international law derived from established custom, from the principles of humanity and from the dictates of public conscience.

(GPII)

THE HIGH CONTRACTING PARTIES,

Recalling that the humanitarian principles enshrined in Article 3 common to the Geneva Conventions of 12 August 1949, constitute the foundation of respect for the human person in cases of armed conflict not of an international character,

Recalling furthermore that international instruments relating to human rights offer a basic protection to the human person,

Emphasizing the need to ensure a better protection for the victims of those armed conflicts,

Recalling that, in cases not covered by the law in force, the human person remains under the protection of the principles of humanity and the dictates of the public conscience, . . .

3. PROHIBITORY RESTRICTIONS

(GCI)

Article 12.

Members of the armed forces and other persons mentioned in the following Article, who are wounded or sick, shall be respected and protected in all circumstances.

They shall be treated humanely and cared for by the Party to the conflict in whose power they may be, without any adverse distinction founded on sex, race, nationality, religion, political opinions, or any other similar criteria. Any attempts upon their lives, or violence to their persons, shall be strictly prohibited; in particular, they shall not be murdered or exterminated, subjected to torture or to biological experiments; they shall not wilfully be left without medical assistance and care, nor shall conditions exposing them to contagion or infection be created.

(GCII)

Article 12.

Such persons shall be treated humanely and cared for by the Parties to the conflict in whose power they may be, without any adverse distinction founded on sex, race, nationality, religion, political opinions, or any other similar criteria. Any attempts upon their lives, or violence to their persons, shall be strictly prohibited; in particular, they shall not be murdered or exterminated, subjected to torture or to biological experiments; they shall not wilfully be left without medical assistance and care, nor shall conditions exposing them to contagion or infection be created.

(GCIII)

Article 13.

Prisoners of war must at all times be humanely treated. Any unlawful act or omission by the Detaining Power causing death or seriously endangering the health of a prisoner of war in its custody is prohibited, and will be regarded as a serious breach of the present Convention. In particular, no prisoner of war may be subjected to physical mutilation or to medical or scientific experiments of any kind which are not justified by the medical, dental or hospital treatment of the prisoner concerned and carried out in his interest.

Likewise, prisoners of war must at all times be protected, particularly against acts of violence or intimidation and against insults and public curiosity.

Measures of reprisal against prisoners of war are prohibited.

(GCIV)

Article 32.

The High Contracting Parties specifically agree that each of them is prohibited from taking any measure of such a character as to cause the physical suffering or extermination of protected persons in their hands. This prohibition applies not only to murder, torture, corporal punishment, mutilation and medical or scientific experiments not necessitated by the medical treatment of a protected person, but also to any other measures of brutality whether applied by civilian or military agents.

4. LIMITATIONS

(H54)

Article 4.

Respect for Cultural Property

1. The High Contracting Parties undertake to respect cultural property situated within their own territory as well as within the territory of other High Contracting Parties by refraining from any use of the property and its immediate surroundings or of the appliances in use for its protection for purposes which are likely to expose it to destruction or damage in the event of armed conflict; and by refraining from any act of hostility against such property.

2. The obligations mentioned in paragraph 1 of the present Article may be

waived only in cases where military necessity imperatively requires such a waiver.

(GCIV)

Article 16.

The wounded and sick, as well as the infirm, and expectant mothers, shall be the object of particular protection and respect.

As far as military considerations allow, each Party to the conflict shall facilitate the steps taken to search for the killed and wounded, to assist the shipwrecked and other persons exposed to grave danger, and to protect them against pillage and ill-treatment.

5. ENCOURAGEMENT/INCENTIVES

(GCIV)

Article 14.

In time of peace, the High Contracting Parties and, after the outbreak of hostilities, the Parties thereto, may establish in their own territory and, if the need arises, in occupied areas, hospital and safety zones and localities so organized as to protect from the effects of war, wounded, sick and aged persons, children under fifteen, expectant-mothers and mothers of children under seven.

Article 24.

The Parties to the conflict shall take the necessary measures to ensure that children under fifteen, who are orphaned or are separated from their families as a result of the war, are not left to their own resources, and that their maintenance, the exercise of their religion and their education are facilitated in all circumstances. Their education shall, as far as possible, be entrusted to persons of a similar cultural tradition.

(H54)

Article 3.

Safeguarding of Cultural Property.

The High Contracting Parties undertake to prepare in time of peace for the safeguarding of cultural property situated within their own territory against the foreseeable effects of an armed conflict, by taking such measures as they consider appropriate.

6. WOMEN

(GCI, GCII).

Article 12.

Women shall be treated with all consideration due to their sex.

(GCIII)

Article 14.

Prisoners of war are entitled in all circumstances to respect for their persons and their honour.

Women shall be treated with all the regard due to their sex and shall in all cases benefit by treatment as favourable as that granted to men.

(GCIV)

Article 27.

Women shall be especially protected against any attack on their honour, in particular against rape, enforced prostitution, or any form of indecent assault.

(GPI)

Article 76

Protection of women.

1. Women shall be the object of special respect and shall be protected in particular against rape, forced prostitution and any other form of indecent assault.

2. Pregnant women and mothers having dependent infants who are arrested, detained or interned for reasons related to the armed conflict, shall have their cases considered with the utmost priority.

7. PILLAGE AND REPRISALS

(HIV)

Article 47.

Pillage is formally forbidden.

Article 25.

The attack or bombardment, by whatever means, of towns, villages, dwellings, or buildings which are undefended is prohibited.

Article 28.

The pillage of a town or place, even when taken by assault, is prohibited.

(GCIV)

Article 27.

Protected persons are entitled, in all circumstances, to respect for their persons, their honour, their family rights, their religious convictions and practices, and their manners and customs. They shall at all times be humanely treated, and shall be protected especially against all acts of violence or threats thereof and against insults and public curiosity.

Article 33.

No protected person may be punished for an offence he or she has not personally committed. Collective penalties and likewise all measures of intimidation or of terrorism are prohibited.

Pillage is prohibited.

Reprisals against protected persons and their property are prohibited.

(GPI)

Article 20.

Prohibition of reprisals.

Reprisals agains the persons and objects protected by this Part are prohibited.

Article 51.

6. Attacks against the civilian population or civilians by way of reprisals are prohibited.

(GO100)

44. All wanton violence committed against persons in the invaded country, all destruction of property not commanded by the authorized officer, all robbery, all pillage or sacking, even after taking a place by main force, all rape, wounding, maiming, or killing of such inhabitants, are prohibited under the penalty of death, or such other severe punishment as may seem adequate for the gravity of the offense.

(H54)

Article 4.

3. The High Contracting Parties further undertake to prohibit, prevent and, if necessary, put a stop to any form of theft, pillage or misappropriation of, and any acts of vandalism directed against, cultural property. They shall refrain from requisitioning movable cultural property situated in the territory of another High Contracting Party.

4. They shall refrain from any act directed by way of reprisals against cultural property.

8. HUMAN RIGHTS MANDATES FROM HAGUE CONVENTIONS

(HIV)

Article 18.

Prisoners of war shall enjoy complete liberty in the exercise of their religion, including attendance at the services of whatever Church they may belong to, on the sole condition that they comply with the measures of order and police issued by the military authorities.

Article 46.

Family honour and rights, the lives of persons, and private property, as well as religious convictions and practice, must be respected. Private property cannot be confiscated.

Article 56.

The property of municipalities, that of institutions dedicated to religion, charity and education, the arts and sciences, even when State property, shall be treated as private property.

All seizure or destruction of, or wilful damage to, institutions of this character, historic monuments, works of art and science, is forbidden, and should be made the subject of legal proceedings.

(HV)

Article 12.

In the absence of a special Convention, the neutral Power shall supply the interned with the food, clothing, and relief required by humanity.

9. HUMAN RIGHTS MANDATES FROM GENERAL ORDER 100

(GO100)

56. A prisoner of war is subject to no punishment for being a public enemy, nor is any revenge wreaked upon him by the intentional inflicting of any suffering, or disgrace, by cruel imprisonment, want of food, by mutilation, death, or any other barbarity.

61. Troops that give no quarter have no right to kill enemies already disabled on the ground, or prisoners captured by other troops.

72. Money and other valuables on the person of a prisoner, such as watches or jewelry, as well as extra clothing, are regarded by the American Army as the private property of the prisoner, and the appropriation of such valuables or money is considered dishonorable, and is prohibited.

75. Prisoners of war are subject to confinement and imprisonment such as may be deemed necessary on account of safety, but they are to be subjected to no other intentional suffering or indignity. The confinement and mode of treating a prisoner may be varied during his captivity according to the demands of safety.

79. Every captured wounded enemy shall be medically treated, according to the ability of the medical staff.

80. Honorable men, when captured, will abstain from giving to the enemy information concerning their own army, and the modern law of war permits no

longer the use of any violence against prisoners in order to extort the desired information, or to punish them for having given false information.

148. The law of war does not allow proclaiming either an individual belonging to the hostile army, or a citizen, or a subject of the hostile government, an outlaw, who may be slain without trial by any captor, any more than the modern law of peace allows such international outlawry; on the contrary, it abhors such outrage. The sternest retalliation should follow the murder committed in consequence of such proclamation, made by whatever authority. Civilized nations look with horror upon offers of rewards for the assassination of enemies as relapses into barbarism.

10. PROTECTION OF INDIVIDUAL

(GCIII)

Article 17.

No physical or mental torture, nor any other form of coercion, may be inflicted on prisoners of war to secure from them information of any kind whatever. Prisoners of war who refuse to answer may not be threatened, insulted, or exposed to unpleasant or disadvantageous treatment of any kind.

(GPI)

Article 75.

2. The following acts are and shall remain prohibited at any time and in any place whatsoever, whether committed by civilian or by military agents:

    a. violence to the life, health, or physical or mental well-being of persons, in particular:

      i. murder;

      ii. torture of all kinds, whether physical or mental;

      iii. corporal punishment; and

      iv. mutilation;

    b. outrages upon personal dignity, in particular humiliating and degrading treatment, enforced prostitution and any form of indecent assault;

    c. the taking of hostages;

    d. collective punishments; and

    e. threats to commit any of the foregoing acts.

(GPII)

Article 4.

2. Without prejudice to the generality of the foregoing, the following acts against the persons referred to in paragraph 1 are and shall remain prohibited at any time and in any place whatsoever:

    a. violence to the life, health and physical or mental well-being of persons, in particular murder as well as cruel treatment such as torture, mutilation or any form of corporal punishment;

b. collective punishments;

c. taking of hostages;

d. acts of terrorism;

e. outrages upon personal dignity, in particular humiliating and degrading treatment, rape, enforced prostitution and any form of indecent assault;

f. slavery and the slave trade in all their forms;

g. pillage;

h. threats to commit any of the foregoing acts.

11. FOOD AND CLOTHING

(GCIII)

Article 20.

The evacuation of prisoners of war shall always be effected humanely and in conditions similar to these for the forces of the Detaining Power in their changes of station.

The Detaining Power shall supply prisoners of war who are being evacuated with sufficient food and potable water, and with the necessary clothing and medical attention. The Detaining Power shall take all suitable precautions to ensure their safety during evacuation, and shall establish as soon as possible a list of the prisoners of war who are evacuated.

Article 26.

The basic daily food rations shall be sufficient in quantity, quality and variety to keep prisoners of war in good health and to prevent loss of weight or the development of nutritional deficiencies. Account shall also be taken of the habitual diet of the prisoners.

The Detaining Power shall supply prisoners of war who work with such additional rations as are necessary for the labour on which they are employed.

Sufficient drinking water shall be supplied to prisoners of war. The use of tobacco shall be permitted.

Article 27.

Clothing, underwear and footwear shall be supplied to prisoners of war in sufficient quantities by the Detaining Power, which shall make allowance for the climate of the region where the prisoners are detained.

(GCIV)

Article 55.

To the fullest extent of the means available to it, the Occupying Power has the duty of ensuring the food and medical supplies of the population; it should, in particular, bring in the necessary foodstuffs, medical stores and other articles if the resources of the occupied territory are inadequate.

Article 89.

Daily food rations for internees shall be sufficient in quantity, quality and variety to keep internees in a good state of health and prevent the development of nutritional deficiencies. Account shall also be taken of the customary diet of the internees.

Sufficient drinking water shall be supplied to internees. The use of tobacco shall be permitted.

Internees who work shall receive additional rations in proportion to the kind of labour which they perform.

Expectant and nursing mothers, and children under fifteen years of age, shall be given additional food, in proportion to their physiological needs.

(GPI)

Article 54.

Protection of Objects Indispensable to the Survival of the Civilian Population.

1. Starvation of civilians as a method of warfare is prohibited.

Article 69.

Basic Needs in Occupied Territories.

1. In addition to the duties specified in Article 55 of the Fourth Convention concerning food and medical supplies, the Occupying Power shall, to the fullest extent of the means available to it and without any adverse distinction, also ensure the provision of clothing, bedding, means of shelter, other supplies essential to the survival of the civilian population of the occupied territory and objects necessary for religious worship.

12. MEDICAL CARE

(GCI)

Article 15.

At all times, and particularly after an engagement, Parties to the conflict shall, without delay, take all possible measures to search for and collect the wounded and sick, to protect them against pillage and ill-treatment, to ensure their adequate care, and to search for the dead and prevent their being despoiled.

Whenever circumstances permit, an armistice or a suspension of fire shall be arranged, or local arrangements made, to permit the removal, exchange and transport of the wounded left on the battlefield.

Article 46.

Reprisals against the wounded, sick, personnel, buildings or equipment protected by the Convention are prohibited.

(GCII)

Article 18.

After each engagement, Parties to the conflict shall, without delay, take all possible measures to search for and collect the shipwrecked, wounded and sick, to protect them against pillage and ill-treatment, to ensure their adequate care, and to search for the dead and prevent their being despoiled.

Whenever circumstances permit, the Parties to the conflict shall conclude local arrangements for the removal of the wounded and sick by sea from a beseiged or encircled area and for the passage of medical and religious personnel and equipment on their way to that area.

Article 47.

Reprisals against the wounded, sick and shipwrecked persons, the personnel, the vessels or the equipment protected by the Convention are prohibited.

(GCIII)

Article 29.

The Detaining Power shall be bound to take all sanitary measures necessary to ensure the cleanliness and healthfulness of camps and to prevent epidemics.

Prisoners of war shall have for their use, day and night, conveniences which conform to the rules of hygiene and are maintained in a constant state of cleanliness. In any camps in which women prisoners of war are accommodated, separate conveniences shall be provided for them.

Also, apart from the baths and showers with which the camps shall be provided, prisoners of war shall be provided with sufficient water and soap for their personal toilet and for washing their personal laundry; the necessary installations, facilities and time shall be granted them for that purpose.

(GCIV)

Article 56.

To the fullest extent of the means available to it, the Occupying Power has the duty of ensuring and maintaining, with the cooperation of national and local authorities, the medical and hospital establishments and services, public health and hygiene in the occupied territory, with particular reference to the adoption and application of the prophylactic and preventive measures necessary to combat the spread of contagious diseases and epidemics. Medical personnel of all categories shall be allowed to carry out their duties.

(GPI)

Article 10.

Protection and Care.

1. All the wounded, sick and shipwrecked, to whichever Party they belong, shall be respected and protected.

2. In all circumstances they shall be treated humanely and shall receive, to the fullest extent practicable and with the least possible delay, the medical care and attention required by their condition. There shall be no distinction among them founded on any grounds other than medical ones.

(GPII)

Article 7.

Protection and Care.

1. All the wounded, sick and shipwrecked, whether or not they have taken part in the armed conflict, shall be respected and protected.

2. In all circumstances they shall be treated humanely and shall receive, to the fullest extent practicable and with the least possible delay, the medical care and attention required by their condition. There shall be no distinction among them founded on any grounds other than medical ones.

13. PRIVATE PROPERTY

(GCIII)

Article 18.

All effects and articles of personal use, except arms, horses, military equipment and military documents, shall remain in the possession of prisoners of war, likewise their metal helmets and gas masks and like articles issued for personal protection. Effects and articles used for their clothing or feeding shall likewise remain in their possession, even if such effects and articles belong to their regulation military equipment.

Sums of money carried by prisoners of war may not be taken away from them except by order of an officer, and after the amount and particulars of the owner have been recorded in a special register and an itemized receipt has been given, legibly inscribed with the name, rank and unit of the person issuing the said receipt.

The Detaining Power may withdraw articles of value from prisoners of war only for reasons of security; when such articles are withdrawn, the procedure laid down for sums of money impounded shall apply.

(GCIV)

Article 97.

Internees shall be permitted to retain articles of personal use. Monies, cheques, bonds, etc., and valuables in their possession may not be taken from them except in accordance with established procedure. Detailed receipts shall be given therefor.

Articles which have above all a personal or sentimental value may not be taken away.

Family or identity documents in the possession of internees may not be taken away without a receipt being given. At no time shall internees be left without identity documents. If they have none, they shall be issued with special documents drawn up by the detaining authorities, which will serve as their identity papers until the end of their internment.

14. PROTECTION OF FAMILY
(GCIV)

Article 82.

Throughout the duration of their internment members of the same family, and in particular parents and children, shall be lodged together in the same place of internment, except when separation of a temporary nature is necessitated for reasons of employment or health or for the purposes of enforcement of the provisions of Chapter IX of the present Section. Internees may request that their children who are left at liberty without parental care shall be interned with them.

Wherever possible, interned members of the same family shall be housed in the same premises and given separate accommodation from other internees, together with facilities for leading a proper family life.

(GPI)

Article 74.

Reunion of Dispersed Families.

The High Contracting Parties and the Parties to the conflict shall facilitate in every possible way the reunion of families dispersed as a result of armed conflicts and shall encourage in particular the work of the humanitarian organizations engaged in this task in accordance with the provisions of the Conventions and of this Protocol and in conformity with their respective security regulations.

Article 77.

Protection of Children.

1. Children shall be the object of special respect and shall be protected against any form of indecent assault. The Parties to the conflict shall provide them with the care and aid they require, whether because of their age or for any other reason.

(GPII)

Article 4.

3. Children shall be provided with the care and aid they require, and in particular:

    a. they shall receive an education, including religious and moral education, in keeping with the wishes of their parents, or in the absence of parents, of those responsible for their care;

    b. all appropriate steps shall be taken to facilitate the reunion of families temporarily separated;

15. LABOR PROTECTIONS

(GCIII)

Article 51.

Prisoners of war must be granted suitable working conditions, especially as regards accommodation, food, clothing, and equipment; such conditions shall not be inferior to those enjoyed by nationals of the Detaining Power employed in similar work; account shall also be taken of climatic conditions.

The Detaining Power, in utilizing the labour of prisoners of war, shall ensure that in areas in which prisoners are employed, the national legislation concerning the protection of labour, and, more particularly, the regulations for the safety of workers, are duly applied.

Prisoners of war shall receive training and be provided with the means of protection suitable to the work they will have to do and similar to those accorded to the nationals of the Detaining Power. Subject to the provisions of Article 52, prisoners may be submitted to the normal risks run by these civilian workers.

Article 62.

Prisoners of war shall be paid a fair working rate of pay by the detaining authorities direct. The rate shall be fixed by the said authorities, but shall at no time be less than one-fourth of one Swiss franc for a full working day.

16. RELIGIOUS FREEDOM

(GCIII)

Article 34.

Prisoners of war shall enjoy complete latitude in the exercise of their religious duties, including attendance at the service of their faith, on condition that they comply with the disciplinary routine prescribed by the military authorities.

(GCIV)

Article 58.

The Occupying Power shall permit ministers of religion to give spiritual assistance to the members of their religious communities.

The Occupying Power shall also accept consignments of books and articles required for religious needs and shall facilitate their distribution in occupied territory.

Article 93.

Internees shall enjoy complete latitude in the exercise of their religious duties, including attendance at the services of their faith, on condition that they comply with the disciplinary routine prescribed by the detaining authorities.

Article 86.

The Detaining Power shall place at the disposal of interned persons, of whatever domination, premises suitable for the holding of their religious services.

(GPII)

Article 5.

1(d) they shall be allowed to practice their religion and, if requested and appropriate, to receive spiritual assistance from persons, such as chaplains, performing religious functions;

17. JUDICIAL PROCESS

(GPI)

Article 85.

4. (e) depriving a person protected by the Conventions or referred to in paragraph 2 of this Article of the rights of fair and regular trial.

(GPII)

Article 6.

Penal Prosecutions.

1. This Article applies to the prosecution and punishment of criminal offences related to the armed conflict.

2. No sentence shall be passed and no penalty shall be executed on a person found guilty of an offence except pursuant to a conviction pronounced by a court offering the essential guarantees of independence and impartiality. In particular:

a. the procedure shall provide for an accused to be informed without delay of the particulars of the offence alleged against him and shall afford the accused before and during his trial all necessary rights and means of defence;

b. no one shall be convicted of an offence except on the basis of individual penal responsibility;

c. no one shall be held guilty of any criminal offence on account of any act or omission which did not constitute a criminal offence, under the law, at the time when it was committed; nor shall a heavier penalty be imposed than that which was applicable at the time when the criminal offence was committed; if, after the commission of the offence provision is made by law for the imposition of a lighter penalty, the offender shall benefit thereby;

d. anyone charged with an offence is presumed innocent until proved guilty according to law;

e. anyone charged with an offence shall have the right to be tried in his presence;

f. no one shall be compelled to testify against himself or to confess guilt.

3. A convicted person shall be advised on conviction of his judicial and other remedies and of the time-limits within which they may be exercised.

(GCIII)

Article 84.

In no circumstances whatever shall a prisoner of war be tried by a court of any kind which does not offer the essential guarantees of independence and impartiality as generally recognized, and, in particular, the procedure of which does not afford the accused the rights and means of defence provided for in Article 105.

Article 86.

No prisoner of war may be punished more than once for the same act or on the same charge.

Article 87.

Collective punishment for individual acts, corporal punishment, imprisonment in premises without daylight and, in general, any form of torture or cruelty, are forbidden. . . .

In no case may a woman prisoner of war be awarded or sentenced to a punishment more severe, or treated whilst undergoing punishment more severely, than a male member of the armed forces of the Detaining Power dealt with for a similar offence.

Article 105.

The prisoner of war shall be entitled to assistance by one of his prisoner comrades, to defence by a qualified advocate or counsel of his own choice, to the calling of witnesses and, if he deems necessary, to the services of a competent interpreter. He shall be advised of these rights by the Detaining Power in due time before the trial.

Failing a choice by the prisoner of war, the Protecting Power shall find him an advocate or counsel, and shall have at least one week at its disposal for the purpose. The Detaining Power shall deliver to the said Power, on request, a list of persons qualified to present the defence. Failing a choice of an advocate or counsel by the prisoner of war or the Protecting Power, the Detaining Power shall appoint a competent advocate or counsel to conduct the defence.

The advocate or counsel conducting the defence on behalf of the prisoner of war shall have at his disposal a period of two weeks at least before the opening of the trial, as well as the necessary facilities to prepare the defence of the accused. He may, in particular, freely visit the accused and interview him in private. He may also confer with any witnesses for the defence, including prisoners of war. He shall have the benefit of these facilities until the term of appeal or petition has expired.

Particulars of the charge or charges on which the prisoner of war is to be arraigned, as well as the documents which are generally communicated to the accused by virtue of the laws in force in the armed forces of the Detaining

Power, shall be communicated to the accused prisoner of war in a language which he understands, and in good time before the opening of the trial. The same communication in the same circumstances shall be made to the advocate or counsel conducting the defence on behalf of the prisoner of war.

Article 108.

A woman prisoner of war on whom such a sentence has been pronounced shall be confined in separate quarters and shall be under the supervision of women.

(GCIV)

Article 71.

No sentence shall be pronounced by the competent courts of the Occupying Power except after a regular trial.

Accused persons who are prosecuted by the Occupying Power shall be promptly informed, in writing, in a language which they understand, of the particulars of the charges preferred against them, and shall be brought to trial as rapidly as possible.

Article 72.

Accused persons shall have the right to present evidence necessary to their defence and may, in particular, call witnesses. They shall have the right to be assisted by a qualified advocate or counsel of their own choice, who shall be able to visit them freely and shall enjoy the necessary facilities for preparing the defence.

Failing a choice by the accused, the Protecting Power may provide him with an advocate or counsel. When an accused person has to meet a serious charge and the Protecting Power is not functioning, the Occupying Power, subject to the consent of the accused, shall provide an advocate or counsel.

Article 73.

A convicted person shall have the right of appeal provided for by the laws applied by the court. He shall be fully informed of his right to appeal or petition and of the time limit within which he may do so.

Article 76.

Protected persons accused of offences shall be detained in the occupied country, and if convicted they shall serve their sentences therein. They shall, if possible, be separated from other detainees and shall enjoy conditions of food and hygiene which will be sufficient to keep them in good health, and which will be at least equal to those obtaining in prisons in the occupied country.

They shall receive the medical attention required by their state of health.

They shall also have the right to receive any spiritual assistance which they may require.

Women shall be confined in separate quarters and shall be under the direct supervision of women.

Proper regard shall be paid to the special treatment due to minors.

Article 100.

The disciplinary regime in places of internment shall be consistent with humanitarian principles, and shall in no circumstances include regulations imposing on internees any physical exertion dangerous to their health or involving physical or moral victimization. Identification by tattooing or imprinting signs or markings on the body, is prohibited.

In particular, prolonged standing and roll-calls, punishment drill, military drill and manoeuvres, or the reduction of food rations, are prohibited.

Article 119.

In no case shall disciplinary penalties be inhuman, brutal or dangerous for the health of internees. Account shall be taken of the internee's age, sex and state of health.

(GPI)

Article 75.

4. No sentence may be passed and no penalty may be executed on a person found guilty of a penal offence related to the armed conflict except pursuant to a conviction pronounced by an impartial and regularly constituted court respecting the generally recognized principles of regular judicial procedure, which include the following:

a. the procedure shall provide for an accused to be informed without delay of the particulars of the offence alleged against him and shall afford the accused before and during his trial all necessary rights and means of defence;

b. no one shall be convicted of an offence except on the basis of individual penal responsibility;

c. no one shall be accused or convicted of a criminal offence on account of any act or omission which did not constitute a criminal offence under the national or international law to which he was subject at the time when it was committed; nor shall a heavier penalty be imposed than that which was applicable at the time when the criminal offence was committed; if, after the commission of the offence, provision is made by law for the imposition of a lighter penalty, the offender shall benefit thereby;

d. anyone charged with an offence is presumed innocent until proved guilty according to law;

e. anyone charged with an offence shall have the right to be tried in his presence;

f. no one shall be compelled to testify against himself or to confess guilt;

g. anyone charged with an offence shall have the right to examine, or have examined, the witnesses against him and to obtain the attendance and examination of witnesses on his behalf under the same conditions as witnesses against him;

h. no one shall be prosecuted or punished by the same Party for an offence in respect of which a final judgment acquitting or convicting that person has been previously pronounced under the same law and judicial procedure;

i. anyone prosecuted for an offence shall have the right to have the judgment pronounced publicly; and

j. a convicted person shall be advised on conviction of his judicial and other remedies and of the time limits within which they may be exercised.

18. CULTURAL RIGHTS

(GCIII)

Article 22.

The Detaining Power shall assemble prisoners of war in camps or camp compounds according to their nationality, language and customs, provided that such prisoners shall not be separated from prisoners of war belonging to the armed forces with which they were serving at the time of their capture, except with their consent.

(GCIV)

Article 38.

With the exception of special measures authorized by the present Convention, in particular by Articles 27 and 41 thereof, the situation of protected persons shall continue to be regulated, in principle, by the provisions concerning aliens in time of peace. In any case, the following rights shall be granted to them:

1. They shall be enabled to receive the individual or collective relief that may be sent to them.

2. They shall, if their state of health so requires, receive medical attention and hospital treatment to the same extent as the nationals of the State concerned.

3. They shall be allowed to practise their religion and to receive spiritual assistance from ministers of their faith.

4. If they reside in an area particularly exposed to the dangers of war, they shall be authorised to move from that area to the same extent as the nationals of the State concerned.

5. Children under fifteen years, pregnant women and mothers of children under seven years shall benefit by any preferential treatment to the same extent as the nationals of the State concerned.

(c) Centres containing a large amount of cultural property as defined in sub-paragraphs (a) and (b), to be known as 'centres containing monuments'.

(PROTOCOL TO H54)

Section I.

Each High Contracting Party undertakes to prevent the exportation, from a territory occupied by it during an armed conflict, of cultural property as defined in Article I of the Convention for the Protection of Cultural Property in the Event of Armed Conflict, signed at The Hague on 14 May 1954.

2. Each High Contracting Party undertakes to take into its custody cultural property imported into its territory either directly or indirectly from any occupied territory. This shall either be effected automatically upon the importation of the property or, failing this, at the request of the authorities of that territory.

19. RIGHTS OF DECEASED

(GCIII)

Article 120.

The detaining authorities shall ensure that prisoners of war who have died in captivity are honourably buried, if possible according to the rites of the religion to which they belonged, and that their graves are respected, suitably maintained and marked so as to be found at any time. Wherever possible, deceased prisoners of war who depended on the same Power shall be interred in the same place.

Deceased prisoners of war shall be buried in individual graves unless unavoidable circumstances require the use of collective graves. Bodies may be cremated only for imperative reasons of hygiene, on account of the religion of the deceased or in accordance with his express wish to this effect. In case of cremation, the fact shall be stated and the reasons given in the death certificate of the deceased.

(GPI)

Article 34.

Remains of Deceased.

1. The remains of persons who have died for reasons related to occupation or in detention resulting from occupation or hostilities and those of persons not nationals of the country in which they have died as a result of hostilities shall be respected, and the gravesites of all such persons shall be respected, maintained and marked as provided for in Article 130 of the Fourth Convention, where their remains or gravesites would not receive more favourable consideration under the Conventions and this Protocol.

20. DISCRIMINATION

(GCIII)

Article 16.

Taking into consideration the provisions of the present Convention relating to rank and sex, and subject to any privileged treatment which may be accorded to them by reason of their state of health, age or professional qualifications, all prisoners of war shall be treated alike by the Detaining Power, without any adverse distinction based on race, nationality, religious belief or political opinions, or any other distinction founded on similar criteria.

(GCIV)

Article 13.

The provisions of Part II cover the whole of the populations of the countries in conflict, without any adverse distinction based, in particular, on race, nationality, religion or political opinion, and are intended to alleviate the sufferings caused by war.

Article 27.

Without prejudice to the provisions relating to their state of health, age and sex, all protected persons shall be treated with the same consideration by the Party to the conflict in whose power they are, without any adverse distinction based, in particular, on race, religion or political opinion.

(GPI)

Article 9.

Field of Application.

1. This Part, the provisions of which are intended to ameliorate the condition of the wounded, sick and shipwrecked, shall apply to all those affected by a situation referred to in Article 1, without any adverse distinction founded on race, colour, sex, language, religion or belief, political or other opinion, national or social origin, wealth, birth or other status, or on any other similar criteria.

Article 75.

Fundamental Guarantees.

1. In so far as they are affected by a situation referred to in Article 1 of this Protocol, persons who are in the power of a Party to the conflict and who do not benefit from more favourable treatment under the Conventions or under this Protocol shall be treated humanely in all circumstances and shall enjoy, as a minimum, the protection provided by this Article without any adverse distinction based upon race, colour, sex, language, religion or belief, political or other opinion, national or social origin, wealth, birth or other status, or on any other similar criteria. Each Party shall respect the person, honour, convictions and religious practices of all such persons.

Article 85.

4. In addition to the grave breaches defined in the preceding paragraphs and in the Conventions, the following shall be regarded as grave breaches of this Protocol, when committed wilfully and in violation of the Conventions or the Protocol:

c. practices of apartheid and other inhuman and degrading practices involving outrages upon personal dignity, based on racial discrimination;

(GPII)

Article 2.

Personal Field of Application.

1. This Protocol shall be applied without any adverse distinction founded on race, colour, sex, language, religion or belief, political or other opinion, national or social origin, wealth, birth or other status, or on any other similar criteria (hereinafter referred to as "adverse distinction") to all persons affected by an armed conflict as defined in Article 1.

Protection of Cultural Objects and of Places of Worship.

Article 82.

The Detaining Power shall, as far as possible, accommodate the internees according to their nationality, language and customs. Internees who are nationals of the same country shall not be separated merely because they have different languages.

(GPI)

Article 53.

Without prejudice to the provisions of the Hague Convention for the Protection of Cultural Property in the Event of Armed Conflict of 14 May 1954, and of other relevant international instruments, it is prohibited:
a. to commit any acts of hostility directed against the historic monuments, works of art or places of worship which constitute the cultural or spiritual heritage of peoples;
b. to use such objects in support of the military effort;
c. to make such objects the object of reprisals.

Article 85.

4(d) making the clearly-recognized historic monuments, works of art of places of worship which constitute the cultural or spiritual heritage of peoples and to which special protection has been given by special arrangement, for example, within the framework of a competent international organization, the object of attack, causing as a result extensive destruction thereof, where there is no evidence of the violation by the adverse Party of Article 53, sub-paragraph (b), and when such historic monuments, works of art and places of worship are not located in the immediate proximity of military objectives;

(GPII)

Article 16.

Protection of cultural objects and of places of worship. Without prejudice to the provisions of the Hague Convention for the Protection of Cultural Property in the Event of Armed Conflict of 14 May 1954, it is prohibited to commit any acts of hostility directed against historic monuments, works of art or places of worship which constitute the cultural or spiritual heritage of peoples, and to use them in support of the military effort.

(H54)

Article I.

Definition of Cultural Property. For the Purposes of the present Convention, the term 'cultural property' shall cover, irrespective of origin or ownership:

a. Movable or immovable property of great importance to the cultural heritage of every people, such as monuments of architecture, art or history, whether religious or secular; archaeological sites; groups of buildings which, as a whole, are of historical or artistic interest; works of art; manuscripts, books and other objects of artistic, historical or archaeological interest; as well as scientific collections and important collections of books or archives or of reproductions of the property defined above;

b. Buildings whose main and effective purpose is to preserve or exhibit the movable cultural property defined in sub-paragraph (a) such as museums, large libraries and depositories of archives, and refuges intended to shelter, in the event of armed conflict, the movable cultural property defined in sub-paragraph (a);

Article 4.

Fundamental Guarantees.

1. All persons who do not take a direct part or who have ceased to take part in hostilities, whether or not their liberty has been restricted, are entitled to respect for their person, honour and convictions and religious practices. They shall in all circumstances be treated humanely, without any adverse distinction. It is prohibited to order that there shall be no survivors.

21. NON-INTERNATIONAL ARMED CONFLICT (GCI, GCII, GCIII, GCIV)

Article 3.

In the case of armed conflict not of an international character occurring in the territory of one of the High Contracting Parties, each Party to the conflict shall be bound to apply, as a minimum, the following provisions:

(1) Persons taking no active part in the hostilities, including members of the armed forces who have laid down their arms and those placed *hors de combat* by sickness, wounds, detention, or any other cause, shall in all circumstances be

treated humanely, without any adverse distinction founded on race, colour, religion or faith, sex, birth or wealth, or any other similar criteria.

To this end, the following acts are and shall remain prohibited at any time and in any place whatsoever with respect to the above-mentioned persons:

a. violence to life and person, in particular murder of all kinds, mutilation, cruel treatment and torture;

b. taking of hostages;

c. outrages upon personal dignity, in particular, humiliating and degrading treatment;

d. the passing of sentences and the carrying out of executions without previous judgment pronounced by a regularly constituted court, affording all the judicial guarantees which are recognized as indispensable by civilized peoples.

(2) The wounded, sick and shipwrecked shall be collected and cared for.

22. DISSEMINATION OF INFORMATION (GPI, GPII)

Resolution 21.

Dissemination of knowledge of international humanitarian law applicable in armed conflicts. The Diplomatic Conference on the Reaffirmation and Development of International Humanitarian Law Applicable in Armed Conflicts, Geneva, 1974–1977,

Convinced that a sound knowledge of international humanitarian law is an essential factor for its effective application,

Confident that widespread knowledge of that law will contribute to the promotion of humanitarian ideals and a spirit of peace among nations, . . .

2. CONFERENCES ON SECURITY AND COOPERATION IN EUROPE (1975, 1983)

INTRODUCTION

The most significant (and most controversial) East-West Agreements on human rights are the Helsinki accord of 1975 and the "follow-up" Madrid accord of 1983. In international law and diplomatic language, they are termed the Final Act of the Conference on Security and Cooperation in Europe (CSCE), entered into in Helsinki on August 1, 1975, and the Concluding Document of the CSCE "review" meeting, signed in Madrid on September 9, 1983.

Concurred in unanimously by thirty-two European nations, the Vatican and both the United States and Canada, these "accords" or "agreements" are not considered binding treaties in international law, although formulated in treaty language. Rather they are "final acts" of diplomatic conferences—examples of classic diplomacy among sovereign states.

Both the Helsinki and Madrid accords are part of the so-called Helsinki process, giving these agreements continuing force and effect. The Final Act at Helsinki included a section labeled "Follow-Up to the Conference." Here the parties "declare their resolve" to implement the terms of the agreement, and "to continue the multilateral process" with a "thorough exchange of views" and a series of meetings. The meetings are designed to assess the extent to which the commitments made in Helsinki have been implemented and to consider what might be done to further the purposes of the CSCE. The first such meeting (which failed to reach any important agreement) was held in Belgrade in 1977. The second opened in Madrid in 1980 and ended with the 1983 Concluding Document. The Madrid accord provides for the continuation of the CSCE review process with a Vienna meeting to begin in November, 1986. An Experts' Meeting on Human Rights is scheduled for Ottawa in 1985. The accords also led to the formation of national "watch committees" to monitor compliance with human rights pledges.

What makes these accords so controversial is the pledge to respect the territorial integrity of the participating states. This has been criticized as "legitimizing" the Soviet Union's annexation of Estonia, Latvia and Lithuania and territories which were once part of Germany, Poland and Rumania. Such pledge was ostensibly made in exchange for promises to respect human rights and fundamental freedoms and to respect the equal rights of peoples and their right to self-determination.

The CSCE accords are subdivided into three parts or "baskets": (I) Questions Relating to Security in Europe; (II) Cooperation in the Field of Economics, of Science and Technology and of the Environment; and (III) Cooperation in Humanitarian and Other Fields.

The basic statements on human rights and self-determination are set forth in Sections VII and VIII of Basket I of the Final Act at Helsinki. These are supplemented and expanded by ten of the nineteen provisions in the Principles section of the Madrid Concluding Document. Here special mention is made of religious liberty, rights of national minorities, trade union freedoms and terrorism.

Section 4 of Basket II at Helsinki called for exchange of information and direct contacts among scientists and technologists. This is restated and somewhat amplified in the first two paragraphs of Madrid's Section 12. Also important is Section 14 of the Madrid document on migrant labor.

It is Basket III, however, which is primarily concerned with human rights. Here is how this part of the Helsinki document is described in the Seventh Semi-Annual Report by the United States President to the Commission on Security and Cooperation in Europe, June 1 to November 30, 1979:

> Basket III is intended to increase the flow of people, ideas, and information between the participating countries and thus to reduce the barriers which have separated the people of Europe since the Second World War. Basket III calls for specific actions on the part of participating governments in the areas of human contacts, information, culture, and education. Basket III and the much broader Principle

Seven of Basket I constitute the major sections of the Final Act which deal with human rights.[70]

Here is how this part of the Madrid document is described in "The Madrid CSCE Review Meeting" report issued by the United States CSCE Commission in November, 1983:

> Throughout the Madrid meeting the West attempted to move forward the Helsinki commitments in Basket III—particularly in the human contacts and information sections—while the East sought to qualify and limit those commitments. Most of the original Western proposals for inclusion in the human contacts section are incorporated, albeit often in diluted form, in the concluding document. Limited improvements over the Final Act have been made in several areas where the participating states have pledged:
> — to "favorably deal with" and "decide upon" applications for family meetings, family reunification and binational marriages. The Final Act provides only that they will "consider" or "deal with" applications in a positive and humanitarian spirit."
> — to decide marriage and family reunification applications "within six months." This reference to a definite time period is a useful improvement over the Final Act commitment merely to decide "as expeditiously as possible."
> — to refrain from actions modifying rights to "employment, housing, residence status, family support, access to social, economic or educational benefits" for those making or renewing application for family reunification. This directly addresses abusive procedures often applied to visa applicants in the USSR and Eastern Europe.
> — to provide the necessary forms and information on emigration procedures and regulations which, up to now, often have been unavailable.
> — to reduce fees charged in connection with emigration "to bring them to a moderate level in relation to the average monthly income." The reference to monthly income provides a new standard by which to judge fee levels which in some cases have been exorbitant.
> — to inform applicants as "expeditiously as possible of the decision" on their cases and, in cases of refusal, to inform them of "their right to renew applications after reasonably short intervals." Both the fact that applicants must be informed of decisions and the recognition of the right to reapply are important in that many applicants in the USSR have been given "final refusals" and told they could not reapply.[71]

There are also several "improvements" in the Madrid statement relating to press freedoms.

The leading work on the subject is *Human Rights, International Law and the Helsinki Accord,* edited by Dean Thomas Buergenthal in 1977. *See* also the important article by A.H. Robertson, *The Helsinki Agreement and Human Rights.*

For additional documentation, *see* the six-volume work on *Human Rights, European Politics, and the Helsinki Accord: The Documentary Evolution of the Conference on Security and Co-Operation in Europe 1973–1975,* edited by Igor I. Kavass, Jacqueline Paquin Granier and Mary Frances Dominick.

The most comprehensive treatment of the Madrid document is found in *The Madrid CSCE Review Meeting,* compiled and edited by the Staff of the Commission on Security and Cooperation in Europe. This is a commission consisting of 12 members of the United States Congress, with one representative of the State, Defense and Commerce Departments in liaison. *See* also "CSCE Followup Meeting Concludes in Madrid," *Department of State Bulletin,* October, 1983.

While the provisions of Basket III remain largely unfulfilled and there are continuing differences between East and West on interpretation and implementation, the CSCE accords must be considered, in Dean Buergenthal's words, a landmark of "ideological tolerance."

CONFERENCE ON SECURITY AND CO-OPERATION IN EUROPE FINAL ACT 1975 (HELSINKI)

(EXCERPTS)

QUESTIONS RELATING TO SECURITY IN EUROPE

I

(A) DECLARATION IN PRINCIPLES GUIDING RELATIONS BETWEEN PARTICIPATING STATES . . .

* * * * * * *

VII. Respect for human rights and fundamental freedoms, including the freedom of thought, conscience, religion or belief

The participating States will respect human rights and fundamental freedoms, including the freedom of thought, conscience, religion or belief, for all without distinction as to race, sex, language or religion.

They will promote and encourage the effective exercise of civil, political, economic, social, cultural and other rights and freedoms all of which derive from the inherent dignity of the human person and are essential for his free and full development.

Within this framework the participating States will recognize and respect the freedom of the individual to profess and practise, alone or in community with others, religion or belief acting in accordance with the dictates of his own conscience.

The participating States on whose territory national minorities exist will respect the right of persons belonging to such minorities to equality before the law, will afford them the full opportunity for the actual enjoyment of human rights and fundamental freedoms and will, in this manner, protect their legitimate interests in this sphere.

The participating States recognize the universal significance of human rights and fundamental freedoms, respect for which is an essential factor for the peace, justice and well-being necessary to ensure the development of friendly relations and co-operation among themselves as among all States.

They will constantly respect these rights and freedoms in their mutual relations and will endeavour jointly and separately, including in co-operation with the United Nations, to promote universal and effective respect for them.

They confirm the right of the individual to know and act upon his rights and duties in this field.

In the field of human rights and fundamental freedoms, the participating States will act in conformity with the purposes and principles of the Charter of the United Nations and with the Universal Declaration of Human Rights. They will also fulfil their obligations as set forth in the international declarations and agreements in this field, including inter alia the International Covenants on Human Rights, by which they may be bound.

VIII. Equal rights and self-determination of peoples

The participating States will respect the equal rights of peoples and their right to self-determination, acting at all times in conformity with the purposes and principles of the Charter of the United Nations and with the relevant norms of international law, including those relating to territorial integrity of States.

By virtue of the principle of equal rights and self-determination of peoples, all peoples always have the right, in full freedom, to determine, when and as they wish, their internal and external political status, without external interference, and to pursue as they wish their political, economic, social and cultural development.

The participating States reaffirm the universal significance of respect for and effective exercise of equal rights and self-determination of peoples for the development of friendly relations among themselves as among all States; they also recall the importance of the elimination of any form of violation of this principle.

II

CO-OPERATION IN THE FIELD OF ECONOMICS, OF SCIENCE AND TECHNOLOGY AND OF THE ENVIRONMENT

The participating States,

*   *   *   *   *   *   *

Have adopted the following:

*   *   *   *   *   *   *

4. Science and technology

* * * * * * *

Forms and methods of co-operation

Express their view that scientific and technological co-operation should, in particular, employ the following forms and methods:
— exchange and circulation of books, periodicals and other scientific and technological publications and papers among interested organizations, scientific and technological institutions, enterprises and scientists and technologists, as well as participation in international programmes for the abstracting and indexing of publications;
— exchanges and visits as well as other direct contacts and communications among scientists and technologists, on the basis of mutual agreement and other arrangements, for such purposes as consultations, lecturing and conducting research, including the use of laboratories, scientific libraries, and other documentation centres in connexion therewith;
— holding of international and national conferences, symposia, seminars, courses and other meetings of a scientific and technological character, which would include the participation of foreign scientists and technologists;
— joint preparation and implementation of programmes and projects of mutual interest on the basis of consultation and agreement among all parties concerned, including, where possible and appropriate, exchanges of experience and research results, and correlation of research programmes, between scientific and technological research institutions and organizations;

* * * * * * *

III

CO-OPERATION IN HUMANITARIAN AND OTHER FIELDS

The participating States,

Desiring to contribute to the strengthening of peace and understanding among peoples and to the spiritual enrichment of the human personality without distinction as to race, sex, language or religion.

Conscious that increased cultural and educational exchanges, broader dissemination of information, contacts between people, and the solution of humanitarian problems will contribute to the attainment of these aims,

Determined therefore to co-operate among themselves, irrespective of their political, economic and social systems, in order to create better conditions in the above fields, to develop and strengthen existing forms of co-operation and to work out new ways and means appropriate to these aims,

Convinced that this co-operation should take place in full respect for the principles guiding relations among participating States as set forth in the relevant document.

Have adopted the following:

1. HUMAN CONTACTS

The participating States,

Considering the development of contacts to be an important element in the strengthening of friendly relations and trust among peoples,

Affirming, in relation to their present effort to improve conditions in this area, the importance they attach to humanitarian considerations,

Desiring in this spirit to develop, with the continuance of détente, further efforts to achieve continuing progress in this field

And conscious that the questions relevant hereto must be settled by the States concerned under mutually acceptable conditions,

Make it their aim to facilitate freer movement and contacts, individually and collectively, whether privately or officially, among persons, institutions and organizations of the participating States, and to contribute to the solution of the humanitarian problems that arise in that connexion,

Declare their readiness to these ends to take measures which they consider appropriate and to conclude agreements or arrangements among themselves, as may be needed, and

Express their intention now to proceed to the implementation of the following:

(a) Contacts and Regular Meetings on the Basis of Family Ties

In order to promote further development of contacts on the basis of family ties the participating States will favourably consider applications for travel with the purpose of allowing persons to enter or leave their territory temporarily, and on a regular basis if desired, in order to visit members of their families.

Applications for temporary visits to meet members of their families will be dealt with without distinction as to the country of origin or destination: existing requirements for travel documents and visas will be applied in this spirit. The preparation and issue of such documents and visas will be effected within reasonable time limits; cases of urgent necessity—such as serious illness or death—will be given priority treatment. They will take such steps as may be necessary to ensure that the fees for official travel documents and visas are acceptable.

They confirm that the presentation of an application concerning contacts on the basis of family ties will not modify the rights and obligations of the applicant or of members of his family.

(b) Reunification of Families

The participating States will deal in a positive and humanitarian spirit with the applications of persons who wish to be reunited with members of their family, with special attention being given to requests of an urgent character— such as requests submitted by persons who are ill or old.

They will deal with applications in this field as expeditiously as possible.

They will lower where necessary the fees charged in connexion with these applications to ensure that they are at a moderate level.

Applications for the purpose of family reunification which are not granted may be renewed at the appropriate level and will be reconsidered at reasonably short intervals by the authorities of the country of residence or destination, whichever is concerned; under such circumstances fees will be charged only when applications are granted.

Persons whose applications for family reunification are granted may bring with them or ship their household and personal effects; to this end the participating States will use all possibilities provided by existing regulations.

Until members of the same family are reunited meetings and contacts between them may take place in accordance with the modalities for contacts on the basis of family ties.

The participating States will support the efforts of Red Cross and Red Crescent Societies concerned with the problems of family reunification.

They confirm that the presentation of an application concerning family reunification will not modify the rights and obligations of the applicant or of members of his family.

The receiving participating State will take appropriate care with regard to employment for persons from other participating States who take up permanent residence in that State in connexion with family reunification with its citizens and see that they are afforded opportunities equal to those enjoyed by its own citizens for education, medical assistance and social security.

(c) Marriage between Citizens of Different States

The participating States will examine favourably and on the basis of humanitarian considerations requests for exit or entry permits from persons who have decided to marry a citizen from another participating State.

The processing and issuing of the documents required for the above purposes and for the marriage will be in accordance with the provisions accepted for family reunification.

In dealing with requests from couples from different participating States, once married, to enable them and the minor children of their marriage to transfer their permanent residence to a State in which either one is normally a resident, the participating States will also apply the provisions accepted for family reunification.

(d) Travel for Personal or Professional Reasons

The participating States intend to facilitate wider travel by their citizens for personal or professional reasons and to this end they intend in particular:

gradually to simplify and to administer flexibly the procedures for exit and entry;

to ease regulations concerning movement of citizens from the other participating States in their territory, with due regard to security requirements.

They will endeavor gradually to lower, where necessary, the fees for visas and official travel documents.

They intend to consider, as necessary, means—including, in so far as appropriate, the conclusion of multilateral or bilateral consular conventions or other relevant agreements or understandings—for the improvement of arrangements to provide consular services, including legal and consular assistance.

*   *   *   *   *   *   *

They confirm that religious faiths, institutions and organizations, practising within the constitutional framework of the participating States, and their representatives can, in the field of their activities, have contacts and meetings among themselves and exchange information.

(e) Improvement of Conditions for Tourism on an Individual or Collective Basis

The participating States consider that tourism contributes to a fuller knowledge of the life, culture and history of other countries, to the growth of understanding among peoples, to the improvement of contacts and to the broader use of leisure. They intend to promote the development of tourism, on an individual or collective basis, and, in particular, they intend:

> to promote visits to their respective countries by encouraging the provision of appropriate facilities and the simplification and expediting of necessary formalities relating to such visits;
> to increase, on the basis of appropriate agreements or arrangements where necessary, co-operation in the development of tourism, in particular by considering bilaterally possible ways to increase information relating to travel to other countries and to the reception and service of tourists, and other related questions of mutual interest.

(f) Meetings among Young People

The participating States intend to further the development of contacts and exchanges among young people by encouraging:

> increased exchanges and contacts on a short or long term basis among young people working, training or undergoing education through bilateral or multilateral agreements or regular programmes in all cases where it is possible;
> study by their youth organizations of the question of possible agreements relating to frameworks of multilateral youth co-operation;
> agreements or regular programmes relating to the organization of exchanges of students, of international youth seminars, of courses of professional training and foreign language study;
> the further development of youth tourism and the provision to this end of appropriate facilities;
> the development, where possible, of exchanges, contacts and co-operation on a bilateral or multilateral basis between their organizations which represent wide circles of young people working, training or undergoing education;
> awareness among youth of the importance of developing mutual

understanding and of strengthening friendly relations and confidence among peoples.

(g) Sport

In order to expand existing links and co-operation in the field of sport the participating States will encourage contacts and exchanges of this kind, including sports meetings and competitions of all sorts, on the basis of the established international rules, regulations and practice.

(h) Expansion of Contacts

By way of further developing contacts among governmental institutions and non-governmental organizations and associations, including women's organizations, the participating States will facilitate the convening of meetings as well as travel by delegations, groups and individuals.

2. INFORMATION

The participating States,

Conscious of the need for an ever wider knowledge and understanding of the various aspects of life in other participating States,

Acknowledging the contribution of this process to the growth of confidence between peoples,

Desiring, with the development of mutual understanding between the participating States and with the further improvement of their relations, to continue further efforts towards progress in this field,

Recognizing the importance of the dissemination of information from the other participating States and of a better acquaintance with such information,

Emphasizing therefore the essential and influential role of the press, radio, television, cinema and news agencies and of the journalists working in these fields,

Make it their aim to facilitate the freer and wider dissemination of information of all kinds, to encourage co-operation in the field of information and the exchange of information with other countries, and to improve the conditions under which journalists from one participating State exercise their profession in another participating State, and

Express their intention in particular:

(a) Improvement of the Circulation of, Access to, and Exchange of Information

(i) Oral Information

To facilitate the dissemination of oral information through the encouragement of lectures and lecture tours by personalities and specialists from the other participating States, as well as exchanges of opinions at round table meetings, seminars, symposia, summer schools, congresses and other bilateral and multilateral meetings.

(ii) Printed Information

To facilitate the improvement of the dissemination, on their territory, of newspapers and printed publications, periodical and non-periodical, from the other participating States. For this purpose:

> They will encourage their competent firms and organizations to conclude agreements and contracts designed gradually to increase the quantities and the number of titles of newspapers and publications imported from the other participating States. These agreements and contracts should in particular mention the speediest conditions of delivery and the use of the normal channels existing in each country for the distribution of its own publications and newspapers, as well as forms and means of payment agreed between the parties making it possible to achieve the objectives aimed at by these agreements and contracts;
> where necessary, they will take appropriate measures to achieve the above objectives and to implement the provisions contained in the agreements and contracts.

To contribute to the improvement of access by the public to periodical and non-periodical printed publications imported on the bases indicated above. In particular:

> they will encourage an increase in the number of places where these publications are on sale;
> they will facilitate the availability of these periodical publications during congresses, conferences, official visits, and other international events and to tourists during the season;
> they will develop the possibilities for taking out subscriptions according to the modalities particular to each country;
> they will improve the opportunities for reading and borrowing these publications in large public libraries and their reading rooms as well as in university libraries.

They intend to improve the possibilities for acquaintance with bulletins of official information issued by diplomatic missions and distributed by those missions on the basis of arrangements acceptable to the interested parties.

(iii) Filmed and Broadcast Information

To promote the improvement of the dissemination of filmed and broadcast information. To this end:

> they will encourage the wider showing and broadcasting of a greater variety of recorded and filmed information from the other participating States, illustrating the various aspects of life in their countries and

received on the basis of such agreements or arrangements as may be necessary between the organizations and firms directly concerned; they will facilitate the import by competent organizations and firms of recorded audio-visual material from the other participating States.

The participating States note the expansion in the dissemination of information broadcast by radio, and express the hope for the continuation of this process, so as to meet the interest of mutual understanding among peoples and the aims set forth by this Conference.

(b) Co-operation in the Field of Information

To encourage co-operation in the field of information on the basis of short or long term agreements or arrangements. In particular:

they will favour increased co-operation among mass media organizations, including press agencies, as well as among publishing houses and organizations;

they will favour co-operation among public or private, national or international radio and television organizations, in particular through the exchange of both live and recorded radio and television programmes, and through the joint production and the broadcasting and distribution of such programmes;

they will encourage meetings and contacts both between journalists' organizations and between journalists from the participating States;

they will view favourably the possibilities of arrangements between periodical publications as well as between newspapers from the participating States, for the purpose of exchanging and publishing articles;

they will encourage the exchange of technical information as well as the organization of joint research and meetings devoted to the exchange of experience and views between experts in the field of the press, radio and television.

(c) Improvement of Working Conditions for Journalists

The participating States, desiring to improve the conditions under which journalists from one participating State exercise their profession in another participating State, intend in particular to:

examine in a favourable spirit and within a suitable and reasonable time scale requests from journalists for visas;

grant to permanently accredited journalists of the participating States, on the basis of arrangements, multiple entry and exit visas for specified periods;

facilitate the issue to accredited journalists of the participating States of permits for stay in their country of temporary residence and, if and when these are necessary, of other official papers which it is appropriate for them to have;

ease, on a basis of reciprocity, procedures for arranging travel by journalists of the participating States in the country where they are exercising their profession, and to provide progressively greater opportunities for such travel, subject to the observance of regulations relating to the existence of areas closed for security reasons;

ensure that requests by such journalists for such travel receive, in so far as possible, an expeditious response, taking into account the time scale of the request;

increase the opportunities for journalists of the participating States to communicate personally with their sources, including organizations and official institutions;

grant to journalists of the participating States the right to import, subject only to its being taken out again, the technical equipment (photographic, cinematographic, tape recorder, radio and television) necessary for the exercise of their profession;

enable journalists of the other participating States, whether permanently or temporarily accredited, to transmit completely, normally and rapidly by means recognized by the participating States to the information organs which they represent, the results of their professional activity, including tape recordings and undeveloped film, for the purpose of publication or of broadcasting on the radio or television.

The participating States reaffirm that the legitimate pursuit of their professional activity will neither render journalists liable to expulsion nor otherwise penalize them. If an accredited journalist is expelled, he will be informed of the reasons for this act and may submit an application for re-examination of his case.

3. CO-OPERATION AND EXCHANGES IN THE FIELD OF CULTURE

The participating States,

*   *   *   *   *   *   *

Express their intention now to proceed to the implementation of the following:

*   *   *   *   *   *   *

Access

To promote fuller mutual access by all to the achievements—works, experiences and performing arts—in the various fields of culture of their countries, and to that end to make the best possible efforts, in accordance with their competence, more particularly:
— to promote wider dissemination of books and artistic works, in particular by such means as:

facilitating, while taking full account of the international copyright conventions to which they are party, international contacts and communications between authors and publishing houses as well as other cultural institutions, with a view to a more complete mutual access to cultural achievements;

recommending that, in determining the size of editions, publishing houses take into account also the demand from the other participating States, and that rights of sale in other participating States be granted, where possible, to several sales organizations of the importing countries, by agreement between interested partners;

encouraging competent organizations and relevant firms to conclude agreements and contracts and contributing, by this means, to a gradual increase in the number and diversity of works by authors from the other participating States available in the original and in translation in their libraries and bookshops;

promoting, where deemed appropriate, an increase in the number of sales outlets where books by authors from the other participating States, imported in the original on the basis of agreements and contracts, and in translation, are for sale;

promoting, on a wider scale, the translation of works in the sphere of literature and other fields of cultural activity, produced in the languages of the other participating States, especially from the less widely-spoken languages, and the publication and dissemination of the translated works by such measures as:

> encouraging more regular contacts between interested publishing houses;

> developing their efforts in the basic and advanced training of translators;

> encouraging, by appropriate means, the publishing houses of their countries to publish translations;

> facilitating the exchange between publishers and interested institutions of lists of books which might be translated;

> promoting between their countries the professional activity and co-operation of translators;

> carrying out joint studies on ways of further promoting translations and their dissemination;

> improving and expanding exchanges of books, bibliographies and catalogue cards between libraries;

— to envisage other appropriate measures which would permit, where necessary by mutual agreement among interested parties, the facilitation of access to their respective cultural achievements, in particular in the field of books;
— to contribute by appropriate means to the wider use of the mass media in order to improve mutual acquaintance with the cultural life of each;
— to seek to develop the necessary conditions for migrant workers and their families to preserve their links with their national culture, and also to adapt themselves to their new cultural environment;
— to encourage the competent bodies and enterprises to make a wider choice and effect wider distribution of full-length and documentary films from the

other participating States, and to promote more frequent non-commercial showings, such as premiers, film weeks and festivals, giving due consideration to films from countries whose cinematographic works are less well known;

— to promote, by appropriate means, the extension of opportunities for specialists from the other participating States to work with materials of a cultural character from film and audio-visual archives, within the framework of the existing rules for work on such archival materials;

— to encourage a joint study by interested bodies, where appropriate with the assistance of the competent international organizations, of the expediency and the conditions for the establishment of a repertory of their recorded television programmes of a cultural nature, as well as of the means of viewing them rapidly in order to facilitate their selection and possible acquisition.

* * * * * * *

4. CO-OPERATION AND EXCHANGES IN THE FIELD OF EDUCATION

The participating States,

* * * * * * *

Express to these ends their intention in particular:

* * * * * * *

(b) Access and Exchanges

To improve access, under mutually acceptable conditions, for students, teachers and scholars of the participating States to each other's educational, cultural and scientific institutions, and to intensify exchanges among these institutions in all areas of common interest, in particular by:

— increasing the exchange of information on facilities for study and courses open to foreign participants, as well as on the conditions under which they will be admitted and received;

— facilitating travel between the participating States by scholars, teachers and students for purposes of study, teaching and research as well as for improving knowledge of each other's educational, cultural and scientific achievements;

— encouraging the award of scholarships for study, teaching and research in their countries to scholars, teachers and students of other participating States;

— establishing, developing or encouraging programmes providing for the broader exchange of scholars, teachers and students, including the organization of symposia, seminars and collaborative projects, and the exchanges of educational and scholarly information such as university publications and materials from libraries;

— promoting the efficient implementation of such arrangements and programmes by providing scholars, teachers and students in good time with more detailed information about their placing in universities and institutes and the programmes envisaged for them; by granting them the opportunity to use relevant scholarly, scientific and open archival materials; and by facilitating their travel within the receiving State for the purpose of study or research as well as in the form of vacation tours on the basis of the usual procedures;

— promoting a more exact assessment of the problems of comparison and equivalence of academic degrees and diplomas by fostering the exchange of information on the organization, duration and content of studies, the comparison of methods of assessing levels of knowledge and academic qualifications, and, where feasible, arriving at the mutual recognition of academic degrees and diplomas either through governmental agreements, where necessary, or direct arrangements between universities and other institutions of higher learning and research;

— recommending, moreover, to the appropriate international organizations that they should intensify their efforts to reach a generally acceptable solution to the problems of comparison and equivalence between academic degrees and diplomas.

CONCLUDING DOCUMENT OF THE MADRID MEETING 1980 OF REPRESENTATIVES OF THE PARTICIPATING STATES OF THE CONFERENCE ON SECURITY AND CO-OPERATION IN EUROPE, HELD ON THE BASIS OF THE PROVISIONS OF THE FINAL ACT RELATING TO THE FOLLOW-UP TO THE CONFERENCE

I

QUESTIONS RELATING TO SECURITY IN EUROPE

* * *

4. The participating States condemn terrorism, including terrorism in international relations, as endangering or taking innocent human lives or otherwise jeopardizing human rights and fundamental freedoms, and emphasize the necessity to take resolute measures to combat it. They express their determination to take effective measures for the prevention and suppression of acts of terrorism, both at the national level and through international co-operation including appropriate bilateral and multilateral agreements, and accordingly to broaden and reinforce mutual co-operation to combat such acts. They agree to do so in conformity with the Charter of the United Nations, the United Nations Declaration on Principles of International Law concerning Friendly Relations and Co-operation among States and the Helsinki Final Act.

5. In the context of the combat against acts of terrorism, they will take all

appropriate measures in preventing their respective territories from being used for the preparation, organization or commission of terrorist activities, including those directed against other participating States and their citizens. This also includes measures to prohibit on their territories illegal activities of persons, groups and organizations that instigate, organize or engage in the perpetration of acts of terrorism.

6. The participating States confirm that they will refrain from direct or indirect assistance to terrorist activities or to subversive or other activities directed towards the violent overthrow of the regime of another participating State. Accordingly, they will refrain, *inter alia*, from financing, encouraging, fomenting or tolerating any such activities. . . .

8. They emphasize that all the participating States recognize in the Final Act the universal significance of human rights and fundamental freedoms, respect for which is an essential factor for the peace, justice and well-being necessary to ensure the development of friendly relations and co-operation among themselves, as among all States.

9. The participating States stress their determination to promote and encourage the effective exercise of human rights and fundamental freedoms, all of which derive from the inherent dignity of the human person and are essential for his free and full development, and to assure constant and tangible progress in accordance with the Final Act, aiming at further and steady development in this field in all participating States, irrespective of their political, economic and social systems.

They similarly stress their determination to develop their laws and regulations in the field of civil, political, economic, social, cultural and other human rights in the fundamental freedoms; they also emphasize their determination to ensure the effective exercise of these rights and freedoms.

They recall the right of the individual to know and act upon his rights and duties in the field of human rights and fundamental freedoms, as embodied in the Final Act, and will take the necessary action in their respective countries to effectively ensure this right.

10. The participating States reaffirm that they will recognize, respect and furthermore agree to take the action necessary to ensure the freedom of the individual to profess and practise, alone or in community with others, religion or belief acting in accordance with the dictates of his own conscience.

In this context, they will consult, whenever necessary, the religious faiths, institutions and organizations, which act within the constitutional framework of their respective countries.

They will favourably consider applications by religious communities of believers practising or prepared to practise their faith within the constitutional framework of their States, to be granted the status provided for in their respective countries for religious faiths, institutions and organizations.

11. They stress also the importance of constant progress in ensuring the respect for and actual enjoyment of the rights of persons belonging to national minorities as well as protecting their legitimate interests as provided for in the Final Act.

12. They stress the importance of ensuring equal rights of men and women;

accordingly, they agree to take all actions necessary to promote equally effective participation of men and women in political, economic, social and cultural life.

13. The participating States will ensure the right of workers freely to establish and join trade unions, the right of trade unions freely to exercise their activities and other rights as laid down in relevant international instruments. They note that these rights will be exercised in compliance with the law of the State and in conformity with the State's obligations under international law. They will encourage, as appropriate, direct contacts and communication among such trade unions and their representatives. . . .

15. They reaffirm the particular significance of the Universal Declaration of Human Rights, the International Covenants on Human Rights and other relevant international instruments of their joint and separate efforts to stimulate and develop universal respect for human rights and fundamental freedoms; they call on all participating States to act in conformity with those international instruments and on those participating States, which have not yet done so, to consider the possibility of acceding to the covenants.

16. They agree to give favourable consideration to the use of bilateral round-table meetings, held on a voluntary basis, between delegations composed by each participating State to discuss issues of human rights and fundamental freedoms in accordance with an agreed agenda in a spirit of mutual respect with a view to achieving greater understanding and co-operation based on the provisions of the Final Act. . . .

II

CO-OPERATION IN THE FIELD OF ECONOMICS, OF SCIENCE AND TECHNOLOGY AND OF THE ENVIRONMENT

* * *

12. The participating States recognize the important role of scientific and technical progress in the economic and social development of all countries in particular those which are developing from an economic point of view. Taking into account the objectives which countries or institutions concerned pursue in their bilateral and multilateral relations they underline the importance of further developing, on the basis of reciprocal advantage and on the basis of mutual agreement and other arrangements, the forms and methods of co-operation in the field of science and technology provided for in the Final Act, for instance international programmes and co-operative projects, while utilizing also various forms of contacts, including direct and individual contacts among scientists and specialists as well as contacts and communications among interested organizations, scientific and technological institutions and enterprises.

In this context they recognize the value of an improved exchange and dissemination of information concerning scientific and technical developments as a means of facilitating, on the basis of mutual advantage, the study and the transfer of, as well as access to scientific and technical achievements in fields of co-operation agreed between interested parties. . . .

III

CO-OPERATION IN HUMANITARIAN AND OTHER FIELDS

The participating States,

Recalling the introductory sections of the Chapter on Co-operation in Humanitarian and other Fields of the Final Act including those concerning the development of mutual understanding between them and détente and those concerning progress in cultural and educational exchanges, broader dissemination of information, contacts between people and the solution of humanitarian problems,

Resolving to pursue and expand co-operation in these fields and to achieve a fuller utilization of the possibilities offered by the Final Act,

Agree now to implement the following:

HUMAN CONTACTS

1. The participating States will favourably deal with applications relating to contacts and regular meetings on the basis of family ties, reunification of families and marriage between citizens of different States and will decide upon them in the same spirit.

2. They will decide upon these applications in emergency cases for family meetings as expeditiously as possible, for family reunification and for marriage between citizens of different States in normal practice within six months and for other family meetings within gradually decreasing time limits.

3. They confirm that the presentation or renewal of applications in these cases will not modify the rights and obligations of the applicants or of members of their families concerning *inter alia* employment, housing, residence status, family support, access to social, economic or educational benefits, as well as any other rights and obligations flowing from the laws and regulations of the respective participating State.

4. The participating States will provide the necessary information on the procedures to be followed by the applicants in these cases and on the regulations to be observed, as well as, upon the applicant's request, provide the relevant forms.

5. They will, where necessary, gradually reduce fees charged in connection with these applications, including those for visas and passports, in order to bring them to a moderate level in relation to the average monthly income in the respective participating State.

6. Applicants will be informed as expeditiously as possible of the decision that has been reached. In case of refusal applicants will also be informed of their right to renew applications after reasonably short intervals.

7. The participating States reaffirm their commitment fully to implement the provisions regarding diplomatic and other official missions and consular posts of other participating States contained in relevant multilateral or bilateral conventions, and to facilitate the normal functioning of those missions. Access by

visitors to these missions will be assured with due regard to the necessary requirements of security of these missions.

8. They also reaffirm their willingness to take, within their competence, reasonable steps, including necessary security measures, when appropriate, to ensure satisfactory conditions for activities within the framework of mutual co-operation on their territory, such as sporting and cultural events, in which citizens of other participating States take part.

9. The participating States will endeavour, where appropriate, to improve the conditions relating to legal, consular and medical assistance for citizens of other participating States temporarily on their territory for personal or professional reasons, taking due account of relevant multilateral or bilateral conventions or agreements.

10. They will further implement the relevant provisions of the Final Act, so that religious faiths, institutions, organizations and their representatives can, in the field of their activity, develop contacts and meetings among themselves and exchange information.

11. The participating States will encourage contacts and exchanges among young people and foster the broadening of co-operation among their youth organizations. They will favour the holding among young people and youth organizations of educational, cultural and other comparable events and activities. They will also favour the study of problems relating to the younger generation. The participating States will further the development of individual or collective youth tourism, when necessary on the basis of arrangements, *inter alia* by encouraging the granting of suitable facilities by the transport authorities and tourist organizations of the participating States or such facilities as those offered by the railway authorities participating in the "Inter-Rail" system.

INFORMATION

1. The participating States will further encourage the freer and wider dissemination of printed matter, periodical and non-periodical, imported from other participating States, as well as an increase in the number of places where these publications are on public sale. These publications will also be accessible in reading rooms in large public libraries and similar institutions.

2. In particular, to facilitate the improvement of dissemination of printed information, the participating States will encourage contacts and negotiations between their competent firms and organizations with a view to concluding long-term agreements and contracts designed to increase the quantities and number of titles of newspapers and other publications imported from other participating States. They consider it desirable that the retail prices of foreign publications are not excessive in relation to prices in their country of origin.

3. They confirm their intention, according to the relevant provisions of the Final Act, to further extend the possibilities for the public to take out subscriptions.

4. They will favour the further expansion of co-operation among mass media and their representatives, especially between the editorial staffs of press agencies, newspapers, radio and television organizations as well as film com-

panies. They will encourage a more regular exchange of news, articles, supplements and broadcasts as well as the exchange of editorial staff for better knowledge of respective practices. On the basis of reciprocity, they will improve the material and technical facilities provided for permanently or temporarily accredited television and radio reporters. Moreover, they will facilitate direct contacts among journalists as well as contacts within the framework of professional organizations.

5. They will decide without undue delay upon visa applications from journalists and re-examine within a reasonable time frame applications which have been refused. Moreover, journalists wishing to travel for personal reasons and not for the purpose of reporting shall enjoy the same treatment as other visitors from their country of origin.

6. They will grant permanent correspondents and members of their families living with them multiple entry and exit visas valid for one year.

7. The participating States will examine the possibility of granting, where necessary on the basis of bilateral arrangements, accreditation and related facilities to journalists from other participating States who are permanently accredited in third countries.

8. They will facilitate travel by journalists from other participating States within their territories, *inter alia* by taking concrete measures where necessary, to afford them opportunities to travel more extensively, with the exception of areas closed for security reasons. They will inform journalists in advance, whenever possible, if new areas are closed for security reasons.

9. They will further increase the possibilities and, when necessary, improve the conditions for journalists from other participating States to establish and maintain personal contacts and communication with their sources.

10. They will, as a rule, authorize radio and television journalists, at their request, to be accompanied by their own sound and film technicians and to use their own equipment.

Similarly, journalists may carry with them reference material, including personal notes and files, to be used strictly for their professional purposes.[72]

11. The participating States will, where necessary, facilitate the establishment and operation, in their capitals, of press centres or institutions performing the same functions, open to the national and foreign press with suitable working facilities for the latter.

They will also consider further ways and means to assist journalists from other participating States and thus to enable them to resolve practical problems they may encounter.

CO-OPERATION AND EXCHANGES IN THE FIELD OF CULTURE

1. They will endeavour, by taking appropriate steps, to make the relevant information concerning possibilities offered by bilateral cultural agreements and programmes available to interested persons, institutions and non-governmental organizations, thus facilitating their effective implementation.

2. The participating States will further encourage wider dissemination of

and access to books, films and other forms and means of cultural expression from other participating States, to this end improving by appropriate means, on bilateral and multilateral bases, the conditions for international commercial and non-commercial exchange of their cultural goods, *inter alia* by gradually lowering customs duties on these items.

3. The participating States will endeavour to encourage the translation, publication and dissemination of works in the sphere of literature and other fields of cultural activity from other participating States, especially those produced in less widely spoken languages, by facilitating co-operation between publishing houses, in particular through the exchange of lists of books which might be translated as well as of other relevant information.

4. They will contribute to the development of contacts, co-operation and joint projects among the participating States regarding the protection, preservation and recording of historical heritage and monuments and the relationship between man, environment and this heritage; they express their interest in the possibility of convening an inter-governmental conference on these matters within the framework of UNESCO.

5. The participating States will encourage their radio and television organizations to continue developing the presentation of the cultural and artistic achievements of other participating States on the basis of bilateral and multilateral arrangements between these organizations, providing *inter alia* for exchanges of information on productions, for the broadcasting of shows and programmes from other participating States, for co-productions, for the invitation of guest conductors and directors, as well as for the provision of mutual assistance to cultural film teams.

6. At the invitation of the Government of Hungary a "Cultural Forum" will take place in Budapest, commencing on 15 October 1985. It will be attended by leading personalities in the field of culture from the participating States. The "Forum" will discuss interrelated problems concerning creation, dissemination and co-operation, including the promotion and expansion of contacts and exchanges in the different fields of culture. A representative of UNESCO will be invited to present to the "Forum" the views of that organization. The "Forum" will be prepared by a meeting of experts, the duration of which will not exceed two weeks and which will be held upon the invitation of the Government of Hungary in Budapest, commencing 21 November 1984.

CO-OPERATION AND EXCHANGES IN THE FIELD OF EDUCATION

1. The participating States will promote the establishment of governmental and non-governmental arrangements and agreements in education and science, to be carried out with the participation of educational or other competent institutions.

2. The participating States will contribute to the further improvement of exchanges of students, teachers and scholars and their access to each other's educational, cultural and scientific institutions, and also their access to open information material in accordance with the laws and regulations prevailing in

each country. In this context, they will facilitate travel by scholars, teachers and students within the receiving State, the establishment by them of contacts with their colleagues, and will also encourage libraries, higher education establishments and similar institutions in their territories to make catalogues and lists of open archival material available to scholars, teachers and students from other participating States.

3. They will encourage a more regular exchange of information about scientific training programmes, courses and seminars for young scientists and facilitate a wider participation in these activities of young scientists from different participating States. They will call upon the appropriate national and international organizations and institutions to give support, where appropriate, to the realization of these training activities.

4. The representatives of the participating States noted the usefulness of the work done during the "Scientific Forum" held in Hamburg, Federal Republic of Germany, from 18 February to 3 March 1980. Taking into account the results of the "Scientific Forum", the participating States invited international organizations as well as the scientific organizations and scientists of the participating States to give due consideration to its conclusions and recommendations.

5. The participating States will favour widening the possibilities of teaching and studying less widely spread or studied European languages. They will, to this end, stimulate, within their competence, the organization of and attendance at summer university and other courses, the granting of scholarships for translators and the reinforcement of linguistic facilities including, in case of need, the provision of new facilities for studying these languages.

6. The participating States express their readiness to intensify the exchange, among them and within competent international organizations, of teaching materials, school textbooks, maps, bibliographies and other educational material, in order to promote better mutual knowledge and facilitate a fuller presentation of their respective countries.

3. EUROPEAN DOCUMENTS ON THE PROTECTION OF HUMAN RIGHTS FROM ACTS OF TERRORISM (1977, 1986)

INTRODUCTION

By convention, declaration and resolutions, the Council of Europe, "mindful of the adherence of the member States . . . to the protection of human rights and fundamental freedoms," has sought methods and procedures to end terrorism. In November, 1976, the Council, enlarging upon the initiative taken by the member states of the Common Market (E.E.C) the preceding June, unanimously adopted a European Convention on the Suppression of Terrorism.

The Convention was ultimately signed by 17 European governments on January 27, 1977. It entered into force less than two years later on August 4, 1978, having secured the necessary five ratifications.

While this pioneer document emphasized the need to combat terrorism and set forth a number of proposals to bring about its end, the 1977 Convention has needed supplementation. This has come in the form of Resolution 863 adopted on September 18, 1986 by the Parliamentary Assembly of the Council of Europe, and the Declaration of the European Conference of Ministers Responsible for Combating Terrorism on November 4 and 5, 1986. This last Declaration incorporates three Resolutions of the ministers.

The European Convention on the Suppression of Terrorism was the first major effort to proscribe specifically enumerated acts of terrorism and severely to limit the so-called political offense exception to general European extradition practice. Despite the fact that it was loosely drafted, the Convention marked a major turning point in Western attitudes toward political criminality. Ideologically motivated offenders are now denied a claim of right to safe haven for certain proscribed offenses.

The 1986 Resolution emphasized "the unreserved condemnation of terrorism, which denies democratic values and human rights," and regretted "the procrastination of European states in reacting multilaterally to the terrorist threat." It also designated Libya, Syria and Iran as nations which "must be politically and morally isolated in all international forums."

Concerted action on the diplomatic front is the keynote of the Declaration and its three Resolutions agreed upon by the Ministers of the Member states of the Council of Europe.

Broad limitations upon the general denial of the political offense exception are maintained by the Convention, based upon "race, religion, nationality, or political opinion . . . " There is no definition of what constitutes a political offense, nor is there a definition of the terrorism itself. A proscribed act apparently becomes a terrorist act through incorporation into the general offense of terrorism as established by the title of the Convention. Moreover, due to fuzzy and ill-defined language, common criminality, such as the crime of extortion, can be construed as a terrorist offense. Thus, the European Convention by its own terminology must invariably be subject to statutory constriction. This may raise as many difficulties as it seeks to remedy.

Despite more than a decade of global terror-violence, the international community has yet to agree upon a universal definition, and the lack of specificity about the subject continues to plague the international community. Likewise, the inability of the United Nations to develop any effective remedial measures allows regional conventions, treaties, and agreements to provide the only useful means of dealing with the international and transnational threat. The real importance of the European Convention on the Suppression of Terrorism is not so much that it sought to limit the parameters of the political offense exception in Western Europe, but that it also sought to develop regional cooperation and collaboration on a formalized basis to meet the expanding terrorist threat. Supplemented by the 1986 documents, it may still be regarded as a model for future cooperation against terrorism.

COUNCIL OF EUROPE

EUROPEAN CONVENTION ON THE SUPPRESSION OF TERRORISM (1977)

The member States of the Council of Europe, signatory hereto,

Considering that the aim of the Council of Europe is to achieve a greater unity between its Members;

Aware of the growing concern caused by the increase in acts of terrorism;

Wishing to take effective measures to ensure that the perpetrators of such acts do not escape prosecution and punishment;

Convinced that extradition is a particularly effective measure for achieving this result,

Have agreed as follows:

Article 1

For the purposes of extradition between Contracting States, none of the following offences shall be regarded as a political offence or as an offence connected with a political offence or as an offence inspired by political motives;

a. an offence within the scope of the Convention for the Suppression of Unlawful Seizure of Aircraft, signed at The Hague on 16 December 1970;

b. an offence within the scope of the Convention for the Suppression of Unlawful Acts against the Safety of Civil Aviation, signed at Montreal on 23 September 1971;

c. a serious offence involving an attack against the life, physical integrity or liberty of internationally protected persons, including diplomatic agents;

d. an offence involving kidnapping, the taking of a hostage or serious unlawful detention;

e. an offence involving the use of a bomb, grenade, rocket, automatic firearm or letter or parcel bomb if this use endangers persons;

f. an attempt to commit any of the foregoing offences or participation as an accomplice of a person who commits or attempts to commit such an offence.

Article 2

1. For the purposes of extradition between Contracting States, a Contracting State may decide not to regard as a political offence or as an offence connected with a political offence or as an offence inspired by political motives a serious offence involving an act of violence, other than one covered by Article 1, against the life, physical integrity or liberty of a person.

2. The same shall apply to a serious offence involving an act against property, other than one covered by Article 1, if the act created a collective danger for persons.

3. The same shall apply to an attempt to commit any of the foregoing

offences or participation as an accomplice of a person who commits or attempts to commit such an offence.

Article 3

The provisions of all extradition treaties and arrangements applicable between Contracting States, including the European Convention on Extradition, are modified as between Contracting States to the extent that they are incompatible with this Convention.

Article 4

For the purposes of this Convention and to the extent that any offence mentioned in Article 1 or 2 is not listed as an extraditable offence in any extradition convention or treaty existing between Contracting States, it shall be deemed to be included as such therein.

Article 5

Nothing in this Convention shall be interpreted as imposing an obligation to extradite if the requested State has substantial grounds for believing that the request for extradition for an offence mentioned in Article 1 or 2 has been made for the purpose of prosecuting or punishing a person on account of his race, religion, nationality or political opinion, or that that person's position may be prejudiced for any of these reasons.

Article 6

1. Each Contracting State shall take such measures as may be necessary to establish its jurisdiction over an offence mentioned in Article 1 in the case where the suspected offender is present in its territory and it does not extradite him after receiving a request for extradition from a Contracting State whose jurisdiction is based on a rule of jurisdiction existing equally in the law of the requested State.

2. This Convention does not exclude any criminal jurisdiction exercised in accordance with national law.

Article 7

A Contracting State in whose territory a person suspected to have committed an offence mentioned in Article 1 is found and which has received a request for extradition under the conditions mentioned in Article 6, paragraph 1, shall, if it does not extradite that person, submit the case, without exception whatsoever and without undue delay, to its competent authorities for the purpose of prosecution. Those authorities shall take their decision in the same manner as in the case of any offence of a serious nature under the law of that State.

Article 8

1. Contracting States shall afford one another the widest measure of mutual assistance in criminal matters in connection with proceedings brought in respect of the offences mentioned in Article 1 or 2. The law of the requested State concerning mutual assistance in criminal matters shall apply in all cases.

Nevertheless this assistance may not be refused on the sole ground that it concerns a political offence or an offence connected with a political offence or an offence inspired by political motives.

2. Nothing in this Convention shall be interpreted as imposing an obligation to afford mutual assistance if the requested State has substantial grounds for believing that the request for mutual assistance in respect of an offence mentioned in Article 1 or 2 has been made for the purpose of prosecuting or punishing a person on account of his race, religion, nationality or political opinion or that that person's position may be prejudiced for any of these reasons.

3. The provisions of all treaties and arrangements concerning mutual assistance in criminal matters applicable between Contracting States, including the European Convention on Mutual Assistance in Criminal Matters, are modified as between Contracting States to the extent that they are incompatible with this Convention.

Article 9

1. The European Committee on Crime Problems of the Council of Europe shall be kept informed regarding the application of this Convention.

2. It shall do whatever is needful to facilitate a friendly settlement of any difficulty which may arise out of its execution.

Article 10

1. Any dispute between Contracting States concerning the interpretation or application of this Convention, which has not been settled in the framework of Article 9, paragraph 2, shall, at the request of any Party to the dispute, be referred to arbitration. Each Party shall nominate an arbitrator and the two arbitrators shall nominate a referee. If any Party has not nominated its arbitrator within the three months following the request for arbitration, he shall be nominated at the request of the other Party by the President of the European Court of Human Rights. If the latter should be a national of one of the Parties to the dispute, this duty shall be carried out by the Vice-President of the Court or, if the Vice-President is a national of one of the Parties to the dispute, by the most senior judge of the Court not being a national of one of the Parties to the dispute. The same procedure shall be observed if the arbitrators cannot agree on the choice of referee.

2. The arbitration tribunal shall lay down its own procedure. Its decisions shall be taken by majority vote. Its award shall be final.

Article 11

1. This Convention shall be open to signature by the member States of the Council of Europe. It shall be subject to ratification, acceptance or approval. Instruments of ratification, acceptance or approval shall be deposited with the Secretary General of the Council of Europe.

2. The Convention shall enter into force three months after the date of the deposit of the third instrument of ratification, acceptance or approval.

3. In respect of a signatory State ratifying, accepting or approving subsequently, the Convention shall come into force three months after the date of the deposit of its instrument of ratification, acceptance or approval.

Article 12

1. Any State may, at the time of signature or when depositing its instrument of ratification, acceptance or approval, specify the territory or territories to which this Convention shall apply.

2. Any State may, when depositing its instrument of ratification, acceptance or approval or at any later date, by declaration addressed to the Secretary General of the Council of Europe, extend this Convention to any other territory or territories specified in the declaration and for whose international relations it is responsible or on whose behalf it is authorised to give undertakings.

3. Any declaration made in pursuance of the preceding paragraph may, in respect of any territory mentioned in such declaration, be withdrawn by means of a notification addressed to the Secretary General of the Council of Europe. Such withdrawal shall take effect immediately or at such later date as may be specified in the notification.

Article 13

1. Any State may, at the time of signature or when depositing its instrument of ratification, acceptance or approval, declare that it reserves the right to refuse extradition in respect of any offence mentioned in Article 1 which it considers to be a political offence, an offence connected with a political offence or an offence inspired by political motives, provided that it undertakes to take into due consideration, when evaluating the character of the offence, any particularly serious aspects of the offence, including:

    a. that it created a collective danger to the life, physical integrity or liberty of persons; or

    b. that it affected persons foreign to the motives behind it; or

    c. that cruel or vicious means have been used in the commission of the offence.

2. Any State may wholly or partly withdraw a reservation it has made in accordance with the foregoing paragraph by means of a declaration addressed to the Secretary General of the Council of Europe which shall become effective as from the date of its receipt.

3. A State which has made a reservation in accordance with paragraph 1 of this article may not claim the application of Article 1 by any other State; it may, however, if its reservation is partial or conditional, claim the application of that article in so far as it has itself accepted it.

Article 14

Any Contracting State may denounce this Convention by means of a written notification addressed to the Secretary General of the Council of Europe. Any such denunciation shall take effect immediately or at such later date as may be specified in the notification.

Article 15

This Convention ceases to have effect in respect of any Contracting State which withdraws from or ceases to be a Member of the Council of Europe.

Article 16

The Secretary General of the Council of Europe shall notify the member States of the Council of:

a. any signature;

b. any deposit of an instrument of ratification, acceptance or approval;

c. any date of entry into force of this Convention in accordance with Article 11 thereof;

d. any declaration or notification received in pursuance of the provisions of Article 12;

e. any reservation made in pursuance of the provisions of Article 13, paragraph 1;

f. the withdrawal of any reservation effected in pursuance of the provisions of Article 13, paragraph 2;

g. any notification received in pursuance of Article 14 and the date on which denunciation takes effect;

h. any cessation of the effects of the Convention pursuant to Article 15.

IN WITNESS WHEREOF, the undersigned, being duly authorised thereto, have signed this Convention.

DONE at Strasbourg, this 27th day of January 1977, in English and in French, both texts being equally authoritative, in a single copy which shall remain deposited in the archives of the Council of Europe. The Secretary General of the Council of Europe shall transmit certified copies to each of the signatory States.

RESOLUTION 863 ON THE EUROPEAN RESPONSE TO INTERNATIONAL TERRORISM (1986)

The Parliamentary Assembly,

1. Recalling its various appeals for the defence of democracy against terrorism in Europe, in particular Recommendation 1024 (1986) on the European response to international terrorism;

2. Renewing its unreserved condemnation of terrorism, which denies democratic values and human rights, and reiterating its conviction that the response of the European democracies to terrorism must be founded on respect for the principles enshrined in their constitutions, in the European Convention on Human Rights and in international law;

3. Regretting the procrastination of European states in reacting multilaterally to the terrorist threat, and the absence up to the present time of a coherent and binding set of co-ordinated measures adopted by common consent;

4. Deeply concerned at the link between terrorism and trafficking in weapons and drugs;

5. Convinced that those states that directly or indirectly support terrorism—

particularly Libya, Syria and Iran—must be politically and morally isolated in all international forums;

6. Welcoming, as a first step in the right direction, the measures set out in the Declaration on International Terrorism adopted in Tokyo on 5 May 1986 by the heads of state or government of the seven major democracies and by the representatives of the European Community;

7. Convinced that the Council of Europe is called upon, by virtue of the wide geographical area it covers, its composition and democratic basis, to define and co-ordinate European action against international terrorism;

8. Welcoming the decision by the Committee of Ministers to convene, on 4 and 5 November 1986, a European Conference of Ministers responsible for Combating Terrorism,

9. Invites the member states of the Council of Europe:

a. to join in imposing on any state they regard as directly or indirectly responsible for abetting terrorism, political and economic sanctions, including:

i. diplomatic measures against the government of that state, involving reduction and eventually severing of diplomatic relations;

ii. suspension of international flights to and from that country;

iii. suspension of trade in military materials;

iv. suspension of all training of military personnel;

v. curtailment of investment;

vi. in appropriate cases, gradual termination of purchases of raw materials and energy products;

b. to reconsider and reduce arms trade with some countries of Africa and the Middle East, since it is in those regions that terrorist groups and the governments that support them procure the means with which to carry out their activities;

10. Urges the governments of the member states of the Council of Europe, which have not yet done so, to ratify the European Convention on the Suppression of Terrorism, and calls upon them, pending this necessary ratification, to co-operate as effectively as possible with the other member states in combating terrorism;

11. Invites the governments of the member states to review and, where possible, to withdraw any reservations made to that convention at the time of signature or ratification;

12. Invites the European Conference of Ministers responsible for Combating Terrorism to consider:

a. inviting member states to reach an agreement, in consultation, on defining terrorism as a crime against humanity;

b. setting up within the Council of Europe, by means of a partial agreement, a co-operation group for combating terrorism, composed of the ministers in the national governments with responsibility in this field, membership of which might be open to other European and non-European democratic states;

c. drawing up criteria on the basis of which Council of Europe member states could define their attitude to states that abuse, in one way or another, their diplomatic immunity in order to promote terrorist acts;

    d. encouraging where necessary, while having full respect for the freedom of the press, the representative professional organisations to work out a code of ethics for the media, in order to define their role and responsibilities in the defence of democracy, particularly against terrorism;

    e. setting up, in the Council of Europe, a study and documentation centre for the prevention and suppression of terrorism, benefiting from the fullest possible governmental and parliamentary support, with the participation of non-governmental organisations.

DECLARATION OF THE EUROPEAN CONFERENCE OF MINISTERS RESPONSIBLE FOR COMBATING TERRORISM (1986)

The Ministers of the member States of the Council of Europe taking part in the European Conference of Ministers responsible for combating terrorism, held in Strasbourg on 4 and 5 November 1986,

Deeply concerned at the upsurge in terrorist acts, which give rise to horror and revulsion;

Expression their total and unanimous condemnation of such acts which endanger or destroy human lives;

Convinced that terrorism in whatever form constitutes a continued aggression against the democratic institutions of all member States of the Council of Europe and a constant threat to them;

Mindful of the adherence of the member States of the Council of Europe to the principles of parliamentary democracy and the rule of law, and of their commitment, under the Statute of the Council, to the protection of human rights and fundamental freedoms;

Convinced of the need to combine measures at national level with reinforced international co-operation in order to counter terrorism more effectively;

Considering that terrorism has no justification whatsoever and resorts to particularly odious means for achieving its aims;

Noting that certain terrorist groups and those who sponsor them do not confine their actions to only one State;

Acknowledging the need for enhanced action based on improved internal security systems and, among others, on co-ordinated judicial and diplomatic measures;

    I. REAFFIRM their will to fight against terrorism in all its manifestations including terrorism in which States are implicated in whatever manner;

    II. STRESS the need further to analyse terrorism in all its forms as well as its links with organised international crime;

    III. CALL on the member States of the Council of Europe to:

1. reinforce and develop bilateral and multilateral co-operation for combating terrorism;

2. improve extradition and mutual assistance procedures;

3. co-operate closely with a view to resolving conflicts of jurisdiction in cases where several States are concerned;

4. adopt a policy of firmness in response to terrorists' demands based on blackmail;

5. act firmly against terrorism involving abuse of diplomatic or consular privileges and immunities and terrorism directed against diplomatic or consular representatives;

6. consider applying the measures to counter terrorism involving abuse of diplomatic or consular privileges and immunities to acts of organised international crime, such as drug or arms trafficking, involving such abuse;

7. endeavour to influence any State supporting or sponsoring terrorist acts to refrain from doing so and to abide by the rules of international law.

RESOLUTION NO. 1 CONCERNING CLOSER CO-OPERATION BETWEEN THE MEMBER STATES OF THE COUNCIL OF EUROPE IN ALL FIELDS RELATING TO THE COMBAT OF TERRORISM

The Ministers of the member States of the Council of Europe taking part in the European Conference of Ministers responsible for combating terrorism, held in Strasbourg on 4 and 5 November 1986;

Considering that the aim of the Council of Europe is to achieve greater unity among its members;

Deeply deploring the resurgence and spread of terrorism;

Bearing in mind the past initiatives of the Council of Europe, including the work of the Parlimentary Assembly, aimed at the suppression of terrorism;

Having regard to the existing co-operation between the member States of the Council of Europe in combating terrorism;

Convinced of the need further to develop and to strengthen such co-operation under the auspices of the Council of Europe;

Bearing in mind the importance of the media in promoting public awareness of the threat which terrorism presents to democracy;

Taking into account the deliberations of the Conference;

I. RECOMMEND to the member States of the Council of Europe:

1. to co-operate more closely in all fields relating to the combat of terrorism, wherever necessary, by:

   a. strengthening and extending existing co-operation between member States of the Council of Europe at the bilateral level or in the framework of groups of member States;

b. developing existing contracts in order to increase efficiency of bilateral and multilateral co-operation;

2. to avail themselves of any assistance which the Council of Europe may provide in establishing closer links of co-operation;

II. RECOMMEND to the Committee of Ministers:

1. to entrust the closest Counsellors of the Ministers responsible for combating terrorism with a study of questions relating to the implementation of the declaration and the resolutions adopted at this Conference.

The Counsellors should, in particular, study with the support of the Secretary General:

a. questions relating to closer co-operation between the member States of the Council of Europe in the combat of terrorism;

b. appropriate ways of impeding the movements of terrorists from one country to another, including questions of their entry and stay;

c. the experience acquired by member States in the field of investigation, prosecution and punishment of acts of terrorism;

d. existing national law in particular in the penal field, and its application to terrorism as well as the question of its progressive harmonisation;

e. the possibility of co-operation between the member States of the Council of Europe and the member States of the European Community in their respective efforts to unite in the struggle against terrorism;

f. the way in which those non-member States which share the common concern about international terrorism shall be kept informed of any development within the Council of Europe in this field;

2. to examine the possibility of extending intergovernmental co-operation to States not members of the Council of Europe in the areas covered by the Resolutions of the present Conference;

3. to examine, in the light of relevant considerations at the national level and the work of the forthcoming Vienna Ministerial Conference on Mass Media Policy, the question of establishing contacts, at the appropriate level, with representatives of the media, with a view to discussing matters relating to the reporting of acts of terrorism and measures to prevent such acts.

RESOLUTION NO. 2 CONCERNING ADHERENCE TO INTERNATIONAL INSTRUMENTS

The Ministers of the member States of the Council of Europe taking part in the European Conference of Ministers responsible for combating terrorism, held in Strasbourg on 4 and 5 November 1986,

Considering that the aim of the Council of Europe is to achieve greater unity between its members;

Convinced that it is important further to develop and strengthen international co-operation in combating acts of terrorism as well as in assisting the victims of such acts;

Emphasising that the principles laid down in the European Convention on Human Rights of 4 November 1950 must be respected when combating terrorism;

Considering that the principle of "aut dedere aut iudicare" might enable the judicial authorities to combat terrorism more effectively and facilitate international co-operation;

Recognising the Council of Europe's achievements in this field, particularly the European Convention on the Suppression of Terrorism of 27 January 1977, the Declaration on terrorism adopted by the Committee of Ministers on 23 November 1978 and Recommendation R (82) 1 of the Committee of Ministers to member States concerning international co-operation in the prosecution and punishment of acts of terrorism;

Taking note of Resolution No 3 adopted by the 15th Conference of European Ministers of Justice (Oslo, June 1986);

Bearing in mind the work of the Parliamentary Assembly in the field of combating terrorism,

    I. RECOMMEND to the member States which have not yet done so to consider the possibility of becoming parties to the relevant European (1) and other international Conventions (2);

    II. RECOMMEND to the member States party to these treaties to consider the possibility of withdrawing some or all of the reservations they may have made;

    III. RECOMMEND to the member States to conclude, if necessary, bilateral agreements on extradition or to strengthen existing agreements by incorporating in them for the most serious crimes, such as acts of terrorism, the principle of "aut dedere aut iudicare".

(1) In particular:

— the European Convention on the Suppression of Terrorism of 27 January 1977;

— the European Convention on Extradition of 13 December 1957, and its additional protocols;

— the European Convention on Mutual Assistance in Criminal Matters of 20 April 1959, and its additional protocol;

— the European Convention on the International Validity of the European Convention on the Transfer of Proceedings in Criminal Matters of 15 May 1972;

— the Convention on the Transfer of Sentenced Persons of 21 March 1983;

— the European Convention on the Compensation of the Victims of Violent Crimes of 24 November 1983.

(2) In particular:

— the Tokyo Convention on offences and on certain other acts committed on board aircraft of 14 September 1963;

— the Hague Convention for the suppression of unlawful seizure of aircraft of 16 December 1970;

— the Montreal Convention for the suppression of unlawful acts against the safety of civil aviation of 25 September 1971;

— the Convention on the prevention and punishment of crimes against internationally protected persons including diplomatic agents of 14 December 1973;

— the International Convention against the taking of hostages of 17 December 1979;

— the International Convention on the physical protection of nuclear materials of 3 March 1980.

RESOLUTION NO. 3 CONCERNING CO-OPERATION IN MEASURES TO COUNTER TERRORISM INVOLVING ABUSE OF DIPLOMATIC OR CONSULAR PRIVILEGES AND IMMUNITIES AND TERRORISM DIRECTED AT DIPLOMATIC OR CONSULAR REPRESENTATIVES

The Ministers of the member States of the Council of Europe taking part in the European Conference of Ministers responsible for combating terrorism, held in Strasbourg on 4 and 5 November 1986,

Deeply concerned at acts of terrorism involving abuse of diplomatic or consular privileges and immunities as well as those directed against diplomatic or consular representatives;

Convinced of the need to develop and strengthen co-operation in measures to counter these forms of terrorism,

HAVE RESOLVED as follows:

Member States will co-operate in measures to counter terrorism involving abuse of diplomatic or consular privileges and immunities and terrorism directed at diplomatic or consular representatives. To this end, they will:

a. give the closest possible scrutiny to any notification of new members of diplomatic missions or consular posts in their country;

b. co-operate in the exchange of information about members of diplomatic missions or consular posts considered as having connections with terrorism;

c. consider not accepting as a diplomatic or consular representative any person with regard to whom they have, as receiving State or State of residence, concrete information implicating him in an act of terrorism;

d. be ready to use their ability under Art. 11 of the Vienna Convention on diplomatic relations and Art. 20 of the Vienna Convention on consular relations to limit the size of diplomatic missions or consular posts in their country. In particular, they will bear in mind that when a member leaves a mission or post it cannot be assumed that that member can automatically be replaced;

e. attach particular importance to the principle that the premises of a diplomatic mission or a consular post must not be used in a manner incompatible with the functions of the mission or post as laid down in the Vienna Conventions on diplomatic relations and consular relations or by other agreements in force between the two States concerned;

f. endeavour to adopt an agreed position with regard to States which encourage these acts of terrorism. If one member of the Council of Europe suffers from such an act, the member States will consider what action in accordance with international and domestic law they might take jointly or individually to respond to this and in particular to make clear to the offending State that such behaviour is unacceptable;

g. facilitate exchanges of information among themselves on threats to diplomatic missions and consular posts located within their country. They will also facilitate exchanges of information about the threat of terrorism against their diplomatic or consular representatives in third countries and about possible security measures to protect them;

h. consult on the application of the Vienna Conventions on diplomatic and consular relations, with a view to adopting a common approach in their joint efforts to combat terrorism.

VII. Constitutions

INTRODUCTION

Of the 170 nations of the world, all but six have written one-document constitutions—either presently in effect or temporarily suspended. And all contain some statement-formulation of human rights. Such promulgations can be found in the constitutions of the one-party authoritarian regimes and the communist states as well as in the constitutions of the democracies. And there are human rights guarantees in the organic laws of the United Kingdom, New Zealand and Israel, states which do not have one-document constitutions, and in the Koran, which is proclaimed as the constitution of Saudi Arabia, Oman and Libya.[72]

While these constitutional pronouncements do not enjoy the same respect in all the governments of the world, they are at least official expressions of the recognition of the basic rights of individuals and groups within each society. Even where these rights statements have little force, they remain as promises.

Constitutions constitute fundamental law; rights statements in constitutions constitute the basis of national rights policies. And of course constitutions provide the framework of government. But they do much more. Constitutions also legitimatize the power of government. They impose restraints upon governmental authority, they provide a national symbol, they declare or infer an official ideology and they may even state societal goals. Constitutions can be mere window-dressing for repressive regimes; but even then they provide a minimum ground for the justification for governance. Most constitutions do set forth clear statements of human rights. True, such statements may be modified or implemented by legislative, executive, judicial or administrative action. But, in any event, they represent the starting point for national rights policies.

The concept of constitutionalism—the shared belief that governmental power is proscribed by the provisions of a constitution—must be present if a constitution is to be an effective source of citizen's rights.[73] Constitutionalism treats a constitution as a form of higher law, drawing on an ancient tradition in Western political thought which reaches back to the late middle ages.[74] In many western nations, constitutionalism rests upon the foundation of liberal political thought derived from the seventeenth century English philosopher John Locke.[75] In others it is the French tradition, heavily influenced by Jean-Jacques Rousseau. The French experience directly influenced the constitution writers in Belgium, the Netherlands, Switzerland, Austria, Italy and the former French colonies, all of whom embraced the 1789 Declaration of the Rights of Man and of the Citizen. This likewise served as a beacon in Latin American constitutional developments.

The other major model of constitutionalism and human rights is the United States Bill of Rights of 1791, likewise a model for constitutional rights throughout Europe, Latin-America and the Third World. A more reticent example is the English model—a cumulative collection of rights statutes. The Magna Carta of 1215, the Petition of Right of 1628, the Habeas Corpus Act of 1641 and the Bill of Rights of 1689 are the basic rights documents providing the key sources of rights policy in England and in nations following the English example. Unfortunately, the export of the French, American and English constitutions to Asia, Africa,

Latin America and the Near East has not always been accompanied by the spirit of constitutionalism.

The other important philosophical source for constitutional rights is found in Marxist theory. Many of the world's nations, regarding themselves as socialist, follow the Soviet model, and although their constitutions resemble western-style constitutions in their rights statements, they often go far beyond the older models in their listings of rights. Note, however, that the purpose and functions of constitutional rights statements are also different. For the countries which follow the Soviet Union's constitutional example do not share Western notions of constitutionalism; they argue that constitutionalism violates the role of the socialist state in its relations with its own people. Their rights statements and rights policies are not meant as negative restraints upon government.

Marx and Engels had little to say about the form of government which would follow the proletarian revolution. Aside from sketchy references to the "dictatorship of the proletariat" and "the withering away of the state," few guidelines were created for the structure of the post-revolutionary society.[76] It was left to Russia—the world's first avowedly Marxist state—to provide a constitutional model. And the important model was the Stalin Constitution of 1936. This was intended as a symbol of progress in the transition from a dictatorship of the proletariat to a socialist state. Civil liberties protections were provided as an indication to the people of the end of purges and unrestrained arbitrary rule.[77] But coupled with the many guarantees was the important phrase indicating that they were made "in conformity with the interests of the working people, and in order to strengthen the socialist system."[78] Thus, the rights granted were necessarily limited to the benefit of the Communist system. Nevertheless, the 1936 Soviet Constitution did set forth a new litany of rights, including the right to rest and leisure, the right to work, the right to maintenance in old age and similar social rights. Non-socialist countries have also included such rights in their constitutions.

Religion has also played a role in constitution-making. The Irish Constitution based its Directive Principles of State Policy on the social doctrines found in the papal encyclicals, *Rerum Novarum* (1891) and *Quadrageisimo Anno* (1931). These encyclicals warn of both the excesses of capitalist competition and Marxian materialism. Catholic doctrines also found their way into the constitutions of Franco Spain and many Latin American constitutions. Similarly, Buddhist doctrines influenced the Burmese and Sri Lanka constitutional formulations. Islamic concepts have been especially significant in the 1980 Iranian constitution, in Pakistan,[79] Saudi Arabia and elsewhere in the Islamic world. Jewish traditions have been important in Israel.

And in the post-World War II world, the United Nations Universal Declaration of Human Rights has been a powerful force. Many newly independent Asian and African states incorporated United Nations principles into their own constitutions. It remains to be seen whether these statements will truly shape the rights practices of these newer nations.

Independence documents also contain meaningful rights statements. While these documents do not carry the same legal force as constitutions, they may present vivid assertions of human rights. Certainly, the American Declaration of

Independence of 1776 with its principles that "all men are created equal" and that they possess the inalienable rights to "life, liberty, and the pursuit of happiness" has provided a justification for human rights policies around the world. Similarly, the 1918 Soviet Union Declaration of the Rights of the Working and Exploited People announced important human rights for "working people" against "exploiters."

ORGANIZATION OF CONSTITUTIONAL MATERIALS

The human rights provisions reprinted here are excerpts from the world's most important constitutions—deleting material which is either irrelevant, redundant or antiquated. Such selections are based upon the influence of the rights statements, the influence of the constitutional documents and the clarity of the presentation. Thus, the selections are far more than samples of constitutional rights; they are the leading expressions of those rights.

The constitutional provisions are set forth in four major categories, each based upon a different concept of human rights. The oldest and most widely accepted of the human rights are political in nature, designated as rights against the state. These include the various individual rights such as freedom of speech, press, assembly, religion and the many protections given individuals accused of criminal offenses. Such rights are found in both the oldest and newest constitutions.

The second category of rights encompasses the economic and social areas. These include the right to work, to medical care, to education, to social security and to minimum wages. Such rights are not mentioned in national constitutions prior to World War I, and are still absent from many constitutions.

The third category of rights—group rights—is a largely post-World War II phenomenon in national constitutions. Multicultural nations have sometimes prescribed special rights or protections for major population groups, based on race, religion, ethnicity or language. Recognition of such rights is still uncommon, but the trend is toward greater awareness and protection of groups qua groups.

The fourth category—denoted as "new rights"—consists of rights derived from the state rather than restrictions against the state. They include rights to a decent environment, to peace to individual and group development and to the enhancement of the quality of life. Viewing human rights in this context, the state has the duty to be an active partner in the emergence of the individual personality.

This is followed by a fifth section on constitutional enforcement procedures.

WRITINGS ON COMPARATIVE CONSTITUTIONAL LAW

The best general study of comparative constitutional rights is Richard P. Claude, ed., *Comparative Human Rights* (Baltimore: Johns Hopkins Press, 1976).

On equality, the best study is T. Koopmans, ed., *Constitutional Protection of Equality* (Leyden, Neth: A.W. Sijthoff, 1975). Walter Murphy and Joseph Tanenhaus, *Comparative Constitutional Law* (New York: St. Martin's Press, 1977) is a useful collection of cases interpreting national constitutional documents. There are several other less useful casebooks on comparative constitutional rights. The best political study of constitutional rights is Ivo Duchacek, *Power Maps: Comparative Politics of Constitutions* (Santa Barbara, CA: ABC Clio Press, 1973). A powerful, but biased, analysis of comparative rights may be found in Kurt Glaser and Stefan Possony's *Victims of Politics: The State of Human Rights* (New York: Columbia University Press, 1979.) Of special interest is Ogi Nwabrese, *Constitutionalism in the Emergent States* (London: C. Hurst, 1973). On freedom of speech and assembly, see Ivo Duchacek, *Rights and Liberties in the World Today: Constitutional Promise and Reality* (Santa Barbara, CA: ABC-Clio Press, 1973) and Frede Castberg, *Freedom of Speech in the West* (New York: Oceana Publications, 1960).

There is a rich national literature on constitutional rights, too lengthy and diverse to be described here. The United States has developed the most detailed constitutional commentary, although India, Germany, Japan, Australia and France have also developed an extensive literature of rights. It is difficult to keep track of national commentaries on constitutional rights, but the best general bibliography may be found within the 18-volume collection edited by Albert P. Blaustein and Gilbert H. Flanz, *Constitutions of the Countries of the World* (Dobbs Ferry, N.Y.: Oceana, 1971—date).

A. RIGHTS AGAINST THE STATE

1. UNITED KINGDOM

INTRODUCTION

While the British have not consolidated the principle elements of their constitution into one document, their law accords constitutional significance to selected major public statutes and agreements. Excerpts from these documents are presented here not only for their significance in the United Kingdom, but also because of the extraordinary importance of developments in Great Britain in the history of human rights.

The Magna Carta, which was forced from King John in 1215 by the English barons, constituted the first great advance in the modern history of human rights. The document itself formulated the substantial limitations upon the powers of the British monarchy. While the immediate beneficiaries of such limitations were the British noblemen and the clergy, portions of Magna Carta also refer to "free men" and use general terminology which created a justification for later broad human rights claims.

The Petition of Right of 1628 was enacted by the British Parliament as part of its historic struggle to increase its powers at the expense of the monarch. Royal taxing power was curtailed as was royal power to conduct political trials and to use the criminal law for repressive purposes. The most important part is clause four which states that "no man . . . should be put out of his lands or tenements, nor taken, nor imprisoned, nor disinherited, nor put to death, without . . . due process of law."[80] This passage became the foundation of subsequent Anglo-American concepts of fair procedure, and the phrase "due process of law" was to be incorporated into the American Constitution 170 years later.

The Habeas Corpus Act of 1641 explicitly dissolved the Court of Star Chamber, the notorious royal tribunal for political trials. More important for the later development of human rights, the Act provided a criminal procedure for the hearing and trying of criminal cases. The Habeas Corpus Act requires an indictment or a presentment of a grand jury to initiate a criminal proceeding and bars the king and his judges from evading the ordinary processes of the criminal law.

The British Bill of Rights of 1689 is a summation of the rights of free Englishmen at the end of the seventeenth century. After the Glorious Revolution of 1688, a special session of Parliament convened to present a statement of rights to William and Mary of Orange. This Bill of Rights formed the cornerstone of the limited monarchy which followed. It was a vivid reminder of the ancient liberties of Englishmen which some monarchs had violated. It also provided the inspiration for many of the phrases and ideas which subsequently found their way into the American Constitution and the constitutions of many other nations.

Taken together these four documents provide a source for basic Western ideals of human rights. While many other rights have been added by various other national constitutions, these British rights documents provide the bedrock of human rights in most of the nations of the world.

MAGNA CARTA (1215)

JOHN, by the grace of God, king of England, lord of Ireland, duke of Normandy and Aquitaine, count of Anjou to the archbishops, bishops, abbots, earls, barons, justiciars, foresters, sheriffs, reeves, servants, and all bailiffs and his faithful people greeting. Know that by the suggestion of God and for the good of our soul and those of all our predecessors and of our heirs, to the honor of God and the exaltation of holy church, and the improvement of our kingdom, by the advice of . . . [twenty-seven barons and church lords] . . . and others of our faithful.

1. In the first place we have granted to God, and by this our present charter confirmed, for us and our heirs forever, that the English church shall be free and shall hold its rights entire and its liberties uninjured; and . . . that the freedom of elections, which is considered to be most important and especially necessary to the English church . . . we will observe and . . . we will shall be observed in good faith by our heirs forever.

We have granted moreover to all free men of our kingdom for us and our heirs forever all the liberties written below . . .

21. Earls and barons shall only be fined by their peers, and only in proportion to their offence.

22. A clergyman shall be fined, like those before mentioned, only in proportion to his lay holding . . .

30. No sheriff or bailiff of ours or anyone else shall take horses or wagons of any free man for carrying purposes except on the permission of that free man.

31. Neither we nor our bailiffs will take the wood of another man for castles, or for anything else which we are doing, except by the permission of him to whom the wood belongs.

32. We will not hold the lands of those convicted of a felony for more than a year and a day, after which the lands shall be returned to the lords of the fiefs . . .

34. The writ which is called *praecipe* shall not be given for the future to anyone concerning any tenement by which a free man can lose his court.

35. There shall be one measure of wine throughout our whole kingdom, and one measure of ale, and one measure of grain, . . . and one width of dyed cloth and of russets and of halbergets . . . ; of weights, moreover it shall be as of measures.

36. Nothing shall henceforth be given or taken for a writ of inquisition concerning life or limbs, but it shall be given freely and not denied . . .

38. No bailiff for the future shall put anyone to his law on his simple affirmation, without credible witnesses brought for this purpose.

39. No free man shall be taken or imprisoned or dispossessed, or outlawed, or banished, or in any way destroyed, . . . except by the legal judgment of his peers or by the law of the land.

40. To no one will we sell, to no one will we deny, or delay right or justice.

63. Wherefore we will and firmly command that the Church of England shall be free, and that the men in our kingdom shall have and hold all the aforesaid liberties, rights and concessions, well and peacefully, freely and quietly, fully and completely, for themselves and their heirs, from us and our heirs, in all things and places, forever, as before said. It has been sworn, moreover, as well on our part as on the part of the barons, that all these things spoken of above shall be observed in good faith and without any evil intent. Witness the above named and many others. Given by our hand in the meadow which is called Runnymede, between Windsor and Staines, on the fifteenth day of June in the seventeenth year of our reign.

PETITION OF RIGHT (1628)

TO THE KING'S MOST EXCELLENT MAJESTY.

Humbly show unto our Sovereign Lord the King, the Lords Spiritual and Temporal, and Commons in Parliament assembled, that whereas . . . by . . . the good laws and statutes of this realm, your subjects have inherited this freedom, that they should not be compelled to contribute to any tax, tallage, aid, or other like charge, not set by common consent in Parliament: . . .

II. Yet nevertheless, of late divers commissions . . . have issued, by means whereof your people have been in divers places . . . required to lend certain sums of money unto your Majesty . . .

IV. And in the eight and twentieth year of the reign of King Edward the Third, it was declared and enacted by authority of Parliament, that no man . . . should be put out of his lands or tenements, nor taken, nor imprisoned, nor disherited, nor put to death, without . . . due process of law:

V. Nevertheless . . . divers of your subjects have of late been imprisoned without any cause showed, and when . . . they were brought before your Justices, . . . no cause was certified, but that they were detained by your Majesty's special command, . . . and yet were returned back to several prisons, without being charged with anything to which they might make answer according to the law.

VI. And whereas of late great companies of soldiers and mariners have been dispersed into divers counties . . . and the inhabitants . . . have been compelled to receive them into their houses . . .

VII. And . . . also by authority of Parliament, in the 25th year of the reign of King Edward the Third, it is declared and enacted, that no man shall be forejudged of life or limb against the form of the Great Charter, and the law of the land . . . ; or by Acts of Parliament . . . nevertheless of late . . . certain persons have been assigned and appointed Commissioners with power and authority to proceed . . . against such soldiers and mariners or other dissolute persons joining with them . . . and them to cause to be executed and put to death, according to the law martial:

VII. By pretext whereof, some of your Majesty's subjects have been by some of the said Commissioners put to death . . .

IX. And also sundry grievous offenders . . . have escaped the punishments due to them by the laws and statutes of this your realm . . . upon pretence that the said offenders were punishable only by martial law . . .

X. They do therefore humbly pray your Most Excellent Majesty, that no man hereafter be compelled to make or yield any gift, loan, benevolence, tax, or such like charge, without common consent by Act of Parliament; and that none by called to make answer, or take such oath, or to give attendance, or be confined, or otherwise molested or disquieted concerning the same, or for refusal thereof; and that no freeman, in any such manner as is before-mentioned, be imprisoned or detained; and that your Majesty will be pleased to remove the said soldiers and mariners, and that your people may not be so burdened in time to come; and that the aforesaid commissions for proceeding by martial law, may be revoked and annulled; and that hereafter no commissions of like nature may issue forth to any person or persons whatsoever . . .

XI. All which they most humbly pray of your Most Excellent Majesty, as their rights and liberties according to the laws and statutes of this realm . . .

[Which Petition being read the 2nd of June 1628, the King's answer was thus delivered unto it:

The King willeth that right be done according to the laws and customs of the realm; and that the statutes be put in due execution, that his subjects may have no cause to complain of any wrong or oppressions . . .

HABEAS CORPUS ACT (1641)

Whereas by the Great Charter many times confirmed in Parliament, it is enacted that no freeman shall be taken or imprisoned, or disseized of his freehold or liberties or free customs, or be outlawed or exiled or liberties or free customs, or be outlawed or exiled or otherwise destroyed, and that the King will not pass upon him or condemn him but by lawful judgment of his peers or by the law of the land; and by another statute . . . no man shall be attached by any accusation nor forejudged of life or limb, nor his lands, tenements, goods nor chattels seized into the King's hands against the form of the Great Charter and the law of the land; and by another statute . . . none shall be taken by petition or suggestion made to the King or to his Council, unless it be by indictment or presentment of good and lawful people of the same neighborhood where such deeds be done, in due manner or by process made by writ original at the common law, and that none be put out of his franchise or freehold unless he be duly brought in to answer and forejudged of the same by the course of the law, and if anything be done against the same, it shall be redressed and holden for none; and by another statute . . . no man of what estate or conditions soever he be shall be put out of his lands or tenements, nor taken nor imprisoned nor disinherited without being brought in to answer by due process of law; and by another statute . . . it is enacted, that no man be put to answer without presentment before Justices or matter of record, or by due process and writ original according to the old law of the land, and if anything be done to the contrary, it shall be void in law and holden for error; and by another statute . . . all please which shall be pleaded in any Courts before any of the King's Justices, or in his other places, or before any of his other ministers, or in the Courts and places of any other Lords within the realm shall be entered and enrolled in Latin; and whereas by the statute made in the third year of King Henry the Seventh, power is given to the Chancellor, the Lord Treasurer of England for the time being, and the Keeper of the King's Privy Seal, or two of them, calling unto them a Bishop and a Temporal Lord of the King's most honorable Council, and the two Chief Justices of the King's Bench and Common Pleas for the time being, or other two Justices in their absence, to proceed as in that Act is expressed for the punishment of some particular offences therein mentioned; and by the statute made in the one-and twentieth year of King Henry the Eighth, the President of the Council is associated to join with the Lord Chancellor and other Judges in the said statute of the third year of Henry the Seventh mentioned: but the said Judges have not kept themselves to the points limited by the said statute, but have undertaken to punish where no law doth warrant, and to make decrees for things having no such authority, and to inflict heavier punishments than by any law is warranted;

II. Forasmuch as all matters examinable or determinable before the said Judges, or in the Court commonly called the Star Chamber, may have their proper remedy and redress, and their due punishment and correction, by the common law of the land, and in the ordinary course of justice elsewhere; and forasmuch as the reasons and motives inducing the erection and continuance of that Court do now cease; and the proceedings, censures and decrees of that Court have by experience been found to be an intolerable burden to the subjects, and the means to introduce an arbitrary power and government; and forasmuch as the Council Table hath of late times assumed unto itself a power to intermeddle in civil causes and matters only of private interest between party and party, and have adventured to determine of the estates and liberties of the subjects, contrary to the law of the land and the rights and privileges of the subject, by which great and manifold mischiefs and inconveniences have arisen and happened, and much uncertainty by means of such proceedings hath been conceived concerning men's rights and estates; for settling whereof and preventing the like in time to come:

III. Be it ordained and enacted by the authority of this present Parliament, that the said Court commonly called the Star Chamber, and all jurisdiction, power and authority belonging unto or exercised in the same Court, or by any of the Judges, Officers or Ministers thereof, be . . . clearly and absolutely dissolved, taken away, and determined; . . . and that all and every Act and Acts of Parliament . . . by which any jurisdiction, power or authority is given . . . unto the said Court . . . shall . . . be . . . repealed and absolutely revoked and made void.

IV. And be it likewise enacted, that the like jurisdiction now used and exercised in the Court before the President and Council in the Marches of Wales; and also in the Court before the President and Council established in the northern parts; and also in the Court commonly called the Court of the Duchy of Lancaster . . . ; and also in the Court of Exchequer of the County Palatine of Chester . . . ' shall . . . be also repealed and absolutely revoked and made void . . . ' and that from henceforth no court, council, or place of judicature shall be erected, ordained, constituted, or appointed within this realm of England or dominion of Wales, which shall have, use or exercixe the same of the like jurisdiction, as is or hath been used, practised or exercised in the said Court of Star Chamber.

V. Be it likewise declared and enacted by authority of this present Parliament, that neither His Majesty nor his Privy Council have or ought to have any jurisdiction, power or authority by English bill, petition, articles, libel, or any other arbitrary way whatsoever, to examine or draw into question, determine or dispose of the lands, tenements, hereditaments, goods or chattels of any the subjects of this kingdom, but that the same ought to be tried and determined in the ordinary Courts of Justice and by the ordinary course of the law.

BILL OF RIGHTS (1689)

Whereas the lords spiritual and temporal and commons assembled at Westminster lawfully, fully and freely representing all the estates of the people of this realm, did . . . present unto Their Majesties, . . . William and Mary, . . . a certain declaration . . . in the words following viz.:

Whereas the late king James the Second by the assistance of divers evil counsellors, judges and ministers . . . did endeavour to subvert and extirpate the Protestant religion and the laws and liberties of this kingdom . . .

And whereas the said late king James the Second having abdicated the government and the throne being thereby vacant, His Highness the prince of Orange . . . did (by the advice of the lords spiritual and temporal and divers principal persons of the commons) cause letters to be written to the lords spiritual and temporal, being Protestants; and other letters to the several counties, cities, universities, boroughs and Cinque ports for the choosing of such persons to represent them, as were of right to be sent to parliament, . . . in order to such an establishment as that their religion, laws and liberties might not again be in danger of being subverted . . .

And thereupon the said lords spiritual and temporal and commons . . . being now assembled in a full and free representative of this nation, taking into their most serious consideration the best means for attaining the ends aforesaid, do in the first place (as their ancestors in like cases have usually done) for the vindicating and asserting their ancient rights and liberties, declare:

That the pretended power of suspending of laws or the execution of laws by regal authority without consent of parliament is illegal.

That the pretended power of dispensing with laws of the execution of laws by regal authority as it hath been assumed and exercised of late is illegal.

That the commission for erecting the late court of commissioners for ecclesiastical causes and all other commissions and courts of like nature are illegal and pernicious.

That the levying money for or to the use of the crown by pretence of prerogative without grant of parliament for a longer time or in other manner than the same is or shall be granted is illegal.

That it is the right of the subjects to petition the king and all commitments and prosecutions for such petitioning are illegal.

That the raising or keeping a standing army within the kingdom in time of peace unless it be with consent of parliament is against law.

That the subjects which are Protestants may have arms for their defence suitable to their conditions and as allowed by law.

That election of members of parliament ought to be free.

That the freedom of speech and debates or proceedings in parliament ought not to be impeached or questioned in any court or place out of parliament.

That excessive bail ought not to be required nor excessive fines imposed nor cruel and unusual punishments inflicted.

That jurors ought to be duly impanelled and returned and jurors which pass upon men in trials for high treason ought to be freeholders.

That all grants and promises of fines and forteitures of particular persons before conviction are illegal and void.

And that for redress of all grievances and for the amending, strengthening and preserving of the laws parliaments ought to be held frequently.

And they do claim, demand and insist upon all and singular the premises as their undoubted rights and liberties and that no declarations, judgments, doings or proceedings to the prejudice of the people in any of the said premises ought in any wise to be drawn hereafter into consequence or example. To which demand of their rights they are particularly encouraged by the declaration of His Highness the prince of Orange as being the only means for obtaining a full redress and remedy therein. Having therefore an entire confidence that His said Highness the prince of Orange will perfect the deliverance so far advanced by him, and will still preserve them from the violation of their rights, which they have here asserted, and from all other attempts upon their religion, rights and liberties, the said lords spiritual and temporal and commons assembled at Westminster do resolve, that William and Mary, prince and princess of Orange, be and be declared king and queen of England, France and Ireland and the dominions thereunto belonging . . .

Upon which Their said Majesties did accept the crown and royal dignity of the kingdoms of England, France and Ireland and the dominions thereunto belonging, according to the resolution and desire of the said lords and commons, contained in the said declaration. And thereupon Their Majesties were pleased, that the said lords spiritual and temporal and commons being the two houses of parliament should continue to sit, and with Their Majesties' royal concurrence make effectual provision for the settlement of the religion, laws and liberties of this kingdom . . . Now in pursuance of the premises, the lords spiritual and temporal and commons in parliament assembled . . . do pray that . . . all and singular the rights and liberties asserted and claimed in the said declaration are the true, ancient and indubitable rights and liberties of the people of this kingdom, and . . . shall be firmly and strictly holden and observed . . . ; and all officers and ministers whatsoever shall serve Their Majesties and their successors according to the same in all times to come. . . .

II. And be it further declared and enacted by the authority aforesaid, that, from and after this present session of parliament, no dispensation by *non obstante* of or to any statute or any part thereof shall be allowed, but that the same shall be held void and of no effect, except a dispensation be allowed of in such statute, and except in such case as shall be specially provided for by one or more bill or bills to be passed during this present session of parliament.

2. UNITED STATES

INTRODUCTION

The 1791 American Bill of Rights—the first ten amendments to the United States Constitution—is based upon the revolutionary American theory that mankind possesses certain inalienable rights granted by God or by nature. These are the self-proclaimed rights of a people as sovereign. And while they have antecedents in English law and history, they are unlike the English in that they are not concessions obtained from hereditary rulers.

This embodiment of the basic rights of the American people was enacted by the Congress and ratified by the states two years after the Constitution was adopted—rectifying the failure of the framers to include such a rights statement in the original document.

Some rights, however, had been set forth in the 1789 constitution. These included "the privilege of the writ of habeas corpus," Art. I, sec. 9(2), and the prohibitions against bills of attainder and ex post facto laws, Art. I, sec. 9(3). There was also a constitutional ban upon religious tests for public office, Art. VI, sec. 3. Yet these were far less significant than those subsequently placed in the 1791 Bill of Rights. James Madison, the Virginia statesman who played such a large part in formulating the American provisions, recognized that a succinct and precise statement of rights was necessary to instill confidence in the new nation and to safeguard the interests of individuals against the incursions of national government.

Significantly, the American Bill of Rights refers solely to the national government. Except for the Tenth Amendment, there is not even mention of state governments. From this fact and from the references to Congress in the First Amendment, Supreme Court Justice John Marshall concluded, in 1833, that the Bill of Rights constrained only the federal government.[81] Technically, this is still the law of the land. But the ratification of the Fourteenth Amendment has resulted in a slow incorporation of the Federal Bill of Rights as a restriction upon the actions of state government.[82]

The rights which James Madison selected for inclusion in the first eight amendments were all taken from the first state constitutions and bills of rights.

Free exercise of religion had been protected in all of these documents and the rights of criminal defendants were likewise well developed in state constitutions. Trial by jury was guaranteed in eleven states; freedom of the press in ten; due process and bail in nine. Freedom of speech and the right against being placed in double jeopardy were elevated to a constitutional plane as a result of Madison's insistence.[83]

The first nine amendments are all addressed to the national government on behalf of the rights of individuals. The Ninth Amendment underscores this emphasis by stating that the enumeration of certain rights "shall not be construed to deny or disparage others retained by the people." The Tenth Amendment, the only one which does not deal with individual rights, reserves to the states all powers not delegated by the Constitution to the national government—with the people retaining residual powers.

The Thirteenth, Fourteenth and Fifteenth amendments added significantly to American freedom. Important matters not mentioned in the 1791 Bill of Rights were made fundamental law. These three amendments, promulgated after the American Civil War, related to the slavery issue. The Thirteenth Amendment, ratified in 1865, freed all the slaves and forbade slavery and involuntary servitude. The Fourteenth Amendment, ratified in 1868, reversed the results of the Supreme Court's notorious Dred Scott[84] decision, making all persons born or naturalized in the United States full citizens, with all of the "privileges or immunities of citizens." The Fourteenth Amendment also guaranteed the "equal protection of the laws" to all citizens, a phrase of enormous significance in subsequent constitutional law decisions. The Fourteenth Amendment also forbids states from depriving persons of "life, liberty or property, without due process of law," providing another potent source of judicially prescribed American rights.

UNITED STATES CONSTITUTION (Original Text, 1787)

Article I, Sec. 9

2. The privilege of the Writ of Habeas Corpus shall not be suspended, unless when in the cases of rebellion or invasion the public safety may require it.

3. No Bill of Attainder or *ex post facto* law shall be passed.

Article I, Sec. 10

1. No State shall enter into any treaty, alliance, or confederation, grant letters of marque and reprisal, coin money, emit bills of credit, make anything but gold and silver coin a tender in payment of debts, pass any Bill of Attainder, *ex post facto* law, or law impairing the obligation of contracts, or grant any title of nobility.

(Bill of Rights, 1791)

Articles in Addition to, and Amendment of, the Constitution of the United States of America, proposed by Congress, and ratified by the Legislatures of the Several States pursuant to the Fifth Article of the Original Constitution:

Article One

Congress shall make no law respecting an establishment of religion, or prohibiting the free exercise thereof; or abridging the freedom of speech, or of the press; or the right of the people peaceably to assembly, and to petition the Government for a redress of grievances.

Article Two

A well-regulated militia, being necessary to the security of a free State, the right of the people to keep and bear arms, shall not be infringed.

Article Three

No soldier shall, in time of peace, be quartered in any house, without the consent of the owner, nor in time of war, but in a manner to be prescribed by law.

Article Four

The right of the people to be secure in their persons, houses, papers, and effects, against unreasonable searches and seizures, shall not be violated, and no warrants shall issue, but upon probable cause, supported by oath or affirmation, and particularly describing the place to be searched, and the persons or things to be seized.

Article Five

No person shall be held to answer for a capital, or other infamous crime, unless on a presentment or indictment of a Grand Jury, except in cases arising in the land or naval forces, or in the militia, when in actual service, in time of war or public danger; nor shall any person be subject for the same offense to be twice put in jeopardy of life or limb; nor shall be compelled in any criminal case to be a witness against himself; nor be deprived of life, liberty, or property, without due process of law; nor shall private property be taken for public use, without just compensation.

Article Six

In all criminal prosecutions, the accused shall enjoy the right to a speedy and public trial, by an impartial jury of the State and district wherein the crime shall have been committed, which district shall have been previously ascertained by law, and to be informed of the nature and cause of the accusation; to be confronted with witness against him; to have compulsory process for obtaining witnesses in his favour, and to have the assistance of counsel for his defense.

Article Seven

In suits at common law, where the value in controversy shall exceed twenty dollars, the right of trial by jury shall be preserved, and no fact tried by a jury shall be otherwise re-examined in any court of the United States, than according to the rules of the common law.

Article Eight

Excessive bail shall not be required, nor excessive fines imposed, nor cruel and unusual punishments inflicted.

Article Nine

The enumeration in the Constitution, of certain rights shall not be construed to deny or disparage others retained by the people.

Article Ten

The powers not delegated to the United States by the Constitution, nor prohibited by it to the States, are reserved to the States respectively, or to the people.

(Civil War Amendments, 1868–1870)

Article Thirteen (1868)

1. Neither slavery nor involuntary servitude, except as a punishment for crime whereof the party shall have been duly convicted, shall exist within the United States, or any place subject to their jurisdiction.

2. Congress shall have power to enforce this article by appropriate legislation.

Article Fourteen (1868)

1. All persons born or naturalized in the United States, and subject to the jurisdiction thereof, are citizens of the United States and of the State wherein they reside. No State shall make or enforce any law which shall abridge the privileges or immunities of citizens of the United States; nor shall any State deprive any person of life, liberty, or property, without due process of law; nor deny to any person within its jurisdiction the equal protection of the laws.

2. Representatives shall be appointed among the several States according to their respective numbers, counting the whole number of persons in each State, excluding Indians not taxed. But when the right to vote at any election for the choice of Electors for President and Vice-President of the United States, representatives in Congress, the Executive and Judicial officers of a State, or the members of the Legislature thereof, is denied to any of the male members of such State, being twenty-one years of age, and citizens of the United States, or in any way abridged, except for participation in rebellion, or other crimes, the basis of representation therein shall be reduced in the proportion which the

number of such male citizens shall bear to the whole number of male citizens twenty-one years of age in such State.

3. No person shall be a Senator or Representative in Congress, or Elector of President and Vice-President, or hold any office, civil or military, under the United States, or under any State, who, having previously taken an oath, as a member of Congress, or as an officer of the United States, or as a member of any State Legislature, or as an Executive or Judicial officer of any State, to support the Constitution of the United States, shall have engaged in insurrection or rebellion against the same, or given aid and comfort to the enemies thereof. But Congress may, by a vote of two-thirds of each House, remove such disability.

4. The validity of the public debt of the United States, authorized by law, including debts incurred for payment of pensions and bounties for services in suppressing insurrection and rebellion, shall not be questioned. But neither the United States nor any State shall assume or pay any debt or obligation incurred in aid of insurrection or rebellion against the United States, or any claim for the loss or emancipation of any slave; but all such debts, obligations, and claims shall be held illegal and void.

5. Congress shall have power to enforce by appropriate legislation the provisions of this article.

Article Fifteen (1870)

1. The right of citizens of the United States to vote shall not be denied or abridged by the United States or by any State on account of race, color, or previous condition of servitude.

2. The Congress shall have power to enforce this article by appropriate legislation.

3. FRANCE

INTRODUCTION

The 1789 Declaration of the Rights of Man and of the Citizen—which preceded and then was part of the French constitutions of 1791, 1793 and 1795— is the most influential of all human rights documents. Such influence contin-ues—especially in France. For while the present French Constitution of 1958 does not have an explicit bill of rights, its Preamble solemnly proclaims the attachment of the French people to the rights of man as set forth in the Declaration. And the language of the French Declaration has been influential in the Netherlands, Belgium, Switzerland, Italy, Austria and in parts of Asia and Africa following the end of French colonial rule.

Prior to the French Revolution, there were no guarantees of the rights of the ordinary citizen. The King could imprison his enemies at will, without trial, through the issuance of Lettres de Cachet. True, the French law courts could protest royal edicts, but the king could and did ignore them. The campaign against this system of arbitrary arrest and imprisonment was begun by a coterie of lawyers and judges, who later combined with other anti-royalty and anti-aristocratic forces leading to the French Revolution and the overthrow of the monarchy.

Within a month after the storming of the Bastille, the National Constituent Assembly met to restructure the basic character of French life. The Assembly decreed the abolition of the feudal system and the privileges of persons and towns. Equality before the law was proclaimed; tithes were supressed.

The task of formulating a Declaration of Rights was seen as a necessary first step prior to the work of the Assembly in framing a constitution. Since the object of a constitution was supposed to be the preservation of the natural rights of man, such Declaration was needed to define those rights. Most of the drafting work fell to Lafayette, Mourier, Talleyrand, Laily-Tollendal and Alexandre de Lameth.[85] The document was completed on August 26, 1789, representing a blending of middle-class individualism with the intellectual ideals of enlightenment thinkers.

The French Declaration makes no mention of a nation or a system of government. It was intended to be, as Mirabeau said, "a declaration applicable to all ages, all peoples, all moral and geographical latitudes." Yet, at the same time, the Declaration has proved to be the most fundamental of all French legal documents.

Article One proclaims that men are equal in rights. This does not mean full political or social equality, but it does signify the termination of privilege. Article Two defines as fundamental the human rights of liberty, property, security and resistance to oppression. Article Three is directed against the royal doctrine that France was the personal property of its kings. Articles Ten and Eleven provide for liberty of speech, press, and religion, subject to legal limitations upon the abuse of these rights. Articles Seven, Eight and Nine deal with protections for persons accused of criminal offenses. The broadest human rights statement is in Article Four which declares that the exercise of national rights is unlimited, except for the need to secure to others the same enjoyment of rights. Limits upon the exercise of rights must be stated in a law.

Lafayette, one of the draftsmen of the French Declaration of the Rights of Man and of the Citizen, was in America when the Declaration of Independence was being prepared and became a friend of its principal author, Thomas Jefferson. He was also familiar with the Virginia Bill of Rights and its author, George Mason. And Thomas Jefferson was the American ambassador in France in 1789 and it is known that Lafayette discussed the wording of the French Declaration with him. A certain amount of borrowing obviously took place, although French scholars dispute the matter.[86]

There was, during this revolutionary period in history, considerable interchange of ideas between France, England and the United States. But France had the furthest to go to achieve liberty for all the people and not just a privileged elite. America had had no experience with feudalism and direct royal absolutism was seldom evident. The French Declaration is more sweeping than the American Bill of Rights because it had to be.

THE DECLARATION OF THE RIGHTS OF MAN AND THE CITIZEN (26 AUGUST 1789)

The Representatives of the French People constituted in National Assembly,

Considering that ignorance, forgetfulness or contempt of the rights of man are the sole causes of public misfortune and governmental depravity,

Have resolved to expound in a solemn declaration the natural, inalienable and sacred rights of man,

So that this declaration, perpetually present to all members of the body social, shall be a constant reminder to them of their right and duties;

So that, since it will be possible at any moment to compare the acts of the legislative authority and those of the executive authority with the final end of all political institutions, those acts shall thereby be the more respected;

So that the claims of the citizenry, founded thenceforth on simple and uncontestable principles, shall always tend to the support of the constitution and to the common good.

Consequently the *National Assembly* recognizes and declares in the presence and under the auspices of the Supreme Being the following rights of man and of the citizen:

1. In respect of their rights men are born and remain free and equal. The only permissible basis for social distinctions is public utility.

2. The final end of every political institution is the preservation of the natural and imprescriptible rights of man. These rights are those of liberty, property, security and resistance to oppression.

3. The basis of all sovereignty lies, essentially, in the Nation. No corporation nor individual may exercise any authority that is not expressly derived therefrom.

4. Liberty is the capacity to do anything that does no harm to others. Hence the only limitations on the individual's exercise of his natural rights are those which ensure the enjoyment of these same rights to all other individuals. These limits can be established only by legislation.

5. Legislation is entitled to forbid only those actions which are harmful to society. Nothing not forbidden by legislation may be prohibited nor may any individual be compelled to do anything that legislation has not prescribed.

6. Legislation is the expression of the general will. All citizens have a right to participate in shaping it either in person, or through their representatives. It must be the same for all, whether it punishes or it protects. Since all citizens are equal in its eyes, all are equally eligible for all positions, posts and public employments in accordance with their abilities and with no other distinctions than those provided by their virtues and their talents.

7. No individual may be accused, arrested or detained except in the cases prescribed by legislation and according to the procedures it has laid down. Those who solicit, further, execute or arrange for the execution of arbitrary commands must be punished; but every citizen charged or detained by virtue of legislation must immediately obey; resistance renders him culpable.

8. The only punishments established by legislation must be ones that are strictly and obviously necessary, and no individual may be punished except by

virtue of a law passed and promulgated prior to the crime and applied in due legal form.

9. Since every individual is presumed innocent until found guilty, legislation must severely repress all use of force beyond that which is necessary to secure his person in those cases where it is deemed indispensable to arrest him.

10. Nobody must be persecuted on account of his opinions, including religious ones, provided that the manifestation of these does not disturb the public order established by legislation.

11. The free communication of thoughts and opinions is one of the most precious rights of man; hence every citizen may speak, write and publish freely, save that he must answer for any abuse of such freedom according to the cases established by legislation.

12. In order to guarantee the rights of man and the citizen, a police force is necessary: it follows that such a force is established for the public weal and not for the private advantage of those to whom it is entrusted.

13. The upkeep of the police force and the expenses of public administration necessitate public taxation. This must be borne by all citizens equally, according to their means.

14. All citizens, individually or through their representatives, possess the right to assure themselves that a need for taxation exists, to accept it by free consent, to monitor the way it is being used and to prescribe the base, the allocation, collection and duration of the tax.

15. Society possesses the right to demand from every public servant an account of his administration.

16. A society in which rights are not secured not the separation of powers established in a society without a constitution.

17. Since property is an inviolable and sacred right, no individual may be deprived of it unless some public necessity, legally certified as such, clearly requires it; and subject always to a just and previously determined compensation.

B. ECONOMIC AND SOCIAL RIGHTS

(First promulgated in the 1917 Mexican Constitution as well as an out-growth of the Soviet revolution of that same year. The U.S.S.R. human rights provisions, originally framed in 1918, were refined in the constitutions of 1936 and 1977.)

1. MEXICO (1917)

INTRODUCTION

Mexico's turbulent history has been punctuated by constitutional change and its revolutionary idealism was manifest in its 1917 Constitution. This constitution reveals a concern for workers and the poor, but is also concerned with foreign investors. Land ownership, an important political issue for gener-ations, is treated in special provisions on land and natural resources. Mexican rights provisions have been influential throughout Latin America and other nations of the Third World. While they have a peculiarly national flavor, they also possess a universal appeal.

Mexican rights provisions are the most elaborate in the world. Lengthy clauses detail the exact extent of rights and obligations as though to place certain issues beyond the reach of shifting majorities. Further, these provisions have been frequently supplemented and altered, adding to the complexity of the texts. Because this detailed elaboration of rights provides a different approach to rights statements, these provisions deserve attention as a matter of form as well as for their substantive content.

Mexico has a strong heritage of anti-clericalism, as a reaction to the policies, power and privileged position of the Catholic Church in the nineteenth century. In addition, Church opposition to the Revolution of 1910 played into the hands of anti-clerical factions. And when the 1916–17 Constitutional Convention met, its members proposed sweeping anti-clerical measures, which were incorpo-rated into the constitution.

Article 3, established "liberty of education" by requiring that all education be secular—a blow against religious education. The provision is quite explicit and reserves to the government the power to prevent the establishment of religious schools. This Art. 3 must be studied in conjunction with Arts. 24, 130 and 27 to understand the Mexican version of church-state relations. Art. 24 authorized government supervision of places of public worship in the name of free exercise of religion. Art. 130 then curtails the power of the Catholic Church over marriage and divorce, and over church property. In addition, it gives the government power to regulate religious denominations and to restrict the rights of ministers to hold property and to receive bequests. And Art. 130 also places stringent restraints upon religious publications and the professional training of ministers. Art. 27 prohibits church ownership of real estate. As a package, this collection of Mexican rights is unique, but they have been nonetheless influential in constitutional deliberations in many other countries.

Article 27, a social guarantee, is one of the most important rights statements in the constitution. Defining the nature of private property, it goes beyond individual rights limiting and regulating ownership and use. It is partially aimed at the problem of land distribution, a severe cause of tension in Mexico as well as elsewhere in Latin-America. Original ownership of Mexican land rests in the nation, but can be transmitted to individuals. The nation can also grant, as owner of the waters and subsoil, certain rights of exploitation. Alien ownership of land is only permitted under the proviso that foreign owners renounce the protection of their own governments. The constitution also lays the foundation for far-reaching agrarian reform and legalizes communal land rights. But the constitution stops far short of social ownership of land and does not accomplish land redistribution.

Article 123, dealing with labor protections, was the world's most advanced when it was adopted in 1917. Frequently amended to expand the rights of labor, it remains fundamental to Mexican law and has provided an inspiration to constitutional draftsmen elsewhere. Art. 28 is an important example of an anti-monopoly provision—a social right rather than an individual right, acclaimed as another pioneering provision of the Mexican Constitution.

MEXICO CONSTITUTION (1917)

Article 4.2

Men and women are equal before the law. The law shall protect the organization and development of the family.

Every person has the right to decide in a free, responsible and informed manner on the number and spacing of their children.

It is the duty of parents to preserve the right of minors to satisfy their needs and to physical and mental health. The law shall determine the support for the protection of minors to be given by public institutions.

Article 5.1

No person can be prevented from engaging in the profession, industrial or commercial pursuit or occupation of his choice, provided it is lawful. The exercise of this liberty shall only be enjoined by judicial order when the rights of third parties are infringed, or by administrative order, issued in the manner provided by law, when the rights of society are violated. No one may be deprived of the fruits of his labor except by judicial decision.

The law in each state shall determine the professions which may be practiced only with a degree, and set forth the requirements for obtaining it and the authorities empowered to issue it. . . .

The State cannot permit the performance of any contract, convenant, or agreement having for its object the restriction, loss or irrevocable sacrifice of the individual freedoms, whether for work, education, or religious vows. The law, therefore, does not permit the establishment of monastic orders, whatever be their denominator or purpose.

A labor contract shall be binding only to render the services agreed on for the time set by law and may never exceed one year to the detriment of the worker, and in no case may it embrace the waiver, loss, or restriction of any civil or political right.

Noncompliance with such contract by the worker shall only render him civilly liable for damages, but in no case shall it imply coercion against his person.

Article 6.1

The expression of ideas shall not be subject to any judicial or administrative investigation unless if offends good morals, infringes the rights of others, incites to crime, or disturbs the public order. The right to information shall be guaranteed by the State.

Article 7

Freedom of writing and publishing writings on any subject is inviolable. No law or authority may establish censorship, require bonds from authors or printers, or restrict the freedom of printing, which shall be limited only by the respect due to the right of privacy, morals, and public peace. Under no circumstances may a printing press be sequestered as the instrument of the offense.

The organic laws shall contain whatever provisions may be necessary to prevent the imprisonment of the vendors, newsboys, workmen, and other employees of the establishment publishing the work denounced, under pretext of a denunciation of offenses of the press, unless their guilt is previously established.

Article 8

Public officials and employees shall respect the exercise of the right of petition, provided it is made in writing and in a peaceful and respectful manner; but this right may only be exercised in political matters by citizens of the Republic.

Every petition shall be replied to in writing by the official to whom it is addressed, and said official is bound to inform the petitioner of the decision taken within a brief period.

Article 24

Everyone is free to embrace the religion of his choice and to practice all ceremonies, devotions, or observances of his respective faith, either in places of public worship or at home, provided they do not constitute an offense punishable by law.

Every religious act of public worship must be performed strictly inside places of public worship, which shall at all times be under governmental supervision.

Article 25

Sealed correspondence sent through the mail shall be exempt from search and its violation shall be punishable by law.

Article 26

No member of the army shall in time of peace be quartered in private dwellings without the consent of the owner, nor may he impose any obligation whatsoever. In time of war the military may demand lodging, equipment, provisions, and other assistance, in the manner laid down in the respective martial law.

Article 27

Ownership of the lands and waters within the boundaries of the national territory is vested originally in the Nation, which has had, and has, the right to transfer title thereof to private persons, thereby constituting private property.

Private property shall not be expropriated except for reasons of public use and subject to payment of indemnity.

The Nation shall at all times have the right to impose on private property such limitations as the public interest may demand, as well as the right to regulate the utilization of natural resources which are susceptible of appropriation, in order to conserve them to ensure a more equitable distribution of public wealth, to attain a well-balanced development of the country and improvement of the living conditions of the rural and urban population. With this end in view, necessary measures shall be taken to divide up large landed estates; to develop small landed holdings in operation; to create new agricultural centers, with necessary lands and waters; to encourage agriculture in general and to prevent the destruction of natural resources, and to protect property from damage to the detriment of society. Centers of population which at present either have no lands or water or which do not possess them in sufficient quantities for the needs of their inhabitants, shall be entitled to grants thereof, which shall be granted to private persons and the Nation will make use of the property and natural resources which are required for these ends.

The use of nuclear fuels for the generation of nuclear energy and the regulation of its application to other purposes is also a function of the Nation. Nuclear energy may be used only for peaceful purposes.

The Nation exercises in an exclusive economic zone situated outside the territorial sea and adjacent thereto the rights of sovereignty and jurisdiction as determined by the laws of the Congress. The exclusive economic zone shall extend two hundred nautical miles, measured from the base line from which the territorial sea is measured. In those cases in which the extension results in a superposition on the exclusive economic zones of other States, the delimitation of the respective zones shall be made as this becomes necessary, by agreement with those States.

II. Religious institutions known as churches, regardless of creed, may in no case acquire, hold, or administer real property or hold mortgages thereon; such property held at present either directly or through an intermediary shall revert to the Nation, any person whosoever being authorized to denounce any property so held. Presumptive evidence shall be sufficient to declare the denunciation well founded. Places of public worship are the property of the Nation, as represented by the Federal Government, which shall determine which of them may continue to be devoted to their present purposes. Bishoprics, rectories, seminaries, asylums, and schools belonging to religious orders, convents, or any other buildings built or intended for the administration, propagation, or teaching of a religious creed shall therefore become the property of the Nation by operation of law, to be used exclusively for the public services of the Federal or State Governments, within their respective jurisdictions. All places of pubic worship hereafter erected shall be the property of the Nation.

* * * *

TITLE VI

Labor and Social Security

Article 123.1

Every person is entitled to suitable work that is socially useful. Toward this end, the creation of jobs and social organization for labor shall be promoted in conformance with the law. The Congress of the Union, without contravening the following basic principles, shall enact labor laws which shall apply to:

A. Workers, day laborers, domestic servants, artisans (obreros, jornaleros, empleados domésticos, artesanos) and in a general way to all labor contracts;

I. The maximum duration of work for one day shall be eight hours.

II.2 The maximum duration of nightwork shall be seven hours. The following are prohibited for minors under sixteen years of age: unhealthful or hazardous work, industrial nightwork, and work (of any kind) after ten o'clock at night.

2. U.S.S.R. (1977)

INTRODUCTION

For more than six decades, the Soviet constitutions of 1918, 1936 and 1977 have provided the model for communist constitutionalism. And for that reason, the human rights concepts set forth in Soviet documents are of great significance for an understanding of rights policies in communist systems. In general, Soviet scholars do not contend that the Communist Constitution is a restraint upon the state on behalf of individual rights. Instead, the Constitution is an expression of "socialist reality," under government which manifests the will of the Communist party and the people.[87]

The 1977 Constitution was promoted by Soviet leader Leonid Brezhnev and approved on October 7, 1977, the 60th anniversary of the October Revolution. This constitution is significantly different from the so-called Stalin Constitution of 1936. And many of the changes were made in the area of human rights. The 1977 Soviet Constitution defines more specifically the economic, social and political rights and freedoms of its citizens and the limitations upon rights are more fully articulated.

In the 1936 Constitution, equal rights were insured for all citizens regardless of sex, nationality or race.[88] At the time, the statement of women's equality was an important pioneering constitutional innovation.[89] An extensive statement as to freedom of expression was also contained in the 1936 Stalin Constitution. But that vital right and other related rights were provided only conditionally, "in conformity with the interests of the working people, and in order to strengthen the socialist system."[90] In practice, this limitation has applied to all rights of consequence, and it is understood that the decision as to what is in the interests of the working people is ordinarily made by the Central Committee of the Communist Party, by the Praesidium—or sometimes by the Soviet judiciary.

Individual rights in the 1977 Constitution, including the right of self-expression, are likewise explicitly subordinated to the broader precepts and goals of communism. The compendium of "Basic Rights, Freedoms and Duties of Citizens of the USSR" is accompanied by the proviso that "enjoyment by citizens of their rights and freedoms must not be to the detriment of the interests of society or the state, or infringe upon the rights of other citizens."[91] This language of Article 59 also provides a clear statement of the limited scope of individual rights in Soviet society.

Both the 1936 and the 1977 Soviet Constitutions create, in addition, specific citizen obligations and duties. The 1977 document includes duties concerning the raising of children,[92] the protection of nature,[93] the preservation of historical monuments[94] and the furtherance of international cooperation.[95] Obviously, these are duties which impinge upon individual freedom of action in the name of greater social good.

The 1977 Constitution lists economic rights ahead of civil rights, following the example of the 1936 Constitution. However, the 1977 Constitution builds upon the economic rights proclaimed by Stalin. Now the right to labor also includes a right to choose a vocation and a minimum wage requirement.[96] The constitutional guarantee of a right to rest and leisure includes a 41-hour work week provision.[97] There now is a specific provision on the right to health protection in place of a narrower protection under the 1936 Constitution.[98] This new economic right includes free health care, improved work safety, environmental protection and preventive health research.[99]

In some respects, the 1977 Constitution expands upon freedom of speech, the press, assembly and public meetings. Article 49 now allows a citizen to criticize his working conditions and prohibits the persecution of any individual for such criticism. Article 58 permits complaints against the actions of public officials and creates a right to compensation for damages resulting from unlawful actions by state organizations and officials. Even though the exercise of freedom of expression is still generally confined to be "in accordance with the interests of the people and in order to stengthen and develop the socialist system,"[100] these new constitutional rights suggest that Soviet government and its officials are not entirely beyond criticism and correction.

U.S.S.R. CONSTITUTION (1977)

II. THE STATE AND THE INDIVIDUAL

CHAPTER 6.

CITIZENSHIP OF THE USSR. EQUALITY OF CITIZENS' RIGHTS

Article 33

Uniform federal citizenship is established for the USSR. Every citizen of a Union Republic is a citizen of the USSR.

The grounds and procedure for acquiring or forfeiting Soviet citizenship are defined by the Law on Citizenship of the USSR.

When abroad, citizens of the USSR enjoy the protection and assistance of the Soviet state.

Article 34

Citizens of the USSR are equal before the law, without distinction of origin, social or property status, race or nationality, sex, education, language, attitude to religion, type and nature of occupation, domicile, or other status.

The equal rights of citizens of the USSR are guaranteed in all fields of economic, political, social, and cultural life.

Article 35

Women and men have equal rights in the USSR.

Exercise of these rights is ensured by according women equal access with men to education and vocational and professional training, equal opportunities in employment, remuneration, and promotion, and in social and political, and cultural activity, and by special labour and health protection measures for women; by providing conditions enabling mothers to work; by legal protection, and material and moral support for mothers and children, including paid leaves and other benefits for expectant mothers and mothers, and gradual reduction of working time for mothers with small children.

Article 36

Citizens of the USSR of different races and nationalities have equal rights.

Exercise of these rights is ensured by a policy of all-round development and drawing together of all the nations and nationalities of the USSR, by educating citizens in the spirit of Soviet patriotism and socialist internationalism, and by the possibility to use their native language and the languages of other peoples of the USSR.

Any direct or indirect limitation of the rights of citizens or establishment of direct or indirect privileges on grounds of race or nationality, and any advocacy of racial or national exclusiveness, hostility or contempt, are punishable by law.

Article 37

Citizens of other countries and stateless persons in the USSR are guaranteed the rights and freedoms provided by law, including the right to apply to a court and other state bodies for the protection of their personal, property, family, and other rights.

Citizens of other countries and stateless persons, when in the USSR, are obliged to respect the Constitution of the USSR and observe Soviet laws.

Article 38

The USSR grants the right of asylum to foreigners persecuted for defending the interests of the working people and the cause of peace, or for participation in the revolutionary and national liberation movement, or for progressive social and political, scientific or other creative activity.

CHAPTER 7.

THE BASIC RIGHTS, FREEDOMS, AND DUTIES OF CITIZENS OF THE USSR

Article 39

Citizens of the USSR enjoy in full the social, economic, political and personal rights and freedoms proclaimed and guaranteed by the Constitution of the USSR and by Soviet laws. The socialist system ensures enlargement of the rights and freedoms of citizens and continuous improvement of their living standards as social, economic, and cultural development programmes are fulfilled.

Enjoyment by citizens of their rights and freedoms must not be to the detriment of the interests of society or the state, or infringe the rights of other citizens.

Article 40

Citizens of the USSR have the right to work (that is, to guaranteed employment and pay in accordance with the quantity and quality of their work, and not below the state-established minimum), including the right to choose their trade or profession, type of job and work in accordance with their inclinations, abilities, training and education, with due account of the needs of society.

This right is ensured by the socialist economic system, steady growth of the productive forces, free vocational and professional training, improvement of skills, training in new trades or professions, and development of the systems of vocational guidance and job placement.

Article 41

Citizens of the USSR have the right to rest and leisure.

This right is ensured by the establishment of a working week not exceeding

41 hours, for workers and other employees, a shorter working day in a number of trades and industries, and shorter hours for night work; by the provision of paid annual holidays, weekly days of rest, extension of the network of cultural, educational and health-building institutions, and the development on a mass scale of sport, physical culture, and camping and tourism; by the provision of neighborhood recreational facilities, and of other opportunities for rational use of free time.

The length of collective farmers' working and leisure time is established by their collective farms.

Article 42

Citizens of the USSR have the right to health protection.

This right is ensured by free, qualified medical care provided by state health institutions; by extension of the network of therapeutic and health-building institutions; by the development and improvement of safety and hygiene in industry, by carrying out broad prophylactic measures; by measures to improve the environment; by special care for the health of the rising generation, including prohibition of child labour, excluding the work done by children as part of the school curriculum; and by developing research to prevent and reduce the incidence of disease and ensure citizens a long and active life.

Article 43

Citzens of the USSR have the right to maintenance in old age, in sickness, and in the event of complete or partial disability or loss of the breadwinner.

This right is guaranteed by social insurance of workers and other employees and collective farmers by allowances for temporary disability; by the provision by the state or by collective farms of retirement pensions, disability pensions, and pensions for loss of the breadwinner; by providing employment for the partially disabled; by care for the elderly and the disabled; and by other forms of social security.

Article 44

Citizens of the USSR have the right to housing.

This right is ensured by the development and upkeep of state and socially-owned housing; by assistance for co-operative and individual house building; by fair distribution, under public control, of the housing that becomes available through fulfilment of the programme of building well-appointed dwellings, and by low rents and low charges for utility services. Citizens of the USSR shall take good care of the housing allocated to them.

Article 45

Citizens of the USSR have the right to education.

This right is ensured by free provision of all forms of education, by the institution of universal, compulsory secondary education, and broad development of vocational, specialised secondary, and higher education, in which instruction is oriented toward practical activity and production; by the development of extramural, correspondence and evening courses; by the provision of state scholarships and grants and privileges for students; by the free issue of school textbooks; by the opportunity to attend a school where teaching is in the native language; and by the provision of facilities for self-education.

Article 46

Citizens of the USSR have the right to enjoy cultural benefits.

This right is ensured by broad access to the cultural treasures of their own land and of the world that are preserved in state and other public collections; by the development and fair distribution of cultural and educational institutions throughout the country; by developing television and radio broadcasting and the publishing of books, newspapers and periodicals, and by extending the free library service; and by expanding cultural exchanges with other countries.

Article 47

Citizens of the USSR, in accordance with the aims of building communism, are guaranteed freedom of scientific, technical, and artistic work. This freedom is ensured by broadening scientific research, encouraging invention and innovation, and developing literature and the arts. The state provides the necessary material conditions for this and support for voluntary societies and unions of workers in the arts, organises introduction of inventions and innovations in production and other spheres of activity.

The rights of authors, inventors and innovators are protected by the state.

Article 48

Citizens of the USSR have the right to take part in the management and administration of state and public affairs and in the discussion and adoption of laws and measures of All-Union and local significance.

This right is ensured by the opportunity to vote and to be elected to Soviets of People's Deputies and other elective state bodies, to take part in nationwide discussions and referendums, in people's control, in the work of state bodies, public organisations, and local community groups, and in meetings at places of work or residence.

Article 49

Every citizen of the USSR has the right to submit proposals to state bodies and public organisations for improving their activity, and to criticise shortcomings in their work.

Officials are obliged, within established time-limits, to examine citizens' proposals and requests, to reply to them, and to take appropriate action.

Persecution for criticism is prohibited. Persons guilty of such persecution shall be called to account.

Article 50

In accordance with the interests of the people and in order to strengthen and develop the socialist system, citizens of the USSR are guaranteed freedom of speech, of the press, and of assembly, meetings, street processions and demonstrations.

Exercise of these political freedoms is ensured by putting public buildings, streets and squares at the disposal of the working people and their organisations, by broad dissemination of information, and by the opportunity to use the press, television, and radio.

Article 51

In accordance with the aims of building communism, citizens of the USSR have the right to associate in public organisations that promote their political activity and initiative and satisfaction of their various interests.

Public organisations are guaranteed conditions for successfully performing the functions defined in their rules.

Article 52

Citizens of the USSR are guaranteed freedom of conscience, that is, the right to profess or not to profess any religion, and to conduct religious workship or atheistic propaganda. Incitement of hostility or hatred on religious grounds is prohibited.

In the USSR, the church is separated from the state, and the school from the church.

Article 53

The family enjoys the protection of the state.

Marriage is based on the free consent of the woman and the man; the spouses are completely equal in their family relations.

The state helps the family by providing and developing a broad system of child-care institutions, by organising and improving communal services and public catering, by paying grants on the birth of a child, by providing children's allowances and benefits for large families, and other forms of family allowances and assistance.

Article 54

Citizens of the USSR are guaranteed inviolability of the person. No one may be arrested except by a court decision or on the warrant of a procurator.

Article 55

Citizens of the USSR are guaranteed inviolability of the home. No one may, without lawful grounds, enter a home against the will of those residing in it.

Article 56

The privacy of citizens, and of their correspondence, telephone conversations, and telegraphic communications is protected by law.

Article 57

Respect for the individual and protection of the rights and freedoms of citizens are the duty of all state bodies, public organisations, and officials.

Citizens of the USSR have the right to protection by the courts against encroachments on their honour and reputation, life and health, and personal freedom and property.

Article 58

Citizens of the USSR have the right to lodge a complaint against the actions of officials, state bodies and public bodies. Complaints shall be examined according to the procedure and within the time-limit established by law.

Actions by officials that contravene the law or exceed their powers, and infringe the rights of citizens, may be appealed against in a court in the manner prescribed by law.

Citizens of the USSR have the right to compensation for damage resulting from unlawful actions by state organisations and public organisations, or by officials in the performance of their duties.

Article 59

Citizens' exercise of their rights and freedoms is inseparable from the performance of their duties and obligations.

Citizens of the USSR are obliged to observe the Constitution of the USSR and Soviet laws, comply with the standards of socialist conduct, and uphold the honour and dignity of Soviet citizenship.

Article 60

It is the duty of, and a matter of honour for, every able-bodied citizen of the USSR to work conscientiously in his chosen, socially useful occupation, and strictly to observe labour discipline. Evasion of socially useful work is incompatible with the principles of socialist society.

Article 61

Citizens of the USSR are obliged to preserve and protect socialist property. It is the duty of a citizen of the USSR to combat misappropriation and squandering of state and socially-owned property and to make thrifty use of the people's wealth.

Persons encroaching in any way on socialist property shall be punished according to the law.

Article 62

Citizens of the USSR are obliged to safeguard the interests of the Soviet state, and to enhance its power and prestige.

Defence of the Socialist Motherland is the sacred duty of every citizen of the USSR.

Betrayal of the Motherland is the gravest of crimes against the people.

Article 63

Military service in the ranks of the Armed Forces of the USSR is an honourable duty of Soviet citizens.

Article 64

It is the duty of every citizen of the USSR to respect the national dignity of other citizens, and to strengthen friendship of the nations and nationalities of the multinational Soviet state.

Article 65

A citizen of the USSR is obliged to respect the rights and lawful interests of other persons, to be uncompromising towards anti-social behaviour, and to help maintain public order.

Article 66

Citizens of the USSR are obliged to concern themselves with the upbringing of children, to train them for socially useful work, and to raise them as worthy members of socialist society. Children are obliged to care for their parents and help them.

Article 67

Citizens of the USSR are obliged to protect nature and conserve its riches.

Article 68

Concern for the preservation of historical monuments and other cultural values is a duty and obligation of citizens of the USSR.

Article 69

It is the internationalist duty of citizens of the USSR to promote friendship and cooperation with peoples of other lands and help maintain and strengthen world peace.

C. GROUP RIGHTS/PROTECTIONS

These protections were developed primarily in the post-World War II era—reflecting a switch from emphasis on individual human rights to the human rights of groups as groups. However, these group rights protections had their pioneer constitutional manifestation in Ireland in 1937. The most comprehensive treatment of such protections is in the 1949 Constitution of the then newly independent India. To understand the transition from traditional human rights thinking to group rights protections, the principal constitutional treatment is in the 1971 revision of the 1831 Belgian Constitution. Another good statement is in the Malaysian Constitution of 1957.

1. IRELAND

INTRODUCTION

There were Irish Free State constitutions in both 1919 and 1923, but it was not until the Constitution of 1937 that constitutional authority over the 26 counties of the Irish Free State was formally established. It was this document that was accepted by the United Kingdom government without protest, although British connections with the Republic of Ireland were not finally severed until 1949.

The Irish Constitution recognized the family group as the natural, primary and fundamental unit of society, possessing inalienable and imprescriptive rights, antecedent and superior to all positive law. This, of course, reflects the influence of the Roman Catholic Church on Irish society. Principles of human rights social policy, intended for the general guidance of Parliament but not cognizable by the courts, may also be found in Article 45 this Constitution. The enumeration of such principles has been followed as a model in the constitutions of India, Nigeria, Liberia and other Third World nations. This Article 45 and its progeny deserve serious attention as a means of setting rights priorities in a flexible manner for the guidance of policymakers.

IRELAND CONSTITUTION (1937)

Directive Principles of Social Policy

Article 45

The principles of social policy set forth in this Article are intended for the general guidance of the Oireachtas. The application of those principles in the making of laws shall be the care of the Oireachtas exclusively, and shall not be cognisable by any Court under any of the provisions of this Constitution.

1. The State shall strive to promote the welfare of the whole people by

securing and protecting as effectively as it may a social order in which justice and charity shall inform all the institutions of the national life.

2. The State shall, in particular, direct its policy towards securing

    i. That the citizens (all of whom, men and women equally, have the right to an adequate means of livelihood) may through their occupations find the means of making reasonable provision for their domestic needs.

    ii. That the ownership and control of the material resources of the community may be so distributed amongst private individuals and the various classes as best to subserve the common good.

    iii. That, especially, the operation of free competition shall not be allowed so to develop as to result in the concentration of the ownership or control of essential commodities in a few individuals to the common detriment.

    iv. That in what pertains to the control of credit the constant and predominant aim shall be the welfare of the people as a whole.

    v. That there may be established on the land in economic security as many families as in the circumstances shall be practicable.

3. 1° The State shall favour and, where necessary, supplement private initiative in industry and commerce.

2° The State shall endeavour to secure that private enterprise shall be so conducted as to ensure reasonable efficiency in the production and distribution of goods and as to protect the public against unjust exploitation.

4. 1° The State pledges itself to safeguard with especial care the economic interests of the weaker sections of the community, and, where necessary, to contribute to the support of the infirm, the widow, the orphan, and the aged.

2° The State shall endeavour to ensure that the strength and health of workers, men and women, and the tender age of children shall not be abused and that citizens shall not be forced by economic necessity to enter avocations unsuited to their sex, age or strength.

2. INDIA

INTRODUCTION

More effort was expended in framing the Constitution of India than in the promulgation of any other national constitution. The result is a unique and elaborate document, consisting of a preamble, 395 articles (divided into 22 parts) and eight schedules—and much of it is devoted to human rights. When India finally achieved independence in 1947, many unresolved social tensions persisted. And fundamental changes would be necessary if India was to achieve a society resting upon individual rights. A social revolution was called for since India was composed of so many minorities, separated by racial, religious, linguistic, social and caste distinctions.

Part III of the Indian Constitution constitutes a bill of rights—a detailed formulation which Indian constitutional draftsmen deliberately developed as a guide to post-independence policymakers.

The list of rights begins with a guarantee of equality before the law, followed by a prohibition against discrimination based upon religion, race, sex, caste or place of birth. Article 17 reaches the single most serious rights abuse in Indian society by abolishing untouchability. Note that the untouchables as a group still face de facto discrimination, although much progress has been made to improve their social and economic conditions.[101]

Articles 29 and 30 are especially important to the complex society that is India. For the preservation of cultural and linguistic minority rights remains a valued objective, even though the conservation of distinctive languages and scripts has complicated Indian education and development.

The statement of fundamental rights contained in Part III of the Constitution was designed to protect Indian citizens from the arbitrary actions of the state. Part IV of the Constitution, however, contains an affirmation of the obligations of the state positively to promote the rights of Indian peoples, i.e., Indian population groupings. Denominated Directive Principles of State Policy, these are the most detailed among the world's constitutions.[102] Most significant is Article 46, which places a duty upon the state to promote the educational and economic interests of the "weaker sections of the people." Thus, the language of this portion of the Constitution permits preferential treatment for certain groups—or a form of positive discrimination which might not be possible where a nation is committed to the equal treatment of all of its citizens.[103]

Article 37 makes it clear that these Directive Principles of State Policy are not enforceable by any court—even though the Indian Constitution recognizes these principles as "fundamental to the governance of the country." The Bill of Rights, on the other hand, is judicially enforceable, and Article 32 gives Indian citizens the right to seek enforcement of its provisions in the Supreme Court.[104] Thus, the Constitution creates two types of fundamental rights, only one of which is judicially cognizable.

Since the Indian Constitution promotes equality on one hand and special group rights on the other, there may be a conflict between Articles 15 and 16. There may be inconsistency between the "special provisions relating to certain classes" (Articles 330 through 342) and the principle of equality. The reconciliation of such conflict is the province of Indian politics and the tensions involved are perhaps beyond the scope of the Indian judiciary.[105]

INDIA CONSTITUTION (1947)

Right to Equality

14. The State shall not deny to any person equality before the law or the equal protection of the laws within the territory of India.

15. (1) The State shall not discriminate against any citizen on grounds only of religion, race, caste, sex, place of birth or any of them.

(2) No citizen shall, on grounds only of religion, race, caste, sex, place of birth or any of them, be subject to any disability, liability, restriction or condition with regard to—

a. access to shops, public restaurants, hotels and places of public entertainment; or

b. the use of wells, tanks, bathing ghats, roads and places of public resort maintained wholly or partly out of State funds or dedicated to the use of the general public.

(3) Nothing in this article shall prevent the State from making any special provision for women and children.

(4) Nothing in this article or in clause (2) or article 29 shall prevent the State from making any special provision for the advancement of any socially and educationally backward classes of citizens or for the Scheduled Castes and the Scheduled Tribes.

16. (1) There shall be equality of opportunity for all citizens in matters relating to employment or appointment to any office under the State.

(2) No citizen shall, on grounds only of religion, race, caste, sex, descent, place of birth, residence or any of them, be ineligible for, or discriminated against in respect of, any employment or office under the State.

(3) Nothing in this article shall prevent Parliament from making any law prescribing, in regard to a class or classes of employment or appointments to an office [under the Government of, or any local or other authority within, a State or Union territory, any requirement as to residence within that State or Union territory] prior to such employment or appointment.

(4) Nothing in this article shall prevent the State from making any provision for the reservation of appointments or posts in favour of any backward class of citizens which, in the opinion of the State, is not adequately represented in the services under the State.

(5) Nothing in this article shall affect the operation of any law which provides that the incumbent of an office in connection with the affairs of any religious or denominational institution or any member of the governing body thereof shall be a person professing a particular religion or belonging to a particular denomination.

17. "Untouchability" is abolished and its practice in any form is forbidden. The enforcement of any disability arising out of "Untouchability" shall be an offence punishable in accordance with law. . . .

Cultural and Educational Rights

29. (1) Any section of the citizens residing in the territory of India or any part thereof having a distinct language, script or culture of its own shall have the right to conserve the same.

(2) No citizen shall be denied admission into any educational institution maintained by the State or receiving aid out of State funds on grounds only of religion, race, caste, language or any of them.

30. (1) All minorities, whether based on religion or language, shall have the right to establish and administer educational institutions of their choice.

(2) The State shall not, in granting aid to educational institutions, discriminate against any educational institution on the ground that it is under the management of a minority, whether based on religion or language. . . .

Right to Constitutional Remedies

32. (1) The right to move the Supreme Court by appropriate proceedings for the enforcement of the rights conferred by this Part is guaranteed.

(2) The Supreme Court shall have power to issue directions or orders or writs, including writs in the nature of *habeas corpus, mandamus,* prohibition, *quo warranto* and *certiorari,* whichever may be appropriate, for the enforcement of any of the rights conferred by this Part.

²(3) Without prejudice to the powers conferred on the Supreme Court by clauses (1) and (2), Parliament may by law empower any other court to exercise within the local limits of its jurisdiction all or any of the powers exercisable by the Supreme Court under clause (2).

(4) The right guaranteed by this article shall not be suspended except as otherwise provided for by this Constitution.

33. Parliament may by law determine to what extent any of the rights conferred by this Part shall, in their application to the members of the Armed Forces or the Forces charged with the maintenance of public order, be restricted or abrogated so as to ensure the proper discharge of their duties and the maintenance of discipline among them. . . .

PART IV

Directive Principles of State Policy

36. In this Part, unless the context otherwise requires, "the State" has the same meaning as in Part III.

37. The provisions contained in this Part shall not be enforceable by any court, but the principles therein laid down are nevertheless fundamental in the governance of the country and it shall be the duty of the State to apply these principles in making laws.

38. The State shall strive to promote the welfare of the people by securing and protecting as effectively as it may a social order in which justice, social, economic and political, shall inform all the institutions of the national life.

39. The State shall, in particular, direct its policy towards securing—
   a. that the citizens, men and women equally, have the right to an adequate means of livelihood;
   b. that the ownership and control of the material resources of the community are so distributed as best to subserve the common good;
   c. that the operation of the economic system does not result in the concentration of wealth and means of production to the common detriment;
   d. that there is equal pay for equal work for both men and women;
   e. that the health and strength of workers, men and women, and the tender age of children are not abused and that citizens are not forced by economic necessity to enter avocations unsuited to their age or strength;

f. that childhood and youth are protected against exploitation and against moral and material abandonment.

40. The State shall take steps to organise village panchayats and endow them with such powers and authority as may be necessary to enable them to function as units of self-government.

41. The State shall, within the limits of its economic capacity and development, make effective provision for securing the right to work, to education and to public assistance in cases of unemployment, old age, sickness and disablement, and in other cases of undeserved want.

42. The State shall make provision for securing just and humane conditions of work and for maternity relief.

43. The State shall endeavour to secure, by suitable legislation or economic organisation or in any other way, to all workers, agricultural, industrial or otherwise, work, a living wage, conditions of work ensuring a decent standard of life and full enjoyment of leisure and social and cultural opportunities and, in particular, the States shall endeavour to promote cottage industries on an individual or co-operative basis in rural areas.

44. The State shall endeavour to secure for the citizens a uniform civil code throughout the territory of India.

45. The State shall endeavour to provide, within a period of ten years from the commencement of this Constitution, for free and compulsory education for all children until they complete the age of fourteen years.

46. The State shall promote with special care the educational and economic interests of the weaker sections of the people, and, in particular, of the Scheduled Castes and the Scheduled Tribes, and shall protect them from social injustice and all forms of exploitation.

47. The State shall regard the raising of the level of nutrition and the standard of living of its people and the improvement of public health as among its primary duties and, in particular, the State shall endeavour to bring about prohibition of the consumption except for medicinal purposes of intoxicating drinks and of drugs which are injurious to health.

48. The State shall endeavour to organise agriculture and animal husbandry on modern and scientific lines and shall, in particular, take steps for preserving and improving the breeds, and prohibiting the slaughter, of cows and calves and other milch and draught cattle.

49. It shall be the obligation of the State to protect every monument or place or object of artistic or historic interest [1][declared by or under law made by Parliament] to be of national importance, from spoliation, disfigurement, destruction, removal, disposal or export, as the case may be.

50. The State shall take steps to separate the judiciary from the executive in the public services of the State.

51. The State shall endeavour to—

a. promote international peace and security;

b. maintain just and honourable relations between nations;

c. foster respect for international law and treaty obligations in the dealings of organised peoples with one another; and

d. encourage settlement of international disputes by arbitration. . . .

PART XVI

Special Provisions Relating to Certain Classes

330. (1) Seats shall be reserved in the House of the People for—
a. the Scheduled Castes;
b. the Scheduled Tribes [except the Scheduled Tribes in the tribal areas of Assam and in Nagaland]; and
c. the Scheduled Tribes in the autonomous districts of Assam.

(2) The number of seats reserved in any State [or Union territory] for the Scheduled Castes or the Scheduled Tribes under clause (1) shall bear, as nearly as may be, the same proportion to the total number of seats allotted to that State or Union territory] in the House of the People as the population of the Scheduled Castes in the State [or Union territory] or of the Scheduled Tribes in the State or Union territory] or part of the State [or Union territory], as the case may be, in respect of which seats are so reserved, bears to the total population of the State [or Union territory].

331. Notwithstanding anything in article 81, the President may, if he is of opinion that the Anglo-Indian community is not adequately represented in the House of the People, nominate not more than two members of that community to the House of the People.

332. (1) Seats shall be reserved for the Scheduled Castes and the Scheduled Tribes, [except the Scheduled Tribes in the tribal areas of Assam and in Nagaland], in the Legislative Assembly of every State * * *.

(2) Seats shall be reserved also for the autonomous districts in the Legislative Assembly of the State of Assam.

(3) The number of seats reserved for the Scheduled Castes or the Scheduled Tribes in the Legislative Assembly of any State under clause (1) shall bear, as nearly as may be, the same proportion to the total number of seats in the Assembly as the population of the Scheduled Castes in the State or of the Scheduled Tribes in the State or part of the State, as the case may be, in respect of which seats are so reserved, bears to the total population of the State.

333. Notwithstanding anything in article 170, the Governor * * * of a State may, if he is of opinion that the Anglo-Indian community needs representation in the Legislative Assembly of the State and is not adequately represented therein, [nominate one member of that community to the Assembly].

334. Notwithstanding anything in the foregoing provisions of this Part, the provisions of this Constitution relating to—
a. the reservation of seats for the Scheduled Castes and the Scheduled Tribes in the House of the People and in the Legislative Assemblies of the States; and
b. the representation of the Anglo-Indian community in the House of the People and in the Legislative Assemblies of the States by nomination,
shall cease to have effect on the expiration of a period of [thirty years] from the commencement of this Constitution:
Provided that nothing in this article shall affect any representation in the

House of the People or in the Legislative Assembly of a State until the dissolution of the then existing House or Assembly, as the case may be.

335. The claims of the members of the Scheduled Castes and the Scheduled Tribes shall be taken into consideration, consistently with the maintenance of efficiency of administration, in the making of appointments to services and posts in connection with the affairs of the Union or of a State.

340. (1) The President may by order appoint a Commission consisting of such persons as he thinks fit to investigate the conditions of socially and educationally backward classes within the territory of India and the difficulties under which they labour and to make recommendations as to the steps that should be taken by the Union or any State to remove such difficulties and to improve their conditions and as to the grants that should be made for the purpose by the Union or any State and the conditions subject to which such grants should be made, and the order appointing such Commission shall define the procedure to be followed by the Commission.

(2) A Commission so appointed shall investigate the matters referred to them and present to the President a report setting out the facts as found by them and making such recommendations as they think proper.

(3) The President shall cause a copy of the report so presented together with a memorandum explaining the action taken thereon to be laid before each House of Parliament.

3. BELGIUM

INTRODUCTION

Belgium contains three distinct linguistic groups within its 11,700 square miles. The Northern Belgian provinces of West-Vlaanderen, Oost-Vlanderen, Antwerpen and Lemberg have been settled primarily by Flemish Dutch speakers. French is the language of the Southern Belgian provinces of Hainait, Namur and Luxemburg. And the eastern portion of Liege has been settled by a German-speaking majority. These linguistic differences, plus the religious and cultural differences which permeate Belgium have given rise to unique constitutional provisions on group rights.

Major changes were made in the Belgian constitution in 1971 to recognize the special rights of the nation's cultural communities. Legislative power over their own regional affairs was given both to the Flemish and to the French-speaking groups, and legislation has been passed to implement applicable constitutional provisions.

Art. 59 is the most lengthly provision concerning cultural and linguistic rights. In spite of—or perhaps because of—the detailed provisions, political strife between linguistic and cultural groups has produced political stalemate in Belgian politics.

BELGIUM CONSTITUTION (1831, REV. 1971)

HEADING I

Concerning the Territory and its Divisions

Article 1.

—Belgium is divided into provinces.

These provinces are: Antwerp, Brabant, West Flanders, East Flanders, Hainault, Liège, Limbourg, Luxemburg, Namur.

It is up to the law, if necessary, to divide the territory into a larger number of provinces.

An act of Parliament may exempt certain territories, whose boundaries it shall determine, from being divided into provinces, place them directly under the executive authority, and subject them to an individual status.

Such an act must be passed by a majority vote in each linguistic group of each of the Houses, on condition that the majority of the members of each group is present and that the total number of votes in favour in each of the two linguistic groups attains two-thirds of the votes cast.

Article 2.

—The subdivisions of the provinces can only be established by law.

Article 3.

—The boundaries of the State, the provinces and the boroughs may only be changed or rectified by virtue of a law.

Article 3b.

—Belgium comprises four linguistic regions: the French language region, the Dutch language region, the bilingual region of Brussels-Capital, and the German language region.

Every commune in the Kingdom belongs to one of these linguistic regions.

The boundaries of the four regions may only be altered or amended by an act of Parliament passed on a majority vote in each linguistic group of each of the Houses, on condition that the majority of the members of each group are present and that the total votes in favour within the two linguistic groups attain two-thirds of the votes cast.

HEADING IB

Concerning the Cultural Communities

Article 3c.

—Belgium comprises three cultural communities: French, Dutch and German.

Each community enjoys the powers invested in it by the Constitution or by such legislation as shall be enacted by virtue thereof.

Article 32.

—The members of both Houses represent the nation, and not merely the province or subdivision of a province which elected them.

Article 32b.

—For those cases prescribed in the Constitution, the elected members of each House are divided into a French-language group and a Dutch-language group in such manner as is laid down by law.

Section III.—Concerning the Cultural Councils

Article 59b.—Section 1.

There is a cultural council for the French cultural community made up of members of the French linguistic group of both Houses, and a cultural council for the Dutch cultural community made up of the members of the Dutch linguistic group of both Houses.

A bill passed on a majority vote within each linguistic group of each of the Houses, subject to the majority of the members of each group being present and providng the total votes in favour in the two linguistic groups attains two-thirds of the votes cast shall determine the procedure whereby the cultural councils exercise their powers with particular reference to articles 33, 37, 38, 39, 40, 41, 42, 43, 44, 59, 70 and 88.

Section 2.

The cultural councils, each in its own sphere, shall determine by decree:
1. cultural matters;
2. education, excluding all matters appertaining to the Schools Covenant, compulsory education, teaching structures, diplomas, subsidies, salaries and the standards governing student population;
3. co-operation between the cultural communities and international cultural co-operation.

A bill passed with the majority specified in Section 1, paragraph 2, shall lay down the cultural matters referred to at 1) above and also the forms of co-operation referred to at 3) of this paragraph.

Section 3.

Moreover the cultural councils, each in its own sphere, shall determine by decree, to the exclusion of the legislator, the use of languages for:
1. administrative matters;
2. the education provided in establishments which are set up, subsidised or recognised by the public authorities;
3. industrial relations between employers and their staff together with such business instruments and documents as are laid down by the law and regulations.

Section 4.

Such decrees as are promulgated in pursuance of Section 2 shall have the force of law respectively in the French language region and in the Dutch language region and also in respect of institutions established in the bilingual region of Brussels-Capital which, by virtue of their activities, must be considered as belonging exclusively to one or other of the cultural communities.

Such decrees as are promulgated in pursuance of Section 3 shall have force of law respectively in the French language region and in the Dutch language region except as regards:

—such communes or groups of communes which are adjacent to another linguistic region and where the law lays down or permits the use of a language other than that of the region in which they are located;

—departments whose activities extend beyond the linguistic region in which they are established;

—national and international institutions referred to in legislation whose activity is common to more than one cultural community.

Section 5.

Initiative is vested in the King and in the members of the cultural councils.

Section IIIc.—Concerning the regional institutions

Article 107d.

—Belgium comprises three regions: the Walloon region, the Flemish region and the Brussels region.

The law confers on the regional bodies which it sets up and which are composed of elected representatives the power to rule on such matters as it shall determine, to the exclusion of those referred to in articles 23 and 59*b*, within such jurisdiction and in accordance with such procedure as it shall determine.

Such law must be passed with a majority vote within each linguistic group of both Houses, providing the majority of the members of each group are present and on condition that the total votes in favour in the two linguistic groups attains two thirds of the votes cast.

4. MALAYSIA

INTRODUCTION

Malaysia has witnessed an economic imbalance between its ethnic Chinese and its ethnic Malays, with the Chinese dominant in finance, commerce and industry. The famous Art. 153 of the Malaysian Constitution was thus developed to safeguard both the special position of the Malays and the native populations of Malaysia's Borneo states of Sarawak and Sabah.

Art. 153 provides special educational and economic opportunities for the Malay group. The singling-out of the Malays (and the natives of Borneo) for special favoritism is an unusual aspect of group rights on a constitutional plane. So important is Art. 153 to Malaysia that it is supported by legislation which makes it unlawful to discuss changes in the article or to challenge its fundamental premises.

(For a useful commentary, *see* Tun Mohanned Suffian, H.P. Lee, and F.A. Trindade, *The Constitution of Malaysia* (Kuala Lumpur: Oxford University Press, 1979).)

MALAYSIA CONSTITUTION (1957)

§153.

Reservation of quotas in respect of services, permits, etc., for Malays and natives of any of the States of Sabah and Sarawak.

(1) It shall be the responsibility of the Yang di-Pertuan Agong to safeguard the special position of the Malays and natives of any of the States of Sabah and Sarawak and the legitimate interests of other communities in accordance with the provisions of this Article.

§(2) Notwithstanding anything in this Constitution, but subject to the provisions of Article 40 and of this Article, the Yang di-Pertuan Agong shall exercise his functions under this Constitution and federal law in such manner as may be necessary to safeguard the special position of the Malays and natives of any of the States of Sabah and Sarawak and to ensure the reservation for Malays and natives of any of the States of Sabah and Sarawak of such proportion as he may deem reasonable of positions in the public service (other than the public service of a State) and of scholarships, exhibitions and other similar educational or training privileges or special facilities given or accorded by the Federal Government and, when any permit or licence for the operation of any trade or business is required by federal law, then, subject to the provisions of that law and this Article, of such permits and licenses.

§(3) The Yang di-Pertuan Agong may, in order to ensure in accordance with Clause (2) the reservation to Malays and natives of any of the States of Sabah and Sarawak of positions in the public service and of scholarships, exhibitions and other educational or training privileges or special facilities, give such general directions as may be required for that purpose to any Commission to which Part X applies or to any authority charged with responsibility for the grant of such scholarships, exhibitions or other educational or training privileges or special facilities; and the Commission or authority shall duly comply with the directions.

§(4) In exercising his functions under this Constitution and federal law in accordance with Clauses (1) to (3) the Yang di-Pertuan Agong shall not deprive any person of any public office held by him or of the continuance of any scholarship, exhibition or other educational or training privileges or special facilities enjoyed by him.

§(5) This Article does not derogate from the provisions of Article 136.

§(6) Where by existing federal law a permit or licence is required for the operation of any trade or business the Yang di-Pertuan Agong may exercise his functions under that law in such manner, or give such general directions to any authority charged under that law with the grant of such permits or licences, as may be required to ensure the reservation of such proportion of such permits or licences for Malays and natives of any of the States of Sabah and Sarawak as the Yang di-Pertuan Agong may deem reasonable; and the authority shall duly comply with the directions.

§(7) Nothing in this Article shall operate to deprive or authorise the deprivation of any person of any right, privilege, permit or licence accrued to or enjoyed or held by him or to authorise a refusal to renew to any person any such permit or licence or a refusal to grant to the heirs, successors or assigns of a person any permit or licence when the renewal or grant might reasonably be expected in the ordinary course of events.

§(8) Notwithstanding anything in this Constitution, where by any federal law any permit or licence is required for the operation of any trade or business, that law may provide for the reservation of a proportion of such permits or licences for Malays and natives of any of the States of Sabah and Sarawak; but no such law shall for the purpose of ensuring such a reservation—

a. deprive or authorise the deprivation of any person of any right, privilege, permit or licence accrued to or enjoyed or held by him; or

b. authorise a refusal to renew to any person any such permit or licence or a refusal to grant to the heirs, successors or assigns of any person any permit or licence when the renewal or grant might in accordance with the other provisions of the law reasonably be expected in the ordinary course of events, or prevent any person from transferring together with his business any transferable licence to operate that business; or

c. where no permit or licence was previously required for the operation of the trade or business, authorise a refusal to grant a permit or licence to any person for the operation of any trade or business which immediately before the coming into force of the law he had been *bona fide* carrying on, or authorise a refusal subsequently to renew to any such person any permit or licence, or a refusal to grant to the heirs, successors or assigns of any such person any such permit or licence when the renewal or grant might in accordance with the other provisions of that law reasonably be expected in the ordinary course of events.

§(8A) Notwithstanding anything in this Constitution, where in any University, College and other educational institution providing education after Malaysian Certificate of Education or its equivalent, the number of places offered by the authority responsible for the management of the University, College or such educational institution to candidates for any course of study is less than the number of candidates qualified for such places, it shall be lawful for the Yang di-Pertuan Agong by virtue of this Article to give such directions to the authority as may be required to ensure the reservation of such proportion of such places for Malays and natives of any of the States of Sabah and Sarawak as the Yang di-Pertuan Agong may deem reasonable; and the authority shall duly comply with the directions.

§(9) Nothing in this Article shall empower Parliament to restrict business or trade solely for the purpose of reservations for Malays and natives of any of the States of Sabah and Sarawak.

§(9a) In this Article the expression "natives" in relation to the State of Sabah or Sarawak shall have the meaning assigned to it in Article 161A.

(10) The Constitution of the State of any Ruler may make provision corresponding (with the necessary modifications) to the provisions of this Article.

D. RIGHTS FROM THE STATE: THE NEW "RIGHTS"

(The early human rights emphasis was on the protection of the individual—or group—from the abuses of state authority. The modern emphasis is on the responsibilities of the state to provide and promote human rights guarantees. In the process, there has been recognition of a new generation of human rights, including the right to peace and the right to development.)

1. JAPAN

INTRODUCTION

The 1947 Constitution of Japan, following military defeat and foreign occupation, was designed to eliminate the authoritarian structure of the past and to pave the way toward political democracy. As part of this process, Japanese citizens obtained new rights. And the Japanese people used their new constitution to renounce war, giving rise to new concepts of rights, including a right to be free from militarism.

The Japanese Constitution, partly prepared by the staff of the occupying American forces,[106] replaced the 1889 Constitution, a nationalistic document which bestowed wide-ranging powers upon the Emperor. Art. 1 of the 1947 Constitution reduces the position and authority of the still-existing Emperor by stating that he derives "his position from the will of the people, with whom resides sovereign power."

The background of Art. 9—the provision against the use of war—is still confused. No one is certain of just how it came to be incorporated into the Japanese Constitution. The Americans, of course, were determined to prevent Japan from waging a future aggressive war. But there was also a Japanese initiative. Prime Minister Shidehara undoubtedly played a large part in the decision to include the Art. 9 renunciation of warfare.[107] (Note that Japan may not maintain land, sea or air forces as a result of this article.)

In addition to the more traditional political rights found in Arts. 10 through 20, the Japanese Constitution provides additional advanced thinking on other rights. Art. 23 guarantees academic freedom; and Art. 25 provides a "right to maintain the minimum standards of wholesome and cultured living." An excellent statement on equality between the sexes is in Art. 24.

JAPAN CONSTITUTION (1947)

Chapter II. Renunciation of War

Article 9.

Aspiring sincerely to an international peace based on justice and order, the

Japanese people forever renounce war as a sovereign right of the nation and the threat or use of force as means of settling international disputes.

In order to accomplish the aim of the preceding paragraph, land, sea, and air forces, as well as other war potential, will never be maintained. The right of belligerency of the state will not be recognized.

Chapter III. Rights and Duties of the People

Article 10.

The conditions necessary for being a Japanese national shall be determined by law.

Article 11.

The people shall not be prevented from enjoying any of the fundamental human rights. These fundamental human rights guaranteed to the people by this Constitution shall be conferred upon the people of this and future generations as eternal and inviolate rights.

Article 12.

The freedom and rights guaranteed to the people by this Constitution shall be maintained by the constant endeavour of the people, who shall refrain from any abuse of these freedoms and rights and shall always be responsible for utilizing them for the public welfare.

Article 13.

All of the people shall be respected as individuals. Their right to life, liberty, and the pursuit of happiness shall, to the extent that it does not interfere with the public welfare, by the supreme consideration in legislation and in other governmental affairs.

Article 14.

All of the people are equal under the law and there shall be no discrimination in political, economic or social relations because of race, creed, sex, social status or family origin.

Peers and peerage shall not be recognized.

No privilege shall accompany any award of honour, decoration or any distinction, nor shall any such award be valid beyond the lifetime of the individual who now holds or hereafter may receive it.

Article 15.

The people have the inalienable right to choose their public officials and to dismiss them.

All public officials are servants of the whole community and not of any group thereof.

Universal adult suffrage is guaranteed with regard to the election of public officials.

In all elections, secrecy of the ballot shall not be violated. A voter shall not be answerable, publicly or privately, for the choice he has made.

Article 16.

Every person shall have the right of peaceful petition for the redress of damage, for the removal of public officials, for the enactment, repeal or amendment of laws, ordinances or regulations and for other matters, nor shall any person be in any way discriminated against for sponsoring such a petition.

Article 17.

Every person may sue for redress as provided by law from the State or public entity, in case he has suffered damage through illegal act of any public official.

Article 18.

No person shall be held in bondage of any kind. Involuntary servitude, except as punishment for crime, is prohibited.

Article 19.

Freedom of thought and conscience shall not be violated.

Article 20.

Freedom of religion is guaranteed to all. No religious organization shall receive any privileges from the State, nor exercise any political authority.

Article 23.

Academic freedom is guaranteed.

Article 24.

Marriage shall be based only on the mutual consent of both sexes and it shall be maintained through mutual cooperation with the equal rights of husband and wife as a basis.

2. With regard to choice of spouse, property rights, inheritance, choice of domicile, divorce and other matters pertaining to marriage and the family, laws shall be enacted from the standpoint of individual dignity and the essential equality of the sexes.

Article 25.

All people shall have the right to maintain the minimum standards of wholesome and cultured living.

2. In all spheres of life, the State shall use its endeavors for the promotion and extension of social welfare and security, and of public health.

Article 26.

All people shall have the right to receive an equal education correspondent to their ability, as provided by law.

2. All people shall be obligated to have all boys and girls under their

protection receive ordinary educations as provided for by law. Such compulsory education shall be free.

Article 27.

All people shall have the right and the obligation to work.

2. Standards for wages, hours, rest and other working conditions shall be fixed by law.

3. Children shall not be exploited.

Article 28.

The right of workers to organize and to bargain and act collectively is guaranteed.

Article 29.

The right to own or to hold property is inviolable.

2. Property rights shall be defined by law, in conformity with the public welfare.

3. Private property may be taken for public use upon just compensation therefor.

2. SPAIN

INTRODUCTION

The 1978 Spanish Constitution, which replaced the authoritarian constitution of the Franco regime, recognizes many of the "new rights" concepts advanced by human rights advocates in the European Community, in the U.N. Human Rights fraternity in Geneva, and in UNESCO in Paris. Art. 43 speaks to the right to health protection, which includes health education, physical education and sports. Art. 44 recognizes the right to culture; Art. 45 pronounces the right to enjoy a suitable environment, and Art. 51 creates a public obligation to defend and protect consumers. For an interesting commentary on these Spanish constitutional provisions, *see* Oscar Alzaga, *La Constitucion Espanola de 1978* (Madrid: Ediciones de Foro, 1978).

SPAIN CONSTITUTION (1978)

Article 43

1. The right to health protection is recognized.

2. It is incumbent upon the public authorities to organize and watch over public health and hygiene through preventive measures and through necessary care and services. The law shall establish the rights and duties of all in this respect.

3. The public authorities shall foster health education, physical education, and sports. Likewise, they shall facilitate adequate utilization of leisure.

Article 44

1. The public authorities shall promote and watch over access to culture, to which all have a right.

2. The public authorities shall promote science and scientific and technical research for the benefit of the general interest.

Article 45

1. Everyone has the right to enjoy an environment suitable for the development of the person as well as the duty to preserve it.

2. The public authorities shall concern themselves with the rational use of all natural resources for the purpose of protecting and improving the quality of life and protecting and restoring the environment, supporting themselves on an indispensable collective solidarity.

3. For those who violate the provisions of the foregoing paragraph, penal or administrative sanctions, as applicable, shall be established and they shall be obliged to repair the damage caused.

Article 46

The public authorities shall guarantee the preservation, and promote the enrichment, of the historical, cultural and artistic patrimony of the peoples of Spain and the property that make them up, regardless of their juridical status and their ownership. The penal law shall punish any offenses against this patrimony.

Article 51

1. The public authorities shall guarantee the defense of the consumers and users, protecting their safety, health and legitimate economic interests through effective procedures.

2. The public authorities shall promote the information and education of consumers and users, foster their organizations and hear them in those questions which could affect them under the terms which the law shall establish.

3. Within the framework of the provisions of the foregoing paragraphs, the law shall regulate domestic commerce and the system of licensing commercial products.

3. PORTUGAL

INTRODUCTION

Portugal's 312-article Constitution of 1976 is the longest of any Western European constitution—exceeded in size only by those of Yugoslavia, India, Malaysia and Papua New Guinea. Its length and complexity is partly explained by the political turmoil which existed during the drafting period as each party and faction strove to cast its policies into permanent constitutional form. Yet the final product is a remarkably cohesive democratic document, safeguarding individual rights and promoting individual economic welfare in expansive ways.

It goes further than most other constitutions in requiring state participation for the fostering of important human rights. For example, Art. 37(4) secures the right of reply as part of freedom of expression and information and Art. 39 provides that "expressing and confronting the various currents of opinion" over television or through other means of public information shall be safeguarded. This includes, in Art. 40, the right of political parties, trade unions and professional organizations to broadcasting time on radio and television.

Other articles protect the freedom of cultural creation and the freedom to learn and teach.

PORTUGAL CONSTITUTION (1976)

Article 35

Use of Data Processing

1. All citizens shall have the right to information on the contents of data banks concerning them and on the use for which it is intended. They shall be entitled to require the said contents to be corrected and brought up to date.

2. Data processing shall not be used for information concerning a person's political convictions, religious beliefs or private life except in the case of non-identifiable data for statistical purposes.

3. Citizens shall not be given all-purpose national identification numbers.

Article 36

Family, Marriage and Filiation

1. Everyone shall have the right to found a family and marry on terms of complete equality.

2. The conditions for and effects of marriage and its dissolution by death or divorce shall be regulated by law without regard to the form of solemnisation.

3. Husbands and wives shall have equal rights and duties with regard to civil and political capacity and the maintenance and education of their children.

4. Children born out of wedlock shall not for that reason be the subject of discrimination; discriminatory designations of filiation shall not be used by the law or by government departments.

5. Parents shall have the right and duty to bring up their children.

6. Children shall not be separated from their parents unless the latter fail to perform their fundamental duties towards the former, and then only by judicial decision.

Article 37

Freedom of Expression and Information

1. Everyone shall have the right to express and make known his thoughts freely by words, images or any other means and obtain information without hindrance or discrimination.

2. The exercise of these rights shall not be prevented or restricted by any type or form of censorship.

3. Offences committed in the exercise of these rights shall be punishable under ordinary law, the courts of law having jurisdiction to try them.

4. The right of reply shall be equally and effectively be secured to all natural and artificial persons.

Article 38

Freedom of the Press

1. Freedom of the press shall be safeguarded.

2. Freedom of the press shall involve freedom of expression and creation for journalists and literary contributors and a place for the former in giving ideological orientation to information organs not belonging to the state or to political parties without any other sector or group of workers having power to exercise censorship or prevent free creativity.

3. Freedom of the press shall involve the right to found newspapers and any other publications without prior administrative authority, deposit or qualification.

4. Periodicals and non-periodical publications may belong to any non-profit-making bodies corporate, journalistic interprises and publishing houses in company form or natural persons of Portuguese nationality.

5. No administrative or fiscal system, credit policy or foreign trade policy shall affect the freedom of the press, directly or indirectly, and the means necessary to protect the independence of the press against political and economic powers shall be safeguarded by law.

6. The television shall not be privately owned.

7. Means of public information, in particular those belonging to the State, shall be regulated by law through an information statute.

Article 39

State's Means of Public Information

1. Means of public information belonging to the state or to bodies directly or indirectly subject to its economic control shall be used in such a way as to safeguard their independence of the government and public administrative authorities.

2. The possibility of expressing and confronting the various currents of opinion in the means of public information referred to in the foregoing paragraph shall be safeguarded.

3. In the means of public information referred to in this article there shall be established information councils comprising proportionate numbers of representatives appointed by those political parties that hold seats in the Assembly of the Republic.

4. The information councils shall have powers to secure a general orientation in keeping with ideological plurality.

Article 40

Right to Broadcasting Time

1. The political parties and trade union and professional organisations shall have the right to broadcasting time on radio and television in keeping with their representativeness, according to criteria to be laid down in the information statute.

2. In election periods the competing political parties shall have the right to regular broadcasting time fairly apportioned.

Article 41

Freedom of Conscience, Religion and Worship

1. Freedom of conscience, religion and worship shall be inviolable.

2. No one shall be persecuted, deprived of rights or exempted from civil obligations or duties because of his convictions or religious practices.

3. The churches and religious communities shall be separate from the state and shall be free to organise and exercise their own ceremonies and worship.

4. The freedom to teach any religion within its own denomination and the use of its own means of public information for the pursuit of its activities, shall be safeguarded.

5. The right of conscientious objection shall be recognised, provided that conscientious objectors shall be required to perform unarmed service for a period identical with that of compulsory military service.

Article 42

Freedom of Cultural Creation

1. Intellectual, artistic and scientific creation shall be unrestricted.

2. This freedom shall include the right to invention, production and dissemination of scientific, literary or artistic works, including legal protection of copyright.

Article 43

Freedom to Learn and Teach

1. The freedom to learn and teach shall be safeguarded.

2. The state shall not arrogate to itself the right to plan education and culture in accordance with any philosophical, aesthetic, political, ideological or religious guidelines.

3. Public education shall not be denominational.

Article 44

Right to Travel and Emigrate

1. The right of all citizens to travel and to settle freely anywhere in the national territory shall be safeguarded.

2. The right to emigrate or leave the national territory and the right to return to it shall be secured to everyone.

Article 45

Right to Meet and Demonstrate

1. Citizens shall have the right to meet peacefully and without arms, even in public places, without requiring any authorisation.
2. The right of all citizens to demonstrate shall be recognised.

Article 46

Freedom of Association

1. Citizens shall have the right to form associations freely and without requiring any authorisation provided such associations are not intended to promote violence and their objectives are not contrary to the criminal law.
2. Associations may pursue their objectives freely without interference by any public authority. They shall not be dissolved by the state and their activities shall not be suspended except by judicial decision in the cases provided by law.
3. No one shall be obliged to join any association or forced by any means to remain in it.
4. Armed, military-type, militarised or para-military associations outside the state and the Armed Forces and organisations which adopt Fascist ideology shall not be permitted.

Article 47

Political Associations and Parties

1. Freedom of association shall include the right to establish or join political associations and parties and through them to work democratically to give form to the will of the people and to organise political power.
2. No one shall be a member of more than one political party simultaneously, or be deprived of the exercise of any right because of membership, or cessation of membership, of a lawfully constituted party.
3. Without prejudice to the philosophy or ideology inspiring their programmes, political parties shall not use names that contain terms directly related to any religion or church or use emblems which may be mistaken for national or religious symbols.

Article 48

Participation in Public Life

1. All citizens shall have the right to take part in political life and the control of the country's public affairs, either directly or through freely-elected representatives.
2. There shall be universal, secret and equal suffrage for all citizens over the age of 18 years, subject to incapacities as provided in general law. Its exercise shall be personal and constitute a civic duty.
3. Every citizen shall have the right to objective information about acts of state and other public bodies and to be informed by the government and other authorities about the management of public affairs.

4. All citizens shall have the right of access to public functions in equal and free conditions.

Article 49

Right of Petition and Popular Action

1. All citizens may individually or collectively submit to the organs of supreme authority or to any authority whatsoever petitions, representations, claims or complaints in defence of their rights, the Constitution, the laws or the general interest.

2. The right to popular action in the cases and on the conditions provided for by law shall be recognised.

Article 66

Environment and Quality of Life

1. Everyone shall have the right to a healthy and ecologically balanced human environment and the duty to defend it.

2. It shall be the duty of the state, acting through appropriate bodies and having recourse to popular initiative to:

   a. prevent and control pollution and its effects and harmful forms of erosion;

   b. have regard in regional planning to the creation of balanced biological areas;

   c. create and develop natural reserves and parks and recreation areas and classify and protect landscapes and sites so as to ensure the conservation of nature and the preservation of cultural assets of historical or artistic interest;

   d. promote the rational use of natural resources, safeguarding their capacity for renewal and ecological stability.

3. Any citizen whose rights under paragraph 1 are threatened or infringed may apply as provided by law for an end to the causes of such violation and for appropriate compensation.

4. The state shall promote the progressive and rapid improvement of the quality of life for all Portuguese.

4. NIGERIA (1979)

INTRODUCTION

Nigeria is by far the most important country in Africa and its constitutional pronouncements are looked to as precedent throughout the continent. The 1979 constitution, the result of years of bitter controversy and civil war, provided a useful model of a balanced approach to human rights. Unfortunately, political turmoil since its promulgation resulted in a military takeover and in 1987 the Constitution was still suspended. While the 1979 Constitution makes broad rights statements, it qualifies them with exceptions for laws which are "reasonably justifiable in a democratic society." The Constitution is also cognizant of group rights and appears to guarantee equal treatment of different communities and ethnic groups, thus reducing some of the tension which nearly resulted in the breakup of the state.

The Nigerian Constitution provides the best modern formulation of human rights concepts available in the international community. The guarantees of Arts. 30 and 31, for example, provide a succinct statement of basic human rights, including the right to life and the right to respect for the dignity of the person.

NIGERIA CONSTITUTION (1979)

Chapter IV

Fundamental Rights

30.

Right to life.

—(1) Every person has a right to life, and no one shall be deprived intentionally of his life, save in execution of the sentence of a court in respect of a criminal offence of which he has been found guilty in Nigeria.

(2) A person shall not be regarded as having been deprived of his life in contravention of this section, if he dies as a result of the use, to such extent and in such circumstances as are permitted by law, of such force as is reasonably necessary—

a. for the defence of any person from unlawful violence or for the defence of property;

b. in order to effect a lawful arrest or to prevent the escape of a person lawfully detained; or

c. for the purpose of suppressing a riot, insurrection or mutiny.

31.

Right to dignity of human person.

—(1) Every individual is entitled to respect for the dignity of his person, and accordingly—

a. no person shall be subjected to torture or to inhuman or degrading treatment;

b. no person shall be held in slavery or servitude; and

c. no person shall be required to perform forced or compulsory labour.

(2) For the purposes of subsection (1) (c) of this section, "forced or compulsory labour" does not include—

a. any labour required in consequence of the sentence or order of a court;

b. any labour required of members of the armed forces of the Federation or the Nigeria Police Force in pursuance of their duties as such or, in the case of persons who have conscientious objections to service in the armed forces of the Federation, any labour required instead of such service;

   c. any labour required which is reasonably necessary in the event of any emergency or calamity threatening the life or well-being of the community; or

   d. any labour or service that forms part of—

     i. normal communal or other civic obligations for the well-being of the community,

     ii. such compulsory national service in the armed forces of the Federation as may be prescribed by an Act of the National Assembly, or

     iii. such compulsory national service which forms part of the education and training of citizens of Nigeria as may be prescribed by an Act of the National Assembly.

34.

The privacy of citizens, their homes, correspondence, telephone conversations and telegraphic communications is hereby guaranteed and protected.

35.

(1) Every person shall be entitled to freedom of thought, conscience and religion, including freedom to change his religion or belief, and freedom (either alone or in community with others, and in public or in private) to manifest and propagate his religion or belief in worship, teaching, practice and observance.

(2) No person attending any place of education shall be required to receive religious instruction or to take part in or attend any religious ceremony or observance if such instruction, ceremony or observance relates to a religion other than his own, or a religion not approved by his parent or guardian.

(3) No religious community or denomination shall be prevented from providing religious instruction for pupils of that community or denomination in any place of education maintained wholly by that community or denomination.

(4) Nothing in this section shall entitle any person to form, take part in the activity or be a member of a secret society, and for the purposes of this subsection, "a secret society" means a society or association, not being a solely cultural or religious body, that uses secret signs, oaths, rites or symbols—

   a. whose meetings or other activities are held in secret; and

   b. whose members are under oath, obligation or other threat to promote the interest of its members or to aid one another under all circumstances without due regard to merit, fair play or justice,

to the detriment of the legitimate expectation of those who are not members.

36.

(1) Every person shall be entitled to freedom of expression, including freedom to hold opinions and to receive and impart ideas and information without interference.

(2) Without prejudice to the generality of subsection (1) of this section, every

person shall be entitled to own, establish and operate any medium for the dissemination of information, ideas and opinions:

Provided that no person, other than the Government of the Federation or of a State or any other person or body authorised by the President, shall own, establish or operate a television or wireless broadcasting station for any purpose whatsoever.

(3) Nothing in this section shall invalidate any law that is reasonably justifiable in a democratic society—

a. for the purpose of preventing the disclosure of information received in confidence, maintaining the authority and independence of courts or regulating telephony, wireless broadcasting, television or the exhibition of cinematograph films; or

b. imposing restrictions upon persons holding office under the Government of the Federation or of a State, members of the armed forces of the Federation or members of the Nigeria Police Force.

37.

Every person shall be entitled to assemble freely and associate with other persons, and in particular he may form or belong to any political party, trade union or any other association for the protection of his interests:

Provided that—

a. the provisions of this section shall not derogate from the powers conferred by this Constitution on the Federal Electoral Commission with respect to political parties to which that Commission does not accord recognition; and

b. a person elected to a legislative house as a candidate who was not sponsored by any political party shall not be entitled to join or declare himself to be a member of a political party until the general election next following his election as such candidate

38.

—(1) Every citizen of Nigeria is entitled to move freely throughout Nigeria and to reside in any part thereof, and no citizen of Nigeria shall be expelled from Nigeria or refused entry thereto or exit therefrom.

(2) Nothing in subsection (1) of this section shall invalidate any law that is reasonably justifiable in a democratic society—

a. imposing restrictions on the residence or movement of any person who has committed or is reasonably suspected to have committed a criminal offence in order to prevent him from leaving Nigeria; or

b. providing for the removal of any person from Nigeria to any other country—

    i. to be tried outside Nigeria for any criminal offence, or

    ii. to undergo imprisonment outside Nigeria in execution of the sentence of a court of law in respect of a criminal offence of which he has been found guilty:

Provided that there is reciprocal agreement between Nigeria and such other country in relation to such matter.

39.

—(1) A citizen of Nigeria of a particular community, ethnic group, place of origin, sex, religion or political opinion shall not, by reason only that he is such a person—

a. be subjected either expressly by, or in the practical application of, any law in force in Nigeria or any executive or administrative action of the government to disabilities or restrictions to which citizens of Nigeria of other communities, ethnic groups, places of origin, sex, religions, or political opinions are not made subject; or

b. be accorded either expressly by, or in the practical application of, any law in force in Nigeria or any such executive or administrative action, any privilege or advantage that is not accorded to citizens of Nigeria of other communities, ethnic groups, places of origin, sex, religions or political opinions.

(2) No citizen of Nigeria shall be subjected to any disability or deprivation merely by reason of the circumstances of his birth.

(3) Nothing in subsection (1) of this section shall invalidate any law by reason only that the law imposes restrictions with respect to the appointment of any person to any office under the State or as a member of the armed forces of the Federation or a member of the Nigeria Police Force or to an office in the service of a body corporate established directly by any law in force in Nigeria.

5. CANADA

INTRODUCTION

The repatriation of the Canadian Constitution took place in April, 1982, ending the system under which Canada had to ask the British Parliament to legislate its constitutional changes. While it absorbed much of the earlier British legislation, the new constitution is autochthonous, recognizing Canada's particular political structure and its multicultural heritage. It contains an affirmation of the existing rights of native peoples; the principle of equalization which fosters the sharing of wealth among the provinces through payments by the federal government; provisions for provincial ownership of particular natural resources and a purely Canadian method for amending the constitution.

Advanced thinking in the field of human rights is reflected in Sec. 15 which authorizes the operation of an affirmative action program on behalf of disadvantaged persons or groups. The right to communicate with government officials is established by Sec. 20 and minority language education is protected by Sec. 23. The equalization of regional economic disparities is provided for in Sec. 36.

CANADA CONSTITUTION (1982)

15.

(1) Every individual is equal before and under the law and has the right to the equal protection and equal benefit of the law without discrimination and, in particular, without discrimination based on race, national or ethnic origin, colour, religion, sex, age or mental or physical disability.

(2) Subsection (1) does not preclude any law, program or activity that has as its object the amelioration of conditions of disadvantaged individuals or groups including those that are disadvantaged because of race, national or ethnic origin, colour, religion, sex, age or mental or physical disability.

Official Languages of Canada

16.

(1) English and French are the official languages of Canada and have equality of status and equal rights and privileges as to their use in all institutions of the Parliament and government of Canada.

(2) English and French are the official languages of New Brunswick and have equality of status and equal rights and privileges as to their use in all institutions of the legislature and government of New Brunswick.

(3) Nothing in this Charter limits the authority of Parliament or a legislature to advance the equality of status or use of English and French.

20.

(1) Any member of the public in Canada has the right to communicate with, and to receive available services from, any head or central office of an institution of the Parliament or government of Canada in English or French, and has the same right with respect to any other office of any such institution where

a. there is a significant demand for communications with and services from that office in such language; or

b. due to the nature of the office, it is reasonable that communications with and services from that office be available in both English and French.

Minority Language Educational Rights

23.

(1) Citizens of Canada

a. whose first language learned and still understood is that of the English or French linguistic minority population of the province in which they reside, or

b. who have received their primary school instruction in Canada in English or French and reside in a province where the language in which they received that instruction is the language of the English or French lingustic minority population of the province,

have the right to have their children receive primary and secondary school instruction in that language in that province.(90)

(2) Citizens of Canada of whom any child has received or is receiving primary or secondary school instruction in English or French in Canada, have the right to have all their children receive primary and secondary school instruction in the same language.

(3) The right of citizens of Canada under subsections (1) and (2) to have their children receive primary and secondary school instruction in the language of the English or French linguistic minority population of a province

a. applies wherever in the province the number of children of citizens who have such a right is sufficient to warrant the provision to them out of public funds of minority language instruction; and

b. includes, where the number of those children so warrants, the right to have them receive that instruction in minority language educational facilities provided out of public funds.

Rights of the Aboriginal Peoples of Canada

35.

(1) The existing aboriginal and treaty rights of the aboriginal peoples of Canada are hereby recognized and affirmed.

(2) In this Act, "aboriginal peoples of Canada" includes the Indian, Inuit and Métis peoples of Canada.

Equalization and Regional Disparities

36.

(1) Without altering the legislative authority of Parliament or of the provincial legislatures, or the rights of any of them with respect to the exercise of their legislative authority, Parliament and the legislatures, together with the government of Canada and the provincial governments, are committed to

a. promoting equal opportunities for the well-being of Canadians;

b. furthering economic development to reduce disparity in opportunities; and

c. providing essential public services of reasonable quality to all Canadians.

(2) Parliament and the government of Canada are committed to the principle of making equalization payments to ensure that provincial governments have sufficient revenues to provide reasonably comparable levels of public services at reasonably comparable levels of taxation.

6. LIBERIA

INTRODUCTION

Following a military coup in 1980, Liberia's 1847 constitution (then the fourth oldest in the world) was suspended. The new military government announced that it desired a return to civilian rule as soon as possible, and in 1981 established a National Constitution Commission to draft a new constitution. Such draft was completed in March, 1983. It was referred to a Constitutional Advising Assembly, which submitted an Approved Revised Draft Constitution in October, 1983. This was approved in a National Referendum in July, 1984.

The Constitution has an unusually comprehensive article on freedom of expression, speech and information. Equal pay for equal work is established as a basic principle. And the rights of accused persons is buttressed by a penalizing provision directed against abuses of official authority. There is also an extension of the right to counsel.

Liberian human rights provisions are addressed to sensitive, but realistic issues of particular importance to Liberians. Especially pertinent is Art. 80 which protects the free competition of ideas by prohibiting laws which would create a one-party state. Also significant are the various provisions regarding emergency powers which limit executive authority to suspend the Constitution. As a means of preventing presidential dictatorship, the constitution "entrenches" an unamendable two consecutive term limit to the president in power.

LIBERIA CONSTITUTION (1984)

Fundamental Rights

Article 15

a) Every person shall have the right to freedom of expression, being fully responsible for the abuse thereof. This right shall not be curtailed, restricted or enjoined by government save during an emergency declared in accordance with this Constitution.

b) The right encompasses the right to hold opinions without interference and the right to knowledge. It includes freedom of speech and of the press, academic freedom to receive and impart knowledge and information and the right of libraries to make such knowledge available. It includes non-interference with the use of the mail, telephone and telegraph. It likewise includes the right to remain silent.

c) In pursuance of this right, there shall be no limitation on the public right to be informed about the government and its functionaries.

d) Access to state owned media shall not be denied because of any disagreement with or dislike of the ideas express. Denial of such access may be challenged in a court of competent jurisdiction.

e) This freedom may be limited only by judicial action in proceedings grounded in defamation or invasion of the rights of privacy and publicity or in the commercial aspect of expression in deception, false advertising and copyright infringement.

Article 21

a) No person shall be made subject to any law or punishment which was not in effect at the time of commission of an offense, nor shall the Legislature enact any bill of attainder or ex post facto law.

b) No person shall be subject to search or seizure of his person or property, whether on a criminal charge or for any other purpose, unless upon warrant lawfully issued upon probable cause supported by a solemn oath or affirmation, specifically identifying the person or place to be searched and stating the object of the search; provided, however, that a search or seizure shall be permissible without a search warrant where the arresting authorities act during the commission of a crime or in hot pursuit of a person who has committed a crime.

c) Every person suspected or accused of committing a crime shall immediately upon arrest be informed in detail of the charges, of the right to remain silent and of the fact that any statement made could be used against him in a court of law. Such person shall be entitled to counsel at every stage of the investigation and shall have the right not to be interrogated except in the presence of counsel. Any admission or other statements made by the accused in the absence of such counsel shall be deemed inadmissible as evidence in a court of law.

d) (i) All accused persons shall be bailable upon their personal recognizance or by sufficient sureties, depending upon the gravity of the charge, unless charged for capital offenses or grave offenses as defined by law.

(ii) Excessive bail shall not be required, nor excessive fines imposed, nor excessive punishment inflicted.

e) No person charged, arrested, restricted, detained or otherwise held in confinement shall be subject to torture or inhumane treatment; nor shall any person except military personnel, be kept or confined in any military facility; nor shall any person be seized and kept among convicted prisoners or treated as a convict, unless such person first shall have been convicted of a crime in a court of competent jurisdiction. The Legislature shall make it a criminal offense and provide for appropriate penalties against any police or security officer, prosecutor, administrator or any other public official acting in contravention of this provision; and any person so damaged by the conduct of any such public official shall have a civil remedy therefor, exclusive of any criminal penalties imposed.

f) Every person arrested or detained shall be formally charged and presented before a court of competent jurisdiction within forty-eight hours. Should the court determine the existence of a prima facie case against the accused, it shall issue a formal writ of arrest setting out the charge or charges and shall provide for a speedy trial. There shall be no preventive detention.

g) The right to the writ of habeas corpus, being essential to the protection of human rights, shall be guaranteed at all times, and any person arrested or detained and not presented to court within the period specified may in consequence exercise this right.

h) No person shall be held to answer for a capital or infamous crime except in cases of impeachment, cases arising in the Armed Forces and petty offenses, unless upon indictment by a Grand Jury; and in all such cases, the accused shall have the right to a speedy, public and impartial trial by a jury of the vicinity, unless such person shall, with appropriate understanding, expressly waive the right to a jury trial. In all criminal cases, the accused shall have the right to be represented by counsel of his choice, to confront witnesses against him and to have compulsory process for obtaining witnesses in his favor. He shall not be compelled to furnish evidence against himself and he shall be presumed innocent until the contrary is proved beyond a reasonable doubt. No person shall be subject to double jeopardy.

i) The right to counsel and the rights of counsel shall be inviolable. There shall be no interference with the lawyer-client relationship. In all trials, hearings, interrogatories and other proceedings where a person is accused of a criminal offense, the accused shall have the right to counsel of his choice; and where the accused is unable to secure such representation, the Republic shall make available legal aid services to ensure the protection of his rights.

There shall be absolute immunity from any government sanctions or interference in the performance of legal services as a counsellor or advocate; lawyer's offices and homes shall not be searched or papers examined or taken save pursuant to a search warrant and court order; and no lawyer shall be prevented from or punished for providing legal services, regardless of the charges against or the guilt of his client. No lawyer shall be barred from practice for political reasons.

j) Any person who, upon conviction of a criminal offense, was deprived of the enjoyment of his civil rights and liberties, shall have the same automatically restored upon serving the sentence and satisfying any other penalty imposed, or upon an executive pardon.

Political Parties and Elections

Article 77

a) Since the essence of democracy is free competition of ideas expressed by political parties and political groups as well as by individuals, parties may freely be established to advocate the political opinions of the people. Laws, regulations, decrees or measures which might have the effect of creating a one-party state shall be declared unconstitutional.

Emergency Powers

Article 85

The President, as Commander-in-Chief of the Armed Forces, may order any portion of the Armed Forces into a state of combat readiness in defence of the Republic, before or after the declaration of a state of emergency, as may be warranted by the situation. All military power or authority shall at all times, however, be held in subordination to the civil authority and the Constitution.

Article 86

a) The President may, in consultation with the Speaker of the House of Representatives and the President Pro Tempore of the Senate, proclaim and declare the existence of a state of emergency in the Republic or any part thereof. Acting pursuant thereto, the President may suspend or affect certain rights, freedoms and guarantees contained in this Constitution and exercise such other emergency powers as may be necessary and appropriate to take care of the emergency, subject, however, to the limitations contained in this Chapter.

b) A state of emergency may be declared only where there is a threat or outbreak of war or where there is civil unrest affecting the existence, security or well-being of the Republic amounting to a clear and present danger.

Article 87

a) Emergency powers do not include the power to suspend or abrogate the Constitution, dissolve the Legislature, or suspend or dismiss the Judiciary; and no constitutional amendment shall be promulgated during a state of emergency. Where the Legislature is not in session, it must be convened immediately in special session and remain in session during the entire period of the state of emergency.

b) The writ of habeas corpus shall remain available and exercisable at all times and shall not be suspended on account of any state of emergency. It shall be enjoyed in the most free, easy, inexpensive, expeditious and ample manner. Any person who suffers from a violation of this right may challenge such violation in a court of competent jurisdiction.

Article 88

The President shall, immediately upon the declaration of a state of emergency, but not later than seven days thereafter, lay before the Legislature at its regular session or at a specially convened session, the facts and circumstances leading to such declaration. The Legislature shall within seventy-two hours, by joint resolution voted by two-thirds of the membership of each house, decide whether the proclamation of a state of emergency is justified or whether the measures taken thereunder are appropriate. If the two-thirds vote is not obtained, the emergency automatically shall be revoked. Where the Legislature shall deem it necessary to revoke the state of emergency or to modify the measures taken thereunder, the President shall act accordingly and immediately carry out the decisions of the Legislature.

Amendments

Article 93

The limitation of the Presidential term of office to two terms, each of six years duration, may be subject to amendment; provided that the amendment shall not become effective during the term of office of the encumbent President.

E. CONSTITUTIONAL ENFORCEMENT
PROCEDURES

INTRODUCTION

Constitutional pronouncements and proscriptions on human rights are seldom self-executing. They require implementation (usually in the form of supplementary legislation) for their enforcement. But the modern constitutions do provide the framework for such implementation, authorizing courts or special agencies to enforce their human rights statements.

Most significant among the older constitutions, which fail to provide specific procedural protection, is the Constitution of the United States of America (1789). In that nation, courts have evolved a bevy of doctrines to avoid major constitutional questions, including rights issues.

First, the litigant must establish a genuine "case or controversy," a real dispute in which rights are being trampled upon or are in imminent danger. Second, the Supreme Court has repeatedly refused to offer advisory opinions on proposed executive action, or legislation, even at the request of the President or Congress. Third, the litigant must show that the right involved is personal to him, and not a general claim available to all citizens or a large group of them. Fourth, a dispute must be "ripe" or "final" before the Supreme Court will hear it. Thus, a litigant must exhaust his administrative or other appeals prior to seeking court action. Fifth, a question presented the Supreme Court must be "justiciable," and not a "political question." This vague doctrine seems to mean that the Supreme Court will avoid direct conflicts with Congress or the President when confronted with a major issue. Constitutional lawyers must also be familiar with other doctrines if they are to gain access to the Supreme Court of the United States.

Courts are usually regarded as the chief protectors of individual rights. The Brazilian Constitution (1977 Amendments) makes this very clear by providing that "the law may not exclude any impairment of individual rights from consideration by the judicial branch." (Article 153, Paragraph 4.) Procedurally, that constitution states, "the institution of proceedings may be subject to the prior exhaustion of administrative channels, provided a cost bond is not required or the period of 180 days for a decision on the petition is not exceeded."

Some constitutions invite more active judicial participation in the implementation of human rights. In West Germany, for example, the Basic Law (1949) looks to the Federal Constitutional Court to take the lead. Article 93 of the Basic Law grants the Court abstract judicial review to interpret rights and duties whenever asked to do so by the federal government, a Land (state) government or by one-third of the members of the Federal Bundestag. The decision, even though non-adversary in nature, is completely binding. The Basic Law also gives private citizens direct access to the Federal Constitutional Court (Art. 93, Sec. 4a). This means that a constitutional complaint can be lodged by any person who claims that any public official has deprived him or her of civil rights guaranteed by the Basic Law. Some 95 percent of the cases brought before the Federal Constitutional Court are in accordance with this procedure.

The Constitution of the Republic of Ireland also permits easy access to the Irish High Court. Article 34 of the constitution expressly confers original jurisdiction in disputes about the constitutionality of a statute. This article has been liberally construed to enable private citizens readily to challenge actions of government.[108] In addition, the President of the Republic may refer any proposed legislation to the Supreme Court for an advisory opinion and, if the Court finds any provision of the bill to be repugnant to the constitution, "the President shall decline to sign such bill." (Article 26.)

The more modern constitutions provide stronger procedural provisions for rights claimants. For example, the 1982 Nigerian Constitution states that "any person who alleges that any (rights provision) is being or is likely to be controvened in any state in relation to him may apply to a High Court in that state for redress." (Article 42.) The national High Court is also given original jurisdiction to hear such cases, subject to rules and procedures made by the Chief Justice of Nigeria. In addition, the Nigerian Constitution provides financial assistance or legal aid for indigent rights claimants.

The Spanish Constitution of 1978 authorizes citizens to make a claim to certain basic rights and liberties before the regular courts "through a process based on the principles of preference and speed." (Article 53.) More important, the new office of Defender of the People, appointed by the General Cortes (legislature), has the task of protecting the general rights and liberties of Spaniards, of supervising the administration, and informing the General Cortes. (Article 54.)

Obviously, the mere listing of rights in a constitution is insufficient to provide enjoyment of those rights. Dictatorial constitutions frequently give lip service to human rights. Unless a tradition of rights recognition and protection has emerged in a nation, as in the United States, the United Kingdom, and Japan, only constitutionally prescribed procedural safeguards can provide genuine enjoyment of rights. Of course, constitutions can be ignored or violated by governments, but at least the citizens can have the bases for eventual human rights reform.

1. UNITED STATES (1787)

Article III

Section 2.[1] The judicial Power shall extend to all Cases, in Law and Equity, arising under this Constitution, the Laws of the United States, and Treaties made, or which shall be made, under their Authority;—to all Cases affecting Ambassadors, other public Ministers and Consuls;—to all Cases of admiralty and maritime Jurisdiction; —to Controversies between two or more States;— between a State and Citizens of another State; —between Citizens of different States; —between Citizens of the same State claiming Lands under Grants of different States, and between a State, or the Citizens thereof, and foreign States, Citizens or Subjects.

2. BRAZIL (1977 AMENDMENT)

Article 153

Paragraph 4. The law may not exclude any impairment of individual rights from consideration by the judicial branch. The institution of proceedings may be subject to the prior exhaustion of administrative channels, provided a cost bond is not required or the period of 180 days for a decision on the petition is not exceeded.

3. FEDERAL REPUBLIC OF GERMANY (1949)

Article 93

4a. on complaints of unconstitutionality, which may be entered by any person who claims that one of his basic rights or one of his rights under paragraph (4) of Article 20, under Article 33, 38, 101, 103, or 104 has been violated by public authority;

4. IRELAND (1937)

Article 34

3. 1° The Courts of First Instance shall include a High Court invested with full original jurisdiction in and power to determine all matters and questions whether of law or fact, civil or criminal.

2° Save as otherwise provided by this Article, the jurisdiction of the High Court shall extend to the question of the validity of any law having regard to the provisions of this Constitution, and no such question shall be raised (whether by pleading, argument or otherwise) in any Court established under this or any other Article of this Constitution other than the High Court or the Supreme Court.

3° No Court whatever shall have jurisdiction to question the validity of a law, or any provision of a law, the Bill for which shall have been referred to the Supreme Court by the President under Article 26 of this Constitution, or to question the validity of a provision of a law where the corresponding provision in the Bill for such law shall have been referred to the Supreme Court by the President under the said Article 26.

Article 26

This Article applies to any Bill passed or deemed to have been passed by both Houses of the Oireachtas other than a Money Bill, or a Bill expressed to be a Bill containing a proposal to amend the Constitution, or a Bill the time for the consideration of which by Seanad Éireann shall have been abridged under Article 24 of this Constitution.

1.   1° The President may, after consultation with the Council of State, refer any Bill to which this Article applies to the Supreme Court for a decision on the Question as to whether such Bill or any specified provision or provisions of such Bill is or are repugnant to this Constitution or to any provision thereof.

2° Every such reference shall be made not later than the seventh day after the date on which such Bill shall have been presented by the Taoiseach to the President for his signature.

3° The President shall not sign any Bill the subject of a reference to the Supreme Court under this Article pending the pronouncement of the decision of the Court.

2.   1° The Supreme Court consisting of not less than five judges shall consider every question referred to it by the President under this Article for a decision, and, having heard arguments by or on behalf of the Attorney General and by counsel assigned by the Court, shall pronounce its decision on such question in open court as soon as may be, and in any case not later than sixty days after the date of such reference.

2° The decision of the majority of the judges of the Supreme Court shall, for the purposes of this Article, be the decision of the Court 'and shall be pronounced by such one of those judges as the Court shall direct, and no other opinion, whether assenting or dissenting, shall be pronounced nor shall the existence of any such other opinion be disclosed.

3.   1° In every case in which the Supreme Court decides that any provision of a Bill the subject of a reference to the Supreme Court under this Article is repugnant to this Constitution or to any provision thereof, the President shall decline to sign such Bill.

2° If, in the case of a Bill to which Article 27 of this Constitution applies, a petition has been addressed to the President under that Article, that Article shall be complied with.

3° In every other case the President shall sign the Bill as soon as may be after the date on which the decision of the Supreme Court shall have been pronounced.

5. NIGERIA (1982)

Article 42.

(1) Any person who alleges that any of the provisions of this Chapter has been, is being or likely to be contravened in any State in relation to him may apply to a High Court in that State for redress.

(2) Subject to the provisions of this Constitution, a High Court shall have original jurisdiction to hear and determine any application made to it in pursuance of the provisions of this section and may make such orders, issue

such writs and give such directions as it may consider appropriate for the purpose of enforcing or securing the enforcement within that State of any rights to which the person who makes the application may be entitled under this Chapter.

(3) The Chief Justice of Nigeria may make rules with respect to the practice and procedure of a High Court for the purposes of this section.

(4) The National Assembly—

a. may confer upon a High Court such powers in addition to those conferred by this section as may appear to the National Assembly to be necessary or desirable for the purpose of enabling the court more effectively to exercise the jurisdiction conferred upon it by this section; and

b. shall make provisions—

  i. for the rendering of financial assistance to any indigent citizen of Nigeria where his right under this Chapter has been infringed or with a view to enabling him to engage the services of a legal practitioner to prosecute his claim, and

  ii. for ensuring that allegations of infringement of such rights are substantial and the requirement or need for financial or legal aid is real.

6. SPAIN (1978)

Article 53

1. The rights and liberties recognized in the second chapter of the present Title are binding on all public authorities. Only by law, which in every case must respect their essential content, could the exercise of such rights and liberties be regulated, and they shall be protected in accordance with the provisions of Article 161, 1 b).

2. Any citizen may make a claim to the liberties and rights recognized in Article 13 and the first Section of the Second Chapter before the regular courts through a process based on the principles of preference and speed and through the recourse "de amparo" before the Constitutional Court. This last recourse shall be applicable to objections of conscience recognized in Article 30.

3. Recognition, respect and protection of the principles recognized in the Third Chapter shall guide positive legislation, judicial practice and the actions by public authorities. They may also be argued before ordinary jurisdiction through procedures established in the laws affecting them.

Article 54

An organic law shall regulate the institution of the Defender of the People as the High Commissioner of the General Cortes, appointed by them for the protection of the rights contained in this Title, for which purpose he may supervise the activity of the administration, informing the General Cortes of it.

VIII. Legislation

1. INDIA

INTRODUCTION

Article 17 of the Indian constitution of 1949 provides in unambiguous terms that, " 'Untouchability' is abolished and its practice in any form is forbidden." The article continues by providing that, "The enforcement of any disability arising out of 'Untouchability' shall be an offence punishable in accordance with law."

The consequent legislation which made the practice of untouchability a penal offense was the Untouchability (Offences) Act, 1955. This was amended as the result of the recommendations in the Report of the Committee on Untouchability, Economic and Educational Development of the Scheduled Caste, 1969. Such amendments provided for more severe punishment for untouchability offenses and eliminated loopholes which the working of the Act had revealed. The amended legislation became the Protection of Civil Rights Act, 1976, now known as the Protection of Civil Rights Act, 1955.

"Prior to British rule," explains Prof. Marc Galanter, "some Indian regimes had actively intervened (on behalf of untouchability practices) to support and enforce privileges and disabilities associated with membership in a particular social group. During the British period, the practice of untouchability and other discrimination by private persons did not enjoy such explicit governmental sanction. Such conduct was not directly prescribed by legislation. But as part of the government's policy of non-intervention in social and religious matters, there was little effort to interfere with their usages."[109]

Comprehensive legislation making it an offense to discriminate against the now one hundred million untouchables began with the Removal of Social Disabilities Act, passed by the Madras legislature in 1938. This was followed by a series of post-World War II Acts in most of the provinces and in many of the larger princely states to afford basic human rights to untouchables. It thus became a crime even prior to Indian independence and the 1949 constitution to prevent untouchables from worshipping in places of public worship, having access to rivers and streams, wells, roads, burial grounds, etc., being admitted to hospitals, schools and hostels, and having the right to purchase goods and services on the same terms as others.

THE PROTECTION OF CIVIL RIGHTS ACT, 1955, 22 OF 1955

(AS MODIFIED UP TO THE 1ST JANUARY, 1978.)
[8th May, 1955]
[Footnotes Renumbered]

An Act to prescribe punishment for the [111][preaching and practice of "Untouchability"], for the enforcement of any disability arising therefrom and for matters connected therewith.

Be it enacted by Parliament in the Sixth Year of the Republic of India as follows:—

Short title, extent and commencement.

1. (*1*) This Act may be called [112][the Protection of Civil Rights Act], 1955.

(*2*) It extends to the whole of India.

(*3*) It shall come into force on such date[113] as the Central Government may, by notification in the Official Gazette, appoint.

Definitions

2. In this Act, unless the context otherwise requires,—

[114][(*a*) "civil rights" means any right accruing to a person by reason of the abolition of "untouchability" by article 17 of the Constitution:]

[115][(*aa*)] "hotel" includes a refreshment room, a boarding house, a lodging house, a coffee house and a cafe;

[116][(*b*) "place" includes a house, building and other structure and premises; and also includes a tent, vehicle and vessel;]

(*c*) "place of public entertainment" includes any place to which the public are admitted and in which an entertainment is provided or held.

Explanation.—"Entertainment" includes any exhibition, performance, game, sport and any other form of amusement;

(*d*) "place of public worship" means a place, whatever name known, which is used as a place of public religious worship or which is dedicated generally to, or is used generally by, persons professing any religion or belonging to any religious denomination or any section thereof, for the performance of any religious service, or for offering prayers therein; [117][and includes—

(*i*) all lands and subsidiary shrines appurtenant or attached to any such place,

(*ii*) a privately owned place of worship which is, in fact, allowed by the owner thereof to be used as a place of public worship, and

(*iii*) such land or subsidiary shrine appurtenant to such privately owned place of worship as is allowed by the owner thereof to be used as a place of public religious worship;]

[118][(*da*) "prescribed" means prescribed by rules made under this Act;

(*db*) "Scheduled Castes" has the meaning assigned to it in clause (24) of article 366 of the Constitution;]

(*e*) "shop" means any premises where goods are sold either wholesale or by retail or both wholesale and by retail [119][and includes—

(*i*) any place from where goods are sold by a hawker or vendor or from a mobile van or cart,

(*ii*) a laundry and a hair cutting saloon;

(*iii*) any other place where services are rendered to customers].

Punishment for Enforcing Religious Disabilities.

3. Whoever on the ground of "untouchability" prevents any person—

(*a*) from entering any place of public worship which is open to other persons professing the same religion[120]* * * or any section thereof, as such person; or

(*b*) from worshipping or offering prayers or performing any religious service in any place of public worship, or bathing in, or using the waters of, any sacred tank, well, spring or water-course [121][river or lake or bathing at any ghat of such tank, water-course, river or lake] in the same manner and to the same extent as is permissible to other persons professing the same religion [3]* * * or any section thereof, as such person;

[122][shall be punishable with imprisonment for a term of not less than one month and not more six months and also with fine which shall be not less than one hundred rupees and not more than five hundred rupees].

Explanation.—For the purposes of this section and section 4 persons professing the Buddhist, Sikh or Jaina religion or persons professing the Hindu religion in any of its forms or developments including Virashaivas, Lingayats, Adivasis, followers of Brahmo, Prarthana, Arya Samaj and the Swaminarayan Sampraday shall be deemed to be Hindus.

Punishment for Enforcing Social Disabilities.

4. Whoever on the ground of "untouchability" enforces against any person any disability with regard to—

(*i*) access to any shop, public restaurant, hotel or place of public entertainment; or

(*ii*) the use of any utensils, and other articles kept in any public restaurant, hotel, *dharmshala, sarai* or *musafirkhana* for the use of the general public or of [123][any section thereof]; or

(*iii*) the practice of any profession or the carrying on of any occupation, trade or business [124][or employment in any job]; or

(*iv*) the use of, or access to, any river, stream, spring, well tank, cistern, water-tap or other watering place, or any bathing ghat, burial or cremation ground, any sanitary convenience, any road, or passage, or any other place of public resort which other members of the public, or [125][any section thereof], have a right to use or have access to; or

(*v*) the use of, or access to, any place used for a charitable or a public purpose maintained wholly or partly out of State funds or dedicated to the use of the general public, or [126][any section thereof]; or

(*vi*) the enjoyment of any benefit under a charitable trust created for the benefit of the general public or of [127][any section thereof]; or

(*vii*) the use of, or access to, any public conveyance; or

(*viii*) the construction, acquisition, or occupation of any residential premises in any locality, whatsoever; or

(*ix*) the use of any *dharmshala, sarai* or *musafirkhana* which is open to the general public, or to [128][any section thereof]; or

(*x*) the observance of any social or religious custom, usage or ceremony or [129][taking part in, or taking out, any religious, social or cultural procession]; or

(*xi*) the use of jewellery and finery;

[130][shall be punishable with imprisonment for a term of not less than one month and not more than six months and also with fine which shall be not less than one hundred rupees and not more than five hundred rupees].

[131][*Explanation.*—For the purposes of this section, "enforcement of any disability" includes any discrimination on the ground of "untouchability".]

Punishment for Refusing to Admit Persons to Hospitals, Etc.

5. Whoever on the ground of "untouchability"—

(*a*) refuses admission to any person to any hospital, dispensary, educational institution or any hostel [132]* * *, if such hospital, dispensary, educational institution or hostel is established or maintained for the benefit of the general public or any section thereof; or

(*b*) does any act which discriminates against any such person after admission to any of the aforesaid institutions;

[133][shall be punishable with imprisonment for a term of not less than one month and not more than six months and also with fine which shall be not less than one hundred rupees and not more than five hundred rupees].

Punishment for Refusing to Sell Goods or Render Services.

6. Whoever on the ground of "untouchability" refuses to sell any goods or refuses to render any service to any person at the same time and place and on the same terms and conditions at or on which such goods are sold or services are rendered to other persons in the ordinary course of business [134][shall be punishable with imprisonment for a term of not less than one month and not more than six months and also with fine which shall be not less than one hundred rupees and not more than five hundred rupees].

Punishment for Other Offences Arising Out of "Untouchability".

7. (1) Whoever—

(*a*) prevents any person from exercising any right accruing to him by reason of the abolition of "untouchability" under article 17 of the Constitution; or

(*b*) molests, injures, annoys, obstructs or causes or attempts to cause obstruction to any person in the exercise of any such right or molests, injures, annoys or boycotts any person by reason of his having exercised any such right; or

(*c*) by words, either spoken or written, or by signs or by visible representations or otherwise, incites or encourages any person or class of persons or the public generally to practise "untouchability" in any form whatsoever; [135][or]

[136][(*d*) insults or attempts to insult, on the ground of "untouchability", a member of a Scheduled Caste;]

[137][shall be punishable with imprisonment for a term of not less than one month and not more than six months and also with fine which shall be not less than one hundred rupees and not more than five hundred rupees].

[138][*Explanation I*].—A person shall be deemed to boycott another person who—

(*a*) refuses to let to such other person or refuses to permit such other person, to use or occupy any house or land or refuses to deal with, work for hire for, or do business with, such other person or to render to him or receive from him any customary service, or refuses to do any of the said things on the terms on which such things would be commonly done in the ordinary course of business; or

(*b*) abstains from such social, professional or business relations as he would ordinarily maintain with such other person.

[139][*Explanation II.*—For the purposes of clause (*c*), a person shall be deemed to incite or encourage the practice of "untouchability"—

(*i*) if he, directly or indirectly, preaches "untouchability" or its practice in any form; or

(*ii*) if he justifies, whether on historical, philosophical or religious grounds or on the ground of any tradition of the caste system or on any other ground, the practice of "untouchability" in any form.]

[140][(*1A*) Whoever commits any offence against the person or property of any individual as a reprisal or revenge for his having exercised any right accruing to him by reason of the abolition of "untouchability" under article 17 of the Constitution, shall, where the offence is punishable with imprisonment for a term exceeding two years, be punishable with imprisonment for a term which shall not be less than two years and also with fine.]

(2) Whoever—

(*i*) denies to any person belonging to his community or any section thereof any right or privilege to which such person would be entitled as a member of such community or section, or

(*ii*) takes any part in the ex-communication of such person, on the ground that such person has refused to practise "untouchability" or that such person has done any act in furtherance of the objects of this Act,

[141][shall be punishable with imprisonment for a term of not less than one month and not more than six months, and also with fine which shall be not less than one hundred rupees and not more than five hundred rupees.]

Unlawful Compulsory Labour When to be Deemed to be a Practice of Untouchability.

[142][7A. (1) Whoever compels any person, on the ground of "untouchability", to do any scavenging or sweeping or to remove any carcass or to flay any animal or to remove the umbilical cord or to do any other job of a similar nature, shall be deemed to have enforced a disability arising out of "untouchability".

(2) Whoever is deemed under sub-section (1) to have enforced a disability arising out of "untouchability" shall be punishable with imprisonment for a term which shall be not less than three months and not more than six months and also with fine which shall not be less than one hundred rupees and not more than five hundred rupees.

Explanation.—For the purposes of this section, "compulsion" includes a threat of social or economic boycott.]

Cancellation or Suspension of Licences in Certain Cases.

8. When a person who is convicted of an offence under section 6 holds any licence under any law for the time being in force in respect of any profession, trade, calling or employment in relation to which the offence is committed, the court trying the offence may, without prejudice to any other penalty to which such person may be liable under that section, direct that the licence shall stand cancelled or be suspended for such period as the court may deem fit, and every order of the court so cancelling or suspending a licence shall have effect as if it

had been passed by the authority competent to cancel or suspend the licence under any such law.

Explanation.—In this section, "licence" includes a permit or a permission.

Resumption or Suspension of Grants Made by Government.

9. Where the manager or trustee of a place of public worship [143][or any educational institution or hostel] which is in receipt of a grant of land or money from the Government is convicted of an offence under this Act and such conviction is not reversed or quashed in any appeal or revision, the Government may, if in its opinion the circumstances of the case warrant such a course, direct the suspension or resumption of the whole or any part of such grant.

Abetment of Offence.

10. Whoever abets any offence under this Act shall be punishable with the punishment provided for the offence.

[144][*Explanation.*—A public servant who wilfully neglects the investigation of any offence punishable under this Act shall be deemed to have abetted an offence punishable under this Act.]

Power of State Government to Impose Collective Fine.

[145][10A. (1) If, after an inquiry in the prescribed manner, the State Government is satisfied that the inhabitants of an area are concerned in, or abetting the commission of, any offence punishable under this Act, or harbouring persons concerned in the commission of such offence or failing to render all the assistance in their power to discover or apprehend the offender or offenders or suppressing material evidence of the commission of such offence, the State Government may, by notification in the Official Gazette, impose a collective fine on such inhabitants and apportion such fine amongst the inhabitants who are liable collectively to pay it, and such apportionment shall be made according to the State Government's judgment of the respective means of such inhabitants and in making any such apportionment the State Government may assign a portion of such fine to a Hindu undivided family to be payable by it:

Provided that the fine apportioned to an inhabitant shall not be realised until the petition, if any, filed by him under sub-section (3) is disposed of.

(2) The notification made under sub-section (1) shall be proclaimed in the area by beat of drum or in such other manner as the State Government may think best in the circumstances to bring the imposition of the collective fine to the notice of the inhabitants of the said area.

(3) (a) Any person aggrieved by the imposition of the collective fine under sub-section (1) or by the order of apportionment, may, within the prescribed period, file a petition before the State Government or such other authority as that Government may specify in this behalf for being exempted from such fine or for modification of the order of apportionment:

Provided that no fee shall be charged for filing such petition.

(b) The State Government or the authority specified by it shall, after giving to the petitioner a reasonable opportunity of being heard, pass such order as it may think fit:

Provided that the amount of the fine exempted or reduced under this section shall not be realisable from any person, and the total fine imposed on the inhabitants of an area under sub-section (1) shall be deemed to have been reduced to that extent.

(4) Notwithstanding anything contained in sub-section (3), the State Government may exempt the victims of any offence punishable under this Act or any person who does not, in its opinion, fall within the category of persons specified in sub-section (1), from the liability to pay the collective fine imposed under sub-section (1) or any portion thereof.

2 of 1974.

(5) The portion of collective fine payable by any person (including a Hindu undivided family) may be recovered in the manner provided by the Code of Criminal Procedure, 1973, for the recovery of fines imposed by a Court as if such portion were a fine imposed by a Magistrate.]

Enhanced Penalty on Subsequent Conviction.

11. Whoever having already been convicted of an offence under this Act or of an abetment of such offence is again convicted of any such offence or abetment, [146][shall, on conviction, be punishable—

(a) for the second offence, with imprisonment for a term of not less than six months and not more than one year, and also with fine which shall be not less than two hundred rupees and not more than five hundred rupees;

(b) for the third offence or any offence subsequent to the third offence, with imprisonment for a term of not less than one year and not more than two years, and also with fine which shall be not less than five hundred rupees and not more than one thousand rupees].

Presumption by Courts in Certain Cases.

12. Where any act constituting an offence under this Act is committed in relation to a member of a Scheduled Caste [147]* * *, the court shall presume, unless the contrary is proved, that such act was committed on the ground of "untouchability".

Limitation of Jurisdiction of Civil Courts.

13. (1) No civil court shall entertain or continue any suit or proceeding or shall pass any decree or order or execute wholly or partially any decree or order if the claim involved in such suit or proceeding or if the passing of such decree or order or if such execution would in any way be contrary to the provisions of this Act.

(2) No court shall, in adjudicating any matter or executing any decree or order, recognise any custom or usage imposing any disability on any person on the ground of "untouchability".

Offences by Companies.

14. (1) If the person committing an offence under this Act is a company, every person who at the time the offence was committed was in charge of, and

was responsible to, the company for the conduct of the business of the company, shall be deemed to be guilty of the offence and shall be liable to be proceeded against and punished accordingly:

Provided that nothing contained in this sub-section shall render any such person liable to any punishment, if he proves that the offence was committed without his knowledge or that he exercised all due diligence to prevent the commission of such offence.

(2) Notwithstanding anything contained in sub-section (1), where an offence under this Act has been committed with the consent of any director or manager, secretary or other officer of the company, such director, manager, secretary or other officer shall also be deemed to be guilty of that offence and shall be liable to be proceeded against and punished accordingly.

Explanation.—For the purposes of this section,—

(a) "company" means any body corporate and includes a firm or other association of individuals; and

(b) "director" in relation to a firm means a partner in the firm.

Protection of Action Taken in Good Faith.

[148][14A. (1) No suit, prosecution or other legal proceeding shall lie against the Central Government or a State Government for anything which is in good faith done or intended to be done under this Act.

(2) No suit or other legal proceeding shall lie against the Central Government or a State Government for any damage caused or likely to be caused by anything which is in good faith done or intended to be done under this Act.]

Offences to be Cognizable and Triable Summarily. 2 of 1974.

[149][15. (1) Notwithstanding anything contained in the Code of Criminal Procedure, 1973, every offence punishable under this Act shall be cognizable and every such offence, except where it is punishable with imprisonment for a minimum term exceeding three months, may be tried summarily by a Judicial Magistrate of the first class or in a metropolitan area by a Metropolitan Magistrate in accordance with the procedure specified in the said Code.

2 of 1974.

(2) Notwithstanding anything contained in the Code of Criminal Procedure, 1973, when any public servant is alleged to have committed the offence of abetment of an offence punishable under this Act, while acting or purporting to act in the discharge of his official duty, no court shall take cognizance of such offence of abetment except with the previous sanction—

(a) of the Central Government, in the case of a person employed in connection with the affairs of the Union; and

(b) of the State Government. in the case of a person employed in connection with the affairs of a State.

Duty of State Government to Ensure That the Rights Accruing From the Abolition of "Untouchability" May be Availed of by the Concerned Persons.

15A. (1) Subject to such rules as the Central Government may make in this behalf, the State Government shall take such measures as may be necessary for ensuring that the rights arising from the abolition of "untouchability" are made available to, and are availed of by, the persons subjected to any disability arising out of "untouchability".

(2) In particular, and without prejudice to the generality of the provisions of sub-section (1), such measures may include—

(i) the provision of adequate facilities, including legal aid, to the persons subjected to any disability arising out of "untouchability" to enable them to avail themselves of such rights;

(ii) the appointment of officers for initiating or exercising supervision over prosecutions for the contravention of the provisions of this Act;

(iii) the setting up of special courts for the trial of offences under this Act;

(iv) the setting up of Committees at such appropriate levels as the State Government may think fit to assist the State Government in formulating or implementing such measures;

(v) provision for a periodic survey of the working of the provisions of this Act with a view to suggesting measures for the better implementation of the provisions of this Act:

(vi) the identification of the areas where persons are under any disability arising out of "untouchability" and adoption of such measures as would ensure the removal of such disability from such areas.

(3) The Central Government shall take such steps as may be necessary to co-ordinate the measures taken by the State Governments under sub-section (1).

(4) The Central Government shall, every year, place on the Table of each House of Parliament, a report on the measures taken by itself and by the State Governments in pursuance of the provisions of this section.]

Act to Override Other Laws.

16. Save as otherwise expressly provided in this Act, the provisions of this Act shall have effect notwithstanding anything inconsistent therewith contained in any other law for the time being in force, or any custom or usage or any instrument having effect by virtue of any such law or any decree or order of any court or other authority.

Probation of Offenders Act, 1958, Not to Apply to Persons Above the Age of Fourteen Years.

20 of 1958.

[150][16A. The provisions of the Probation of Offenders Act, 1958, shall not apply to any person above the age of fourteen years who is found guilty of having committed any offence punishable under this Act.

Power to Make Rules.

16B. (1) The Central Government may, by notification in the Official Gazette, make rules to carry out the provisions of this Act.

(2) Every rule made by the Central Government under this Act shall be laid, as soon as may be after it is made, before each House of Parliament while it is

in session for a total period of thirty days which may be comprised in one session or in two or more successive sessions, and if, before the expiry of the session immediately following the session or the successive sessions aforesaid, both Houses agree in making any modification in the rule or both Houses agree that the rule should not be made, the rule shall thereafter have effect only in such modified form or be of no effect, as the case may be; so, however, that any such modification or annulment shall be without prejudice to the validity of anything previously done under that rule.]

Repeal.

17. The enactments specified in the Schedule are hereby repealed to the extent to which they or any of the provisions contained therein correspond or are repugnant to this Act or to any of the provisions contained therein.

2. UNITED STATES

INTRODUCTION

The general compliance with the provisions of the United States Civil Rights Act and the routine litigation over interpretations of its fine print cloud recollections of the political and legal controversy which surrounded its passage.

Two days before Independence Day in 1964, Congress finally enacted the legislation which was designed to clarify, extend and enforce the general terms of the Constitution's Thirteenth, Fourteenth, and Fifteenth Amendments intended to confer equal rights upon the nation's black population. A bipartisan majority in the House of Representatives had passed the measure on February 10, and it then became the chief order of business in the Senate for the next four months. Passage was not assured until June 10 when supporters rallied sufficient votes to choke off an extended filibuster by southern Senators.

This was the first time since 1917, when the Senate had initially adopted rules for limiting debate, that cloture was successfully invoked for a civil rights measure.

Structured to insure maximum rights for blacks in as many areas of public life as could be encompassed by legislation, the Act generally provides for the following:

1. A broadening of the powers of the Civil Rights Commission.

2. The establishment of a Community Relations Service, the job of which is to conciliate racial disputes.

3. A prohibition on discrimination based on race, color, sex, religion, or natural origin either by employers or by labor unions in larger businesses.

4. The creation of a Federal Fair Employment Practices Commission (FEPC) to administer the employment provisions of the act.

5. A prohibition on voting registrars to prevent them from applying different standards to white and black applicants. Literacy tests were

required to be in writing, with a sixth-grade education a "rebuttal assumption" of literacy.

6. Permission for the attorney general to bring suit on behalf of injured individuals in order to secure desegration of facilities owned, operated, or managed by state or local governments.

7. A granting of power to the president to halt any federal aid funds to public or private programs in which racial discrimination is practiced.

8. Complete prohibition of discrimination in "public accommodations" because of "race, religion, color, or national origin" in hotels, restaurants, theaters, and all other public facilities that affect interstate commerce.

9. A granting of power to the attorney general to file enforcement suits against owners of public accommodations who continue to discriminate and also to sue on behalf of any persons against whom other illegal forms of discrimination are practiced.

Section 101, dealing with voting rights, was strengthened by the Voting Rights Act of 1965 which suspended literacy tests in twelve states and imposed upon them a federal registration system. 42 U.S.C §§ 1781–1783.

Because of the unusual importance of this law, the Supreme Court took speedy action to decide the cases testing its constitutionality. Congressional authority was upheld in *Heart of Atlanta Motel* v. *United States*, 379 U.S. 241 (1964), decided only five months after the act was passed.

The meaning and effect of the Civil Rights Act is analyzed in detail in a publication of the United States Commission on Civil Rights: *Federal Civil Rights Enforcement Effect*, published by the Government Printing Office in 1973. Two other important works are: Harrell R. Rodgers, Jr. and Charles J. Bullock III, *Law and Social Change: Rights, Laws and Their Consequences*, New York: McGraw-Hill Book Company, 1972; and James Coleman, Sarah D. Kelley and John Moore, *Trends in Social Segregation, 1968–1973*, Washington, D.C.: Urban Institute, 1975.

CIVIL RIGHTS ACT OF 1964 (As Amended) 42 U.S.C. S 1971 ET SEQ. (EXCERPTED)

An act to enforce the constitutional right to vote, to confer jurisdiction upon the district courts of the United States to provide injunctive relief against discrimination in public accommodations, to authorize the Attorney General to institute suits to protect constitutional rights in public facilities and public education, to extend the Commission on Civil Rights, to prevent discrimination in federally assisted programs, to establish a Commission on Equal Employment Opportunity, and for other purposes

Be it enacted by the Senate and House of Representatives of the United States of America in Congress assembled, That this Act may be cited as the "Civil Rights Act of 1964."

TITLE I

VOTING RIGHTS . . .

Section 101.

. . . (2) No person acting under color of law shall—

A. in determining whether any individual is qualified under State law or laws to vote in any Federal election, apply any standard, practice, or procedure different from the standards, practices, or procedures applied under such law or laws to other individuals within the same county, parish, or similar political subdivision who have been found by State officials to be qualified to vote;

B. deny the right of any individual to vote in any Federal election because of an error or omission on any record or paper relating to any application, registration, or other act requisite to voting, if such error or omission is not material in determining whether such individual is qualified under State law to vote in such election; or

C. employ any literacy test as a qualification for voting in any Federal election unless (i) such test is administered to each individual and is conducted wholly in writing, and (ii) a certified copy of the test and of the answers given by the individual is furnished to him within twenty-five days of the submission of his request made within the period of time during which records and papers are required to be retained and preserved pursuant to title III of the Civil Rights Act of 1960 (42 U.S.C. 1974—74e; 74 Stat. 88): *Provided, however,* That the Attorney General may enter into agreements with appropriate State or local authorities that preparation, conduct, and maintenance of such tests in accordance with the provisions as are necessary in the preparation, conduct, and maintenance of such tests for persons who are blind or otherwise physically handicapped, meet the purposes of this subparagraph and constitute compliance therewith.

Title II—Injunctive Relief Against Discrimation in Places of Public Accommodation

Section 201.

(a) All persons shall be entitled to the full and equal enjoyment of the goods, services, facilities, privileges, advantages, and accommodations of any place of public accommodation, as defined in this section, without discrimination or segregation on the ground of race, color, religion, or national origin.

(b) Each of the following establishments which serves the public is a place of public accommodation within the meaning of this title if its operations affect commerce, or if discrimination or segregation by it is supported by State action:

1. any inn, hotel, motel, or other establishment which provides lodging to transient guests, other than an establishment located within a building which contains not more than five rooms for rent or hire and

which is actually occupied by the proprietor of such establishment as his residence;

2. any restaurant, cafeteria, lunchroom, lunch counter, soda fountain, other facility principally engaged in selling food for consumption on the premises, including but not limited to, any such facility located on the premises of any retail establishment; or any gasoline station;

3. any motion picture house, theater, concert hall, sports arena, stadium or other place exhibition or entertainment; and

4. any establishment (A)(i) which is physically located within the premises of any establishment otherwise covered by this subsection, or (ii) within the premises of which is physically located any such covered establishment, and (B) which holds itself out as serving patrons of such covered establishment.

(c) The operations of an establishment affect commerce within the meaning of this title if (1) it is one of the establishments described in paragraph (1) of subsection (b); (2) in the case of an establishment described in paragraph (2) of subsection (b), it serves or offers to serve interstate travelers or a substantial portion of the food which it serves, or gasoline or other products which it sells, has moved in commerce; (3) in the case of an establishment described in paragraph (3) of subsection (b), it customarily presents films, performances, athletic teams, exhibitions, or other sources of entertainment which move in commerce; and (4) in the case of an establishment described in paragraph (4) of subsection (b), it is physically located within the premises of, or there is physically located within its premises, an establishment the operations of which affect commerce within the meaning of this subsection. For purposes of this section, "commerce" means travel, trade, traffic, commerce, transportation, or communication among the several States, or between the District of Columbia and any State, or between any foreign country or any territory or possession and any State or the District of Columbia, or between points in the same State but through any other State or the District of Columbia or a foreign country.

(d) Discrimination or segregation by an establishment is supported by State action within the meaning of this title if such discrimination or segregation (1) is carried on under color of any law, statute, ordinance, or regulation; or (2) is carried on under color of any custom or usage required or enforced by officials of the State or political subdivision thereof; or (3) is required by action of the State or political subdivision thereof.

(e) The provisions of this title shall not apply to private club or other establishment not in fact open to the public, except to the extent that the facilities of such establishment are made available to the customers or patrons of an establishment within the scope of subsection (b).

Section 202.

All persons shall be entitled to be free, at any establishment or place, from discrimination or segregation of any kind on the ground of race, color, religion, or national origin, if such discrimination or segregation is or purports to be required by any law, statute, ordinance, regulation, rule, or order of a State or any agency or political subdivision thereof.

Section 203.

No person shall (a) withhold, deny, or attempt to withhold or deny, or deprive or attempt to deprive, any person of any right or privilege secured by section 201 or 202, or (b) intimidate, threaten, or coerce, or attempt to intimidate, threaten, or coerce any person with the purpose of interfering with any right or privilege secured by section 201 or 202, or (c) punish or attempt to punish any person for exercising or attempting to exercise any right or privilege secured by section 201 or 202.

Section 204.

(a) Whenever any person has engaged or there are reasonable grounds to believe that any person is about to engage in any act or practice prohibited by section 203, a civil action for preventive relief, including an application for a permanent or temporary injunction, restraining order, or other order, may be instituted by the person aggrieved and, upon timely application, the court may, in its discretion, permit the Attorney General to intervene in such civil action if he certifies that the case is of general public importance. Upon application by the complainant and in such circumstances as the court may deem just, the court may appoint an attorney for such complainant, and may authorize the commencement of the civil action without the payment of fees, costs, or security. . . .

Section 206.

(a) Whenever the Attorney General has reasonable cause to believe that any persons or group of persons is engaged in a pattern or practice of resistance to the full enjoyment of any of the rights secured by this title, and that the pattern or practice is of such a nature and is intended to deny the full exercise of the rights herein described, the Attorney General may bring a civil action in the appropriate district court of the United States by filing with it a complaint (1) signed by him (or in his absence the Acting Attorney General), (2) setting forth facts pertaining to such pattern or practice, and (3) requesting such preventive relief, including an application for a permanent or temporary injunction, restraining order or other order against the person or persons responsible for such pattern or practice, as he deems necessary to insure the full enjoyment of the rights herein described. . . .

TITLE III—DESEGREGATION OF PUBLIC FACILITIES

Section 301.

(a) Whenever the Attorney General receives a complaint in writing signed by an individual to the effect that he is being deprived of or threatened with the loss of his right to the equal protection of the laws, on account of his race, color, religion, or national origin, by being denied equal utilization of any public facility, which is owned, operated, or managed by or on behalf of any State or subdivision thereof, other than a public school or public college as defined in section 401 of title IV hereof, and the Attorney General believes the complaint is meritorious and certifies that the signer or signers of such complaint are unable, in his judgment, to initiate and maintain appropriate legal proceedings for relief and that the institution of an action will materially further the orderly progress of desegregation in public facilities, the Attorney General is authorized to institute for or in the name of the United States a civil action in any appropriate district court of the United States against such parties and for such relief as may be appropriate, and such court shall have and shall exercise jurisdiction of proceedings instituted pursuant to this section. The Attorney General may implead as defendants such additional parties as are or become necessary to the grant of effective relief hereunder.

(b) The Attorney General may deem a person or persons unable to initiate and maintain appropriate legal proceedings within the meaning of subsection (a) of this section when such person or persons are unable, either directly or through other interested persons or organizations, to bear the expense of the litigation or to obtain effective legal representation; or whenever he is satisfied that the institution of such litigation would jeopardize the personal safety, employment, or economic standing of such person or persons, their families, or their property. . . .

TITLE IV—DESEGREGATION OF PUBLIC EDUCATION

DEFINITIONS

Section 401.

As used in this title—

(a) "Commissioner" means the Commissioner of Education.

(b) "Desegregation" means the assignment of students to public schools and within such schools without regard to their race, color, religion, sex or national origin, but "desegregation" shall not mean the assignment of students to public schools in order to overcome racial imbalance.

(c) "Public school" means any elementary or secondary educational institution, and "public college" means any institution of higher education or any technical or vocational school above the secondary school level, provided that such public school or public college is operated by a State, subdivision of a State, or governmental agency within a State, or operated wholly or predominantly from or through the use of governmental funds or property, or funds or property derived from a governmental source.

(d) "School board" means any agency or agencies which administer a system of one or more public schools and any other agency which is responsible for the assignment of students to or within such system. . . .

Technical Assistance

Section 403.

The Commissioner is authorized, upon the application of any school board, State, municipality, school district, or other governmental unit legally responsible for operating a public school or schools, to render technical assistance to such applicant in the preparation, adoption, and implementation of plans for the desegregation of public schools. Such technical assistance may, among other activities, include making available to such agencies information regarding effective methods of coping with special educational problems occasioned by desegregation, and making available to such agencies personnel of the Office of Education or other persons specially equipped to advise and assist them in coping with such problems. . . .

Grants

Section 405.

(a) The Comissioner is authorized, upon application of a school board, to make grants to such board to pay, in whole or in part, the cost of—

4. giving to teachers and other school personnel inservice training in dealing with problems incident to desegregation, and

5. employing specialists to advise in problems incident to desegregation.

(b) In determining whether to make a grant, and in fixing the amount thereof and the terms and conditions on which it will be made, the Commissioner shall take into consideration the amount available for grants under this section and the other applications which are pending before him; the financial condition of the applicant and the other resources available to it; the nature, extent, and gravity of its problems incident to desegregation; and such other factors as he finds relevant. . . .

TITLE VI—NONDISCRIMINATION IN FEDERALLY ASSISTED PROGRAMS

Section 601.

No person in the United States shall, on the ground of race, color, or national origin, be excluded from participation in, be denied the benefits of, or be subjected to discrimination under any program or activity receiving Federal financial assistance.

Section 602.

Each Federal department and agency which is empowered to extend Federal financial assistance to any program or activity, by way of grant, loan, or contract other than a contract of insurance or guaranty, is authorized and directed to effectuate the provisions of section 601 with respect to such program or activity by issuing rules, regulations, or orders of general applicability which shall be consistent with achievement of the objectives of the statute authorizing the financial assistance in connection with which the action is taken. No such rule, regulation, or order shall become effective unless and until approved by the President. Compliance with any requirement adopted pursuant to this section may be effected (1) by the termination of or refusal to grant or to continue assistance under such program or activity to any recipient as to whom there has been an express finding on the record, after opportunity for hearing, of a failure to comply with such requirement, but such termination or refusal shall be limited to the particular political entity, or part thereof, or other recipient as to whom such a finding has been made and, shall be limited in its effect to the particular program, or part thereof, in which such noncompliance has been so found, or (2) by any other means authorized by law: *Provided, however,* That no such action shall be taken until the department or agency concerned has advised the appropriate person or persons of the failure to comply with the requirement and has determined that compliance cannot be secured by voluntary means. In the case of any action terminating, or refusing to grant or continue, assistance because of failure to comply with a requirement imposed pursuant to this section, the head of the Federal department or agency shall file with the committees of the House and Senate having legislative jurisdiction over the program or activity involved a full written report of the circumstances and the grounds for such action. No such action shall become effective until thirty days have elapsed after the filing of such report.

Section 603.

Any department or agency action taken pursuant to section 602 shall be subject to such judicial review as may otherwise be provided by law for similar action taken by such department or agency on other grounds. In the case of action, not otherwise subject to judicial review, terminating or refusing to grant or to continue financial assistance upon a finding of failure to comply with any requirement imposed pursuant to section 602, any person aggrieved (including any State or political subdivision thereof and any agency of either) may obtain judicial review of such action in accordance with section 10 of the Administrative Procedure Act, and such action shall not be deemed committed to unreviewable agency discretion within the meaning of that section. . . .

TITLE VII—EQUAL EMPLOYMENT OPPORTUNITY

* * *

Discrimination Because of Race, Color, Religion, Sex, or National Origin

Section 703.

(a) It shall be an unlawful employment practice for an employer—
1. to fail or refuse to hire or to discharge any individual, or otherwise to discriminate against any individual with respect to his compensation, terms, conditions, or privileges of employment, because of such individual's race, color, religion, sex, or national origin; or
2. to limit, segregate, or classify his employees or applicants for employment in any way which would deprive or tend to deprive any individual of employment opportunities or otherwise adversely affect his status as an employee, because of such individual's race, color, religion, sex, or national origin.

[Public Law 92–261]

(b) It shall be an unlawful employment practice for an employment agency to fail or refuse to refer for employment, or otherwise discriminate against, any individual because of his race, color, religion, sex, or national origin, or to classify or refer for employment any individual on the basis of his race, color, religion, sex, or national origin.

(c) It shall be an unlawful employment practice for a labor organization—

1. to exclude or to expel from its membership or applicants for membership, or otherwise to discriminate against, any individual because of his race, color, religion, sex, or national origin;

2. to limit, segregate, or classify its membership, or to classify or fail or refuse to refer for employment any individual, in any way which would deprive or tend to deprive any individual of employment opportunities, or would limit such employment opportunities or otherwise adversely affect his status as an employee or as an applicant for employment, because of such individual's race, color, religion, sex, or national origin; or

3. to cause or attempt to cause an employer to discriminate against an individual in violation of this section.

(d) It shall be an unlawful employment practice for any employer, labor organization, or joint labor-management committee controlling apprenticeship or other training or retraining, including on-the-job training programs to discriminate against any individual because of his race, color, religion, sex, or national origin in admission to, or employment in, any program established to provide apprenticeship or other training. . . .

Equal Employment Opportunity Commission

Section 705.

(a) There is hereby created a Commission to be known as the Equal Employment Opportunity Commission, which shall be composed of five members, not more than three of whom shall be members of the same political party. Members of the Commission shall be appointed by the President by and with the advice and consent of the Senate for a term of five years. Any individual chosen to fill a vacancy shall be appointed only for the unexpired term of the member whom he shall succeed, and all members of the Commission shall continue to serve until their successors are appointed and qualified, except that no such member of the Commission shall continue to serve (1) for more than sixty days when the Congress is in session unless a nomination to fill such vacancy shall have been submitted to the Senate, or (2) after the adjournment sine die of the session of the Senate in which such nomination was submitted. The President shall designate one member to serve as Chairman of the Commission, and one member to serve as Vice Chairman. The Chairman shall be responsible on behalf of the Commission for the administrative operations of the Commission, and, except as provided in subsection (b), shall appoint, in accordance with the provisions of title 5, United States Code, governing appointments in the competitive service, such officers, agents, attorneys, administrative law judges and employees as he deems necessary to assist it in the performance of its functions and to fix their compensation in accordance with the provisions of chapter 51 and subchapter III of chapter 53 of title 5,

United States Code, relating to classification and General Schedule pay rates: *Provided*, That assignment, removal, and compensation of administrative law judges shall be in accordance with sections 3105, 3344, 5362, and 7521 of title 5, United States Code. . . .

(g) The Commission shall have power—

1. to cooperate with, and, with their consent, utilize regional, State, local, and other agencies, both public and private, and individuals;

2. to pay to witnesses whose depositions are taken or who are summoned before the Commission or any of its agents the same witness and mileage fees as are paid to witnesses in the courts of the United States;

3. to furnish to persons subject to this title such technical assistance as they may request to further their compliance with this title or an order issued thereunder;

4. upon the request of (i) any employer, whose employees or some of them, or (ii) any labor organization, whose members or some of them, refuse or threaten to refuse to cooperate in effectuating the provisions of this title, to assist in such effectuation by conciliation or such other remedial action as is provided by this title;

5. to make such technical studies as are appropriate to effectuate the purposes and policies of this title and to make the results of such studies available to the public;

6. to intervene in a civil action brought under section 706 by an aggrieved party against a respondent other than a government, governmental agency or political subdivision. . . .

Prevention of Unlawful Employment Practices

Section 706.

(a) The Commission is empowered, as hereinafter provided, to prevent any person from engaging in any unlawful employment practice as set forth in section 703 or 704 of this title.

(b) Whenever a charge is filed by or on behalf of a person claiming to be aggrieved, or by a member of the Commission, alleging that an employer, employment agency, labor organization, or joint labor-management committee controlling apprenticeship or other training or retraining, including on-the-job training programs, has engaged in an unlawful employment practice, the Commission shall serve a notice of the charge (including the date, place and circumstances of the alleged unlawful employment practice) on such employer, employment agency, labor organization, or joint labor-management committee (hereinafter referred to as the "respondent") within ten days, and shall make an investigation thereof. Charges shall be in writing under oath or affirmation and shall contain such information and be in such form as the Commission requires. Charges shall not be made public by the Commission. If the Commission determines after such investigation that there is not reasonable cause to believe that the charge is true, it shall dismiss the charge and promptly notify the person claiming to be aggrieved and the respondent of its action. In determining whether reasonable cause exists, the Commission shall accord substantial weight to final findings and orders made by State or local authorities in proceedings commenced under State or local law pursuant to the requirements of subsections (c) and (d). If the Commission determines after such investigation that there is reasonable cause to believe that the charge is true, the Commission shall endeavor to eliminate any such alleged unlawful employment practice by informal methods of conference, conciliation, and persuasion. Nothing said or done during and as a part of such informal endeavors may be made public by the Commission, its officers or employees, or used as evidence in a subsequent proceeding without the written consent of the persons concerned. Any person who makes public information in violation of this subsection shall be fined not more than $1,000 or imprisoned for not more than one year, or both. The Commission shall make its determination on reasonable cause as promptly as possible and, so far as practicable, not later than one hundred and twenty days from the filing of the charge or, where applicable under subsection (c) or (d), from the date upon which the Commission is authorized to take action with respect to the charge. . . .

Section 707.

(a) Whenever the Attorney General has reasonable cause to believe that any person or group of persons is engaged in a pattern or practice of resistance to the full enjoyment of any of the rights secured by this title, and that the pattern or practice is of such a nature and is intended to deny the full exercise of the rights herein described, the Attorney General may bring a civil action in the appropriate district court of the United States by filing with it a complaint (1) signed by him (or in his absence the Acting Attorney General), (2) setting forth facts pertaining to such pattern or practice, and (3) requesting such relief, including an application for a permanent or temporary injunction, restraining order or other order against the person or persons responsible for such pattern or practice, as he deems necessary to insure the full enjoyment of the rights herein described. . . .

Effect on State Laws

Section 708.

Nothing in this title shall be deemed to exempt or relieve any person from any liability, duty, penalty, or punishment provided by any present or future law of any State or political subdivision of a State, other than any such law which purports to require or permit the doing of any act which would be an unlawful employment practice under this title.

Investigations, Inspections, Records, State Agencies

Section 709.

(a) In connection with any investigation of a charge filed under section 706, the Commission or its designated representative shall at all reasonable times have access to, for the purposes of examination, and the right to copy any evidence of any person being investigated or proceeded against that relates to unlawful employment practices covered by this title and is relevant to the charge under investigation. . . .

Veterans' Preference

Section 712.

Nothing contained in this title shall be construed to repeal or modify any Federal, State, territorial, or local law creating special rights or preference for veterans. . . .

Nondiscrimination in Federal Government Employment

Section 717.

(a) All personnel actions affecting employees or applicants for employment (except with regard to aliens employed outside the limits of the United States) in military departments as defined in section 102 of title 5, United States Code, in executive agencies (other than the General Accounting Office) as defined in section 105 of title 5, United States Code (including employees and applicants for employment who are paid from nonappropriated funds), in the United States Postal Service and the Postal Rate Commission, in those units of the Government of the District of Columbia having positions in the competitive service, and in those units of the legislative and judicial branches of the Federal Government having positions in the competitive service, and in the Library of Congress shall be made free from any discrimination based on race, color, religion, sex, or national origin. . . .

3. UNITED KINGDOM

INTRODUCTION

Britain's Race Relations Act of 1976 was passed during a period of racial confrontation and protest rivaling the urban unrest which spread through the United States in the 1960's. The approximately 1.7 million Blacks and Asians in the United Kingdom were living in largely inadequate housing, were subject to discriminatory treatment and police harassment and were the victims of the ever-widening gap between the salaries available for white and non-white co-workers.

Parliament had already responded to some of these problems with Race Relations Acts in 1965 and 1968, but these had proved inadequate. Decisions by the House of Lords—Britain's highest appellate court—had interpreted provisions of these acts narrowly. And, among other things, the new legislation was designed to reverse the effect of at least four prior judicial determinations.

The 1976 Race Relations Act provided for more effective enforcement machinery. But it went further than that. It made unlawful not only overt and deliberate discrimination, but also any conditions or requirements that in effect discriminate or are likely to discriminate against any particular racial group. This

indirect discrimination encompasses the imposition of a condition or requirement on a racial group with which few can comply. It also encompasses
victimization, i.e., treating a member of a particular racial group less favorably
than another person in the same circumstances.

In preparing this legislation, explains Anthony Lester, then Special Adviser
to the Secretary of State for the Home Department, "the British Government
was influenced by the way in which the concept of discrimination had been
developed by the United States Supreme Court in interpreting the Civil Rights
Act of 1964."[151]

Unlawful discrimination now applies to nationality as well as race. And the
scope of discrimination now covers contract workers, partnerships and clubs
with 25 or more members.

The Act created a new administrative board, the Commission for Racial
Equality, which replaced both the Race Relations Board and the Community
Relations Commission. The new commission has new powers and functions; its
duties include working towards elimination of discrimination, promoting equality of opportunity and good relations between different racial groups, and
keeping under review the workings of the Act. The new commission is
authorized to give direct assistance to complainants. It can also issue non-
discrimination notices and seek injunctions to stop persistent discrimination.[152]

RACE RELATIONS ACT 1976 CHAPTER 74 [EXERPTED]

An Act to make fresh provision with respect to discrimination on
racial grounds and relations between people of different racial groups;
and to make in the Sex Discrimination Act 1975 amendments for
bringing provisions in that Act relating to its administration and
enforcement into conformity with the corresponding provisions in this
Act. [22nd November 1976]

Be it enacted by the Queen's most Excellent Majesty, by and with the
advice and consent of the Lords Spiritual and Temporal, and Commons, in this present Parliament assembled, and by the authority of
the same, as follows:—

PART I

DISCRIMINATION TO WHICH ACT APPLIES

1. Racial Discrimination.

(1) A person discriminates against another in any circumstances relevant for
the purposes of any provision of this Act if
a. on racial grounds he treats that other less favourably than he
treats or would treat other persons; or
b. he applies to that other a requirement or condition which he
applies or would apply equally to persons not of the same racial group
as that other but—
i. which is such that the proportion of persons of the same racial

group as that other who can comply with it is considerably smaller than the proportion of persons not of that racial group who can comply with it: and

ii. which he cannot show to be justifiable irrespective of the colour race, nationality or ethnic or national origins of the person to whom it is applied: and

iii. which is to the detriment of that other because he cannot comply with it.

(2) It is hereby declared that, for the purposes of this Act, segregating a person from other persons on racial grounds is treating him less favourably than they are treated.

2. Discrimination by Way of Victimisation.

(1) A person ("the discriminator") discriminates against another person ("the person victimised") in any circumstances relevant for the purposes of any provision of this Act if he treats the person victimised less favourably than in those circumstances he treats or would treat other persons, and does so by reason that the person victimised has—

a. brought proceedings against the discriminator or any other person under this Act; or

b. given evidence or information in connection with proceedings brought by any person against the discriminator or any other person under this Act; or

c. otherwise done anything under or by reference to this Act in relation to the discriminator or any other person; or

d. alleged that the discriminator or any other person has committed an act which (whether or not the allegation so states) would amount to a contravention of this Act,

or by reason that the discriminator knows that the person victimised intends to do any of those things, or suspects that the person victimised has done, or intends to do, any of them.

(2) Subsection (1) does not apply to treatment of a person by reason of any allegation made by him if the allegation was false and not made in good faith.

3. Meaning of "Racial Grounds" "Racial Group" Etc.

(1) In this Act, unless the context otherwise requires—"racial grounds" means any of the following grounds, namely colour, race, nationality or ethnic or national origins;

"racial group" means a group of persons defined by reference to colour, race, nationality or ethnic or national origins, and references to a person's racial group refer to any racial group into which he falls.

(2) The fact that a racial group comprises two or more distinct racial groups does not prevent it from constituting a particular racial group for the purposes of this Act.

(3) In this Act—

a. references to discrimination refer to any discrimination falling within section 1 or 2; and

b. references to racial discrimination refer to any discrimination falling within section 1,
and related expressions shall be construed accordingly.

(4) A comparison of the case of a person of a particular racial group with that of a person not of that group under section 1(1) must be such that the relevant circumstances in the one case are the same, or not materially different, in the other.

PART II

DISCRIMINATION IN THE EMPLOYMENT FIELD

Discrimination by employers

4. Discrimination Against Applicants and Employees.

(1) It is unlawful for a person, in relation to employment by him at an establishment in Great Britain, to discriminate against another—
a. in the arrangements he makes for the purpose of determining who should be offered that employment; or
b. in the terms on which he offers him that employment: or
c. by refusing or deliberately omitting to offer him that employment.

(2) It is unlawful for a person, in the case of a person employed by him at an establishment in Great Britain, to discriminate against that employee—
a. in the terms of employment which he affords him; or
b. in the way he affords him access to opportunities for promotion, transfer or training, or to any other benefits, facilities or services, or by refusing or deliberately omitting to afford him access to them; or
c. by dismissing him, or subjecting him to any other detriment.

(3) Except in relation to discrimination falling within section 2, subsections (1) and (2) do not apply to employment for the purposes of a private household.

(4) Subsection (2) does not apply to benefits, facilities or services of any description if the employer is concerned with the provision (for payment or not) of benefits, facilities or services of that description to the public, or to a section of the public comprising the employee in question, unless—
a. that provision differs in a material respect from the provision of the benefits, facilities or services by the employer to his employees; or
b. the provision of the benefits, facilities or services to the employee in question is regulated by his contract of employment; or
c. the benefits, facilities or services relate to training.

5. Exceptions for Genuine Occupational Qualifications.

(1) In relation to racial discrimination—
a. section 4(1)(*a*) or (*c*) does not apply to any employment where being of a particular racial group is a genuine occupational qualification for the job; and
b. section 4(2)(*b*) does not apply to opportunities for promotion or transfer to, or training for, such employment.

(2) Being of a particular racial group is a genuine occupational qualification for a job only where—

    a. the job involves participation in a dramatic performance or other entertainment in a capacity for which a person of that racial group is required for reasons of authenticity; or

    b. the job involves participation as an artist's or photographic model in the production of a work of art, visual image or sequence of visual images for which a person of that racial group is required for reasons of authenticity; or

    c. the job involves working in a place where food or drink is (for payment or not) provided to and consumed by members of the public or a section of the public in a particular setting for which, in the job, a person of that racial group is required for reasons of authenticity; or

    d. the holder of the job provides persons of that racial group with personal services promoting their welfare, and those services can most effectively be provided by a person of that racial group.

(3) Subsection (2) applies where some only of the duties of the job fall within paragraph (*a*), (*b*), (*c*) or (*d*) as well as where all of them do.

(4) Paragraph (*a*), (*b*), (*c*) or (*d*) of subsection (2) does not apply in relation to the filling of a vacancy at a time when the employer already has employees of the racial group in question—

    a. who are capable of carrying out the duties falling within that paragraph; and

    b. whom it would be reasonable to employ on those duties; and

    c. whose numbers are sufficient to meet the employer's likely requirements in respect of those duties without undue inconvenience.

6. Exception for Employment Intended to Provide Training in Skills to be Exercised Outside Great Britain.

Nothing in section 4 shall render unlawful any act done by an employer for the benefit of a person not ordinarily resident in Great Britain in or in connection with employing him at an establishment in Great Britain, where the purpose of that employment is to provide him with training in skills which he appears to the employer to intend to exercise wholly outside Great Britain.

7. Discrimination Against Contract Workers.

(1) This section applies to any work for a person ("the principal") which is available for doing by individuals ("contract workers") who are employed not by the principal himself but by another person, who supplies them under a contract made with the principal.

(2) It is unlawful for the principal, in relation to work to which this section applies, to discriminate against a contract worker—

    a. in the terms on which he allows him to do that work; or

    b. by not allowing him to do it or continue to do it; or

    c. in the way he affords him access to any benefits, facilities or services or by refusing or deliberately omitting to afford him access to them; or

d. by subjecting him to any other detriment.

(3) The principal does not contravene subsection (2)(*b*) by doing any act in relation to a person not of a particular racial group at a time when, if the work were to be done by a person taken into the principal's employment, being of that racial group would be a genuine occupational qualification for the job.

(4) Nothing in this section shall render unlawful any act done by the principal for the benefit of a contract worker not ordinarily resident in Great Britain in or in connection with allowing him to do work to which this section applies, where the purpose of his being allowed to do that work is to provide him with training in skills which he appears to the principal to intend to exercise wholly outside Great Britain.

(5) Subsection (2)(*c*) does not apply to benefits, facilities or services of any description if the principal is concerned with the provision (for payment or not) of benefits, facilities or services of that description to the public, or to a section of the public to which the contract worker in question belongs, unless that provision differs in a material respect from the provision of the benefits, facilities or services by the principal to his contract workers. . . .

Discrimination by Other Bodies

10. Partnerships.

(1) It is unlawful for a firm consisting of six or more partners, in relation to a position as partner in the firm, to discriminate against a person—

> a. in the arrangements they make for the purpose of determining who should be offered that position; or
>
> b. in the terms on which they offer him that position; or
>
> c. by refusing or deliberately omitting to offer him that position; or
>
> d. in a case where the person already holds that position—
>> i. in the way they afford him access to any benefits, facilities, or services, or by refusing or deliberately omitting to afford him access to them; or
>>
>> ii. by expelling him from that position, or subjecting him to any other detriment.

(2) Subsection (1) shall apply in relation to persons proposing to form themselves into a partnership as it applies in relation to a firm.

(3) Subsection (1)(*a*) and (*c*) do not apply to a position as partner where, if it were employment, being of a particular racial group would be a genuine occupational qualification for the job.

(4) In the case of a limited partnership references in this section to a partner shall be construed as references to a general partner as defined in section 3 of the Limited Partnerships Act 1907.

11. 1907 c. 24.

Trade unions etc.

(1) This section applies to an organisation of workers, an organisation of employers, or any other organisation whose members carry on a particular profession or trade for the purposes of which the organisation exists.

(2) It is unlawful for an organisation to which this section applies, in the case of a person who is not a member of the organisation, to discriminate against him—

a. in the terms on which it is prepared to admit him to membership; or

b. by refusing, or deliberately omitting to accept, his application for membership.

(3) It is unlawful for an organisation to which this section applies, in the case of a person who is a member of the organisation, to discriminate against him—

a. in the way it affords him access to any benefits, facilities or services, or by refusing or deliberately omitting to afford him access to them; or

b. by depriving him of membership, or varying the terms on which he is a member; or

c. by subjecting him to any other detriment. . . .

Police

16.

(1) For the purposes of this Part, the holding of the office of constable shall be treated as employment—

a. by the chief officer of police as respects any act done by him in relation to a constable or that office;

b. by the police authority as respects any act done by them in relation to a constable or that office.

(2) There shall be paid out of the police fund—

a. any compensation, costs or expenses awarded against a chief officer of police in any proceedings brought against him under this Act, and any costs or expenses incurred by him in any such proceedings so far as not recovered by him in the proceedings; and

b. any sum required by a chief officer of police for the settlement of any claim made against him under this Act if the settlement is approved by the police authority.

(3) Any proceedings under this Act which, by virtue of subsection (1), would lie against a chief officer of police shall be brought against the chief officer of police for the time being or, in the case of a vacancy in that office, against the person for the time being performing the functions of that office; and references in subsection (2) to the chief officer of police shall be construed accordingly.

(4) Subsection (1) applies to a police cadet and appointment a police cadet as it applies to a constable and the office of constable.

(5) In this section—"chief officer of police"—

a. in relation to a person appointed, or an appointment falling to be made, under a specified Act, has the same meaning as in the Police Act,

b. in relation to any other person or appointment, means the officer who has the direction and control of the body of constables or cadets in question;

1964 c. 48. 1967 c. 77.

"the Police Act" means, for England and Wales, the Police Act 1964 or, for Scotland, the Police (Scotland) Act 1967;
"police authority"—
a. in relation to a person appointed, or an appointment falling to be made, under a specified Act, has the same meaning as in the Police Act,
b. in relation to any other person or appointment, means the authority by whom the person in question is or on appointment would be paid;
"police cadet" means any person appointed to undergo training with a view to becoming a constable;
"police fund" in relation to a chief officer of police within paragraph (*a*) of the above definition of that term has the same meaning as in the Police Act, and in any other case means money provided by the police authority;

1829 c. 44. 1839 c. xciv.

"specified Act" means the Metropolitan Police Act 1829, the City of London Police Act 1839 or the Police Act.

PART III

DISCRIMINATION IN OTHER FIELDS

Education

17. *Discrimination by Bodies in Charge of Educational Establishments.*

It is unlawful, in relation to an educational establishment falling within column 1 of the following table, for a person indicated in relation to the establishment in column 2 (the "responsible body") to discriminate against a person—
a. in the terms on which it offers to admit him to the establishment as a pupil; or
b. by refusing or deliberately omitting to accept an application for his admission to the establishment as a pupil; or
c. where he is a pupil of the establishment—
i. in the way it affords him access to any benefits, facilities or services, or by refusing or deliberately omitting to afford him access to them; or
ii. by excluding him from the establishment or subjecting him to any other detriment. . . .

Goods, Facilities, Services and Premises

20. *Discrimination in Provision of Goods, Facilities or Services.*

(1) It is unlawful for any person concerned with the provision (for payment or not) of goods, facilities or services to the public or a section of the public to

discriminate against a person who seeks to obtain or use those goods, facilities or services—

a. by refusing or deliberately omitting to provide him with any of them; or

b. by refusing or deliberately omitting to provide him with goods, facilities or services of the like quality, in the like manner and on the like terms as are normal in the first-mentioned person's case in relation to other members of the public or (where the person so seeking belongs to a section of the public) to other members of that section.

(2) The following are examples of the facilities and services mentioned in subsection (1)—

a. access to and use of any place which members of the public are permitted to enter;

b. accommodation in a hotel, boarding house or other similar establishment;

c. facilities by way of banking or insurance or for grants, loans, credit or finance;

d. facilities for education;

e. facilities for entertainment, recreation or refreshment;

f. facilities for transport or travel;

g. the services of any profession or trade, or any local or other public authority.

21. Discrimination in Disposal or Management of Premises.

(1) It is unlawful for a person, in relation to premises in Great Britain of which he has power to dispose, to discriminate against another—

a. in the terms on which he offers him those premises; or

b. by refusing his application for those premises; or

c. in his treatment of him in relation to any list of persons in need of premises of that description.

(2) It is unlawful for a person, in relation to premises managed by him, to discriminate against a person occupying the premises—

a. in the way he affords him access to any benefits or facilities, or by refusing or deliberately omitting to afford him access to them; or

b. by evicting him, or subjecting him to any other detriment.

(3) Subsection (1) does not apply to a person who owns an estate or interest in the premises and wholly occupies them unless he uses the services of an estate agent for the purposes of the disposal of the premises, or publishes or causes to be published an advertisement in connection with the disposal.

22. Exception from ss. 20(1) and 21: small dwellings.

(1) Sections 20(1) and 21 do not apply to the provision by a person of accommodation in any premises, or the disposal of premises by him, if—

a. that person or a near relative of his ("the relevant occupier") resides, and intends to continue to reside, on the premises; and

b. there is on the premises, in addition to the accommodation occupied by the relevant occupier, accommodation (not being storage accommodation or means of access) shared by the relevant occupier with other persons residing on the premises who are not members of his household; and

    c. the premises are small premises.

(2) Premises shall be treated for the purposes of this section as small premises if—

    a. in the case of premises comprising residential accommodation for one or more households (under separate letting or similar agreements) in addition to the accommodation occupied by the relevant occupier, there is not normally residential accommodation for more than two such households and only the relevant occupier and any member of his household reside in the accommodation occupied by him;

    b. in the case of premises not falling within paragraph (*a*), there is not normally residential accommodation on the premises for more than six persons in addition to the relevant occupier and any members of his household.

23. Further Exceptions from ss. 20(1) and 21.

(1) Sections 20(1) and 21 do not apply—

    a. to discrimination which is rendered unlawful by any provision of Part II or section 17 or 18; or

    b. to discrimination which would be rendered unlawful by any provision of Part II but for any of the following provisions, namely sections 4(3), 5(1)(*b*), 6, 7(4), 9 and 14(4).

(2) Section 20(1) does not apply to anything done by a person as a participant in arrangements under which he (for reward or not) takes into his home, and treats as if they were members of his family, children, elderly persons, or persons requiring a special degree of care and attention.

24. Discrimination: Consent for Assignment of Sub-Letting.

(1) Where the licence or consent of the landlord or of any other person is required for the disposal to any person of premises in Great Britain comprised in a tenancy, it is unlawful for the landlord or other person to discriminate against a person by withholding the licence or consent for disposal of the premises to him.

(2) Subsection (1) does not apply if—

    a. the person withholding a licence or consent, or a near relative of his ("the relevant occupier") resides, and intends to continue to reside, on the premises; and

    b. there is on the premises, in addition to the accommodation occupied by the relevant occupier, accommodation (not being storage accommodation or means of access) shared by the relevant occupier with other persons residing on the premises who are not members of his household; and

    c. the premises are small premises.

(3) Section 22(2) (meaning of "small premises") shall apply for the purposes of this as well as of that section.

(4) In this section "tenancy" means a tenancy created by a lease or sub-lease, by an agreement for a lease or sub-lease or by a tenancy agreement or in pursuance of any enactment; and "disposal", in relation to premises comprised in a tenancy, includes assignment or assignation of the tenancy and sub-letting or parting with possession of the premises or any part of the premises.

(5) This section applies to tenancies created before the passing of this Act, as well as to others.

25. Discrimination: Associations Not Within s. 11.

(1) This section applies to any association of persons (however described, whether corporate or unincorporate, and whether or not its activities are carried on for profit) if—

a. it has twenty-five or more members; and

b. admission to membership is regulated by its constitution and is so conducted that the members do not constitute a section of the public within the meaning of section 20(1); and

c. it is not an organisation to which section 11 applies.

(2) It is unlawful for an association to which this section applies, in the case of a person who is not a member of the association, to discriminate against him—

a. in the terms on which it is prepared to admit him to membership; or

b. by refusing or deliberately omitting to accept his application for membership.

(3) It is unlawful for an association to which this section applies, in the case of person who is a member or associate of the association, to discriminate against him—

a. in the way it affords him access to any benefits, facilities or services, or by refusing or deliberately omitting to afford him access to them; or

b. in the case of a member, by depriving him of membership, or varying the terms on which he is a member; or

c. in the case of an associate, by depriving him of his rights as an associate, or varying those rights; or

d. in either case, by subjecting him to any other detriment.

(4) For the purposes of this section—

a. a person is a member of an association if he belongs to it by virtue of his admission to any sort of membership provided for by its constitution (and is not merely a person with certain rights under its constitution by virtue of his membership of some other association), and references to membership of an association shall be construed accordingly;

b. a person is an associate of an association to which this section applies if, not being a member of it, he has under its constitution some or all of the rights enjoyed by members (or would have apart from any provision in its constitution authorising the refusal of those rights in particular cases).

26. *Exception From s. 25 for Certain Associations.*

(1) An association to which section 25 applies is within this subsection if the main object of the association is to enable the benefits of membership (whatever they may be) to be enjoyed by persons of a particular racial group defined otherwise than by reference to colour; and in determining whether that is the main object of an association regard shall be had to the essential character of the association and to all relevant circumstances including, in particular, the extent to which the affairs of the association are so conducted that the persons primarily enjoying the benefits of membership are of the racial group in question.

(2) In the case of an association within subsection (1), nothing in section 25 shall render unlawful any act not involving discrimination on the ground of colour. . . .

PART IV

OTHER UNLAWFUL ACTS

28. *Discriminatory Practices.*

(1) In this section "discriminatory practice" means the application of a requirement or condition which results in an act of discrimination which is unlawful by virtue of any provision of Part II or III taken with section 1(1)(*b*), or which would be likely to result in such an act of discrimination if the persons to whom it is applied included persons of any particular racial group as regards which there has been no occasion for applying it.

(2) A person acts in contravention of this section if and so long as—
    a. he applies a discriminatory practice; or
    b. he operates practices or other arrangements which in any circumstances would call for the application by him of a discriminatory practice.

(3) Proceedings in respect of a contravention of this section shall be brought only by the Commission in accordance with sections 58 to 62.

29. *Discriminatory Advertisements.*

(1) It is unlawful to publish or to cause to be published an advertisement which indicates, or might reasonably be understood as indicating, an intention by a person to do an act of discrimination, whether the doing of that act by him would be lawful or, by virtue of Part II or III, unlawful.

(2) Subsection (1) does not apply to an advertisement—
    a. if the intended act would be lawful by virtue of any of sections 5, 6, 7(3) and (4), 10(3), 26, 34(2)(*b*), 35 to 39 and 41; or
    b. if the advertisement relates to the services of an employment agency (within the meaning of section 14(1)) and the intended act only concerns employment which the employer could by virtue of section 5,

6 or 7(3) or (4) lawfully refuse to offer to persons against whom the advertisement indicates an intention to discriminate.

(3) Subsection (1) does not apply to an advertisement which indicates that persons of any class defined otherwise than by reference to colour, race or ethnic or national origins are required for employment outside Great Britain.

(4) The publisher of an advertisement made unlawful by subsection (1) shall not be subject to any liability under that subsection in respect of the publication of the advertisement if he proves—

    a. that the advertisement was published in reliance on a statement made to him by the person who caused it to be published to the effect that, by reason of the operation of subsection (2) or (3), the publication would not be unlawful; and

    b. that it was reasonable for him to rely on the statement.

(5) A person who knowingly or recklessly makes a statement such as is mentioned in subsection (4)(*a*) which in a material respect is false or misleading commits an offence, and shall be liable on summary conviction to a fine not exceeding £400.

30. Instructions to Discriminate.

It is unlawful for a person—

    a. who has authority over another person; or

    b. in accordance with whose wishes that other person is accustomed to act,

to instruct him to do any act which is unlawful by virtue of Part II or III, or procure or attempt to procure the doing by him of any such act.

31. Pressure to Discriminate.

(1) It is unlawful to induce, or attempt to induce, a person to do any act which contravenes Part II or III.

(2) An attempted inducement is not prevented from falling within subsection (1) because it is not made directly to the person in question, if it is made in such a way that he is likely to hear of it.

32. Liability of Employers and Principals.

(1) Anything done by a person in the course of his employment shall be treated for the purposes of this Act (except as regards offences thereunder) as done by his employer as well as by him, whether or not it was done with the employer's knowledge or approval.

(2) Anything done by a person as agent for another person with the authority (whether express or implied, and whether precedent or subsequent) of that other person shall be treated for the purposes of this Act (except as regards offences thereunder) as done by that other person as well as by him.

(3) In proceedings brought under this Act against any person in respect of an act alleged to have been done by an employee of his it shall be a defence for that person to prove that he took such steps as were reasonably practicable to prevent the employee from doing that act, or from doing in the course of his employment acts of that description.

33. Aiding Unlawful Acts.

(1) A person who knowingly aids another person to do an act made unlawful by this Act shall be treated for the purposes of this Act as himself doing an unlawful act of the like description.

(2) For the purposes of subsection (1) an employee or agent for whose act the employer or principal is liable under section 32 (or would be so liable but for section 32(3)) shall be deemed to aid the doing of the act by the employer or principal.

(3) A person does not under this section knowingly aid another to do an unlawful act if—

a. he acts in reliance on a statement made to him by that other person that, by reason of any provision of this Act, the act which he aids would not be unlawful; and

b. it is reasonable for him to rely on the statement.

(4) A person who knowingly or recklessly makes a statement such as is mentioned in subsection (3)(*a*) which in a material respect is false or misleading commits an offence, and shall be liable on summary conviction to a fine not exceeding £400.

PART V

CHARITIES

34. Charities.

(1) A provision which is contained in a charitable instrument (whenever that instrument took or takes effect) and which provides for conferring benefits on persons of a class defined by reference to colour shall have effect for all purposes as if it provided for conferring the like benefits—

a. on persons of the class which results if the restriction by reference to colour is disregarded; or

b. where the original class is defined by reference to colour only, on persons generally;

but nothing in this subsections shall be taken to alter the effect of any provision as regards any time before the coming into operation of this subsection.

(2) Nothing in Parts II to IV shall—

a. be construed as affecting a provision to which this subsection applies; or

b. render unlawful an act which is done in order to give effect to such a provision.

(3) Subsection (2) applies to any provision which is contained in a charitable instrument (whenever that instrument took or takes effect) and which provides for conferring benefits on persons of a class defined otherwise than by reference to colour (including a class resulting from the operation of subsection (1)).

(4) In this section "charitable instrument" means an enactment or other instrument passed or made for charitable purposes, or an enactment or other

instrument so far as it relates to charitable purposes, and in Scotland includes the governing instrument of an endowment or of an educational endowment as those expressions are defined in section 135(1) of the Education (Scotland) Act 1962.

1962 c. 47.

In the application of this section to England and Wales, "charitable purposes" means purposes which are exclusively charitable according to the law of England and Wales.

PART VI

GENERAL EXCEPTIONS FROM PARTS II TO IV

35. Special Needs of Racial Groups in Regard to Education, Training or Welfare.

Nothing in Parts II to IV shall render unlawful any act done in affording persons of a particular racial group access to facilities or services to meet the special needs of persons of that group in regard to their education, training or welfare, or any ancillary benefits.

36. Provision of Education or Training for Persons not Ordinarily Resident in Great Britain.

Nothing in Parts II to IV shall render unlawful any act done by a person for the benefit of persons not ordinarily resident in Great Britain in affording them access to facilities for education or training or any ancillary benefits, where it appears to him that the persons in question do not intend to remain in Great Britain after their period of education or training there.

37. Discriminatory Training by Certain Bodies.

(1) Nothing in Parts II to IV shall render unlawful any act done in relation to particular work by a training body in or in connection with—
    a. affording only persons of a particular racial group access to facilities for training which would help to fit them for that work; or
    b. encouraging only persons of a particular racial group to take advantage of opportunities for doing that work,
where it appears to the training body that at any time within the twelve months immediately preceding the doing of the act—
    i. there were no persons of that group among those doing that work in Great Britain; or
    ii. the proportion of persons of that group among those doing that work in Great Britain was small in comparison with the proportion of persons of that group among the population of Great Britain.
(2) Where in relation to particular work it appears to a training body that although the condition for the operation of subsection (1) is not met for the whole of Great Britain it is met for an area within Great Britain, nothing in Parts

II to IV shall render unlawful any act done by the training body in or in connection with—

a. affording persons who are of the racial group in question, and who appear likely to take up that work in that area, access to facilities for training which would help to fit them for that work; or

b. encouraging persons of that group to take advantage of opportunities in the area for doing that work.

(3) In this section "training body' means—

a. a person mentioned in section 13(2)(*a*) or (*b*); or

b. any other person being a person designated for the purposes of this section in an order made by the Secretary of State.

38. *Other Discriminatory Training Etc.*

(1) Nothing in Parts II to IV shall render unlawful any act done by an employer in relation to particular work in his employment at a particular establishment in Great Britain, being an act done in or in connection with—

a. affording only those of his employees working at that establishment who are of a particular racial group access to facilities for training which would help to fit them for that work; or

b. encouraging only persons of a particular racial group to take advantage of opportunities for doing that work at that establishment.

where any of the conditions in subsection (2) was satisfied at any time within the twelve months immediately preceding the doing of the act.

(2) Those conditions are—

a. that there are no persons of the racial group in question among those doing that work at that establishment; or

b. that the proportion of persons of that group among those doing that work at that establishment is small in comparison with the proportion of persons of that group—

   i. among all those employed by that employer there; or

   ii. among the population of the area from which that employer normally recruits persons for work in his employment at that establishment.

(3) Nothing in section 11 shall render unlawful any act done by an organisation to which that section applies in or in connection with—

a. affording only members of the organisation who are of a particular racial group access to facilities for training which would help to fit them for holding a post of any kind in the organisation; or

b. encouraging only members of the organisation who are of a particular racial group to take advantage of opportunities for holding such posts in the organisation,

where either of the conditions in subsection (4) was satisfied at any time within the twelve months immediately preceding the doing of the act.

(4) Those conditions are—

a. that there are no persons of the racial group in question among persons holding such posts in that organisation; or

b. that the proportion of persons of that group among those holding such posts in that organisation is small in comparison with the proportion of persons of that group among the members of the organisation.

(5) Nothing in Parts II to IV shall render unlawful any act done by an organisation to which section 11 applies in or in connection with encouraging only persons of a particular racial group to become members of the organisation where at any time within the twelve months immediately preceding the doing of the act—

    a. no persons of that group were members of the organisation; or

    b. the proportion of persons of that group among members of the organisation was small in comparison with the proportion of persons of that group among those eligible for membership of the organisation.

(6) Section 8 (meaning of employment at establishment in Great Britain) shall apply for the purposes of this section as if this section were contained in Part II.

39. *Sports and Competitions.*

Nothing in Parts II to IV shall render unlawful any act whereby a person discriminates against another on the basis of that other's nationality or place of birth or the length of time for which he has been resident in a particular area or place, if the act is done—

    a. in selecting one or more persons to represent a country, place or area, or any related association, in any sport or game; or

    b. in pursuance of the rules of any competition so far as they relate to eligibility to compete in any sport or game.

40. *Indirect Access to Benefits Etc.*

(1) References in this Act to the affording by any person of access to benefits, facilities or services are not limited to benefits, facilities or services provided by that person himself, but include any means by which it is in that person's power to facilitate access to benefits, facilities, or services provided by any other person (the "actual provider").

(2) Where by any provision of this Act the affording by any person of access to benefits, facilities or services in a discriminatory way is in certain circumstances prevented from being unlawful, the effect of the provision shall extend also to the liability under this Act of any actual provider.

41. *Acts Done Under Statutory Authority Etc.*

(1) Nothing in Parts II to IV shall render unlawful any act of discrimination done—

    a. in pursuance of any enactment or Order in Council; or

    b. in pursuance of any instrument made under any enactment by a Minister of the Crown; or

    c. in order to comply with any condition or requirement imposed by a Minister of the Crown (whether before or after the passing of this Act) by virtue of any enactment.

References in this subsection to an enactment, Order in Council or instrument include an enactment, Order in Council or instrument passed or made after the passing of this Act.

(2) Nothing in Parts II to IV shall render unlawful any act whereby a person discriminates against another on the basis of that other's nationality or place of ordinary residence or the length of time for which he has been present or resident in or outside the United Kingdom or an area within the United Kingdom, if that act is done—

a. in pursuance of any arrangements made (whether before or after the passing of this Act) by or with the approval of, or for the time being approved by, a Minister of the Crown; or

b. in order to comply with any condition imposed (whether before or after the passing of this Act) by a Minister of the Crown.

42. Acts Safeguarding National Security.

Nothing in Parts II to IV shall render unlawful an act done for the purpose of safeguarding national security.

PART VII

THE COMMISSION FOR RACIAL EQUALITY

General

43. Establishment and Duties of Commission.

(1) There shall be a body of Commissioners named the Commission for Racial Equality consisting of at least eight but not more than fifteen individuals each appointed by the Secretary of State on a full-time or part-time basis, which shall have the following duties—

a. to work towards the elimination of discrimination;

b. to promote equality of opportunity, and good relations, between persons of different racial groups generally; and

c. to keep under review the working of this Act and, when they are so required by the Secretary of State or otherwise think it necessary, draw up and submit to the Secretary of State proposals for amending it.

(2) The Secretary of State shall appoint—

a. one of the Commissioners to be chairman of the Commission; and

b. either one or more of the Commissioners (as the Secretary of State thinks fit) to be deputy chairman or deputy chairmen of the Commission.

(3) The Secretary of State may by order amend subsection (1) so far as it regulates the number of Commissioners.

(4) Schedule 1 shall have effect with respect to the Commission.

(5) The Race Relations Board and the Community Relations Commission are hereby abolished.

44. Assistance to Organisations.

(1) The Commission may give financial or other assistance to any organisation appearing to the Commission to be concerned with the promotion of equality of opportunity, and good relations, between persons of different racial groups, but shall not give any such financial assistance out of money provided (through the Secretary of State) by Parliament except with the approval of the Secretary of State given with the consent of the Treasury.

(2) Except in so far as other arrangements for their discharge are made and approved under paragraph 13 of Schedule 1—

    a. the Commission's functions under subsection (1); and

    b. other functions of the Commission in relation to matters connected with the giving of such financial or other assistance as is mentioned in that subsection,

shall be discharge under the general direction of the Commission by a committee of the Commission consisting of at least three but not more than five Commissioners, of whom one shall be the deputy chairman or one of the deputy chairmen of the Commission.

45. Research and Education.

(1) The Commission may undertake or assist (financially or otherwise) the undertaking by other persons of any research, and any educational activities, which appear to the Commission necessary or expedient for the purpose of section 43(1).

(2) The Commission may make charges for educational or other facilities or services made available by them.

46. Annual Reports.

(1) As soon as practicable after the end of each calendar year the Commission shall make to the Secretary of State a report on their activities during the year (an "annual report").

(2) Each annual report shall include a general survey of developments, during the period to which it relates, in respect of matters falling within the scope of the Commission's functions.

(3) The Secretary of State shall lay a copy of every annual report before each House of Parliament, and shall cause the report to be published. . . .

PART VIII

ENFORCEMENT

General

53. Restriction of Proceedings for Breach of Act.

(1) Except as provided by this Act no proceedings, whether civil or criminal, shall lie against any person in respect of an act by reason that the act is unlawful by virtue of a provision of this Act. . . .

PART IX

INCITEMENT TO RACIAL HATRED

70. *Incitement to Racial Hatred. 1936 c. 6 (1 Edw. 8 & 1 Geo. 6).*

(1) The Public Order Act 1936 shall be amended in accordance with the following provisions of this section.

(2) After section 5 there shall be inserted the following section:—

5A.—(1) A person commits an offence if—

    a. he publishes or distributes written matter which is threatening, abusive or insulting; or

    b. he uses in any public place or at any public meeting words which are threatening, abusive or insulting.

in a case where, having regard to all the circumstances, hatred is likely to be stirred up against any racial group in Great Britain by the matter or words in question.

(2) Subsection (1) above does not apply to the publication or distribution of written matter consisting of or contained in—

    a. a fair and accurate report of proceedings publicly heard before any court or tribunal exercising judicial authority, being a report which is published contemporaneously with those proceedings or, if it is not reasonably practicable or would be unlawful to publish a report of them contemporaneously, is published as soon as publication is reasonably practicable and (if previously unlawful) lawful; or

    b. a fair and accurate report of proceedings in Parliament.

(3) In any proceedings for an offence under this section alleged to have been committed by the publication or distribution of any written matter, it shall be a defence for the accused to prove that he was not aware of the content of the written matter in question and neither suspected nor had reason to suspect it of being threatening, abusive or insulting.

(4) Subsection (3) above shall not prejudice any defence which it is open to a person charged with an offence under this section to raise apart from that subsection.

(5) A person guilty of an offence under this section shall be liable—

    a. on summary conviction, to imprisonment for a term not exceeding six months or to a fine not exceeding £400, or both;

    b. on conviction on indictment, to imprisonment for a term not exceeding two years or to a fine, or both;

but no prosecution for such an offence shall be instituted in England and Wales except by or with the consent of the Attorney General.

(6) In this section—

    'publish' and 'distribute' mean publish or distribute to the public at large or to any section of the public not consisting exclusively of members of an association of which the person publishing or distributing is a member;

    'racial group' means a group of persons defined by reference to colour, race, nationality or ethnic or national origins, and in this definition 'nationality' includes citizenship;

'written matter' includes any writing, sign or visible representation."
(3) In section 7(2), after the words "section 5" there shall be inserted the words "or 5A".

PART X

SUPPLEMENTAL . . .

RACE RELATIONS ACT: c. 74   II.

PART I

Discrimination to Which Act Applies

PART II

Discrimination in the Employment Field

Discrimination by Employers

Discrimination by Other Bodies

Police

PART III

Discrimination in Other Fields

Education

RACE RELATIONS ACT 1976
ARRANGEMENT OF SECTIONS

PART III

Discrimination in Other Fields

PART IV

Other Unlawful Acts

77. Financial provisions
78. General interpretation provisions
79. Transitional and commencement provisions, amendments and repeals.
80. Short title and extent
SCHEDULES:
Schedule 1—The Commission for Racial Equality
Schedule 2—Transitional provisions
Schedule 3—Minor and consequential amendments
Schedule 4—Amendments of Sex Discrimination Act 1975
Schedule 5—Repeals

4. FRANCE

INTRODUCTION

In response to a felt need to extend and expand the human rights principles set forth in the 1789 Declaration of the Rights of Man and of the Citizen and the 1958 Constitution of the Fifth Republic, all of France's major political parties have introduced proposed constitutional laws in the National Assembly.

These new constitutional laws incorporate advanced and progressive ideas on human rights which reflect the thinking expressed in human rights debates and discussions at UNESCO in Paris and the Council of Europe in Strasbourg, France.

Human rights in these legislative proposals include the right of the individual to both international peace and civil peace. Recognized in these documents is both the right to resources assuring a minimum well-being and the right to a balanced healthy environment. They provide that manual workers and intellectual workers are equal in dignity and possess the same rights.

The latest version of France's Draft Constitution Law on the Liberties and Rights of Man was incorporated in Report No. 3455 of 1977 of the Commission on Constitutional Law of the National Assembly, a body especially created to study such legislation. The National Assembly failed to act and the proposal became inactive at the end of the legislative term. But its provisions are still the subject of discussion in human rights circles and will certainly come before the National Assembly (and the French people) in the future.

DRAFT CONSTITUTIONAL LAW ON THE LIBERTIES AND RIGHTS OF MAN No. 3455, 1977

TITLE I

FRATERNITY

Article 1.

Every man has the right to international peace. Wars of aggression in violation of this right is a crime.

Genocide and all other crimes against humanity, war crimes, and crimes against peace are indefensible.

Military force, assuring territorial integrity and national independence, may not be employed against the liberty of any people.

Article 2.

Every man has the right to civil peace. Public authority may have recourse to force only as a last resort and to the extent necessary to assure respect for law. All violence for private or partisan ends shall be suppressed by law.

Article 3.

Every citizen shall have the right and the duty to serve the community and the nation. No one may be constrained to bear arms in violation of his moral or religious convictions.

Article 4.

Every citizen has the duty to contribute to public expenses according to his means and his status. Fiscal justice, particularly progressive taxation of revenue and cognizance of family responsibilities, shall be assured by law. The law shall protect taxpayers from all arbitrary measures.

Article 5.

France conceives of liberty as the common property of all men; she affirms that the liberty of man is inseparable from solidarity among peoples. Contribution to the progress of developing countries, while respecting their sovereignty, shall be a national and international duty.

Article 6.

Any person who is persecuted because of activity for liberty or peace shall have the right to asylum on the territory of the Republic. Such person shall be obliged to respect the laws and shall enjoy the status of political refugee.

Extradition for political or military reasons shall be forbidden. It must be authorized by judicial decision.

Article 7.

No French citizen may be deported.

Article 8.

Everyone has the right to resources assuring a minimum well-being.
Everyone has the right to social security.

In this spirit, regarding members of society whose situation so requires, society shall be mutually responsible.

Article 9.

The family, which is the fundamental element of society, shall be protected by law. All children shall have the right to the special protection which their condition requires.

Article 10.

Every man shall have the right to a balanced, healthy environment, and he shall have the duty to defend it.

In order to assure the qualify of life of present and future generations, the State shall protect nature and ecological balances. The State shall supervise the rational exploitation of natural resources.

Article 11.

The right to housing shall be guaranteed by law under conditions favoring individual prosperity, development of human relations, and development of community life. The State, banishing all segregation of all kinds, shall assure proper surroundings through city planning, territorial planning, and appropriate equipment.

Article 12.

The French Republic, one and indivisible, shall recognize and protect diversity of cultures, customs, and ways of life. Everyone has the right to be different and to appear publicly as such.

TITLE II

EQUALITY

Article 13.

All human beings are born, and remain, free and equal in their rights. All forms of segregation shall be prohibited.

Article 14.

All citizens are equal before the law, before justice and public service, without distinction as to origin, opinion, belief, or social situation. The organization of society shall foster equality of opportunity and conditions.

Article 15.

Men and women shall possess equal rights. Any discrimination which violates this principle shall be suppressed by law.

Article 16.

The Republic shall outlaw and suppress racism in all forms and all manifestations.

Article 17.

Manual workers and intellectual workers shall be equal in dignity and shall possess the same rights. All discrimination toward young workers, whether they be professionals or students, shall be prohibited.

Article 18.

Foreign workers contribute to the national effort. They shall enjoy the same liberties and the same economic, social, familial and cultural rights as French citizens.

In those areas, they shall have the same duties.

TITLE III

LIBERTY

Article 19.

The liberty of each person may be limited only by law in order to assure the liberty and security of all.

Article 20.

Every man has the right to life and to physical and moral integrity.

Article 21.

No one may be subjected to torture nor to cruel, inhuman, or degrading punishment. All acts of torture shall be punished by criminal penalties.

Article 22.

Parents shall have decision-making power on matters regarding their children.

Article 23.

Every man shall have the right to the protection of his private life.

The law shall guard particularly against the dangers which may be involved in information processing, as well as techniques of collecting, preserving and use of information.

Article 24.

The domicile shall be inviolable. No search may be conducted without a judicial warrant.

Article 25.

Privacy of correspondence and telecommunications shall be guaranteed by law; this may be removed only under conditions defined by law for investigation of infractions or for the needs of national defense.

Article 26.

The law shall guarantee the security of citizens from all abusive or arbitrary detention. Those who detain persons by reason of origins, opinions, or beliefs shall be held personally responsible.

Punishment which deprives the convicted person of liberty must aim at rehabilitation and a return to society.

The law shall protect against any arbitrary placement in a caretaking establishment. No one may be placed against his will except in exceptional cases which are subject to the supervision of the judicial authority.

Article 27.

The law shall assure the continued development of democratic liberties.

Political parties and groups shall be formed and shall freely engage in their activities.

There is no democracy without freedom to travel, without freedom of opinion, expression, religion and belief, association, assembly and demonstration, and without freedom for labor unions.

There is no liberty without respect for the law by the judge and by the administration.

Article 28.

Everyone shall have the right to seek, receive and propagate information and ideas by any means of his choice. The Republic shall assure access to administrative documents, within conditions compatible with public security and public order.

Article 29.

Free enterprise shall be guaranteed by law.

The law shall take the necessary measures so that private, national and international economic powers do not elude the discipline required by general interest. The law shall encourage cooperatives and associated enterprises to the extent compatible with economic rationality.

Article 30.

Private property shall be guaranteed. No one may be expropriated arbitrarily or without a fair prior indemnity. Transmittal of property by inheritance shall be guaranteed by law.

Article 31.

Any enterprise whose business activity has, or acquires, the character of national public service or monopoly must become collective property.

Article 32.

The participation of everyone in decisions of concern to him in all sectors of political, economic, social and cultural life shall be guaranteed and facilitated by law.

Article 33.

Every man shall have the right to engage in work, freely accepted, to assure his existence and his dignity. The Republic shall guarantee this right particularly through the application of a policy of full employment and fight against unemployment.

Freedom of work for everyone shall be guaranteed by law. No one may be disturbed in his work because of opinions which he professes.

Article 34.

Everyone has the right to a remuneration corresponding to his level of responsibility and qualifications.

The law shall assure security and hygiene at work, with the widest participation of the interested parties and their representatives. Victims of working accidents and illnesses shall have the right to full reparations.

Everyone shall have access to professional training and to continued training during his active life.

Article 35.

Free time shall be recognized as a right indispensable for the growth of the human person.

Every man has the right, in freedom, to rest, vacation, and to leisure.

Article 36.

The law shall assure the free exercise of the right to strike within the limits required by State security and the protection of people and property.

Article 37.

Every man has the right to education, to continued training, and to culture.

Public education, respecting all convictions, shall be free of charge. Freedom of education and freedom within education shall be assured by law.

Culture, which is inseparable from liberty, shall assure a full personal life and the development of personal relations, while respecting the right to be different. Culture must be available to everyone and must be given resources for expansion.

Article 38.

Radio and television shall perform a mission of public service.

They shall be obliged to give information in a spirit of objectivity and to guarantee expression and confrontation of currents of opinion. The right to respond shall be guaranteed.

Freedom of the press is a fundamental right. Its effective exercise shall be assured by law.

A statute regarding journalists shall guarantee their freedom of conscience.

Article 39.

Every man shall have the right to protection of his health. Medical privacy and free choice of a doctor shall be guaranteed.

FINAL PROVISION

The Declaration of 1789 and the Preamble to the Constitution of 1946, on which is based the Preamble to the Constitution of October 4, 1958, shall retain their constitutional force in all of their provisions which are not contrary to this constitutional law.

IX. JUDICIAL DECISIONS

1. England

BUSHELL'S CASE (1670)

More than any international covenant, more than any constitution, more than any legislative enactment, the freedom and independence of the judicial *process* in the common law comes from a judicial opinion: the precedent-setting *Bushell's Case*, decided in 1670.

For until *Bushell's Case*, the crown-designated judges of the common law courts (as well as the Star Chamber) asserted the power to fine or imprison jurors with whom they disagreed. That ended with *Bushell's Case* which arose out of the famous trials of the Quakers, William Penn and William Meade. They were tried at the Court of Oyer and Terminer at London's Old Bailey before the Lord Mayor and the Recorder, sitting as judges of a superior court of record.

The Recorder of London directed the jury that as a matter of law the Quakers were guilty. The jury refused to follow such direction and rendered an acquittal. And "the jury not finding them guilty as the Recorder and Mayor would have had them, they were kept without meat and drink some three days, till almost starved, but would not alter their verdict; so fined and imprisoned."[153]

The jurors were then brought before the Court of Common Pleas on a writ of habeas corpus and discharged. Writing the opinion in *Bushell's Case*, Chief Justice Vaughan held that no judge had the right to fine or imprison a jury for disobeying his direction on a point of law—for every case depended on the facts and on matters of fact the jurors were the sole judges.

Once freed, one of the members of the jury brought an action against the Lord Mayor and the Recorder of London based on false imprisonment. The argument was that they were liable for having exceeded their jurisdiction. Now the court held against the juryman. True, the Recorder had no jurisdiction to fine or imprison the jurors; he had made a mistake as to the scope of his jurisdiction. But he was acting—though erroneously—in the bona fide exercise of his office and under the belief that he had such jurisdiction. The court held that a judge was immune from liability for damages while acting as a judge or performing a judicial act.[154]

CASE OF THE IMPRISONMENT OF EDWARD BUSHELL, FOR ALLEGED MISCONDUCT AS A JURYMAN:

22 Charles II. A.D. 1670. [Vaughan's Reports, 135.] [Excerpted]

This important Case, which arose out of the preceding, is thus reported by Chief Justice Vaughan: [Extracts.]

The King's Writ of Habeas Corpus, dat. 9 die Novembris, 22 Car. 2. issued out of this court directed to the then Sheriffs of London, to have the body of Edward Bushell, by them detained in Prison, together with the day and cause of his caption and detention, on Friday then next following, before this court, to do and receive as the court should consider; as also to have then the said writ in court. . . .

The Writ of Habeas Corpus is now the most usual remedy by which a man is restored again to his liberty, if he have been against law deprived of it. . . .

In the present case it is returned that the prisoner, being juryman, among others charged at the session court at the Old Baily, to try the issue between the King and Penn and Meade, upon the indictment for assembling unlawfully and tumultously, did against the full and manifest evidence openly given in court, acquit the prisoners indicted in contempt of the King, etc. . . .

[T]he verdict of a jury, and evidence of a witness are very different things, in the truth and falsehood of them. A witness swears but to what he hath heard or seen, generally or more largely, to what hath fallen under his senses. But a juryman swears to what he can infer and conclude from the testimony of such witnesses, by the act and force of his understanding, to be the fact enquired after; which differs nothing in the reason, though much in the punishment, from what a judge, out of various cases considered by him, infers to be the law in question before him. . . .

[T]he judge, qua judge, cannot know the fact possibly, but from the evidence which the jury have, . . . and consequently he cannot know the matter of fact, nor punish the jury for going against their evidence, when he cannot know what their evidence is. It is true, if the jury were to have no other evidence for the fact, but what is deposed in court, the judge might know their evidence, and the fact from it, equally as they, and so direct what the law were in the case; though even when the judge and jury might honestly differ in the result from the evidence, as well as two judges may, which often happens.

But the evidence which the jury have of the fact is much other than that: for,

1. Being returned of the vicinage, whence the cause of action ariseth, the law supposeth them thence to have sufficient knowledge to try the matter in issue (and so they must) though no evidence were given on either side in court, but to this evidence the judge is stranger.

2. They may have evidence from their own personal knowledge, by which they may be assured, and sometimes are, that what is deposed in court, is absolutely false; but to this the judge is a stranger, and he knows no more of the fact than he hath learned in court, and perhaps by false depositions, and consequently knows nothing.

3. The jury may know the witnesses to be stigmatized and infamous, which may be unknown to the parties, and consequently to the court.

4. In many cases the jury are to have view necessarily, in many, by consent, for their better information; to this evidence likewise the judge is a stranger.

5. If they do follow his direction, they may be attainted, and the judgment reversed for doing that, which if they had not done, they should have been fined and imprisoned by the judge which is unreasonable.

6. If they do not follow his direction, and be therefore fined, yet they may be attainted, and so doubly punished by distinct judicatures for the same offence, which the common law admits not. . . .

7. To what end is the jury to be returned out of the vicinage whence the

cause of action ariseth? To what end must hundredors be of the jury, whom the law supposeth to have nearer knowledge of the fact than those of the vicinage in general? To what end are they challenged so scrupulously to the array and poll? To what end must they have such a certain freehold, and be *probi & legales homines*, and not of affinity with the parties concerned? To what end must they have in many cases the view for their exacter information chiefly? To what end must they undergo the heavy punishment of the villanous judgment, if after all this they implicitly must give a verdict by the dictates and authority of another man, under pain of fines and imprisonment, when sworn to do it according to the best of their knowledge?

A man cannot see by another's eye, nor hear by another's ear, no more can a man conclude or infer the thing to be resolved by another's understanding or reasoning; and though the verdict be right the jury give, yet they being not assured it is so from their own understanding, are forsworn, at least *in foro conscientiae*.

[Note: There is no number 8 in the opinion.]

9. It is absurd a jury should be fined by the judge for [not] going against their evidence, when he who fineth knows not what it is, as where a jury find without evidence, in court on either side. [S]o if the jury find upon their knowledge, as the course is if the defendant plead *solvit ad diem* to a bond proved, and offers no proof. The jury is directed to find for the plaintiff, unless they know payment was made of their own knowledge, according to the plea. . . . And it is absurd to fine a jury for finding against their evidence, when the judge knows but part of it; for the better and greater part of the evidence may be wholly unknown to him.

[The jurors were discharged.]

2. UNITED STATES

BROWN v. BOARD OF EDUCATION (1954, 1955)

The greatest judicial landmark in the struggle for racial equality was the 1954 United States Supreme Court case of *Brown* v. *Board of Education*. There, a unanimous court struck down all state-imposed racial discrimination as unconstitutional *per se* under the equal protection clause of the Fourteenth Amendment of the United States Constitution. See Part Four, Ch. I. It was a decision which climaxed two centuries of litigation on the legal status of black Americans and opened a new era in the law affecting all aspects of racial rights.

Probably no decision in the history of the United States Supreme Court has directly affected so many individuals. At the time of this unanimous decision, school segregation was required or permitted by law in 17 states and the District of Columbia. This involved more than 8,000,000 white and 2,500,000 black pupils, enrolled in 35,000 white schools and 15,000 black schools.

The rationale of the decision—valid for its own day, but questionable in the era of equal rights for women—was as follows: (a) since all legislation necessarily involves classification, the equal protection clause of the Fourteenth Amendment cannot demand absolute equality; state laws and practices protecting people according to age, sex, and the like are constitutionally valid; (b) discriminatory state action will be upheld providing that it is reasonable; a statute devoted exclusively to regulating the working hours of women is not violative of the equal protection clause, because of the real differences between male and female and the reasonableness of the legislative purpose in protecting the latter; (c) discriminatory racial practices are inherently unreasonable; a racial classification can have no reasonable relation to any legislative purpose; therefore any state-imposed classification based on race is unconstitutional *per se* as violative of the equal protection mandate.

While the *Brown* case declared invalid discrimination required or permitted by the states, it did not encompass the school segregation situation in the District of Columbia. This is because the District is under federal authority, and the actions of the United States government are not restricted by the equal protection clause found in the Fourteenth Amendment. But the Supreme Court, on the same day, reached the same unamimous conclusion on federal authority, holding discrimination in the schools of the District invalid under the Fifth Amendment's due process clause.[155]

The 1954 determinations set forth the constitutional principles, but said nothing about enforcement. The implementation decision was handed down a year later.[156] This was the mandate ordering school desegregation "with all deliberate speed," requiring "good faith compliance at the earliest practicable date."

But the implementation problem could not and did not end with the *Brown* decision of 1955. On the contrary, the efforts to achieve school desegregation became the central concern of the federal judiciary for the next three decades. And two United States presidents, Dwight D. Eisenhower and John F. Kennedy, supported the *Brown* decisions by calling out the federal troops to overcome local opposition.

In the deep South the fierce opposition was at first followed by mere token integration, but mixed classes eventually became a reality throughout the Southern public school systems as various evasionary schemes were invalidated by the courts.

It has been far more difficult to eliminate school segregation in the North. Court-ordered busing has been the major method of implementation since *Alexander* v. *Holmes County Board of Education.*[157] That case also held, 15 years after *Brown*, that the delays permissible under the "with all deliberate speed" mandate were ended and that segregation was to end in all schools immediately.

The issue is still not fully resolved. Some pockets of school segregation still remain in the United States, the result of private patterns of housing and economics. While the *Brown* case eliminated *de jure* segregation, *de facto* segregation unfortunately continues. But this, too, is being attacked on a case by case basis wherever an intentional discrimatory racial purpose can be demonstrated. Such invidious discriminatory intent may be evident or may be "inferred from the totality of the relevant facts."[158]

For a study on the meaning of *Brown* v. *Board of Education* from the perspective of its time, see Desegregation and the Law by Albert P. Blaustein and Clarence Clyde Ferguson, Jr., Rutgers University Press, 1957, second edition revised, Vintage, 1962, Rothman Reprint, 1985. The leading work exploring the history and influence of the case is *From Brown to Baake: The Supreme Court and School Integration, 1954–1978*, by J. Harvie Wilkinson, Oxford University Press, 1979.

BROWN v. BOARD OF EDUCATION OF TOPEKA

Supreme Court of the United States, 347 U.S. 483 (1954). [Footnotes, which are renumbered and appear in the Footnotes, are an integral part of opinions.]

Opinion on Segregation Laws

No. 1 Appeal from the United States District Court for the District of Kansas.[159]

MR. CHIEF JUSTICE WARREN delivered the opinion of the Court.

These cases come to us from the States of Kansas, South Carolina, Virginia, and Delaware. They are premised on different facts and different local conditions, but a common legal question justifies their consideration together in this consolidated opinion.[160]

In each of the cases, minors of the Negro race, through their legal representatives, seek the aid of the courts in obtaining admission to the public schools of their community on a non-segregated basis. In each instance, they have been denied admission to schools attended by white children under laws requiring or permitting segregation according to race. This segregation was alleged to deprive the plaintiffs of the equal protection of the laws under the Fourteenth Amendment. In each of the cases other than the Delaware case, a three-judge federal district court denied relief to the plaintiffs on the so-called "separate but equal" doctrine announced by this Court in *Plessy* v. *Ferguson*, 163 U.S. 537. . . . Under that doctrine, equality of treatment is accorded when the races are provided substantially equal facilities, even though these facilities be separate. In the Delaware case, the Supreme Court of Delaware adhered to that doctrine, but ordered that the plaintiffs be admitted to the white schools because of their superiority to the Negro schools.

The plaintiffs contend that segregated public schools are not "equal" and cannot be made "equal," and that hence they are deprived of the equal protection of the laws. Because of the obvious importance of the question presented, the Court took jurisdiction.[161] Argument was heard in the 1952 Term, and reargument was heard this Term on certain questions propounded by the Court.[162]

Reargument was largely devoted to the circumstances surrounding the adoption of the Fourteenth Amendment in 1868. It covered exhaustively consideration of the Amendment in Congress, ratification by the states, then existing practices in racial segregation, and the views of proponents and opponents of the Amendment. This discussion and our own investigation convince us that, although these sources cast some light, it is not enough to resolve the problem with which we are faced. At best, they are inconclusive. The most avid proponents of the post-War Amendments undoubtedly intended them to remove all legal distinctions among "all persons born or naturalized in the United States." Their opponents, just as certainly, were antagonistic to both the letter and the spirit of the Amendments and wished them to have the most limited effect. What others in Congress and the state legislatures had in mind cannot be determined with any degree of certainty.

An additional reason for the inconclusive nature of the Amendment's history, with respect to segregated schools, is the status of public education at that time.[163] In the South, the movement toward free common schools, supported by general taxation, had not yet taken hold. Education of white children was largely in the hands of private groups. Education of Negroes was almost nonexistent, and practically all of the race were illiterate. In fact, any education of Negroes was forbidden by law in some states. Today, in contrast, many Negroes have achieved outstanding success in the arts and sciences as well as in the business and professional world. It is true that public school education at the time of the Amendment had advanced further in the North, but the effect of the Amendment on Northern States was generally ignored in the congressional debates. Even in the North, the conditions of public education did not approximate those existing today. The curriculum was usually rudimentary; ungraded schools were common in rural areas; the school term was but three months a year in many states; and compulsory school attendance was virtually unknown. As a consequence, it is not surprising that there should be so little in the history of the Fourteenth Amendment relating to its intended effect on public education.

In the first cases in this Court construing the Fourteenth Amendment, decided shortly after its adoption, the Court interpreted it as proscribing all state-imposed discriminations against the Negro race.[164] The doctrine of "separate but equal" did not make its appearance in this Court until 1896 in the case of *Plessy* v. *Ferguson, supra,* involving not education but transporation.[165] American courts have since labored with the doctrine for over half a century. In this Court, there have been six cases involving the "separate but equal" doctrine in the field of public education.[166] In *Cumming* v. *County Board of Education,* 175 U.S. 528, and *Gong Lum* v. *Rice,* 275 U.S. 78, the validity of the doctrine itself was not challenged.[167] In more recent cases, all on the graduate school level, inequality was found in that specific benefits enjoyed by white students were denied to Negro students of the same educational qualifications. *Missouri ex rel. Gaines* v. *Canada,* 305 U.S. 337; *Sipuel* v. *Oklahoma,* 332 U.S. 631; *Sweatt* v. *Painter,* 339 U.S. 629; *McLaurin* v. *Oklahoma State Regents,* 339 U.S. 637. In none of these cases was it necessary to re-examine the doctrine to grant relief to the Negro plaintiff. And in *Sweatt* v. *Painter, supra,* the Court expressly reserved decision on the question whether *Plessy* v. *Ferguson* should be held inapplicable to public education.

In the instant cases, that question is directly presented. Here, unlike *Sweatt* v. *Painter,* there are findings below that the Negro and white schools involved have been equalized, or are being equalized, with respect to buildings, curricula, qualifications and salaries of teachers, and other "tangible" factors.[168] Our decision, therefore, cannot turn on merely a comparison of these tangible factors in the Negro and white schools involved in each of the cases. We must look instead to the effect of segregation itself on public education.

In approaching this problem, we cannot turn the clock back to 1868 when the Amendment was adopted, or even to 1896 when *Plessy* v. *Ferguson* was written. We must consider public education in the light of its full development and its present place in American life throughout the Nation. Only in this way can it be determined if segregation in public schools deprives these plaintiffs of the equal protection of the laws.

Today, education is perhaps the most important function of state and local governments. Compulsory school attendance laws and the great expenditures for education both demonstrate our recognition of the importance of education to our democratic society. It is required in the performance of our most basic public responsibilities, even service in the armed forces. It is the very foundation of good citizenship. Today it is a principal instrument in awakening the child to cultural values, in preparing him for later professional training, and in helping him to adjust normally to his environment. In these days, it is doubtful that any child may reasonably be expected to succeed in life if he is denied the opportunity of an education. Such an opportunity, where the state has undertaken to provide it, is a right which must be made available to all on equal terms.

We come then to the question presented: Does segregation of children in public schools solely on the basis of race, even though the physical facilities and other "tangible" factors may be equal, deprive the children of the minority group of equal education opportunities? We believe that it does.

In *Sweatt* v. *Painter, supra,* in finding that a segregated law school for Negroes could not provide them equal educational opportunities, this Court relied in large part on "those qualities which are incapable of objective measurement but which make for greatness in a law school." In *McLaurin* v. *Oklahoma State Regents, supra,* the Court, in requiring that a Negro admitted to a white graduate school be treated like all other students, again resorted to intangible considerations: " . . . his ability to study, to engage in discussions and exchange views with other students, and, in general, to learn his profession." Such considerations apply with added force to children in grade and high schools. To separate them from others of similar age and qualifications solely because of their race generates a feeling of inferiority as to their status in the community that may affect their hearts and minds in a way unlikely ever to be undone. The effect of this separation on their educational opportunities was well stated by a finding in the Kansas case by a court which nevertheless felt compelled to rule against the Negro plaintiffs:

Segregation of white and colored children in public schools has a detrimental effect upon the colored children. The impact is greater when it has the sanction of the law; for the policy of separating the races is usually interpreted as denoting the inferiority of the negro group. A sense of inferiority affects the motivation of the child to learn. Segregation with the sanction of law, therefore, has a tendency to [retard] the educational and mental development of negro children and to deprive them of some of the benefits they would receive in a racial[ly] integrated school system.[169]

Whatever may have been the extent of psychological knowledge at the time of *Plessy* v. *Ferguson,* this finding is amply supported by modern authority.[170] Any language in *Plessy* v. *Ferguson* contrary to this finding is rejected.

We conclude that in the field of public education the doctrine of "separate but equal" has no place. Separate educational facilities are inherently unequal. Therefore, we hold that the plaintiffs and others similarly situated for whom the actions have been brought are, by reason of the segregation complained of, deprived of the equal protection of the laws guaranteed by the Fourteenth Amendment. This disposition makes unnecessary any discussion whether such segregation also violates the Due Process Clause of the Fourteenth Amendment.[171]

Because these are class actions, because of the wide applicability of this decision, and because of the great variety of local conditions, the formulation of decrees in these cases presents problems of considerable complexity. On reargument, the consideration of appropriate relief was necessarily subordinated to the primary question—the constitutionality of segregation in public education. We have now announced that such segregation is a denial of the equal protection of the laws. In order that we may have the full assistance of the parties in formulating decrees, the cases will be restored to the docket, and the parties are requested to present further argument on Questions 4 and 5 previously propounded by the Court for the reargument this Term.[172] The Attorney General of the United States is again invited to participate. The Attorneys General of the states requiring or permitting segregation in public education will also be permitted to appear as *amici curiae* upon request to do so by September 15, 1954, and submission of briefs by October 1, 1954.[173]

It is so ordered.

BOLLING v. SHARPE

Supreme Court of the United States, 347 U.S. 497 (1954).

MR. CHIEF JUSTICE WARREN delivered the opinion of the court.

This case challenges the validity of segregation in the public schools of the District of Columbia. The petitioners, minors of the Negro race, allege that such segregation deprives them of due process of law under the Fifth Amendment. They were refused admission to a public school attended by white children solely because of their race. They sought the aid of the District Court for the District of Columbia in obtaining admission. That court dismissed their complaint. The Court granted a writ of certiorari before judgment in the Court of Appeals because of the importance of the constitutional question presented. 344 U.S. 873. . . .

We have this day held that the Equal Protection Clause of the Fourteenth Amendment prohibits the states from maintaining racially segregated public schools.[174] The legal problem in the District of Columbia is somewhat different, however. The Fifth Amendment, which is applicable in the District of Columbia, does not contain an equal protection clause as does the Fourteenth Amendment, which applies only to the states. But the concepts of equal protection and due process, both stemming from our American ideal of fairness, are not mutually exclusive. The "equal protection of the laws" is a more explicit safeguard of prohibited unfairness than "due process of law," and, therefore, we do not imply that the two are always interchangeable phrases. But, as this Court has recognized, discrimination may be so unjustifiable as to be violative of due process.[175]

Classifications based solely upon race must be scrutinized with particular care, since they are contrary to our traditions and hence constitutionally suspect.[176] As long ago as 1896, this Court declared the principle "that the constitution of the United States, in its present form, forbids, so far as civil and political rights are concerned, discrimination by the general government, or by the states, against any citizen because of his race."[177] And in *Buchanan* v. *Warley*, 245 U.S. 60, . . . the Court held that a statute which limited the right of a property owner to convey his property to a person of another race was, as an unreasonable discrimination, a denial of due process of law.

Although the Court has not assumed to define "liberty" with any great precision, that term is not confined to mere freedom from bodily restraint. Liberty under law extends to the full range of conduct which the individual is free to pursue, and it cannot be restricted except for a proper governmental objective. Segregation in public education is not reasonably related to any proper governmental objective, and thus it imposes on Negro children of the District of Columbia a burden that constitutes an arbitrary deprivation of their liberty in violation of the Due Process Clause.

In view of our decision that the Constitution prohibits the states from maintaining racially segregated public schools, it would be unthinkable that the same Constitution would impose a lesser duty on the Federal Government.[178] We hold that racial segregation in the public schools of the District of Columbia is a denial of the due process of law guaranteed by the Fifth Amendment to the Constitution.

For the reasons set out in *Brown* v. *Board of Education*, this case will be restored to the docket for reargument on Questions 4 and 5 previously propounded by the Court. 345 U.S. 972. . . .

It is so ordered.

BROWN v. BOARD OF EDUCATION OF TOPEKA

Supreme Court of the United States, 349 U.S. 294 (1955).

Enforcement Decree

No. 1 Appeal from the United States District Court for the District of Kansas.[179]

MR. CHIEF JUSTICE WARREN delivered the opinion of the Court.

These cases were decided on May 17, 1954. The opinions of that date[180] declaring the fundamental principle that racial discrimination in public education is unconstitutional, are incorporated herein by reference. All provisions of federal, state, or local law requiring or permitting such discrimination must yield to this principle. There remains for consideration the manner in which relief is to be accorded.

Because these cases arose under different local conditions and their disposition will involve a variety of local problems, we requested further argument on the question of relief.[181] In view of the nationwide importance of the decision, we invited the Attorney General of the United States and the Attorneys General of all states requiring or permitting racial discrimination in public education to present their views on that question. The parties, the United States, and the States of Florida, North Carolina, Arkansas, Oklahoma, Maryland, and Texas filed briefs and participated in the oral argument.

These presentations were informative and helpful to the Court in its consideration of the complexities arising from the transition to a system of public education freed of racial discrimination. The presentations also demonstrated that substantial steps to eliminate racial discrimination in public schools have already been taken, not only in some of the communities in which these cases arose, but in some of the states appearing as *amici curiae*, and in other states as well. Substantial progress has been made in the District of Columbia and in the communities of Kansas and Delaware involved in this litigation. The defendants in the cases coming to us from South Carolina and Virginia are awaiting the decision of this Court concerning relief.

Full implementation of these constitutional principles may require solution of varied local school problems. School authorities have the primary responsibility for elucidating, assessing, and solving these problems; courts will have to consider whether the action of school authorities constitutes good faith implementation of the governing constitutional principles. Because of their proximity to local conditions and the possible need for further hearings, the courts which originally heard these cases can best perform this judicial appraisal. Accordingly, we believe it appropriate to remand the cases to those courts.[182]

In fashioning and effectuating the decrees, the courts will be guided by equitable principles. Traditionally, equity has been characterized by a practical flexibility in shaping its remedies[183] and by a facility for adjusting and reconciling public and private needs.[184] These cases call for the exercise of these traditional attributes of equity power. At stake is the personal interest of the plaintiffs in admission to public schools as soon as practicable on a nondiscriminatory basis. To effectuate this interest may call for elimination of a variety of obstacles in making the transition to school systems operated in accordance with the constitutional principles set forth in our May 17, 1954, decision. Courts of equity may properly take into account the public interest in the elimination of such obstacles in a systematic and effective manner. But it should go without saying that the vitality of these constitutional principles cannot be allowed to yield simply because of disagreement with them.

While giving weight to these public and private considerations, the courts will require that the defendants make a prompt and reasonable start toward full compliance with our May 17, 1954, ruling. Once such a start has been made, the courts may find that additional time is necessary to carry out the ruling in an effective manner. The burden rests upon the defendants to establish that such time is necessary in the public interest and is consistent with good faith compliance at the earliest practicable date. To that end, the courts may consider problems related to administration, arising from the physical condition of the school plant, the school transportation system, personnel, revision of school districts and attendance areas into compact units to achieve a system of determining admission to the public schools on a nonracial basis, and revision of local laws and regulations which may be necessary in solving the foregoing problems. They will also consider the adequacy of any plans the defendants may propose to meet these problems and to effectuate a transition to a racially nondiscriminatory school system. During this period of transition, the courts will retain jurisdiction of these cases.

The judgments below, except that in the Delaware case, are accordingly reversed and the cases are remanded to the District Courts to take such proceedings and enter such orders and decrees consistent with this opinion as are necessary and proper to admit to public schools on a racially nondiscriminatory basis with all deliberate speed the parties to these cases. The judgment in the Delaware case—ordering the immediate admission of the plaintiffs to schools previously attended only by white children—is affirmed on the basis of principles stated in our May 17, 1954, opinion, but the case is remanded to the Supreme Court of Delaware for such further proceedings as that Court may deem necessary in light of this opinion.

It is so ordered.

3. CANADA

RONCARELLI v. DUPLESSIS (1959)

Roncarelli v. *Duplessis* is the judicial cornerstone of the "rule of law" in Canada, setting forth via the judicial process a fundamental principle of human rights which is not specified either constitutionally or legislatively. Public officials in Canada are not free, in the name of the public interest, to use any procedural means to pursue public goals. Rather, officials must carry out the law as it is written, and when a public official ignores or goes beyond his authority, he will be held legally accountable just as a private individual. The effect of the case is to place limits on the discretionary acts of public officials.

The losing party in this case was the Premier of Quebec himself, Maurice Duplessis. He had been instrumental in the cancellation of the liquor license of a restaurant proprietor who was a bondsman for his co-religionists in the Jehovah's witnesses. Because Duplessis could cite no legal basis for his action he was held accountable personally for $25,000 in damages.

RONCARELLI v. DUPLESSIS

[1959] S.C.R. 121; 16 D.L.R. (2d) 689 Supreme Court of Canada [Excerpted]

Abbott J.: In his action appellant claimed from respondent the sum of $118,741 as damages alleged to have been sustained as a result of the cancellation of a licence or permit for the sale of alcoholic liquors held by appellant. The action was maintained by the learned trial judge [[1952] 1 D.L.R. 680] to the extent of $8,123.53. From that judgment two appeals were taken, one by respondent asking that the action be dismissed in its entirety, the other by appellant asking that the amount allowed as damages be increased by an amount of $90,000. The Court of Queen's Bench [[1956] Que. Q.B. 447] allowed the respondent's appeal, Rinfret J. dissenting, and dismissed the action. The appeal taken by appellant to increase the amount of the trial judgment was dismissed unanimously. The present appeals are from those two judgments.

The facts are these. On December 4, 1946, appellant was conducting a restaurant business in the City of Montreal, a business which he and his father and mother before him had been carrying on continuously for some 34 years prior to that date. The restaurant had been licensed for the sale of alcoholic beverages throughout the entire period.

In 1946 and for many years prior thereto, persons operating establishments of this kind and selling alcoholic beverages had been required to obtain a licence or permit under the Alcoholic Liquor Act, R.S.Q. 1941, c. 255. Unless granted for a shorter period, these were annual licences and expired on April 30th in each year. Moreover, s.35(1), of the Act provides as follows: "The Commission may cancel any permit at its descretion." The Commission referred to is the "Quebec Liquor Commission" established as a corporation under the Act in question and, generally speaking, it has been entrusted by the Legislature with the responsibility of directing and administering the provincial monopoly of the sale and distribution of alcoholic beverages.

On December 4, 1946, without previous notice to the appellant, his licence to sell alcoholic beverages was cancelled by the Quebec Liquor Commission, and at about 2 p.m. on that date the stock of liquor on his premises was seized and removed. The licence was not restored and after operating for some months without such a licence, in 1947 appellant sold the restaurant and the building in which it was located.

Appellant learned from press reports either in the afternoon of December 4th or early the following day, that his licence had been cancelled and the stock of liquor seized because he was an adherent of a religious sect or group known as the Witnesses of Jehovah. It soon became clear from statements made by the respondent to the press and confirmed by him at the trial as having been made by him, that the cancellation of the licence had been made because of the appellant's association with the sect in question and in order to prevent him from continuing to furnish bail for members of that sect summoned before the Recorder's Court on charges of contravening certain city by-laws respecting the distribution of printed material.

It might be added here that in December 1946 and for some time prior thereto the Witnesses of Jehovah appear to have been carrying on in the Montreal district and elsewhere in the Province of Quebec, an active campaign of meetings and the distribution of printed pamphlets and other like material of an offensive character to a great many people of most religious beliefs, and I have no doubt that at that time many people believed this material to be seditous.

The evidence is referred to in detail in the courts below and I do not propose to do so here. I am satisfied from a consideration of this evidence: First; that the cancellation of the appellant's license was made for the sole reason which I have mentioned and with the object and purpose to which I have referred; Second: that such cancellation was made with the express authorization and upon the order of the respondent; Third; that the determining cause of the cancellation was that order, and that the Manager of the Quebec Liquor Commission would not have cancelled the licence without the order and authorization given by the respondent.

There can be no question as to the first point. It was conceded by respondent in his evidence at the trial and by his counsel at the hearing before us. As to the second, and third points, I share the view of the learned trial judge and of Rinfret J. that both were clearly established.

The religious beliefs of the appellant and the fact that he acted as bondsman for members of the sect in question had no connection whatever with his obligations as the holder of a licence to sell alcoholic liquors. The cancellation of his licence upon this ground alone therefore was without any legal justification. Moreover, the religious beliefs of the appellant and his perfectly legal activities as a bondsman had nothing to do with the object and purposes of the Alcoholic Liquor Act, and the powers and responsibilities of the Manager of the Quebec Liquor Commission are confined to the administration and enforcement of the provisions of the said Act. This may be one explanation of the latter's decision to consult the respondent before taking the action which he did to cancel the appellant's licence.

At all events a careful reading of the evidence and a consideration of the surrounding circumstances has convinced me that without having received the authorization, direction, order, or "approbation énergique" of the respondent— however one chooses to describe it—the Manager of the Quebec Liquor Commission would not have cancelled the licence.

The proposition that in Canada a member of the executive branch of Government does not make the law but merely carries it out or administers it requires no citation of authority to support it. Similarly, I do not find it necessary to cite from the wealth of authority supporting the principle that a public officer is responsible for acts done by him without legal justification. I content myself with quoting the well-known passage from *Dicey's Law of the Constitution*, 9th ed., at 193–4, where he says: "Every official, from the Prime Minister down to a constable or a collector of taxes, is under the same responsibility for every act done without legal justification as any other citizen. The Reports abound with cases in which officials have been brought before the courts, and made, in their personal capacity, liable to punishment, or to the payment of damages, for acts done in their official character but in excess of their lawful authority. A colonial governor, a secretary of state, a military officer, and all subordinates, though carrying out the commands of their official superiors, are as responsible for any act which the law does not authorize as is any private and unofficial person."

In the instant case, the respondent was given no statutory power to interfere in the administration or direction of the Quebec Liquor Commission although as Attorney-General of the Province the Commission and its officers could of course consult him for legal opinions and legal advice. The Commission is not a Department of Government in the accepted sense of that term. Upon the Alcoholic Liquor Act the Commission is an independent body with corporate status and with the powers and responsibilities conferred upon it by the Legislature. The Attorney-General is given no power under the said Act to intervene in the administration of the affairs of the Commission nor does the Attorney-General's Department Act, R.S.Q. 1941, c. 46, confer any such authority upon him.

I have no doubt that in taking the action which he did, the respondent was convinced that he was acting in what he conceived to be the best interests of the people of his Province but this, of course, has no relevance to the issue of his responsibility in damages for any acts done in excess of his legal authority. I have no doubt also that respondent knew and was bound to know as Attorney-General that neither as Premier of the Province nor as Attorney-General was he authorized in law to interfere with the administration of the Quebec Liquor Commission or to give an order or an authorization to any officer of that body to exercise a discretionary authority entrusted to such officer by the statute.

It follows, therefore, that in purporting to authorize and instruct the Manager of the Quebec Liquor Commission to cancel appellant's licence, the respondent was acting without any legal authority whatsoever. Moreover, as I have said, I think respondent was bound to know that he was acting without such authority.

The respondent is therefore liable under art. 1053 of the Civil Code for the damages sustained by the appellant, by reason of the acts done by respondent in excess of his legal authority.

In my opinion before a public officer can be held to be acting "in the exercise of his functions", within the meaning of art. 88 C.C.P., it must be established that at the time he performed the act complained of such public officer had reasonable ground for believing that such act was within his legal authority to perform: *Asselin v. Davidson* (1914), Que.K.B. 274 at 280. In the instant case, as I have said, in my view the respondent was bound to know that the act complained of was beyond his legal authority.

Rand J. (Judson J. Concurring): In these circumstances, when the *de facto* power of the Executive over its appointees at will to such a statutory public function is exercised deliberately and intentionally to destroy the vital business interests of a citizen, is there legal redress by him against the person so acting? This calls for an examination of the statutory provisions governing the issue, renewal and revocation of liquor licences and the scope of authority entrusted by law to the Attorney-General and the Government in relation to the administration of the Act.

The liquor law is contained in R.S.Q. 1941, c.255, entitled An Act Respecting Alcoholic Liquor. A Commission is created as a corporation, the only member of which is the General Manager. By s.5: The exercise of the functions, duties and powers of the Quebec Liquor Commission shall be vested in one person alone named by the Lieutenant-Governor in Council, with the title of manager. The remuneration of such person shall be determined by the Lieutenant-Governor in Council and be paid out of the revenues of the Liquor Commission.

The entire staff for carrying out the duties of the Commission are appointed by the General Manager—here Mr. Archambault—who fixes salaries and assigns functions, the Lieutenant-Governor in Council reserving the right of approval of the salaries. Besides the general operation of buying and selling liquor throughout the Province and doing all things necessary to that end, the Commission is authorized by s.9(e) to "grant, refuse, or cancel permits for the sale of alcoholic liquor or other permits in regard thereto, and to transfer the permit of any person deceased". By s.12 suits against the General Manager for acts done in the exercise of his duties require the authority of the Chief Justice of the Province, and the Commission can be sued only with the consent of the Attorney-General. Every officer of the Commission is declared to be a public officer and by the Public Officers Act, R.S.Q. 1941, c.10, s.2 holds office during pleasure. By s.19 the Commission shall pay over to the Provincial Treasurer any moneys which the latter considers available and by s.20 the Commission is to account to the Provincial Treasurer for its receipts, disbursements, assets and liabilities. Section 30 and 32 provide for the issue of permits to sell; they are to be granted to individuals only, in their own names; by s.34 the Commission "may refuse to grant any permit"; (2) provides for permits in special cases of municipalities where prohibition of sale is revoked in whole or part by by-law; sub-s. (3) restricts or refuses the grant of permits in certain cities the council of which so requests; but it is provided that "If the fyling of such by-law takes place after the Commission has granted a permit in such city or town, the Commission shall be unable to give effect to the request before the first of May next after the date of fyling." Subsection (4) deals with a refusal to issue permits in small cities unless requested by a by-law, approved by a majority vote of the electors. By sub-s. (6) special power is given the Commission to grant permits to hotels in summer resorts for five months only notwithstanding that requests under sub-ss. (2) and (4) are not made. Section 35 prescribes the expiration of every permit on April 30th of each year. Dealing with cancellation, the section provides that the Commission may cancell any permit at its discretion." Besides the loss of privilege and without the necessity of legal proceedings, cancellation entails loss of fees paid to obtain it and confiscation of the liquor in the possession of the holder and the receptacles containing it. If the cancellation is not followed by prosecution for an offence under the Act, compensation is provided for certain items of the forfeiture. Sub-section (5) requires the Commission to cancel any permit made use of on behalf of a person other than the holder; s.36 requires cancellation in specified cases. The sale of liquor is, by s.42, forbidden to various persons. Section 148 places upon the Attorney-General the duty of:

1. Assuring the observance of this act and of the Alcoholic Liquor Possession and Transportation Act (c.256), and investigating, preventing and suppressing the infringements of such acts, in every way authorized thereby;

2. Conducting the suits or prosecutions for infringements of this act or of the said Alcoholic Liquor Possession and Transportation Act.

The provisions of the statute, which may be supplemented by detailed Regulations, furnish a code for the complete administration of the sale and distribution of alcoholic liquors directed by the Commission as a public service, for all legitimate purposes of the populace. It recognizes the association of wines and liquors as embellishments of food and its ritual and as an interest of the public. As put in McBeth, the "sauce to meat is ceremony," and so we have restaurants, cafes, hotels and other places of serving food, specifically provided for in that association.

At the same time the issue of permits has a complementary interest in those so catering to the public. The continuance of the permit over the years, as in this case, not only recognizes its virtual necessity to a superior class restaurant but also its identification with the business carried on. The provisions for assignment of the permit are to this most pertinent and they were exemplified in the continuity of the business here. As its exercise continues, the economic life of the holder becomes progressively more deeply implicated with the privilege while at the same time his vocation becomes correspondingly dependent on it.

The field of licensed occupations and businesses of this nature is steadily becoming of greater concern to citizens generally. It is a matter of vital importance that a public administration that can refuse to allow a person to enter or continue a calling which, in the absence of regulation, would be free and legitimate, should be conducted with complete impartiality and integrity; and that the grounds for refusing or cancelling a permit should unquestionably be such and only such as are incompatible with the purposes envisaged by the statute: the duty of a Commission is to serve those purposes and those only. A decision to deny or cancel such a privilege lies within the "discretion" of the Commission; but that means that decision is to be based upon a weighing of considerations pertainent to the object of the administration.

In public regulation of this sort thre is no such thing as absolute and untrammelled "discretion," that is that action can be taken on any ground or for any reason that can be suggested to the mind of the administrator; no legislative Act can, without express language, be taken to contemplate an unlimited arbitrary power, exercisable for any purpose, however, capricious or irrelevant, regardless of the nature or purpose of the statute. Fraud and corruption in the Commission may not be mentioned in such statutes but they are always implied as exceptions. "Discretion" necessarily implies good faith in discharging public duty; there is always a perspective within which a statute is intended to operate; and any clear departure from its lines or objects is just as objectionable as fraud or corruption. Could an applicant be refused a permit because he had been born in another Province, or because of the colour of his hair? The ordinary language of the Legislature cannot be so distorted.

To deny or revoke a permit because a citizen exercises an unchallengeable right totally irrelevant to the sale of liquor in a restaurant is equally beyond the scope of the discretion conferred. There was here not only revocation of the existing permit but a declaration of a future, definitive disqualification of the appellant to obtain one: it was to be "forever." This purports to divest his citizenship status of its incident of membership in the class of those of the public to whom such a privilege could be extended. Under the statutory language here, that is not competent to the Commission and *a fortiori* to the Government or the respondent" *McGillivray v. Kimber* (1915), 26 D.L.R. 164, 52 S.C.R. 146. There is here an administrative tribunal which, in certain aspects, is to act in a judicial manner; and even on the view of the dissenting Justices in *McGillivray*, there is liability: what could be more malicious than to punish this licensee for having done what he had an absolute right to do in a matter utterly irrelevant to the Alcoholic Liquor Act? Malice in the proper sense is simply acting for a reason and purpose knowingly foreign to the administration, to which was added here the element of intentional punishment by what was virtually vocation outlawry.

It may be difficult if not impossible in cases generally to demonstrate a breach of this public duty in the illegal purpose served; there may be no means, even if proceedings against the Commission were permitted by the Attorney-General, as here they were refused, of compelling the Commission to justify a refusal or revocation or to give reasons for its action; on these questions I make no observation; but in the case before us that difficulty is not present: the reasons are openly avowed.

The act of the respondent through the instrumentality of the Commission brought about a breach of an implied public statutory duty toward the appellant; it was a gross abuse of legal power expressly intended to punish him for an act wholly irrelevant to the statute, a punishment which inflicted on him, as it was intended to do, the destruction of his economic life as a restaurant keeper within the Province. Whatever may be the immunity of the Commission or its member from an action for damages, there is none in the respondent. He was under no duty in relation to the appellant and his act was an intrusion upon the functions of a statutory body. The injury done by him was a fault engaging liability within the principles of the underlying public law of Quebec: *Mostyn v. Fabrigas* (1774), 1 Cowp. 161, 98 E.R. 1021, and under art, 1053 of the Civil Code. That, in the presence of expanding administrative regulation of economic activities, such a step and its consequences are to be suffered by the victim without recourse or remedy, that an administration according to law is to be superseded by action dictated by and according to the arbitrary likes, dislikes and irrelevant purposes of public officers acting beyond their duty, would signalize the beginning of disintegration of the rule of law as a fundamental postulate of our constitutional structure. An administration of licences' on the highest level of fair and impartial treatment to all may be forced to follow the practice of "first come, first served," which makes the strictest observance of equal responsibility to all of even greater importance; at this stage of developing government it would be a danger of high consequence to tolerate such a departure from good faith in executing the legislative purpose. It should be added, however, that the principle is not, by this language, intended to be extended to ordinary governmental employment: with that we are not here concerned.

It was urged by Mr. Beaulieu that the respondent, as the incumbent of an office of state, so long as he was proceeding in "good faith," was free to act in a matter of this kind virtually as he pleased. The office of Attorney-General traditionally and by statute carries duties that relate to advising the Executive, including here, administrative bodies, enforcing the public law and directing the administration of justice. In any decision of the statutory body in this case, he had no part to play beyond giving advice on legal questions arising. In that role his action should have been limited to advice on the validity of a revocation for such a reason or purpose and what that advice should have been does not seem to me to admit of any doubt. To pass from this limited scope of action to that of bringing about a step by the Commission beyond the bounds prescribed by the Legislature for its exclusive action converted what was done into his personal act.

"Good faith" in this context, applicable both to the respondent and the General Manager, means carrying out the statute according to its intent and for its purpose; it means good faith in acting with a rational appreciation of that intent and purpose and not with an improper intent and for an alien purpose; it does not mean for the purposes of punishing a person for exercising an unchallengeable right; it does not mean arbitrarily and illegally attempting to divest a citizen of an incident of his civil status.

MARTLAND J., KERWIN C.J.C., and LOCKE J. also concurred.
TASCHEREAU, Cartwright, and FAUTEUX JJ. dissented.

4. COMMONWEALTH

BRIBERY COMMISSIONER v. RANASINGHE (1965)

Constitutional guarantees are immune from acts of Parliament. A legislature does not possess the inherent power to disregard the constitutional mandate. Possibly the most fundamental of the fundamental rights is the inviolability of constitutional protection against temporary legislative majorities and their shifting policies.

So ruled the Privy Council of the House of Lords hearing the case of *Bribery Commissioner v. Ranasinghe*, on appeal from Ceylon (now Sri Lanka) in 1964. It was an interpretation of the Constitution of Ceylon—which, as in all the other Commonwealth nations save New Zealand and the United Kingdom itself, was promulgated as a single document to represent the nation's highest law. Struck down as a violation of the constitutionally protected judicial structure and due process of law was the legislatively created bribery commission and its procedures.

This would not be the law in the United Kingdom where the Mother of Parliaments is empowered to change the nation's constitutional structure by a simple majority vote. The same is true in New Zealand. But it is the law throughout the rest of the Commonwealth that a measure violative of the existing constitution requires a constitutional amendment to become valid.

BRIBERY COMMISSIONER v. RANASINGHE

House of Lords and Privy Council (On Appeal from the Supreme Court of Ceylon) 1965 Appeals Cases 172 [Excerpted. Footnotes renumbered.]

May 5. The judgment of their Lordships was delivered by Lord Pearce. The appellant is the Bribery Commissioner of Ceylon on whom lies the duty of bringing prosecutions before the Bribery Tribunal which was created by the Bribery Amendment Act, 1958. The respondent was prosecuted for a bribery offence before that tribunal. It convicted and sentenced him to a term of imprisonment and a fine. On appeal the Supreme Court declared the conviction and orders made against him null and inoperative on the ground that the persons composing the Bribery Tribunal which tried him were not lawfully appointed to the tribunal. In the present case, as in some earlier reported cases, the court took the view that the method of appointing persons to the panel from which the tribunal is drawn offends against an important safeguard in the Constitution of Ceylon.

The Constitution is contained in the Ceylon (Constitution) Orders in Council, 1946 and 1947. There is no need to refer in detail to the various Acts and Orders that established the independence of Ceylon. Viscount Radcliffe in *Attorney-General of Ceylon v. de Livera*[185] said of the Constitution, "although there are many variations in matters of detail, its general conceptions are seen at once to be those of a parliamentary democracy founded on the pattern of the constitutional system of the United Kingdom."

The Constitution does not specifically deal with the judicial system which was established in Ceylon by the Charter of Justice of 1833 and is dealt with in certain Ordinances, the principal being the Courts Ordinance, cap. 6. The power and jurisdiction of the courts are thereafter not expressly protected by the Constitution. But the importance of securing the independence of judges and of maintaining the dividing line between the judiciary and the executive was appreciated by those who framed the Constitution. See the Ceylon Report of the Soulbury Commission on Constitutional Reform, Appendix I (I), paragraphs 27 and 28, and Appendix I (II), sections 68 and 69. Part 5 of the Constitution is headed "The Executive" and Part 6 "The Judicature." Part 6 deals with the appointment and dismissal of judges. The judges of the Supreme Court are not removable except by the Governor-General on an address of the Senate and the House of Representatives (section 52). So far as concerns the judges of lesser rank, section 55 provided that "The appointment, transfer, dismissal and disciplinary control of judicial officers is hereby vested in the Judicial Service Commission." The Commission consists of the Chief Justice as chairman and a judge of the Supreme Court and "one other person who shall be, or shall have been, a Judge of the Supreme Court" [section 53 (1)], and no Senator or Member of Parliament shall be appointed. Thus there is secured a freedom from political control, and it is a punishable offence to attempt directly or indirectly to influence any decision of the Commission (section 56).

The questions before their Lordships are whether the statutory provisions for the appointment of members of the panel of the Bribery Tribunal otherwise than by the Judicial Service Commission conflict with sections 55 of the Constitution, and, if so, whether those provisions are valid.

In 1954 the Bribery Act was passed in order to meet a social need. It gave to the Attorney-General or officers authorised by him power to direct and conduct the investigation of any allegation of bribery, and certain powers for securing information and assistance. If there was a prima facie case, he was empowered to indict offenders who were not public servants before the ordinary courts. Offenders who were public servants might either be so indicted or be arraigned before a Board of Inquiry constituted from certain panels to which members were appointed by the Governor-General on the advice of the Prime Minister. It had to decide whether the accused was guilty and it could order the guilty to pay the amount of the bribe as a penalty. A finding of guilt resulted in automatic dismissal and certain disqualifications and incapacities.

The Bribery Act of 1954 was treated by the legislature as coming within section 29 (4) of the Constitution, which deals with any amendments to the Constitution, and there was endorsed on the bill, when it was presented for the Royal Assent, the necessary certificate of the Speaker. That Act also contained a section as follows: "2. (1) Every provision of this Act which may be in conflict or inconsistent with anything in the Ceylon (Constitution) Order in Council, 1946, shall for all purposes and in all respects be as valid and effectual as though that provision were in an Act for the amendment of that Order in Council enacted by

Parliament after compliance with the requirement imposed by the proviso of subsection (4) of section 29 of that Order in Council. (2) Where the provisions of this Act are in conflict or are inconsistent with any other written law, this Act shall prevail."

In 1958 radical changes were made. The Bribery Amendment Act, 1958, swept away the Boards of Inquiry which dealt with public servants and created Bribery Tribunals for the trial of persons prosecuted for bribery with power to hear, try, and determine any prosecution for bribery made against any person before the tribunal. The Bribery Commissioner was brought into being and was empowered to prosecute persons before the tribunal. All the offences of bribery specified in Part II of the Act, punishable with rigorous imprisonment for a term not exceeding seven years or a fine not exceeding Rs.5000 or both became triable by the tribunal. Whether the effect was that the offences of bribery under Part 2 of the Act "were no longer triable by the courts" as was said by Sansoni J. in *Senadhira v. Bribery Commissioner*[186] or that, as is contended by Mr. Lawson on behalf of the Bribery Commissoner, the courts and the tribunal have concurrent powers, is immaterial. No doubt, even if Mr. Lawson's contention on his behalf be correct, the practical effect would be to supercede the court's jurisdiction in bribery cases to a large extent. . . .

There is, therefore, a plain conflict between section 55 of the Constitution and section 41 of the Bribery Amendment Act under which the panel is appointed. What is the effect of this conflict? The Supreme Court has held that it renders section 41 invalid. Mr. Lawson, however, contends on behalf of the Bribery Commissioner that, since the Act has been passed by both Houses and received the Royal Assent, it is a valid enactment and has the full force of law, amending the Constitution if and in so far as necessary. If, he argues, there has been a defect in procedure, that does not make the Act invalid, since the Ceylon Parliament is sovereign and had the power to pass it. Nor are the courts able to look behind the Act to see if it was validly passed.

The voting and legislative power of the Ceylon Parliament are dealt with in sections 18 and 29 of the Constitution.

"18. Save as otherwise provided in subsection (4) of section 29, any question proposed for decision by either Chamber shall be determined by a majority of votes of the Senators or Members, as the case may be, present and voting . . . "

"29—(1) Subject to the provisions of this Order, Parliament shall have power to make laws for the peace, order and good government of the Island.

"(2) No such law shall—(a) prohibit or restrict the free exercise of any religion;"

There follow (b), (c) and (d), which set out further entrenched religious and racial matters, which shall not be the subject of legislation. They represent the solemn balance of rights between the citizens of Ceylon, the fundamental conditions on which inter se they accepted the Constitution; and these are therefore unalterable under the Constitution.

"(3) Any law made in contravention of subsection (2) of this section shall, to the extent of such contravention, be void.

"(4) In the exercise of its powers under this section, Parliament may ammend or repeal any of the provisions of this Order, or of any other Order of Her Majesty in Council in its application to the Island:

"Provided that no Bill for the amendment or repeal of any of the provisions of this Order shall be presented for the Royal Assent unless it has endorsed on it a certificate under the hand of the Speaker that the number of votes cast in favour thereof in the House of Representatives amounted to not less than two-thirds of the whole number of Members of the House (including those not present).

"Every certificate of the Speaker under this subsection shall be conclusive for all purposes and shall not be questioned in any court of law."

The Bribery Amendment Act, 1958, contained no section similar to section 2 of the Act of 1954, nor did the Bill bear a certificate of the Speaker. There is nothing to show that it was passed by the necessary two-thirds majority. If the presence of the certificate is conclusive in favour of such a majority, there is force in the argument that its absence is conclusive against such a majority. Moreover, where an Act involves a conflict with the Constitution, the certificate is a necessary part of the Act-making process and its existence must be made apparent.

The fact that the 1958 Bill did not have a certificate and was not passed by the necessary majority was not really disputed in the Supreme Court or before their Lordships' Board, but it has been argued that the court, when faced with an official copy of an Act of Parliament, cannot inquire into any procedural matter and cannot now properly consider whether a certificate was endorsed on the Bill. That argument seems to their Lordships unsubstantial, and it was rightly rejected by the Supreme Court. Once it is shown that an Act conflicts with a provision in the Constitution, the certificate is an essential part of the legislative process. The court has a duty to see that the Constitution is not infringed and to preserve it inviolate . . .

[A] legislature has no power to ignore the conditions of law-making that are imposed by the instrument which itself regulates its power to make law. This restriction exists independently of the question whether the legislature is sovereign, as is the legislature of Ceylon, or whether the Constitution is "uncontrolled," as the Board held the Constitution of Queensland to be. Such a Constitution can, indeed, be altered or amended by the legislature, if the regulating instrument so provides and if the terms of those provisions are complied with: and the alteration or amendment may include the change or abolition of those very provisions. But the proposition which is not acceptable is that a legislature, once established, has some inherent power derived from the mere fact of its establishment to make a valid law by the resolution of a bare majority which its own constituent instrument has said shall not be a valid law unless made by a different type of majority or by a different legislative process. And this is the proposition which is in reality involved in the argument.

It is possible now to state summarily what is the essential difference between the *McCawley* case[187] and this case. There the legislature, having full power to make laws by a majority, except upon one subject that was not in question, passed a law which conflicted with one of the existing terms of its Constitution Act. It was held that this was valid legislation, since it must be treated as pro tanto an alteration of the Constitution, which was neither fundamental in the sense of being beyond change nor so constructed as to require any special legislative process to pass upon the topic dealt with. In the present case, on the other hand, the legislature has purported to pass a law which, being in conflict with section 55 of the Order in Council, must be treated, if it is to be valid, as an implied alteration of the Constitutional provisions about the appointment of judicial officers. Since such alterations, even if express, can only be made by laws which comply with the special legislative procedure laid down in section 29 (4), the Ceylon legislature has not got the general power to legislate so as to amend its Constitution by ordinary majority resolutions, such as the Queensland legislature was found to have under section 2 of its Constitution Act, but is rather in the position, for effecting such amendments, that the legislature was held to be in by virtue of its section 9, namely, compelled to operate a special procedure in order to achieve the desired result. . . .

The legislative power of the Ceylon Parliament is derived from section 18 and section 29 of its Constitution. Section 18 expressly says "save as otherwise ordered in subsection (4) of section 29." Section 29 (1) is expressed to be "subject to the provisions of this Order." And any power under section 29 (4) is expressly subject to its proviso. Therefore in the case of amendment and repeal of the Constitution the Speaker's certificate is a necessary part of the legislative process and any Bill which does not comply with the condition precedent of the proviso, is and remains, even though it receives the Royal Assent, invalid and ultra vires.

No question of sovereignty arises. A Parliament does not cease to be sovereign whenever its component members fail to produce among themselves a requisite majority, e.g., when in the case of ordinary legislation the voting is evenly divided or when in the case of legislation to amend the Constitution there is only a bare majority if the Constitution requires something more. The minority are entitled under the Constitution of Ceylon to have no amendment of it which is not passed by a two-thirds majority. The limitation thus imposed on some lesser majority of members does not limit the sovereign powers of Parliament itself which can always, whenever it chooses, pass the amendment with the requisite majority.

The case of *Thambiayah v. Kulasingham*[188] is authority for the view that where invalid parts of the statute which are ultra vires can be severed from the rest which is intra vires it is they alone which should be held invalid.

Their Lordships therefore are in accord with the view so clearly expressed by the Supreme Court "that the orders made against the respondent are null and inoperative on the grounds that the persons composing the Bribery Tribunal which tried him were not lawfully appointed to the Tribunal."[189] They will accordingly humbly advise Her Majesty to dismiss this appeal. In accordance with the agreement between the parties the appellant will pay the costs of the respondent.

5. FEDERAL REPUBLIC OF GERMANY

MEPHISTO CASE

What should be the decision when two fundamental human rights collide? Few court opinions are available on this fascinating issue. But it is one which the West German Federal Supreme Court squarely faced involving the protection of the dignity and privacy of the individual confronting the conflicting right of artistic expression. As the case indicates, there may be situations in which the publication of a book may be banned. One must examine with care the weights given to the competing rights in the majority and two dissenting opinions.

The *Mephisto Case* arose out of a novel written by Klaus Mann in which his former brother-in-law, Gustaf Gruendgens, is portrayed as a Nazi collaborator of the most corrupt and cynical sort. The character's name was changed to Hendrik Hoefgen, but the figure of Hoefgen was readily identifiable as Gruendgens, who had died prior to the case.

Suit was brought by Gruendgens' adopted son in an attempt to enjoin publication as defaming his father's memory. The publisher filed a constitutional complaint in the Constitutional Court, claiming that the judgment of lower German courts which forbade distribution of the book violated Article 5, par. 3, sent. 1 of the Basic Law: "Art and science, research and teaching, shall be free."

This case involves more than the civil law of libel. It illustrates the delicate task of resolving an individual right which is infringed by the exercise of another individual right. Whether Klaus Mann the novelist had a greater right than the son of the allegedly defamed man is a matter which goes beyond the doctrines of the laws of tort. At stake are two sections of a constitutional text which was intended generously to protect human rights.

MEPHISTO CASE

30BVerfGE 173 (1971) West German Constitutional Court [Excerpted] [Footnotes Renumbered.] [Opinion of Court] Reasons. . . .

III. . . .

. . . Art. 5, par. 3, sent. 1, contains first of all an objective norm that regulates relationships between the realm of the arts and the State and decides between values. At the same time, this provision guarantees everyone who is active in this sphere an individual right to freedom.

1. . . . The essential characteristic of artistic activity is free creative shaping in which the artist's impressions and experiences are given immediate expression through a specific form of language. . . .

2. . . . Even if the artist describes events of real life, this reality is

"poeticized" in a work of art. The real event is detached from empiric-historical reality and brought into new relations that are governed . . . by artistic rules of graphic description. The truthfulness of an individual event can and sometimes must be sacrificed to artistic uniformity.

The essence and purpose of the basic right of Art. 5, par. 3, sent. 1, are to keep processes, modes of behavior, and decisions based on the inherent laws of art and determined by aesthetic considerations independent of limits set by public authorities. The manner in which an artist encounters reality and describes events that he experiences in this encounter cannot be prescribed for him if the process of artistic creation is to develop freely. Only the artist himself can decide the "rightness" of his attitude toward reality. In this respect, the guarantee of artistic freedom constitutes a prohibition against influencing methods, contents, and tendencies of artistic activity and, in particular, against restricting the sphere of artistic creativity or prescribing generally binding rules for this creative process. For the epic work of art, the constitutional guarantee includes free choice of a subject and free shaping of that subject.

3. Art. 5, par. 3, sent. 1, comprehensively guarantees freedom of artistic activity. As far as public media are necessary to establish relations between the artist and the public, the guarantee of artistic freedom therefore also protects persons who exercise such an intermediary function. . . . The complainant, being the publisher of the novel, can therefore rely on the basic right from Art. 5, par. 3, sent. 1. . . .

4. Art. 5 guarantees autonomy of the arts without reservation. Attempts to restrict that guarantee by limiting the concept of art, be extending interpretations, or by analogy to clauses restricting other constitutional provisions, all fail because of Art. 5's clear instructions.

. . . The genesis of Art. 5, par. 3, offers no basis for assuming that the authors of the Constitution considered freedom of the arts as a sub-category of freedom of expression. . . .

The opinion that Art. 2, par. 1, second half of the sentence, restricts freedom of the arts by the rights of others, the constitutional order, and the moral code must also be rejected. This view is inconsistent with the subsidiary position of Art. 2, par. 1, as compared to the speciality of individual rights of liberty, which have been consistently recognized by the Federal Constitutional Court. . . .

5. On the other hand, the right of artistic liberty is not unlimited. Like all basic rights, the guarantee of liberty in Art. 5, par. 3, sent. 1, is based on the Basic Law's image of man as an autonomous person who develops freely within the social community. But the unconditional nature of basic rights means that limits on artistic freedom can be determined only by the Constitution itself. Since freedom of the arts does not contain any reservation for the legislator, it cannot be restricted by the general legal system or by an indefinite clause which . . . endangers values necessary for the existence of a national community. A conflict respecting artistic freedom must rather be solved by interpreting the Constitution according to the value order established in the Basic Law and the unity of its fundamental system of values. Freedom of the arts is closely related to the dignity of man guaranteed in Art. 1, which, as the supreme value,

governs the entire value system of the Basic Law. But the guarantee of freedom of the arts can conflict with that latter constitutionally protected sphere since a work of art can also produce social effects. Because a work of art acts not only as an aesthetic reality, but also exists in the social world, an artist's use of personal data about people in his environment can affect their social rights to respect and esteem. . . .

6. In order to judge the protective effects arising from the personality sphere of the late actor Gruendgens, the courts properly referred to Art. 1, par. 1. It would be inconsistent with the constitutionally guaranteed right of the inviolability of the dignity of man, upon which all basic rights are based, if man . . . could be degraded or debased in this right to respect even if only after his death. Accordingly, the obligation imposed on all State authority in Art. 1, par. 1, to protect the individual against attacks on his dignity does not end with death. . . .

7. The solution to the conflict between protection of one's personality and the right to artistic freedom must therefore not only refer to the effects of a work of art in the extra-artistic social sphere, but must also take art-specific aspects into account. The image of man upon which Art. 1, par. 1, is based is influenced by the guarantee of liberty in Art. 5, par. 3, sent 1. The individual's social right to respect and esteem is just as little superior to the freedom of the arts as the arts can summarily override man's general right to respect.

The decision whether an artistic presentation's utilization of personal data threatens such a grave encroachment upon the protected private sphere of the described person that it could preclude publication of the work of art can only be made after carefully weighing all the facts of individual cases. It must be taken into account whether and to what extent the "image," because of the artistic shaping of the material and its incorporation into and subordination to the overall organism of the work of art, appears as so independent from the "original" that the individual, personal-intimate aspects have been rendered objective in favor of the general, symbolic character of the "figure." If such a study . . . reveals that the artist has given or even wanted to give a "portrait" of the "original," then the answer depends on the extent of artistic abstraction or the extent and importance of the "falsification" of the reputation or memory of the person concerned.

IV.

The Federal Constitutional Court thus must decide whether the courts, when weighing the personality sphere of the late Gustaf Gruendgens and his adopted son . . . against freedom of the arts . . . took these principles into account. The Senate was divided equally on this question. Pursuant to Art. 15, par. 2, sent. 4, of the court's jurisdictional statute, it could not be found that the challenged judgments violate the Basic Law. . . .

2. . . . [T]he Supreme Court of Hamburg and the Federal Supreme Court assumed that protection of Gruendgen's right to respect continues in the social sphere. In this regard the Federal Supreme Court correctly considered that the need for protection—and accordingly the obligation to protect—diminishes as the memory of the deceased person fades. . . . On the other hand, the courts also assumed that Klaus Mann's novel constitutes a work of art in the sense of Art.

5, par. 3. . . . The Courts tried to solve this conflict by weighing the conflicting interests against each other.

3. The Federal Constitutional Court has consistently held that in deciding a constitutional complaint court decisions can be reviewed only within narrow limits. In particular, establishment and evaluation of facts, interpretation of laws and their application to individual cases are the business of regular courts and cannot be reviewed by the Federal Constitutional Court. These principles apply here, namely, weighing conflicting rights of the parties. . . . This weighing is primarily assigned to the competent courts that interpret and apply the civil law. In such cases, the civil judge's task is to appraise and weigh the facts of the individual case, taking into consideration the general prohibition against arbitrariness, and then defining the limits of the respective spheres of the basic rights of the two parties. The basic right of the defeated party is not violated merely because the judge's weighing of conflicting interests might attach too much or too little importance to his interests. . . . The Federal Constitutional Court is not empowered to substitute its own valuation of individual cases as if it were a court of appeal. . . . In such cases, it can declare a violation of the basic right of the defeated party only if the competent judge did not recognize that it is a matter of weighing conflicting spheres of basic rights or if his decision is based on a fundamentally incorrect conception of the significance of one or the other of the basic rights, in particular the extent of their protective spheres.

. . . Judging these decisions in their overall context, it cannot be found that they are based on a fundamentally incorrect conception of the significance and extent of the spheres protected by the two basic rights. The decisions do not demonstrate any incorrect conception of the essence of the basic right that was defeated. . . . The courts not only attached importance to the novel's effects in the extra-artistic social sphere, but also took art-specific aspects into account. They explained carefully and in detail that the novel's character Hendrik Hoefgen corresponds so clearly in so many details to Gruendgens that a considerable number of readers had no difficulty recognizing Gruendgens in Hoefgen. Whether this is correct is not for the Federal Constitutional Court to decide; in any event, the courts' decisive valuation of the facts in that the artistic treatment of the material and its incorporation into and subordination to the overall organism of the novel did not make the "image" Hoefgen independent enough from the "original" Gruendgens and did not artistically transcend the representation, so that the individual, personal-intimate aspects do not appear sufficiently objectified in favor of the general, symbolic character of the "figure." The courts also discussed in detail the fact that the author painted a basically negative picture of the personality and character of Hoefgen and thus of the late Gruendgens, a picture that is in many details enriched by untrue, invented acts that negatively characterize the person's attitude . . . and contains verbal insults and calumnies that are inflicted on Gruendgens through the person of Hoefgen. The Supreme Court of Hamburg designated the novel—without objection from the Federal Supreme Court—as a "libelous pamphlet in the form of a novel." There are no sufficient reasons to oppose this evaluation. . . .

Finally, the conclusion of the courts . . . cannot be challenged by an argument that the ban on publication is out of proportion to the encroachment on the late Gustaf Gruendgens' right to respect. It is true that the Federal Constitutional Court has repeatedly emphasized that the principle of proportionateness* has constitutional rank and must therefore be considered in all encroachments by public authority on the citizen's sphere of liberty. But here it is not a matter of such an encroachment. The courts only had to judge a civil law claim made by one citizen against another, that is, to give concrete definition to a civil law relationship in an individual case. . . . ± The primary function of law is to solve conflicts between interests of persons of equal legal status in as appropriate a manner as possible. Therefore, the Federal Constitutional Court can review the ban on publication only to the extent of determining whether the constitutional provision regarding equality before the law was observed (Art. 3, par. 1). This question must be answered in the affirmative. . . .

Dissenting opinion of Justice Dr. Stein

In the foregoing decision only the view of three judges is presented in [Sec. IV]. . . . Being one of the three other judges . . . I give the following reasons for my dissent. . . .

I. . . .

In the present trial, the Federal Constitutional Court should independently review the challenged court decisions to determine, among other things, whether civil courts in the required framework of weighing interests sufficiently considered the special laws inherent to the novel of Klaus Mann as a work of art which, according to the value decision in Art. 5, par. 3, must also be taken into consideration vis-à-vis the protected interests of Gustaf Gruendgens' personality sphere. For the content and scope of the constitutional guarantee of Art. 5, par. 3, sent. 1, and its relation to the other value decisions of the Basic Law are immediately affected if a civil law decision does not correctly determine the effect of the basic right on civil law and thus misinterprets the Constitution's value hierarchy. Such a misinterpretation would violate the basic right whose judicial protection Art. 1, par. 3, declares to be a constitutional right. . . . Whether and to what extent within the scope of the civil law order the conflict between clashing interests occurs because of "emissive effects" from the value system of the Constitution itself . . . cannot be established in the abstract. . . . Thus, on the basis of the concrete facts of the case at hand, the Federal Constitutional Court must examine the compatibility of the challenged decisions with the constitutional guarantee of freedom of the arts. By so doing, the Federal Constitutional Court does not weigh the interests on the level of ordinary law, nor does it usurp the functions of a court of appeal. Rather, it establishes only the protective scope of basic rights and their effect on the civil law in the case to be decided. Thus the Court only fulfills the function assigned by the Constitution to supervise application of constitutional norms by judicial organs. If in cases such as this the Federal Constitutional Court's competency for reviewing were . . . restricted to the narrow question of whether the courts recognized and considered the influence of basic rights and did not violate the general prohibition of arbitrariness . . . then the Federal Constitutional Court would not do justice to its task as guardian of basic rights. . . . In its judgments . . . this

Court has consistently refused to limit itself to abstract declarations, but has considered itself competent to substitute its own evaluations for those of civil and criminal courts. . . .

II.

1. The required weighing of interests . . . must correspond in all respects to the Constitution's value decisions. If the obligatory weighing of interests disregards this specific constitutionally imposed relationship, as in [the official opinion], freedom of the arts as guaranteed by Art. 5, par. 3, sent. 1, is violated. The evaluation of the interests . . . by the Supreme Court of Hamburg and the Federal Supreme Court fundamentally misjudged this relationship to art which the Constitution demands. . . .

Neither court sufficiently considered that a work of art . . . has reality not only in the extra-artistic sphere . . . but predominantly on the aesthetic level. The courts one-sidedly considered only tensions in the social sphere and, in so doing, ignored the novel's aesthetic aspect. This one-sided consideration affected the weighing of interests. . . . They compared the appearance and behavior of the fictitious Hendrik Hoefgen with the personality of Gustaf Gruendgens only from the viewpoint of readers who take the novel for reality. . . .

This approach may be appropriate for a documentary or biography. . . . But a novel's artistic intent is not a realistic, truth-oriented description of historical events, but a substantial, descriptive shaping of material by the writer's imagination. A judgment on a novel solely on the basis of effects that it produces outside its aesthetic existence neglects the specific relationship of art with reality and thus unlawfully restricts the right guaranteed by Art. 5. . . .

2. A work of art like the novel by Klaus Mann aspires to a "more realistic reality" that is independent from real reality. . . . In a novel, time and space are different than in real life. A "photograph" of reality is not the novel's artistic goal. Even if, as here, the author refers to real historical facts, there occurs a transcendence of these events . . . into the work of art's own "aesthetic reality" created by the artist's imagination. The artistic representation cannot, therefore, be measured by standards of the real world, but only by an art-specific, aesthetic standard. Data taken from reality and transformed can still be "truthful" with reference to artistic intent even if they, with reference to only the real world, "falsify reality." In aesthetic reality, facts and fiction are mixed without being separated; they do not lead a cumbersome coexistence, but form an inseparable union; everything is a free, "artistic game." . . .

A comparison of Hendrik Hoefgen and Gustaf Gruendgens . . . is on principle irrelevant to the "rightness" or "trueness to reality" of the fictitious character Hendrik Hoefgen in the aesthetic reality of the novel *Mephisto*. . . .

Tensions between an individual whose dignity is to be respected by everyone and the artist's concern are a constituent part of literature. . . . Regardless of their classification among the so-called *roman à clef*, their artistic quality is uncontested, like, among others, the works of: Goethe . . . G. Keller . . . Th. Fontane . . . L. Quidde . . . Thomas Mann . . . H. Hesse . . . G. Flaubert . . . Leo Tolstoy . . . [or] Simone de Beauvoir. . . . These few examples show that real persons have at all times been used even in literature to represent human weaknesses and abysses, and in particular to demonstrate the struggle with the demoniacal in man; persons were "abstracted" by the artist, but could be recognized by anyone familiar with the circumstances. In this connection it is important to note that as early as publication of the novel in the *Pariser Tageszeitung* in Paris in 1936, Klaus Mann protested in a letter to the editors of that newspaper against a remark in the preliminary announcement written by the editors that *Mephisto* was a *roman à clef* concerning the person of G. Gurendgens. He wrote . . .

I am compelled to declare solemnly: When I wrote *Mephisto—Roman einer Karriere*, I was not interested in writing the story of a certain person. I was interested in representing a type, and . . . the sociological and intellectual conditions that made his career possible. . . .

An exclusion of the arts from this sphere of experience would affect their very core. . . . If the arts were thus restricted, they would not be free in the sense of Art. 5, par. 3, sent. 1. The Basic Law's guarantee of freedom of the arts permits neither a restriction of the artist's possible subjects nor a prohibition of certain means or methods of expression. Neither can the artist be required, in particular not by the State, to abstract personal data . . . to prevent identification of a person used as a model. . . . No binding rules can be established for what can be demanded aesthetically, nor can they be established in a liberal State by State authorities. . . .

The Supreme Court of Hamburg, with no objection from the Federal Supreme Court, has ignored the autonomy of artistic processes in its demand that after the end of the war Klaus Mann should have changed his novel *Mephisto*, taking the latest findings about Gruendgens into consideration. Aside from the fact that the novel could only be written under the impression of a very definite, individually experienced situation and cannot be repeated at will independent of the place and time of its creation . . . the courts' unreasonable demand . . . constitutes an unconstitutional encroachment on freedom of artistic creation. . . .

3. . . . The courts' determination that Gruendgens very obviously served as a model for the novel's Hoefgen is correct, but irrelevant. . . . What is decisive is whether the picture of the fictitious Hoefgen has its own function within the world of the novel through which it becomes independent of Gruendgens. . . . The relation of the fictitious Hoefgen with the individual personality of Gruendgens is so strongly superimposed by the artistic conception and symbolic treatment that Gruendgen's personality recedes into the background. At the forefront is the "phenomenon of the intellectual hanger-on." . . . This interpretation was also expressed in reviews which were submitted during the trial. In this connection, contemporary history and cultural history must be taken into consideration. . . . *Mephisto* is a work of exile literature whose subject, structure and language can be correctly judged only under the pressure of the political, social and psychological state of emergency emigration. It is the artistic expression of the profound pain of an outcast who no longer hears news from home except as an echo of madness and terror. He waits for the unknown event that will call him back. . . .

4. Furthermore, in the required weighing of interests, the Federal Supreme Court and the Supreme Court of Hamburg overemphasized the detrimental effects of the novel on the protected sphere of Gustaf Gruendgen's personality. . . .

In this connection it must also be considered that as the memory of the deceased person fades, so does the danger of an adverse effect on the protected personal sphere. These aspects were emphasized, it is true, in the challenged decisions; but they ignored the fact that general interest in persons who are not part of *general* contemporary history but like Gustaf Gruendgens became prominent in a narrower field of public life of their period decreases more quickly after their deaths and that danger of an identification of Gustaf Gruendgens with the novel's character Hendrik Hoefgen . . . is thus smaller.

. . . For those circles who are really interested in Gruendgens, for the connoisseurs of recent theatrical history, the image of Gruendgens' personality is so firmly established that it can no longer be seriously shaken by publication of this novel in 1971. . . .

. . . Also, due to its structure and publications in 1936 and 1956, the novel can today be expected to be of interest only to a limited group of readers who are mostly of the better educated classes . . . [and] know that a novel does not claim to be truthful in the sense of a documentary or a biography, further reducing fear that this novel might be taken literally. . . . This productive and imaginative cooperation of the reader who realized the unity and imminent connections of the work of art is not given any weight at all in the decisions appealed from. On the other hand, one must recognize a justified interest of the public familiar with and interested in literature to know *Mephisto* as a significant work by one of the main representatives of exile literature, what is more, by a member of the Mann family. . . .

When weighing conflicting interests in the sense of constitutional value decisions, impairment of the deceased's personal dignity cannot be so weighty that it could justify a ban on publication.

5. In addition, the foreward reduced possible adverse effects on Gustaf Gruendgens' personal dignity to such an extent that . . . the ban on publication violates the constitutional principle of proportionateness. . . .

Dissenting opinion of Justice Rupp v. Brunneck

I endorse the dissenting opinion of Justice Dr. Stein and would only like briefly to emphasize and add the following:

1. The denial of the constitutional complaint is based on a restrictive interpretation of the Federal Constitutional Court's competency for review which constitutes a break with past decisions and may lead to very serious consequences. . . .

2. The challenged decisions did not sufficiently consider the effect of the basic right guaranteed in Art. 5, par. 3, on the conflict of interests to be decided here. . . .

3. If under certain conditions a restriction of the basic right to artistic freedom comes into question because of protection of the dignity of man in Art. 1, freedom of the arts must nevertheless remain less restricted than if the

restrictions of Art. 5, par. 2, were applied: The encroachment made in the interest of protection of personality must not be more than a slightly restrictive exception. . . .

4. . . . Even if . . . examination is based on the criteria applied in the challenged judgments, the special situation of the author at the time of writing and first publishing the novel must be fully considered. It is well known that Klaus Mann suffered particularly strongly from his fate as an emigrant and that at the same time he was one of the few emigrants who . . . devoted their strength to the intellectual fight against the unlawful National-Socialist regime. In the Schmid-Spiegel case ‡. . . the Federal Constitutional Court held that in a press feud even strong polemics are justified if they correspond to the manner of the opponent's attack and serve a justified interest in exerting an influence on public opinion. I want to refer here also to the extremely generous decisions of the Supreme Court of the United States, which in regard to persons and matters of contemporary life always values the general interest in free public discussion more highly than personal interests . . . as long as there is no "actual malice" involved. _Mephisto_ presents more than a conflict of opinions in the usual frame; rather, it is a form of resistance to an inhuman, unlawful, and unconstitutional regime. . . . If, in the circumstances of that time, a writer employed intellectual weapons that were at his disposal on behalf of a good cause, if he expressed thoughts and feelings not in a political pamphlet, but in the supposedly more effective form of a novel and modeled the plot on a widely known person of contemporary history who because of his high position was regarded as a cultural representative of the opposed regime, then the existing emergency justifies his actions even if he should have made a mistake in the choice of his means. This consideration also remains valid for republication of the novel at the present time. With increasing distance from the historical occasion and with political changes that have occurred, protection of the personality concerned might have relatively more weight, but this is outweighed again by the decrease in need for protection since today a large part of the novel's potential readers no longer associate anything with the name and person of Gustaf Gruendgens. On the whole, the continuing . . . significance of the events of the National-Socialist period and the part of Klaus Mann's artistic message that transcends the concrete occasion make the private and general interest in the novel's publication today seem more worthy of protection than protection from a possible, comparatively small, impairment of Gustaf Gruendgens' memory.[190]

6. INDIA

BENNETT COLEMAN & CO. v. INDIA

Freedom of expression faces barriers in the Third World nations unknown to the prosperous countries of North America and Western Europe—where there are a superabundance of radio and television channels and sets, a superabundance of printing presses and, of course, no shortage of newsprint stock.

But there cannot be that nearly unlimited freedom of press (as in the United States under its First Amendment) where there is a scarcity of the raw materials necessary for the actual printing. Importation of newsprint plus demands on limited foreign exchange and the expenditure means the sacrifice of other needs and wants.

Nowhere is this problem more pressing than in India—a poor nation with a rich tradition in freedom of expression. In order to preserve its scarce foreign exchange, the government concluded that it had to limit the importation of newsprint. This was accompanied by a government order rationing that newsprint. The 1972–73 rationing scheme placed a 10-page limitation upon all newspapers. And it was the constitutionality of this order which was at issue in *Bennett Coleman & Co. v. India.*

The majority conclusion was expressed by Justice Ray in these words: "The power of the Government to import newsprint cannot be denied. The power of the Government to control the distribution of newsprint cannot equally be denied. It has, of course, to be borne in mind that the distribution must be fair and equitable."

BENNETT COLEMAN & CO. v. INDIA

Supreme Court of India AIR 1973 SC 106 (Excerpted)

The Judgment of the Court was delivered by

RAY, J.:—(on behalf of S. M. Sikri, C. J., P. Jaganmohan Reddy, J. and himself): These petitions challenge the Import Policy for Newsprint for the year April 1972 to March 1973. The Newsprint Policy is impeached as an infringement of fundamental rights to freedom of speech and expression in Article 19(1) (a) and right to equality in Article 14 of the Constitution. Some provisions of the Newsprint Control Order 1962 are challenged as violative of Article 19(1) (a) and Article 14 of the Constitution.

2. The import of newsprint is dealt with by Import Control Order, 1955 (referred to as the 1955 Import Order). The 1955 Import Order is made in

exercise of powers conferred by Sections 3 and 4A of the Imports and Exports Control Act, 1947 (referred to as the 1947 Act). Section 3 of the 1947 Act speaks of powers of the Central Government to prohibit, restrict or otherwise control imports and exports. Section 4A of the 1947 Act comtemplates issue or renewal of licences under the 1947 Act for imports and exports. Item 44 in Part V of Schedule I of the 1955 Import Order relates to newsprint. Newsprint is described as white printing paper (including water lined newsprint which contained mechanical wood pulp amounting to not less than 70% of the fibre content). The import of newsprint is restricted under the 1955 Import Order. This restriction of newsprint import is also challenged because it infringes Article 19(1) (a). It is said that the restriction of import is not a reasonable restriction within the ambit of Article 19(2).

3. The Newsprint Control Order 1962 (referred to as the 1962 Newsprint Order) is made in exercise of powers conferred by Section 3 of the Essential Commodities Act 1955 (referred to as the 1955 Act). Section 3 of the 1955 Act enacts that if the Central Government is of opinion that it is necessary or expedient to do so for maintaining or increasing supply of essential commodities or for securing their equitable distribution and availability at fair prices, it may, by order, provide for regulating or prohibiting production, supply and distribution and trade and commerce therein. Section 2 of the 1955 Act defines "essential commodity". Paper including newsprint, paper board and straw board is defined in S. 2(a) (vii) of the 1955 Act to be an essential commodity. . . .

6. The Newsprint Policy of 1972–73 referred to as the Newsprint Policy with white printing paper (including water lined newsprint which contained chemical wood pulp amounting to not less than 70 per cent of the fibre content). Licences are issued for newsprint. The validity of licences is for 12 months. The Newsprint Policy defines "common ownership unit" to mean newspaper establishment or concern owning two or more news interest newspapers including at least one daily irrespective of the centre of publication and language of such newspapers. Four features of the Newsprint Policy are called in question. These restrictions imposed by the Newsprint policy are said to infringe rights of freedom of speech and expression guaranteed in Article 19(1) (a) of the Constitution. First, no new paper or new edition can be started by a common ownership unit even within the authorised quota of newsprint. Secondly, there is a limitation on the maximum number of pages to 10. No adjustment is permitted between circulation and the pages so as to increase the pages. Thirdly, no interchangeability is permitted between different papers of common ownership unit or different editions of the same paper. Fourthly, allowance of 20 per cent increase in page level up to a maximum of 10 has been given to newspapers with less than 10 pages. It is said that the objectionable and irrational feature of the Newsprint Policy is that a big daily newspaper is prohibited and prevented from increasing the number of pages, page area and periodicity by reducing circulation to meet its requirement even within its admissible quota. In the Newsprint Policy for the year 1971–72 and the earlier periods the newspapers and periodicals were permitted to increase the number of pages, page area and periodicity by reducing circulation. The current policy prohibits the same. The restrictions are, therefore, said to be irrational, arbitrary

and unreasonable. Big daily newspapers having large circulation contend that this discrimination is bound to have adverse effects on the big daily newspapers.

7. The Newsprint Policy is said to be discriminatory and violative of Article 14 because common ownership units alone are prohibited from starting a new paper or a new edition of the same paper while other newspapers with only one daily are permitted to do so. The prohibition against interchangeability between different papers of the same unit and different editions of the said paper is said to be arbitrary and irrational, because it treats all common ownership units as equal and ignores pertinent and material differences between some common ownership units as compared to others. The 10 page limit imposed by the policy is said to violate Article 14 because it equates newspapers which are unequal and provides the same permissible page limit for newspapers which are essentially local in their character and newspapers which reach larger sections of people by giving world news and covering larger fields. The 20 per cent increase allowed for newspapers, whose number of pages was less than 10 is also challenged as violative of Art. 14 by discriminating against newspapers having more than 10 pages. The difference in entitlement between newspapers with an average of more than 10 pages as compared with newspapers of 10 or less than 10 pages is said to be discriminatory because the differentia is not based on rational incidence of classification. . . .

29. The power of the Government to import newsprint cannot be denied. The power of the Government to control the distribution of newsprint cannot equally be denied. It has, of course, to be borne in mind that the distribution must be fair and equitable. The interests of the big, the medium and the small newspapers are all to be taken into consideration at the time of allotment of quotas. In the present case, there was some dispute raised as to whether there should be more import of newsprint. That is a matter of Government policy. This Court cannot adjudicate on such policy measures unless the policy is alleged to be mala fide. Equally, there was a dispute as to the quantity of indigenous newsprint available for newspapers. This Court cannot go into such disputes.

30. The petitioners raised a question as to whether the Newsprint Control Policy is a newsprint control or a newspaper control. Mr. Palkhivala characterised the measure to be newspaper control with degrees of subtlety and sophistication. Rationing of newsprint is newsprint control. That is where quota is fixed. Newspaper control can be said to be post-quota restrictions. The post-quota restrictions are described by Mr. Palkhivala to be newspaper control. The newspaper control, according to the petitioners, is achieved by measures adopted in relation to common ownership units owning two or more newspapers. These common ownership units are not allowed to bring out newspapers or new editions of their dailies. These are not to have interchangeability of quota within their unit. In addition large papers are not allowed to have more than 10 pages. It was said that in the past several years Newsprint Control Policy worked remarkably without any challenge.

31. Article 19(1) (a) provides that all citizens shall have the right to freedom of speech and expression. Article 19(2) states that nothing in subclause (a) of clause (1) shall affect the operation of any existing law, or prevent the State from

making any law, in so far as such law imposes reasonable restrictions on the exercise of the right conferred by the said sub-clause in the interests of the security of the State, friendly relations with foreign States, public order, decency or morality, or in relation to contempt of court, defamation or incitement to an offence. Although Article 19(1) (a) does not mention the freedom of the Press, it is settled view of this Court that freedom of speech and expression includes freedom of the Press and circulation. . . .

34. Publication means dissemination and circulation. The press has to carry on its activity by keeping in view the class of readers, the conditions of labour, price of material, availability of advertisements, size of paper and the different kinds of news comments and views and advertisements which are to be published and circulated. The law which lays excessive and prohibitive burden which would restrict the circulation of a newspaper will not be saved by Article 19(2). If the area of advertisement is restricted, price of paper goes up. If the price goes up circulation will go down. This was held in Sakal Papers case (1962) 3 SCR 842 = (AIR 1962 SC 305) (supra) to be the direct consequence of curtailment of advertisement. The freedom of a newspaper to publish any number of pages or to circulate it to any number of persons has been held by this Court to be an integral part of the freedom on speech and expression. This freedom is violated by placing restraints upon it or by placing restraints upon something which is an essential part of that freedom. A restraint on the number of pages, a restraint on circulation and a restraint on advertisements would affect the fundamental rights under Article 19(1) (a) on the aspects or propagation, publication and circulation. . . .

64. . . . The policy prescribed by the Government of fixing the maximum page limit at 10 is described by the petitioners to hit the big dailies and to prevent the newspapers to rise above mediocrity. It is true that the Government relied on an historical reason. It is said to prevent big newspapers from getting any unfair advantage over newspapers which are infant in origin. It is also said that the Government policy is to help newspapers operating below 10 pages to attain equal position with those who are operating above 10 page level. But this intention to help new and young newspapers cannot be allowed to strangulate the freedom of speech and expression of the big dailies.

65. The Government has sought to justify the reduction in the page level to 10 not only on the ground of shortage of newsprint but also on the grounds that these big dailies devote high percentage of space to advertisements and therefore the cut in pages will not be felt by them if they adjusted their advertisement space. In our judgment the policy of the Government to limit all papers at 10 pages is arbitrary. It tends to treat unequals as equals and discriminates against those who by virtue of their efficiency, standard and service and because of their All-India stature acquired a higher page level in 1957. The main source of income for the newspapers is from advertisements. . . .

133. MATTHEW, J. (concurring) . . . The matter can be looked at from another angle. The constitutional guarantee of the freedom of speech is not so much for the benefit of the press as it is for the benefit of the public. The freedom of speech includes within its compass the right for all citizens to read and be informed. . . .

135. If the right of the public to hear and be informed is also within the concept of the freedom of speech, the government, when it insists upon the newspapers concerned maintaining their present level of circulation does not abridge the freedom of speech but only enriches and enlarges it. In other words, under the theory of the freedom of speech which recognises not only the right of the citizens to speak but also the right of the community to hear, a policy in the distribution of newsprint for maintenance of circulation at its highest possible level, as it furthers the right of the community to hear, will only advance and enrich that freedom.

136. At present, our circulation is only 1.3 copies for every 100 people and 4.6 copies for every 100 literates in the country. Circulation must be doubled if the press is to reach all the literates in the country. This is a sufficient justification for a circulation-oriented policy. Newsprint which is in short supply must be used so as to help to achieve the widest possible dissemination of news and at the same time meet the demands of the press as a whole.

137. Under Art. 41 of the Constitution the State has a duty to take effective steps to educate the people within limits of its available economic resources. That includes political education also.

138. Public discussion of public issues together with the spreading of information and any opinion on these issues is supposed to be the main function of newspaper. The highest and lowest in the scale of intelligence resort to its columns for information. Newspaper is the most potent means for educating the people as it is read by those who read nothing else and, in politics, the common man gets his education mostly from newspaper.

139. The affirmative obligation of the Government to permit the import of newsprint by expending foreign exchange in that behalf is not only because press has a fundamental right to express itself, but also because the community has a right to be supplied with information and the Government a duty to educate the people within the limits of its resources. . . .

7. AUSTRALIA

KOOWARTA v. BJELKE-PETERSEN

A 1982 pronouncement of the Supreme Court of Australia has provided precedent for the principle that international law can be a basis for legislation expanding human rights on a domestic level. It concluded that international human rights had been incorporated into local law.

At issue was the refusal of the Minister of Land of the State of Queensland in Australia to grant a proposed land lease to plaintiff Koowarta, an aboriginal. The professed reason was that aboriginals already possessed sufficient lands.

Koowarta's case was based on the Australian Race Discrimination Act of 1975—passed to give effect to the United Nations' International Convention on the Elimination of All Forms of Racial Discrimination which had been ratified by Australia. Pursuant to the preamble of this Convention, the national government created broad new rights.

The preamble to the Convention encompasses a resolution to adopt all necessary measures to eliminate racial discrimination in all its forms and manifestations. And this was the objective of the Australian act.

In the Australian text was the incorporation of Article 2 of the United Nations Convention pledging the parties to protect specified rights. These included "the right to own property alone as well as in association with others" and "the right to freedom of peaceful assembly and association."

The State of Queensland took the position that the Australian Race Discrimination Act was unconstitutional as exceeding legislative powers granted by the Australian National Constitution. Such constitutionality hinged on the question of whether the act could be internal in effect—for federal governmental powers are external in character. Was the federal government empowered to act in regard to internal lands under state authority?

The Supreme Court responded affirmatively—holding that Australia's parliament had the requisite "external affairs" powers, pursuant to ratification of the International Convention. True, the decision does not make the external affairs power available to national government to create rights policies "merely because Australia enters into an international agreement, or merely because a subject matter excites international concern." But, as Justice Stephen concluded on behalf of the majority, Australia is bound "in common with other nations to enact domestic legislation in pursuit of the common objective of the elimination of all forms of racial discrimination."

KOOWARTA v. BJELKE-PETERSEN

Supreme Court of Australia, 56 Australian L. L. 625 (1982)

(The complicated legal issues in this case resulted in six separate judicial opinions, discussing issues of federalism, property, immigration and procedure as well as human rights. Excerpts from Justice Stephen's majority opinion sustaining the validity of the statute involved on the basis of human rights follow:)

Stephen, J. The Constitution confers upon the Parliament of the Commonwealth power to make laws for the peace, order and good government of the Commonwealth with respect to "The people of any race for whom it is deemed necessary to make special laws"—s.51 (26) and with respect to "External affairs"—s. 51 (29). These actions raise for decision the content of these two grants of legislative power. They do so by reference to challenges to the validity of Commonwealth legislation, the Racial Discrimination Act 1975.

In Koowarta v. Bjelke-Petersen and Others the plaintiff alleges breaches of the Racial Discrimination Act, claiming to be a person aggrieved under the Act and accordingly entitled to seek in his action the several remedies claimed in his statement of claim. The defendants by their defence and demurrer challenge the validity of the Act as well as denying that the plaintiff is a person aggrieved or has any locus standi to sue. In State of Queensland v. The Commonwealth of Australia the plaintiff State challenges the validity of many provisions of the Racial Discrimination Act and seeks a declaration of the invalidity of the Act as a whole or of certain of its provisions.

Since I have concluded that in Mr. Koowarta's action he does have standing to sue, I turn immediately to the constitutional questions, deferring for the moment my reasons for according him locus standi. An appreciation of the constitutional questions is aided by some indication of the circumstances in which Mr. Koowarta's action arises. It is common ground that in 1975 the Aboriginal Land Fund Commission, a body corporate under Commonwealth legislation, contracted to buy a Crown leasehold pastoral property in northern Queensland; that it was a term of the contract and a consequence of the Land Act 1962 of Queensland that transfer of the Crown lease would require the permission of the State's Minister for Lands; that consent to that transfer was sought from but was refused by the Minister; and that a reason for his refusal was that the settled policy of the Queensland Government was to view unfavourably proposals to acquire "large areas of additional freehold or leasehold land for development by Aborigines or Aboriginal groups in isolation."

The Minister's refusal to consent to the transfer of this Crown leasehold led to Mr. Koowarta's action, in which he alleges that that refusal constituted a breach of provisions of the Racial Discrimination Act. Although the proposed transferee was the Commission, not Mr. Koowarta, it seems that it was he who was active in procuring the Commission to arrange for its purchase and that he did so so that, together with other Aborigines, he might have the use of the property for pastoral purposes once it was acquired by the Commission. This aspect will require closer examination when Mr. Koowarta's standing to sue comes to be examined.

The Parliament, in enacting the Racial Discrimination Act, prefaced the terms of the enactment itself by the following recitals:

"Whereas a Convention entitled the 'International Convention on the

Elimination of all Forms of Racial Discrimination' (being the Convention a copy of the English text of which is set out in the Schedule) was opened for signature on 21 December 1965:

And whereas it is desirable, in pursuance of all relevant powers of the Parliament, including, but not limited to, its power to make laws with respect to external affairs, with respect to the people of any race for whom it is deemed necessary to make special laws and with respect to immigration, to make provisions contained in this Act for the prohibition of racial discrimination and certain other forms of discrimination and, in particular, to make provision for giving effect to the Convention."

It is, then, primarily, upon the grants of legislative power expressly referred to in the third recital, those contained in pars. (26), (27) and (29) of s. 51 of the Constitution, that the Act relies. However those provisions of the Act which are supported by s. 51(27), the immigration and emigration power, are not presently in issue; it is exclusively with par. (26) and (29) of s. 51 that this judgment will deal. . . .

Although it is people of "any" race that are referred to, I regard the reference to special laws as confining what may be enacted under this paragraph to laws which are of their nature special to the people of a particular race. It must be because of their special needs or because of the special threat or problem which they present that the necessity for the law arises; without this particular necessity as the occasion for the law, it will not be a special law such as s. 51(26) speaks of. No doubt it may happen that two or more races will share particular problems within the Australian community and that this will make necessary the enactment of one law applying equally to those several races; such a law will not necessarily forfeit the character of a law under par. (26) because it legislates for several races. A law will, however, not possess that character if it legislates for all peoples of the Commonwealth, regardless of race, who happen to be confronted with or to present particular problems deemed to call for legislative action. Nor will a law attain that character merely because the problem with which it deals is one of discrimination on the ground of race; it will not be enough that the law is about one race, the coincidence that its subject-matter happens to match one of the words in par. (26) will not of itself bring it within power.

To be within power under par. (26) a law must be special in the sense that it is the particular race, or races, for whom it legislates that gives rise to the occasion for its enactment. The Racial Discrimination Act is not such a law. True, it legislates about race and proscribes discrimination upon the basis of race. But it is a perfectly general law, addressed to all persons regardless of their race and requiring that the members of all races shall be free from discrimination on account of race. It protects no particular race or races. As its recitals attest, its purpose is to give effect to the International Convention, a copy of which is scheduled to the Act. That Convention, in its opening recitals, stresses the promotion of universal respect for human rights and fundamental freedoms for all without distinction; universality of application lies very much at its heart. The Act takes from the Convention this quality, thereby denying to it the character of a special law in which par. (26) refers. . . .

. . . The real issue in these cases is confined to the question whether this power to implement treaty obligations is subject to any and if so what overriding qualifications derived from the federal nature of our Constitution. It is such qualifications which, in my statement of a highest common factor, have led to the introduction of the phrases "matters international in character" and "legitimately the subject of agreement between nations."

The need for such qualifications is said to arise in this way. Whereas, read in isolation, par. (29) would seem to authorize legislation to give effect municipally to each and every international obligation which Australia may incur, yet Australia is a federation possessing a constitution which assigns carefully limited legislative power to the federal legislature, leaving the undefined residue of legislative competence to the States. The power of the federal Executive to conclude treaties upon any subject-matter it sees fit is undoubted. If it can thereby at will create such "external affairs" as it wishes and if par. (29) then confers power upon the federal legislature to legislate with respect to whatever external affair has thus been brought into being, this may place in jeopardy the federal character of our polity, the residuary legislative competence of the States being under threat of erosion and final extinction as a result of federal exercise of the power which par. (29) confers.

The authorities have made quite clear two things about the limits of the "External affairs" power. First, the few express restrictions upon legislative power which appear in the Constitution restrict the ambit of the power conferred by par. (29); like all other paragraphs of s. 51, par. (29) is expressed to be "subject to this Constitution" and its grant of power must be read as subject to the restraints upon legislative power imposed, for example, by ss. 92, 99, 114, 116 and 117 of the Constitution. Secondly, the grant of power conferred by par. (29) is plenary in the sense that it is not to be restricted by reference to the limited legislative competence conferred by the other paragraphs of s. 51. What however remains unclear is the extent to which the federal nature of the Constitution requires that limits be imposed upon the broad power to implement international obligations seemingly conferred by par. (29), thus ensuring that exercise of that power will not destroy the federal character of the polity. . . .

The great post-war expansion of the areas properly the subject-matter of international agreement has, as Henkin points out and as J. A. Thomson emphasizes in his article, at pp. 164–166, made it difficult indeed to identify subject-matters which are of their nature not of international but of only domestic concern—see also Howard, *Australian Federal Constitutional Law* (2nd ed., 1972) pp. 445–446. But this does no more than reflect the increasing awareness of the nations of the world that the state of society in other countries is very relevant to the state of their own society. Thus areas of what are of purely domestic concern are steadily contracting and those of international concern are ever expanding. Nevertheless the quality of being of international concern remains, no less than ever, a valid criterion of whether a particular subject-matter forms part of a nation's "external affairs." A subject-matter of international concern necessarily possess the capacity to affect a country's relations with other nations and this quality is itself enough to make a subject-matter a part of a nations's "external affairs". And this being so, any attack upon validity, either in what must be the very exceptional circumstances which could found an allegation of lack of bona fides or where there is said to be an absence of international subject-matter, will still afford an appropriate safeguard against improper exercise of the "External affairs" power. . . .

That prohibition of racial discrimination, the subject-matter of the Racial Discrimination Act, now falls squarely within that concept I regard as undoubted. That a consequence would seem to be an intrusion by the Commonwealth into areas previously the exclusive concern of the States does not mean that there has been some alteration of the original federal pattern of distribution of legislative powers. What has occurred is, rather, a growth in the content of "External affairs." This growth reflects the new global concern for human rights and the international acknowledgement of the need for universally recognized norms of conduct, particularly in relation to the suppression of racial discrimination.

The post-war history of this new concern is illuminating. The present international regime for the protection of human rights finds its origin in the Charter of the United Nations. Prominent in the opening recitals of the Charter is a re-affirmation of "faith in fundamental human rights, in the dignity and worth of the human person, in the equal rights of men and women." One of the purposes of the United Nations expressed in its Charter is the achieving of international co-operation in promoting and encouraging "respect for human rights and for fundamental freedoms for all without distinction as to race . . . "— Ch. I, Art. 1:3; see too Ch. IX, Art. 55(c). By Ch. IX, Art 5.6 all member nations pledge themselves to take action with the Organization to achieve its purposes. The emphasis which the Charter thus places upon international recognition of human rights and fundamental freedoms is in striking contrast to the terms of the Covenant of the League of Nations, which was silent on these subjects.

The effect of these provisions has in international law been seen as restricting the right of member States of the United Nations to treat due observance of human rights as an exclusively domestic matter. Instead the human rights obligations of member states have become a "legitimate subject of international concern . . .' "

These matters having, by virtue of the Charter of the United Nations, become at international law a proper subject for international action, there followed, in 1958, the Universal Declaration of Human Rights and thereafter many General Assembly resolutions on human rights and racial discrimination. A full catalogue of the various international instruments in this area can be found in a United Nations publication, Human Rights: A Compilation of International Instruments (1978). There have also been various regional agreements on human rights, perhaps the leading example being the European Convention for the Protection of Human Rights and Fundamental Freedoms of 1950.

It was in 1965 that the Assembly unanimously adopted the International Convention on the Elimination of All Forms of Racial Discrimination. . . .

. . . [T]he Convention apart, the subject of racial discrimination should be regarded as an important aspect of Australia's external affairs, so that legislation much in the present form of the Racial Discrimination Act would be supported by power conferred by s. 51(29). As with slavery and genocide, the failure of a nation to take steps to suppress racial discrimination has become of immediate relevance to its relations within the international community. . . .

In the present cases it is not necessary to rely upon this aspect of the external affairs power since there exists a quite precise treaty obligation, on a subject of major importance in international relationships, which calls for domestic implementation within Australia. This in itself, without more, suffices to bring the Racial Discrimination Act within the terms of 51(29). I mention in passing that in these cases it is common ground that the provisions of the Racial Discrimination Act now under challenge do give effect to those terms of the International Convention on the Elimination of All Forms of Racial Discrimination which Australia, as a party to the Convention, is bound to implement municipally. . . .

. . . Agreement by nations to take common action in pursuit of a common objective evidences the existence of international concern and gives the subject-matter of the treaty a character which is international. I speak of course of a treaty which is genuine and not of a colourable treaty, if that can be imagined, into which Australia has entered solely for the purpose of attracting to the Commonwealth Parliament the exercise of a legislative power over a subject-matter not specifically committed to it by the Constitution. . . .

On the broad view which I take of the power it extends to the implementation of the International Convention on the Elimination of All Forms of Racial Discrimination. It is an international treaty to which Australia is a party which binds Australia in common with other nations to enact domestic legislation in pursuit of the common objective of the elimination of all forms of racial discrimination. . . .

The point of all this, so it seems to me, is that the community of nations, or at least a very large number of them, are vigorously opposed to racial discrimination, not only on idealistic and humanitarian grounds, but also because racial discrimination is generally considered to be inimical to friendly and peaceful relations among nations and is a threat to peace and security among peoples. . . .

All the materials indicate that the United Nations consider racial discrimination to be abhorrent conduct which, posing a threat to international peace and security, should be eliminated. At the level of international law the means chosen to attain this end was the formulation of the Convention. It imposes on each of the many parties to it an obligation to eliminate racial discrimination in its territory. The failure of a party to fulfil its obligations becomes a matter of international discussion, disapproval, and perhaps action by way of enforcement. Viewed in this light, the subject-matter of the Convention is international in character. . . .

X. MISCELLANEOUS DOCUMENTS

1. DECLARATION OF INDEPENDENCE OF THE UNITED STATES OF AMERICA (1776)

INTRODUCTION

The words of the United States Declaration of Independence have echoed and still echo in innumerable international covenants, independent documents and constitutions throughout the world. For the Declaration literally resounds in freedom. But even more significant than its language has been its concepts and visions—inspirations for liberation and freedom movements for more than two centuries.

The actual writing of the document was the handiwork of Thomas Jefferson, one of a five-member committee designated by the Continental Congress to prepare such a declaration. The others were John Adams, Benjamin Franklin, Roger Sherman and Robert R. Livingston.

Radical as the document was to the world of 1776, Jefferson did not attempt to set forth novel principles or new arguments on behalf of liberty. Rather, he saw the Declaration of Independence as an accurate expression of the American mind and will—as a codification of common American agreement.

The Declaration of Independence was preceded by a month by the Virginia Bill of Rights. It, too, was predicated by the doctrine that all men possessed inherent rights which could not be taken from them by government. The Virginia declaration spoke of life, liberty and property; language derived directly from the English political philosopher John Locke. However, Thomas Jefferson substituted the phrase "pursuit of happiness" for "property" in drafting the Declaration of Independence. This was a revolutionary shift, and suggested that human rights in American were much broader than they had been in England, or, for that matter, anywhere else in the world.

THE DECLARATION OF INDEPENDENCE

When in the Course of Human Events it becomes necessary for one people to dissolve the political bands which have connected them with another, and to assume among the Powers of the earth, the separate and equal station to which the Laws of Nature and of Nature's God entitle them, a decent respect to the opinions of mankind requires that they should declare the causes which impel them to the separation.

We hold these truths to be self-evident, that all men are created equal, that they are endowed by their Creator with certain unalienable Rights, that among these are Life, Liberty and the pursuit of Happiness.

That to secure these rights, Governments are instituted among Men, deriving their just powers from the consent of the governed, That whenever any Form of Government becomes destructive of these ends, it is the Right of the People to alter or to abolish it, and to institute a new Government, laying its foundation on such principles, and organizing its powers in such form, as to them shall seem most likely to effect their Safety and Happiness. Prudence, indeed, will dictate that Governments long established should not be changed for light and transient causes; and accordingly all experience hath shown, that mankind are more disposed to suffer, while evils are sufferable, than to right themselves by abolishing the forms to which they are accustomed. But when a long train of abuses and usurpations, pursuing invariably the same Object evinces a design to reduce them under absolute Despotism, it is their right, it is their duty, to throw off such Government, and to provide new Guards for their future security.—Such has been the patient sufferance of these Colonies; and such is now the necessity which constrains them to alter their former Systems of Government. The history of the present King of Great Britain is a history of repeated injuries and usurpations, all having in direct object the establishment of an absolute Tyranny over these States. To prove this, let Facts be submitted to a candid world.

He has refused his Assent to Laws, the most wholesome and necessary for the public good.

He has forbidden his Governors to pass Laws of immediate and pressing importance, unless suspended in their operation till his Assent should be obtained; and when so suspended, he has utterly neglected to attend to them.

He has refused to pass other Laws for the accommodation of large districts of people, unless those people would relinquish the right of Representation in the Legislature, a right inestimable to them and formidable to tyrants only.

He has called together legislative bodies at places unusual, uncomfortable, and distant from the depository of their Public Records, for the sole purpose of fatiguing them into compliance with his measures.

He has dissolved Representative Houses repeatedly, for opposing with manly firmness his invasions on the rights of the people.

He has refused for a long time, after such dissolutions, to cause others to be elected; whereby the Legislative Powers, incapable of Annihilation, have returned to the People at large for their exercise; the State remaining in the mean time exposed to all the dangers of invasion from without, and convulsions within.

He has endeavoured to prevent the population of these States; for that purpose obstructing the Laws of Naturalization of Foreigners; refusing to pass others to encourage their migrations hither, and raising the conditions of new Appropriations of Lands.

He has obstructed the Administration of Justice, by refusing his Assent to Laws for establishing Judiciary Powers.

He has made Judges dependent on his Will alone, for the tenure of their offices, and the amount and payment of their salaries.

He has erected a multitude of New Offices, and sent hither swarms of Officers to harrass our People, and eat out their substance.

He has kept among us, in times of peace, Standing Armies without the Consent of our legislature.

He has affected to render the Military independent of and superior to the Civil Power.

He has combined with others to subject us to a jurisdiction foreign to our constitution, and unacknowledged by our laws; giving his Assent to their acts of pretended legislation: For quartering large bodies of armed troops among us:

For protecting them, by a mock Trial, from Punishment for any Murders which they should commit on the Inhabitants of these States: For cutting off our trade with all parts of the world: For imposing Taxes on us without our Consent: For depriving us in many cases, of the benefits of Trial by Jury: For transporting us beyond Seas to be tried for pretended offences: For abolishing the free System of English Laws in a neighbouring Province, establishing therein an Arbitrary government, and enlarging its Boundaries so as to render it at once an example and fit instrument for introducing the same absolute rule into these Colonies: For taking away our Charters, abolishing our most valuable Laws, and altering fundamentally the Forms of our Governments: For suspending our own Legislature, and declaring themselves invested with Power to legislate for us in all cases whatsoever.

He has abdicated Government here, by declaring us out of his Protection and waging War against us.

He has plundered our seas, ravaged our Coasts, burnt our towns, and destroyed the lives of our people.

He is at this time transporting large armies of foreign mercenaries to compleat the works of death, desolation and tyranny, already begun with circumstances of Cruelty and perfidy scarcely paralleled in the most barbarous ages, and totally unworthy the Head of a civilized nation.

He has constrained our fellow Citizens taken Captive on the high Seas to bear Arms against their Country, to become the executioners of their friends and Brethren, or to fall themselves by their Hands.

He has excited domestic insurrections amongst us, and has endeavoured to bring on the inhabitants of our frontiers, the merciless Indian Savages, whose known rule of warfare, is an undistinguished destruction of all ages, sexes and conditions.

In every stage of these Oppressions We have Petitioned for Redress in the most humble terms: Our repeated Petitions have been answered only by repeated injury. A Prince, whose character is thus marked by every act which may define a Tyrant, is unfit to be the ruler of a free People.

Nor have We been wanting in attentions to our British brethren. We have warned them from time to time of attempts by their legislature to extend an unwarrantable jurisdiction over us. We have reminded them of the circumstances of our emigration and settlement here. We have appealed to their native justice and magnanimity, and we have conjured them by the ties of our commond kindred to disavow these usurpations, which, would inevitably interrupt our connections and correspondence. They too have been deaf to the voice of justice and of consanguinity. We must, therefore, acquiesce in the necessity, which denounces our Separation, and hold them, as we hold the rest of mankind, Enemies in War, in Peace Friends.

We, therefore, the Representatives of the UNITED STATES OF AMERICA, in General Congress, Assembled, appealing to the Supreme Judge of the world for the rectitude of our intentions, do, in the Name, and by Authority of the good People of these Colonies, solemnly publish and declare, That these United Colonies are, and of Right ought to be FREE AND INDEPENDENT STATES; that they are Absolved from all Allegiance to the British Crown, and that all political connection between them and the State of Great Britain, is and ought to be totally dissolved; and that as Free and Independent States, they have full Power to levy War, conclude Peace, contract Alliances, establish Commerce, and to do all other Acts and Things which Independent States may of right do. And for the support of this Declaration, with a firm reliance on the Protection of Divine Providence, we mutually pledge to each other our Lives, our Fortunes and our sacred Honor.

2. CZECHOSLOVAKIA. CHARTER 77

INTRODUCTION

The most significant human rights document from behind the Iron Curtain is the New Year's manifesto promulgated by a group of 241 Czechoslovakian dissidents in the first week of 1977—named simply Charter 77 to mark the date of its issuance. It called upon the authorities to respect the terms of the United Nations International Covenant on Economic, Social and Cultural Rights, signed on behalf of the Czechoslovakian government in 1968 and confirmed by the Helsinki Accords in 1975. (Part Three, Ch. II.)

As stated in the document:

> Charter 77 is a free and informal and open association of people of various convictions, religions and professions linked by the desire to work individually and collectively for respect for human and civil rights in the world and in Czechoslovakia . . . It represents a general declaration of human rights.

While the signers of Charter 77 had expected the Prague government to reject the manifesto, they had not anticipated that the reaction would be so extreme. Within hours after its publication in Western European newspapers, police had arrested a number of prominent Czechs involved in the charter drafting. On January 10th, as the government continued to denounce the charter, four of the signers were detained and charged with "serious crimes against the Republic."[191]

Then, in March, 1977, the government summoned 47 workers, writers and party officials to a press conference to denounce the charter, claiming that its supporters were in the pay of Western reactionaries and in league with Western intelligence agencies. The journalists in attendance questioned the credibility of the press conference when it was noted that the Prague government had forbidden the publication of Charter 77 in Czechoslovakia—raising doubts that the press conference participants had even read the document they were condemning.

Ex-Czechoslovakian Foreign Minister Jiri Hajek, one of the first signers and one of the first detainees, asserted that the government feared a revival of the "Prague Spring" of 1968. It was then that some liberalization of Communist rule began under the leadership of Alexander Dubcek, prompting the Soviet invasion of Czechoslovakia and Dubcek's removal.

The Czechoslovakian government newspaper *Rude Pravo* confirmed that assessment with this statement: "The year 1968 will not be repeated . . . these Don Quixotes want to sow the seeds of a new counterrevolution and throw our socialist society into chaos and uncertainty."[192]

Charter 77 remains a rallying point in the fight for freedom in Eastern Europe. Six important dissidents were convicted of "subversion of the Republic" in November, 1979, and were sentenced to a combined total of 19 1/2 years in prison. But the publicity surrounding this trial and the continuing campaign against the other dissidents has only increased the number of its supporters.[193] For a comprehensive background analysis, see Skilling, H. Gordon, *Charter 77 and Human Rights in Czechoslovakia*, 1981).

CHARTER 77 (1977)

Law No. 120 of the Czechoslovak Collection of Laws, published October 13, 1976, includes the text of the International Covenant on Civil and Political Rights, and the International Covenant on Economic, Social and Cultural Rights, both signed in behalf of our Republic in 1968 and confirmed at the 1975 Helsinki Conference. These pacts went into effect in our country on March 23, 1976; since that date our citizens have had the right, and the State has had the duty, to abide by them.

The freedoms guaranteed to individuals by the two documents are important assets of civilization. They have been the goals of campaigns by many progressive people in the past, and their enactment can significantly contribute to a humane development of our society. We welcome the fact that the Czechoslovak Republic has agreed to enter into these covenants.

Their publication, however, is at the same time an urgent reminder of the many fundamental humane rights that, regretably, exist in our country only on paper. The right of free expression guaranteed by Article 19 of the first pact, for example, is quite illusory. Tens of thousands of citizens have been prevented from working in their professions for the sole reason that their views differ from the official ones. They have been the frequent targets of various forms of discrimination and chicanery on the part of the authorities or social organizations; they have been denied any opportunity to defend themselves and are practically the victims of apartheid. Hundreds of thousands of other citizens have been denied the "freedom from fear" cited in the Preamble to the first pact; they live in constant peril of losing their jobs or other benefits if they express their opinions.

Contrary to Article 13 of the second pact, guaranteeing the right to education, many young people are prevented from pursuing higher education because of their views or even because of their parents' views. Countless citizens worry that if they declare their convictions, they themselves or their children will be deprived of an education.

Exercising the right to "seek, receive and impart information regardless of frontiers and of whether it is oral, written or printed," or "imparted through art,"—Point 2, Article 13 of the first pact—can result in persecution not only outside the court but also inside. Frequently this occurs under the pretext of a criminal indictment (as evidenced among other instances, by the recent trial of young musicians).

Freedom of speech is suppressed by the government's management of all mass media, including the publishing and cultural institutions. No political, philosophical, scientific, or artistic work that deviates in the slightest from the narrow framework of official ideology or esthetics is permitted to be produced. Public criticism of social conditions is prohibited. Public defense against false and defamatory charges by official propaganda organs is impossible, despite the legal protection against attacks on one's reputation and honor unequivocally afforded by Article 17 of the first pact. False accusation cannot be refused, and it is futile to attempt rectification or to seek legal redress. Open discussion of intellectual and cultural matters is out of the question. Many scientific and cultural workers, as well as other citizens, have been discriminated against simply because some years ago they legally published or openly articulated views condemned by the current political power.

Religious freedom, emphatically guaranteed by Article 18 of the first pact, is systematically curbed with a despotic arbitrariness. Limits are imposed on the activities of priests, who are constantly threatened with the revocation of government permission to perform their function; persons who manifest their religious faith either by word or action lose their jobs or are made to suffer other repressions; religious instruction in schools is suppressed, et cetera.

A whole range of civil rights is severely restricted or completely suppressed by the effective method of subordinating all institutions and organizations in the State to the political directives of the ruling Party's apparatuses and the pronouncements of highly influential individuals. Neither the Constitution of the CSSR nor any of the country's other legal procedures regulate the contents, form or application of such pronouncements, which are frequently issued orally, unbeknown to and beyond the control of the average citizen. Their authors are responsible only to themselves and their own hierarchy, yet they have a decisive influence on the activity of the legislative as well as executive bodies of the State administration, on the courts, trade unions, social organizations, other political parties, business, factories, schools and similar installations, and their orders take precedence over laws.

If some organizations or citizens in the interpretation of their rights and duties, become involved in a conflict with the directives, they cannot turn to a neutral authority, for none exists. Consequently, the right of assembly and the prohibition of its restraint, stemming from Articles 21 and 22 of the first pact, the right to participate in public affairs, in Article 25, and the right to equality before the law, in Article 26—all have been seriously curtailed.

These conditions prevent working people from freely establishing labor and other organizations for the protection of their economic and social interests, and from freely using their right to strike as provided in Point 1, Article 8 of the second pact.

Other civil rights, including the virtual banning of "willful interference with private life, the family, home and correspondence" in Article 17 of the first pact, are gravely circumscribed by the fact that the Interior Ministry employs various practices to control the daily existence of citizens—such as telephone tapping and the surveillance of private homes, watching mail, shadowing individuals, searching apartments, and recruiting a network of informers from the ranks of the population (often by illegal intimidation or, sometimes, promises), etc.

The Ministry frequently interferes in the decisions of employers, inspires discrimination by authorities and organizations, influences the organs of justice, and even supervises the propaganda campaigns of the mass media. This activity is not regulated by laws, it is covert, so the citizen is unable to protect himself against it.

In the cases of politically motivated persecution, the organs of interrogation and justice violate the rights of the defendants and their counsel, contrary to Article 14 of the first pact as well as Czechoslovakia's own laws. People thus sentenced to jail are being treated in a manner that violates their human dignity, impairs their health, and attempts to break them morally.

Point 2, Article 12 of the first pact, guaranteeing the right to freely leave one's country, is generally violated. Under the pretext of "protecting the State security," contained in Point 3, departure is tied to various illegal conditions. Just as arbitrary are the procedures for issuing visits to foreign nationals, many of whom are prevented from visiting Czechoslovakia because they had some official or friendly contact with persons who had been discriminated against in our country.

Some citizens—privately at their places of work, or through the media abroad (the only public forum available to them)—have drawn attention to these systematic violations of human rights and democratic freedoms and have demanded a remedy in specific cases. But they have received no response, or have themselves become the objects of investigation.

The responsibility for the preservation of civil rights naturally rests with the State power. But not on it alone. Every individual bears a share of responsibility for the general conditions in the country, and therefore also for compliance with the enacted pacts, which are as binding for the people as for the government.

The feeling of this coresponsibility, the belief in the value of civic engagement and the readiness to be engaged, together with the need to seek a new and more effective expression, gave us the idea of creating Charter 77, whose existence we publicly announce.

Charter 77 is a free and informal and open association of people of various convictions, religions and professions linked by the desire to work individually and collectively for respect for human and civil rights in Czechoslovakia and the world—the rights provided for in the enacted international pacts, in the First Act of the Helsinki Conference, and in numerous other international documents against wars, violence and social and mental oppression. It represents a general declaration of human rights.

Charter 77 is founded on the concepts of solidarity and friendship of people who share a concern for the fate of ideals to which they have linked their lives and work.

Charter 77 is not an organization; it has no statutes, permanent organs or registered membership. Everyone who agrees with its ideas and participates in its work and support it, belongs to it.

Charter 77 is not intended to be a basis for opposition political activity. Its desire is to serve the common interest as have numerous similar organizations of civic initiative East and West. It has no intention of initiating its own programs for political or social reforms or changes, but it wants to lead in the sphere of its activity by means of a constructive dialogue with the political and State authorities—and particularly by drawing attention to various specific violations of civil and human rights, by preparing their documentation, by suggesting solutions, by submitting various more general proposals aimed at furthering these rights and their guarantees, by acting as a mediator in the event of conflict situations which might result in wrongdoings, etc.

By its symbolic name, Charter 77 stresses that it has been established on the threshold of what has been declared the year of political prisoners, in the course of which a meeting in Belgrade is to review the progress—or lack of it—achieved since the Helsinki Conference.

As signatories of this declaration, we designate Dr. Jan Patocka, Dr. Vaclav Havel and Professor Jiri Hajek to act as spokesmen for Charter 77. These spokesmen are authorized to represent Charter 77 before the State and other organizations, as well as before the public at home and throughout the world, and they guarantee the authenticity of its documents by their signatures. In us and other citizens who will join Charter 77, they will find their collaborators who will participate in the necessary negotiations, who will accept partial tasks, and will share the entire responsibility.

We trust that Charter 77 will contribute to making it possible for all citizens of Czechoslovakia to live and work as free people.

3. LUSAKA MANIFESTO ON SOUTHERN AFRICA

INTRODUCTION

Africa's ultimate statement on racism[194] and colonialism—the Lusaka Manifesto—was issued as the final communique of the fifth conference of Heads of State and Government of East and Central African States, held in Lusaka, Zambia, in April, 1969. Fourteen nations, six represented by their heads of state, attended the conference, and all but Malawi joined in support of the Manifesto.

Condemnation of British, French and Portuguese colonialism was joined by condemnation of apartheid and other forms of racial discrimination. And the Lusaka signatories announced their refusal to enter into any dialogue with the minority regimes in Southern Africa since those regimes had rejected the principle of human equality.

While the Manifesto was directed against white racism, the eighth paragraph pointed out that the conference was not advocating "a reversal of the existing racial domination." Here is the key sentence: "We believe that all the peoples who have made their homes in the countries of Southern Africa are Africans, regardless of the colour of their skins; and we would oppose a racialist majority government which adopted a philosophy of deliberate and permanent discrimination between its citizens on grounds of racial origin."

Zambia's President Kenneth Kaunda, in his opening address, praised the record of the Black African nations in regard to racism. "Nowhere in independent Africa has a nationalist government taken vengeance and victimized its minority groups. Nowhere in Africa has an African government driven or even threatened to drive a racial minority into the sea."

While the nations pledged to increase both moral and material support for African liberation movements, the twelfth paragraph emphasizes that, "We have always preferred, and we still prefer, to achieve liberation without physical violence." "We would prefer to negotiate rather than destroy, to talk rather than kill."

The objectives of the Manifesto were adopted in September, 1969, by the Assembly of Heads of State and Government of the Organization of African Unity. Then, on November 20th, the United Nations General Assembly adopted Resolution 2ʳ   (XXIV) welcoming the Manifesto and commending it to the attention "oⁱ   .ates and peoples." The resolution expressed "once again the firm intenti.jn of the United Nations, acting in cooperation with the Organization of African Unity, to intensify its efforts to find a solution to the present grave situation in southern Africa."

For further data on the Lusaka Manifesto, *see* Colin Legum, *Africa Contemporary Record, Annual Survey and Documents, 1969–70, pages C39–C41.*

THE LUSAKA MANIFESTO ON SOUTHERN AFRICA (1969)

Adopted by the Conference of East and Central African States, held in Lusaka in April, 1969. It was subsequently approved by the Heads of State and Government of the O.A.U. in September, 1969, and then endorsed by the U.N. General Assembly in November of the same year in resolution 2505 (XXIV).

1. When the purpose and the basis of States' international policies are misunderstood, there is introduced into the world, a new and unnecessary disharmony, disagreements, conflicts of interest, or different assessments of human priorities, which provoke an excess of tension in the world, and disastrously divide mankind, at a time when united action is necessary to control modern technology and put it to the service of man. It is for this reason that, discovering widespread misapprehension of our attitudes and purposes in relation to Southern Africa, we, the leaders of East and Central African States meeting at Lusaka, on 16 April 1969, have agreed to issue this Manifesto.

2. By this Manifesto, we wish to make clear, beyond all shadow of doubt, our acceptance of the belief that all men are equal, and have equal rights to human dignity and respect, regardless of colour, race, religion or sex. We believe that all men have the right and duty to participate, as equal members of the society, in their own Government. We do not accept that any individual or group has any right to govern any other group of sane adults, without their consent, and we affirm that only the people of a society, acting together as

equals, can determine what is, for them, a good society and a good social, economic, or political organization.

3. On the basis of these beliefs we do not accept that any one group within a society has the right to rule any society without the continuing consent of all the citizens. We recognize that at any one time there will be, within every society, failures in the implementation of these ideals. We recognize that for the sake of order in human affairs, there may be transitional arrangements while a transformation from group inequalities to individual equality is being effected. But we affirm that without an acceptance of these ideals—without a commitment to these principles of human equality and self-determination—there can be no basis for peace and justice in the world.

4. None of us would claim that within our own States we have achieved that perfect social, economic and political organization which would ensure a reasonable standard of living for all our people and establish individual security against avoidable hardship or miscarriage of justice. On the contrary, we acknowledge that within our own States the struggle towards human brotherhood and unchallenged human dignity is only beginning. It is on the basis of our commitment to human equality and human dignity, not on the basis of achieved perfection, that we take our stand of hostility towards the colonialism and racial discrimination which is being practised in southern Africa. It is on the basis of their commitment to these universal principles that we appeal to other members of the human race for support.

5. If the commitment to these principles existed among the States holding power in southern Africa, any disagreements we might have about the rate of implementation, or about isolated acts of policy, would be matters affecting only our individual relationships with the States concerned. If these commitments existed, our States would not be justified in the expressed and active hostility towards the régimes of southern Africa such as we have proclaimed and continue to propagate.

6. The truth is, however, that in Mozambique, Angola, Rhodesia, Namibia and the Republic of South Africa, there is an open and continued denial of the principles of human equality and national self-determination. This is not a matter of failure in the implementation of accepted human principles. The effective administrations in all these territories are not struggling towards these difficult goals. They are fighting the principles; they are deliberately organizing their societies so as to try to destroy the hold of these principles in the minds of men. It is for this reason that we believe the rest of the world must be interested. For the principle of human equality, and all that flows from it, is either universal or it does not exist. The dignity of all men is destroyed when the manhood of any human is being denied.

7. Our objectives in southern Africa stem from our commitment to this principle of human equality. We are not hostile to the administration of these States because they are manned and controlled by white people. We are hostile to them because they are systems of minority control which exist as a result of, and in the pursuance of, doctrines of human inequality. What we are working for is the right of self-determination for the people of those territories. We are

working for a rule in those countries which is based on the will of all the people and an acceptance of the equality of every citizen.

8. Our stand towards southern Africa thus involves a rejection of racialism, not a reversal of the existing racial domination. We believe that all the peoples who have made their homes in the countries of sourthern Africa are Africans, regardless of the colour of their skins; and we would oppose a racialist majority government which adopted a philosophy of deliberate and permanent discrimination between its citizens on grounds of racial origin. We are not talking racialism when we reject the colonialism and apartheid policies now operating in those areas; we are demanding an opportunity for all the people of these States, working together as equal individual citizens, to work out for themselves the institutions and the system of government under which they will, by general consent, live together and work together to build a harmonious society.

9. As an aftermath of the present policies, it is likely that different groups within these societies will be self-conscious and fearful. The initial political and economic organizations may well take account of these fears, and this group self-consciousness. But how this is to be done must be a matter, exclusively for the peoples of the country concerned, working together. No other nation will have a right to interfere in such affairs. All that the rest of the world has a right to demand is just what we are now asserting, that the arrangements within any State which wishes to be accepted into the community of nations must be based on an acceptance of the principles of human dignity and equality.

10. To talk of the liberation of Africa is thus to say two things. First, that the peoples in the territories still under colonial rule shall be free to determine for themselves their own institutions of self-government. Secondly, that the individuals in southern Africa shall be freed from an environment poisoned by the propaganda of racialism, and given an opportunity to be men, not white men, brown men, yellow men or black men.

11. Thus the liberation of Africa for which we are struggling does not mean a reverse racialism. Nor it is an aspect of African imperialism. As far as we are concerned the present boundaries of the States of southern Africa are the boundaries of what will be free and independent African States. There is no question of our seeking or accepting any alterations to our own boundaries at the expense of these future free African nations.

12. On the objectives of liberation as thus defined, we can neither surrender nor compromise. We have always preferred, and we still prefer, to achieve it without physical violence. We would prefer to negotiate rather than destroy, to talk rather than kill. We do not advocate violence, we advocate an end to the violence against human dignity which is now being perpetrated by the oppressors of Africa. If peaceful progress to emancipation were possible, or if changed circumstances were to make it possible in the future, we would urge our brothers in the resistance movements to use peaceful methods of struggle even at the cost of some compromise on the timing of change. But while peaceful progress is blocked by actions of those at present in power in the States of southern Africa, we have no choice but to give the peoples of those territories all the support of which we are capable in their struggle against their oppressors.

This is why the signatory States participate in the movement for the libertion of Africa under the aegis of the Organization of African Unity. However, the obstacle to change is not the same in all the countries of southern Africa, and it follows therefore that the possibility of continuing the struggle through peaceful means varies from one country to another.

13. In Mozambique and Angola, and in so-called Portuguese Guinea, the basic problem is not racialism but a pretence that Portugal exists in Africa. Portugal is situated in Europe; the fact that it is a dictatorship is a matter for the Portuguese to settle. But no decree of the Portuguese dictator, nor legislation passed by any Parliament in Portugal, can make Africa part of Europe. The only thing which could convert a part of Africa into a constituent unit in a union which also includes a European State would be the freely expressed will of the people of that part of Africa. There is no such popular will in the Portuguese colonies. On the contrary, in the absence of any opportunity to negotiate a road to freedom, the people of all three territories have taken up arms against the colonial Power. They have done this despite the heavy odds against them, and despite the great suffering they know to be involved.

14. Portugal, as a European State, has naturally its own allies in the context of ideological conflict between West and East. However, in our context, the effect of this is that Portugal is enabled to use her resources to pursue the most heinous war and degradation of man in Africa. The present Manifesto must, therefore, lay bare the fact that the inhuman commitment of Portugal in Africa and her ruthless subjugation of the people of Mozambique, Angola and so-called Portuguese Guinea are not only irrelevant to the ideological conflict of power politics, but also diametrically opposed to the politics, the philosophies and the doctrines practised by her Allies in the conduct of their own affairs at home. The peoples of Mozambique, Angola and Portuguese Guinea are not interested in communism or capitalism; they are interested in their freedom. They are demanding an acceptance of the principles of independence on the basis of majority rule, and for many years they called for discussions on this issue. Only when their demands for talks was continually ignored did they begin to fight. Even now, if Portugal should change her policy and accept the principle of self-determination, we would urge the liberation movements to desist from their armed struggle and to co-operate in the mechanics of a peaceful transfer of power from Portugal to the peoples of the African territories.

15. The fact that many Portuguese citizens have immigrated to these African countries does not affect this issue. Future immigration policy will be a matter for the independent Governments when these are established. In the meantime, we would urge the liberation movements to reiterate their statements that all those Portuguese people who have made their homes in Mozambique, Angola or Portuguese Guinea, and who are willing to give their future loyalty to those States, will be accepted as citizens. An independent Mozambique, Angola or Portuguese Guinea may choose to be as friendly with Portugal as Brazil is. That would be the free choice of a free people.

16. In Rhodesia the situation is different in so far as the metropolitan Power has acknowledged the colonial status of the territory. Unfortunately, however, it has failed to take adequate measures to reassert its authority against the

minority which has seized power with the declared intention of maintaining white domination. The matter cannot rest there. Rhodesia, like the rest of Africa, must be free, and its independence must be on the basis of majority rule. If the colonial Power is unwilling or unable to effect such a transfer of power to the people, then the people themselves will have no alternative but to capture it as and when they can. Africa has no alternative but to support them. The question which remains in Rhodesia is therefore whether Great Britain will reassert her authority in Rhodesia and then negotiate the peaceful progress to majority rule before independence. In so far as Britain is willing to make this second commitment, Africa will co-operate in her attempts to reassert her authority. This is the method of progress which we would prefer; it could involve less suffering for all the peoples of Rhodesia, both black and white. But until there is some firm evidence that Britain accepts the principles of independence on the basis of majority rule and is prepared to take whatever steps are necessary to make it a reality, Africa has no choice but to support the struggle for the people's freedom by whatever means are open.

17. Just as a settlement of the Rhodesian problem with a minimum of violence is a British responsibility, so a settlement in Namibia with a minimum of violence is a United Nations responsibility. By every canon of international law and by every precedent, Namibia should now have been a sovereign, independent State with a government based on majority rule. South West Africa was a German colony until 1919, just as Tanganyika, Rwanda and Burundi, Togoland and Cameroon were German colonies. It was a matter of European politics that when the mandatory system was established after Germany had been defeated, the administration of South West Africa was given to the white minority Government of South Africa, while the other ex-German colonies in Africa were put into the hands of the British, Belgian or French Governments. After the Second World War every mandated territory except South West Africa was converted into a Trust Territory and has subsequently gained independence. South Africa, on the other hand, has persistently refused to honour even the international obligation it accepted in 1919 and has increasingly applied to South West Africa the inhuman doctrines and organization of apartheid.

18. The United Nations General Assembly has ruled against this action, and in 1966 terminated the Mandate under which South Africa had a legal basis for its occupation and domination of South West Africa. The General Assembly declared that the territory is now the direct responsibility of the United Nations, and set up an ad hoc committee to recommend practical means by which South West Africa would be administered, and the people enabled to exercise self-determination and to achieve independence.

19. Nothing could be clearer than this decision, which no permanent member of the Security Council voted against. Yet, since that time no effective measures have been taken to enforce it. Namibia remains in the clutches of the most ruthless minority Government in Africa. Its people continue to be oppressed, and those who advocate even peaceful progress to independence continue to be persecuted. The world has an obligation to use its strength to enforce the decision which all the countries co-operated in making. If they do this there is hope that the change can be effected without great violence. If they

fail, then sooner or later the people of Namibia will take the law into their own hands. The people have been patient beyond belief but one day their patience will be exhausted. Africa, at least, will then be unable to deny their call for help.

20. South Africa is itself an independent, sovereign State and a member of the United Nations. It is more highly developed and richer than any other nation in Africa. On every legal basis its internal affairs are a matter exclusively for the people of South Africa. Yet, the purpose of law is people and we assert that the actions of the South African Government are such that the rest of the world has a responsibility to take some action in defence of humanity.

21. There is one thing about South African oppression which distinguishes it from other oppressive régimes. The apartheid policy adopted by its Government, and supported to a greater or lesser extent by almost all its white citizens, is based on a rejection of man's humanity. A position of privilege or the experience of oppression in the South African society depends on the one thing which is beyond the power of any man to change. It depends upon a man's colour, his parentage and his ancestors. If you are black you cannot escape this categorization, nor can you escape it if you are white. If you are a black millionaire and a brilliant political scientist, you are still subject to the pass laws and still excluded from political activity. If you are white, even protests against the system and an attempt to reject segregation will lead you only to the segregation and the comparative comfort of a white jail. Beliefs, abilities, and behaviour are all irrelevant to a man's status; everything depends upon race. Manhood is irrelevant. The whole system of government and society in South Africa is based on the denial of human equality. The system is maintained by a ruthless denial of the human rights of the majority of the population and thus, inevitably, of all.

22. These things are known and are regularly condemned in the United Nations and elsewhere. But it appears that for many countries international law takes precedence over humanity; therefore no action follows the words. Yet even if international law is held to exclude active assistance to the South African opponents of apartheid, it does not demand that the comfort and support of human and commercial intercourse should be given to a Government which rejects the manhood of most humanity. South Africa should be excluded from the United Nations agencies, and even from the United Nations itself. It should be ostracized by the world community. It should be isolated from world trade patterns and left to be self-sufficient if it can. The South African Government cannot be allowed both to reject the very concept of mankind's unity and to benefit by the strength given through friendly international relations. Certainly Africa cannot acquiesce in the maintenance of the present policies against people of African descent.

23. The signatories of this Manifesto assert that the validity of the principles of human equality and dignity extend to South Africa just as they extend to the colonial territories of southern Africa. Before a basis for peaceful development can be established on this continent, these principles must be acknowledged by every nation and in every State there must be a deliberate attempt to implement them.

24. We reaffirm our commitment to these principles of human equality and human dignity and to the doctrines of self-determination and non-racialism. We

shall work for their extension within our own nations and throughout the continent of Africa.

4. UNIVERSAL ISLAMIC DECLARATION OF HUMAN RIGHTS

INTRODUCTION

Based on the Holy Qur'an and the Sunnah, a Muslim statement on human rights was promulgated in 1981. It was preceded by a Universal Islamic Declaration announced at the International Conference on the Prophet Muhammad and His Message in 1980 in London. The human rights compliation was made by eminent Muslim jurists and other scholars, together with the collaboration of representatives of various Islamic movements.

In Islam, human rights have a devine origin. This means that such rights are obligitory on all Muslim goverments and all organs of Muslim society. Consequently, no Muslim ruler can violate or even curtail such rights and no Muslim can surrender them.

UNIVERSAL ISLAMIC DECLARATION OF HUMAN RIGHTS (1981)

PREAMBLE

WHEREAS the age-old human aspiration for a just world order wherein people could live, develop and prosper in an environment free from fear, oppression, exploitation and deprivation, remains largely unfulfilled;

WHEREAS the Divine Mercy unto mankind reflected in its having been endowed with super-abundant economic sustenance is being wasted, or unfairly or unjustly withheld from the inhabitants of the earth;

WHEREAS Allah (God) has given mankind through His revelations in the Holy Qur'an and the Sunnah of His Blessed Prophet Muhammad an abiding legal and moral framework within which to establish and regulate human institutions and relationships;

WHEREAS the human rights decreed by the Divine Law aim at conferring dignity and honour on mankind and are designed to eliminate oppression and injustice;

WHEREAS by virtue of their Divine source and sanction these rights can neither be curtailed, abrogated or disregarded by authorities, assemblies or other institutions, nor can they be surrendered or alienated;

Therefore we, as Muslims, who believe

  a. in God, the Beneficient and Merciful, the Creator, the Sustainer, the Sovereign, the sole Guide of mankind and the Source of all Law;

  b. in the Vicegerency (Khilafah) of man who has been created to fulfil the Will of God on earth;

  c. in the wisdom of Divine guidance brought by the Prophets, whose mission found its culmination in the final Divine message that was conveyed by the Prophet Muhammad (Peace be upon him) to all mankind;

d. that rationality by itself without the light of revelation from God can neither be a sure guide in the affairs of mankind nor provide spiritual nourishment to the human soul, and, knowing that the teachings of Islam represent the quintessence of Divine guidance in its final and perfect form, feel duty-bound to remind man of the high status and dignity bestowed on him by God;

e. in inviting all mankind to the message of Islam;

f. that by the terms of our primeval covenant with God our duties and obligations have priority over our rights, and that each one of us is under a bounden duty to spread the teachings of Islam by word, deed, and indeed in all gentle ways, and to make them effective not only in our individual lives but also in the society around us;

g. in our obligation to establish an Islamic order:

　i. wherein all human beings shall be equal and none shall enjoy a privilege or suffer a disadvantage or discrimination by reason of race, colour, sex, origin or language;

　ii. wherein all human beings are born free;

　iii. wherein slavery and forced labour are abhorred;

　iv. wherein conditions shall be established such that the institution of family shall be preserved, protected and honoured as the basis of all social life;

　v. wherein the rulers and the ruled alike are subject to, and equal before, the Law;

　vi. wherein obedience shall be rendered only to those commands that are in consonance with the Law;

　vii. wherein all worldly power shall be considered as a sacred trust, to be exercised within the limits prescribed by the Law and in a manner approved by it, and with due regard for the priorities fixed by it;

　viii. wherein all economic resoures shall be treated as Divine blessings bestowed upon mankind, to be enjoyed by all in accordance with the rules and the values set out in the Qur'an and the Sunnah;

　ix. wherein all public affairs shall be determined and conducted, and the authority to administer them shall be exercised after mutual consultation (*Shura*) between the believers qualified to contribute to a decision which would accord well with the Law and the public good;

　x. wherein everyone shall undertake obligations proportionate to his capacity and shall be held responsible pro rata for his deeds;

　xi. wherein everyone shall, in case of an infringement of his rights, be assured of appropriate remedial measures in accordance with the Law;

　xii. wherein no one shall be deprived of the rights assured to him by the Law except by its authority and to the extent permitted by it;

　xiii. wherein every individual shall have the right to bring legal action against anyone who commits a crime against society as a whole or against any of its members;

xiv. wherein every effort shall be made to

a. secure unto mankind deliverance from every type of exploitation, injustice and oppression,

b. ensure to everyone security, dignity and liberty in terms set out and by methods approved and within the limits set by the Law;

Do hereby, as servants of Allah and as members of the Universal Brotherhood of Islam, at the beginning of the Fifteenth Century of the Islamic Era, affirm our commitment to uphold the following inviolable and inalienable human rights that we consider are enjoined by Islam.

I Right to Life

a) Human life is sacred and inviolable and every effort shall be made to protect it. In particular no one shall be exposed to injury or death, except under the authority of the Law.

b) Just as in life, so also after death, the sanctity of a person's body shall be inviolable. It is the obligation of believers to see that a deceased person's body is handled with due solemnity.

II Right to Freedom

a) Man is born free. No inroads shall be made on his right to liberty except under the authority and in due process of the Law.

b) Every individual and every people has the inalienable right to freedom in all its forms—physical, cultural, economic and political—and shall be entitled to struggle by all available means against any infringement or abrogation of this right; and every oppressed individual or people has a legitimate claim to the support of other individuals and/or peoples in such a struggle.

III Right to Equality and Prohibition Against Impermissible Discrimination

a) All persons are equal before the Law and are entitled to equal opportunities and protection of the Law.

b) All persons shall be entitled to equal wage for equal work.

c) No person shall be denied the opportunity to work or be discriminated against in any manner or exposed to greater physical risk by reason of religious belief, colour, race, origin, sex or language.

IV Right to Justice

a) Every person has the right to be treated in accordance with the Law, and only in accordance with the Law.

b) Every person has not only the right but also the obligation to protest against injustice; to recourse to remedies provided by the Law in respect of any unwarranted personal injury or loss; to self-defence against any charges that are preferred against him and to obtain fair adjudication before an independent judicial tribunal in any dispute with public authorities or any other person.

c) It is the right and duty of every person to defend the rights of any other person and the community in general (*Hisbah*).

d) No person shall be discriminated against while seeking to defend private and public rights.

e) It is the right and duty of every Muslim to refuse to obey any command which is contrary to the Law, no matter by whom it may be issued.

V Right to Fair Trial

a) No person shall be adjudged guilty of an offence and made liable to punishment except after proof of his guilt before an independent judicial tribunal.

b) No person shall be adjudged guilty except after a fair trial and after reasonable opportunity for defence has been provided to him.

c) Punishment shall be awarded in accordance with the Law, in proportion to the seriousness of the offence and with due consideration of the circumstances under which it was committed.

d) No act shall be considered a crime unless it is stipulated as such in the clear wording of the Law.

e) Every individual is responsible for his actions. Responsibility for a crime cannot be vicariously extended to other members of his family or group, who are not otherwise directly or indirectly involved in the commission of the crime in question.

VI Right to Protection Against Abuse of Power

Every person has the right to protection against harassment by official agencies. He is not liable to account for himself except for making a defence to the charges made against him or where he is found in a situation wherein a question regarding suspicion of his involvement in a crime could be *reasonably* raised.

VII Right to Protection Against Torture

No person shall be subjected to torture in mind or body, or degraded, or threatened with injury either to himself or to anyone related to or held dear by him, or forcibly made to confess to the commission of a crime, or forced to consent to an act which is injurious to his interests.

VIII Right to Protection of Honour and Reputation

Every person has the right to protect his honour and reputation against calumnies, groundless charges or deliberate attempts at defamation and blackmail.

IX Right to Asylum

a) Every persecuted or oppressed person has the right to seek refuge and asylum. This right is guaranteed to every human being irrespective of race, religion, colour and sex.

b) Al Masjid Al Haram (the sacred house of Allah) in Mecca is a sanctuary for all Muslims.

X Rights of Minorities

a) The Qur'anic principle "There is no compulsion in religion" shall govern the religious rights of non-Muslim minorities.

b) In a Muslim country religious minorities shall have the choice to be governed in respect of their civil and personal matters by Islamic Law, or by their own laws.

XI Right and Obligation to Participate in the Conduct and Management of Public Affairs

a) Subject to the Law, every individual in the community (*Ummah*) is entitled to assume public office.

b) Process of free consultation (*Shura*) is the basis of the administrative relationship between the government and the people. People also have the right to choose and remove their rulers in accordance with this principle.

XII Right to Freedom of Belief, Thought and Speech

a) Every person has the right to express his thoughts and beliefs so long as he remains within the limits prescribed by the Law. No one, however, is entitled to disseminate falsehood or to circulate reports which may outrage public decency, or to indulge in slander, innuendo or to cast defamatory aspersions on other persons.

b) Pursuit of knowledge and search after truth is not only a right but a duty of every Muslim.

c) It is the right and duty of every Muslim to protest and strive (within the limits set out by the Law) against oppression even if it involves challenging the highest authority in the state.

d) There shall be no bar on the dissemination of information provided it does not endanger the security of the society or the state and is confined within the limits imposed by the Law.

e) No one shall hold in contempt or ridicule the religious beliefs of others or incite public hostility against them; respect for the religious feelings of others is obligatory on all Muslims.

XIII Right to Freedom of Religion

Every person has the right to freedom of conscience and worship in accordance with his religious beliefs.

XIV Right to Free Association

a) Every person is entitled to participate individually and collectively in the religious, social, cultural and political life of his community and to establish institutions and agencies meant to enjoin what is right (*ma'roof*) and to prevent what is wrong (*munkar*).

b) Every person is entitled to strive for the establishment of institutions whereunder an enjoyment of these rights would be made possible. Collectively, the community is obliged to establish conditions so as to allow its members full development of their personalities.

XV The Economic Order and the Rights Evolving Therefrom

a) In their economic pursuits, all persons are entitled to the full benefits of nature and all its resources. These are blessings bestowed by God and for the benefit of mankind as a whole.

b) All human beings are entitled to earn their living according to the Law.

c) Every person is entitled to own property individually or in association with others. State ownership of certain economic resources in the public interest is legitimate.

d) The poor have the right to a prescribed share in the wealth of the rich, as fixed by Zakah, levied and collected in accordance with the Law.

e) All means of production shall be utilised in the interest of the community (*Ummah*) as a whole, and may not be neglected or misused.

f) In order to promote the development of a balanced economy and to protect society from exploitation, Islamic Law forbids monopolies, unreasonable restrictive trade practices, usury, the use of coercion in the making of contracts and the publication of misleading advertisements.

g) All economic activities are permitted provided they are not detrimental to the interests of the community (*Ummah*) and do not violate Islamic laws and values.

XVI Right to Protection of Property

No property may be expropriated except in the public interest and on payment of fair and adequate compensation.

XVII Status and Dignity of Workers

Islam honours work and the worker and enjoins Muslims not only to treat the worker justly but also generously. He is not only to be paid his earned wages promptly, but is also entitled to adequate rest and leisure.

XVIII Right to Social Security

Every person has the right to food, shelter, clothing, education and medical care consistent with the resources of the community. This obligation of the community extends in particular to all individuals who cannot take care of themselves due to some temporary or permanent disability.

XIX Right to Found a Family and Related Matters

a) Every person is entitled to marry, to found a family and to bring up children in conformity with his religion, traditions and culture. Every spouse is entitled to such rights and privileges and carries such obligations as are stipulated by the Law.

b) Each of the partners in a marriage is entitled to respect and consideration from the other.

c) Every husband is obligated to maintain his wife and children according to his means.

d) Every child has the right to be maintained and properly brought up by his parents, it being forbidden that children are made to work at an early age or that any burden is put on them which would arrest or harm their natural development.

e) If parents are for some reason unable to discharge their obligations towards a child it becomes the responsibility of the community to fulfil these obligations at public expense.

f) Every person is entitled to material support, as well as care and protection, from his family during his childhood, old age or incapacity. Parents are entitled to material support as well as care and protection from their children.

g) Motherhood is entitled to special respect, care and assistance on the part of the family and the public organs of the community (*Ummah*).

h) Within the family, men and women are to share in their obligations and responsibilities according to their sex, their natural endowments, talents and inclinations, bearing in mind their common responsibilities toward their progeny and their relatives.

i) No person may be married against his or her will, or lose or suffer dimunition of legal personality on account of marriage.

XX Rights of Married Women

Every married woman is entitled to:

a) live in the house in which her husband lives;

b) receive the means necessary for maintaining a standard of living which is not inferior to that of her spouse, and, in the event of divorce, receive during the statutory period of waiting (*Iddah*) means of maintenance commensurate with her husband's resources, for herself as well as for the children she nurses or keeps, irrespective of her own financial status, earnings, or property that she may hold in her own right.

c) seek and obtain dissolution of marriage (*Khul'a*) in accordance with the terms of the Law. This right is in addition to her right to seek divorce through the courts.

d) inherit from her husband, her parents, her children and other relatives according to the Law;

e) strict confidentiality from her spouse, or ex-spouse if divorced, with regard to any information that he may have obtained about her, the disclosure of which could prove detrimental to her interests. A similar responsibility rests upon her in respect of her spouse or ex-spouse.

XXI Right to Education

a) Every person is entitled to receive education in accordance with his natural capabilities.

b) Every person is entitled to a free choice of profession and career and to the opportunity for the full development of his natural endowments.

XXII Right of Privacy

Every person is entitled to the protection of his privacy.

XXIII Right to Freedom of Movement and Residence

a) In view of the fact that the World of Islam is veritably *Ummah Islamia*, every Muslim shall have the right to freely move in and out of any Muslim country.

b) No one shall be forced to leave the country of his residence, or be arbitrarily deported therefrom, without recourse to due process of Law.

EXPLANATORY NOTES

1 In the above formulation of Human Rights, unless the context provides otherwise:

a) the term 'person' refers to both the male and female sexes.

b) the term 'Law' denotes the *Shari'ah*, i.e. the totality of ordinances derived from the Qur'an and the Sunnah and any other laws that are deduced from these two sources by methods considered valid in Islamic jurisprudence.

2 Each one of the Human Rights ennunciated in this Declaration carries a corresponding duty.

3 In the exercise and enjoyment of the rights referred to above every person shall be subject only to such limitations as are enjoined by the Law for the purpose of securing the due recognition of, and respect for, the rights and freedom of others and of meeting the just requirements of morality, public order and the general welfare of the Community (*Ummah*).

4 The Arabic text of this *Declaration* is the original.

Glossary of Arabic Terms

SUNNAH   The example or way of life of the Prophet (peace be upon him), embracing what he said, did or agreed to.

KHILAFAH   The vicegerency of man on earth or succession to the Prophet, transliterated into English as the Caliphate.

HISBAH   Public viligance, an institution of the Islamic State enjoined to observe and facilitate the fulfilment of right norms of public behaviour. The "Hisbah" consists in public viligance as well as an opportunity to private individuals to seek redress through it.

MA'ROOF   Good act.

MUNKAR   Reprehensible deed.

ZAKAH   The 'purifying' tax on wealth, one of the five pillars of Islam obligatory on Muslims.

'IDDAH   The waiting period of a widowed or divorced woman during which she is not to re-marry.

KHUL'A   Divorce a woman obtains at her own request.

UMMAH ISLAMIA   World Muslim community.

SHARI'AH   Islamic law.

NOTE: *The Roman numerals refer to the topics in the text. The Arabic numerals refer to the Chapter and the Verse, of the Qur'an, i.e. 5:32 means Chapter 5, Verse 32.*

5. DECLARATION ON DEMOCRATIC VALUES

INTRODUCTION

On June 8, 1984, the leaders of the seven major industrial democracies issued a 500-word Declaration on Democratic Values. Their document was a product of the Tenth Economic Summit Meeting of representatives of Canada, France, the Federal Republic of Germany, Italy, Japan, the United Kingdom and the United States.

Free elections and free expression were described as fundamental to the maintenance of democracy.

Emphasizing the relationship between democracy and economic progress, the document called for "governments to set conditions in which there can be the greatest possible range and freedom of choice and personal initiative." It also called upon the wealthy nations to meet their moral obligations to the world-wide fight against hunger and poverty.

DECLARATION ON DEMOCRATIC VALUES (1984)

We, the heads of state or government of seven major industrial democracies, with the president of the Commission of the European Communities, assembled in London for the 10th economic summit meeting, affirm our commitment to the values which sustain and bring together our societies.

We believe in a rule of law which respects and protects without fear or favor the rights and liberties of every citizen, and provides the setting in which the human spirit can develop in freedom and diversity.

We believe in a system of democracy which insures genuine choice in elections freely held, free expression of opinion and the capacity to respond and adapt to change in all its aspects.

We believe that, in the political and economic systems of our democracies, it is for governments to set conditions in which there can be the greatest possible range and freedom of choice and personal initiative, in which the ideals of social justice obligations and rights can be pursued, in which enterprise can flourish and employment opportunities can be available for all, in which all have equal opportunities of sharing in the benefits of growth and there is support for those who suffer or are in need, in which the lives of all can be enriched by the fruits of innovation, imagination and scientific discovery and in which there can be confidence in the soundness of the currency. Our countries have the resources and will to jointly master the tasks of the New Industrial Revolution.

We believe in close partnership among our countries in the conviction that this will reinforce political stability and economic growth in the world as a whole. We look for cooperation with all countries on the basis of respect for their independence and territorial integrity, regardless of differences between political, economic and social systems.

We respect genuine nonalignment. We are aware that economic strength places special moral responsibilities upon us. We reaffirm our determination to fight hunger and poverty throughout the world.

We believe in the need for peace with freedom and justice. Each of us rejects the use of force as a means of settling disputes. Each of us will maintain only the military strength necessary to deter aggression and to meet our responsibilities for effective defense. We believe that in today's world the independence of each of our countries is of concern to us all. We are convinced that international problems and conflicts can and must be resolved through reasoned dialogue and negotiation and we shall support all efforts of this end.

Strong in these beliefs, and endowed with great diversity and creative vigor, we look forward to the future with confidence.

XI. FOOTNOTES

Chapter I, Introduction

1. Covenant of the League of Nations, Part I of the Treaty of Peace Between the Allied and Associated Powers and Germany, Article 22, U.S. Senate, Treaties, Conventions, International Acts, Protocols and Arguments Between the United States of America and Other Powers 1910–1923, Vol. III 3329, 3342 (U.S. Government Printing Office, 1923).

2. Statute of the International Court of Justice, Art. 38. See 3 Bevans, Treaties and Other International Arguments of the United States of America 1776–1949, pp. 1153, 1187. U.S. Dept. of State, 1969.

3. Falk, *On the Quasi-Legislative Competence of the General Assembly*, 60 Am. J. Int'l L. 774, 786 (1966).

4. On the juridicial nature of the documents in this area see, generally, A. D'Amato, *The Concept of Custom in International Law* (1971); J. Casraneda, *Legal Effects of United Nations Resolutions* (1969); O. Asamoah, *The Legal Significance of the Declarations of The General Assembly of the United Nations* (1966); H. Bokor-Szego, *The Role of the United Nations in International Legislation* (1978). The views we have expressed in this Note are substantially supported by the Reporters' Notes in American Law Institute, Restatement of the Law, Foreign Relations Law of the United States (Revised), Tentative Draft No. 1 at 31–33 (1980).

5. Preamble

6. Preamble

7. See, United Nations Charter, Articles 1 and 55. See, e.g., United Nations Office of Public Information, The International Bill of Human Rights (includes Universal Declaration of Human Rights, International Covenant on Economic, Social and Cultural Rights, International Covenant on Civil and Political Rights and Optional Protocol thereto), United Nations, New York, 1978.

8. Universal Declaration of Human Rights, Preamble, G. A. Res. 217A (III), 3(1) U.N. GAOR Res. 71, U.N. Doc. A/810 (1948).

9. For excellent introductions to the activities of the UN in the field of human rights, see A. Mower, *The United States, the United Nations and Human Rights* (1979); V. Van Dyke, *Human Rights, the United States and World Community* (1970); J. Green, *The United Nations and Human Rights* (1956); M. Moskowitz, *The Politics and Dynamics of Human Rights* (1968). There is a mine of rich source material both in L. Sohn and T. Buergenthal, *International Protection of Human Rights* (1973), and in R. Lillich and F. Newman, *International Human Rights: Problems of Law and Policy* (1979).

Two extremely useful UN publications on the area are United Nations Action in the Field of Human Rights, U.N. Pub. Sales No. E.74XIV.2 (1974) and M. Ganji, Special Rapporteur, "The Realization of Economic, Social and Cultural Rights: Problems, Policies, Progress," U.N. Doc. E/CN.4/1108/Rev.1, E/CN.4/1131/Rev.1 (1975).

The classic study of Article 2.7 is M. Rajan, *United Nations and Domestic Jurisdiction* (2nd. ed. 1961).

Chapter I, Section B. 3

10. The Optional Protocol to the International Covenant on Civil and Political Rights, reproduced in Chapter IV (A.6) is sometimes treated as part of the International Bill of Rights also.

11. "Permanent Sovereignty over Natural Resources," G.A. Res. 1803 (XVII), U.N. GAOR, Supp. (No. 17) 15, U.N. Doc. A/5217 (1962). Document I.L.1.

Chapter I, Section G

12. Filartiga vs. Peña-Irala, 630 F.2d 876 (2d Cir. 1980).

Chapter I, Section L

13. The Resolution is often referred to as a Declaration, although that term is not used in its title; the final preambular clause does use the word "Declares."

14. C. N. Brower, "The Future for Foreign Investment—Recent Developments in the International Law of Expropriation and Compensation," in *Private Investors Abroad-Problems and Solutions in International Business in 1975* (V. Cameron ed. 1976). See also F. G. Dawson and B. A. Weston, "Prompt, Adequate and Effective: A Universal Standard of Compensation," 30 *Fordham L. Rev.* 727 (1962).

15. Ernst-U. Petersmann, "The New International Economic Order: Principles, Politics and International Law," in The *International Law and Policy of Human Welfare* 449 at 462 (R. MacDonald, D. Johnston and G. Morris, eds. 1978).

Chapter IV, Introduction

16. We have not included in our selection procedures or agencies that deal with the activities of a particular state. Thus, for example, we have not included the relevant documents of two very important bodies dealing with the actions of South Africa, the Special Committee on Apartheid and the United Nations Council for Namibia.

17. There is much useful practical material on many of the U.N. procedures (some of it a little dated) in G. Da Fonseca, *How to File Complaints of Human Rights Violations: A Practical Guide to Inter-Governmental Procedures* (1975).

Chapter IV, Part B, Introduction

18. For assistance in obtaining this material and that pertaining to the Committees on the Application of Conventions and Recommendations, the authors are indebted to Nicolas Valticos, Assistant Director-General and Adviser for International Labour Standards of the International Labour Office.

Chapter IV, Part B, Section 2

19. See paragraph 100 of Volume A of the Committee of Expert's report.

20. This year the sessions involved would be the 56th–63rd Sessions (1971–77). No Conventions or Recommendations were adopted at the 57th Session (1972).

Chapter IV, Part B, Section 6

21. See First Report of the Committee, paragraph 24; see also 29th Report of the Committee, paragraphs 4 and 5.

22. Decisions taken by the Committee at its 19th Session (February 1958).

23. Ibid.

24. Ibid.

25. See First Report of the Committee, paragraphs 119–142.

26. See First Report of the Committee, paragraph 25.

27. See 127th Report of the Committee, paragraph 25.

28. See 127th Report of the Committee, paragraph 27.

29. Ibid., paragraph 28.

30. See First Report of the Committee, paragraph 25.

31. See, in this connection, 157th Report, Case No. 812 (Spain), Case No. 763 (Uruguay) and Case No. 823 (Chile); 158th Report, Case No. 774 (Central African Republic); 160th Report, Case No. 842 (Argentina); 161st Report, Case No. 823 (Chile); 163rd Report, Case No. 763 (Uruguay); 164th Report, Case No. 750 (Spain); 165th Report, Case No. 842 (Argentina); 166th and 169th Reports, Cases Nos. 685, 781, 806, 814 (Bolivia); 172nd Report, Case No. 824 (Benin); 175th Report, Case No. 842 (Argentina); 176th Report, Case No. 823 (Chile); 177th Report, Case No. 823 (Chile) and Case No. 829 (Jordan); 181st Report, Case No. 897 (Paraguay); 183rd Report, Case No. 763 (Uruguay); 184th Report, Case No. 842 (Argentina); 187th Report, Case No. 840 (Sudan), Case No. 885 (Ecuador), Case No. 823 (Chile), Case No. 854 (Paraguay), Case No. 861 (Bangladesh), Case No. 899 (Tunisia); 188th Report, Case No. 763 (Uruguay); 189th Report, Case No. 842 (Argentina).

32. 178th Report, Case No. 814 (Bolivia).

33. Decision taken by the Governing Body at its 123rd Session (November 1953); see Ninth Report of the Committee, para. 29.

34. See 111th Report, paragraphs 9 to 11.

35. See 127th Report, paragraph 15.

36. See 111th Report, paragraph 19.

37. See 127th Report, paragraphs 16 to 19.

38. See 164th Report, paragraphs 23 and 24.

39. See 127th Report, paragraphs 25, 27 and 28.

40. See 29th Report, paragraphs 12 and 13. See also, in this connection, para. 24 below.

41. See 43rd Report, paragraphs 4 and 5.

42. See 127th Report, paragraphs 20 and 21.

43. See 164th Report, paragraph 27.

44. See 155th Report, paragraph 9; 177th Report, para. 12.

45. See First Report, paragraph 142.

46. See 179th Report, paragraph 20.

Chapter IV, Part C, Introduction

47. Article 8 of the Convention itself provides for the reference of disputes concerning the "interpretation or application" of the Convention to the International Court of Justice, apparently with the consent of all parties to the dispute. Like Similar provisions in numerous UN treaties it appears to be a dead letter.

Chapter V, Part A.1, Section 1

48. As amended by Protocols Nos. 3 and 5, which entered into force on September 21, 1970 and December 20, 1971 respectively.

49. As amended by Protocol No. 5, which entered into force on December 20, 1971.

50. As amended by Protocol No. 3, which entered into force on September 21, 1970.

51. As amended by Protocol No. 3, which entered into force September 21, 1970.

52. As amended by Protocol No. 3, which entered into force September 21, 1970.

53. As amended by Protocol No. 5, which entered into force on December 20, 1971.

Chapter V, Part A, Section 4

54. Treaty Series No. 42 (1955), Cmnd. 9512.

55. Ibid., p. 50.

56. Miscellaneous No. 1 (1957)', Cmnd. 41.

Chapter V, Part B, Introduction

57. Organization of American States, *Handbook Existing Rules Pertaining to Human Rights,* 1978, p. 4.

58. Review of the International Commission of Jurists, No. 21, December, 1978, p. 27.

59. Ibid.

Chapter V, Part B, Section 6

60. Amended by Resolution 625 (XII-0/82) of the twelfth Regular Session of the OAS General Assembly.

61. Ibid.

Chapter V, Part B, Section 7

62. As amended by the Court, January 22nd, 1981.

Chapter V, Part C, Introduction

63. Organization of African Unity (Hereafter OAU) Document AHG-115 (XVI).

64. OAU Doc. CM-1149 (XXXVI) 2 (1981).

65. OAU Diary No. 6, June 21, 1981.

66. OAU Doc. CM-Plen Draft Rept. (XXXVII) 60 (1981).

67. Ibid.

68. OAU Diary No. 6, June 21, 1981.

Chapter VI, Part 7, Section a

69. H. Doc. 551, Vol. 7, p. 14.

Chapter VI, Part 7, Section b

70. United States Department of State. Seventh Semi-Annual Report by the President to the Commission on Security and Cooperation in Europe, June 1 to November 30, 1979, p. 13.

71. United States Congress, Commission on Security and Cooperation in Europe. "The Madrid CSCE Review Meeting," November, 1983, p. 17.

Chapter VI, Part 7, Section b

72. In this context it is understood that importation of printed matter may be subject to local regulations which will be applied with due regard to the journalists' need for adequate working material.

Chapter VII, Part 1

73. See William G. Andrews, *Constitutions and Constitutionalism* (Princeton, N.J.: D. Van Nostrand, Inc., 1961), pp. 9–16.

74. Charles Howard McIlwain, *Constitutionalism: Ancient and Modern* (Ithaca, N.Y.: Cornell University Press, 1948).

75. See Edward S. Corwin, "The 'Higher Law' Background of American Constitutional Law" (Ithaca, N.Y.: Cornell University Press, 1955).

76. Henry B. Mayo, *Introduction to Marxist Theory* (New York: Oxford University Press, 1967).

77. Andrews, *op. cit.,* p. 146.

78. Article 129 of the 1936 Constitution extends freedom of speech, press, assembly and demonstrations in this conditional fashion.

79. The 1960 Constitution of Pakistan enumerated many rights, liberties and welfare guarantees. But preceding the list was the statement that, "No law should be repugnant to Islam," a statement of growing importance in other Islamic nations.

Chapter VII, Part 2, Section a

80. Britain, Petition of Right, clause four (1628).

Chapter VII, Part 2, Section b

81. Barron vs. Baltimore, 7 Peters 243 (1833).

82. During the 1920's, the Supreme Court of the United States began to hold that specific guarantees of the Bill of Rights were so fundamental as to be protected by the Fourteenth Amendment against impairment by the states. This incorporation was greatly expanded by later court decisions after 1962.

83. Bernard Schwartz, *The Great Rights of Mankind* (New York: Oxford University Press, 1977), pp. 88–90.

84. Dred Scott vs. Sanford, 19 How. 393 (1857). In this case the Supreme Court held that a native-born Negro was not a citizen, against the generally understood principle of English law that birth in a country conferred citizenship.

Chapter VII, Part A, Section 3

85. See, Albert Godwin, *The French Revolution* (Dover, N.H.: Hutcheson Education, 1984).

86. See Emile Boutny, "La Declaration des droits de l'homme et du citoyen et M. Jellinek," *Annales des Sciences Politique* 18 (1902), pp. 415–443.

Chapter VII, Part B, Section 2

87. See S. Rusinov and V. Rianzhin, Sovetskoe Konstitutzionoe Pravo (Soviet Constitutional Law) (Leningrad; Izdatel'stvo Leningradskogo Univer-Siteta, 1975), pp. 8–9.

88. Articles 122 and 123, 1936 Constitution.

89. Article 122 states the "women in the USSR shall be granted equal rights with men in all domains of economic, state cultural, and socio-political life."

90. Article 125, 1936 Constitution.

91. Article 39, 1977 Constitution.

92. Ibid., Article 66.

93. Ibid., Article 67.

94. Ibid., Article 68.

95. Ibid., Article 69.

96. Ibid., Article 40.

97. Ibid., Article 41.

98. Article 120 of the 1936 Constitution gives a right to "financial security . . . in the event of an illness."

99. Article 42, 1977 Constitution.

100. Ibid., Article 50.

Chapter VII, Part C, Section 2

101. Statutes have been passed giving untouchables the legal right to enter any temple, draw water from any tap or well, or use any public restaurant. Yet there are reports of the shooting and harassment of untouchables. Prime Minister Indira Ghandi had pressed for land distribution to untouchables.

102. The Irish Constitution also contains Directive Principles of State Policy which has had an influence upon the Indian practice, even though the Irish Principles were strongly influenced by Catholic doctrine. Bangladesh and Nigeria, among others, have used the same constitutional device.

103. Considerable constitutional controversy over preferential programs for minorities has occurred in the United States.

104. Concurrent jurisdiction is given the High Courts by Art. 226.

105. See Marc Galanter, *Competing Equalities: The Indian Experiment with Compensatory Discrimination*, Chapter 2, unpublished manuscript. Professor Galanter is at the University of Wisconsin Law School.

Chapter VII, Part D, Section 1

106. The American version is set forth in Government Section, Supreme Commander for the Allied Powers, *Political Reorientation of Japan: September 1945 to September 1948*. (Washington: U.S. GPO, 1949).

107. See Kenzo Takayanagi, "Some Reminiscences of Japan's Commission on the Constitution," in Dan Fenno Henderson, ed., *The Constitution of Japan* (Seattle, Wash.: University of Washington Press, 1968), pp. 71–88. Dr. Takayanagi who was chairman of the Commission on the Constitution from 1957 to 1964, insists that Art. 9 was first suggested by Prime Minister Shidehara, not by U.S. General Douglas MacArthur.

Chapter VII, Part E

108. *Mart Act Case* (1970) I. R. 317.

Chapter VIII, Part 1

109. Galanter, "Caste Disabilities and Indian Federalism," 3 *Jour. Ind. L. Inst't.* 205, 208 (1961). See also Galanter, "Temple-Entry and the Untouchability (Offences) Act, 1975," 6 *Jour. Ind. L. Ins't.* 185 (1964).

110. Extended to Goa, Daman and Diu with modifications by Regulation 12 of 1962, section 3 and Schedule, to Dadra and Nagar Haveli by Regulation 6 of 1963, section 2 and Schedule I (with effect from 1st July, 1965) and to Pondicherry by Regulation 7 of 1963, section 3 and Schedule I (with effect from 1st October, 1963).

111. Subs. by Act 106 of 1976, s. 2 for "practice of 'Untouchability'" (w.e.f. 19–11–1976).

112. Subs. by s. 3, *ibid.*, for "the Untouchability (Offences) Act" (w.e.f. 19–11–1977).

113. 1st June, 1955, *vide* Notification No. S.R.O. 1109, dated the 23rd May, 1955, Gazette of India, 1955, Extraordinary, Part II, Section 3, Page 971.

114. Ins. by Act 106 of 1976, s. 4 (w.e.f. 19–11–1976).

115. Clause (a) was relettered as clause (aa) by s. 4, *ibid*. (w.e.f. 19–11–1976).

116. Subs. by s. 4, *ibid*., for cl. (b) (w.e.f. 19–11–1976).

117. Subs. by s. 4, *ibid*., for certain words (w.e.f. 19–11–1976).

118. Ins. by Act 106 of 1976, s. 4 (w.e.f. 19–11–1976).

119. Subs. by s. 4, *ibid*., for certain words (w.e.f. 19–11–1976).

120. The words "or belonging to the same religious denomination" omitted by s. 5, *ibid*. (w.e.f. 19–11–1976).

121. Ins. by s. 5, *ibid*. (w.e.f. 19–11–1976).

122. Subs. by s. 5, *ibid*., for certain words (w.e.f. 19–11–1976).

123. Subs. by s. 6, *ibid*., for certain words (w.e.f. 19–11–1976).

124. Ins. by s. 6, *ibid*. (w.e.f. 19–11–1976).

125. Subs. by Act 106 of 1976, s. 6, for certain words (w.e.f. 19–11–1976).

126. Subs. by Act 106 of 1976, s. 6, for certain words (w.e.f. 19–11–1976).

127. Subs. by Act 106 of 1976, s. 6, for certain words (w.e.f. 19–11–1976).

128. Subs. by Act 106 of 1976, s. 6, for certain words (w.e.f. 19–11–1976).

129. Subs. by s. 6, *ibid*., for "taking part in any religious procession" (w.e.f. 19–11–1976).

130. Subs. by Act 106 of 1976, s. 6 . . . for certain words (w.e.f. 19–11–1976).

131. Ins. by s. 6, *ibid*. (w.e.f. 19–11–1976).

132. The words "attached thereto" omitted by s. 7, *ibid*. (w.e.f. 19–11–1976).

133. Subs. by s. 7, *ibid*., for certain words (w.e.f. 19–11–1976).

134. Subs. by s. 8, *ibid*., for certain words (w.e.f. 19–11–1976).

135. Ins. by Act 106 of 1976 (w.e.f. 19–11–1976).

136. Ins. by Act 106 of 1976 (w.e.f. 19–11–1976).

137. Subs. by s. 9, *ibid*., for certain words (w.e.f. 19–11–1976).

138. Re-numbered by s. 9, *ibid*. (w.e.f. 19–11–1976).

139. Re-numbered by s. 9, *ibid*. (w.e.f. 19–11–1976).

140. Re-numbered by s. 9, *ibid*. (w.e.f. 19–11–1976).

141. Subs. by Act 106 of 1976, s. 9, for certain words (w.e.f. 19–11–1976).

142. Ins. by s. 10, *ibid*. (w.e.f. 19–11–1976).

143. Ins. by s. 11, *ibid*. (w.e.f. 19–11–1976).

144. Ins. by s. 12, *ibid*. (w.e.f. 19–11–1976).

145. Ins. by s. 13, *ibid*. (w.e.f. 19–11–1976).

146. Subs. by Act 106 of 1976, s. 14, for certain words (w.e.f. 19–11–1976).

147. The words "as defined in clause (24) of article 366 of Constitution" omitted by Act 106 of 1976, s. 15 (w.e.f. 19–11–1976).

148. Ins. by s. 16, *ibid*. (w.e.f. 19–11–1976).

149. Subs. s. 17, *ibid*., for s. 15 (w.e.f. 19–11–1976).

150. Ins. by Act 106 of 1976, s. 18 (w.e.f. 19–11–1976).

Chapter VIII, Part 3

151. Lester, "Fundamental Rights in the United Kingdom: The Law and the British Constitution," 125 *U. Pa. L. Rev.* 337, 354 (1976).

152. Preliminary Note to the Act in Halsbury's *Statutes of England*, v. 6, p. 389.

Chapter IX, Part 1

153. Holdsworth, *A History of English Law*, 3d ed., vol. 1, p. 345.

154. Hamond vs. Howell, 1 Mod. 119, 184 (1676), 2 Mod. 218, 219 (1677).

Chapter IX, Part 2

(Footnotes 155 to 184 are an integral part of the *Brown* and *Bolling* decisions.)

155. *Bolling* v. *Sharpe*, 347 U.S. 497 (1954).

156. *Brown* v. *Board of Education of Topeka*, 349 U.S. 294 (1955).

157. 396 U.S. 19 (1969).

158. *Washington* v. *Davis*, 426 U.S. 229, 240 (1976).

159. Together with No. 2, *Briggs et al.* v. *Elliott et al.*, on appeal from the United States District Court for the Eastern District of South Carolina, argued December 9–10, 1952, reargued December 7–8, 1953; No. 4, *Davis et al.* v. *County School Board of Prince Edward County,*

Virginia, et al., on appeal from the United States District Court for the Eastern District of Virginia, argued December 10, 1952, reargued December 7–8, 1953; and No. 10, *Gebhart et al.* v. *Belton et al.*, on certiorari to the Supreme Court of Delaware, argued December 11, 1952, reargued December 9, 1953.

160. In the Kansas case, *Brown* v. *Board of Education*, the plaintiffs are Negro children of elementary school age residing in Topeka. They brought this action in the United States District Court for the District of Kansas to enjoin enforcement of a Kansas statute which permits, but does not require, cities of more than 15,000 population to maintain separate school facilities for Negro and white students. Kan.Gen.State.§ 72–1724 (1949). Pursuant to that authority, the Topeka Board of Education elected to estabilsh segregated elementary schools. Other public schools in the community, however, are operated on a nonsegregated basis. The three-judge District Court, convened under 28 U.S.C. § 2281 and 2284, found that segregation in public education has a detrimental effect upon Negro children, but denied relief on the ground that the Negro and white schools were substantially equal with respect to buildings, transportation, curricula, and educational qualifications of teachers. 98 F.Supp. 797. The case is here on direct appeal under 28 U.S.C. § 1253.

In the South Carolina case, *Briggs* v. *Elliott*, the plaintiffs are Negro children of both elementary and high school age residing in Clarendon County. They brought this action in the United States District Court for the Eastern District of South Carolina to enjoin enforcement of provisions in the state constitution and statutory code which require the segregation of Negroes and Whites in public schools. S.C.Const., Art. XI, § 7; S.C.Code § 5377 (1942). The three-judge District Court, convened under 28 U.S.C. § 2281 and 2284, denied the requested relief. The court found that the Negro schools were inferior to the white schools and ordered the defendants to begin immediately to equalize the facilities. But the court sustained the validity of the contested provisions and denied the plaintiffs admission to the white schools during the equalization program. 98 F.Supp. 529. This Court vacated the District Court's judgment and remanded the case for the purpose of obtaining the court's views on a report filed by the defendants concerning the progress made in the equalization program. 342 U.S. 350. On remand, the District Court found that substantial equality had been achieved except for buildings and that the defendants were proceeding to recitfy this inequality as well. 103 F.Supp. 920. The case is again here on direct appeal under 28 U.S.C. § 1253.

In the Virginia case, *Davis* v. *County School Board*, the plaintiffs are Negro children of high school age residing in Prince Edward County. They brought this action in the United States District Court for the Eastern District of Virginia to enjoin enforcement of provisions in the state constitution and statutory code which require the segregation of Negroes and whites in public schools. Va. Const., of 140; Va. Code § 22–221 (1950). The three-judge District Court, convened under 28 U.S.C. § 2281 and 2284, denied the requested relief. The court found the Negro school inferior in physical plant, curricula, and transportation, and ordered the defendants forthwith to provide substantially equal curricula and transportation and to "proceed with all reasonable diligence and dispatch to remove" the inequality in physical plant. But as in the South Carolina case, the court sustained the validity of the contested provisions and denied the plaintiffs admission to the white schools during the equalization program. 103 F.Supp. 337. The case is here on direct appeal under 28 U.S.C. § 1253.

In the Delaware case, *Gebhart* v. *Belton*, the plaintiffs are Negro children of both elementary and high school age residing in New Castle County. They brought this action in the Delaware Court of Chancery to enjoin enforcement of provisions in the state constitution and statutory code which require the segregation of Negroes and whites in public schools. Del. Const. Art. X, § 2; Del.Rev.Code § 2631 (1935). The Chancellor gave judgment for the plaintiffs and ordered their immediate admission to schools previously attended only by white children, on the ground that the Negro schools were inferior with respect to teacher training, pupil-teacher ratio, extracurricular activities, physical plant, and time and distance involved in travel. 87 A.2d 862. The Chancellor also found that segregation itself results in an inferior education for Negro children (see note 10, *infra*), but did not rest his decision on that ground, *Id.*, at page 865. The Chancellor's decree was affirmed by the Supreme Court of Delaware, which intimated, however, that the defendants might be able to obtain a modification of the decree after equalization of the Negro and white schools had been accomplished. 91 A.2d 137, 152. The defendants, contending only that the Delaware courts had erred in ordering the immediate admission of the Negro plaintiffs to the white schools, applied to this Court for certiorari. The writ was granted, 344 U.S. 891. . . . The plaintiffs, who were successful below, did not submit a cross-petition.

161. 344 U.S. 1, 141, 891.

162. 345 U.S. 972. The Attorney General of the United States participated both Terms as *amicus curiae*.

163. For a general study of the development of public education prior to the Amendment, see Butts and Cremin, *A History of Education in*

American Culture (1953), Pts. I, II; Cubberley, Public Education in the United States (1934 ed.) cc. II-XII. School practices current at the time of the adoption of the Fourteenth Amendment are described in Butts and Cremin, *supra*, at 269–275; Cubberley, *supra*, at 288–339, 408–431; Knight, Public Education inthe South (1922), cc. VIII, IX. See also H. Ex. Doc.. No. 315; 41st Cong., 2d Sess. (1871). Although the demand for free public schools followed substantially the same pattern in both the North and the South, the development in the South did not begin to gain momentum until about 1850, some twenty years after that in the North. The reasons for the somewhat slower development in the South (*e.g.*, the rural character of the South and the different regional attitudes toward staté assistance) are well explained in Cubberley, *supra*, at 408–423. In the country as a whole, but particularly in the South, the War virtually stopped all progress in public education. *Id.*, at 427–428. The low status of Negro education in all sections of the country, both before and immediately after the War, is described in Beale, A History of Freedom of Teaching in American Schools (1941), 112–132, 175–195. Compulsory school attendance laws were not generally adopted until after the ratification of the Fourteenth Amendment, and it was not until 1918 that such laws were in force in all the states. Cubberley, *suprea*, at 563–565.

164. *Slaughter-House Cases*, 16 Wall. 36, 67–72 (1873); *Strauder* v. *West Virginia*, 100 U.S. 303, 307–308 (1880): "It ordains that no State shall deprive any person of life, liberty, or property, without due process of law, or deny to any person within its jurisdiction the equal protection of the laws. What is this but declaring that the law in the States shall be the same for the black as for the white; that all persons, whether colored or white, shall stand equal before the laws of the States, and, in regard to the colored race, for whose protection the amendment was primarily designed, that no discrimination shall be made against them by law because of their color? The words of the amendment, it is true, are prohibitory, but they contain a necessary implication of a positive immunity, or right, most valuable to the colored race,—the right to exemption from unfriendly legislation against them distinctively as colored,—exemption from legal discriminations, implying inferiority in civil society, lessening the security of their enjoyment of the rights which others enjoy, and discriminations which are steps towards reducing them to the condition of a subject race." See also *Virginia* v. *Rives*, 100 U.S. 313, 318 (1880); *Ex parte Virginia*, 100 U.S. 339, 344–345 (1880).

165. The doctrine apparently originated in *Roberts* v. *City of Boston*, 59 Mass. 198, 206 (1850),

upholding school segregation against attack as being violative of a state constitutional guarantee of equality. Segregation in Boston public schools was eliminated in 1855. Mass. Acts 1855, c. 256. But elsewhere in the North segregation in public education has persisted in some communities until recent years. It is apparent that such segregation has long been a nationwide problem, not merely one of sectional concern.

166. See also *Berea College* v. *Kentucky* 211 U.S. 45 (1908).

167. In the *Cumming* case, Negro taxpayers sought an injunction requiring the defendant school board to discontinue the operation of a high school for white children until the board resumed operation of a high school for Negro children. Similarly, in the *Gong Lum* case, the plaintiff, a child of Chinese descent, contended only that state authorities had misapplied the doctrine by classifying him with Negro children and requiring him to attend a Negro school.

168. In the Kansas case, the court below found substantital equality as to all such factors, 98 F.Supp. 797, 798. In the South Carolina case, the court below found that the defendants were proceeding "promptly and in good faith to comply with the court's decree." 103 F.Supp. 920, 921. In the Virginia case, the court below noted that the equalization program was already "afoot and progressing" (103 F.Supp. 337, 341); since then, we have been advised, in the Virginia Attorney General's brief on reargument, that the program has now been completed. In the Delaware case, the court below similarly noted that the state's equalization program was well under way. 91 A.2d 137, 149.

169. A similar finding was made in the Delaware case: "I conclude from the testimony that in our Delaware society, State-imposed segregation in education itself results in the Negro children, as a class, receiving educational opportunities which are substantially inferior to those available to white children otherwise similarly situated." 87 A.2d 862, 865.

170. K. B. Clark, "Effect of Prejudice and Discrimination on Personality Development" (Midcentury White House Conference on Children and Youth, 1950); Witmer and Kotinsky, *Personality in the Making* (1952), c. VI; Deutscher and Chein, "The Psychological Effects of Enforced Segregation: A Survey of Social Science Opinion," 26, *J. Psychol.* 259 (1948); Chein, "What are the Psychological Effects of Segregation Under Conditions of Equal Facilities?" 3 *Int. J.. Opinion and Attitude Res.* 229 (1949); Brameld, "*Educational Costs, in Discrimination and National Welfare* (MacIver, ed.), 1949), 44–48; Frazier, *The Negro in the United States* (1949),

674–681. And see generally Myrdal, *An American Dilemma* (1944).

171. See *Bolling* v. *Sharpe, Post*, p. 497, concerning the Due Process Clause of the Fifth Amendment.

172. "4. Assuming it is decided that segregation in public schools violates the Fourteenth Amendment

"(*a*) would a decree necessarily follow providing that, within the limits set by normal geographic school districting, Negro children should forthwith be admitted to schools of their choice, or

"(*b*) may this Court, in the exercise of its equity powers, permit an effective gradual adjustment to be brought about from existing segregated systems to a system not based on color distinctions?

"5. On the assumption on which questions 4(*a*) and (*b*) are based, and assuming further that this Court will exercise its equity powers to the end described in question 4(*b*).

"(*a*) should this Court formulate detailed decrees in these cases;

"(*b*) if so, what specific issues should the decree reach;

"(*c*) should this Court appoint a special master to hear evidence with a view to recommending specific terms for such decrees;

"(*d*) should this Court remand to the courts of first instance with directions to frame decrees in these cases, and if so what general directions should the decrees of this Court include and what procedures should the courts of first instance follow in arriving at the specific terms of more detailed decrees?"

173. See Rule 42, Revised Rules of this Court (effective July 1, 1954).

174. *Brown* v. *Board of Education*, 347 U.S. 483.

175. *Detroit Bank* v. *United States*, 317 U.S. 329; *Currin* v. *Wallace*, 306 U.S. 1, 13–14; *Steward Machine Co.* v. *Davis*, 301 U.S. 548, 585.

176. *Korematsu* v. *United States*, 323 U.S. 214, 216; *Hirabayashi* v. *United States*, 320 U.S. 81, 100.

177. *Gibson* v. *Mississippi*, 162 U.S. 565, 591, Cf. *Steele* v. *Louisville & Nashville R.R. Co.*, 323 U.S. 192, 198–199.

178. Cf. *Hurd* v. *Hodge*, 334 U.S. 24.

179. Together with No. 2, *Briggs et al.* v. *Elliot et al.*, on appeal from the United States District Court for the Eastern District of South Carolina; No. 3, *Davis et al.* v. *County School Board of Prince Edward County, Virginia, et al.*, on appeal from the United States District Court for the Eastern District of Virginia; No. 4, *Bolling et al.* v. *Sharpe et al.*, on certiorari to the United States Court of Appeals for the District of Columbia Circuit; and No. 5, *Gebhart et al.* v. *Belton et al.*, on certiorari to the Supreme Court of Delaware.

180. 347 U.S. 483; 347 U.S. 497.

181. Further argument was requested on the following questions, 347 U.S. 483, 495–496,n. 13, previously propounded by the Court:

"4. Assuming it is decided that segregationin public schools violates the Fourteenth Amendment

"(a) would a decree necessarily follow providing that, within the limits set by normal geographic school districting, Negro children should forthwith be admitted to schools of their choice, or

"(b) may this Court in the exercise of its equity powers, permit an effective gradual adjustment to be brought about from existing segregated systems to a system not based on color distinctions?

"5. On the assumption on which questions 4(a) and (b) are based, and assuming further that this Court will exercise it equity powers to the end described in question 4(b),

"(a) should this Court formulate detailed decrees in these cases;

"(b) if so, what specific issues should the decrees reach;

"(c) should this Court appoint a special master to hear evidence with a view to recommending specific terms for such decrees;

"(d) should this Court remand to the courts of first instance with directions to frame decrees in these cases, and if so what general directions should the decrees of this Court include and what procedures should the courts of first instance follow in arriving at the specific terms of more detailed decrees?"

182. The cases coming to us from Kansas, South Carolina, and Virginia were originally heard by three-judge District Courts convened under 28 U.S.C. 2281 and 2284. These cases will accordingly be remanded to those three-judge courts. See *Briggs* v. *Elliot*, 342 U.S. 350.

183. See *Alexander* v. *Hillman*, 296 U.S. 222, 239.

184. See *Hecht Co.* v. *Bowles*, 321 U.S. 321, 329–330.

Chapter IX, Part 4

185. (1963) A.C. 103, 118; (1962) 3 W.L.R. 1413; (1962) 3 ALL E.R. 1066, P.C.

186. (1961) 63 N.L.R. 313, 314.

187. (1920) A.C. 691.

188. (1948) 50 N.L.R. 25.

189. Id. at 37.

Chapter IX, Part 5

190. Translation and excerpts from *Comparative Constitutional Law* by Walter F. Murphy and Joseph Tanenhaus (New York; St. Martin's Press, 1977), pp. 538–545.

Chapter X, Part 2

191. *New York Times*, Jan. 11, 1977, p. 1. c. 1.

192. *New York Times*, Jan. 13, 1977, p. 3, c. 4.

193. "A Stalin Era Trial in Prague," *Newsweek*, Nov. 5, 1979, p. 68.

Chapter X, Part 3

194. The Manifesto uses the equivalent British word, "racialism."

XII. BIBLIOGRAPHY

Aggarwal, N., "Press Freedom: A Third World View," 4 *The Independent* 1 (1977).

Alcock, A., *History of the International Labour Organization* (1971).

Alzaga, G., *La Constitucion Espanola de 1978* (1978), 710 American Law Institute, Restatement of the Law, Foreign Relations Law of the United States (Revised), Tentative Draft No. 1 (1980).

Andrews, W., *Constitutions and Constitutionalism* (1961), 630; *The Anti-Slavery Reporter and Aborigine's Friend*, Volitz, No. 5 (1976).

Asamoah, O., The Legal Significance of the Declarations of the General Assembly of the United Nations (1966), 7 Association Internationale de Droit Penal, Special Issue of the Revue Internationale de Droit Penal, Nos. 3 and 4, The Prevention and Suppression of Torture (1977).

Bassiowni, M., *International Criminal Law*, Vol. I, *Crimes*, 1986.

Bergsten, F., *Toward a New International Economic Order* (1975).

Blaustein, A. P. and Flanz, G., *Constitutions of the Countries of the World* (1971–date).

Blaustein, A. P. and Ferguson, C. C. Jr., *Desegregation and the Law*, 2d. ed. (1982).

Bokor H.-Szego, *The Role of the United Nations in International Legislation* (1978).

Brower, C. N., "The Future for Foreign Investment—Recent Developments in the International Law of Expropriation and Compensation," in *Private Investors Abroad—Problems and Solutions in International Business in 1975* (1976).

Buergenthal, T., *Human Rights, International Law and the Helsinki Accord* (1977).

Burke, K., "New United Nations Procedure to Protect Prisoners and Other Detainees," 64 *Calif. L. Rev.* 201 (1976).

Carey, J., *U.N. Protection of Civil and Political Rights* (1970).

Castaneda, J., *Legal Effects of United Nations Resolutions* (1969).

Cassese, A., "The Admissability of Communications to the United Nations on Human Rights Violations," 5 *Human Rights Journal* 375 (1972–73).

Castberg, S., *The European Convention on Human Rights*, Leyden (1974).

Castberg, S., *Freedom of Speech in the West* (1960).

Clark, R., *A United Nations High Commissioner for Human Rights* (1972).

Clark, R., "The United Nations Declaration on the Elimination of All Forms of Intolerance and of Discrimination Based on Religion and Belief," *Chitty's Law Journal* (1984).

Clark, R., "The United Nations and Religious Freedom," 11 *New York University Journal of International Law and Politics* 197 (1978).

Clark, R., and Berman, M., *State Terrorism: Disappearances*, 13 Rutgers, L. J. 531 (1982).

Clark, R. and Nevas, L., *The First Twenty-Five Years of the Universal Declaration of Human Rights and the Next*, 48 Conn. B. J. 111 (1974).

Claude, R. ed., *Comparative Human Rights* (1976).

Claydon, J., "Internationally Uprooted People and the Transitional Protection of Minority Culture," 24 *N.Y. Law Sch. Rev.* 125 (1978).

Coleman, J.; Kelley, S. D.; and Moore, J., *Trends in Social Segregation 1968–1973* (1975).

Corwin, E., *The "Higher Law" Background of American Constitutional Law* (1955).

D'Amato, D., *The Concept of Custom in International Law* (1971).

Da'Fonesca, G., *How to File Complaints of Human Rights Violations: A Practical Guide to Inter-Governmental Procedures* (1975).

Dawson, F. G.; and Weston, B. A., "Prompt, Adequate and Effective: a Universal Standard of Compensation?" 30 *Fordham L. Rev.* 727 (1962).

Denoon, D. ed., *The New International Economic Order: A U.S. Response* (1979).

Duchacek, I., *Power Maps: Comparative Politics of Constitutions* (1973).

Duchecek, I., *Rights and Liberties in the World Today: Constitutional Promise and Reality* (1973).

El-Ayouty, Y., *The United Nations and Decolonization: The Role of Afro-Asia* (1971).

Emerson, R., *Self-Determination Revisited in an Era of Decolonization* (1964).

Falk, R., "On Quasi-Legislative Competence of the General Assembly," 60 *A. J. Int'l L.* 774 (1966).

Falk, R.; Kolko, G.; and Lifton, R., *Crimes of War* (1971).

Fawcett, J. E. S., *The Application of the European Convention on Human Rights*, Oxford, (1969).

Federal Civil Rights Enforcement Effect (1973).

Galanter, M., "Caste Disabilities and Indian Federalism," 3 *Journ. Ind. L. Ins't.* 185 (1964).

Galanter, M., *Competing Equalities: The Indian Experiment with Compensatory Discrimination* (unpublished manuscript).

Galanter, M., "Temple-Entry and the Untouchability (Offences) Act, 1975," 6 *Jour. Ind. L. Ins't* 185 (1964).

Ganji, M., Special Rapporteur, "The Realization of Economic, Social and Cultural Rights: Problems, Policies, Progress," U.N. Doc. E/CN. 4/1108/Rev.1,E/CN.4/1131/rev.1 (1975).

Gaspard, A., "International Action to Preserve Press Freedom," in *The International Protection of Human Rights* 183 (E. Luard ed. 1967).

Government Section, Supreme Commander for the Allied Powers, Political Reorientation of Japan: September 1945 to September 1948 (1949).

Grahl-Madsen, A., *The Status of Refugees in International Laws* (1966).

Green, J., *The United Nations and Human Rights* (1956).

Haas, E., *Beyond the Nation—State* (1964).

Hass, E., *Human Rights and International Action: The Case of Freedom of Association* (1970).

Hannum, H., ed., *Guide to International Human Rights Practice* (1984).

Henderson, D. F., ed., *The Constitution of Japan*, (1968).

Holborn, L., *Refugees: A Problem of Our Time. The Work of the United Nations High Commissioner for Refugees 1951–1972* (1975).

Hollsworth, *A History of English Law*, 3d ed.

Human Rights in Europe, 2d ed., Manchester, (1977).

Human Rights In National and International Law, Manchester, (1908).

Inter-American Yearbook on Human Rights, 1969–1970 (1976).

Jenks, C. Wilfred, *Human Rights and International Labor Standards* (1960).

Jhabvala, F., "The Practice of the Covenant's Human Rights Committee, 1976–1982: Review of State Party Reports," 6 *Human Rights Q.* 81 (1984).

Kaufman, S., "The Necessity for Rules of Procedure in Ad Hoc United Nations Investigations," 18 *American U.L. Rev.* 739 (1968–69).

Kavass, I.; Granier, J.; and Dominick, M., *Human Rights, European Politics, and the Helsinki, Accord: The Documentary Evolution of the Conference on Security and Co-Operation in Europe, 1973–1975.*

Koopmans, T., ed., *Constitutional Protection of Equality* (1975).

Lador-Lederer, J., "An International Human Rights Committee for Slavery," 3 *Israel L. Rev.* (1968).

Landy, E., *The Effectiveness of International Supervision: Thirty Years of I.L.O. Experience* (1966).

Lauterpacht, H., *International Law and Human Rights* (1950).

Legam, C., *Africa Contemporary Record, Annual Survey and Documents*, (1969–1970).

Lester, "Fundamental Rights in the United Kingdom: The Law and the British Constitution," 125, *U. Pa. L. Rev.* 337 (1976).

Lillich, R. and Newman, F., *International Human Rights: Problems of Law and Policy* (1979).

Lipiz, M., "The Protection of Universal Human Rights; The Problem of Torture," Vol. 1, No. 4 *Universal Human Rights* 25 (1979).

McIlwain, C., *Constitutionalism: Ancient and Modern* (1948).

McKean, W., "The International Law of Non-Discrimination," in *Essays on Race Relations and the Law in New Zealand* (McKean ed. 1971).

Marks, S., "UNESCO and Human Rights: The Implementation of Rights Relating to Education, Science, Culture and Communication," 13 *Texas Int'l L.J.* 35 (1977).

Mayo, H., *Introduction to Marxist Theory*, (1967).

Moskowitz, M., *The Politics and Dynamics of Human Rights* (1968).

Mower, A., *The United States, the United Nations and Human Rights* (1979).

Murphy, W. and Tanenhaus, J., *Comparative Constitutional Law* (1977).

Mutharika, A., *The International Law of Development* (4 vols) (1978).

Mutharika, A., *The Regulation of Statelessness Under International and National Law* (1976 with 1978 Supp.).

Nanda, V. and Bassiouni, M., "Slavery and the Slave Trade; Steps Toward its Eradication," 12 *Santa Clara Lawyer* 434 (1972).

Nedjati, Z., *Human Rights Under the European Convention*, North-Holland (1978).

Nivabrese, O., *Constitutionalism in the Emergent States* (1973).

Okolie, C., *International Law Perspectives of the Developing Countries: The Relationship of Law and Economic Development to Basic Human Rights* (1978).

The Organization of American States and Human Rights: Activity of the Inter-American Commission on Human Rights, 1960–1967 (1972).

Petersmann, Ernst-U., "The New International Economic Order: Principles, Politics and International Law," in *The International Law and Policy of Human Welfare* 449 (R. MacDonald, J. Johnson, and G. Morris ed. 1978).

Phelen, E., *Yes and Albert Thomas* (1936).

Possony, S., *Victims of Politics: The State of Human Rights* (1979).

Rajan, M., *United Nations and Domestic Jurisdiction* (2nd. ed. 1961).

Ramcharan, B., *Implementing the International Covenants on Human Rights, in Human Rights: Thirty Years After the Universal Declaration* 159 (B. Ramcharan ed. 1979).

Ramcharan, B., ed., *International Fact-Finding in the Field of Human Rights* (1982).

"Report of the United Nations Special Rapporteur on Slavery," 243. Awad, Mohamed, U.N. Doc. E/4168/Rev. 1 (1966).

Robertson, A. H., *The Helsinki Agreement and Human Rights*.

Rodgers, H. R., Jr., and Ballock, C. J. III, *Law and Social Change: Rights, Laws, and Their Consequences*, (1972).

Rusinov, S. and Rianzhin, V., *Sovetskow Konstitutzione Pravo* (1975).

Schwebel, S., "The Story of the U.S.'s Declaration on Permanent Sovereignty Over Natural Resources," 49 *Am. Bar Assoc. J.* 463 (1963).

Skilling, Gordon, H., *Charter 77 and Human Rights in Czechoslovakia*, (1981).

Skoler, D., "World Implementation of the United Nations Standard Minimum Risks for the Treatment of Prisoners," 10 *J. Int'l L. and Econ.* 453 (1975).

Sohn, L., "A Short History of United Nations Documents on Human Rights," in *Commission to Study the Organization of Peace, the United Nations, and Human Rights*, 39 (1968).

Sohn, L. and T. Buergenthal, *International Protection of Human Rights* (1973).

Stoessinger, J., *The Refugee and the World Community* (1956).

Saffian, T. M.; Lee, H. P.; and Trindade, F. A., *The Constitution of Malaysia* (1979).

Sureda, A., *The Evolution of the Right of Self-Determination: A Study of United Nations Practice* (1973).

Tardu, M., *1 Human Rights: The International Petition System* (1979).

Toussaint, C., *The Trusteeship System of the United Nations* (1956).

Umozurike, U., *Self-Determination In International Law* (1972).

"United Nations Action in the Field of Human Rights," U.N. Pub. Sales No. E. 74XIV.2 (1974).

United Nations Department of Political Affairs, Trusteeship, and Decolonization, *Fifteen Years of the United Nations Declaration on the Granting of Independence to Colonial Countries and Peoples*, Decolonization Vol. II No. 6 (December 1975).

Valticos, N., "The International Labor Organization," in *The Effectiveness of International Decisions* 134 (S. Schwebel ed. 1971).

Valticos, N., "The Role of the ILO: Present Action and Future Perspectives" in *Human Rights: Thirty Years After the Universal Declarations* (B. Ramchoran ed. 1979).

Van Dyke, V., *Human Rights, The United Nations and World Community* (1970).

Van Dyke, V., "Human Rights Without Distinction," 67 *Am. Pol. Sci. Rev.* 1267 (1973).

Van Dyke, V., "Human Rights Without Distinction as to Language," 20 *Int'l Studies* Q.3 (1976).

Weil, G. L., *The European Convention on Human Rights*, Leyden, (1963).

Wilkinson, J. H., *From Brown to Bakke: The Supreme Court and School Integration, 1954–1978* (1979).

Yearbook of the European Convention on Human Rights.

INDEX